RED VELVET SEAT

RED VELVET SEAT

Women's Writings on
the First Fifty Years of Cinema

Edited by Antonia Lant

with Ingrid Periz

VERSO

London · New York

For Caspar

First published by Verso 2006

Verso
UK: 6 Meard Street, London W1F 0EG
USA: 180 Varick Street, New York, NY 10014–4606

Verso is the imprint of New Left Books

ISBN-10   1–84467–119–4 (hbk)
ISBN-10   1–85984–722–6 (pbk)
ISBN-13   987–1–84467–119–9 (hbk)
ISBN-13   978–1–85984–722–0 (pbk)

British Library Cataloguing in Publication Data
A catalogue record for this book is available from the British Library

Library of Congress Cataloging-in-Publication Data
A catalog record for this book is available from the Library of Congress

Designed and typeset in Monotype Joanna
by illuminati, Grosmont, www.illuminatibooks.co.uk
Printed and bound in Great Britain by Bell & Bain, Scotland

Contents

PART THREE   Cinema as a Power

PART FIVE   Cinema as a Job

THE DIRECTOR

WORKING IN THE AUDITORIUM

Acknowledgments

Several individuals played a key role in launching this project. Edward Dimendberg initially suggested an application to the National Endowment for the Humanities, which Miriam Hansen and Doug Armato endorsed, and Margaret Cordi and Ann Greenberg of the Office of Sponsored Programs at New York University supervised. At the Endowment, special thanks to Elizabeth Arndt, David Wise, and Margot Backas. Mary Lea Bandy at the Museum of Modern Art gave the project early and timely support. The project was first funded by a New York University Research Challenge Fund Award—Jennifer Wicke assisted in the success of this grant application. Andrew Brower also helped in the initial stages.

As N.E.H. consultant for the book, Anthony Slide was ever generous and encouraging. Among many other contributions, he suggested researching Film Weekly, prompted attention to Nerina Shute, Gladys Hall, Alice Guy Blaché, and others, many of whom ultimately failed to make the cut, and manually retrieved and transcribed rare materials. Lea Jacobs, Charlene Regester, Heide Schlüpmann, and Stephen Bottomore, also N.E.H. consultants, all played a significant part in shaping the work. Coming aboard at a later stage, Colin Robinson, formerly at Verso, deserves very special thanks. Designer Lucy Morton was heroic. Other contributors at Verso were Jane Hindle, Tim Clark, and Rowan Livingstone. Amy Scholder, until recently publisher at the New York Verso office, singlehandedly and dramatically revived the book, at death's door at the press. For that eternal gratitude.

This project entailed a long period of research, assisted by the staff of the Fales Collection, Bobst Library, New York University; the Chicago Public Library, Harold Washington Branch, and Woodson Regional Library, Vivien G. Harsch Collection; the Chicago Historical Society, Manuscripts Division; Evelyn Cunningham of The Pittsburgh Courier; Shiela Scott of the Baltimore Afro-American; John H. Bracey, Jr. (General ed. NAACP papers); the Division of Motion Pictures and Recorded Sound of the Library of Congress, and especially Madeline Matz; the Museum of Modern Art Film Library and Film Study Center in New York, especially Charles Silver and Jytte Jensen; the British Film Institute Library, and the National Film Archive, London, and especially Elaine Burrows and Janet Moat; the British Newspaper Library at Collingdale; and the British Library, London. I also received help at the University of Southern California, Film Library, Special Collections, from Ned Comstock; at the Academy Library of Motion Picture Arts and Sciences, Los Angeles, particularly from Sam Gill; from Genette McLaurn and the staff of the Schomburg Branch of the New York Public Library; from the Special Collections Division of the Library of the University of California at Los Angeles, and especially Brigitte Kneppers of the Arts Library Special Collections; from Dr. Mayme Clayton; from Catherine Fox of the Center for American History at the University of Texas; from Harold L. Miller of the State Historical Society of Wisconsin; from the Fawcett Library, London; and from Anne Summers and Pam Porter, who advised me on the Marie Stopes papers at the Manuscripts Division, British Library. Without Linda Johnson and the staff of the Inter-Library Loan office of Bobst Library, as well as Jennifer Vinopal and the Humanities Services Visual Laboratory of Bobst Library, New York University, this project would have have been impossible.

I enthusiastically thank the following individuals for suggesting particular texts for inclusion: Mary Carbine, for Minnie Adams' "In Union is Strength"; Katie Trumpener, for Ada Negri's "The Movies" and Winifred Holtby's "Missionary Film"; Richard Crangle, for Virginia, "The Diary of a Daughter of Eve"; Stephen Bottomore, for "The Matinee Girl," Mrs. Henry Mansergh's "An Idyll of the Cinematographe," Marian Bowlan's monologue, Mrs. Whitby's "The Future of the Cinematograph," and Jessica Borthwick's "A Girl Cinematographer at the Balkan War"; Guiliana Bruno, for Matilde Serao's "A Spectatrix is Speaking to You"; Charlene Regester, for articles by Fredi Washington, Eva Jessye, and Lillian Johnson; Cari Beauchamp, for Frances Marion's "Why Do they Change the Stories on the Screen"; Karen Mahar, for Clara Beranger's "Feminine Sphere in the Field of Movies is Large Indeed"; Heide Schlüpmann for the essays and excerpts by Lu Märten, Malwine Rennert, Emilie Altenloh, Resi Langer, and Milena Jesenska; Miriam Hansen for the essays by Mary Heaton Vorse and Olivia Howard Dunbar; Annie Hill for Fannie Hurst's "An Author is the Person Who Wrote the Story"; Christopher Davis for the Emily Post excerpts and Florence M. Osborne's editorial; Kevin Hagopian for Ruth Suckow's essay; and Gerald Peary for Alice Guy Blaché's "Woman's Place in Photoplay Production" and Joy Davidman's "Women: Hollywood Version."

The following scholars directed me to fruitful areas of research, if not in person, then through their publications: Richard Koszarski, to the female directors interviewed in Film Daily; Ian Taylor, to Winifred Horrabin; Katherine Biers, to Djuna Barnes; John Belton, to Frances Taylor Patterson; Sabina Lenk, to Sarah Bernhardt; Alice Black, to Asta Nielsen's translated memoir at the Museum of Modern Art; Dan Streible, to Alice Rix and Lillie Devereux Blake; Sam Gill, to Anzia Yerzierska; and Leslie Hall, to Marie Stopes.

In addition to all the individuals mentioned above, I have benefited from discussions, encouragement, and advice from Richard Abel, Richard Allen, Kay Armatage, Mary Carbine, Hazel Carby, Oksana Chefranova, Lizabeth Cohen, Don Crafton, Jane Gaines, Marguerite Engberg, David Francis, Anthony Gibbs, Wolfgang

Greisenegger, Alison Griffiths, Ann Harris, Scott Higgins, Renata Jackson, Margot Jefferson, Phyllis Klotman, Brian Larkin, Anna McCarthy, Alison McMahan, Michelle Mednick, Annette Michelson, Susan Ohmer, Steffen Pierce, Dana Polan, Mary Poovey, Eric Santner, David Schwarz, Robert Sklar, Raphael Tennenbaum, Kim Tomadjoglou, Yuri Tsivian, and David Williams. Consultations with Charles Musser and Paul Spehr (about Antonia Dickson), Tom Gunning (about Jessie Dismorr's poem), Lee Grieveson (about the Hull House nickelodeon), Richard Maltby (about the League of Nations), Peter de Cherney (about Iris Barry), Eric Smoodin (about Walt Disney's Night), and Pearl Bowser (about The Half-century Magazine), were particularly helpful, as were discussions with Laura Marcus. Marty Broan assisted in obtaining a copy of Laura Riding's Literal Solutions: Len Lye and the Problem of Popular Films, while Andrew Broan assisted in researching Germaine Dulac; Frederick Felman gave computer help; G. M Loreto, G. V. Hoyer, and staff gave practical support, as did Chris McCauliffe; Anthony Kaes gave timely advice on translating from German; Jeanette and Laurie Gwen Shapiro helped with Anzia Yezierska; Eddie Sutton and Carol Jenkins assisted with sources; Heike Klippel provided biographical summaries of the lives of Resi Langer and Lu Märten, while Michael Loebenstein also assisted on the latter; Heide Schlüpmann provided biographical information for Malwine Rennert, and Roland Cosandey did so for Emilie Altenloh and Malwine Rennert.

For assistance with illustrations I would like to thank: Bill Ford and Julie Copenhagen, of Olin Library, Cornell University; Ted Barber; Stephen Bottomore; Wendy Holliday for Sarah Y. Mason; Alison McMahan for suggesting the photograph of Alice Guy Blaché; Mary Fisher of the Chicago Historical Society; the James Ford Library at the University of Minnesota Library, and especially Susan Stekel Rippley; the Jackson Library at the University of North Carolina Library at Greensboro, and especially Carolyn Shankle; Randy Roberts, Curator of Special Collections at Pittsburg State University Library, Kansas; and Kathryn Hodson, Special Collections Department Manager, University of Iowa Libraries. The organizers of the Pordenone International Silent Film Festival in 2000 first drew my attention to the poster adapted for the cover of Red Velvet Seat.

I would also like to thank the many research assistants who have contributed at different points: Jim Latham, (especially for forming the bibliographical database), Alice Black (for massive amounts of typing), Noah Tsika (for indexing), Torey Liepa, Augusta Palmer, Louisa Shein, Ray Uzwyshyn, Jackie Joyce, Derek Kane-Meddock, Federico Windhausen, Cynthia Lourdan, Talitha Espiritu, Sabrina Zanella-Foresi, and Ragan Rhyne.

In a year of writing, as Associate of the Carpenter Center at Harvard University, I benefited from the kind support of Chris Killip and the faculty and staff of the Department of Environmental and Visual Studies, from fruitful discussions with Robert Brain, Mary Hamer, and Alfred Guzzetti, and from the local cameradierie of Sabrina Zanella-Foresi, Katie Trainor, and Heidi Bliss. The Institut für Film-, Theater-, und Medienwissenschaft at the University of Vienna, under Wolfgang Greisenegger, generously hosted me at a later phase. My own Department of Cinema Studies at New York University has consistently backed this long effort, and in this regard I particularly

thank my chair, Chris Straayer. I also acknowledge the New York University's Emergency Research Challenge Fund for its contribution to printing and illustration costs.
  I would like to thank the student participants in a 1990s graduate seminar at New York University, and especially Ingrid Periz, who researched writings by women for the class, and later sketched drafts for sections of the editorial essays accompanying Parts Two, Three, and Four in an early incarnation of the book. Ingrid Periz also contributed to the bibliography, biographies, and annotations.
  The completion of this book has only been possible thanks to the volumes of personal support I have received since it began. I acknowledge: Klemens Gruber, for his permanent encouragement and loyalty in all domains; Lynn Siefert and Mitch Nides, for their welcomes in Los Angeles; Herbert Habersack and Lydia Miklautsch, for good spirits while writing in Vienna; Gaby Aahs, Irene Zeindlhofer, Beatrix Eugen, Babette Brose, Steffi Rappl, Eva Stockinger, and Doris Schaffler for their gifts as au pairs; and the numerous parents who have taken Caspar under their wing so I could return to the office (the Mandells, Sydels, Dreschers, Schiffman-Butterfields, Yacubs, Grubers, Scaife-Lounsberys, Kings, Normarks—former gardeners of Triphammer Road—as well as Naomi Pierce, Melissa Franklin, and Holly and Libby in Cambridge). I thank above all Beryl Lant for looking after Caspar during umpteen work stints on both sides of the Atlantic. More recently, Claude Bertemes has unstintingly contributed his many talents to getting this book out of the house. For this we will all be endlessly grateful.

                                                          Antonia Lant, New York, 2006

  I have endeavored to contact all copyright holders of items reprinted here, and acknowledge the following: CMG Worldwide for excerpts from Lillian Gish's "Beginning Young"; Washington University and Brandeis University who co-own copyright for Fannie Hurst; Reprinted by permission of The Peters Fraser and Dunlop Group Limited on behalf of: © Rebecca West, "Preface" from *Keeping it in the Dark or the Censor's Handbook*, by Causton, Bernard & G. Gordon Young, and "New Secular Forms of Old Religious Ideas"; Reprinted by permission of The Peters Fraser and Dunlop Group Limited on behalf of Rose Macauley; Jean Faulks for Ethel Mannin; Djuna Barnes reprinted with permission from the Authors' League Fund; the British Library for Marie Stopes' letter, Add. MS 58545, ff. 56–56v; "Movie," from *The Collected Poems of Muriel Rukeyser*, 1978, McGraw-Hill, New York City, © Muriel Rukeyser, by permission of William L. Rukeyser; Carcanet Press Limited for Dilys Powell and C.A. Lejeune's "Humoresque"; "Movies" from *The Freud Journal of Lou Andreas-Salomé* by Stanley A. Leavy, translator, copyright © 1964 by Basic Books, Inc., reprinted by permission of HarperCollins Publishers, Inc., and "Movies," taken from *The Freud Journal* by Lou Andreas Salomé, published in the UK by Quartet Books Ltd. in 1987; Dorothy Richardson, "Women in the Arts" reprinted with permission from *Vanity Fair*; articles by Barbara Deming, Cecilia Ager, and Elinor Gibbs, originally published in *Vogue*, republished courtesy the Condé Nast Publications, Inc.; Ada Negri, "The Movies" (27 November 1928), translated by Robin Pickering-Iazzi. Reprinted by permission of The Feminist Press at the City University of New York, from

Printed with a subvention from the Emergency Research Challenge Fund at New York University.

List of Illustrations

General Introduction

Cinema-going was the most important way in which women joined in the urban mass culture of the first half of the twentieth century. As film patrons, actresses, directors, and critics, they engaged with film as the most prominent medium of their age. They spoke of it as a precious refuge of their modern landscape, as a force of political change, as a pictorial mode, and as an opportunity both for education and for emotional transport; cinema "makes itself her weepery," as Dorothy Richardson put it.[1]

Women published their film opinions in a host of venues—daily newspapers, parent monthlies, art and literary journals, the fashion press—and in writing styles from the highbrow modernist's to the agony aunt's. Gay women, straight women, black women, white women, old women, young women, all wrote in response to film, women as unalike as social reformer Jane Addams, gossip columnist Louella Parsons, Imagist poet H.D., and internationally read Italian short-story writer Ada Negri, as well as black performer Fredi Washington, early sex-educator Catheryne Cooke Gilman, labor organizer Mary Heaton Vorse, birth-control pioneer Marie Stopes, and American suffragist Lillie Devereux Blake. Such a diverse group in itself testifies to the breadth of cinema's impact, but also points to cinema's propensity for multiple rather than singular response—there was no *one* female view of the cinema.

Filmmakers and exhibitors consciously targeted women from the start; by the 1920s popular wisdom had it that films were for women, and that they formed the majority of audiences. These regular filmgoers further shaped cinema's fortunes in their buying of, and written responses to, film magazines, the act of reading about cinema became an intrinsic part of consuming it. "The kinema must please the women or die," was C.A. Lejeune's portentous conclusion.[2] Cinema was certainly chiefly made by men, but from the 1910s into the mid 1920s, a substantial corpus of women directly contributed to moviemaking in both Hollywood and Europe. Another sector of women, particularly highly organized within the United States, attempted to modify films' effects through forming activist groups that might educate

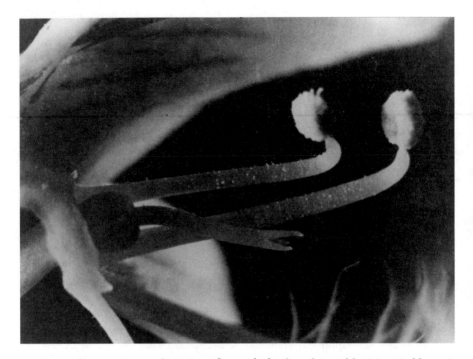

Fig. 1   Frame enlargement from *Life of a Plant*, directed by Mary Field, 1926.

viewers as well as movie executives. Studios were acutely interested in female taste, particularly as it concerned moral and stylistic matters—and several newsreel companies and cinemagazines covered fashions for women— and yet, paradoxically, scant evidence of women's views of cinema from this era survives today. Writings that might record and flesh out their reactions have escaped collection and critical attention, and the rare books of women's film journalism that were once assembled are almost entirely out of print.[3] The silent era is at the point of memory's eclipse, and women's reflections remain dispersed and unremembered, veiled by historical opinions formed through the texts of men.

The years covered by this collection—1895 to 1950—are significant for the sweeping historical and cultural phenomena they encompass; for the distinctiveness of change in women's lives they saw; and as they bear on the history of cinema itself.

The First and Second World Wars, the Depression, and the rise of fascism were events of such magnitude as to impinge on all writers. Modernist movements in art and literature (generated by Britain's Vorticist and Bloomsbury groups, for example, or in the Harlem Renaissance in the United States) left their marks on female film response, as did the political currents of communism, suffrage, Prohibition, and progressivism. This half-century spawned the spread of electrification, the commercialization of the telegraph and telephone, automobile mass production, and the invention of the airplane. (Automobile and plane races were a form of live entertainment frequently recorded on film for further profit.) Recent inventions which separately graphed or recorded sound and motion fed the nineteenth-century disciplines of psychology, and time-and-motion studies, enabling scientists to pursue new, intensive investigations of human physiology and sense perception, as they also feverishly examined processes of biological inheritance. Streamlined printing methods nurtured a tabloid press, the eruption of hoardings in the landscape, and the full-scale arrival of consumer culture, with its instruments of promotion.[4]

Vachel Lindsay characterized modernity as an explosion of images. America had been a "word-civilization" that, through the commercials "in the back of the magazines and on the bill-boards and in the street-cars," and through "the acres of photographs in the Sunday papers," was growing "more hieroglyphic every day."[5] Films, and their attendant trade and fan magazines, lobby cards, tie-ins, and programs, were part of this avalanche. Women wrote of the foyer's luxurious and vibrant collage of print and light, while its novel visual impact also disturbed female propriety: Mrs J.T. Bowen sneered at the "lurid advertisements and sensational posters," while, for cleaning up the cinema, the *Woman's Home Companion* urged they be replaced by "announcements," for, as reform-minded E. Margery Fox lamented in 1916, "the posters ... in many cases ... are even worse than the real thing."[6]

These fifty years brought momentous changes to the lives of women: the vote, significant victories in the birth-control movement, divorce reform, and reduced maternal and infant mortality rates.[7] (The right to belong to an official paramilitary organization was won in Britain in 1917, with full military status granted to two women's services in 1941.) Women's dress altered radically: the bustle and corset departed; bloomers teamed with bicycle-riding; Poiret robes swooped and draped from the shoulder and breast. The institution of the eight-hour working day and the continued trend toward more women working away from home demarcated leisure time as never before.[8] As one commentator of 1927 noted, "If in imagination we place ourselves at the year 2000, and ask what was the outstanding feature of human events in the first quarter of the twentieth century, we shall see that it was not the World War, nor the Russian Revolution, but the change in the status of women."[9]

The fifty-year span covered by this book also saw the birth of cinema, in around 1895; the growth and global expansion of the studio system in the United States following the First World War, with a rise in Hollywood's output to 500 feature-length movies annually in the 1930s (plus thousands of shorts); the year of peak movie attendance in Britain and the United States in 1946; and the decline of Hollywood and filmgoing culture from the late 1940s onwards, resulting from anti-trust suits, demoralizing and damaging Cold War government investigations, competition from television, and modified demographic habits accompanying post-war suburbanization.[10] Women's filmmaking also peaked and shrank during these years; as cinema grew into a rationalized, centralized industry following the First World War, female participation narrowed to the roles of screen actress and filmgoer, as opportunities

Fig. 2   Portrait of Ruby Berkley Goodwin in 1950.

in screenwriting, production, and direction dwindled—only one woman, Dorothy Arzner, had any prominence directing in Hollywood by the 1930s.

Research so far suggests a close synchrony between women's enthusiasms for the film medium and its economic fortunes, a historical basis for Julie Burchill's hunch that the movies went bad when they stopped making them for women.[11] If we do not have the evidence to say that the rising and falling graph of cinema's success over fifty years coincided with a similar curve in actual female attendance (let alone with women's work in the film industry), it certainly tallied with a widely documented shift in perceptions: a change from the view that women were the primary market for exhibitors, since they were the primary consumers of film (a view that held for most of the period covered by this book), to the view, held mainly after 1950, that women were less significant, and that other audience groups, such as teenagers, mattered more.[12] In the words of one journalist writing in 1950, "sometimes it seems Hollywood has clean forgotten that girls and women still make up the majority of theater audiences."[13] Even now, when Hollywood remembers its female viewers, astounding box office revenue follows: the romantic comedy *Ghost* was, until the appreciation of *Titanic* by teenage girls, the second highest grossing film of all time (behind *E.T.* and ahead of *Star Wars*).[14]

These years also witnessed the emergence and demise of the most fruitful engagement of African Americans with film (that is until the more recent efflorescence of black cinema). The relative lack of standardization of industry jobs (which also allowed entry for women), and the relative inexpensiveness of film production and exhibition before sound technology arrived in the late 1920s helped to make participation possible. The segregation of audiences, and outrage at film stereotyping, ironically fuelled an energetic and specifically African-American film culture around so-called "Race Films," films portraying black life, films advertised and reviewed in papers such as *The Chicago Defender*, *The Pittsburgh Courier*, and *The Baltimore Afro-American*.[15] In these publications, and elsewhere, in local columns and art magazines, African-American women responded to the medium. Eloyce Gist, a black Southern director of religious melodramas who musically accompanied her screenings in churches, apparently left no published account of her opinions of cinema, but Geraldine Dismond, entertainment journalist for *The Pittsburgh Courier*, and writer-cum-publicist-cum-actress Ruby Berkley Goodwin did (See Fig. 2).

For many observers, including Will Durant, quoted above, the modernity of America expressed itself quintessentially in the activity and visibility of its women. Jane Addams wrote in 1909 that, "Never before in civilization have such numbers of young girls been suddenly released from the protection of the home and permitted to walk unattended upon city streets and to work under alien roofs; for the first time they are being prized more for their labor power than for their innocence, their tender beauty, their ephemeral gaiety."[16] When Hugo Münsterberg, the German-born Harvard psychologist who would later write *The Photoplay: A Psychological Study*, penned his reflections on the United States in 1901, it was educated women who had made the greatest impact upon him: "There are beautiful and brilliant and clever and energetic women the world over, but the college girl is a new type to us, and, next to the twenty-four storey buildings, nothing excites our curiosity more than the women who have their bachelor's degrees."[17] Münsterberg simultaneously lamented another feminine type, however, the woman teacher: "the disappearance of the man from the classroom, not only of the lower schools, but even of the high schools, is distinctly alarming. The primary school is today absolutely monopolized by women teachers, and in the high school they have the overwhelming majority."[18] Women also disagreeably imposed on him at plays, where "theater managers claim that eighty-five percent of their patrons are women."[19] And Münsterberg derided "the half-educated woman [who] cannot discriminate between the superficial and the profound, and [who], without the slightest hesitation, ... effuses, like a bit of gossip, her views on Greek art or on Darwinism or on the human soul, between two spoonfuls of ice-cream."[20] He feared that "the whole situation militate[d] against the home and against the masculine control of higher culture" and was "therefore antagonistic to the health of the nation.... If the whole national civilization should receive the feminine stamp, it would become powerless and without decisive influence on the world's progress."[21]

Feminization was afoot, by almost any account.[22] And such a negative evaluation of its effects was by no means confined to studies of the United States. As Andreas Huyssen has observed, the idea that mass culture would overwhelm "real, authentic culture ... the prerogative of men," was also elegantly argued by Nietzsche.[23] However, when we look to the evidence of women's actual written engagement with the movies, we find a situation more complex and multifaceted than these malignant descriptions would suggest: women expressed as much disdain, amazement, curiosity, glee, stridency, and perplexedness towards film as those supposedly feminine reactions of weeping, emotionalism, and, in this context, vulgarity. Among female viewers was the scrutinizing reformer. If she had inherited the feminine Victorian mantle of moral guardianship, she was now armed with the organizational skills of suffrage and temperance, and could orchestrate an incisive, critical, and consequential response towards cinema, incarnating a side of modernity apparently less visible to male pundits, as well as less appetizing to later feminist scholars.

German critics Walter Benjamin and Siegfried Kracauer, writing in the 1920s and 1930s, as well as the American Gertrude Stein, have most famously articulated the ways in which cinema perfectly embodied the changing phenomena of modern life and their effects.[24] These writers focused, on the one hand, on cinema's repeating, copying form, which playfully rearranged time and location, and eroded the stability and uniqueness of images. On the other hand, they wrote of the habits this entertainment induced, and on the needs it met, which bore on the repetitive labor patterns of filmgoers, and spoke to modernity's conditions of fleetingness, decenteredness, and loss. But it seems that, for some female commentators, cinema was also emblematic of modernity precisely because recent transformations of womanhood confronted them there most starkly. Their prose explored the intertwined propositions that cinema was modern; that women had become modern; that the cinema was for women; that women were for the cinema. Even as early as 1894, Antonia Dickson (together with her brother, W.K.L.) could find in the film inventions of Thomas Edison the promise of "new forms of social and political life" based in new possibilities of collaboration between the sexes.[25] And when C.A. Lejeune penned her regular column for the *Guardian* in January 1926, and called it The *Women*, she seemed not be reviewing an upcoming movie so much as attempting to describe a powerful and syncretic web spanning the distance between the screen, with its abundance of female images, and the female appreciators arrayed across the auditorium.[26] Her title lay deliberately across these two sets of women.

Where Münsterberg had espied American women's prominence from the vantage point of cultural displacement and international comparison (he was writing about a visit he had paid to the United States from Germany in 1901), and had feared its consequences, increased female visibility pointed to enfranchisement, pleasure, and expansiveness for many female writers.[27] Violet Taylor concluded in 1930 "that

Fig. 3   Watercolour attributed to Jules Chéret, c. 1896,
for promotion of Lumière Bros films..

the cinema has contributed, in no small measure, towards the rapid strides made of late in the progress of woman's emancipation."[28] Alma Taylor, one of Britain's first film stars, seconded her view, proclaiming that cinema had "completed Mrs Pankhurst's work by establishing the Modern Girl's right to a good time and evoking her capacity for enjoying one. Women and films have been closely associated from the commencement of moving pictures. With the invention of the cinema, women secured, for the first time, a form of entertainment which was peculiarly their own."[29] Giving closer argumentation, Taylor optimistically expanded: "Already weakening, the authority of fathers, husbands and brothers over their womankind came definitely to an end with the opening of the cinema."[30]

The tone of these texts suggests that cinema made women's new participation in public life evident and concrete as nothing before it had; that the female collectivity of the auditorium was part of female suffrage; that, in some way, cinema expressed that women had arrived.[31]

The emphases of women's discussions about modernity and women at the movies varied greatly. Both Violet and Alma Taylor stressed the overtly feminist import of

Fig. 4 "If the Strike Fever Hits the Movies," by Ethel Plummer, *Shadowland*, December 1919.

the movie theater's new aggregations, finding them proof that the cinema was for women. Others, such as Catherine de la Roche, Cecelia Ager, E. Arnot Robertson, and Joy Davidman, called for new screen representations commensurate with recent alterations in gender roles.[32] De la Roche, referring above all to upheavals consequent on World War II, asserted that "Our epoch has produced probably the most fundamental changes in the relationship between men and women ever known," even as movie scripts failed to register them.[33] Still another group of women wrote of the relief cinema brought, from modern drudgery and the labors of motherhood, offering female workers, as well as the masses generally, respite from long factory hours of regimentation.[34]

Another strand of discussion, less specifically tied to femininity, described the malaise of modernity's unmoored, lusterless being, one who existed in a culture of jazz, cynicism, and sensationalism, and who, in Barbara Low's view, demanded "easy and effortless" diversion.[35] Cinema both expressed and mollified this being's condition. In 1931, June Head proposed that "in its development, the cinema has been intrinsically bound up with the development of general thought and feeling during the last fifteen years. By virtue (or vice) of the combination of emotional stimulus and relaxation which it affords, it is completely in accord with the spirit of the age, which is all for violent superficial activity cloaking a period of mental enervation."[36] Iris Barry, comparing cinema to theater, found that cinema "soothed and drugged … after the feverish activity of a day of modern life.… Humanity has almost forgotten how to wonder, to dream for itself: it ought to thank heaven for providing it the constant sedative, the escape from the self, which it so direly needs, in the little cheap shadowy picture houses."[37] Barry found in cinema a needed and compelling suspension of modernity's onrush, one profoundly new in its structure and forms of reception. This brief sampling of women's commentaries

on cinema and modernity can end with Dorothy Richardson, who, together with Maboth Moseley, appreciated the medium as an avenue to worldliness and other forms of indiscrete knowledge appropriate to the new age.[38] In fact, Richardson's investigations into the phenomenon of cinema might be compared with those of Siegfried Kracauer of the same era; she wrote of the "new mental climate" she lived in, born of "uncertainty, noise, speed, movement, rapidity of external change," and of the cinema itself, which contributed "more than any other single factors ... to the change in the mental climate wherein Everyman has his being."[39]

All in all, with its extraordinary capacity to reproduce and rearrange time and space, with its sudden effects, and what Miriam Hansen has termed its "peculiar interpenetration of public and private realms," as well as its inviting, communal, ritual form, women claimed cinema as the art by which to recognize, enjoy, cope with, and even have illustrated, the contemporary.[40]

There was never a cinema without women. On 20 May 1891, Mrs Thomas Edison invited 147 club women to her husband's laboratory to view a Kinetoscope prototype.[41] Writing of a screening at Charles Aumont's fashionable brothel that had opened on 22 June 1896, Maxim Gorky irksomely recalled the "provoking laughter of a woman" alongside him.[42] In 1897, Dr. John Macintyre demonstrated X-ray cinematographic loops of frog leg motion to the Glasgow Philosophical Society's Ladies' Night.[43] Reports of Kinetoscope parlors in 1894 illustrated women staring into peepholes, while the earliest Lumière posters, of 1896, showed hatted women before the screen.[44] In advertising film equipment, female imagery allegorized cinema's spirited, technological power; a woman's sinuous figure might entwine with the apparatus or, as in an Italian promotional slide of the late 1890s, the projected image might emanate uncannily from her opened cape.[45] (See Fig. 3) And female performers were among the first subjects of the first moving films, soon coming to dominate the screen.[46] (See Fig. 4.6)

The effects of feminine prominence (before the screen, on the screen, and in advertising) snowballed until journalists could write of the "petticoat policies" of Los Angeles, "a city that worships women and women's beauty," and fans could proclaim Mae West as a single-handed inspiration for the National Legion of Decency.[47] A cartoon published following America's Red Summer of 1919 imagined the film industry decimated if women were also to strike.[48]   (See Fig. 4)

Women confronted this plethora of images dominated by themselves every day, and in ways and to an extent that they had never had to before. A widespread and elaborate entangling of movies, stardom, and womanhood ensued, expressed through a fully ramified fan culture. It entailed, among other things, confessions and newspaper debates about racial passing, in both film and life.[49] In describing "an experimental film programme" shot in Vugiri (in Tanganyika, present-day Tanzania) in 1935 by a white missionary crew, Marcus Garvey—the black nationalist leader who had inspired a "Back to Africa" movement in the United States—hinted at some repercussions for women of living in this image maze.[50] As editor of *The Black Man*, where his commentary appeared, Garvey wrote of the experimental film that, "all actors in the films … [were] natives [but] one of the difficulties was to find women actors. [For], unlike their Western sisters, the African women [had] no film star complex, and in many cases female parts had to be taken by boys" (this lack of bedazzlement was one of the reasons that there seemed, as yet, modest hope of "unearthing an African Garbo").[51] Garvey understood that African women's distance from modernity's picture bombardment also distanced them from developing the fan's appetite to be on screen, while his remarks simultaneously suggested the profound impact these feminine hieroglyphs had on African-American women (and at least by inference, on their white sisters).[52] He described the circuitry by which the movie-struck girl desired to fashion herself after the screen in her makeup and clothing, to the point of even wishing to appear in the movies, while drawing our attention to a geographical and cultural circumstance in which the circuit had, as yet, failed to complete itself.

Models for emulation came from screen hairstyles, costuming, and roles—as one critic put it, the movies "furnish a complete record of etiquette."[53] Western filmgoers invested weekly (or even nightly) to slake their thirst, and read fan magazine tales (synchronized to specific film releases) of rapid success, class mobility, and phenomenal fortune.[54] Margaret Turnbull's adventure-romance *The Close-Up* pursued these themes in tracing a young woman's journey down the feminine image stream.[55] Set in 1916, the novel describes Kate Lawford's rags-to-riches rise from secretary in the East to star in the West. Jilted by her boyfriend Jeffrey Grace, who, unbeknown to her, suffers from TB and wants to spare her the nursing-duty consequences, Lawford heads to California from New York with a new film company as their stenographer. There she is spotted by the director, hits the big time, has the "facts of her life as might be colored to interest the public spread before them in motion picture and other magazines," and abandons all when the miraculously clear-chested Jeffrey (now working as a secret agent) triumphs in arresting German spies.[56] As war for the United States is declared, Kate and Jeffrey are retiring (presumably temporarily) to a cabin in the redwoods.

Right from the start, from its epigraph, the novel signals its interest in the relation of women to images, and particularly their own image: "'A close-up?' repeated Kate, 'I don't think I understand.' 'It's a movie term. You've seen a face so magnified that it filled the whole screen?' Kate nodded. 'Well, that's a close-up.'" When Kate sees rushes of her first, own close-up, later in the book, she sees "horrible caricature. Every fault that she knew from long study of and familiarity with her face was suddenly made public property."[57] From now on, the novel tells us, she had to examine her walk, the fit of her dress, the motion of her face as she talked. A parallel shock was experienced by ingénue Queenie, heroine of Zelda Fitzgerald's "Our Own Movie Queen," who "gasped as there was a sudden close-up of herself" on the screen; Dorothy Richardson suspected that a film titled "*A Mirror of Audiences*, with many close-ups," might quiet voluble female filmgoers, presumably also because of the shock they would suffer at seeing themselves displayed and enlarged.[58]

For cinema's first avant-garde, and particularly the filmmakers Jean Epstein, Dziga Vertov, and Sergei Eisenstein, magnification through the film lens constituted a singular and supremely modern mode of scrutinizing and exposure—a revelatory epistemology via an optical machine. But where they celebrated the close-up's unmasking power, female response was often ambivalent.[59] Actresses Asta Nielsen and Betty Balfour spoke of the close-up's challenges to acting, while school teacher E. Margery Fox, out to protect her students from cinema in 1917, found close-ups particularly revolting: "faces are so large that you can see the pores of the skin."[60] Perhaps, for Fox, the close-up epitomized cinema's overall disrespect for time-honored codes of interpersonal distance and decency. The close-up's pillowing flesh and breathing stomata were tantamount to pornography. For Kate Lawford, the multiplication and enlargement of her person effected through the close-up, held under the eyes of a thousand consuming stares, was the wellspring of commodification, escorting the erstwhile uniqueness of her face off into circulated infinity.

These women emphasize above all the shock of witnessing one's own face, as if cinema sundered the integrity of the self by splitting identity from likeness, essence from appearance. Such close-ups may also have triggered, in viewers, recollections of methods of criminology, phrenology, and racial classification, by which photographed serried heads, accompanied by measurements and descriptions, had built up data banks of types and their tendencies, procedures which had motivated the Biograph Company's one-shot, 1904 motion picture, *Photographing a Female Crook*. In this short film, as the camera approaches a close-up of the suspected woman, she, restrained by policemen, but forced to confront the lens, contorts her face in attempting to camouflage her identity. Perhaps these actresses' sights of themselves, expanded and projected on screen, were redolent of such judgemental uses of the photographed face.

Close-ups were the most gigantic countenances popularly seen, save those gracing ancient monuments and modern billboards.[61] If, as Jean Cocteau once suggested, to look in the mirror was to see death at work, the scrutiny of the face enacted in the cinematic female close-up exposed precisely femininity's dance with mortality.[62] C.A. Lejeune described the way audiences of the 1920s traced and remembered their own lengthening years by the measure of movie star maturation, a process we still feel intensely in the television ritual of Academy Award ceremonies with their phalanxes of former celebrities.[63] Rebecca West attributed an (undocumented) diminution in the use of the close-up in the late 1920s precisely to the ageing of cinema's first generation of female stars, so as to let "the experienced actress reap the benefit of her years" without sharing her wrinkles and lines.[64] Cinema was a medium haunted by the image of the mirror, with its camera's peering intrusiveness into detail; in all of film's vocabulary, the close-up was the figure most reminiscent of this mirror for the female actress (as we might also imagine it was for women filmgoers).

If cinema was felt to be for women, was felt to be used predominantly by them, and was drenched with the female image—most intensely in the stunning impact of the female close-up—we can see why the image itself also came to seem feminine. So closely entwined were women and cinema that a description of women's new sartorial freedoms might have announced the power of film itself: "the modern girl is boldly emancipated from the dignified impediments and impenetrable accoutrements that once chained her into a breathless immobility."[65] While casting Kate as too morally "good" to submit to movie stardom or succumb to the seductions of its wealth (Jeff is, of course, always against her lipstick), Margaret Turnbull's perceptiveness about the impact of the enlarged visage in The Close-Up, and of images in general in young women's lives, surely corralled the latter as readers. Kate's journey pointed to that of all women—outside Tanganyika—as they adapted and transformed in the face, the most prominent and literal face, of twentieth-century iconic life.

Why have women written on film? What can we make of what they have said? Have black and white women had different things to say? Does this writing differ from that of male observers?

Compiling this collection provokes endless queries, and significantly renews opportunity for examining feminine typicality—a controversial proposition, dismissed by some for its essentialism, but pursued at various times by Susan Gubar and Sandra Gilbert, and Hélène Cixous, to name but three, with vigor.[66] With a sample of 160-odd items, Red Velvet Seat asks us to mull the potential for a distinctly feminine film-writing with more evidence.[67] While sexual roles of men and women were changing during this era, they were still, typically, quite dissimilar from one another, perhaps more so than differences between one woman and another. Women had a structurally different experience of modernity: they experienced different social duties and biological capacities; different, and usually narrower means of access to culture, knowledge, and public life; and different work patterns, not least in that the jobs accessible to men and to women were different. It seems possible, given all these distinctions, that women's essays about film would exhibit their own flavor.

Women wrote on film for a host of reasons. For some, it was a form of activism, as in the coordination and orchestration of efforts to reform motion pictures. For others, it was a lucrative career. Mary Roberts Rinehart submitted her stories and essays (on film among other topics) to popular journals geared to female audiences, reaping a fortune. Conversely, Alice Guy Blaché penned her autobiography (published posthumously) to restore the memory of her forgotten film-directing career (see Fig. 5). Class consciousness, or at least class interests, impelled other writing: Minnie Pallister complained that "the reason why so much nonsense is written about cinemas is because the wrong people write about them" (although this couldn't "be helped," she added, "because the only people who really know what cinemas are, are, as a rule, inarticulate"), while Marie Stopes called on the privileged to neglect film no longer.[68] Cinema offered a tourism of the lower orders, those of concern to educators like Jane Addams, E. Margery Fox, and Louise de Koven Bowen, as well as to novelist Matilde Serao, who visited the cinema to discover how she should write for it.[69] Harriette Underhill and Fannie Hurst professed to disdain film's association with this class, but others relished the chance the cinema gave to observe the classes—but not the races—mingling.[70]

The journal Close Up's raison d'être was to write criticism which might bring a new cinema culture into being. Bryher and H.D. wrote for this cause as Close Up editors, while Iris Barry posed a similar sentiment in her own book, urging her readers to support the "non-sentimental, the experimental films, the ones that cause new blood to come into the unwieldy carcass of cinematography."[71] Other women wrote to protect their medium against film. Dorothy L. Sayers vigorously defended her detective thrillers against weak screen interpretations.[72] Others wrote of film, even though it threatened their livelihoods. Modernist writers might have feared film for this reason, even if, as Dorothy Richardson was to argue, filmgoing promised to send audiences back to live theater.[73] But these writers' formal interests—in instantaneity, simultaneity, and duration—drew them to a medium portending to evoke, in extraordinary new ways, consciousness in operation.[74] Here lay Dorothy Richardson's love of cinema. Laura Riding, typically an abstruse author, was sufficiently taken with film to pen a screenplay for Alexander Korda. Even Virginia Woolf, who hardly went to the movies, was compelled by the idea of cinema.

A motion picture arguably inspired Rebecca West's two-volume epic on Yugoslavia, which she began by recounting her eagerness to see the newsreel of the 1934 assassination in Marseilles of Alexander Karageorgevitch, King of Yugoslavia, as she was recovering from an illness.[75] West writes of arranging a private screening (the film had completed its regular run), which she "peered at ... like an old woman reading the tea-leaves in her cup."[76] After repeated viewings, and after writing three pages of detailed description of the film's frames (a technique scholars have subsequently come to term "close analysis"), she remains unable to make sense of them—the unreeling celluloid will not explain its recorded act of violence, will not yield history.[77] West wrote the rest of her book to release this blockage.

But the modernist and populist strands of written female response to film are not readily separable: Margaret Anderson, in the Little Review she founded, with its small circulation and passion for formal innovation, explored the genre of the fan magazine letter; and Djuna Barnes found aesthetically inventive ways of producing nevertheless publishable film journalism by typesetting her writing in smatterings of different typographic styles, and sprinkling it with doodles and drawings.[78]

Most African-American women wrote about cinema impelled by its promised democracy; it offered the possibility of representation. Suffering the violence and privations of racism, they proclaimed the need for blacks to be seen, and not simply as white fantasies imagined them. At a banquet given in April 1939 in honor of Jesse A. Graves, "colored official" of the Screen Actors' Guild, Graves had put the argument this way:

> Never in the history has a large number of people assembled, nor a street scene where there wasn't some negroes present.... We are entitled to more employment and realism in pictures. Not just some far-fetched ideas thrust upon the American people. We spend enough money to warrant employment of colored actors in all pictures, and many should be stars. I cannot recall any historical movement or any economic endeavor that has affected the entire nation that didn't affect the American Negro.[79]

Fredi Washington wrote approvingly of Jules Dassin's *The Naked* City (a police investigation movie shot on location in New York in 1946) because it "cast negro actors in bit parts." As she went on,

> Nowhere will you go in all of New York City where you will not find negroes in all capacities. Street, elevator, subway, department stores, private and civil offices, in fact anywhere you look in New York, you will find a negro, so why not make films realistic by using negroes wherever and whenever they can be used? It would make for better and more normal films, to say nothing of the experience and badly needed work it will give the negro actor.[80]

The engagement of female black writers with film, from Minnie Adams's urging that more blacks should be loyal to black-owned cinemas, to the black cosmetician's protest that, "I am not judging a whole race of people by the ideas of a moving picture producer—my knowledge comes from living with them," is, above all, contestatory, bearing on the racist conditions surrounding the screen, as conveyed in the black newspaper phrases, "sepia Hollywood," and "sepia Cinderella," the latter a term for the fleeting possibilities of black female stardom.[81] Black women's urgent interest in the relation of film to life accounts for their relative prominence in the fourth section of this book, that part which assembles women's film criticism, with its analyses of film's images and plots. Such an approach to understanding cinema gave greatest purchase on the burning question of race representation, the question of whose version of black life was to be produced and seen.

In departing this brief survey of why women have written on film (a question answered throughout this collection), we should pause to reflect on the status of this writing. What kind of things can it tell us? What can it not?

These writings do not generate a picture of mass taste. Although authors mention box office hits, such as *Gone with the Wind* and *Imitation of Life*, and while superstar Rudolph Valentino's name crops up more than once, we would not guess from the opinions expressed here that romances, comedies, and the so-called woman's film were the most popular genres of feature film for women during these years, while "babies and battleships" were their preferred items in newsreels.[82] Emilie Altenloh's survey of German audiences in 1913 comes closest, in this collection, to satisfying any query into overall audience preference, but the bulk of selections convey more individuated opinions. From the comments of Janet Flanner and Ada Negri, for example, we might conclude a feminine partiality for Westerns.[83] Certainly, Gladys Hall, Harriette Underhill, and Colette can stand for the many women (not collected here) who focused their writing on screen stars, fashion, luxury, diet, and shopping (interests of the female audience at large), but the demands of E. Arnot Robertson, Madeleine Carroll, Catherine de la Roche, Cecelia Ager, and Joy Davidman for expanded female screen roles, and Iris Barry's and Barbara Deming's disappointments at couple-centered plots, may well represent idiosyncratic appetites.[84]

As we try to grasp why the cinema has been so important to women, perusing women's writings can offer clues irrecoverable in any other way. Their chronicles offer a potentially more historically valid and nuanced method for understanding film reception than the practice of hypothesizing old films' meanings for an earlier female audience solely through reanalyzing the film texts themselves (though this technique has certainly brought results). That said, we should also remember that these writings are retellings, a discourse on viewing, a retrospective published version, often commissioned or paid for by a magazine, a product of professional or volunteer reform activity, and not the experience of viewing itself. But though we can never recapture any "pure" instance of original reception—no direct source is, or ever will be available to us of the Ur-moment of historical consumption—we might appreciate the relatively short temporal gap that intervened between actually going to the movies, and these accounts. These are writings done at the time, not autobiographical texts penned, or remembered orally, forty years on. This does not make them truer, or more honest, than a film outing recalled much later (in an oral history interview, for example), but it makes them different, accounts inviting us to reflect on the significance of cinema for these women, recorded as it entered their lives, without the benefit of hindsight. These opinions, in their details of seating design, screen glamor, and star "suction," are a residue of a particularly evanescent social form, a small trace of the massive scale and diversity of women's passion for film.[85]

Many of the topics covered in women's film journalism suggest no obvious, immediate relation to gender. It seems that, for both men and women, film unavoidably summoned discussion of nationality, and especially Americanness. Women's writings, as men's, engaged the gross political movements of the day—Anderson and Flanner vied with Prohibition, while Marie Stopes and Margherita G. Sarfatti likened cinema's power to that of the Russian Revolution.[86] Central public figures appear, from Mussolini to Eleanor Roosevelt; we gain a feeling for the era, its incidents, and its major metropolises, as well as its films.

Primitiveness, as a concept, assisted both male and female writers in their efforts to describe cinema. This theme had shaped discussions (and the making) of modern European art, where, in the painting and sculpture of Henri Matisse and Pablo Picasso, and the German Expressionists, for example, it described a revolutionary plastic and pictorial vocabulary of design and drawing, adapted and borrowed from African and other sources.[87] In writing on cinema, its use was somewhat different; ideas of the ancient or primitive explained the reception of film more than its creation, illuminating relations between audience and screen rather than the director and his or her set. In linking the movie theater to the Attic temple, H.D. compared the film star to the pagan idol; B. Bergson Spiro Miller discussed a female spectator, "face raised and serious," as one who "might have been staring through the symbols of some shrine at a life remote, mysterious and inexpressibly beautiful."[88]

If primitivism did shed light on the medium's form, such explanations ultimately still drew on the movies' deep appeal. Lillian Gish connected film's universal success to a basis in Aboriginal communication.[89] Cinema's global popularity was "proof" of the elemental nature of film's mode of telling.[90] The medium's transparency (its verisimilitude) resembled the assumed simple-mindedness of the non-Western audience.[91] It was heir to antique pictographic systems of visual communication, and thus a contemporary instantiation of cultural beginnings.[92] Iris Barry even found the photogenetic significance that objects acquired on screen to be a leftover from animism, a form of belief practiced outside the cinema only by children and the unsophisticated.[93]

In a strand of sometimes earnestly appreciative appraisal, several writers, including Barbara Deming, Iris Barry, Ruth Suckow, H.D., and Rebecca West, proposed that the oldest foundations of human culture had not disappeared with the onset of modernity, but rather were to be found, and satisfied, at the cinema; the cinema answered essential but now buried psychological needs.[94] For West and Suckow, cinema reinvented, or replaced religious ritual, while filmgoing worship and indulgence salved the new age's ills. Our modern selves, unable to dream (Barry) and overrationalized (C.P. Gilman) found succor in film spectatorship, which offered images and fantasies otherwise denied in the onward force of rationalization.[95] Cinema offered magic to a disenchanted world.

The vocabulary of evolution haunted such accounts of cinema's atavism. Mechanisms of heredity had been so ubiquitously debated throughout the nineteenth century that the conceptual underpinnings of the arguments had become second nature—Darwinism went with ice cream, as Münsterberg had noted.[96] In order to understand Elizabeth Bowen's "racial child," who re-emerged before the cinema screen, for example, we might recall ingrained neo-Lamarckian principles of the day—notions that ontogeny recapitulated phylogeny, that intraorganismal development, the growth of the child, replayed, in miniature, the complex patterns and vast sweep of biological history, and that milieu and environment were critical to these unfoldings, in that they could bring about a heritable change in the structure and functioning of human organs.[97] Under the conditions of cinema—in everything from its "dim sapphire gloom" to the semaphoric gestures of its screen—the original stirrings of a human being, incipient and black (as the phrase "racial child" hints) are to be seen and felt again.[98] Bowen valued the attention and massage this early child received; it was one of the reasons she went. For Virginia Woolf, the peculiar qualities of life ("the antics of our kind") were generalized and distilled in being processed by cinema, so that looming screen figures, in their actions, expressions, and motions, appeared archetypal. Watching them from a distance—the inevitable condition of the film viewer for Woolf—we could "endow one man with the attributes of the race."[99] Like Bowen, Woolf also characterized moviegoers as twentieth century savages, analogizing current film production to the ignorant hammering and thumping of "bright-eyed, naked men" on sophisticated musical instruments.[100]

For all these writers, cinema unavoidably brought back into view a history of development that modern efforts of invention might have been expected to banish. It revealed, in the links between its screen forms and its reception, the erupting continuation of unshed origins. This aspect of these texts—when writers broach these themes—offends on grounds of racism, as indeed Dorothy Richardson's review of Hearts of Dixie recently has.[101] Because of the era's widespread practices of imperialism and colonialism, fed by disciplines also informed by racially hierarchical principles, the human race, as referred to in Bowen's "racial child," or in Woolf's observation of the screen's condensation of "the attributes of the race," is always in some oblique, if not antagonistic relation to "the race" summoned by Minnie Adams, as she promotes the formation of black audiences.[102] Such rhetorics are a rampant and unavoidable trait of writings of the period, even if some of their unacceptability arises in part from the very ambivalence of the meanings they construe: does "the race" include or exclude certain races? Rather than desist from reprinting such items, Red Velvet Seat aims to encourage examination of this context. Comparison and interaction of opinions on cinema, as they bear on race and primitivism, will ultimately widen and illuminate discussion of the ways in which cultural perceptions of race and gender have shaped discourse about the cinema, and vice versa.[103]

Is there a difference between men and women's writings on the cinema? The absence of a collection of men's writings from this era, one compiled from publication sources comparable to the ones used here, mitigates against a certain straightforward, if perhaps superficial evaluation of similarities and differences, by which the attraction of certain stars to the male or female pen might be discerned, for example. In addition, Red Velvet Seat's claim that there was not a historical female spectator makes it eager to stress dissimilarities among women, and chary of generalizing. But let us make some observations.

While women sometimes found cinema to harbor a residual primitive force, they also understood it as intimately linked to a new kind of historical sense, one born of modernity's great convulsion, World War I.[104] This had erased the massive empires of Central and Eastern Europe, left 10 million dead, and wrought such chaos as to pull in its wake the catastrophe of World War II. Both wars altered the demographics of cinema's clientele while boosting attendance. (During World War I, the appeal of actuality films attracted more middle-class filmgoers to the cinema in Great Britain, while women's filmgoing went up during both wars—the Great War left a surplus of women quite palpable in European accounts of movie congregations.[105]) Belligerence prevailed during most of the period covered by this book (there were the Spanish-American, Balkan, and Spanish civil wars, besides the two world wars). We might imagine that the traumatic setting of mass death had very different consequences for non-combatant and mourning women than for soldiers, and it does indeed seem that women's remove from the field of battle shaped their understanding of cinema. Both metaphorical and literal references to war's distance (or intrusion) mark their discourse on cinema.[106]

The direct interaction of war and cinema was high on women's agendas: Marie Stopes, writing during the First World War, found cinema's potency in constructing a nation's "conception of the universe" a threat grave enough to warrant extreme vigilance over the importation of foreign films, while Mary Losey, during the Second World War, planned a study on "Films for the Community at War."[107] Women (as well as men) enthusiastically debated whether filmed images of war might incite or inhibit aggression, especially in the young and sheltered (audiences above all under women's charge).[108] War lay just off-stage in Lillie Devereux Blake's visceral response to the violence of a boxing picture, fought while the Spanish-American War also raged.[109]

War was the unavoidable benchmark of the real, making cinema's luxury glitter more brilliantly in Colette's besieged Paris, and making the deluded screen aspirations of an ageing contralto-manqué pall in comparison with the losses of bereft mothers of sons in Dieppe in Katherine Mansfield's London.[110] Malwine Rennert hoped that cinema might tap war's high-flying energy in order to nourish the inner, spiritual worlds of returning soldiers; war was transforming German audiences from mere onlookers into fully living and "experienced" citizens—there was no knowing what greatness they might now demand of modernity's only invention that did not serve destructive ends.[111]

The very possibility of filming war made Florence Kiper Frank "shudder at sophistication," at the terrifying spatial and temporal implosion of witnessing material acts of war from afar.[112] Her poem records her watching newsreels of Belgian refugees escaping bursting shells, while she simultaneously listens to a cameraman, standing live before her, in the auditorium, as he recalls the very same battlefield (now seen on the screen), as he had filmed it but three weeks ago. For Frank, the heretofore unimaginable scope of war's awfulness was made legible by the newmedium—cinema could press the fighting front into the home front, fuse two geographical points, interleave and transfer consciousnesses and fears.

Lu Märten and Virginia Woolf came to their very conceptions of cinema through war. Märten's Marxism shaped her analysis of the power of art: "After all, if the claim that things determine our consciousness and not the consciousness the things

Fig. 5   Alice Guy Blaché directing *My Madonna*, 1915.

is rightfully part of our scientific foundations, we must conclude that our sensory reactions, too, can change, and do not forever remain the same."[113] For Märten, part of film's essential character lay in its unique capacity to represent mass events and mass experience, setting them against "vast spatial backgrounds in general."[114] Her chief example of this new, epic subject matter was the industrial carnage of World War I, "which could only be portrayed through film."[115] For Woolf it was the spatio-temporal remove of cinematic form that evoked the enormity of war's rupture, rather than any verisimilitudinous capacity it might have for grasping war's gigantic scale and substance. The absentness of film (it was but a record of an event, now reduced to flickering light across a wall) reverberated with that abyss, which cut off, forever, a former way of life, a world "gone beneath the waves."[116] This temporal and spatial dislocation resulted in a "queer sensation," as Woolf put it, an experience of viewing stamped by loss, for, if war had been unbearably real, by 1926 (the date of Woolf's essay) it was becoming something else, a marker of past deaths, of innocence erased.[117] Where Märten had emphasized the cinema as the best medium for permanently witnessing, for the public, measureless, modern events, Woolf wrote as a lonely, single viewer, tracing over the gap between what she now knew of the past and what the screen had preserved—brides were now mothers; ushers, once ardent, were now silent.[118]

Some writers of the era speculated as to whether women's perceptions functioned differently from men's for biological or cultural reasons. One notion, with some currency, posed that women thought habitually in pictures, while men naturally aspired to abstract concepts: "When men think pictorially they unsex themselves," wrote Holbrook Jackson in 1938, attacking the extent of illustrations and graphics in London tabloids.[119] In 1894, the Dicksons, closely associated with Thomas Edison's laboratory, proposed that this sort of difference could be harmonized through marriage, which united "woman's perceptive wisdom with the rational wisdom of the man."[120] Variants of this idea supported subsequent claims that cinema was a career for women: June Mathis found women to be the best screenwriters because they thought in pictures; Florence Osborne found women "good at picturization"; Barry found women "more visually-minded on the whole"; while director Alice Guy Blaché suggested that women were uniquely suited to photoplay production because they were used to thinking of things, including themselves, in terms of looking at them.[121]

The invocation of sex-linked characteristics should not surprise us, for this was also, after all, the era of the emergence of psychoanalysis, a discipline acutely attentive to the social and psychological aspects of sexual identity, and one arising (not coincidentally) in an age which was roundly challenging gender roles. The historical confluence of the beginnings of cinema and psychoanalysis in the late nineteenth century—endeavors born of the same cultures, fantasies, and pressures—had made psychoanalysis visible and available as a creative tool for understanding film as early as the 1920s. Sigmund Freud's core concepts were so familiar in the United States by that time that writers as unalike as Anzia Yezierska and Charlotte Perkins Gilman could refer to them when discussing film while omitting Freud's name.[122] Barbara Low, one of the first British Freudians, examined the effects of cinema in psychoanalytic terms, publishing an article on the subject in the journal Close Up in 1927 (itself an organ substantially shaped by psychoanalytic theory and analysis), while the notion of the still camera as a phallic symbol was also well established by this date.[123] Rebecca West deployed a psychoanalytic framework for explaining the transfer and survival of European rituals in the United States in the 1920s, paying special attention to film, while Helene Deutsch, reading films as indicative of human psychological traits, found "numerous pictures in popular movies or magazines" (above all the representation of King Kong) to express feminine passive and masochistic longings.[124] Interestingly, Deutsch is the only female writer of the period who overtly draws on psychoanalysis and cinema in order to answer a question about gender—West was interested in cultural and national traits (though the female star played a special role in her schema), Low in child development in general. These women often wrote with deep awareness of themselves as female, consuming a screen that may have forgotten them (Powell went to films, "however manly"), but psychoanalysis did not immediately appear to them to be the key to unlocking and explaining female spectatorship in particular, as it was to beckon later on.[125]

Sometimes women used the language of geometry to specify a sexual dimension for cinema (as did men). If this amounted to little more than the commonplace search for plots with "a feminine slant" or "feminine angle," occasionally it reached into understandings of the screen's attraction, motion, and form.[126] In Cecelia Ager's words, "there is something about curved lines, Miss [Mae] West finds, that gets the roving eye. Straight lines, she has noticed, seem to lead it elsewhere."[127] Colette mourned the waning of West's curves, as she lost weight between 1934 and 1938, while, in conversation with her "familiar," dressed as a cavalier, Lotte Reiniger proffered that a platform of her film art lay in its curves, soft and feminine, as they played against its direct and masculine diagonals, a combination orchestrated across the flat surface of the paper on which she positioned her silhouetted paper shapes (as well as in the deep space of the ballet stage she wished to evoke).[128]

But women's writing of cinema's sexual dimensions did not remain within the banal frame of geometry, or, indeed, within the screen's frame with its various versions of the star's body. Judging from the figures of speech, and suggestive wording they chose, many women experienced filmgoing itself to be an eroticized affair. Elizabeth Bowen described movie entrances as "voluptuously promising," and wrote of feeling "home again" when settled in her seat; Zelda Fitzgerald's characters became "rigid with excitement" as "the red velvet curtains parted to show the screen," while C.A. Lejeune found "the small cushioned seats" of the cinema to have a feminine build, the picture palace's furry velour metonymically securing a woman's entitlement to sit there.[129] Once the picture begins, continued Lejeune, "a woman can get into close touch with the shadows she has longed to meet, can seem to know them, ... share with them the most intense experiences."[130]

We find andrological, spermatic locutions: in 1908, Lucy France Pierce described the illumination of a theater's exterior as a "fascinating ribbon of incandescent light [which] wriggles around and around the word 'motion'"; Virginia Woolf fell upon an eruptive description for fluff, trapped in the projector's gate, which cast upon the screen a "monstrous, quivering tadpole," that "swelled to an immense size, quivered, bulged, and sank back again into non-entity"; Jessie Dismorr, in her poem "Matinee," watched "shapes quicken and pass."[131] Women's rapture, according to these writings, lay in venturing through the cinema's outer portal, nestling in a seat, observing curtains open, and sensing the onset and process of projection. Their sensual phrasing vividly communicates an adventure in sentience, a thrill merely deepened in the screen's voyeuristic play of light.[132]

The representation of female sexuality—in films about abortion, birth, birth control, and sexual hygiene, for example—was also of concern to female writers, as well as filmmakers.[133] Lois Weber's film *Where Are My Children?* (1916) criticized abortion as a means of dealing with unwanted pregnancy. It attracted the scrutiny of the British Board of Film Censors as well as the ire of British birth control pioneer Marie Stopes, who penned a letter, destined for the London *Times*, seeking to have the film banned.[134] Winifred Ray, Bryher, and "Norma Mahl" all wrote about Goskino's *Abortion* (1924), Ray dubbing it "the famous film, *Abort*," a film which was very popular with Soviet audiences, and a financial success but which we since seem to have forgotten.[135] Dr. Marthe Ruben Wolff introduced *Abortion* to the World League for Sexual Reform Congress in London in 1929, and advised viewers that, while they should "not expect to see the fine photography and technical treatment of an Eisenstein or Pudovkin film" (since the film was "about six years old"), they should note "how in Soviet Russia the greatest artists, painters, actors, and so on, are not ashamed to serve the commission for public health."[136]

Heralded advances in Soviet health care caught the attention of women on both sides of the Atlantic. Abortion was illegal in Britain and the United States, although it played a significant, if hidden role in Hollywood, where studios kept abortion doctors on retainer so that forced abortions of inconvenient impregnations, even of married stars, might keep industry schedules and financial ambitions protected.[137] It is in this context that we must understand these writers' appetites for discussing this theme in Soviet film, whether they came across it in the largely documentary form of *The Abortion*, or in fictional dramas like Abram Room's *Bed and Sofa* (1927), which the *Close Up* editorial team reviewed in great detail. The film portrayed a *menage à trois* in which Ludmilla became pregnant by Vladimir, her husband Nikolai's friend. While waiting in a private hospital for an abortion (a choice and service needed by a myriad types of women, the film shows us), Ludmilla decides to have the child but leave both men; as the nurse informs Nikolai and Vladimir as they arrive later to collect Ludmilla from the ward, "she changed her mind." On account of its "non-propagandistic" method, *Close Up* pronounced the film "one of the most momentous contributions to film progress yet achieved," adding, "We would remind *Close Up* readers again, that birth control is completely legalised in Russia. Films, showing in detail the dangers of irregular abortion are freely shown, and all information supplied." It was with this film that Bryher "discovered Russia" and began to "see every Russian film available," for *Bed and Sofa* was the first film to attack life itself.... It was this world taking a step forward." While she found Ludmilla's final choice implausible—here Room fails—Bryher concluded, in her 1929 book on Soviet cinema that it "must remain one of the great films of the world."[138] We can conclude that, for women, Soviet film was clearly of interest as much for its subject matter, mode of address, and goals of education, as for its experimental style.

Left-wing journalist Agnes Smedley, reporting on the German Association of Educational and Cultural Films Congress held in Berlin in May 1926, discussed *False Shame*, a venereal disease film produced under the auspices of the Berlin Board of Health, which combined shots of actual patients with fictional footage.[139] For Smedley, the film was "intimately connected with a romance to hold the attention of the public," for while it was "in places a study by diagrams, ... running throughout it [was] a drama that at times threatened to be a tragedy." Smedley added that the "deeply human truths" of the film safeguarded it from misinterpretation, or the possibility of suggestiveness: "It is not possible to view it in a vulgar light, for its nature is so serious and scientific that even the foul-minded could see it and profit."[140]

Whatever the "deeply human truths" of such films, however, reception could not be fully controlled (*vide* Stopes's response to Weber's well-intentioned *Where Are My Children?*). One way of shoring up the intended meaning of such a film was to accompany the screening with a lecture, to direct audience understanding (a widespread practice of cinema's earliest years). Yet this too could fail, even when the viewer clearly grasped the initial goal. A letter to the *Birth Control Review* described such an outcome in Berlin in 1927:

> I heard a lecture by a population booster the other day. Seeing a poster advertising a film called *The Hygiene of Marriage* I went to it. An old man professor gave a running talk not much of which I could follow. The printed remarks on the screen sufficiently explained the pictures. The play could be summed up about like this:—Only wealthy people should marry; the chief happiness of marriage is in plenty of children who must be well looked after and carefully brought up.... It all looked so easy. The ideal mother is shown with six or seven children playing around, while she does the family wash under the apple trees in bloom. ... I spoke to the lecturer afterwards, but he did not know English, and when in bad German I asked him what about the problem of having too many children as we had in England, he lost all interest and looked as much to say: "Don't come preaching that doctrine here." The impression I got was that if the ideas contained in the film are common here, then they intend to go ahead and have as many healthy Germans as possible, confident that either they will have a war and defeat France, or that Germans will penetrate the sparsely peopled countries like Australia, South America, etc.[141]

If films could fictionalize the dilemma of a pregnant woman's choice, as in *Bed and Sofa*, or document the workings of a liberal health system, as in *The Abortion*, they might also help improve the conditions of birthing itself, by displaying the life processes in newly magnified ways, for instance. Winifred Holtby emphasized this power of cinema when reporting on how she had assiduously queued for a private Kensington screening of a Soviet Health Department instructional film about giving birth.[142] But *Cosmos*, a German scientific film purportedly about humanity's origins, disappointed Bryher deeply. It abstained from any representation of human development. As she dryly noted, after the great effort of arranging a screening of the banned film,

> I know it is the unwritten rule that the difficulties of child-birth are never to be mentioned before unmarried women because of their possible effect on the birth rate. But is this any way to deal with the problem? If the money spent on building one cruiser or the training of one army division were to be devoted to research into the problems of painless child-birth probably many of the difficulties would be solved by this time.[143]

Bryher's complaint adds yet one more element to the impressive complex of concerns adhering to women's discussions of female sexuality on film: censorship and freedom of speech; militarism and national strength; women's health; the control of scientific knowledge; the changing map of gender; and film form itself.

But let us turn to one last topic in this assessment of what might distinguish women's writings on cinema from men's, a topic, as it turns out, intimately linked to the foregoing discussion: women's written responses to films of plant growth.

Mary Field made a film of this subject (see Fig. 1, *Life of a Plant* (1926)), Germaine Dulac seems to have made one, *Germination d'un Haricot* (1928), though it is lost, and, along with Colette, Agnes Smedley, Lu Märten, and Isabel Bolton, they both wrote vividly of viewing projections of vegetal dramas.[144]

The planting of a bean and the observation of its growth were, in the first half of this century (if they are not still) a staple of kindergarten life, as well as a standard fixture in film's introduction to school, as Mary Field was to remind an interviewer.[145] Colette enjoyed her bean film at a special educational screening, one attended mainly by children, who saw "the birth of [the seed's] tunneling radicelles, the avid yawning of the cotyledons from which sprung up, throwing its serpent's head like a spear, the first sprout."[146] Colette watched the children too, who, in their fascination, imitated this searching ascent, arising and craning from their seats. In effect, the bean film invited Colette to describe the motion shared between body and screen, to model their porous interaction. (As an aside, we might note that part of Colette's figure of spectatorship had already been catalogued, in an altogether different account of expectant viewing: "The old lady sat up so erect and full of anticipation that, what with her crainy neck and her pert little upstanding toque, she looked like something that had begun to sprout."[147])

Lu Märten, writing on behalf of workers' culture, took the example of "the life of a plant from sprouting to withering" to demonstrate the way in which cinema could make "a vivid impression ... [of] invisible movements ... through time exposure," and could make widely available a process heretofore confined to the scientist's bench, or to overspecialized books.[148] Her analysis suggests, yet again, arguments made by both Béla Balázs and Walter Benjamin as to the power of film, according to which (particularly through the techniques of the close-up and slow motion) film could disclose unknown facets of natural phenomena, features invisible to the naked eye, a kind of unconscious knowledge.[149] The appeal of such films, which initiated the public into the intimate lives of plants, may well also have been linked in Märten's mind to this same public's need for illumination in other hidden, or over-academicized matters of development, above all in sex education, a project thoroughly familiar to her through her general concern with proletarian well-being.

Filming the process of seed germination tapped the unique capacities of cinema, particularly its ability to manipulate time, so that events which took days to unfold might now be seen in seconds and minutes. This subject matter pointed to the ways in which film projection itself was a process of metamorphosis. On more than one occasion Dulac wrote of the swelling and pushing of the grain, the tenuous clinging of the roots, and the hungry rising of the stalk which, "in an instinctive yearning ... lunges hopelessly for the sun," before "the era of verticals" ends.[150] As Dulac favorably concluded: "The cinema, by capturing these unconscious, instinctive, and mechanical movements," as well as "the psychology of that movement ... allows us to witness plant life's unseen aspirations toward air and light ... producing, in graceful contours, the drama and physical pleasure of growth and blossoming." Dulac included a shot of a bean sprouting in water in her short experimental film *Thèmes et Variations* (1929), and followed this shot with a time-lapse sequence in which three bean vines wind gracefully around a pole in movements likened, through montage, to the languid, searching gestures of a ballerina's hands and arms. Dulac would apparently screen her nature film *Germination d'un Haricot* to illustrate her lectures on cinema's expressive power, while Le Corbusier described such films as "miraculous."[151]

A fascination with witnessing concealed biological struggles also characterized Mary Field's account, which pointed to "the ultra-slow photography which enables one to see plants growing, roots spreading" and which showed "root tips actually feeling and directing operations" so that we might "appreciate how marvellous is the instinct behind each of what one might have been inclined to regard as blind growths."[152] Field explained that the cinematic technique for capturing this process required directing root growth down between two peat layers, hinged together, layers which had to be opened by clockwork to expose regularly to the camera the probing root doing its business between the blankets.

If there is a sexual suggestiveness to these descriptions, it was supported by a relatively recent insight of evolutionary biology: that plants had an elaborate sex life.[153] And it it is still more evident in Isabel Bolton's account of a spectatrix being moved to poetry at the "heavenly" time-lapsed sight of an opening rose: it "silently, precisely, unfolded its matchless and immaculate petals, laying one over upon another until all the delicate threadlike stamens were exposed and each, tipped with its divine essential grain of pollen, quivering, shivering there before her eyes."[154] Following the "infernal" suffering of war-zone footage—she is at a lunchtime, New York, newsreel—the slowly choreographed floral emergence lifted the woman into "a state of the highest excitement," releasing three lines of a stanza. When further "miracles of nature" flowed—a whale film, "one picture dissolving quickly into the next"—she spewed verse of "aqueous copulations."[155]

In trying to account for these women's eager interest in kinetic biology, we can look to personal biography, as well as to wider intellectual trends. Colette was aware of the work of foremost entomologist, Henri Fabre, recently deceased, who had researched the worlds of insect development and pollination, and was reminded of his endeavors when watching science documentaries, films Colette summarized as "inexhaustible luxury."[156] Dulac was responding to a strong French tradition of the analysis of movement, exemplified in the nineteenth-century career of Etiènne-Jules Marey, as well as to Bergsonian concepts of life force (*élan vital*), which the moving, tumescent vegetable would seem perfectly to instantiate.[157] Märten's interest in life-of-the-plant films might be linked to *Neue Sachlichkeit* photography, such as the still plant images of Albert Renger-Patzsch, or to the impact of the work of Karl Blossfeldt, whose *Urformen der Kunst/Art Forms in Nature*, a book of 120 austere, gravure plates, emphasizing the geometry of plant structure, catapulted him to international fame in 1928.[158] Mary Field's botany films certainly grew out of her collaboration with Percy Smith, with whom she directed and wrote *The Secrets of Nature* (1922–33) films, and whose cinematography also belonged within this broader European context of investigating and illustrating life processes.

However, in order to support a claim for erotic content in these writings, we also need to contemplate more diffuse forces, ones resulting from the different lives women lived from men in the first half of the twentieth century. Women were still largely cut off from opportunities for viewing images of sexual activity (film pornography was an arena not marketed for their pleasure), and indeed their presence before nude presentations (or the nude in art school) still caused a stir. (Part One discusses the attraction of boxing pictures for women at the turn of the century, as exceptional vistas of male nakedness.) It seems that the elegant opening of a bloom, with its fanning array of petals and powdered, protruding stamens, as well as the formal composition of seed germination unfolding on screen, with its fleshy central mass, hard, ultimately discarded seed coating, "tiny rootlets plunging their way into the ground," and searching cotyledons, may have conjured up a rare sexual display, replete with the invitation to envision male and/or female parts.[159] This alone may have delighted women. But seed footage may also have hinted at expanding foetal imagery. Formaldehyde specimens, serially arranged in museums, displayed embryonic stages, but no medium was as yet able to record such human development in motion. Film frames of eggs developing into tadpoles, and grains germinating into adult plants, pointed to and foreshadowed the cinematic portrayal of the life of the womb.

Germination films arrayed complex sequences of divergent yet simultaneous motions: tendrils unfurling; stems elbowing; roots spreading and descending. Depth of field was usually very shallow, so that fuzzy, dark hollows loomed around and behind these more legible structures (See Fig. 1). Viewers of these films may readily have recalled an idiom of the day, the saying that women "bloom" as they mature through adolescence. (Dulac in her experimental film Etude cinématograph sur an arabesque (1929) paralleled, through intercutting, a time-lapse opening anemone with a relaxing veiled woman luxuriating outdoors on a chaise longue.) The expression linked women to natural beauty, but also suggested that the female sex emerged from a concealed, hitherto unobserved state (the bud), to become seen, and even eye-catching. These films represented such growth with intimate skill and precision. They made visible a development which had remained invisible, and in this sense mapped a path from interiority to exteriority which may have had uncanny resonance for female viewers. In their revelation of the unseen, they may have pointed to the putative interiority of women. Perhaps these bean scenes, in their curving motion, and in their status as hidden knowledge, viewed unawares, even evoked women's own shaky grasp of their own interiors, so long described by medicine and other branches of science in mysterious and enclosed terms.

As presiders over gestation, as well as over the household, as harbingers of monthly cycles, and by dint of being the sex that gave birth, as well as being the sex valued for youth and beauty, women of the first half of this century attended daily to physiological temporalities (especially those conducted cutaneously, and in utero). In the intricate image of angiosperm expansion these women may have sensed a representation of the properties and metamorphoses, the branching, indirect paths of their own lives.

These speculations as to the feminine significance of bean films arise from having used gender as a criterion for aggregation; by collecting women's writings on cinema together, women's recurring enthusiasm for germination films has the chance of appearing before the reader and researcher. In other words, the method by which this collection has been assembled has precipitated out a marginal detail, which has then triggered the imaginative work of historical explanation, as offered in the foregoing paragraphs. The workings of this process suggest a *mode d'emploi* for *Red Velvet Seat* in general. Images, metaphors, and concerns which course between writings furnish the possibility of deepening and building insight into women's engagement with cinema. The red velvet seat itself commanded attention through a similar pelmanism.

Compiling this book has been a tale of systematicity and randomness. Intimate combing of entire runs of certain journals followed sporadic checks of others. Clues as to likely sources came from letterheads, from other scholars, from indexes.[160] Examined were the women's press, suffrage weeklies, African-American publications, Little Magazines.[161] Collections of women's papers were consulted.[162] Research was hampered, or blocked, by absence of bylines and by the use of pseudonyms. Standard bibliographies were unreliable.[163] Loss of records contributed to the research challenge, most markedly in looking for black women's writings.[164] It also contributed to loss of meaning. The very *au courant* jottings of journalism traded on the moment, but, as novelty has ebbed, the specialized vocabulary developed in responding to film has become opaque: the nomenclature "The Fifth Estate" regularly ennobled film against the press, while the terms the "Sixth" and indeed the "Seventh" art for the film medium were commonplace; Lillian Wald used "play" to mean "film" in 1915; Flanner used "cinema" in 1918 to mean an individual film; Dickson used "mimic life" in 1895, Devereux Blake used "mimic scene" and "mimic audience" in 1899, while Addams used "mimic stage" in 1910, all to refer to the emerging new form; and, finally, Lucy France Pierce used "motography" in 1908 to refer to both cinema and cinematography, an expression recalling Edison's first name for his new invention, the "motograph" (one he abandoned for the word "kinetoscope").[165]

The annotations aim to restore these meanings, while biographies of the authors give readers further assistance. In most cases, selections have been reprinted in full, and have included several illustrations that accompanied the original publications. Excerpting for readability is indicated by ellipses thus [...].

Five editorial essays proffer the context and significance of the collection, although they do not (and could not) attempt to interpret fully its contents. In fact, the foregoing discussion of female response to filmed germination serves as a salutory indication of what might have happened, had these essays more full-bloodedly taken that route.

Research for this book yielded well over a thousand writings, a haul demanding careful triage. While a wealth of non-English material exists, the collection focuses mostly on women's writings in English.[166] However, two essays by Germaine Dulac have been translated from the French, and a group by Resi Langer, Lu Märten,

Malwine Rennert, Milena Jesenská, and Emilie Altenloh from the German, partly to encourage the production of similar anthologies for other languages or regions (Germany and Italy apparently offering the richest seams). A translation of part of Emilie Altenloh's On the Sociology of Cinema was particularly warranted since she was perhaps the first sociologist of the film audience, and because her work is frequently cited in English-language texts.[167] Two Italian women's writings are here, those of Matilde Serao and Ada Negri, the former because of the extreme relevance of her topic, "La Spettatrice," and the latter because of her widespread popularity in the silent era—she was translated into fourteen languages, and accumulated such power as to be responsible for silent star Pola Negri's name change from Appolonia Chalupek.[168]

In choosing texts those from rare sources have been privileged to enhance access. That a writing must be about cinema has been an almost inflexible criterion for inclusion—that a writing must be by an actual woman has been, paradoxically, a criterion applied with slightly more latitude.[169] As previously mentioned, the use of pseudonyms camouflages authorship—when men took female pseudonyms, their views would typically have been understood as expressing a woman's opinion.[170] In the case of female stars, whose opinions were often ghostwritten, sometimes by men, these opinions would also have become part of the female star's image.[171] For these reasons, the use and inadvertent inclusion of pen names creates not such a methodological flaw, or trauma. As the exception that proves the rule, Zelda Fitzgerald's short story "Our Own Movie Queen," which was initially published under F. Scott Fitzgerald's name, is reprinted here.[172]

The collection largely omits fiction, chiefly because excerpting from it disengages that writing too strongly from its context, and because the lengths of excerpt needed are too cumbersome. However, its distinction from documentary writing is often hard to discern: two of the earliest authors (the Matinee Girl and Virginia, the Daughter of Eve) fictionalized their identities so as to enhance their flânerie, as they segue from fashion shopping to film viewing, adopting the diary format to knit their filmgoing into their other weekly habits. Winifred Holtby's short story "Missionary Film" tangibly evokes the spectator's place within the auditorium in ways very similar to those found in the more ostensibly reportage descriptions of the cinema crowd by Elizabeth Bowen, Janet Flanner, and Dorothy Richardson.[173]

Also omitted are film scenarios, and what Nettie Palmer once referred to as "the cinematic in writing," the stylistic mark of modernist, stream-of-consciousness prose to be found in the literature of Virginia Woolf, Djuna Barnes, and Gertrude Stein, among others.[174] Also not here are jointly authored works, in which one contributor was male, rendering texts by Martha Wolfenstein and Nathan Leites, or Laura Riding's "Film-Making: Movement as Language," co-authored with Len Lye, ineligible.[175] (At first glance this impermissibility gives ludicrous weighting to anatomical difference, but that difference has had its consequences, and those are not too absurd to study.) Many other women are omitted from the volume because of a lesser interest of available pieces of their writing, or a lack of appropriate length of writing sample, or merely, inevitably, because of page limitations.[176] Zora Neale

Hurston and Dorothy Parker are among the many women who would seem to have expressed their views on cinema, but for whom sadly there is no contribution here, either because their opinions remained unpublished, took fictional form, or were apparently never penned.[177]

Although prompted in part by the richness of private recollections, this volume does indeed concentrate on public discourse—only previously published writings have been selected.[178] By holding to this criterion, one can materially make the case for the existence and substantial scale of public and professional reaction by women, even *among* women, to film.[179]

This volume is arranged thematically, according to five key areas of response, each group of selected writings building on the prior one, with several bridges forming across and between sections.[180] The areas are: Part One, "The Red Velvet Seat"; Part Two, "What Was Cinema?"; Part Three, "Cinema as a Power"; Part Four, "The Critic's Hat"; Part Five, "Cinema as a Job." Part One assembles women's written accounts of filmgoing. Here women survey the varied attractions of going—to have a quiet cry, to be moved by music, to interrupt the working day, to "pass an hour or two" with a friend, to enact the rights of one's race.[181] When women took on this subject, their attention fanned out across the auditorium, as they observed differences within and among audiences, according to class, and urban, rural, and metropolitan geography.[182] They spotted the "gent," front row boys (the audience of the future), and "the salesman."[183] They spoke of films watched in "Gracie Fields country," or in a Tuscan hill town; and they specified particular reactions to the rendition of a song at an individual film show. [184] The movie auditorium emerges as a physical entity, of seating, bodies, screen, and air, a volume crisscrossed by smells, sounds, looks, tastes and tactility. The network of participants' glances, built up through these descriptions, encompasses the writer herself, as she pauses to remark on her own presence before the screen.

Several women mull cinema's utopian promise of female *flânerie*—the hall and screen as an arena of meandering contemplation, free from returned scrutiny.[185] They invite us to construe a varied and lively idea of female spectatorship, in contrast to that developed in some subsequent film scholarship which characterizes spectators (their attitudes imputed or inferred from the structure and content of screen offerings) as passive, regressed, and subject to the dictates of the film apparatus, particularly female viewers, described occasionally as incapable of detached viewing, as too glued to the screen to analyze it.[186] These earlier women's interest in each fold and wrinkle of their favorite cinema, and its particular inhabitants, itself an expression of their active engagement with that space, is summed up in Mary Heaton Vorse's confession, "I had gone, as they had, to see pictures, but in the end I saw only them."[187]

In Part Two, "What Was Cinema?", a title honoring André Bazin's famous earlier inquiry, women compare cinema to the other arts, and debate cinema's mingling of art forms, and its particular bonds to musical and performative rhythm.[188] As with their writing on the culture of filmgoing, they approach the aesthetic concerns of the cinema as embodied spectators, finding particular explanatory value in likening film to dance, itself a form of expression residing in, and emanating from, the body. They probe the different ways in which cinema engaged the faculties of sight, hearing, and intellection, noting a cleaving of the ear's from the eye's attention, for example, a separation Marie Seton later found to be rebalanced in the medium of television.[189] And a number of them gave the cinema a particularly visionary cast, as they wondered how film conveyed thought, whether it portended dreaming, a new emotional realm, or a form of non-verbal communication in the chance witnessing of ephemeral moments. Overall, these women rarely systematically analyzed film's formal and expressive vocabulary, and never detached it from their own presence before the screen. In this regard, their writing lies closer to that of Jean Epstein than Rudolph Arnheim, among male writers on film of the era.[190]

In Part Three, "Cinema as a Power," women wrote of the effects of all this looking. Where, in Part One, women had found the cinema to house new audiences in a new social setting, and where, in Part Two, they had found it to announce a new expressive means, the psychologists and reformers of Part Three (who typically bought their movie ticket to do upaid work at the cinema, not to relax) treated future effects, educational effects, and turpitudinous effects of film, spilling much ink in designing ways to control the industry. Their divergent views on censorship, as both watchful angels and free-lovers, dramatically exhibit the range of opinion possible among women: for Rebecca West and Anita Loos, censorship created scandal; for numerous other women, it ensured against it.[191]

While for some women cinema was the "modern child trap," others envisaged a medium whose tremendous global force might be tamed.[192] They labored to turn cinema's attractiveness to a greater, restorative good, finding educative potential (towards moral reform, socialization, and general instruction) in the most mundane of film productions—where some reformers rued cinema's power in disclosing the existence, if not the specific pleasures of sexual life, these women prized the screen's buffet of sophisticated knowledge.[193] Arguing that audiences themselves had agency, women developed classes in ciné-literacy (for developing audience taste and aesthetic judgement), that acts of patronage might improve film culture.[194] Film director Dorothy Arzner, lecturing to students at the University of California at Los Angeles in the 1950s, promulgated the widely and long-held view that it was the medium's primacy of sight which made it a new pedagogical tool: "the moving picture, and now TV, through the simultaneous appeal to mind, heart, and eye, has a greater power of suggestibility than either the press or the radio. What the eye sees in pictures often leaves a deeper and more permanent imprint on the retina of the soul than the printed or spoken word."[195]

While commentators have often noted the early abundance of female film critics, their work remains largely uncollected and unread. In revisiting their writing, and the numerous arenas in which it appeared, the editorial essay for Part Four, "The Critic's Hat," highlights the vitality of their practice. It notes the flexibility of the review format (from Dorothy Richardson's regular, "Continuous Performance" column to Lejeune's ironic poem on the woman's film, Humoresque), and points to women's interests in the phenomena of stardom and genre, and in film as a key to interpreting society. Writing in the second half of the 1940s (on both sides of the Atlantic, in venues ranging from *Mademoiselle* and *The Penguin Film Review* to *New Masses* and *Vogue*), women were increasingly discontented with Hollywood's treatment of women, both on screen and in terms of how it made film appealing to women (some argued that the event of the war had thrown into intolerably stark relief discrepancies between the lives of actual women, and what the screen offered them).[196] When writing his first book, in 1950, André Bazin, analysing the demise of Rita Hayworth in *The Lady from Shanghai*, was to remark that, "for some years, the misogyny of the American cinema has become a commonplace of intellectual criticism."[197] He might well have been referring to the journalism of Deming, Ager, de la Roche, and Davidman, which predated, by a quarter of a century, similar criticism born of the second women's movement.[198]

The fifth and final section, "Cinema as a Job," assembles printed responses to the labor of filmmaking, film exhibition, and, ultimately, writing on film. The editorial essay delineates the striking range of women's participation in cinema's first fifty years, from the role of director to that of manager and cinema studies scholar. It reflects on women's fluctuating fortunes in filmmaking, and their relation to historical change itself, as well as on changing perceptions of the links between womanhood, technology, and artistic creativity. The story told reminds us that things do not necessarily get better—that there were more female directors working in Hollywood in the late 1910s and early 1920s than at any time since, and that more women received Academy Awards for writing in the 1930s and 1940s than in the 1980s or 1990s.

The timeliness of making this archive accessible is clear. For the female filmgoer, it consolidates a passionate history whose elements have been dispersed or are in the process of being discarded. On the academic front, this collection redefines the field we know as classical film theory. It challenges the contours of that canon by revealing a greater diversity of accounts and formulations about film, and by stretching our notions of where, how, and why writing about film has taken place. Some might argue that both theory and history are absent from the women's texts selected for this collection, but, rather, that they appear here in a different writerly form. Antonia Dickson's account of the kinetoscope, and Lucy France Pierce's report on "The Nickelodeon," both included in Part Four, are examples of popular reporting, yet they are important as early endeavors to express the invention and short career of the cinema through writing.[199] In a parallel way, it is through the accumulation of Dorothy Richardson's multiple investigations into the phenomenology and materiality of filmgoing that we might come to find her writing indispensable in efforts to characterize the place and pull of cinema. We also learn from this collection that women were in the thick of debates about cinema's social and public import. As Joan Scott reminds us, by adding women to history you occasion its rewriting.[200]

Two questions remain. One is, what happened next? *Red Velvet Seat*'s assortment and analysis cease in approximately 1950, but the next twenty years (up to the late 1960s and early 1970s, when the journals *Silent Picture* and *Women and Film* first appeared) were apparently yet more barren than the previous fifty—*pace* Pauline Kael, female-authored publications about cinema were still rarer, although the young industry of television was offering new opportunities for female employment, and recruiting some former screenwriters. Only more research can reveal how just this impression is, and what its significance is. By concluding around 1950, this book leaves to be considered what two-decade bridge, if any, links this anthology's contents to the critical writing that began in the late 1960s, when the study of cinema developed an academic profile, and when female writers gained more voice, both in the media and in scholarly debate.

The other question is, what effect did all this writing have? For this, there is no neat answer, in part because more research needs to be done, in part because the evidence needed to answer does not survive, and also because the range of women's responses to cinema cannot be unified and synthesized into one conclusion. Writing about cinema was a critical factor in the construction and perpetuation of its powerful effect, and some women's pen power was mighty. Louella Parsons and Hedda Hopper, the most widely known of any film reporters of cinema's first half-century, were heard to claim a global readership of seventy-five million.[201] Club women directly shaped the operations of Hollywood through their publications, and other work.[202] Sometimes their impact was repressive, but at other points these women were credited with increasing the numbers of females employed in Hollywood.[203] It was even mooted, in 1925, that women's presence in American film production, and their louder voices in American culture more generally, might explain the international dominance of American cinema; in Europe women had less say.[204]

The ultimate effect, however, was that, collectively, such women's publications attested to film's existence in a public space resoundingly marked by feminine presence. Their writing was a vital aspect of their public involvement in twentieth-century life, and recorded as well as contributed to a film culture since largely lost or overlooked, one which, once re-engaged, strikes us again and again with the realization that women were there—they linger in the seated vocabulary of their writing.

PART ONE
The Red Velvet Seat

Fig. 1.1   Mabel Dwight, "The Clinch," lithograph on stone, 1928.

PART ONE

Introduction

One way of answering the question, "What did the cinema mean to women?" is to read what they have had to say about filmgoing. This topic frequently drew their attention. They found the cinema's murky assembly of friends and strangers striking and newsworthy, and often described the intermixing of women into this crowd, if it was not their outright focus. This is literature by women, writing about women at the cinema, often for a female readership. It is triply swirled with an alertness to gender.

The cinema, as a novel method of recording, storing, and delivering moving images, had rapidly become a commercial industry, bringing into being a newly minted space of social congregation, and even, some will argue, new modes of perception. And women were claiming this genderless technology for themselves. However, exactly what percentage of film audiences were female remains elusive. This has been a notoriously difficult, if not impossible, figure for scholars to calculate or research, in part because of contingent factors affecting individual screenings, and in part because of the idiosyncratic ways in which producers and exhibitors have, historically, acquired their notions of who was watching.[1]

The fifty-year period covered by this collection saw enormous changes in the ways films were consumed. For the first ten years or so, until about 1905, they typically appeared as part of a show that included live entertainments; they were sometimes custom-edited by their exhibitor, embellished by live sound effects, or altered by a lecturer or narrator's voice emanating from alongside or behind the screen.[2] Venues for film included vaudeville houses, fairgrounds, circuses, wax museums, opera houses, and scientific demonstrations, but not purpose-built cinemas. During the next few years, known as the nickelodeon era in the United States, many storefront cinemas opened, usually comprising one simple, fairly low-ceilinged, unraked, undecorated room, furnished with wooden benches, with the projector boxed-off or perched at the back. Reformers, pushing for fire regulation and censorship, hastened the nickelodeon's demise, and the arrival of the more salubrious motion picture palace of the 1910s and 1920s. Especially in cities, luxurious, extravagantly designed auditoria replaced the airless, spartan shopfront theaters. And from the late 1920s into the 1930s, modernist theater design challenged the indulgently tactile palace environments, a transformation accompanied by synchronized sound; "foyers once crimson and richly stuffy are air-conditioned and dove-grey," wrote Elizabeth Bowen of the trend toward new, cool sensibleness in London's super cinemas.[3]

However, both Olivia Howard Dunbar's and Marian Bowlan's accounts remind us that the variety format—film combined with live elements and knockabout comedy—still thrived in 1913 on Manhattan's East Side, and in Chicago.[4] Changes in patterns of exhibition did not follow a uniform timetable convenient to historians. Instead, each cinema-going expedition was a unique encounter, despite the mass-reproductive methods of the medium. The moviegoing milieu remained heterogeneous and subject to any number of influences: theater proprietorship, neighborhood location, the time of day and week of the screening (not to mention the year), the price zone of the theater in which you sat, and your own age, gender, experience, and so on. African Americans owned and operated small neighborhood theaters from the 1910s onwards, but no picture palaces; where a male clientele apparently dominated later evening shows, noon was strongly favored by women in the silent era. ("Nooning" defined skipping lunch to slide into a nickelodeon[5]).

The impression that women comprised the majority of filmgoers derived from the sources Hollywood used to gain an idea of its audience. Until the mid 1930s, when studios and other organizations conducted more "scientific" surveys (using sampling on the basis of gender, age, income, etc.), fan mail was the chief indicator of attendance. Since women wrote most of these letters, women seemed to be in the majority of those present in the movie house. In journalism of the 1920s and 1930s, the scale of the female audience, while fluctuating wildly from writer to writer, became impressively large, occasionally hitting 83 per cent,[6] with women almost always constituting "the great majority of filmgoers."[7] A subset of this writing pointed out that many men were, for statistical purposes, women. As Lillie Messinger put it, describing her work as a star scout:

> I believe that all film-testing is woman's work. Not because I am an ardent feminist, but because it is women who finance the motion picture industry. All the greatest stars, male or female, are women's ideal types, rather than men's. Nearly always, when a man goes to the cinema, it is a woman who chooses the picture he will see.[8]

In a similar vein, Miles Mander estimated that, in 1934, while 65 per cent of filmgoers were women, of the 30 per cent men (the other 5 per cent were children), one-third were there at the behest of women.[9]

This picture of an overwhelmingly female audience ended with the introduction of more systematic surveying, in the late 1930s, in which "highly structured empirical methods supplanted the personal, impressionistic studies of film audiences that had characterized the first two decades of the century."[10] By the beginning of the decline of the Golden Age of Hollywood at the end of the 1940s, most evaluators reckoned the ratio of the audience was 50:50 male-to-female.

Whatever the actual numbers of female ticket-holders, women have had a disproportionate impact on people's idea of cinema. Writers on film audiences endlessly remarked on its feminine contigent, and their significance for film fortune. Even before the turn of the century, exhibitors discussed needing to appeal to female customers; by 1908 this effort was openly tied to cleaning up the reputation of nickelodeons; and by 1915 Anna Steese Richardson's urging of managers and producers to know "the taste of women customers" was typical.[11]

Women's writing on film was undoubtedly motivated by a sense of the impressiveness of feminine scale, and by the unprecedented cultural and social possibilities film seemed to indicate. Indeed, the extraordinary novelty of moviegoing for women, and for those observing them, cannot be overestimated. Where before had droves of women been allowed, indeed invited, to amass, to stare, to assemble in darkness, to risk the chance encounter, the jostling and throng of the crowd? Via cinema, they saw, alone, or in groups, largely without censure, and publicly, images not slated for their gaze, as well as towering icons of femininity, and tales of female derring-do. They committed a myriad female types of filmgoer to paper: the preview huntress, the shop girl, Mrs Fitton caparisoned in her Sunday hat, the typist "in search of a thrill," the immigrant Austrian viewer.[12] Dorothy Richardson, in particular, calibrated women's voices, their burdens, their walks, their lonelinesses, the visits of all those "weary women of all classes for whom at home there is no resting-place."[13] Indeed, one of the fascinations of Richardson's writing on film lies in its kaleidoscopic display of such optical and acoustic fragments, highly tuned to female presence.

Where some writings by women give prominence to idiosyncratic viewers, others find interest in the coalescence of beings into a crowd. For Holtby, this emerged in the synchronous motion of eyes, in laughter rippling across faces as wind through corn.[14] In Serao and Langer, writing of the early 1910s, it lay in the transient, cross-class fusion effected before the screen.[15] For Vorse, it had specific dimensions of ethnicity and citizenship: "There they were, a strange company of aliens—Jews, almost all.... The American-born sat next to the emigrant."[16] Horrabin chose "comrade" as the ideal term for her fellow filmgoer and loyal reader.[17] Dunbar puzzled the obscure pleasures of this indifferent, "emotionless," "phlegmatic," "random assemblage," while Barry sketched its elusive appeal thus: "a cinema audience is not a corporate body, like a theater audience, but a flowing and inconstant mass."[18]

A web of observations as to the smells, sounds, tastes, feelings, and sights of moviegoing fingers its way through these texts. Women record the cinema's throw of light into the street outside, its "incidental interests," its missing "zodiacal goats" and "seat phones," and its scent of "warm humanity and muddy boots," the usher's tip dropping in "your bag like divers with lead helmets on."[19] Viewers swim in and out of focus, as they enter, sit, watch, and leave, caught up in the particular aspects of the town, neighborhood, village, or country hosting the experience. It was as if moviegoing unleashed in these writers (as in their fellow audience-members) an awareness of the dawning of a new sensory culture, the specific movie being screened—the "adolescence of an oyster," "The Drama of the Dessert"—remaining but one strand of the warp and weft of cinematic texture.[20]

The palpable sense of a particular writer, sitting before the screen, pervades these commentaries.[21] This writer records and attaches a temporality to film which was not that of the duration of the feature, nor that of the storyline, but that of the somatic experience of watching. And this interest in conveying, through words, a phenomenology of this writing viewer's physical observations and responses in turn drew its momentum from the medium's power for expanding and rearranging the sensorium of daily life. More and more different kinds of women attempted to record the significance of this ceremony, drawn ever deeper into explaining why they went. Over the decades, the climate of filmgoing changes, but the nature and subtlety of those changes defy recapture. Such women's essays aid us in leaving us tangible clues as to its earlier character, while reminding us what an ephemeral culture this has been. When was the last time "there was quite audible sobbing all over the house?"[22]

Female authors approached this arena with a variety of writing styles. The travelogue was one, often a search for distinction in regional or national film consumption. Langer's sketches of two different Berlin neighborhoods fit this mold, as does Cecilie Leslie's 1931 month-long series "A Thousand Miles of Filmgoing," begun in Glasgow, where the "big super cinema" had not yet displaced the Black Cat Picture House with its hard seats, gas jet lights, tarred brick walls, and afternoon screening of an eight-reeler "in complete silence, the only accompaniment being the whir of the projection motors from the back."[23] Leslie journeyed on to Edinburgh, Manchester, Liverpool, Leicester, and finally London, concluding (pace Sir James Barrie) that "you can buy happiness in this world, but in one place only—the cinema."[24] Janet Flanner's reports on Turkey and Montmartre (where "the cinemas along the notorious Boulé Miché ... are shoe shops or old bakeries, slightly made over") belong to this genre, as does Mary Heaton Vorse's venturing into movie parlors on Manhattan's Bowery and Houston Street.[25]

Curiosity about cinema's crowds generated two of the oldest commentaries here—"The Matinee Girl" and "Alice Rix at the Veriscope"—both of which describe a screening of Jim Corbett's long-anticipated fight against Robert Fitzsimmons in 1897, the first widely known fight film, a battle ultimately fought for the camera.[26] "The Matinee Girl" attended an afternoon show, and refers to the female audience as a group, "us," the fans of Corbett. Alice Rix's much longer treatment appeared in the colorful Sunday supplement of Hearst's San Francisco Examiner (an addition to the paper aimed at increasing female readership), and introduced itself as a quest for the rumored female audience.[27] Screenings of the Corbett–Fitzsimmons Fight, premièred in New York in 1897 at the Academy of Music in Union Square, and eventually spread across the United States and abroad, to both opera houses and fairgrounds, road-showing through the turn of the century and amassing the film's sponsors a fortune. The experience of watching this film was extraordinary, for its length (at about 100 minutes, when each three-minute round was unspooled in sequence, it constituted the first full-length performance devoted exclusively to motion pictures), and for its visual impact (the reels were shot and projected using a wide (63 mm), large-format film stock, reminiscent of a modern widescreen ratio, designed specifically for this event, so that it could embrace the ring with ease, while the arching sky and glittering Western light, flooding the vast, purpose-built, Carson City, open-air stadium, further enhanced the spectacle of agile, sparring antagonists).[28]

This fight film was no normal outing to the movies for women. Indeed, it may well have constituted these women's "first memorable contact with cinematic presentations."[29] In attending, these women entered a controversial male milieu, and availed themselves, in mixed company, of sights usually denied.[30] In this, as Charles Musser has pointed out, they were asserting their independence, and loosening the codes of conduct that typically circumscribed their lives, while their enthusiasm for these films, unanticipated and unintended, accounts for the historical record they (and others) have left of this unique moment of film spectatorship.[31] This chance for looking at boxing had been invented by the cinema, an entertainment that still had unclear conventions of attendance, especially for women, while the medium also increased the material's sexual charge, by displaying, up close and exposed Caucasian, male physiques (including that of matinée idol "Pompadour Jim," who was known to women from the theater stage, but not the ring), packaging them as a show.[32] In the film, Corbett takes the corner nearest the camera, a position enhancing display of his strikingly cutaway shorts; carving the contour of the gluteas maximus, the bobbing juxtaposition of Corbett's miniscule dark trunks against his white cheeks provides the moment of greatest visual contrast on the screen, one strengthening the spectacle's capacity to mesmerize.[33]

Concern for the film crowd spawned another, quite different, mode of writing: the analytical audience survey. Studios and distributors solicited such inquiries to improve commercial performance. Government offices also did so, to help determine how to "reach" specific audiences at times of crisis. Scholars, investigative individuals, and philanthropic groups also used surveys, to study cultural fluctuations and preferences, perhaps in aiming to elevate standards.[34] Mary Field used infra-red photography in the late 1940s to record children's facial expressions, in order to calculate the educational impact of a screening.[35] Aspects of these methods still have currency, especially in efforts to tap the opinion of populations not generally able to find public expression.[36]

Emilie Altenloh's doctorate, written under national economist and cultural sociologist Professor Alfred Weber, in 1913, was one of the earliest analyses of the film audience.[37] Her method resembled that used by Marie Bernays, who wrote a dissertation on factory workers' culture in Germany at about the same time, a project which, like Altenloh's, found women of special interest.[38] Although Bernays conducted her work under Alfred, the latter's brother Max Weber was her real, shadow advisor, an arrangement which may also have pertained to Altenloh's studentship. (Through similar connections, it is likely that Hugo Münsterberg was aware of Altenloh's project, since he visited both Weber brothers in Heidelberg during the summers.) Altenloh understood cinema as a new social forum, shaped and driven by the capitalist market of which it and its audiences were part, and she travelled to Paris, visiting Pathé Frères (whose films knew worldwide domination at the time) to inform herself of the vigorously growing film industry.[39] Her method was to sort and interpret 2,400 questionnaires, collected in Heidelberg and Mannheim with the help of Else Biram-Bodenheimer. She paid attention to movie theater statistics, and to distinctions of class, sex, age, marital status, religious denomination, political leanings, and professional background in what Miriam Hansen has termed "with all due scepticism due to empirical studies … one of the most differentiated sources on spectator stratification available."[40]

Altenloh wrote of the hard-working lives of many patrons, transformations in their home setting, and the fragmentation of street existence in modernity. She was particularly curious as to possible divergences between female and male tastes, and among tastes of different classes (troubling the widely held view that cinema was chiefly a working-class amusement), and while she identified the young, single male factory worker as one of cinema's most regular customers, she gave ample room to female viewers, writing of the salesgirl, the secretary, the working-class woman, and the bourgeois housewife, as well as the familiar sight of mothers with small children in cinemas. One of her more intriguing observations concerns the appeal of operatic scores for young female filmgoers, whose pleasure arose from a transporting combination of aural and visual elements, such that they recalled vivid impressions of music, but only vague ones of films in their questionnaires.

Altenloh, like Malwine Rennert and Milena Jesenská, penned her account in the midst of Germany's cinema reform movement, whose proponents debated cinema's potential as an art form, one with its own, distinctive authors, and one which might accomplish feats as refined and distinguished as those of theater or opera.[41] However, unlike many critics participating in this discussion, who described women only to disapprove of their behavior, Altenloh insisted on female presence as a central ingredient of any socially nuanced picture of contemporary film recreation. As a result, her book possesses a relative neutrality, even to the point of emphasizing the remarkable passion for cinema (and especially for Asta Nielsen) shared by women across the class divide.[42]

Only six of the twenty-eight writings selected here belong to the talkie era. While this may have resulted from biases in collecting, it more interestingly suggests that the silent era's massing of viewers might have been more startling, and worthier of note, that it might have had more feminine significance.[43] Tinges of regret certainly accompanied much female response to the arrival of commercial, synchronized sound after 1926.

Women's commentaries alight on the paradox of mute cinema's noises, which took umpteen forms.[44] H.D. enjoyed the murmur and chatter of a tiny, provincial, lakeside movie house in Switzerland in 1927. As the audience burbled along in the dark, in German, French, and English, H.D. felt its "languages filter into my consciousness."[45] Marian Bowlan built a monologue sketch around "Minnie," a movie natterer, and the trigger for a group of vignettes on the Chicago "city woman."[46]

Another chatterer, also apparently female (and reported in an anonymous column of 1921), talked unendingly for two hours, starting in the street outside the cinema, not ceasing while happening upon a Douglas Fairbanks film inside, and continuing as she departed again.[47] She was a vocal source regularly lambasted in the movie trade papers, but one whom Dorothy Richardson, hesitatingly, came to appreciate: "I have learned to cherish her. For it's she at her most flagrant that has placed the frail edifice of my faith in woman at last upon a secure foundation."[48] Richardson treasured her refusal to shut up and sit meekly in silence before the silent screen (the attitude demanded by the "Early Father" to whom Richardson attributed her Latin epigraph, "*animal impudens*"), for this irritating female (a woman clearly very different from herself) possessed an admirable measure of spunk.[49]

There was also the sound of music. Women wrote of its somnolent or emotional appeal, Altenloh's research even indicating, as mentioned above, that women sought out the film auditorium as much for its music as for its pictures.[50] Janet Flanner poked fun at silent cinema's scores, cynically suggesting that filmgoers might forgo viewing, and simply read the pianola player's cue sheet as it supplied intertitles, timing, and mood. The words of songs, playing in viewer's heads, prompted by musical cues, as well as the musical themes themselves, would shape and aid perceptions so efficiently as to make the screen redundant.[51] Iris Barry mourned the coming of sound specifically on musical grounds; she had revelled in the delicious and unexpected association of live accompaniment and recorded image, teamed together in a way now being lost: "Should we never again experience the same pleasure that *Intolerance*, *Moana*, or *Greed* had given with their combination of eloquent silence, visual excitement and that hallucinatory 'real' music from 'real' orchestras in the movie theaters which buoyed them up and drifted us with them into bliss?..."[52] For other writers lamenting the new technology, unpleasantness lay in the intrusion of speech.[53] Reporting from Los Angeles in 1926, Grace Kingsley remained skeptical of the "new talking machine": "It isn't likely that the talking pictures will be a reality, because nobody wants to hear pictures talk! The charm about pictures, in this age of noise, is their restful silence."[54] Laura Whetter pined for the "silent strong man" now replaced with a "poor mutt," the hero who talked, and, at best, sang and danced, her derogatory mongrel reference echoing Dorothy Richardson's interpretation of sound cinema as a form of miscegenation.[55]

Richardson herself valued the gravity of film's silence, which could "translate" the spectator to a "peculiar ... individual intensity of being."[56] In recalling that "life's 'great moments' are silent," she speculated that the experience of a silent film was one of solitude, a state to be treasured, while the sound film had the far more common-or-garden talent of producing "association," taking spectators "out of themselves."[57] In 1931, Djuna Barnes was still hoping for minimal dialogue in her filmgoing (the kind she found in Joseph von Sternberg's *Morocco*): "I like my human experience served up with a little silence and restraint. Silence makes experience go further and, when it does die, gives it that dignity common to a thing one has touched but not ravished."[58]

Talking, whether a source of enjoyment or dismay at the cinema, was not cinema's only engagement of the mouth.[59] Women's writings also recorded other rhythms of oral satisfaction, rising and falling with the film drama's emotional surges: a viewer is "peeling her chocolate box"; an audience "contentedly chews its gum"; and a "tension created by the film gives rise to the unconscious, infantile sucking habit," so that a "sudden frenzy of chocolate eating and cigarette lighting immediately accompanies an emotional climax."[60] Horrabin "got so excited" at the wartime British documentary drama *Target For Tonight* that she "bit through an unlighted cigarette."[61] In B. Bergson Spiro Miller's auditorium, "Organ-bees distil long notes of honey, drip long, drip sweet.... Paper bags rustle to the seeking fingers, yearning of the void wet tender mouth: munchy soft squashy toffee. Or nervous inbreathing of cigarette's tantalizing tang. Old man, dimly pipe-sucking. Enlapped baby, clasped by heedless mother, all warm and drowsed and softly soother-suckling...."[62]

This indubitable sensuousness appalled reformers such as Marjorie Fox, who, in her survey of the movies, had witnessed schoolchildren, "sated with sensationalism ... placidly gnaw[ing] chocolate and suck[ing] oranges."[63] The metaphor of the "child caught at the jampot" conveyed the risqué pleasure of cinemagoing for a Boston "Lady Correspondent" in 1908, while for Janet Flanner the movie theater was "dark as a jam-closet."[64] Bowen found suspect pectin remains while smoking in her "sticky velvet seat."[65] In this clinging tactility, and the sweet arousal of taste and touch, lay a cinema for trysting and sex.

Women feasted on describing the movie theater interior's pile seating, its absorbent lining, cupping and rimming the hall. Returning to it with uncanny regularity, they verbally explored the seat's contours, colors, and embrace, tracing over its form with feeling. Sometimes it is a "Stammsessel": Gertie Slayback, has, with her husband Jimmie Batch, for two years and eighteen months of Saturday nights, dined for one hour, and sixty cents, at the White Kitchen, before taking the tenth from last row at the De Luxe Cinematograph on Broadway, to feel "the give of velvet-upholstered chairs, perfumed darkness, and any old love story moving across" the screen; seventy-year-old Miss Felicia Bodwell always took the same seat, and hadn't missed a change of program in three years.[66] These women claim their familiar chair, the individual film being "more or less ... neither here nor there."[67]

Where, during the first fifteen years of cinema, the obtruding hat had been the sign of female presence (a theme taken up later in this essay), in the age of the picture palace a different but parallel figuration, suggesting a lower area of the woman's body, persisted in women's ubiquitous references to plush banquettes. Lejeune says as much: "the small cushioned seats are women's seats; they have no masculine build."[68] Her assessment joins Marian Spitzer's "deep-piled velvet divans," Miller's "soft plush cushions," Langer's "soft, velvety chair," Hurst's "fauteuils of marshmallow plush," and Macaulay's "plush" ones.[69] This collection's title, *Red Velvet Seat*, plumbs this synechdochal female fundament, and the feminine occupation of cinema it underscored.

Concentric waves of written architectural detail encircle and envelop these thrones, as women, through writing, find ways of grasping the *whole* space of the cinema; it was as if, through articulating the infinitely varied details of its sensations and materials, cinema's full social and emotional significance might be exposed. Holtby entered a "big, crowded super-cinema," past "a 'jungle' of artificial reeds and dried grasses," arrayed under a massive, adventure film hoarding, replete with stills of a blonde "in a brief skirt of monkey fur."[70] A rural Wisconsin picture palace beckoned with an "arched white and gold entrance, a flood of amber light stream[ing] across the pavement. The girl ticket seller [stood] in a domed oriental booth.... Tricolored posters in violent drawing advertise[d] the nightly change of bill."[71] The outer hall of a Berlin UFA cinema was "flooded with a straight line light thrown from the walls," while "square cubes of light enframe[d] the two girls who [sold] tickets"; inside serenity abounded, in the spare luminiscent lines dividing the "blue and white petunia" color scheme. Dorothy Woodman, visiting this cinema in Fall 1931 (the same season as Holtby's brush with a window-dresser's jungle), contrasted it to "the extravagantly—often vulgarly—decorated entrance halls of English super-cinemas," her distaste resembling Fannie Hurst's for the American movie hall.[72]

Most of the essays collected here leave a strong impression of the particular theater being visited, but Dorothy Richardson and Nell Shipman offered especially graphic assessments of architectural structure. The former challenged conventional layouts: front-row seats (those with the poorest view, where you were "the proverbial fly" who had no idea about "the statue over which he crawls") stole space from more appropriate uses (for entrances and ushers), and should be replaced by increased lateral seating, possible if one shifted the screen to the auditorium's longer wall—a film glanced tangentially, from middle or back pews, was still "excellent."[73] Shipman, fictionalized as the character Joyce Jevons, an actress, writer, and director with her own production company, experienced the peripheral view of the screen "five-times daily" in New York, in the 1920s, while promoting her latest film.[74] She "waited back-stage while the last reel of her picture unwound.... Standing in the entrance she could see the screen, distorted by the close, oblique angle, so that the actors were strange, elongated objects. And she waited lonesomely," since there were no live acts, and even the audience itself seemed dead.[75]

Where Shipman likened this scene to that of a hauntingly still pool, other substances came to mind for other writers: in L'Electric-Palace, Paris, the cinema's atmosphere was "chemically past expressing by anything but laboratory signs"; at a London newsreel theater the "packed audience in the hot, tobacco-clouded theater [grew] tense" as Gandhi responded to the question of whether he would be prepared to die for his cause.[76] In Berlin, the "ozone dispenser" combed the aisles, while the Viennese "squirt gun" spritzed "with a mixture that smelled of herbs to clear away the smoke."[77] Elsewhere, "the cinema smelt of poor people," or spectators were "sprayed, as a festal touch, with strong, inalienable scent."[78] A "perfume cloud of seductive Khasana [hung] oppressively" over other, paired cinemagoers.[79] In Holtby's fictional "Missionary Film," pungent, nostalgic smells emanated from the screen's reed-thatched huts in a synaesthetic effect.[80]

The cinema's ether was pending, heavy, "coiled away in that round tin box," as the celluloid waited "for the hour when the film's uncoiling could begin, when its dreamy poison would grow and unfold and thickly blossom in the hothouse darkness congenial to its strange erotic sensibility."[81] Such descriptions (especially when taken together with women's renderings of hearing, tasting, speaking, and feeling at the movies) pinpoint the manner by which these writings seem to seize hold of movie house volume as tangible stuff. Auditorial space becomes filled, named as a substance through and against which bodies moved; it was perceptibly "air," wrote Langer, not the clean brew of the mountains, "but something dense, something that [took] your breath away."[82] Antonia and W.K.L. Dickson concluded their adulatory biography of Edison with millennial praise for "the man who, in his own peculiar line of thought, has done more than any other to neutralize the gross fixity of matter, to extend the limited range of the senses, and to furnish a plastic basis for the incoming spiritual forces."[83] We can only wonder at how many subsequent women actually took up Edison's invitation, in stalking the sentient palpability of the cinematic outing.

"Why did the movie audience assemble?" When black female writers answered, the politics of race took center stage, for cinema-going was, first and foremost, a matter of identifying. Minnie Adams pushed her readers to "care for the welfare of our own" by patronizing the black-owned Pekin theater in Chicago, instead of its numerous, white-owned neighbors.[84] Writing nine years later, in 1921 (the peak year of silent, independent black film production), Rose Atwood asked black audiences to stay away from white-made movies: "White people seldom go to see a Colored moving picture production. Why? Because they do not feel that the life and actions of the Negro are of any interest to them. They do not believe they can be benefited [sic] or pleased by seeing a Colored show. Is it not possible that we can develop the same attitude in the minds of our own people against white shows after they shall have become accustomed to seeing first-class Colored pictures?"[85]

Segregation of audiences, while illegal in the northern United States, was a widespread phenomenon, limiting black access to cinema.[86] Local censorship boards (particularly in the South) routinely excised scenes of black performers, further minimizing the opportunity of both blacks and whites to see them. Jim Crow laws, combined with screen racism, created uniquely difficult conditions for black viewers; Mrs Charles Merriam's campaign against children going to the cinema at all, or the anti-censorship Better Films Movement's argument that "patronage makes production" scarcely constitute a parallel politics of filmgoing expressed among white women's writings.[87] Bryher insisted that film choice was a political freedom, while Barry and Lejeune, among many others, urged the film fan to vent her discontentment, for this would bring change.[88] And Celia Harris even made a vast historical comparison between the Elizabethan theater audience and that for film in the 1920s, reminding readers that the former "proved to have a force which called their own playrights into being," causing the phenomenon of Shakespeare, as it were.[89] All these white writers made the case for the agency of

Fig. 1.2   "A Theater Built for Mothers," *Photoplay*, November 1919, p. 50.

collectivity, but only to this extent is a comparison with the predicament of black viewers relevant.

Women formulated other theories as to why people gathered before the screen, most of them not specifically aimed at explaining female attendance, or uniquely expressed by women. Filmgoing was for "solace and distraction" (Jane Addams), and fulfilled social and emotional needs born of modernity.[90] It was a safety valve, for "most of us are not able to be as rude (thus working off our aggressions) as

THE WORLD'S LEADING MOVING PICTURE MAGAZINE

PHOTOPLAY

Vol. XVI   AUGUST, 1919   No. 3

The Lonely Girl

*P*ERHAPS *the war sent her to the city as a worker. Perhaps it was the Big Adventure, which makes geniuses and breaks the weak on the same wheel. Perhaps she has always been in but not of the city—and still is lonely.*

At any rate, she doesn't mind it so much between breakfast and dinner, for she's striving with the rest of her kind for a living, or a little more than a living.

But after the day-ending meal—what? If she isn't a hibernating animal she doesn't wish to sleep the clock around every night. She can't always go to church. She can't always be reading. She hasn't the money for expensive drama. Neither can she pile a cargo of overstudy on a deep freighting of daily labor.

Of course, pleasant evenings she might go out in the streets, but—

Boys can find so many things to do outdoors, at night, that girls can't do. It is one of the vulgarities of our day—and many other days—that the evening girl who strolls alone is the legitimate subject for indignity that would not dare proffer itself in the fair light of the sun.

It may be idle to speculate on the number of girls that blessed refuge, the photoplay, has saved from actual harm. It is not speculation that it has saved hundreds of thousands from the mental weariness that breeds defeat. It has opened windows into fresher airs. It has rekindled the lamp of inspiration in the darkness of solitude. Through its window has flashed the rosy dawn of many a new inspiration.

Think of the lonely girl when next you hear that the "Sunday movie" is unrighteous and unlawful.

Fig. 1.3 "The Lonely Girl," Photoplay, August 1919, p. 27.
(See Annotations, Part One, p. 135 for "Sunday Movie.")

often as we should like to be, for fear of the consequences, such as the loss of our jobs."[91] It offered escapism, from the ambiguities of life (Jesenská), from the life of demands (Dunbar), from a humdrum life (Rennert).[92] Cinema's novel and disjunct temporality contributed to this release: "Here, for three hours, is a new time, self-sufficient, unrelated: the march of actual time artificially broken, and synthetically replaced, dream-potent."[93] Its dreams attracted Hattie Loble, who spoke on cinema's remedies to the Daughters of the Confederacy in Montana in 1912.[94] She took heart in the medium's recently arrived maturity (its longer running times, "high class" subjects—from Dickens to Dante—appearances from renowned stage performers, and educational efforts), and, in her closing poem, ranked the power and satisfaction of filmgoing over that of fireside dreaming.[95] An incessant anti-depressant, cinema wicked away loneliness in its unending chains of scenes, and, Loble implies, through its assembling of crowds.[96]

Women writers were also, however, as we might expect, interested to record more particular reasons as to why *women* might go to the pictures. The movies, unlike theater, were hospitable to infants—some halls provided a crying room.[97] The cinema was a baby-sitter, buying a mother a moment's nap.[98] (The provision of checkrooms for baby carriages and even, sometimes, for children themselves were part of exhibitors' efforts in the 1910s to improve the cinema's standing by increasing its appeal to mothers.[99]) For the young, single woman, it was a more salubrious entertainment venue than other options (dance halls and down-market cafés), inexpensive and less risqué.[100] In a one-page layout, *Photoplay* defended "The Lonely Girl"'s pleasure, reminding reformers that the cinema kept her off the streets.[101] *Photoplay*'s plea to leave her in peace comes in response to the recent intensification of the city's reputation as a sexualized setting, for, as many scholars have observed, immigration and migration to cities in the 1880s and 1890s had suddenly swelled the urban US female labor force, so that now large numbers of women publicly walked the avenues, buying, peramulating, going, and coming to work. The arrival of cinema, and its use by "bachelor girls," were part and parcel of these grosser changes and adjustments.[102] And it was an entertainment readily integrated into women's daily routines of shopping, socializing, and child-rearing. David Lean's *Brief Encounter* (1945) relishes such patterns by linking two very female middle-class activities of the period—lunch in town, followed by the cinema—both through the main female character's (Laura Jesson) movement from the Kardomah tea room to the supercinema on one particular afternoon, and through the working life of the female musician who both plays the cello during Laura's lunch at the Kardomah, and later the organ in front of Laura's movie screen on the same afternoon.

Reasons to go to the cinema escalated in wartime. Many women recorded increased enjoyment at viewing glamor under siege.[103] Such pleasures caused the British government to reverse its ruling, after only three weeks, on the forcible closure of all cinemas and sports stadia (for fear of extreme casualties during air raids) during the Second World War.[104] During the Great War, the female employee, "who has gone to work in the Munition Factory out of a grim determination to share, as far as she is allowed, in the work her man is doing in the trenches, can for a space, as she watches some thrilling picture drama, forget the War, and the terrors that haunt her every night."[105] Also during this campaign, aristocratic women held London matinée fund-raising screenings of captured foreign films for their afternoon circles.[106] Other writers mention women's interest in newsreels, a crucial source of information whether in wartime or not in households where "the morning paper is seized upon by the lord and master at breakfast and taken off to the city train."[107]

Reports of women availing themselves of the movies for crying are abundant.[108] Shedding tears alongside the unaffected, let alone those laughing, triggered a quiet gender war; sexual isolation was the most urgently needed reform, wrote one—let us "have separate cinemas for men and women."[109] Luxuriating in the lachrymose, Gabriel Costa shared her fellow Jewess's delight at the "onion films" that "will cause her tears to fall copiously for the remainder of the evening."[110] Barnes recounted the Hollywood manager's etiquette of allowing patrons to "repair the ravages of emotion" by keeping the lights down until some time after the film had ended, a courtesy omitted in Langer's Berlin movie house.[111]

Other writers allude, if infuriatingly vaguely, to a new emotional register reached by the cinema. This terrain exceeded the domain of identifying with characters and situations on-screen. It had to do with an affective realm that, until the cinema, was possibly only reached by music. Writing before the arrival of sound, Iris Barry, for instance, linked the cinema's emotional appeal specifically to its visuality:

> because the motion picture speaks direct to the eye, it is a powerful form of communication ... even in the crudest films something is provided for the imagination, and emotion is stirred by the simplest things—moonlight playing in a bare room, the flicker of a hand against a window ... the finest films are as lovely to the eye as they are moving to the emotions.[112]

If the cinema had established "the Modern Girl's right to a good time," perhaps what she might lay claim to there was "an education in feeling".[113]

Barry found that "the best films are the ones with little or no conventional sentiment in them," while Maya Deren wished to make a film that would affect the viewer by being "about the inner experiences of a human being," for film was not "bound by the astronomy of clocks and calendars, [but] could make manifest the astronomy of the heart and mind."[114] Laura Riding asserted that "films ... expose to view, magically, the actual movement of emotions through all the daily turns of human life," while Woolf suspected cinema might give access to emotions hitherto unrepresented, portend ones that "may, in time to come, be composed."[115] All these women accord film's capacity to engage and release the emotions an intriguing, positive value.

The moved female viewer is as much a part of cinema furniture in this writing as the female cashier. Altenloh observed, by way of wrapping up her study, that the sight of women in the cinema, crying or not, rivalled the attraction of the film itself.[116] Altenloh's comment reminds us that looks and glances striated the entirety of cinema's space; that cinemagoers looked at the movie, and at each other; that if cinema unleashed a plethora of sights, some of these lay off-screen. Vision has claimed the attention of scholars and critics of cinema before any of the other senses, and women's writings of the era certainly do not fail us in this regard. They harness a vale of imagery for the unique patterns of illumination falling upon customers, whose "pallid ovals," "sheened" in "the half-light," with a "self-protective surface of apparent torpor," lifted "a foolish gaze towards the glare."[117] The screen's "pallor" might fall on an "eagerly gazing row," or on "dull eyes unresponsively meeting the shadowy grimaces on the flickering 'film.'"[118] Women were also among the many who discussed cinema's appeal to the eye over the intellect, and its optical consequences: the damp "moving-picture eye," "the movin' pitcher squint," and the "permanently injur[ed]" oculus.[119] And women parsed eyes: the practical, "English unaesthetic eye" that kept one safe; "the too synthetic eye," inadequate to the medium's demands.[120]

Women's initial observations of the sense of sight at the movies aggregated around the themes of looking and being looked at, seeing and being seen. As Shelley Stamp points out, such gazing was nourished through the rich decorative schemes of picture palaces from the early 1910s onwards, which adopted the styles of department stores and theater foyers with their gilded mirrors and sweeping lobby staircases.[121] The prospect of the theater or gallery dissected by gazes, especially gazes travelling between the sexes, interested several independent painters of the 1870s and 1880s, including Mary Cassatt, Pierre Renoir, and Edgar Degas, all of whom crisscrossed their pictorial compositions of loges, salons, and opera boxes with studied and absent stares, binoculared or lorgnetted, focused near or far. The illustration accompanying Alice Rix's boxing report recalled this iconography, in its proposal of cinema's multi-directional invitations to look (See Fig. 1.7). It shows a seated woman craning intently toward the screen, where a sketchy Corbett (identifiable by his shorts) maneuvers, the gauze of the woman's hat veiling full disclosure of her interest. The standing, "disinterested" woman turns away, looking uphill, toward the higher reaches of the theater, apparently studying the audience, perhaps anxious at being seen, or, as Dan Streible suggests, maybe she represents "a chaperone's sense of social impropriety."[122] Rix writes of the discomfort of being observed at the Veriscope at all, a discomfort presumably exacerbated by being witnessed while taking in the erotic delights of Corbett disrobing down to his buttock-revealing trunks, pleasures etched by the spectacle of violence (his defeat in a knockout).[123]

Several of women's earliest accounts of filmgoing associated looking with desire, by likening viewing to window-shopping; discussion of the new medium erupted into weekly fashion and theatergoing columns, amid consumer reports on metropolitan life.[124] Virginia, of "The Diary of a Daughter of Eve" (1896), longed for a cinematograph for her private use, so she might secrete her lust, while The Matinee Girl, in 1897, recounted hiding from the other girls she knew in the audience, when visiting the Corbett prizefight film.[125] The frisson of risk (attached both to clandestine and to exposed gazing) present in these primordial stirrings of the spectatrix was to stamp itself on women's discoursing about their own

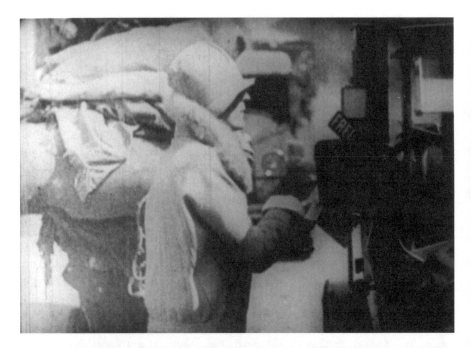

Fig. 1.4   Frame enlargements from Walter Ruttmann,
Berlin: Symphony of a Great City, 1927.

viewing for a couple more decades: in 1908, a female Boston journalist described the embarrassment of a woman friend of hers, glimpsed going to the movies, and wrote both of not wanting to confide her own "liking of this sort of thing," and of her satisfaction and relief in learning that others like her went too.[126]

This anxiety was partly attributable to the newness of the setting, for women who attended such public events would have been suspect as prostitutes, almost by definition. In addition, as mentioned in the earlier discussion of prize fight pictures, conventions of female behavior at the movies did not yet exist. Rix searches for such guidelines in her focus on decorum: "They take off their hats, after deliberation. A woman across the aisle watches them. Then she takes off hers."[127] Hats were, indeed, a particular challenge.[128] Assessing the impact of feminism, one writer in 1910 disparaged those types of women who were always discontent "unless they *dope* themselves with amusement," women "who have put their sex to shame in the last year or two by the wild vulgarity of their silly, and hideous, and selfish hats."[129] Rinehart recounted her part in a hat battle in a Viennese movie house, while a mind-your-manners glass slide (designed to punctuate a nickelodeon show) illustrated a male customer scaling, by step ladder, the mushrooming woman's headgear before him.[130] Another such slide asked "Ladies Under Forty-Five" to remove their chapeaux. Women's bonnets, swelling to monstrous size, with their strident and even emancipatory significance, elicited not only comment but also legislation. An Atlanta city ordinance of 1910 compelled the removal of large hats in theaters; motion picture managers demanded the ordinance's annulment, since "women [were] staying away from their houses, rather than remov[ing] their hats."[131] As a *Vogue* advice column later put it, "hats are emotional stuff."[132]

These millinery disputes were a symptom of the intrusiveness of women's very visibility; the enlarged hat was an index of her presence; the hidden ocular drama sheltered under the hat brim or behind the veil asked: if women are present, what are they seeing? After the later 1910s, as picture hats shrank to cloches (was women's fashion accommodating itself to the movies?) commentary on the anxiety of being witnessed (especially outside or on entering the cinema), all but vanished, while accounts of the pleasures of being only dimly seen inside, and of the reconfigured power of looking effected by the dark, took over.[133] Several medium close-ups of urban women in cloches in Walther Ruttmann's film essay of the German capital, *Berlin: Symphony of a Great City/Berlin. Die Sinfonie der Großstadt* (1927), seem bewitched by the new dynamics of looking enabled by this modernist headgear, which, in its shape and name echoed the phonograph's sound-gathering bells (also typically referred to as cloches). In this film, the camera seeks to peer around and under the cloches' shading felt, as if to discover exactly how this or that woman was taking in the city. The cloche's deep, snug-fitting prow shielded women's eyes from onlookers, and hence also denied them, these curious onlookers, knowledge of the precise objects these fashionable women were espying. On the other hand, pulled hard down, these molded, brimless forms framed a woman's field of view, up close, severely limiting peripheral vision. If the cinema, by the early 1920s, had become a venue for female flânerie, in wearing a cloche, the woman took her cinema out and about with her.[134]

American artist Mabel Dwight took on moviegoing in her lithographs and drawings. As in all her work as a printmaker and illustrator of urban life, her images of cinema betray her fascination with the variegated crowd, and the quality of human contact it supported. During 1928 and 1929, at around the time of her first solo exhibition, Dwight completed three works on the movie audience, treating three film genres: the Western; the "oriental thriller"; and the romance. Each composition balances architectural details (pillars, balconies, proscenium, curtains) against the irregular forms of seated or standing spectators, gazing towards the screen. In "Mott Street Movies," a pencil-and-crayon drawing, the Chinese-American audience views from two levels; a woman holds a child behind the back rows, the steeply raked auditorium pitching down towards the organist's squat, silhouetted form, while a string of other viewers juts forwards from an upper, cantilevered ledge. A film, The Spiders, unfolds before them.[135] In "The Clinch," through soft Conté on stone, Dwight accumulates another audience's physical mass, its hunched shoulders, craning necks, and gawping faces caught in the screen's reflected glow.[136] (See Fig. 1.1). One or two people rise to leave, obstructing the view of other, rapt spectators. In departing, they will intersect the projector's dusty shaft, which elsewhere flickers across boxes, indirectly limning the proscenium and curtain swags with light. It is the climax of the film. Two stars (modelled on Vilma Banky and Rudolph Valentino, or perhaps John Gilbert) sway in a gripping embrace. They draw the crowd's focus, but the schmozzle of viewers entering and leaving (a door is uncurtained at the rear) makes the screening imperfect and unique, only one facet of the show's entertainment.[137]

Dwight's pictures encapsulate visually the mood of much of the writing in Part One. They convey the febrile, constantly shifting atmosphere of cinema's culture of darkness. In each of these twenty-nine accounts, we enter the cinema in the "celluloid twilight," the film en marche.[138] Women writers remark on missing the film's beginning, or, more often, on the succession of different kinds of film unspooling through the auditorium, arrangements making the point of entry somewhat insignificant. Instead, it was the "fantastic elves, dancing," the ushers' flashlights, that marked the start.[139] Janet Flanner reported them "lighting your entire front," making her an outsider, "for a few moments … a public character," before the darkness joined her to the crowd.[140] Dorothy Richardson's spectators "creep" as Barry's "slink," arriving into a gloom which defined, this writing suggests, the distinctiveness of the venue."[141] And while Negri expanded on the attractive shivers of accidental contact this promoted, Emilie Post instructed us on how to avoid them.[142]

Negri's spectator "graze[d] the arm of some invisible person" as she entered in the dark, but later, in the light, she did not look at them, for "to look at someone means to be looked at.… If only it were possible in life to be close to someone all the time without seeing each other."[143] This is the critical option the cinema

Fig. 1.5   Mabel Dwight, "Mott Street Movies,"
pencil and black crayon drawing, 1929.

promised women, inviting looking without being seen to be doing so, and without being looked at in return.[144] At the cinema women engaged an endlessly changing stream of images and tales of femininity, while sampling the (utopian) potential of their own disappearance—while still looking. This may be one reason why the otherwise limited figure of the harem woman held peculiar allure—veiled, she saw from the vantage of invisibility. Among the many screen incarnations of her persona, that of Howard Hawks's *Fazil* taps the fantasy most directly. After briefly touring the empty desert sand with his camera, in an opening sequence, Hawks cuts to a single, stationary, interior shot of a woman gazing through a square-framed opening, within an arabesque. Her back largely to us, her shrouded body is motionless in dark silhouette. We never see her again. She plays no role in plot or character. Rather, her early presence on the screen, as the first human figure of the film, conjures up the waiting female audience, shadowy before it.

Gertrude Koch has pondered why women have gone to the pictures at all, given the broad cultural taboo against female voyeurism.[145] But it seems that the film setting, over time, conditionally and partially modified this social code, so that women might imagine they eluded witness. It is in this sense that Lejeune could write that "the darkness, the sleepy music, the chance to relax unseen are all women's pleasures which no man, however tired he may be, can ever quite appreciate or understand," and that Richardson could enjoy jewels, "fair face," and an "exquisite toilet" rendered invisible in a gloaming of informality: "to the movies you may go just as you are—within and without."[146] If Post pondered why it might sometimes be acceptable for women to go to a matinée with a man, but not lunch with him, she overlooked entirely the attractions of cinema's "unaccompanied pleasures."[147] Here women might possess an unseen eye, a glance and an appearance cloaked in auditorial dusk. Cinema offered a disruption of, if not an escape from, the daily sightlines that impinged on women. Simultaneously, of course, the screen's stars offered templates for female emulation and enjoyment, and aids to examination of appearance, as the lobby mirrors did. Women's attraction to the cinema might be explained by these peculiar fluctuations: its valences of collectivity sheltering anonymity, of visibility within hiddenness, of publicness blended with privacy; its strange, amoebic drift from isolation towards coagulation, and back. But this slender, limited opportunity to view unseen was something revolutionary, a facet of modernity women's writings urge us to remember.

Part One's gathering of twenty-six spectatrixes echoes a more recent invitation from the journal *Camera Obscura* in 1989, in which sixty women answered a questionnaire about female spectatorship.[148] The inquiry was consequent on dissatisfactions with existing scholarship, which had overlooked the historical existence of the female viewer, and instead had invented an evolving but abstract model of her; it had become clear that there was a powerful dissonance between women's lively and varied responses to film, and the space allotted them in academic study. In the latter domain, female spectators had existed only as a theoretical construction, and even then one entering but as an afterthought—the female spectator of the 1970s and 1980s had been determined (one might even say overruled) by study of the film itself. Such opinion could only flourish in the anaerobic climate of inaccessible earlier female writing on film. It was only in the late 1980s, when revisionists embraced the Valentino cult, the three-hanky movie, and interviewed Scarlett's women, that we glimpsed again the spectatrix of yore.[149]

According to Laura Mulvey's extremely influential initial formulations, Hollywood cinema offered its spectators only a male position from which to view, regardless of any spectator's actual sex.[150] This was largely because active screen characters were male, passive ones were female; understandings of the cinematic apparatus as having the power to reproduce patterns of bourgeois subjectivity supported the proposal. Spectators entered the world of the film via an attraction to predominantly white, male dynamism, and readily sank, while watching, into primal habits of vision from childhood: the cinema (with its glamor, possibilities of peeking in the dark, and so on) set in motion activities of voyeurism and fetishism, so that identification occurred both with characters on screen and with the apparatus itself.[151]

In the psychoanalytical theories deployed by Mulvey and others for these analyses of cinema, a person's adult sense of subjecthood originated in the perception of sexual difference. However, this perception, devolving as it did on the unveiling of female genitals, became misunderstood as a difference between male and castrated male. The way in which the male child came to understand who he was was bound to this visual moment, which spurred visual processes (of voyeurism and fetishism, techniques for covering up for the lack of a penis, means to cope with castration fear) encouraged again by cinema.

One central aspect of this theory was soon challenged with the question, "Is the gaze male?"[152] Was there any way to look at film without being interpolated as male? Freudian psychoanalysis had provided no account as to what the female child did with that foundational moment of the sight of the mother's "absent penis." Gaylyn Studlar, among others, explored the possible consequences of women's masochistic attachment to the passive female character on screen.[153] When Mulvey revised her account a few years later, the female spectator still had to assume a masculine position, but now more awkwardly, less successfully, with, seemingly, more room for variations in pleasure: "the female spectator's phantasy of masculinization is always to some extent at cross purposes with itself, restless in its transvestite clothes."[154] Mary Ann Doane's analysis of femininity as "masquerade" posed another alternative, arguing that femininity emerged separately from those drives characterizing the male spectator, with the consequence that the gap between the image and the self necessary for voyeurism and fetishism was diminished at the cinema: "For the female spectator, there's a certain over-presence of the image—she is the image." According to Doane, drawing on an essay by Joan Rivière of 1929, the woman overcame this overidentification with the image, this lack of distance, through performing a masquerade by which the very history of the construction of femininity—both on screen and in society—was revealed.[155]

To this point, female spectators had only been associated with awkwardness and misfit, despite empirical evidence that they reaped multiple delights at the cinema. A universalizing psychoanalytic history had isolated them from any social setting, leaving nuances of historical change within audiences, and within viewing circumstances impossible to register.[156] In seeking a way out of this impasse—the collision between theoretical models of viewing and empirical spectators—Annette Kuhn proposed the paired categories "film audience" and "film spectator."[157] The former were historically and physically present at the cinema, flesh and blood, while the latter were products of film texts and the apparatus, and addressed by them. This, among many steps taken by numerous scholars—including Doane and Mulvey, and including ethnographic investigation of female audiences, via questionnaires or interviews—challenged the hegemonic grip of "spectator-positioning," as the theory, in shorthand, had come to be known.[158] It was a move paralleled in literary studies, and indeed in cultural studies, in which the ideal reader came under challenge from the consumer.[159]

The distinction between spectator and audience, while enabling the development of recent feminist scholarship, is not readily apparent in women's earlier writings—indeed, it is remarkable how absent an abstract account of spectatorship is. Insistent, rather, is the presence of the spectator as clearly one with the writer, named often as "I," and described as variously integrating with, or observing, the larger audience. Dunbar must take some distance from the "persons of a certain degree of simplicity" attending the movies; Lejeune, though willingly there, is also apart from the women she describes; Serao finds her status vis-à-vis the crowd shifting, and growing warmer, in the time elapsing between entering the cinema, settling in, and later being moved to tears; Bowen is intent on attaching herself to the throng to become one of the "sophisticates," although she then insists, in one of the least generalizing of the essays, "I go to please myself, and when I sit opposite a film the audience is me."[160]

Where a uniformity had descended upon the spectatorship of recent theory, with all females squashed into the same theoretical box as the male (having to put on male clothes there sometimes, but any option beyond this binarism being foreclosed), earlier accounts display as much variation as there are writers. We cannot speak of the spectator, as suggested by psychoanalytic theory, but rather of a wide variety. With both periods of enquiry motivated by the same question—"what happens at the cinema?"—the focus in the 1970s and 1980s had been on the unconscious hold film-watching had over viewers (explained in terms of ideological critique and psychoanalytic development), while earlier female writers answered through an endlessly proliferating attention to the observed minutiae of filmgoing. Against the one-dimensional, spectatorial hook of gaze theory, one finds the full sensorium at work. For earlier writers, vision—that facet of cinema most frequently discussed by their descendants—was always in play with the other senses. Cinemagoing entailed, and invited, a new kind of balancing, even collision of sensory activities, of looking, listening, smelling, touching, and tasting, accompanied perhaps by only intermittent attentiveness to the screen. Delight and interest lay more in the "pulse" of the film setting, and in the flickering of the filmic image, glimpsed with a "casual glance," than in the armature of the film's narrative, the element most responsible for pinning down spectatorial position more recently.[161]

But let us not overstate the case. Among writings by women on the film audience from the first fifty years of cinema, there is some interest in delineating a structure for female spectatorship, and among these lie antecedents for later theoretical work. Cecelia Ager railed against the manipulative masochism through which movies reached towards women: "their heartbreak is what the ladies really enjoy and remember."[162] Spectators overidentify with the screen: Ada Negri, in her "explosively popular" fiction column, published on the cultural page of the Milan evening daily, described the forlorn addiction of a lonely secretary who ultimately blended the film with the street outside—"she doesn't know where she is"—throwing herself in front of a car.[163] (Although we also read of the alternative scenario: Virginia Woolf suffering the "queer sensation" of knowing that "the wave will not wet our feet" when we sit before the pictured ocean, or, to refer to those crowds watching the platform at La Ciotat in a Lumière film in 1895, that the train arriving at the station will not run us down.[164]) However, descriptions of extreme and disorienting emotional attachment to the screen are as likely to pertain to men as to women, at least in written accounts dating into the early 1920s. Men and boys suffered "movanic odeonum," or were "filmaniacs."[165] They were casualties of "photobia," or "filmitis," or might be a "poor moth," or victim of "cinemania," duped into believing in a film career.[166] (Later, this pathological cathexis came more to characterize a feminine response—an ancestry for the masquerading spectatrix—a habit supported between screenings by writing to stars via fan magazines, or merely basking in magazine pages.[167] By the late 1930s, fans had become "girls mostly, with a sprinkling of loungers."[168])

Winifred Holtby's fictional "Missionary Film" delineated a relation between viewer and screen with more dynamic consequences in her making of a mild case for cinema's politically galvanizing effect, in that Mr Grant is spurred on by film-viewing to return to his South African missionary work.[169] However, this was not a description of female spectatorship, nor was it formulated in stringent, diagrammatic terms—the tale appeared as one of seven stories in the "Exotic" section of Holtby's collection, Truth is Not Sober.[170] Dunbar quizzed the odd, "unnatural 'continuousness'" of movie presentation, finding that it ultimately explained cinema's hold over its patrons: "It makes no demand whatever upon its audiences, requiring neither punctuality—for it has no beginning—nor patience—for it has no end—nor attention—for it has no sequence."[171] In paralleling the formlessness of film entertainment to the apathetic, inexpressive attitude of viewers, Dunbar conceptualized a reciprocal relation of crowd (though not specifically of women) to projection.

It was Dorothy Richardson who probed female filmgoing most thoroughly in this era, testing a number of possible relations of viewer to screen. However, her accounts remain far from generalizable, and do not derive primarily from on-screen events or structures of looking governed by the apparatus, but rather rest on fragile links between the picture and the community of the auditorium, evoked in ethnographic and architectural detail. For example, in one of Richardson's descriptions, viewer and screen feed off one another in an interdependent, fluctuating equilibrium: "In she comes and the screen obediently ceases to exist.... She maintains a balance, the thing perceived and herself perceiving.... [She] testifies that life goes on, art or no art, and that the onlooker is a part of the spectacle."[172] Elsewhere Richardson described this bond as one of "attention and collaboration," and, in another formulation, suggested that "the film, by setting the landscape in motion and keeping us still, allows it to walk through us."[173]

Richardson's most recurrent interest lay in describing the varied spectatorial attitudes cinema's "apparitional quality" invited.[174] She identified meditative viewing via incidentals; states of contemplation before the screen; and the silent screen's active encouragement, as "collaborator," of "the imagination of the onlooker."[175] Of the young slum dweller she wrote, "There is in the picture that which emerges and captures him before details are registered and remains long after they are forgotten."[176] The closing of the silent era provoked Richardson, retrospectively, into defining contemplation as a specifically feminine pleasure in cinema (one now ruined), a pleasure which resided, Richardson suggested, in the spectatrix's scanning of the screen, her eye wandering across it as if aggregating details across a surface, without direction or plan.[177] Traversing the gap between viewer and screen on the brink of sound, Richardson warned that the linearizing, plot-regulating forces of synchronized sound were now channeling and constraining these feminine habits. With the coming of sound, a new code of manners would quiet this viewer's flooding, ebullient, self-expressivity.[178]

The diffuseness and expansiveness of cinematic reception captured Richardson. Cinema took us all in, from "the dustman's wife" to "that pleasant intellectual."[179] This "strange hospice risen overnight" met practical needs of retreat and shelter.[180] If her writing *does* suggest a continuity with later efforts, then it is through descriptions of female spectatorship as mobile. But a structural or abstract approach to the question of spectating would have entirely missed what she relished within it, those very shifting states of consciousness and awareness it brought into being, for an expanding array of publics.

As an answer to the quest for knowledge about female spectators of the past, this writing showers us with individuated and abundant verbal images. Indeed, this editorial essay has been organized by grouping together detailed observations, and distilling some of their possible meanings. Attention to the contingencies of viewing might be precisely what most distinguishes this earlier writing from later theories.[181] Naomi Schor has argued that the detail has been "doubly gendered as feminine," first through its association with ornamentation and decoration (from not seeing the bigger picture, "the proverbial forest for the trees," or worse, "the tree for the leaves"), and second, through its links to proliferation, the everyday, and domestic life.[182] As the work of anthropologist Sherry Ortner and others has suggested, as social beings women have been "seen as more embedded in the concrete and particular than man," even saving man from this fate.[183] While we might think of women as the more sheltered sex of the day, it was men, above all, who were protected from the debilitating deluge of details and differentiated responsibilities of quotidian life, concluded Dorothy Richardson in her essay on women in the arts.[184] If the research of *Red Velvet Seat* links women once again to the detail, is this writing then of lesser significance, slighter than general theories of cinema?[185]

In finding the opportunity to publish (and sometimes make films), the women in this collection were journalists, child-rearers, caretakers, housekeepers, partners, and more. Certainly, Virginia Woolf and, particularly, Catheryne Cooke Gilman were never far from a servant, but, in general, the roles of mother and wife were held uneasily alongside acts of writing or filming. If women lived in the thickness of materiality, should we not be attentive to this in their writing?

As a photographic medium, cinema could not help but register stray incidents erupting before the lens. (As Mary Ann Doane has put it, cinema had the capacity to record "whatever happens to be there at the moment.")[186] As a technically more demanding medium than still photography, cinema required yet more preparation and defence against chance—the wind that might rustle the curtain, lift the hair, blow the leaves. But an attraction of the screen for women seems to have been precisely the possibility of alighting on these effects: "the gardener mowing the lawn," seen through the window, the star wearing imitation chinchilla, the diffuse "aesthetic sensations" of nature on-screen, detached from any particular plot, title, or place.[187]

Perhaps we might understand this characteristic of women's writings—the recording of both the particularity of the auditorium, and of passing effects on-screen—in two opposing, yet related, ways. First, they echo tendencies of film itself, even to the point of rivaling them; they inscribe, in the way film could, had to, the unique and contingent over the universal and general. Yet were these writers not relishing exactly that which feature cinema was learning to eschew? While film's appetite for chance was alive and well in travelogues and newsreels, fiction films lay saturated with techniques for minimizing mishaps. The details of the auditorium strewn through, and even comprising, women's discourse rival filmic content, as indeed the shards of accidental events within an individual film rival the central, planned event of the narrative. The film unfolding in the dark, inexorably unwinding and all but insensitive to the specific constellations of that day's viewing audience, tracked the pacing onbeat of time, furnished a backdrop for the scattered minutiae of that particular screening occasion. The film's planar, inorganic yet moving indifference was a measure of the auditorium's contrasting Brownian motion. Writers of the detail restored, if not to the medium, then to its display, the stuff of life that the continuity system was working to strain out. In recording the cinema in its fullest aggregations, these authors produced the kind of evidence of its sensuality and chaos that the film camera itself was straining to leave out, but might have been capable of suggesting, had it been set loose, turned in another direction.

Seeing or Being Seen

Picture Shows Popular in the "Hub" (1908)
Lady Correspondent of the *Boston Journal*

Have you contracted the moving picture show habit yet? Most of the folks I know have, though for some reason they one and all seem loath to acknowledge the fact. Perhaps it is because it seems a childish pastime and not just the form of amusement one would expect worldly men and women to patronize to any extent. The man or woman who occupies a desk at your elbow may be a regular attendant upon these instructive and wholly entertaining little picture performances of an hour's duration. You will not know it unless by chance you happen to see him or her buying an admission at the window, or after groping your way to a seat in the dark find one or the other filling the chair at your side.

Visiting the little theaters that offer an attractive assortment of pictures has long been a custom of mine, though curiously enough I have not confided my liking for this sort of thing to even my intimate friends. In the past I have paid my admission, and slipping into a seat, watched whatever the screen had to offer. Yesterday afternoon, quite by accident, I learned that a congenial friend of mine had the same interest in these fascinating views of foreign shores; of mirth-provoking happenings and of events in the news which form the basis of the entertainment, so we made an appointment to attend one.

While waiting the young lady's arrival, I lingered in the entrance and for the brief space of ten minutes was absorbed in watching the manner of men and women who singly and in groups approached the box office and paid their admittance fee of a dime. All kinds were represented in the steady throng that sought an entrance. The first man who held my attention looked as though he might be a bank official or broker. He had that cast-iron, blank expression that attaches itself to men who constantly handle money or constantly think about it in the day's work. The next were a family party of three—father, mother and a two-year-old child.

Then came a woman who looked as though she might be employed in one of the great department stores. She was followed by another group of three, all women, winding up an afternoon's shopping in town with a few moments' recreation before returning to their homes to preside over their own supper tables and afterward put the babies to bed.

Next came two men whom I know by sight and reputation. They are partners in a flourishing business in the down-town section. I caught sight of a doctor next, whose name proclaims him prominent in his realm of endeavour, and then of a man of whom I have bought steaks and chops and other good things for several years. Beside those whom I recognized or had some inkling of their object in life, there were twenty others as interesting and as different in appearance as those I have described.

I was about to give my friend up and venture in alone when another figure loomed before me which made me feel quite conscious. It was that of a woman friend of mine who seemed to shrink within herself when she saw me. She felt as I felt no doubt—like a child caught at the jampot. We smilingly exchanged greetings, she murmured something about "enjoying them so much," to which I promptly responded, "So do I." The friend whom I had been expecting pushed me through the door, brandishing the tickets as she did so, and we gave ourselves up to the enjoyment of an entertainment that appeals to all sorts, rich and poor, intelligent and unintelligent, which is instructive and helpful as well as amusing.

[quoted in *The Moving Picture World* (New York), 16 May 1908, p. 433.]

The Diary of a Daughter of Eve (1896)
Virginia

TUESDAY. No house is complete without a cinematographe. I yearn for one for my private use, and I revelled in the show at the Empire last night. Julia suggests that as I never move I should have small service for such a toy; she even ventured to observe that my tastes were childish, my joy in the performance reminding her of nothing but the enthusiasm I was wont to exhibit at a Punch and Judy show. Julia's stupidity really begins to bore me. The charm of the cinematographe to me is that it showed me life as I know it. I like things I know—the inexplicable has no charms for me; a conjuror is my *bête-noir*—I detest a person who can do the things I cannot. Which reminds me that I really detest Julia, for she can walk down the most attractive streets, gaze into all the shop windows, and desire nothing. This, she thinks, marks her as superior; while I am convinced it simply stigmatises her as an inferior animal, with no possible appreciation of beauty, but scant taste, and small ambition. Fashion is very pleasing to me this year; its main characteristic is its flimsiness: the softest and thinnest of fabrics are used, and the embroideries are of the same diaphanous type. The tulle and chiffon cravats and vests will in their short life inspire the repetition of the well-known baby's epitaph: "Since they are so quickly done for,/ We wonder what they are begun for."

[*Black and White* (London), 4 April 1896, p. 442, excerpted.]

The Matinee Girl (1897)
The Matinee Girl

[...] I saw the prize-fight at the Academy last week. Of course I mean the Veriscope.[1] I saw lots of girls I knew there, but I didn't pretend to notice they were there. I felt just as much ashamed of it as they were!

It is a pity Corbett doesn't win.[2] He is a great favorite with us, but he's been knocked out of our hearts by his recent defeat.

Mr. Brady will have to give away some very expensive souvenir if he ever expects to have his star regain his popularity with the Saturday afternoon audiences.[3] Fitzsimmons isn't pretty—but Oh, my![4]

[*New York Dramatic Mirror* (New York), 12 June 1897, p. 14, excerpted.]

Alice Rix at the Veriscope (1897)[1]
Alice Rix

Well?

Where is she?

Where is woman at the prize fight?

Where is that fierce, primitive, savage thing, that harpy, that bird of prey, that worse-than-man who was expected to sit six rows deep before the Veriscope at the Olympia and gloat over the bloody sport of the ring? Where is the brute?

I do not see her on Monday night. But then, as somebody reminds me, Monday is Press night.

It is on Tuesday then that I may expect her?

Yes, certainly. She will be there on Tuesday.

Various simple ostriches of my acquaintance assure me there will be a crush of women at the Olympia every night and a bigger crush still at the matinees. That is woman's first opportunity, you know, to see a prize fight with the blessing of the world upon her head and she would rather lose the head than miss it. Why? Look at her in New York where the Veriscope was running at the Academy of Music. I saw her at the Veriscope in New York, of course, sitting fierce-eyed and dry-mouthed before the screen with her thumbs down? No? I read about her, then? And saw the pictures in the papers?

Well, it would be the same thing here.

"Women, you know, are the same everywhere."

Oh, simple ostrich! In Persia woman is called the Eternal Disappointment.

"There'll be a hot time down there tonight," said a man on the dummy.

"You bet!" said the man with him.

"Turn women loose on the chance of seeing a prize fight without getting herself talked about and there'll be no holding them back."

Fig. 1.6 "The Interested and the Disinterested," Original illustration from "Alice Rix at the Veriscope," 18 July 1897.

"You bet," said the other man.

I see these men again at the entrance to the Olympia. They are waiting there, as one of them remarks, to watch the women pour in.

I look up and down the block. There is only one woman in sight, and she seems to be pouring in the opposite direction. Still it is early—only a little after eight.

A few men clutter the lobby—men, the florid sort with short, harsh, hair-cuts and natty-noisy clothes—if the world will admit that style in clothes—and it will have to, since there is no other name by which they can be made to sound as they seem.

A short line forms before the box office. There is not a woman in it.

"You can sit anywhere," says the usher. "There's plenty of room."

I look for a place near some women. There is [sic] only a few here as yet. Apparently the hot time is not quite hot. I find a seat in front of a family party—mother, father and two girls—and wait for the time to warm.

The Olympia is a huge, white-painted wooden circus, and little groups of persons freckle its big, round face with dark, irregular patches that do not, in some way, relieve the whiteness of it. The women present are dressed down and sit quietly, speaking little. All the color is concentrated in a corner where the costumes of the mandolin players splash blood-red across the white beyond and suggest uncomfortable symbols. Everything else is coldly white. The big screen stands out white against white, the big lights shine down white over white. The place is singularly chill and singularly still. People whisper. A man laughs out once and the effect is like a shot in the night.

"Ain't it quiet here?" says the woman behind me—the mother of the two girls.

She is a middle-aged woman with a wide, sweet, kind, complacent face. She looks like a woman who would step over an ant and pick a fly out of a cream jug as much for the sake of the fly as for the cream. And the simple ostrich told me this was the worst kind. It will be interesting, I think, to watch the harpy spirit keening over such a face as this. The girls are young—at the impressionable age. I change my seat to have a fair look at all three when the fight is on.

There is a little flutter at the door and the men in the body of the house crane their necks and smile expectantly. A string of society girls file down the aisle and take the chairs in front of mine. They are companioned by the very young men who make gayety of the seasons in the Western social year and irreproachably gooseberried by Papa and Mamma. The girls look quietly over the house, as much as they can see of it without turning their well-bred heads beyond the right angle of manners, whisper with the very young men, consult Mamma, deliberate, titter and finally take off their hats. A woman across the aisle watches them. Then she takes off hers.

"Do you suppose," asks one of the girls, "that it will be much fun?"

"I don't see anyone here," answers the other girl.

A few young men in dress suits saunter in and sit staring before them at the big ocean across the stage. The short-haired sporting men incline to the boxes. The gallery is only half-filled. The seats at the back of the house are all empty. There are altogether about a thousand people and only sixty of these are women.

The mandolins tinka-tinkle through a few tunes with a vigorous piano behind them. Then there is a long pause. Then a man in a dress suit appears at the side of the screen and introduces the Veriscope. Then the lights go down and the single light boxed in the gallery reaches out over the house and burns on the canvas screen. The audience is shrouded in the silent dark. The light widens on the canvas and suddenly the screen is alive with the figures of men, moving, gesticulating, smiling, speaking, without sound. It is weird, peculiar, a little uncomfortable—a grayish shuddering semblance of humanity, neither shadow nor substance, neither quick nor dead.

It is very trying to the eyes, but it is even more bewildering to the brain. One cannot but seek to liken it to something—and it is like nothing in all the world. It is like nothing I have ever thought of as belonging to other worlds. These silent, moving shapes are neither ghostly nor shadowy. They are fully featured and of the earth. Their unreality is in their grayish color, their strange silence and the eternal blinding, flickering light that plays over them as at the morgue water runs over the faces and bodies of the dead.

This is not a pretty simile, but the Veriscope is not an entirely pretty exhibition. It is in its way a little awful.

I am reminded suddenly of a long-forgotten childish terror on the Magic Lantern show. The drawing-room in darkness, the ghastly white plain stretching away into the unknown world of shadows. It was all very well to call it a linen sheet, to say it was stretched between innocent familiar folding doors. It nevertheless divided the known and safe from the mysterious beyond where awful shadows lived and moved with a frightful rapidity and made no sounds at all.

And they were always awful, no matter how grotesquely amusing the shape they took, and they followed me to the nursery in after hours and sat on my heart and soul the black night through. And sometimes even morning light could not drive them quite away, and now forsooth, it seems they have withstood the years.

I would not go to see the Veriscope often. It is, as one of the girls in front of me said, "A little too leary for me."

The man in the dress suit explained the progress of the fight.

"That is Mr. Corbett on the right," he said. "And that is Mr. Fitzsimmons on the left."[2]

"Yes, that's old Fitz," said a man in the audience. "That's old lanky Fitz."

Old lanky Fitz was pacing restlessly back and forth at his side of the ring with his snake-like head thrust forward and his feet dragging a little as he walked. Pompadour Jim danced around the center of the ring and tried the ground with his feet and laughed and waved his hand to a friend outside the ropes and talked voicelessly with his attendants.[3] The giddy films lent both men strange flickering distorted features. With faces turned to the front they grimaced horribly: their profiles broke in wavering lines from brow to chin. Now and then a stretch of clean limb, a head well outlined, a swift, sharp impression cut through the vague, flying picture, just enough to show what the Veriscope will accomplish with time and mechanical perfection.

The man in the dress suit stood at the side of the screen and called off the rounds.

"Round one!"

The principals came out of their bathrobes, the gong sounded, the shapes danced up to each other, sparred, retreated, advanced, clinched, sprang apart and went through the process over and over again. The gong sounded again. A shape climbed under the ropes and a phantom chair swung up over them. The principals retreated into their corners and their attendants shut them out behind a flopping screen of towels.

"Is that all?" said one of the society girls. "Who won?"

"That's only one round," explained one of the very young men.

"Well, I know that," said the girl. "I meant who won that round?"

The picture-life shuddered on over the screen. The principals took their one minute's rest. Their attendants rubbed and fanned. The crowd beyond the ropes at the back swayed in its seats. A few men visible on the side nearest the house smoked and scribbled on note-books and went through their soundless motions of talk and laughter. The audience sat unexcitedly waiting for more.

"Round two!"

The shapes bobbed into the ring and the dancing and sparring began again.

"They don't seem to hurt each other much," said one of the society girls.

"You can't hear 'em hit in this," answered one of the very young men. "That's half the fun."

"Ugh!" answered the girl. "I should think it would be horrid."

The light flashed out on the screen and on over the house.

I looked to see how the complaisant woman was taking the fight. She sat with her hand over her eyes. One of the girls gave her arm a tender little nudge. "You can look now mamma. It's out."

"Don't it hurt your eyes, father?" asked the complaisant woman. But father shook his head.

"It's a bum way to see a fight, though," he answered discontentedly.

"Ain't it just like it was up there?" asked one of the girls.

Father laughed. "Not much it ain't," he said, "not much."

"Why," persisted the girl, "its all photographed. It must have looked just the same."

"Well," said the father, slowly, "It ain't all looks in a fight."

"Round three!"

Round three was rather brisk and the film showed fair. The house warmed perceptibly. The sporting men reminisced.

"That's it! That's the way Jim landed him that one in the jaw. I bet you that was pretty work!"

But the women said nothing. During the next intermission they yawned and moved about restlessly in their chairs.

The man in the dress suit made some remark about Mr. Hannman's hat and the questionable propriety of his using it as a signal to his principal each time before the gong sounded to end a round.

"The idea!" said one of the girls behind me. "If he's on Fitzsimmon's side why shouldn't he help him all he can?"

The shades on the screen were fighting in earnest now. They fought with each other and with the imperfections in the film. A line cut the lank Cornishman suddenly in two and his lean halves came together again like a pair of shears. His left hand shot out from his shoulder and Corbett doubled and slid under it like a snake and came up smiling on the other side.

"Good duck," called a voice from the gallery. And the house applauded.

When the Californian put the Cornishman on his knees in the famous sixth round the man in the gallery called out:

"Good boy, Jim!" And the house applauded again.

When the fourteenth and last round was fought and the Veriscope, which does not lie, showed Fitzsimmons landing a blow on the jaw of the man who had one knee and one glove on the floor, the man in the gallery groaned. But this time the house did not respond. I was rather sorry—for the sake of the man in the gallery as well as for the honor and glory of California, whose world's champion lay in the dust—but especially for the sake of the man in the gallery. I felt that he should have been encouraged in his enthusiasms, whichever way they led him. Other men who were present had none. If they were a shade more interested in the exhibition than the women who yawned through it, that was only because they were better informed concerning what they saw and the unexciting pleasures of memory were theirs.

The Veriscope is a bloodless battle, fought on canvas by the wraiths and shades of men.

"You don't hear the blows in this," said the very young man.

It is a faithful picture of the great Carson contest.[4] "But," as father said, "looks ain't everything in a fight."

Suspense is. Or nearly everything. The rest is the sight of blood and the magnetism of the personal fury behind the blows.

The San Francisco woman sat calmly before the Veriscope.

So did the San Francisco man.

[*San Francisco Examiner*, 18 July 1897, p. 22.]

Touring the Audience

Some Picture Show Audiences (1911)
Mary Heaton Vorse

One rainy night in a little Tuscan hill town I went to a moving-picture show. It was market-day: the little hall was full of men in their great Italian cloaks. They had come in from small isolated hamlets, from tiny fortified towns perched on the tops of distant hills to which no road led, but only a *salita*. I remember that there was in the evening's entertainment a balloon race, and a pilgrimage to the Holy Land, and a mad comic piece that included a rush with a baby carriage through the boulevards of Paris; and there was a drama, "The Vendetta," which had for its background the beautiful olive terraces of Italy.

I had gone, as they had, to see pictures, but in the end I saw only them, because it seemed to me that what had happened was a latter-day miracle. By an ingenious invention all the wonderful things that happened in the diverse world outside their simple lives could come to them. They had no pictures or papers; few of them could read; and yet they sat there at home and watched the inflating of great balloons and saw them rise and soar and go away into the blue, and watched again the strange Oriental crowd walking through the holy streets of Jerusalem. It is hard to understand what a sudden widening of their horizon that meant for them. It is the door of escape, for a few cents, from the realities of life. It is drama, and it is travel, and it is even beauty, all in one. A wonderful thing it is, and to know just how wonderful I suppose you must be poor and have in your life no books and no pictures and no means of travel or seeing beautiful places, and almost no amusements of any kind; perhaps your only door of escape or only means of forgetfulness more drink than is good for you. Then you will know what a moving-picture really means, although you will probably not be able to put it into words.

We talk a good deal about the censorship of picture shows, and pass city ordinances to keep the young from being corrupted by them; and this is all very well, because a great amusement of the people ought to be kept clean and sweet; but at the same time this discussion has left a sort of feeling in the minds of people who do not need to go to the picture show that it is a doubtful sort of a place, where young girls and men scrape undesirable acquaintances, and where the prowler lies in wait for the unwary, and where suggestive films of crime and passion are invariably displayed.[1] But I think that this is an unjust idea, and that any one who will take the trouble to amuse himself with the picture show audiences for an afternoon or two will see why it is that the making of films has become a great industry, why it is that the picture show has driven out the vaudeville and the melodrama.

You cannot go to any one of the picture shows in New York without having a series of touching little adventures with the people who sit near you, without overhearing chance words of a *naïveté* and appreciation that make you bless the living picture book that has brought so much into the lives of the people who work.

Houston Street, on the East Side, of an afternoon is always more crowded than Broadway. Push-carts line the street. The faces that you see are almost all Jewish—Jews of many different types; swarthy little men, most of them, looking undersized according to the Anglo-Saxon standard. Here and there a deep-chested mother of Israel sails along, majestic in *sheitel* [sic] and shawl.[2] These are the toilers—garment-makers, a great many of them—people who work "by pants," as they say. A long and terrible workday they have to keep body and soul together. Their distractions are the streets, and the bargaining off the push-carts, and the show. For a continual trickle of people detaches itself from the crowded streets and goes into the good-sized hall; and around the entrance, too, wait little boys—eager-eyed little boys—with their tickets in their hands, trying to decoy those who enter into taking them in with them as guardians, because the city ordinances do not allow a child under sixteen to go in unaccompanied by an older person.

In the half-light the faces of the audience detach themselves into little pallid ovals, and, as you will always find in the city, it is an audience largely of men.[3]

Behind us sat a woman with her escort. So rapt and entranced was she with what was happening on the stage that her voice accompanied all that happened—a little unconscious and lilting *obbligato*. It was the voice of a person unconscious that she spoke—speaking from the depths of emotion; a low voice, but perfectly clear, and the unconsciously spoken words dropped with the sweetness of running water. She spoke in German. One would judge her to be from some part of Austria. She herself was lovely in person and young, level-browed and clear-eyed, deep-chested; a beneficent and lovely woman one guessed her to be. And she had never seen Indians before; perhaps never heard of them.

The drama being enacted was the rescue from the bear pit of Yellow Wing, the lovely Indian maiden, by Dick the Trapper; his capture by the tribe, his escape with the connivance of Yellow Wing, who goes to warn him in his log house, their siege by the Indians, and final rescue by a splendid charge of the United States cavalry; these one saw riding with splendid abandon over hill and dale, and the marriage then and there of Yellow Wing and Dick by the gallant chaplain. A

Fig. 1.7   "The Line at the Ticket Office," drawing by Wladylsaw T. Benda
illustrating "Some Picture Show Audiences."

guileless and sentimental dime novel, most ingeniously performed; a work of art;
beautiful, too, because one had glimpses of stately forests, sunlight shifting through
leaves, wild, dancing forms of Indians, the beautiful swift rushing of horses. One
must have had a heart of stone not to follow the adventures of Yellow Wing and
Dick the Trapper without passionate interest.

But to the woman behind it was reality at its highest. She was there in a fabled
country full of painted savages. The rapidly unfolding drama was to her no make-
believe arrangement ingeniously fitted together by actors and picture-makers. It had
happened; it was happening for her now.

"Oh!" she murmured. "That wild and terrible people! Oh, boy, take care, take
care! Those wild and awful people will get you!" "*Das wildes und grausames Volk*," she
called them. "Now—now—she comes to save her beloved!" This as Yellow Wing
hears the chief plotting an attack on Dick the Trapper, and then flies fleet-foot
through the forest. "Surely, surely, she will save her beloved!" It was almost a
prayer; in the woman's simple mind there was no foregone conclusion of a happy
ending. She saw no step ahead, since she lived the present moment so intensely.

When Yellow Wing and Dick were besieged within and Dick's hand was wounded—

"The poor child! how can she bear it? To see the *geliebte* wounded before one's very eyes!"

And when the cavalry thundered through the forest—

"God give that they arrive swiftly—to be in time they must arrive swiftly!" she exclaimed to herself.

Outside the iron city roared; before the door of the show the push-cart vendors bargained and trafficked with customers. Who in that audience remembered it? They had found the door of escape. For the moment they were in the depths of the forest following the loves of Yellow Wing and Dick. The woman's voice, so like the voice of a spirit talking to itself, unconscious of time and place, was their voice. There they were, a strange company of aliens—Jews, almost all, haggard and battered and bearded men, young girls with their beaus, spruce and dapper youngsters beginning to make their way. In that humble playhouse one ran the gamut of the East Side. The American-born sat next to the emigrant who arrived but a week before. A strange and romantic people cast into the welter of the terrible city of New York, each of them with the overwhelming problem of battling with strange conditions and an alien civilization. And for the moment they were permitted to drink deep of oblivion of all the trouble in the world. Life holds some compensation, after all. The keener your intellectual capacity, the higher your artistic sensibilities are developed, just so much more difficult it is to find this total forgetfulness—a thing that for the spirit is as life-giving as sleep.

And all through the afternoon and evening this company of tired workers, overburdened men and women, fills the little halls scattered throughout the city and throughout the land.

There are motion-picture shows in New York that are as intensely local to the audience as to the audience of a Tuscan hill town. Down on Bleecker Street is the Church of Our Lady of Pompeii. Here women, on their way to work or to their brief marketing, drop in to say their prayers before their favorite saints in exactly the same fashion as though it were a little church in their own parish. Towards evening women with their brood of children go in; the children frolic and play subduedly in the aisles, for church with them is an every-day affair, not a starched-up matter of Sunday only. Then, prayers finished, you may see a mother sorting out her own babies and moving on serenely to the picture show down the road—prayers first and amusement afterwards, after the good old Latin fashion.

It is on Saturday nights down here that the picture show reaches its high moment. The whole neighborhood seems to be waiting for a chance to go in. Every woman has a baby in her arms and at least two children clinging to her skirts. Indeed, so universal is this custom that a woman who goes there unaccompanied by a baby feels out of place, as if she were not properly dressed. A baby seems as much a matter-of-course adjunct to one's toilet on Bleecker Street as a picture hat would be on Broadway.

Every one seems to know everyone else. As a new woman joins the throng other women cry out to her, gayly:

"Ah, good-evening, Concetta. How is Giuseppi's tooth?"

"Through at last," she answers. "And where are your twins?"

The first woman makes a gesture indicating that they are somewhere swallowed up in the crowd.

This talk all goes on in good North Italian, for the people on Bleecker Street are the Tuscan colony. There are many from Venice also, and from Milan and from Genoa. The South Italian lives on the East Side.

Then, as the crowd becomes denser, as the moment for the show approaches, they sway together, pushed on by those on the outskirts of the crowd. And yet everyone is good-tempered. It is—

"Not so hard there, boy!"

"Mind for the baby!"

"Look out!"

Though indeed it doesn't seem any place for a baby at all, and much less so for the youngsters who aren't in their mothers' arms but are perilously engulfed in

Fig. 1.8 "They Were Permitted to Drink Deep of Oblivion of All the Trouble in the World," drawing by Wladyslaw T. Benda illustrating "Some Picture Show Audiences."

the swaying mass of people. But the situation is saved by Latin good temper and the fact that every one is out for a holiday.

By the time one has stood in this crowd twenty minutes and talked with the women and the babies, one has made friends, given an account of one's self, told how it was one happened to speak a little Italian, and where it was in Italy one had lived, for all the world as one gives an account of one's self when traveling through Italian hamlets. One answers the questions that Italian women love to ask:

"Are you married?"

"Have you children?"

"Then why aren't they at the picture show with you?"

This audience was an amused, and an amusing audience, ready to laugh, ready to applaud. [...]

Throughout the whole show, [...] there was one face that I turned to again and again. It was that of an eager little girl of ten or eleven, whose lovely profile stood out in violent relief from the dingy wall. So rapt was she, so spellbound, that she couldn't laugh, couldn't clap her hands with the others. She was in a state of emotion beyond any outward manifestation of it.

In the Bowery you get a different kind of audience. None of your neighborhood spirit here. Even in what is called the "dago show"—that is, the show where the occasional vaudeville numbers are Italian singers—the people seem chance-met; the audience is almost entirely composed of men, only an occasional woman.

It was here that I met the moving-picture show expert, the connoisseur, for he told me that he went to a moving-picture show every night. It was the best way that he knew of spending your evenings in New York, and one gathered that he had tried many different ways. He was in his early twenties, with a tough and honest countenance, and he spoke the dialect of the city of New York with greater richness than I have ever heard it spoken. He was ashamed of being caught by a compatriot in a "dago show."

"Say," he said, "dis is a bum joint. I don't know how I come to toin in here. You don't un'erstan' what the skoit's singin', do you? You betcher I don't!"

Not for words would he have understood a word of the inferior Italian tongue.

"I don't never come to dago moving-picter shows," he hastened to assure me. "Say, if youse wanter see a real show, beat it down to Grand Street. Dat's de real t'ing. Dese dago shows ain't got no good films. You hardly ever see a travel film; w'en I goes to a show, I likes to see the woild. I'd like travelin' if I could afford it, but I can't; that's why I like a good travel film. A good comic's all right, but a good travel film or an a'rioplane race or a battle-ship review—dat's de real t'ing! You don't get none here. I don't know what made me come here," he repeated. He was sincerely displeased with himself at being caught with the goods by his compatriots in a place that had no class, and the only way he could defend himself was by showing his fine scorn of the inferior race.

You see what it means to them; it means Opportunity—a chance to glimpse the beautiful and strange things in the world that you haven't in your life; the gratification of the higher side of your nature; opportunity which, except for the big moving picture book, would be forever closed to you. You understand still more how much it means opportunity if you happen to live in a little country place where the whole town goes to every change of films and where the new films are gravely discussed. Down here it is that you find the people who agree with my friend of the Bowery—that "travel films is de real t'ing." For those people who would like to travel they make films of pilgrims going to Mecca; films of the great religious processions in the holy city of Jerusalem; of walrus fights in the far North. It has even gone so far that in Melilla there was an order for the troops to start out; they sprang to their places, trumpets blew, and the men fell into line and marched off—all for the moving picture show. They were angry—the troops—but the people in Spain saw how their armies acted.

In all the countries of the earth—in Sicily, and out in the desert of Arizona, and in the deep woods of America, and on the olive terraces of Italy—they are making more films, inventing new dramas with new and beautiful backgrounds, for the poor man's theater. In his own little town, in some far-off fishing village, he can sit and see the coronation, and the burial of a king, or the great pageant of the Roman Church.

It is no wonder that it is a great business with a capitalization of millions of dollars, since it gives to the people who need it most laughter and drama and beauty and a chance for once to look at the strange places of the earth.

The Outlook (New York) 98, 24 June 1911, pp. 441–7, excerpted.]

The Lure of the Films (1913)
Olivia Howard Dunbar

Adventures to discover how and where the rest of the world amuses itself are rarely as jocund as they sound. But the adventurer of proper spirit is usually content in witnessing the riotous joy of the multitude, however grimly unmoved his own less facile springs of mirth. Oddly enough, an attempt to share in the delights of "moving pictures," widely accepted as the most popular of amusements, can scarcely be counted upon to produce even this vicarious satisfaction. For if the adventurer himself gives no sign of being entertained by the "photoplay" or the "art film," neither, to his amazement, does the close-packed audience that surrounds him—a fact that is at first inexplicable.[1]

Does all the world demand the "film-show" and then withhold its approval from sheer caprice? And why does it throng so steadily today to the very performance whose lack of stimulus it must have discovered yesterday and the day before?

On the other hand, if a random assemblage of this sort gives mysteriously few evidences of active enjoyment, it gives fewer still of displeasure or ennui. To watch it is to discover that it is infinitely tolerant; completely and blessedly immune to boredom. It even betrays no annoyance on being gently approached from behind by some deputy of the management, and sprayed, as a festal touch, with strong, inalienable scent. Daily and hourly—for their patronage is so great that they open either at noon or at nine in the morning—these theaters offer thousands of cases in disproof of all that has been fallaciously said in regard to the restless energy of the American. You wonder how it can be possible, in an alleged busy world, to secure this magnificent total of leisure—to assemble daily, and for long, blank periods, so many people who have nothing to do and who are obviously not worrying about it. Every day, under these roofs, has the stagnant and misleading air of a holiday. And while it may be true that shirking housewives and truant children are never missing, it is nevertheless an interesting fact that three-fourths of the spectators are always men.[2]

Rarely does such an audience betray animation, scarcely ever awareness. Its posture is indifferent and relaxed; its jaws moving unconcernedly in tune with the endlessly reiterated ragtime ground out by some durable automaton—at least, one prefers to believe it an automaton; its dull eyes unresponsively meeting the shadowy grimaces on the flickering "film."

Fig. 1.9   "There is not so much as a change of expression, much less a sign of applause," drawing by Wilson C. Dexter illustrating "The Lure of the Films."

Are these pleasure-seekers resolutely disguising their enjoyment? Or are they, as they appear to be, half asleep? It is true that all the conditions conduce to semi-somnolence—the unbroken whine of the ragtime; the unnatural "continuousness" of the exhibition, hour after hour, without a moment's interval; the lack of sequence or climax, as of one oddly literal dream succeeding another—varied, at long intervals, by a bolder picture that introduces the strange, noiseless turbulence of nightmare.

In spite of the lack of enthusiasm, there is an indefinable atmosphere of experience and accustomedness. Nobody but yourself is unfamiliar and inquiring. There is rather less suspense and excitement than you will encounter in a trolley-car. You begin to suspect that the phlegmatic audience, having come a great many times before, is quite prepared for the fact that nine-tenths of the programme will be padding and that it does not mind in the least. There is not so much as a change of its expression, much less a sign of applause, as companies of shadow-soldiers are assembled and drilled; parades of a dozen kinds trail their blurred length across the curtain; foreign cities flash out glimpses of their characteristic scenes; ships are launched, cornerstones are laid, medals are presented, and laboratory experiments demonstrating some feature of popular science are painstakingly performed. All "films," in fact, that may be classed as educational or even indirectly instructive, as well as the occasional ones that are of a genuinely artistic interest, meet with frank but unrebellious indifference.

For an hour this may continue. Then you are conscious of a stir in the chairs behind you, and a man's didactic voice begins to enlighten the woman who is with him, in precisely the same fashion that the couple who have sat behind you at the theater all your life have gratuitously explained and perfunctorily listened. You rouse yourself, look about, even glance at the forgotten curtain to discover what it is that has relieved an apathy so general and so profound; and discover that, far from being some unimagined marvel, it is merely a street scene in New York. And you wonder why the "Film Trust" should go to the trouble of contriving historical "playlets" in costume, through which the audiences sleep contentedly, when what really stirs them is the representation of something that they see every day of their lives—the life-size figure of a policeman, a trolley-car, a crowd on Broadway.[3] But this is not, after all, a new phenomenon. The ecstasy experienced by persons of a certain degree of simplicity in recognizing on the stage a familiar object or character has never been explained, although producers must long have realized and catered to it, as an incident in many kinds of drama. It has so often been apparent that audiences betrayed a keener delight in the introduction into a play of a cow or a horse than in the exploits of the most accomplished actor. During one long afternoon of widely varied cinematographic devices, the only genuine success was achieved by a youth who came out before the curtain and—made a sound like an automobile! This bit of simple realism did wake the sleeping audience from its dreams and gave them an unmistakably poignant pleasure which they expressed without restraint.

These flashes of sympathetic response are rare and fleeting, but may always be evoked by one other element—the broadly farcical. And it is perhaps unnecessary to explain that, the more nearly this unliteral comedy (for realism plays no part here) approaches that of the comic supplement, the wilder and more immediate its success. An altercation, a practical joke, a chase, are of course the unvarying themes, a chase of anything by anybody, however meaningless, being the acknowledged favorite. Unfailingly popular are the pictured disputes between an impossible mistress and an unnatural servant, in which the maid tumultuously triumphs; or farcical interruptions of the love-making of an ill-suited couple; or rowdy street scenes in which people tumble over each other and somebody gets beaten for an offense he didn't commit, while the culprit leers from a neighboring corner. All this is, of course, more or less vulgar, but in the highly unrealistic sense that the comic supplement is vulgar—a harsh, unlovely, shadow-land, repellent, one would suppose, to intelligence and sanity.

The merriment that was set free by the pictured conflict of boy and policeman subsides again into apathy when the first scene in the more ambitious "photoplay" is flashed upon the curtain. For these fragmentary echoes of melodrama seem to be accepted merely as echoes, dim and undisturbing. Their warmed-over quality enables the spectator to remain entirely cool and disillusioned. And yet these plays often present not only the same type of heroine and villain that the old plays did, but the same actors—one would swear to it. The villain's throwing back his head in cruel, contemptuous laughter is a trick he must have learned and often practised on Fourteenth Street.[4] And the malign deliberation of his walk is full of an ancient theatric significance that could scarcely be felt by any traditionless cub, hired to play in pantomime before the camera. On the other hand, that intemperate use of the telephone that characterizes the moving-picture play was of course unknown to melodrama.

The "Indian play"—indeed, the Wild West drama generally—is understood to be a commodity that is ordered in large quantities for contemporary audiences; but the result produces no apparent excitement. While a red man discovers a child left alone in a prairie cabin, and, brandishing cruel weapons, pursues the child through various shadow-scenes, the audience contentedly chews its gum. Further scenes are revealed in which the child's father appears, rescues the child and slays the Indian—but the onlookers are still unmoved. Even the dramatic adventures of the simpering young girl who is menaced by a nondescript villain and rescued at the critical moment by the humble but hitherto neglected suitor are accepted with complete nonchalance. Endangered girlhood is, however, so frequently and persistently presented that the theory must exist that it is a favorite stimulus with these stodgy audiences.

Yet these apathetic groups who now appear, except for their occasional bursts of unjoyous mirth, emotionless, are the same men and women who only a few years ago thronged constantly to the melodramas at the urge of what seemed to be an elemental need, the need of wholesome emotional exercise. No audience was ever disappointed in one of these eminently reliable performances; none was ever bored or critical or sleepy. One knew what one had come for and settled down comfortably to enjoy it. It was of relatively little importance whether the central figure in the tangle of love, danger, sacrifice, villainy, heroism, disaster, and triumph was Nellie, the Beautiful Cloak Model, or Bertha, the Sewing-Machine Girl—the succession of thrills was of practically the same character and intensity. What these audiences unconsciously demanded was an excuse to laugh, weep, pity, resent, condemn, and admire, all in strict conformity with the orthodox moral code; and it was this that was abundantly furnished them. It would surely be a psychological marvel if so deep a need could have vanished as the coincidence of a mere change of fashion in entertainments.

But the best and most satisfying feature of the melodramas was their imaginative scope, their denial of logical limitations. The simple, normal mind while it has felt a childlike delight in the occasional realistic detail, has probably always been charmed by the theater in proportion as its spectacle, as a whole, transcended reality. A world as unfettered as the world of faery, whose characters should have the shape and speech of the ordinary wage-earner, would have at any time a compelling appeal. "What attracted me so strongly to the theater," Wagner says, speaking of his childhood, "was ... the fascinating pleasure of finding myself in an entirely different atmosphere, in a world that was purely fantastic and often gruesomely attractive. Thus to me ... some costume or a characteristic part of it seemed to come from another world, to be in some way as *attractive as an apparition*." There is no doubt that this is the expression of a universal experience; and that if a sensitive, impressionable child of six or seven could define and express the emotions (too vaguely recalled by the adult) aroused by its first theater, this would form a human document of thrilling interest. And it may be that melodrama at its best supplied multitudes of adult children with an approximation of this delicious and memorable experience of infancy.

In comparison with the popular drama that it has succeeded and supplanted, the motion picture of course provides little or no emotional outlet. It is far from attempting to "purge with pity and terror" the casual multitudes that it attracts. In most cases the interest that it excites, when it excites any, is shallow, fleeting, two-dimensional, like the pictures themselves. It offers no illusion and no mystery. What is left to those who have had to accustom themselves to this thin and un-satisfying form of recreation, but to acquire, as they have, a self-protective surface of apparent torpor?

It is easy, of course, to recall conspicuously exceptional cases. There is now and then a feverish desire to see the pictured record of some current event of especial interest, particularly when it has to do with sports. But the kind of excitement that would be aroused by the records of a baseball or football game is a very special thing, and is infinity [sic] removed from the mere normal desire for amusement. Yet it is fully shared, as everybody knows, by sophisticated childhood. Indeed, the overpowering desire felt by youthful East Side citizens to see certain celebrated "movies" has more than once led them into tragic difficulty. Not many months ago, just after a much advertised prize-fight, two little boys, whose uncontrollable longing for the admission fee to a picture-hall had led them to upset a grocer's display and barter his goods independently, were brought to the Children's Court. "The price of admittance was five cents?" inquired the judge, examining them. The smaller boy, who was very small indeed, quickly raised his thin, tense face. "Oh, but it was ten cents to see the big fight, judge!" he cried, hoarsely, the tremendous intensity of his manner and expression at once defining the almost irresistible character of his temptation and what he felt to be the manly magnitude of his crime.

But even though its imagination starve, a disaster of which it can scarcely be conscious, it is not difficult to understand why the vast, simple, unexigent public so faithfully follows up the moving picture. Almost any institution that cost so little would probably be patronized, even though the most it did was to provide a convenient and often comfortable lounging place, and, in the poorer quarters of the city, to provide an excuse for social contact. After all, there is no question but that the equivalent of a nickel is usually supplied. Beyond this, there is the fascination of never knowing what one is going to see, which is a far greater lure than an exact knowledge of what is forthcoming. But its strongest hold must be the fact that it makes no demand whatever upon its audiences, requiring neither punctuality—for it has no beginning—nor patience—for it has no end—nor attention—for it has no sequence. No degree of intelligence is necessary, no knowledge of our language, nor convictions nor attitude of any kind, reasonably good eyesight being indeed the only requisite. In the world of amusement, no line of less resistance than this has surely yet been offered.

[*Harper's Weekly* (New York) 57, 18 January 1913, pp. 20, 22.]

The Street Cinema (1931)
Winifred Holtby[1]

[...] As we drank our coffee, however, we became aware that something strange was happening in the crowd opposite. All faces were raised; all eyes moved together, as eyes move watching the play at the centre court at Wimbledon. Once or twice a ripple of laughter crossed all the faces at once, like wind across corn. At last we rose to investigate. Above our heads, above the awning over our tables, a sheet had been stretched and on it, from the café opposite, came the beam of a cinema lantern. It was a device for attracting custom to the café. There one could sit at little tables and see plates flung, goats devouring boots, bridegrooms dropping rings, and all the other delights of slap-stick comedy which apparently appeal to universal humour. And there we stood, until we decided that St. Lunaire was not even Dinard, and that somewhere beyond sea and land, there lay our beds. We hired our motor boat; we telephoned for our taxi; we went home. [...]

[From "My Weekly Journal 9: Rain Over Brittany," *The Schoolmistress* 50: 2592, 13 August 1931, pp. 533, 539, excerpted.]

From Northern Berlin and the Surrounds (1919)
Resi Langer

Yes, it's the far north. True to life, right down to "the northern lights"—little lamps that herald the cinema in the evenings. During the day, it's the screamingly kitschy posters, whose palette, spanning the entire color spectrum, from yellow through red and green to blue and even beyond, celebrates wild orgies. They resoundingly bellow the embarrassing title of some "sensational drama" or "highly suspenseful novel" at us, with their abundant array of images.

With her plump fingers the young woman in the ticket booth or "Cassa" (whose outward appearance has so often been faithfully rendered by Heinrich Zille) plucks at a block of identically colored perforated tickets.[1] They will grant entrance to the inner sanctum.

A green woollen curtain is pulled back, and the perception is "air." Entirely unlike the kind found in the high Swiss mountains (oh, that one could can it like milk and sell it in tins!), but something dense, something that takes your breath away. Eventually one gets used to that, too.

A man with an electric flashlight directs someone to a seat. Above it is posted a sign with the suggestive inscription: "lst Place." We sit, and a filmstrip rolls on the screen in front. It's a bit worn away by the loving embrace of too many projectors, but that doesn't lessen the enjoyment. It is over, and the room lightens. Many a "smoocher" settles fully back into his seat (which he only half made use of in the dark) and here and there a bun is laboriously pinned back up. A faint sigh about the indiscreet lighting passes through the room, followed by a second, a third, and sometimes even a whole string of them. Up front, in the first row, a young woman's head turns around; turquoise earrings and a matching brooch tear pale blue holes in the dirty, yellow-gold lighting. The man with the ozone dispenser goes up and down, and is somewhat abusively teased by several particular wisecrackers, on account of his odd occupation. There, up the middle aisle, comes someone with a sailor's gait—no, let's take the youth with a "coffee roaster" (as people have mischievously dubbed the stiff brown head-covering) and beautifully adorned with paper underwear ("I've worn them for seven years. I'll wear them no more—" etc.). He spits on the floor, because it is expressly forbidden, and then sits down in an orchestra seat. For some reason he gets into a tiff with his neighbor and the following exchange is heard: "Man, you don't need to puff yourself up. Can't you be no gentleman?" "Shut up, or I'll rearrange your face!" answers his equally unchivalrous interlocutor. At that point, Miss Turquoise tunes in with the highest soprano: "Hey, did they drop you at birth? Whatya want from Will?" "Look, the tame little thing is trying to pull something," chimes another feminine voice.

The piano stifles this deft repartee and a "singer" (once upon a time!) appears, not on, but in front of the screen, illuminated by the footlights. He boldly states: "There lies a crown in the deepest Rhine!" People seem to believe him—that a crown lies down there—because he extends this positive certainty through four stanzas and leaves the podium accompanied by applause.

Meanwhile, the shuttle service (managed by cyclists) which smaller store-front theaters organize together in order to make the acquisition of film less expensive, has arrived with the next box office hit and done its duty.

Next a notice of the police prohibition appears on the screen: no children may remain on the premises past nine o'clock. A band of girls and boys walks towards the theater exit. Well, tomorrow, having ingested Demon Jealousy, they will fail to perform their lessons to the satisfaction of their teachers; in the end, they will have helped to make a hit out of the country uncle, Uncle Rohrstock. Now that the wheat has been separated from the chaff, one new screen wonder can follow the next: seriousness alternates with humor, and over the darkened room, the love god (even if only as a plaster mock-up) brandishes his torch, smiling happily. Hand finds hand and, most likely, mouth finds mouth, and a giggle erupts as, in their tender play, they miss the film's ending and the harsh light illuminates a sweet love scene.

["Aus dem Berliner Norden und da Herum", Kinotypen: Vor und Hinter den Filmkulissen (Zwölf Kapitel aus der Kinderstube des Films) (Hannover: Der Zweemann Verlag, 1919), pp. 21–5. Translated by Patti Duquette, with the assistance of Christine Haas and Sarah Hill.]

In the Movie Houses of Western Berlin (1919)
Resi Langer

An oasis of light in a Berlin street! Aha! A nickelodeon [Kientopp] (Karl Kraus). In western Berlin it is known as a "movie house," "movie theater," even "film art show." That is, when the temple of mute Thalia has not been dubbed some other characteristic or appropriately catchy name.[1]

It is foggy in the Decemberish streets, and you escape from the un-Christmassy weather to search out a safe little spot for yourself in a soft, velvety chair, or behind the balcony banister of our numerous fashionable cinemas. You sink into contemplation of the types making up the audience.

One catches your eye right by the entrance; she isn't actually part of the audience but a more permanent (not literally, of course) fixture of the theater—the cashier.

That one is beautiful! That she is! Of course, say the envious, the exception that again proves the rule.

Her hair is well-kempt—perhaps she has touched it up a bit, but so what. It becomes her. With well-manicured white hands she dispenses the colorful tickets (which are in no way inferior to real theater tickets) to those who desire them. An eternal "Thank you!" floats over the beautifully reddened lips. Perhaps a little Leichner red deepens the shade—perhaps it's natural.[2] The effect is good. All wishing to partake of the film goodies awaiting inside are dammed up in front of her little glass house.

There is the "gent." Fur, of course! Sable! God, he's got it! "Fashionable"—top hat. He takes the most expensive seat. After tossing away his cigarette he surrenders the gorgeous fur cloak and stiff head ornament to the plump arms of the friendly, smiling wardrobe girl. His cutaway disappears behind the balcony door, in front of which a violet- or perhaps green-uniformed attendant is still recovering from his tip.

A lady. Every inch a lady! The ash-colored, lolling plume flatters not only the fabulous hat brim, but also the nose of the person standing behind (who sometimes protests with a very distinct, powerful, masculine sneeze). The lady, an inveterate filmgoer, naturally has a regular seat in the balcony boxes. Her alluring, violet dress glitters alongside the aforementioned cutaway, and over them both a perfume cloud of seductive Khasana oppressively hangs.

The couple. Him and Her. He: (monocle, wonderfully slicked-down parting, oozing with pomade, diamond pin on the necktie) "Which seat? A balcony box?" She: "Oh, Darling no ... I prefer to sit in the orchestra." He (turning to the cashier, playing with a piece of gold): "Miss, two orchestra seats, please!" You ask yourself, why? An impish voice answers you: Ha, she wants to show off her "bob" as "the latest thing" in fashion, and therefore sheds the protective aigrette.

The country uncle has come. With very heavy steps his clodhoppers trample the soft down of the red Smyrna runner. And at the ticket window at the top of the steps he demands his (ever stylish) orchestra ticket. Oh yes! (His twinkling, happy, piggy eyes tell all as they scan the scene). He must, of course, have something of the "joys of the big city" to report to his cronies back home. Marveling, the country-ears of dear fellow citizens (usually it is 7,999, so the little hometown counts its inhabitants at 8,000) listen and take their fearless XYZ for, at the very least, a North Pole explorer. He thinks himself important, to be the gentleman from "somewhere"; he wants to observe, but is only observed—even making an unseemly sight of himself here and there. He moves somewhat insecurely along the narrow orchestra aisle. The button on his sleeve is forward enough to start a "dalliance" with the lace collar of a woman's blouse, while his shoe marked with the size "next-number-belongs-outside" lands on another trotter.[3] A not too loud, but definitely penetrating "Ouch!" followed by "Damn!", drives the minor, provincial foot off the big city instep, and in the maneuver, the button takes off a piece of the lace collar. He isn't familiar with the convention of "right" and "left." He chases the occupant of Nr. 114 from his seat and proclaims his right to it. (He has been directed by an usher to the right side, where the second Nr. 114 is located.) The country uncle always laughs, and of course in the most inappropriate places (even sometimes at sentimental moments), thereby attracting the most bitter contempt of the female audience.

The salesman and the shop girl. They are allowed—oh noble boss—to leave work one quarter hour earlier and feel themselves among human beings. Under her white cambric blouse, a feeling heart fervently beats for the peculiar fate of the film hero, and the frozen red hand of the salesman gently rests on her gold-ringed hand; across his lips passes the shaky sentimental murmur: "Do you like it, Fräulein?" Her nodding "yes" unleashes a tear from the prison of her lashes, landing on the frozen hand—a quiet tribute to emotion.

The familiar clatter of the film's motion stops, and tasteful lamps stream brightness over excited faces, ruthlessly exposing yet more damp eyes. Then, accompanied by music, everyone streams towards the exits, and what was once a whole disintegrates into atoms, for today. Perhaps tomorrow each one will once again form a vital part of the whole and allow itself to be caught up in another light oasis.

["In den Lichtspielhäusern des Berliner Westens," Kinotypen: Vor und Hinter den Filmkulissen (Zwölf Kapitel aus der Kinderstube des Films) (Hannover: Der Zweemann Verlag, 1919), pp. 26–31. Translated from German by Patti Duquette, with the assistance of Christine Haas and Sarah Hill.]

My Experience in the Movies (1920)
Mary Roberts Rinehart

Now about eleven years ago we—the family—spent a winter in Vienna. And re-member, please, that moving pictures were a comparative novelty then. I remember the dark, ill-ventilated little theatres in Vienna, made out of former shops. The men smoked and wore their hats, and in between times a boy with an apparatus which was merely some sort of squirt gun went round spraying the air with a mixture that smelled of herbs, to clear away the smoke.

I remember the Head requesting a gentleman in a tall silk hat to remove it, so the children could see, and his surly refusal. Probably it was a new hat, or perhaps he was bald. There are always reasons. He refused, so we got up and sat in front of him; and as I was at that time wearing the largest hat the city of Vienna had ever produced, I sat directly in front of the obstructor. There followed an exchange of civilities which grew less and less civil, and the Head took off his gloves, because they were new and he did not want to split them.

However, no blows were struck, because if a foreigner in those days was assaulted by a Viennese the foreigner was immediately locked up, and it took an appeal to the British Embassy to get him out.

[*The American Magazine* (New York) 90, October 1920, p. 76, excerpted.]

Missionary Film (1927)
Winifred Holtby

Mr. Grant, cycling along the country road, felt too happy even to whistle. Security intoxicated him. He drank it from the green twilight that tasted of new-ploughed stubble, wet straw and smouldering wicks. He heard it in the soft clashing of dead leaves below his wheel, and in the hollow cropping sound of ewes among the turnips. He saw it in the vision of his wife as he had left her, reading aloud to cousin Lucy and Ellen Deane in the fire-lit cottage, the lines of fear soothed from her darling face. Sight, sound and scent flowed together in the pervading consciousness of safety. Not a voice spoke, not a bird twittered in the darkened trees, but they brought the reassurance of familiarity. He was at home. In every cottage of the valley lived men and women who had known his father. He passed his brother's farm, and the graveyard where his forefathers rested. Death brought nothing for sorrow, when it meant only closer communion with the familiar earth. This was his world; these were his friends. Never, never would he leave these things again.

The cottages crouched nearer to the road. Light suddenly gleamed on scattered pools. Mr. Grant rode into the Street of Market Brindle. A jolly little street he thought it, where friends called greetings to him from the glowing doors of little shops. He told the pork butcher about Mrs Brown's old sow, and teased the grocer about his part in the new play run by the "Lit. and Phil." He bought corn for his hens from the dealer whose second cousin married his Aunt Jennie's niece. He talked to every one.

In the market place the cinema beckoned to him, flaring with joyous light, festooned with small electric bulbs like jewels, emerald green and ruby stars. Such stars, thought Mr. Grant, set all the Sons of God shouting for joy.

He paid eightpence and went in.

The honest friendly darkness engulfed him, but against the flickering pallor of the screen he saw the clear outline of Mrs. Fitton's Sunday hat. He liked Mrs. Fitton; he liked the rural English audience; the scent of warm humanity and muddy boots reminded him of Sunday school treats in his childhood. The orchestra, a local pianist, and a girl playing the violin, broke out into Mendelssohn's "Spring Song." Bending to light his pipe, Mr. Grant missed the first title of the film. He read only "...missionary propaganda, but rather education in the broadest sense." He felt a twinge of disappointment, for he did not want to be educated. Above all, he did not want to be reminded of a man who had once been a missionary educationalist. He wanted to see Harold Lloyd or Tom Mix.

"The first sight of land which thrills the heart of the traveller," he read with faint distaste. What trash about travellers. The best thing about travel was the last mile on the way home. He wanted to see Charlie Chaplin; but he saw instead a line of flat-topped hills, mottled about their base with little houses, and towering starkly over a placid sea.

He sat up rigidly, frowning.

"Adderly Street," danced the caption.[1] "The gateway to a continent." Tall buildings, faint against the sunlight; dark trees tossing in dusty wind; bearded farmers in knee breeches; Indian schoolgirls with prim plaits of hair hanging down muslin dresses; a market-gardener swinging baskets of melons and yams; pretty typists in sleeveless summer frocks; here they came. Then a couple swaggered down the road, the wind flapping in their ragged coats and wide trousers. They carried canes, and wore handkerchiefs in their breast pockets. Their black faces grinned, growing larger and larger until they filled the screen, blotting out towers and trams and all the paraphernalia of the European.

Click! They had gone. The orchestra began to play Liszt's Hungarian Rhapsody. A train started up from the veldt like a frightened snake and slid out of the picture. An ox-wagon lumbered between the scorching hills and twisted thorn bushes. A naked boy with a round, gleaming belly ran ahead of the beasts. Mr. Grant could hear the creak of the leather and the grinding of heavy wheels on the dry red soil.

A group of women stooped beside the spruit washing sweet potatoes.[2] Their white bead anklets clanked as they moved. Water dripped from black wrists and flat pink palms. One carried on her head a blanket in which two fowls roosted cackling.

Mr. Grant's pipe had gone out. He sat clutching the plush arm rest of his eightpenny chair. The sweat round his lips tasted salt and cold.

He saw raw mud huts thatched with reeds. From their gaping doors came a hot, acrid smell, a hateful savage smell. Chickens prinked themselves on a pile of mealie cobs, and two curs fought over a piece of goat-flesh. In the white shimmering light a man was dancing. His flat, hard feet struck the burnt soil; his black body glistened with sweat; brass ear-rings swung like little censers as he leapt forward, free, free, free, dancing in the sunlight, glorying in his black naked body, in the dry crumbling earth, in the hot valley.

The valley disappeared. Mr. Grant saw a row of tin and concrete huts leaning against the wall of the mine compound. A kaffir in rags sat laboriously pedalling a sewing machine. The steel jaws of the engines chewed shrieking stone; the orchestra played "Valencia," but Mr. Grant could hear nothing but the huge inhuman din of the machines. The caption explained that the mines of the Transvaal were very hygienic and that the men had Every Comfort. A black policeman with bare feet below his puttees walked through the location.

The orchestra played, "Jesus shall reign where'er the sun," and the picture shifted to the Missionary Settlement at Lovedale. Below a dim arcade of oak trees, the black school children were singing hymns. Half a mile away a girl leaned her back against the hut; her baby lay between her pendulous breasts; she pushed mealie-meal porridge into its reluctant mouth. Mr. Grant knew all about her. Three of her children had already died. Her husband was away at the mines. The goats had eaten all the grass on the common land. "Each year," said her mother, "the common grows smaller, the goats are fewer, and the mouths to fill grow more. How can we pay taxes?"

"The House of Assembly, Cape Town," ran the caption. But Mr. Grant did not see the film before him. He saw the table of the committee room covered with papers about his own case. He heard the voice of Authority telling him, "Of course we shall be sorry to lose your services, Grant, but if you feel you must take this line of action ... " He saw his wife entering the low house near Pretoria. She folded her parasol, and stood fingering a little spray of plumbago. "I can't bear it," she said. "They called you a race-traitor. I'm never going to a tea-party again." Mr. Grant remembered the Bishop's worried gentleness. "Of course I honour you motives, Mr. Grant. The Church has fought long and loyally on this very ground. But experience teaches us that we must proceed with caution. We have the weaker brethren to consider." And all that he had done was to protest against the slamming of a door in the face of educated natives, boys and girls whom he had taught in his own mission school. He had protested until his name was the signal for laughter or abuse, until he himself was subjected to quiet, relentless pressure. Until his wife had said that she could bear no more. It was all very well to be a martyr; but has one the right to offer up one's family as a sacrifice?

"End of Part I. Five minutes interval."

The lights sprang up, Mrs. Fitton turned round. "Well, I thought I should see you here. And how's your wife? Very interesting, very, isn't it? Especially to you, with your knowledge of South Africa. Do you ever want to go back?"

Mr. Grant mumbled a reply and made for the door. He found his bicycle entangled in a jungle of steel in the stableyard. The night closed in upon him down the country road, but he no longer tasted its sweet autumnal scents. His nostrils burned with a harsh acrid smell. He fled between the elm trees. Dead leaves like small birds floated round his shoulders. How could he take his wife again from this sweet safety? How could he snatch her from the chicken farm, where people were kind and friendly, and where the only problems lay in the market for eggs? He passed his brother's farm again, but only saw the men and women crouched on sodden bundles waiting for the midnight train. It was, as usual, two hours late. The platform became strewn with nut-shells and mealie cobs. A woman on a pile of blankets suckled her child. A man played a mouth organ. Mr. Grant heard again the clicking guttural speech. His head ached with the attempt to understand.

The Administrator said, "But, my dear fellow, don't be quixotic. You can do nothing against economic forces and race prejudice."

"You can do nothing," Mr. Grant repeated menacingly. "You have tried before and failed. It will kill Laura. You can't go back again."

Irrelevantly, he remembered that his brother and sister-in-law were coming to Sunday night's supper. He could not tell them. He could not leave his family again. And yet. And yet. In his vision, the train crawled into the dark station. The men and women shouldered their bundles and rose from the ruins of their orange skins and mealie cobs, and in rising looked at him with dumb reproach for his desertion, then one by one sat down again. What was the use of their attempt to move forward if their friends deserted them? Yet how could he sacrifice his family, or how desert them in order to return to these black men and women who were nothing to him?

"...And he looked round on those which sat round him and said, 'Behold my mother and my brethren.'"

Mr. Grant rode home to tell his wife that he was going back to his mission work in South Africa.

[From *Truth is Not Sober*, (London: William Collins, 1934), pp. 108–13.]

At Public Gatherings (1923)
Emily Post

GOOD MANNERS AT THE THEATER

In passing across people who are seated, always face the stage and press as close to the backs of the seats you are facing as you can. Remember also not to drag anything across the heads of those sitting in front of you. At the moving pictures, especially when it is dark and difficult to see, a coat on an arm passing behind a chair can literally devastate the hair-dressing of a lady occupying it.

If you are obliged to cross in front of some one who gets up to let you pass, say "Thank you," or "Thank you very much" or "I am very sorry." Do *not* say

"Pardon me!" or "Beg pardon!" Though you can say "I beg your pardon." That, however, would be more properly the expression to use if you brushed your coat over their heads, or spilled water over them, or did something to them for which you should actually beg their pardon. But "Beg pardon," which is an abbreviation, is one of the phrases never said in best society. [...]

As a matter of fact, comparatively few people are ever anything but well behaved. Those who arrive late and stand long, leisurely removing their wraps, and who insist on laughing and talking are rarely encountered; most people take their seats as quietly and quickly as they possibly can, and are quite as much interested in the play and therefore as attentive and quiet as you are. A very annoying person at the "movies" is one who reads every "caption" out loud. [...]

[From Mrs. Price Post, Etiquette: in Society, in Business, in Politics and at Home (New York: Funk & Wagnalls, 1923), pp. 40–41, 42, excerpted.]

The Chaperon and Other Conventions (1923)
Emily Post

FREEDOM OF THE CHAPERONED

To be sure the time has gone by when the presence of an elderly lady is indispensable to every gathering of young people. Young girls for whose sole benefit and protection the chaperon exists (she does not exist for her own pleasure, youthful opinion to the contrary notwithstanding), have infinitely greater freedom from her surveillance than had those of other days, and the typical chaperon is seldom seen with any but very young girls, too young to have married friends. [...]

There are also many occasions when a chaperon is unnecessary! It is considered perfectly correct for a young girl to drive a motor by herself, or take a young man with her, if her family know and approve of him, for any short distance in the country. She may play golf, tennis, go to the Country Club, or Golf Club (if near by), sit on the beach, go canoeing, ride horseback, and take part in the normal sports and occupations of country life. Young girls always go to private parties of every sort without their own chaperon, but the fact that a lady issues an invitation means that either she or another suitable chaperon will be present.

CONVENTIONS THAT CHANGE WITH LOCALITY

In New York [...], no young girl of social standing may, without being criticized, go alone with a man to the theater. Absolutely no lady (unless middle-aged—and even then she would be defying convention) can go to dinner or supper in a restaurant alone with a gentleman. A lady, not young, who is staying in a very dignified hotel, can have a gentleman dine with her. But any married woman, if her husband does not object, may dine alone in her own home with any man she pleases or have a different one come in to tea every day in the week without being criticized.

A very young girl may motor around in the country alone with a man, with her father's consent, or sit with him on the rocks by the sea or on a log in the woods; but she must not sit with him in a restaurant. All of which is about as upside down as it can very well be. In a restaurant they are not only under the surveillance of many eyes, but they can scarcely speak without being overheard, whereas short-distance motoring, driving, riding, walking or sitting on the seashore has no element of protection certainly. Again, though she may not lunch with him in a restaurant, she is sometimes (not always) allowed to go to a moving picture matinée with him! Why sitting in the dark in a moving picture theater is allowed, and the restaurant is tabu is very mysterious.

[From Mrs. Price Post, Etiquette: in Society, in Business, in Politics and at Home (New York: Funk & Wagnalls, 1923), pp. 288–89, 293, excerpted.]

Why We Go to the Movies

A Western Woman's Opinion of Pictures (1912)
Hattie M. Loble

I sat by the fireside dreaming of days long ago,
And pictures seemed to form in the midst of the ember's glow
But faded e'er I could catch them, the coals to ashes died,
E'en as my hopes had perished and the heart within me sighed.

I left the dying firelight, and the lonely, cheerless room
And wandered down the avenue, seeking to lift the gloom
When I heard the sound of music, saw countless lights agleam
And suiting an idle fancy, I entered as in a dream.

I entered into darkness, but sudden, before my eyes
On a curtain of white, came pictures and I stared in mute surprise,
Pictures that world! In wonderment I quite forgot my pain.
Pictures that lived! And with them I lived my youth again.

The North, the South, the East, the West were all at my command;
The whole world came before me, at touch of an unseen hand.
Ah, the pictures by the fireside may fade and die away,
But those on the magic canvas live anew for me every day.

[Moving Picture World (New York) 12:9, 1 June 1912, p. 820, excerpted.]

In Union is Strength (1912)
Minnie Adams

It is a shame so great that we should blush when we realise how little we care for the welfare of our own. The efforts of individuals for the betterment and the pleasure of the race should be met by the hearty co-operation of every man and woman. My reason for saying the above is the outcome of viewing the patrons of the theaters along the stroll.[1] We are being censured daily by all races for our lack of unity and prognosticators say, "It is not in us to help one another, and that we never will do it." And every day we are proving their words true. On State street are four excellent playhouses. Please observe which of the four is the least frequented. Very little observation is needed, and we should hang our heads in shame when we are compelled to confess the Pekin is the neglected one. One might argue that the offerings at the above named house were not creditable, perhaps not at all times, but on whom can the blame be laid? By all means on the community. Give the theater your support and watch its policies improve. What other house has given our local talent as much consideration as the Pekin? And for that reason if no other, it should have our approval and patronage. Many theaters in the city we go to and are admitted on sufferance and more than apt to be relegated to the rear of the house, but we grin and bear it. Is the propensity to be charitable to outsiders so deep rooted in our natures that we will ever play the fool and be the cat's paw for those who only laugh in your face for your coin and then are willing to lynch you if given half a chance, or, if they become prosperous after having bled you sufficiently they will turn you down. With all due respect for the theaters on State street, and their managers, I wish to say that I feel they are of the opinion that a race is crazy who would not assist to upbuild its own and feel a pride in doing so. There are sufficient of the race in Chicago to give to each of the theaters excellent box office receipts, so that all might live and flourish. I approve of all the playhouses, the Grand and Monogram are delightful places of amusement. The plays are fine and the managements are in the hands of men who are courteous and desirous of placing before us the best talent possible; and why? Because we make it easy for them. Now, if we would do our duty by the Pekin it would be enabled to do likewise. In saying these things we seek not to take away patronage from any house, but simply to show to the people the selfishness which is slowly but surely sapping the life's blood of our independence. In conclusion, we wish to say, "It is our most ardent wish that all the theaters be prosperous on the stroll, but do urge and entreat the people to wake up to the fact that they are not letting 'charity begin at home.'"

[*Chicago Defender*, 24 February 1912, p. 6.]

The Onlookers of Life at the Cinema (1914–15)
Malwine Rennert

I recently came across the following statement about pleasure in an entertainment magazine: all people strive for pleasure, even in material things. They want not only to eat, but also to take in food that tastes good. So it is also in the spiritual domain: the hunger is there, the soul wants to take—but what does it take in, in most cases? Sweet poison.

These simple words contain a truth at the heart of all the earth's evils: our dreadful ignorance in the realm of the spiritual.

Humanity has come so far over many thousands of years because it knows what is physically beneficial—how mankind should eat, drink, live, and move. Our fiercest ambition is now to put all classes in a position where hygiene is possible. But we have only the dimmest knowledge and legends about the inner world, the soul; the experiences of the privileged few can't serve as the general rule.

But the spiritual hunger is there—that longing for pleasurable indulgence. Happy were the Greeks who enjoyed existence as a vision of beauty, the first Christians who lived and died in moral rapture, and the men of action of the middle ages. Is it not also a pleasure when Orientals huddle together of an evening under a starry sky and smoke and tell stories?

How do Europeans enjoy their life since European culture has been marked by the bourgeoisie? (Let us leave the moral question aside.) He who has ears to hear with and eyes to see with, and who has seen many peoples such that he can make comparisons, will not be able to rid himself of the perception that Europeans are famished, and that many reach for poison in their hunger. It came about in the name of freedom—political and occupational freedom—with thunder and crushing blows, and settled on souls like a paralyzing net, bringing commercial calculation and the gravity and weight of technology into the inner world.

Many soldiers perceive this war as a liberation from the banality of everyday life, despite the dangers, drudgery, and privations. Suddenly they sense the wonderful energy that lies in their souls that they carry as if on wings. Where earlier they could take only fearful, measured steps, where scornful and smug neighbors jeered and stifled their power, now they can spread their wings and rise to the light. Therein lay the peril: the ruling system had paralyzed the will and the spirit, reason presided as absolute ruler—and the senses…

Today there are no more political events, no elections brought about through long speeches and much money; no more outdoor folk festivals where joy and grace step out. Instead there are stuffy beer halls and dance halls with vulgar dances. For the middle class there are tight circles with predetermined social schedules—so much for dinner, for the wine. One hand washes the other: no one belongs who cannot equally return the favor—everything personal, lovable, and uncalculated is eliminated. Senseless norms are honored like divine laws or accepted as physical necessities. For reading: novels from family magazines reflecting the same life; blinders against everything that doesn't concern the chosen circle. People, be it in

England, France, Germany, Sweden, or Holland, experienced nothing. They worked, most of them, very hard, but they experienced nothing. And they had no opportunity to break out of the circle. Women could at most tend to their moods, or choose the free love of the art world as their *modus vivendi*, only to be destroyed by it.

The turmoil of the demimonde lies under this half-petrified bourgeois strata. Contemporary novels and plays reflect bourgeois spiritual poverty.

One can say that most people have only been onlookers of life; they have had an inkling that life could be more beautiful and finer, even more noble. They have gone all over the place—anywhere they could hope to satisfy their hunger for life; one takes up surrogates and counterfeits when the genuine item is lacking.

They filled, and fill, the cinemas, always in hope of life. Can one then demand serious art there when people don't go there for art at all? The Bedouins who huddle together under the starry skies telling stories to each other would be astonished if an aesthete stepped up to them asking: are you telling artistic stories? It inevitably happens, however, that from time to time a poet sits among them, a good storyteller who holds his own against the critics, and one to whom the listeners would particularly enjoy listening. The elders of the tribe—if they are wise—will keep watch that the stories don't offend decency, but they won't drive theories of art between storyteller and listener.

This war is destroying Europe's well-being. All reserves are being exhausted and that means starting from the beginning. It remains to be seen whether those returning home, the core of the people, will be able to put powerful will and winged soul to use for peaceful purposes, and establish new and better conditions. They are no longer onlookers of life; they have experienced, and we don't know yet how they will react to the cinema. But in any case, the cinema will continue to exist and the very question of cinema will bear on the welfare of youth, and the well-being of the people into the future. While our troops heroically fight and suffer the unspeakable, those at home can and want to work, so that upon their return the troops will find the ground prepared, not full of thorns and thistles.

It seems to me that the question of whether a ciné-drama might be possible is of purely aesthetic interest. It is much more important for our time, a time in which we have regressed to a primitive state, to promote presentations other than scientific and landscape films, perhaps in the form of plays, or illustrated novels, or historical events which can be viewed as healthy nourishment for the soul. Otherwise we will be overwhelmed with trash. The future of our nation is a serious matter, and it makes no sense that we should act less energetically with respect to the inner world than we would with regard to military life, simply in order to please a couple of dozen speculators or even the mob.

When we free ourselves from formulas and judge the latest arrival according to its own laws, then we must admit that the cinema has created many beautiful things. How many great actors have we seen in brilliant performances; how many outstanding sets that attain even greater atmospheric value through the plot. It is entirely inconsequential whether the film held its own within the existing categories of drama, the novel, and other forms, as long as it was beautiful. The often cited

Atlantis was no high point; it was rather a low point, a complete failure, and may not be taken as a standard. There are a slew of beautiful film creations—French, American, Italian, along with German—that would be worth preserving in a museum; let's not condemn the cinema entirely. Once the life of the individual is enriched, when there aren't so many onlookers of life anymore, then the flocking to the cinema will desist; the cinema will be forced to change.

Besides, might one not wish that some philistines, some pedants, went to a good movie more often? Perhaps the atrophication and sclerosing of their inner lives would be somewhat stemmed. Moralists and aesthetes fight the trash film; the pedant fights all films, for he is blind and deaf to each and every art.

All other inventions of the last decades serve destruction—even the airship, as it turns out in this war. Yes, since man conquered the air, humanity must hide away in the cellars. Why should we then fight film when it offers so many good and beautiful possibilities for edifying the inner life? We only want to be sure to watch over and protect film so that it doesn't become a destroyer of inner values, the way cabaret singing has become. Cabaret singing, so it appears, has proliferated so wildly in the midst of war, that the daily newspapers must lift their voices in warning. The worst dirt is brought to some military hospitals under the pretense of entertainment.

When the riders of the apocalypse tear across the earth and the most noble men die, this becomes possible in Germany.

["Die Zaungäste des Lebens im Kino", Bild und Film (Berlin), 4, 1914/15, pp. 217–18. Translated from German by Patti Duquette, with the assistance of Christine Haas and Sarah Hall.]

Cinema (1920)
Milena Jesenská

I am always perplexed when I read of the cinema being compared to the theater. Someone condemns or defends a performance, weighs one against the other, speaks of the artistry, or lack thereof, in the cinema. Many interesting things can be said about the cinema—e.g. about its sexual effect upon the masses (more so than about its moral or aesthetic effect), its propagandistic function, or taste and decoration, in some instances also about its technical and, in many instances, its provocative side—but the insistence upon a rivalry with theater strikes me as downright exaggerated, and perhaps also superficial.

If such a competition exists, it remains only apparent: we can refer to the cost of a ticket, to the length and variety of the programs, to the heated spaces, to the low and high cost of entertainment (which corresponds to the strata of the audience), to milieu, to a hundred other external things. But to cite an inner and artistic competition would not be appropriate since with the cinema the artistic presents only limited

Fig. 1.10   Milena Jesenská in the early 1920s.

possibilities and these have nothing in common with the theater. When we speak of art in the context of theater, we refer to the author, the drama, the language, the problem, the depth of the idea, its connection to life. If we speak about art in the cinema, we can speak of the technical achievement that may be exemplary—whether it be the photography, the director, the actors or the subject matter—but always in the sense of pure reproduction. In the theater we do not enjoy ourselves; in the theater we listen, compare, learn and look. In the worst case, we are interested. In the cinema? That is it precisely: What do we do in the cinema?

I know people who sit everyday from noon until night in coffeehouses. It is not as if they don't have a living room at home, that they don't have anything to eat, that they cannot cook, or find a quiet place. Nowadays all these excuses do not apply to the people I mean. Before the war, they sat in the coffeehouse (the difference being that they sat there longer because they were open longer), and they sit there after the war, too. I don't mean the loungers and idlers who are useless by any standard. Many coffeehouse patrons are excellent artists who give daily form to ideas and notions through their particular media. Many pursue their bourgeois labor and spend the rest of the day in the coffeehouse. That isn't an unrespectable life; it is the search for a neutral milieu; the opportunity to forget—not to have to think about oneself; the need to exist as a private ego as little as possible—a relief from life.

Now yes! I know people who can go to the movies everyday. It's not that they don't want to work or have nothing to do. Rather it is because it is a comfort to the soul to sit in the movies.

Everything we see seems to be life. And nevertheless such a powerful—and such a comfortable—difference. In the movies, it's about love and hate, good and evil, honesty, and depravity. Here, a villain appears, rolls his eyes, clenches his fists. Everyone knows with certainty that this man will be captured in the end, and that nothing bad will befall the innocent girl who is ardently in love with a poor young man. The poor young man is true to her and does well for himself. Isn't that nice? Nothing can happen to the girl, otherwise it wouldn't be ethical, otherwise the film would not be approved by the censor. Here there are bad women in negligees who smoke, reclining on an ottoman, and good women, who darn laundry, read books, play the piano, or hug curly-haired children. We know with certainty that they are good and that it is entirely impossible to discover anything bad in their souls; and about the evil ones, we know that they are evil and, therefore, that they have earned our contempt and absolutely no sympathy. We need not fear committing an injustice against them, and can rest assured that they will be punished before we leave the cinema, and that the punishment will be just. Here heroic, honorable men risk their lives for the beloved woman—they risk honor, possessions, health, existence. While the others, who simply want to possess a woman, approach her from behind and grab her shoulders in a devilish way. If they should be rejected, they bow their heads elegantly; if not, they sit "afterwards" in an easy chair. But in every case they smoke a cigarette out of the corner of their mouths, which lends an air of cynicism. They have pyjamas and black hair. We recognize them immediately and disdain them with utter loathing.

Really, how nice the world would be, if it were so. How comfortable it would be, if a person were either guaranteed good or evil, if the women were bad or noble, true or untrue, seducible or chaste, goodhearted or rotten! How lovely, how compassionate the world is in the movies, where simple dimensions appear in pure form that we never see, never comprehend, never fathom in life. In our world, people are simultaneously good and bad, true and untrue, reviled and proud. Every heart is complicated, every life is difficult and unresolved; happiness is moody, independent of good or evil acts. Everything is a thousand times different from what we know. We cannot flee at the last minute out of the window of a high tower on a hundred meter rope that we have spun from our own shirt. We cannot, happily in the instances when we are good, or unhappily in those instances when we are bad, jump over the tops of moving trains or throw ourselves from bridges into the water. No villains immure our rightful inheritance in underground chambers and await our legacy, and the prostitutes whom we encounter are not demonic women, nor are they women with tragic fates who stir our hearts with their frantic laughter. Our husbands betray us without being the scum of human society, and our lovers are entirely ordinary officials, businessmen, ministers, and actors, not seductive and undependable rascals.

We puzzle over the meaning of our existence. And look, at the movies the puzzle is solved, and done so with all the falseness of our fantasies about life. How pleasant! How charming! How comfortable! How sweet it is to think for a time with the mind of screen heroes, to take a break from the problems of one's own life, and to see a clear, self-evident life made up of light-phantoms; to experience great passion with the strong, unproblematic, uncomplicated hearts of figures who stride about beautifully turned out (even when there is nothing to eat), lit by the shimmer of fantastic scenery and accompanied by waltz melodies strummed by an orchestra.

Cinema is somewhat different from entertainment. We can compare cinema with a drinker's alcohol, with an addict's opium—it is something that allows forgetting, pleasantly tickles, and rocks one to sleep. Cinema is something to which we cowards happily give ourselves in order to better endure life; it is something easier to bear, because in the face of our misshapen lives we are impotent.

["Kino," *Tribuna* (Prague), 15 January 1920. Translated from German by Patti Duquette, with the assistance of Christine Haas and Sarah Hall.]

A Spectatrix is Speaking to You (1916)
Matilde Serao

Before the war, novelists, poets, and playwrights could not avoid noticing the impetuous and incessant agitation of the curious, even anxious crowds created by the cinema. Some of these writers became fiercely indignant, showing deep contempt for such inferior spectacles; others, more numerous, shrugged their shoulders, whispering *que faire?*—unfortunately the usual outcome of common delusions in art; finally, others, more eclectic, gradually came to exercise their talent in this popular, or, to put it more pointedly, this universal form of expression. Then came the war: novels and poems fell into neglect, and those who wrote them became discouraged and confused. To compose old dramatic works for an audience so capricious was useless and dangerous; but movie theaters were full to bursting, more than ever....

"So, let's make these *movies*"—novelists, poets, and playwrights mused, and then decided—"let's make them, but let's also uplift the cinematographic art by lofty, poetic, and sublime stories; let's elevate the silent art [*l'arte muta*[1]] to the illustrious skies of poetry, grant an uncommon nobility and crystalline purity to these dark and trivial exhibitions, and throw all those *scriptwriters*—paid (and worth) no more than a few lire per story—to mediocrity, ineptitude, and inconsistency. Let us show who *we* are, poets, playwrights, and novelists, and show what happens when all those low and cheap things of the cinema meet the magic touch of our pen."

My friends, brothers, and colleagues, you cannot deny you have said all this, you, who do the same job as I, who have talked to me about this a hundred times in the past; and I listened to you, without answering; or I happened to agree, by nodding carelessly, with complacency…. But now your long research, initially quite serene, has become more and more anxious and concerned: "What *newer, different, and more impressive* could be done? What could one find in the old stories, in the great poems, which could turn out unprecedented, wonderful, and appealing? What other *novelty, beauty, or long forgotten antiquity* could be shown for the first time? Dante's *La Vita Nuova*? The second part of Goethe's *Faust*? Heine's *Almansor*? Moore's *The Loves of the Angels*, or Milton's *Paradise Lost*? The *Romance of the Rose*? One of Tennyson's *Idylls of the King*? Alexander Dumas (senior) *Le Corricolo*? The expedition to Sapri, with Pisacane and Nicotera? Lamartine's *Graziella*? What, what, what?

And I don't deny that the novelist and writer named above—myself—has, with her companions in the very same toil, often vigorously discussed potentially remarkable and beautiful but utterly forgotten stories from the names that live on in literary history; stories which for the most part flash across the reality of the cinema like an immense rocket on a summer night, momentarily lighting the firmament only to leave behind a denser darkness and the stink of burned gun powder. …

Then, for months and months, and with a feeling of sincere humility, I did only one thing: I went to the movies to take up my role of spectatrix [*spettatrice*]. With my mortal eyes, I went to see, for a few cents, or even less, whatever might please, amuse, or move me in a film show. I sat in a corner, in the dark, silent and still, like all my neighbors; and my anonymous and unknown persona became like many others, anonymous and unknown, who were sitting in front of, behind, or beside me. I was like them, an ordinary spectator, without preconceptions, without prejudices, without any sort of bond to anything or anybody. I did not have any ideas or opinions, nothing of anything crammed my mind, which became pure and childlike, spending so little money, staying in that darkness, in that silent and stationary anticipation. And do you know what happened? I experienced the very same impressions felt by my neighbor on my right, who was, I suppose, a shop assistant; the same ones felt by my neighbor on my left, who, now urbanized, had formerly been, I think, a little provincial. And when the lady sitting in front of me laughed, I laughed too because in the dark everybody was laughing; and if the lady behind me cried, I started crying like her and like all the others who were doing the same.

And so I became a perfect spectatrix, by going from show to show, watching all those stories on the white screen, startling at a sudden appearance or a threatening danger, a-throb with the anguish freezing heroes of an unknown drama, or with the mortal risk run by a sweet character, destined to expire. This spectatrix became convinced of a truth—let us say an eternal truth—that the audience of the cinematograph is made of thousands of simple souls, who were either like that in the first place or made simple by the movies themselves. For one of the most bizarre miracles occurring inside a movie theatre is that everybody becomes part of one single spirit. This common spirit gets bored with, or angry at the characters' entanglements, the intricate episodes, the written and often fleeting intertitles, which force it into extremely rapid mental effort. In addition, it is impressionable and tender, sensitive to real and sincere affections; honourable and right—perversity and meanness astonish, yet outrage it. Attracted, but not deceived by the exterior beauty of actors and actresses, it is disappointed if their acts and faces reveal no interior life. Plain but highly sentimental forces like love and pain can deeply affect such an innocent being.

Oh, poets, novelists, playwrights, and brothers of mine, we should not strive so anxiously and painfully for rare and precious scenarios for our films! Let's just go to the truth of things and to people's naturalness. Let's just tell plain good stories, enriching our craft from life itself and take on that elusive but passionate aura of poetry, which springs from our overflowing heart. Stories in which every man and woman would be human, in the widest and humblest meaning of the word; stories in which the slings and arrows of reality would be intense and powerful; stories in which tragic, dramatic, ironic, and grotesque performances would merge in that unlikely harmony of human events. Dearest friends, it is a spectatrix speaking to you, a spectatrix who now asks herself, in retrospect, the reasons for her tears, her smiles, her boredom. This woman who is speaking to you is a creature of the crowd, it is she whom you should move, whom you should please....

["Parla una Spettatrice," *L'Arte Muta* (Naples, Italy) 1:1, 15 June 1916, pp. 31–2. Translated from Italian by Giorgio Bertellini].[1]

Cinema (1936)
Rose Macaulay

Never a dull moment! From a bright foyer we descend in darkness down a slope lit by the flashing torches of fantastic elves, dancing ahead like wills-o'-the-wisp until they settle, pointing us to seats in the middle of an eagerly gazing row of persons, past whom we push, to subside into plush chairs and eagerly gaze too. There is a news reel on; ships are being launched, royalties visit cities and are met by mayors; football is played in the rain before vast crowds, tennis flashes by like lightning, and is repeated in slow motion, horses race and leap, troops walk past with that jerky gait peculiar to animated photography, Signor Mussolini, roaring wide-mouthed like a bull of Bashan, harangues the people of Italy; all is bustle and energy. One feels that ours is a busy world, wherein humanity scuttles about like ants, each bearing his little burden. It is not very like the world which we see about us; still it is a little too like to be really good entertainment, and we are pleased when it abruptly ceases and the screen burgeons into the colour and fantastic nonsense of a Silly Symphony.[1] This is what films ought to show us; they should assist in the process of apotheosising the absurd. This is, indeed, what they do throughout, even when they mimic life, and this is why I prefer them to flesh and blood miming on the stage, which is often so near life as to be tedious. This flat, two-dimensioned moving photography can never be at all like life; it is the most charming, the most bizarre, the most ludicrous convention. See how flowers ring bells and sing, how trees turn into forest demons, how hares play lawn tennis, leaping over the net to take the ball they have served! And, the Silly Symphony over, the Big Picture begun, how the photographs representing persons run about, emitting, in metallic, hollow voices and the lilt of the Californian tongue, the most improbable remarks. Those young British officers, trained at Sandhurst and pursuing their vocation on the Indian frontier, have obviously profited by a career of film-seeing, for they speak the purest Hollywood. So does the little Scottish minister, which is stranger, for he lived before films were. So too does that Roman Empress, and the proud patrician Marcus, but that is all right; if you translate the speech of foreigners, it may as well be into American as into English. The remarkable thing is that any of these photographs should speak at all. It is like women preaching, or dogs walking on their hind legs.

See how that daring young man leaps from his aeroplane in mid air, sailing in his parachute so as to alight on the roof of the house in Chinatown where the gangsters have the girl tied up. Can you beat it? Certainly not on the stage; probably not in life. That is the beauty of the films; they expand life, puff it up into a ludicrous, incredible, magnificent balloon, set it soaring through space, cut loose from the ropes which tie it down to fact. Then, how well they photograph raging seas, glaciers, deserts, mountain peaks, penguins, grasshoppers, and wild beasts prowling through jungles. Battles, too; here are Waterloo and Plassey [sic] in little, terrible with battling elephants and upping Guards.[2] Had Shakespeare known of such a way of miming Agincourt, how he would have rejoiced! And in what unearthly, horrid and transparent shapes would his ghosts have revisited the glimpses of the moon, in place of the too solid flesh in which perforce dead Caesar and King Hamlet stalked the boards and stalk them to this day. As to his fairies, in what elegant and dainty minuteness would Titania and Oberon meet and square, while their elves for fear crept into acorn cups and hid them there.

There is, to be sure, one thing that moving photography should never attempt; that is to portray serious and actual human drama, the relations between human creatures. Indeed, why should they? These we can see all about us in life, and very weary of them we get. To be confronted with them again on the screen would be too much. Indeed, I seldom am so, since I choose my films with care. They should be funny, fantastic, exotic, anything they like, but not human. Love they should shun like the devil; it is not for photographs, however animated, nor for mechanically recorded voices, however Hollywood, to mime this universal terrestrial passion. Let the films know their business, and lead us tip-toe through strange fantastic realms, soaring above the clouds, burrowing in the bowels of the earth, galloping across cactus deserts among mesquite and Gila monsters, pursued by Sheriffs, zig-zagging in wild and rickety cars pursued by the constabulary, grappling with monsters of the deep or of the trackless jungle, wooing humour with the suave voice and face of Mr. Laughton, the impassivity of Mr. Harold Lloyd, the rolling eyes of Mr. Cantor, improbable legs and the impossible figure of Mr. Jack Hulbert and Miss Courtneidge, the imbecility of Mr. Ralph Lynn, the glitter of Miss Lyn Fontaine.[3] Once they stoop, or attempt to stoop to realism, they are undone, these wonderful contrivances. Heavens above, is there not enough realism in life, that our moving photographs should ape it?

Come away: a gripping drama has begun. Out, past still eagerly gazing rows; out into the night. If we must have gripping dramas, we prefer to see them in the world at large, where, alas, they are all too common. Our comic fairyland falls shattered about us at so crude a trumpet blast. We will adjourn to the Café Royal and consume sandwiches and bock.[4]

[From *Personal Pleasures*, (London: Macmillan, 1936), pp. 135–38.]

Why I Go to the Cinema (1937)
Elizabeth Bowen

I go to the cinema for any number of different reasons—these I ought to sort out and range in order of their importance. At random, here are a few of them: I go to be distracted (or "taken out of myself"); I go when I don't want to think; I go when I do want to think and need stimulus; I go to see pretty people; I go when I want to see life ginned up, charged with unlikely energy; I go to laugh; I go to be harrowed; I go when a day has been such a mess of detail that I am glad to see even the most arbitrary, the most preposterous pattern emerge; I go because I like bright light, abrupt shadow, speed; I go to see America, France, Russia; I go because I like wisecracks and slick behaviour; I go because the screen is an oblong opening into the world of fantasy for me; I go because I like story, with its suspense; I go because I like sitting in a packed crowd in the dark, among hundreds riveted on the same thing; I go to have my most general feelings played on.

These reasons, put down roughly, seem to fall under five headings: wish to escape, lassitude, sense of lack in my nature or my surroundings, loneliness (however passing) and natural frivolity. As a writer, I am probably subject during working hours to a slightly unnatural imaginative strain, which leaves me flat and depleted by the end of a day. But though the strain may be a little special in nature, I do not take it to be in any way greater than the strain, the sense of depletion, suffered by other people in most departments of life now. When I take a day off and become a person of leisure, I embark on a quite new method of exhausting myself; I amuse myself through a day, but how arduous that is; by the end of the day I am generally down on the transaction—unless I have been in the country.

I take it that for the professional leisured person things, in the long run, work out the same way. Writers, and other inventive workers, are wrong, I think, in claiming a special privilege, or in representing themselves as unfairly taxed by life: what is taken out of them in some ways is saved them in others; they work, for the most part, in solitude; they are not worn by friction with other people (unless they choose to seek this in their spare time); they have not to keep coming to terms with other people in order to get what they have to do done. They escape monotony; they are sustained in working by a kind of excitement; they are shut off from a good many demands. Their work is exhausting, and by human standards unnatural, but it cannot be more exhausting than routine work in office, shop, or factory, teaching, running a family, hanging on to existence if one is in the submerged class, or amusing oneself. I make this point in order to be quite clear that my reasons for cinema-going are not unique or special: they would not be worth discussing if they were.

I am not at all certain, either, that the practice of one art gives one a point of vantage in discussing another. Where the cinema is concerned, I am a fan, not a critic. I have been asked to write on "Why I Go to the Cinema" because I do write, and should therefore do so with ease; I have not been asked to write, and am not writing, as a writer. It is not as a writer that I go to the cinema; like everyone else, I slough off my preoccupations there. The film I go to see is the product of a kind of art, just as a bottle of wine is the product of a kind of art. I judge the film as I judge the bottle of wine, in its relation to myself, by what it does to me. I sum up the pleasure it gives. This pleasure is, to an extent, an affair of my own palate, or temperament, but all palates and temperaments have something in common; hence general "taste," an accepted, objective standard in judgement of films or wine. Films, like wines, are differently good in their different classes; some of us prefer to seek one kind, some another, but always there is the same end—absolute pleasure—in view.

Cinemas draw all sorts. In factory towns they are packed with factory workers, in university cities with dons, at the seaside with trippers (who take on a strong, though temporary character), in the West End with more or less moneyed people with time to kill, in country towns and villages with small tradespeople and with workers scrubbed and hard from the field. Taste, with these different audiences, differs widely, but the degree of pleasure sought is the same. A film either hits or misses. So affectable are we that to sit through a film that is not pleasing the house, however much it may happen to please one personally, causes restless discomfort that distracts from one's pleasure. [...] This works both ways: the success of a film with its house communicates a tingling physical pleasure—joining and heightening one's private exhilaration—a pleasure only the most weathered misanthrope could withstand—and your misanthrope is rarely a cinema-goer. There is no mistaking that tension all round in the dark, that almost agonised tension of a pleased house—the electric hush, the rapt immobility. The triumphantly funny film, hitting its mark, makes even laughter break off again and again, and the truly tragic suspends the snuffle.

The happily constituted cinema-goer learns to see and savour a positive merit in films that may do nothing to him personally, films whose subjects, stars or settings may to him, even, be antipathetic. To reject, as any kind of experience, a film that is acting powerfully on people around seems to me to argue poverty in the nature. What falls short as aesthetic experience may do as human experience: the film rings no bell in oneself, but one hears a bell ring elsewhere. [...] I speak of the happily constituted cinema-goer—I mean, perhaps, the happily constituted, and, therefore, very rare person. The generality of us, who hate jokes we cannot see and mysteries we are out of, may still hope to become sophisticates in at least this one pleasure by bringing with us, when we go to a cinema, something more active, more resourceful than tolerance. [...]

Films have—it is a truism of the trade—a predetermined destination. Every film made makes a bid for the favour of certain localities whose taste has been gauged in advance, correctly or not. Local appeal, at its strongest, is strongly delimited. If one is to go to a film for its popularity-interest, one should go to it in its own country—its areas may be social, not geographic, though largely they *are* geographic, for climate and occupation do condition an audience. For instance, my great respect for Miss Gracie Fields does not alter the fact that I would not willingly see, for its own sake, at my nearest London cinema, a film in which she appeared.[1] But I should feel I had missed something if I missed seeing a Gracie Fields film in the Gracie Fields country. There she operates in full force, and I cannot fail to react—to the audience, if not to her. [...] The determining factor must, I think, be social: hard-living people like to have some one to admire; they like what is like themselves. The sophisticated are attracted, titillated, by what is foreign, outrageous, by what they may half deplore.

But it would be misleading, as well as precious, to overstress this rest-of-the-audience factor in my reaction to films. I do really only like what I like. I go to please myself, and when I sit opposite a film the audience is *me*. My faculties are riveted, my pleasure can only be a little damped down or my disappointment added to by the people cheek by jowl with me in the dark. I expect a good deal, when I go to the cinema; my expectations absorb me from the moment I enter. I am giving myself a treat—or being given a treat. I have little spare time or money, the cinema is my anodyne, not my subject, and my objective interest in its emotional mechanics is not really very great. Nine times out of ten, it is alert, exacting expectations of pleasure that carry me to the cinema. The tenth time I may go from abstract curiosity, or at random—as when I have hours to pass in a strange town where it is raining or there are no buildings to see. [...]

I expect, then, to enjoy myself. This end I do all I can to further by taking as good a seat as my purse, that day, will allow. [...] Cramp or any other physical irritation militates quite unfairly against the best film: if a film is worth seeing at all they seem to me worth avoiding. [...] Anyhow, I seek comfort—and how important smoking is. I start slightly against the best film in a foreign cinema where I am unable to smoke. Very great films (generally Russian) and moments in any good film do suspend my desire to smoke; this is the supreme test.

I have—like, I suppose every other filmgoer—a physical affection for certain cinemas. In London the "Empire" is my favourite; when settled down in there I feel I am back in the old home, and am predisposed to happiness. May it never come down. I suppose I could rationalise my feeling for the Empire by saying I like Metro-Goldwyn-Mayer films—but though I have enjoyed these all over Europe, the last drop of pleasure is added by being at the Empire. However, one must take films not only as but where one finds them. In the provinces, I have often had to desert my favourite cinema in order to see a promising film elsewhere; this gave the evening, though the film might prove excellent, an undertone of nostalgia: "I wish this were at the Such-and-Such." The sentiment was absurd and is only mentioned because I think it is general. Pleasure is at its best when it has in it some familiar element. [...]

I hope I never go to the cinema in an entirely unpropitious mood. If I do, and am not amused, that is my fault, also my loss. As a rule, I go empty but hopeful, like someone bringing a mug to a tap that may not turn on. The approach tunes me up for pleasure. The enchantment that hung over those pre-War facades of childhood—gorgeously white stucco facades, with caryatids and garlands—has not dissolved, though the facades have been changed. How they used to beam down the street. Now concrete succeeds stucco and chromium gilt; foyers once crimson and richly stuffy are air-conditioned and dove-grey. But, like a chocolate-box lid, the entrance is still voluptuously promising: sensation of some sort seems to be guaranteed. How happily I tread the pneumatic carpet, traverse anterooms with their exciting muted vibration, and walk down the spotlit aisle with its eager tilt to the screen. I climb over those knees to the sticky velvet seat, and fumble my cigarettes out—as I used not to do.

I am not only home again, but am, if my choice is lucky, in ideal society. I am one of the millions who follow Names from cinema to cinema. The star system may be all wrong—it has implications I hardly know of in the titanic world of Hollywood, also it is, clearly, a hold-up to proper art—but I cannot help break it down. I go to see So-and-So. I cannot fitly quarrel with this magnification of personalities, while I find I can do with almost unlimited doses of anybody exciting, anybody with beauty (in my terms), verve, wit, style, *toupet* and, of course, glamour. What do I mean by glamour? A sort of sensuous gloss: I know it to be synthetic, but it affects me strongly. It is a trick knowingly practised on my most fuzzy desires; it steals a march on me on my silliest side. But all the same, in being subject to glamour I experience a sort of elevation. It brings, if not into life at least parallel to it, a sort of fairy-tale element. It is a sort of trumpet call, mobilizing the sleepy fancy. If a film is to get across, glamour somewhere, in some form—moral, if you like, for it can be moral—cannot be done without. The Russians break with the bourgeois-romantic conception of personality; they have scrapped sex-appeal as an annexe of singularising, anti-social love. But they still treat with glamour; they have transferred it to mass movement, to a heroicised pro-human emotion. I seek it, in any form.

To get back to my star: I enjoy, sitting opposite him or her, the delights of intimacy without the onus, high points of possession without the strain. This could be called inoperative love. Relationships in real life are made arduous by their reciprocities; one can too seldom simply sit back. The necessity to please, to shine, to make the most of the moment, overshadows too many meetings. And apart from this—how seldom in real life (or so-called real life) does acquaintanceship, much less intimacy, with dazzling, exceptional beings come one's way. How very gladly, therefore, do I fill the gaps in my circle of ideal society with these black-and-white personalities, to whom absence of colour has added all the subtleties of tone. Directly I take my place I am on terms with these Olympians; I am close to them with nothing at all at stake. Rapture lets me suppose that for me alone they display the range of their temperaments, their hesitations, their serious depths. I find them not only dazzling but sympathetic. They live for my eye. Yes, and I not only perceive them but *am* them; their hopes and fears are my own; their triumphs exalt me. I am proud for them and in them. Not only do I enjoy them; I enjoy in them a vicarious life.

Nevertheless, I like my stars well supported. If a single other character in the film beside them be unconvincing or tin-shape, the important illusion weakens; something begins to break down. I like to see my star played up to and played around by a caste that is living, differentiated and definite. The film must have background, depth, its own kind of validity. [...] There is family-feeling inside a good film—so that the world it creates is valid, water-tight, *probable*.

What a gulf yawns between improbablity—which is desolating—and fan-tasy—which is dream-probabilty, likeliness on an august, mad plane. Comedy films show this fantasy element more strongly than tragedies, which attempt to approach life and fail too often through weakness and misrepresentation; comedies are thus, as a rule, better. A really good comic (a Laurel and Hardy, for instance) is never simply improbable: it suspends judgement on the workaday plane. Comedy-drama needs some verisimilitude.

When I say verisimilitude, I do not mean that I want the film to be exactly *like* life: I should seldom go to the cinema if it were. The effective film (other, of course, than the film that is purely documentary) must have at least a touch of the preposterous. But its distance from life, or from probability, should stay the same throughout: it must keep inside its pitch. The film that keeps in its pitch makes, and imposes, a temporary reality of its own.

Any cinema-goer, however anxious for peace and for his own pleasure, may detect in a film a gaff that he cannot pass. I quarrel most, naturally, with misrepresentation of anything that I happen to know about. For instance, I have, being Irish, seen few films about Ireland, or set in Ireland, that did not insult and bore me. (*The Informer* was one remarkable exception.) But I could sit through a (no doubt) equally misrepresenting film about Scotland, which I do not know, without turning a hair. [...] As a woman, I am annoyed by improbability in clothes: English films offend rather badly in this way. Dressy at all costs, English heroines hike, run down spies or reclaim lovers from storm-girt islands in their Kensington High Street bests. An equal unlikeliness blights the English film interior: I revolt from ancestral homes that are always Gothic, from Louis Seize bedrooms in poverty-stricken manors, from back-street dwellings furnished by Mr. Drage. The frumpy and unsatirical flatness of the average English stage-set is almost always transferred by the English film to the screen. The French make *genre* films in which every vase, tassel and door-handle thickens the atmosphere, makes for verisimilitude and adds more to the story: why cannot we do the same?

Why are there so few English *genre* films? All over this country, indoors and out, a photographable drama of national temperament is going on, and every object has character. By-passes, trees on skylines, small country town streets with big buses pushing along them, village Sundays, gasometers showing behind seaside towns, half-built new estates, Midland canals, the lounges of private hotels, stucco houses with verandas, rectory tea-tables, the suburban shopping rush, garden fêtes and the abstract perspectives of flyblown, semi-submerged London are all waiting the camera and are very dramatic. English interiors are highly characterised; English social routine is romantically diverse. As it is, the same few shots—which might, from their symbolic conventionality, have been made to be exported to Hollywood—drearily reappear, to give English films their locality: Westminster Bridge, crazy gables stuck with oak beams, corners of (apparently) Oxford Colleges masquerading as Great Homes, clotted orchards (that might be faked with a few rolls of crêpe paper), the spire of always the same church, and those desolating, unconvincing, always-the-same rooms. There are exceptions to this—Anthony Asquith shows feeling for landscape, and Hitchcock gets humour into interiors—but not nearly enough exceptions. Generally speaking, English films lack humour in the perceptive, sympathetic and wide sense. They lack sensibility; they do not know how to use objects. Are we blind to our country? Too many English films are, humanly speaking, dead. Character in them is tin-shape and two-dimensional. The whole effect is laborious, genteel, un-adult and fussy. Comedies, technically "clean," are unbearably vulgar; there is no fun, only knockabout and facetiousness. It is true that we are beginners, that we have admittedly much to learn, still, in the way of technique. But we fail in more than technique; we fail, flatly and fatally, in conception.

At present it appears, discouragingly enough, that to make outstanding films one must either be sophisticated, like some Americans; disabused and witty, like the French; vividly neurotic like the Germans; or noble, like the Russians. [...]

I am discussing, throughout, the "story" film. That is the film I go to see; I go to see the cinema for amusement only; my feeling for it may be exceptionally frivolous. I more than admire, I am often absorbed, by good "interest" or documentary films that may occur in a programme, but as these are not the films I seek I do not feel that I am qualified to discuss them. I go for what is untrue, to be excited by what is fantastic, to see what has never happened happen. I go for the fairy story. [...] I have very little curiosity, and an inordinate wish to be entertained. If many more cinema-goers were as lazy-minded and fantasy-loving as I am what a pity it would be—but I take it that I am in a minority. I hope that the cinema may develop along all lines, while still giving me many more of the films I like—grown-up comedies, taut thrillers, finished period pieces and dashing Westerns. I want no more American tragedies, Russian comedies or crepitating Teutonic analysis. I should like still more dramatic use of landscape and architecture. I like almost any French film—perhaps I have been lucky. I have rather dreaded beforehand, as one dreads drastic experience, any Russian film I have seen; have later wished, while it lasted, to protract every moment, and finally found it, when it was over, more powerful than a memory—beside everything else, there had been so much more fun than one foresaw.

I am shy of the serious aspect of my subject, and don't want to finish on an unnaturally high note. It is, of course, clear to me that a film, like any other attempt on art, or work of art—all being tentative—can have in it germs of perfection. Its pretension to an aesthetic need be no less serious than that of a poem, picture, or piece of music. Its medium, which is unique to it, is important; fluid pattern, variation of light, speed. In time, the cinema has come last of all the arts; its appeal to the racial child in us is so immediate that it should have come first. Pictures came first in time, and bore a great weight of meaning: the "pictures" date right back in their command of emotion: they are inherently primitive. A film can put the experience of a race or a person on an almost dreadfully simplified epic plane.

We have promise of great art here, but so far few great artists. Films have not caught up with the possibilities of the cinema: we are lucky when we get films that keep these in sight. Mechanics, the immense technical knowledge needed, have kept the art, as an art, unnaturally esoteric; its techical progress (more and more discoveries: sound, now colour) moves counter to its spiritual progress. An issue keeps being obscured, a problem added to. Yet we have here, almost within our grasp, a means to the most direct communication possible between man and man. What might be a giant instrument is still a giant toy.

How much I like films I like—but I could like my films better. I like being distracted, flattered, tickled, even rather upset—but I should not mind something more; I should like something serious. I should like to be changed by more films, as art can change one; I should like something to happen when I go to the cinema.

[From *Footnotes to the Film*, ed Charles Davy. London: Lovat Dickson, 1937, pp. 205–20.]

Woman and the Film (1947)
E. Arnot Robertson

Before the war there was a yearning song-hit: "I dunno why I love you like I do. I dunno why, I just do—hoo." Roughly it summed up then, and it sums up now, my feelings towards the cinema.

Indeed, I dunno!

There are plenty of reasons for my being enormously interested in the cinema. As a citizen, aware that this is probably the most powerful agent there is to-day for forming standards of public taste and behaviour. As a private individual, wanting—definitely needing at times—the relief of laughter or of being moved by human circumstances which aren't my own. As a writer, because this is a most exciting and malleable art form: there seems, at present, to be no limit to its possibilities, the heights to which it can rise, the depths to which it can sink, the people it can reach and influence. But to love it, when I think of the things it has done to me in the past—without hope, too, that it will refrain from doing as bad or worse in the future—as a woman I can't explain that: I suppose I just do-hoo.

There is, in real life, a particular kind of boredom—lover's boredom—which has never, I believe, been adequately dealt with in literature or anywhere else: the awful blankness of the whole world, because it doesn't visibly contain at the moment the only creature worth containing; the almost unbearable triviality of human faces and shapes which don't happen to be the right ones. This is the only kind of boredom I have ever known—the positive sort, when it ceases to be an absence of interest and becomes an active mental pain—which can compare with the boredom I have endured from films like The Hoodlum Saint, or the one about the child who wanted her adopted daddy to love her, so she pretended to "mother"him and hold conversations with his dead wife, till he strangely weakened in his resolve to send her to boarding school (my memory, flinching, refuses to supply the title), or Love Letters—all pictures in which, after the first five minutes, I not only didn't care what was going to happen to the characters, obvious as this was, I passionately didn't care. The reason, of course, is that both are lover's boredom. It is only because the cinema is so supremely worth-while when it is good that it is so exasperating to see a rewarding medium used shoddily or dishonestly. In fact, probably the best measure of how much one cares about it is the amount of anger which a bad film can arouse.

It is as a woman, though, not as a writer, citizen, etc., that I most easily get annoyed in the audience. Identifying myself for the moment with the heroine on the screen, as the female part of a good audience is supposed to do, I feel it is high time I was allowed to do something besides looking cute in order to inspire true love, of the undying variety, in the hero. Still, in ninety-nine films out of a hundred I don't have to do anything, say anything or be anything endearing; I just look cute. (By the same means I, incidentally, inspire the villain with emotion which has exactly the same symptoms, but this, I understand, is mere lust, and quite, quite different somehow.) Here the cinema has lagged far behind contemporary feeling in its handling of motive. With certain glorious exceptions like Brief Encounter, blessedly adult, truthful and contemporary, everything to do with love in the cinema is early Victorian, adolescent at that. Apart from appealing to the eye, all I may show, in place of character, are a few "accomplishments" in the young Victorian sense: that is if the picture is a musical I may help myself to catch the hero's approving glance by singing and dancing. Isn't it time the cinema grew up a bit about love? Not only about sexual love, which in most cases in real life is plainly not as much as 99 per cent physical attraction, or most of us wouldn't have the wherewithal to get any at all; but also about maternal love. Any good, honest mother knows that the most pleasing sight in the world is the back-view of her children going off almost anywhere (so long as it's safe and they don't actively dislike it, in order that she shan't have to worry about them or even think of them at all) for several hours, in which she will not have to answer their questions or subordinate her interests to theirs. And she admits that all school holidays seem much too long. Has there ever been a film which reflected this prevalent feeling? No, screen mothers enjoy the company of their young twenty-four hours a day, God and the directors alone know how.

[From *Penguin Film Review* (London) 3, August 1947, pp. 31–3, excerpted.]

The Week on the Screen: *The Women* (1926)
C.A. Lejeune

It is strange how few people in the motion picture industry know anything about the minds of women. You would think that, coming into contact with women every day, watching them individually and in the mass, listening to their comments through the varied experiences of years, the showman of pictures would have finished his study in complete understanding. But he has not. He still blunders on in the face of woman's prejudices. He still grounds his appeals to woman on a misconception of her tastes. He still brings her tidbits that she despises, and protects her from the pleasures that she loves. When she wants to see horses he gives her children, when she longs for dogs he smothers her with babies. Instead of the romance that tickles every homebound fancy, he expects womanly things to please the women most. For adventure, domesticity; for the gun, a Paris gown; for the boar-hound, a Pekingese; in every way the showman provides his woman patrons with the things that have for them the least appeal.

If the time should ever come when the men inside the kinema discover the tastes and inhibitions of the women outside it—find that slapstick bores them, incidental noises enrage them, scenes of cruelty make them sick,—if they learn what women really think of freaks and deformities, of beatings and brandings and death-scenes, there will be such a turmoil, such a scuffling to and fro to revise the kinema as that complacent industry has never known before.

For the kinema must please the women or die. The vast majority of picture-goers are women and always will be. The time of day is in their favour, to steal an odd hour from the afternoon; and woman, whose work lies at home, is just as glad of the opportunity to escape from home for an hour as man, whose work lies outside, is glad of the opportunity to be in it. The price, too, is a woman's price, easily found. When a man spends money, he likes to feel he is spending: when a woman spends money, she likes to feel she is not. The small cushioned seats are women's seats; they have no masculine build. The warmth in winter, the coolness in summer, the darkness, the sleepy music, the chance to relax unseen are all women's pleasures which no man, however tired he may be, can ever quite appreciate or understand.

But the main attraction of the kinema for women rises out of a common factor in their natures. Woman is fiercely, desperately personal, and the kinema the most personal of all the arts. Through it a woman can get into close touch with the shadows she has longed to meet, can seem to know them, can follow them through the whole gamut of their moods and share with them the most intense experiences. For women and because of women the "star" system has grown up in the kinema. It is nothing more or less than a commercial means of giving women the most of what they want—personality. Books, pictures, music, dancing cannot do it. The theatre satisfies only the front rows of stalls. But the kinema brings personal contact to everybody, rich or poor; individual contact, isolated in the heart of a crowd; and, bringing it, brings, too, the allegiance of the most loyal public any art could desire.

The ordinary woman, who has neither time nor inclination to be very clever, who has a home to run, and children, who has a typewriter to drive perhaps, or a dinner to cook, a market basket to fill, a counter of goods to sell, has made her shadow friends in the kinema long ago and finds happiness in them, in seeing them every now and then, reading of what they are doing, remembering what they have done. She is no fool, this woman, no sluggard in criticism. The first to notice the inconsistencies of a production, the bad workmanship, the flaws in thought, she has no illusions about her screen friends and their quality. She knows when their work is bad just as surely as she knows when the film around them is bad. She knows every one of their faults and weaknesses—knows that this one is ugly, this one miscast, that this one cannot act. She knows and does not care. Criticism, in the face of friendship, loses all its sting. Let no one mock at this personal loyalty in women. It is sprung, more often than men can understand, from the keenest intuition. It is full of a shrewd pity that a shrewder wisdom hides. It is incorruptible and the source of endless power. And if, because of it, no art has ever yet been woman born, through it, and out of it, and by the grace of it each and every art has come to be born of man.

[*Manchester Guardian* (Manchester), 16 January 1926, p. 9.]

The Spectatrix

The Movies (1928)

Ada Negri

She's just a typist, closer to forty than to thirty, not quick and shrewd like so many other working-class women. She slouches a little, and invariably dresses in steel gray or dark brown, with a small felt hat pulled tightly down over her forehead so its shadow will cover her eyes and thin lashes. She's had her hair bobbed like other women, but only so her fine hair—so limp it seems pasted to her head and so thin her braided bun slides out of the hairpins—won't dangle down her neck anymore and embarrass her. Short dresses don't look good on her. They betray her skinny legs, with her nylons obstinately sagging, especially at the ankles. There's nothing that spoils a woman's appearance and makes her more homely than nylons that sag at the ankles.

She lives alone. Her parents are dead, and no young man has ever liked her pale little face, shrivelled like an old apple, as if she'd been born with wrinkles. The business office where she works is gloomy, with its electric lights turned on even in the daytime to struggle with the sticky, ashen light coming in the windows overlooking a downtown alley. There's the smell of paper, old and new; numbers; copying ink; of meagre, penned-in lives revolving around the daily schedule and payday, the twenty-seventh of the month. The handful of employees have eyes only for the second typist—an adolescent, practically. She has her hair bobbed too, but her lips are lacquered with lipstick, her eyelashes heavy with black mascara, and for a dress she wears a kind of knit beach cover-up that doesn't reach her knees, and clings so tightly to her small breasts and supple hips that it looks as if it were wet.

On Thursday or Saturday evenings, and sometimes on Sunday afternoons, too, the poor little clerk with the wrinkled, applish face goes to the movies.

The other days of the week she thinks about what she saw at the movies, and gets ready for the joy of the next movie.

She goes to the movies without girlfriends, because she doesn't have any. She never looked for friends and didn't find any, not even when she was a little girl going to school. She was always held back by a shyness she couldn't overcome, and also, perhaps, a vague sense of inferiority, an inborn restraint that kept her from opening up about herself, from confiding in someone, from asking for anything. There are some people born with an air that attracts others, and some people born with an air that drives others away. Then there are people with neither one nor the other, and they are the most miserable and lonely of all. Even her name is pitiful: Bigia, which in the Lombard dialect is the corrupted form of the name Luigia, and brings to mind fog, twilight, and rain.

She only wants to go to the best movie theaters where they play the best shows, and that's where she ends up spending half her salary. But isn't it like travelling, after all? Like taking voyages around the world? The only way to travel is first class, with all the comforts. The novelty of it and the feeling of leisure begin at the entrance, in the lobby, which is usually spacious and adorned with columns, lit by heavy, luxurious chandeliers, and decorated with broad stucco mouldings, and publicity posters with gigantic headlines and colored drawings done to the nth degree of brightness, a loud, garish style. The film has almost always started already, and, in pitch darkness, the main floor seats seem empty, occupied only by an immense breath of suspense. Sitting in the dark, she often happens to graze the arm of some invisible person; each time the same shiver runs through her. She can't tell whether it's a woman or a man. It's a living being, whose presence she feels, for now, without seeing its face, or being seen herself, and she's not sorry about it. At the intermission, when the lights suddenly come on in the theater, she can see the profile of the man or woman next to her, but she's not interested anymore. To look at someone means to be looked at. She's aware of how shabby and plain she looks. If only it were possible in life to be close to someone all the time without seeing each other!

At the movies she prefers to see dramas in which the most unlikely adventures intertwine and whirl in a vortex around astonishing love affairs. Perhaps this need for flights of fantasy is born from the barrenness and poverty of her own destiny. If she were rich and educated, she'd go to the theater. But being the way she is, the theater—opera or plays—couldn't give her coarse tastes and uncultivated mind the kind of nourishment she relishes at the movies. A fitful, capricious, and often poisoned nourishment. She's not aware of how it happens, but beginning with the first scenes, she completely identifies with the leading lady's character. She enters her world; she loves and hates, sins and takes risks, is joyful, suffers and triumphs, entirely absorbed within the character. For two or three very long and very fleeting, eventful hours, she has Mary Pickford's sweet, affectionate face, Mae Murray's golden halo of hair and wide triangular nostrils, Greta Garbo's lithe body, ambiguous grace, and magical, light blue eyes. She is Pola Negri, she is Bebe Daniels, not as they really are, but as they bring to life the characters they play.[1]

For two or three very long and very fleeting hours she lives in countries she's never seen before but recognizes at first sight and where she feels at ease, as though she'd always lived there. She crosses these lands in luxurious cars and lightning-fast trains, or flies over them in gliders. She stays at hotels worthy of queens and kings, and receives genteel ladies and gentlemen in drawing rooms full of precious objects, she herself adorned and bejewelled, like an idol. Or else, dressed in a low-cut bodice, with a checkered scarf around her neck and a carnation in her hair, she greets adventurers, gold seekers, and jailbirds in a rough American saloon at the edge of the Western prairie. She shakes with fear and fights in worldly intrigues; she risks her life and wins it back; she disappears and reappears. If he's not a Fairbanks-style cowboy or a Ghione-style hoodlum, the man she loves usually behaves nobly and has refined manners, a clean-shaven and perfect face with an enigmatic, scowling smile, and a nervous tic in the left or right corner of his lips.[2] An Anglo-American type, he vaguely resembles the young boss in her office. But her boss is thousands of miles away from her, even when they're separated only by the narrow space between his desk and her typewriter table. Instead, the other man—oh, the other man—is so close to her that she feels the warmth of his breath, and with him she can run away to the farthest ends of the earth.

To run away, to run away to the sea! She's never been there. The only sea she knows is the sea in the movies. She knows it so well that she hears the rhythmic breaking of waves on the beach, she breathes in its saltiness, she relishes its freedom. Only she's bothered by the constant fury of the waves, one rolling in right after the other. Is the sea always so restless, even when it's calm? Everything on the screen happens so fast; the people's gestures, the going, the coming, the crying, the laughing, the rhythm of work, embracing, committing crimes. Everything unfolds in high speed. At the climactic moments of the film, if the theater weren't immersed in darkness, Bigia would see, in the orchestra seats, rows of faces, with their expressions distorted by the rush of blood and the nervous agitation. If she saw herself in a mirror, even her own face would look like this.

If only real life were like life in the movies! With doors that fling open by themselves; paths of water, land, and air, waiting there to rescue whoever is in danger; distances reduced to a dot; nothing forbidden, everything made possible and easy, obeying the crazy whims of fantasy and passion.

But isn't it all lies? And isn't a lie something bad? If Bigia's mother were still alive, it would frighten her. She'd say, "Just look at yourself." But nowadays girls don't listen to their mothers. They say, "I make my own money, so I'll do what I want." But then, Bigia's mother isn't there anymore. No one is there for Bigia, there never will be anyone. A passion burns inside her—although she's never even admitted it to herself and she shows no sign of it; that passion is appeased by the fantastic happenings she enjoys and endures on the screen, and is channeled off in a thousand different directions. She lives two parallel existences; she has two distinct souls. Except that for some time now the parallel lives have gone astray, they've caught up with each other and intersected. These two souls struggle with one another. When she gets home from the movies, her skin is burning and she has a rapid pulse that comes and goes with a nervous fever. She's not able to fall asleep; she keeps thinking and thinking about images that have the clarity, intensity, and sharpness of hallucinations. Toward dawn, worn out, she finally grows drowsy. But in her sleep, as she dreams, she relives the fable of the weaver who through the magic of love becomes a duchess, or the billionaire who runs away from the splendors of her palace to follow the handsome knight, or the robot woman who's more seductive than a woman of real flesh and blood and drags multitudes to ruin.[3]

It's difficult to wake up again. Her tongue is swollen, her memory tangled, her will weak. In the office she's distracted and sits motionless at the typewriter, daydreaming. She makes mistakes with the figures, amounts to be carried over, and columns. She isn't herself anymore. But maybe she's ill. This is the only thought that keeps the boss from firing her.

One Saturday evening around eleven, she comes out of the Helios movie theater with dazed eyes and a confused buzzing in her ears, her wrinkled applish face transformed by some spellbinding thought that completely absorbs her. In the square, the comings and goings of people pouring out of the nightclubs: they cross each other's paths, horns honk, the haunting glare of signs all lit up in white, purple, deep blue, some in long ribbons, some fanning out, others turning round, like wheels. The car headlights are shining on the wet asphalt. Lights above, lights below. Illusion. She doesn't know where she is. She doesn't know who she is. The climax of the romantic story that elated her just moments ago won't stop playing over and over in front of her eyes and in her mind. Her name is Ginevra. She's twenty years old, in love, desperate. She's waiting on a boulevard in Paris for her lover's car to go by, so she can throw herself in front of it and be crushed. Her lover! He doesn't love her anymore, because he doesn't believe her anymore. Her lover! What sweetness, what pangs, to have a lover, to suffer for love, to cry for him, to say to herself, "Now I'm going to kill myself for him." But not really to die, of course. Instead, she'd be gathered up in his arms, saved by him, and he'd believe in her again, love her again. The heroines in the movies don't actually die, do they?

The scene unfolds as if it were a movie. People pass by and don't look; they're indifferent, in a hurry. Shining lights; vehicles speeding by; everything moving along quickly, without obstacles, as in a dream. Bigia—Ginevra knows she's beautiful, and so elegant, like a porcelain figurine in a Russian gray–squirrel fur coat with soft silver flecks, with her legs veiled in a delicate gray mesh, and light pearl gray suede shoes that look like jewels in the mud. She isn't wearing anything on her head. She has a full head of curly blonde hair. Where did she get that blonde head of hair? And how can she see it, if she doesn't have a compact and all the shop windows are shuttered up?

But she's beautiful, elegant, and in love, ready to kill herself.

A fast car swerves sharply but isn't able to avoid the determined victim in time! A scream. Two policemen compassionately lift a woman's body up from the ground. Her shabby little dark brown dress has climbed up to her shoulders in all the havoc, leaving her injured torso and broken legs almost naked. They take her to the hospital in the same car that ran over her. The throng of curious people stares after her. Then they disperse, going their own ways, in different directions.

Someone sighs, "Poor creature!" And another person says, "Who could it be?"

No one. Not really anyone. Just a typist who lived alone and had only one passion—the movies.

[Originally titled "Cinematografia," *Corriere della Sera* (Milan), 27 November 1928, p. 3. Translated by Robin Pickering-Iazzi.]

Continuous Performance (1927)
Dorothy Richardson

...So I gave up going to the theatre. Yet I had seen one or two who possessed themselves upon the stage and much good acting, especially of character parts; but I have never been on my knees to character acting. The one or two I saw again and again, enduring for their sakes those others, many of them clever, all keyed up for their parts, all too high-pitched, taking their cues too soon. It was not that the pain of seeing them lose all our opportunities—their own and with them ours who were the audience—outweighed the joy of recreation at the hands of those others, makers and givers of life, but rather that on the whole the sense of guilt, of wasted performance for players and audience alike was too heavy to be borne. Waste and loss that could, it seemed to me, with ever so little control of the convulsionaries, be turned to gain.

Lured back by a series of German plays zestfully performed by a small and starless group, I found at once my persuasion confirmed that the English, whose very phlegm and composure is the other side of their self-consciousness and excitability, do not make actors. Watching for foreigners I saw a few French plays, saw Bernhardt and was more than ever ashamed of the remembered doings of the English casts. Not even the most wooden of those selected to surround and show up the French star could produce anything to equal the sense of shame and loss that at that time overshadowed for me all I saw on the English stage that was not musical comedy with its bright colour for the soul and its gay music for the blood. The dignity of the French art and the simplicity of the German restored my early unapprehensive enthusiasm for the theatre, even for the pillared enclosure, the draped boxes, the audience waiting in the dim light to take their part in the great game. I went to no more English plays. And for a long time there were no foreign ones to see. But photoplays had begun, small palaces were defacing even the suburbs. My experience with the English stage inhibited my curiosity. The palaces were repulsive. Their being brought me an uneasiness that grew lively when at last I found myself within one of those whose plaster frontages and garish placards broke a row of shops in a strident, north London street. It was a Monday and therefore a new picture. But it was also washing day, and yet the scattered audience was composed almost entirely of mothers. Their children, apart from the infants accompanying them, were at school and their husbands were at work. It was a new audience, born within the last few months. Tired women, their faces sheened with toil, and small children, penned in semi-darkness and foul air on a sunny afternoon. There was almost no talk. Many of the women sat alone, figures of weariness at rest. Watching these I took comfort. At last the world of entertainment had provided for a few pence, tea thrown in, a sanctuary for mothers, an escape from the everlasting qui vive into eternity on a Monday afternoon.

The first scene was a tide, frothing in over the small beach of a sandy cove, and for some time we were allowed to watch the coming and going of those foamy waves, to the sound of a slow waltz, without the disturbance of incident. Presently from the fisherman's hut emerged the fisherman's daughter, moss-haired. The rest of the scenes, all of which sparked continually, I have forgotten. But I do not forget the balm of that tide, and that simple music, nor the shining eyes and rested faces of those women. After many years during which I saw many films, I went, to oblige a friend, once more to a theatre. It was to a drawing-room play, and the harsh bright light, revealing the audience, the over-emphasis of everything, the over-driven voices and movements of all but the few, seemed to me worse than ever. I realised that the source of the haunting guilt and loss was for me, that the players, in acting *at* instead of *with* the audience, were destroying the inner relationship between audience and players. Something of this kind, some essential failure to compel the co-operation of the creative consciousness of the audience.

Such co-operation cannot take place unless the audience is first stilled to forgetfulness of itself as an audience. This takes power. Not force or emphasis or noise, mental or physical. And the film, as intimate as thought, so long as it is free from the introduction of the alien element of sound, gives this co-operation its best chance. The accompanying music is not an alien sound. It assists the plunge into life that just any film can give, so much more fully than just any play, where the onlooker is perforce under the tyranny of the circumstances of the play without the chances of escape provided so lavishly by the moving scene. The music is not an alien sound if it be as continuous as the performance and blending with it. That is why, though a good orchestra can heighten and deepen effects, a piano played by one able to improvise connective tissue for his varying themes is preferable to most orchestral accompaniments. Music is essential. Without it the film is a moving photograph and the audience mere onlookers. Without music there is neither light nor colour, and the test of this is that one remembers musically accompanied films in *colour* and those unaccompanied by music as colourless.

The cinema may become all that its well-wishers desire. So far, its short career of some twenty years is a tale of splendid achievement. Its creative power is incalculable, and its service to the theatre is nothing less than the preparation of vast, new audiences for the time when plays shall be accessible at possible rates in every square mile of the town. How many people, including the repentent writer, has it already restored to the playhouse?

[*Close Up* (Territet, Switzerland) 1:1, 1927, pp. 34–7.]

The Wanton Playgoer (1931)
Djuna Barnes

Out in Hollywood, the managers of picture houses leave the lights off several moments at the close of a sad or harrowing film that the audience—film stars and beauties of all kinds, and sorts—may repair the ravages of emotion (if any) without being observed of the vulgar public. I have been puzzled all my life as to why I never wanted to be an actress, and now I know. When I cry, low lights or high, it's one and the same. Cry I will and let who will be handsome.

[*Theatre Guild Magazine* (New York), September 1931, p. 21, excerpted.]

On the Sociology of Cinema (1914)
Emilie Altenloh

GIRLS' TASTE

The gushingly sentimental films that appeal to adolescent girls are rarely presented—especially not at children's shows. When girls go to a show, it is not so much out of the pure interest a particular program has occasioned. Rather, they enjoy the program just as they do the numerous other entertainments their parents take them to. Boys, on the other hand, go to the movies of their own accord and they particularly enjoy going with their peers. Also, girls don't become as entirely engrossed in these experiences, and it seems that the excitement won at the theater or concerts is repressed to a lesser degree—especially in productions reminiscent of fairy tales—and hence occupies them more strongly than those in any film show.

The music in the cinema appears to be the main attraction for them, and therein lies a characteristic common to nearly all female moviegoers. The variety of the programs appears to confuse them, and they could no longer recall specific pieces from the flow of presentations. They made only very general statements like "I liked the little jokes" or "the stories" or "when it made me laugh"; a more specific taste with regard to film doesn't seem to exist. Perhaps they have allowed themselves to be influenced in their tastes and preferences by the teachers who have carried out a campaign against the cinema, which later led to the complete prohibition of children going to the movies in many cities.* Shows specifically for children from which the censor has edited all exciting material run on afternoons when there is no school. These are considered "boring" by true city boys; they always find the ways and means to stay in the cinema, even late into the night.

---

* A short time before this survey, an ordinance of this kind was issued by the police authorities in Mannheim according to which children under the age of 16 were no longer admitted to the regular shows.

Beyond these findings, the statistics about movie attendance show the extent to which youth participate in the expansion of the cinematographic theater. On many days, the number of children exceeded the number of adult moviegoers. If the losses due to child prohibition were not so considerable, then theater owners wouldn't feel obliged to mount the endless protests directed at having these regulations repealed. All possible arguments are brought to that end—above all, that of the transgression of police authority upon parental control. But one can hardly speak of such an infringement in relation to those children and young people for whom the cinema threatens to become the sole authority. It is they, if anyone, who are in need of the state's tutelage.

WORKING WOMEN

All the differentiating factors that shape various types of working-class men—the enthusiastic theatergoer, the union member—are absent from women of the same class. Women constitute a far more unified picture than men because their interests lie primarily in two areas—the theater and the cinema. The latter, especially as a form of entertainment, is most significant. Visits to the theater are still on average a little more common among women than among men. Concerts and lectures trail far behind. The academic or party interests that take up a great deal of men's free time are lacking, so to speak, in women. To the extent that women belong to social-democratic organizations, they are enthusiastic party supporters. Occasionally, some women have gone to meetings and lectures. In general, however, the drive to acquire the solid knowledge that could serve as a basis for a political position is extremely weak.[1] In this context it is understandable that the cinema plays an important role, especially for women who don't have a profession. Once they are done with their housework, there are relatively few convenient opportunities for enriching their free time. They go to the cinema more often out of boredom, rather than out of any genuine interest in the program. While the men are attending political meetings, women visit the movie theater next door where they'll be met by their spouses when the screening is over. Gradually, however, this stop-gap activity becomes an essential part of their daily lives. Before long, they are seized by a veritable passion for the cinema, and more than half of them try to gratify that passion at least once a week. During the screening they live in another world, in a world of luxury and extravagance which makes them forget the monotony of the everyday.

By comparison, all other attractions appear meaningless; the number of those who have been to the theater only on occasion and who otherwise go only to the movies, is relatively large.[*]

---

[*] This finding appears to contradict observations made during visits to the movie theater in which the audience was predominantly male. But it is at best further proof for both assertions made above: (i) that with the increase in political interest, interest in the cinema recedes. In a certain sense, those surveyed here fit this description because they are organized in unions, and this circumstance explains their relatively few visits to the movies. The main body of the male

At best, musical content comes to the fore here again, as one might infer from the operas frequently mentioned [in the survey]. In addition to Wagner, Bizet and Mozart, composers who were not mentioned by men, figure more prominently. Still, it cannot first and foremost be strictly the music that motivates operagoing, for then concerts would also enjoy greater patronage. It appears rather that the simultaneous effect on the eye and ear, the musical interpretation of the plot which opera and ciné-drama have in common, appeals particularly to the taste of women. The same coincidence of a preference for opera and film music also repeats itself particularly often among salesgirls.

FEMALE SHOP ASSISTANTS

Just as among tradesmen, so it appears that among young women the appeal of going to the movies chiefly corresponds to a certain age, but it then gradually loses its importance. However, in those years of active cinema patronage, going to the movies never becomes in and of itself as important a part of their lives as it is for young men. Of all those surveyed, only 63 per cemt of women went to the movies as compared to 79 per cent of the male shop assistants.[†] The much diminished interest comes to light even more clearly when one compares the numbers of regular patrons. They stand at 11:21. The cause for this finding certainly lies in part in the greater dependency of young women. The daughter is always more closely bound to the framework of the family, and parents have a lot to say about how she spends her free time. She will hardly ever undertake anything completely on her own. From time to time, she too goes to the movies with her family, and in later years she will go more frequently with her "boyfriend" or "acquaintance," more rarely with female friends. It certainly appears that (this greater dependency that stands in the way of regular moviegoing aside) actual interest is not so great—otherwise, later, at times of higher earnings and correspondingly greater independence, an increased intensity of moviegoing would emerge, as is the case among male shop assistants. Quite to the contrary, the highest rate of visits occurs among fourteen- to fifteen-year-olds, dwindling with each year thereafter.

They patronize almost exclusively the better theaters. This is because their programs rarely mention robber and detective dramas—as rarely as films of the *Asphaltpflanze* or *Sündige Liebe* type.[2] Young women also display only meager enthusiasm for Westerns [*Indianerstücke*] and historical things. Already among fourteen-year-olds, love stories qualify as the main interest, and primarily those films closest in content to their own lives, or that reflect back to them an image of the wider world. The

---

moviegoing public draws more from the younger generations and the politically indifferent; and (ii) that unmarried, working women are not independent enough to go the movies alone. If the percentage of moviegoers was as high in general as it is among married women, then women would dominate the movie audience even more.

[†] Missing [from these percentages] is the heavy impact of those who live in the country. They produce the lower attendance average among business pupils who form the basis of this study—especially among the younger male classes, and almost entirely in the female section. The majority of the pupils have resided in Mannheim for a while.

story is usually about the fate of a common woman; after much confusion it ends in either moral ruin or "a quiet happiness." Most dramas of this kind are distinguished by their strong sentimental bent, obvious already from their characteristic titles, the string here taken from the answers of female shop assistants: "The Rose of the Mother," "Miss Lady," "The Suffering of a Woman," "The Female Clerk," "Women's Fate." In all these, conflict of a woman's heart is the centerpiece. Accordingly, it is obvious that Asta Nielsen (in films by Urban Gad) should be extraordinarily pleasing and inspire tremendous adoration.[3] The passionate temperament of the heroine, and the guilt and fate in which she becomes entangled correspond to the image these girls have of life, making them able to put themselves completely in her position.

Aside from the dramas, nature spectacles inspire an equally strong interest in women as in their male colleagues. But their attitude towards them seems to differ from that of men. Young men name more footage of foreign countries and scientific pictures. An interest in content is absolutely fundamental. Young women answer more generally. Their preferences appear to be rooted primarily in aesthetic sensations. For example, they often mention images of water and the ocean such as "Italian Waterfalls" or "Waterfalls and Wave Movement" and "Drifting Ice-Floes" without adding any more precise description.

Comic pictures are, by comparison, less popular among young women than among their male coworkers. In general, the level of interest in distinct subjects of cinematographic presentations is equally present for both, but among young women it is expressed more weakly. The preference for dramas is more pronounced only among upper-class apprentices. A more active theater and concert attendance corresponds to lukewarm interest in the movies. Still, even in these areas, characteristically, taste is only marginally defined. Apparently, fourteen- and fifteen-year-old girls have seen on average more films than boys the same age. From the outset, girls' taste develops strongly along musical lines. In this way, they take a different road in obtaining pleasures for themselves than boys. For the latter, at age fourteen, music means military music. Hence, in addition to the musical experience, patriotic feelings are also released. Girls entirely lack this characteristic. From the outset, opera melodies appeal more to their taste. In addition to Wagner's music, which is valued to about the same degree by young male shop assistants, the romantic operas, such as *Mignon*, *Martha* and *Tosca*, are mentioned by girls much more often. The soft music of the cinema orchestra is very popular, and to a still greater degree than for male apprentices, the orchestra constitutes the decisive factor in girls' choice of cinematographic theater. However, this delight in music leads just as infrequently among them as among lower- and middle-class women to a deepening and development of their taste. Concerts are patronized more often by women than by men. However, they rarely ever mention specific musical pieces and favorite composers. Among women, a purely emotional experience—which has nothing to do with reason—appears to associate itself with music, so much so that even the titles remain an aside. With regard to subjects that are to be grasped through the intellect, young women remain behind their male coworkers. This disposition, which is oriented less toward the real and the concrete aspects of life, corresponds to their very limited interest in lectures and scientific films. Only very few attend lectures.

In general, their taste doesn't tend towards the high and serious zones; nor does it get lost in the lowlands of decidedly bad taste. Among them one finds neither those who show an interest in Bach, Beethoven, religious questions, and social problems—inasmuch as they are not concretized by film dramas—nor those who limit their standards to acrobats, marches, and detective dramas.

THE REMAINING CLASSES

Essentially the same goes for women of the upper classes—insofar as one is not dealing with a small intellectual elite here—as for the young female shop assistants (who have been considered separately here), except that upper-class women go to the cinema even more often, unless they, too, are limited in their free time by a job. It is particularly because of the Asta Nielsen dramas and historical films that they attend the shows. And the more uncomplicated and worry-free their actual lives are, the more they seek to integrate some extraordinary moments into them by empathizing with particular films. Cinema brings to the small towns a reflection of the wider world, showing women how they dress in Paris, what kinds of hats they wear. With thrills, great and small, the cinema helps pass away the many empty hours of the day which, with the progressive simplification of housework, are becoming ever more numerous. The cinematic presentation must be especially easily accessible to the female sex, of whom it is generally said that they always take in an impression in its entirety, purely and emotionally. In contrast, it appears difficult for very educated, intellectual people to lose themselves in the separate, often disjunctive, successive plots. Repeatedly, people who are used to dealing with everything in a purely intellectual manner say that it is extraordinarily difficult for them to apprehend the coherence of a film plot.

With respect to cinematographic presentation, one can hardly speak of the taste of adult members of the upper class. They have none, save an attitude toward the cinema as a general phenomenon. Tellingly, the question about particularly popular pieces was rarely answered by regular moviegoers, who would seem to have refined their opinions precisely on this matter.

Film is generally rejected from an artistic perspective.[*] And as to the nature pictures, they ascribe to them only a certain didactic value—especially for the lower classes. But, all the same, they go—and rather often—to the cinema.

They go in the evening if nothing else is on the agenda, but they prefer to go to the movies in the afternoon after shopping. They relax there, rather than in a café, escaping the bustle of the department store. With regard to this, of 100 people,

---

[*] Only here and there (mostly among the younger people) does one find the opinion that noteworthy achievement in props and costumes and the expressiveness of famous film actors might lead much further to a new kind of interpretive art.

over 80 have gone to the cinema at least once under these circumstances, and 60 go regularly. The latter come exclusively from the class of officers and businessmen, while the academic professions (including students) show proportionally the lowest number of movie patrons overall, as well as of weekly patrons. Whether in view of their other intellectual interests, the need for light entertainment is not as strong among these classes, or whether it is found in another form that replaces the cinema is difficult to determine. Perhaps the abstract mode of thought involved in these professions makes it easier to relax during free time, even while doing something more difficult. No greater exertion of concentration is required.

However, the employees of those professions whose activity is oriented more toward immediate practical and graspable ends are in a position to enjoy art once they have undertaken an absolutely new orientation in their way of thinking. Doing so, however, requires an intellectual exertion. Therefore, they prefer to resort to very light entertainment in their leisure time in order to take themselves out of the complex of thinking of the occupational context.* "At night I'm too tired to give myself over to such difficult things as theater and concerts," was a frequent answer, "and, therefore, I go to a cinematographic theater."

Next to professional exertion, hundreds of other things lay claim to people—community activities, social responsibilities—and their need to be on top of the latest onrush of offerings in the theaters and art museums and in command of (to a certain degree) politics, and modern literature. All members of this class have responsibilities of this kind, and, to the extent to which the various interests of men pull them in different directions, the need grows for a counterbalance of some kind that doesn't make any demands on the individual. Light forms of entertainment, from which there is nothing further to be gained, become a necessity. Others, on the other hand, who have much time and few interests for filling it, find in cinema the appropriate surrogate for distracting themselves in order to experience sensations. Something must be out there to satisfy these diverse needs: the wish to distract oneself, to relax from the demands of modern life, to satisfy boredom and the hunger for sensation. And had the cinematograph not been invented, then some other possibility would have had to have taken its place. Perhaps cafés with artists' troupes or variety shows would have experienced still greater new development. But in cinema the appropriate medium has been found, one which has acquired power and meaning far beyond the framework of the entertainment apparatus to date. If thereby it infringes upon related areas, and also draws the public away from going to the theater and concerts—which appears to be the case according to the complaints of theater directors about their worsening business ventures—then only those masses are to blame for whom the theater and concert were nothing more than a temporary distraction. But it is precisely this which all members of the upper classes desire from the cinema—nothing more than simple entertainment, the

---

* The need for a counterweight of this kind that in no way places further demands on the individual but simply distracts is mostly apparent among businesspeople, engineers, and officers. The active patronage of the cinema among the last group is explained by the fact that their profession leaves them more free time than the two other groups.

opportunity for once to laugh heartily; but, for them, it ought not to and cannot in any way replace the theater or other forms of artistic experience. The cinema appeals on the whole to very different kinds of needs. Thus, when it ventures upon the solution of higher, more artistic projects, the cinematograph appears to many people ill-suited. From this perspective, they also view the attempted elevation of the level of performance through the co-operation of famous artists as experimentation with an unsuitable object. Such an attempt would eliminate the pleasant naïveté and simplicity of the presentation, unless the reduction of artistic work to the flatness of the average achievement were its only success. Still, in no way does the average film correspond to the far from moderate demands of the upper class, and that which is aesthetically bearable for the cultivated city dweller is by no means equal to the standard of the average film. "The sentimental tendency of films, the exaggeration of gestures," and the often tasteless packaging insult many viewers. Others even experience the inherent character of cinema, with its swift, jarring alternations of happy and sad, as unbearable.

For the majority, the quality of films is not at all significant because their impression doesn't survive for more than a moment. Instead, other interests determine whether they go to the cinematograph theater. Real interest in the presentations is most often still the true stimulus for business people and women. But for very few is the joy found there strong enough to prompt them to go to the cinema alone; only a few bachelors reach for this emergency remedy out of boredom. Among married couples, the wife (more often among young people) motivates the couple to go. For the man who accompanies her, "she" is ostensibly more the object of observation than the goings-on on the white screen. "She is always moved to tears," and psychological studies of the spectator—especially the female spectator—are, for many people, far more amusing than the films themselves, and reason enough to spend an hour in the cinema once in a while.

Ask all these patrons why they really go to the movies, and most will shrug their shoulders. "*Faute de mieux*," a woman once answered. This "*mieux*," however, has as many different faces as individual spectators. In any case, the cinema succeeds in addressing just enough of those individuals' needs to provide a substitute for what would really be "better," thus assuming a powerful reality in relation to which all questions as to whether the cinema is good or evil or has any right to exist are rendered moot.

[From *Zur Soziologie des Kino: Die Kino-Unternehmung und die sozialen Schichten ihrer Besucher* (On the Sociology of Cinema: Film Entertainment and the Social Classes of its Patrons) (Jena: Eugen Diederichs, 1914), pp. 62–3, 78–9, 88–91, 91–4, excerpted. Translated from German by Patti Duquette, with the assistance of Christine Haas and Sarah Hall.]

Minnie at the Movies (1913)
Marian Bowlan

CHARACTER: MINNIE MURRAY, *an independent and emotional follower of the film drama.*
SCENE—*a neighborhood nickel theater.*
MINNIE MURRAY *charges down the aisle and expounds:*

Go on down in front, Tillie, and never mind raspin' about where that fly usher plants yu. Well, if there ain't that sassy bunch o' kids with Jimmie Casey from the flat below us amonopolizin' the front row!

(*Seating herself*) What's that name o' the reel that's on now? Oh, ya-ah, Elmer's Fall! Jimmie Casey, you turn right around and the very next time you holler "Archer Avenue (*or name local street of corresponding type*) Belle" at me when I'm leavin' for a dance, I'll report yu to the station.

(*To Tillie*) Ain't it funny you never see any kids in real life like the children in the movin' pitchers? Look at them two little boys in sailor suits asingin' hymns on their mother's knees in the twilight. One of 'em is hung in the last act? Don't you get fresh and stuff me, Jimmie Casey, like the way you was tryin' last week to tell me them Western Injun and cowboy pitchers was taken in Evingston (*name local suburban town*).

Whatyuthink Gus and me did Sunday, Tillie? We took in all the fi'cent theeayters between (*two widely separated streets embracing neighborhood of Archer Avenue type*). Honest! And the next mornin' when I shows up to work, the Boss says what's the matter with my eyes and before I got a chanct [sic] to answer that flip bookkeeper speaks up and says, "Who, Min? Oh, she's got the movin' pitcher squint!"

What's the name o' this fillum? *The Drama of the Desert.* Say, I wonder if A-rabs always wears white; the laundries must work over time. Say, Til, how 'dju like to wear a veil over your jaw like that there A-rab lady?—though there is some girls of my acquaintance that does need a gag for the mouth and no mistake, Ruby Clancy, fer instance. She's sore because I met Gus at her house and he's been just about livin' at our flat ever since. There's not a mornin' I gets to the office but what Ruby dislocates her neck alampin' my lef' hand. Gus is in a awful unusual business. He makes costumes for circuses and has always got his pockets full o' samples o' dazzling red and green. Gus says he ain't acomin' to the nickel show no more, cause he's gettin' knock-kneed from fallin' over the baby carriages out front.

I gotta yawn. These pitchers they got on now—a ancient ruined city it says—are turr'ble dry. The music is good, though; that's the Chicle Rag. But who wants to look at a pile o' old stones? My brother'n-law works in a quarry.

Here comes that swell baritone with all the diamonds, Tillie. Don't his vest glitter, though? I'm just crazy about the way he sings Red, Red, Roses. Ya-ah, he rolls his eyes sump'n grand in the chorus. (*Flustered*) He's lookin' straight at us, Til. (*Nudging her*) Ain't he, huh? Whatya gettin' so embarrassed about?

That fellah at the snare drum works in a boiler factory daytimes. He has awful pow'rful arms; the man'ger o' the show is crazy about him because there's the elevated and the night freight and the river tugs has to be drowned out while the show is goin' on.[1] I usta know the fella that played the coronet. He was a gen'lman—give me and Ma passes twice ever' evenin'.

That girl at the piano remin's me o' the new girl who's moved into the flat acrost the hall from us. She's turr'ble entertainin', Til. She's a waitress, uhuh, a waitress in a restaurant. And say, some o' the things she can tell about the way they cook in those swell places! Her advice to ever'body that's partic'lar is: "Cut out hash, don't think o' stew, and for heaven's sake never touch a chicken croquette. "No," she sez, "far better a cheese sandwich and a egg nogg at home; you know what you're gettin'."

This one is the big fillum that they've got them thrillin' blue and yellow pitchers of outside, the Horse Thief's Revenge. That's it. There's the hero-een with the long braid down her back. Ain't she sweet? The girl's brother is plottin' against the cowboy because he seen him stealin' the horse out of the coral. The cowboy—ain't he handsome in a dress suit?—is goin' for a ride up the mountain and I bechu anything the bonehead brother'ull way-lay him. I seen him on his hands and feet around them rocks a minute ago. Look at the dagger, will yu! (*Covers face with hands*) Did they stab him, Tillie? (*muffled*) Did they? Oh, I wisht I was home! Is they blood comin? (*Taking hands down from face*).

Part II! She's goin' to him—the girl's goin' to him. Ain't you crazy about the way she fixes her hair? I'm goin' to try mine that way when I get home. Look at her horse goin' lickety-cut. Yu can hear the hoofbeats just as plain. Do yu think she'll get there in time? Say, Til, do yu? She does. Gee, I'm glad.

But it ain't all over yet. There comes that half breed sneakin' out from those trees. He draws a gun. Look, Til, he's goin' to shoot. (*She covers her face with her hands*) Gosh, I swallowed my gum! And the hero knocks the gun out o' the half-breed's hands. Then my gum went for nothin'.

(*Rising*) That last reel just took ever'thing out of me. My forehead is wringin' wet. Ever' time I come to this nickel show I gotta be almost carried to the drug store across the street. The man there allus expects me now. I feel it so. Now, I just imagined I was that girl in *The Horse Thief's Revenge*. It's awful.

(*Starting for exit*) I sez to Gus... at the movies... (*Exit*).

[*Minnie at the Movies: A Monologue* (in the series *Denison's Monologues*) (Chicago: T.S. Denison, 1913), pp. 3–8.]

Continuous Performance VIII (1928)
Dorothy Richardson

> *Animal Impudens....*
> (Early Father, conditioned reflex of,)[1]

Amongst the gifts showered upon humanity by the screen and already too numerous to be counted, none has been more eagerly welcomed than the one bestowed upon the young woman who is allowed to shine from its surface just as she is. In silent, stellar radiance, for the speech that betrayeth is not demanded of her and in this she is more fortunate than her fellows upon the stage. Yet even they—even those who are mere stage effects, a good deal less than actors and, since they are ambulatory, rather more than properties—are, for some of us, magical and songworthy. And to those film-stars who are just ambulatory screen effects many of us have paid homage to the point of willingness to die for their sweet sakes, and all of us partly on account of their silence but largely for the Film's sake, have suffered them more or less gladly.

But it is not only upon the screen that this young woman has been released in full power. She is to be found also facing it, and by no means silent, in her tens of thousands. A human phenomenon, herself in excelsis; affording rich pasture for the spiritual descendants of Messrs Juvenal and Co.[2] And thus far the lady is beneficent. But there are others together with her in the audience. There are for example those illogical nice creatures who, while they respectfully regard woman as life's supreme achievement, capping even the starfish and the stars, are still found impotently raging when in the presence of the wonders of art she remains self-centred and serenely self-expressive. Such, meeting her at her uttermost, here where so far there is not even a convention of silence to keep her within bounds, must sometimes need more than all their chivalry to stop short of moral homicide.

I must confess to having at least one foot in their camp. I evade the lady whenever it is possible and, in the cinema, as far as its gloom allows, choose a seat to the accompaniment of an apprehensive consideration of its surroundings, lest any of her legion should be near at hand. Nevertheless I have learned to cherish her. For it's she at her most flagrant that has placed the frail edifice of my faith in woman at last upon a secure foundation. For this boon I thank her, and am glad there has been time for her fullest demonstrations before the day when the cinema audience shall have established a code of manners.

That day is surely not far off. One of the things, perhaps so far, the only thing, to be said for the film that can be heard as well as seen is that it puts the audience in its place, reduces it to the condition of being neither seen nor heard. But it may be that before the standard film becomes an audible entertainment it will occur to some enterprising producer, possibly to one of those transatlantic producers who possess so perfectly the genial art of taking the onlookers into their confidence and not only securing but conducting their collaboration, to prelude his performance by a homily on the elements of the technique of film-seeing; a manual of etiquette for the cinema in a single caption, an inclusive courteous elegant paraphrase of the repressed curses of the minority:

> Don't stand arguing in the gangway, we are not deaf.
> Crouch on your way to your seat, you are not transparent.
> Sit down the second you reach it.
> Don't deliver public lectures on the film as it unfolds.
> Or on anything else.
> Don't be audible in any way unless the film brings you laughter.
> Cease, in fact, to exist except as a contributing part of the film, critical or otherwise,
> and if critical, silently so.

If this minimum of decent consideration for your neighbours is beyond you, go home.

An excellent alternative would be a film that might be called *A Mirror of Audiences*, with many close-ups.

Meanwhile here we are, and there she is. In she comes and the screen obediently ceases to exist. If when finally she attends to it—for there is first her toilet to think of, and then her companion, perhaps not seen since yesterday—she is disappointed, we all hear of it. If she is pleased we learn how and why. If her casual glance discovers stock characters engrossed in a typical incident of an average film, well known to her for she has served her enthraled apprenticeship and is a little blasé, her conversation proceeds uninterrupted. And to this we do not entirely object. The conversation may be more interesting than the film. But, so long as she is there, gone is the possibility of which any film is so delightfully prodigal: the possibility of escape via incidentals into the world of meditation or of thought. And, whatever be the film so long as she is close at hand there is no security. Odd fantasy, a moving drama well acted, a hint of any kind of beauty, may still her for a while. But there is nothing that can stem for long the lively current of her personality. Her partner follows her lead after his manner, but quietly, unless his taste is for commentary displaying his wisdom or his pretty wit.

Let us attend to her, for she can lead her victim through anger to cynicism and on at last to a discovery that makes it passing strange that no male voice has been raised save in condemnation, that no man, film-lover and therefore for years past helplessly at her mercy, has risen up and cried Eureka. For she is right. For all her bad manners that will doubtless be pruned when the film becomes high art and its temple a temple of stillness save for the music that at present inspires her to do her worst, she is innocently, directly, albeit unconsciously, upon the path that men have reached through long centuries of effort and of thought. She does not need, this type of woman clearly does not need, the illusions of art to come to the assistance of her own sense of existing. Instinctively she maintains a balance, the thing perceived and herself perceiving. She must therefore insist that she is not unduly moved, or if she be moved must assert herself as part of that which moves her. She takes all things currently. Free from man's pitiful illusion of history, she sees everything in terms of life that uncannily she knows to be at all times fundamentally the same. She is the amateur realist. Not all the wiles of the most perfect art can shift her from the centre where she dwells. Nor has she aught but scorn for those who demand that she shall be so shifted. And between her scorn and the scorn we have felt for her who shall judge?

Down through the centuries men and some women have pathetically contemplated art as a wonder outside themselves. It is only in recent years that man has known beauty to emanate from himself, to be his gift to what he sees. And the dreadful woman asserting herself in the presence of no matter what grandeurs unconsciously testifies that life goes on, art or no art and that the onlooker is a part of the spectacle.

[*Close Up* (Territet, Switzerland) 2:3, March 1928, pp. 51–5.]

The Public's Pleasure (1926)
Iris Barry

[...] Now one thing never to be lost sight of in considering the cinema is that it exists for the purpose of pleasing women. Three out of every four of all cinema audiences are women. I suppose all successful novels and plays are also designed to please the female sex too. At any rate the overwhelming, apparently meaningless, and immensely conventional love interest in the bulk of films is certainly made for them. Disguise it how they may, practically every film pretends to be "about a man and a woman." This is true of farces (remember Chaplin, Keaton and Lloyd, who all have their pretty young women companions), true of big spectacles like the *Sea Beast*, *The Covered Wagon*, as well as the plainly amatory picture. Somebody must marry somebody before the piece is through, or must fall into somebody's arms.

The insistence on marriage, or conjunction of male and female, as the end of difficulties is of course due to the fact that in actual experience we find it the beginning of difficulties. The symbolic importance of marriage is also to be found in folk tales such as those trimmed up in the Contes de Perrault (a man sets out to seek his fortune and wins a bride: a princess sets out to escape parental tyranny or after injustice at home and after vicissitudes is "recognized" and wedded by a prince and enjoys riches). Also in savage folk tales, though mingled here with even more resentment and fear of parental or heavenly authority and power. It is absent from much great literature, Homer, Quixote, Aesop, "Pilgrim's Progress," the Bible. In these, though the sexual relation is a story theme it is not romanticized, falsified or castrated, as it is in popular legend and the popular movies.

The relation of man and woman, and of men and women to the home (i.e., society) or to parents and religion (i.e., to eternity) is a theme for any art. The superficiality of courtship and wedding bells is not. It is only a daydream for the dissatisfied.

The dissatisfied (i.e., the "people") have foisted their empty dreams and discontents on civilisation since the early nineteenth century, yet it is the concepts of the aristocrats like Shakespeare which penetrate the masses and make artistic creation possible. This penetration from above the cinema overlooks: yet it is necessary.

Really it is not the whole function of woman to get herself married, nor her sole possible interest. But no doubt because it is the only thing most women ever do bring off successfully, the only thing they realize they want, this business of love (leading to marriage, *of course*), is the one preponderating subject of the movies. Cowboys, business-men, mechanics—they all go the same way on the stage or the screen, straight into some woman's arms, and then no one cares any more about either him or her. Any kind of relationship that leads to no marriage, be it business association, friendship or what not, is of no interest either.

I am blaming all this on the American films, and I think with reason. English films too are almost all love romances in some form or another, except for the straight travel films. But then English films do not bulk very large anyhow. But when you come to consider the Continental films, you notice a difference at once. Continental films are (when they are worth seeing at all) hardly ever love romances in the American sense. Take for instance, a few examples:

FRANCE

Coster Bill of Paris.
The Call of Motherhood.
Mother (Visage d'Enfants).
The Wheel.
The Three Masks.
Koenigsmark.
Le Miracle des Loups.
Les Miserables.
The Late Matthew Pascal.

None of these [is] concerned with the business of getting a man and a girl married up at all. Coster Bill was a character study of an old man, or an essay about legal justice. The Call of Motherhood was concerned with the relations of man and woman after marriage. Mother tells of children's feelings towards a stepmother. The Wheel is a picture poem to the railway, and such frustrated love as there is goes unluckily and in the end tragically. The Three Masks is a tale of revenge and the sentiment holds between father and son, not man and woman. The love interest in Koenigsmark, shocking as it was, was illicit, the passion of a boy of eighteen for a woman of forty. And the emotion in Le Miracle des Loups was patriotism, not love. In all of them, family life is obviously far more important than sexual passion: the French are happily able to take sex for granted and put their artistic imagination to work in other fields.

Now for:

GERMANY

The Golem.
The Niebelungs.
Destiny.
The Last Laugh.
The Street.
Warning Shadows.
Caligari.
Nju.
Peter the Great.
Cinderella.
Vaudeville.
The Ancient Law.
Dr. Mabuse.

Never in any of these is "love and marriage" the theme. Even in The Niebelungs the love of Siegfried and Kriemhild is only one little thread in the great canvas of magic and war and hatred.* *Warning Shadows* and *Nju* were again tales of married life, not of the business of getting married. They assumed no conventions, were plain tales of emotional crises, such as occur, or might well occur, in any home. They were truth and not fiction. *The Last Laugh* had no love interest at all: it was a character study, and so at heart was *The Street*. Character is what counts in all of them, not marriage lines.

I have only seen one Russian film—*Polikushka*, and there was nothing about love in it as anyone will know who has read the masterly short story of Tolstoi, on which it was founded. Swedish and Danish films, again, though I do not remember many of them very distinctly, follow the Continental, not the Anglo-Saxon tradition. *Thy Soul Shall Bear Witness* had no love in it.

"Well," the reader might say here, "that's all very well, but if you say that the cinema has artistic possibilities and virtues solely because of its size, that its size is due to the American output, and the American output is based on the public's pleasure, what then? If the public want love stuff, the girl and the man, the marriage achieved, and so forth, why grumble?"

Well, to begin with, I am not at all convinced that the public as a whole do want love stuff and love stuff only. I think the love stuff is overdone. It's at such a pass now that you can't have a woman nestle in any man's arms without the collective audience reaching for its hat under the impression that the finale is due. I concur that a love interest would always be useful and necessary in seven-eighths of all films. But not *such* a love interest. Not this cheap business of just getting oneself married, not this insistence on the feminine power of attracting a man till he finds her bed and board till the end of her days without her making one effort to deserve it.

And if it is so, then let us unite quickly to do something about bringing the great Anglo-Saxon races to an end. For if the adult population of England, America, Canada, Australia and S. Africa think that the main thing on earth is for a woman to get herself married off, then the sooner the end the better. If I thought it, I wouldn't be concerned about picking the cinema out of the mud, I'd be manufacturing bombs and dropping germs into the biggest reservoirs. I suppose we have all liked Jane Austen for ridiculing this "getting married" business. But women in those days really had some excuse for feeling so urgent about matrimony. It was the only career open to them. To-day, thank heaven, we're crawling out of that bog! There are a good many things women can do, including the making of good wives, the kind of wives who are more than food-dispensers and child rearers, who are human beings with some individuality of their own as well. Also we are beginning to realize that a woman who isn't well—I mean who doesn't feel she is doing the best that's in her—inside marriage, is best out of it. But it's hard to get people to admit this, even if they believe it, for "popular opinion" is against them. Now popular opinion is really just nothing but a lot of lies boosted in the form of soothing syrup by the printing press and the film factory, to give people false dreams for fear they kick at true facts.

---

* In twenty-four reels of *Fredericus Rex* there is the smallest possible proportion of erotic sentiment.

I admit it began with the printing-press. For years, thousands of sloppy stories, poems, articles, plays and novels have been pouring out into the world harping on this great love and marriage business. But it is soothing syrup, not reality, all the same. What if we all do (the women) wish we were the heroine in *The Blue Lagoon*, or the heroine in any magazine story, or the heroine in any musical comedy? We jolly well know we aren't and sometimes we recognize that if we were we wouldn't like it. Do women usually marry the first young man they meet under suitable circumstances? No, they don't, and they tend to do so less every year. They look around. It is all very well to lull oneself from the age of sixteen to sixty with "sweet love stories," but do we act up to them? No, we don't.

We might as well, then, do something about persuading the film producers not to drop treacle into our mouths any more. It is bad for us.

If one out of ten of all the women who go to the movies here and in America would write a nice little letter to the manager of their pet cinema and tell him they're tired of just nothing but unreal love-stuff, they'd get something else. They certainly would. If one out of ten of them asked for more films like:

Abraham Lincoln
Her Sister from Paris
Forbidden Paradise
Pearls and Savages
The Woman of Paris
College Days
The Marriage Circle
The Last Laugh
Don Q.
The Black Pirate
Stella Dallas
Skinner's Dress Suit
The Monkey's Paw
The Tower of Lies
Vaudeville
The Unholy Three
Nell Gwyn
Dr. Mabuse
Her Big Night

they'd get them. If they asked for slow-motion sports pictures, or films about people's lives, or about ideas like revenge, parental responsibility, a desire for self-expression, or what not, they'd get them. The films would be every bit as competent, every bit as entertaining as they now are. There'd still be love interest, of course, but it would not queer everything as it now does.

One moment! Remember that *Robin Hood*, *Way Down East*, *The Ten Commandments*, *The Hunchback of Notre Dame*, were big successes. Remark also that the love interest in them was very slight. Why there's even money in films that aren't entirely about love!

And then we might get some films about the people who fall in love, not just about their getting caught up together; real romance these might be, palpitating bits of sentiment. But real. For after all, what's interesting in a love story is not the fact that a man loves the girl, but (a) the circumstances they are in, the adventures they have, and (b) in their own characters and the change their sentimental relationship makes in them.

There always will be plays, novels, stories and films simply about courtship; there is a demand for them. People know that they are "nice" just as they know jokes about fleas and boarding houses are "funny." Such sentiment indeed represents an ideal, another waking dream. All that I suggest is that out of the billions of people who do go to the pictures there exist some millions who tire of false sentiment, and I earnestly beg everyone who does so tire of it to join me and some others in a fight for variety. I say false sentiment advisedly for the majority of the films of sentiment *are* false and correspond to nothing in the actual erotic experience of anyone.

Also the cinema must develop or die, and it is remarkable that all the best films are the ones with little or no conventional sentiment in them. The best that the enlightened public can do is to boost the non-sentimental, the experimental films, the ones that cause new blood to come into the unwieldy carcase of cinematography.

The cinema runs after the public: it does not spring from the public.

We must remember that all the stories we love best in the world are not stories of sentiment. Dickens does not rely on his sentiment for his power, he only threads it delicately into his plot. Shakespeare's themes are of emotion, other than love: in Hamlet, Macbeth, Lear, for instance. Or when he writes most freely of love, it is of tragic love in Romeo. Homer, longest lived of all, writes of men's adventures and exploits, and again only threads in the heart interest.

The public's pleasure is not, however, solely concerned with sentiment. It is odd to see how well the cinema has incorporated many ingredients of the circus, the music-hall and the popular theatre. What are the farce comedians, Keaton and the Sennett Company, but circus clowns? What are Harold Lloyd's (and other people's) staggerings along narrow parapets but a combination of Blondin and the old circus clown?[1] Or if you like, they are the music-hall low comedian too: as Chaplin is, as Fatty Arbuckle was. The cowboys are relatives of the circus bushriders, too; I mean that the public like them for the same reason, for the pleasure of participating, at second-hand, in the apparently thrilling horsemanship, the exhilarating sense of movement, the physical prowess, the neat wildness and the efficiency.

From the popular theatre come all the melodramas which form so solid a bulk in cinema programmes. Here D.W. Griffith is king. *Way Down East* and *Broken Blossoms*, *The White Rose* (a little watered, this) are fine and magnificent melodrama. But the Vitagraph Company have also a special line in melodramas, of which even the titles are reminiscent of vanished theatre hoardings. And Drury Lane has been run out of town with the "catastrophe" film—the railway smash, the aeroplane accident, the burst dam, the toppling pine tree, the shipwreck, and so forth.[2] How the public dotes on catastrophes! Cathedrals totter (*Ten Commandments*), cities finish

(*Sodom and Gomorrah*), forests are burnt up (any Western "super"), homes are razed to the ground, bombs go off (in farces even), scores of people are cast away. It's adventure, lots of it, in safety, for 1s. 2d. It stimulates the glands, jostles up the emotions, and it's the public's pleasure.

How they love money! Poverty is sometimes forced on heroes and heroines to "purify" them, but no one (except Chaplin) stays poor long. Every young man sets out to make his fortune, and makes it. Every girl marries well. It's as old as fairy stories and as wholesome. It is also as monotonous. But it is the kind of monotony no one minds, if it is ingeniously varied.

Splendour is another beloved theme. Cecil de Mille is perhaps pre-eminent at this, but the constant presence of palatial homes on the screen everywhere is only a gift of free evanescent gorgeousness to the public. It is part of the desire for heaven-sent wealth. Is there anyone whose income is under £8,000 a year who doesn't sometimes dream of unexpected inheritances, hidden treasure, and the rest? The films flatter these dreams and make the poorest inhabit marble halls for a few hours.

And what stay-at-home does not also dream of travel? Even those who get no further than Hampstead or perhaps Blackpool, Douglas and Southend, love to fancy themselves further afield, in the arid desert, on mountain peaks, far out at sea, or beneath the palms of a tropical island. The films also supply this want. They take their uninspired heroine and characterless hero to the most unlikely spots before they set the antique machinery of courtship going: the kiss of betrothal is generally exchanged by a rocky seashore, in a forest of pines, on a yacht, in a native hut, or in the (equally romantic) slums of New York.

This is the great strength of the cinema, that it caters for daydreams—surface sentiment, riches, travel, splendour and wild excitement—more thoroughly, more generously, more convincingly than any other known form of entertainment, and offers it in the most effortless way, under the best circumstances, to music, in a twilight solitude, with no mental effort demanded of those for whom it caters.

Howls of dismay are always rending the air of Los Angeles because the public tire of first one thing and then another. The howls generally show, not the fickleness of the public, but the density of film producers who are really so stupid that they imagine, if one film about the Argentine is a success, that they are perfectly safe in turning out a dozen more films set in the Argentine, quite forgetting that: (1) it may not have been the setting at all but some other peculiarity of the film which made it enjoyable, and (2) that their Argentine imitations will not necessarily be equally successful, even if the setting was the *bonne bouche* of the original picture, if stupid stories, particularly improbable Spanish castes, bad continuity, poor psychology and a half-dozen other common faults drown the one merit of colourful scenes. They behave, in fact, like manufacturers who think a trade mark is all that is sufficient to ensure the sale of their goods, and neglect to make their goods saleable.

The public is not fickle. It is the most ridiculously faithful of animals, as every innovator knows. It has, for instance, enjoyed low comedy, universal satires (I mean satire on the foibles of humanity, not those of some clique) and heartrending melodrama since, at least, the sixteenth century. And it still likes all these things. But the fact that it may love one low comedy in which a dog steals some sausages does not mean that you have only to show a dog stealing sausages in any low comedy in order for it to be successful. This simple fact eludes the somewhat extraordinary brain of many who make films.

But I wish the public could, in the midst of its pleasures, see how blatantly it is being spoon-fed, and ask for slightly better dreams.

[From *Let's Go to the Pictures*, (London: Chatto & Windus, 1926), pp. 59–73, excerpted.]

PART ONE

Annotations

The Lonely Girl

1. Sunday Screening. In the late 1920s, a number of local laws in different American states attempted to restrict Sunday film screenings. In an effort to thwart these measures, exhibitors made a particular effort to schedule educational films on Sunday.

The Matinee Girl

1. Veriscope. An extra-wide-format camera-projector using $2^3/_{16}$ inch (68 cm) film stock, employed by Enoch Rector for the Veriscope Company to film the Corbett–Fitzsimmons fight on 17 March 1897 in Carson City, Nevada.
2. Jim (James) Corbett (1866–1933). American boxing champion who was the first to win a heavyweight title under Marquess of Queensberry Rules. Known as "Gentleman Jim" because of his erect, clean-cut stance, Corbett brought an image of respectability to professional boxing while popularizing it through his subsequent theatrical appearances.
3. William A. Brady (1863–1945). American boxing promoter, theatrical personage, and major Broadway producer. Father of actress Alice Brady.
4. Robert Fitzimmons (1862–1917). British boxer who won world titles at the middleweight (1891), heavyweight (1897), and light heavyweight (1903) divisions. Like Jim Corbett, he gave sparring matches on stage.

Alice Rix at the Veriscope

1. Veriscope. An extra-wide-format camera-projector using $2^3/_{16}$ inch (68 cm) film stock, employed by Enoch Rector for the Veriscope Company to film the Corbett–Fitzsimmons fight on 17 March 1897 in Carson City, Nevada.
2. Jim (James) Corbett (1866–1933). American boxing champion who was the first to win a heavyweight title under Marquess of Queensberry Rules. Known as "Gentleman Jim" because of his erect, clean-cut stance, Corbett brought an image of respectability to professional boxing while popularizing it through his subsequent theatrical appearances.
   Robert Fitzimmons (1862–1917). British boxer who won world titles at the middleweight (1891), heavyweight (1897), and light heavyweight (1903) divisions. Like Jim Corbett, he gave sparring matches on stage.
3. Pompadour Jim. Jim Corbett.
4. Carson City, Nevada, the site of the Corbett–Fitzsimmons match. Nevada was, at this time, one of the few American states (New York state being another) that tolerated boxing with gloves—that is, boxing according to Marquess of Queensbury rules.

Some Picture Show Audiences

1. Research so far indicates that the first city to pass a local ordinance to control film screenings by requiring police permits was Chicago, on 4 November 1907. The New York City Board of Censorship was set up in 1909.
2. Sheitel [sic]. A *sheitel* is a wig worn by orthodox Ashkenazi Jewish women upon marriage.
3. Vorse's description of the audience as predominantly male is noteworthy. Most observers writing at this time remark on the strength of female presence in the movie theater. However, recent research has shown how specific individual audiences were for the silent cinema, varying in composition according to geographical location and time of day, for example.

The Lure of the Films

1. "Art film." Filmed versions of dramatic or literary classics, such as those produced by the French company Films d'Art or Vitagraph's costume pictures. These constituted an effort on the part of producers to attract a middle-class audience. Dunbar later refers to these films as historical "playlets."
2. While most observers from this period remark on the strength of female presence in the movie theater, men clearly constituted part of the audience. Recent research shows how specific individual audiences were for the silent cinema, varying in composition according to geographical location and time of day, for example.
3. "Film Trust." A combine of nine film producers—Edison, Biograph, Vitagraph, Essanay, Kalem, Selig, Lubin, Pathé Frères, and Méliès—and one importer, George Kleine, formed the Motion Picture Patents Company in December 1908 to secure a monopoly on all motion-picture activity in the United States through control of film stock, film exchange (distribution), and exhibition.
4. 14th Street was the center for New York vaudeville while also being home to high-class shopping and entertainment, the Academy of Music, dime museums, nickelodeons, and hotels.

The Street Cinema

1. Holtby arrives in Brittany from Southhampton in her "Weekly Journal" of the previous week ("My Weekly Journal 8: The Emerald Coast," *Schoolmistress*, 6 August 1931: 513, 528). Elsewhere in this "Weekly Journal" we learn that Holtby is dining at the Duchesse Anne restaurant in St. Malo, Brittany, having reached there via Dinard in a taxi, and then via a motor launch. Holtby and her companions had been listening to a flute player outside the restaurant when they noticed "that something strange was happening in the crowd opposite."

From Northern Berlin and the Surrounds

1. Heinrich Zille (1858–1929). German draughtsman, printmaker and photographer who exhibited at the Berlin Secession and was known for his sympathetic depictions of the Berlin working class.

In the Movie Houses of Western Berlin

1. Karl Kraus (1874–1936). Acerbic Viennese satirist, playwright and journalist who founded the journal *Die Fackel* (The Torch) in 1899.
   Kientopp. German term for a nickelodeon, a store-front, cheap cinema, made from a converted shop, numerous in the years 1904–10.
   Thalia was the Greek muse of comedy.
2. Leichner. Brand of cosmetics.
3. The "next-number-belongs-outside" means that such shoes are so big they cannot fit in the store.

Missionary Film

1. Adderly Street is the main thoroughfare through the downtown heart of Cape Town, running from the harbor up towards Table Mountain.
2. *Spruit*: Afrikaans for rivulet, brook, or creek.

In Union is Strength

1. The Stroll. The "Stroll" was located on Chicago's South State Street, between 26th and 39th Streets, and was the center of the business and leisure activities of the city's African-American community. The Pekin Theatre was located on the corner of State and 27th Streets and, unlike the rival and newer Grand Theatre, was owned by an African American, Robert T. Motts, who opened for business in 1904. The Pekin Theatre became America's best-known black-owned and -operated theater, so that dozens of other black-only movie and vaudeville houses copied its name. It was a regular news item in the Chicago Broad-Ax, and when Motts died in mid 1911, it was the subject of several front-page stories.

A Spectatrix is Speaking to You

1. L'Arte Muta: Rassegna della Vita Cinematografica was a Neopolitan monthly film periodical, published between 15 June 1916 and 30 April 1917. Lavishly illustrated with photographs and Art Nouveau drawings and decoration, the periodical combined sophisticated contributions from well-known writers such as Serao with special inserts for readers. Arte muta (silent art), together with teatro muto, dramma muto, and scena muta, were elevated Italian critical terms used to describe the specific qualities of film. While the French terms art muet and art silencieux, expressions attempting to define the same aspects of film, were fairly uncommon, in Italy arte muta was widely used in the second half of the 1910s.

Cinema

1. Silly Symphony. The Silly Symphonies were a series of Disney cartoons animated to music. The first in the series was Skeleton Dance, made in 1929.
2. Plassey. 1757 battle in which Clive defeated the nawab of Bengal and paved the way for British rule in India.
3. Mr. Laughton [Charles Laughton] (1899–1962). British actor and director who worked in Hollywood and achieved his greatest popular success in the 1930s. His films include The Private Life of Henry VIII (1933), Mutiny on the Bounty (1935), Ruggles of Red Gap (1935), and Rembrandt (1936).
Mr. Cantor [Eddie Cantor]. Jack Hulbert (1892–1978). British stage entertainer, immensely popular during the 1930s, who also appeared in films.
Miss (Cicely) Courtneidge (1893–1980). British stage and music hall star who also worked in films. Wife of Jack Hulbert and his stage partner.
Ralph Lynn (1881–1962). English actor of stage and screen who also directed films.
Lyn Fontaine [Lynne Fontanne] (1887–1983). American actress who starred with her husband Alfred Lunt.
4. Bock. A strong, dark-colored variety of German beer.

Why I Go to the Cinema

1. Gracie Fields [Grace Stansfield] (1898–1979). Popular British stage and recording star who achieved the height of her success in a series of musical film comedies in the 1930s. Born in the textile milling area of Lancashire, Fields, who had the persona of an ordinary working-class woman who overcame adversity, became a cultural icon for British people.

The Movies

1. Mae Murray (1883–1965). American actress known as the "gardenia of the screen," Murray had become especially famous for her role in Eric von Stroheim's The Merry Widow (1925).
Pola Negri (Appolonia Chalupek) (1894–1987). Polish-born actress who made her film debut in 1914, who took her name from the popular Italian writer Ada Negri, and who appeared in several of Ernst Lubitsch's early German films. Bella Donna, Negri's first successful American film, was made in 1923, but sound ended her career there and she returned to filming in Europe.
Bebe Daniels (1901–1971). A child actress, Daniels was a very popular star of the silent period, appearing as Harold Lloyd's leading lady and as Cecil B. De Mille's star, becoming a major musical star with the coming of sound. Her career included films such as Why Change Your Wife? (1920), Reaching for the Moon (1931), and 42nd Street (1933). From the mid 1930s, she pursued

a successful music-hall and radio career in England with her husband Ben Lyon, and in the 1950s created the popular radio show, *Life with the Lyons*.

2. Emilio Ghione (1879–1930). Italian film director, actor, screenwriter and producer who created the character "Za-la-Mort" in his *Nelly la Gigolette ovvero La danzatrice della Taverna Nera* in 1915. Ghione described "Za-la-Mort," a slang underworld expression roughly translated as "long live death," as a "romantic apache." He played the character in the serial *La Banda delle Cifre* (1915), which he also directed and in which he introduced a female companion, "Za la Vie." Two serials based on the "Za-la-Mort" type of character, *I Topi grigi* (*The Grey Rats*, in eight parts) and *Il Triangolo giallo* (*The Yellow Triangle*, in four parts), produced from 1917 to 1919, enjoyed tremendous success and several films featuring "Za la Mort" and "Za la Vie" were produced in the 1920s, and indeed after Ghione's death.

3. Negri is possibly referring here to Fritz Lang's robot Maria in *Metropolis* (1927).

On the Sociology of Cinema

1. German women were first to vote in the 1919 elections.

2. *Asphaltpflanze*: a young proletarian girl growing up in the asphalt jungle of the big city who has become a prostitute, or is in danger of becoming one. The term was a euphemism for a street-walker. *Asphalt* means tarmac and *Pflanze* is a plant or blossom, so the term suggests an exotic plant blossoming under neon lights on tarmac. *Sündige Liebe* means sinful love, and revers to either incest or adultery. Both words are probably—definitely in the second case—movie titles from the period of Aufklaerungsfilme ("sex education" films, i.e. soft-core sensationalist sex films), and the fact that Altenloh refers to them in inverted commas suggests she is using specific film titles in order to refer to a genre or type of sexploitation film.

3. Asta Nielsen (1881–1972). Danish stage actress who made over seventy silent films, most of them produced in Germany, and achieved world renown for an acting style characterized by energy, precision, and realism. Most of her films made up to 1914 were directed by her husband, Urban Gad, whom she divorced in 1914. Nielsen, known internationally as "die Asta," formed her own production company in 1920, but her film career did not survive the transition to sound. Her films include *The Abyss* (1910), *The Suffragette* (1913), *The Eternal Night* (1914), *Intoxication* (1919), *Lulu* (1923), *Hedda Gabler* (1924), and *The Joyless Street* (1925).

Minnie at the Movies

1. Elevated. The loop of the elevated train circumscribed the chief white entertainment district of Chicago.

Continuous Performance VIII

1. "Animal impudens" might be translated as "shameless creature." See also n49, p. 740.

2. Juvenal (c. 60–140). Roman poet and satirist who wrote verse which denounced the political and social conditions of Rome.

The Public's Pleasure

1. Charles Blondin [Jean-Françcois Gravelet] (1824–1897). French daredevil who crossed Niagara Falls on a tightrope four times.

2. Drury Lane. London street associated with theater.

PART TWO

What Was Cinema?

Fig. 2.1 Actress and inveterate traveler Lillian Gish blows a goodbye kiss to friends in Czechoslovakia as she leaves for the USA in 1938, shortly before Hitler occupies Prague.

PART TWO

Introduction

Many writers welcomed cinema during the first part of the twentieth century by comparing it to the other arts. Sometimes they examined the constituent features of the film medium and, finding them different to those of the other arts, emphasized cinema's singularity. At other times they sought interaction among cinema and the other arts, thereby establishing cinema intrinsically as an art. This range of responses forms the core literature of an area of scholarship frequently referred to as "classical film theory" (though many of its concerns continue to the present day).

Few of the authors gathered in Part Two would have argued that their primary aim, in discussing film, was to itemize the medium's aesthetic properties. Dorothy Richardson and H.D. regularly contributed opinions on film to the Anglo-European art cinema journal *Close Up*, but this attention merely punctuated their long literary careers focused elsewhere.[1] Maya Deren and Germaine Dulac wrote extensively about cinema alongside their filmmaking, but not to provide primers of film form.[2] Only Iris Barry, in her capacity as first curator of the new Film Library at the Museum of Modern Art from 1935 was professionally charged with defining cinema's place as an art. But almost half the women collected in "What Was Cinema?" earned their living, sometimes meagerly, in the day-to-day creation of it.

There is an absence here of the kind of systematic analysis to be found in the writing of Rudolph Arnheim, for example, who reflected long on cinema's means of expression, on everything from its black-and-whiteness to its perspectival consequences; or that of Hugo Münsterberg, who made blow-by-blow comparisons between the structure of human thinking and filmic devices (likening the close-up to mental attention, for example), coming to the conclusion that film had modeled itself on the functioning of the mind.[3] This seems to have been a task of writing about the cinema of lesser appeal to women, for they penned infinitely less about it than they did about cinema's social and psychological power, for example, where they were prolific (see Part Three), while their writing as film critics was also voluminous (see Part Four).

Lu Märten sketched an aesthetic of film which linked the "struggle" for film form to the political and cultural struggles of the German working class. She wrote that the cinema, and only the cinema, was capable of fulfilling this class's desire, and that through film all previous efforts for cultural knowledge on the part of this class would at last be realizable (though changes in programming, subject matter, and the conception of the feature picture would be necessary for any such achievement). Film was accessible both physically and mentally in a way that the theater, the lecture, and the library were not. Its proclivity for the grand scale was, Märten argued, determined by the distinguishing feature of the historical moment of its development, namely the mass age.[4]

J. Cogdell, like Märten, wrote about film in terms of the needs of a specific audience, here the largely black readership of The Messenger in the United States.[5] Her argument ranged from Robeson to Joyce, from jazz to Mary Pickford, refusing the categories of high and low culture—she assigns a place with the other dramatic arts in her fourfold schema of artistic expression (art expresses itself literarily, pictorially, musically, dramatically). Cogdell found American cultural life in thrall to Puritanism, stymied by censorship, and overwhelmingly repressed—the two exceptions were "Negro Folk Music, the only real music America ha[d] yet produced," and the energizing effect of the "dramatic feeling of the Negro" in American theater.[6] Even cinema, the "youngest of the dramatic arts," was, paradoxically, already decadent, dishonest in its methods of literary adaptation, sentimentalizing and Christianizing, and false in its representation of class and race.[7] Comparing Lubitsch's The Loves of Pharaoh (which she described as an American production) with the Italian spectacular Cabiria, she argued that the former made the characters of the Ethiopian King and princess "intentionally ... ridiculous," while the latter showed the Ethiopians strong and proud—she apparently perceived Machiste, the lead performer, as black.[8] When Cogdell condemned the American cinema and the popular press, it was because they had no purchase on those "universal" "verities" such as truth and beauty that were necessary to art and that transcended national and racial differences. At the same time she was aware that nations create forms of expression particular to themselves: "M. Anatole France speaks for France but not for America. D'Annunzio strikes the Roman chord, but it is not the scale of America." When she wrote that "we would prefer to hear what American artists have to say about the vital functions of life," the participation of African-American artists is implicit, as her comments on American music and the theater confirm.[9] While some observers from this period wrote of the movies, however critically, as a quintessentially American art form, Cogdell seems to discount the possibility that the cinema could ever constitute a significant form of art, even if, through the contribution of blacks, it became American.

Female performers Betty Balfour and Asta Nielsen, and director and performer Leontine Sagan stressed the absence of a live audience when they wrote about making cinema.[10] In front of the screen actress was a camera which hypostatized the difference between theater and film, placing new demands on her as she forewent her voice and operated without benefit of immediate audience response. Denied speech and what Balfour described as the "vitality" the public gives, Balfour and Nielsen had to rethink their craft.[11]

The silent screen relied above all on the mute face, and particularly the eyes, as the source of expression. Through the close-up—an increase in the proximity and size of the expressive facial gesture impossible in the theater—the actor's performance was tested, an effect not lost on these women.[12] Unlike the non-performers Balázs, Vertov, and Epstein, who wrote of the camera's superior visual capacity in terms of its "capture" and "revelation" of the truth of a facial expression, these women pointed out that the camera caught any lapse in concentration or effort, revealing flaws that might pass unnoticed in live theater where the actress was more physically distant from her audience.[13] For the twenty-year-old Balfour, a lack of "personality," which could be compensated for in the theater, would not escape the camera's gaze because the new medium demanded "sincerity."[14] For Nielsen, the cinema required "soul," but this inwardness, unlike in theater, paradoxically had to be objectified for the camera: "I saw ... the main demand of film in the purely visual, in letting face and motions alone give expression to the soul, in letting the spirit become visible."[15] Lastly, for Sagan, a film director with twenty years' experience as a stage actress and director, the camera demanded a spontaneous unselfconsciousness difficult for performers to achieve. The camera's detective work provoked a new self-scrutiny as Nielsen and the neophyte actress Resi Langer noted.[16] In her autobiography, Nielsen recalls that on seeing her first film appearance, in The Abyss (1910), she became instantly aware of her shoulder shrugging, an oft-criticized habit of her theatrical performance. She immediately stopped herself: "From now on in similar situations I gave my shoulders a downward motion, a reaction that soon became not only natural but typical for me. What the director had tried for years in vain to correct was done by only one frame of film."[17]

If the movie camera demanded more of the performer by dissecting her performance (in effect, by seeing more than the live audience), these texts by women evidence an anxiety that, at the same time, the camera saw less, creating new, almost contradictory demands. Its superiority of vision was not total. It could not register the spontaneity that Balfour claimed was apparent on stage, and certain gestures could fail to register cinematically (although these, Balfour suggested, could be improved by experience and training).[18] The "soul" of an actor was a "piece of art to which the fullest expression cannot be given by the camera," wrote Sagan, suggesting, like Balfour and Nielsen, that there was an aspect of performance that escaped the camera.[19] The qualm here is that the camera exposes "sincerity," as Balfour herself observed of the technical basis of on-screen naturalism, as an effect of the performance rather than a quality of the performer.[20] This was why Sagan suggested that the film director work with untrained actors who did not "carry on their faces the ... sensitive mask, trained to portray a hundred different expressions."[21] The camera in close-up tore from an actor's face "its inner truth," a truth that was the product of the actor's training, leaving it impossible "to say where illusion end[ed] and reality beg[an]."[22] As women who were ever attentive to the way in which their appearance produced meaning, they recognized that the camera might reveal less the truth of any facial expression than the effort of producing it.

Sagan's argument derived from her sense of cinema's mechanical basis, which, while it had negative consequences for performance, also made possible something new. The camera had the special capacity of producing a visual realness in objects of the mise-en-scène, one impossible in the theater where such objects remained merely props. The camera grasped the unposed aspects of those natural elements and objects which it "pierce[d]" visually.[23] Given the inability of film to support properly the art of acting, combined with this positive affinity for nonhuman elements, Sagan suggested that the "highest kind of film" would be the one in which the actor's personality would be reduced to the point of recalling a tree or animal in his or her unselfconsciousness before the camera—an unselfconsciousness that still preserved individuality. She saw this quality realized in the films of René Clair and Charlie Chaplin, where the actor became objectified in a game of catch between camera and director. In their minimization of dramatic craft, and emphasis on physicality and movement, these were the most "film-like" films of all.[24]

Sagan argues that the Chaplin and Clair films share their qualities of physicality, movement, humor, and broadly drawn rather than individuated characters with the popular Italian theatrical form, commedia dell'arte. Both the commedia and silent cinema relied on conventionalized gestures and an exaggerated physicality that dispensed with the spoken word. (The pantomimic mode of their respective performance styles was noted by many other writers of the time, including literary historian Beatrice Corrigan.[25]) Chaplin is mentioned more than any other actor by writers in Red Velvet Seat. For Sagan, this tremendous popularity attests to the widespread appeal of acting styles based on bodily expression and gesture, repeating the success of the earlier commedia dell'arte.

Sagan and Corrigan applauded the physicality of film comedy, Sagan because it complemented the distinctive realism of objects and bodies in the cinema, and Corrigan because this basis in the human body made possible an international art form. For Janet Flanner, anticipating a film version of Uncle Tom's Cabin in 1918, nineteenth-century melodrama served as the point of dramatic comparison. Melodrama had also been popular, having flourished "ever since it became customary to dramatize women's woes," and was vigorous, "absurd and satisfying."[26] In Flanner's grand phrase, melodrama was "the breath of the stage and [...] the light in the celluloid."[27] Here she diverged from Virginia Woolf, who, writing in the same year, aligned melodrama with film (as she knew it) and dismissed them both accordingly.[28] Woolf's occasion for writing was a review of the Sylvia Scarlett series of novels by Compton MacKenzie. She criticized the heroine's character and the series' plots for being overemotional and excessively action-oriented at the expense of psychology and character motivation. Understanding melodrama in the late-nineteenth-century sense of perilous adventure and sensation, Woolf equated it with the cinematic; the incessant action of the Sylvia Scarlett plots echoed film chase scenes. And the very robustness of the melodramatic form (which Flanner described appreciatively as a force for social cohesion) failed, in Woolf's eyes, to allow the spectator any imaginative or empathetic engagement with fictional characters.

Dance also interested women as a point of comparison with cinema. This is especially evident in the writing of Iris Barry, Mary Ellen Bute, Maya Deren, and Germaine Dulac.[29] Women gravitated toward the language of dance in their discussions of film for a number of reasons: dance, like music, was one area in which women could claim some expertise, given the middle- and upper-class practice of raising daughters with dancing lessons; as a metaphor, it facilitated discussions of film's qualities of rhythm, musicality, and sequencing of expressive motion, thereby offering a rudimentary language for discussion of film form; by linking expression, emotion, and music—topics which Altenloh's research suggested to have had particular resonance for female film spectators—the language of dance itself provided a means by which women could begin to approach and link these topics in their own written responses to film; and, unlike literature or painting, dance was a form of expression residing in the body—as this book suggested in Part One, and will at various points, women tended to approach the cinema as embodied spectators.[30]

Lotte Reiniger compared the visual patterns of dance to those of film, and described herself as a choreographer organizing movements in time in such a way that the "artificial" motions created in animation realized the "possibilities of screen rhythm."[31] However, her conception of the frame was particularly dynamic: she contrasted the horizontal patterning of ballet to the vertical one of film, differentiating the horizontal ground of the dance floor from the vertical surface of the screen, while at the same time never abandoning the animator's peculiarly aerial axis of observation from above the camera stand.[32] As a consequence, her directive to choreographers and filmmakers alike was, "Underline your climax with a diagonal!" a slogan which recalled that of Sergei Eisenstein, with whom she shared an interest in Baroque aesthetics.[33]

Music was another art sustaining fruitful comparisons with cinema for women writers. Janet Flanner wrote critically of the conventionality and predictability of silent screen accompaniment, in which music ruled when cueing the audience's emotional responses or providing atmosphere.[34] Music could have such force that, according to Flanner, after reading the cue sheet, "the naked plot of the play stands out to the reader ... as though he had written the scenario."[35] What was at issue here was the balance of the relationship of musical sound to image. Flanner implied that while music should assist the film, music's emotional and associative power was such that it ended up dominating it instead. Mary Ellis Opdycke considered the issue from the point of view of musical integrity. Film needed music, she wrote—without it, stars shrink to "two-dimensional shadow dolls with white blood like fishes."[36] However, a common practice of cinema exhibitors and their musicians entailed fragmenting well-known musical pieces, and then welding them for new purposes extrinsic to the original musical scores themselves. While quotations from Shakespeare did no harm to the author, Opdycke found this not true of music: music was not an idea that could be relocated and recontextualized, but an "emotional process" that derived its meaning from its place in a sequence.[37] Without duration, music's climaxes, which were born of thematic development, were neither possible nor perceptible. With popular excerpting, witheringly described as done by "vivisectionists," climaxes, though present, became unreadable.[38]

Opdycke suggested that, in the final instance, music didn't need images in the way that filmed images needed music. This relationship—music and image—was not one of equals; the image was parasitical because it had the capacity to subvert music's meaning. If the *Allegretto* of Beethoven's *Seventh Symphony* could bury "babies and hopes, Civil War veterans and autumn leaves," the singularity of Beethoven's intention came undone.[39] Where Flanner had argued that music cued the audience's emotional response, Opdycke saw the image track as determining all, because the perceptions of the eye overrode what the ear heard.

From writings that compare film to another art in order to trace shared affinities between them, in Opdycke we have a comparison that holds them separate. Iris Barry, Irene Nicholson, and Mary Ellen Bute referred to theater, Post-Impressionist painting, and the planar and temporal arts, as well as music and ballet in this manner, to show how film extended the possibilities or superseded the limitations of those earlier artistic forms.[40]

Writing one of the earliest popular guides to film appreciation, Iris Barry largely based her arguments on her experience as a film critic. But she hedged at the category "Art." "Art-speak about the cinema," she wrote, was the domain of critics who have yet to catch up with the "monster public" in its unselfconscious enthusiasm for film and its "simple intelligence."[41] However, in spite of her posture of deferring to others the task of critical elaboration, Barry developed an understanding of spectatorial pleasure grounded in a distinctly aesthetic account of the cinema. She compared it to the theater and painting in turn, and found the cinema capable of achieving effects impossible in these media, effects which might account for cinema's popularity in modern society. In the movie theater one saw people doing things, instead of simply talking about them, as in theater, and this dominant visuality more than compensated for the physical absence of the on-screen performer.[42] The cinema allowed a greater intimacy with the actor—through the close-up his or her thoughts were revealed and he or she was seen more intently.[43] Reiterating an observation made by Sagan, Barry noted that on film, objects, landscape, and architecture acquired a realness and consequently a significance impossible in theater.[44] Barry's description of the world of the film as unbounded and freed from spatio-temporal limitations while resolutely factual in appearance approximated the dreamscape, and it was in the dream that she found one of her metaphors for spectatorial experience, for she wrote that, unlike the theater audience, the cinema audience experienced no separation from the image on screen. In this dream-like state, in which the ego was liberated and all conflicts resolved, lay an escape from a modernity burdened with "too much actual experience."[45]

Through her comparison with painting, Barry elaborated on the "good to look at" quality of film.[46] Film's aesthetic was based on movement, and because of this it was able to continue the task of advanced (Cubist and post-Cubist) painting, tracing rhythms of interrelated motion, be they of objects and people within a scene, or of the camera, or of shot transitions made through editing. Barry listed the range of movements possible in the cinema and found there a "fugitive and unanalysable beauty, similar to the ballet" (the separation and hierarchization of the arts was an ideal not always realizable), a "harmonious succession of movements of free, not arrested, motion in which the line of beauty follow[ed] the passage of matter in space and in which pleasure [was] given by the spectacle of lively units harmoniously changing their relative positions to each other and to the whole composition."[47] The camera was not merely a recording tool but an "instrument of organization" which, in conjunction with the work of the editor, created the film's "pictorial organization" and "unconscious time and space–time rhythms," so that the film cohered through shape or "unity."[48] The pleasure or satisfaction produced through cohesive film form was of a different order to that "liberation of the ego" effected in the darkened movie theater; for Barry it was the possibility of achieving the former that determined the cinema's singular aesthetic, while it was the possibility of the latter that suited it to the modern consumer.[49]

Barry explained that the cinema's expressive armature was richer and more complex than those of either realistic traditional painting or the international avant-garde. While film's particular beauty was obedient to their laws of pictorial organization, it was nonetheless greater than the possibilities accounted for by those laws. Irene Nicholson would take this even further in arguing that the cinema's formal properties exceeded those of all pre-existing media, that it inherited and synthesized the "dimensions" of all these art forms, noting that film's basis was to be found precisely where the limits of other media were exceeded.[50] The most striking consequence of Nicholson's, admittedly abbreviated, schema was her suggestion that film's photographic base did not determine its aesthetic. The camera, the celluloid, and the fact of projection were, for her, "no more than … mechanics."[51]

Nicholson was writing in 1935, for a magazine audience highly informed about theories of Soviet montage. By proposing that the camera and the film strip did not determine film's formal properties, she offered an alternative to Soviet discussions of shot fragments and their juxtaposition. Through her argument, she punctured montage, with its stress on the abstract concept realized in the collision of two individual shots, in order to reiterate the importance of communicable expression of personal experience as a defining quality in the work of art (although she can offer no real inkling of the form this would take in the cinema). It is film's synthesis of the planar and temporal arts that will determine its subject matter, a subject matter glimpsed in Basil Wright's *Song of Ceylon*, where "an almost mystic insight into the life of a people" is attained.[52]

This prospective tone was echoed by filmmaker Mary Ellen Bute in a statement of aesthetic principles for what she called Absolute Film. Like Nicholson, and unlike Barry, Bute confined discussion of cinema to its formal means. In a manner recalling the manifestoes of early modernism, and the arguments for a "pure cinema" made by Jean Epstein and Germaine Dulac in the 1920s, Bute described the Absolute Film as a nonrepresentational interrelation of light, form, movement, and sound.[53] Freed from representational, literary, or symbolic meaning, the Absolute Film stimulated purely an "aesthetic idea" in the spectator.[54] In a subsequent article Bute explained the aspirations of Absolute Film from the filmmaker's point of view: "I wanted to manipulate light to produce visual compositions in time continuity much as a musician manipulates sound to produce music."[55] (Again, the complementary analogy with music.) Bute cited Cézanne and Cubism as important precursors, and developed a concept of synaesthesia drawn from Richard Wagner as well as Wassily Kandinsky, who had used a chromatic scale to determine painterly composition. This description of Absolute Film's synaesthetic aspirations entailed a model of filmic effect in which the eye and ear were interrelatedly addressed (rather than the intellect), and in which the film worked as a stimulant, producing visual and aural sensations directly—new, synthetic sensations, in which the eye saw as the ear heard, and vice versa.

In Bute's reckoning, movement made up a quarter of film's expressive capacity. Iris Barry and Germaine Dulac each accorded movement an even more significant place. According to Barry, because the motion picture recorded movement, it realized the aims of Cubism and made the continued practice of this form of painting redundant.[56] More importantly, film's ability to capture movement and to create movement within itself established the basis of film's specific beauty, one greater than that of the ballet "because less stereotyped, and more spiritual."[57] The spirituality and beauty of motion were equally at the heart of Dulac's concept of abstract or "integral" cinema, which refused narrative or theatrical representation in favor of forms "divested of all literal meaning," and was grounded in the recording of movement, the recording of its duration, and its interrelationships (the most important of which was rhythm).[58] Dulac illustrated her case through the example of germination. Writing in the single published issue of her film journal *Schémas*, Dulac proposed that filmed sprouting showed a "pure movement which unfold[ed] according to the continuous logic of its dynamic force"; it showed organic drive or vegetal instinct, and, by combining the "sentimental and suggestive with the material theme," produced an emotional response in the viewer, a "purely visual emotion."[59]

It is arguable that, when women approached the question, "What was cinema?" the most complex and interesting answers arose in their detailed consideration of sound and silence—and for some writers, this *was* a relationship with gendered contours. The majority of texts that analyze the consequences of sound here are concerned above all with sound's effect on the spectator; they stress the different cognitive operations triggered through the faculties of hearing and seeing as the key to grasping the expressive possibilities of sound and silence.

In "The Art of Cinema" Betty Balfour wrote of the positive consequences of the absence of speech in film, since this encouraged one to "dispossess oneself of all thoughts" of the other arts, when in the presence of cinema.[60] The cinema's silence was again turned to advantage by Lillian Gish, and others, who saw in the freedom from the national and ethnic limits of spoken language the promise of a new art of universally intelligible expressive means, an "esperanto of the eye."[61] Gish argued that, unlike music, drama, or the visual arts, the silent cinema transcended national borders because it relied on two fundamental and overlapping elements of human perception and comprehension: a pantomimic mode of expression, and pictorial representation. Gish was joining what Umberto Eco has described as the "philanthropic impulse and the non-confessional religious spirit" that had animated the growth of Esperanto since it was first proposed in 1887.[62] Heralded as a "peacemaker," film promised to "provide deciding influence against wars for the future."[63] This idea, which intensified after the carnage of World War I, was linked to the general hope of resolving conflict through new international bodies such as the League of Nations (which formally came into existence on 10 January 1920). The July 1919 issue of Photoplay, self-billed as "the world's leading moving picture magazine," editorialized that before the ideal of brotherhood could be realized, "all peoples must get acquainted."[64] Only the motion picture was capable of tying "country to country ... in the bonds of understanding"; the motion picture, "a Universal Visitor," could show "other human beings of like mind." "We must," the editorial concluded, "back up the League of Nations with a League of Sunshine."[65] In an accompanying illustration, Atlas taped the globe back together with celluloid ribbons.[66]

Proof of film's bonding power lay in the worldwide popularity of Chaplin, Pickford, and Fairbanks, alongside the apparently unlimited intelligibility of American pictures.[67] But the eclipse of silent film challenged this belief: national differences now asserted themselves audibly. In D.W. Griffith's famous summation, war was caused by "too many languages," where silent film transcended linguistic, national, and racial distinctions.[68] Mary Pickford was among the many who feared that sound film would curtail the motion picture's ability to bring "us close to natives of every corner of the world."[69] Worse, not only would the message of the talking picture be limited to speakers of the same language, but even within this group, "some of those who understand the words may resent our intonation, accent and idiom."[70] In a 1934 report of the Cinema and Broadcasting Commission of the International Women's Council, Laura Dreyfus-Barney put it this way:

> The image, this universal language, lost something of its power. From being purely international, the film tended to become national again, when the word began to assume an equal place with the image. The drawback was so widely felt that various processes and plans were evolved to abolish the watertight compartments of different languages.[71]

Henrietta Grayne, reporting on a British Esperanto convention in 1930, speculated that the adoption of such a language by motion pictures would enable them to recapture their former accessibility.[72] Writing in the twilight of silent cinema's "precious universality" in 1932, G. Moulan could still remain hopeful: "Thus we may look forward to the day when every people will have a realistic knowledge of the life of other peoples and will have but one ideal, that is to live in peace with other nations knowing how alike their ideals are to its own."[73]

Dreyfus-Barney's reference to universal means of communication was widespread in descriptions of the cinema in the 1910s and 1920s, as already touched on in the General Introduction. H.D.'s poem "Projector" took up this theme by acknowledging the flooding power of the ray of light that was the primal source of all cinema's images. In "Projector," H.D. ennobled light, hellenizing and deifying it as a male god (Helios/Apollo). But cinema also gave light a new attribute, enabling it to breach discord and champion beauty, giving "with new vision fresh hope to the impotent."[74] The poem valorized light's healing qualities, naturalized it by coupling it with the sun (still more so in the poem "Projector II (Chang)", and rendered the cinema hall viewing space as a beam of light thrown across a darkened room, redolent of the temple pierced by light's beneficent power. In her description of the totality of the cinematic sensorium—the theater's light, warmth, and pulse—she noted that the redemptive capacity of light was shared by both cinema and church; with its play of smoke and half-light, the cinematic "temple" acceded to the sacred and invited worship.[75] In sum, the light of "Projector" made possible both new ways of seeing and new images—"islands arise where never islands were."[76]

An earlier poem of H.D.'s had prompted Ezra Pound to coin the term "Imagism," and in her privileging of sight in "Projector" we still see the importance of clear and accurate images for this member of the group of poets who came to be called "Imagists."[77] Sight continues to be the dominant sense in "The Mask and the Movietone," the final part of her "The Cinema and the Classics" trilogy of essays for *Close Up*. Here H.D. asks whether the commercial ascendance of synchronized sound—perhaps the single most important technical development influencing film aesthetics before 1950—serves any artistic purpose, and, like many within the European avant-garde, she answers no. Her reasoning parallels Rudolph Arnheim's repudiation of sound technology as a move toward reduced (because imitative) rather than expanded expressive means, but her formulation of the viewing experience in the silent cinema is quite different from his. For Arnheim, the "gap" between cinematic representation and visible (or audible) reality was where artistic devices could be developed.[78] For H.D., this "gap" was where spectatorial investment took place. H.D. recalls the recorded performance of the singer Raquel Meller, likening her filmed image to a marionette. Using the metaphor of the doll throughout her essay, she writes that the Movietone's sound is not "wedded" to the image; instead, sound and image operate against each other in a "diabolic fashion."[79] Speech renders the cinematic doll in turn mechanical, robotic, and ultimately demonic. Singly, either image or sound would be sufficient for H.D.'s pleasure, but when joined so that vision seems capable of speech, H.D. is robbed of her enjoyment at the cinema.

H.D.'s extreme argument against the sound film has two related aspects. In the first, the absence of sound affords a particular opportunity for spectatorial involvement. (In her words, the viewer wants to "help" the film and sound precludes this.[80]) In the second, the mechanical perfection glimpsed in the Movietone has the effect of confusing the represented with the real so that (and here she invokes the analogy of the temple again) the cinema audience risks idolatry in its devotion to the now more fully embodied, simulacral stars of the screen instead of their voiceless pictures. The "gods" of the cinema are not its stars but their onscreen images, or what she refers to as their masks. The audience knew, before the arrival of sound, that "these symbols were utterly divorced from reality."[81] With the ascent of the Movietone, the separation of symbol from reality becomes confused, and cinematic art loses its potentially sacred nature. H.D. is left pleading for the maintenance of the difference between the represented and the real, the image and its referent, because it is only through this difference that she will be able to continue to "drape ... devotions" on the cinematic image.[82]

Although the Movietone's mechanical perfection denied the possibility of a "divinity" behind the mask of appearance, it had potential to serve another, albeit non-aesthetic, purpose for H.D.: that of propaganda in the cause of promoting international understanding; the filmed records of statesmen's speeches would offer "bottled" distillations of national character, marked perhaps by "turns of wrists (and) intonations of voices."[83] Where we might see here in H.D. an alarming naïveté, her optimism was also a very late expression of those hopes for universal intelligibility and international understanding held for the now lost silent film following the trauma of the First World War.

Dorothy Richardson, like H.D., was a frequent contributor to Close Up. In her thirteen-volume stream-of-consciousness novel Pilgrimage (1915–67), Richardson had set out to express what she described as the "woman consciousness" in the "feminine equivalent of the current masculine realism."[84] Reviewing Revolving Lights, the seventh volume of Pilgrimage, in 1923, Virginia Woolf wrote that Richardson had developed the "psychological sentence of the feminine gender," capable of capturing "not states of doing" but "states of being."[85]

Fundamental to Richardson's approach to film was her investigation of the relationship of women to language, now foregrounded in the conjunction of the female audience attending the talkies. She wrote with the knowledge that, in 1932, the silent film had been superseded, even though in becoming audible film "doubtless" fulfilled its masculine "destiny" and would become an instrument of propaganda and persuasion.[86] This realization afforded Richardson a modicum of optimism, for the sound film could provide the means by which female voices might be permitted a hearing, or female ears a listening, but Richardson in general is wry in her rejoicing in the new cinema's prospect of a "fair field and no favour" for women.[87] She questions the historical necessity of film's latest development, if only through irony. Because women have little faith in speech as a medium of communication, they excel at what Richardson calls "memory proper."[88] When they do speak, in that specifically feminine mode of utterance called chat, they do so for the purposes of façade or dissembling. Richardson assigned a particular silence to femininity, one distrustful of speech, and transposed the value of this femininity on to the silent film itself, which she named "essentially feminine."[89] She suggested silent film had resisted the instrumentalization which was now to be the fate of the sound film as the latter became the "battle-ground of rival patterns, plans, ideologies in endless succession and bewildering variety."[90] The sound film, of necessity, spoke to the nation or language group, whereas the silent film bespoke an internationalism, indeed a universalism, although one, paradoxically, feminine.

Richardson's conceptualization derived from two orders of movement within film: the minute movement between each frame—a motion which was never detectable—and the larger movements of camera, bodies, and scenes.[85] While the sound films had these orders of movement, their expressive potential was reduced by the textual dominance of audible speech. The soundtrack plotted a linearity upon the diffuse topos of the silent film, seeking to create conviction where once was the space of contemplation.

Her feminine characterization of the silent film—"its power to evoke ... something of the changeless being at the heart of all becoming"[91]—cannot be divorced from Richardson's concept of a specifically female mode of historical consciousness, already explored in Pilgrimage, and subsequently illuminated through critic Julia Kristeva's notion of "women's time."[92] For Kristeva, the female experience of temporality is marked by repetition and eternity, the twin poles of the cyclical (modeled on biological rhythm) and the monumental. Female subjectivity "becomes a problem with respect to a certain conception of time: time as project, teleology, linear and prospective unfolding; time as departure, progression and arrival—in other words, the time of history."[93] The relation of Richardson's refusal of masculine "straight-line thinkers" to the distinctive, meandering sentence structure of her fiction is further edified by Kristeva's observation that the linear time of history is also that of the enunciation of sentences.[94] Following Richardson's critical comments on the sound film, we might say that the silent film, for her, had no sentence. Refusing the figures of linear temporality, Richardson describes the silent film spatially, "nowhere and everywhere."[95] It lacked the verb function that would make possible direction, plan, instrumentality—all that which was designated by Richardson's word "destiny."[96]

Mary Ellis Opdycke also found a gendered incompatibility of sound and image, one operating in a different way from Richardson's. She feminized music, calling her a "spinster" who did not marry well to words or images.[97] The use of music as accompaniment to the screen constituted a "double standard," where the screen, having "the benefit of the doubt" was able to determine meaning, riding roughshod over "his" bride.[98] Were music to be written specifically for films, it would be prostituted—the "slender virgin that has served Beethoven and Brahms will be painted and peroxided [made over into a star] and will carry a xylophone and three wind machines."[99] Opdycke's insistence on music's intrinsic meaning is couched in the language of feminist resistance, as a refusal to be subordinate to the implicitly masculine domain of the visual.[100]

The gendering of sound takes a slightly different form in Fannie Hurst's plea for a revitalization of the cinema along the lines that the Little Theater movement offered the stage.[101] Hurst is skeptical about the "mechanical maturity" of the sound motion picture, calling the new form a "Frankenstein" who can speak.[102] While sound may add dimension to the cinema screen, she suggests this new Frankenstein of "steel flesh" is soulless, in an echo of H.D.'s terms of disapprobation we have noted in H.D.[103] To both women, the sound film is machine-like, monstrous. However, Hurst's real criticism of the cinema's audible dimension is reserved for the musical component of elaborate film programs that combined music, dance, singing, "violinists, whistlers and tumblers" in a moviegoing experience where the feature film was, as she put it, "so much junk."[104] At issue for Hurst was not the quality of the musical program but the fact that, along with the rococo finery and gilt of the picture palace, the music contributed to an artificial experience. Hurst described this in explicitly feminine terms: the picture palace drowns the viewer in "fauteuils of marshmallow plush" where the "dolled up" motion picture is a "gross over dressed strumpet."[105] Where Opdycke invoked rape to describe the relationship between music-made-for-film and the film itself, Hurst sketches a bordello scene to suggest the parallel prostitution of music and film in contemporary production and exhibition practices.

Hurst wants to set the cinema on a better path. So, too, Germaine Dulac, who, in "The Music of Silence," issues a fourfold plan of action to save the cinema from that which does not properly belong to it, namely literary and dramatic adaptation.[106] As she put it, "If ... cinema should occupy itself with telling stories, ... I doubt that it will have achieved its aim."[107] Dulac's essay employs sound metaphorically to clarify her point. Taking music as a model of film form, she writes (in terms similar to Richardson's valorization of the silent film) that cinema should "suggest rather than specify," create, following the example of music, "through particular chords, that which is imperceptible."[108] She also makes an analogy between musical harmony—the principles of tonal relationships and their arrangement—and the filmmaker's analysis and orchestration of movement on celluloid.

If Dulac suggests that there is no place for sound in a cinema that wishes to remain true to its essentials—for its "true logic" lies "in its exclusive address to sight"—Laura Riding was to argue that sound could strengthen the experience generated in watching a film.[109] She claimed that films performed something new by making visible "the actual movement of emotions through all the daily turns of human life."[110] The "masses" go to the cinema for stimulation of their own "life-interest," for confirmation of their own reality, for easement, and for a sense of meaning beneath life's surface, a formulation reminiscent of Dulac's call to allow cinema to render perceptible what extends beneath the story's surface.[111]

For Riding, the audience's experience of this "emotional evidence of reality" could be enhanced by the right kind of musical sound which gave these impressions a tempo or sequence, a sense of temporality and instantaneousness that complements the way the cinema appeared to unfold in the continuous present, to show life in "the immediate process of occurrence," unlike the theater, which seemed to lift a curtain on the past.[112] She explains:

Films feed their [the masses'] appetite for emotional evidence of the reality of life from one moment to the next; and everything brought into a film must therefore be presented to them [the masses] as newly alive, if it is to provide genuine satisfaction. The sound in a film must give the effect of being newly made, as if heard for the first time; just as the action must seem newly sprung, precipitated into visible being as if for the first time.[113]

In addition to assisting this sense of film's unfolding in the present, sound helps the audience by reinforcing what they saw. However, most musical accompaniment impeded this process because the associations it brought competed with the image on-screen. As Opdycke also noted, music stimulated moods on its own account, independently of the meaning of the on-screen image. These moods blurred the "visual clarity" of the film and, more importantly, impeded the audience's contact with the screen.[114] According to Riding, jazz was uniquely suited to provide cinema's musical sounds, because jazz had the "emotional integrity and simplicity," the flexibility and subtlety, as well as the necessary rhythm, to enable it to assist the creation of the film's "spell."[115] Jazz was "contemporary in the emotional sense," and its extemporaneous characteristic suited film's quality of continual unfolding in the present better than the fixedness of what Riding called "conventional" music.[116] This premeditated quality of both non-jazz music and diegetic sound effects often failed to convey the "inner intensity of the story."[117] However jazz, thanks to its pliability, could be built into film as an integral element of its dramatic actualities and expressive techniques.[118]

Riding differentiated historically between live musical accompaniment in the silent film and the use of recorded music in the sound film. Repeating H.D.'s distinction between silent cinema's "dolls" and sound cinema's "idols," she suggested that the silent-film audience had accepted the complete artificiality and disjunctive character of accompaniment.[119] By contrast, the sound-film audience experienced a new and more complete illusory world on screen; any off-screen, or non-diegetic music or sound effects threatened its integrity because the audience now sought to place them either within screen events or in the auditorium itself, making them like "concert-hall effects," contradicting the illusion induced by the screen.[120]

Riding's solution was to advocate a use of sound accompaniment that was anti-realist in conception, one that would be determined formally rather than diegetically, as part of an entire sound composition for the story. But there is a paradox in her argument: sound nevertheless had to contribute to the audience's complete absorption by the film. Here is no Brechtian motivation for anti-realism, for the purpose of creating critical awareness in the audience. Indeed, Riding writes that through the sound track, the audience must not be permitted a moment of reflection.[121] The sound track should thus be a fully integrated part of the film, inseparable, in any scene, from vision and color. Echoing the synaesthetic aspirations of Bute, Riding insists that every single aspect of the film "permeates sympathetically" every other, taking the audience fully into the film.[122]

Riding's sense of sound working to bind the audience into the world of the film in such a way that any self-reflection is impossible suggests a potentially harmonious relationship between sound and image. But whether writers pitched for harmony or discord between sound and image, the coming of sound challenged the primacy of vision in the cinema. Many writers lamented the imminent extinction of the language of the body developed by performers for the silent screen. In a 1935 review of *A Midsummer Night's Dream* (1935), Colette extolled the virtues of Reinhardt's *mise-en-scène* for those rare moments "when we are touched simply by the ... opportunity for silence, movement, and immobility," and praised the chittering of Mickey Rooney's Puck precisely because his bodily animism existed, for her, outside the domain of spoken language:

> His voice will doubtless sound around the world. It is the true voice of Oberon's forest messenger, a voice that has never battered itself against the walls of human habitation, a voice as raucous as a peacock's call ... But above all one must hear it as it drones out onomatopoeias that the child has perhaps invented for himself, snuffles of a little boar, chattering of a squirrel, and especially a rising laugh, victorious, impossible to describe, and more savage than all his other sounds.[123]

From this passage looms the threat that sound film represented for many: the cinema now as a rising babble, booming triumphant, trampling both internationalism and private reverie around the world.

In their effort to analyze sight and hearing in the cinema, writers had called in a third domain—in Riding it was 'an education in feeling"; in H.D. it was the spectatorial propensity to invest devotions; in Woolf it will be the brain.[124] However expressed, and whether oriented toward emotion or intellection, toward Clara Beranger's ideal of "absolute self-forgetfulness" or Richardson's "intensity of contemplation," this third domain can be understood as an attempt to articulate the means by which the cinema grasped and entertained the spectator.[125]

Some writers, in tackling the third register, suggested that vision was itself split between an eye that was pragmatic and protective, and one that operated for pleasure. Virginia Woolf, for example, referred to the governessing function of the former and characterized it as "English" and non-aesthetic in its orientation, while Barry (though without preference) split off a kind of looking to follow the plot from the eye's enjoyment of non-narrative or aesthetic elements.[126] One consequence of this division of the eye is that it made possible for Woolf and Barry a concept of film form largely independent of notions of language, whether spoken or merely thought. Here their texts become most prospective, almost spectral: Barry imagines films "throughout which pictures of ineffable loveliness melt into each other"; Woolf writes of a cinema in which "thought in its wildness, in its beauty" would be visible; Deren describes non-representational "inner realities" achievable only through filmic form; and Bute conjures up the non-literary, post-Wagnerian synaesthesia of Absolute Film.[127]

Another consequence of these efforts to tease apart eye and eye, eye and ear, eye and brain, perception and cognition, is to bring into view the relationship between film and certain mental processes, a road well traveled by film theorists of this era.[128] Writers conjecture the relationship between film and thought in at least four ways: film can represent thought, perhaps, as Balfour and Nielsen suggest, by tracing its inscription on the performer's face; film's picture-making capacity duplicates that of certain mental processes; the radical discontinuities produced by editing analogize the operations of the unconscious; and film viewing creates a unique kind of attentiveness. Lou Andreas-Salomé, in a diary entry written while studying the new science of psychoanalysis with Freud in Vienna in 1913, noted that the cinema's "rapid sequence of pictures approximates [the] imaginative faculty."[129] Dorothy Richardson, drawing attention to the contemplative state of the film spectator, claimed that this state could be induced by any film because a film was structured, "arranged and focussed," to do this.[130] The viewing experience created a sense of wholeness in which the filmed "fragments in their own moving reality" were disported around, and through the viewer.[131] Virginia Woolf writes of the as yet unrealized possibilities of seeing emotions and "thought itself" imaged on-screen; Fannie Hurst suggested that the motion picture would only attain its legitimate status as an art form when it "spanned the entire octave of human response."[132]

Filmmaker Maya Deren described "thinking" in film as a process projected, via the camera, from the artist to the audience.[133] Like animator Reiniger, with whom she shared an interest in dance and a strongly anti-realist conception of film form, Deren would have refused the label "theory" for her discussion in "Magic is New" (yet her anecdotal account of the difficulties of describing and achieving her mode of film practice indicates how closely interrelated the activities of theorizing and filmmaking were for her).[134] Her most complete elaboration of film form is developed in her 1946 pamphlet *An Anagram of Ideas on Art, Form, and Film*.[135] *Anagram* is a nine-part interwoven complex of ideas on nature and its mechanics, the character and methods of man, and the means of discovery and invention, threaded through an aesthetics and history of art, which includes the cinema. As Deren intended, the structure of *Anagram* precludes any meaningful excerpting and in its place *Red Velvet Seat* includes a very different text by her.[136] "Magic is New" was published in *Mademoiselle*, a women's fashion magazine, and Deren, who wrote to make money to further her filmmaking, altered her writing style accordingly. The opening narrative of indeterminacy—Deren is neither amateur nor professional, her films are neither educational nor commercial—describes an expressive artist whose work resists easy classification. She writes as one who uses film to answer "some requirement of the imagination," rather than to turn away from thought, as Hollywood film might be accused of doing.[137]

Through the camera, Deren claims to realize imaginative concepts and createa reality that is only possible filmically. But her text here points to a paradox. On the one hand Deren relies on the iconic and indexical strength of the filmic image when she writes of her attraction to the medium: "For if the tree in the scene was real and true, the event which one caused to occur beneath it seemed also real and true."[138] On the other hand, she diminishes the role of representational content in the production of filmic meaning in favor of camera techniques and editing strategies: the camera should be used to make a thing look like "what the audience should feel about it."[139] She indicates that, at least as far as her own practice is concerned, the camera's real purpose is not the creation of verisimilitude but, through the deployment of its unique qualities, the engendering of emotional states in the audience.

For Deren, in order to think cinematically one must overcome the tendency to think in verbal terms. Rather than "contriving an image to illustrate a verbal idea," the filmmaker must start with an image that "contains within itself such a complex of ideas that hundreds of words would be required to describe it."[140] Deren's comments raise the question of the relationship between cinematic signification—the way in which films produce meaning—and language. Her discussion suggests that both the emotional states experienced by viewers and the filmmaker's creative conception of the work exist outside language. The filmmaker must think pictorially, not verbally, and the spectator must experience the film similarly.

The cinema's possibilities for suggesting thought and experience pictorially (rather than verbally) are underlined in Virginia Woolf's account of viewing The Cabinet of Dr. Caligari. Woolf recalls that while watching Caligari, an unexpected shadow had trembled on the screen and this shadow, which appeared to her like the monstrous imaginings of a lunatic, seemed to express not the statement "I am afraid" but "fear itself": "If a shadow at a certain moment can suggest so much more than the actual gestures and words of men and women in a state of fear [she is writing of the silent cinema], it seems plain that the cinema has within its grasp innumerable symbols for emotions that have so far failed to find expression."[141] For Woolf, these symbols are necessarily abstracted; anger "is, perhaps, a black line wriggling upon a white sheet."[142]

Woolf proposes the existence of an emotive domain which, while unspoken, could be made visible, and she raises a question, one with a considerable legacy in the literature of philosophy and film theory: Can a thought be made known or given form without the help of words? Is thinking itself a verbal or non-verbal activity?[143] Like Dulac, Woolf argues that the cinema must free itself from contamination with the verbal, and in order to do this it should concentrate on what it does best. Film is ideally suited to capture the passage of time and what she calls the "suggestiveness" of reality, and its particular beauty is realized in the quotidian, those aleatory moments that escape our attention, which Siegfried Kracauer later called "the unstaged."[144] Filmmakers, however, have regrettably ignored these sources of cinematic interest, writes Woolf, causing eye and brain to be "torn asunder ruthlessly as they try vainly to work in couples."[145] Discussing a filmed adaptation of Anna Karenina, she argues that the (literate) spectator "knows" Anna's thoughts, for this is what literature speaks of, but that the cinema can in no way show "the inside of her mind."[146] Confined to the visible, the cinema can only give us her pearls, her teeth and her velvets, as if this were all this Anna amounted to. But cinema and literature are equally ill-served by this union. Literature is impoverished, being reduced to a display of egregious materiality, while the cinema is forced into a mode of speech it can only jabber. Woolf condemns efforts at cinematic symbolism—the equation of a kiss with love and a broken cup with jealousy—as "the scrawl of an illiterate schoolboy," one who is ignorant of the classics and unable to use his new pen.[147]

Underwriting Woolf's efforts to distinguish the literary from the cinematic, the verbal from the visual, is a distinction between cognition and perception, or brain and eye. Woolf's idealized or uncontaminated cinema, free from literature, storytelling and symbolism, appeals to the eye that thinks visually, but not just for utilitarian purposes, so that "the body does not fall down coal holes."[148]

Woolf finds material for this truly visual eye in what she calls an "accidental scene," where the cinema reveals what it "might do if left to its own devices."[149] Discussing the filmed version of Tolstoy's novel again, she recalls seeing a gardener incidentally mowing a lawn while Anna and Vronsky kiss.[150] It is not only chance that is valued here—that the gardener should happen to be in frame at that particular moment; the incidental fact of the gardener's appearance also registers the cinema's capacity to capture that "suggestiveness of reality" which lies apart from language.[151] This is what the cinema could reveal if filmmakers would resist the impulse to "connect the pictures with the book."[152]

Woolf's phrase "the suggestiveness of reality" offers little by way of conceptual clarity; its rhetorical value lies instead in its own power for suggestion. The plenitude of cinematic images perhaps heightened the sense of reality's "suggestiveness," its propensity to escape the grasp of language. Indeed, this plenitude perhaps rendered language insufficient—words were inadequate to describe either the new reality of the cinema, or reality itself. The cinema functioned as an exemplary instance of reality's "suggestiveness," by refusing closure and a singular meaning.[153] Or, alternatively, we might consider that, by fixing on the incidental as the locus of film's potential, Woolf adopted a spectatorial pose contrary to that ostensibly invited by Hollywood's standard fare. This passing over the obvious to look away from the stars' kiss to a figure at the edges of the frame has been described by Roger Cardinal as a "posture of refusal" which he likens to "peripheral looking," one in which the eye roams across the frame, attentive to ground rather than figure.[154] Most interesting, in the case of Woolf, is Cardinal's suggestion that this mode of looking might be associated with "non-literacy" and to habits of looking more akin to touching, a haptical look.[155]

For Woolf, writing of silent film, it would seem that the "accidental scene" was the locus of a certain kind of specifically cinematic spectatorial pleasure. The cinema allowed for a continually changing relationship of figure and ground, or part to whole. The spectatorial eye could roam the frame, alighting (and delighting) where it chose. Dorothy Richardson describes how the spectator seated in the auditorium becomes the "motionless observing center" of "a moving reality," which is usually only seen in fragments.[156] Film's power, she claims, "rests on leading "the observer to the condition that is essential to perfect contemplation."[157] This condition makes the spectator experience herself as the cohesive center of a moving, fuller represented world.

More recent critics have argued that this imposition by the camera of a spectatorial sense of centeredness and cohesion is nothing but the operation of bourgeois ideology, interpolating, or producing the individual subject's sense of her or his own singular personhood.[158] But for Richardson it is the contemplative state induced in the viewer which is paramount: in this state the spectator is able to become reacquainted with the customary and to see its "lost quality" restored.[159]

And here we return to the silent cinema again, for this perfect contemplation is only possible when film is mute. In "A Tear for Lycidas," written in 1930, Richardson remembers that the secret of silent film's power was its "undiluted appeal to a single faculty."[160] Replaying the kinds of distinctions that Woolf had employed in her discussion of eye and brain, she finds sound and vision cannot work together—one or the other will always lead. As if to support this claim, she notes that moments of intense concentration on the audible demand a cessation of visual impulses: the listener closes her eyes the better to listen. But while hearing is the dominant sense in daily life, she argues, the screen reverses this. On screen, sight leads, and is capable of summoning the other faculties. Thus, in the case of musical accompaniment, Richardson decides that the film uses music, not music the film. Further, the silent film returns the spectator to an "individual intensity of being," in large part because, in Richardson's claim, "Life's 'great moments' are silent."[161] The spectatorial experience of a silent film is one of solitude, whereas the sound film produces "association," taking spectators "out of themselves."[162]

Film Aesthetics
and the Other Arts

The Art of the Cinema (1923)
Betty Balfour

Mr. St. John Ervine, in a recent appreciation of Duse, wrote, "It was not necessary to understand what she was saying because we understood what she was feeling."[1] In other words, a writer, than whom there is no more obstinate traducer of the Art of the Cinema, has set a seal of greatness upon an art that can dispense with language. He implies, in fact, that Duse would have been a great film actress. Her art is, indeed, the art of self-expression so perfected that the voice is unnecessary, the self-same art that we practise in the films. To appreciate or try to understand Cinema Art one must dispossess oneself of all thoughts of the theatre in particular and of literature and other forms of art in general. Critics whose only knowledge is of the theatre, or of literature or other arts, have no right or qualification to criticise an art of which they are entirely ignorant, and which frequently they do not even attempt to study. Too much damage has been done by those people, they prejudice appreciation of the cinema as an art, and even mislead film artists, both producers and players, into trying to adapt stage technique to the requirements of the film, between which there is little connection. They are, in fact, widely different.

The cinema is an entirely new medium of expression, and perhaps the most wonderful of all. It is an art and not a trick, as many people would have you believe. Film artists are not puppets—things without soul—neither is their art merely a matter of grimacing. The puppets, the *poseurs*, the persons who merely grimace, are speedily discovered by the most stern and rigid of judges, the camera, and are inevitably consigned to eventual oblivion.

Sincerity is the keynote of Cinema Art; it is impossible to progress on sham and artificiality. A film artist must live the part—actions and expressions are useless without feeling. Much of the action of a film plot is conveyed not by movement but through the eyes alone, which are the mirror of the soul, and will unfailingly betray any lack of brain effort or sincerity. The strain and concentration thereby imposed is both heavy and of a very different character from the physical and mental strain of playing before an audience. Stage artists who come to the film studio immediately discover that their greatest difficulty is to find some influence to compensate for that of the missing audience. The reason is that a theatre audience gives its vitality to the stage artist, whereas the film artist has to give his or her vitality to the inanimate and unresponsive camera—there is no telepathy of goodwill from the audience. I had a remarkable experience of this not long ago when playing a music-hall scene in the Welsh–Pearson film, *Love, Life and Laughter*. When Mr. [George] Pearson was photographing the big views of this scene, I played before an audience. At the end of a whole day's work I was not a bit tired and could have gone on playing for hours. Subsequently, I had to play in "close-up" scenes without the audience, and I found one "close-up" more exhausting than all the rest of the scenes put together.

Consider the character of the "audience" before which a film artist plays—the camera—a one-eyed, deaf and dumb spectator, incapable of imparting vitality or encouragement, but an uncompromising detector of flaws in appearance, personality and performance. One cannot challenge the opinions of this critic, its record is final. On the stage distance lends enchantment, but the film artist cannot keep at a distance; talent may compensate for personality behind the footlights, but the artist without personality gets a chilly reception from the camera; "theatricalities" may succeed with an audience, but the camera shows them up for what they are. Your one-eyed spectator is at a disadvantage in that it cannot with its one eye take in as much action as can a spectator with two eyes; and so that he does not miss anything of importance, the film artist is obliged to be particularly careful to see that the essential action "registers." The art of cinema-acting is to appear natural, but a comprehensive knowledge of technique is required to produce the desired effect, and in this technique the matter of timing is all-important. Spontaneity registers on the stage and in life, but it does not register on the cinema screen. Improper timing may produce totally unexpected and ineffective, if not contrary, results—serious action easily becomes humorous, and *vice versa*, through being played too fast or too slow. The "swift, sudden right" of a boxing hero, if played naturally, does not register at all except as a jerky, incomprehensible movement, so that the blow has to be delivered more slowly than it would be naturally, but not so slowly as to appear ludicrous. It is not, however, so simple a matter to judge the correct timing of the blow as it might seem, and the difficulty is increased enormously when the action to be registered is entirely a matter of expression and not of physique. To appreciate this point one has only to stand before a mirror and discover what different action may be conveyed by different timings of a glance. Timing is just like shorthand — incorrect timing, like an imperfectly made stroke, may convey an entirely different meaning. […]

So a film artist must first completely master the details of screen technique and thereafter constantly study their application, as a *prima ballerina* constantly practises elementary movements, and the *prima donna* or the *virtuoso* constantly practise their scales.

Unqualified critics sometimes suggest that there is no art in the cinema and that it is all a trick, meaning thereby that it is a product of mechanics. Mechanics are essential to any art, and the mechanics of Cinema Art are merely the material with which the artist works. The painter works with canvas, palette and pigment, but what he produces with them is the result of his own artistic endeavour. A film producer may tell his architect to design a room, give instructions to the carpenter to build it, the decorator to embellish it, the property man to furnish it, and the electricians to provide lamps to light it; but how these materials are utilised to make a screen picture is entirely a matter of the producer's own art. Every development of photography helps him, and through it the cinema offers greater scope than any other art. It is an art of suggestion which stimulates imagination (in spite of Mr. St. John Ervine's opinion to the contrary), and its possibilities for symbolism are wonderful. Even fantasy lies within the immediate bounds of its possibilities, and very soon it will achieve even the effective creation of a Barrie atmosphere.[2] [...]

The cinema is the greatest of modern gifts to mankind. As an educational factor its importance is scarcely yet realised, but as entertainment it has seized upon the imagination of all races, and its appeal to democracy is greater by far than that of any other medium of expression that the world has ever known.

[from *The English Review* (London) 37, September 1923, pp. 388–91, excerpted.]

Courage in Production (1933)
Leontine Sagan

When I began to work with the sound film I threw myself head over heels in this new adventure. I lived in the cinemas; I started thinking only in terms of camera positions and cuts; I hunted for film stories. It made one rather uneasy not to be able to collect in the twinkling of an eye an amount of new experience to correspond with twenty years of work on the stage. But on the other hand, it was exciting to explore new country. I had to quieten my conscience with the thought that intuition must stand for experience. As it is, it often happens that in artistic professions instinct goes further than learning. Instinct is an unconscious wisdom about things, together with a strong sympathy. I felt a strong sympathy with the film because it furnished new means of expression; because it made things visible that until now had remained invisible; but most of all because it put me personally before a new task.

Yet I could not entirely lay aside the spectacles of a person coming from the legitimate stage, and whilst I was working in the studio I struggled hard with myself *against* the movies and for the stage and for the movies *against* my own prejudices.

Stage technique in its best period was modest rather than elaborate in decorative scenery. The spoken word reigned supreme. The most impressive performances were often played in front of a mere curtain. It was not done to make a virtue out of necessity, but it was intended to give a definite style to the acting. Poet and players were to contrast clearly with a mutual background without the eye being distracted. In the film I found I had plunged right into the other extreme. There was no need for limitation. Everything was to be had. Money was no object. Not only real furniture and properties were to be had but also real landscapes, architecture and types of people in all variations. While on the stage, the play was limited and enclosed by the wall of the curtain, it could in the film break through space and time and get into the open. It could be expanded and it could be narrowed-in. It could even be interrupted by something entirely different—by a close-up of a head, a tower or a detail of nature. It was like roaming in the universe. But where was the idea of the creator to end? Where was the limit? ... These were the surprises that occurred in a brain accustomed to stage methods. [...]

There was much else in my film work that puzzled me. Here, for example, was the scene set up in the studio: a scene taken out of the script without any connection with what had preceded and what was to follow it. As is well known, all the shots that are played in one scenic set are taken in sequence, irrespective of their logical connection. Actors and director have to imagine the connections for themselves by the utmost concentration. Seen purely from the creative point of view, such a procedure must seem quite absurd: the dramatic atmosphere is utterly broken up each time and has to be created afresh. That the scenes were later to be given their original continuity of content and form through montage and cutting could help me but little in the hours when I wished to bring these bits to life. Accustomed as I was to work vitally in the theatre, both the actress and the producer in me objected at first to the mechanical fixing of such scenes. In the theatre I had been accustomed to keep the scenes fluid until the evening of the performance. Even then, one experienced surprises both of the pleasant and unpleasant sort; for the players are subject to the changes of their own temperament. Spontaneity in art does not lend itself to being fixed. The actor's art depends on the spontaneity of the spectator. Sudden surprises, sudden emotions, everything that in the theatre is awakened by the magnetic contact between the two sides of the footlights, must, in the case of the film, be provided afterwards during editing. But this again is a mechanical process of the scissors, carried out by the cutter or the director, and not the spontaneous contact between player and spectator.

So it almost appeared to me at first as if the actors were not by any means the first artistic necessities of a film, but rather were only a detail of the whole, in the same way as, for example, an aeroplane or a submarine; and it even became a matter for consideration whether the camera did not pierce further into the aeroplane or the submarine than it could pierce the shell of the actor. For such objects remain unself-conscious while they are being photographed; but how is the human actor to be spontaneously unself-conscious, to express the final truth in his features, when he has to experience utterly disconnected situations before a merciless camera? One may even feel inclined to ask, as some do, whether it is not really better to work with people who are not professional actors, but have the expressive features of lay folk who do not carry on their faces the complicated, sensitive mask, trained to portray a hundred different expressions. Flaherty, Murnau and the Russian directors have done so.[1] In that approximation to reality, the camera is not only to be brought literally close to the actor's face, but it is also to tear from it its inner truth.... But who is to say where illusion ends and reality begins? The soul of the actor is a piece of art to which the fullest expression cannot be given by the camera: it is like a symphony that is played on one instrument only and is not given its full value.

Everything becomes easier and more natural when one goes with the camera into the open and leaves to it the selection. Trees, water, animals do not let themselves be posed. They preserve their own individuality; and it almost seems as if the players too become infected by this atmosphere, as if they were dissolved into nature. In the studio, it is more difficult to bring them to the complete freedom which takes away poses and photographic attitudes. This is indeed the highest kind of film in which, as in the Commedia del'Arte, the actor becomes, as it were, a fascinating ball thrown backwards and forwards between the director and the camera—where catch-ball is played with him in the jolliest way and where everything turns round with him in a mad whirl. These are the films of Chaplin and René Clair.[2] These are the most film-like of all films.

The difficulty begins when the sound film starts to deal with problems, and it is not satisfied only in providing entertainment: when it approaches the great general questions of society and education. The tremendous popularity of the cinema gives the film a corresponding power as an influence. Since the film has begun to talk, it appears to be becoming almighty. And even if, as has been maintained, it has lost thereby its artistic worth, it has certainly gained ten-fold in vitality. Now players are not confined to gestures only on the screen, like beautiful animals, but can express themselves in speech. And as the art of the film stands so much nearer to the world of everyday life than does the theatre, which is a world of fancy, scenarios dealing with the burning questions of the day ought to spring up like mushrooms. The film might educate the public to think for itself by confronting it with questions it must solve for itself. Because the camera can probe in everywhere and can disclose things at their roots, the number of possible subjects is unlimited. Only, in this connection, I do not believe that the manuscript or scenario can be regarded as a mere detail. It needs strong personalities to select and to form material, strong personalities to give it visible shape. It also needs complete freedom within the limits imposed by art and conscience. For this, courage is necessary, courage all along the line: courage on the part of those responsible for creating, and readiness on the part of the public to recognise and support their courage.

[from Cinema Quarterly (Edinburgh), Spring 1933, pp. 140–43, excerpted.]

Comments on the Screen (1918)

Janet Flanner

[...] Metcalfe, drama critic of *Life*, somewhat acridly observes that the cinema and its scope differs completely from the stage and its requirements and in the making of the observation, he attempts not to flatter the film world.[1] The cinema demands an excellent, romantic and gripping plot for its basic ingredient, just as the stage does for its greater successes and if the two differ in technique, let Mr. Metcalfe recall that the technique of the photoplay is so much more intricate, astute, comprehensive and complex than the simpler technique of the spoken drama, that it makes Pinero, Jones and Scribe seem nicely limited by comparison. They find themselves singularly limited by conventions both of the audiences and of the stage. The camera is unlimited. It can employ as many scenes as it desires, also as many characters and it can skip blithely from Spain to Maine and finally deposit the heroine happily in Madagascar if it chooses.

This ought to be much more in the camera's favor than usually it is.

However, in the case of subject matter, surely the stage and screen are not so far apart as Mr. Metcalfe hopes. The gulf, which he believes, yawns forbiddingly between the two can and is bridged by a point in similarity—usefulness of melodrama. Melodrama has flourished on the stage ever since it became customary to dramatize woman's woes. The fifth act—they had time to spare in those days and could afford to be generous—has contained denouements and crises no more absurd and satisfying than the situations frequently found in the films today—situations repugnant to Mr. Metcalfe's sensitive eyes. Melodrama is the breath of the stage and is the light in the celluloid. What more could be said? What more does he want?

Frightfulness and thrills do not constitute a melodrama, the film producers are admitting. Melodrama is composed of suspense on the part of the audience, directed towards an emotional situation grasping the principal actors and over which they have, to a large extent, no control. *Uncle Tom's Cabin* is a splendid melodrama.[2] It was so on the stage and likely will prove to be so on the screen.

It contains besides an element of nationalism—for the North—which is very pleasing to the people, all the robust ideals of the melodrama which constitute the greatest check on our rapidly dissolving social sensibilities. The vast majority of the people, and it is the vast majority who attend the screen, found for years Topsy an ideal in low comedy, Uncle Tom a representative pillar of uncomplaining long suffering—a perfect exposition of the beatitudes—little Eva as near an angel as she could be and escape heaven until the last act, and Legree a complete villain. So doubtless the millions who enjoyed the play on the stage will continue to so to do when it comes on the screen, and if the two versions are anything at all alike, as will be extremely likely, Mr. Metcalfe of *Life* will be displeased.

[*Indianapolis Star*, (Indianapolis) 7 July 1918, Section 6, p. 1, excerpted.]

Film as Ballet (1936)
Lotte Reiniger

A DIALOGUE BETWEEN LOTTE REINIGER AND HER FAMILIAR

(Scene: *Covent Garden Market. It is a summer night, and another performance of the Ballets Russes has just come to a triumphant conclusion.*[1] *Enter Lotte Reiniger accompanied by her familiar in the guise of a cavalier. They pick their way gingerly between the crates and the carts, discussing the spectacle they have just seen.*)

FAMILIAR

Do you know, I have always felt that there is a close relationship between ballet and the trick film? For instance, just as ballet leans on certain types of music, using the metrical pattern as a scaffolding and crossing its own motion in space with music's emotion in time, so your films seem to rely increasingly on sound to provide them with their own characteristic rhythm. It would interest me to know what style of music you have found most congenial to accompany the action of your silhouettes.

LOTTE REINIGER

I have always been regarded with much suspicion by the film trade, because I have never disguised my preference for eighteenth-century music. I have acted on the assumption that in the cinema this music would sound unusual and remote, churchlike to some, almost revolutionary to others, whereas actually it is as clear as water and underlines with perfect discretion the very formal style of silhouette movement and action. For instance, I was proud to hear from those who make it their business to help German workers appreciate good music that these men have shown a marked preference for my film *Ten Minutes with Mozart*. Usually such people are bored by concerts and classical music; but they all agreed that this film had made them understand and enjoy Mozart's music for the first time.

FAMILIAR

That was certainly a fine compliment. I am glad to hear you say that you prefer working with eighteenth-century music—not that I think music of that era should be looked on as *Gebrauchsmusik*, but because I always feel that the extra-musical emotion of the nineteenth century vitiated and obscured true musical emotion and unfitted the music of that subjective age for some of its noblest tasks.[2]

LOTTE REINIGER

But you can have little idea how difficult it is to fit a thoroughly worked-out musical score to the direct narrative action of a film, which advances breathlessly and at every climax insists on its own rhythm like a crying child.

FAMILIAR

Of course, music progresses according to laws of its own. For instance, repetition both literal and implied is an essential part of it. But I always think that the film

Fig. 2.2   Photograph of Lotte Reiniger collaborating with Berthold Bartosch on *The Adventures of Prince Achmed* in 1926 in Potsdam.

of action accelerates to its climax by a series of wave-movements, until the seventh wave lands it more or less safely on the beach. It has no time for repetition: it is far too busy growing in fast motion. You must have felt the drag between these two factors especially strongly in *Papageno*, where you used Mozart's score with only a minimum of cuts.

Lotte Reiniger

Certainly! A devilish lot of mathematical reflection was needed to portion out the endless Papageno–Papagena dialogue (which from the musical point of view cannot possibly be cut) and to translate all this into an action as light and delicate as the music itself. The successful way in which this sequence of operatic numbers was turned into a sound film has entirely changed my style of film composition. Formerly I used to begin by thinking out a plot that would suit me, and then I looked round for music to accompany it: nowadays I search for my music first and invent the necessary action afterwards.

Familiar

It is curious that the arrival of the sound film should have driven your trick films away from realistic narrative action to a more formalised condition approaching that of ballet, especially since the contrary is to a certain extent true of ordinary films. When the cinema was still silent, artists like Charlie Chaplin or Buster Keaton were compelled to invent and rely on a highly artificial style of movement and rhythm to bring off their effects. The coming of sound has led the cinema into a blind alley of realism from which only you and a few others seem to know how to escape.

LOTTE REINIGER

In the days of the silent film the cinema set out to tell its stories by movement alone, and the good film actor invented his own rhythm and was loved for it. Those unforgettable steps of Chaplin which he used for walking into and out of his films were one of the greatest inventions of this phase of cinema which has passed away only too quickly, becoming one of the lost arts. And what rich variations this hopeless, world-forlorn gipsy developed from such a simple theme! One of the wittiest was in *The Pilgrim*, when he straddled along the border with one foot in Mexico and the other in the United States. And all the other artists who discovered and developed the voices of their bodies—why have they had to disappear with the coming of sound? They may try to do justice to that change by singing and dancing; but, apart from the surrealist Marx Brothers and certain other rare exceptions, they have lost the strong personal touch. A different kind of movement must be found to-day, and there the example of the ballet in extending the human body to music is an excellent mentor and guide.

FAMILIAR

The problem of extension is certainly fascinating. Just as in classical ballet the dancers are turned out in movement and in repose, so the silhouette figures in your films are extended, too: they stand and move in bold profile often reminiscent of the conventions of Egyptian art.

LOTTE REINIGER

It's curious, you know, how the anatomy of my figures has to differ from that of human beings if they are to be capable of carrying out real silhouette movements. Their construction must sometimes be changed for musical reasons, too: a figure that moves to a waltz tune has to be jointed quite differently from one that performs to a minuet. And then you must remember that I can perform my ballets, not only with human beings whose movements after all are familiar to most of us, but also with animals. In fact, I may say that God's Zoological Garden lies open before me with all the world's animals and their myriad ways of moving to be carefully studied and worked out. For instance, you or anyone else might be forgiven for thinking that a horse is a horse anywhere and at any time; but I (alas!) know from bitter experience that this is untrue. When I tried to depict the history of vehicular traffic in *The Rolling Wheel*, I thought for one blissful moment that half a dozen horses would suffice for all the various historical episodes of that film. How sadly and completely was I disillusioned! The frisky steeds that dashed through the desert dragging Egyptian chariots behind them were utterly useless when I tried to trick them out for more pompous service with the Roman quadrigas. The team of Roman horses I cut were far too noble to do duty for the hacks that had to draw the heavy medieval travelling coaches through mud and mire. And so on, through all our artificial periods, until my studio was a stables and my fingers exhausted from working out the trot, canter and gallop of at least two hundred different legs.

FAMILIAR

Of course, all those numbers sound very impressive, but aren't they just a little misleading? Although it must be a finicky task to move the legs of so many frisky steeds and to take care that they don't get entangled with each other, surely the real problem arises when a single figure stands alone and has to play (or, if you prefer it, dance) a scene—like an aria in classical opera?

LOTTE REINIGER

To tell the truth, although I had to put so much painstaking work into those tiresome horses, I always looked on them as being of secondary importance. Their main purpose was to introduce a carriage, and that carriage had to appear in a part of the screen where movement was most easily noticed This field of intensive vision is severely restricted—in fact, you might say that as a general rule I have to avoid placing any important movement or action within an imaginary margin that surrounds the important central core of the screen like a frame. I think it will be quite easy for you to understand what I mean if I tell you that the spectator's eye, being accustomed to read from left to right...

FAMILIAR (interrupting)

What about the Jews and the Japanese?

LOTTE REINIGER (ignoring this tactless remark)

...has a natural tendency to react in a similar way to the screen image, and consequently the upper and lower parts of the screen form a kind of no-man's-land. When I want to start an important gesture, I have to place my figure towards the centre of the screen but slightly above the imaginary horizontal line that bisects it. The horses' legs in *The Rolling Wheel* moved far below this intensive zone; but the carriage they so triumphantly drew crossed it. You must always remember, however, that this film was cultural in its tendency and needed no great artistry on my part in the movement of the figures. It is entirely different in a "danced" film or one conceived in terms of ballet. There my most important effect, the thing I am most anxious to hammer into the heads of my audience, is the expression of my leading figure. I try to establish this key impression at the earliest possible moment by means of a solo scene. Thereby the spectator is not only enabled to understand that figure's character, but is also plunged right into the heart of the story; and then, the solo theme having been stated, a world of variation opens.

FAMILIAR

I'm sorry I interrupted you with that foolish remark about the Japanese; but I was particularly interested in what you said about screen-reading from left to right. I think an analogy could be drawn between this and the importance when criticising pictures (especially portraits) of remembering that more than ninety per cent. of the world's artists have been right-handed. And in considering the sensitive screen zone, I think you should also remember that the black edge of the frame exerts a kind of a capillary attraction on the neighbouring portions of the film and sometimes distorts them even to the point of absorbing their significance—and I mention this without taking into account the optic and optical distortion exercised by the human eye and the lens of the projector. But to return to our solo dancer and the *pas seul*—In ballet (and in your silhouette films too) a solo dancer has the possibility of lateral movement; but on the stage there is also the possibility of movement in depth and, more important still, a combination of these two movements along the two stage diagonals. These diagonals are the longest straight lines on the ground-plan of the stage, they intersect in the stage-centre, and they form the axes for all choreographic movements of any complexity. To take another analogy from painting, Baroque artists such as Rubens and El Greco exploited to the full the importance of the diagonal in perspective and often strung the multitudinous figures in their swarming canvases along double recessional diagonals. To these various aspects of movement one should add those proud moments of elevation in ballet when the ballerina is raised, held aloft by her partner and expands in the limelight like a flower on a stalk.

LOTTE REINIGER

If the intersection of these two diagonals forms the crux of the matter, the same point is certainly the centre of a circle or oval that circumscribes this framework. It is the combination of curve and diagonal which gives the sweet softness and startling directness to ballet and film.

FAMILIAR

These are feminine and masculine elements that play into each other's hands.

LOTTE REINIGER

Precisely! And to continue:—If you draw a line to follow the steps of ballet dancers as they move through the rarified space of the stage, you create an arabesque of ornaments—in the case of classical ballet, of baroque ornaments which are the quintessence of Europe's purest and most characteristic art phase since the Renaissance. Where ballet traces these patterns on a horizontal ground, the screen tilts the whole thing onto a vertical plane. My figures, instead of being depressed by the law of gravity with all its attendant disadvantages, lie flat on the trick table, completely at their ease. My camera, instead of confronting them in the normal way, looks down on them from above. One of the best pieces of advice you can give a choreographer or film-producer is "Underline your climax with a diagonal!" and it is to the cinema's special advantage that its very nature makes it possible to use a unique kind of space–time diagonal. The simplest illustration of this is to be found in the ordinary American montage formula for a chase, in which pursuers and pursued establish the right each to one of the screen's diagonals and the pursuit is cut into short scenes and cross-mounted.

FAMILIAR

I should like to take this opportunity to propound a pet theory of mine about "black and white and cutting in between." Just as in the case of your films there are two main screen areas, black and white, and they are bounded by the outline, so in music there are sound and silence, separated from each other by the soft line of cessation and the sharp line of attack. But the theory isn't really very important, except in so far as it emphasises the role played by unoccupied space and the musical caesura.

LOTTE REINIGER

I hate all theories and have none! As soon as some disturbing theory casts its nightmare shadow across my mind, I do my best to exorcise the devil! But I must admit that I have often been preoccupied with this problem of musical cessation (as you call it) and of how to fit the movements of my figures to music's prolonged and dying falls. Most people would be astonished if they could hear recorded music played backwards, for then they would begin to realise that each note, each chord, is like a flag straining from its staff in the wind of time.

FAMILIAR

I wish I'd thought of that myself! But to return to our discussion of film as ballet, what would you say was the equivalent in ballet to the close-up in film?

LOTTE REINIGER

Don't let us look for any exact equivalent, my dear familiar, but let us rather take an illustration from one of the ballets we saw this evening. Undoubtedly the most charming episode in The Good-Humoured Ladies is the merry meal where the servants eat and drink with wildly exaggerated gestures, until the delicious good-humour of this scene bursts into the unforgettable flame of Danilova's coloratura solo.[3] Were I to aim at the same climactic effect in one of my films, I should have to proceed by entirely different methods. The motion of eating and drinking would have to be rendered as natural as possible, and the scene would probably be clinched by a slow deliberate close-up. You see, a close-up intensifies film action by focusing attention on the dramatic key-point, and this effect is obtained by the utmost economy of action within the close-up itself.

FAMILIAR

It's curious to reflect that where puppets do their best to behave like normal human beings in order to please their audience, apparently human actors have to exaggerate and stylise their movements until they approach the condition of puppets.

LOTTE REINIGER

I think on the whole it's easier for the puppet to please than for the actor. But in any case I'm delighted the Russian Ballet has had the courage and good sense in spite of years of exile never to disown the country of its adoption and the country from which it still draws its spiritual impulse.

FAMILIAR

Do you mean France?

LOTTE REINIGER

No, Russia. But you were right to mention France, for the art of the Russian dancers has only truly blossomed and reached its fullest perfection in the West. I really believe they have taken the whole of Europe in their embrace and found their most faithful audience in England. And this makes me happy, for though my poor trick films have little tradition behind them, no assured audience before them and an uncertain future, yet they are based on the same essential principles as the Russian ballet.

FAMILIAR

And have won for themselves a secure niche...

LOTTE REINIGER

No compliments, please! Now I think I shall go home.

(*They hail a taxi; but although the taxi drives off, there is nothing to show whether they may not have slipped out the other side before it started and disappeared down one of London's darker and more mysterious side-streets.*)

[from *Life & Letters Today* (London) 14:3, 1936, pp. 157–63.]

Dolls and Dreams (1926)
Iris Barry

Some glib fraud long ago invented that detestable phrase "the silent drama" to describe cinematography, as though the cinema were nothing more than the theatre docked of its words. This dishonest and unintelligent view is persistent: one of its most patent results is the awful habit of adapting stage plays to the cinema, in the same form in which they were presented in the theatre, the dialogue still preserved and printed out in sub-titles. *The Only Way* is a good example of the horrors that result, though it is a curious fact that some pretty poor plays have made such good films that only an author would have recognized that both film and play arose out of the same material. Actually, if a play has to be transferred to the screen it ought first to be turned inside out and transmuted out of talk into pictures. But in spite of all this "silent stage" nonsense, I really believe that partisan comparisons between stage and cinema are actually unfair to the stage, in that the cinema has so much wider a range. It alone can handle natural history, anthropology and travel, which lie far beyond the capacity of the theatre. The cinema can more fully than the stage, much more convincingly, develop parable, fairy-story and romance. Still, there remains a common ground of comparison. Both theatre and cinema do express farce, comedy, tragedy and melodrama, and over this ground they may properly and I think usefully be compared.

Now in presenting a play, the theatre has certain advantages. The most obvious is that the actors are present in the flesh. Those who saw, say, Sarah Bernhardt in *Queen Elizabeth* (a film exhibited, as far as I can remember, in 1913) felt the loss of her physical presence.[1] Her acting was Bernhardt's acting. But it was not merely her voice that lacked: it was an emanation of personality. She of course did not know how to "express" herself in a strange and novel medium: but, even if she had, she still would have been "absent." Then, secondly, the very concentration and confinement of the actors on the stage gives an enviable intensity to what they do there. The atmosphere is one so gem-like and fierce that the audience, dazzled by that brilliant cube beyond the footlights, is given a lasting impression of light and activity. They forget that the theatre is as dark as the picture palace, and that the acting on the stage is static compared with film-acting. For in some ways the stage is more real-seeming than the screen-image. Thirdly, the stage has colour. The screen very rarely has and I myself sometimes hope coloured films will never become general. The fourth advantage of the theatre I consider a difference and not really an advantage: that of the spoken word. Since there are excellent plays in which the dialogue has no literary merit, the literary part of a play, the peculiar beauty of the most exalted form of the drama is not an essential part of a play, not, I mean, of a play given in a theatre. And even if it were, then, ideally, the visual beauty of the best films should be the aesthetic alternative to the stage's beauty of language. The most beautiful plays are good to listen to: the most beautiful films are good to look at. There is no rivalry here. I can indeed conceive of films throughout which pictures of ineffable loveliness should continually melt into each other. There have already been promises: in one flash of conscious pictorial organization in *Rosita*, in the perspectives and architecture of *Caligari*, in the co-ordinated movement on many planes of the crowds in the *Golem*, in a certain dramatic and sharp focusing of attention on the rushing mob (seen obliquely through a narrow window) in *Orphans of the Storm*, in many feet of *Anne Boleyn*, in a treatment of landscape in *The White Sister*. *The Last Laugh* and *Vaudeville* were exciting to the eye a dozen times. There was also *The Niebelungs*, which in spite of its lack of dramatic interest, I rather fancy will be considered a classic for many years to come, because it so strove to be pleasing visually. Indeed, it contained a short dream-picture of white and black birds which was one of the finest moving pictures that has yet been achieved.

Of course the cinema has its own peculiar advantages. Visual imagery, less primitive and more sophisticated than auditory imagery, is also sharper, more

Fig. 2.3   Pencil, ink, and watercolor drawing by Wyndham Lewis, titled
"Iris Barry Seated" (1921)

rapidly apprehended, though not richer in association, and more permanent. The
eye, that is, can take in more and more definite impressions in a given time, and
can associate ideas more quickly than can the ear. Tests have shown, besides, that
a moving image is apprehended 20 per cent. more effectively than a static one. The
makers of films have been slow to admit this, but the moment will soon arrive
when the bulk of films will take advantage of the sharpness of visual imagery and
then, when the films are tuned up to the acute visual machinery of the audience,
I think it will be a very exceptional stage-play indeed which will give in dialogue
anything like the diverse, minute and intuitive flashes into behaviour by which
the films of the future will, solely by means of pictures, express drama. *The Woman
of Paris, The Street, The Last Laugh* and *The Marriage Circle*, were, in their very different
ways, valuable experiments in this kind.

Now the personal presence of the actors, so important to the theatre, is, I think,
compensated by the cinema's increased intimacy, by the possibility of seeing the
actor's very thoughts as well as his eloquent gestures and his changes of expression.
Opera glasses are not necessary in the movies, you are saved the trouble of using
them by close-ups: but in the theatre if you want to observe the acting, you are
practically forced either to sit in the front row of the stalls, which many of us

cannot afford to do, or else to hire some glasses, which is very damnable for the eyes. And even then you cannot, as you can in the cinema, see into the minds of the actors, save through their words. And their words, I find myself at least on the English stage, you very often cannot hear.

The world of the screen is also a much wider world than that of the stage: it is not spatially confined, it has, besides an infinite variety of scenes, endless angles of vision and of focuses: you can look down on the action, or up to it, from behind or before. It also includes as part of itself all the riches of landscape or architecture, which are not, as they are in the theatre, mere conventionalized hints. The landscape and the architecture play a definite rôle on the screen: they can even be the chief characters. And the camera brings out an enormous and dramatic significance in natural objects.* Chairs and tables, collar-studs, kitchenware and flowers take on a function which they have lost, save for young children, since we abandoned animism in the accumulating sophistications of civilization. The dramatic advantage of having Desdemona's handkerchief a protagonist, as it can be on the screen, not merely a property, is obvious.

And then, if the cinema has not, ordinarily, colour, it has something very much more important, which is tone. I shall speak about the value of tone in the next chapter ["Art?", following in this volume].

But there are deeper disparities than those I have so far mentioned. The cinema is not, as I have already urged, merely drama with the words left out. It is a vision of people doing things. Now the theatre is by no means that. It is, on the whole, a hearing of people talking about what they have been or are doing. On the stage generally people do very little or nothing: they far more often have something done to them. All the mysterious chemical changes wrought in them by fate or circumstance are registered in words. Of course this is a convention. In life people are not so explicit. Folks do not argue, or soliloquize, or convey precise information in life as dramatists are forced to make them do on the stage. Everything is in the language. What events there are are conventionalized—the air is filled with menace before Oedipus kills his mother. An actress it is true falls when stabbed, poisoned or shot. But of itself this is nothing. She is still a woman who palpably breathes in her mock death. Her murder does not wring us. It is the hero's words, or the old servant's words, that, letting us down into their grief, make the tears spring in our own eyes and lift us by every association of sound and word-choice and cadence to a celestial sphere of exalted pity. It is as though animated dolls jigged stiffly while through their painted lips poured a heavenly and articulate music.

The stage dolls live in a box. The front slides up and there they strut in their nice toy-house, which has an exaggeratedly high ceiling to allow the human beings in the gallery to get an oblique look down into the scene. The side walls are oddly slanted, and there is almost no depth from back to front. All that is concrete is unimportant. The furniture and things might almost as well not be there. There

---

* On this subject I warmly recommend sections of Vachell [sic] Lindsay's "The Art of the Moving Picture" [1915; 1922].

are generally no shadows in the dolls' house, everything is vivid with sharp lights pouring from invisible and unnatural sources. The front of the house slides down: after tedious pauses and muffled bumps from behind, it rises again. The dolls are in another kind of box now—a boxed off bit of the out-of-doors with a blue cloth sky and wooden trees with cloth leaves. Nothing is real: the audience doesn't think it is real. It concentrates on listening for the sound that will let them down into the depth of human emotion. They certainly do watch the stage, but I doubt if a blind person misses much. I was much struck by this on hearing the two first broadcast plays, written specially by Mr. Richard Hughes for the British Broadcasting Company. Though my only theatre was a pair of head-phones, I saw in imagination at least, the flooded mine, the three people trapped there, saw the girl turn to her sweetheart as vividly as I could ever have done in a playhouse. And when listening-in, just as in the theatre, one's anxiety was: What is life doing to these people?

The cinema "stage" has all the latitude of a world of imagination. No longer are the protagonists confined within a lighted box, no longer may we watch them only fixed at one point in space at a certain distance from us. On the screen the hero and heroine move freely in a vast unbounded world of what seems like fact. Their ship, we know because we are allowed to see it from all sides, is a real, not a *papier mâché* vessel: it rides over real waves, not painted ones. The hero grows large as a giant, he becomes as small as a pea. He walks upstairs, enters a room, and we know he has walked upstairs because we have seen it, almost done it ourselves, whereas on the stage, though he says he has walked upstairs, we know he has just come from his dressing-room. In the cinema we are free to follow him everywhere, from below or above as we choose. Space as a limitation is banished: it becomes not a convention but a factor. Time as a limitation is destroyed too. In a flash we can be seven thousand years back, a century forward, in a thousand ages and areas. And all the while there is something to look at. It moves. People are doing something. We see them do it: even if they are only thinking or feeling (as in *Vaudeville* and *The Big Parade*), we still see it, either in their changing expressions or by seeing their thoughts themselves.

A cinema audience is not a corporate body, like a theatre audience, but a flowing and inconstant mass. I fancy that we associate the picture-house with darkness, though the theatre is dark too, because the stage is a lighted dolls' house: our minds project themselves into the light, leaving the body behind in its seat (as happened to the man in the Hans Andersen fairy-story when he wandered through the hearts of his neighbours). The stage of the cinema is in the minds of the spectators. There is no such sense of separation as the theatre-goers experience. To go to the pictures is to purchase a dream. To go to the theatre is to buy an experience, and between experience and dream there is a vast difference. That is why when we leave the theatre, we are galvanized into a strange temporary vigour, why so many people run home and act and strut in their own rooms before the wardrobe mirror. But we come out of the pictures soothed and drugged like sleepers wakened, having half-forgotten our own existence, hardly knowing our own names. The theatre is a tonic, the cinema a sedative. The cinema is a liberation of the ego, the theatre an enrichment of it. And that is why, after the feverish activity of a day of modern life, the screen calls to us more strongly than the footlights. It is not merely that the cinema is cheap, accessible, a popular not a social entertainment, and that you don't have to put your best clothes on to see Harold Lloyd fall off a sky-scraper. After the agitation of a day which includes catching buses, trams or tubes, manipulating typewriters or telephones or lathes or the machines that make clothing and nails, a rest in the picture-house with all its flattering dreams is better for one than the more disturbing experiences in the theatre. We get too much actual experience and not enough dreams.

I admit, of course, that by reason of the absence of language, there are some subtleties, intellectual subtleties, which you cannot get on the screen: for words mean such very different things. I doubt if there is any such *double entendre* in vision. At the same time I think there are emotional subtleties which are better conveyed by the cinema than the theatre, and that in some respects character can be better portrayed there. There is an intimacy, a reality in the illusion of the cinema which the theatre cannot attain. At the pictures, we are all Paul Prys: we go round to the kitchen, we see the heroine's underwear, we see what her young man is up to a hundred miles away. Of course, it is equally true that broadcast plays make us just as much like people listening at keyholes. But looking is more convincing than listening.

It seems, then, idle to insist that the cinema is inherently inferior to the stage artistically: as idle, since the difference is one of medium, as to claim that Tchekov is a greater artist than Van Gogh. There are certainly ugly and idiotic films, but what of *Tons of Money*, *White Cargo*, and plays of that kind?[2]

It is by no mere accident that films are so well adapted to treat fantasy and dream: the art of the cinema offers the world that escape from everyday life, that rationalization of conflicts which lifts the audience so completely out of themselves to a region that other ages found to lie somewhere about an altar, but which we, with our wise freedom from superstitions, our cheap agnosticism and common sense are denied. Humanity has almost forgotten how to wonder, to dream for itself: it ought to thank heaven for providing it the constant sedative, the escape from the self, which it so direly needs, in the little cheap shadowy picture houses. The cinema provides us with the safe dreams we want: and if our dreams are often not worth having, it is because we demand no better.

[from *Let's Go to the Pictures* (London: Chatto & Windus, 1926), pp. 23–33, excerpted.]

Art? (1926)
Iris Barry

In the preceding chapter I was concerned only with one function of the film—the dramatic or story-telling one. But it has another, which is to be something to look at. The mere fact that it moves compels us to look at it, just as we cannot help staring at the moving electric signs in Piccadilly. They catch the eye. Anything that moves catches the eye because it is the eye's business to guard the body against being hit by a falling star or a coco-nut, against being pounced on by a jaguar, bitten by a bug, or stopped by a flag-day collector. That which moves is looked at.

But from being always on the look-out, the eye has learnt another habit, the enjoyment of vision, which is a very different thing. When I look from a hill down into the valleys and sigh with contentment at the green landscape below, I am not concerned—consciously at any rate—with spying for enemies ambushed in the distant hedgerows. I enjoy seeing for its own sake. No doubt the primitive men who drew the first pictures on stones and rocks were partly concerned with telling a story. But the habit of looking at paintings and drawings has generated another necessity—that of looking at pictures for their own pleasure-giving qualities apart from their story-telling value or symbolism. In my championship of the cinema, I wish to examine this "good to look at" quality and to examine in what the moving picture differs from the static picture, and to discover what reason those people have who believe or state that the moving pictures can have no real aesthetic value.

They usually begin by saying that films cannot be art because they are photography. Now, the prejudice against photography is a very queer one. A Man from Mars would have some difficulty in seeing where lay the qualitative superiority of, say, the best and most pleasing exhibits in the annual Salon of photography and the average paintings in the Royal Academy. Yet it is the same people who sincerely admire the Academicians' work (and admire it the more, the more realistic it is, the more you could "eat" the grapes on the canvas) who are so contemptuous of photographs. It is true the photographs are not coloured, and the paintings are, but both of them are an arrangement (those so-natural paintings of flowers and household utensils are very much arranged, of course), both are slightly untrue to appearance, for the camera's one eye distorts every whit as much as does a painter's fancy. But unfortunately for the denigrators of cinematography, they forget that a film is not just photography, but moving photography, which is another thing altogether.

A draughtsman's talent really lies not so much in his ability to represent nature accurately, that is, not merely in his technical ability, as in giving an appearance of life to a non-living representation of life. He is also concerned with form and volume, with the use of light and shade to give an appearance of three dimensions to that which is in fact flat. The moving picture has light and shade and looks three-dimensional. But in giving an appearance of life, the moving picture and the artist are on unequal terms. The artist has eternally to arrest movement in such a way that the action which has gone before and that which will succeed the actual moment depicted are both somehow suggested. The film, on the other hand, uses motion as one of its mediums, very unlike the artist who can only suggest the life-quality by convention. So that, in this sense, the film approximates very much more to the ballet or dance-drama. Take away the story-telling quality of a ballet, and what is it? It is a harmonious succession of moments of free, not arrested, motion in which the line of beauty follows the passage of matter in space and in which pleasure is given by the spectacle of lively units harmoniously changing their relative positions to each other and to the whole composition; also in the various rhythms of speed. This is exactly the case with a film, though less noticeably, because attention is drawn primarily to the dramatic element. It is most appreciated consciously in the pictures of crowds, such as *Intolerance*, *Orphans of the Storm*, *The Ten Commandments*. But it is present in all films: whether there is a good or a bad rhythm, whether the composition of movement is harmonious or not. Now the whole tendency of modern painting has been an attempt to fix eternally—that is, in the only way open to a painter—that rhythm of inter-related movement of lively units. The artists have generally gone about it by utilizing the shapes and the rhythms of machinery, because machines are static lively objects impregnated with internal movement, symbols, that is, of a free motion they do not actually possess themselves. Now the cinema, because it is not static, can take up that part of the modern artist's problem where he is forced to leave off.

In all films, even the most naturalistic and the dullest, there may be these related speed-rhythms, however awkward and inharmonious they be. But in recent German films there has been, together with a pleasing use of these time-rhythms, a use of space–time rhythms that have indeed taken up the painter's problems and worked them out more freely than can ever be done on canvas. I refer now to such films as the over-famous *Caligari*, *The Golem*, to Lubitsch's *Rosita*, if one may call that German, *The Street* and to *Warning Shadows*. There have been others but unfortunately they have not been seen in England. *The Golem* stood alone in that it used the crowds moving in the specially designed, rather distorted and angular alleyways and steep paths of the Ghetto exactly as the dancers in a ballet are moved, to emphasize a pattern. The same structure, without the movement of crowds, was noticeable in *Destiny*, where flights of steps and balconies, not merely as symbols, but as directions of movement, were used for all emotional scenes. *Caligari*, while more interesting architecturally (if one can call "architecture" an arrangement of canvas and paint and shadows to give an appearance of architectural form and volume) did not so noticeably use crowds in counterpoint against and with the scenery, except for one short but important episode—a scene of a fair-ground, with roundabouts turning in one direction, streams of people coming and going, more roundabouts at different speeds and on different planes—an almost indescribable use of movement to convey a definite atmosphere. Films like *The Street* and *Kean* and *Coster Bill of Paris*, by using composite photography to depict mental impressions, came very close in appearance to modern painting, and any moment of those composite photographs was singularly like the paintings of Braque or any other of the cubists. But although I instance these exceptionally original films, all films are full of (generally unconscious and often bad) pictorial organization and full, too, of unconscious time and space–time rhythms. The film director, or perhaps rather, his camera-man and the person who cuts and edits the final form of the film, is nearly always an artist, a *half* artist, working in a new medium that neither he nor anyone else understands yet—the medium having quite a new aesthetic which is concerned with movement.

I know it has often been said that the camera coming between a producer and his imaginative concepts restricts the possibility of his doing fine work. It seems to me to be as true that the canvas of an artist hampers him. Surely it is a much righter view to regard the camera as an instrument of organization, through which the producer is content to sift his studio-scene.

And, by the way, is it not a curious thing that realism is often achieved by cunning rather than by a use of real things? The Niebelungs, a film in which the producer was so anxious to make good to look at that he quite subordinated the story to the scene, demonstrated this. There were mists, real, clinging mists, under trees, real tall, shadow-throwing trees. The mists and the trees were manufactured, not real, however. There are great possibilities in store for future producers who will continue to experiment along the lines of this impressive film.

It is almost impossible for a non-expert to analyse this new visual quality of the films. But, to make a clumsy beginning, you are given a flat surface, two dimensional, on which you are free to represent three-dimensional objects in motion. The third is, as in painting, indicated by the use of light and shade, of form (the film is much more stereoscopic than the still photograph). But another description of the third dimension, impossible to painting, enters: this is the delineation of planes by the free movement of the objects in the picture. The objects, seen in the round in a sense, move not only on their own axes but also in free orbit, and the line of their motion describes the depth of the scene. It may be objected that the objects are not seen in the round because the screen is flat. But in order to assure oneself that the Venus de Milo is not hollow behind, it is not necessary to walk round her. It is sufficient if she is revolved for us. And this is what happens on the screen; the objects are revolved for us.

The emphasis and description of receding planes by the motion of the objects goes on at the same time as the changing of their relative positions, and their changed positions in regard to the whole composition. In these movements, I consider, as much as in the more obvious "scene" as a whole, lies the beauty of cinematography. It is true that each scene, or each second of time, can be aesthetically beautiful in itself in the same way as a painting can: but all the scenes can also be beautiful in relation to each other, and in the passage from scene to scene, from moment to moment, detail by detail, as well as en masse, is a fugitive and unanalysable beauty, similar to that of the ballet, but still richer because less stereotyped, and more spiritual. I wonder sometimes why the Montmartre cubists go on cubing when the cinema exists.

❦

Now the cinema does not generally employ colour. Why? Well, first of course because even now the best of the processes for getting coloured films is not wholly satisfactory. But really I am not yet convinced that there is any reason why colour should ever be utilized generally. As I said in Chapter II [reprinted in this volume as "Dolls and Dreams"], while the film has no colour, it has something much more important, which is tone. Now colour without tone has no aesthetic value at all, any more than noise without music has. That is where the stage decorators and of course house-decorators too, go so woefully wrong. They juxtapose vermilion with lemon and harsh blue with veridian, irrespective of the surface on which they are displayed, irrespective of the tonal qualities of the colours employed, and believe they have been very clever—(I think it is called creating "a gorgeous riot of colour." It certainly is a riot, all right)—as though a child should assemble at random letters of the alphabet and think it had spelt words. Colour without form and colour without tone are meaningless. Consider for a moment, our knowledge of the Old Masters. I think we know most of them by black and white reproductions. But because they have "tone" the very colours are somehow implicit in the blacks and whites and greys. Put a reproduction of a Signorelli beside a Rembrandt, a Corot, a Hogarth and *see*. I have heard the opinion expressed, indeed, that no art critic should be allowed to function until he can, from a black and white photograph of a painting of which he has never seen the original, accurately determine the true colours in which it is painted. Now the cinema has the all-important tone-value, and I think the absence of colour is relatively unimportant. In the harmony of shades between the fullest blacks and the sharpest whites in a well-photographed film, there is an orchestra of tones which can give to everyone, I think, the keenest delight. Think too, what horrible colours we may get if the films are to be dyed—imagine the sort of sickly sweet greens and pinks. Can we trust the taste for colour of ... I won't mention names, but I think most of the producers you've heard about? About eighty per cent. of artists are quite unable to colour their pictures decently nowadays, so why in heaven's name should we expect any better of producers?

However, supposing by some means satisfactory colour could be assured, there is this to be said in its favour, that colour tends to enhance the stereoscopic quality of film-photography. This was noticeable in Fairbanks' *The Black Pirate*, far and away the best colour-film made. After a few moments it ceased to trouble the eye, and dramatically it is obvious that in pirate films when seas are green and blood really red there is definite point in chromatics.

❧

Should films preserve as closely as possible some convention of space and time? It is remarkable at any rate that some of the most important films, from a directional or technical angle, have done so with excellent effect. Of "serious" films one has only to recall Nju, *Warning Shadows*, *The Goose Hangs High*, and of comedies, *Her Night of Romance*, and many another Chaplin, Douglas Maclean and Reginald Denny comedy, to recognize how a sensation of ease and brilliance is secured by limiting the action of the drama depicted to very little more than the time taken actually to exhibit the film itself, how one's attention is held because no breaks occur to bring one back to reality and how the illusion of participating in the action is thereby increased.[1] It limits the action of the film, of course, to the expansion of one incident, on the lines of a certain kind of short story, and it allows no room for the *development* of character. On the other hand, because of the simplicity of the plot, it leaves plenty of room for the exhibition of character and consequently for good acting and it makes it possible to limit the subtitles to a minimum of bare conversation.

Now one of the distinguishing marks of the film is its unruliness, its power to soar beyond all limits of possibility, to depict the passage of years, to step over oceans and mountain ranges, to double back on itself and show what happened before the action commenced, to interpolate dreams and fantastic sequences. But at the same time all the various elements are made more or less successfully to cohere, if only because there are no actual breaks in a film such as you get in a play—no "acts" and intervals. I know some Continental pictures stick "Act I," "Act II" and so forth, into their pictures, but this is simply a piece of mistaken folly and doesn't count. And on the whole the more successfully a film does cohere, the better. In other words, a film should have form. Though it is difficult at first to see how the best pictures have form, on examination one finds that all satisfying films have one cohesive force which holds the whole in shape. The formless-seeming Chaplin comedies, like The Gold Rush, are unified by the "character" of Chaplin: the film is a theme on that character alone. The comedies of Harold Lloyd on the other hand are unified by a gradually accelerated pace: they begin slowly, to end in a riot of fast movement, and it is this, not the rather colourless personality of Lloyd (who functions largely as a metronome) which gives his pictures their peculiar form. I admit that in College Days a touch of pathos in the comedian gave the typically mechanical Lloyd a tinge of Chaplinism: but his picture was still a theme on accelerated motion.[2] Other pictures again, Abraham Lincoln, The Lady, So Big, A Lost Lady and Stella Dallas, take the shape of biography, all the incidents being strung on a life-story. Germany has often used the triptych form, not an ideal method, but one which held the three parts of Destiny and Waxworks together. Pictures expressive of a mood, like The Street, have a better shape. The Last Laugh was the development of character, in two contrasted aspects—jocose pride and baffled humiliation, and was further held together by unity of place; the theme being life in an hotel as well as the emotions of an ageing workman. The worst possible unity is a common one: a false emotional crisis or conflict such as one gets in the innumerable American pictures with heroines who have pasts, or are played some rough trick by circumstances and are too spiritless to fight it. The real raison d'être of these pictures is that they give a female star plenty of opportunity for appearing on the screen, and whether she is taking the place of her fallen twin-sister, or engaged in secret business which enrages her husband, but is in reality innocence itself, or does unaccountable things to bring happiness to her little daughter, the picture sags and oozes beyond anything that can be called true form.

The unity of space is more often kept in films than one notices: the action often takes place about one building though not in one room of it. Yet as the camera can catch the building from all sides so that the eye can grasp its identity the effect is of unity. Even the action being confined to one village or street may amount to the same thing if the audience is allowed to grasp the continuity of space over which the action takes place. It is not a convention to be respected overmuch, however. Contrasts of land and water, contrasts of town and country, of open air and indoors, are useful not only to refresh and divert the eyes and to give an impression that the action really takes place in the everyday world we know, but even, too, in bringing out light and shade in character. A good example of this was in *He Who Gets Slapped*, not a first-rate picture, except for one scene, where the hero and heroine steal away from the circus to the woods one spring day and conduct their courtship under the fluttering sun-riddled leaves. The contrast with the sawdust of the circus life was reflected in the changed demeanour of the lovers, much more natural and much shyer under the trees than among their associates and in their daily haunts.

Another trick was tried in this picture: that of unifying it by the repeated interpolation of a symbolical clown, on the lines, of course, of Griffith's cradle-rocking woman in *Intolerance*, and repeated again in a smartly made but silly piece, *Time, the Comedian*. In *Intolerance* it was justified because it held together vastly different elements, but there was no use for it in *He Who Gets Slapped* or the other picture. It is when film producers start being arty that the worst happens, and this is true of German and American producers alike. The less the magnates of films talk of art the better; the critics hold a brief to do all the art-talk necessary about the cinema.

[From *Let's Go to the Pictures* (London: Chatto & Windus, 1926), pp. 37–49, excerpted.]

Film—Its Basic Structure (1935)
Irene Nicholson

It constantly happens that the technique of the moment is confused with a whole art medium, and exterior traditions are condemned because they do not conform to fashion. This has happened in the film today; and ironically the Russian montage theory, which grew out of a necessity to "get across" a few elemental concepts to varied and often uneducated audiences, has, outside Russia, become a "cut for the cut's sake" dilettantism.[1] The achievements of the Russians lead us to assume that the whole of cinema can be contained in this theory, or in that part of it which is based on the assumption that visual shot + visual shot = abstract concept. While we have certainly forgotten, if we ever knew, that film is many things beside an art. It is a whole new means of communication between people.

Film is a new means of education, of propaganda, of recording events and processes, of entertainment and of the perpetuation of experience (art). Each use must evolve its own technique; but for many reasons, principally economic, the director's purpose often remains obscure. It is therefore one of the film critic's most difficult tasks to discover this purpose and to find within the film itself his standards of criticism. Imposed standards are simply useless.

For non-aesthetic ends it is sufficient for the directors and critics to explore the possibilities of technical innovations as they arrive. For aesthetic ends it is important, since art always piles tradition upon tradition, that the first bricks should be laid on the right foundation. The essential basis of film must be discovered: what is film that other media are not?

Film is a new synthesis of dimensions—height, breadth and time.*

The capabilities of every art are determined primarily by its dimensions and only secondarily by its material and tools. The arts existing before the film may be divided into groups, each under a general common aesthetic, as follows:—

Plane surface—drawing, painting, etching, carpet weaving etc. Concerned with the discovery of a permanent reality underlying transitory nature, a discovery which is completely possible in two dimensions only, since a series of views of an object presents to the senses a series of realities, related but not identical.

Spatial—architecture, sculpture, pottery, landscape gardening etc. Arising from the desire to inscribe (architecture) and describe (sculpture) the infinite and illimitable qualities of space. In this connection it may be noted how space forces itself as an active material upon the sculptor or architect. The draughtsman seems (though only to the superficial observer) to consider the paint or pencil alone, whereas space to the architect and sculptor is necessarily as plastic as stone.

Life dimensions (space with direction in time)—ritual, ballet, sport etc. The ordering of muscular reaction to external facts and internal emotions.

Temporal—music, poetry, novel etc. The architectonics of time—necessity to fix the infinite quality of time, to inscribe it (rhythm) and describe it (pitch, tone and image). A philosophy of metamorphosis, within limits conceivable by the human mind (literature) and the intuition (music). Note that in poetry, and rhythmic literature generally, mind and intuition are in varying degrees fused.

These groups require fuller definition, but they are given here simply to show how the dimensions of an art absolutely determine its ideal content, whereas its materials only modify this content in course of presentation.

Film may now be considered as a synthesis of plane and temporal art. The photographic film has a sufficiently sensory illusion of space (shadows presuppose three dimensions) to relate it to the aesthetics also of space, but this illusion must be considered only as one of many possible modifications of film by specific materials and tools, and not as an essential of the medium. The true ideal content of the

---

* Fairthorne notes, in his article in this issue, that film may be used as a four dimensional tracing paper—but the fourth dimension is created by an illusion only. Suppositions such as these—let x = any given quantity, let a perspective line = the dimension of depth, let 1" = 1 mile, are allowable in all non-artistic communication for the sake of brevity and to reduce to symbols the cumbersome materials of life. But it is the very essence of art that the presentation is itself the idea, and imagination as the mathematician knows it does not exist. To contemplate art it is necessary to have sufficient imagination to negate one's own and accept another's, an act of which most people are more or less incapable, their own imaginations being taught and therefore rigid. It is easier to imagine X as any given quantity, a taught feat analogous to reading the alphabet, than to imagine a bowl of sunflowers as Van Gogh imagined one, which is a "seeing into" (as distinct from a "looking at") a simple enough act but one for which the speed of contemporary life allows no time.

cinema has yet to be analysed. But first it must be stressed that the camera, the celluloid base, the method of projection, are no more than the mechanics which have made this new synthesis for the first time possible. When film is defined by its bare essentials then all technical innovations will either be easily absorbed in its aesthetic or will be manifestly not film at all but simply a new means of giving shape to some other art. Colour will belong to the former,* stereoscopy to the latter class; for the colour film will bear the same relationship to the monochrome film as crayon to pencil drawing, whereas stereoscopy will be not film, but a new and multiple theatre.

The film as we know it today is a very small thing. Apart from a few cartoons (and an occasional experiment like *Night on the Bare Mountain*) only one of its surface media—the photographic—has been explored.† While within the photographic only one technique—that of the Russian montage school—has even approached perfection. It is not to be wondered at, therefore, that this lonely off spring of contemporary cinema, a technique (of cutting) within a technique (of photography) within an aesthetic (of height, breadth and time) which is itself only the artistic use of this new method of communication, should so often be confused with the whole medium.

It is time we took our eyes off the branch and attempted to explore the wood. Montage is important to us because it is the contemporary technique [of] film, as free verse is the contemporary technique of poetry. But blank verse did, it must be admitted, achieve a little; and no doubt there will be other rhythms in future. Nor must we forget that words and film are used for other things but art.

Most important of all, we must remember that form exists in art as the outward, communicable expression of an intuition—the perpetuation of an experience which would otherwise die in the mind that conceived it. Without intuition there is no reason why any shape should be thus and thus; without it we may as well cease at once to talk of dimensions, montage, photography and every other part of the film's outward paraphernalia; we may as well scrap the cinema houses and their degenerate audiences (who are there only to look for synthetic sensation or, on the other hand, to perform intellectual gymnastics) and get down once more to the business of living.

But so long as there are such films being made as *Dawn to Dawn* and *The Song of Ceylon* (which attains an almost mystic insight into the life of a people), we believe there is hope for the film.

[*Film Art* (London) 2, Autumn 1935, pp. 54–6.]

---

* It is worth noting, however, that sculptors have, for the most part, found that colour confuses the simple relationship of planes and shadows, two essentials of the photographic film in which colour becomes, therefore, an almost certain redundancy.

† See article by Leonard Hacker in this issue. At a recent presentation of a G.P.O. experiment in colour, by Len Lye, it was announced that no camera had been used in its making; whereupon the audience shrieked with ridiculous laughter.

Light * Form * Movement * Sound (1941)
Mary Ellen Bute

The Absolute Film is not a new subject. It is concerned with an art which has had as logical [a] development as other arts, perhaps slowly but naturally.

This art is the interrelation of the light, form, movement and sound—combined and projected to stimulate an aesthetic idea. It is unassociated with ideas of religion, literature, ethics or decoration. Here light, form and sound are in dynamic balance with kinetic space relations.

The Absolute Film addresses the eye and the ear. Other motion pictures, although making use of the sensations of sight and sound, address not the eye and the ear but the intellect. For example, in realistic films, the onlooker is expected to enjoy the clever imitation of nature—to be deceived into thinking the living prototype is before him. Whereas the Absolute Film stimulates our visual and aural senses directly with color, form, rhythm and sound. In realistic films, the medium is subordinate to story, symbol or representation. We view an Absolute Film as a stimulant by its own inherent powers of sensation, without the encumbrance of literary meaning, photographic imitation, or symbolism. Our enjoyment of an Absolute Film depends solely on the effect it produces; whereas, in viewing a realistic film, the resultant sensation is based on the mental image evoked.

Cinematographers, painters and musicians find a common enthusiasm in the Absolute Film. Through using the motion picture camera creatively, cameramen find a seemingly endless source of new possibilities and means of expression undreamed of while the camera was confined to use merely as a recording device. But we must turn back to painters and musicians to find the ideas which probably motivated the Absolute Film into a state of being.

Work in the field of the Absolute Film is accelerating both here and abroad. The foundations for it were laid years ago and it was more recently anticipated by Cézanne and his followers with whom we have an abstract art of painting taking form.[1] Cézanne used the relationships between color and form, discarding the former mixture of localized light and shade. By stressing relationship, he lifted color from imitating objective nature to producing a visual sensation in itself. His paintings of still-lifes: apples and tablecloth, are not conceived in a spirit of objective representation; they are organized groups of forms having relationships, balanced proportions and visual associations. His use of color on a static surface reaches a point where the next step demanded an introduction of time sequence and a richer textural range.

The Cubists tried to produce on a static surface a sensation to the eye, analogous to the sensation of sound to the ear. That is, by the device of presenting simultaneously within the visual field the combined aspects of the same object viewed from many different angles or at different intervals. They tried to organize forms distantly related to familiar objects to convey subjective emotions aroused by contemplation of an objective world.

Fig. 2.4 Photograph of Mary Ellen Bute with one of her electronic machines (1954).

The element of music appears in the painting of Kandinsky.[2] He painted abstract compositions based on an arbitrary chromatic scales of senses.

The word color occurs often in the writing of Wagner.[3] In the "Reminis of Amber" [sic] (1871) he writes: "Amber made his music reproduce each contrast, every blend in contours and color—we might almost fancy we had actual music paintings."

There is simply no end to the examples which we might cite. Some musicians have gone on record as having color associations with specific instruments.

These experiments by both musicians and painters, men of wide experience with their primary art material, have pushed this means of combining the two mediums up into our consciousness. This new medium of expression is the Absolute Film. Here the artist creates a world of color, form, movement and sound in which the elements are in a state of controllable flux, the two materials (visual and aural) being subject to any conceivable interrelation and modification.

[*Design* (Indianapolis) 42:8, April 1941, p. 25.]

From Sentiment to Line[1] (1927)
Germaine Dulac

Rivarol has said: "When you can see sense twenty-four hours before the rest of humanity, you are judged to have lost your senses for those hours."[2]

When the idea of abstract cinema is put before the majority of the public, and even before many intellectuals and professional filmmakers, it is received with scepticism, if not downright hostility; this new Art—whose expression comprises the visual capture of pure movement beyond existing aesthetics—may be permitted to evolve, providing that in its striving for perfection it does not overstep the formal boundaries of tradition that have already enclosed it.

But suddenly dedicated filmmakers from around the globe, without contact or discussion, isolated in the silent thoughts and intuitions of identical lines of research, have converged at the same frontier. "Utopia!" will cry the host of those whose judgements come to a stop precisely at the limits of well-established structures. "Truth!" will reply the theorists who see in everything but an ephemeral stage of transformation.

When one brain sprouts a new concept, it is a dream, and yet the seed of progress. But when several minds conceive of a similar inspiration, a nucleus is created and, from that, a reality.

Abstract or "integral" cinema should therefore be subject neither to doubt nor disdain since, latent within the constructive energy of some, and in the already significant proclamations of others, it exists by virtue of this very fact. Conceived, welcomed, and already concretely formulated in several works, it has emerged from a limbo of nebulous theories into the material domain of expression. Embryonic, certainly, but tangible, it will mechanically assert itself via the rising pressure animating all living principles, this offspring of collective instinct.

The opinion of this minority may not prevail immediately, but should be recognized as a germinating truth, an anticipated ideal of the future.

I don't mean to say that "integral cinema"—whose expression comes through visual rhythms materializing in forms divested of all literal meaning—should be the "only cinema" but merely that "integral cinema" is the *very essence of cinema* considered in its broadest sense: its inner reason for being, its direct manifestation, independent of the dialectics and plasticity of the other arts.

It was by means of a slow evolution, based in experience, that I first arrived at the concept of the visual symphony, and then at the stronger, more synthetic concept of "integral cinema," music of the eye.

Like others, I used to hold that creations for the screen should stem from the development of an action, a feeling—through the mirage of capturing direct or reconstituted life—of one or many human faces and their emotive qualities issuing from the selective juxtaposition of animated images whose intrinsic and successive mobility led to a result more intellectual than physical.

Movement, considered in and of itself, in its dynamic force and diverse measured rhythms, did not yet seem to me a "perceptible element" worthy of presentation on its own.

But soon it became evident to me that the expressive quality of a face lay less in the attitude of its features themselves than in the mathematical duration of the reactions they registered. In other words, the full meaning of a muscle tensed or contorted in shock lay in the long or short measure of the movement performed.

Since the shrinking or extending motion of a physiognomic muscle can evoke abstract thought, without the whole face needing to move, wouldn't visual drama depend on the intervening rhythm in the development of the movement? A hand placed on another hand. Movement. Dramatic line analogous to a geometric line connecting one point to another. *Action*. But, should this hand enact its gesture quickly or slowly, *the rhythm gives the movement its inner meaning*. Fear, doubt, spontaneity, firmness, love, hate. Diverse rhythms in the same movement. Let us consider cinematically the various stages of germination of a wheat grain buried in the earth. On the same plane we have a view of pure movement which unfolds according to the continuous logic of its dynamic force and whose rhythms, inspired by the difficulties of integral development, will mingle the sentimental and suggestive with the material theme.

The grain swells, pushing aside earth particles. In height and in depth it traces its path. Here its roots grow longer, branch out, cling tenuously; there the stalk rises hungrily for air and light in an instinctive yearning. The upright stem lunges hopelessly for the sun, stretches wildly towards it; the roots establish themselves, the ear reaches maturity. The movement changes course. The era of verticals is over. Movement opens onto other directions. Should an outside influence hinder this happy blossoming, should the stem deprived of sun seek its warm and regenerative source in vain, the plant's anguish will be expressed through halting rhythms, changing the movement's significance. Roots and stalk create harmonies. The movement and its rhythms, already purified in form, determine the emotion, *the purely visual emotion*.

Flowers or leaves. Growth, fullness of life, death. Anxiety, joy, sorrow. Flowers and leaves disappear. The spirit of movement and rhythm alone remain.

Should a muscle play across a face, should a hand place itself on another, should a plant grow, drawn to the sun, or crystals augment, should an animal cell evolve, we find at the source of these mechanical manifestations of movement a perceptible and suggestive impulse—the life force—expressed and communicated in rhythm. Whence emotion.

From plants and minerals, lines, volumes, and less precise forms right through to integral cinema is but a short step because only movement and its rhythms create feelings and sensations. When a spiralling circle whirls through space and disappears, as though thrown beyond our range of vision by the force and strength of its movement, we create a sensitive impression if the rhythms of speed are coordinated by a clearly defined inspiration.

The concept of emotion is not exclusively tied to the evocation of precise actions, but to every expression which affects human beings in the duality of their physical and moral life.

If, to better please the public, cinema should occupy itself with telling stories, with glorifying events and inventing others, I doubt that it will have achieved its aim. Cinema captures movement. Certainly a human being travelling from point to point is movement, as is the projection of that same being in time and space, and also his moral evolution. But already the blossoming of a wheat grain seems to us a more perfect and precise cineographic idea, *in that it gives greater significance to the mechanical movement of logical transformation*; by means of its unique vision such a film creates a new drama of the mind and senses.

Followers of "integral" cinema are considered Utopians. Why? For myself, I'm not arguing the need for emotional values in the conception of a work. The creative will should reach the public's understanding by means of a perceptible line which unites them. What I oppose is the narrow idea that people generally have of movement. Movement is not merely displacement, but also, and above all, evolution and transformation. So, why banish it from the screen in its purest form, which, perhaps better than others, hides within itself the secret of a new art form. Lines, volumes, surfaces, light, depicted in their constant metamorphosis are as capable of gripping us as the plant that grows, if we know how to organize them corresponding to the needs of our nerves and imagination. Because movement and rhythm remain in any case—even in the more material and significant embodiment—the intimate and unique essence of cineographic expression.

I conjure up a dancer! A woman? No. A leaping line of harmonious rhythms. I conjure up a luminous projection on voile. Precise matter! No. Fluid rhythms. Why deny the screen pleasures that movement procures at the theater. Harmony of line; harmony of light.

Lines, surfaces, volumes, evolving in the logic of their forms directly, without contrivance, stripped of their all-too-human meanings, the better to aspire toward abstraction and give more space to feelings and dreams—INTEGRAL CINEMA.

["Du sentiment à la ligne," *Schémas* 1 (Paris: Imprimateur Gutenberg), February 1927, pp. 26–31. Translated by Leslie Camhi.]

Workers and Film[1] (1928)
Lu Märten

One of modern society's fundamental contradictions was, and still is, that the vast masses of the working class have no part, or only a small part, in the culture of their time. This not only means that they do not share in the fruits of culture, but also that they are not adequately party to *knowledge* about it; nor do they participate in *surveying* it and its far-reaching associations. Since entering into political history around 1844, the working class has tried many times to overcome these challenges. Consider the older *worker education programs*: the group lessons, the libraries, the exhibitions, the popularization of many sciences, and lastly, the founding of theaters—and now consider what a small stratum has been reached by all of this. Consider also the fact that the practical value of all of these most noble, well-intentioned attempts has remained contingent upon the social conditions shaping workers' lives. Among these the factor of *time*, in and of itself, is still of fundamental importance. Time means not only time in the sense of leisure time. It also means—in terms of the *opportunity to receive and to absorb information*—distance from the particular educational facilities, and all of the associated preparations, among other things. The most essential conveyor of the cultural values in question has been the *word*, verbal documentation through lectures or books. But as far-reaching as this means of communication essentially is—as much as it can accomplish in regard to a certain kind of knowledge—faced with the multiplicity of *phenomena* in culture as a whole, lectures can still only cover certain aspects or topics. Plus, the number of books from various subject areas that can relate these phenomena to us is limitless. Whether one is striving to learn in detail about something very specific, or about the grand scheme of things; whether one is trying to grasp the fundamental principles of economy, history, philosophy, technology, or the sciences; it all requires, even for the layman, a kind of formal study. It is quite understandable, therefore, that only a few workers can achieve this type of learning, and this particular kind of effort. When the working class finally created theaters by itself and for itself, these became an important means of exposure to fiction, plays, and concerts. Thanks especially to peripheral factors, cheap tickets above all else, it became a medium accessible to many.[2]

But can it be a means to transmit culture, to the extent that our definition of culture demands? Under this collective term we include more than certain arts and specific kinds of intellectual concepts; we understand the term "culture" to encompass the technical and material evolution from which—as in radio and film today—we have witnessed the growth of important intellectual institutions. We also understand it to mean the past values that help us to make sense of the ideas of the past, as well as those of the present, which make many current events comprehensible. We not only understand it to mean the evolution and essence of our culture and of modern cultures, but also those of foreign peoples. Finally, we not only understand it to include things and ideas engendered through, and originating from, human labor, but also those generated by nature and its forces. Our discovery of them and our *way* of discovering and using them are all part of human knowledge. Our history and our labor are part of culture. Hence, we understand culture to mean the *results* and *interrelationships* of developments up until now, as well as the *contradictions and problems* inherent in all of these developments.

Let us take as our foundation this approximate survey of a truly gigantic subject, which has for decades only gained in richness and complexity as well as in contradictions of all kinds. Looking from this vantage point at what have so far been the workers' only *means* of gaining access to all these things, we almost have to despair about the chances of success (and would even if the factors of time and money, i.e. the living situation of the worker, had been completely different). Many of you probably know what Marx has proven about history: a decisive demand for time could never be met until the appropriate means or tools for doing so had been perfected. And so, for example, the numerous machines invented over the course of almost three centuries did not bring about revolution in the entire basis of production. Instead, it was achieved by the invention of the steam engine as the driving force for all the others. In terms of demands made by workers with regard to culture and knowledge, I believe that one should not view film today as a medium rendering all former efforts useless. Rather, this medium will enable those efforts to achieve their actual aims. The strong interest the working class is taking in film—the interest of a more conscious class as well as that of any human hungry for knowledge and life—might contain the germ for this still distant, but nevertheless verifiable, fact.

Because what exactly is film? And what can it accomplish? Film is an instrument for the transmission of pictures. Its significance, and hence its effectiveness, are dependent on the image. But this brand of image possesses new dimensions: expansion into depths, heights, and surfaces, like the "old" picture. And a similar but new dimension—that of motion. Film is able to capture even those things and movements that are invisible to our normal vision, for the camera is armed with slow motion and micro-vision. Therefore this image-apparatus relates to the simple miniatures of the old days, and to past photography in the way that a state-of-the-art machine relates to a simple tool. And yet this highly developed image-apparatus is so easily transportable, so flexible, too, that it is, in its places of its presentation, itself like a simple tool. This physical mobility of film, as well as its accessibility, distinguish it from all other, older cultural forms. Suddenly, spontaneously, without preparations of any kind, we can go—workers can go—to the movies.

The true, inner essence of film is the moving image. That alone already determines its superiority in relation to older image options. This is why we can demand from it the broad dissemination of culture. Primitive peoples were able to communicate by way of simple, archaic drawings. Higher and highly developed societies developed writing out of drawings. Thus writing and language became the most perfect means for the communication and representation of things and thoughts. Consider that in spite of the invention of printing, and all the developments in circulation and exchange, the worker's access to writing is still impeded; in all circumstances a picture makes the conceptualization of a given thing *easier*. While the image in and of itself cannot replace the word, the *moving* image in its new, dynamic form—the image that captures every object—might do so.

We may consider whether its abilities are limitless in this capacity. And in the course of this consideration, we might be able to clear up the false notion held abroad today by those who consider film to be a form of theater with slightly altered technical foundations. Take any given process with which you want to familiarize yourself, such as, for example, the life of a plant from sprouting to withering. A book—its words and language—can describe this process; but we do not really get a vivid impression, because we are confronted here with invisible movements. Film can show these invisible movements through time exposure, whether the action is unfolding in the air, on the bottom of the ocean, or in foreign regions.

Until now no medium has been able to offer this to us. So far, the microscopic results have been confined to the workshops of the scientists. And if they made it into books, there again they could only serve to prove isolated points of a process, as opposed to its overarching context. Choose (since I do have time to cite examples) any subject matter from the cultural realm, in order to consider whether it could be represented by film. In what film offers *today*, we can only catch glimpses of its actual cultural tasks. The so-called "culture films" (*Kulturfilme*), which are, with respect to subject matter and images, already often of good quality, are but temporary engagements within regular programming, and are therefore restricted in their scope, and random in their topics.[3]

But it is not what film offers today that justifies our interest and our demands; they are justified by what it is suited to offer. Working class friends of mine have often commented on the nonsense usually offered by cinema, and I have heard them mock those who impulsively run to the movies—just like that—with neither standards nor a critical attitude. But the effect of bad film on all these people who simply enjoy going to the movies is but one of the motivations for the intensification of our struggle over, as well as our investigation into, the value of the film-object. It is proven that these classes are affected by the appeal of the image and the way pictures make it easier to grasp many things. The ease with which we can reach people via pictures, though, encourages us to conceive of film projects which might make even more complicated intellectual notions more comprehensible through images, the more so since nowadays sound has been added to the visuals. It is true that the movie industry remains convinced it can impose upon its audience a two-hour movie that is for the most part bad or trivial. While, on the other hand, it cannot offer a two-hour-long non-fictional or truly cultural film (a form which does not really exist yet anyway, except for a couple of expedition films). Here, the demands and the positive, concrete critique of the workers, who are by far the largest consumer group when it comes to film, should be deployed with much more force than has been done until now. The mania for feature films has grown stronger with the advent of sound, but their overall quality has not improved.

Why is that? Because film is mainly regarded as a reproductive medium and simply as theater, which veils its original, specific nature. Of course, film is able to reproduce everything that has been treated earlier in fiction and art. And it does this, for one, because it is impossible, and maybe never will be possible, to create as many original feature films as there are possibilities for representation. Connected with this is the fact that film still has to search for subject matter, although a vast sum of elemental subjects and cultural value lies right under its nose. The more conscious working class is interested in the feature film, but only when its demands and interests are linked to feature films that correspond to its ideology.

At this point we can clarify the nature of film versus that of theater. Even an ideological workers' film can be a good film if it is created in accordance with the nature of film—if its subject matter corresponds to the essential laws of film. Not all narratives reflecting aspects of the life and struggle of the working class require film. But just as contemporary narratives deal ever more emphatically with mass-events, mass-identity, and [mass] experience—and since the backdrop for such events is of an elemental nature (i.e. it demands oceans, continents, vast spatial backgrounds in general, since these are part of the design and the effect of the whole to a monumental extent)—here the film medium is superior to theater. Think for a moment now about the design and effect of Potemkin, one of the best, and—I would hazard—best known of all films. The theater could never render it in this form, since it is not just the sets nor the highest accomplishments of the actors that determine its impact. Only by encapsulating all its essential elements, and, yes, even their rhythm, was it able to transform a revolutionary episode into a work of symbolic dimensions. And all that completely without sound.

On the other hand, through its own means of production, the theater allows other essential qualities of the worker's life and struggle to be portrayed effectively, as for example in Cyankali.[4] This statement holds true especially when language is required to make certain designs and tendencies comprehensible. Hence, thus far, film has gained no ground on theater when more intimate settings and individual performances have been required. The ideological topic of the workers can only be treated perfectly in film if its subject matter is filmic in nature—as in, for example, the tremendous epic and drama of the world war, which could only be portrayed through film. It is thus evident, even within the feature film, within the feature film genre, that film's superiority is determined precisely by its ability to grasp the elemental and the original, and thereby, the force of reality itself. But in the current mass production of feature films, film is gambling away these—its wonderful dimensions—in order to make banalities appealing.

I hope you will not misunderstand this delimitation and critique of the issue of film. In contrast to everything that deserves to be called a non-fictional [Sachfilm], or true culture film [Kulturfilm], feature films dominate the movie schedules today. Nevertheless, this should not impede our recognition of the true significance of film. Only this certain recognition can reveal the great importance film holds for the workers' demands and duties, even those that are not yet evident. This discussion does not even approach the legitimacy of light-hearted and funny, animated pictures either. Animation film in particular has developed out of the technology of film. It offers us light entertainment in a silly and non-committal manner, and it is quite possible that one day it could be used to treat satirical and other subject matter. But the vast majority of feature films have attained dominance not by virtue of filmic qualities, but by virtue of the performance of the actors. Apart from a few serious crime stories, the comedy film rules these days. Does this not demonstrate the embarrassing incompetence of the film industry, which, in spite of tremendous expenditure on labor, amenities, and energy for feature films, is never, or hardly ever, capable of producing anything remarkable in this realm? This flaw is not attributable to the difficulties of portraying the unique world and ideology of workers. It is rooted more deeply in the fact that a feature film, a good feature film, can be no more mass-produced than a theater play; it can be just as much a quality work as any piece of literary writing; and this type of film is but one of cinema's functions, not its only one, and not its most essential. The workers' demands and criticism on this point should be much more direct than has been the case up until now.[*]

Music, which has been dragged into cinema in abundance via the sound apparatus, also has nothing to do with the essence of film—it does not serve to make

---

[*] The preceding paragraph appears on a separate page at the end of the account. A note indicates that its insertion was intended here.

film complete. It is simply that here, as in radio, very good vocal and other musical achievements are being made accessible to a broader audience. In silent films, music's role was to accompany and emphasize, because music is movement—and the moving image could find its rhythm. But the best music cannot rescue a bad film. Hence, music is never in and of itself a compliment to the film. The soundtrack, however, as word and sound, does expand the qualitative expectations of the feature film and is important, above all, with respect to the intended cultural mission. As a means of presenting natural sounds, however, sound in film gains ever greater importance when its succeeds through radio-technical means to capture inaudible noises for us.

All of this should only enrich and strengthen the conception of film as one of the most wonderful tools for the final transmission of culture according to the sensibility and aspirations of the working class. Therefore, the struggle for the good film is, on the part of the workers as well as elsewhere, the struggle for film itself.

["Arbeiter und Film" [1928], from Formen für den Alltag: Schriften, Aufsätze, Vorträge, ed. Rainard May (Dresden: Verlag der Kunst, 1982). Translated by Patti Duquette, with the assistance of Christine Haas and Sarah Hall.]

Truth in Art in America (1923)
J. Cogdell

First, what is Art? It is a mirror that reflects the world of thought and action colored by the individual character of the artist who holds the mirror. Truth is necessary to Art since that which is Art must have a universal appeal, and only the verities are universal. Art has four different methods of expressing itself; literarily (poetry and prose), pictorially (engraving, carving, painting, sculpture), musically (voice, instrumental), dramatically (tragedy, comedy), each division and sub-division serving varying sets of senses in an effort to express the phenomena of life.

THE QUALITIES OF AN ARTIST

On their positive side the Arts help to clarify and intensify Life, thereby emphasizing the experience of existence. On their negative side they are a means of balance and expression to artist and public alike. In essence, it may be said, they are not only radically individualistic but radically social as well: all the "art for art's sake" to the contrary. The artist differs from other men in the strength of his emotions. The average man has only sufficient energy to steer his own craft: the artist manages his own craft with enough remaining energy to steer the world besides. Two, seemingly opposed, fundamental human qualities drive him forward to concrete expression: a strong feeling of individual power and a desire to exhibit this power: and a strong feeling of insufficiency and a desire for security: both in their formal result are Social since they require participation of others for proper demonstration. The artists in general have repudiated the label of

"Social" upon Art—understanding in its limited sense to mean the morals of their particular epoch. But a work of art may be immoral in its period and essentially social in its reach. In France, Ro[u]sseau was "immoral" religiously and politically during his lifetime, ostracized and exiled for his opinions, though these opinions formed the morals of the succeeding epoch. The artist is obsessed by the Perfect and the Absolute, and therein is Social. Always restless under any given form of society because of its clumsy inadequacy he is always the progressive pioneer of his time, in seeking a better way. He is the Pathfinder and should be allowed to stride unshackled in his search. But in every age there are always those who are comfortable and wish to maintain their comfort at any cost since they are usually also selfish, for comfort does not sharpen the acuteness of pity. And these Comfortable Ones, possessed of economic power, either try to seduce the artist by gifts into celebrating the Comfortable, or failing, pile obstacles in his path to discourage him. The more this discouragement succeeds the blacker is the night in which that particular civilisation stumbles. The Middle Ages in Europe are a terrible example of the suppression of artistic liberty. Life does not stand still and the civilisation that refuses to see itself in the mirror of artistic truth retrogresses. The thwarted genius of the Middle Ages turned his energy from love of the Perfect into hate and capricious destruction of all life. The People having no healthy expression of their instincts secretly indulged themselves in Witches' Sabboths [sic], and those who had not even this outlet became mad or epileptic. That liberty, civic health, progress, and art are closely related is obvious.

"OLD MAIDS" MAKE ART BACKWARD

It may be said that America is still restrained by the vestiges of the Middle Ages. The Puritans brought with them here, to our misfortune, the narrow cramping morals of the Middle Ages, the inquisitive methods of the church from which they had revolted, and more bigotry and ignorance of nature than the Church of Rome ever possessed, lacking even a Witches' Sabboth. Modern America still labors under these taboos. Moral prohibition falls most directly and heavily upon the feminine sex here, then rebounds onto the artist and the general public. The part of our populace who have the time and money to cultivate themselves, and in so doing encourage or restrict Art we find are mostly women: middle-aged wives and spinsters are our "Leisure Class." Perhaps this is the reason Art is considered effeminate in America. These women, forced by custom to suppress their natural instincts are, because of their very respectability, almost without exception neurotic, and in turn relentlessly force their unnatural taboos upon Art, in consequence soldering fast the door by which they, and more agreeably their children of the next generation, might escape into a healthier existence. Thus they perpetrate their weakness. Our literature, painting, drama, and shadow stage are censored with fanatic intolerance by the male sex brought up on the fears of these neurotic mothers. That most magnificent and powerful instinct, the Reproductive urge, must walk among us masked and only in the laboratory or saloon may it ever be lifted with impunity, in the one for sterilization, in the other for brutalization. The Artist whose business it is to beautify life for Mankind, by purifying its instincts with palatable truth and glorifying them with passion, must keep his hands off.

THE CURSE OF CENSORSHIP

In Literature we find abortive censorship. For passages describing and interpreting everyday facts of life mailing privileges are denied and the authors even face imprisonment. Take Theodore Dr[ei]ser's *Genius*, suppressed mainly because it describes the phenomenon of the male's interest in the well-formed limbs of the female, although this fact supplies the material for one-half of our vaudeville jokes, and is substantiated by every "Girl Show" in the country, where the only possible attraction is supplied by the exposed limbs of the chorus.[1] But *that* is a different matter; our average business man who, knowing nothing of culture and art despises and ignores them—is interested here, so for his delectation the bars are let down. Besides, too, a chorus in no way disputes the prevailing moral standard, in fact affirms it: for what average wife or business man does not regard the chorus girl as on the "other side of the line"? Also we admit the sale of foreign masters who have already achieved great reputations, and who, like Rabelais and Boccaccio, or moderns like Anatole France and Gabriel D'Annunzio, furnish us realistic descriptions of the most intimate human proclivities. These are permitted because otherwise we fear to be styled "boors" by Europe should we publicly refuse to admit literary masterpieces: but most of our libraries are "protected" from them by carrying the original and not the translation. That which has not yet attained the stamp of the mighty, but is nevertheless truthful and perhaps more vital to us, is forbidden, or sold secretly at exorbitant prices, making their reading a sort of Upper-Class vice: money here as elsewhere forming a class barrier. Putting such historical records as *The Worship of the Generative Powers* by Knight under the ban of secrecy is a dastard act of bigotry since the book effectually clears up many otherwise puzzling customs of today.[2] Psychoanalytic text books are sold at such prices that the public, who is in need of them, never see them. Only "Physicians" may purchase certain books, while if the public were permitted them the former might largely be dispensed with. Although we are thankful for the European masterpieces suffered us, we would prefer to hear what American artists have to say about the vital functions of life. M. Anatole France speaks for France but not for America. D'Annunzio strikes the Roman chord, but it is not the scale of America. What are the hopes, fears and desires of America, what has it to say on Love and Individualism, the two pivots of existence? But our corseted middle-aged purity squad cannot bear the undisguised mention of either. A remarkable book has lately been secretly (or "privately") published in America: only the very rich can afford the forty dollars for which it sells. But it is a book which every adult not only should be allowed but forced to read. Wealthy perverts will wallow in its frankness, although the book far from being amatory is a revolt against all sex. However, they will see only the details and their meaning will entirely escape them. The book was written by a well known American, the

Purity Squad cannot arraign the author of Ulysses but it can that of Fantazius Mallare, and so I believe, has already been the case.[3] The author's penetration into human instincts, the uncompromising strength of his style and his audacious self-assertion mark this book as a departure and a new beginning in American literature. For, though forced underground, its influence will be manifest sooner or later.

NUDE PAINTINGS

The plastic and pictorial arts are in the same dilemma as are the literary arts. The incoherency of "Modern Art" is something like revenge. What truth may not this scrawling confusion utter with no one the wiser? It is an unconscious effort at freedom comparable to hysterics, the result of an age of standardization and repression. A free age would not think in such terms. It is interesting psychologically and it is possible that fantastic and mystical subjects which do not lend themselves gracefully to the formal touch may now possess a medium. Our savage ancestors employed a similar method of symbolization of the "unutterables" which later evolved into orthography. Certainly if some of them are not pictures some indeed make very agreeable designs. The nude is allowed—properly removed—because it is traditional; describe the same nude in literature and you run a risk. "Why are our censors so afraid of the body?" one asks, "Because they fear themselves," says Freud. Now that we know that even the mental processes take place throughout the body and are not centered in the brain, what are we going to do?

HANDICAPS OF THE STAGE

The stage has much more to put up with. Drama, which should surge with the pulse of the people since it is more directly connected with them, limps along twenty to fifty years behind literature. The closer the Tree of Art grows to the People the faster fly the pruning scissors of the purity maniacs. It is amusing to note that the opera is permitted many of the "unconventionalities" in plot denied the speaking stage—but no one understands, so where's the harm?

The most radically worthwhile recent plays have been: The Circle, where for once the man who "breaks up" the home actually is not a villain at all but a delightful lover, and the heroine dares to do what the courageous woman always does; The First Fifty Years, showing what everyone knows to be the average lot of marriage these days; The Hairy Ape and The Fool, the one brutal and the other idealistic, but both powerfully dealing with present social conditions; Heartbreak House, the best thing Shaw has ever done; Kolb and Dill's Give and Take, inartistic and inaccurate, but appearing a sincere effort to solve the industrial problem; The Passion Flower, revealing the jealous enmity between mother and daughter where the affection of a man is concerned, a general phenomenon; and The Emperor Jones, chiefly remarkable in that it is written about a Negro of virile masculinity and individualism, with the difficult role portrayed by a Negro.[4] The significance of this is sweeping; it opens up an entirely new field to literature and the stage. The tenor of The Emperor Jones is not flattering to the Negro race, but it is the necessary intermediary step.

The dramatic feeling of the Negro is sadly needed on the American stage. For years he has dominated the minstrel and comedy in spirit: he was even permitted to "Personally" make a fool of himself—as long as you can laugh at him he is harmless! The ability of Bert Williams was no challenge, but Mr. Gilpin challenges subtly behind the lines of his part.[5]

These, our most advanced dramas, are yet, philosophically speaking, far behind our literature, and are merely the recounting of what we all already know.

THE DECADENT MOVIES

Last is the youngest of the dramatic arts, the cinema, and the most starved for truth, at present exceptional in that it is the only known sphere of existence where virtue is always rewarded. It runs parallel with the newspapers in the dishonesty of its methods: likewise everything it touches comes out changed and cheapened. History and the most sacred literature is twisted to suit current propaganda. The tenth-rate scenario and magazine writers, who supply its plots, search frantically among the great masters for material that may serve them without condemning them; in the pursuit of swiping they are dexterous: nowhere else. Everything must have a happy ending (evidently they feel America needs encouragement), and but for the Bolsheviks, Germans, and Darker Races, this is the "best of all possible worlds"! The fabrication of the "Nationalization of Russian Women" although refuted by the United States Government, has, notwithstanding, been used several times, spreading this false idea among the Public who innocently but restlessly swallow all they are told. Miss Norma Talmadge lends her presence to the glorification of such falsehood.[6] One expected better things of her. Even the Ku Klux Klan unblushingly idealizes its absurdities and brutalities for public consumption. *Hungry Hearts*, for instance, whose vital significance dwells in its tragedy is given a happy ending: thereby converting it into a mere character and dialect study.[7] Or take *Tess of the Storm Country*, admirably acted by Miss Pickford; but what about all those "Tesses" who, lacking Miss Pickford's beauty, are unable to charm rich men into liberality? How many "Squatter's Villages" not possessing a Miss Pickford are permitted their poor existence against the wishes of a wealthy antagonist? These tales are untold. Even Omar Khayyam must be sacrificed: he who is magnificently pagan in spirit must be Christianized to agree with the idea that nothing could possibly be great that disagrees with popular religious notions. In fact, censorship, direct and indirect, has reduced the cinema to such puerilities in thought and plot, and such subterfuges in action, that even the average intelligence, in the habit of accepting everything, begins to criticize them. The foreign pictures brought in are so popular because of their greater integrity that they have seriously damaged the American product in its own field. The German company producing the series of pictures, among them *Deception*, was brought to America because of the popularity of these films, but there they produce *The Loves of Pharaoh*, which is a dismal failure: in fact, absurd in the extreme.[8] Oh, the spectacles are magnificent, much money was spent upon them, more than on the European productions: but remark its philosophy?—and the "Loves," where are the "Loves"? There weren't any! No, that would be *a-little-bit-riské*! But then, in titles more liberty is allowed: that endangers nothing and bait is necessary, and the public doesn't know the difference until after its money is spent. *A little piece of American hypocritical meanness was observed in the character of the Ethiopian King and his daughter: they were intentionally made ridiculous.* In Cabiria, the Italian picture, there is a noticeable difference: the two main male parts are Ethiopians and are portrayed with all the strength and pride of Ethiopia. But what can you expect when even the Sheik must be half-English: and the "Young Rajah" half-"European," although the Arabs and Hindus are of Caucasian stock. But their color is darker and here is the prick! Credit must be given Mr. Valentino for bringing passion into cinema love: even the censors cannot take the feeling of this away from his pictures. Anglo-Saxons are ashamed of emotion: proper young business men love—but with caution and economy! Much to their chagrin it has been found that American women prefer Valentino.

THE "DIVINITY OF JAZZ"

Only at Comedy may we gaze without becoming intellectually nauseated. Much is permitted the laugh that is denied the tear. The laugh ends with itself: the tear is a scorching reproach.

Music in America, because it speaks another language, is given license where the other Arts are denied truth. Our prohibited instincts riot disgustingly here like thirsty men in a desert oasis: we revel in "Jazz." This "lets off steam" but it deplorably cheapens our instincts and corrupts the true spirit of music. Jazz is essentially a capitalistic production, it steals its melodies from all sources, the Masters, the Negroes, the Orient, with naive greed and unconcern, then proceeds to ruin them. It is as noisy and rapacious as the system that creates it. (*Broadway jazz must not be confused with Negro Folk Music, the only real music America has yet produced.*)

Are we to remain a nation of "Peeping Toms" and "Jazz Jumpers"? We cannot suppress Nature: we can only pervert it. *Where is the Culture that our politicians tell us we must fight to save?* The Movies? The Newspapers? The Jazz? Art and Truth are outlawed. Would it not be far wiser and nobler to admit life as it is and then glorify it with our tenderness and passion?

[*The Messenger* (New York) 5:3, March 1923, pp. 634–6.]

A Universal Language (c. 1930)
Lillian Gish

The motion picture, by virtue of its intrinsic nature, is a species of amusing and informational Esperanto, and, potentially at least, a species of aesthetic Esperanto.[1] Of all the arts, if it may be classified as one, the motion picture has in it, perhaps more than any other, the resources of universality. Even a simple waltz by Johann

Strauss may remain alien and unassimilable to the musical ear of the Chinese; a Michelangelo fresco may fail to impress its significant beauty upon a Japanese or Hindu; a drama by Ibsen may remain completely unintelligible, even in competent translation, to a maharaja of India, just as Chinese music must ever remain strange, peculiar and incomprehensible to the Anglo-Saxon ear. But the motion picture art of Charlie Chaplin will inevitably make a Japanese laugh as heartily as a Dane.

The reason is simple. Pantomime is the aboriginal means of human communication and intercourse, and pictures bring to a child his first acquaintance with and understanding of the world about him. The motion picture, combining the two, is thus addressed to a common human understanding. It begins with the elementals of human perception and comprehension; it starts at the outset with the advantage of the fundamentals of human intercommunication and explicitness. It is for this reason that the moving picture has spread through the world and has been accepted far and wide in what has seemed an unbelievably short space of time.

The motion picture tells its stories directly, simply, quickly and elementally, not in words but in pictorial pantomime. To see is not only to believe; it is also in a measure to understand. In theatrical drama, seeing is closely allied with hearing, and hearing, in turn, with mental effort. In the motion picture, seeing is all—or at least nine-tenths of all.

This, of course, is the screen in its fundamental aspect. This is the motion picture simple and unsophisticated. This is the universal *engine* that is the cinema. The motion picture, plainly enough, in certain of its manifestations may remain largely vague and ambiguous to a people alien to the source of its imagination, preparation and making. But the motion picture in itself and in the aggregate is based upon materials of easy, common appreciation. Love, hate, desolation, despair, joy, ecstasy, defeat, triumph—these are universal emotions. Conveyed by words, as drama conveys them, they may offer difficulties to remote and various peoples. But conveyed by the movements of the human face and body, by smiles and tears, troubled brows and dejected shoulders, sparkling eyes and fluttering hands, they are immediately recognizable. A laugh or a sob is the same the world over. They need no words to explain them.

In another phase of the cinema, the so-called news-reel has already proved itself to be a form of journalistic Esperanto, just as the so-called educational moving picture has shown itself to be a form of informational Esperanto. The news-reel has brought to the far corners of the earth the life and daily activities of all nations and people. The educationals, as they are known, have acquainted the audiences of the world with various phenomena associated with invention, manufacture, discovery, ingenuity and enterprise peculiar to a certain country. The news-reel has informed every country of its neighbour, his leaders, his achievements, his troubles, his pleasures, his problems. It has spread a direct acquaintanceship with alien lands, peoples and customs to other lands. It has provided an international newspaper self-adapted to the understanding of all peoples, and a running commentary on contemporaneous history.

The motion picture is at once the common story-book, newspaper and text-book of the 20th century. In its loftier aspects, it may conceivably elude the comprehension of audiences remote from its birthplace. That is, when it abandons its more elemental nature and strives for isolation as an art form. But that is the fate of art, all art, wherever it be found. Art is for the few, unfortunately; the generality of people have difficulty in taking it into their understanding. Shakespeare and the Orient may remain strangers; Leonardo and Dostoievsky may find no sympathy and hospitality in the consciousness of half a dozen lands. But there is probably no land where the spectacle of soldiers marching off to war or a fat man being struck with a custard pie is not instantaneously hailed with understanding. It is in *elementary* excitements and humours such as these, together with the thousand and one others that they connote, that the motion picture, reaching constantly after higher things, finds the mainspring of its wide and comprehensive appeal. It deals for the most part with primitive instincts, primitive impulses, primitive human peace and alarm, happiness and ache, ambition and dream. These may be dressed in strange costumes and may be shown through strange peoples, but underneath they are the emotions and inspirations and trials of all the human race. The backgrounds may be unfamiliar, but the hearts that beat and struggle, triumph or fall, are the hearts of all mankind. And so the world laughs with Chaplin and Lloyd, cries with Seastrom and Murnau and Griffith, startles at the revelations of Eisenstein, gasps pleasurably at Fairbanks and Valentino, feels tenderness with Mary Pickford and warms to the homely lovableness of Wolheim and Beery.[2]

[Contribution to *The Theatre and Motion Pictures: A Selection of Articles from the New 14th Edition of the Encyclopedia Britannica* (New York and London: Encyclopaedia Britannica, 1929–33), pp. 33–34.]

Projector[1] (1927)
H.D.

Light takes new attribute
and yet his old
glory
enchants;
not this,
not this, they say,
lord as he was of the hieratic dance,
of poetry
and majesty
and pomp,
master of shrines and gateways
and of doors,
of markets
and the cross-road
and the street;

not this,
they say;
but we say otherwise
and greet
light
in new attribute,
insidious fire;
light reasserts
his power
reclaims the lost;
in a new blaze of splendour
calls the host
to reassemble
and to readjust
all severings
and differings of thought,
all strife and strident bickering
and rest;
O fair and blest,
he strides forth young and pitiful and strong,
a king of blazing splendour and of gold,
and all the evil
and the tyrannous wrong
that beauty suffered
finds its champion,
light
who is god
and song.

He left the place they built him
and the halls,
he strode so simply forth,
they knew him not;
no man deceived him,
no,
nor ever will,
with meagre counterfeit
of ancient rite,
he knows all hearts
and all imagining
of plot
and counterplot
and mimicry,
this measuring of beauty with a rod,

no formula
could hold him
and no threat
recall him
who is god.

Yet he returns,
O unrecorded grace,
over
and under
and through us
and about;
the stage is set now
for his mighty rays;
light,
light that batters gloom,
the Pythian
lifts up a fair head
in a lowly place,
he shows his splendour
in a little room;
he says to us,
be glad
and laugh,
be gay;
I have returned
though in an evil day
you crouched despairingly
who had no shrine;
we had no temple and no temple fire
for all these said
and mouthed
and said again;
beauty is an endighter
and is power
of city
and of soldiery
and might,
beauty is city
and the state
and dour duty,
beauty is this and this and this dull thing,
forgetting who was king.

Yet still he moves
alert,

invidious,
this serpent creeping
and this shaft of light,
his arrows slay
and still his foot-steps
dart
gold
in the market-place;
vision returns
and with new vision
fresh
hope
to the impotent;
tired feet that never knew a hill-slope
tread
fabulous mountain sides;
worn
dusty feet
sink in soft drift of pine
needles
and anodyne
of balm and fir and myrtle-trees
and cones
drift across weary brows
and the sea-foam
marks the sea-path
where no sea ever comes;
islands arise where never islands were,
crowned with the sacred palm
or odorous cedar;
waves sparkle and delight
the weary eyes
that never saw the sun fall in the sea
nor the bright Pleiads rise.

[*Close Up* (Territet, Switzerland), 1:1 July 1927, pp. 46–51.]

The Mask and the Movietone (1929)
H.D.

The problem arises (it has been dogging us for some time): is the good old-fashioned conventionalised cinema product a more vivid, a more vital, altogether in many ways a more inspiring production than his suave and sometimes over-subtelised offspring? Our hero with sombrero, our heroine with exactly set coiffure, each in himself, in herself a mask of himself or herself, one with sleek dutch-doll painted in black cap of piquante elf like mahogany coloured hair, another with radiant curls, so many dolls, are treasures—boy dolls in sombreros—are they to be discarded, are we going to be asked to discard them for another set of boxes, containing such intricate machinery, such suave sophistication of life that we wonder if we really want them? Do we want little ivory balls for instance, pretty as they are, fitting into ivory balls, and the intricate paraphernalia of meccano or jigsaw puzzle to tax our little minds to breaking?[1] Don't we really want what we know, what we see, what intellectually we can aptly "play" with? Don't we? Or do we? I mean do we really want to give up curls and painted-in dutch-doll fringes, and beautifully outlined eyes and eyelashes and doll-stuffed bodies (doing for instance trapeze turns just like real circus people) for something perhaps "better"? Do we really want to discard our little stage sets and all the appliances that we have grown so used to for something more like "real" life? Well, do we or don't we? Please answer me. I am at my wits' end. Do we or don't we want to scrap our old dolls? The problem reasserted itself with renewed force at a New Gallery demonstration of the Movietone.[2]

Here we have our little people. Here comes our heroine. Truly it is not the heroine exactly of our most, most vapid romances, of our most, most old box of dolls and paper-dolls but it is the sort of toy that we are used to, a doll, a better doll, a more highly specialised evolved creation but for all that a doll (Raquel Meller) steps forward.[3] It bows, it smiles, it is guaranteed to perform tricks that will shame our nursery favourites *but do we want it?*

The doll in question, a Spanish doll this time, done up in Castillian embroidery, not over exaggerated with suitable *décor* of operatic street scene and so on, steps out smiles pathetically, tragically, or with requisite pathos, familiar gestures but somehow sensitized, really our old bag of tricks. And then wonder of wonders, the doll actually lifts its eyes, it breathes, it speaks—it *speaks*. This is no mechanical voice off, it is the vision itself, the screen image actually singing with accuracy and acumen, with clear voice and beautiful intonation, singing and moving, moving and singing, voice accurately registering the slightest change of expression (Raquel Meller with her *Flor del Mar* and *La Tarde del Corpus*) each tiny fall and lift of note following raised eyebrow or curl of lip or dejection of drooping shoulder. Voice follows face, face follows voice, face and voice with all their subtle blending are accurately and mechanically welded. They are *welded*—that is the catch. The catch is that the excellent actress with all her beauty and her finished acting had a voice as beautifully finished as her screen image but it was (wasn't it?) *welded* to that image. Her voice and herself moving with so finished artistry were welded not (and this seemed some odd catastrophe) *wedded*. The projection of voice and the projection of image were each in itself perfect and ran together perfectly as one train on two rails but the rails somehow though functioning in perfect mechanical unison, remained a separate,—separate entities, fulfilling different mechanical requirements. It seemed to me, astonished as I was at both (beauty of face and

Fig. 2.5   Photograph of H.D. (Hilda Doolittle) in Egypt, 1923

mellow finish of song) that each in some diabolic fashion was bringing out, was understressing mechanical and artificial traits in the other. Each alone would have left us to our dreams. The two together proved too much. The screen image, a mask, a sort of doll or marionette was somehow mechanized and robbed of the thing behind the thing that has grown to matter so much to the picture adept. A doll, a sort of mask or marionette about which one could drape one's devotions, intellectually, almost visibly like the ardent Catholic with his image of madonna, became a sort of robot. Our old doll became replaced by a wonder-doll, singing, with musical insides, with strings that one may pull, with excellent wired joints. But can we whisper our devotion to this creature? Are we all beings of infinite and pitiful sentiment? I didn't really like my old screen image to be improved (I might almost say imposed) on. I didn't like my ghost-love to become so vibrantly incarnate. I didn't like to assert my intellect to cope with it any more than I should have liked Topsy (of the old days) suddenly to emerge with wired-in legs and arms and with sewed-on bonnet and really grown-up bead bag dangling (also sewed on) from one wrist. We want, don't we, our old treasures? Or do we want a lot of new toys, mechanical and utterly proficient?

O well, there it is. I know and see and admire. I do think it is wonderful to hear and see. "Speaks for Itself" reads the slogan on the folder. But do we want our toy dog to "speak for itself"? Do we really want our rag doll to stand up and utter? Don't we, like the pre-fifth peoples of Attica, of Crete, of the Cyclades treasure old superstitions (even the most advanced of us) and our early fantasies? Take away our crude upright pillar, take away our carved symbols of Demeter and our goat-herd chorus, said pre-fifth century Athenians and you rob us of our deity. Haven't we been just a little hurt and disappointed that our dolls have grown so perfect?

Well, that is for you to say and you to say and you to say. We each have an idea and a sentiment. We are all sentiment when it comes to discarding dolls for (it seems incredible) robots. Don't look so nice, and sing so nicely at the same time, I want to scream at Raquel Meller, for I seem to be about to be done out of something. She is doing everything. I want to help to add imagination to a mask, a half finished image, not have everything done for me. I can't help this show. I am completely out of it. This acting, singing, facial beauty is perfected. This screen projection is not a mask, it is a person, a personality. That is just it. Here is art, high art, but is it our own art? Isn't cinema art a matter (or hasn't it been) of inter-action? We have grown so used to our conventions, our intellectual censors have allowed us to acclaim such silly and sometimes vapid figures. You may fall in love said our censor with things so patently outside the intellectual scope of your realities. You may fall in love with gilt curls or a sailor doll or a brainless sombrero image. For these were masks, images of man, images of women, the feminine, the masculine, all undistressed, all tricked up with suitable accoutrements. Then we sank into light, into darkness, the cinema palace (we each have our favourite) became a sort of temple. We depended on light, on some sub-strata of warmth, some pulse or vibration, music on another plane too, also far enough removed from our real artistic consciousness to be treated as "dope" rather than accepted in any way as spiritual or intellectual stimulus. We moved like moths in darkness, we were hypnotised by crosscurrents and interacting shades of light and darkness and maybe cigarette smoke. Our censors, intellectually off guard, permitted our minds to rest. We sank into this pulse and warmth and were recreated. The cinema has become to us what the church was to our ancestors. We sang, so to speak, hymns, we were redeemed by light literally. We were almost at one with Delphic or Elucinian candidates, watching symbols of things that matter, accepting yet knowing those symbols were divorced utterly from reality. The mask originally presented life but so crudely that it became a part of some super-normal or some sub-normal layer of consciousness. Into this layer of self, blurred over by hypnotic darkness or cross-beams of light, emotion and idea entered fresh as from the primitive beginning. Images, our dolls, our masks, our gods, Love and Hate and Man and Woman. All these attributes had their more or less crude, easily recognised individual complements. Man and Man and Man. Woman and more and more and more Woman. Bits of chiffon became radiantly significant, tiny simple and utterly trivial attributes meant so much. Or didn't they? I mean that is what the moving pictures have done to us sometimes. We are like pre-fifth Athenians waiting for our Aeschylus, our Sophocles, our Euripides. We are being told that the old gods won't do and we know they won't do really. We must have refinement and perfection and more intricate machinery. Now I know that this is quite right. I do know. I know and utterly appreciate for instance the immense possibilities of the Movietone in certain circumstances. If it were used properly there would be no more misunderstandings for instance (or there shouldn't be) of nations. I mean that five minutes of what I call "bottled" America should do more for the average intelligent English mind than ten weeks on that continent. Look at "Lindy".[4] Now we have all seen this charming gentleman, alighting, arising, swooping a little, crowded and pushed and pulled here and there and which way. But did we know "our Lindy" till we saw him, till we heard him at the New Gallery Movietone performance? "Colonel Lindberg's departure for Paris and reception in Washington" read the second number on our programme. The first bit ("departure for Paris") showed blatantly the flaws of the excellent Movietone. I mean the crowds came up in funny little squeaks and whistles and gasps. Someone whistling (I suppose at random) somewhere, cut across vital and exaggerated while more important factors of group surge and voice rhythm were blurred over utterly. The buzz and whirr of the plane wheels was excellent but we were not particularly impressed by that as we have been so long familiar with the same sort of thing adequately represented "off" at the average cinema. The plane buzzed off dramatically but the slice "departure for Paris" was really only the somewhat usual topical budget number somewhat more skilfully presented.[5] But that "reception in Washington" should teach statesmen better. I mean look and look and look at what I call "bottled" America and look and look and look. Turn on that reel ten thousand times and then talk to me of international understanding. Does the average Englishman understand the average American (I say average) and vice versa? Can they? Do they? If you want to understand America, I feel like saying to Lord Birkenhead (who made an address, 5 on our excellent programme) go (or come) and look and look and look at this particular reel, "and reception in Washington."[6] Nations should understand (but they won't, with the best intentions, do) nations. It would make life so simple really if we really wanted really, really to understand anybody. Where would be our speeches and our receptions and our conferences and our gatherings? Half of life would be out of an occupation. If we could not sit up nights hating Englishmen or Frenchmen or Italians or Spaniards or Americans (or Americans) where, where would all our energy and our spirit flow to? I mean where would we get to? We would be, like pre-Periclean Athenians, I fear, really ready for an Art Age.

Art, art, ahrt and arrt and AHRT age. Yes, we would be ready for an art age. Turn on a thousand times and go on turning bits of "bottled" Germany, and "bottled" America, kings and presidents and the reception by varied peoples of varied kings and generals and senators and presidents and we will understand each other. Nations are in turns of wrists, in intonations of voices and that is where the Movietone can do elaborate and intimate propaganda. Peace and love and understanding and education could be immensely aided by it. The Movietone outside the realm of pure sentiment, treated from a practical viewpoint is excellent in all particulars. Oh, how we could understand if only we wanted to understand, each other. Take the president's voice for instance. In it is an America (or should I say the America) that many of us, even though natives of its eastern sea-coast never meet with. The words of President Coolidge cut across London mist and our Europeanized consciousness like dried brush crackling in a desert.[7] Arid, provincial, pragmatic and plain it held singular vitality. I mean (speaking all too personally) Lord Birkenhead, standing in a garden before a hedge of oak trees (or it ought to have been, if it wasn't, oak trees) was really bottled "England" just as the president with his arid talk of republicanism and his "man of the people" stunt was "bottled" and then distilled America. The Germans we are told, are delighted and rock with mirth at the screen aspect of the French president. Well, let us rock and scream and laugh at one another. Laughter precludes a sort of affectionate acceptance. Let us laugh but let it be in temples, in gatherings, the group consciousness is at the mercy of Screen and Movietone. Let us understand one another. Let the Movietone become a weapon in the hand of a Divinity.

UNDERSTANDING was the deity of Athens, Mind and Peace and Power and Understanding. Know thyself (we all know) says the deity of Delphi, who is Beauty and Inner Understanding (which is mantic) and more Beauty and Art in the abstract that we all hope for. This new invention seems an instrument of dual god-head. A miracle is literally unrolled before our eyes. We are too apt to take divinity for granted. Understanding, Athene with her olive wreath, another sort of understanding, Helios with his justice and his power of divination, are both eager for new neophites [sic]. Here is an instrument of twin divinity. Tone and vision, sight and sound, eyes and ears, the gate ways to the mind are all appealed to. We are visionaries, we may become prophets. We are adepts, moving at will over foreign lands and waters, nothing is hidden from us. Apply the Movietone to questions of education and international politics and you will do away with revolutions. Well, there it all is in a nut-shell, "bottled". But are we ready for so suave simplification? Some of us will grow in outer and in inner vision with the help of this invention. Others will be left cold as they would be left inert before another Mons or Marathon. Yet it stands to reason that a new world is open, a new world of political understanding, of educational reform, or art (in its pure sense) even. Art, I repeat unparenthetically, may in its pure essence be wedded not merely welded to art. I felt frankly disappointed in Raquel Meller. By some ironic twist of psychic laws, it seems impossible to be luke-warm, to be "almost good enough", Madame Meller does not lack power and personality. But some genial sub-strata of humour or humanity seemed wanting. Mechanical efficiency, technique carried to its logical conclusion do not make divinity. I felt however in Nina Tarasova and Miss Gertrude Lawrence (numbers 7 and 11 on our programme) a full-blooded vitality that nothing can diminish.[8] Madame Tarasova registered sorrow and despair with almost oriental subtlety; though her gesture was obvious, her real artistry redeemed her curious appearance her bulk, unwieldy as our now familiar *Chang* elephants only served by some ironic twist of circumstance to increase our appreciation. The grandeur of voice in this case seemed healing and dynamic. Madame Tarasova, magnified to the size of Big Ben almost, became as hugely interesting. One laughs (or used to) at scientific projections, lizards like dinosaurs, beetles exaggerated out of recognition, gargantuan nightmoths, flower petals that would enclose Cleopatra's Needle. We used to laugh hysterically at these things, but now we take them for granted. So for the moment the spectacle of an operatic singer complete with voice strains our credulity. Voice and body beat and pulsed with what dynamic energy. We laughed of course. But as I say, didn't we use to laugh in somewhat the same fashion at the exaggerated antics of enormous ants and hornets? We are used to nature, expanded and ennobled past all recognition, now we must again readjust and learn to accept calmly, man magnified. Man magnified, magnified man, with his gestures, his humors, his least eccentricities stressed to the point of almost epic grandeur. Art to conceal art. Is there any more damaging revelation than art revealed? Art is cut open, dissected so to speak by this odd instrument. Movietone creates and recreates until we feel that nothing can remain hidden, no slightest flaw of movement or voice or personality undetected. It is odd how damaging this double revelation is to some otherwise (we should think) unassailable artistes, while others apparently not so fine, emerge unscathed and smiling. Gertrude Lawrence for instance endured this double ordeal with wit and subtlety. The screen Gertrude Lawrence, at first sight a slim mannequin, became animated with fluid inspiration. Her gesture and her speech blended, in this case completely *wedded*. The pure artist perhaps cannot be assailed, and certainly Madame Tarasova and Miss Lawrence stood this trying ordeal valiantly.

There it is. We stand by our own gods, like or dislike, there is no possible strict standardization to be arrived at. We cannot weigh and measure our affections, we cannot count and label our wavering emotions. I like this, you like that, X or Y or Z like something different. Personally, though I admit the brilliance of this performance, I was not totally won over by it. I think for a long time we have perhaps unconsciously, accepted, as I said earlier, the cinema palace as a sort of temple. So I say yes to anything having to do with reality and with national affairs and with education then the Movietone is perfect. The outer vision, yes, should be projected, the outer sound, yes, should be amplified and made accessible. Everyone should have access to great music as easily as to books in libraries. This Movietone places people and things, catalogues them. It is excellent as a recorder, as a corrective of technical flaws, or as a means of indefinitely protracting artistic perfection. Art under this magnascope can be dissected and analysed. As an instrument of criticism, yes, as an instrument of international understanding, yes and yes and yes. As a purveyor of ideas and even ideals, yes. But somehow no. There is a great no somewhere. The Movietone has to do with the things outside the sacred precincts. There is something inside that the Movietone would eventually I think, destroy utterly, for many of us. That is the whole point really of the matter. Is our temple, our inner place of refuge, to be crowded out with gods like men, not masks, not images, that are so disguised, so conventionalized that they hold in some odd way possibility of some divine animation? If I see art projected too perfectly (as by Raquel Meller) don't I feel rather cheated of the possibility of something more divine behind the outer symbol of the something shown there? The mask in other words seems about to be ripped off showing us human features, the doll is about to step forward as a mere example of mechanical inventiveness. We cannot worship sheer mechanical perfection but we can love and in a way worship a thing (like Topsy with her rag arms) that is a symbol of something that might be something greater.

We feel fearful that our world may be taken from us, that half-world of lights and music and blurred perception into which, as I said earlier the being floats as a moth into summer darkness. Like a moth really we are paralysed before too much reality, too much glamour, too many cross currents of potentialities. There is too much really for the soul to cope with and all these out-reaching odd soul-feelers that you and I and Tom Jones and the shop girl and the barber and the knife boy have sometimes felt threatened with odd maladies. We want healing in blur of half tones and hypnotic vibrant darkness. Too mechanical perfection would serve only I fear, to threaten that world of half light. We hesitate to relinquish our old ideals and treasures, fearing we may lose our touch with mystery by accepting the new (this sort of Euripidean sophistication) in place of the old goat-herd and his ribald painted chorus.

["The Cinema and the Classics III: The Mask and the Movietone,"
Close Up (Territet, Switzerland) 1:5, November 1927, pp. 18–31.]

New Films for Old (1929)
Fannie Hurst

The Little Motion Picture Theatre has come of age. These tiny temples have emerged from the back-streets and the sub-cellars in the same fashion that the back-street and the sub-cellar phase of the so-called legitimate Little Theatre one day asserted its important little self.[1]

Just as new light, new beauty and new courage have been injected into the American drama through the precious medium of the Little Theatre so, by that same token, must those same qualities eventually infiltrate to the screen.

The mighty minority is the ultimate monitor of public taste.

In the City of New York, two small and very special and very beautiful motion picture houses, Little Carnegie Playhouse and Film Guild Cinema are opening their esoteric doors this winter, under the avowed principles of dedicating themselves to pictures outside the box-office pale; those which rise above the average sentimental garbage which is offered nightly at the modern movie palaces which line and make bright the Main Streets of the land.[2]

It is a gallant revolt and a mammoth enterprise.

There is little doubt that in these small clearing houses lie the white hope for the self-respect of the motion picture. Toward that end, every one who is intelligent or hopes to be intelligent, should be pricked with the urge to seek out the kind of motion picture theatre which, it is to be hoped, will follow the wake of Little Carnegie Playhouse and Film Guild Cinema.

There is a great deal of justifiably excited and exciting optimism abroad today over the steady and amazing development of the sound-dimension in pictures. For all its stumbling, wayward childhood, the juvenile motion picture is now on the brink of at least its mechanical maturity. With the introduction of the dimension of sound to the flat surface of the screen, every technical difficulty is about to be overcome—for better or for worse.

Frankenstein now has a set of vocal chords. And they work! Frankenstein can squeak. There remains little doubt that in an astonishingly short time the remaining mechanical difficulties of the Frankenstein voice will be conquered, just as the mechanical difficulties of his arms and legs were overcome. But in all the hullabaloo, nobody has had time to bother much over Frankenstein's soul.

And he needs it more than he does his voice.

But as if to cover up the embarrassing, the tiresome, and the fundamental fact that the motion picture, soulless, is a bunch of elaborate junk, higher, finer, and more rococco are becoming the motion picture palaces which present these adventures in mediocrity.

To venture into one of the "toney" picture palaces of New York today is like forging your way through the marshmallow heart of a gigantic wedding cake. Atmosphere flows like marshmallow ooze. Gilt icing ripples and twists. The patisserie auditorium punctures space and repose with stalactites and drowns you in fauteuils of marshmallow plush.

One city block from where you are seated, beyond a double symphony orchestra, three organs, foliage and illuminated pillars, lurks the motion-picture screen. From behind ornate overtures of orchestra, ballet-dancing tableaux, singers, dancers, violinists, whistlers and tumblers there finally emerges, drenched in the odor of Hollywood, pretty as bisque and all dolled up, the kind of motion picture which it is the function of the Little Motion Picture house to reject as so much junk.

The gross, over-dressed strumpet, which in so many ways the motion picture feature film has become, is not un-understandable. Here is a new-born art happening along at an immense interval after her last sister and with an appeal so wide that it is practically limitless. It has none of the more precious exclusiveness of painting or music or drama. It combines all three. It must span the entire octave of human response. It must cater to the man in the street, the man who laid the macadam of that street and the man who dwells high above the street.

It is the most limitless of the arts, and at this moment in its development, the most limited. And since the great common denominator of the masses to which it caters is mediocrity, picture-piffle has been the almost inevitable commercial result.

The average programme picture that unwinds itself across the silver-plated sheets of this country is Dime Novel standard. All dressed up and no place to go.

Superb photography, expensive actors, mawkish sentimentality, tinned emotions, fear-of-truth, fear of box-office. Frankenstein put together so skillfully that he even says "Ma-Ma, Pa-Pa," but in the soulless voice of a poll parrot.

Obviously, the spiritual, educational, and aesthetic fulfillment of the motion-picture does not lurk in the steel flesh of the latest inventions. [...]

There is little doubt, judging from the experience of the theatre, and from certain precedents in the motion picture world itself, that the so-called non-box-office picture has a public. And a bigger one than realized. We all know the moss-grown credo of the commercial producer: "The public is mentally eleven years old." The average commercial producer thereupon proceeds, with the same astuteness which prompts a tenement mother to feed her baby bananas because it cries for them, to stuff the retarded child of a public with marshmallow.

It will be interesting to observe these small theatres, which are offering adult entertainment to adults on the startling assumption that even a retarded fourteen-year-old mind can develop if given the opportunity.

Caligari, The Last Laugh, Sunrise, Potemkin have, it is true, proved esoteric and indigest-ible diet for the fourteen-year-old mental digestion. But that does not mean, Little Motion Picture Movement to the vanguard, that taste for intelligence and courage cannot be cultivated.

That is the tremendous chore for that tremendous trifle, the Little Theatre, to perform.

More power to these small crucibles of idealism.

["New Films for Old: The Little Cinema Movement Offers Something to Those Whose Taste Has Been Formed by Competent Artists," *Theatre Guild Magazine* (New York), January 1929, pp. 11–13, excerpted.]

The Film Gone Male (1932)
Dorothy Richardson

Memory, psychology is to-day declaring, is passive consciousness. Those who accept this dictum see the in-rolling future as living reality and the past as reality entombed. They also regard every human faculty as having an evolutionary history. For these straight-line thinkers memory is a mere glance over the shoulder along a past seen as a progression from the near end of which mankind goes forward. They are also, these characteristically occidental thinkers, usually found believing in the relative passivity of females. And since women excel in the matter of memory, the two beliefs admirably support each other. But there is memory and memory. And memory proper, as distinct from a mere backward glance, as distinct even from prolonged contemplation of things regarded as past and done with, gathers, can gather, and pile up its wealth only round universals, unchanging, unevolving verities that move neither backwards nor forwards and have neither speech nor language.

And that is one of the reasons why women, who excel in memory and whom the cynics describe as scarcely touched by evolving civilisation, are humanity's silent half, without much faith in speech as a medium of communication. Those women who never question the primacy of "clear speech", who are docile disciples of the orderly thought of man, and acceptors of theorems, have either been educationally maltreated or are by nature more within the men's than within the women's camp. Once a woman becomes a partisan, a representative that is to say of one only of the many sides of question, she has abdicated. The battalions of partisan women glittering in the limelit regions of to-day's world, whose prestige is largely the result of the novelty of their attainments, communicating not their own convictions but some one or other or a portion of some one or other of the astonishing varieties of thought-patterns under which men experimentally arrange such phenomena as are suited to the process, represent the men's camp and are distinguishable by their absolute faith in speech as a medium of communication.

The others, whom still men call womanly and regard with emotion not unmixed with a sane and proper fear, though they may talk incessantly from the cradle onwards, are, save when driven by calamitous necessity, as silent as the grave. Listen to their outpouring torrents of speech. Listen to village women at pump or fireside, to villa women, to unemployed service-flat women, to chatelâines, to all kinds of women anywhere and everywhere. Chatter, chatter, chatter, as men say. And say also that only one in a thousand can talk. Quite. For all these women use speech, with individual differences, alike: in the manner of a facade. Their awareness of being, as distinct from man's awareness of becoming, is so strong that when they are confronted, they must, in most circumstances, snatch at words to cover either their own palpitating spiritual nakedness or that of another. They talk to banish embarrassment. It is true they are apt to drop, if the confrontation be prolonged, into what is called gossip and owes both its charm and its poison to their excellence in awareness of persons. This amongst themselves. In relation to men their use of speech is various. But always it is a façade.

And the film, regarded as a medium of communication, in the day of its innocence, in its quality of being nowhere and everywhere, nowhere in the sense of having more intention than direction and more purpose than plan, everywhere by reason of its power to evoke, suggest, reflect, express from within its moving parts and in their totality of movement, something of the changeless being at the heart of all becoming, was essentially feminine. In its insistence on contemplation it provided a pathway to reality.

In becoming audible and particularly in becoming a medium of propaganda, it is doubtless fulfilling its destiny. But it is a masculine destiny. The destiny of planful becoming rather than of purposeful being. It will be the chosen battle-ground of rival patterns, plans, ideologies in endless succession and bewildering variety.

It has been declared that it is possible by means of purely aesthetic devices to sway an audience in whatever direction a filmateur desires. This sounds menacing and is probably true. (The costumiers used Hollywood to lengthen women's skirts. Perhaps British Instructional, with the entire medical profession behind it, will kindly shorten them again).[1] It is therefore comforting to reflect that so far the cinema is not a government monopoly. It is a medium, or a weapon, at the disposal of all parties and has, considered as a battlefield a grand advantage over those of the past when civil wars have been waged disadvantageously to one party or the other by reason of inequalities of publicity, restrictions of locale and the relative indirectness and remoteness of the channels of communication. The new film can, at need, assist Radio in turning the world into a vast council-chamber and do more than assist, for it is the freer partner. And multitudinous within that vast chamber as within none of the preceding councils of mankind, is the unconquerable, unchangeable eternal feminine. Influential.

Weeping therefore, if weep we must, over the departure of the old time films['] gracious silence, we may also rejoice in the prospect of a fair field and no favour. A field over which lies only the shadow of the censorship. And the censorship is getting an uneasy conscience.

["Continuous Performance: The Film Gone Male," *Close Up* (London) 9:1, March 1932, pp. 36–8.]

The Music of Silence (1928)
Germaine Dulac

There was a time, not so long ago, when the art of cinema sought not to define itself, as it does today, hopelessly through the mistakes of commercial interpretation. It found satisfaction through form of an almost traditional kind, one that allowed for its technical evolution toward a considerable degree of perfection while remaining unconcerned with its higher aesthetic.

By cinema's technique we mean the scientific aspect of its material expression: photography. By its aesthetic we mean the inspiration that deploys technique for spiritual expression.

And while the great masters of this evolution recognized that conceptions of lighting, optics and chemistry might undergo transformation, being subject to progress, they utterly rejected the thought of a parallel moral evolution.

The combination of sensitive film stock and an appropriate mechanism meant we could now photograph life and record its diverse manifestations and movements. To photograph, one aimed the lens in the direction of tangible forms in motion within or toward a goal. Apart from these same forms, the idea of photographing the *imperceptible* would have been considered folly.

I say *imperceptible* and not invisible. The invisible, the materially existent that lies beyond our visual perception has long been caught by the cinema. The informed use of technique can, for example, record each stage of a plant's germination or flowering, producing, in graceful contours, the drama and physical pleasure of growth and blossoming.

It is of the invisible that I speak when slow motion, augmenting the number of recorded images, allows us to analyze the logic of a movement's beauty, by revealing the fine details of its synthesis; this, too, I call "invisibility."

Now, each new discovery has modified, and continues to modify, the conditions of visibility. One discovery affects proportionality and delves into space, thereby impressing our vision. Another, by increasing film stock's sensitivity, makes it possible to register color in more delicate shades, rendering gentler and more subtle contrasts of black and white. Other improvements in lighting enable the projection of vibrations with a more powerful effect on our vision.

When cameras decompose movement in exploration of Nature's realm of the infinitely small, it is to instruct us visually of the beauties and the dramas which our hypersynthesizing eye cannot see. For example, a horse clears a gate; our eye gauges his effort synthetically. The same holds true for our gauging of the growth of a germinating grain of wheat. The cinema, in decomposing movement, *makes us see* the beauty of a leap analytically, through the succession of rhythms that compose a rhythmic whole. And when we focus on germination we get not only the synthesis of growth in movement but the psychology of that movement. We sense visually the effort involved in the emergence of a plant's stem from the earth and in its flowering. The cinema, by capturing these unconscious, instinctive, and mechanical movements, allows us to witness plant life's unseen aspirations toward air and light.

Visually, through its rhythms and line—straight and curvilinear— movement gives us a relation to a life of complexity.

Thus, we observe that each scientific discovery is directed toward the improvement of visual perception: significance. The cinema wants to make us "see this," "see that." Throughout its technical development it constantly adresses our eye so as to affect our understanding and sensibility. Its true logic would then seem to lie in its exclusive address to sight, similar to music's address to our faculty of hearing.

I have constantly on my lips—and with no fear of contradiction—the words *visual, visually, sight, eye, look*. However, there does exist a factor of contradiction. Although cinema may, in its technique, be solely visual, it happens that by virtue of its moral aesthetic, it disdains the purely visual image. Rather, it focuses on the representation of expression in which the image may take the first, but not the most important, place.

For example, the cinema records frames, not in order to move "visually," but so as to narrate or enhance episodes created for reading or hearing, rather than essentially for viewing.

Current work focuses not on the value of the image or on its rhythmic movement, but on silent dramatic action. There is a world of difference between silent dialogue and the music of silence. Until now cinema has tended to be silent dialogue rather than music. Two actors in a scene talk to each other. This is wrong; only their silent facial expressions will be visual. But, sadly, in dramatic films the factual counts more heavily than the expressive.

To sum up; the cineographic instrument is conceived in its scientific potential for one purpose; cineographic inspiration pursues another goal. Where lies its truth? In the technical instrument that has created the seventh art. "But why," you will ask, "this duality of purpose?" Because of the basic error that governed the writing of the first scenarios, the prejudice in favor of the dramatic action that could develop only like that of a novel or play—that is to say, through factual precision rather than suggestion.

Human action—since it is to be caught live—consists of gestures, of comings and goings, races and battles, and since for this external action, some supporting pretext must be found, the word goes out: "Let's adopt works of literature and of theater, works requiring no effort and of proven popularity." The result is our current cinema.

When we directors are asked to make a film, the producer doesn't say, "Have you a visual idea? Do you know how your scene will unfold visually?" Instead, he says, "Make an adaptation of this action drama or that best-selling novel," and it is the story that give literature a visual element that is sought.

Should we not take up the struggle? (1) For the extreme thematic simplicity that favors the meaningful image—that is, visual expression? (2) For simplification of décor? Bear in mind that a set is visually static, not dynamic, that the cinema is motion and that, despite popular opinion, a film's artistic value is not determined by its set. (3) For the idea that cinema, in the clarity of its images should suggest rather than specify, creating, like music, through particular chords, that which is imperceptible? (4) For the rejection of any guiding idea for a film incapable of emotional development exclusively through the image, in the silence of the eye?

The cinema can certainly tell stories, but we must remember that the story is nothing but a surface. The seventh art, the art of the screen, lies in the depth beneath this surface, in musical imperceptibility.

["La Musique du Silence," Cinégraphie 5, 15 January 1928, pp. 77–8. Translated by Annette Michelson.]

What the Movies Have Done to Music (1922)
Mary Ellis Opdycke

We all know what music does to the movies. We have felt the great emptiness that ensues when Miss Smith's memory fails her at the Main Street Moving Picture Palace piano, and our hearts have sunk to realize that without music even our favorite stars are only two-dimensional shadow dolls with white blood like fishes. Then again, when some prolonged climax has been whipping us up to frenzy, when Lillian is cavorting on her ice cakes, or Doug is beating somebody to it through several reels, we try to tell our neighbor of our own particular brand of thrill, and suddenly note that the music has also been growing up with the excitement to a fortissimo fever and conversation is prohibited.[1]

But what do movies do to music? That is a question which we hear less about. Messrs Griffith and Zukor may arise and demand appropriate musical backgrounds for their films, but Messrs. Beethoven and Tschaikowsky must remain unheard.[2] Even if their favorite pieces be dissected and torn to tortured fragments to provide love interest for a close-up, they remain to suffer silently in their shrouds. Vivisectionists may invade Valhalla, but no musician appears to cry: Murder.[3] It is a muted as well as a mooted question.

Those film producers who hold their business as a sacred, if lucrative, mission, insist that the movies extend music to fields where it would otherwise be unheard. They proudly quote the overtures given between films at metropolitan theaters and the suites which are visually demonstrated by a backdrop that deepens into purple during the storm section and blushes rosy at the final cadence. But this is not strictly movie music. It is possible only in theaters which own an orchestra, and is frankly a musical intermission. It is a very desirable feature from the musical point of view, and if members of the audience choose to change seats or go out to smoke cigarettes at that particular point, it is not the fault of the conductor or of the music itself. But music between films is merely an accessory, and not always a welcome one.

Movie music is quite another matter. Here we have fragmentary selections welded loosely together for a purpose outside of the music itself. The music is frankly subordinate. And yet the musical producer assures one that his snatches are also contributing a definite help to musical education in the public. "The averaged [sic] unenlightened listener," he says, "will not listen to music, since he has nothing to relate it to. Especially in the better music he lacks the associations and imagination to make mental pictures to fit the music. When he is given a simultaneous picture on the screen, he carries the musical theme away with him from the theatre [sic] with a definite illustration in his mind. The music means something to him, and that something is a picture."

Admitting for the moment that the average movie fan will carry away any memory of the music that has been subconsciously lining his visual perceptions, one may question the desirability of a definite picture accompanying a piece of music. In cases where the composer permitted a definite title to his piece and where that title is carried out in the picture, an authentic impression might result. Grieg's Morning Voices might be brought home to the unmusical person by a sunrise, and the novice might be taught that Debussy's Iberia meant Spain, if there were plenty of mantillas and bulls on the screen.

But where there is a definite title, there exists also a definite idea, at least as definite as the impression which the composer sought to convey. Even without a photographic background, the listener may be guided toward the fields where the composer has wished him to disport himself.

Then again it is improbable that the picture has been made with the idea of following the music step by step. Although movies and music have in common that continuous motion which is shared by none of the other arts, they do not flow in the same ways. The three eternal principles of music are repetition, development and contrast. Movies admit no repetition, except short retrospective sections, and their development is a development of character and action rather than of theme. Nor is it conceivable that they should be manipulated, even were it possible, with the primary idea of enhancing the effect of the music.

Turning to the so-called absolute music in which there are no tags, no directions for the imagination outside of the line of the melody or the harmonic progress, one meets a deeper problem. The movies exploit this music for a thousand different ends. A stormy passage may be chosen to accompany a storm at sea, a rise of Ku Klux Klansmen, a triangular bedroom melee [sic], or a foreign invasion. The slow movement of the Fifth Tschaikowsky Symphony has exemplified religious piety and domestic affection. The Allegretto of Beethoven's Seventh has buried babies and hopes, Civil War veterans and autumn leaves. In other words, the movies stuff so many notions of the meaning of a given piece of music into the brains of an audience that if any of them stick they are as likely as not to be the farthest from the composer's original inspiration. Is no idea better than a wrong idea, especially when there is no particularly right idea? Thus asks the musical movie producer, while no composer of absolute music—and there are a few of them left today—arises to give a proud "Yes."

Far more heinous than this rather ambiguous harm of tagging music is the sin of cutting up and mutilating musical masterpieces to make a movie holiday. One can quote Shakespeare, and the quotations lose no truth in the telling, but one can't quote Beethoven without hurting him. That there is a subtle difference should be clear to any moving picture expert. How much thrill can one work up in the eight seconds of next week's film that is flashed on without music as an advertisement? Even the death-grip climaxes have a sort of comic impropriety. An idea, pure and simple, may be torn from its environment and lose no power, but one can't transplant an emotional process without caring for its roots and soil. Some music gains its essential mood by contrast with what has preceded it. A sudden change of key may work wonders with a feeling. To this end composers study the delicate psychology of transposing toward the flat or sharp keys. They note that too much contrast undermines all feeling of contrast; that too much minor mode weakens the minor effect.

In steps the musical manager of a screen theatre. "How do you arrange to transpose from one key into another without losing time during the picture?" he is asked.

"Oh well, the pieces always seem to fit together somehow," is the answer.

No matter how adroitly the operation is performed, something is lost in the process. Music demands stretches of gradual incline to heighten the climaxes. The listener who hears only the first explosion of the theme, and no development, hits so many high spots that he seems on a level plain. His first valid symphonic experience in Carnegie Hall would seem like the school-child's Hamlet—so full of quotations that he would have no attention for what came between them.

Apart from the irrelevancy of musical quotation, and apart from the undue emphasis on thematic climax, there is another sin committed by the movies in the name of musical enlightenment. In the production of historical pictures there is often an elaborate pretense of musical research. The audience is led to think that the music is strictly contemporary. A recent film dealing with the life of Henry VIII was accompanied, for example, with a Bach suite. Now Bach was born over a hundred years after Henry's death, but that didn't matter to the producer. The effect was "quaint," even "classical," and the audience was led to think it accurate, so many carefully worked details having been advertised by the manager.

No musician could regret hearing a Bach suite well performed at a motion picture theatre, but many a musician would sigh to think that several thousand people had been deluded into a false association, that their future hearings of that particular piece, and probably of all Bach music in the same spirit would summon up the picture of a lascivious court quite unknown to the God-fearing composer of Leipsic [sic].

But these are minor offenses, and will in time be doubtless cured if the same scholarship that is already applied to scenery and costume be turned to music. The cardinal sin remains, and sometimes it looks as if the present-day composer were about to canonize it.

Music is a spinster. Her nature is emotional and intellectual, more the former under Tschaikowsky, more the latter under Bach, but always a mixture of the two. If you marry her off, one side of her nature suffers. Marry her to a poem, and the poem overshadows her entirely, or else her form is weakened. The perfect song is a perfect union, but it is not perfect music.

Marry her to a libretto, and if it is a true love match, as with Wagner, she is lost in serving her verbal master, or else she rides supreme over his lines and forthwith appears in a divorced version on the concert stage.

Marry her to the dance. Notice how unobtrusively she follows her more blatant companion. See how her essential characteristics are twisted and reread and interpreted and then shadowed by the bright light that shines beyond her upon the stage.

Marry her to the movies. Drag her, faltering, to that altar which has only front and sides. Pick her to little pieces and file them away under "love interest," "same … passionate," "nature music, soft," "nature music, stormy." Label all her throbbing nerves. Then remove her brain, curve away her form, her development, her sequence, her vital tissue. Say that accompaniment is music's highest function: that there is no place for her like the film. Set up a double standard where the screen has the benefit of the doubt. And what music is left?

Some day we may have music that is especially written for the films. It will probably be very sensational, with emphasis on the orchestral battery. The slender virgin that has served Beethoven and Brahms will be painted and peroxided and will carry a xylophone and three wind machines. She may be happy as she plays these instruments. She will be a Famous Player, anyhow.[4] But until she appears her sisters must suffer, her spinster sisters begotten by Weber or Dvorak, Mozart or Moussorgsky [sic]. They must serve with rent limbs and broken bows, fractured themes and amputated climaxes, any lurking sign of intelligence sacrificed to the thrills of a movie audience. This is the slaughter that the movies have done to music.

["What the Movies Have Done to Music: A New View of the Relationship between Music and the Screen," Filmplay (New York) 2:1, July 1922, pp. 16–17.]

Comments on the Screen (1918)
Janet Flanner

A strong paternal feeling exists in the heart of the filmmaker for his children, the exhibitors. Almost tenderly he supplies them with their little needs. Each cinema goes to the exhibitor with an accompaniment of press sheets and music cue papers which tell the cinema displayer all he need ever know.[1] The press sheet informs him as to the plot so that he may be relieved of the necessity of seeing his own pictures; a brief perusal of this paper, his feet on the desk, and he is familiar with the most delicate of the play's situations. The music cues tell him how suitably to chaperone the cinema with dulcet and appropriate sounds.

While the screen drama is silent, we all know the theater in which it is given is not. Music fills the air as he and she, on the sheet, quarrel and make up, go out into the cold storm with their children or hunt for the papers in the safe. This last, especially if the hunter is in a hurry and is using an electric flash to see his way around the dining room, would require from the orchestra or lonely pianola player, the use of what is, in professional musical parlance, called an "agit." This is brief for agitato—music of a hasty and exciting caliber.

❦

Besides "agits"—though they are the most popular and nearest capable, each time they are played, of making the shivers go down the spines of the paid spectators—other well-known varieties of music are mentioned on the orchestral sheet. In order that the exhibitor's way may be made as smooth for him as glass, these various types of music are employed and indicated by the filmmaker and tacked onto the sub-titles in a printed schedule of the play sent out regularly to the prospective displayer. This cue-sheet, as it is called, is a marvel of conventionality. It is also a potent indicator of the melodramatic merits of the play. If it has many "andante dramaticos" or "allegro appassionatos," the exhibitor can get ready to hang out the s.r.o. sign and look for a full house.[2] The music follows the play as meekly as Mary was ever followed by her lamb; where the plot goes, it goes; its people are the plot's people and naught shall come between them.

❦

Illustration makes everything clear. The cue-sheet given out with Her One Mistake, a cinema where, one supposes by the title, though titles are misleading now-a-days, as we find out, the heroine comes supplied with a past, is a delightful case in point. The naked plot of the play stands out to the reader after peeking at its cue-sheet as plainly as though he had written the scenario or helped direct the show. No imagination is needed to become fully acquainted with the meaning of the play. Like high-lights, the music cues with their associating subtitles, plucked from the film show up everything. To proceed:

Reel 1: At screening, advice is given to play an allegro vivace, 2–4. This cinema begins brightly; light stimulating music leads up to whatever may follow. "At Silver Beach," the second cue, demands and gets, let us hope, a lento, 6–8; the use of a flute here would be pretty; doubtless a moonlight scene, made at a California studio anytime between 10 a.m. and 4 p.m. before the actors go home from work, is utilized at this juncture and the first stage tradition for romance steps into the play. Then the heroine says: "I'm awfully tired, mother." Apparently things are going badly for her; she's young; we suspect a villain. She gets an andantino con expressione, [sic] 4–8; a girl's best friend is her mother.

☙

Reel 2: "Enter Mr. Scully." Ah! He comes! The kingly male! He comes and as he does it he is accompanied by Andantino con expressione [sic], but with 9–8, the highest fractional average any one has received so far. On his second appearance we become more intimate with him; the Mr. is dropped. "When Scully Enters Rooms" Andantino Appassionato 4–4 is played. Appassionato! We are thrilled! Is he villain or hero? Both become passionate at times. Just when we are all agog to sound his identity and grow intimate with his moral values, delay is introduced into the film to whet our appetite by suspense—another old trick. "Five Years Later"—Andante 2–4, we are informed. How quiet and introspective this music must be; what ravages time can make. Then "When Charlie Plays the Piano" we are to hear "Mother o' Mine."[3] We are "on" to Charlie; the films are full of him. He is part of every play. He sits in a disreputable boarding house and idly strums the battered keys of an old Chickering cornered in a dirty living room.[4] He sentimentally thinks of his gray-haired mother as he plays—the music tells you so—and the spectator weeps.

"The Bulls Have Found Us," the next title, puts us all off the scent. Is this a Mexican play or one of the underworld? We don't know where we stand. When young, we thought bulls were animals; familiarity with cinemas entitles us now to the knowledge that bulls may also be the O'Learies and Reillies called, during Robert Peel's unpopular administration, "peelers."[5] "Won't You Let Me Say Good-by?" is answered by "I'm Coming Tonight." Both get Andantes. Then "When Miss Gordon Enters Charlie's Rooms"—we fear Charlie has forgotten his gray-haired mother at this crisis in his life—Andante Dramatico sets the pulses going. "At Struggle" Allegro 4–4. This is a fifty–fifty affair. We grip our chairs.

☙

Allegro! How suitable that it should be followed by Il Penseroso. Life is sunshine and shadow. "And then—Half an Hour Later"—the dashes are not our own—we know the worst. "Adagio Cantabile, Segue into Dramatico Andante." Cantabile means singingly. Perhaps, on second thought, it was not so bad as we feared when we first got excited. Maybe Charlie had honorable intentions, after all, with Miss Gordon, and has made the girl superlatively happy. Singingly—life is not so bad. We get hopeful; if the cantabile on the cue-sheet had been replaced by a patetico we might still have grounds for our opening suspicions, but this play has a happy ending; we can see it from here. Cantabile told the tale.

❦

A valse triste, 3/4 a dram. Tension, 9–8—this must be Mr. Scully again; that was his batting average—and a moderato, 4–4, finish reel 5. An even balance prevails at the last moment of the cinema, from which we infer a promise of marriage is received and carefully retained. A little excitement precedes its coming—dram. Tension—and a little sentimentality comes before that. A valse triste is a very moving strain of music. All get ready for the final embrace. Five hundred feet more and it comes twenty feet long.

What would we do without music? We would be bereft of one of our greatest sensory advisors. Her One Mistake, melodically speaking, is a successful one. In her second and third she could do no better, we are assured. Miss Gordon must rest content. One is often enough for any one—but a cinema star.

[Indianapolis Star (Indianapolis), 21 July 1918, section 5, pp. 33, 38.]

Magic is New (1946)
Maya Deren

"I am making a 16 mm film. I understand that, in order to use a tripod in Central Park, I need a special permit."

"That's correct," the girl at the information desk said. "You can pay your fee and get your permit at the third office down the hall."

"Oh, I didn't know there was a fee."

"Oh, yes, all commercial photographers must pay a fee."

"But I am not a commercial photographer."

"Amateurs don't need permits, as long as they do not use a tripod, clutter the walks or frighten the animals in the zoo."

"But I have to use a tripod for these shots."

"What kind of films are these?"

"I suppose you could call them experimental."

"About what kind of experiments?"

"They are not *about* experiments. They are themselves experiments—experiments with the form of film itself."

"Whom do you work for?"

"For nobody. That is, I work for myself."

"Then it is a hobby?"

"Well, not exactly. The films are shown at universities and other places."

"Then they are educational documentaries?"

"Well, no. They are certainly not documentaries. Or rather, they are documentaries of the interior, in a sense. And they are educational only in the sense that art is always educational."

'What did you say?"

"I said that ... well, perhaps I had better see the educational division."

She was glad to be rid of me. At the educational office we covered approximately the same ground and tried to go on from there.

"What is the purpose of these films?"

"That's a little difficult to explain. Really, there is no purpose, except to make a film."

"Well, in that case, they're commercial, entertainment films. You can get your permit and pay your fee at the third office to the left of the foyer."

"But they're not commercial and they don't mean to entertain, exactly. That is, I don't make them to make money. As a matter of fact they cost me money to make," I said frantically.

With the attitude of someone trying to prevent a scene, the girl pulled herself together to deal with me as gently as possible.

"Suppose you tell me what they are about."

"Well, that's a little difficult to explain. They're not about any specific subject." I tried again. "You see, they are about the inner experiences of a human being."

"I see. Well, now, this one, for instance. What is the story about?"

"Well, there is no literary story. You see, I believe that cinema, being a visual medium should discover its own, visual integrity—in cinematic terms."

"What was that?"

"I said, its hard to explain in words because it's so visual."

"I see. Now which part of the park did you want to photograph?"

"It doesn't really matter. The least traveled parts. It isn't the park so much. It's a matter of having a countryside-like background without actually having to take my friends, who are in it, out to the country."

"Then it's a film about your friends."

"Well, not exactly. They're doing the acting for me."

"So there is a plot. What is the plot about?"

"No, there isn't a literary plot."

Her patience was growing thin.

"Look, Miss ... er, Deren. I am trying to help you out. I have to fill out this questionnaire for your permit. Maybe we could get at it if you tried to tell me *why* you make these films?"

"I wonder myself. It's awfully hard work sometimes."

My attempt at levity fell completely flat. There was a long pause, during which we stared at each other helplessly. Then, speaking slowly and distinctly, as if to a foreigner who had just landed in America, she said:

"Miss Deren, I have to fill out the blanks on this questionnaire in order to have the permit signed by the proper authorities. I cannot give you a permit unless you can say something about the films which I can write down. Do you think you can say anything about the films which I can write down?"

"Write down 'psychological,'" I said desperately. "It won't take long and I won't clutter the walks and there are just a few people in the scene. Just write down 'psychological.'"

She looked at me intently for a moment.

"Yes," she said, half to herself. "That's what it is ... psychological."

"Miss Deren," she called after me as I was leaving, "do they wear ... normal clothes?"

"Yes," I assured her, "Everything will be quite normal."

This conversation, which took place last summer, brought forcibly to my attention the fact that, after three years and five films, I still had no succinct term or formula to describe their nature. My work has constituted an exploration of the medium of film rather than the fulfilment of a preconceived goal. I am fascinated precisely by those aspects and methods of cinema which are as yet undefined and rarely exploited. I am concerned with it as a creative art form, and so I have tried to work as an artist, and independently of all the terminology, methods and institutions which are already established.

❧

In the beginning I was ignorant also of the material and physical problems of film production, which begin after the creative labor of conceiving the film is already achieved. And I am convinced that this foolhardy naiveté is to some extent responsible for the fact that the films have actually been made. Now, after considerable experience, I deliberately ignore the infinite number of complications which threaten the production of a film. For I have found that the first shot is always the most difficult; once one has plunged in, the problems can be dealt with as they come up.

I have met numbers of talented people who tell me of scripts which they have written and filed away as a "some time" project. They await financial backing, for most people have permitted themselves to assume the prerequisite of an elaborate budget to provide for much film, complex studio sets, intricate equipment. There is, moreover, no institution which at the moment subsidizes cinema as an art form, in spite of the fact that it is more expensive than most other art forms.[1]

My films have been paid for by that part of the personal budget which is usually set aside for entertainment, such as going to the movies, and the fund for small luxuries. The limitations of such a small budget can be compensated for by the exercise of imagination and ingenuity and physical exertion. Instead of attempting to pay salaries to professional actors, I use my friends and act in the films myself. And since the burden of the meaning and the emotional projection of the film is carried actually by the visual effects of the camera and cutting, I have found these non-professionals more than adequate to my needs. Instead of dreaming up a set which would cost hundreds of dollars to build and more hundreds to light, I conceive the films in terms of interesting landscapes and locales which, though sometimes accessible only by great physical effort, are always convincingly real as well as naturally lit, and all free for the asking. As for interiors, I have turned my own home into a studio, photographed in the apartments of indulgent friends, worked in the Metropolitan Museum of Art, in the unrented ballroom of a hotel.

The equipment, also, is extremely simple, and here especially imagination and ingenuity not only compensate for its seeming limitations but, on the contrary, the very absence of gadgets and mechanical paraphernalia inspires an exploitation and creative use of some of those basic capacities of the camera which, being so taken for granted, have been greatly neglected by professionals. Furthermore, when the mechanical means remain simple, the camera does not become a monster which reduces the artist to impotent awe.

Free time is another thing that these "some time" scripts are waiting for. Yet the first film, Meshes of the Afternoon, was photographed in two weeks. At Land was shot on weekends, over the course of three summer months. And the dance film was photographed whenever Talley Beatty, who dances in it, had some spare time left over from teaching classes, taking classes and rehearsing for a Broadway production.

Or perhaps the prospective film is postponed until one can "learn some technique." This is perhaps the most destructive of all misconceptions about film. The actual operation of a motion picture camera is very simple and consists largely of pressing a button. All the rest is achieved best if it is developed, as one goes along, in answer to some requirement of the imagination. There is nothing more deadening to the development of a form than the technician who takes his instrument and its means so much for granted that he never attempts anything new.

In the final analysis the only critical requirement is the determination to make a film. Only an obsessed determination can account for the kind of effort which my films have sometimes required of me. I have spent hours walking the midsummer pavements of New York, tracking down a hundred-foot roll of film in the midst of the film shortage. For each scene of At Land, Hella Hamon and I had to carry the equipment two and a half miles (part of it over sand dunes) and row an hour and a half in order to reach this desolate but beautiful beach.[2] I have stood in October ocean water for hours to get certain tidal effects. It was inevitable that in some of these most uncomfortable moments I should ask myself with considerable anguish, "Why, oh why do I do this?"

I am driven by that which motivates any artist or writer—the conviction that his medium has infinite potentialities for conveying his particular perceptions of life. And because I came to cinema not as to an industry in which to find a lucrative position but from a background which had included a preoccupation with poetry, dance, music, I brought to it some of these basic esthetic criteria.

What particularly excited me about film was its magic ability to make even the most imaginative concept seem real. For if the tree in the scene was real and true, the event which one caused to occur beneath it seemed also real and true. And so one could create new realities which, being rendered visible, could stand up to the challenge of "Show me!" We are moved by what we see, according to how we see it. And the film maker, by controlling what the audience sees, is also, therefore, in control of what the audience feels. The creative effort should be directed not at making a thing look like itself, but at using the capacity of the camera to make it look like what the audience should feel about it. Here was a medium which, instead of being bound by the astronomy of clocks and calendars, could make manifest the astronomy of the heart and mind—that which knows an evening as endless, or the walk back always being shorter than the first walk there. Here was a medium which could project in real terms those inner realities by which people truly live. For we act and suffer and love according to what we imagine to be true, whether it is really true or not. And since the cinema seemed peculiarly qualified to project those inner realities, I had always been impatient with what I felt was a criminal neglect of that potent magical power.

It was in such a mood of impatience that I met my husband. I was at a Hollywood cocktail party where a sympathetic friend, wishing, no doubt, to avert a scene in which I would vehemently denounce the star and story approach to film, introduced me to Alexander Hackenschmied who, as my friend put it, "would probably agree with me."[3] He had been making films for over ten years in Czechoslovakia but was known here largely as codirector and photographer of the documentaries, Crisis, Lights Out in Europe and Forgotten Village. We did agree, profoundly, in our concept of the direction that film should take. No doubt this encouraged us to discover other agreements, which culminated, so to speak, in our marriage.

❧

It was not until 1943, two years later, that we acquired a small, 16 mm camera. Since Sasha was working during the day, my original intention was to make a film by myself. I started out by thinking in terms of a subjective camera, one that would show only what I could see by myself without the aid of mirrors and which would move through the house as if it were a pair of eyes, pausing with interest here and there, opening doors, and so on. The beginning developed into a film about a girl who fell asleep and saw herself in her dream, and it soon became obvious that I could not both photograph and act myself, so I waited until my husband was free to develop the concept of the film and execute it with me.

Meshes of the Afternoon does start with a subjective camera sequence in which only the feet and shadow of the girl are visible. For the rest the film is the result of one of those perfect collaborations in which an idea advanced by either person is spontaneously accepted by the other or immediately reconsidered and rejected by both. It was a far cry from story conferences in which the sensitive and delicate intuitions which give real vitality and meaning are somehow lost under the welter of arguments, justifications and analyses. Meshes of the Afternoon is concerned with the inner realities of an individual and the way in which the subconscious will develop, interpret and elaborate an apparently simple and casual occurrence into a critical emotional experience. It is culminated by a double ending, in which it would seem that the imagined achieved, for the protagonist, such force that it became reality. Using cinematic techniques to achieve dislocations of inanimate objects, unexpected simultaneities etcetera, this film establishes a reality which, although based somewhat on dramatic logic, can exist only on film.

That summer my husband went to work as motion picture director for the Overseas Motion Picture Division of the Office of War Information, and I decided to go on by myself here in New York. *The Witch's Cradle* (which was never completed for various reasons) was photographed in the Art of This Century gallery, where the architecture, designed by Frederick J. Kiesler, and the paintings and objects by the foremost modern artists seemed to me to constitute a strange, magic world.[4]

This effort to make a film quite by myself—to direct, photograph and light it without any assistance or previous experience—served as an invaluable lesson. In the first film the task of lighting and photographing in such a way as to realize on the screen the vision we had conceived, had fallen to my husband. In the course of this second film I began to understand, at first hand, how important every visual detail is in those films which rely entirely upon the visual image to convey meaning and continuity, rather than upon some plot behind the image. I came to understand the difference between contriving an image to illustrate a verbal idea and starting with an image which contains within itself such a complex of ideas that hundreds of words would be required to describe it. This is the central problem of thinking in cinematic terms, for our tendency is to think in verbal terms. One writes: "She felt frightened and alone." But the impact of this statement lies in the word-idea of "fright" and "alone" and the image contrived to express that would always be less satisfactory than the verbal statement. On the other hand, if one begins with an image of a small person standing in the corner of a large room, which is made to seem empty by dusters thrown over the furniture, this conveys, in a visual moment, a whole complex of ideas which would take many contrived sentences to describe.[5]

I pondered these problems and by the following summer I was anxious to develop the idea of cinematic magic in terms of space and time, for film is a time–space art. I was fortunate in meeting Hella Hamon who, although attending City College during the week, was anxious enough to learn about film to spend all her summer weekends as a camerawoman. *At Land* strives for the elimination of literary-dramatic lines and tries to discover, instead, a purely cinematic coherence and integrity. It presents a relativistic universe—one in which the locations change constantly and distances are contracted or extended; in which the individual goes toward something only to discover upon her arrival that it is now something entirely different; and in which the problem of that individual, as the sole continuous element, is to relate herself to a fluid, apparently incoherent, universe. It is in a sense a mythological voyage of the twentieth century. This sense of the active, fluent universe was achieved largely by the technique of beginning some simple movement in one place and concluding it in another. Thus the integrity of human movement was used to relate unrelated places, and this concept was even further developed in the dance film which followed. *A Study in Choreography for Camera* was made by Talley Beatty as dancer, and by me as director and photographer. I had felt that in most dance films the restiveness of the camera—with its closeups, its views from the wings, etcetera—served merely to destroy choreographic patterns which had been carefully conceived for a theatre stage space and a fixed-front audience. In this film, on the other hand, cinematographic space—the entire world—becomes itself an active element of the dance rather than an area in which the dance takes place. And the dancer shares, with the camera and cutting, a collaborative responsibility for the movements themselves. This results in a film dance which could not be performed except on film.

I am now engaged in a new film, as yet untitled, which is the most elaborate of my productions.[6] In order to be able to concentrate creatively on the direction of the film, I have had most of the acting done by friends. It is only in the increased number of actors and in such physical details, however, that this film is more elaborate. What still inspires me most is the capacity of cinema to create new, magic realities by the most simple means, with a mixture of imagination and ingenuity in about equal parts.

For example, to achieve on film the sense of an endless, frustrating flight of stairs, the great Hollywood studios would probably spend hundreds on the building of a set. You, however, can do it for just the price of the film required to photograph any ordinary stairway three times—the first angle shows all but the top landing, the second angle shows the flight without any landings included, and the third angle shows the flight with the top landing. If the actor climbs the visible portion of the stairs three times at a consistent rhythm, you will succeed in having created a stairway three times as long as the real one. By such exercise of ingenuity, using even the most modest camera and equipment, you can create whole worlds for just the cost of the film.

For more than anything else, cinema consists of the eye for magic—that which perceives and reveals the marvelous in whatsoever it looks upon.

[*Mademoiselle* (New York), January 1946, pp. 181, 260–65.]

The Movies and Reality (1926)[1]
Virginia Woolf

People say that the savage no longer exists in us, that we are at the fag-end of civilization, that everything has been said already, and that it is too late to be ambitious. But these philosophers have presumably forgotten the movies. They have never seen the savages of the twentieth century watching the pictures. They have never sat themselves in front of the screen and thought how, for all the clothes on their backs and the carpets at their feet, no great distance separates them from those bright-eyed, naked men who knocked two bars of iron together and heard in that clangor a foretaste of the music of Mozart.

The bars in this case, of course, are so highly wrought and so covered over with accretions of alien matter that it is extremely difficult to hear anything distinctly. All is hubble-bubble, swarm and chaos. We are peering over the edge of a cauldron in which fragments of all shapes and savors seem to simmer; now and again some vast form heaves itself up, and seems about to haul itself out of chaos. Yet, at first sight, the art of the cinema seems simple, even stupid. There is the King shaking hands with a football team; there is Sir Thomas Lipton's yacht; there is Jack Horner winning the Grand National. The eye licks it all up instantaneously, and the brain, agreeably titillated, settles down to watch things happening without bestirring itself to think. For the ordinary eye, the English unaesthetic eye, is a simple mechanism, which takes care that the body does not fall down coal-holes, provides the brain with toys and sweetmeats to keep it quiet, and can be trusted to go on behaving like a competent nursemaid until the brain comes to the conclusion that it is time to wake up. What is its surprise, then, to be roused suddenly in the midst of its agreeable somnolence and asked for help? The eye is in difficulties. The eye wants help. The eye says to the brain, "Something is happening which I do not in the least understand. You are needed." Together they look at the King, the boat, the horse, and the brain sees at once that they have taken on a quality which does not belong to the simple photograph of real life. They have become not more beautiful, in the sense in which pictures are beautiful, but shall we call it (our vocabulary is miserably insufficient) more real, or real with a different reality from that which we perceive in daily life? We behold them as they are when we are not there. We see life as it is when we have no part in it. As we gaze we seem to be removed from the pettiness of actual existence. The horse will not knock us down. The King will not grasp our hands. The wave will not wet our feet. From this point of vantage, as we watch the antics of our kind, we have time to feel pity and amusement, to generalize, to endow one man with the attributes of the race. Watching the boat sail and the wave break, we have time to open our minds wide to beauty and register on top of it the queer sensation—this beauty will continue, and this beauty will flourish whether we behold it or not. Further, all this happened ten years ago, we are told. We are beholding a world which has gone beneath the waves. Brides are emerging from the Abbey—they are now mothers; ushers are ardent—they are now silent; mothers are tearful; guests are joyful; this has been won and that has been lost, and it is over and done with. The War sprung its chasm at the feet of all this innocence and ignorance, but it was thus that we danced and pirouetted, toiled and desired, thus that the sun shone and the clouds scudded up to the very end.

But the picture-makers seem dissatisfied with such obvious sources of interest as the passage of time and the suggestiveness of reality. They despise the flight of gulls, ships on the Thames, the Prince of Wales, the Mile End Road, Piccadilly Circus. They want to be improving, altering, making an art of their own—naturally, for so much seems to be within their scope. So many arts seemed to stand by ready to offer their help. For example, there was literature. All the famous novels of the world, with their well-known characters, and their famous scenes, only asked, it seemed, to be put on the films. What could be easier and simpler? The cinema fell upon its prey with immense rapacity, and to this moment largely subsists upon the body of its unfortunate victim. But the results are disastrous to both. The alliance is unnatural. Eye and brain are torn asunder ruthlessly as they try vainly to work in couples. The eye says: "Here is Anna Karenina." A voluptuous lady in black velvet wearing pearls comes before us. But the brain says: "That is no more Anna Karenina than it is Queen Victoria." For the brain knows Anna almost entirely by the inside of her mind—her charm, her passion, her despair. All the emphasis is laid by the cinema upon her teeth, her pearls, and her velvet. Then "Anna falls in love with Vronsky"—that is to say, the lady in black velvet falls into the arms of a gentleman in uniform, and they kiss with enormous succulence, great deliberation, and infinite gesticulation on a sofa in an extremely well appointed library, while a gardener incidentally mows the lawn. So we lurch and lumber through the most famous novels of the world. So we spell them out in words of one syllable written, too, in the scrawl of an illiterate schoolboy. A kiss is love. A broken cup is jealousy. A grin is happiness. Death is a hearse. None of these things has the least connection with the novel that Tolstoy wrote, and it is only when we give up trying to connect the pictures with the book that we guess from some accidental scene—like the gardener mowing the lawn—what the cinema might do if it were left to its own devices.

But what, then, are its devices? If it ceased to be a parasite, how would it walk erect? At present it is only from hints that one can frame any conjecture. For instance, at a performance of Dr Caligari the other day, a shadow shaped like a tadpole suddenly appeared at one corner of the screen. It swelled to an immense size, quivered, bulged, and sank back again into nonentity. For a moment it seemed to embody some monstrous, diseased imagination of the lunatic's brain. For a moment it seemed as if thought could be conveyed by shape more effectively than by words. The monstrous, quivering tadpole seemed to be fear itself, and not the statement, "I am afraid." In fact, the shadow was accidental, and the effect unintentional. But if a shadow at a certain moment can suggest so much more than the actual gestures and words of men and women in a state of fear, it seems plain that the cinema has within its grasp innumerable symbols for emotions that have so far failed to find expression. Terror has, besides its ordinary forms, the shape of a tadpole; it burgeons, bulges, quivers, disappears. Anger is not merely rant and rhetoric, red faces and clenched fists. It is perhaps a black line wriggling upon a white sheet. Anna and Vronsky need no longer scowl and grimace. They have at their command—but what? Is there, we ask, some secret language which we feel and see, but never speak, and, if so, could this be made visible to the eye? Is there any characteristic which thought possesses that can be rendered visible without the help of words? It has speed and slowness; dartlike directness and vaporous circumlocution. But it has also, especially in moments of emotion, the picture-making power, the need to lift its burden to another bearer; to let an image run side by side along with it. The likeness of the thought is, for some reason, more beautiful, more comprehensible, more available, than the thought itself. As everybody knows, in Shakespeare the most complex ideas form chains of images through which we mount, changing and turning, until we reach the light of day. But, obviously, the images of a poet are not to be cast in bronze, or traced by pencil. They are compact of a thousand suggestions of which the visual is only the most obvious or the uppermost. Even the simplest image: "My luve's like a red, red rose, that's newly sprung in June," presents us with impressions of moisture and warmth and the glow of crimson and the softness of petals inextricably mixed and strung upon the lilt of a rhythm which is itself the voice of the passion and hesitation of the lover. All this, which is accessible to words, and to words alone, the cinema must avoid.

Yet if so much of our thinking and feeling is connected with seeing, some residue of visual emotion which is of no use either to painter or to poet may still await the cinema. That such symbols will be quite unlike the real objects which we see before us seems highly probable. Something abstract, something which moves with controlled and conscious art, something which calls for the very slightest help from words or music to make itself intelligible, yet justly uses them subserviently—of such movements and abstractions the films may, in time to come, be composed. Then, indeed, when some new symbol for expressing thought is found, the film-maker has enormous riches at his command. The exactitude of reality and its surprising power of suggestion are to be had for the asking. Annas and Vronskys—there they are in the flesh. If into this reality he could breathe emotion, could animate the perfect form with thought, then his booty could be hauled in hand over hand. Then, as smoke pours from Vesuvius, we should be able to see thought in its wildness, in its beauty, in its oddity, pouring from men with their elbows on a table; from women with their little handbags slipping to the floor. We should see these emotions mingling together and affecting each other.

We should see violent changes of emotion produced by their collision. The most fantastic contrasts could be flashed before us with a speed which the writer can only toil after in vain; the dream architecture of arches and battlements, of cascades falling and fountains rising, which sometimes visits us in sleep or shapes itself in half-darkened rooms, could be realized before our waking eyes. No fantasy could be too far-fetched or insubstantial. The past could be unrolled, distances annihilated, and the gulfs which dislocate novels (when, for instance, Tolstoy has to pass from Levin to Anna and in so doing jars his story and wrenches and arrests our sympathies) could, by the sameness of the background, by the repetition of some scene, be smoothed away.

How all this is to be attempted, much less achieved, no one at the moment can tell us. We get intimations only in the chaos of the streets, perhaps, when some momentary assembly of color, sound, movement suggests that here is a scene waiting a new art to be transfixed. And sometimes at the cinema in the midst of its immense dexterity and enormous technical proficiency, the curtain parts and we behold, far off, some unknown and unexpected beauty. But it is for a moment only. For a strange thing has happened—while all the other arts were born naked, this, the youngest, has been born fully clothed. It can say everything before it has anything to say. It is as if the savage tribe, instead of finding two bars of iron to play with, had found, scattering the seashore, fiddles, flutes, saxophones, trumpets, grand pianos by Erard and Bechstein, and had begun with incredible energy, but without knowing a note of music, to hammer and thump upon them all at the same time.

[The New Republic (New York), 4 August 1926, pp. 308–10.]

Movies (1913)[1]
Lou Andreas-Salomé

The discussion on the evening of February 19, was devoted to Dr. Weiss's lecture on rhyme and refrain which Freud praised rather half-heartedly and about which he had not much else to say.[2] The next-to-last lecture on Saturday, February 22, was omitted on account of the exhibition of photographs of the latest Roman excavations. Tausk and his boys and I indulged in a more-or-less kindred pleasure at the Urania Theater.[3] The movies really play a role of no small significance for us and this is not the first time I have thought about this fact. A few purely psychological considerations deserve to be added to the many things that might be said in vindication of this Cinderella of aesthetic criticism. One has to do with the fact that only the technique of the film permits the rapid sequence of pictures which approximates our own imaginative faculty; it might even be said to imitate its erratic ways. Part of the weariness to which we finally succumb in seeing works of art performed in the theater results not on account of the effort nobly expended in artistic enjoyment, but because we tire of making allowances for the clumsy way in which the illusion of movement is represented on the stage. Spared this effort in the movies we are free to bestow the mass of our uninhibited devotion to the illusion. The second consideration has to do with the fact that even though the most superficial pleasure is involved, we are presented with an extraordinarily abundant variety of forms, pictures, and impressions. Only the film is in itself able to provide some faint trace of artistic experience for both the workman in the stultifying monotony of his daily work and the intellectual worker bound to his vocational or mental treadmill. Still the two thoughts make us ponder whether this consideration for our mental state might not mean the future of the film in the theater, the little golden slipper for the Cinderella of art. Here in Vienna it was Tausk who took me to the movies despite work, weariness, and lack of time. Often we can spare only a half hour, and I always have to laugh at this activity in which we indulge.

[From The Freud Journal of Lou Andreas-Salomé (London: Quartet Books, 1987), 100–101, excerpted.]

A Tear for Lycidas (1930)[1]
Dorothy Richardson

During last year's London season we saw and heard one Talkie, *Hearts in Dixie* and wrote thereof in *Close Up* and foreswore our sex by asserting, in bold, masculine, side-taking, either-or fashion, that no matter what degree of perfection might presently be attained by the recording apparatus we were certain that the talkie, as distinct from the sound-film, will never be able to hold a candle to the silent film.

This year, therefore, though we knew there must be small local halls still carrying on, and hoped that our own little Bethel, which we had left last autumn ominously "closed for repairs," might have taken courage to re-open, we felt that we were returning to a filmless London. Resignedly.

There was, there always is, one grand compensation: we came fully into our heritage of silent films. "The Film," all the films we had seen, massed together in the manner of a single experience—a mode of experience standing alone and distinct amongst the manifolds we assemble under this term—and with some few of them standing out as minutely remembered units, became for us treasure laid up. Done with in its character of current actuality, inevitably alloyed, and beginning its rich, cumulative life as memory. Again and again, in this strange "memory" (which, however we may choose to define it, is, at the least, past, present and future powerfully combined) we should go to the pictures; we should revisit, each time with a difference, and, since we should bring to it increasing wealth of experience, each time more fully, certain films stored up within. But to the cinema we should go no more.

Arriving, we found our little local hall still wearing its mournful white lie. All over London we met—there is no need to describe what we met, what raucously hailed us from the façade of every sort of cinema. Our eyes learned avoidance, of façade, newspaper column, hoarding and all the rest.

But ears escape less readily and we heard, as indeed, bearing in mind the evolution of pianola and gramophone, we had expected to hear, of the miracles of realism achieved by certain speech-films. Of certain beautiful voices whose every subtle inflection, every sigh, came across with a clarity impossible in the voice speaking from the stage. People who last year had wept with us had now gone over to the enemy and begged us to see at least this and that: *too* marvellous. Others declared that each and every kind of speech film they had seen had been *too* dire.

We accepted the miracle so swiftly accomplished, the perfected talkie, but without desire, gladly making a present of it. Wishing it well in its world that is so far removed from that of the silent film. Saw it going ahead to meet, and compete with, the sound-film. Heard both rampant all over the world.

Driven thus to the wall, we improvised a theorem that may or may not be sound: that it is impossible both to hear and to see, to the limit of our power of using these faculties, at one and the same moment. We firmly believe that it is sound.

The two eloquences, the appeal to the eye and the appeal to the ear, however well fused, however completely they seem to attain their objective—the spectator-auditor—with the effect of a single aesthetic whole, must, in reality, remain distinct. And one or the other will always take precedence in our awareness. And though it is true that their approximate blending can work miracles the miracle thus worked is incomparably different from that worked by either alone.

Think, for example, of the difference between music heard coming, as it were, out of space and music attacking from a visible orchestra. Recall that an intense concentration on listening will automatically close the eyes. That for perfect seeing of a landscape, work of art, beloved person, or effectively beautiful person, we instinctively desire silence. And agree, therefore, that there neither is, nor ever can be, any substitute for the silent film. Agree that the secret of its power lies in its undiluted appeal to a single faculty.

It may be urged that to the blind the world is a sound-film whose images must be constructed by the extra intelligent use of the remaining senses helped out by memory, while to the deaf it is a silent film whose meaning cannot be reached without some contrived substitute for speech. That deaf people are more helpless and are usually more resentful of, less resigned to, their affliction than are the happier blind. And that therefore the faculty of hearing is more important than that of sight: the inference being that the soundless spectacle is a relatively lifeless spectacle.

Those who reason thus have either never seen a deaf spectator of a silent film or, having seen him, have failed to reflect upon the nature of his happiness. For the time being he is raised to the level of the happy, skilful blind exactly because his missing faculty is perfectly compensated. Because what he sees is complete without sound, he is as one who hears. But take a blind man to a never so perfect sound-film and he will see but little of the whole.

In daily life, it is true, the faculty of hearing takes precedence of the faculty of sight and is in no way to be compensated. But on the screen the conditions are exactly reversed. For here, sight *alone* is able to summon its companion faculties: given a sufficient degree of concentration on the part of the spectator, a sufficient rousing of his collaborating creative consciousness. And we believe that the silent film secures this collaboration to a higher degree than the speech-film just because it enhances the one faculty that is best able to summon all the others: the faculty of vision.

Yet we have admitted, we remember admitting, that without musical accompaniment films have neither colour nor sound! That any kind of musical accompaniment is better than none. The film can use almost any kind of musical accompaniment. But it is the film that uses the music, not the music the film. And the music, invisible, "coming out of space," enhances the faculty of vision. To admit this is not to admit the sound-film as an improvement on the silent film though it may well be an admission of certain possible sound-films as lively rivals thereof.

Life's "great moments" are silent. Related to them, the soundful moments may be compared to the falling of the crest of a wave that has stood poised in light, translucent, for its great moment before the crash and dispersal. To this peculiar intensity of being, to each man's individual intensity of being, the silent film, with musical accompaniment, can translate him. All other forms of presentation are, relatively, diversions. Diversions in excelsis, it may be. But diversions. Essential, doubtless, to those who desire above all things to be "taken out of themselves," as is their definition of the "self."

Perhaps the silent film is solitude and the others association. [...]

["Continuous Performance: A Tear for Lycidas," *Close Up* (Territet, Switzerland and London) 7:3, September 1930, pp. 196–202, excerpted.]

Narcissus (1931)
Dorothy Richardson

Discontent may be rooted in the contempt of one who believes mankind to be on its way to a better home and thinks, or most oddly, appears to think, that he honours that home by throwing mud at this. Or it may be just the natural mysterious sense of incompleteness haunting those for whom at times, haunting even those for whom all the time, life is satisfying beyond measure. More generally it is the state of having either lost or never fully possessed the power of focusing the habitual.

From this kind of discontent, escape by flight is impossible. Another house, another town, country, planet, will give only a moment's respite, for each in turn, and each with more swiftness than the last, will close in and become odious while, perversely, those left behind will mock the fugitive by revealing, with an intensity that grows as it recedes further and further into the distance, the qualities that once had charmed him.

It is customary to account for this distressing experience by the part played by distance, to say that distance lends enchantment and to talk of the transforming power of memory.

But distance *is* enchantment. It is a perpetual focus. And escape from the obstructive, chronic discontent we are considering the state of deadness to the habitual, whether that habitual to good or bad, is possible only to those who by nature or by grace have the faculty of ceaseless withdrawal to the distance at which it may be focused.

Some kind of relinquishment is implied: an abandonment of rights that reproduces on a very humble level the saint's *salto mortale*. Something of the kind must take place before surroundings can be focussed. It may be enforced. By illness, for example. The sick man, recovering, returns from his enforced detachment to a world transformed. But his freshness of vision is for a while only, unless his experience has taught him the secret of withdrawal. Or by a disinterested observer, through whose eyes what had grown too near and too familiar to be visible is seen with a ready-made detachment that restores its lost quality.

An excellent illustration of the operation of this casual gift is afforded by the story of the man who grew weary of his house, put it up for sale and, soon after, reading in his newspaper amongst descriptions of properties on the market a detailed account of a residence whose enumerated features, attracting him more and more as he read on, presently forced upon his attention the fact that it was his own house he was contemplating, was filled with remorse and telephoned to the agent to cancel the offer.

And what has all this moralising to do with the film? Everyone knows that amongst its thousand and one potentialities the film possesses that of being a mirror for the customary and restoring its essential quality. But must we not, to-day, emerge from our small individual existences and from narcissistic contemplation thereof? Learn that we are infinitesimal parts of a vast whole? Labour and collaborate to find salvation for a world now paying the prices of various kinds of self-seeking? And, for the re-education of humanity, is any single instrument more powerful than the film that is here offered merely as a provider of private benefits?

True. But the everlasting WE who is to accomplish all this remains amidst all change and growth a single individual.

Even so, is this so obvious mirror-focus quality a point worth insisting upon in relation to an art that has now passed so far beyond photographic reproductions of the familiar and, in so far as it remains documentary, registers—if we except Dziga-Vertoff and his followers engaged in directly representing anything and everything without selective interference beyond that dictated by the enchanted eye—only "interesting" or "instructive" material?[1]

I believe it is immensely worth making and insisting upon. I believe that mirroring the customary and restoring its essential quality is and remains the film's utmost. Remains *Borderline*'s utmost as well as that of *The Policeman's Whistle*.[2]

An early "animated picture," a little fogged and incessantly sparking, of a locomotive in full steam making for the enchanted spectator, a wild-west film complete with well-knit story on a background that itself is an adventure, a psychological drama all situations and intensities, a film that concentrates on aesthetic beauty or on moral beauty, an abstract film that must be translated by the mind of the onlooker, a *surréaliste* film produced by the unconscious alone, all these, every imaginable kind of film, talkies included in their utmost nearness to or distance from stage-plays, reduces or raises, as you please, the onlooker to a varying intensity of contemplation that is, in a way that cannot be over-estimated, different from the contemplation induced by a stage-play just because, whatever the ostensible interest of the film, it is arranged and focussed at the distance exactly fitting the contemplative state.

And this not only because it is a finished reproduction that we are seeing, so that part of our mind is at ease as it can never be in the play that is as it were being made before our eyes in a single unique performance that is unlike any other single performance, and the faculty of contemplation has therefore full scope, but also because in any film of any kind those elements which in life we see only in fragments as we move amongst them, are seen in full in their own moving reality of which the spectator is the motionless, observing centre.

In this single, simple factor rests the whole power of the film: the reduction, or elevation of the observer to the condition that is essential to perfect contemplation.

In life, we contemplate landscape from one point, or, walking through it, break it into bits. The film, by setting the landscape in motion and keeping us still, allows it to walk through us.

And what is true of the landscape is true of everything else that can be filmed.

["Continuous Performance: Narcissus," *Close Up* (London) 8:3,
September 1931, pp. 182–85, excerpted.]

PART TWO

Annotations

The Art of the Cinema

1. Eleonora Duse (1858–1924). Nicknamed "The Duse," Italy's foremost theater actress achieved international fame and was considered a rival to Sarah Bernhardt. Her single film appearance was in *Cenere* (1916).
2. Sir James Matthew Barrie (1860–1937). Scottish dramatist and novelist, best known for *Peter Pan, or The Boy Who Would Not Grow Up* (1904).

Courage in Production

1. Robert J. Flaherty (1884–1951). American documentary pioneer who was originally an explorer. His films include *Nanook of the North* (1922), *Moana* (1926), *Tabu* (1931) (co-directed with F.W. Murnau), *Man of Aran* (1934), *The Land* (1942), and *Louisiana Story* (1948).
   F.W. Murnau (1888–1931). German director who worked in the United States from 1927 until 1931. His films include *Nosferatu* (1921), *The Last Laugh* (1924), *Faust* (1926), *Sunrise* (1927), and, with Robert J. Flaherty, *Tabu* (1931).
2. René Clair (1898–1981). French director of comedy whose films include *Paris Qui Dort* (1923), *Sous les Toits de Paris* (1930), *Le Million* (1931), *A Nous la Liberté* (1931), and *The Ghost Goes West* (1935).

Comments on the Screen

1. James Metcalfe, the drama critic for *Life*, whose views were noticeably anti-semitic, occasionally reviewed films in the 1910s.
2. *Uncle Tom's Cabin*. Abolitionist novel by Harriet Beecher Stowe. A bestseller when first published in 1852, the novel was adapted for the stage by George L. Aiken in the same year, and for over ninety years the play was in continuous production in the United States. Several silent-film versions were made, including ones by Edwin S. Porter and Pathé, and in 1918 a feature-length film version starring Marguerite Clark in the dual roles of Topsy, a wilful young slave girl who achieves redemption through Christianity, and Eva, the saintly fair white child who expires young.

Film as Ballet

1. Ballets Russes. Ballet company founded by Serge Diaghilev in Paris in 1909, the Ballets Russes inspired major writers, composers, painters, choreographers, and dancers and is generally considered the birthplace of modern ballet.
2. *Gebrauchsmusik*. Literally "music for use" or "functional music," a term first defined by Heinrich Besseler in 1925 to refer to music designed to be socially relevant. Composers of *Gebrauchsmusik*

aimed at a simple style, direct expression and practical use. They composed for film, radio, schools, dance halls, and so on, as well as for proletarian uses such as fight songs.

3. *The Good-Humoured Ladies (Les femmes de bonne humeur).* One-act comedy ballet debuted by the Ballets Russes in 1917, based on Carlo Goldoni's play, the complicated love affair *Le donne di buon umore.*
Danilova (Alexandra Dionisyevna Danilova) (1903–97). Russian-American dancer and teacher engaged with George Balanchine by Diaghilev for his Ballets Russes, she was one of the most popular dancers of her time. She also wrote on film.

Dolls and Dreams

1. *Queen Elizabeth (Les amours de la reine Elizabeth).* (1912, Film d'Art) Sarah Bernhardt is in the title role.
2. *Tons of Money* (1922). Play written by Will Evans and "Valentine." First of the "Aldwych Farces."
White Cargo (1923). Sensationalist melodrama written by Leon Gordon.

Art?

1. Douglas Maclean (1890–1967). Silent-era actor who starred in light comedies and turned to producing after the advent of sound.
Reginald Denny (1891–1967). English actor best known for a string of successful silent comedies for Universal.
2. *College Days* (1925) was the British release title for *The Freshman.*

Film—Its Basic Structure

1. "The Russian montage theory." Through the restricted and occasionally controversial exhibition of films by Sergei Eisenstein, Alexander Dovzhenko, Vsevolod Pudovkin, and Dziga Vertov, and the translation of texts on film aesthetics by Eisenstein in particular, developments in Soviet film were made available to a British audience. This audience was comprised of workers' film groups, members of the London Film Society, filmmakers, and art-cinema patrons. The term "montage" encapsulated their conception of Soviet film form and particularly film editing at this time.

Light * Form * Movement * Sound

1. Paul Cézanne (1839–1906). French Post-Impressionist painter whose pictures were constructed from a rhythmic series of colored planes and marks, and whose method inspired Cubism.
2. Wassily Kandinsky (1866–1944). Russian abstract painter, teacher, printmaker and theorist who, in his 1912 treatise *Concerning the Spiritual in Art,* advocated an art reliant on expressive power and color rather than descriptive prowess or recognizable subject matter.
3. Richard Wagner (1813–1883). German composer, conductor, and writer. His "Reminiscences of Auber," an obituary to the French composer Daniel-François-Espirit Auber, was published in November 1871.

From Sentiment to Line

1. Dulac's title, "Du sentiment à la ligne" puns on the French journalistic expression of payment, "à la ligne," equivalent in English to being paid "per 1,000 words" perhaps; as in English, her "à la ligne" also implies a political line, a new tack; she also uses its most straightforward meaning of a geometric line.
2. Antoine Rivarol (1753–1801). French writer who wrote on language during the last two decades of the eighteenth century.

Workers and Film

1. Lu Märten, "Arbeiter und Film," from *Lu Märten: Formen für den Alltag: Schriften, Aufsätze, Vorträge,* ed. Rainhard May (Dresden: Verlag der Kunst, 1982) pp. 116–22. This is one of sixteen essays Märten wrote on film, and one of five that she wrote on workers and film. According to Rainhard May, this essay (item no. 30 in the Lu Märten Archive, LM-A Sign. 30) was not

published, but has a note appended to it saying "Rundfunk Berlin 1928." The overall tone of Märten's essay and its mode of address suggest that she broadcast it. After 1924 Märten gave many public lectures and readings, and wrote and gave radio presentations, on the topic of workers and film, among others. (See *Formen für den Alltag*, p. 182.)

2. These were the Volksbühne, "people's stages" or independent workers' theaters founded with social-democratic and socialist tendencies in Berlin in 1890.

3. Culture films (Kulturfilme). General education films, often of a scientific nature, produced by UFA (Universum Film Aktien Gesellschaft), the chief German film production company, which was founded in 1917.

4. *Cyankali* (1929). Anti-abortion play written by socialist realist playwright Friedrich Wolf (1888–1953).

Truth in Art in America

1. Theodore Dreiser (1871–1945). American novelist and journalist associated with naturalism. His novel *Sister Carrie* was withdrawn from circulation for immorality when it was first published in 1900. His novel *Genius* was published in 1915. Dreiser's biggest success came with *An American Tragedy* (1925).

2. Richard Payne Knight (1751–1824), *The Worship of the Generative Powers*, also known as *Two Essays on the Worship of Priapus* (1786; reprinted 1865), possibly co-authored with Thomas Wright.

3. *Fantazius Mallare, a Mysterious Oath* (1922), a supernatural and occult novel written by Ben Hecht (1893–1964). In March 1918, Margaret Anderson's *Little Review* began serializing James Joyce's *Ulysses*. Over the next few years, copies of the journal were seized and burnt four times by the United States Post Office on the grounds of obscenity. In 1920 Anderson and co-editor Jane Heap were charged with obscenity, found guilty, and fined $100. The Society for the Suppression of Vice, headed by John Sumner, was a key antagonist in Anderson's travails.

4. *The Circle* (1921); *The First Fifty Years* (1922); *The Hairy Ape* (1922); *The Fool* (1922); *Heartbreak House* (1919); *Give and Take* (1922); *The Passion Flower* (1920).
The Emperor Jones (1920). A successful Eugene O'Neill play, revived three times in the 1920s; it starred Charles Gilpin in the 1920 production, and Paul Robeson in both the 1925 revival and the 1933 film version.

5. Egbert Austin "Bert" Williams (1876–1922). Highly successful African-American entertainer and songwriter, longtime-featured comedian in the *Ziegfeld Follies* during the 1910s.
Charles S. Gilpin (1878–1930). African-American actor who played Brutus Jones in *The Emperor Jones*.

6. One of the more reactionary responses in the West to the 1917 Soviet Revolution was the assertion that, under Bolshevism, all women would become the common property of all men, becoming in effect the property of the state. In 1919 several American films were made on this premise, among them *Bolshevism on Trial*, *Everybody's Business*, *Common Property*, *The World and the Woman*, and *The New Moon* which featured Norma Talmadge and was made by the Norma Talmadge Film Corporation.

7. D.W. Griffith's *Birth of a Nation* (1915) had endorsed the Ku Klux Klan, the white supremacist group founded during Reconstruction. In the process of filming *Hungry Hearts* (based on Anzia Yezierska's 1920 collection of short stories about her immigrant experiences in New York's Lower East Side), *Potash and Perlmutter* author Montague Glass was hired to alter Yezierska's own screen adaptation by making the film shorter and more humorous. For Yezierska's experiences in Hollywood, see her "This is what $10,000 Did to Me," reprinted in this volume.

8. *The Loves of Pharaoh* (1921) was made in Germany with E.F.A. (Europeanischen Film-Allianz) money, but released in the United States before its release in Berlin. This production and marketing strategy was developed after the American success of Ernst Lubistch's *Madame DuBarry* (a.k.a. *Passion*) in 1920.

A Universal Language

1. Esperanto. The most well known of numerous attempts to construct a language of international intelligibility, it was first proposed by Dr Ledger Ludwik Zamenhof, writing as "Dr Esperanto," in 1887.

2. Victor Seastrom (Sjostrom) (1879–1960). Swedish director with stage experience who worked

in the United States from 1923 to 1928. Lillian Gish acted for Seastrom in *The Scarlet Letter* (1926) and *The Wind* (1928).

F.W. Murnau (1888–1931). German director who worked in the United States from 1927 until 1931. His films include *Nosferatu* (1922), *The Last Laugh* (1924), *Faust* (1926), *Sunrise* (1927), and, with Robert J. Flaherty, *Tabu* (1931).

Louis Wolheim (1880–1931). German-born character actor known for his thuggish roles, and best remembered for his part in *All Quiet on the Western Front* (1930).

Wallace Beery (1885–1949). American actor best known for his role as a boxer in *The Champ* (1931).

Projector

1. This is the first of the two parts comprising the poem. The second, "Projector II: Chang," was published in *Close Up* I:4 (October 1927), pp. 35–44.

The Mask and the Movietone

1. Meccano. A metal construction system patented by Liverpool entrepreneur Frank Hornby in 1901, which became a household name as an educational toy, and which spawned many derivatives, including the Erector set in the United States.
2. Movietone. Earl Sponable and Theodore Case developed an optical sound-on-film process in the late 1920s, one acquired by Twentieth Century Fox and named Movietone. It allowed for audio recording directly onto the filmstrip.
3. Raquel Meller (1888–1962). Spanish singer, music-hall star, and recording artist who was signed to record two Movietone shorts in 1926, as part of Fox's efforts to bring high class appeal to the new format. In the 1920s, Meller was very popular among the intelligentsia on both sides of the Atlantic.
4. "Lindy". Charles A. Lindbergh (1902–1974). American aviator who in 1927 became the first person to fly solo across the Atlantic. Leaving New York on 20 May, he arrived in Paris the next day to great public adulation.
5. Topical Budget. A British newsreel produced from September 1911 to March 1931, usually consisting of five one-minute items released in two bi-weekly programs.
6. Lord Birkenhead (1872–1930). Frederick Edwin Smith, first Earl of Birkenhead. English Conservative statesman and lawyer renowned for brilliant oratory and wit, he played a major part in the Irish settlement of 1921 and was appointed Secretary of State for India (1924–28).
7. President Coolidge (1872–1933). Thirtieth American President from 1923 to 1929. Republican Governor of Massachusetts from 1919 to 1920, Vice-President from 1921 to 1923. On President Harding's death, he was appointed President and re-elected in 1924.
8. Gertrude Lawrence (1898–1952). British revue star of the 1920s who occasionally appeared in films.

New Films for Old

1. The Little Theatre. An amateur theatrical movement, beginning in the United States in the late 1800s and early 1910s, which was influenced by the social mission of some of the advanced European drama of the same time, a dissatisfaction with commercial theater, and a passionate belief that the arts and crafts of theater could be grasped by enthusiastic non-professionals seeking self-expression.
2. The Little Carnegie Playhouse was one of a group of cinemas under the direction of Michael Mindlin. Its interior was designed by Wolfgang Hoffmann, Pola Hoffmann, Inc. The Film Guild Cinema, designed by the Viennese architect Frederick Kiesler, was located on Manhattan's West 8th Street. It was under the direction of Symon Gould for the Film Arts Guild. In 1926–27, Gould helped pioneer the little cinema movement in America with a series of presentations of American and foreign films at the Cameo Theatre in New York.

The Film Gone Male

1. British Instructional. British educational and documentary film production company founded by Harry Bruce Woolfe in 1919. British Instructional's first film, *The Battle of Jutland* (1921) an animated model and map film made with minimal resources, was a critical and commercial

success. The company attracted naturalists interested in cinematography, and, in 1922, the nature film series "Secrets of Nature" was initiated. By the end of the decade, almost one hundred of these had been produced. In November 1925, the Educational Department, headed by Mary Field, was founded to supply educational films.

What the Movies have Done to Music

1. In a famous scene from D.W. Griffith's *Way Down East* (1920), Lillian Gish raced across frozen sections of a raging river. (For Gish's account of the production trials of this film, see an excerpt from her "Beginning Young," reprinted in this volume.) Douglas Fairbanks was renowned for the swashbuckling athleticism he displayed in any number of films.
2. Adolph Zukor (1873–1976). Hungarian-born American film pioneer who distributed the French film *Queen Elizabeth*, starring Sarah Bernhardt, enabling him to found Famous Players Film Corporation in 1912. Zukor had commissioned a score for the film by composer Joseph Carl Breil. In 1913, Zukor distributed Edwin S. Porter's *Prisoner of Zenda*, also with a Breil score. Breil worked closely with director D.W. Griffith on the score for *The Birth of a Nation* (1915).
3. Valhalla. The hall assigned to those who have died in battle in Old Northern myth and the setting of the home of the gods for Richard Wagner's opera *Die Valküre* from his Ring Cycle. Composer Joseph Carl Breil worked with D.W. Griffith on the specially commissioned score for *The Birth of a Nation*, and he used parts of Wagner's "Ride of the Valkyries" from *Die Valküre* to accompany scenes depicting the ride and rescue by the Ku Klux Klan. Many observers have commented on the Wagnerian motifs in this part of the score and assumed a simple transposition on Breil's part. However, recent work by music scholar Martin Miller Marks shows precisely how Breil manipulated Wagner's music for the film's purposes. Breil also used passages from Tchaikovsky's *1812 Overture*, Grieg's *In The Hall of the Mountain King*, and Beethoven's *Sixth Symphony*.
4. Famous Players. Production company founded by Adolph Zukor in 1912 to produce film versions of classic plays using leading theatrical talent.

Comments on the Screen

1. "Cinema" is Flanner's term for films in this column.
2. "s.r.o.". Standing room only.
3. "Mother o' Mine." Song especially popular from 1903 to 1927.
4. Chickering. American firm of piano manufacturers who pioneered the use of cast-iron frames for the grand piano in 1843 and whose products were internationally acclaimed during the second half of the nineteenth century. By the early 1910s, however, the company had fallen on hard times and Flanner's reference here suggests the quaint, out-of-dateness of the Chickering product.
5. Peelers. Name given to Irish and British police forces after Sir Robert Peel who established the Irish constabulary in 1818 and the London Police in 1829. Since the end of the nineteenth century, Irish Americans had played an important role in the police forces of major American cities.

Magic is New

1. In 1946, Deren became the first filmmaker to be awarded a grant from the John Simon Guggenheim Foundation.
2. Hella Hamon. Hella Heyman, who was cinematographer for *At Land* (with Alexander Hammiid) and *Ritual in Transfigured Time*.
3. Alexander Hackenschmied (Hammid) (1910–2004). Czech documentarist and filmmaker who was married to Deren from 1942 to 1947, and with whom she collaborated.
4. Frederick Kiesler (1890–1965). Viennese-born architect who was a member of the Dutch De Stijl group. After emigrating to the United States in 1926, he designed the Film Guild Cinema (1929), and Peggy Guggenheim's "Art of this century" Gallery in New York (1942).
5. Reference to a sequence in *At Land* (1944).
6. This film is *Ritual in Transfigured Time* (1946).

The Movies and Reality

1. This essay exists in two other versions: "Cinema," *Arts* (New York) 9:6 (June 1929), pp. 314–16; and "The Cinema," *The Nation & Athenaeum* (London) 39:13 (3 July 1926), pp. 381–8.

Movies

1. First published in Lou Andreas-Salomé, *In der Schule bei Freud* (Zurich: Max Niehaus Verlag, 1958); first publication in English in Lou Andreas-Salomé, *The Freud Journal of Lou Andreas-Salomé*, translated and with an introduction by Stanley A. Leavy (New York: Basic Books, 1964).
2. Karl Weiss. A physician in Vienna who published this lecture in in *Imago* II (1913), pp. 552–72, a journal founded in 1912. See Salomé, *The Freud Journal of Lou Andreas-Salomé*, pp. 196, 200.
3. Victor Tausk (1878–1919). Lawyer, journalist, and student of medicine. A member of the Vienna Psychoanalytic Society from 1909 until his death by suicide in 1919. He was one of Andreas-Salomé's lovers.

A Tear for Lycidas

1. *Lycidas*. A pastoral elegy by Milton first published in 1638. It was prompted by the early death of a young friend, Edward King, who had shown intellectual and poetic promise.

Narcissus

1. Dziga Vertov (Dennis Kaufman) (1896–1954). Soviet filmmaker and documentary theorist who founded the Kino-Eye Group. His films include *One-Sixth of the World* (1926), *The Man with the Movie Camera* (1929), and *Three Songs of Lenin* (1934).
2. *Borderline* (1930) was an independently produced silent film of approximately seventy minutes, made by the POOL group of Bryher, H.D., and Kenneth MacPherson in Switzerland, and featuring Paul Robeson, his wife Esland Goode Robeson, and H.D. The story of an interracial love triangle, the film was influenced by theories of intellectual montage and by Freudian psychoanalysis. *Borderline* attracted the support of Lotte Eisner and G.W. Pabst, but the film was not a public success. In the United States, it was impounded by the US Customs Service, and it had very limited exhibition in Europe. The Museum of Modern Art holds a print of *Borderline*.
Policeman's Whistle. We have been unable to find any reference to this film.

Cinema as a Power[1]

Fig. 3.1 Group portrait of the International Federation of Catholic Alumnae reviewers, with Mrs Mary Looram (*back row, right*), in the 1940s

Introduction

When Marie Stopes pronounced, in 1918, that the cinema was "the greatest social influence since the discovery of printing," such a view was no longer news.[2] Large claims had been made for cinema since its inception. Edison imagined the filmic rendering of grand opera, performed by artists since deceased, and the Dicksons (Antonia and her brother, W.K.L.) anticipated the recording and transmission of historical events through film.[3] The device that sent audiences screaming in December 1895 drew millions daily within a span of a decade and a half.[4] Cinema's attraction for these masses would not be disputed; what was at issue were its scope and effects. Cinema *was* a power, but what kind of power did it represent, who was susceptible to it, and how could it be regulated, resisted, or marshaled for good?

Female writers discussed this matter in terms of its impact on the intellect (cinema as instructor), opinions (cinema as persuader), morality and behavior (cinema as guardian, role-model, or corruptor), and emotions (cinema as heightened, new, transporting, or vicarious experience). They attended more to the public than the private consequences of viewing. They occasionally discussed women (Moseley, Diehl, Field, de Koven Bowen, Addams), an audience sector of which they were all, of course, a prismatic part, but more often singled out the child (Elie, Addams, Low, Merriam, Fox, de Koven Bowen), or wrote about the crowd (Stopes, Snow, Pallister, Repplier, Dorothy Richardson). Their tone ranged from patronizing antagonism to philanthropic empathy and compassionate kinship. Some suggested film worked "insensibly" (Dorothy Richardson), "indiscreetly" (Dulac), or "homeopathically" (Elie); it rekindled ills (Washington), retarded infancy (Low), expanded the mind (Perkins Gilman); it induced a passive response (Fox), an imitative one (de Koven Bowen), or a worldly one (Moseley, Dorothy Richardson); it taught what was inaccessible (Stopes, Dorothy Richardson, Dulac), what the eye could not see (Dulac, Field), what should be left unseen (Mansergh, Stopes, West, Merriam), or what the word taught less effectively (Dulac, Weber, Bryher, Perkins Gilman, Stopes, Colette).

Selecting texts for Part Three, "Cinema as a Power" was especially challenging since, during the cinema's first fifty years, women wrote most often on this topic, and most consciously as women. When they took up the pen explicitly as women, female writers readily inhabited a culturally and socially designated niche—that of speaking on behalf of the inarticulate and unempowered: children, immigrants, laboring youth, the family, adolescents.[5] This possibility emerged from two, fused assumptions: that women's innate moral superiority or particularity of experience qualified them especially (even uniquely) to give voice to those in need of protection; and that such a response was women's distinct civic duty. (Cinema audiences included more children, and a greater proportion of the working class than theater audiences, therefore seeming to warrant greater vigilance and supervision.) Not only were women able and allowed to speak, they were impelled as women to do so.[6] Agnes Repplier summarized this status as "the ennobling and purifying influence of woman."[7]

Burgeoning scholarly interest in film censorship is only just beginning to examine the particular role women have played.[8] Feminists have generally averted their gaze from this activity, although it represents (in America at least) a central element of film's social history. Women "mothered the movies," as Alison M. Parker puts it, through the agency of religious groups, professional bodies, child matinée societies, and parents' organizations. They used existing nationwide networks of women's clubs (the Daughters of the American Revolution, the General Federation of Women's Clubs, and the International Federation of Catholic Alumnae, among others) to channel views back to, and away from, Hollywood's offices.[9] While their impact might be viewed as negligible (in terms of affecting film content), or essentially negative—punitive rather than creative—the public expression of female opinion on movie culture was loudly heard. Besides, as Marina Warner has observed, a woman's right of prohibition has traditionally been "an enormous source of female power."[10]

American women's responses to cinema inherited the largely female activism that had underwritten two of the most important reformist movements of the turn of the century: suffrage and prohibition. These efforts had lent the club woman a dynamic and modern image, one now forgotten. As Rebecca West once reported, "the number of serenely energetic American women between forty-five and sixty-five far surpasses the number in England who manage to preserve the integrity of their nervous system"; West appreciated their clubs as breeding grounds for mid-life activism.[11] In 1910, another commentator had described the

> Countless Woman's Clubs, composed of middle-aged women, sprung into eager
> existence in the last twenty years: they are admirable and helpful organizations,
> but they all express in one way or another the restlessness of growth, a restlessness
> infinitely removed from the old content of a generation ago. The "club-woman," as
> she likes to call herself, has none of her mother's placid content with things as they
> are, any more than she has the pretty little accomplishments of her mother's youth,
> or her small conventional charities, or her sweet and gracious and dutiful living.[12]

Club women extended the ideal of female social service, of "municipal housekeeping," into the newly emergent public sphere of the cinema.[13] Their efforts to control and shape this realm took them beyond the confines of home and hearth as they addressed studio heads, picketed screenings, organized Saturday film programs and film evaluation panels, and challenged film distribution systems.[14] Remarkably few expressed, in public, the sense of desperation conveyed by Mrs Winter, in her 21 September 1934 letter to Will Hays, writing as representative for women's groups as part of his Studio Relations Committee in Hollywood:

> A very large part, perhaps a majority, of picture audiences are made up of women. The whole set-up of the previewing service [performed by women's groups] is based upon this fact and the additional fact that women influence the attendance of men and children. You could not get any bodies of men to contribute the kind of help these groups are giving you all over the country merely as a piece of social service, with no returns to themselves. Then why in heaven's name don't you recognize the women's point of view in the creation of standards of production?[15]

While some women went to the pictures after work (as Vorse, Dunbar, and other writers from Part One detail), women of Mrs Winter's ilk went to the movies *as* work, as volunteers for a civic duty without pay.

Club women were not exclusively white; a similar movement existed among middle-class African Americans.[16] The United States National Association of Colored Women, founded in Boston in 1895, with its motto "lifting as we climb," was instrumental in organizing the International Council of the Darker Races in 1920. In 1921, prior to the Third International Convention of Negroes, African-American women were being exhorted to greater community activity, for "no race rises higher than its women."[17] But gender did not provide black women with a source of moral authority and a license to speak in the same way that it did white. A recent study of the community work and social activism of black women in North Carolina during the early part of this century suggests that, typically, communal and racial concerns overrode any perceived to be defined by gender alone.[18] Certainly, the effects of cinema were a vital topic of discussion for women in the African-American press, as a number of pieces in this collection evidence. But it seems that black women's clubs did not organize networked responses to film, partly, no doubt, on account of their smaller scales of operation, and also because of the greater urgency of problems of poverty and poor education. In addition, segregation, not only of cinemas but also of the women's club movement itself, mitigated against black women's activism in this area.[19]

❧

Several women wrote futuristic visions of film, finding it, variously, potentially beneficial, dubiously intrusive, or highly destructive. Mrs Whitby's assessment pointed prophetically to a practical education based on the teaching demonstration: filmed surgery would reach students remote from the classroom; the filmed record of a skill would enable a new level of self-examination.[20] On the other hand, in her short story from 1898, about an affianced couple who have been separated for fifteen years by the demands of imperial service, Mrs Mansergh questioned the new medium's virtue.[21] In her tale film provided surreptitious evidence of the withered charms and dissolute living of the respective parties, images proving too shocking to the ties of affection.

Mansergh imagined an advanced form of cinema; she blended the motion picture with magic lantern slides, and implied a film of thirty minutes' length, not the typical product of 1898.[22] Technical and aesthetic fantasies aside, her romance manqué cloaks the familiar outlines of the detective story, but the "who" of this whodunit is time, whose effects emerge via the detective villain's movie machine.[23] But, in her closing, nuptial remarks, Mansergh queries the value of this lens's sight in suggesting that it may offer only a partial index of truth—that there is a knowledge (of the affections) that escapes that produced by cinematic vision.

That the cinema should be the instrument of such doubt in the visible might strike us as an overly postmodern inflection, but it was precisely this question—what was the reality of screened images and how did they function in the mind of the spectator—that writing on the power of cinema attempted to engage.[24] Of paramount concern was the way in which cinema seemed to test, or even erase, the distinction between public and private worlds. (In Mansergh's fiction, cinema has intruded into two lives which would have been happier left alone.) In her optimistic and visionary essay "Mind-stretching," Charlotte Perkins Gilman found that cinema collapsed the category of the private entirely.[25] She conceived film and the brain as sharing a functional similarity: they were both picture-making faculties. Through this likeness, the mental "spaces" of the individual viewer became one with the larger space on screen, the cinema "stretching" and "unstinting" the mind, stuffing it with endlessly new, proliferating sights, enlarging its activity with minimum effort.[26] This made cinema a superior instructor, one especially stimulating to the child's imagination in that "ability ... to set up some inner picture."[27]

Where for Virginia Woolf (among other writers) the cinema comprised an indexical, photographic link to what had been (was a record of what had existed in front of the camera), Gilman understood the image as prophecy: by showing us "what has not been," the cinema could show us what would be.[28] Her future needed cinema for the transformation of human consciousness, but also to implement a program of reform—her future was rationalist, ruled by technocrats and far-sighted individuals, "city planners, sanitarians, and advanced educators," with film assisting in showing the evils of deforestation and the benefits of energy efficiency and modern dress.[29] By keeping this world and its needs firmly in view (literally by seeing them on screen), the individual and collective "mental area" would be freed to inhabit the universe, indeed would become "coterminous" with it, and would no longer occupy the "parlor" (consciousness) or "cellar" (the unconscious) of Gilman's domestic topography of mental operations.[30]

Screenwriter and director Marguerite Bertsch[31] put the photodrama in the service of a Christian millennialism. This entailed empathetic understanding, the desire for good, and the individual's recognition of a personal conscience. Filmed drama, according to the concluding chapter of her 1917 best-selling guide, enabled viewers to foresee the consequences of their actions, correcting or warning them, and allowing them to experience vicariously the full range of human emotions, living, surviving, and learning from "life's great refining tragedies."[32] As with Gilman, Bertsch's faith in the motion picture as a tool of human perfectibility and as a route to utopia rested on a perceived similarity between the picturing operations of film and humans, and a doing away with the private boundaries of the mind. For both writers, the moving image offered a kind of second sight, either for building a progressive future (Gilman) or for developing moral reasoning and *caritas* (Bertsch).[33]

Marie Stopes also proposed that film duplicated the visualizing capacity of thinking (like Germaine Dulac and Mary Field as well), adding that it was film's capacity to record movement that gave it superior representational force.[34] Cinematic records of motion created "vivid mental images of facts" which endured in memory where verbal representations did not.[35] Stopes, writing during the First World War (as was Bertsch, though she wrote from the United States), also argued that cinema made possible "an extended conception of the human race"—the masses, hitherto denied that potential through their limited education, were glimpsing a wider world.[36] But Stopes's cinematic power was broader and less explicitly instrumental than Gilman's; even the most frivolous picture—to which Gilman referred disdainfully—had value in making worldliness familiar.[37]

The moving picture as a mode of transnational communication portending mutual understanding was a common feature of writing about cinema until at least the late 1920s and the arrival of sound, as noted in Part Two. But this optimistic internationalism was riven with contradiction; if films might show the essential similarity of human kind, their documentary quality might also reveal the other in all the authenticity of his or her alienness, even if this better enabled the viewer to grasp human variety. The newsreel, according to Frances Diehl, showed "all men and all women that other nations are interestingly different but basically and profoundly kin."[38] If seeing the screen could make all men brothers—or all women sisters—this force might equally lead to ill. Films might inspire imitation in their public. If filmed images were indeed experienced as fact, the consequences of viewing American melodramas could only be baneful, and the potential for cinematic propaganda, for misprision, enormous.[39]

Authors who tackled this latter aspect of cinematic power worried that viewers' brains were too passive, held in thrall to the screen and the lure of the auditorium. The gray matter was not "filled" or "stretched," as in Gilman's vision, but a tabula rasa, waiting to be written upon by on-screen events which would then provide a script for future action. Jane Addams was particularly mindful of such dangers. She assessed the cinema with the experience of twenty years of settlement work behind her. In September 1889, with college friend Ellen Starr, she had founded Hull House in a poor and largely immigrant section of Chicago. Initially organized to provide neighborhood entertainment, the House quickly became a center for improving general working and living conditions; Addams and her colleagues agitated against child labor, for the provision of playgrounds and public recreational facilities, for the development of kindergartens and adult education programs, and for the establishment of juvenile courts.[40]

In her popular 1909 study of juvenile delinquency and public morality, *The Spirit of Youth and the City Streets*, Addams reported on the plight of urban adolescents—among them "wayward girls" and "girls gone wrong."[41] In discussing their quest for entertainment, she alighted on drinking, dance halls, sex, baseball, Wild West Shows, parades, cricket, golf, parks, baths, municipal gymnasia, and music in the streets, as well as cinema. For Addams, the latter offered crude fantasies to audiences hungry for release; young folk looked to film for what "reading and reverie" did for the undeprived child.[42] However, decline in moral instruction and parental supervision (a consequence of weakened family structures generated by industrialism and immigration) made the poor, urban audience vulnerable to cinema's illusory worlds. In addition, when immigrant children watched on-screen behavior abhorrent to their elders, without parental consent, their sense of ethnic heritage diminished in inverse proportion to their favorable reception of that before them. Also (and here Addams was criticizing not only film content but its manner of articulation), the chains of cause and effect meanings of dramatic structure gave "a man the thrilling conviction that he may yet be master of his fate," a prospect of self-determination eluding her charges, as Addams was well aware.[43] Ultimately, according to Addams, film promised only to foster a sense of alienation and a "skepticism of life's value."[44]

When Addams wrote that dramatic scenes became the foundation of "working moral codes," and then recounted poor or criminal behavior modeled on film viewing, she was apparently describing a process of mirroring; youth copies the screen, theater forecasts life.[45] In subsequent writing on white slavery, Addams put it this way: "So closely is child life founded upon the imitation of what it sees that the child who knows all evil is almost sure in the end to share it."[46] But Addams's thinking was arguably more complex. By acknowledging the adolescent's conscious search for role models, she granted a spectatorial force beyond the mere act of aping. Her sympathetic account of this audience's need for recreation, discussed in terms of a complex of economic, industrial, and social factors, explains why Addams did not join, outright, the Chicago reformers who wished children banned from cinemas, or who wished nickelodeons themselves shut down. (In fact, Chicago was the first city in the USA to attempt to regulate its moving picture theaters through official censorship, when, on 4 November 1907, pressure from Addams, de Koven Bowen, and a coalition of other influential reformers resulted in a city ordinance requiring police permits for all locally screened films.[47])

When taking this broader view, critics like Addams could see that cinema's appeal resided as much in its setting (its physical and social space) as in its programs, and that both should be regulated; protection from noxious images and themes was a concern, but of equal and possibly greater menace was the communion among variously aged and classed men, women, and children that the darkened interior and garishly postered foyer enhanced.[48] Louise de Koven Bowen's report of a 1909 Juvenile Protective Association investigation of Chicago nickelodeons, and its 1911 follow-up study, is but one example of the growing monitoring of leisure activities of children and the working class in the United States at this time, and a classic text in its negative response to such mingling.[49] For de Koven Bowen, who provided financial support to Hull House and to whom Addams dedicated The Spirit of Youth and the City Streets, nickelodeon entrances were the gates of hell.[50] Late hours and cheap admissions fueled a social mix toxic to the child. Attracted by lurid advertisements, children risked molestation. Physical threats were among the numerous violations of safety codes recorded by the investigation.

Like Addams, de Koven Bowen recounted behavior imitated from the screen, that "fire" for childish imagination, and criticized amateur nights for appealing to "girls [who] in their craving for excitement are only too anxious to appear in public."[51] Her report ended on a clarion call. Following a compendium of worthwhile films as a guide to the wary, she listed needed reforms: theater licensing, prohibition of amateur night, improvement in interior lighting, and censorship of lobby hoardings. Such changes would enable movie theaters to assume their proper role in the city's social life, to play their part as agencies of "wholesome recreation, culture and education" in expanding a program of civic righteousness.[52]

Presenting a paper in England a few years later, in the era of the "picture palace," British headmistress E. Margery Fox stridently concluded that film vitiated life "physically, intellectually, and morally."[53] (The Great War palpably added urgency to Fox's discussion, as if her sense of a threat to British children came in response to the attrition of British men.) Cinematic power—emanating for her more from the screen than from its surroundings—was a particular danger when her charges were unaccompanied (as Addams and de Koven Bowen had similarly found). For Fox, films' illogical aggregation of disparate scenes impeded child learning. (This was in contrast to Addams, for whom films' narrative coherence facilitated spectatorial misidentification.) Further, the passivity of children's viewing jarred with modern conceptions of pedagogy which stressed the centrality of the child's activity in comprehension.[54]

On the other hand, film could also overexcite, threatening nervous disorders—its extreme sensationalism, with impossible situations presented as normal, could be excessively arousing.[55] This tension in Fox's understanding of cinematic effect was paralleled by one present in her research method, which committed her to umpteen insalubrious screenings over several years. (In her submission to the Cinema Commission of Inquiry in 1917, Fox was to retort to one questioner, who had asked her whether she had seen "the picture of the Tanks," a war documentary: "No; I only go to the bad cinemas, those I think are going to be bad."[56]) Bracketing off the possibility of an educative use of the cinema entirely, Fox ultimately concluded that a film's manner of presentation could override its intended meaning, noting her own sympathy for criminals in films whose moral would otherwise suggest that crime does not pay.[57] If a headmistress was not immune to such fabrications, what hope had children? Regulation, an expression of "decent thinking people," should control attendance of those under eighteen.[58]

In the late 1920s and early 1930s, with a rearmed Germany and renewed prospect of large-scale unrest in Europe, another dimension of cinema's power came into focus. War had set a standard of realism against which cinema's images continually failed; war had fueled discussion of film as a universal language; and the use of film as war propaganda had made claims for silent film's transparency and truthfulness dubious. Now, European debates clustered about the influence of war films on children, and the problem of the continued viability of "ciné-internationalism." War films were a limit case, in that their power ran in two opposing directions (they might incite either pacifism or belligerence) and because the thematic stakes were so high: individual life and death; national security; world peace.

The most conspicuous site for these discussions was the International Institute of Educational Cinematography (IIEC), established in Rome in 1928 "to develop an international collaboration in the educational field by means of the educational film."[59] The official publication of the IIEC, The International Review of Educational Cinematography, appeared in English, Spanish, French, Italian, and German editions, the linguistic spectrum underscoring its view of cinema's mission.[60] In 1931, the IIEC hosted the fourth meeting of the International Council of Women's Commission of the Cinema, in Rome, a conference on cinematography and broadcasting attended by delegates from fifteen countries.[61] By way of introducing the subsequently published conference proceedings, Institute director Dr. Luciano de Feo itemized the feminine aspects of the job of developing cinema's peacemaking potential: "Women can fulfil two functions in Cinematographic affairs: take care of those moral principles upon which social life is based, and contribute to the realisation and development of the educational and instructional possibilities of the Cinema."[62] While de Feo noted conflicting opinions—cinema was both dangerous to "human dignity" and capable of refining the purpose of life—women might resolve these contradictions: they were practical (unlike men, who were preoccupied with work or study); they had a natural authority to intervene in matters of private and public morality (and were thus ideally suited to the task of censorship); and because "in every woman there is a mother's heart," women could "smooth and soften" the perpetual struggle of humanity.[63]

De Feo's invocation of the special qualities of womanhood (including women's separation from the world of business) echoed the Italian Fascist state's delimitation of women's role to those of helpmeet and childbearer, even as women themselves sought a more far-reaching purpose; instead of soothing war's struggle, they would end it—while the International Council of Women's Commission of the Cinema was meeting in Rome to discuss movies, the International Council of Women was collecting signatures for arms control. The following year, 1932, the Peace and Disarmament Committee of the International Council of Women presented a petition of six million names to the League of Nations Conference on the Reduction and Limitation of Arms in Geneva.[64] The simultaneity of these events correctly indicates the interrelatedness of two facets of female activism, coalescing under the auspices of the League of Nations: the inquiry into cinematic power, and the drive for international peace. Women were precisely concerned with peace through cinema, or in the face of cinema.[65]

Among the published Rome conference papers was that of Countess Apponyi of Hungary. For her, the cinema was an educator and propagandist, able to make apparent the "solidarity of the whole of human society" and so "unite nations by that sympathy which alone can bring about the security and peace so necessary to the progress of humanity."[66] But war films ran contrary to this great collaborative effort, irrespective of their type; the horror of documentary damaged a child's nervous system, while fictional portrayals "only pervert[ed] the natural judgement of the child on that most terrible of human ills."[67] By contrast, Madame Costanzi-Masi, a member of the National Council of Italian Women, in classifying a range of types of war film, found one category of benefit:

> With regard to the continuance of friendly relationships between the nations, the Italian National Committee is of the opinion that those war films treating recent events should not be shown, for they can bring about bad feeling between the nations. Historical films of a warlike nature, referring to events in the past, however, may contain the principles of virile national education.[68]

The 1931 Rome meeting ultimately approved a compromise resolution favoring the exclusion of films promoting racial and national antagonism, while recommending that "special encouragement be given to producers in every country to assist the development of films that make known the individual characteristics of their own nations."[69] The women's decision attempted to balance the conflicting aims of promoting international understanding and perpetuating national identity, the latter already quite evident in Mussolini's Rome setting.

As part of a series of inquiries into cinema's effect on children, IIEC was to sponsor, in 1931, a questionnaire survey of 200,000 schoolchildren in Rome, as well as one in Belgium, probing the basic question of whether bellicose representations promoted pacifism or militarism in the young.[70] In 1930, Eva Elie of Switzerland had argued that war films might serve a "homeopathic" function, inducing in the child "an intelligent as well as an instinctive horror of war."[71] (She was thereby suggesting that film made its appeal at both a conscious and an unconscious level, and that both tiers needed to be persuaded if a new generation was to be inured.) However, the inconclusive results of the IIEC enquiry, published in the first five issues of the *Review* in 1932, forced Elie to reconsider. In her 1932 "Open Letter to the Director of the IIEC," Elie found that war films were instructive to Italian children but that they were not, as she had anticipated, terrified by their images.[72] Further, exposure to war pictures seemed to promote Italian children's willingness for patriotic sacrifice.[73]

Heeding the flexing of Fascist muscles, Maria Martinez Sierra of Spain revisited the issue a year later, in 1933, noting that the anti-war film (that is, a film using scenes of war with a pacifist intent) could only achieve its aim with an adult audience, for the child was too inexperienced to feel empathy, that particular emotion which a film had to engage if it was to succeed in its pacifist mission.[74]

Children, particularly impressionable and unable to distinguish fact from fiction, fully embraced on-screen characters (a process compared in Sierra's discussion with the overidentification of poorly educated women, who "when they read a novel weep real tears ... at the troubles of the heroine") and identified with the hero (who inevitably survived the battles of war unscathed), for the child directed its imperious ego solely toward self-preservation and sought to suppress anything opposed to it.[75] Given all these conditions and susceptibilities, Sierra suggested the pacifist cause was better served by exploiting the child's imitative instincts: a child "will feel sympathy with an Eskimo or an Indian if he sees them petting their dogs like he pets his own."[76]

Addams, de Koven Bowen, Field, and the League of Nations women had focused on the danger of film to the child audience, but others focused on films that were powerful enough to summon up childish impressionability in adults. Lillie Devereux Blake, Lillian Wald, Fredi Washington, and Marie Stopes all wrote on controversial films (or proposed films) whose contentiousness stemmed from their treatment of race, reproduction, and violence (many such films also either directly represented, or suggested, war), and was heightened by the historical moments of their reception: wartime.[77] They analyzed specific films and recounted specific occasions of viewing, using these case studies to delineate the medium's broader power: cinema could activate otherwise repressed sentiments, adversely expanding audiences both numerically and in terms of worldliness, displaying material and ideas best left unknown. Wald and Blake witnessed instances of bridled or aggressive reception, and reported on this inflammatory atmosphere in order to press home the authenticity, accuracy, and relevance of critical response derived from first-hand knowledge.[78] (Their accounts also suggest the daring of their very presence among an audience.)

Sixty-year-old suffragist Devereux Blake reported on the hideous brutality of boxing pictures when attending a screening of the *Jeffries–Sharkey Contest* (1899), a prizefight fought live in Coney Island, and recorded by American Mutoscope and Biograph Co. (and also, surreptitiously, by the Edison Company) in which white heavyweight champion Jeffries held his title. Boxing films (a vital sub-genre of early cinema) had been protested on account of their violence and possible illegality ever since their first commercial exhibition, when Edison's Kinetoscope parlors offered "Gentleman Jim" Corbett sparring against Peter Courtney at five cents a round, or thirty cents for all six, in 1894. Prizefights had been banned in most of the United States by 1896 for their ghastliness (deaths on the ropes were not uncommon) and on account of their unsavory ringside pall—they were to be suspended in New York in 1900.

Devereux Blake abhorred cinema's power to amplify and transform the prizefight spectacle. Cinema prompted restagings of fights (although not in the case of the specific film she was viewing), effectively changing, even inventing, the event to be filmed—the profilmic material—while it also swelled audiences to include women, and those tens of thousands of film spectators living in states in which live prizefighting was illegal. The recording, reduplicating capacity of film staged the opportunity for the violence welling up in the audience around Blake. The black and whiteness of the image, for all its initial clean classicism, merely postponed the details of damage from eventually seeping through. Dismayed, Blake speculated that either the nation's belligerent mood (a reference to the Spanish–American War), or women's diminished vigilance, were responsible—as for others of her generation, protecting the domestic fabric was, for her, women's work.

The need to stop the spreading of damnable imagery led Lillian Wald to campaign against D.W. Griffith's The Birth of a Nation (1915), a film notorious for its approbation of the Ku Klux Klan and denigrating depiction of blacks. She joined a nationwide crusade to bar the film from exhibition, an effort which united black community leaders and white reformers in common cause. (The most intense struggles—in New York, Boston, and Chicago—ultimately failed to prevent screenings, although the NAACP did succeed in delaying showings and in obtaining excisions.)[79] One racist irony pointed out by the film's antagonists was that the Sims Act (an act passed in 1912, after heavyweight black boxer "Jack" Johnson's successive triumphs over white opponents, which prohibited interstate transportation of prizefight films as well as their importation, and which effectively suspended the movie business's lucrative creation of this genre) now protected audiences from the sight of blacks overcoming whites, while the inverse, as represented in Griffith's film, was being championed by the screen.[80]

Head of New York's Lower East Side Henry Street Settlement, and writing on behalf of herself and Jane Addams, Wald argued that a "grave injustice" was done by the film's historical falsity and appeal to "hate."[81] The period of Reconstruction, still within living memory, was too recent to be shown filmically without risk of reviving its incendiary sentiments of racial antagonism and putting its unificatory goals at risk.[82] Fredi Washington identified a similar relation between past and present in her condemnation of MGM's planned but unproduced 1944 film, Uncle Tom's Cabin, fearing the project would re-arouse attitudes best forgotten.[83] Having reread Harriett Beecher Stowe's 1852 abolitionist novel, Washington echoed the opinions of W.E.B. DuBois in pointing out that racial attitudes of white America had not changed since Stowe's time.[84] A new film version of the play would firm up these prejudices by giving them renewed commercial form, bolstering them rather than dispelling them in the minds of white spectators. In a context in which black soldiers were dying for a democracy which underrepresented them—by fighting in the Second World War—Washington argued that "the Negro" needed a positive representation of his or her modernity, not the revival of outmoded thinking which would retard his or her advancement to full equality.

War, too, played its role in Marie Stopes's drafting of her letter protesting Lois Weber's 1916 anti-abortion film Where are My Children? Released in the United States in May 1916, and in the United Kingdom on 8 November 1916, the picture was originally titled The Illborn. We glimpse the role of eugenics, and, indirectly, racial hierarchy, both in the film's British exhibition history—it was shown under the auspices of the National Council of Public Morals as an explanation for the decline of the British birth rate—and in Stopes's reception of its theme, for, as a member of the Eugenics Society, she envisaged birth control as improving the national stock.[85] Stopes was not generally in favor of censorship (indeed, as representative of the Society of Authors on the Cinema Commission of Inquiry in 1917, she was to have the first of her many clashes with T.P. O'Connor MP, the Chief Film Censor), but she found Weber's film dangerous in that its very news of abortion as a means of reproductive management might damage the birth-control movement. Like Wald, who found The Birth of a Nation's presentation of black males during the Civil War and Reconstruction incomplete in not reporting that there were no recorded instances of black men attacking white women, Stopes posited that what a film does not show renders it factually inexact, and thereby risks dangerous distortion in argument: Weber had failed to show the real economic and social reasons for the dwindling birth rate.[86] Ironically, Stopes's final criticism was strikingly prescient of the conservative reaction her own book, Married Love, was to suffer, for she faulted Weber for making available knowledge—abortion as a method of population limitation—better kept secret, not least because it made a work sensational.[87]

Before considering the ways in which women argued for curtailing access to such knowledge, we need to recall the ways in which women, as 89 per cent of the nation's teachers, considered cinema as an instructor for good.[88] "Enlightment without tears," Dorothy Richardson's evocation of cinema's educational style, reminds us that the audience sucking oranges before the screen (Fox) might also be the audience at school.[89] Optimistic pronouncements of cinema's role often included an educational dimension. Hattie Loble even proffered that it might "suggest normal thought to the insane."[90]

It is probably impossible for us now to comprehend the initial excitement of seeing distant lands become mobile and proximate on the screen. Cinema afforded a touristic (some will say internationalist) acquaintance with the world. When exploring a specific opportunity for learning, writers often latched onto this cartographic bounty. In a 1916 letter written to an early British film magazine, a "governess" hoped that film might transform geographic instruction, for if her charge, "Betty," could see "real little Japs and wee Hindoos running about at play in their respective countries, the crack-jaw names of their mountains and rivers would stick in her mind ever so much more easily, because she would realize that Japan and India were actual places where boys and girls not so very unlike herself ... lived."[91] As Stopes, Diehl, and others also hoped, the cinematic image taught likeness more than difference, from which came understanding (although, as discussed in the context of the war film, this interpretation was not automatic, and the opposite result could ensue).

The governess's letter also made clear geography's place in imperial education:

> As things are, Betty will have to commit laborious lists of exports to memory, and the chances are that she will forget on some critical occasion that tea comes from India, or coffee from Ceylon. If she could go to a Cinema, and watch the natives ... working in the tea plantation, or attending to the coffee plants, she would get the facts firmly fixed in her head for the rest of her natural life.[92]

Colette's account of children before a fast-motion germinating bean echoed the Governess' faith: "I saw children get up, imitate the extraordinary ascent of a plant climbing in a spiral ... groping over its trellis: 'It's looking for something! It's looking!' cried a little boy.... These spectacles are never forgotten and give us the thirst for further knowledge."[93] Indeed, educational filmmaker Mary Field quipped to an interviewer that such films might surpass features in their excitement: "Thrills? What screen romance can compare with the sight of tiny rootlets plunging their way into the ground, or the baby chickens growing within the egg."[94]

Cinema's capacity to picture plantations, or to display invisible, temporal processes—be they the trajectory of evolutionary change (for Perkins Gilman), or the maturation of a legume (for Colette, Field, and Dulac)—had ramifications for the curriculum beyond geography or biology. In reporting on Lois Weber's intention to direct a series of educational films in 1934, journalist Winifred Aydelotte cited a new pleasure in learning based on the general principle that moving images remain longer in the mind than facts acquired by rote, an argument already outlined by "the Governess," as well as Bertsch, Perkins Gilman, and Stopes. Learning would no longer be "a monotonous routine of study and recitations," but would become "a continuous succession of vivid experiences."[95]

Writing in 1910, Jane Elliott Snow even appreciated the educational consequences of ordinary nickelodeon attendance.[96] Motion pictures provided necessary relaxation at day's end, effortlessly "broadening" the laborer's world.[97] Repeating the kind of transposition found in Gilman's "Mindstretching," Snow described this person's "views of life" as expanded by the consumption of new, filmic locales.[98] And, referring to entertainment bills combining actuality and fiction film (fairly standard fare in 1910), she proposed that the cinema's value as an educator lay in its cheapness, its proximity, and its fusion of amusement and instruction.[99] Mary Field valued the entertainment film for similar reasons and, in an observation we see repeated, held that the young learned poise in their film viewing—a factory girl could now know how to act in a European Grand Hotel.[100] Like the woman mentioned by Stopes, who incidentally gleaned the existence of abortion by watching Weber's film, such viewers could not have come by their knowledge in any other way. Dorothy Richardson was one of the many writers who cast this chance education extremely positively. In taking up the cause of the great unwashed in "The Cinema and the Slums," she argued that cinema assisted the masses more than either philanthropy or compulsory education, in part because it was untainted by altruism—it had no mission to help, required no gratitude.[101] She conjured up a cinematic power as pervasively polyvalent as the beneficence she claimed for it; accidental instruction for her amounted to far more than merely learning some manners. This "civilising agent" extended "cramped" lives by putting them "into communication with the general life."[102]

A portion of Richardson's argument was undoubtedly rhetorical. As much as she proposed the integrity of commercial exchange (money for entertainment, no do-gooding strings attached), she was equally against a narrowly instrumental view of cinema as uplift, disliking the purposeful instructional film, and favoring the more variable, incidental knowledge of the feature (like Field). In fact, cinema taught everything that formal education did not—it made concrete how the other half lived. Where Barbara Low was to cite a Birmingham investigation to argue that the dangers "of the Cinema providing an *effortless* way of acquiring *superficial* knowledge must always be guarded against if the Cinema is to be of real educational value," Richardson subtly refashioned the problem of audience passivity, writing that, because film bestowed its gifts unawares, the audience retained them all the more.[103] Not being "spoon-fed," not simply looking and listening, viewers learned "the gift of quiet, of attention, and concentration, of perspective," as well as an "awareness of alien people and alien ways."[104] They gained a training both in spectatorship and in the film's content, being suffused with unsuspected effects. Occupied by and with the screen, they were themselves "cultivating and improving the medium from which they ha[d] drawn life."[105]

Agnes Repplier shared Richardson's sense that cinema's greatest power lay in its chance rather than intended effects; the "uncounted throngs" did not go to the movies to be educated, and neither did the movies pretend to educate them, but films had an unplanned "unconscious humor" in their divergence from life.[106] However, where Richardson evaluated this power in positive (if vague) terms, Repplier, while accepting as legitimate the world's need for entertainment, mocked the movies' pretensions to broach international understanding, detailing their sentimentality and inflated ambitions, their condescension to viewers, and the gap between their idealized representations and spectatorial knowledge of what she referred to as "the pure drama of life," the very gap between them being productive of unconscious humor.[107] The power of cinematic realism was inherently compromised (as was intuitively apparent to her viewers); films were a symptom of the age, not the operation of a threatening force in need of control, for how could censors "destroy realism in what [was] already unreal"?[108]

Addams's argument in "The House of Dreams" had not precluded her own selective use of film, even if her appreciation of cinema caught some off-guard.[109] She was not against cinema *per se* so much as the way in which popular dramatic forms profited from and exploited the legitimate "childish eagerness for pleasure."[110] In her history of Hull House, Addams described the settlement's short-lived, second-floor, safe cinema, a model nickelodeon offering educational and higher-brow fiction pictures in 1907.[111] In return for Carl Laemmle's largesse (he supplied her films for free), Addams allowed her name and views to embellish his advertising (which in turn helped him in his battle to stop the Edison empire from encircling the so-called "Independent" filmmakers and distributors).[112] While foreseeing a positive role for cinema in schools and churches, Addams's Laemmle letter suggested that cinema's worth stretched far beyond the particular lessons of individual films, for, in its very representation of daily life, cinema laid forth the unsuspected "inner beauty" of the familiar.

Addams grapples here for language found in later arguments made by Woolf and others articulating, however vaguely, the penetrating and revelatory power of the camera's eye. For Field, a co-director of the famous British *Secrets of Nature* series (which also recorded leguminous growth), newsreels and documentaries were the most instructive of readily available films. Of particular force were disaster scenes, inspiring empathetic response to human suffering, although the magazine structure of programming, in its chop and change fashion—volcanic eruptions tucked among car races—tended to interrupt or dilute this emotional identification.[113] Germaine Dulac also had high praise for the newsreel and the scientific film, both of which showed "images of life in its various instinctive movements."[114] The cinema news theater (a new type of auditorium devoted exclusively to newsreels and linked to the Parisian daily press) was "the great social educator," providing immediate images of nation and race, which, in their precision, would develop familiarity and thence sympathy in their audience.[115]

According to Dulac, the newsreel's method of instruction was "indiscreet"; it taught "without form or methodology," putting the spectator in "direct relations with the events, beings, ideas and objects of the whole world."[116] Viewers became part of the world depicted on-screen. This model of movie power might be slighted for its idealism, for it implied that what a filmgoer saw was the real world, but perhaps something more interesting is at hand. Simply by witnessing filmed "movements" of national society, the spectator was taught, recognizing his or her place in the general "movement" of modernity: as Dulac put it, "the cinema teaches life."[117]

Both Field's and Dulac's discussions of films' educational role emerge from the context of nurturing film culture.[118] Both wrote as experienced filmmakers: Field was already known for her nature films, and, at the time of publication, in 1934, was producing shorts for schools at Gaumont British; Dulac had established a reputation in the 1920s as an avant-garde director, but her filmmaking had, by now, included newsreel production.[119] She had earlier been active in the French ciné-club movement, traveling, lecturing, and presenting films since the early 1920s, and had founded the (single-issue) journal *Schémas* in 1927.[120] Both women expounded a broad concept of education through film by analyzing the medium itself as much as the uses to which it had been put. Field wrote that film viewing was not an innate activity but a learned one, to be improved through hard work, so that we gradually came to see and understand more.[121] Stressing film's mechanical basis, Dulac described the camera as "a powerful eye added to our own."[122] By making the very small and imperceptible apparent, cinema benefited both artistic sensibility and scientific knowledge. It revealed on both the grand and the small scale, showing the "great and effective lines" of life of other races, creating common understanding by teaching the similarity of different lives (an argument heard across this collection).[123] Echoing Perkins Gilman's vision of a collective mind coterminous with the universe, Dulac wrote of cinema's consequences, "When children or adults have been visually educated ... they will understand that nature outstrips imagination and that the duty of the latter is simply to join the dream to the reality. When penetrated with the profound sense of the Cinema, they [children and adults] will become the public of tomorrow."[124]

Within this mission, avant-garde practitioners had a crucial, dual role: their work was a testing ground for the development of cinema as a whole—and in this way truly experimental—and was an instructor for the public in learning about the nature of film itself.[125] This twin pedagogical function, this doubling of cinema's power, developed both through repeated viewings, through which the invisible within film emerged (as both Field and Dulac noted), and in those avant-garde assays through which cinema found new expressive means (as Dulac suggested).[126]

Barbara Low's writing stands in stark contrast to all this enthusiasm. Her "Mind-Growth or Mechanization?" formulates one of the most sophisticated theories of cinema's power to be found in this part of the collection. A lay analyst and pedagogue, she was concerned specifically with the child audience and its psychological growth. She argued that watching films confirmed in the child an illusory sense of omnipotence and, as such, was inherently regressive, stymying the child's development. Making these claims independently of what was on the screen (it was "the method of the cinema" that produced this result), she observed that spectatorial affect overrode factual content; film's exclusive appeal to visuality kept the child at an infantile level of curiosity, providing immediate gratification through sight, without effort.[127] In contrast to Perkins Gilman's view, Low's cinema operated in "a mechanical universe," unfolding in the constant present, retarding the development of the child's conception of time; film denied the experience of bodily duration, forestalling the child's acceptance of death, a prerequisite for successful maturation.

Like de Koven Bowen and Addams, Low berated the cinema as generally bad for children, but this time because of the "lack of emotional contact" it fostered.[128] The apparatus's retention of both adult and child in a state of infantile narcissism was more serious for children because, by keeping them at this level, the cinema was producing adults who were really, emotionally and mentally, children. In these ways, by meeting the twentieth century's newly childish desire for instant gratification, cinema contributed to Low's dismal view of modernity.

Another way of characterizing the kinds of distinction these writers were making—between the blatant and the peripheral, the planned and the accidental, the intelligent and the instinctive (Elie), glamour and life, or even the conscious and the unconscious—is in terms of the Gestalt relation of figure to ground.[129] Many of these women understood cinema to produce a diffuse meaning, a quality as much the result of the nature of cinema itself (its picture-making capacity in Woolf, its odd difference from reality in Repplier, its "indiscreet" confrontations in Dulac) as of film audiences' viewing habits, or of specific screen imagery and plots. Two of the most literary observers, Woolf and Richardson, argued most strongly against an approach to examining film that would stress its "obvious" dramatic content, even as American high school English teachers were beginning to institute precisely such an approach.[130] Efforts to insist on the distinction between figure and ground (rather than notice these levels' elusive, symbiotic, shifting exchanges), to control both the planned and accidental lessons of cinema, are in large part the story of censorship.

Underlying women's individual and collective attempts to tame cinematic might ran a fear that neither the industry, nor the meanings of its films, nor the culture of moviegoing were controllable, a fear balanced by the hope, if not belief, that intervention by consumer groups or the state might reign in influence and harness bad effects. Proponents of censorship sought to regulate both at the point of production, through scrutiny of scripts, and at the point of exhibition, through excision of material. Both activities aimed to protect by removing contact with threatening images and language. Those anti-censorship (Rinehart, Merriam, Field, Lejeune, and Diehl are among those considered here) expressed faith in a different dimension of consumer power. Concentrating on the process of reception, they argued for training the viewer to see critically, and thus to internalize safety measures; armed with a method, and knowledge to resist screen maleficence, audiences would vote with their feet and effect a market-driven check.[131] (Early high school film appreciation courses in America were part of this movement.) For all the writers admiring the medium's power, there is, therefore, in this final grouping, a counter-investment in setting up discursive, institutional, legal, and inculcated constraints.

The Church played a key role wherever control meant the protection of vulnerable groups: in the United Kingdom, through the Bishop of Birmingham, Russell Wakefield, who was President of the Cinema Commission of the National Council of Public Morals in the late 1910s, for example; and in the United States, in an infinitely more far-reaching case, through the Catholic Church and its participation in the National Legion of Decency's drive to influence the motion picture industry, as well as in the film previewing activities of the all-female International Federation of Catholic Alumnae (IFCA). The Catholic magazine *Extension* debated the degree of moral guilt (mortal or venial) an adult incurred by deliberately patronizing a film condemned by the Legion of Decency, concluding that "in most cases, the harm done is gradual, and by way of general tendency," and does not result from a single infraction.[132]

The rhetoric of maternalism clarified woman's special fitness to censor: woman was the guardian of the family, and, since the motion picture was one of the greatest influences on family life, its regulation was her legitimate concern. Censorship boards in Italy and Australia required the presence of a mother to operate, while, in 1912, in the United Kingdom, the cabinet recommended that one of the four censors of the newly forming British Board of Film Censors (BBFC) should be a woman, if not a mother.[133] In 1911, reporting on similar developments in the USA, the *Illustrated London News* published a drawing of censors screening films at the New York People's Institute[134] (See Fig. 3.2). The drawing showed the New York Board of Censors (which was led at the time by the secretary of the People's Institute, and had been operating since March 1909) to be comprised, on this occasion, of one hatted woman, sitting prominently in the foreground, and three men. Perhaps the woman was Miss M. Serena Townsend, of the Woman's Municipal League, who had been selected for the Board at its inception.[135]

Maternalism was a legacy of the nineteenth-century doctrine of separate spheres (in which men and women attended to, and lived in separate realms), but also indicated the burgeoning professionalization of the maternal role, one simultaneously expressed in the growth of female employment in social work, teaching, and nursing. The related notions that women had superior judgement in matters of taste and "art" (their male counterparts approached art "with the mind of a prurient greengrocer"), and heightened perception of emotional nuance and morality, also qualified them better for censoring—as well as for, paradoxically, the job of screenwriter.[136]

American women's groups were enormously active ranking, surveying, censoring, and generally working to "improve" film during the late 1910s, 1920s, and early 1930s; from cursory research into the question, it seems that British women were also moderately active.[137] The scale of women's activism in British film reform was certainly sufficient to make Caroline Denton-Smyth, secretary to "the Christian Cinema Company formed for the Purification of British Film," and the eponymous heroine of Winifred Holtby's satirical novel Poor Caroline, a recognizable figure.[138]

One important distinction between the British and American film businesses was economic. As Annette Kuhn has noted, in Britain films made money through marketing rather than production (given the high proportion of foreign, and especially American films shown on British screens, a rate often running at 75 per cent). In Britain, therefore, censorship usually had to operate at distribution and exhibition points rather than at earlier stages in a film's life, as the letter published here by Marie Stopes suggests.[139] Much of the shaping and curtailing of films shown in Britain had already been accomplished in the United States, by organizations and industry discussions acting nearer the point of production, although cooperation between the two nations' censorships took tangible, concrete form at times.[140]

The only writing included here that extensively discusses British censorship is Rebecca West's preface to Bernard Causton and G. Gordon Young's Keeping it Dark, or the Censor's Handbook, and it is anomalous on several counts. Anti-libertarian, repressive, and we might now say homophobic in its overall approach, West's essay is one of only two non-fictional reflections on film she penned.[141] A cursory glance suggests that, despite her general argument against censorship (which we might expect, given West's earlier career of radical suffrage journalism), movies constituted "cheap and ugly and depressing" offerings, the audible realism of a chorus girl's hiccup (newly intrusive on account of the coming of sound) eliciting particular disgust.[142] However, West's ultimate target is the system of restraint which indirectly nurtured such representation; the girl's involuntary spasm seems, in West's essay, to be a metonym for what must break through under repressive conditions (and an event that might be likened, in its status of uncontrolled release, to the sneeze in Edison's kinetoscope film Fred Ott's Sneeze (1894), a film which Linda Williams has interpreted within the pornographic genre).[143] The hiccup simply proves West's thesis that censorship sensationalizes that which it seeks to bury; the imposition of rules nourishes corporeal offense.

The case of homosexuality proves this, above all: despite a relentless ban on its discussion over the last thirty years, since the Oscar Wilde trial of 1895, "homosexuality has enormously increased."[144] Efforts to censure it have backfired, producing a martyr in Wilde, and, more recently, in Radclyffe Hall (whom West elsewhere described as "a very beautifully made sporting rifle or golf club").[145] According to West, censorship has both failed to contain the supposedly objectionable, and hidden the very clinical knowledge that West believed would have been able to stem the behavior—parental reticence has stimulated the next generation's interest.[146]

The very arrangement of West's case seems to undo her point. There is little way of comparing the increasing visibility of homosexuality, as a response to the Wilde trial, with a female film sound effect; in terms of West's argument, suppression of information provokes the first, its excess the second. In writing that cinema produces sounds and images better left unheard and unseen, West seems to recommend the very procedure of occlusion she criticizes. What was it that caused film to overstep a threshold, for West, and so warrant oversight? Or, to put it another way, what was causing these inconsistencies in West's argument? West suggests that cinema invites addiction, like drugs or alcohol, that its show of movement, its "writhing," lay on the verge of indecency, and that its advertising was more powerfully misleading than literature's. All these might contribute to an answer, in addition to her remarks that modern life drove her to the movies, for she now needed their soothing convenience, cheapness, and informality, even though it was precisely such casual, unplanned attendance which put her, the young, and the masses at risk.

By the early 1920s, the central symbol of cinematic vice was Hollywood itself. Several events had exacerbated this impression: Mary Pickford's quickie divorce and remarriage to Douglas Fairbanks (1920); the trial of Roscoe "Fatty" Arbuckle for the murder of Virginia Rappe (1921); the announcement of the (accidental) drug addiction of the apparently clean-living, all-American matinée idol Wallace Reid; the death from drugs of Jack Pickford's wife Olive Thomas; and the murder of director William Desmond Taylor (1922) (Mabel Normand and Mary Miles Minter, who had enjoyed sexual relations with him, were implicated in the case). In the resulting scandals several careers expired, as daily reporting conflated the bad behavior and illicit lifestyles of movie folk with the salacious content of motion pictures generally. This blending—the stock-in-trade of the popular press, as Anita Loos and Katharine Fullerton Gerould observed—effectively doubled a filmic force already widely perceived as malignant.[147]

The film-reforming club women tackling this evil garnered an unflattering profile. A religious journal dubbed them "deluded women"; elsewhere they were "dyspeptic middle-aged souls who dislike lithe, willowy ladies on principle"; in 1940 they received advice to "weep no more" over their failure to understand the movie business.[148] Some activities of organized women's groups were undoubtedly puritanical: they attempted to stop Sunday film screenings, advised parents to keep their children completely out of cinemas, and reported suggestive lobby cards to

Fig. 3.2   "'Redfords of the Screen: Censors of Living Pictures,' the work of the New York Board of Censors at the People's Institute," *Illustrated London News*, 22 April 1911

local censor boards.[149] But it is important to recall the wider context in which club women understood their cinematic mission, and to recognize their substantial legacy of literature on film culture.

Mrs Thomas Edison treated 147 presidents from the General Federation of Women's Clubs to a display of her husband's "new Kinetograph" in his laboratory in 1891.[150] While their scrutinous gazes were presumably as yet undeveloped for celluloid—the picture they saw was of the gentlemanly W.K.L. Dickson in tie and waistcoat doffing his hat—it seems hardly fortuitous that such is the first known news record of a film audience. Club women's interest in film intensified during two subsequent historical periods. In 1908, the New York Women's Municipal League, in partnership with the progressive People's Institute, undertook a study of movies, and, while deploring exhibition conditions, praised films in their resulting report for supplying "healthy and even educational amusement."[151] When the New York Board of Censorship was formed a year later—partly as an industry response to

Mayor McClellan's closure of New York City's nickelodeons, as dangerous amusement, on Christmas Eve of 1908—the Women's Municipal League was one of the civic organizations represented, as mentioned above.[152]

The second period of fervent female activity occurred during the 1920s, coinciding with the Hollywood scandals and the proliferation of local censorship boards, boards which were weakening the effectiveness and image of the National Board of Review (formerly the New York Board of Censorship), and swelling the general climate of public concern about moviegoing practices.[153] There were growing calls for federal intervention; the passing of censorship legislation in New York State in 1921 was one of many red flags (to the industry), warning of the "slide towards government control."[154] When Will Hays (former chairman of the Republican party and Postmaster General in president Warren G. Harding's cabinet) took up the post of President of the newly formed Motion Picture Producers and Distributors of America (MPPDA) in 1922, to rescue the situation, he made one of his first orders of business the establishment of a Public Relations Committee, for which, to the skepticism of some, he solicited representatives from various women's organizations.[155] The history of the emergence of a Hollywood censorship code from the early 1920s onwards was, at one level, a response to public, and women's groups' discontent. It was also, first and foremost, the industry's attempt to set down what was likely to be banned, or to provoke actions from state censorship boards.[156] The MPPDA adopted a so-called "Thirteen Points" of proscribed elements for film in 1924, embellishing it in 1927 with a series of "Don'ts and Be Carefuls." The Production Code of 1930 ratified the do's and don'ts, and, through a series of rewritings (there is no definitive text of the Code because it was continually being refined and revised), gave rise to the establishment of the Production Code Administration (PCA) in 1934.[157] Under these rules, Mae West's It Ain't No Sin would be retitled Belle of the Nineties.

Widespread public perception was that industry efforts at movie clean-up of the early 1920s had been a sham. Among the series of subsequent modifications and adjustments engineered by the movie business, led by Hays, was the establishment, in March 1925, of a Department of Public Relations, dubbed the "Open Door," which replaced the Committee on Public Relations.[158] Its name was to evoke an image of unimpeded and helpful exchange between public and industry. The Hays Office now worked very hard at appearing to include female opinion, even if only as a public relations exercise, further nurturing its relationships with women's groups. Mrs Frances White Diehl, in her office as chairman of Motion Pictures at the General Federation of Women's Clubs (GFWC) for example, was to formalize official contact with the Hays Office in 1927. Hays also conspicuously reached out to women in New York in September 1929, at a meeting attended by film industry executives, lawyers, and religious leaders, as well as women's groups. The four-day conference was titled "The Community and the Motion Picture."[159] There, Mrs Alice Ames Winter, former president of the GFWC, became official liaison to the industry on behalf of ten million other women, serving on the Studio Relations Committee. She had an office alongside the Production Code staff, was on their payroll, and earned the moniker "Lady Czar of the Movies."[160]

Frances White Diehl's "Women and the Cinema" of 1934 summarizes her much fuller exposition of club women's aims and methods, delivered at the Rome Conference of October 1931, where she had spoken as representative of the United States National Council of Women (a group composed of twenty-three different women's organizations with a combined membership of several million), and as Chairman of its Motion Pictures Department.[161] Although an American organization, the National Council of Women assumed a global responsibility for motion pictures, recognizing the dominance of American film on the world scene, and believing that "considerations which inspire women to exert their influence on the medium of the screen are universal."[162] Diehl argued that motion pictures should represent woman "with true proportionate stress on the great urges that motivate her life" (a reference presumably to motherhood above all) rather than showing her "solely in the role of sex protagonist."[163] Drawing up a balance sheet on cinematic influence, the promotion of world peace headed the ledger's positive side: "I place that first," Diehl declared, "because no topic is dearer to the hearts of women.... There is no division among women. With every fiber of our beings we are against war; we are for peace."[164]

Diehl and the organizations she represented were, of course, concerned with the ledger's negative side, especially with those films "anti-social in their influence," which violated "cherished moral or cultural values."[165] Censorship, however, was not the answer. Noting the current failure of Prohibition to instill temperance, Diehl knew that law did not make men good. Rather than legislative fiat, she recommended educating public taste, as well as industry cooperation with women's groups which might "analyse and regulate" films' effects.[166] To this end, she published a regular column in Ladies' Home Journal during 1932 titled "Recommended Motion Pictures." In her later, 1934 essay, "Women and the Cinema," as in her 1931 speech, Diehl triumphantly attributed recent improvements in American film to the activities of American club women; dubious of Mrs Catheryne Cooke Gilman, she especially complimented A.A. Winter, claiming that the women of America were "in large part responsible" for the (recently reinforced) Production Code, even if motion picture attendance remained, in its influence in family life, "our great and most immediate social problem."[167]

Diehl's speech was widely reported (and later published), inspiring a number of headlines upsetting to the industry, such as "Woman Urges Movie Reform," and "Calls Movie Censorship a Complete Failure."[168] Richard Maltby's research has revealed that Frederick Herron, Head of the MPPDA's Foreign Department, reported to Will Hays that Diehl had "done as bad a job in Rome as it is possible for anyone to have pulled off," and that she had been quoted in the New York Times as claiming, "I do not believe ... that the mothers of civilized countries will stand for the trash which most motion picture producers are now giving us."[169] Hays and Herron were evidently incensed by Diehl's apparent insults to the MPPDA, and by the Congress's further resolution to end block-booking and establish an international convention on censorship, both gestures towards curtailing American movie influence. Her speech was, in actuality, far more moderate than the reactions provoked, pointing to the tangible force of women's opinions when expressed in such public fora for the MPPDA.

Civic leaders like Diehl believed that reformers' collective responsibility overrode that of individual parents', for unsupervised children needed to be "protected and guided toward the proper type of picture."[170] If club women could claim any influence on the increased production of this type of picture, this was due, in part, to their recognition of the economic realities of the motion picture industry. As Diehl put it, it was not sufficient to condemn bad products—club women had to create demand for better. One activity that had emerged to this end was the Better Films Movement, established in 1917.[171] Club women had, from the start, proffered this system as an alternative to government intervention in filmmaking. (As a representative and member of the National Committee for Better Films, Louise Connolly traveled through Georgia and North Carolina in 1921 to stave off official intervention, and addressed the Committee on Education of the House of Representatives in 1926 with the same goal, contributing to the aversion of federal censorship.[172]) Richard Kozsarski has described the Movement's activities as "ambitious, well-organized, and certainly the earliest national effort to promote film as a medium of social and artistic importance," setting the "national agenda for serious film study during this period."[173] Some Better Films groups formed independently, while others arose as a result of National Board of Review policy. Interestingly, in that it indicates yet again women's significance in these matters, the large-scale female involvement in these latter groups triggered criticism that the Board was "the biggest woman's club machine in the country."[174]

Just such a Better Films Service was run as part of the Good Citizenship Bureau of *Woman's Home Companion*; director of the Bureau, Anna Steese Richardson, touted hers as the first general magazine to offer this resource.[175] Through the publication of booklets, her Bureau instructed on the operation of government, provided lists of approved fiction, and assisted club women in matters of procedure and coordination. It occasionally advised readers on proposed legislation affecting women and children. The Better Films Service published lists of recommended films, reviewed by an "expert," and, in 1923, the Good Citizenship Bureau announced the first of an anticipated series of *Woman's Home Companion* films: "This Wife's Business" was claimed to be "as wholesome as the fiction in the magazine, and as gay and entertaining as real-life comedy can make them, in no way propaganda, but with a real thought in back of them."[176]

The Better Films Service aimed to involve the entire community, and trumpeted successful cooperation between women's clubs, theater management, chambers of commerce, religious groups, and service organizations from the Rotarians to the Boy Scouts. Such community-oriented activities exploited cinema's civic potential, aiming to siphon its attractiveness into the new role of "grand social worker," while also working to improve the medium itself by educating public taste.[177] In 1919, Janet Priest, sketching a range of initiatives undertaken by individual cities nationwide in cooperation with the Better Photoplay League of America (another splinter of the Better Films Movement), had outlined the philosophy: "Are you

Fig. 3.3   Frances White Diehl in 1930

interested in your city's welfare? The officials of the cities … are a few of those who are really concerned in the well-being of the commonwealths they represent. And their attitude represents … a definite 'platform' for pictures of the better type. Clean streets, clean yards, clean houses," mattered little, she argued, if people did not have "clean minds, and to a large extent the minds of Americans of to-day are guided by the motion pictures they see. Clean films are essential to the welfare of every community."[178]

In 1925, Zelda Fitzgerald included a film service—the fictional "Our Own Movie" committee of New Heidelberg—in her short story "Our Own Movie Queen."[179] It is possible to interpret this inclusion as a satire on the hubristic and naïve aspirations of some branches of the Better Films Movement. However, writing in the same year, film actress and director Leah Baird could surmise that women's work in Better Film departments (by then established in "all of the units of the National Federation of Women's Clubs") had been "indirectly responsible" for a "drastic and interesting change": "what began to be known as 'the Woman's Point of View'" had led to "added responsibilities" being "given to the women of the industry in the belief that they could better gauge the pulse beat of women in general. In doing this the producers [had] acted on the theory that the larger portion of a picture audience [is] made up of women."[180] Club women's attention to the screen had, according to Baird, indirectly increased female employment in Hollywood.

The most influential and largest of the women's film reviewing services was the International Federation of Catholic Alumnae (IFCA).[181] (See Fig. 3.1) Founded in 1912, IFCA drew membership from female alumnae of Catholic high schools, colleges, and universities, upholding the ideals of Catholic womanhood, and extending Catholic education through literature, motion pictures, and social service. It was among the more than two hundred civic, religious, educational, and service institutions that had attended a special emergency conference called by Hays in 1922, in the infancy of the Open Door initiative, and became one of those groups officially responsible for registering objections to films with the MPPDA, and for encouraging public support of worthwhile pictures.[182] From 1924 onward, the all-woman Federation began compiling and distributing lists of recommended films to Catholic schools through its Motion Pictures Department, reviewing up to eleven thousand films annually, including shorts, documentaries, and foreign films.[183] It held to a philosophy of informed choice, and did not make consumers pledge not to see certain pictures, as the League of Decency was to do in the next decade. A *Woman's Home Companion* article on Hays's September 1929 crisis meeting (a meeting precipitated in part by the new challenges to morals sound film presented) reported that the Federation had been cited, among volunteer organizations, for performing "the most effective and consistent work in film betterment for the community."[184]

Another volunteer group largely staffed by women and concerned with film was the National Congress of Parents and Teachers, which, between 1922 and 1924, published its pamphlet of approved films, *Endorsed Films*, guiding parent-teacher associations nationwide.[185] Mrs Charles E. Merriam, Chairman of the Better Films Committee of the National Parent–Teacher Association, and of the Parent–Teacher Association of Chicago in 1924, recommended drastic action in her "Solving the Motion Picture Problem."[186] Parents should keep children out of motion picture theaters as much as possible; instead children might do dramatics, an activity profiting from their natural desire to act. (Others were to recommend music lessons as an antidote to moviegoing: "every piano keyboard kept in practical use is a barrier against the dangerous misuse of leisure time in adult life."[187]) Children's viewing, when it did occur, should be parentally supervised and limited to endorsed films.

Merriam resigned from her chairmanship the year her article was published, in 1924. Richard de Cordova has noted a change in the PTA attitude toward film at this point, corresponding perhaps to the recommendations of Merriam's successor, Mrs Elizabeth Kerns, who did not favor denigrating individual films, believing this served as free publicity.[188] One problem beleaguering reform groups was precisely their industry-encouraged policy of backing the best and ignoring the rest. Could groups remain easy pretending ignorance of films left off their lists? Another difficulty was the corollative perception that reformers were in thrall to Mr. Hays.[189] Catheryne Cooke Gilman's "Better Movies—But How?", of 1930, illuminated one side of this struggle in its complete refutation of cooperation.

Gilman pitted the humanitarian aims of women's groups against the "unhealthy" commerce of a profit-seeking industry, criticizing women's volunteer reviewing as mere surface public relations, performed at the industry's bidding.[190] She saw the Better Films Movement as tinkering, and the Open Door policy and appointment of Winter as a betrayal of "the women of this country."[191] Improvements in motion pictures would only come with changes to the system of production, she argued, which would lead to adjustment in the nature and treatment of topics filmed, as well as to the system of distribution. (Current practices of block-booking and blind bidding meant that individual theaters could exercise no choice in their offerings.)[192]

After Diehl's Rome performance of 1931, Herron had sardonically quipped to Hays that "next time, perhaps, it would be better to send Mrs Gilman on these tramping tours. At least we will know what she is going to say."[193] The devil-you-know, Gilman, had been one of the MPPDA's most outspoken opponents. President of the Motion Picture Committee of the National Council of Women (Diehl's predecessor), and future chairman of the Motion Picture Committee of the National Congress of Parents and Teachers (as of 1932), Gilman had had extensive settlement house experience, had fought for child welfare legislation, was interested in problems of delinquency, and was an early sex educator.[194] Her article appeared in The Woman's Journal, a suffrage paper founded in Boston in 1870, whose original editors had included Julia Ward Howe and Lucy Stone. In 1928, on its relocation to New York City, the journal readopted its original title and emphasized its fighting flavor of old, a setting fitting to Gilman's excoriation.

Gilman proposed government supervision through a commission which would operate along the lines of commissions recently established to regulate interstate commerce and food standards. A year later, she was to repeat this call for "intervention by a centralized power outside the motion picture industry," which would "bring about fundamental and permanent changes in the character and treatment ... of motion picture production."[195] And her challenge continued in her proposal of "new production, distribution and exhibition companies ... operated as civic enterprises ... by groups from the fields of science, art, education, and technical mechanics."[196]

This radical kind of reorganization (and the production censorship it implied) was anathema to club women's Hollywood representative, Alice Ames Winter, as well as to the MPPDA. Her remarkably conciliatory reply, in The Woman's Journal's next issue, reminded Gilman of cinema's broad appeal, of its massive audiences and its huge influence on their conduct, and of its collaborative manufacture.[197] Winter acknowledged industry "mistakes" but scotched censorship, pointing to the folly of the present undemocratic system of local board cutting. Any proposed system of federal oversight (such as the Hudson Bill currently under discussion, which would, had it been passed, have legally enforced the "Thirteen Points") was anti-Republican government meddling.

For Winter, there was a reciprocal relationship between motion pictures and audience; because film was cheap, accessible, and easy to understand, everybody must have a voice in its future. She saw her role as one of strengthening relations between these two sides. If the industry were to cater to "special groups" (i.e. those advocating censorship), film would depart from its essentially democratic character. Winter forecast that sound cinema would bring a new "psychology" and sophistication of the motion picture.[198] The consequent deepening of the "consciousness of obligation" of the industry to its millions of ticket holders would improve its "new young giant" where censorship could not.[199]

Mary Roberts Rinehart, an enormously popular writer, with Hollywood experience, had also hoped for a democratic form of constraint, to be expressed through withdrawal of patronage and protest to exhibitors, rather than via the censor's knife.[200] Sketching an apparently divided audience, one part discriminating and calling for reform, the other inarticulate and seeking "lurid thrills," who liked "life represented in the raw," she protested that this latter, larger component was nonetheless also "militantly moral."[201] All audiences converged in "the great body of the people," which was "dependable, clear in its judgements and sure in its verdicts"—the production of censorable films thus constituted a misreading of the greater unity of public opinion.[202] Rinehart's article, published in 1921, three months before the Arbuckle affair broke, and six months before the appointment of Will Hays, pleaded that the public should have faith in Hollywood's current attempt to police itself (since 1919 the National Association of the Motion Picture Industry, NAMPI, forerunner of the MPPDA, had been organizing for self-censorship), and pay heed to producers' promises of "cleaner and better pictures."[203] This would also reduce the casualty list of mutilated films, a triage of obvious concern to Rinehart the screenwriter.

As we have already seen, in our discussion of the opinions of Catheryne Cooke Gilman and Alice Ames Winter, critics might disagree as to what extent the relationship between audience and industry demanded supervision, but there was general consensus that power lay somewhere within this delicate balance, and, in all likelihood, with the consuming millions. The motion picture business, wrote Katharine Fullerton Gerould in 1922, was now everybody's business, and increased calls for censorship were punishment for rampant Hollywood wealth.[204]

Like Rinehart the year before, Gerould argued against censorship, but where Rinehart had conferred an essential goodness on the mass audience, Gerould was more sanguine, if not patronizing, inferring that Hollywood's self-censorship resulted from the small-town mentality's petty-mindedness, that it was really a form of prurience. Recalling the impact of women, she satirized the reformist impulse, taking particular aim at the watchdog's stance of knowing better than a parent the needs of a child.[205] Expansively defining movies to include the off-screen life of performers, Gerould explained that, through the fan magazine and its trade in gossip, viewers sensed intimacy with stars, making Hollywood's scandals no longer local but national in their impact.[206] This was an extremely important insight—cinema's power grew not only from the totality of filmed images, but from star power trafficked through press and posters. As Anita Loos was also to remark, with pithy and ironic demolition, film journalism was a critical factor in the stabilization or inflation of cinema's moral temperature.[207]

Dorothy Richardson's fantasy of symbiosis—the cinema giving life to the slum audience who would cultivate it in return—also expressed the aspiration of improving film in the process of reception. A.S. Richardson, writing from a position far removed from her English namesake, but in the same pre-Code era, touched on

Fig. 3.4   Alice Ames Winter (inset), and, above, on the Warner Bros. set in 1930 (extreme left) with, from left to right: Mrs Coolidge, Calvin Coolidge, Mary Pickford, Jack L. Warner and director Alan Crosland

this model when observing the failure of other types of reform: "all efforts of organized groups could not prevail against the wishes of theater-goers as expressed in box-office returns."[208] It was the 115 million weekly attendees of the cinema who determined what was made in Hollywood, not "groups of welfare workers nor magazine editors."[209]

Despite all this reflection on reception, however, it seems rarely to have occurred to pedagogues and activists that one and the same film might garner different interpretations, let alone that film might not have the power claimed for it. No terrain existed for an exchange of views between Catheryne Cooke Gilman and Laura Whetter, for example, who complained in 1930 that screen virtue was triumphant and cinematic vice "as innocuous as rice pudding."[210] Only occasionally, in Gerould and Loos, do we get a sense that writers might have found pronouncements of influence ridiculous. And relatively rare is discussion of what we would now call "resistant" reading, that delight in indirect, contrary attention to the screen, as in a 1931 report on the work of the IIEC, which concluded with teachers' doubts as to the efficacy of film's pedagogical use: "School films do not altogether fulfil their pedagogical function, because by their instructional aim and purpose they arouse an instinctive opposition in the child and thus have less effect than they should."[211] The overall scarcity of such opinion, however, was not simply a question of the reforming ken's lack of levity. Rather, these protagonists' conceptions of cinematic power were so determining as to preclude a benign regard for the movies. Indeed, such a perspective was part of the "problem" reformers were trying to overcome.

The involvement of organized women in Hollywood's affairs ebbed after the mid 1930s, in part because their brothers in the Catholic Legion of Decency were to influence the Hays Office so effectively, and in part because of the increasingly effective aura of the Code as an earnest industry response to public disquiet with the movies, from 1930 onwards. Sophonisba Breckenridge's history of women in the twentieth century, written in 1933, inadvertently suggests another reason, however: by 1933, membership of the GFWC was shrinking, perhaps because of a general increase in educational opportunities for women, "so that the literary programs [of the GFWC] are no longer attractive to so many women, and with a similar increase in recreational facilities in movies, athletics, in bridge clubs, the social features no longer seem necessary."[212] This is the only mention of cinema in Breckenridge's book.

Adela Rogers St. Johns recounted in her autobiography how, as an experienced but young reporter (she was in her mid twenties) she was dared to debate the formidable Mrs Winter on the topic "Is Modern Woman A Failure?"[213] St. Johns claimed that the newly enfranchised sex had achieved nothing if she used her freedom to roll in the same gutter as men; running after false gods, she was ignoring home, social, and religious culture, and the education of her children. Winter, more than twice St. Johns's age, spoke of modern women's new fields of endeavor and new continents of learning, even remarking that women's presence gently improved the marketplace. The judges ruled St. Johns the winner.

Female attention to cinema took place within the context of vast transformations in women's lives, and indeed some contributors suggestively wrote that cinema's problems were bound up with some unnamed modernity. Both Repplier and Low discerned an infantilization within the contemporary, a process to which the cinema contributed, and of which its appeal was symptomatic. For Repplier, this amounted to a lowering of intellectual standards, an increase in sentimentality, and a deliberate condescension to the audience. For Low, it was cinema's form, and the desire it gratified, that belonged to the current moment:

> most competent observers agree that the present age, in spite of its virtues, is a period of easily-fatigued attention, of inability to concentrate on slow laborious processes whether of mind or body, of inability to take long views and hold them with particular persistency—a period, in fact, which may be characterized in many respects as childish, emotionally and mentally.[214]

Repplier and Low made similar indictments of cinema from radically different starting points: Low was a feminist and Freudian who supported avant-garde literature; Repplier saw no need for suffrage, disdained modernist fiction, and argued for maintaining the reticence around sexuality that popular Freudianism destroyed.[215]

These two sets of comparisons—St. Johns vs. Winter, Repplier vs. Low—caution us to resist any uniform verdict on what cinema's power looked like to women. In the former example, inverting our historical expectation perhaps, the flapper generation fan magazine writer plays moral guardian, while the indomitable club woman endorses change. They beg the question as to how to characterize this effort. Was it a reactionary, progressive, or critical activity? Was the reformist impulse underwriting so much female response a legacy of nineteenth-century platforms, with their ethos of women's innately superior morality?[216] Or was it part of the "feminization of American culture" that, as Ann Douglas has argued, began in the post-Civil War period, and that was a crucial aspect of modernization?[217] Lauren Rabinovitz posits that efforts to ban amateur night seemed to educate women in the theater's trade in their displayed bodies, raising consciousness of their pivotal, objectified place within commercial entertainment.[218] In her study of American club women, Blair has argued that the national acceptance of Franklin D. Roosevelt's ideal of federal intervention in the early 1930s was predicated on the prior achievements of female reform.[219] Could the female activism prompted by the cinema similarly constitute something new and modern in women's scope of influence? The Progressive Era was riven with contradictions in its precarious balancing of social control with social justice: Marie Stopes's eugenicism accompanied her desire to bring birth control to poor women; the specter of containment lay within Jane Addams's vision for the working class; Progressives instituted child labor laws and prison reform while banning liquor, and aimed to police servicemen's sexuality and recreation during the First World War through the Commission on Training Camp Activities.[220] Whereas we may abhor some of these women's acts as meddlesome and closed-minded, we might also see that they constituted an amplification of the number of channels by which women could shape cinema, making particularly vivid women's general engagement with their century's most powerful mass medium.

A monumental feature of both the urban and rural terrain, cinema's intrusive insistence left no woman alone. Even Marie Stopes, at age thirty-seven, who had already completed a study of Japanese theater and a paleobotanical monograph for the British Museum, who had founded and edited *The Sportophyte: A British Journal of Botanical Humor*, who was working on coal research for the British Home Office, and who was eagerly seeking a publisher for *Married Love*, felt compelled to pen "Cinema as a Power."[221] Stopes was undoubtedly exceptional, but her span of activities hints at the complex circumstances in which many women came to formulate their sense of cinema's effects. Merely in turning to the pen, as well as in protesting, speech-making, pamphleteering, and organizing, these women's "service" constituted an engaged and alert reception, one which challenges any simple idea of the female spectator as a passive consumer buying an afternoon of easy leisure, free of demands. Their response unsettles a habitual simile of that era, that mass culture was feminine (an idea by which pulp fiction, serialized romances, and magazines, and the broad masses who consumed them, were consistently perceived as subjective, emotional, trivial, banal, and ominously expanding and engulfing—all qualities attached to the feminine.)[222] The opinions and actions of many of these women call for a refiguring of the career of this idea, for, at least in terms of cinema's reception, the maintanance of the simile "mass culture as feminine" must have entailed a veiling over of the multiplicity and complexity of women's social and cultural response to it, in an instance of neglect or blinkeredness that the recollection of these women's writings makes explicit—the climate of female reception they register must have constituted a simultaneous undertow to the simile's opening years. Some women certainly feared cinema for its "feminine" qualities, but others spoke of its use for instruction in life and the future, for its value in survival. For none of them was dreaming sessile before the screen the extent of their movie world.

Futurology

An Idyll of the Cinematographe (1898)
Mrs. Henry Mansergh

There are some people who require a course of education before an idea penetrates to their brain; there are others who clutch greedily at a discovery while it is yet in the air, and are instant to realise the service which it may render to themselves.

Mark Robson belonged to the latter class. He was a private detective, moderately successful in business, yet cherishing a grudge against fate, inasmuch as he found himself at a constant disadvantage as compared with his brothers of the magazines. Lords and ladies consulted him in his office, but showed no disposition to take him to their social bosoms: there was no intelligent young gentleman ready to share his midnight journeys and play the part of assistant, free of charge: while, so far from being pressed to relate his experiences, his friends yawned and showed unmistakable signs of boredom when he threatened a recital. But, as has been said, Mark Robson was a sharp fellow, and his day was coming. He studied the newspapers assiduously, digesting the news of the nations with an undercurrent of questioning as to how he could make any particular event serve his own ends, which, as every sensible person knows, is the only spirit by which a business man can hope to make his way in the world. And suddenly he had a brilliant inspiration. The cinematographe was the novelty of the hour; all the world was flocking to see it; Mark Robson flocked with the rest; and it was while watching the entrance of the Czar and the Czarina into Paris that he suddenly clapped his hands together, to the amazement of the beholders, took up his hat and rushed hurriedly from the building.

Two days later a large-typed announcement was added to Mark Robson's advertisements in the London dailies—

> Cinematographic Slides of private individuals taken without their knowledge, and forwarded secretly to any quarter of the globe.

After fifteen years of hard labour beneath an Indian sun, John Webb found himself in the position to fulfil his engagement to Daisy May. Fifteen years before he had said "good-bye" to Daisy in the drawing-room of the old house at Liverpool, and again in the cab—because she ran down to the gate at the last moment and refused to be left behind—and again on the landing-stage, and again—oh, the knell-like sound of that bell!—when the very last moment had come, and the tender was about to return to the shore. He had leant over the side of the vessel gazing at Daisy as the tender bobbed up and down, and Daisy had held out her arms to him with a gesture of longing so child-like and winsome that he had groaned aloud, and hidden his head in his hands. Fifteen years ago! And he had written to Daisy once a week ever since: "My own precious darling!" "Darling Daisy!" "Dearest Daisy!" "My dear girl!" ... Ah me! if we could only eat our cake while the appetite is keen. Fifteen years is a long time, and a continued course of curry has a hardening effect on the masculine mind.

John had just written home asking Daisy to come out to be married in the following autumn, and though this was the object for which he had been working for so many years, it is certain that his difficulty in composing the letter was caused less by excess of rapture than by the problem of making the request sufficiently warm to please Daisy, and at the same time honest enough to satisfy his own conscience. After the letter was finished he took up the latest photograph which he had received from his fiancée, and studied it with critical eyes. Daisy had been a pretty girl, and the face which looked at him now seemed almost as young as the one which he had kissed in farewell.

"But it's all nonsense!" grumbled John to himself. "I know these 'present-day' photographs. She will be forty in a couple of years, and it stands to reason that she can't look like this. Why does she always send vignettes? Can it be that she is growing—fat? She was always a trifle inclined that way; and if there is one thing more than another that I do bar—Fat, fair and forty! O Lord!" He threw the photograph on the table, and picked up the newspaper with an expression anything but appropriate for a bridegroom-elect, and the first thing on which his eye lighted was the advertisement of Mark Robson, with that insidious large-typed addition!

When the "boy" came in an hour later to collect the sahib's mail he carried away two letters addressed to London, one of which bore the name of Miss Daisy May and the other that of Mr. Mark Robson, the detective. To such depths of iniquity will men descend when temptation is pressing and the chance of discovery remote!

Some months later a carefully-packed box was delivered at Mr. Webb's residence in Calcutta, and a local photographer was summoned, who busied himself in preparing a magic-lantern exhibition of such enthralling interest to the master of the house that he denied himself to all visitors, and was fairly apoplectic with excitement before the critical moment arrived.

Whir-r! A curious rattling noise came to his ear, and there upon the sheet was the picture of the old-fashioned English room where he had wooed his love. The chintz-covered chairs and the maidenhair ferns under the glass domes were there all complete, not a detail was changed, from the beadwork bannerette pendant from the mantlepiece to the case of stuffed birds on the chiffonnier. How was it possible for furniture to stand so still while the world moved so fast? Webb felt that he had lived through a dozen incarnations since he had looked his last upon this old-world scene. And Daisy—poor little loyal Daisy, with her petals already beginning to wither and lose their dainty flush! In what a narrow garden she had passed her youth! It was a touching thought, and John's heart swelled with a throb of the old devotion to the love of his youth. What if she had lost some of the early bloom? Could such a trifle as that weigh against the faithful devotion of a lifetime? The lines of a sweet old ballad came into his head, and he hummed them in tender tones—

> Thou would'st still be mine own, as this moment thou art,
> Let thy loveliness fade as it will;
> And around the dear ruins each wish of my heart...

The whirring sound continued, and curious spots and blemishes appeared upon the sheet. It was by no means a perfect exhibition, but accurate enough for the purpose for which it was required. And presently the door opened and a stout lady came into the room. She wore a dark dress, which fitted closely to her exuberant figure, and her hair was coiled tightly round her head. There was no nonsense about this good lady, no dallying in dressing-gowns, no waste of time with curling-tongs or crimping-irons; from the bunch of keys which hung at her side to the pile of account-books under her arm everything breathed of method, order and decorum. The stout lady drew a chair to the table, and dipped her pen in the ink. It was evident that she was about to overlook her weekly accounts; but it was not until she bent forward to take a book from a shelf on the wall, and in so doing turned her face more fully towards him, that John Webb realised that this was Daisy—this stout, bustling, middle-aged woman, the little Daisy with the withered petals and the drooping head, about whom he had been sentimentalising a moment before!

From out the magic sheet she stared at him, sentient, breathing, the keen eyes fixed, the lips pressed together in frugal calculation. At the sight of the figures at the bottom of the page a frown contracted her forehead and her fingers rapped the table: anon she smiled, and a network of wrinkles showed round her eyes.

The photograph had lied—basely lied! She looked older than her age, and old with a cut-and-dried, old-maid-like severity which struck ice into Webb's soul. Fifteen years of bachelor life in India, no woman in the house to consider, what in the world would—er—Daisy! [Why could not people christen their children by sensible names?] have to say to his free and easy ways? John Webb lay back in his chair and stared at his fiancée, and his fiancée went on with her work in methodical unconsciousness. The little books were checked off one by one; she drew the ledger towards her and began fumbling about in her pockets, and clapping her hands over various parts of her dress as if in search for some article which persistently refused to be found. Something in her gestures brought a vivid recollection of his old mother to Webb's mind, and his heart beat with a sickening fear. Could it be that Daisy——? Already? Alas! it was but too true. The good lady produced a leather case from some hidden receptacle and fitted a pair of spectacles over her ears. Daisy—in spectacles! If she had looked her age before she looked fifty now—sixty—a hundred—any age you liked to mention, and formidable enough into the bargain to frighten the life out of a poor defenceless bachelor.

The writing was finished. Miss May put away the ledger and rose to cross the room. Her figure advanced towards him, nearer and nearer, larger and larger, with such startling, convincing reality, that he seemed to hear the tread of her feet, the rustling of her garments. The spectacles were still on her nose; the short skirts stood out well round the stout figure. She tried to take a short cut between the chiffonnier and the table, and failed because—O, Daisy, Daisy!

Webb burst into a roar of hysterical laughter. "The dear ruins!" he cried aloud. "My dear ruins!" and clapped his hands together like a maniac.

"That's all, sir," said the photographer, coming forward into the room. "The impressions don't go any farther."

Now Mark Robson, as has been said, was a shrewd man of business, and when he received a commission from India to secure a cinematographic photograph of Miss Daisy May, he reasoned with himself that if Mr. Webb were interested in Miss May, Miss May would naturally be interested in Mr. Webb, and that it was absurd to be satisfied with one client, when it was possible to secure two. He therefore selected one of his most specious circulars, in which special reference was made to agencies in India and the Colonies, posted it to the lady's address in an envelope marked "private," and awaited the course of events. Miss May read the circular, re-read the circular, and carried it away to show her bosom friend.

"It doesn't seem altogether fair," she said. "I don't like the idea of spying upon him unawares; but still—"

"But still, my dear, when the happiness of a whole life is concerned," said the bosom friend solemnly. "I am told men degenerate terribly in India."

"He asks me to come out in October," faltered the fiancée. "He has always been most kind and thoughtful, and I have no reason to believe—"

"You see this Mr. Robson says that his agents arrange with the servants, by means of a small—er—gratuity, to introduce the camera into the room, so that Mr. Webb would be none the wiser. Marriage is a serious step."

"It is, Maria, it is. And I am such a wretched sailor—I am afraid the fee would be very high!"

"It would be cheaper than a trousseau, and the fare out—and back again, if he ill-used you. It seems to me like a leading of Providence."

"Poor dear Jack!" sighed Miss May pensively, for ladies may still cherish sentimental memories though they be stout and middle-aged. Daisy had a tender place in her heart for the love of her youth, but fifteen years—that dreadful voyage—and at the other end the heat, the discomfort, the—serpents, worst of all the strange man, who might turn out to be so painfully different to the Jack of her dreams...

"I'll do it!" she cried desperately, and Mr. Robson reaped a handsome profit by her decision, the black "boy" in Calcutta also, though his sahib was far from suspecting his business one evening, five or six weeks later on, when he roared at him to cease fidgeting about the room and to take himself off to his own quarters.

The days of John Webb's bachelorhood were drawing to a close, and he set ever-increasing store upon those long lazy evenings, when he could loll at ease, undisturbed by feminine prejudice. It was not precisely the moment he would have chosen, however, in which to make his appearance before the two maiden ladies at home, who had spent their lives in a narrow and rigid environment.

Miss May started violently as she beheld the counterfeit presentment of her lover, and the surprise did not apppear to be pleasurable.

"He is—a great deal changed! He used to be such a—pretty boy!" she faltered. ... "I never thought he would grow so plain.... He is getting bald. He used to have such lovely hair, Maria—all little, tight, curling rings, like a woolly lamb." Then her eyes wandered round the room. "I don't see the chair-back I sent him, or the sofa blanket.... Is that my portrait on the table? Your eyes are better than mine."

"She has on a white dress. I don't think you were ever taken in white, dear," said the bosom friend sweetly. "Had he always that very—er—cadaverous appearance?"

"It's the liver, I suppose. They suffer from it in India," said the fiancée sadly.... "I wish he wouldn't crumple up those cushions. It's a shame to treat them like that—such handsome embroidery.... Dear me, he is terribly thin. Do you think he can be quite strong? A delicate man is a great responsibility.... I tell you solemnly, Maria, that if he had walked on board the boat to meet me I should not have known him from Adam.... Here's the native servant coming to see what is wanted.... Poor benighted heathen! I hope Jack is kind to him, and remembers that if he is black, we are all brothers.... O Maria! O heavens! How could he do it? ... To throw the book at the poor creature's head in that savage manner.... It's sinful. If I had not seen it with my own eyes I never would have believed it.... A brandy bottle! Why, he has just finished what was in the glass! I thought it was lemonade. No wonder his liver is out of order. And then that cigar...."

"They will never get the smell of smoke out of those curtains," said the bosom friend. "I know what it is. You will find it a little difficult to get him into your ways, dear, but you must be firm. Those violent tempered men always give in in the end, if you worry long enough.... Now he is falling asleep.... Very dangerous lying there, with his head hanging over the chair.... I shouldn't wonder if he had apoplexy some night and died off suddenly.... There! I knew he would waken himself if he nodded like that.... Here's the black man again.... He keeps calling for him all the time. You will never be able to keep your servants.... What is it he wants? *Another brandy and soda!*.... My poor, dear Daisy!"

"It's the second he has had in the last half hour!" cried Miss May wildly, and burying her face in her hands, she burst into a passion of tears.

Miss May wrote to Calcutta to state that, upon mature reflection, she had come to the conclusion that it would be wiser to bring the engagement to an end—lapse of time, change of disposition, etc.—and John Webb sent back a straightforward, manly letter, commending her candour, and agreeing in the wisdom of her decision.

For the time being both are inclined to bless Mr. Robson and the cinematographe for being the means of their deliverance, but, as the years pass by one is inclined to doubt whether they will remain of the same opinion. The loss of the weekly letters will make a blank in Webb's life, and there may come an hour when the joys of a solitary life pall upon him, and he thinks longingly of Daisy—poor Daisy, who was faithful to him for fifteen long years! And Daisy too may weary of her account-books, and her dusting and mending and polishing up, for, ah, dear me, however well garnished the house, it is bare indeed if love be not in it, and companionship, and sympathetic smiles. She is bound to think of Jack, and to torment herself by useless questionings, for she is a woman, and he was the lover of her youth. Was she right in playing the coward at the last moment? "For better, for worse." He was all alone, poor fellow, and she might have helped him....

But Mark Robson, the detective, grows fat and flourishes.

[*The Windsor Magazine* (London) 7, February 1898, pp. 363–8.]

Mind-Stretching (1925)
Charlotte Perkins Gilman

"Once upon a time there was," begin the stories of our childhood; wonderful, beautiful, exciting; and the child wishes he had lived then, wishes he could go back, finds the present dull.

"Once upon a time there will be," is an opening for stories which may be far lovelier and more stimulating; and when the child desires such surroundings, such events, we can say that they may be had for the making.

Genealogy has a profound interest for some of us. We dig among the dry bones as far back as we can find the faintest trace of our progenitors, and form proud societies based on dead men. One long-buried ancestor means more to us than a hundred unborn descendants. History is a favorite study, especially ancient history. If we can exhume an extinct civilization, we are widely delighted. There has been more intense interest in the unearthed treasures of Tut-ankh-Amen, that godsend to weary designers, than in the organization of the world today.[1]

What is the matter with our minds that they only stretch one way? Our mental area is coterminous with the universe. It is capable of thinking backward to the nebular hypothesis, and forward to the hypothesis of eternity, but this capacity is not used. We, who can hold earth and sky in easy range, live in a few rooms. We are "kitchen-minded," "parlor-minded," "nursery-minded," and "office-minded," with a weekly excursion heavenward and a few disconnected ideas on politics. [...]

Moreover, with the increasing sum of knowledge, we specialize more closely, and stretch our minds in a single line. [...]

Quite apart from special learning, vitally necessary as it is, the great mass of us could, if we chose, enlarge our mental activity to an unknown extent by no more difficult method than a little gentle exercise. So far, those who come to us with propositions for mental improvement offer either to put in more information or to train the memory with due allowance for the drug-givers, the bringers of mental anesthesia, who seek to make us impervious to human pain by denying that there is any.

As for exercising the brain, widening its range, strengthening its action, we make no effort in this direction. The truth is, we do not occupy our own minds. We are like the owner of a dozen palaces living in a three-roomed flat. Perhaps we have, in addition to the little flat, a lot of mental furniture in storage, and certain jewels of faith which are kept in a vault, to be worn only on Sundays. But for daily use we occupy cramped quarters of which we inevitably weary.

Then comes the demand of the imperfectly used mind for extra stimulus, for amusement, change, excitement, and we eagerly greet each new theory which, for a time at least, gives relief to the crumpled organ. At present the favorite line of diversion is what we glibly term "the subconscious."

The three-roomed flat is now supplied with a mysterious cellar, a sub-cellar, of unknown extent, into which we cannot penetrate, but out of which arise the most amazing appearances, the more unpleasant the better. It certainly is appealing. One is constantly peering and listening down the cellar stairs, wondering what reptile will come up next.

The subconscious mind is that part of our mind which we are not using. The brain receives impressions from infancy, stores them all, and brings forward into use those which we need at the time. When we are playing chess, bridge is relegated to "the subconscious," and *vice versa*; we should be poor players if we were thinking about both at once. It is as desirable to ignore that part of our mental supply which we are not using as it is to ignore dancing steps while running the typewriter.

It is quite true that the subconscious mind is of great importance. There is much more in it than in that lighted workroom in front where we do things. The strength of the great man largely consists in clearing that room of every unnecessary thing, and then pouring all his strength along the line of the work he is doing. Concentration, we call it.

But it is bad indeed for the great man if all those other things are thrown down cellar and forgotten, and if, having finished his period of labor, he finds but an empty mind, like the "tired business man": this gentleman, having succeeded in forgetting everything he ever knew except business, having kept his nose to the grindstone with commendable vigor all day, leaves the grindstone at evening, and, since nature abhors a vacuum, seeks to refill that vacant mind with something light and pleasant, like ladies' legs, set to music.

Most of what we are forced to learn as children is promptly relegated to the subcellar. [...]

It is a singular process of education, laboriously pushing into unwilling minds what we know will not stay there, merely something children are expected to go through with, like the measles. There is this further amusing feature in our system of early mental training, that what we teach is not at all what the little sufferer will need to use in later life, and that what we do most seriously need we are not taught. The difficulties, disappointments, and dangers which await us are in uncharted seas. "Children will not take advantage of the experience of their elders," we say, but, as a matter of fact, we do not teach them that experience. [...]

The child's first years are passed in company with the "kitchen-minded" and "parlor-minded" mother; his first impressions of ethics are wholly "nursery-minded," and the laborious years of study are spent in stocking "the subconscious" with disconnected masses of information. Then he must needs settle into some business or trade, and she usually into the kitchen or parlor, and we have the world as it is, with the vast, clear, luminous spaces of the human mind unoccupied, forgotten.

☙

Consider for a little what we might have in our minds, all of us.

There is a wonderful new art in the world which we, with these little-used minds of ours, have utterly failed to appreciate. We have at last the universal language so long sought, a method of communication which reaches every race and class and age, the cinema. This is the greatest medium of education since the printing-press; indeed, it is even greater in some ways. The book is for him who has learned to read in its language, who has time to read, and who likes to read. The moving picture needs neither learning nor translator, it takes little time, and for one who likes reading there are hundreds, perhaps thousands, who like "the pictures."

That this prodigious gift to the world has been prostituted to the cheapest, coarsest tastes of amusement-peddlers is no discredit to the art, only to the peddlers. Pornographic books or collections of low jokes do not discredit the art of literature, nor the Sunday supplements the art of painting.

We have, it is true, a struggling subdivision of what we call "educational" pictures, failing to see that all pictures are educational, for good or bad. Let us now stretch our minds a little to see how limitlessly the moving picture may enlarge the mind of the world.

The world we live in is the world we know. It was large when men thought it small, round when men thought it flat, but their minds were affected by what they thought it, not by what it was. We endeavor to teach geography to children; some of us can remember when that alluring science was given in a wide, thin book that began with the tempting bit of knowledge, "Geography is derived from two Greek words, *ge*, the earth and *grapho*, to write." It is taught far better now, but the average child has still only a dim notion of his world.

When the screen replaces the school-book in most of the informative fields of education, a child of ten may know more about the world than any but the wisest geographers. In happy groups, for periods not requiring too prolonged attention, children may see before them the world as it slowly grew. This calls for the work of the cartoonist, by which mysterious process we see happen what the artist makes.

Where now a map is a mystery to many a childish mind, one flight in an airplane would give to each a bird's-eye view of city and country, and the bird's-eye view seen in the pictures would turn into a map, with no confusion. With the round earth spinning before him, with the power of the "close-up" not spent on glycerin tears and tedious kisses, but used to make the river, first seen as on a map, come nearer and nearer till it was recognizable water; the face of the earth, shown far off and then brought close—we could give to all our children all their world. As mere mind-stretching, this would be most valuable to us all. For the world, once seen, need never be dropped into that subcellar.

With this for background, we could go on and give the child the unspeakably thrilling story of unfolding life on earth. Bare rock, creeping lichen, low moss, uprising ferns and cycads, the rich profusion of the coal-making period, the appearance of new kinds of trees and flowers—no fairy-story that ever was told is more wonderful and lovely than this transformation scene. By the power of the artist and the cinema we can *see* evolution.

If the background of astronomy, [...] the base of geology, and the unfolding of our wonder-world of plant and flower are interesting to eager young eyes, what delight remains for them in animal development! From weak and tiny wigglers in warm water, they can watch life grow on and out into types of fish and shell-fish; from small land-creepers [...] to insect, reptile, bird, and beast.

Then man—man as first discernible, beginning to stand erect, having an opposable thumb, using a club, throwing a stone, unmistakably *genus Homo*. So the real story of human growth, the vivid, thrilling, spectacular series of discoveries, inventions, achievements which make us human; a continued story, opening day after day, chapter after chapter, overflowing with adventure, danger, surprise, and triumph; a story that was all illustration, the greatest story that ever was—and a true one. [...]

To see the story of humanity, like this, would be not only ceaselessly interesting in detail and valuable in sum; but its largest benefit is that, however much might be forgotten, no child could forget that *life moves*. When older students came to more specific history, the same enchantment would open wide the door of the past. Race after race, nation after nation, would move before us. We could see Babylon in all her glory, the rise of Athens, and the fall of Rome.

The same magic would give to all the rudimentary knowledge of many arts and sciences, of handicrafts and trades. As the child grew old enough to specialize in taste, to plan for this work or that, the whole course of it could be shown, its length and breadth and bearing on human life. In "the subconscious" of the average citizen we could implant a range of knowledge hardly possessed by any of us to-day, and that without the grinding effort now demanded of the child mind.

❧

A general knowledge of the past, a broad acquaintance with the present, would become common knowledge. What of the future? All the learning here indicated and far more is of no benefit to us at all unless we use it to improve human life.

Just knowing things is of no value. [...] All our power to receive, retain, and collate impressions is utterly useless unless we can apply them to conduct.

What we have done in our whole past is as irrelevant as the number of ounces in Betelgeuze unless it applies to what we are going to do in the future. The future ought to be the main concern of every intelligent person. The past we cannot help. The present slips from under our feet even while we mention it. To "live in the present" is like standing on a rolling barrel; you must move in order to stand still.

Our blank indifference to our own future is difficult to understand. [...]

If we read to a child some exciting tale, he cannot bear to leave the book; he is eager know what happened next. We ourselves seem to have no curiosity about what is going to happen next. If life grew progressively worse as we advanced, it might be wise not to look forward, or even if we were powerless to affect events; but the contrary is true.

From age to age we move faster, move farther, and the world blossoms into numberless amazing inventions; also from age to age we are increasingly more able to "remould it nearer to our hearts' desire." Then why, in the name of reason, do we not stretch our minds forward? We have even a definite philosophy of what we call "living from day to day." We are definitely told by religion to "take no thought for the morrow." If we took no thought for the morrow, there would not be a house built or a road made. [...]

But with this moving-picture teaching of life we shall at last see that it does move, that every difference between us and our hairy progenitors is a step of change, of doing something that never was done before. Up to date we have come a long way indeed, but are we satisfied? Does the world as it is please us entirely? Are the average health and beauty of human beings a credit to us?

❧

Would it not be worth while for thinking people to stop muck-raking in "the subconscious," and use "the conscious" to more purpose? We might make the initial step in mind-stretching by grasping this not too difficult thought, that things do not need to remain as they are. The world has changed, the world can change, and we can change it. [...]

We have injured our country by deforesting greedily and carelessly; we can improve our country by reforesting better than before. Our cities are ugly and diseased, swollen, bloated things, necessarily criminal and morbid; but they do not have to stay so. We made them; we can remake them, and make them differently.

We waste our soil, we waste our food, we waste our resources of coal and oil and gas; we are, as a people, precisely like an ignorant, slovenly housewife, too slack and lazy to "keep house" decently. In the matter of coal, [...] our method of burning it wastes the larger part of its heat, and our foolish dragging it about over the face of the earth adds enormously to its cost. Coal should be burned scientifically, near the mine, or [...] carried to a city and burned in one place, and the heat and power transmitted. This would mean a vast saving in money, and again a saving in sparing our cities and our lungs from the tons upon tons of coal-dust now poured into them.

But our minds, accustomed only to a view of coal limited to one stove or furnace, find difficulty in considering it as a national asset. A sailor may be able to walk for hours on the planks of his vessel, and yet become exhausted by one straight mile on land. We are so accustomed to think only of little short-range things that it tires us to consider large ones; our minds need stretching. [...]

Our uproar over the troubles of life is as disconnected and futile as if no one had ever lived before, and would resolve itself into definite action to remove those troubles if we would but stretch our minds to see them as due merely to our own action or lack of action.

Observe the anxiety, the labor, and the expense poured out by intelligent human beings in trying to change their clothes as swiftly as is demanded by those who sell them. The earnest young people take "the fashions" as seriously as their heartaches, as if they were something new. The cinema could do great service here in giving us a connected view of the evolution of costume. Once the story of dress had become common knowledge, we should have some ground for judgement in regard to it. It would make a lovely picture: breech-clout, moccasin, legging, shirt; the shirt growing longer to make a robe, the robe cut in two to make a skirt, the upper half longer again in various over-tunics and draperies.

Separate parts could be shown in all their vagaries, as the sleeve, tight, loose, flowing till it hung to the ground, slit and scalloped and trimmed with lace, puffed to the "leg-o'-mutton," shrunk so bindingly that the wearer must put her hat on before her "basque," removed entirely. We could show the voluminous, sweeping draperies of one period, as in France before the Revolution, rapidly reduced to the brief, scant, tenuous muslins of the empire, then swelling again to the nineteenth-century grotesques, the time when a girl wore nine starched white petticoats to a party and found the "crinoline" a blessing by contrast. If the last sixty years were shown in their changes of women's dress on the same figure, swelling and shrinking, rising and sinking, trailing on the ground, cut off to the knee, wasp-waist and no waist, high collar and naked back; if the thing were presented as a whole, with its increased speed of change, the human body within utterly ignored and often injured, then we might be able to stretch our minds wide enough to ask why we must thus spin like a top under the lash of a salesman.

Is the human brain really incapable of any choice in costume, even a choice of evils? Are the only persons to think about clothes those who design, make, and sell them; while those who wear them never once use their minds on the subject, asking only what is the latest change ordered?

Within the limits of those orders we do take pleasure in planning a new dress. Why not take more pleasure in studying what is the most beautiful kind of clothing, what is most comfortable and becoming to ourselves, and facing a lifetime of peace and beauty, ease and economy, all the variety one desires, each individually dressed; with a large number of persons now engaged in making us change our clothes whether we wish to or not, forced to take up a more useful business? That we are such helpless puppets in the hands of clothes-dictators is merely because we do not use our own minds on the subject at all.

If we widen the range of mental activity to a degree quite possible to civilized beings, we shall then have room to place the facts of life in true relation. No man who is forced to live in a closet can take much interest in city-planning. But the closet is not locked.

No unusual power or genius is needed. The human brain is specially developed to think for humanity; that is what it is for. If it is cramped and stunted, there is nothing to prevent our freeing and developing it as soon as we choose. There is nothing to prevent any one from beginning a course of mind-stretching. No law can stop it, nobody need know we are doing it; it can be done alone, without noise or commotion, while awake in the night or drowsing under a dull sermon. We can think as far as we please. And day by day, as we use it, the mind will stretch farther, rise higher, grow stronger, by use. [...]

Upon those who ask permission to poke about in our subcellars and drag out into prominence such undesirable discards as are to be found there, we may shut the door, telling them that we are too much occupied with learning and doing to pay attention to what is best forgotten. [...]

By the normal use of the human mind, by enlarged and applied intelligence, we can make of ordinary life something so pleasant that it will require no effort at all to think of good; there will be more good to think about.

["Mind-Stretching: The Mental Area Can Be Made Coterminous with the Universe," *The Century Magazine* (New York) 3, December 1925, pp. 217–24, excerpted.]

The Unsuspected Future of the Cinema (1918)[1]
Marie Stopes

The greatest social influence since the discovery of printing is the Cinema. It is yet in its infancy, but as almost every country in the world can testify, it is already pushful and with a power well-nigh incredible in one so young. The "Intelligentsia" on the whole have despised and ignored it, and the creation of the moving pictures which move millions of the "common people" to laughter or to tears has mainly been left to those who are not creators in the divine sense in which a poet or great author is a creator, but who make these pictures as a commercial enterprise which pays.

You, reader, may not agree with my first sentence, you may even have thought so little of the Cinema that its claim may outrage you; but it is true. Mere figures seldom convey anything in one's mind, but the fact that in England, America, and the cities of most countries in the world, the attendances at Cinema shows run into incredible millions every year, indicates how widespread is the appreciation of the Cinema. The point of importance in this is that the people who go most are not the people who read books to any great extent, and the Cinema often represents to them all the arts; it is the avenue through which they glimpse a vista of all the wide Universe beyond the corner wherein they dwell.

We of the class who read literature and history and have trained imagination, have always had minds stored with pictures of the outstanding human triumphs throughout the ages; we were from our childhood linked in thought with Caesar, Leonardo da Vinci, Shakespeare, with the majestic procession of great minds each the centre of human achievement and the triumph of a human passion for beauty. Thus our conception of human life has been indefinably great, incredibly rich in variety and potentiality, and we have had the exhilarating sense of being linked, through knowledge of their existence and their thoughts, with a myriad varieties of humanity.

But through the ages there have always been, hitherto, large masses who led the narrow lines of barely literate workers to whom no extended conception of the human race has been possible. To them, at last, has come the Cinema with its rich variety of pictures of life. The workers can see daily in moving pictures phases of life utterly remote from their uninstructed imaginings. The pictures present not only a host of intimate interiors of luxurious or beautiful houses, the wild life of cow-boys and savages but also, with increasing frequency fine presentations of the great civilisations of the past, the rich wonders of Babylon, the sheer beauty of Greece. That hitherto many of the modern dramas have been trivial or sordid, and that nearly every picture has lacked the dignity and moving power of life as portrayed by a master mind is our fault, not the fault of the Cinema itself, which is a tool of magic potentialities. Nevertheless, even with its tawdriness and defects, the Cinema has meant to the masses of the people a measureless expansion of interest and of awareness.

By presenting pictures biased to illustrate any particular view for some time, it would be possible to create a biased public opinion. He who held the Cinema shows in his power could at will create a revolution.

At present the Cinema trade is largely an unevolved chaos of individual firms each out to make its own success by "appealing to the public taste," but a unity and a policy is rapidly crystallising and I see the menace of a danger that before the public is aware of it, public opinion will be being controlled if not created by a trade, the trade which makes the pictures.

In England some people have begun to consider a few of the immense numbers of problems raised by the growth of this vital but undirected new force, and the National Council of Morals has convened a Commission of men of weight under the presidency of the Bishop of Birmingham to consider particularly the cinema in its relation to the child.[2] Though I have the honour of being a member of the Commission, I am writing this article entirely as a private individual because I believe I go very much further in my views of the importance and potential power of the Cinema than do my colleagues.

My own opinion is strengthened by a paragraph translating a German official statement as follows:[3]

> The immense importance of the film as a means of propaganda, makes it neces-
> sary that so important an instrument of Kultur should be placed only in select and
> suitable hands. At the same time, that licensing is made compulsory, efforts will be

made greatly to multiply the cinematograph theatres, and if necessary this movement will be promoted officially.

While I should be the last to advocate bureaucratic and repressive methods towards this vital and growing influence, yet I think it should be clearly realised that it is only at the risk of possible peril to national thought that any country can ignore the Cinema, and can allow the unscrutinised importation of foreign films with their necessarily foreign standards. The pictures shown day after day to any people, are incessantly, though imperceptibly, forming the very fibre of that nation's conception of the universe.

As to the future, in my opinion, there are four principal fields of operation for the cinema: 1. purely recreative; 2. purely educational; 3. national; 4. commercial.

Of the first, the Recreative film, little need be said, for that is the type of film with which most of us are acquainted, and that is the film which those who run picture houses for private profit will always find their mainstay. That such films improve from year to year is known to everyone, and that they could improve still more rapidly than they are doing, is thought by many. They may be left to take care of themselves in their purely recreative capacity, but it must never be forgotten that even the most frivolous film is always teaching something, even though it be only accustoming the poorer classes to imagine the rich as always living in the ugly ostentation of the cinema room, and as spending their lives in the absurd way characteristic of cinema people. How this may help to spread "revolutionary" ideas should be seriously considered. In so far as the cinema picture creates in the minds of the populace most vivid, though often false views of another class or another country, the Recreative cinema becomes a national concern.

2. The Educational film which is now used to some extent in America and Western Europe, should have an immense future before it, but its place is not in the ordinary cinema house. For one reason, to be really educational, it should be accompanied by carefully planned lectures or explanations, which could not be organised by the ordinary cinema palace; for another, the audience of an ordinary cinema show resents being academically instructed when it goes for recreation and amusement. But in schools, universities and technical colleges, the Educational film should find its way subsidised by educational authorities. What teacher, were he gifted with the eloquence of a poet, could explain to little children living in a flat country the appearance of the Niagara Falls, in such a way that the children had as vivid a picture of the Falls as they would get from three minutes of a cinema representation of them?[4]

What class of thirty clumsy little boys, even if their teacher had immense influence over them, could all be enabled to see simultaneously, wriggling out of its old skin, the winged Dragon Fly? And yet the Cinema can show this to them all, and shew it, magnified to a size sufficient for their unaccustomed eyes and brains to grasp the beauty of its every detail. What surgeon would allow a hundred students to crowd round him and peer at the minute nerves and blood vessels of a subject on whom he is performing a rare operation? And yet the Cinema will record it so that not once, for a few fleeting minutes, but repeated innumerable times, students may learn from the master touch. Such illustrations could be multiplied indefinitely, and we can all think of wonderful things in motion which our brains can record, and which the cinema could photograph, but the impression of which a volume of words would fail to convey.

Acquaintance with such natural or man-created phenomena is an essential part of the education of the young, so that suitable films, planned by those who understand each subject, should be available to supplement every teacher's verbal teaching. Some who specialise in education condemn the cinema, saying that it makes for superficiality of mind, but because the cinema will not do for us the necessary mental grind of adding two and two and of learning to spell, they should not overlook its power to create vivid mental images of facts we all ought know.

A teacher of geography, whom someone was trying to persuade to look favourably upon the cinema, said: "If I wanted to explain to my children what a hill was like, I should take them to the nearest hill," but he had no answer when asked, "If you wanted to shew your children what the wild penguins at the South Pole are like, would you take them to the South Pole?" But the cinema takes us there, and explorers can now bring home the very places to which they, and perhaps which they alone, have been.

A selected "library" of really valuable educational films should, in my opinion, be in the possession of every central educational authority, and these should be circulated to every school in the country. Possibly they should be accompanied by lecturers or teachers specially trained to supplement their usefulness, but on the other hand, as the average teacher has readily picked up the knack of using lantern illustrations, so the average teacher on Geography and Natural History, could readily learn to use cinematograph illustrations.

3. This War has seen the beginning of the national use of the Cinema. "War films," official pictures of the Somme and of the many fields of fighting, have been organised and distributed by almost all the belligerent Governments. A great extension of Governmental use of the cinema should come in the future; for it is to be hoped that though the War will unite in one aspect of Brotherhood all the well intentioned nations, yet the national feeling of each country should be enhanced and encouraged. Nothing could do this better than by each nation making known to itself its own chief achievements. So it is to be hoped that all possible events of national importance will be properly "filmed" and the film shown up and down the country. Ramifying from this use of the film comes (to some extent already, and it will inevitably grow), the use of the film for direct national propaganda. The War Savings Committee have their special films today. In times of Peace, why should not any aspect of a national life which requires collaborated action, be brought home to each member of the community in a telling and vivid way, by picture?

4. Increasingly, trade is of world importance, and firms today spend on advertisements for the selling of their goods, more than the whole turnover of corresponding firms a generation ago, and certainly one of the best and most telling forms of advertisement for many articles will be the cinema. Immensely complicated machinery which would require innumerable expensive drawings, (and

then if it were novel might still not be vividly realised), can be shewn in action in a cinematograph representation. Particularly for dealers in heavy machinery, and plant of all kinds, the cinematograph offers not only a wonderfully persuasive form of advertisement, but a handy one, likely to save much labour and expense. But the benefits which the cinematograph can confer on trade are perhaps principally indirect. If the popular heroine of a play rides in a certain kind of a motor-car, or lives in a certain kind of house, that very fact is likely to spread the wish for similar things in the community. And this, in turn, links itself on to the National use of the cinema, for, if one nation is scattering over the world immense numbers of attractive cinematograph films, even if they be nominally purely recreative, that nation is impressing on others its standard of living and its ideas and thus indirectly fostering its own Trade wherever that film penetrates.

There are other ways in which the Cinema may be used, both by artists as a medium for the expression of beauty, by reformers to transmit their propaganda, by cranks and faddists of all kinds,—there is no need to elaborate the innumerable openings for this wonderful new invention in the complex life of civilisation. It has come, not only to stay, but to influence the future history of the world.

[*The New East* (Tokyo) 3:1, July 1918, pp. 26–28.]

Motion Pictures: The Greatest Educational Force of All Times (1917)
Marguerite Bertsch

For centuries we have dreamed of a millennium. Great minds have planned and tried to put into practice their schemes for a Utopia, a land of love and harmony. It is not in any geographical location that such dreams come true, nor is it in the firm resolve of individuals who band themselves together that their ideal may be achieved. Such a determination is a man-made resolve; it can move never more than a limited number and these only partially. There are bigger forces at work in humanity; forces God implanted, on which our very beings are founded. What would advance the world and sweep us sixteen hundred million strong toward a millennium must be based on life's propelling force. Before the bewildered mind of a child can arrive at any order in its chaos, it can understand through the extent of its little being approval or disapproval. All of us, as we come from God, have implanted in us the desire to do what according to our lights or the lights of humanity is thought good. Whether this impelling power express itself in martyrdom for a cause, or in the tear quickly wiped away that moistens for a moment the eye of the criminal in the presence of a gentler influence, it is one and the self-same force. Guidance for this invincible power, enlightenment, is the cry of the world. How often we hear the expression: "If you could only have been there,—if you could only have heard her side of the story, how differently you would feel toward the stand she has taken." It is the photodrama that takes us "there;" it is these picture plays that give us the other side of the story; that teach us to understand our neighbour as ourselves and ourselves so much the better. They develop in us that greatest agent for good, a wholesome imagination. How many little thoughtless acts we perform and then stand back aghast and oh, so sorrowful, to think how deeply we have hurt a very dear friend. If we could have known before the careless act was performed just how much suffering it would bring, the same would never have occurred. If we could imagine in taking another man's property the harrowing grief of the loss of a life-time's saving, we could not take the dishonest step. From day to day we hear the expression: "I can sympathise with you for I have been through just such a sorrow myself." We must really live through a great grief, or even through a petty annoyance, before we can appreciate what the same will mean to another. Life holds for each of us but a limited amount of actual experience. To run the whole gamut of joys and sorrows would exhaust that vitality which belongs to us for the world's work. We must get the greater part of our experiences, therefore, at second hand, through pictures, stories, and through the lives of our neighbours as interpreted by a sympathetic understanding. All that we so glean helps us to imagine, or to conjure up mentally, the reaction on others of every deed we perform. When any one hurts our feelings, we smart under the blow and in our hearts we cannot realise how any one could have ruthlessly inflicted so much pain. That is because we know ourselves and love ourselves, rejoice and sorrow with ourselves. If we knew and learned to love others even as we do ourselves, we would suffer with them beyond the possibility of harming them, and rejoice with them to the utmost extent of our power to help them. This is the great work of the photodrama. Reaching all classes and vivid as life in its graphic portrayals, it causes its spectators not only to hear of, but actually to live, life's great refining tragedies. It gives us a thousand lives in the span of "three score years and ten."

No one is so heavily encumbered as he who would mount to success with a body exhausted by its own infirmities. A cancer in an otherwise wholesome body, rendering all infirm, is that element in society that blocks the path of upward progress. As a millstone about our necks is the truth that "one half of us do not know how the other half lives." Toward the ultimate effect which we speak of as our millennium, we must advance all in all or not at all. Nothing at any time in the world's history has been so influential in the letting in of light into dark places, as has the photodrama. Nothing has been so helpful in giving us all the data from which we can glean those eternal underlying principles in harmony with which, and not otherwise, we can attain the highest in human perfection. It is to this greatest of all fields that we may well dedicate our most earnest and inspired efforts, giving all our strength to that cause which must eventually bring it to pass, through enlightenment, that we shall do to others as we would they should do unto us, and that we shall love our neighbour as ourselves,—the achievement of the millennium.

[From *How to Write for Moving Pictures: A Manual of Instruction and Information* (New York: George H. Doran, 1917), pp. 272–75, excerpted.]

Captive Minds

The House of Dreams (1909)
Jane Addams

[...] "Going to the show" for thousands of young people in every industrial city is the only possible road to the realms of mystery and romance; the theater is the only place where they can satisfy that craving for a conception of life higher than that which the actual world offers them.[1] In a very real sense the drama and the drama alone performs for them the office of art as is clearly revealed in their blundering demand stated in many forms for "a play unlike life." The theater becomes to them a "veritable house of dreams" infinitely more real than the noisy streets and the crowded factories.

This first simple demand upon the theater for romance is closely allied to one more complex which might be described as a search for solace and distraction in those moments of first awakening from the glamour of a youth's interpretation of life to the sterner realities which are thrust upon his consciousness. These perceptions which inevitably "close around" and imprison the spirit of youth are perhaps never so grim as in the case of the wage-earning child. We can all recall our own moments of revolt against life's actualities, our reluctance to admit that all life was to be as unheroic and uneventful as that which we saw about us, it was too unbearable that "this was all there was" and we tried every possible avenue of escape. As we made an effort to believe, in spite of what we saw, that life was noble and harmonious, as we stubbornly clung to poesy in contradiction to the testimony of our senses, so we see thousands of young people thronging the theaters bent in their turn upon the same quest. The drama provides a transition between the romantic conceptions which they vainly struggle to keep intact and life's cruelties and trivialities which they refuse to admit. A child whose imagination has been cultivated is able to do this for himself through reading and reverie, but for the overworked city youth of meager education, perhaps nothing but the theater is able to perform this important office.

The theater also has a strange power to forecast life for the youth. Each boy comes from our ancestral past not "in entire forgetfulness," and quite as he unconsciously uses ancient war-cries in his street play, so he longs to reproduce and to see set before him the valors and vengeances of a society embodying a much more primitive state of morality than that in which he finds himself. Mr. Patten has pointed out that the elemental action which the stage presents, the old emotions of love and jealousy, of revenge and daring take the thoughts of the spectator back into deep and well worn channels in which his mind runs with a sense of rest afforded by nothing else. The cheap drama brings cause and effect, will power and action, once more into relation and gives a man the thrilling conviction that he may yet be master of his fate. The youth of course, quite unconscious of this psychology, views the deeds of the hero simply as a forecast of his own future and it is this fascinating view of his own career which draws the boy to "shows" of all sorts. They can scarcely be too improbable for him, portraying, as they do, his belief in his own prowess. A series of slides which has lately been very popular in the five-cent theaters of Chicago, portrayed five masked men breaking into a humble dwelling, killing the father of the family and carrying away the family treasure. The golden-haired son of the house, aged seven, vows eternal vengeance on the spot, and follows one villain after another to his doom. The execution of each is shown in lurid detail, and the last slide of the series depicts the hero, aged ten, kneeling upon his father's grave counting on the fingers of one hand the number of men that he has killed, and thanking God that he has been permitted to be an instrument of vengeance. [...]

Is it not astounding that a city allows thousands of its youth to fill their impressionable minds with these absurdities which certainly will become the foundation for their working moral codes and the data from which they will judge the proprieties of life?

It is as if a child, starved at home, should be forced to go out and search for food, selecting, quite naturally, not that which is nourishing but that which is exciting and appealing to his outward sense, often in his ignorance and foolishness blundering into substances which are filthy and poisonous.

Out of my twenty years' experience at Hull-House I can recall all sorts of pilfer-ings, petty larcenies, and even burglaries, due to that never ceasing effort on the part of boys to procure theater tickets.[2] I can also recall indirect efforts towards the same end which are most pitiful. I remember the remorse of a young girl of fifteen who was brought into the Juvenile Court after a night spent weeping in the cellar of her home because she had stolen a mass of artificial flowers with which to trim a hat.[3] She stated that she had taken the flowers because she was afraid of losing the attention of a young man whom she had heard say that "a girl has to be dressy if she expects to be seen." This young man was the only one who had ever taken her to the theater and if he failed her, she was sure that she would never go again, and she sobbed out incoherently that she "couldn't live at all without it." Apparently the blankness and grayness of life itself had been broken for her only by the portrayal of a different world.

One boy whom I had known from babyhood began to take money from his mother from the time he was seven years old, and after he was ten she regularly gave him money for the play Saturday evening. However, the Saturday performance, "starting him off like," he always went twice again on Sunday, procuring the money in all sorts of illicit ways. Practically all of his earnings after he was fourteen were spent in this way to satisfy the insatiable desire to know of the great adventures of the wide world which the more fortunate boy takes out in reading Homer and Stevenson.

In talking with his mother, I was reminded of my experience one Sunday afternoon in Russia when the employees of a large factory were seated in an open-air theater, watching with breathless interest the presentation of folk stories. I was told that troupes of actors went from one manufacturing establishment to another presenting the simple elements of history and literature to the illiterate employees. This tendency to slake the thirst for adventure by viewing the drama is, of course, but a blind and primitive effort in the direction of culture, for "he who makes himself its vessel and bearer thereby acquires a freedom from the blindness and soul poverty of daily existence." [...]

And while many young people go to the theater if only to see represented, and to hear discussed, the themes which seem to them so tragically important, there is no doubt that what they hear there, flimsy and poor as it often is, easily becomes their actual moral guide. In moments of moral crisis they turn to the sayings of the hero who found himself in a similar plight. The sayings may not be profound, but at least they are applicable to conduct. In the last few years scores of plays have been put upon the stage whose titles might be easily translated into proper headings for sociological lectures or sermons, without including the plays of Ibsen, Shaw and Hauptmann, which deal so directly with moral issues that the moralists themselves wince under their teachings and declare them brutal. But it is this very brutality which the over-refined and complicated city dwellers often crave. Moral teaching has become so intricate, creeds so metaphysical, that in a state of absolute reaction they demand definite instruction for daily living. Their whole-hearted acceptance of the teaching corroborates the statement recently made by an English playwright that "The theater is literally making the minds of our urban populations today. It is a huge factory of sentiment, of character, of points of honor, of conceptions of conduct, of everything that finally determines the destiny of a nation. The theater is not only a place of amusement, it is a place of culture, a place where people learn how to think, act, and feel." Seldom, however, do we associate the theater with our plans for civic righteousness, although it has become so important a factor in city life.

One Sunday evening last winter an investigation was made of four hundred and sixty six theaters in the city of Chicago, and it was discovered that in the majority of them the leading theme was revenge; the lover following his rival; the outraged husband seeking his wife's paramour; or the wiping out by death of a blot on a hitherto unstained honor. It was estimated that one sixth of the entire population of the city had attended the theaters on that day. At that same moment the churches throughout the city were preaching the gospel of good will. Is not this a striking commentary upon the contradictory influences to which the city youth is constantly subjected?

This discrepancy between the church and the stage is at times apparently recognized by the five-cent theater itself, and a blundering attempt is made to suffuse the songs and moving pictures with piety. Nothing could more absurdly demonstrate this attempt than a song, illustrated by pictures, describing the adventures of a young man who follows a pretty girl through street after street in the hope of "snatching a kiss from her ruby lips." The young man is overjoyed when a sudden wind storm drives the girl to shelter under an archway, and he is about to succeed in his attempt when the good Lord, "ever watchful over innocence," makes the same wind "blow a cloud of dust into the eyes of the rubberneck," and "his foul purpose is foiled." This attempt at piety is also shown in a series of films depicting Bible stories and the Passion Play at Oberammergau, forecasting the time when the moving film will be viewed as a mere mechanical device for the use of the church, the school and the library, as well as for the theater.

At present, however, most improbable tales hold the attention of the youth of the city night after night, and feed his starved imagination as nothing else succeeds in doing. In addition to these fascinations, the five-cent theater is also fast becoming the general social center and club house in many crowded neighborhoods. It is easy of access from the street, the entire family of parents and children can attend for a comparatively small sum of money, and the performance lasts for at least an hour; and, in some of the humbler theaters, the spectators are not disturbed for a second hour.

The room which contains the mimic stage is small and cozy, and less formal than the regular theater, and there is much more gossip and social life as if the foyer and pit were mingled. The very darkness of the room, necessary for an exhibition of the films, is an added attraction to many young people, for whom the space is filled with the glamour of love making. [...]

The young people attend the five-cent theaters in groups, with something of the "gang" instinct, boasting of the films and stunts in "our theater." They find a certain advantage in attending one theater regularly, for the habitués are often invited to come upon the stage on "amateur nights," which occur at least once a week in all the theaters.[4] This is, of course, a most exciting experience. If the "stunt" does not meet with the approval of the audience, the performer is greeted with jeers and a long hook pulls him off the stage; if, on the other hand, he succeeds in pleasing the audience, he may be paid for his performance and later register with a booking agency, the address of which is supplied by the obliging manager, and thus he fancies that a lucrative and exciting career is opening before him. Almost every night at six o'clock a long line of children may be seen waiting at the entrance of these booking agencies, of which there are fifteen that are well known in Chicago.

Thus, the only art which is constantly placed before the eyes of the "temperamental youth" is a debased form of dramatic art, and a vulgar type of music, for the success of a song in these theaters depends not so much upon its musical rendition as upon the vulgarity of its appeal. [...]

This spring a group of young girls accustomed to the life of a five-cent theater, reluctantly refused an invitation to go to the country for a day's outing because the return on a late train would compel them to miss one evening's performance. They found it impossible to tear themselves away not only from the excitements of the theater itself but from the gaiety of the crowd of young men and girls invariably gathered outside discussing the sensational posters.

A steady English shopkeeper lately complained that unless he provided his four daughters with the money for the five-cent theaters every evening they would steal it from his till, and he feared that they might be driven to procure it in even more illicit ways. Because his entire family life had been thus disrupted he gloomily asserted that "this cheap show had ruined his 'ome and was the curse of America." This father was able to formulate the anxiety of many immigrant parents who are absolutely bewildered by the keen absorption of their children in the cheap theater. This anxiety is not, indeed, without foundation. An eminent alienist of Chicago states that he has had a number of patients among neurotic children whose emotional natures have been so over-wrought by the crude appeal to which they had been so constantly subjected in the theaters, that they have become victims of hallucination and mental disorder. The statement of this physician may be the first note of alarm which will awaken the city to its duty in regard to the theater, so that it shall at least be made safe and sane for the city child whose senses are already so abnormally developed.

This testimony of a physician that the conditions are actually pathological, may at last induce us to bestir ourselves in regard to procuring a more wholesome form of public recreation. Many efforts in social amelioration have been undertaken only after such exposures; in the meantime, while the occasional child is driven distraught, a hundred children permanently injure their eyes watching the moving films, and hundreds more seriously model their conduct upon the standards set before them on this mimic stage.

Three boys, aged nine, eleven and thirteen years, who had recently seen depicted the adventures of frontier life including the holding up of a stage coach and the lassoing of the driver, spent weeks planning to lasso, murder, and rob a neighborhood milkman, who started on his route at four o'clock in the morning. They made their headquarters in a barn and saved enough money to buy a revolver, adopting as their watchword the phrase "Dead Men Tell no Tales." One spring morning the conspirators, with their faces covered with black cloth, lay "in ambush" for the milkman. Fortunately for him, as the lariat was thrown the horse shied, and although the shot was appropriately fired, the milkman's life was saved. [...]

In so far as the illusions of the theater succeed in giving youth the rest and recreation which comes from following a more primitive code of morality, it has a close relation to the function performed by public games. It is, of course, less valuable because the sense of participation is largely confined to the emotions and the imagination, and does not involve the entire nature.

We might illustrate by the "Wild West Show" in which the onlooking boy imagines himself an active participant.[5] The scouts, the Indians, the bucking ponies, are his real intimate companions and occupy his entire mind. In contrast with this we have the omnipresent game of tag which is, doubtless, also founded upon the chase. It gives the boy exercise and momentary echoes of the old excitement, but it is barren of suggestion and quickly degenerates into horse-play.

Well considered public games easily carried out in a park or athletic field, might both fill the mind with the imaginative material constantly supplied by the theater, and also afford the activity which the cramped muscles of the town dweller so sorely need. Even the unquestioned ability which the theater possesses to bring men together into a common mood and to afford them a mutual topic of conversation, is better accomplished with the one national game which we already possess, and might be infinitely extended through the organization of other public games.

The theater even now by no means competes with the baseball league games which are attended by thousands of men and boys who, during the entire summer, discuss the respective standing of each nine and the relative merits of every player. During the noon hour all the employees of a city factory gather in the nearest vacant lot to cheer their own home team in its practice for the next game with the nine of a neighboring manufacturing establishment and on a Saturday afternoon the entire male population of the city betakes itself to the baseball field. [...] The enormous crowd of cheering men and boys are talkative, good-natured, full of the holiday spirit, and absolutely released from the grind of life. They are lifted out of their individual affairs and so fused together that a man cannot tell whether it is his own shout or another's that fills his ears; whether it is his own coat or another's that he is wildly waving to celebrate a victory. He does not call the stranger who sits next to him his "brother" but he unconsciously embraces him in an overwhelming outburst of kindly feeling when the favorite player makes a home run. Does not this contain a suggestion of the undoubted power of public recreation to bring together all classes of a community in the modern city unhappily so full of devices for keeping men apart? [...]

Many Chicago citizens who attended the first annual meeting of the National Playground Association of America, will never forget the long summer day in the large playing field filled during the morning with hundreds of little children romping through the kindergarten games, in the afternoon with the young men and girls contending in athletic sports; and the evening light made gay by the bright colored garments of Italians, Lithuanians, Norwegians, and a dozen other nationalities, reproducing their old dances and festivals for the pleasure of the more stolid Americans. Was this a forecast of what we may yet see accomplished through a dozen agencies promoting public recreation which are springing up in every city of America, as they already are found in the large towns of Scotland and England?

Let us cherish these experiments as the most precious beginnings of an attempt to supply the recreational needs of our industrial cities. To fail to provide for the recreation of youth, is not only to deprive all of them of their natural form of expression, but is certain to subject some of them to the overwhelming temptation of illicit and soul-destroying pleasures. To insist that young people shall forecast their rose-colored future only in a house of dreams, is to deprive the real world of that warmth and reassurance which it so sorely needs and to which it is justly entitled; furthermore, we are left outside with a sense of dreariness, in company with that shadow which already lurks only around the corner for most of us—a skepticism of life's value.

[From *The Spirit of Youth and the City Streets* (New York: Macmillan, 1909), pp. 75–103, excerpted.[1]]

Five and Ten Cent Theatres (1909 & 1911)[1]
Louise de Koven Bowen

32,000 Children Attend Chicago Theatres Daily In every large city thousands of young people, eager for pleasure, constantly attend the theatres. It is estimated that in the United States 750,000 people attend daily the regular theatres, while two and a quarter million attend the motion picture shows. Of this number 400,000 are children. In Chicago the theatres seat 93,000 people and about 32,000 children attend them daily.

Conditions of Theatres in 1909 In 1909 there were in Chicago 41 first-class theatres and 405 five and ten cent theatres. At that time the Juvenile Protective Association endeavoured to get an idea of the conditions existing in the theatres, and for this purpose their officers made 1,156 visits to them.[2] Part of this investigation was made in two evenings, when all of the officers of the Association and 120 volunteers visited 298 cheap theatres. This investigation showed a demoralized condition of affairs and 216 violations of the law were reported to the police, the building and fire departments and the state factory inspector.

Crowds of Children Around Theatre Entrances The observation of the investigators was that outside the theatres there was always a crowd of children who were attracted by the lurid advertisements and sensational posters, and these crowds were often worked by evil-minded men, who are generally to be found where little girls congregate.

Evil Minded Men and Young Girls The boys and men in such crowds often speak to the girls and invite them to see the show, and there is an unwritten code that such courtesies shall be paid for later by the girls.

Late Hours and Cheap Tickets In most of the theatres the hours were late, because they offered at the close of the evening three admissions for ten cents, or sometimes two for five cents, and the children stood around pilfering or begging in order to obtain the price of admission.

Physical Conditions Bad   Inside the theatres the ventilation was bad, the air was vitiated, the exits were inadequate, and the darkness afforded a cover for familiarity and sometimes even for immorality. The buildings frequently did not comply with the building and fire ordinances.

Pictures Uncensored   The motion pictures thrown upon the screens were demoralizing. The imagination of the boy who attended these shows was fired by what he saw. The gentlemanly burglar, the expert safe blower, the daring train robber, the reckless scout, all filled his ideas of what a hero ought to be. At one time, after a set of pictures had been given on the West Side which depicted the hero as a burglar, thirteen boys were brought into court, all of whom had in their possession house-breakers' tools, and all stated they had invested in these tools because they had seen these pictures and they were anxious to become gentlemanly burglars.

Crime Made Attractive   The pictures not only showed crime of all kinds, but scenes of brutality and revenge calculated to arouse coarse and brutal emotions. One set of pictures, for instance, would show Indians on the warpath. It would detail with great accuracy the torturing and burning and horrible scenes attendant upon a massacre. Another set, called The Gypsies' Revenge, represented a band of gypsies robbing a man and then, because he resisted, binding him and hanging him by a rope over a precipice. As the picture showed vividly the body dangling between heaven and earth and being plucked at by vultures, the shudder of horror which passed over the audience was quite obvious. Another set of films was called School Children's Strike. It showed a school principal reprimanding a pupil, who, in revenge, organized all the other children in the school into a revolt. They all went on strike, seized all the furniture in the schoolroom, piled it in the middle of the floor and set it on fire. This was continued until the building was a heap of ashes.

Many Films Brutalising   The names and a partial description of some of the films shown at that time were: Black Hand's Revenge—showed explosion of bomb, a killing, a fire, a robbery and at [sic] attack on a woman. Conscience showed a hanging; then a husband killing his wife; boy arrested for the crime, later acquitted, but was tortured by robbers on the way to his father's deathbed.

Difficult to Remove Bad Films   Such pictures could not fail to have an injurious effect upon young people, and the Juvenile Protective Association would report a film of this kind to the Chief of Police and it would be removed at once, but it would turn up shortly in another part of town, and would again be reported. The Association, feeling that it was necessary to take some decisive step in the matter, found that an ordinance had been passed previously which provided that a censorship committee should be appointed by the Chief of Police and that every film should be passed on by this committee and signed by the Chief before it could be shown in a theatre; also that a license to show the film should be posted in the theatre.

Formation of Censorship Bureau   Representatives of the Association and of the City Club went to the Chief of Police and urged that this ordinance be put in force.[3] This was done, and Lieutenant McDonnell, who afterward was succeeded by Sergeant O'Donnell, was appointed by the Chief of Police to see to its enforcement.

615 Films Rejected by Bureau   This department since its inception has discarded 615 films (each film averages about 950 feet) and made 50 cut-outs comprising 14,950 feet. This censorship committee does not allow scenes of murder or robbing or abduction to be shown upon the screens, and in consequence the motion picture shows of Chicago are now very decent. Occasionally a film gets by the censorship committee, but it is immediately reported by the officers of the Juvenile Protective Association and is at once removed. [...]

License raised from $100 to $200   In 1909 the licenses of the smaller theatres were raised from $100 to $200, and thereby the number of 5 and 10 cent theatres was reduced from 425 to 335, and at present is only 298.

Conditions in 1911   The Juvenile Protective Association undertook a recent investigation of the Chicago theatres in the late winter of 1911. They discovered that Chicago now has 383 theatres. Of these 50 might be called first class, 35 second class and 298 third class. The Association has just completed its investigation of the 298 third-class theatres. These comprise all of the 5 and 10 cent shows and this investigation shows great improvement in every way. The posters were found to be good in 220 theatres, fair in 50 and bad in 11 only. When we see crowds of children looking with absorbed interest at these posters we realize how necessary it is that they should not be suggestive or vulgar.

Many Bad Conditions Improved or Eliminated   The conduct of the "barker" outside the theatre is important, as his utterances have great weight with the crowds of children waiting for admission. Out of the 87 theatres who employed "barkers" only 6 were bad. At all but 20 theatres there were crowds, although the condition was good in 270 and bad only in 8. The employees inside the theatres were good in 270 cases, fair in 12 and bad in 13. At three theatres there were no employees, the owners acting as ushers, etc. There was no ventilation whatever in 29 theatres and in 71 the air was bad; all the others were good. The fire protection in all the theatres was excellent, only 12 exits being found locked and 28 unlighted. Out of the 298 theatres 77 were found to be without dressing rooms, but in most of these theatres motion pictures were shown; in the other theatres where there were dressing rooms five were found unsafe; three dirty and eight had no privacy.

Only Eight Violations of Child Labor Law and None of These on the Stage   This investigation showed only eight violations of the child labor law; 4 girls under 14 were found selling theatre tickets; 2 were vendors of candy and gum in the theatres and 2 were ushers. Not a child was found on the stage, which shows that the theatrical people and the public have at last accepted and recognized the fact that our admirable Child Labor Law does not permit children upon the stage. This Association is convinced that any attempt to break down this law will work a great injury to children. In 288 theatres motion pictures were shown; 251 of these were good; 33 were fair, and 4 bad.

Many Films of Educational Value   A large number of the films shown are historical and have an educational value; 32 belong to this class. Some of the films shown were *King Henry the Seventh, Napoleon and Princess Hatzfeld, The Discovery of America, The War of 1861*, etc. Many of the films consist of scenes in foreign countries and are very beautiful, such as *Trip Through Switzerland, A Trip to Mexico, Discoveries at the North Pole, Life and People South of the Equator, A Tour of Athens, A Trip to Norway*. There were 18 of this kind.

Religious and Bible Stories   The pictures vary with the season of the year, those shown during the season of Lent consisting largely of religious subjects or Bible stories such as *The Queen of Judea, The Story of Moses* and so on.

Stories from Classics   A large number are taken from well known novels and tell the story in an interesting way. The best known being *Tale of Two Cities, Ramona, The Vicar of Wakefield, Ben-Hur*, etc. Many shown were taken from plays such as Rostand's *Chanticleer* and *Mme. Sans-Gene*.

Hygiene and Health   Others deal with matters which are injurious to health and cannot fail to make an impression upon the people present, such as *The Acrobatic Fly*. Many are simply humorous and these are the most popular, comprising 188 out of the 288 shown; they are silly, but harmless, and include among others the following: *How Humorous Rastus Gets His Turkey, An Animated Armchair, Bridget and the Egg, The Crazy Razors, In Search of a Husband*, etc.

Many Melodramas   A large number are drama or melodrama, all of a rather lurid type and sometimes showing criminal adventures. *The Red Man's Revenge, Kit Carson, Buffalo Bill*, and *The Gipsy's Love Story*. Others are full of homely sentiment, such as *Poor Little Match Girl, Breaking Home Ties* and *The Old Family Bible*. There are also a large number which cannot be classified. Many of these are very instructive, such as *The Japanese Fishery, Gathering Coconuts, The Diver, The Flight of an Airship, Clouds and Icebergs, The Pepper Industry*, etc. The vaudeville also shows great improvement. Instead of having coarse and vulgar scenes, many of the theatres now produce acts from grand operas, which are given in costume and fairly well sung; of these, *The Bohemian Girl, Faust* and *Macbeth* are the most prominent.

General Condition Encouraging   The investigation of these 298 theatres show general improvement, which is encouraging. Yet one difficulty apparently insuperable, is the fact that many of them are situated in undesirable localities and although the theatre itself may be well managed, it nevertheless attracts a number of young girls and boys into a neighborhood to which they would otherwise have no occasion to go. The theatre itself is often situated next door to a saloon or a transient rooming house. In fact, it is so often in the same building with the latter that the phrase "A Five Cent Theatre Hotel" has become current. It seems quite impossible to control the location of these Five Cent Theatres. There are, however, many more improvements which should be made.

License for Place Instead of Person   We need; first, an ordinance which would require a theatre to obtain a license for the place and not for the person who operates it. If this were done it would prevent a repetition of the following incident: About a year and a half ago at a theatre on the North Side the proprietor was in the habit of enticing little girls into the theatre, promising if they would do a little work, such as dusting or sweeping, he would give them tickets for the evening performance. Under this pretence he assaulted 14 little girls. He was arrested and prosecuted by the Juvenile Protective Association, which had many witnesses to testify against him. The case was continued from time to time and finally the jury disagreed. Although a year and a half has now elapsed, the case has not come to trial; the proprietor has been out on $6,000 bail, and, although he was forbidden by the judge to go inside his theatre, he has been seen repeatedly in the neighborhood by officers of the Association conversing with young girls. After his arrest in the first place the license for the theatre was revoked at the request of the Juvenile Protective Association, but a few days later was issued to his wife, who connived at his immoralities. If a place, not a person, were licensed, it would be impossible after the revocation of a license to have it taken out again by a friend or relative.

Amateur Nights Should be Prohibited   Second, the amateur nights, which were very popular and which are occasionally to be found in the 5 cent theatres, should be abolished. Girls in their craving for excitement are only too anxious to appear in public. They give the little stunts which they have learned and, if they please the audience, are sometimes rewarded by pennies which are thrown to them. If they fail to please, they are pulled off the stage by a large hook. The amateur nights are often coarse and vulgar. The theatres should not be permitted to allow the children to appear.

Lighting Bad   Third, the strain on the eyes in the cheap theatres from watching the motion pictures is bad. They should be shown in well-lighted halls. This is perfectly possible now owing to a new device, and if it were put into use it would do away with many opportunities for familiarity now afforded by the darkness.

Censorship Should be Extended to Advertisement and Posters   Fourth, all posters or advertisements shown outside theatres, or advertisements of plays, musical performances, operas, etc., should be passed upon by the censorship committee and signed by the Chief of Police before being shown or posted in any part of the city.

The theatre is a permanent institution which plays a large part in the social life of every city. It should be encouraged and supported, but freed from all objectionable features and made an agency for wholesome recreation, culture and education rather than for vice, disorder and delinquency.

[Five and Ten Cent Theatres: Two Investigations (Juvenile Protective Association of Chicago, 1909 & 1911), excerpted.]

Children and Picture Palaces (1916)*
E. Margery Fox

I

Our President has asked me to raise the question of the attendance of children at picture palaces. I am not now going to discuss whether they may ever be made means of educational good or whether, as the Head Master of Eton pointed out in the Hibbert Journal of July, 1913, they are not, in their very essence uneducational. They are with us, and they have come to stay. We may differ among ourselves as to the recreative or educational value of picture palaces properly run; I do not believe there can be much divergence of opinion in any Conference of Educators as to the perniciousness of the present frequent attendance of children of elementary or secondary school age.

On the analogy of magic lantern slides and dissolving views, the pictures are considered to afford pleasure and education to juveniles especially, and parents who would not dream of allowing their children to go unchaperoned to the legitimate drama will send them to a "turn" at the picture palace: a turn consisting of from six to twelve plays, of the plots of all of which the parents are ignorant.

The cost of a theatre seat is often prohibitive. At no other place of amusement can be obtained for the outlay of 2d. such comfort of seats, such length of performance, and such variety of sensation as at the palaces. Neither is a theater always available, but every town has one or more picture show. A town of under seven thousand inhabitants has three palaces, all with continuous performances in afternoon and evening; all doing well and apparently, numbering among their shareholders, doctors, and committee members a large proportion of the population. The audience at all performances consists largely of children, as a rule unaccompanied by their parents. To this rule there is, however, an exception. At ten o'clock at night, I have frequently observed in the spacious lobby of one palace, well known to me, as many as fifty empty perambulators, whose proper occupants are wailing in the vile atmosphere in order that their mothers may enjoy the show.

* A paper read at the Headmistresses' Conference, January 1916.

During the last two years I have made detailed notes of one hundred picture plays, chosen as a fair average of those shewn in palaces around London, Paris and two provincial English towns. With the graver issues I have in view, it may seem meticulous to comment on the bad English style, spelling and grammar of the legends before each scene. But in all but ten of my hundred examples I have noted something in these directions that would be objected to by the ordinary person (not a pedant nor a purist).

Only twenty of my hundred examples seemed to me to pass muster on the grounds of taste and morality. They are the botanical pictures shewn at a well known London palace, travel scenes and patriotic turns. Even here is the trail of artificiality. At a moment when every school-girl is learning First Aid, I have been amazed that the film companies could not master the best way to carry a wounded man, either from a Swiss glacier or the field of battle.[2] They seem as a rule to have unlimited funds and expert advice at their elbow. The only other objection to this type of films, as indeed to every other, is the grotesque effect due to the apparent proximity of the audience to the characters and scenes: the unpleasantness of seeing people "larger than life." The child is introduced to people performing impossible exploits, and dressed in absurd clothes. All this is not in the garb of romance but presented in a modern environment and gravely put forward as practicable. This note of unreality is heard very strongly in all quasi-historical plays, whether based on history or the plot of a novel. Here I put Kenilworth and Ivanhoe with ill-judged scenes of which Scott could not have been guilty, and The Tale of Two Cities with a happy ending.

Far worse, to my mind, than the artificiality is the extreme sensationalism displayed. This is worse than that seen in the poorest form of melodrama, because so much is made in the nature of dummies and various illusion. Also all the killing must be done before the audience. Nothing (since there is no dialogue) can be left to the tale of messengers or the reports of other characters.

Taking them all round, the worst play in my mental "Chamber of Horrors" shewed the attempted escape of a fugitive from justice. He jumped on an engine, killed the driver, and so was in ignorance of the fact that the line was up only a few yards further on. When the train came to the spot, he (by means, of course, of a dummy) was hurled over the cliff to a death which I must admit from the rest of his actions was well deserved. The worst feature was the position from which the film had been taken. For some distance the excited audience were, so to speak, standing on the line a few feet away from that onrushing engine with the swaying and distorted figure. A child in front of me shrieked and was carried out. When we remember that one of the classic causes of epilepsy as of allied nervous diseases is the recurrence in a delicate brain of acute excitement, especially that of fright, we may well tremble for the future. To the last generation no excitement was possible which may be compared to that of the pictures in this.

This love of sentimentality is exploited on the hoarding and the audience is disappointed if the plays do not fulfil their promise. I, myself, overheard one boy tell another not to go to a particular palace, since there was no murder there that night.

But, of course, the gravest harm of all is done to the child's moral sense. In 75 of my examples the moral lesson is wrong. The portrayal of vice triumphant, the sinister suggestion that righteousness does not pay and that luck is worth more than perseverance: these are the lessons, presented in a psychologically indelible form, which daily counteract the wholesome teaching in our schools. And the thing becomes an obsession. Magistrate after magistrate discovers that first offenders pilfer in order to have money to go to the "Movies." In a London suburb recently, a policeman informed the Bench that a boy's ingenious plan of breaking into a shop was directly taken from the local films.

Nor is this all: there is a constant outcry about the risks a child may run from the open bookstall, or the conversation of a coarse schoolfellow. I have seen plays in provincial palaces rightly banned by more enlightened municipal bodies, where the marriage vow is a subject of a jest, filial obedience made a mockery, and domestic intimacies shewn merely to be derided. More than half of my hundred examples contain actions and scenes condemnable at any rate by their suggestiveness. No dangers from loose companionship need be feared for the children who frequent picture palaces. There is nothing left for them to learn.

Some of you who live in large cities under vigilant Watch Committees, will not burn as I burn when I think of these things, and may consider the proposal at the Association of Headmasters adequate.[3] But Watch Committees as at present organised in many provincial towns are worse than no use. They do not know what to condemn.

We need first a passionate and reasoned expression of the concerted opinion of decent thinking people. We need the regulation of the attendance of all children of school age (i.e., to 16 or 18.) Thirdly, we want a Committee in every town of rational and educated men and women to act as Censors. The present system of allowing the Association to pass their own films is worse than useless. Censorship, although it may be delegated to local Committees, should be in the hands of the central authority.

Dr. Abernethey, mindful of the changes and chances of life, and the temptations of a medical career, is reported to have said to a theatre full of students: "Good God! gentlemen, what will become of you all!" How much more may we utter such a despairing thought when we see children thronging the ill-ventilated palaces, wearing out their eyes by staring in concentrated attention at the bright scenes before them: fascinated by their terrors. Perhaps those are [a]n even worse case, who sated with sensationalism can placidly gnaw chocolate and suck oranges while the most thrilling tragedy is performed before them. Their imagination and affections are blunted before anything in life has roused them to a real vital energy: honour, virtue and truth, have become but a show.

II

My special concern with picture palaces is their effect on children, and especially on children in small provincial towns. Children are sent because the cinemas are ubiquitous, one country town of under 7,000 inhabitants, e.g., having three such palaces; all with continuous performances from 3 o'clock, all doing well. The supply creates the demand. They go because the admission is cheap. Even with the new Amusement Tax, such a degree of warmth, such luxury of seats, such variety of entertainment can be procured nowhere else at the price.[4] The connection with the magic lantern shows and dissolving views of the past makes people deem the pictures pre-eminently fit for children. I maintain on the contrary that cinemas are most unsuitable for children. Anything is bad which encourages children to stay in doors when they might be out enjoying the extra hour of daylight in summer time. I admit that schools oblige children to stay in, but the schools are airy and well ventilated, while cinemas are from their very nature unhygienic. I have never seen the cinema which may be flushed with fresh air, or flooded with sunshine: the result is a germ-laden, foul, stale atmosphere harmful to health, especially of the growing child. Theatres have about the same atmosphere, but, owing to the prohibitions of etiquette and price, children do not go to theatres with the same freedom or frequency.

The constant movement of the film has a bad effect on the eyes. This is the opinion of more than one able oculist. It is to be compared with the eye-strain and consequent fatigue caused by looking out of the carriage window on a long railway journey.

Far more serious than these physical drawbacks is the damage done to intellectual interest and to taste, which is the essence of morality.

All modern educators treat the child as an active agent in his own education, no longer as a passive recipient. The pictures treat children as purely passive, and no demands on his mental activity being made, he ceases to use any. This reacts on his habitual attitude at school and at home.

Bad for the training of his logical feeling is the inconsequent diversity of the films shewn. A good play has, like any other work of art, a logic of its own; the films have none. The attention of the child is taken from one action to another with no idea of connection.

We apprehend the real world by many senses. To make its appeal, since no other sense helps that of sight; the cinema must be intensely vivid, all gestures are exaggerated, there is a horrible accentuation of every detail, objects sometimes of the most terrifying nature are presented as nearer to the spectator than they could ever be in real life. In order to arrest the attention, human abnormalities and deformities are constantly portrayed—far more so now than when I first began my minute investigation about three years ago. The common place and the normal are implicitly despised.

For the sake of sensationalism, crime is freely exploited. The moral of the film is, I must admit, usually good. But which of us ever pays attention to the moral? Interest is centred in the life of reckless crime, and interest results frequently as the daily papers shew, in imitation. I have seen murder, arson and burglaries freely portrayed in such a way that my own sympathies invariably and involuntarily go to the criminal. I have no doubt those of the children do as well.

The lighter element is provided by scenes shewing grossly comic features; filial obedience, and conjugal fidelity are honoured rather in the breach than in the observance, and the breach is felt to be a matter not of distress but of ribald merriment. The great mysteries of birth, suffering and death; the relation of man and woman, are treated either with coarseness, or with a mawkish sentimentality between which there is little to choose for the harm they must do to an impressionable and ignorant mind.

All these characteristics are either inherent, or are logical consequences, of the very existence of picture palaces, which must exaggerate either the pathos or the comedy of life to make their appeal. Many accidental defects I have also noted: the most constant indelicacy of the mottoes: the realism which is only mock realism: as when XVIII. century battles are fought in XVII. century costume: wounded soldiers are carried by Red Cross men from the line of battle, or patients are carried to the operating theatre in a way which could only lead to immediate harm. Religious services of various denominations are performed with a total disregard of laws of ritual and ceremony. If, as I have frequently been told, historians of the future are to use our present day films as their material, posterity will have a curious impression of our manners and customs.

I have heard it urged that provision is made for the suppression of any abuse. No adequate censorship at present exists. Local bodies with all the good will in the world have not the knowledge requisite. I know of one county town where a few zealous folk prevailed on the Watch Committee to submit a certain notorious film to a private view before being publicly shewn. It was passed by the entire Committee, either because it was innocuous or because it was no worse than many others. A local Committee is under disability in the provinces at least. Small country towns are still marvellously self-contained, and it is difficult to agitate against cinemas without finding oneself in antagonism to shareholders or members of Committees. "There is no Wealth but Life," and these plays are vitiating that life, physically, intellectually, morally, at the very source.

[*The Parents' Review* (London) 27:9, September 1916, pp. 700–06.]

Should War Films be Seen by Children? (1930)
Eva Elie

This question has now been answered in the affirmative by some countries, but in others school censorship committees still forbid boys and girls under 16—unaccompanied—to witness war-films, which are thus, in fact if not with intention, placed on the same footing as demoralising and pernicious films.

This absolute veto, which even applies to an impartial document like *Verdun* by Léon Poirier, is obviously inspired by the best intentions. Taking into consideration the extreme sensibility of children and the suggestive influence of the cinema on many highly nervous temperaments, these "protectors" of children leave to the parents alone the responsibility of revealing through the screen the most terrible of all calamities, *fratricidal war*, the odious conflict of human bodies and human souls.

And what is the parents' decision? Will they not naturally prefer *Shoulder Arms!* to *The Big Parade*, in other words, the comic to the tragic? No doubt, laughter and gaiety are as necessary for children as they are for adults, but what idea of war will the men and women of to-morrow derive from all these scenes of "fun in the trenches" with Charlie Chaplin in the midst of it, *if the other side of the picture is not shown?* If you ask them what war is, they will imitate a soldier turning a somersault or parody the man who surprises the enemy by camouflaging himself as a tree. Are they to learn the meaning of war from buffoonery of this kind, more ridiculous than the wildest Punch and Judy shows at a village-fair? This might be all very well, if no children were over 10, at which age they may well be kept ignorant of passion and bloodshed. There are, however, others who, without being trained in a militarist sense, must be prepared for the struggle of life. By showing to the young the sad scenes of farewell, the tears of those who are left behind, the endless fields of wooden crosses where the golden corn should be waving in the breeze, are we not applying the homeopathic remedy of driving out one evil by means of another? In the case in point, we have to create an intelligent as well as an instinctive horror of war by cinematographic documents borrowed from war itself. By the time that the whole of the next generation all over the world is imbued with the spirit of peace nurtured by hatred of slaughter and when the right to live confronts the helmeted spectre of death, will it not be more difficult for conflicts to arise out of some slight to a country's amour-propre or from some economic or financial cause? Will not the old antagonisms yield to a single strong and unanimous determination—the overwhelming and righteous desire for peace? The cinema can contribute towards this new ideology and morality by a wise choice of war-films, the aim of which will be the pacification and transfiguration of mankind.

It is the mission of the Educational Cinematographic Institute first to collect and then to disseminate all films of a nature to create the new spirit.[1] Backed by a special visa granting them customs exemption at frontiers, these films should be shown in schools the same way as historical, scientific and travel films, censorship committees in each district being, of course, the ultimate judges as to the expediency or otherwise of showing the film.

[*International Review of Educational Cinematography* (Rome) 2, October 1930, pp. 1177–78.]

Brutality in Prize Fight Pictures (1899)
Lillie Devereux Blake

"SHE SEES THE SHARKEY-JEFFRIES BIOGRAPH EXHIBITION AND COULDN'T STAND THE HIDEOUS BRUTALITY"

In the far-off long ago I remember the interest taken by my boy cousins in the prize fights that from time to time occurred. As their comrade and friend I, too, listened to the story of "manly sport," as they told it, until one day I read for myself the account of a famous "mill." It was a hideous recital, and I turned to one of the "boys" reproachfully, but found little sympathy in my protests, as he strove to silence my objections with tales of gladiatorial heroism and Homeric deeds.

During the years that followed, the contests of the arena were few and far between and with what seemed advancing civilization it grew more and more difficult to find any place in this great, as we hoped, enlightened Union, where such deeds might be done. At last, when a regulation prize fight was to be "fought to a finish" no State could be found willing to permit such a contest within its borders except distant Nevada, where the Apaches still celebrated their wild dances of the sun.[1]

But on a sudden a new interest in pugilism awoke, perchance with the sound of the war trumpet that roused the peaceful valleys of our land a year ago.[2] It was discovered that "glove fights" were within the law, and lately we have had contests that were in every detail prize fights within the limits of our own city. True, the contestants wore five-ounce gloves, but they fought for a purse, and great crowds cheered them through the battle, which left one or both more or less disabled.

AGAIN THE GLADIATORS

All this was defended by some men who commanded the respect of the community. When I protested against the new innovation I was met with the assurance that there was nothing in the spectacle that was really objectionable, and the ancient gladiators were once more invoked so that the distant echoes of the voices of my boy cousins seemed to come to me, as they sang the great deeds of the mighty Hercules, or chanted the memories of the Greek wrestlers.

A friend assured me that there was nothing in the least revolting in such a scene and declared that he thought me too fair-minded to object to what was only a development of the athletics in which I professed to believe. I was even assured that there was much that was fine in a wrestling match and that these encounters were in reality but little more than that.

Nay, presently, I was told that the whole of the last encounter could be seen without any of the disagreeable details, and, since it was not fair to denounce that of which I knew nothing, I was urged to view the scene as it was depicted by a biograph. It has never seemed to be fair to denounce any act without full information, and I consented to look in on the exhibition.

Last night on the great screen at the New York Theatre I saw the railed platform on which stood two contestants, splendid specimens of manhood, looking in the black and white of the pictures like shapes of chisselled marble.[3] Because of this fact that the scene was an animated engraving and showed none of the colors of life, the early details of the fight had nothing revolting in them. As the two men moved over the stage they recalled some of the famous statues of the Old World, not so much in perfection of outline as in litheness of motion. Then the rush of the seconds from the corners at the end of the round was amusing as they violently fanned the pugilists with towels, and the people in the mimic audience were a curious study.

But presently the combat deepened. There was a violent exchange of blows. The faces grew set. The antagonists rushed at each other like angry bulls. They struck fiercely with clenched fists. One man seemed to be hurt, and there was a shout of laughter from the audience. It was enough, and I hurried from the scene that was already growing abhorrent. A great roaring, cheering crowd was howling with delight over some especially cruel blow as the exhibition went on.

How hideous it must have been when the two men repeated in the mimic scene all the details of the combat as they inflicted and suffered wounds and pitiful injuries.

SERIOUS QUESTIONS RAISED

And the original actions of this demoralizing picture actually took place here in the limits of this great city, which boasts equally of its charities and of its refinement! Are there no kind hearts here? Or have all gentleness, humanity, lofty thought and aspiration vanished from the popular mind and brutal sports become the ideals of our manhood both young and old? Is it the war spirit that has done this? Are the women of the land to be blamed? Surely there was a time not very long ago when the community would not have endured these prize fights within our doors and the repetition of the bloody spectacle as an attractive performance. Can it be that we are deteriorating?

No, let us rather hope that the national conscience is for the moment sleeping, and that it can be roused in time to stop this demoralization. All that is really noble, all that is really valiant, all that is really high-hearted, should unite to put a stop to whatever fosters the brutality which still lurks in humanity, and restore the ideals of knightly courage and gentleness.

[*New York Journal* (New York) 21 November 1899, p. 7.]

Grave Injustice to Colored People (1915)[1]
Lillian D. Wald

Miss Jane Addams[2] of Hull House, Chicago, and I saw a performance of the second act of the film drama called *The Birth of a Nation*. We were both painfully exercised over the exhibition.

I should say that the authors' interpretation of the period of reconstruction and its presentation at this time is a grave injustice to the colored people and to my mind is fraught with danger to any community that permits it to be given.

The play purports to be history and even if it were accurate it is too near the painful period that it depicts to be given without danger of inciting hate, hostility, prejudice and sectionalism.

Lillie Devereux Blake

Fig. 3.5   Drawing illustrating Lillie Devereux Blake, "Brutality in Prize Fight Pictures."

It cannot be a sincere attempt to depict history or something would be indicated of the fact that nowhere is there record of any outrage upon white women by the colored men during the entire war time. Nowhere in the film is there any reference to the faithfulness and loyalty and protection by the colored men of the families committed to their charge while the white men were at war.[3]

On the other hand the colored men are shown to be beasts and a type to be feared and detested.

The audience indicated by its applause reaction to the appeals to their prejudice and the hate of the black people.

New York's colored population succeeded admirably in controlling disapproval and protest against the film. They have presented a dignified contrast to the incendiarism exhibited at the Liberty Theatre, but I doubt whether it is reasonable to expect further forbearance of their part.[4]

Having seen the film play I feel it right to urge responsible officials to withhold permission for the presentation of the second act, or at least to insist upon elimination of the objectionable and inciting features.

LILLIAN D. WALD
Head Resident, Henry Street Settlement
New York.[5]

[From *Fighting a Vicious Film: Protest Against "The Birth of a Nation"* (Boston: National Association for the Advancement of Colored People, Boston Branch, 1915), p. 18.]

Where Are My Children? (1917)[1]

Marie Stopes

Sir, Civilized womanhood must protest against the morbid, sensational and untrue film, *Where Are My Children?* which is being forced upon London in the name of the NCPM [National Council on Public Morals], in spite of its suppression under protest in Birmingham.[2]

The film is false in implication and untrue to the known facts of life in this country. The decline in the birthrate is due to at least three other causes in a far greater degree than it is due to the fractional percentage of the population comprised by wealthy women who resort to illegal operations. Venereal disease renders many a home childless through no fault of the wife. The miserable salaries paid to the professional classes together with an increased sense of parental responsibility, and the lateness of marriage this involves forms another serious impediment to the bearing and rearing of children. It is admitted that parents limit their families of deliberate purpose, and *by mutual consent*, but they employ preventive and not criminal methods of doing so.

In the artisan and laboring classes prevention is also practised to an ever increasing degree, and the main motive is the lack of housing accommodation. Landlords refuse to let houses to parents with large families and where houses are obtainable sufficient bedroom accommodation for the decent sleeping of children of both sexes of adolescent years cannot be found within the means of the respectable working class parents.

None of these contributory causes to the decline of the birthrate are indicated in the film story.

No one will deny that there are a few cases of the kind pictured in the film, but they are few indeed in comparison with the luck of British mothers, moreover they do not come to see the film. It would be more use to exhibit it in the drawing room of the class of women to which it obviously refers, and not to the general public. Even in the class of society of that frivolous description, it is not women alone who object to have families. There is much evidence of the dislike of men to incur the expense which might involve limitation of their hunting, golf, etc. and well-to-do women have said "I simply dare not tell my husband that I am enceinte again." It does sometimes happen, in such cases also, that means to destroy the child are resorted to. But the exaggeration of these causes of the decline of the birthrate and the suppression of all mention of other causes at the same time and place, produces in the minds of people such a sense of the want of proportion of the whole thing that any good the film might possibly do is seriously diminished.

Further, any such small good is far overweighted by the suggestion to the minds of many who were before unaware of it, of the possibility of such a crime. Of this there is actual evidence [...] One woman in the audience was heard to say, "I did not know before that if you were in trouble you could get out of it in this way."

[draft of a letter (c. July 1917) protesting the screening of Lois Weber's film *Where Are My Children?* Intended for publication in *The Times* in 1917.]

Uncle Tom's Cabin (1944)
Fredi Washington

There is hardly a person in these United States who has not at one time or another in his lifetime read Harriet Beecher Stowe's novel, *Uncle Tom's Cabin* and the only thing which I dare say people remember about the story is those vivid characters, Topsy, Eva, Simon Legree and Uncle Tom.[1] In most cases, we have made Uncle Tom a selfish, back-bending, "white-folks loving" yard man. When I read the announcement in the daily press last week that *Metro–Goldwyn–Mayer* intended making a picture of this well-known novel by one of the finest women ever to fight the cause of Negro slaves, my first reaction was to become incensed.[2] And then I tried to remember something about the story other than these above-mentioned characters and could only remember the brutality of Legree to his slaves, the saint-like life of little Eva and Eliza's escape across the frozen river.

Realizing that I had seen on numerous occasions these characters burlesqued in this sketch or that, I decided to sit down and reread the book before spouting off at the mouth about Uncle Tom selling us Negroes out. Well, after I'd finished I commenced to think that it wouldn't be a bad idea if we all would refresh our memories on the subject. I didn't find Tom to be the scoundrel we have made him to be. In the book, he is a living saint. The story is one of the most eloquent pleas for the abolition of slavery which probably has ever been written.

While the book is informative and positive propaganda against the vicious practice of slavery which is still a blot on our country, I most definitely am against any picturization of it by MGM or any other studio.

When you realize that the country is still full of potential slave holders (could you think of Congressman Rankin from Mississippi as anything else?) you can understand why it would be suicide to show Negroes at this time on the screen under the bondage of slavery, illiterate, childlike and docile.[3] Conditions for the Negro in the South and in many spots in the north are not too far removed from conditions which existed under actual slavery. Does not the South still keep the Negro from voting; from getting an equal education; refuse war contracts because whites refuse to train or work with Negroes; make the Negro soldier ride in the back of their conveyances, if at all?

Can anyone forget the Louisiana town where Negro soldiers were shot down like dogs in the public square? (This is the same state which is noted for its public auction blocks for the sale of human "articles.") And take the north. Why has it been necessary for the President to issue an executive order on fair employment practices for such states as New York, Oregon, Pennsylvania? Why do you suppose Negroes right in Westchester County have had crosses burned on the lawns of homes they have purchased? And why the Detroit riots?[4]

I dare say every Negro and many whites know the answer to these questions. White America has not accepted the emancipation of the Negro. And for white America to see parade across the silver screen Negroes as they would like to see them—in their so-called places—would tend to bring to the surface many of those inhibitions which have been laying dormant in their breasts. There would be a field day for the South. I daresay the South would give MGM a medal for such a picture.

If MGM has the notion that to make *Uncle Tom's Cabin* would be a plea for the Negro, let him forget such fantastic ideas. The plea for the Jew against his oppressors has, I believe, certainly not helped him with the American people (and there are an alarming number scattered throughout this country who are against him). Instead, Hitler's atrocities have given voice to what were whispers before. I remember when I first started going to Hollywood, various people with whom I came into contact, whispered in unpleasant terms about the Jew owning the town and then I noticed that after Hitler got away with his viciousness against these people, the voices grew continuously louder and more abusive. And so it goes.

Anything the picture industry does in regards to the Negro today must be of a militant nature. America has got to realize that Black America is dying on the battlefields, buying war bonds, paying taxes, helping to hold down the homefront and turning out implements of war, not to be tolerated or handled with kid gloves, but by God, for freedom from want, from discrimination—to be treated like men and women in a free democracy—for an opportunity for education, etc. Why must the moviemakers always dig back into the files and drag out something which they feel will please the bigots? Why cannot there be a picture made which will show the New Negro! It's about time that the pussy-footing stopped. That stories based on some of our accomplishments be made.

[*The People's Voice* (New York), 5 February 1944, p. 22.]

Enlightment without Tears

Letter (1907)
Jane Addams

To whom it may concern:—

The five cent theatre opened by Hull-House in the summer of 1907 depended for its many picture films altogether upon the generosity of Mr. Carl Laemmle of 196 Lake St., Chicago.[1] From his large list of subjects we were able to select fairy stories which delighted the children, foreign scenes which filled our Italian and Greek neighbors with happy reminiscences, dramatizations of great moral lessons contained in such stories as Uncle Tom's Cabin and the Bishop's candlesticks, modern heroism as portrayed by the fireman and the life saving corps, as well as that multitude of simpler domestic scenes which fascinates the spectator, through their very familiarity because they reveal an inner beauty, not suspected before.

It is unfortunate that the five cent theatre has become associated in the public mind with the lurid and unworthy. Our experience at Hull-House has left no doubt in our minds that in time moving pictures will be utilized quite as the Stereopticon is at present, for all purposes of education and entertainment and that schools and churches will count the films as among their most valuable equipment.

Jane Addams
    President Hull-House,
        Chicago.

[Letter printed in Show World (Chicago), 3 August 1907, p. 32, as part of an advertisement for the Laemmle Film Service.]

The Future of the Cinematograph (1900)
J.E. Whitby

Certainly few people, if any, can have foreseen in the invention of the cinematograph that which would to a great extent revolutionise the world of teaching; and yet this is precisely what the instrument promises to do, though originally offered to the public only as a toy, an amusement for an idle hour, in the form of a superior magic-lantern combining motion with pictorial effect.

The cinematograph—with several variations of name, but based on similar principles—has already excited considerable attention and popular favour, by bringing scenes of national and stirring interest before spectators prevented from seeing the actual occurrences, and with a promptitude which made the representation more valuable. Now it appears about to enter on a path of usefulness the extent and value of which it is impossible to estimate; for it has been recognised that as an unrivalled means of demonstration for the use of teachers, and in cases where the eye and hand require to be educated and trained, there is unmistakable evidence that before long its application will be widely established. Every one will understand the enormous advantage, to those engaged in imparting instruction, of a demonstrator which can be called upon to repeat the examples required to explain a lesson whenever and as often as may be required, and can, moreover, be depended upon to reproduce the examples in precisely the same way. The latter attribute makes the cinematograph extremely useful, especially in cases where delicate and exact manipulation is required, and gives the instrument an enormous advantage over a mere flesh-and-blood performer, whose fatigue, state of health, the weather, and numberless other circumstances might cause variations. The use of the cinematograph, by which moving reflections of the subject under consideration will be distinctly seen by all, also enables a much larger number of students to assist at an illustrated lecture, and to derive benefit from the demonstrations. In addition, the lecturer—whether he be the author of the examples or not, and no matter how practised and expert he may be—might be expected to give a far more clear and lucid interpretation of his subject if freed from the embarrassment of simultaneous performance.

To students unable to attend the lectures of the cleverest and ablest professors, as well as those whom fate compels to reside at some distance from the centres of education, the cinematograph in its new function will come as an incalculable boon; for it will be possible by its aid to repeat the illustrative action of the greatest authority on any given subject, and by means of an accompanying lecture to repeat the lesson not only as many times as may be required, but in as many different places. This will enable the poor as well as the rich, the country as well as the town mouse, to enjoy the same high advantages.

It has always been acknowledged that "example is better than precept," and a moment's consideration will help any one realise the vast field for instruction thus opened, for there is scarcely any branch of instruction that does not require a certain amount of demonstration; and the pupil can be so thoroughly familiarised with the movements required for any special purpose, through constant repetition by mechanical means, that there will be far less difficulty experienced in practical work than if the ordinary methods of teaching were followed.

That the same illustrations may be given again and again is an economic advantage which will be apparent to all. Thus, the movements required for swimming might be studied, before the pupil entered the water, by means of a representation of a swimmer actually breasting the waves; cooking classes could be held and lessons given without fire; dancing could be taught, and gymnastics imitated; in fact, there is no end to the subjects which could be treated. It would also be possible, and might be advantageous, for pupils to compare the methods of different demonstrators; while the demonstrators themselves might gain by being able to see and judge of themselves and their actions when imparting instruction.

Useful as all this undoubtedly promises to be, the cinematograph, however, proposes to make its greatest mark in the science of surgery, and by its illustrative power to add immensely to the knowledge of that science, as well as to simplify the means of acquiring it. All centres of medical education possess amphitheatres in which is carried on the practical study of those surgical operations to which poor suffering humanity has to submit. These studies are usually practised on corpses; and though this may be highly necessary in the interests of all, and for the promotion of science, it is a gruesome idea, and most people will hail with satisfaction the news that the use of the cinematograph will do away with or at least lessen the necessity for dissection. No demonstration, however clearly given, on a dead body can possibly equal all that may be learnt from studying the same operation performed on a living patient; and it is just this which the cinematograph will ensure. Even when it is possible for students to watch an operation on a patient, a large number of spectators is impossible, while for various reasons those present must keep at a distance, and thus have a difficulty in seeing the operations. All these disadvantages the cinematograph promises to remove; the benefits to be derived from its employment as a demonstrator in surgical lectures being proved on its exhibition before the British Medical Association when in Edinburgh.[1] There seems to be little doubt, therefore, that the cinematograph is destined to become a recognised factor in the course of surgical instruction. Amongst others who will benefit by its introduction may also be reckoned those people—and there are many such nowadays—who, although not actually following the profession of medicine or surgery, interest themselves in assisting the suffering, as they will thus acquire a knowledge of certain facts of immeasurable importance in a moment of urgency.

It has also been suggested that, by familiarising people with the sights the cinematograph might show, much of the terror felt regarding a surgical operation could be dispelled; while the apparent precision and care with which everything is done, as well as the calmness of the surgeon and his assistants, would induce a feeling of confidence.

Enough has, perhaps, been said to prove that the cinematograph has a future of usefulness totally unsuspected by those who first launched it, and of an extent no one in these days of marvellous discoveries can possibly foretell; while, in addition, there is stimulus given to, and the change likely to result in, the art of photography, of which the cinematograph is a part.

[*Chambers's Journal* (London and Edinburgh), 1 June 1900, pp. 391–92.]

The Workingman's College (1910)
Jane Elliott Snow

"What is the workingman's college?"

Why, the moving picture show.

"How can that be?"

Let us see.

In the first place it is the workingman's college because he can thereby acquire a broad and liberal education.

"A liberal education from that nonsense!" I hear some one say.

But the moving pictures are not wholly made up of nonsense; far from it. There is some to be sure, but

"A little nonsense now and then."

Is relished by the best of men."

Besides it is good for one. Cold indeed must be the heart of the man who doesn't respond to a bit of humor, at least at times. Life is quite too serious for one to wholly ignore its funny side.

"Laugh, and the world laughs with you;

Weep, and you weep alone."

One of the best known and best loved men of all time was Mark Twain, whose humor has kept the world in smiles for many years and will continue to keep it smiling while our literature endures.[1]

Even, the great Dr. Lyman Beecher saw the necessity of humor.[2] His daughter tells us that when the distinguished divine was preparing one of his soul-stirring sermons he devoted all his energies to it; he thought of nothing but his sermon until he had delivered it. Then he went home, brought out his violin, and drew forth from its well toned chords some lively music, which helped to relax the strain to which his nerves had been so long subjected.

The daughter speaks of this last proceeding as her father's method of "letting himself down." While his preparation for the final delivery of his sermon was the act of "winding himself up."

The budget of Lincoln stories bids fair never to become exhausted, which proves that our immortal War President was endowed with a greater sense of humor than that possessed by the ordinary man. This gift no doubt helped to lighten the enormous burden of responsibility and care, which the exigencies of the times imposed upon him.

So much for the funny, the humorous side of the moving picture show. As to the objection sometimes raised that they (the shows) are harmful, they cannot be, since the National Board of Censors have placed their ban upon everything of that character.[3] Some of the film producers are now particular to inform the writers of their scenarios that no scenes of crime, or violence, or anything suggestive of immorality will be permitted.

The workingman, while he is acquiring his higher education at the moving picture show needs the amusing features of it to relax his wearied muscles after his day of toil in the shop or factory.

As he enters the theater he sees thrown upon the canvas possibly a scene where people get into all sorts of amusing situations, they run, fall down, tumble over each other, fall into holes, into water, scramble out and create such hearty laughter that the workman forgets his weariness and is prepared to fully enjoy and appreciate the graver, or the more educational subjects which follow.

He visits different countries; he sees the Fetish worshippers in "Darkest Africa." He sees the Hindoo prostrating himself before his gods; the muezzin calling the faithful to prayer; he sees the Chinaman with his queue and the Turk in his flowing robes. He realizes as never before that this is a great world, and that people of varied ideas, customs and manners inhabit it.

He witnesses the process of some new industry—new to him at least—and then changes off the literature, or possibly to a story taken from Greek mythology.

His mind may be narrow, cramped, but in spite of all he is gaining ideas; his views of life are broadening, and ere long he will become a pretty well educated man.

Indeed it is questionable if since time began there was ever a simple instrumentality that would compare with the moving picture in its work of educating the masses.

I say masses, because the masses are in attendance at the moving picture show, and the masses represent those who toil with their hands.

The workingman cannot attend the professional ball games because it takes half a dollar just to get into the grounds, and in addition it requires the loss of half a day's time. He cannot attend the high class concerts because neither his purse nor his time will admit of it, nor, for the same reasons, can he travel to any great extent, but he can visit the moving picture shows, and there he can travel through all lands and learn the condition of people in all climes.

Who then can say that the moving picture show is not the workingman's college? The medium through which he may rise to the rank of a broad-minded, well-educated man.

[*Moving Picture World* (New York) 7:9, 27 August 1910, p. 458.]

Mind-Growth or Mind-Mechanization?
The Cinema in Education (1927)
Barbara Low

An interesting viewpoint which, though not altogether in accordance with our own beliefs, yet states one side of the educational question with thoroughness and insight. Miss Low is a Member of the British Psychological Society, Executive Member of the Committee for Psychological Research and the Author of "An Outline of the Freudian theory," etc. etc.

The art of the Cinema and its swift development may be ranked as one of the most remarkable features of our latter-day civilization. No one can dispute, nor would even wish to, the enormous hold the "Pictures" exert upon the minds and interest of the adult population—whether white, black, or of any intervening shade—the world over; nor can there be a question as to the new spheres of experience opened up by means of this medium; nor the high degree to which human skill and creative power have developed in this connection. Whether we appreciate it or not, this fact is overwhelmingly established, that the Cinema-art has made a place for itself as a rival to—it may be a triumphant victor over—all the various other arts which make appeal to mankind, and has even surpassed in strength and extent that appeal to a degree hitherto unknown. So far, so good; or, if not so good in all eyes, it is a situation to be accepted, studied, and turned to the very best account. Humanity, in all ages, has pursued its pleasure and will continue so to do, in the mass aiming at the greatest amount of satisfaction with the least output of effort, a goal most satisfactorily achieved via the path of the "Pictures". If in addition, wider experience, more accurate realization of life in its various manifestations, more ready power of contact can be obtained, few will deny the legitimacy of this form of pleasure-getting by the adult man or woman, the *adult*—and here we are face to face with the problem: is the adult's fare necessarily nourishment for the *child*?

The idea of the child as the "little man"—the adult in a backward stage—has long been abandoned by all who can observe and judge, and the profounder aspects of mind which the psychology of the unconscious has revealed must convince us that the child has its own destiny to fulfil, and if it misses essential phases of childhood-development it will inevitably suffer loss, and may be, serious disharmony, when adult. The truth grasped by the Jesuits, namely, that the early years are all-important in shaping character-trends, has been so amply reinforced by modern science that we are forced to value educational methods and agencies according as they help or hinder the developing mind: yet it is notable that such a valuation has hardly been considered by the enthusiasts, educational and "lay", who wholeheartedly welcome the Cinema for educational usage.

Perhaps the first problem is to understand the meaning of the demand for the Cinema-entertainment, to what this is a reaction. Some answer is afforded by study of adult modern communities in which we see a widespread demand for easy and effortless entertainment characterized by incessant variety and sensationalism. The vastly popular variety entertainment, the cabaret show, the jazzband, the modern dance, much of the drama of the moment, pictorial art and literature, and, above all, the contemporary Press bear the characteristics already mentioned. In the individual we can note much the same: that is the demand for, and enjoyment of, sensationalism, alternating with a negativism or so-called cynicism covering a strong but repressed emotional attitude. Thus we may see in the excessive demand for the Cinema, both a *symptom* of this prevalent attitude, and a *gratification* of the wishes creating that attitude: it is by investigating along these lines that we may come to understand some of the deeper significance of the problem.

But before dealing with these more complex issues let us consider a moment the more obvious aspects. Everyone agrees on certain predominant characteristics of the Cinema-entertainment: Its overpowering appeal to the eye and correspondingly small demand upon intellectual processes: its arbitrary, and therefore false, simplification: its confusion of values; the film knows no light and shade; features which are striking to the eye, however superficial or trivial in content, however subsidiary to the main theme, may equal in value or even submerge the really significant aspects: its perpetual variety: and finally the illusion of timelessness due in the first place to the fact that real human beings are never present, only simulacra, and in the second place to swiftly culminating happenings without intermediate phases of slow elaboration.

In the face of this we must ask, is this type of experience, with such characteristic features, suited to either the demand of the child-mind or to its harmonious development. The child as such must learn to develop beyond its purely visual pleasures—a pleasure which along with taste and touch predominates in the first stages of life: it must gain power of concentration, of continuity of interest, in place of the appeal made by variety. As a child it is incapable of a true sense of proportion or understanding of slow development leading towards a wished for goal: but it is just these capacities we must seek to develop if the child is to become adult in the true sense of the word, instead of that product so prevalent in the modern world, the Peter Pan type, the man with the child-mentality.

And now to return to those influences and reactions which are still more significant—concealed from ordinary observation. In the human being's development, one of the most important stages is that of belief in magic, a stage characteristic of the infant, the very young child, the primitive and to some extent, though disguised, of the "Civilized" adult. It is the stage named by Ferenczi, the famous Hungarian psycho-analyst, "the period of unconditional omnipotence," a period wherein life and all its dearest needs and wishes are maintained from some mysterious external source, without human effort.[1] It is clear that such a condition is an actuality in the earliest months of life; a little later this stage is sadly left behind and the child must learn through bitter necessity that achievement is reached only through effort; yet there remains still, and throughout life, some of this "omnipotence" wish (manifested for instance, in such forms as the universal interest in gambling, in fortune-telling, in prophesy, in "luck"). Now it is a matter vitally affecting harmonious development how far such an attitude becomes dominant, for it is one based on the pleasure-principle and antagonistic to reality. Those who cling to their "Omnipotence" stage with the accompanying egocentricity, never get reconciled to the renunciation of their unconscious irrational wishes and "on the slightest provocation feel themselves insulted and slighted and regard themselves as step-children of fate, because they cannot remain her only or favourite children."

It is not difficult to see that the characteristics of the Cinema referred to above are just those which must foster and develop this magic "omnipotence" sense, to a greater degree than is possible in the case of fairy-tale, novel, drama, or picture, and does so independently, to a large degree, of the theme dealt with by the film. It is the method of the moving picture which brings about so vividly the sense of wish-fulfilment as by magic. The Cinema's business is to give a solution to all problems, an answer to all questions, and a key to every locked door. Real life is complex, unselective, often baffling to our curiosity and regardless of our desires: the Film's simplifications and problem-solving creates the fantasy that the spectator's wishes are or can be, fulfilled, and this helps to maintain his omnipotence and narcissism, leading to a regressive attitude: That is to say a return to the pleasure-seeking infancy with its magically fulfilled desires, since it is always easier for the Ego to retread known paths which have already yielded pleasure than to go forward on paths yet untried and calling for effort. But this latter process is essential to the child's development and through it alone can he attain to mental maturity. An even more serious consequence is the disintegration which must result from the failure of the pleasure-impulse to reach to, and co-operate with, the level of development attained by the rest of the personality—that "split" which is so marked a feature of the neurotic. By an emotional expenditure of an infantile nature only (that is, narcissistic emotion unrelated to external reality and very easily obtained) the emotional life remains undeveloped: inadequate and extravagant at one and the same time.

It will, perhaps, appear startling to class together those films which are true to human and scientific reality and the crudely false melodrama or romance. Undoubtedly there is a world of difference as regards the consciously-felt effects, but it is possible for the same unconscious effects to be produced in both cases since the mechanism at work is identical. In the film of the Scott Expedition, than which nothing could be more beautiful and more moving as far as the pictures themselves are concerned all the elements of magic achievement, of simplification, of rapid solution are present just as in other films.[2] And this criticism holds good, though to a far less degree, in nature films, geographical films, and films illustrating mechanical processes. A small investigation recently carried out among school children of different types, and of ages varying from eight to twelve, revealed interestingly the child's capacity for distortion: seventy per cent of the children believed that such processes as the development of the chick from the egg, of the fish from the spawn, of the pearl within the oyster, of nest-building and so forth, took just the time which elapsed in the showing of the films, even though each step in the process was elaborated. And this is inevitable since the film, operating in a mechanical universe, fills the gaps, rounds all corners, and presents persons and events in the neatest way, like so many brown paper parcels: as result, there is lack of emotional contact both in the production and the spectator. Closely related to the above is another aspect of the film which has much significance for the deeper human impulses, namely its relation to time. Research into the unconscious of man has revealed that the idea of time (and its twin-companion death) is among the most deeply-repressed material of the mind, and it is only by the process of becoming adult that a realization and acceptance of time becomes possible. If from a very early stage the child is strengthened in his repression so much the more difficult for him is recognition of reality. Bearing upon another of the most powerful impulses is that character of the film, already referred to, which demands from the spectator an almost exclusive visual attention. The powerful rôle played by curiosity in the early life of the child, developed and gratified by seeing and looking, is maintained by means of the films' dominant appeal, and in thus obtaining and continuing his gratification he is assisted in remaining at the infantile curiosity-level.

In the light of such effects, conscious and unconscious, (and I have here space to touch upon a few only) produced by the film it is surely worth while to consider whether, and to what degree, we are prepared to make it a part of our educational system. The adult, educated or ignorant, in virtue of being adult, must be free to choose his own pursuits and pleasures, but in educating the child we are forcing upon him experience which he is not in [a] position to evaluate: the justification is if our wider and deeper experience convinces us that what we offer will assist the best and truest development of the child.

Can we be satisfied that the Cinema is a method of promoting mind growth rather than one of mechanizing mentality?

[*Close Up* (Territet, Switzerland) 1:3, September 1927, pp. 44–52.]

Can the Film Educate? (1934)
Mary Field

When people talk about the educational influence of the films they are apt to quote the old saying, "Seeing is Believing". [...] I do not think that, with the evidence at present at our disposal, we can speak authoritatively on the influence of the film for good or evil, or on its power to impart knowledge; but my own opinion is that while the cinema can have a great ethical value and can be widely employed for education in both its widest and narrowest sense, each individual can only get from a film in the same proportion as he gives to it. Before we can hope to use films to their best advantage we must learn to look and see and realize what we are seeing—and then we may safely believe and learn. [...] We are taught how to read and to use books to their best advantage. Those of us who are lucky enough are also taught how to listen to music or how to look at pictures: and we cannot expect the cinema to teach us without effort on our part. If the film is to be anything more than a sensuous pleasure and a means of "escape", then we must learn how to look.

The younger generation is learning to look. We call them "film-conscious", but this means only that they have learned to look at moving pictures, whereas the eyes of older people are trained chiefly to look at still pictures or at print. Listen to the children in the cinema! The films are speaking to them in a language they understand completely. They know all the film conventions and appreciate the 'fade-out' or the "mix" or "close-up" as we appreciate the meaning of the paragraph or asterisks. They can pick up a story quickly, can appreciate subtleties, do not require points to be laboured in order to get them over. With regard to films the majority of young people have reached the same stage as the person who has learned to read fluently and must now learn to read with judgement. They "see" fluently and some few are learning to "see" with judgement.

Now to anyone trained to see there is a great deal to be learnt from the ordinary entertainment picture. Experiments with educational films have shown that the outstanding thing about moving pictures is that they give a sense of experience. It is as if one were actually in the scene, not merely a looker-on. Therefore if we go to plenty of films we enlarge our experience. We most of us now know what it is like to be in a submarine or to go up in an aeroplane. People who can't afford to go on a charabanc trip to the seaside have a very good idea of how to travel on a luxury European train, or an Asiatic express. [...] If a girl from a cigarette factory found herself suddenly transported into the halls of a Grand Hotel anywhere in Europe she would know exactly how to behave. [...] I think myself that the poise and self-possession of young people at the present day is due to the fact that through the films they have a store of experience of life in the wide sense. No environment in which they may find themselves is really strange to them, because they have 'seen it on the films', and, believing it, accept it as a matter of course when they meet it in real life. They have learned from films something they could have learned in no other way. Yet, of course, there is another side to the question of whether the entertainment film has educational value or not. Frequently these films are inaccurate; but I do not think that inaccuracies are important so long as the general impression given by the picture is correct. [...]

There are [...] inaccuracies of customs, manners, and above all behaviour, which leave a definitely wrong impression on the minds of those who see the films. And, if we took our ideas only from films, we should have some very odd ideas of how the nations live. We should, I suppose, be inclined to regard America as a country given over to gangsters and—what is hardly less dangerous—to uncontrolled flappers. France, as interpreted by René Clair, we should imagine to be populated by people who, with an over-developed sense of rhythm, move entirely to music.[1] In Germany the sun is always low and the shadows long and heavy; while all Russia is divided into two parts, people who like tractors and machinery, and people who don't, the latter group being much given to eating and drinking till their mouths run over at the corners. Certainly it would not do for us to believe everything we see in entertainment pictures. We must see, use our judgement, and draw our own conclusions; but this applies equally to other forms of art. We cannot believe everything we read in books, and we must take the personality of the author into consideration. [...] By the majority of people the director is overlooked, but actually he usually puts the stamp of his personality on his work. Thus you can be certain that a Von Stroheim picture is definitely anti-monarchist, that a de Mille picture has a touch of the sadist, and so forth.[2] To get the best from a film, then, you must have some idea of the personalities behind its production and make due allowances for them, just as we make allowances for Bernard Shaw in St. Joan.[3] To sum up, in order to get the most from an entertainment film you have got to give a good deal of intelligence, information and attention, and you will get a great deal back in return. [...]

The ethical value of the ordinary theatrical film is difficult to estimate. On the whole they are like the old melodramas and penny dreadfuls—vice triumphs temporarily, but virtue usually conquers in the end. Their moral is therefore a sound one. A little boy asked what lesson he had drawn from the films, replied that he had learned that it did not do to steal because you were found out. Certain "Society" dramas, where the line between social and anti-social conduct is not very clear, are possibly as pernicious as many welfare workers say they are, but again you get from a film what you yourself bring to it. If you have no learning towards orchids and ermine and what Charles Laughton as "Nero" calls "delicious debauches", that type of film bores you and you stay away.[4] If your weakness lies in that direction you would indulge it anyhow with books whose titles are something like Sin and Satan. The only difference is that film with movement and sound makes the illusion greater than a book can ever do, and therefore the bad influence of a film may be stronger. A film which illustrates excellently what I mean about getting from a film what you give is The Sign of the Cross. I know people who have some knowledge of the historical period in question and who think the censor should never have passed the film in its present condition; on the other hand, I have heard of people who have gone more than once because they enjoyed the questionable character of some of the scenes. I know one man who sat through it twice because he enjoyed the cruelty of the arena scenes; another man did not realize they were cruel but considered them an extremely amusing circus. Some women and men are awestruck with the courage of the Christians, others weep over a broken romance. What is the ethical value of that film? One can only say that it proves the vast power of the film for good or evil ... but one cannot say which.

The cinema remains a place of recreation, and most people go there not to exercise their brains, but to rest, and be entertained. If you take your cinema seriously, you will be dissatisfied with the entertainment film as it is at present, for very few films have a definite message and most of them are "escapist"—a means by which people can temporarily forget the world they live in and their anxieties and project themselves into another world of imagination. The cinema helps people to hypnotize themselves in this way, for they sit gazing fixedly at a light concentrated in one place in a dark hall. If you are a realist you will disapprove of this undirected entertainment, and feel that films should be modelled more on the lines of Pabst's *Kameradschaft* or the productions of Pudovkin.[5] This is a question of personal opinion, and I merely put forward for your consideration that there is no reason why, in time, every film should not be a definite contribution to knowledge and have a clearly defined message. But you will have to educate your cinema-going public up to wishing to be instructed and made to use its brains, before that can be accomplished.

In the ordinary programme of a cinema theatre, the most instructive item is undoubtedly the news-reel. That it is popular, the appearance and continuance of 'news' theatres gives ample proof. The value of the news-reel is the same as that of the best feature films—it enables us to "experience" what otherwise would be quite beyond our powers to conceive. I remember particularly some years ago there was a very bad volcanic eruption in Sicily, and the headlines of the newspapers recorded thousands killed and tens of thousands homeless. To most people these figures meant nothing. There had been a terrible earthquake and a volcano was active, but that was just a news item. In the news-reel about a week later there were scenes of lava rolling forward, knocking down walls and burying houses. A gasp of horror went up in the theatre—the audience realized what a volcano in action meant. In the same way we can realize what industrial strife, revolutions, explosions, fire and floods mean to the people who are actually experiencing them; and there is no doubt that the news-reel is a magnificent means of teaching contemporary history; only its value has not yet been fully realized. I am convinced we ought to have more and better news-reels—not better from the cinematic point of view, for the photography is often superb and the camera-men reckless in their efforts to be first with the news; but better in the sense that there should be better editing, more attention given to providing the public with real news in pictures and better arrangement of the items, so that we should not be asked to switch our minds over from the rescue of the victims of a mine disaster to, say, a comic motor race in California.

There is now a tendency to give pictures of experiences we don't want to see. Some of these are not educative but appeal to the spirit which leads people to go to see accidents, not with a view to helping but just to see the mess. There has been correspondence in the papers on this subject—about the recent revolution in Cuba, for instance.[6] In the film of this Cuban revolution there was shown the expression of horror on the face of a man about to be shot; and it is contended that the sufferings of human beings should not be exploited for financial gain. Some people would reply to this that it is good for us to see these happenings, that we should be able to stand them, and that if we cannot bear them we can always shut our eyes. Others are of opinion that such things should not be shown unexpectedly or on the same programme as entertainment films. A further point to consider is that while some people who see that type of film and have imagination will be suitably shocked by it, others may become brutalized.

Sometimes sandwiched in after the news-reel, sometimes by itself in the pro-gramme is the documentary film, [...] a film that aims at showing the truth, and that has no fiction or propaganda in it. These films deal chiefly with travel, industry, science and nature study, and to watch a good documentary is perhaps one of the most pleasant ways of getting instruction. The value of the documentary picture is that it enables you vicariously to experience, to travel, to go round a factory, to watch birds. It is with such films as these that the educational value of the film is most apparent. But instructive as they are, [...] I must remind you not to believe the documentary picture blindly. Wherever a human being comes into the making of a picture, there is danger of distortion. In the documentary film the personality of the director must definitely be reckoned with, for the director is deliberately trying to tell you the truth as seen through his eyes. For instance Flaherty is a sentimentalist, Rotha holds strong views on the position of the workers—these views colour their work.[7] In some cases strong views distort documentary films, in others quite unconsciously a wrong impression is given by editing. [...] I once saw a rough cut of an industrial film where, to shorten action in a workshop, the editor had cut in a close-up of a man at work. The man was, as many people are, very nervous of being filmed, and had sweated with fright. The close-up gave the uninitiated the impression that the workshop was very hot, which it was not. [...] I do warn you, therefore, when you see a documentary film, to believe it, but with reservations. The only films in which you can really believe without any reserva-tion, are the purely educational ones such as Dr. Canti's films on Cancer, or Percy Smith's *Woodwasps and its Parasite*.[8] These films are the record of the camera employed as a scientific eye, and while they are completely true, they are extremely difficult to believe because they are so surprising. The human eye is erratic, roving (in the better sense), easily tired and capable of seeing only movements of a certain speed; but the eye of the camera never relaxes its steady gaze. The limited vision of the camera is not always easily explained to people who have not used the instrument very much, and they do not realize how, unlike the human eye, it is difficult to keep pulling it in and out of focus. But, within its limitations it is amazingly efficient. It will watch day and night for weeks on end, and will exactly record what it has seen. It can observe faithfully movements that are so slow that even when they are speeded up one hundred thousand times we can hardly see them. It can analyse an action that is too quick for us to see. It can already watch in the dark, and when the new infra-red photography is more commonly used, it will not only photograph easily in the dark but in the fog as well. It is by photography of this kind that the film makes its most serious contribution to learning. Those of you who have seen Dr. Canti's film on the treatment of cancer by radium will know that in that you can actually witness the strengthening of the body tissue to resist the attacks of cancer. [...]

The analysis of movement by slow-motion film on ultra-rapid photography is now familiar to most of us. The usual speed for photographing and projecting films for talking pictures is twenty-four pictures a second. By filming and projecting at the same speed we get normal movement on the screen; but if we take between two and three hundred pictures to the second and show them at the rate of twenty-four, we get a perfectly smooth action, but slowed down to about one-tenth of its natural speed. [...] Very valuable work can be done in vocational guidance by means of films showing, for instance, the elimination of industrial fatigue by slow-motion pictures of movements of good and less efficient workers. In fact if you want to know anything about movement, the slow-motion camera is invaluable. You can see and you can believe.

But equally instructive, and to my mind almost more marvellous, is the ultra-slow photography which enables one to see plants growing, roots spreading, the growth of the embryo in an egg. This effect is of course obtained by photographing one picture at a time every ten minutes, half an hour, hour, or numbers of hours as the speed of movement demands. The camera is worked by clock-work, and every picture is taken in darkness by artificial light, so that the final film, taken day and night, is of the same density. Roots are photographed by making them grow between two pieces of peat, or a similar substance, which are hinged together and opened by clock-work at stated intervals. If it were not for this contrivance we should not know that the tip of the root was really the intelligent part of the root and directed growth, but you have to see the root tips actually feeling and directing operations to appreciate how marvellous is the instinct behind each of what one might have been inclined to regard as blind growths. Of course the intimate knowledge one gains of plants changes one's point of view towards them. Poets and writers probably have no idea of the implications of their descriptions of their heroines as flower-like, "fresh as a daisy" or "innocent as a snowdrop". Actually plants are completely ruthless in their struggle for existence, and no one who has ever seen a tiny cress seedling reach over for its next-door neighbour, seize it around the stem and behead it, would ever wish to be compared to anything in the vegetable world. "Smug as a house leek" would be a fine description of someone who cares nothing for the sufferings of others so long as he is all right. "Resourceful as grass" would fit a man who is prepared for almost every emergency.

The film is valuable in enabling us to watch the finest efforts of experts at their jobs. Slow motion and close-views of athletics are frequently seen in theatres, but very few people have seen films of surgical operations. These films enable medical students to see expert surgeons at work, and also to preserve records of rare operations. [...] Also they show the movement of the hands in close-ups which the ordinary eye in an operating theatre could not do. Very little has been done with films of music but I am convinced that films of the finger-movement of masters would be of the greatest assistance to students say of piano and violin. The films of great orchestras which are showing in theatres at the moment suggest what could be done in this direction. [... T]wo experimental talking films recently made (King's English and 48 Paddington Street) indicate that the film would be an excellent medium for teaching foreign languages, showing as it does the jaw and lip movements. Tongue movements would have to be shown by means of moving diagrams, and here we reach a field in which the film is triumphant, the animated cartoon. For showing how machinery works, how bulidings are balanced and planned, how chemical reactions take place and how trade movements are directed, there is nothing to compare with the animated cartoon, and we have hardly yet begun to experiment with its uses in instruction.

The film has a vast potentiality for instruction both direct and indirect, but we have not yet learned to use it. Firstly we have got to learn to see. Many teachers are afraid of using the film because they say that it is too easy a medium for instruction—that their pupils will only sit and look at pictures and tend to become lazy. But those who have experimented with the use of films for teaching are unanimous in agreeing that they mean very hard work on the part of both teacher and pupils. And it is the same for the ordinary filmgoer. To get the best from a film is real hard work. You can see a piece of film thirty or forty times, and then suddenly discover something that you have not noticed before. There are things in a film that you will see but not be conscious of until someone else calls your attention to them. [...] [W]ith films as with books, we shall learn from them both good and evil in proportion to our knowledge, attitude of mind and disposition. The film can do nothing by itself, but we can do much with it; and even, when we are trained to use it, we shall still have cases like the little boy of nine who, when asked what he had learned from films that he had not known before, replied, "I have learned the Art of Making Love."

[From For Filmgoers Only, ed. R.S. Lambert (London: Faber & Faber with British Institute of Adult Education, 1934), pp. 48–61, excerpted.]

The Educational and Social Value
of the News-Reel (1934)
Germaine Dulac

[...] In the beginning, the motion picture was too young an invention to be considered in its early manifestations as an expression of thought. It became intellectual bit by bit, without any definite policy or intention, while its economic bases grew continually more solid.

It reached the zenith of its financial and popular success before its spiritual character was properly defined. The businessmen created the *need* of the film before the artists were able to meditate over its possibilities.

There is no use in going into here the matter of the dramatic films which were produced by commercial organizations. The taste of the public sought to elevate these pieces to the dignity of an art-cinema expression. There is an error here, which it [is] necessary [to] point out. The dramatic film is an application of the cinematographic art, but not the expression of its inner truth, which is better illustrated by the scientific film or the news-reel.

These two kinds of film, one as a result of its demonstrative capacity, the other through its social value, have seized the intimate meaning and essence of the motion

Fig. 3.6   Germaine Dulac, 1920s.

picture much better, giving us images of life in its various instinctive movements. Freed from all commercial interference, and developed in an atmosphere far from cine-theatrical works, having no limit to their expression of thought, such films have given us sincerer models than the regular drama with a more universally human character.

The dramatic film developed with commercial aid far more rapidly than the educational film or the news-reel which has always remained within the cycle of cinema life as a form of propaganda, teaching and distributing of news, almost without considering the question of profit. For this reason the distribution of such films remains still uncertain. The exhibitors take little interest in pictures of this kind, which find favour practically only with the managers of the recently built news-reel theatres.[1]

Notwithstanding this, the cinema news theatre which we are discussing is really the great social educator.

It puts the most opposed mentalities into communication, and joins in a magnetic current the most divergent races of the world. It shows every spectator the real aspect of far off countries and men, without the official mask of tradition and historic fantasy.

Like the scientific film, the news-reel reveals the truth of life which one could not know otherwise than through books, newspapers and manuals. Thus considered, it becomes an individual experience which allows everyone to see it, live it and not only fancy it. The news-reel unites, without any need of intermediaries, classes and races, sentiments, joys and happinesses so that humanity is uplifted above its individual characteristics, and through a gradual comprehension of life begins to forget and forego its hates.

The news-reel is made day by day, and cannot therefore be thought of as a premeditated thing. It seizes events of which it becomes a truthful mirror. It illustrates persons and facts. It even goes so far as to seek the intimate reason of their moral and sentimental motives. It is the mirror of any country, its pleasures and efforts, its joys and sorrows, and in this way it can lead to accord and disaccord. In the farthest off parts of the world, in all latitudes and longitudes, the news-reel remains what it is, a fragment of the world's sincerest life, beliefs, struggles, woes and ideals.

All the news events of the world are, as a rule, gathered together in the news-reel programmes, edited in the forms of regular papers or bulletins composed by a large number of photographic reporters. They cover all fields of activity national and international, political, judicial, scientific or artistic.

Thanks to the news-reels, we are able to become familiar not only with the outstanding figures of our national world, but with the figures of the international chess-board. Cases have occurred where men who have been unpopular with the public of certain foreign countries have won sympathy there owing to a frequent appearance of their pictures in the news-reels.

The public even comes to recognize changes in their habits, dress and manner. Sympathy is born from familiarity, and perhaps an understanding of other peoples' ideas. A knowledge of men and things teaches us to reason better, and the walls of ignorance and hatred fall. The vagueness of words can be harmful; the precision of the motion picture image brings clarity and truth.

Thanks to the news-reel, we can penetrate into the heart of diplomatic debates, see something of the alliance and disputes of nations, their ways of living. We can see how men live in various climates. Little incidents and observations of small account which have often nothing to do with the major problems of the day sometimes help to create bonds and promote understandings. Whether we want it or not, owing to the operation of news-reels, ideas circulate, sorrows become common, less strange and less abstract. The news-reel helps by giving us a wider knowledge of the world to free the senses of the individual and tune his spirit with the general universality of mankind.

The news film reflects also industry and arts. We can learn through it the efforts and skill required in the manufacture of a certain product which may come to us perhaps from some distant corner of the globe. We can place objects in their ideal and natural surroundings. A sense of fraternity arises from these circumstances.

Hygiene, sport, scientific discoveries, new educational methods come within the scope of the news-reel in all countries. It is the mirror of all civilizations in all parts of the world. It is an expression of enthusiasm and misery which every country offers us in its films. It is life itself.

The news-reel breaks down barriers. By its nature it must be indiscreet and varied. It teaches without form or methodology.

All national inventions can be made international through the operation of the film news programmes, as can all the conquests of the spirit and science. Formerly the latter were the exclusive property of specialists and students. Today they [are] at the disposal of the humblest and least cultured spectator who sits in his chair in the cinema hall and observes.

The following reflection may be made. If we tell a story, we surround it with fantasy, and therefore, in a way, we deform it. In the case of the news-reel, the spectator who has paid for his seat in the picture palace is in direct relations with the events, beings, ideas and objects of the whole world, with universal ideas. His relationship is so direct that often the anonymous spectator is inclined to manifest his approval or disapproval in the face of certain happenings or events. He feels that he is part of the events himself, since it is the whole life of the world which passes across the motion picture screen in the brief quarter of an hour reserved to the news-reels. Regular currents of sympathy and antipathy are formed in this way. [...]

News-reels form the most successful means of correspondence and understanding between different peoples and different classes. They constitute the best propaganda agent of culture and progress, and the events they show remain much better impressed on the mind than those read in any newspaper. To see a current happening means for any of us to witness an event and live it through. It means participating in the life of the whole world. It is therefore internationally and socially that we must face the questions of the news-reel which contains the real spirit of the cinema.

[*International Review of Educational Cinematography* (Rome)
6, August 1934, pp. 545–50, excerpted.]

The Cinema in the Slums (1928)
Dorothy Richardson

At the moment of reaching perfection as territory sacred to horror, slumdom produced a novelist who featured with all his mind and all his heart and all his soul the lives of its inhabitants, awakening official expediency and unofficial solicitude and driving the oblivion of the general public into a timely grave.[1] And the day that saw compulsory education snatching the children for a while from the worst, saw also philanthropy grown fashionable, slumming adding meaning to the lives of charitable unemployed and bands of devoted people weaving a network of settlements, missions, and institutions of all kinds over those areas of the larger cities that hitherto had been left undisturbed, save for an occasional forced raid, even by the police, and unproductive save for their disproportionate contribution of disease and crime and the endless procession of half-starved labourers of all ages and both sexes available for exploitation in the basements supporting the British empire.

But slumdom, though not quite what it was, continues to flourish and will continue, however rehoused and state-aided and generally disciplined, if they are right who see its problem as a biological problem, its habitants as a recruited army, an army ceaselessly recruited from above and to disappear only when we make up our minds to weed out undesirable types. And though wonders have been worked, as all may see who can remember the children haunting the by-ways even twenty years ago, there is still a vast army living, except for the all-too-short school years, in a state of mental and moral constriction, pressed upon and paralysed by circumstance and there is its off-shoot, the battalion of half-crazed intelligentsia dreaming of salvation to be reached one by a banding together for destruction.

All these people like all the rest of us are preached at by doctrinaires of all kinds and mostly by heavily interested doctrinaires who from the midst of ease—though many of them are hard workers, at jobs chosen and beloved—rate these state-pampered idlers for their thriftlessness, quote the perilous budgets of exceptionally heroic family chancellors—oh those budgets detailed from margarine to skimmed milk—upon which appears no single one of the necessary superfluities whose rôle in creating the cheerfulness of the complacent judges is ignored by them because it is permanent.

And almost everything that comes to this segregated army from without, teaching, preaching, state-aid, welfare-work, art-galleries and suchlike cultural largesse is tainted more or less, not always hopelessly but always tainted, by the motive of interest. Is not, cannot be, entirely above suspicion. Even the most devoted resident missioners are there with an aim, the confessed aim of betterment, of bringing light into darkness and comfort where no comfort was. It would be monstrous to attempt to decry the motives and the labours of these noble people and absurd to deny their great fruitfulness. And though there may be amongst them numbers of pitying souls who would be left at a loss if there were no one to rescue, there are also those whose labours are carried on in the spirit of an invitation to the dance of life. These bring charm. But their power is akin to that of the kindly host. Contact with them may be for the lost a tour of paradise; but it is a conducted tour.

And now, as it were over-night, there has materialised a presence subsuming all these others and, by reason of its freedom from any ulterior motive beyond that of its own need to survive, immeasurably more powerful as a civilising agent than any one of them. It says of course aloud for all to hear as it opens its doors conveniently in the manner of the gin-palace at every corner: it's your money we want. It does not say we want to help you. Yet it offers as many kinds of salvation as all previous enterprises combined and offers them impersonally, more impersonally than even the printed page. It illustrates. And its illustrations are encountered innocently, unguardedly, in silence and alone.

It is said that the cinema offers nothing to nobody save spiritual degradation. There are clamourings too, and secret whisperings of the enormous power of the film rightly used, used that is to say according to the speaker's idea of what is right. But both these claims ignore what is inherent in pictures, ignore that which exerts its influence apart from the intention of what is portrayed. Mankind's demand for pictures, like the child's demand, is much more than a childlike love for representation. There is in the picture that which emerges and captures him before details are registered and remains long after they are forgotten. And this influence, particularly in the case of the contemplators we are considering, is exercised as potently by a photograph as by a "work of art" and by a moving photograph, if it be the work of an artist, much more potently. Imagination fails in attempting to realise all that is implied for cramped lives in the mere coming into communication with the general life, all that results from the extension of cramped consciousness. But it is not merely that those who are condemned with no prospect of change to a living death, are lifted for a while into a sort of life as are said to be on the great festivals the souls in hell. It is that insensibly they are living new lives. Growing. Gathered spontaneously and unsuspecting before even the poorest pictures, even those that play deliberately upon the passions of the jungle, the onlookers are unawares in an effectual environment. While they follow events they are being played upon in a thousand ways. And all pictures are not bad or base or foolish. But even the irreducible minimum of whatever kind of goodness there is in any kind of picture not deliberately vicious, is civilisation working unawares.

["Continuous Performance: The Cinema in the Slums," *Close Up*
(Territet, Switzerland) 2:5, May 1928, pp. 58–62.]

Sunday Cinemas (1930)
Minnie Pallister

The reason why so much nonsense is written about cinemas is because the wrong people write about them. This can't be helped, because the only people who really know what cinemas are, are, as a rule, inarticulate. The people who live in real homes, whose lives are filled with interesting work, who read widely, dine decorously and decoratively, and who take as a matter of course a background of amenities and refinements, know nothing of cinemas.

To appreciate a cinema at its true value one must live in a mean house in a mean street; one must wear cheap clothing, and eat rough food; one must know the unutterable boredom and discomfort of evenings spent in stuffy rooms, rooms always too hot or too cold or too draughty or too crowded. One must know the misery of cold and damp faced with inadequate equipment, the fatigue of monotonous work, the absence of a warm-scented bathroom, the absence of intellectual stimulus, the absence of grace, colour, romance, change, and travel.

To the vast masses who live such lives the cinema is a fairy tale come true. It is not an entertainment only; it is vicarious life. It is luxury, warmth, comfort, colour, travel; it is scent, romance, mystery, sunshine. It is escape.

Before the cinema there were two avenues of escape for people whose lives cried out to be escaped from—beer and chapel. Beer was never a beverage only; it was escape. The public-house gave warmth and comparative comfort. There were always colonies of people, however, who did not drink. Their leisure centred round the chapel. There they found companionship and music, they listened to sermons and lectures, they spent long Sundays and week evenings in their places of worship.

Many still flock to church on Sunday; the week-night gatherings have been perhaps less in favour—not so much, we may reflect, because of the cinema, but because of the wireless. (Have not the churches in America had to change the times of their prayer-meetings, to avoid clashing with two famous comedians' daily back-chat?)[1]

In fact, to-day the Church must draw its crowd by means of its own virtue. The preacher with something to say can fill a church to-day as easily as ever. Men still cry out for spiritual and moral guidance. The Church which does its duty and takes its part in the solution of world problems has its place, but the Church is no longer the only alternative to the public-house; it is no longer needed as an avenue of escape from boredom and wet streets.

A recreative Sunday seems, on the surface, to mean a lessening of religious sense. In reality, Religion may have simply changed its form. A rigid Sunday religion, in the past, too often meant a religion confined to Sunday. Punctilious attendance at church too often meant a religion which went no further than church.

A religion of water-tight compartments is of no use to-day. What we need is religion diffused through every part of our economic, social, and political life, not one which is kept for stated hours and times and has no bearing on everyday life.

If the Church meets the need of the people, and fulfils the function which gives her the right to exist, she need not fear Sunday cinemas; she will never lack support.[2]

[*The New Leader* (London), 19 December 1930, p. 5.]

Films Have Taught Us What Life Means (1931)
Maboth Moseley

Those who attack the cinema on moral grounds generally admit that films might be of great educational value. These critics confuse education with encyclopaedic knowledge.

Scientific, historical, natural history—in fact, any type of educational film is looked upon as a bore and a delusion. The public is much more interested in the (screen) romances of Marlene Dietrich than in the birth and life of the tsetse fly. Not without reason.

I have yet to be convinced that there is something more *usefully* instructive in knowing the habits of a tropical insect than in trying to assimilate the worldliness and *savoir-faire* of a very accomplished actress.

Education, to my mind, does not end with one's schooldays, but continues until death. Education is not confined to cramming the brain with facts and figures. Education *should* produce cultivated, sensible, open-minded men and women.

A scholar, knowing everything there is to know about vitamin D, the solar system, the habits of aborigines, or the fourth dimension, is probably as helpless as a child in matters affecting his own welfare and happiness.

His knowledge may be vital to the progress of science and the human race, but it is useless to himself as a human being.

The majority of us, fortunately or unfortunately, are merely human beings. We only want to learn the things that will help us to lead wider, better, or more interesting lives.

We learned the three R.'s and a few other things at school. But we know there are far more subjects than reading, writing, and arithmetic in the great world of adult life. Until films made their appearance the majority of people were destined to live and die in ignorance of these subjects.

My generation has been more fortunate. We were brought up with the films. We cannot remember a time when there was not a convenient cinema in which we could be excited, terrified, and enchanted in turn by the exploits of dashing cowboys, fainting maidens, and sinister red-skins.

Critics still find pleasure in attacking our precocity, our "shamelessness" (in other words, our spirit of enterprise), and our sophistication.

I would wager, however, that my generation is more capable and sensible than any previous one. I would go further, and say that films have been largely responsible for this capability.

Films have revealed to us many aspects of life. We have become so accustomed to seeing on the screen wickedness as well as virtue that we accept, as a matter of course, the fact that rotters do exist, and we are on our guard in consequence.

Contrary to critical supposition, we are not quite so depraved that we are incapable of distinguishing vice and virtue; we are merely enlightened, that is all. And, surely, enlightenment is of greater value than ignorance?

Film plots cover the whole gamut of human emotions. Sacrifice is a favourite theme. The mother sacrifices herself for her child, the husband for his wife, the mistress for her lover, and so on. Sacrifice is a noble quality. So are many others beloved of film producers.

In nine out of ten films virtue proves triumphant. Moralising critics often adopt a highbrow pose. They describe immorality on the screen as vulgar and debasing.

Yet I have read highbrow books that were more disgusting and immoral than the worst film ever produced.

The difference between highbrow efforts and immorality on the films is that highbrow immorality is regarded as experimental; on the screen it is incidental to the plot. It is incidental in the lives of all normal, decent-minded people. Hence my view that films are less harmful than a number of so-called artistic literary productions.

Superior people try to justify their efforts by adopting a jargon consisting of "isms" and "ologies," and talking about giving full expression to their desires.

They suceed only in being more revolting and hypocritical than the lowest-minded film producer.

Elstree and Hollywood do not pretend to offer anything more than well-acted, well-produced, well-photographed, competent pieces of entertainment.[1]

Without attempting to educate, film producers have educated millions—in the way of worldliness, broad-mindedness and common sense. They have succeeded in showing half the world how the other half lives: and if that is not a form of education I should like to know what is.

Proselytisers may argue that we are surfeited with films of gangster life, of back-stage sordidness, of marital infidelity.

The answer to that is: Chicago's name is, or was, a by-word; touring with a fifth-rate theatrical company, in England or America, is not exactly like attending a vicarage garden party; the divorce courts are overflowing with undefended petitions.

These things happen in real life. That being the case, they are fit subjects for dramatic interpretation.

If people like to close their eyes to the "facts of life" they are fools and hypocrites. In any case, no one insists on their going to cinemas against their own inclinations.

Cranks and busybodies insist that sex knowledge is harmful. They try to abolish this and reform that. They never seem to realise that the one thing they cannot change is human nature.

This being the case, it is surely more to our social welfare that young people should possess this knowledge than to be, as they were a generation ago, in complete ignorance? I would remind outraged critics that to be forewarned is to be forearmed.

Films, owing to their world-wide appeal, have been responsible for this change. They have educated the uneducated. They have revealed aspects of life hitherto unheard of by the worker in the factory, the housewife in the home, the servant in the kitchen, and the young man in his first job.

Every human being is entitled to a knowledge of life. Where highbrows and cranks go wrong is in trying to pretend that sex is a prerogative of certain classes of society, whereas it is the one thing in which all men and women are equal.

Films have already taught us much, but we can learn a great deal more.

By watching Greta Garbo we begin to understand that restraint and dignity are more pleasing qualities than sex-appeal; from Ruth Chatterton we can learn how to combine sophistication with simplicity; Marlene Dietrich can teach us that fluency in a foreign language is a highly desirable accomplishment; with George Arliss we can learn to grow old gracefully; Will Rogers convinces us that the art of repartee is worth cultivating: and so on, endlessly.[2]

Via the screen we are transported to tropical forests and deserts, to foreign ports and dockside gambling hells, into millionaires' homes and into tenements. We are made aware of the things that make life worth living, and those that make it hell upon earth. All these form a part of our adult education.

In short, films have produced world-wide sophistication. That quality may be alien to Christian precepts, but it is essential if one is not to starve amidst the competitive elements of this over-civilised modern world.

[*Film Weekly* (London), 25 July 1931, p. 9.]

The Unconscious Humor of the Movies (1925)[1]
Agnes Repplier

There are two classes of people who write about moving pictures, and both of them write a great deal, having always a keen and attentive public. The first class tells us of the marvels of mechanism and the dizzy cost of production; the second class, of the lofty ideals which animate producers, and of the educational value of films. We hear of pictures costing well over a million dollars, "and every dollar showing," and of cameras so immense that they cannot be worked for less than a thousand dollars a minute. These details are very satisfactory. Every true American likes to think in terms of thousands and millions. The word "million" is probably the most pleasure-giving vocable in the language.

But when we leave business for benefactions, when we cease to contemplate vast expenses and vaster revenues, and are solemnly assured that "the impression made by the films is greater and deeper than that of any other circulating medium," we ask ourselves what on earth this impression is, and of what value to those who are impressed. We are even more at sea when a contributor to *Current History*, who is obviously serious, and obviously sincere, assures us that the picture-hall is the "people's university," and that the picture itself is "an instrument destined to take its place alongside of the written alphabet and the printed word, as among the modern world's most far-reaching social forces."

This is saying so much that it is but fair to conclude that some meaning underlies the words. The alphabet and the printing press gave form and substance to the secret thinking of humanity, carrying it through space and time to the bookshelf on our wall, so that the least and last of us may, if he so chooses, live under "the distant influence of exalted minds." What have the moving pictures done to so vivify the world? Mr. Hays and Mr. Fairbanks are the only enthusiasts I know who courageously face this question, and they make the same reply.[2] The film is to be the peacemaker of the future. Mr. Hays says that it "will do more than any other existing agency to unite the peoples of the earth, to bring understanding between men and women, and between nation and nation." He does not, however, make clear the character of this understanding, nor explain how the battling nations and the battling sexes are to be turned into friends by the good offices of the cinema. Mr. Fairbanks is more explicit. He says that the film—the American film especially—will go further than the Geneva Conference in establishing international relations, because it represents "the pure drama of life," and because it shows the inhabitants of countries far remote "how alike we all are."[3]

If Mr. Fairbanks means that people in moving pictures are alike, he is correct. They are. They even look alike, the women especially, because they all paint their mouths the same shape, which is not the shape that any human mouth (a self-revealing feature) was ever known to be. But if he means that living people all over the world *are* alike, he is in error. They are not. If ever they come to love, or even to tolerate one another, it will not be on a basis of similarity.

No Oriental, for instance, would understand the *Thief of Bagdad*. He would recognize its setting, its fantasies, the marvellous adroitness with which a difficult tale is told; but not the pure American sentiment which is the keynote of the telling. The ennobling and purifying influence of woman, a commonplace with us, is unfamiliar to the East. It took the wise Scheherazade a thousand and one nights to tame her ferocious lord and save her neck from the bowstring; but one look at a beautiful princess turns the Thief of Bagdad, like the good American he is, into the paths of righteousness and knight-errantry.

So firmly established is this feminine tradition, this simple and amiable reverence for woman as the nursery governess of the Western world, that a sorrowing critic in Argentina has recently censured our moving pictures because they fail to support so noble and consolatory a creed, because they do not consistently present, "the splendid characteristics of American women." It is hard to portray the "pure drama of life," and keep in mind an especial line of guaranteed virtues. The millionaire's wife who, in the movies, neglects her little golden-haired boy (a nice, clean, gracefully affectionate little boy who wants her to hear him say his prayers) for the pursuit of fashionable dissipation may represent "the pure drama of life," but not "the splendid characteristics of American women." The millionaire's daughter (the moving-picture world is congested with millionaires) who abandons the sumptuous home of her unscrupulous father, and a perfectly new ermine coat, to live in a flat with the young husband of her choice, and do her own housework in a costume of studied simplicity and with a coiffure of studied elegance, may represent "the splendid characteristics of American women," but not "the pure drama of life." And neither can do much toward uniting the nations of the world in a bond of friendly and sympathetic understanding.

As a matter of fact, historical and informatory films are not the ones which travel most successfully from continent to continent. Charlie Chaplin is the delight of Arab children. Jackie Coogan is the delight of French, Belgian, English and Irish adults.[4] It was impressive to read in all our papers that the League of Nations knocked off work when Jackie visited Geneva, that he was honourably received by Sir Eric Drummond and photographed under the memorial tablet to President Wilson.[5] If there were anything in Mr. Hays's theory of moving pictures and a cemented world, surely the United States would have entered the League the next day.[6]

Mary Pickford is as overwhelmingly popular in Europe as at home. A fair proportion of the eight hundred thousand letters which she has received in the past five years, and which have failed to depress her spirits or destroy her belief in the sanity of the human race, have come from foreign enthusiasts. But only two years ago *The Birth of a Nation*, one of the most successful of American films, was suppressed in France; perhaps out of deference to the black troops, perhaps from fear lest it should suggest to some imitative madman the murder of the French president. It was richer in knowledge and understanding than ninety-nine out of a hundred moving-picture plays; but it did not present itself as a bond of sympathy between the American and the Gallic mind, nor as a welcome proof of "how alike we are."

It would be unwise and ungrateful to doubt the educational value of the film. Only an expert can speak with assurance on this point. Since I read in the veracious pages of the *Nineteenth Century* that "slow-motion" illustrations of lawn tennis have helped players to improve their stroke, I am prepared to respect any utility claim. But education is a side issue in the gigantic business of making moving pictures. It is not to educate the public that billions of dollars are invested in this industry. The million-dollar film, "with every dollar showing," is not an educational film. The fabulous salaries are not paid to men, women, and children who are imparting information. The uncounted throngs who go to moving-picture halls do not go to be educated. The uncounted halls make no pretense of educating them.

Whatever is meant by the phrase "people's university," it must not be taken to imply any avenue to knowledge. "Le monde où l'on s'amuse" is now everybody's world; and the task of amusing everybody, apart from the task of educating anybody, is the biggest business going.

There is nothing reprehensible about the daily search for amusement, if it is not called education. There is nothing repellent about the childishness of the average film, if it is not called an influence. The unconscious humor of the movie consists often in the contrast between the thing as we know it and the thing as we have it described to us. Sentimentalism is not a regenerative force, any more than debauched history is a source of universal enlightenment. If, by the rarest of all rare chances, a film is produced which is beautiful, interesting, and accurate, the producers, doubtful of our capacity to appreciate its worth, proceed to insult our intelligence by advertising it in terms which are reminiscent of Barnum in the forties.[7]

A case in point is *Grass*, the most remarkable performance ever achieved by the camera. It tells a tale of sober truth which is as adventurous as an epic. It shows us, with a wealth of beautiful detail, the migration of the Baktyari, a nomadic Persian tribe of unknown ancestry, in search of food for their herds; of the perils they brave, the hardships they endure, the traditions they follow. Nothing simpler or more serious could be conceived. Nothing bolder or more determined could be recorded.

Is it really necessary to headline this accurate narrative as "'written by an angry God, staged by fear, adapted by disaster'"? Is it well to describe the stars as "doubting," the sun as "laughing in cynical glee," the snow as "burning like the fires of Hell," the sunshine as "freezing the blood in the veins," the herdsmen themselves, who do as their fathers did before them, as "fighting a finish battle with a Mad

God, on a battlefield planned by the hand of cruel destiny, and commanded by the angel of disaster"?

This is a deplorable way to write. [...] The habit of ascribing to God our own point of view is not, as we might suppose, confined to simple savages. Highly educated people are sometimes content that He should supplement their intelligence. Mrs. Stowe ascribed to Him the authorship of Uncle Tom's Cabin.[8]

Her only excuse for the statement is that she meant it to be complimentary.

If we heard less about the making of films, we should probably be more contented when we see them. If we were not led to expect the impossible, we should never dream of asking it. [...]

❧

It is the habit of moving-picture magnates to lay the blame for most of their absurdities on the shoulders of the censors, who are the privileged meddlers and muddlers of the country. A big New York producer said last year that no Pennsylvanian had any business to find fault with the movies, because he or she had yet to see one as it emerged unspoiled from the studio. We have no doubt that the unconscious humor of the censor rivals, though it cannot surpass, the unconscious humor of the producer. [...] A valiant effort was made recently in Philadelphia to film a sermon, to illustrate with pictures the preaching of a highly successful evangelist who had been telling—or rather reminding—a forgetful world that the wages of sin is death. The Pennsylvania Board of Censors, disliking or distrusting sermons out of church,—and who can blame them?—cut these pictures so liberally that they had no story at all, and left a bored and mystified audience in doubt as to the lesson they were meant to convey.

When Tess of the D'Urbervilles was produced, a strange rumor went the rounds that Tess was hanged in one state and reprieved in another, according to the prejudices of the censors. The Pennsylvania Board has been known to strike out the word "anarchist" and substitute the word "fanatic" as illustrating its own standpoint; while in Ohio a parrot was prohibited from saying "Give him hell, Dickey!" lest, if scandalize the ears of maturity.

But after all what is [...] a hanging, or a sermon, or a swearword, more or less? Mrs. Gerould is doubtless right when she says that nobody fit to be a censor would ever consent to be a censor.[9] [...] Few reformers bring to their work anything but good intentions; and good intentions have gone a long way toward wrecking the happiness of men and the blessed simplicities of freedom.

At their worst, however, the blunders of the censors are incidental. They can be trusted to spoil a scene or two, but they cannot destroy realism in what is already unreal. The blunder of the producer is fundamental. It is contempt for the public's intelligence. [...] Ever and always the managers and producers of motion pictures act on the assumption that their public, if not actually feeble-minded is

> ...idiotically sane,
> With lucid intervals of lunacy.

Even the captions seem written for the blackboard of a child's school rather than for the "people's university." "The winter was long in passing, but it passed" (*Tides of Passion*), swings us back to the chapter on "Verbs and Their Tenses" in our first little grammar. "Like a knight of old, inspired by a shining star, Jimmy ventures forth to slay the Dragon" (*Bad Company*), has the familiar inaccuracy of a second reader. If, as *Current History* tells us, "the movies are peculiarly fitted to the age in which we live," what is the intellectual status of our day?

[*Atlantic Monthly* (Boston), 136, November 1925, pp. 601–07, excerpted.]

Means of Control

Keeping it Dark (1929)
Rebecca West

[... T]here can be no doubt that the censorship is a moral danger of the same nature as those which it attempts to suppress.

There is a point, and it is reached much more easily than is supposed, where interference with freedom of art and literature becomes an attack on the life of society. This freedom is as necessary to the mental survival of a society as a satisfactory sanitary system is to its physical survival. Turn, if you doubt it, to that interesting description of youth in modern Russia, Ognyov's *Diary of a Communist Undergraduate* which was issued some time ago by the active and intelligent Mr. Gollancz.[1] There you will see how a state has bled away its intellectual vitality by suppressing free expression of thought, although it was moved to do so by the very highest motives. It believes it has found the perfect way of living in Communism. It therefore turns into a privileged class all those who were willing to make public avowals that they also believed Communism to be the perfect way of living; and it forbids all others to express their points of view. The result is that the smallest failure on the part of Communism to tally with man's brightest vision of the millennium is the cause of endless agonising conflicts in all persons concerned. The Anti-Communists are filled with gall and venom as they note it because they cannot arise and show that they are right in their dissent. The Communists writhe as they note it because it hints at a flaw in what they have been assured is an inimitable and perfect dispensation, and their intellectual honesty must fight out the question of discussing it with the instinct of self-preservation which urges them not to surrender their privileges by doing any such things; and the political executive which finds the drive of its impetus checked by these perturbations naturally acts in an erratic way. That exactly the same effect follows from the use of a similar technique in Fascist Italy, where the protected orthodoxy is of a different nature, shows that we have nothing here that can be referred to Communism. Whenever the principle of censorship is let loose society becomes as uncomfortable and as unhealthy as we all were a couple of winters ago when our water-pipes and drain-pipes were choked, and we could keep clean neither our homes nor ourselves; and anyone who tries to block up the channels of free discussion that irrigate and drain society, is as dangerous a lunatic as any man who tries to destroy the water supply of a great city.

But it is held by many that though this holds good of political and religious matters, it does not apply to that which touches the sphere of sexual morality. Their theory is that the free discussion of sexual matters is likely to influence the public imagination, and lead to an abandonment of the restraints that the community has agreed are necessary. But this theory does not seem to hold water when we test it in reference to the form of sexual behaviour of which it is quite certain the mass of the community disapproves; for I imagine that few will dispute that the mass of the community do disapprove of homosexuality. I also imagine that few will dispute that during the past thirty years homosexuality has enormously increased. It is impossible for the unbiased observer not to connect this increase with certain events proceeding from the prosecution of Oscar Wilde in 1895, which was conducted by the community with a regrettable lack of the calm that the orthodox can surely permit themselves. Instead of saying quietly, "This middle-aged gentleman cannot be allowed to go about thrusting his peculiarities on minors in this way, so he must be shut up, and we must ask our psychologists to try and give us some idea why people who get shut up in our prisons and asylums for suborning the young behave as they do," it pretended that he was a monster who had invented a new vice (which was far from being the case) and it was the duty of all right-thinking human beings to bare their teeth and howl like a dog at the thought of him. It is hardly necessary to say that all discussion of homosexuality in newspapers, journals, magazines, novels, plays, and scientific publications was discouraged. This ban was relentless: it hit at game as big as Mr. Havelock Ellis and Mr. D.H. Lawrence, and it did not fail throughout the years, as is shown by the recent prosecution of The Well of Loneliness.[2] But it was more than countered by other forces. The more spirited of the younger generation, always critical of its elders, regarded their vehemence with disgust; and sensitive or not, its curiosity was stimulated by their refusal to allow Oscar Wilde to be mentioned, or his offence to be named or analysed, and its chivalry was aroused by the plight of a man of great gifts who in one day was thrown from the heights to the depths. In fact a movement was inaugurated, and given an excellent send-off with a first-rate martyr. In no time homosexuality was given a status as a form of revolt against the Philistine decrepit and thereafter was bound to drum up plenty of recruits.

Now, not only has censorship in this instance failed to check a form of sexual behaviour considered objectionable by the mass of the community; it has also suppressed the only forces that did seem likely to check it. For among the material regarding homosexuality which it prevented from coming to light was a considerable mass of material which, had it been generally accessible, might have diminished the epicene pretensions of the new movement. Quite a number of psychologists have been working industriously on the problem of late years, and have come to the conclusion that the homosexual is not a fixed type, but simply an individual who has for some reason failed to develop past a stage common to the immaturity of everybody, when the companionship of persons of the same sex is found preferable. He is doing nothing unthinkably abominable, and nothing heroic. He is simply seeking to satisfy an adult appetite where it is natural to exercise only less specifically mature interests. A view not less wounding to homosexual pride has been expressed by a certain number of novels in other languages in which candid artists have represented the homosexual as the tragically or comically odd fish whom nobody would want to be. Thus it appears that the case against homosexuality has been suppressed by the censorship, and if it be claimed that at least the case for it was also silenced, since The Well of Loneliness was homosexual propaganda, this must be regretfully denied. That novel's expectation of life would in normal circumstances have been something well under six months, and in that brief span would not have focused much attention. But its suppression (as well as providing the homosexual movement with a handsome, distinguished, and estimable martyr) gave the lower sections of the Press power to disseminate the subject matter of The Well of Loneliness to the greater extent which was represented by the difference between fifteen shillings (which was the price of the novel) and two pence (which is the price of a Sunday paper).[3] Thanks to Lord Brentford there are now but few children old enough to read who are not in full possession of the essential facts regarding female homosexuality; and it is probable that the event which will recall the delicious fact of his being to a future generation will be the unveiling of a statue to him by an exceedingly odd-looking group of people.[4] It throws light upon an essential weakness of any system of censorship that the newspaper could not have used The Well of Loneliness as an excuse to broadcast particulars about homosexuality had it not been (from the censorship point of view) deserving of suppression. If the book had been against homosexuality the newspapers could obviously not have attacked it in the wholehearted way that alone is useful to them; and its message would have remained in its proper place between the boards of a book, unlikely to fall into the hands of persons too young or too uninstructed to cope with it. It was because the book was for homosexuality that the newspapers were able to cram crudely written information about homosexuality down the throats of their unselected public, on the pretext of serving morality. In other words, the censorship can inflict the gravest damage on the community when it is being at its most efficient. This fact is disquieting.

When we consider the recent activities of the censorship we cannot but feel that Mr. Causton and Mr. Young are dealing with an important issue. Society should aim above all at the establishment of a state of decorum, in which nothing occurs that might violently excite the minds of its members on these matters which have least been brought under the control of reason. We do not want sudden presentations of the more acute problems of sexual behaviour that rouse primitive fantasies in the common mind, and lead to regressions from conduct appropriate to reality. When we think of the girls who respond to any newspaper exploitation of the white slave motif by telling stories of kidnapping and assault, we can perceive the kind of damage to sanity that is done. From this point of view censorship is a constant danger, since it is always likely to raise a scandal; and since each time it raises a scandal the community in alarm silences all discussion of these matters even of the most serious kind, it postpones still further the time when they will be brought under the control of reason. There is a case for the relegation of the censorship to a decent obsolescence which cannot justly be answered by the prophecy that if that were done, the world would be flooded with indecent art and literature. But, curiously enough, the world seems already to be as much in that condition as it can be. There are several streets in London I can think of which are lined with bookshops offering pictures and literature that no reasonable person could fail to regard as dealing with the human body and its functions in an ugly and offensive way. But as this is in many ways a free country, I have never been forced to enter one of these shops and acquaint myself with their contents. Nor does there appear to exist in me any compulsive appetite which forces me to do so of my own accord; and since these shops are neither large nor prosperous, and since in the course of a fairly wide experience I have never come across a fortune that could be attributed to this trade, I must conclude that the mass of the population is in the same case. We are not in the presence of a human weakness so widespread and so devastating—such as the desire of alcohol and drugs—that the good sense of the community is forced to recognise its practical effects and organise for their elimination; for there is no reason why these shops should not be as widely spread and as freely patronised as public houses, except the relative failure of their good to make a popular appeal. We can therefore safely say that, though the law must obviously have power to deal with such situations as the thrusting on children of books and pictures presenting sex in a way likely to shock and hurt them, it can well afford to abandon a weapon such as the censorship, which increases instead of allaying public excitement concerning these matters. Particularly is it to be recommended that the law should do this in view of the peculiar, almost magical, inefficiency of this weapon. I have said that since this is a free country I have never been forced to go into a shop and buy pornographic literature. I have, however, been brought into involuntary contact with the indecent on frequent occasions when the human need for entertainment has driven me to the cinema. Only the other day I was the embarrassed spectator of a young woman writhing across a bed in an erotic dream, which was not only exhibited to my eye but was explained to my ear in case I had missed anything.[5] I have also shuddered while modern science triumphantly recorded a drunken chorus girl's hiccough, but found it far from being the most unpleasant incident in the tale of her deliberations as to whether or not she should become a prostitute. I found these things cheap and ugly and depressing, and I am sure that most of the other people in the audience felt the same. I imagine that to the young they must have been troubling and wounding. Yet the art of the cinema is conceived and nourished within the bosom of the censorship. These films had been made at Hollywood under the censorship administered by Mr. Will Hays, and had passed the British Board of Film Censors;

and there can be no doubt that they had complied with the letter of regulations as strict as could be made without obvious oppression.[6] This perplexing fact alone should make us grateful to Mr. Causton and Mr. Young for collecting information about the censorship.

["Preface" to Bernard Causton and G. Gordon Young, *Keeping it Dark, or the Censor's Handbook* (London: Mandrake Press, 1929), pp. 7–13, excerpted.]

The Nemesis of the Screen (1922)
Katherine Fullerton Gerould

[...] It can be contended that the output of the studios is curiously fluid, and hard to put one's finger on; that by the time enlightened public opinion has caused an objectionable film to be withdrawn in one town the same film has already corrupted the audiences of a thousand less enlightened centers; that you may perhaps count on the ladies of Crippsville, Alabama, to keep Crippsville, Alabama, safe, but that there are Crippsvilles in forty-seven other states, and that perhaps the ladies of those other towns cannot be counted on. Nothing, according to that argument, will serve but official censorship.

The answer to that argument is not an impassioned defense of the morals of all Crippsvilles; the answer is the mere statement that never in history has censorship worked properly. Censorship, as practiced in modern societies, serves neither morals nor art. Censors are never—even when they are not appointed for obscure political reasons—fit for their job. No one who is fit for the job is ever willing to be a censor. The things that get by are as absurd as the things that are held up, and vice versa. Censorship, properly managed, demands an immense store of knowledge, long experience of literature and art, extremely wise judgement, entire lack of prejudice, and a profound acquaintance with human psychology. In all these gifts professional reformers are rather notoriously lacking. This is not the place to enter into a discussion of the reforming instinct; but it might be said in passing that, more than most contemporary types, the reformers cry out to be psychoanalyzed.

Must we then, doing without censors, allow our children to be corrupted? is the next query to be met, I suppose. The real answer to that is, of course, that movies are no more the place for children than the theater is the place for them, or than the files of the average newspaper are—if you will pardon the locution—the place for them. If the people who talk censorship would, instead, talk ordinances to the effect that no child should be allowed to enter a moving-picture theater unless accompanied by a responsible adult, or even ordinances to the effect that children should be barred from all movies not especially constructed for them, there would be more point in it. But I doubt that would be to the taste of the producers, any more than to the taste of the censorship addicts. It would offend the former because they want the whole family at the movies; and it would offend the latter because they are not so much out to protect the children as desirous of seeing their own opinions prevail over the parents' opinion—indeed over everyone's opinion.

Being a parent myself I incline to believe that even a stupid parent usually has a keener sense of what will corrupt his child than any board of censors likely to be constituted in any state. Parents are careless; but if they were really shocked I fancy you could count on them, were they themselves present, to take their children out. It may be, again, that I have too much faith in producers; but I certainly do not believe that the more respectable ones are going to antagonize Crippsville if they can help it. The advocates of censorship have, obviously, a low opinion of our citizenry, and think that the average man or woman cannot be trusted to turn down an immoral show.

Still, you are not going to silence easily any cry that is based, whether rightly or wrongly, on the welfare of the children. The movie magnates wanted the whole family to go to the movies; they have got the whole family there, and they are paying for their success. Someone was sure to kick up a row because, as we have said, with the whole family there the movies became everybody's business, and a matter of public interest. If the reformers have never got very far with the legitimate drama in America, that is because the legitimate drama catered to a much smaller group. It was not everybody's business; as a problem it did not exist in Crippsville. You must make no mistake, you captains of the motion-picture industry: What you are up against is the state of mind that never worried half so much about the cocktail in the club as about the workingman's glass of beer—simply because there were fewer cocktails and more glasses of beer. The clubmen could perhaps have been left to the judgement of God: but the corner saloon must go. The reformer yearns, by definition, you might say, for the vast arena and the large effects. Like some of you, he prefers to stage a superproduction. You invited all this when you invaded all the Crippsvilles of the land. It is only with immoderate good fortune that Nemesis concerns herself.

Nor is the censorship of films the only thing success has let the producers in for. Mr. David W. Griffith a few days ago made a pathetic appeal at a public luncheon for tolerance toward men and women engaged in picture making. "The power of the sincere, fanatical minority is tremendous," said Mr. Griffith; and he cited witch hunting as a parallel to the present persecution. Mr. Griffith is doubtless quite right; yet how can one keep from smiling? "Vous l'avez voulu, George Dandin." In other words, Mr. Griffith, it is your own fault. You and your kind have created not only a popularity for your product but a publicity for your personnel that are almost incredible. And this is the price you pay.

What official ever barred a play because an actor or actress was vaguely suspected of being, in private, immoral? Yet America at large may fairly be said to be moral, if not straight-laced; and it has never had any too good an opinion of the profession. We will not name names; or, rather, we will name only one. That supreme actress, Sarah Bernhardt, has never made a secret, I believe, of her theories concerning the relations between men and women, or of her fidelity to her theories.[1] Did America ever turn Sarah Bernhardt down? On the contrary, when she acted in places that did not boast huge auditoriums she acted in a circus tent—to accommodate the crowds. Yet within a fortnight, on the basis of suspicion only, certain towns—I refer you to the daily papers—have banned films showing any actress who is known ever to have written a letter to the late Mr. Taylor.[2]

I have seen it stated somewhere that good behaviour is often, nowadays, put into a motion-picture actor's contract. Funny? It is to scream. Unfair? Certainly, but logical all the same. First, they achieved popularity for the film; then they created publicity for the star. You cannot make it your boast that you cater to the whole family, that you bring joy to every home, without letting yourself in for the corollaries of your success. When a motion-picture star does anything sensationally wrong the act reverberates to a million firesides. If it were suddenly proved overnight, and headlined in the morning papers, that Ivory Soap was 99 per cent impure, the shock would not be more widely felt than when a film favourite goes astray.

Those of us to whom the movies are a phenomenon rather than a habit do not easily realize with what passionate personal interest the public takes the screen star. It seems odd, at first, that anyone whom you have never seen in the flesh, and probably never will see, can be so humanly real to you as all that. Such, however, I am constrained to believe is the case. These shadows are not shadows to the men and women who go three times a week to the movies. No actor or actress of the legitimate stage is half so intimately known, as a human being, to his or her public, as the favorites of the screen to theirs. Whether it be the producers themselves or their allies, someone has seen to it that every sort of intimate gossip concerning these heroes and heroines shall be furnished to Crippsville. The little girl who has a crush on an actor of the legitimate stage may wait for years before she reads an interview with him, a description of his home, an account of his personal tastes. But she can find out anything she wants to know about a movie actor in a very short space of time. By means of the publicity created for him he becomes more real to her even than the actor she has seen with her own eyes, in three dimensions, treading the stage.

If you doubt me, take a little excursion among the various magazines that are devoted to motion pictures and motion picture folk. They will dispose of any notion you may have had that the moviegoing public considers its heroes and heroines as mere creatures of photography. Most illuminating of all features is, perhaps, the department of answers to questions, which most of these magazines maintain. One sympathizes with the oracular editor who cried out to a correspondent: "What kind of talcum powder does Rudolph Valentino use? Have a heart!" They evidently want—these people who beset the editors—every conceivable kind of information. They want not only the life history of the star in every detail: they want to know his or her height, weight and complexion; they want a list of all the pictures he or she has appeared in; they want—always—the star's address; and sometimes they want advice as to whether or not they had better write him or her a letter. They want also to give their opinions; to say that A would have made love better than B, or that C falls off a cliff more gracefully than D. They are insatiably interested in these people whom they see upon the screen. The rest of the magazine ministers to the same intense personal interest; article upon article, profusely illustrated, not only implies but takes for granted the exceeding importance to the public of these personalities. One gathers that a popular screen star receives daily at least a hundred fan letters, and weekly a hundred requests for his or her photograph.

No one whom you write letters to, even though the letters are destined to be unanswered, is unreal to you; and writing an address on an envelope creates a human relation of sorts.

So it is that when C, who falls off cliffs with peculiar grace, shoots up an obscure enemy, or E, who weeps more beautifully than anyone else, is dragged into some other woman's divorce suit, Crippsville feels a personal shock or expresses a personal loyalty. Unless it had happened in Crippsville itself it could not have come nearer home. Hollywood, you see, is not simply a suburb of Los Angeles; it is a suburb of every town in the country. [...]

[*Saturday Evening Post* (Philadelphia), 8 April 1922, pp. 12, 157, excerpted.]

In Defense of Hollywood (1922)[1]

Anita Loos

So much has been said on the subject of Hollywood morality that one might think the fate of nations hung on the vital matter of Californian purity.

As a matter of fact, the movies, and even the world at large will go on much the same, although as many as a dozen of the 250,000 people engaged in making motion pictures may get themselves into scrapes during the next year.

However, the popular attitude toward the subject seems to resolve itself into the following logic: Where there is no scandal, there is no immorality, but where there is a scandal, there is immorality; consequently the immorality of a community is in direct proportion to the amount of publicity given to the sinners of that community; but the citizens of Hollywood, instead of suppressing their scandals, denounce the culprits from the housetops in the most foolish and public-spirited manner, and even evoke the law—ergo, the citizens of Hollywood are guilty, one and all, of fostering immorality, and the town should be burned in accordance with Biblical precedents.

This all seems very clear to me and I should only like to add the suggestion that the citizens of all those other saintly towns which are 100 percent moral because they are too small to support a news syndicate correspondent, be canonized at the earliest possible moment.

[Contribution to "In Defense of Hollywood: Prominent Figures in the Film World Rise to Refute the Exaggerated Reports of Motion Picture Morals," *Filmplay* (New York) 1:2, May 1922, p. 21.]

Women and the Cinema (1934)
Frances White Diehl

THE WOMEN OF THE WORLD UNITE IN CINEMATOGRAPHIC INTEREST

Women of all nations possess the legitimate right to be concerned with influences which affect their homes and the character building of the family. It is natural therefore that women throughout the world are making it their business to throw the spotlight on the Cinema and seek to know the true power and effect of this universal form of recreation and entertainment.

That the motion picture has an influence on our social thinking and social problems is obvious. We have had many expressions of opinion regarding the Cinema and its relation to social problems, but we have not had enough established scientific facts to substantiate them.

There is a variance of scientific opinion as to degree and power of the screen's influence, but we, as women, have felt a decided influence in our family lives, brought about by attendance at motion picture houses; therefore, we are determined to analyze and regulate the effect. It is our right to make our influence felt on all those phases of life which concern the happiness of our homes and our children. Truly, as women, this is our great and most immediate social problem. [...]

There are tendencies and dangers in motion pictures today that we must not minimize, and valuable experiments for their betterment are being carried on by women in various countries of the world. Responsible persons are exerting every effort to bring to the consciousness of those who make and exhibit motion pictures how great an opportunity is theirs for advancing knowledge and raising the ideals common in the hearts of nations the world over. We believe, as we note certain changes that have taken place in recent years, that the women of America with their constructive programme, have exerted a powerful influence to improve films. It is not the occasional critical and prejudiced voice that brings results, but rather the combined efforts of women in thousands of communities throughout the world whose influence cannot fail to be recognized.

The motion picture has found its way to the ends of the earth. Its dramatic appeal is universal.

In our complex and intense modern life, entertainment has become indispensable, and we must join forces to insure the portrayal of proper social and cultural values on the screen.

SAFE-GUARDING THE YOUNGER GENERATION

Naturally the interest of women in the Motion Picture Problem centers about its reaction upon children.

The commercial picture has only occasionally been adaptable to children, therefore it seems logical psychology that children should be given special shows and should be discouraged from a general attendance. This has promoted many local movements for Children's Matinées and Family Night Programmes.

Careful parents are thoughtful as to the influences on coming generations and exercise supervision over their children's recreation and cinema experience, but unfortunately we have a large percentage of neglectful parents—mothers who too frequently utilize the neighbourhood theatre as a day nursery and, regardless of the attraction, permit their offspring to spend hours in cinema houses. Therefore we must, as a civic duty, assist in protecting the unprotected child. This subject has been given much thought and study by most countries and by all conscientious individuals honestly concerned with the welfare of young people. The answer seems to lie in the necessity of demanding general improvement in film production.

It is a sad fact that the public does not always respond to the best in pictures any more than it responds to the best in literature, paintings or stage plays, so we must seek encouragement for worthwhile productions, which has been the fundamental reason for the organization throughout the country of hundreds of Community Better Film Councils and similar groups, to teach discrimination in motion picture attendance and to preview and bulletin the best pictures suitable for family patronage.[1]

There have been endless surveys and attempted analyses of the effect of the Cinema "on children". After carefully studying dozens of such so-called surveys and reading innumerable statements on the subject, we are of the opinion that no one knows the exact extent of the influence of the Cinema or its results. Some authorities insist that the so-called "War" pictures are an influence for peace and give children an aversion to war, other psychologists are positive they create interest and inclination toward the excitement and thrill of war.

Dr. Phyllis Blanchard, of the Philadelphia Child Guidance Clinic,[2] has gone on record with the following opinion:

> Numerous studies made by scientists have failed to establish any appreciable contribution to delinquency from motion pictures, but we do find the motion picture to be helpful in many ways.
>
> The overwhelming cause of child delinquency is maladjustments or neglect of training in home life. The plain truth is that the child's behaviour patterns are formed before the age of picture attendance, and that at least 85 per cent of child delinquency is traceable to home influence which took shape in a generation before the motion picture's popularity afforded a convenient alibi for those who do not, or cannot, provide helpful stimuli for their children.

Others believe the reverse is true. Nevertheless, we must "play safe" with the future generations and every school, association and organization should unite in a definite and concentrated effort to demand that motion picture producers, produce "up to the classes instead of down to the masses" and insist that the industry realize and recognize its obligation as an influence for good as well as for recreation and amusement.

The problem of children and their attendance at pictures is a problem which every father and mother might settle but which, unfortunately, they do not settle. Those children must be protected and guided toward the proper type of motion pictures. They are going to see pictures of course. Every child considers that his or her right. Our duty is to see that what the child sees is in keeping with its needs for wholesome amusement and fun, and at the same time that it is clean and suitable. We cannot shift all the responsibility on to the producers or the exhibitors; we can only share responsibility with them. [...]

CINEMA INFLUENCE ON WORLD PEACE AND UNDERSTANDING

It has been said: "The cinema is a real League of Nations, binding the World together."[3] The Newsreels teach all men and all women that other nations are interestingly different, but basically and profoundly kin. We know it to be a world-wide vehicle of ideas and information. The great goodwill of the screen is its constant introduction of the peoples of the world to one another. School children feel that they have met Mussolini and heard him speak; they feel acquainted with all the great world figures in current events, with the type of building, the natural geography, the customs of the people in all the important nations of the world, even with the games the children play.

The Cinema has proven a potent purveyor between nations of intellectual ideas and national ideals. Through war-realism films, inter-racial friendship and the sympathetic portrayal of peoples, we have been taken out of our provincialism into the area of world affairs. We learn to know the great leaders of thought and government throughout the world and become intimate with the world and its problems.

There is no doubt that motion pictures have been a definite force contributing to world peace. However, we feel the recognition of the power of this contribution has been slow in coming from leaders in the peace movement. Impressions of the stupidity, the futility and waste of war have reached more people through the screen than would have been possible from any other source. It has brought out the sensitiveness of nationalism in the world today. No producer would dare to caricature or misinterpret the nationals of another country or show them only in their worst light. So, in general, pictures place their emphasis on the best to be found among the people of other races.

Travel films have helped wonderfully in internationalization, for vast numbers of people travel the world over today and learn the habits and customs of those of other countries. The great value of many of these so-called travel films lies in the fact that not only are the physical aspects of a country shown, but also the thoughts and habits of the national mind are made clear. [...]

INDICATIONS OF ADVANCEMENT TOWARD
HIGHER PRODUCTION STANDARDS

[...] There is no question but that pictures are improving, but they will continue to improve only in proportion to the public demand and support of better pictures. [...]

The results of the current depression have been reflected in recent motion pictures—the re-establishment of family life on a saner basis. A simpler and less luxurious home life is now being depicted. Another hopeful sign in the development of the motion picture is the recent tendency to deal honestly and realistically with important subject matter.

It is true, however, that people want to see the bright side of life on the screen—the way the other half live—not the drab pictures of life they live themselves. They find on the screen liberation from daily cares and personal problems.

With additional leisure, due to shorter working hours, attendance in picture houses is increasing, and it becomes more than ever important that socially-minded individuals and organizations unite in their programmes for collecting and distributing cinema information to serve as a reliable guide to the family in selecting its motion picture entertainment.

It is particularly significant, in view of the growing demand for more pictures suitable for children, that this year's production in American contained 72 pictures endorsed by the previewing groups as suitable for juveniles, and that 71% of the total year's product for 1933 was passed on as proper cinema entertainment for general distribution.

We have shown that the best way to insure high class motion picture productions is to create a taste for them, and we are glad to report that our hope to do so is being realised, while future production lies in the fact that hundreds of thousands of men and women throughout the country are working earnestly to make America's most democratic amusement conform to the highest standards of taste.

[International Review of Educational Cinematography (Rome)
6, June 1934, pp. 400–05, excerpted.]

Solving the Moving Picture Problem (1924)
Mrs Charles E. Merriam

SUGGESTIONS FOR LOCAL PARENT-TEACHER ASSOCIATIONS AND MOTHERS

Keep your babies away from the motion-picture theater. Do not give them the movie habit. Habits are hard to break. A community nursery is vital today.

If you do not have a law to prohibit the showing of improper films for your boys and girls to see, then work for such a law, or else a law that will prohibit your boys and girls from attendance at any shows unless accompanied by an adult.

Organize worth-while recreation for your children from five to ten years of age. Keep them wholesomely busy after school hours, playing games, reading good books, skating, athletics, and last, but not least, organize classes in dramatics. They love to act. Give them this chance. It will do more than anything else to keep them away from the movies.

Patronize only the indorsed films when you do go to the movies.[1] Always go with your children if you possibly can. Do not think of the theater as a safe place to send them alone. It is not. It may take you a year to undo all they learn in one afternoon, so you are really making work for yourself instead of getting a few hours' rest as you suppose.

When a bad film comes to town, give a party for your children and their friends. And don't forget the little boy just around the corner, who needs your help and sympathy most. Help him to avoid the vicious show. Help him to make good. There are too many ready to help him to go wrong, too few to give him the helping hand.

Remember that patronage makes production. Whenever you attend a show, the exhibitor and producer of that show consider your presence an approval of that show. Whenever you stay at home, they consider it a disapproval.

[The Journal of the National Education Association (Washington, DC), 13:5, May 1924, p. 167, excerpted.]

Better Movies—But How? (1930)
Catheryne Cooke Gilman

This is first of two articles in answer to the question, Shall women's organizations cooperate with the motion-picture industry in an effort to get better pictures? This answer this time is by Mrs. Robbins Gilman, president of the Federal Motion Picture Council in America. She says No. Next month Mrs. Thomas G. Winter, now associated with the motion-picture industry as women's representative, will say Yes.

This is not a discussion of motion pictures, but of methods proposed to improve them. It is no longer necessary to argue whether pictures are satisfactory or not. The facts are before the world. The industry claims that it has twenty million people viewing films a day. These people cannot go to motion pictures for one month without realizing that the worst accusations that have been made are self-evident in the moving picture theatre. There is no need to prove—even if this writer were willing to present the sordid details—that, even with due regard for good pictures, the screen is permeated by exaggerated sex appeal, criminal practices, ridicule of marriage, disregard for law enforcement, desecration of religious ideals and questionable ethics. [...]

It would seem that the motion picture people themselves do not disagree with their critics. They have organized and are spending millions of dollars in plans to secure the cooperation of women's and religious organizations, according to their own statements, to secure better pictures. The spokesman for the industry, Mr. Will Hays, recently claimed that "more than thirty million members of individual church and civic organizations are acting as advisers to the industry in an effort to keep objectionable material off the screen."[1] Yet the evidence in almost any motion picture theatre would lead to the conclusion that the advice of these eminent millions is really bad or they are engaged in inconsequential cooperation.

A short sketch of the twenty years of continuous cooperation of social, civic and religious organizations with the motion picture industry may serve to point the answer to the Journal's question.

The demand for better motion pictures came to the attention of the public in this country in 1908 when the Mayor of New York City closed all motion picture houses because the pictures were unclean and immoral. In 1909 a group of organizations offered to cooperate with the agents of the industry by advising them concerning the type of pictures desirable for public welfare. "Cooperation" has been the watchword since that time.

The groups offering their services in 1909 were given opportunity to censor pictures, but had no power to enforce their recommendations. They were provided by the industry with secretarial help and other expenses. They were called the National Board of Censorship. In a comparatively short time the members of the Board realized that their obligation to the industry reduced their power to *endorsement* of pictures.

The result was unsatisfactory to the public and a new demonstration of unrest then became evident. Some of the members of the Board of Censorship withdrew and the industry proposed cooperation and a reorganization of the Board. A new slogan was adopted, "Selection not censorship," and the old Board became the National Board of Review. Instead of the former financial arrangement, the Board was now paid a fixed sum per reel for reviewing pictures.

In the course of a few more years the public again resented the fact that improvement in motion pictures was deplorably slow. The industry was charged with bad faith as well as with producing, distributing and exhibiting bad films.

Legislatures were interested, and in one year censorship legislation was introduced in thirty-two states and approximately one hundred and seventy-five cities. The situation was serious for the industry. One of the largest producing companies made a clever counterproposal to the effect that "the industry clean up from within." A carefully worded pledge was made public to this effect. It claimed that the producers would produce pictures according to specific standards and "agree to eliminate all objectionable material from pictures." This pledge is known in the literature of the motion-picture industry as the famous "Thirteen Points," announced in 1921.[2] Through these points the industry disapproved pictures emphasizing sex appeal in suggestive forms; showing commercialized vice; making illicit love affairs attractive; showing people scantily clad; needlessly prolonging demonstrations of passionate love; dealing primarily with vice and crime; showing drunkenness, gambling, use of narcotics, etc. in attractive guise; showing vulgarity, improper gestures and attitudes, etc.

The public, however, was still restless, and many organizations increased their activities to promote state censorship. The producers themselves demanded an organization for their combined protection. In 1922 the Motion Picture Producers and Distributors of America, Incorporated, came into existence, with a leader, Mr. Will Hays, selected from a prominent government position. The new organization reaffirmed and signed the famous "Thirteen Points." They became the pact between the producers and the public.

The new agency took steps immediately to enlist the cooperation of sixty-four national groups, representing social, religious and civic organizations. The group was known as the Public Relations Committee. The announcement was received with high hopes and the opposition again relaxed. The Public Relations Committee was to furnish "a previewing," "a reviewing," "an advisory," "an interpreting" and "a disseminating service for the industry."

The members of the cooperating groups on the Public Relations Committee expected results. They sincerely desired better pictures. They grew impatient with the dilatory tactics of the industry, and with the inaction of their own national boards. Group after group—including the National Congress of Parent-Teachers' Associations and the General Federation of Women's Clubs, withdrew in disappointment, disapproval or disgust until the Motion Picture Producers and Distributors of America, Incorporated, hastily announced that the Public Relations Committee, having accomplished its task, would be disbanded.

Two other groups then reorganized their programs. One was formed by those interested in legal censorship. It was independently supported and worked for state and Federal censorship.[3] The other was promoted by the cooperating volunteer censorship groups of the Better Films Committee of the National Board of Review, which was still supported by previewing the industry's films.[4]

This volunteer censorship movement shifted the opposition from the Motion Picture Producers and Distributors to the National Board of Review. The ruse was successful for the time. Women's organizations were flooded with propaganda for better films by the Better Films Committee. In every town where a woman's club could be located, and even in rural districts where names of women could be obtained, appeals by letter or in person were made to rally support for this new cooperative program. Women were feeling keenly the need for better pictures for their children and young people. The offer seemed plausible, the plan simple and the opportunity great.

The result was intoxicating to the industry, but a bromide to women's organizations. The plan promised a false security. The new slogan was "Endorse the best and ignore the rest." This jingle captivated the imagination and stilled the opposition. It was called "constructive cooperation." More men and women from prominent positions were employed by the Motion Picture Producers and Distributors to take charge of the business of cooperation. Some of the employees were politicians, some were attorneys, some educators and others were religious leaders—all were citizens of ability and influence.

But all the time objectionable films continued to flood the country.

The industry took occasion, because of the renewed confidence, to establish a Public Relations Department with an "Open Door Policy." The organization was shifted from New York to Hollywood. Instead of representatives of national boards it was composed of a paid staff and a group of cooperating endorsers. The endorsers were unofficial representatives of women's organizations appointed by the industry. The "Open Door Policy"—in Mr. Hays's words—was an invitation to the public "to come to us frankly and unhesitatingly with your constructive and helpful suggestions and advice." It was a flattering appeal and effective. The work of the Better Films Committee, amply financed and ably directed, flourished for a time, but the result was inevitably the same. The new slogan for this period was "The Formula—for preventing the filming of unwholesome books." Yet producers continued to produce films of books banned by public libraries.

It would seem that no new personality employed by the industry nor new plan of cooperation could revive confidence in cooperation for securing better motion pictures. However, that is being tried. New propaganda with the old "formula" has appeared and the question is whether the industry's latest attempt to betray the women of this country, by installing a woman as official representative of organized women at Hollywood, will succeed.[5] It has aroused the old inquiry as to whether women's organizations should cooperate with the motion-picture industry in the hope of securing better pictures. [...]

As the history shows, the industry has consistently led the cooperating groups to try volunteer censorship. At the same time it has loudly vilified as un-American, unconstitutional and prudish reform all others efforts to regulate and supervise it as a public utility. Apparently it has terrified the press and the radical magazines by pronouncing as censorship all efforts to bring the motion-picture industry under the same or similar statutory regulations that govern the trade practices and industrial promotion of railroads, radios, Federal banks and food packers and producers.

The groups cooperating have tried volunteer censorship under the guise of many names, but *always under the leadership of paid agents of the industry* [...]

The fundamental cause of the increase of undesirable pictures after years of slavish cooperation is found in the fact that cooperation proposed by the industry applies its remedy at the point of exhibition and not at the point of production and distribution where the trouble exists. The causes are in the selection and treatment of subject material during the process of production and in the methods used by the industry for distributing or marketing the product. This latter cause seems little understood by the cooperating groups.

Distribution is through a system of block booking and blind booking under the so-called uniform contract with an unjust arbitration clause. Under block booking distributors must contract to take blocks of pictures selected by the producers and must then load them off on the exhibitor in blocks that may contain seventeen or seventy-seven pictures in a lot. The exhibitor must sign the uniform contract, which provides no appeal through the court, to get on the film circuit. Blind booking means what the name implies—the booking of films before they are produced and their distribution without opportunity to see them. These and other trade practices make it impossible for the exhibitors to be amenable to the demands of the public with or without cooperation.

It is evident, again, that women's organizations are not, and in the nature of things can not be held, responsible for the conduct of the industry. The producers are solely responsible.

The basic objectives of women's organizations and the motion-picture industry are essentially dissimilar. Producers work exclusively, according to their own statement, for profits, the box office receipts and the value of their stock upon the exchange. Improved mechanics and techniques may yield immediate profits while welfare measures may not respond so noticeably. Profits may or may not be legitimate in any business, and being legitimate they may or may not be in accord with the general welfare of citizens. Women's organizations are notably humanitarian. They measure their successes by the welfare of citizens in their own and neighboring countries. They emphasize the needs of youth and specialize in securing its protection. There is no doubt as to the legitimacy of the purposes of women's organizations. Their methods and judgements may at times be questioned, but their objectives are pre-eminently sound. Women's organizations have sacrificed profits for welfare. The motion-picture industry has sacrificed welfare for profits, hence the difficulty of cooperation for the improvement of pictures. [...]

To the independents, meaning those who declare for dissociation from the industry, as opposed to those who cling to cooperation to secure better pictures, the solution lies in what is called the Hoover Doctrine; namely, a "government by commission." The Federal Trade, the Pure Foods, the Radio, Interstate Commerce and other commissions, established by the Government, provide adequate precedents for a Federal Motion-Picture Commission.

It seems clear that pictures are unwholesome and unsatisfactory for interstate or foreign commerce. Cooperation with the industry has been unsuccessful after a conscientious and continuous trial of twenty years. A public utility in its activities is beyond the range of unofficial and volunteer action of any group, however well intentioned. Just as the peace movements needed the Kellogg–Briand peace pact and other enabling acts, just as prohibition demanded an amendment to the Constitution and supporting legislation, so the motion-picture problem requires national legislation, probably international treaties and articles of interpretation and enforcement.[6]

[*The Woman's Journal* (New York) 15:2, February 1930, pp. 10–12, 34–35 excerpted.]

And So to Hollywood (1930)
Alice Ames Winter

Shall women's organizations cooperate with the motion-picture industry to get better pictures? Last month Mrs. Robbins Gilman said No. In this article Mrs. Winter, Associate Director of Public Relations of the Association of Motion Picture Producers, says Yes.

[...] There are plenty of things wrong with movies. In fact one grows a little pessimistic about the intellectual diversions of our country when one surveys the lines of magazines that display themselves luridly along every street, or glances into the daily papers, or listens to the radio, or purchases the latest novel or buys a ticket to the most talked-of play. But for some reason the bad things and the inane things hit us harder when they appear in the moving picture, perhaps because we recognize the fact that no other single form of expression has so wide a circulation as this; that it probably does more to determine ordinary folks' standards of conduct, of fashion, of art and architecture than any other single influence; that it catches men and women and children in those moods when they are most susceptible, that is, when they are seeking lightheartedness.

Small wonder then that blots on its escutcheon afflict us even more than those in other forms of literary or artistic expression. It is the nearest to the democratic heart of all of them, the product of many minds, not of a single creator, the plaything of the whole race today.

Whose fault is it that there are mistakes—sometimes sad and bad mistakes? And what are we going to do about it? To the first question, the reply seems to be that part of the fault lies with the industry and part with the public. To the second question we may give one of two replies; the answer of autocracy is the answer of democracy, censorship or cooperation. [...]

I suppose if I thought censorship would really give us a clean bill of health so far as the movies are concerned, I might be tempted by it although the principle of it does not seem to me in accordance with our national or our racial methods. With all our faults in actual performance, we still believe in the rule of law. Censorship is setting up of the opinion of a single person or a small group of persons as dictatorship. So it does not "set well" with our scheme of government. Even if it could be ideally constituted this would be true.

But besides the fallacy of the idea there are the piled-up difficulties of administration. How shall we keep it out of politics? We can't. Who shall decide as to the standards of morals or vulgarity? These things are not like stealing or murder or any crime, matters of fact, but they are matters of opinion except in those extreme cases where all society is practically agreed. Seven states have censorship laws, and no two of them agree in their findings.[1] The situation even becomes ludicrous when a city notorious for its corrupt government bans the showing of a film that has in it a grafting politician. It can stand the reality but objects to talking about it. Chicago has forbidden all references to crime, carrying firearms, bootlegging, thus securing for itself a higher standard of municipal life than other towns. And a picture with a grafting politician was kept out by that city for six weeks. The difficulty in reaching to the heart of the problem is shown by the single instance of the banning by police officers of a highly intellectual city of the performance of a play that, as a work of art, had received the highest award, while in the same town the same police raised no objection to semi-nudity on the stage.

In practical working, censorship shows itself as a sort of embodiment of conventionality. It is afraid of all things new. What else can you expect of it when it lies in the hands of political appointees, who are not, by the nature of things, critics of art or of thought? [...]

What we, as a nation, think of the idea of censorship when we get a chance at expressing ourselves is perhaps well illustrated by the action of Massachusetts, where the question of to censor or not to censor was decided not by legislative act but by popular vote. The legislature of that state had put through a censorship law which was vetoed by the then Governor Coolidge.[2] A petition drew it into the realm of a referendum vote, and the citizens defeated it by 553,173 to 208,252.

Over the country there is, very wisely, a growing opposition to government by Federal Commissions. Commissions are rightly used for special and brief pieces of work, but as permanent government bodies we look at them warily. Nor are we favorable to the tendency to "federalize" all ruling power. The glory of America is that she has worked out a way to combine imperial power with local responsibility and sense of community and individual independence. That is too precious a thing to lose. So to the idea of censorship, federal control adds the further objection of federalization.

There are special objections to the so-called Hudson Bill recently introduced to provide for Federal Control of Motion Pictures.[3]

It is customary for commissions to be appointed by the President with the advice and consent of the Senate. This bill provides that the commission shall be appointed by the Secretary of the Interior with no necessary advice and consent of anyone else—an entirely irresponsible method of appointing, and therefore full of political snags. This is the first violation of our American traditions and precedents. It is political appointment with a vengeance, responsible to neither the Government nor the people.

It is customary for commissioners to receive appointments for a limited time. This bill provides for tenure of position for good behavior (which is a different thing from fitness for the job)—a second provision for irresponsibility, and a second violation of our national traditions and precedent.

It is customary for Congress to keep its control over all federal agencies by holding the purse strings, and making it impossible for any group to go on without the sanction that goes with an appropriation. This bill provides that all the expenses of the commission shall be met by a levy on the industry. This is the third provision for irresponsibility. It lifts the commission out of congressional control. Again it violates our national tradition and precedent.

The bill provides that not more than one of the commissioners shall be a person who has had practical experience in the motion picture business, which is about as sensible as it would be to create a book commission out of people who know nothing about literature and publishing, a music commission out of people who know nothing of the theory of music.

There are other glaring defects in the proposed bill, but these are enough. They embody principles that, if introduced into our government, would lay all forms of business and industry open to killing government control.

Whether one calls this censorship or federal control, it is in essence censorship, and it adds the above objections to those that belong to local efforts to regulate thought, art, morals by law. [...]

Late last September there was held in New York a conference that was concerned with the motion picture and the community. To it came a variety of people with a variety of points of view, producers and executives and lawyers, professors,

psychologists and scientific men, priests and ministers, and women who were
leading members of eleven national organizations. After two days of many-sided
discussions Mrs. Sippel, the president of the General Federation of Women's Clubs,
made a suggestion that if a woman who knew women's point of view were placed
in organic relation with the administrative end of the motion picture industry,
she might do two things: First, voice the opinions, the criticisms, the suggestions
of her own particular public in places where they would do the most good (and
women are seventy-five percent of the movie audiences); and, second, give back
to her own particular public more reliable information as to the facts of the case.
The women, in conclave, chose the writer of this article. And the industry accepted
the challenge by giving official recognition, an office—a very delightful office—in
conjunction with their Hollywood office, secretarial help, all the paraphernalia—and
the name of Associate Director of Public Relations. [...]

Of my position the head office said: "While the industry makes it possible for
Mrs. Winter to do her work, she is the women's ambassador to the inner circle.
We don't expect her to 'yes' us on pictures, but to interpret frankly and fearlessly
your mass point of view. She is answerable not to the industry for her work but
to the women of the United States and to them only."

Hollywood is a place to itself, backed by mountainous hills, and with whiffs
of the sea—and with some psychologic flavor all its own. It behooves one coming
to it all green to the movies to taste its savor warily, to learn at least a few facts
and touch a few activities before one begins to have opinions and judgements. But
one thing came driving in every day, and more every next day. This is a time of
upheaval, of flux—when the old motion picture world has passed into silence, and
a new motion picture world is being born. [... T]he industry is beginning to find
itself and learn how to use its new tools.

The bringing in of sound means a vast deal more than merely the adding of
a voice to films. It means the reconstruction of all technique. [... T]he day of
drama has begun. A great range of interests is now possible; intricacies of plot
and intricacies of thought, all the stock in trade of story and play and opera. The
philosophizing about life and fate is now the movies' stock in trade, where two
years ago it lived within the stockade of silence. So the structure as well as the
themes must be changed. [...]

So the next epoch begins. If it were just a bigger and better and brighter and
noisier movie, that would be one thing. But there is a psychology going with it.

There seem to me still stupid uninteresting stories being filmed. There are
revolting single scenes in otherwise good plays. There is an occasional wholly
undesirable picture, and short subjects that have to be lived through, and advertising
that maligns instead of lures. I greatly dislike these things. But I turn to marvels
of flight, and marvels under the sea, and delicate transformations of modern plays
and stories—and see the other side of the picture. Sound makes bad things worse
and good things better. Which does the public want? Censorship and control never
help and always hinder the creative spirit. Yet only the creative spirit can keep this
most democratic of the arts alive. [...]

To strengthen that attitude of mind, to convince the producers, most of whom would like to give us cleaner and cleaner and lovelier and lovelier pictures—to convince them that they have support for such pictures for a clean-minded public, is one of the jobs in which I am glad to have a small share.

There are other stories of Hollywood that interest me; of women's part in the industry; of the greatest casual employment office in the world, the Casting Bureau, to which thirty thousand applicants a year come, and which is run by a woman, Miss Marian Mel. There are the 150 women drawn from five women's organizations who divide themselves into daily squads to see and evaluate the pictures day by day as they come from the studios and who send their findings out to many thousands of their constituent groups over the land. They meet with me once a month and I am getting up a course of critical lectures to help them to understand and judge better. There is the big question of children and the movies—though children are only eight percent of the audience. There is the more critical question of the adolescent.

But behind everything this question, here at the source, how can one help to deepen the consciousness of obligation in its production of this new young giant in the world who already holds the eyes and ears and plays on the emotions of millions upon millions? How can closer relations between its public and itself be brought about, each reacting on the other to the advantage of both? It can be done.

[The Woman's Journal (New York) 15:3, March 1930, pp. 7–9, 45–46, excerpted.]

PART THREE

Annotations

Mind-Stretching

1. Tutankhamen's tomb was discovered by Howard Carter in November 1922.

The Unsuspected Future of the Cinema

1. A draft version of this text appears in Stopes's hand under the title "The Cinema as a Power" in the British Library, Department of Manuscripts, Stopes Papers, Add. 58545.
   The New East was a monthly, bilingual (Japanese, English) Tokyo publication. Self-described as a "review of thought and achievement in the Eastern and Western worlds," the first issue was published in June 1917, in the midst of World War I. The publication was directed at "thinking men and women," and it aimed "to press home the lessons of the Disaster which has overtaken Europe," and "to bring a view of the history, the tradition, the achievement, the aims, the ideals and the methods of the Continent [Asia]" in which it was published. See "the Faith of The New East," The New East (Tokyo) I:1, June 1917, pp. 1–2.

2. The National Council of Public Morals (NCPM) was founded in 1911 with the objective of "the regeneration of the race—spiritual, moral and physical." Concerned with issues of public morality, eugenics and social reform, in late 1916 the NCPM established the Cinema Commission of Inquiry, partly as a result of its experience promoting Lois Weber's film Where Are My Children? (1916), to examine the social and moral influence of the cinema. The Commission heard evidence from a range of witnesses about the effects of cinema attendance and published its findings as The Cinema: Its Present Position and Future Possibilities, London: William & Norgate, 1917. The Lord Bishop of Birmingham, Russell Wakefield, was chairman of the NCPM and president of the Cinema Commission. He and Stopes became personal friends.

3. In the manuscript version of this essay, Stopes gives the source of this quotation as "a paragraph in the [London] Times of the other day (July 24)." Stopes, "Cinema as a Power," British Library, Department of Manuscripts, Stopes Papers, Add. 58545. She interlocutes here with the Kino Reform movement of Germany.

4. Stopes illustrated her own natural history lectures with film clips. According to her notes, her 21 March 1918 lecture at Cardiff, "The Cinema and the Naturalist," was illustrated with moving pictures of crystallization, a volvox, a running horse, patterns of shifting sand, bird studies, and a film of the life of a spider. See British Museum, Marie Stopes Papers, Manuscript Division, Add. 58545. See also Marie Stopes, "A Real Use of the Cinema," Bioscope (London), 2 September 1915, pp. 1028–9, for which she interviewed zoologists, plant pathologists, botanists, archaeologists, and geologists, among others, about their use of film in education.

The House of Dreams

1. While Addams's use of the term "theater" is often ambiguous in this text, "mimic theater" and the "five-cent theater" do refer explicitly to the cinema.

2. Hull House. Settlement house established by Addams and Ellen Starr in Chicago's 19th ward in September 1889.
3. Juvenile Court. Chicago pioneered the separate treatment of juvenile offenders by establishing the Juvenile Court in 1899. Here miscreant children were treated as delinquent, and in need of care and correction, rather than as criminal and in need of punishment. The Juvenile Court was established by a private committee, which, for some years, bore many of its costs. In 1907 the Juvenile Court Committee was reformed as the Juvenile Protective Association, whose aim was to keep children out of court by improving conditions around them.
4. Through the Juvenile Protective Association, Addams and her friend Louise de Koven Bowen were both active in the crusade against children performing in the theater, and against child labor in general.
5. Wild West Show. Established by American frontiersman and showman William F. Cody ("Buffalo Bill") in 1883, the Wild West show was an outdoor exhibition that combined Native Americans, buffaloes, and cowboys in a dramatized view of Western life. It toured nationally and internationally for thirty years.

Five and Ten Cent Theatres

1. While de Koven Bowen uses the term "theater" to refer to both the cinema and the stage, the "five-cent theater" (the nickelodeon) refers unquestionably to the cinema.
2. Juvenile Protective Association. Founded in Chicago in 1907 after the reformulation of the Juvenile Court Committee, the Association worked closely with Jane Addams's Hull House Settlement to investigate and remove conditions contributing to juvenile delinquency. De Koven Bowen was its founding president.
3. Women's City Club of Chicago, founded by Mrs Wilmarth, and active in municipal reform issues prior to and after the granting of female suffrage. De Koven Bowen was its president 1914–24. On 4 November 1907, Chicago established police licensing of motion pictures, under the direction of Major M.L.C. Funkhouser.

Children and Picture Palaces

1. Head Master of Eton. Fox is referring to Edward Lyttleton, "Note on the Educational Influence of the Cinematograph," *The Hibbert Journal* (London), July 1913, pp. 851–5.
2. Fox is writing during World War I.
3. The British Board of Film Censors (BBFC) was established in 1912, partly as an effort to protect the exhibition trade from the problem of local variations in the definition of an "undesirable" film. Its operation had not placated local authorities however, who, with the assistance of concerned citizens organized into Watch Committees, could nevertheless move to prevent films from being screened in their area of jurisdiction. In 1916, as Fox's article indicates, the workings of the BBFC were subject to much public criticism, particularly with regard to films screened for children. Ten years later, in 1926, this criticism re-emerged when the National Association of Head Teachers sent a deputation to the BBFC arguing the need for greater control of films screened for audiences under sixteen.
4. Amusement tax. The Entertainments Tax was introduced as a wartime measure to increase government revenue. It was still in operation in 1929.

Should War Films Be Seen by Children?

1. Educational Cinematographic Institute. The International Institute of Educational Cinematography was established in Rome in 1928 to develop international collaboration in the educational field by means of the educational film. The Institute was under the authority of the Council of the League of Nations. Elie's article was published in its journal.

Brutality in Prize Fight Pictures

1. Nevada. In the United States, New York was the first state to permit boxing with gloves, in 1896, followed shortly by Nevada.
2. War. The Spanish–American war lasted from April to July 1898.
3. The Sharkey–Jeffries fight was filmed on 3 November 1899 at the Coney Island Sporting Club with an audience of 10,500. Biograph shot the twenty-five round fight with 70 mm film, and

on 20 November the filmed fight opened a program of Biograph films in New York. Blake is responding to this screening. The Edison Company had also, surreptitiously, filmed this fight.

A Grave Injustice to Colored People

1. When The Birth of a Nation was shown in Boston in April 1915, indignation at the film's appeal to racial hatred led to a series of public meetings. These meetings were organized by the Boston branch of the National Association for the Advancement of Colored People (NAACP), which sought to prevent further screenings of the film in that city. A new Censor Law for the City of Boston was proposed and secured in the legislature, but it failed to stop the film's continued run. To assist other cities' efforts to suppress Griffith's film, the Boston branch of the NAACP published Fighting a Vicious Film: Protest Against "The Birth of a Nation" (1915), a volume of letters, resolutions and speeches written during the Boston protest. Wald's statement is reprinted from this collection.

2. Jane Addams (1860–1935). American social reformer, pacifist and settlement house worker who established the Hull House settlement with Ellen Starr in Chicago's 19th ward in September 1889.
   Lillian D. Wald and Jane Addams were both board members of the National Association for the Advancement of Colored People. Addams' objections to the film, essentially the same as those of Wald, were published as "Jane Addams Condemns Race Prejudice Film," The Evening Post (New York), 13 March 1915, p. 4. Wald and Addams saw the film in New York.

3. Possibly because Wald reports only on the second act of the film, she overlooks the film's references to such loyalty.

4. Liberty Theater. The NAACP only managed to delay The Birth of a Nation's opening in New York, from 3 March at the Liberty Theater, to 15 March. "Incendiarism" refers to reactions to the New York-based National Board of Censorship's (later the National Board of Review) apparent initial enthusiasm for the film.

5. Henry Street Settlement. Wald began what came to be known as the Henry Street Settlement at 27 Jefferson Street, when she moved to New York's Lower East Side to take up settlement house work and nursing in 1893. In 1895, a residence at 265 Henry Street was added to the settlement and this address gave Wald's enterprise its name.

Where Are My Children?

1. This undated letter, marked "re Where Are My Children," is contained in the British Library, Department of Manuscripts, as item number Add. MS 58545, ff.56–56v. It is in Marie Stopes's hand and is interleaved with her correspondence with Catherine L. Osler, President of the Birmingham Branch of the Women's Suffrage Society, whose neighboring letters date from 2 July and 6 July 1917. The Stopes letter ends with the note, "Mrs. C. Ring, Secretary, Birmingham Women's Suffrage Society," perhaps indicating that Stopes sent (or intended to send) the letter to Mrs. Ring for further work and circulation, as Catherine Osler had suggested in her letter of 6 July 1917.
   Osler's 2 July correspondence confirms that the written protests of her Birmingham group to the Bishop of Birmingham had "secured the failure and withdrawal ... of that most objectionable film" from Birmingham. In her 6 July letter to Stopes she writes further:

   > I received your express letter ... [and] decided to bring your proposal before the Executive Council of the National Union of the Women's Suffrage Society [in London] as a matter of urgency. They undertook to draw up a letter to The Times—a resumé of ours to the Bishop of Birmingham—and to try to get it signed by a representative and weighty list of women. The difficulty is that people naturally hesitate to sign a protest against something they have not seen, and time is so short! (I don't know whether the film is to be shown longer than this week). But if a few well-known names can be obtained the letter will be far more effective than one signed for instance only by Mrs Ring and myself, and the National Union may succeed in getting it accepted [by The Times perhaps], where we probably might not.

   The draft letter we reproduce may be a version of Stopes's proposal sent to Catherine Osler for further action. Stopes appends a list of signatories at the end of her letter, again in her own hand, prefaced by the statement:

Protest to the Bishop was signed by: Margaret Ashley, president of the National Union of Women's Workers; Lydia Bowler, Headmistress, Pupil Teacher's Centre; S. Butler, President, Federation of Sisterhoods; Elsie Cadbury (Mrs. G. Cadbury); Geraldine Cadbury, Women's Adult Schools; C. Osler, President, Women's Suffrage Society; K. Lythleftus, President, National Union of Women Workers; Janet Clarkson, President, Birmingham Branch of British Women's Temperance Association; M.A. Marston, on behalf of the whole women teachers' Association; and heaps of others of all sorts of women's societies and unions.

This list probably refers to signatories to the letter organized by Osler to protest the Birmingham showings of Weber's film, to which she refers in her letter to Stopes of 2 July 1917, mentioned above.

Lois Weber's film was made in Hollywood in 1916, and premiered in England on 8 November 1916.

2. In an effort to explain the precipitous decline in the British birth rate, the National Council of Public Morals was sponsoring the exhibition of *Where Are My Children?*

Uncle Tom's Cabin

1. Harriet Beecher Stowe (1811–1896). American writer whose abolitionist novel *Uncle Tom's Cabin* was a bestseller when first published in 1852.
2. This film was not made, following a protest campaign let by the NAACP..
3. Congressman Rankin. John Rankin, a decorated World War I veteran and Mississippi congressman from 1921, was a renowned racist, anti-Communist and anti-Semite. He was to be the driving force behind the House Committee on Un-American Activities Committee (HUAC) investigations of suspected Communists in Hollywood in 1947.
4. In early March 1942, rioting occurred when black tenants attempted to move into the Sojourner Truth housing project in Detroit and met with white opposition. The Sojourner Truth project was built specifically to house black workers, many of whom had moved to Detroit as a consequence of wartime labor demands.

Letter

1. Carl Laemmle (1867–1939). German-born American film mogul who established the largest film distribution concern in the United States, based in Chicago (1906–09), and founded Universal Pictures in 1912.
   Hull House. Chicago settlement house founded by Jane Addams and Ellen Starr in Chicago's 19th ward in September 1889.

The Future of the Cinematograph

1. According to Ian Christie, films of the French surgeon Eugène-Louis Doyen operating were shown at the British Medical Association's 1898 congress in Edinburgh. *The Last Machine: Early Cinema and the Birth of the Modern World* (London: British Film Institute, 1994), pp. 99–100.

The Workingman's College

1. Mark Twain [Samuel Langhorne Clemens] (1835–1910). Popular American humorist whose most famous works, *The Adventures of Tom Sawyer* (1876) and *The Adventures of Huckleberry Finn* (1885), were based on his own childhood experiences growing up in Missouri.
2. Dr Lyman Beecher. Yale-educated Connecticut preacher, theologian and reformer, father of American writer and abolitionist Harriet Beecher Stowe (1811–1896).
3. National Board of Censors [National Board of Censorship]. Established by the People's Institute, a Progressive social research organization, in New York in March 1909, the National Board of Censorship was made up of individuals representing a range of civic organizations. From 1915, it was known as the National Board of Review.

Mind-Growth or Mind-Mechanization?

1. Sandor Ferenczi (1873–1933). Psychoanalysit. An early disciple of Sigmund Freud.

2. Possibly Herbert G. Ponting's early documentary of the Scott expedition, *With Captain Scott R.N. to the South Pole* (1913).

Can the Film Educate?

1. René Clair (1898–1981). French director of comedy whose films include *Paris Qui Dort* (1923), *Sous les Toits de Paris* (1930), *Le Million* (1931), *A Nous la Liberté* (1931), and *The Ghost Goes West* (1935).
2. De Mille. [William C. de Mille] (1878–1955). American director, producer, playwright, and screenwriter, brother to Cecil B. His directorial credits include *Miss Lulu Bett* (1921), *What Every Woman Knows* (1921), and *Nice People* (1922).
3. George Bernard Shaw (1856–1950). Irish-born playwright, critic, and polemicist whose satirical and incisive plays attacked social hypocrisy and challenged conventional theatrical values.
4. Charles Laughton (1899–1962). British actor and director who worked in Hollywood and achieved his greatest popular success in the 1930s. His films include *The Private Life of Henry VIII* (1933), *Mutiny on the Bounty* (1935), *Ruggles of Red Gap* (1935), and *Rembrandt* (1936).
5. G.W. Pabst (1885–1967). German director whose films include *Joyless Street* (1925), *Secrets of a Soul* (1926), *The Love of Jeanne Ney* (1927), *Pandora's Box* (1928), *Diary of a Lost Girl* (1929), *The Threepenny Opera* (1931), *Kameradschaft* (1931), and *L'Atlantide* (1932).
   Vsevolod Pudovkin (1893–1953). Soviet film theorist, writer, actor, and director whose films include *Mother* (1926), *The End of St. Petersburg* (1927), and *Storm over Asia* (1928).
6. The recent revolution in Cuba. In September 1934, Sgt. Fulgenico Batista (1901–1973) had led a revolt against Cuban president Carlos Manuel de Céspedes, who was overthrown and replaced by Dr Ramón Grau San Martín. Batista was president of Cuba 1940–44, 1952–59.
7. Robert J Flaherty (1884–1951). American documentary filmmaker whose films include *Nanook of the North* (1921), *Moana* (1926), *Tabu* (1931) (co-directed with F.W. Murnau), *Man of Aran* (1934), *The Land* (1942), and *Louisiana Story* (1948).
   Paul Rotha (1903–1984). British documentary theorist and filmmaker who made *The Face of Britain* (1935) and many other documentaries during the 1930s.
8. Ronald J. Canti's film *Cultivation of Living Tissue Cells Including Cancer* (c. 1933) documented cancer research undertaken at Strangeways Research Hospital, Cambridge, and St. Bartholomew's, London. Canti presented this film to an audience of British ophthamologists in 1932.
   Percy Smith. British pioneer of microcinematography, Smith worked with Mary Field on the *Secrets of Nature* film series where he specialized in plant and underwater photography. With Field he wrote several works of popular cine-biology including *Secrets of Nature* (1939).

The Educational and Social Value of the News-Reel

1. In the early 1930s the majority of the Paris dailies operated cinemas devoted specifically to newsreels. The first of these were the five "Cinéac-Le Journal" cinemas opened in 1931.

The Cinema in the Slums

1. Charles Dickens (1812–1870). Famous Victorian British novelist whose impoverished childhood inspired him to write on themes of social injustice, child exploitation, and class distinction.

Sunday Cinemas

1. Two famous comedians' daily back-chat. At the time of Pallister's writing, the "Amos 'n' Andy" radio show (which ran from 1928 to 1960) could be heard six nights a week, from 7:00 p.m. to 7:15 p.m. Amos Jones (played by Freeman F. Gosden) and Andrew H. Brown (played by Charles Correll) were two luckless, lovable black guys in Chicago. In the United States, a third of the nation, including the president, were apparently tuning in; factories staggered shifts so that workers could listen.
2. According to Rachael Low, the issue of Sunday screenings was not a particularly lively one in Great Britain between 1918 and 1929. Although some unions opposed it on the grounds that they lengthened the working week of those employed in cinemas, the Labour Party was generally in favor of them. In 1932, the Sunday Entertainments Act was introduced, allowing cinemas to operate on Sundays subject to the discretion of local authorities.

Films Have Taught Us What Life Means

1. Elstree Studios was a production facility located at Borehamwood, north of London.
2. Ruth Chatterton (1893–1961). New York-born actress, nominated for an Academy Award for Best Actress for her role in *Sarah and Son* (1930).
   George Arliss (1868–1946). Distinguished British stage actor who embarked on a successful film career in middle age. His performance in *Disraeli* (1929) won him an Academy Award.
   Will Rogers (1879–1935). American comedian who was a former *Ziegfeld Follies* star. His career included silent and sound films, among them *Jubilo* (1919), *The Cowboy Sheik* (1924), *A Connecticut Yankee* (1931), *State Fair* (1933), *Judge Priest* (1934), and *Steamboat 'Round the Bend* (1935).

The Unconscious Humor of the Movies

1. Unconscious humor. In *Life and Habit* (1877), a study broadly concerned with evolution, Samuel Butler (1835–1902) looked at the workings of the unconscious and the way it often revealed itself in an uncanny manner. He noted, for instance, that strident insistence often concealed doubt and that the things we know best are very often the things of which we are least (consciously) aware. Working from this, he suggested that the best humor is generally unconscious or unintentional. Repplier's use of the term here in her treatment of Hollywood acknowledges Butler's sense of the unintentional, unselfconscious nature of true humor as well as his inference that conscious processes could mask the complex, indeed contradictory, unconscious truth of a subject.
2. Will Hays (1879–1954). President Hardings's postmaster general was invited by the major studios in 1922 to head the Motion Picture Producers and Distributors of America (MPPDA) in an effort to defeat calls for federal film censorship legislation. In 1930 the industry adopted the Hays-authored Production Code which imposed strict limitations on the content of both pre-production scripts and the finished films themselves. Hays was president of the MPPDA from 1922 to 1945.
3. Geneva Conference. In Geneva at the Arms Traffic Convention on 17 June 1925, representatives of eighteen countries, including the United States, had signed agreements which called for the supervision of the international armaments trade, recognized the illegality of chemical and bacteriological warfare, and prohibited the use of poisonous gases in war.
4. Jackie Coogan (1914–1984). Child actor best known for his role opposite Charlie Chaplin in *The Kid* (1921).
5. League of Nations. An international organization formed after World War I to "promote international cooperation and security." Based in Geneva, it functioned from 1920 until it was dissolved in 1946.
   President (Woodrow) Wilson (1856–1924). Twenty-eighth US president (1913–21), Wilson is remembered as a statesman whose high-minded idealism eventually committed his country to World War I, and who became the leading advocate for the League of Nations at the Paris Peace Conference.
   Sir Eric Drummond. First Secretary General of the League of Nations.
6. In spite of the efforts of President Wilson, the United States never joined the League of Nations.
7. Barnum (Phineas Taylor Barnum) (1810–1891). American entrepreneur whose circus known as "The Greatest Show on Earth" traveled around the world to great fame and fortune.
8. Harriet Beecher Stowe (1811–1896). American writer whose abolitionist novel *Uncle Tom's Cabin* was published in 1852.
9. Mrs Gerould. Katherine Fullerton Gerould (1879–44), American short story writer, novelist and essayist. Her "The Nemesis of the Screen," a 1922 article on censorship of which Repplier was aware, is excerpted and reprinted in this volume.

Keeping it Dark

1. N. Ognyov (a pseudonym for Mikhail Grigorevich Rozanov), *Diary of a Communist Undergraduate* (London: Gollancz, 1929).
2. Havelock Ellis (1859–1939). British essayist and physician who studied human sexual behavior. The publication of the first volume of his seven-volume *Studies in the Psychology of Sex* (1897–1928) resulted in an obscenity trial in which the presiding judge refused all claims made for the

book's scientific value. Until 1935, further volumes were only available to the medical profession.

D.H. Lawrence (1885–1930). British writer whose novels The Rainbow (1915) and Lady Chatterley's Lover (1928) were banned as obscene. The latter appeared in an expurgated version in England in 1932.

Radclyffe Hall's novel The Well of Loneliness (1928) was condemned by Sunday Express editor James Douglas and was the subject of an obscenity trial.

3. In the press brouhaha following the condemnation of The Well of Loneliness, Radclyffe Hall was often photographed wearing a wide-brimmed Montmartre hat over her Eton crop and with a cigarette stuck jauntily between her teeth. Hall's grandfather had been knighted, and she could claim familial links to both Charles II and Shakespeare.

4. Lord Brentford (Sir William Joynson-Hicks, popularly known as "Jix"). British Home Secretary in the 1920s. As Home Secretary, Jix was effectively a national censor, empowered to withhold permission to private societies wishing to screen films and to define publications as "obscene" and therefore liable to criminal prosecution. Jix refused private showings of Potemkin in 1929 and, in the same year, advised Jonathan Cape to withdraw publication of Radclyffe Hall's novel, a work he judged "inherently obscene."

5. West's phrasing suggests that, in 1929, the sound film was, for some viewers at least, still something of a novelty.

6. Will Hays (1879–1954). President Hardings's postmaster general was invited by the major studios in 1922 to head the Motion Picture Producers and Distributors of America (MPPDA) in an effort to defeat calls for federal film censorship legislation. In 1930 the industry adopted the Hays-authored Production Code which imposed strict limitations on the content of both pre-production scripts and the finished films themselves. Hays was president of the MPPDA from 1922 to 1945.

British Board of Film Censors (BBFC). British body established in 1912 to approve films for public viewing. The BBFC's recommendations were still subject to regional variance because, under the Cinematograph Act of 1909, local authorities had been granted the right to ban films. In 1921, however, the London County Council enacted bylaws which specified that licensed cinemas could only screen films passed by the BBFC, and most other municipal authorities throughout Great Britain eventually followed this lead. The BBFC worked separately from both the cinema trade and the government, but tried to maintain good relations with both, as well as to be responsive to the opinions of local authorities. Like the Hays Office of the MPPDA, the BBFC lacked any statutory power.

The Nemesis of the Screen

1. Sarah Bernhardt [Rosine Bernard] (1844–1923). Internationally famous French actress, often called the "divine Sarah." Bernhardt made her stage debut in 1862, and appeared in a small number of films.

2. William Desmond Taylor [William Deane Tanner] (1867–1922). An Irish-born ex-officer of the British Army, Taylor was one of Hollywood's leading directors when he was murdered under suspicious circumstances. His death was just one of many industry scandals involving Paramount employees of the period, including Roscoe "Fatty" Arbuckle and Wallace Reid.

In Defense of Hollywood

1. Other contributors to the article were William de Mille, Rupert Hughes, Rita Weiman, and Constance Talmadge. Loos is described as "the dean of scenario writers," while all are referred to as "serious-minded workers in the film world" who have been asked by Filmplay "to give the lie to the false impressions created by the newspapers." The lead-in paragraph mentions the murder of William Desmond Taylor (1867–1922) as among the recent happenings in Hollywood fuelling sensation writers.

Women and the Cinema

1. Community Better Film Councils. The National Committee for Better Films was established by the National Board of Review (then known as the National Board of Censorship) in 1914. From 1917, and particularly after 1922, community groups across the United States encouraged

the idea of better films at a local level through special screenings, selective patronage, and subscription to the publications of the National Board of Review.

2. Dr Phyllis Blanchard. Author of *The Adolescent Girl: A Study from the Psychoanalytic Viewpoint* (New York: Moffat Yard, 1920), and *The Child and Society: An Introduction to the Social Psychology of the Child* (New York: Longman's, Green, 1928), among many other books.

3. The League of Nations. An international organization formed after World War I to "promote international cooperation and security." Based in Geneva, it functioned from 1920 until it was dissolved in 1946.

Solving the Motion Picture Problem

1. An endorsed film displayed the seal of the National Board of Review, signifying that it had been passed for exhibition.

Better Movies—But How?

1. Will Hays (1879–1954). In an effort to defeat calls for federal film censorship legislation in 1922, Will Hays, President Harding's postmaster general, was invited by the major studios to head the Motion Picture Producers and Distributors of America (MPPDA). In 1930 the industry adopted the Hays-authored Production Code, which imposed strict limitations on the content of both pre-production scripts and the finished films themselves.

2. Thirteen Points. A list of proscribed topics designed to prevent films from dealing with potentially offensive material, the "thirteen points" was one of Will Hays's early initiatives for the Motion Picture Producers and Distributors of America (MPPDA), introduced in 1922, rather than 1921 as Gilman writes.

3. Individual states and municipalities could impose their own censorship over films passed by the National Board of Review. The latter enjoyed no legislative status.

4. National Board of Review. Established in 1909 in New York as the National Board of Censorship by the People's Institute, a Progressive social research organization. The National Board of Review established the National Committee for Better Films in 1914 and, from 1917, community groups across the United States encouraged the idea of better films at a local level through special screenings, selective patronage, and subscription to the publications of the National Board of Review.

5. Alice Ames Winters, former president of the General Federation of Women's Clubs, had recently been appointed Associate Director of Public Relations of the Association of Motion Picture Producers and Directors of America (MPPDA). Winters was appointed to represent the concerns of American women to the film industry. Her response to the question posed by *The Woman's Journal* is also reprinted here.

6. Kellogg–Briand peace pact. An agreement signed in Paris by fifteen nations, including the United States, on 27 August 1928 which renounced war as an instrument of national policy. Most nations subsequently signed the agreement.

And So to Hollywood

1. Among the states with their own censorship boards in 1930 were New York, Maryland, Virginia, Ohio, Pennsylvania, and Kansas. Boston and Chicago also maintained municipal censor boards.

2. Governor Coolidge of Massachusetts. Calvin Coolidge (1872–1933), the thirtieth President of the United States, from 1923 to 1929, and Republican Governor of Massachusetts, from 1920 to 1921.

3. Hudson Bill. A bill (H.R. 13686) sponsored by United States Congressman Grant M. Hudson of Michigan, which sought to enforce legally the "Thirteen Points" adopted by the Motion Picture Producers and Distributors of America in 1922. Under the terms of the bill the motion picture industry would have been declared a public utility, supervised and regulated by a Federal Government Commission. The bill was not passed.

PART FOUR
The Critic's Hat

Fig. 4.1   Louella Parsons and Hedda Hopper at a party in 1960.

PART FOUR

Introduction

The hat. It has been, first and foremost, *the* sign of femininity at the movies. The striking picture bonnet, obstructing our view, beribboned and plumed, announced women's presence before the film. "Through the huge hat, with its wilderness of bedraggled feathers, the girl announces to the world that she is here."[1] But this hat was also *on* the screen, abundantly in Asta Nielsen's piled up, overflowing creations as *The Suffragette* (1913). In 1920, actress Elsie Ferguson's headgear rapidly migrated from the screen to appear throughout mid-town Manhattan.[2] Such dispersal indicated the alacrity with which women bought up the screen's stylistic offerings through shopping, while also suggesting the ways in which moviegoing shaped women's views of themselves, and guided them into seeing themselves as images, delineating different niches for the sexes, while also offering new visual themes for self-invention. With time, millinery became the emblem of the critic herself; Howard Hawks adapted Adela Rogers St. Johns's veiled toque (and pin-striped suit) for ace newspaperwoman Hildy Johnson in *His Girl Friday* (1940), (Fig. 4.2, 4.3) and many are the hatted critics illustrated on the pages of this collection.[3]

Idiomatically speaking, to wear a hat is to take up a role; this hat, donned and removed, was certainly the critic's, for she was rarely, if ever, only a columnist—the working lives of at least half the writers here also encompassed magazine editing, and acting, as well as poetry or fiction writing, or other kinds of journalism, and political work. To keep something under one's hat is also to harbor secrets until divulgence proves possible or expedient. This was yet another facet of the critic's practice. Hollywood commentator—and hat lover—Hedda Hopper named her autobiography *From Under My Hat*, reminding us that her work traded in a combination of strategy and gossip.[4]

Highlighting the critic's hat means pointing, deliberately, to the gendered aspects of critical writing on film. Women dominated this area in numbers and in cliché. They were some of the first film reviewers, key Hollywood columnists, and acolytes in that temple of celebrity, the fan magazine.[5] Particularly in Britain, in the careers of C.A. Lejeune and Dilys Powell, the critical film scene was dominated by two

Fig. 4.2   Adela Rogers St. Johns in her signature striped suit.

women, a situation mirrored in America, in the careers of Hedda Hopper, Louella Parsons, and Pauline Kael. One source estimated that, in 1943, approximately 75 per cent of the hundred-odd fan magazine writers of the time were female, "and the rest men, or at least people who wear trousers."[6] Why this preponderance?

Writing about film (initially, if not perpetually) had low status, requiring little or no training, offering women one of the easiest entrees into journalism, as well as a source of income. Irene Thirer, movie critic for almost forty years, and chairman of the New York Film Critics in 1957, began at the New York *Daily News* straight out of high school, where she wrote photocaptions. She moved to reviewing after four years, where she helped to develop the one-two-three-four star method of film rating.[7] *New Yorker* luminaries Janet Flanner and Mollie Panter-Downes had early stints as film critics (Flanner at the *Indianapolis Star* and Panter-Downes at the British *Film Weekly*), as did novelists Sally Benson and Katharine Anne Porter.[8] (The young medium might also have appealed in that it invited the invention of new vocabulary: a "nickelodeon" interior might be a "spectatorium"; a "gladys glycerine"

Fig. 4.3 Rosalind Russell as reporter Hildy Johnson in *His Girl Friday* (1940), wearing a suit modeled on columnist Adela Rogers St. Johns's.

a well-paid screen actress; "films of the soil" a new genre type.[9]) Women also got these jobs because editors thought their sex *should* cover a medium whose scale of female audience was legendary, an assumed reciprocity between writer and audience being the minimum qualification for the rookie reporter. And editors encouraged the opportunity film brought to discuss feminine concerns: fashion, weight, and diet; ageing youth; the movies women wanted; sex roles on film. Sometimes women made a point of reviewing women's work: Evelyn Gerstein assessed Olga Preobrashenskaya's *The Village of Sin*, Madeleine Carroll reflected on Dorothy Arzner's *Sarah and Son* and Winifred Holtby reported at length on Leontine Sagan's *Mädchen in Uniform*.[10]

Other historical circumstances facilitated this career option for women: Elsie Cohen, later manager of the Academy Cinema, London, remembered landing her job at *Kinematograph Weekly* in 1915 because men had gone to war.[11] Louella Parsons recalled getting the same kind of break in the 1910s.[12] Further, the rise of film-making occurred during the daily press's most energetic years. A myriad small and large newspapers would appear, mornings and afternoons, all across small towns and cities. The first film trade journal in the United States, *Views and Film Index*, started publication on 25 April 1906, in response to the nickelodeon boom, and was followed in 1907 by *Moving Picture World* and *Moving Picture News*, as well as Chicago's *The Show World*, which also covered stage. Such organs gave plot summaries and sometimes reviewed films, although opinion was mostly anonymous, as indeed it was in the daily press, where regular review columns started in about 1911, and usually lacked a byline until 1915.[13] Pseudonymous writing was common from the start, male writers sometimes taking female pseudonyms, and vice versa: there were the "Daughter of Eve" of 1896; "Mae Tinee" (Frances Smith) of the *Chicago Tribune*, and "Cal York" (who included various female as well as male writers, reporting on California and New York) of *Photoplay* in the 1910s and 1920s; the crasser "Morphia Money," a satirical reviewer advertised in *Film Weekly* in the 1930s; "H.D." and "Bryher," names concealing Hilda Doolittle's and Winifred Ellerman's sex; and Norma Mahl, pseudonym for Robert Herring of *Close Up*, as he described the screening of a Russian abortion film.[14] "Filmore," writer of a regular "Inside Film Talk" column for *Moving Picture News*, teased readers in 1911 that "Filmore MAY be a female."[15] Namelessness (as well as the use of pen names) means that we will never establish how many women wrote about film, particularly before 1920, but it was a burgeoning field that certainly concealed female authorship.[16]

Women acted out their own modernization through journalism, in feats of physical and emotional courage: Annie Laurie was the first columnist of either sex to reach the Galveston Flood of 1900; Nellie Bly, plucky girl recorder for *The New York World* (who, at age twenty-five, was to circle the globe as a news stunt in 1890), feigned insanity in 1887 to write about asylums; in 1914 Djuna Barnes subjected herself to force-feeding to cover imprisoned suffragists.[17] The emergence of the intrepid female reporter accompanied that of the sob sister, whose "cathartic style," in which "the news event did not count so much as the writer's reaction to it, ... involved the reader in pity, fear, and remorse."[18] While the former were above all associated with Joseph Pulitzer's leadership at the *Morning World* in New York (where Nellie Bly, Polly Pry, and Elizabeth Jordan started out), it was William Randolph Hearst who developed the sob sisters' new "female" voice, a style feeding directly into the development of film fan magazines, and reaching an apotheosis in the pained and empathetic coverage of Rudolph Valentino's sudden death at thirty-one, in 1926.

Writing about film belonged within this modern matrix: Alice Rix's venturing, in 1897, to report on the boxing spectatrix was sensationalist journalism; Alison Smith and Mabel Condon traveled on assignment for stories on the East and West Coast film industries in the 1910s.[19] Rather than Louis Delluc, it was Colette who, on 28 May 1917, initiated the film criticism column for *Le Film*, the journal which helped hatch the French avant-garde film movement, while her earlier review of Cecil B. DeMille's *The Cheat* rocketed the picture to prominence, such that Delluc later recorded that it had persuaded him to become a film critic.[20] Film lay within the professional range of other ground-breaking female journalists: pioneer women sports writers Harriette Underhill and Ruth Hale also covered film; Agnes Smedley, labor writer and radical who filed on the Chinese Revolution and was the only Western journalist to have lived with Communist-led Chinese troops during World War II, discussed UFA's *Kulturfilme* for a Calcutta-based English-language review; and Alice Dunnigan, the first African-American woman to cover the Capitol, reviewed cinema in Washington, DC, in the 1950s.[21]

Some women's careers were prodigious: Edith Nepean published her first column for *Picture Show* on 20 November 1920, and was still writing for it when it ceased publication in 1960; Adele Whitely Fletcher became editor of *Motion Picture Magazine* in February 1920, subsequently editing *Movie Weekly* and *Photoplay* (1948–52), and continuing to contribute articles to film magazines into the 1970s; Ruth Waterbury was associated with *Photoplay* for fifty years, from 1922 onwards, both as a regular contributor and as an editor (1935–40); Radie Harris, who summarized her New Yorker's vision of Hollywood in her autobiography, *Radie's World*, and who was famous for her wooden leg as well as her film journalism, began her reporting career at age seventeen, writing for the New York *Morning Telegraph* in the 1930s before starting on *The Hollywood Reporter* in 1940 (and also writing a regular column for *Photoplay*); and Dylis Powell described Caroline A. Lejeune, whose writing on film spanned forty years (1921–60) as the "true creator of British cinema criticism."[22]

Women's routes in and out of film journalism were varied and pragmatic. Some wrote on cinema as voluntary work for women's clubs, as described in Part Three. Film journalism certainly attracted women because it could lead to industry work. It had been Anna Steese Richardson (whose career moved from film journalism in the 1910s to the promotion of the education of film audiences in the later 1920s) who had proposed in 1921 that "Women should go into photoplay writing from journalism."[23] Critic Marian Spitzer became assistant producer at Paramount, and reviewer Sally Benson later wrote screenplays. Others traveled in reverse, most notably Hedda Hopper, a former actress, and Louella Parsons, a former scenario writer.[24] Film journalist Ida Zeitlin was also the translator (from German) of Vicki Baum's Hollywood novel *Falling Star*, about the travails of the fictional Phoenix Picture Corporation.[25]

Women were certainly also attracted to writing about films for the intricate relationship they held to life (as indeed were men). This provided the dominant framework for film reviewing, as it still does. The medium's appearance of verisimilitude irresistibly drew critics to contemplate its purchase on reality. Winifred Horrabin, assessing *The Sheik* and *The Son of the Sheik*, appreciated the image of perfection in Valentino's pressed riding breeches, improbable in a desert, but despised the dream *rapprochement* of capital with labor of Lang's *Metropolis*.[26] Reporting on Paris during the Great War, in a land of "worn-out jackets and spongy, broken-down shoes," Colette rated both the cinema's contrasting luxury, and the surging wellspring of the crowd's desire.[27] Djuna Barnes relished disclosing Hollywood's manipulative inside workings, in its physical infiltrations into reality (through tie-in scams), while Muriel Rukuyser called on readers to resist the cardboard fakery of film.[28]

Precisely on account of cinema's unavoidable relation to life, and thence nation, film criticism was not rendered superfluous by war. While Louella Parsons might report, after the Italian sacking of Albania in 1939, that the week's "deadly dullness ... was lifted today when Darryl Zanuck admitted he had bought all rights to Maurice Maeterlinck's *The Bluebird* for Shirley Temple," other writers found a particular urgency to their task under crisis conditions.[29] For black women—and black men—cinema's relation to reality held particular potence (a power which partly accounts for the relative numerousness of their contributions in Part Four, by comparison with other parts of the collection). A film's perceived proximity to life provided a means of critical evaluation, its distance a reason for enjoyment or disparagement. Jesse Graves could criticize films for not representing black life as lived, focusing his ire on crowd scenes, for these never reflected the proportion of black Americans to be seen on the streets about the theater.[30] Judgement of a film frequently rested on its representativeness of black subjects, although this did not lead to uniformity of opinion, as the opposing views of Fay Jackson and Hazel Washington regarding *Imitation of Life* illustrate.[31]

Whatever women's actual numbers in this field, film criticism was popularly imagined a female province. Ishbel Ross, in her comprehensive historical survey of women in American journalism, published in 1936, noted that while there were few female dramatic critics, "the motion picture field is virtually their monopoly."[32] In addition to the "sob sisters" and "agony aunts" of the Hollywood gossip columns, female film journalists were sufficiently numerous to warrant epithets such as "flicker" or "vulture."[33] One article reported "the smell" of the female fan magazine writer to be so "lousy" as to repel tough sports correspondents, who decamped as she settled at their press luncheon table.[34] And the readership of these women was vast: at the height of their careers, the two women who most popularly typify the female film writer—Hedda Hopper and Louella Parsons—claimed a combined global audience of many millions.[35]

And yet women have a scant presence in the many published collections of film criticism, one editor even assuming that anonymous reviews were male-authored.[36] The over forty examples of women's film criticism assembled here show the range of women involved, from full-time professionals to fledgling reporters and even an undergraduate winning a competition with her (possibly singular) essay on film.[37] The selection also illuminates stylistic range—poetry, prose, doggerel verse—and geographical spread: fashion and music magazines, literary journals, socialist weeklies, and middle-brow monthlies, published in Baltimore and Indianapolis, as well as in the film metropolises of Chicago, Los Angeles, New York, and London. The analytical armature and text length of writers like Barbara Deming and Ruth Suckow allowed them a degree of critical reflection and the chance to develop and articulate a methodology.[38] This was not true of the newspaper critic, who generally had neither the intellectual need nor the column length; back from her vacation, and with a persona of chatty expertise, Powell had taken herself off to "the cinema of savagery," she said, merely against her better judgement.[39] However, such differences do not automatically lead to a difference of significance. The hoary distinction between film criticism and reviewing has not determined the arrangement of Part Four, or interpretation of these items. Meaghan Morris has suggested that reviewing depends on the day-to-day activity of the industry, where criticism does not. As such, reviewing produces novelty, and assumes that the reader has not seen the film, while criticism takes it that the reader has, will, or should have. Criticism refers to the film retrospectively, reviewing prospectively.[40] For many of the examples here, however, these differences remain hard to specify, as an individual writer takes the opportunity of a particular film's première, or a particular screening, to comment on war, critical standards, or the significance of film sound. Perhaps, for reasons related to the rapidly developing history of the medium as well as to that of journalism and the impact of international events, the style, terms and range of discussion of film writing during cinema's first half-century seem to have been broader and more open-ended than they are now.

The first grouping in Part Four, "Naming the Object," comprises very early accounts of two new media: cinema, here named the kinetoscope and then the nickelodeon; and television. The writers' interests roam among technology, audiences, and the mechanics of screening and programming, refusing to be limited by the image on screen. In "Reviewing," an account of a particular film might be the premise for writing, but it is again rarely the sole focus. In Jessie Dismorr's poem "Matinee" there may be no film at all.[41] The "Croisette" which trembles in her first line may be the broad promenade running beside the beach at Cannes.[42] Perhaps, despite "efficient machinery ... mint[ing] satisfactions" through "sparkling and gesticulating dust," Dismorr merely sits in a boulevard café, not a cinema, delighting in her consciousness (as did other literary modernists). Dismorr's alternation between mental images and those apparently in the external world suggests a homology between the activity of aware thinking (figured as a succession of images) and the unspooling of life itself, perhaps via cinema. Her poem's dancing motes may lie within a projection beam, or in filtered sunlight—it is this dissolving of materiality that is the actual subject of her work. In her first review of a talkie, *Hearts in Dixie*, Dorothy Richardson's interest lies in the changes the arrival of sound brings to spectatorial experience, recounted in the vicissitudes of her own reception of the newly audible image; she does not mention the film's title—*pace* her own column title, "Dialogue in Dixie"—until the last third of her essay.[43] Instead, like Dismorr, she traces out the back and forth motion between her own responses and the vision in front of her, in this case the racially charged instance of one of Hollywood's first all-black-cast sound films.

Djuna Barnes's allusory and febrile account of Walt Disney's cartoon *Night* is also far from a straightforward review, unexpectedly anchoring this film, one of the very few "Silly Symphony" films actually directed by Disney, deep within psychical and artistic history.[44] Barnes was a novelist, poet, playwright, and artist, as well as a journalist. In her column for *Theatre Guild Magazine*, "Playgoer's Almanac" (which was followed by one titled "The Wanton Playgoer," the two appearing sequentially during 1930–31), Barnes regularly covered the film world, alongside theater, in a subsection titled "Personal Eclipses," commenting on personalities (Anita Loos, Greta Garbo, Eisenstein arriving in Hollywood, P.G. Wodehouse's visit there, Joan Crawford, Chaplin, Tallulah Bankhead being drawn by Augustus John, and so on) and current topics (plastic surgery for screen acting, "it," musicians in Hollywood). Barnes's *Ladies Almanack* had recently been privately published in Paris, under the authorship of "A Lady of Fashion." This first edition of her *roman à clef* of the expatriate lesbian community (among those women featured was Janet Flanner) mimed the properties of the Elizabethan chapbook—popular, cheaply printed volumes composed in semi-verse.[45] In this *Almanack*, as in her "Playgoer's Almanac," including her review of *Night*, Barnes experimented with mock archaisms in combining text and graphics, and in using a profusion of idiosyncratic typographies replicating the look of hand-set type; extra-marginal artwork (in the form of bats, blots, moons, stars, and zodiacs) illustrated Barnes's movie observations.

Over her long career, Lejeune frequently varied her reviewing mode, using poetry and dialogue as well as prose. On occasion she incorporated poetry by others into her work, as in her insertion of Iris Barry's poem on the British cinema industry crisis into her own article on the topic.[46] Her verse about Warner Bros.' *Humoresque* constituted her second review of the film (on its suburban and provincial release in England). The germ for the poem lay within her prose review of the première written a few weeks before; Lejeune had earlier rendered the "one moment of good sense," of the poem, as: "she [Joan Crawford] mixed her drinks, put on a black sequin gown, and walked straight into the Atlantic. It seemed to me the only sensible thing she or anyone else did in the whole course of the film."[47] Through poetry, Lejeune revived her interest in the task of appreciation, while tersely truncating, through her superior and erudite poise, the film's melodramatic reach.

Reviews and criticism taking poetic form, while quite common in cinema's first half-century, have all but disappeared.[48] Another outmoded reviewing style is that represented by Margaret Anderson's letter on a filmed version of Ibsen's *Ghosts*.[49] Writing in the pages of the literary review she founded in 1914, her "Dear Mr. Ibsen" both invents a mock familiarity with the playwright, and apes the fan mail genre, creating a modernist parody of a lowly epistolary form, itself but a few years old.

In contrast to the above examples, a particular value of Colette's review of *The Cheat*, or of Evelyn Gerstein's reports on new Soviet films, lay in the way each writer's detailed descriptions evoked the film itself. An energetic American film and theater critic, Evelyn Gerstein followed her passion for Soviet cinema to Moscow, in 1935, to report on Eisenstein's latest shoots.[50] Her readers, living in the days before video, would probably never see these films. Soviet films of the 1920s and 1930s rarely enjoyed theatrical release abroad, and were often banned or censored for their radical content. *The Cheat* also suffered at the hands of the censor.[51] The evocation of rare prints and screenings, through words, was another important and influential service run by critics.

Arguably the most prolix film reporters of cinema's first half-century were Louella Parsons and Hedda Hopper. Parsons's and Hopper's careers were defined by, and intimately bound to, the film industry's changing fortunes, to ownership of the press, to their knowledgeable personal relationships with the famous and powerful, and to their own media images. And their significance lay less in any individual words they wrote than in their mass, and in the particular contours of their individual histories and public personas—for these reasons, the selection of a few lines from the many thousands they penned seems more arbitrary than for any other contributors to this collection.

Parsons, born in 1880, described her journalistic ethos as being "the first to know."[52] She began newspaper work on the Dixon (Illinois) Star, and then, in around 1910, moved to a stereopticon company in Chicago, thereafter joining the syndication room of the Chicago Tribune while crafting motion picture scenarios at night. In the early 1910s she was a story editor and writer for Essanay productions in Chicago, and in 1915 wrote a screenplay guide, How to Write for the "Movies".[53] After its serialization in the Tribune, demand merited a revised edition in 1917.

Parsons was well situated in Chicago. The city ran second only to New York as a center for filmgoing and other forms of mass entertainment. It was a transcontinental railway hub, and thus the ideal city from which to interview celebrities in transit.[54] Its geographical importance enhanced its development as a film distribution center, and, before the westward move of most film companies during the 1910s, as a center for film production. As mentioned in Part Three, Chicago distributor Carl Laemmle, future president of the Universal Picture Company, started his empire by opening nickelodeon theaters there early in 1906.

Parsons claimed later that she had written the original motion picture gossip column while working at the Chicago Record-Herald in 1915–17.[55] She ran her "Seen on the Screen" review column there, and "Answers to Questions," replying to readers' queries about performers, while also contributing to the Chicago Tribune. In May 1918 William Randolph Hearst's American absorbed the Record-Herald, and a month later Parsons took Richard Watts's place as motion picture editor of the New York Morning Telegraph. (Watts had been called up for the war effort.) A press release announcing the appointment stressed "live current gossip" and advised that "everyone with a motion picture secret to tell can send or give it to Miss Parsons."[56] In November 1923, Parsons was named motion picture editor of the American in New York, and by 1926, the year she actually moved to Los Angeles, she was motion picture editor for Hearst's Universal News Service.[57] Her columns were now being carried by the Los Angeles Examiner, the Denver Post, the Seattle Post-Intelligencer, the Portland (Oregon) Journal, and the Indianapolis Star, among others. In the 1930s, her weekly radio program inspired the Warner Bros. film Hollywood Hotel, in which Parsons got to play herself.

Hedda Hopper was five years younger than Parsons, born in 1885. At twenty-two she moved from Pennsylvannia to New York to act on stage and in film. In 1923, after divorcing her husband, and with a small son in tow, she moved to Hollywood where a meager film career followed—by the mid 1930s she was agreeing to work for $1,000 per picture, a sum she had earlier received per week.[58] Hopper and Parsons had met in New York, and after Hopper moved West she would write gossipy letters to Parsons, elements of which proved fertile to Parsons's column. (Hopper's tongue was sufficiently notorious to incite a Hollywood article about it well in advance of her writing career.[59]) In 1935, after dabbling in real estate, working for the cosmetics manufacturer Elizabeth Arden, and in radio, Hopper started a weekly column on Hollywood fashion for the Washington Post. Though short-lived, in 1937 the Esquire Features Syndicate approached her for another, "Hedda Hopper's Hollywood," which was quickly picked up by, among other papers, the Los Angeles Times.[60] In 1939 Hopper played a gossip columnist in George Cukor's filmed adaptation of Clare Booth Luce's The Women, a part she may have landed on the strength of her real-life reputation as much as on her acting talent.[61]

There has been much pondering and consideration of Parsons's and Hopper's relationship, and their much vaunted feuds. George Eells, their joint biographer, suggests that when Parsons's initial encouragement of her one-time source waned, the women's friendship ebbed, to be replaced by a professional rivalry in which each tried to out-scoop the other.[62] As recounted by Cari Beauchamp, the launch of Hopper's column in 1937 assumed a pre-existing antagonism with Parsons, who stayed away from the inaugural party.[63] A recent telemovie, in which Elizabeth Taylor took the part of Parsons, implied that the two women colluded in the public performance of their disagreements to advance their individual careers. Parsons's relationship with actress Marion Davies, long-time mistress of her employer William Randolph Hearst, has similarly fed the rumor mill. Although it is not clear whether Parsons was in fact privy to potentially scandalous information Hearst wished contained, Parsons actively promoted Davies in her columns, and loyally followed Hearst's editorial line.[64]

One power of all this gossip was its mirroring effect. By effectively playing Hopper and Parsons at their own game, the speculation undermined these women's professionalism, making them over into grotesque caricatures of prying and censorious femininity. In Jules Dassin's purported view, the way they "harried" filmmakers for over a quarter of a century was nothing less than a "tragedy."[65] Both were small-town born and bred, beginnings apparent in their approach to their work. By perfecting the gossip column format, subsequently used by reporters like Walter Winchell, Parsons (who favored items of romantic interest) was simply adapting the local social page with which she had opened her career. Hopper, in pursuit of controversy, but also motivated by personal animus and conservative convictions, assumed, in Eells's words, "the outlook of a small-minded, small-horizoned Hollywood provincial."[66] In their caricatures they emerged as narrow, ignorant, vindictive moral policewomen, a profile not dissimilar from that adhering to the middle-aged, film-reforming clubwomen discussed in Part Three; like this clubwoman stereotype, they hunted out scandal and the immorality it ostensibly portended.

Two stories exemplify the reportorial style that fed this reputation: Hopper's support of Joan Barry in her paternity suit against Charlie Chaplin in 1943/44, an opportunity for exercising her right-wing loathing of the Tramp, as well as for digging up dirt near the studio practice of forcing abortions on female stars; and Parsons's scoop on Ingrid Bergman's adulterous pregnancy (a child fathered by Roberto Rossellini) in 1949.[67] Their very public disclosure of these two conceptions is mindful of the traditional village figures of the gossip and scold: "gossips" were childbed helpers who, in the course of their work, acquired information on every man in a particular locality; the "scold" was a more vicious female whose tongue "harmed her man, her neighbors and by extension good moral order in the community."[68] Although both women worked in and with the products of the mass media, in positions and settings undeniably modern, their textual personas were Chaucerian. Wearing the pre-modern mantle, they became privy to intimate, potentially damaging acts of Hollywood village life, and bent on trading on their worth. Taking their careers overall, it is impossible to judge whether one was more the helper (as the gossip to women in childbirth), and the other more the harmer (as the scold who harmed everyone).

However parochial Parsons's and Hopper's outlook might have been—and Parsons never pretended otherwise, writing "Hollywood is my Podunk. I love it"—thanks to the dominance of American film, interest in their particular town was global.[69] As Katharine Fullerton Gerould had put it in the early 1920s, Hollywood's success had made it "a suburb of everytown in the country," requiring a phalanx of journalists to feed public appetite.[70] At its peak, over four hundred accredited reporters worked in Hollywood, producing 100,000 words per day, a figure only exceeded by the American political capital.[71]

The fan magazine came into being fueling and satiating this hunger. Inaugurated in 1911, in James Stuart Blackton's The Motion Picture Story Magazine (1911–1914), the format spawned titles on both sides of the Atlantic: Photoplay (1911–40, and, combined with Movie Mirror, 1941–46), Shadowland (1919–23), Filmplay (c. 1922), Screenland (from 1920), Screen Play (from 1925) Screen Stories (1929–75), Motion Picture Classic (1915–31), Movie Weekly (1921–25), Modern Screen and Movies (both from 1930), and Picture Play (1915–59, occasionally appearing under the alternate titles Charm, and Your Charm), among others, in the United States; and The Cinegoer (1916), Film Weekly (1928–1939, when it merged with The Picturegoer), The Picturegoer (under various titles, 1913–60) and Screen Pictorial (1931–39), among others, in Britain. Although fan magazines reviewed films (a practice by all accounts first introduced by Julian Johnson to Photoplay in November 1915), they had begun as story digests, gradually developing a focus of cultivating fan response by spreading word on stars—indeed, the rise of the fan magazine followed swiftly on the heels of the emergence of the star system itself, so that Gladys Hall was able to build her entire career interviewing celebrities.[72]

In 1922, a year of keen public interest in Hollywood in light of a succession of movie colony scandals, Photoplay claimed a circulation of two million per month.[73] Fan magazines were generally affordable at five cents to twenty-five cents per copy, and by the late 1910s and 1920s had built up a typically female audience of writers of the "mash note," "hypnotized" by the screen.[74] In addition to stories and photographs of the stars at home, their love life, and wardrobes, fan magazines offered beauty hints and fashion stories (often based on a particular performer's latest role), as well as fiction, and a plethora of advertising. Their built-in feedback mechanisms allowed fans to write to their favorite performers, respond to articles or questionnaires, and to enter competitions; the magazines then published their letters.[75] The resulting aura of amateurism and reader participation resembled the women's magazine itself, and, judging by both the advertising and the types of stories featured, it seems clear that the principal audience of the fan magazine was also female. Some, such as *Eve's Pictorial News, Women's Filmfare,* and *Girls' Cinema* (1920–32) addressed women and girls in their titles.[76] *Ivy Crane Wilson's Hollywood Album* might also have particularly invited female readership, even though its well-known namesake wrote on behalf of all film fans.[77]

Fan magazines additionally promised *savoir faire,* sometimes mapping knowledge of femininity onto knowledge of the movies themselves. The British magazine *Film Weekly* regularly published articles with this flavor, including discussion of the effects of images of women on real women watching, thereby deliberating on the representation of women.[78] Its columns argued that cinema had changed women generally, by teaching them forms of worldliness they could acquire by no other means, and by making them more independent and more equal partners of men.[79] At the same time, other writers chastised film for failing to represent the achievements and activities of contemporary women, and for ignoring the desires of their principally female audience (arguments later articulated by Joy Davidman for *New Masses* and Catherine de la Roche for the *Penguin Film Review*).[80] In "The IT-Less British Girl," May Edginton discussed British actresses' lack of a sex appeal that would register on film, pointing to the gap between the face before the camera and its filmed image, insisting that certain qualities of performers were not inherent but produced, the result of lighting, coiffure, make-up, and so on.[81] It seems that readers were allowed, even encouraged, to look critically at the medium, and to develop expertise and specialized viewing competence. An article might embrace and enjoy Hollywood illusion, but, at the same time, and sometimes in the same article, understand illusion to be just that.

It was in examining the phenomenom of the film star that writers appealed most strongly to this sophistication in readers, in distinguishing among stars' different constituent elements: their persona, including its material aspects; the instanciation of this persona in a specific performance; the human being (the unprocessed, if unreachable person) upon whose daily existence the star persona rested. In her short column on female vaudeville impersonator Julian Eltinge, now working on the screen (from about 1917 to 1920, and then briefly in 1925), Louella Parsons, in itemizing his efforts at shopping, wardrobing, and rehearsing, exposed the work entailed in the production of any femininity. (In 1919 Eltinge was to write a one-act farce with June Mathis, in which he also appeared, changing glamorous costumes for a show that combined live and filmed performance.[82]) Hedda Hopper displayed a comparable wisdom, this time of feminine millinery semaphore, in her autobiographical essay on the acting phase of her career, "The Hats in My Life."[83] The competing readings of Mae West's corsetting offered by Cecelia Ager and Colette also exemplify the way in which significance condensed above all onto the star's body, Colette's genuine appreciation of Mae West's mobile sexiness contrasting with Cecelia Ager's archness in sending West up.[84]

Freda Bruce Lockhart's obituary on Jean Harlow traced a working life in which "the real Jean Harlow," an "actual, plebian American girl … the simple sane person she really was," gradually emerged in the later films, after she had established a clause in her contract protecting her hair from ever being platinum again.[85] This effort to get to the "real" individual was an unrealizable task more typically forgone in favor of analysing and understanding a star personality as the historical product of a cocktail of roles, performances, and publicity machine maneuvers, in which any individual film was but one of a star's many manifestations. A fudging of the distinction between the working actress and her succession of working-girl roles was common in reports of Joan Crawford's and Bette Davis's careers. As Catherine de la Roche commented, "publicity saw to it that their [the stars'] private lives were an extension of their film roles."[86] Simone de Beauvoir's 1959 essay on Brigitte Bardot did not search for an underlying, real BB.[87] On the contrary, in her discussion of Roger Vadim's *And God Created Woman*, de Beauvoir's analysis alternates between Juliette, the character, and Bardot, the actress-cum-sex symbol, such that the two become almost melded.[88]

In some accounts, the star embodied Hollywood history: both Ruth Suckow and C.A. Lejeune found Mary Pickford to symbolize the audience's own, youthful filmgoing and, by extension, an earlier, simpler, and idealised Hollywood; while, for Suckow, Clara Bow was its "precocious adolescence," and Garbo, its "neurotic adolescence" and fluctuating love affair with the Old World.[89] Similarly, in a 1941 gloss on Gloria Swanson, *Vogue* critic Allene Talmey detailed Swanson's self-creation from Mack Sennett bathing beauty to sophisticated comedienne and minor European royalty, calling her a "mirror of the movies," one reflecting the movies' own current sense of "paralysing dignity."[90] Swanson's path paralleled the film industry's maturation from shop-front dive to cultural fixture of self-importance. Suckow's was a particularly distinctive and lengthy examination of stardom, one which berated the conventions of fan magazine discourse for conflating the personal and the factual in a refusal of the real tasks of criticism.[91] Suckow found female stars to bear the bulk of the burden of manifesting latent ideals on screen, of calibrating American values, but the essential quality of the American star system lay in the "jeering reduction to the bottom level" running through its journalism, which constrained the motion picture to the status of "unconscious social document" rather than art.[92]

Suckow's analysis illustrates an approach to film criticism that continues to flourish: film as the national barometer.[93] Whether referring to one film, none, or many, this discourse treated cinema as a mirror (however murky), or as a lens of national consciousness, or as a set of images which failed, whether by accident, design, or inevitability, to represent the truth of the country. Stars, for example, either incarnated ideals and trends already present, or distorted, flouted or even dangerously camouflaged national conditions, bringing new fantasies into being. In 1923, writing shortly after the scandals, Gerould found Hollywood to be "a symptom, not a cause; a state of mind, not a geographical entity."[94] In star preoccupation (which she found to be expressed through the fan papers, as Suckow had done, in a discourse she explicitly feminized by likening it to the "philosophy" of women's magazines) she saw nothing less than the twentieth century's attack on the puritan values of hard work, sacrifice, and deferred gratification. As a magnifying glass rather than a mirror, Hollywood advertised an imaginary geography, in which "the young and the ignorant expect to get the triumph without the toil, ... the reward without the sacrifice, the knowledge without the study."[95] (The wit of Barnes's "Ye Gossip's Tayle" lay in its deflationary confrontation with a fantastic geography of canted angles that existed nevertheless, recorded as she stumbled through a highly coded hierarchy of ethnic building styles in Hollywood.[96])

Individual film titles played no part in Gerould's analysis, but many other critics, interested to read the cinema's pressure gauge, turned precisely to screen renderings. In an early example of genre and mise-en-scène criticism, Flanner charged that the Western exposed a national hypocrisy; just as reformers were clinching the deal for prohibition, thousands were thrilling to William S. Hart's drinking. In the barroom counter scene and the hero's style of imbibing lay the country's "suppressed desires."[97] The Western's "picturization" of a "brave life of freedom" satisfied the audience's yearning for the same, perpetuating the false image of America as free, an ideology that could not be done without.[98]

Such critical unpacking of the American imaginary through cinema interested foreign observers as much as Americans. In a sweeping survey of two decades of American films, twenty-two-year-old British critic Penelope Houston looked to Hollywood for a "reflection of recent history, and a picture, idealised or realistic, of what the average American wants and fears."[99] She found two apparently different but "curiously similar" views dominating: an "unconfused" liberalism, and the Capraesque optimism of average Americans.[100] Together, these were working to make Hollywood both the national conscience and the national comforter. It showed problems, but resolved them by film's end, reflecting what "people believe to be the truth about themselves."[101] Houston's method made possible the critical premise of a national cinema, the films of which functioned as a mirror whose distortions the astute observer could interpret.

Rebecca West, travelling in the States in the late 1920s, found in American secularism forces which had taken religious form in Europe. Hollywood exemplified this displacement, both in the popular devotion it directed towards its idols, and in its deifying terminology.[102] (Gladys Hall's eulogy to Valentino would have exemplified this phenomenon in its immortalizing of stars.[103]) In also noting that this practice amounted to a modernization of Greek mythology, one which met a deep-seated and enduring need for female sacrifice, West's becomes one of several works to evaluate the movies as a representational system belonging to and helping to create a national mythos whose values contain either a general sexual pathology or a particularly gendered decay. For Barbara Deming, the "deeper story" of a group of recent Hollywood films, which intensified on-screen battles between men and women, "shadow[ed] forth deep-felt insecurity among us," symptoms of strained contemporary relations between the sexes, an observation Dilys Powell, interpreting the emerging phenomenon of film noir, was to share.[104] Her article on "The Black Film" details the maturing transposition of post-war male trauma into the manly codes of film noir.[105] Using the language of popular Freudianism, Deming's "Love Through a Film" spoke to Vogue readers of film's "compulsion to picture" and of "dream-reversal."[106] Her methodology proposed that while an isolated film portrayal might be trivial, "observed together," films were revelatory, making apparent underlying cultural and psychical patterns and desires.[107] (Here her contemporary association with Siegfried Kracauer is particularly palpable.[108])

The notion of cinema as a dream purveyor also interested anthropologist Margaret Mead, who looked to films "for indications of the way our national daydreams are developing and changing."[109] Hortense Powdermaker's book-length anthropological study of the movies, Hollywood, the Dream Factory also took the dream model, but instead of looking at Hollywood's images, she focused on the industry—the place and the people.[110] An anthropologist writing in the late 1940s, she explicitly refused the mirror analogy, for Hollywood was not a reflection "but a caricature of selected contemporary tendencies, which, in turn, leave their imprint on the movies."[111] By way of illustrating her method of relating Hollywood's product to its industrial and economic history, and to national culture generally, she proposed that the movies' pervasive happy endings served much more than the need for narrative closure; they betrayed studio executives' failures of nerve. The current Hollywood panic (due to economic uncertainty, McCarthyism and blacklisting, and labor unrest) was part of general post-war anxiety. In her final damning assessment, Hollywood was totalitarian, power-hungry, and amoral, manipulating people as property, and driven by a crisis mentality, all patterns echoed in wider American society.[112]

When Louella Parsons ignored the violent annexation of Albania when penning her film column in April 1939, she was roundly chastized; "In the Shadow of War," the next section of Part Four, displays critical personae far less tempered and casual. These writers identified and positioned themselves geographically, temporally, racially, and politically, as well as the cinemas they were assessing. Urgency replaced currency, and (in theory) the gossip of entertainment. Reporting on film culture in Berlin in 1932–33, Bryher argued that "the choice of films to see" was a matter of "respect for intellectual liberty" and, therefore, a relevant factor in the world's prospects for peace.[113] Aside from a cursory reference to Sagan's Mädchen in Uniform, and Pabst's Kameradschaft, she made no mention of particular titles.[114] Her task was rather to be critical of English interest in German film (a curiosity which she herself had fostered in writing for the international readership of Close Up), for such attention might eclipse concern for social and political conditions. When reporting on a Berlin film festival just two years previously, she had written: "I am back in Berlin and that means always a reawakening of life."[115] Now, in 1933, after the arrival of Adolf Hitler as National Socialist leader, Bryher replaced her exultation at Berlin's light-filled architecture with eyewitness accounts of fleeing refugees. In 1927, she had argued that filmed images of war could reveal war's true meaning.[116] Now, six years later, representation was not the issue. Rather, by exercising choice in "refusing to see films that are merely propaganda for any unjust system," patrons might incorporate cinemagoing into their protests against barbarism.[117]

Also reporting from Berlin, for the pacifist newspaper The New World in 1931, Dorothy Woodman compared German troops marching to battle in the First World War in the film Douamont with the sunbathing members of Germany's youth movement, pausing to note their curious, ominous silence, now that they were in the cinema with her, watching this account of their national past.[118] Ethel Mannin, in Paris reviewing Pabst's *Kameradschaft* six months later, linked the brotherhood of the French and German working classes, shown soldiering and mining in the film, to the hopeful, nascent internationalism of the contemporary French audience, but then reflected on the disarmament talks breaking down as she wrote.[119] Establishing this film (set immediately after the First World War) as "anti-war propaganda," she enlarged upon the theme, stitching features of the present (British dole queues, battle cruisers at harbor, the capitalist system, arms limitation) into an argument that refused "politician-made wars" in favor of a worker's revolution.[120]

Writings by African-American women also displayed such expansion from discussion of a particular film to that of pressing contemporary issues, the film seeming to disappear as the object of critical attention. In their columns reprinted here, neither Lillian Johnson nor Fredi Washington perform the basic task of reviewing: Johnson details African-American objections to the screening of *Gone with the Wind* (in relation to racial politics at home), while Washington evaluates stage and screen representations of African Americans in the light of a new European war.[121] As was the case for Bryher, here an audience's choice of film has a political significance beyond the meaning of any individual title; the fundamental concern is survival of democracy.

Johnson argued that the protest tactic of African-American picketing of *Gone with the Wind* was shortsighted in favoring immediate and possibly insignificant gains over lasting change—*Gone with the Wind*, whatever its limitations, was not the real "wolf" for the black audience. (Although Johnson does not mention it, no doubt some anger at the film derived from the unprecedented marketing campaign that had surrounded it, which had made it, in Tino Balio's words, the movie that "created the block-buster syndrome."[122]) African Americans (as all patrons), were having to pay jacked-up prices to this show, even as they were seeing it a year late (screening runs typically catered to white audiences first). One week later, in response to a reader's letter, Johnson pressed home her point that true criticism of the film could only come from those who had seen it; protesting in ignorance risked becoming protest because of ignorance, precisely the sort of ignorance that lay at the root of prejudice. She argued for a range of informed opinion, such as that her column and its exchange with readers made possible; variety was democracy's keystone.

Johnson was writing during the opening year of World War II, before Pearl Harbor. Invocation of democratic principles became yet more insistent once African Americans saw military action; they were fighting to defend countries, many of which colonized other blacks, in the name of a democracy in which they were second-class citizens. These circumstances prompted a new self-awareness, a demand for "militant" films showing the "New Negro," a pressure for new roles for black performers.[123] As Fredi Washington insisted, film would be part of this home-front battle.

Analysts of color had long been aware of films' profound racio-political dimensions.[124] In 1935, Loren Miller had written:

Fig. 4.4   Fredi Washington seated at typewriter, c. 1930s.

> English and American producers will not, indeed cannot afford, to make an honest
> picture dealing with so-called subject races. The whole future of the English capital-
> ist structure, with which the filmmakers are allied, depends to a great degree on
> the maintenance of "imperial authority" just as the American structure depends on
> "keeping the Negro in his place."[125]

But war stepped up demands for change. Critics argued that existing pictures of
African Americans were unusable in the struggle for democracy; needed instead
were images obeying a standard of veracity determined by black potential and
achievement, not by white-nurtured stereotypes. In addition, the war was giving
American blacks a new visibility, and a new international significance; they would be
"the yard stick by which freedom and equality will be measured for the oppressed
Negroes of British and French rule."[126]

Neither Johnson nor Washington hid their personae behind these arguments—
indeed both writers grounded their opinions in their own particular experience.
Johnson wrote of her Southern heritage, giving her analysis a class edge, while
Washington acknowledged criticism of her earlier, now questionable, acting roles.
(Perhaps here she refers to controversy over her mulatta character, Peola, in the
1934 film adaptation of Fannie Hurst's novel Imitation of Life.) Both of them take on
a superficial cinema divorced from black life.

Two other texts, written earlier, develop another, highly sophisticated reading
of film as the national barometer, in which film fuels a potent racial fantasy for
whites. While she does not mention film specifically, Eulalia Proctor's critical frame
in "The Bronze Age" in 1925 is echoed in Ruby Berkeley Goodwin's 1929 analysis
of Hollywood's recent fixation with "'pure' Negro types," published in the black
weekly, Flash.[127] Both satirically dismiss the "color fad"—white society's flirtation
with negritude in the 1920s—as a movement born of white enthrallment with the
image rather than the reality of African-American life, and assess it as yet another
empty trend, promising no lasting change for blacks.[128]

The entry of sound technology into these discussions, beginning in the late 1920s,
was contentious, and complex. Though some circles despised the talkie (including a coterie of Close Up writers), Geraldyn Dismond's careful cataloging of black
performers in American film, published in Close Up in 1929 (for its predominantly,
if not exclusively, international white audience) was decidedly optimistic, as were
many other responses.[129] Of Hearts in Dixie, white critic Robert Benchley wrote,

> It may be that the talking-movies must be participated in exclusively by Negroes,
> but, if so, then so be it. In the Negro the sound-picture has found its ideal pro-
> tagonist.... There is a quality in the Negro voice, an ease in its delivery and a sense
> of timing in reading the lines which make it the ideal medium for the talking-pic-
> ture.[130]

Blackness had been on the talkie agenda from the start, with Al Jolson's black-faced
utterance of "Mammy" in The Jazz Singer in 1927, popularly held to be the first sound
film. Discussion of voice and blackness was then to swirl around two films in
particular: Hearts in Dixie, touted as the first all-black musical, starring Stepin' Fetchit

and Clarence Muse, and *Hallelujah*, the second all-singing black cast motion picture, both being made in 1929, by Fox and MGM studios respectively.[131] In historical fact, sound was disastrous for African-American film culture: sound films were more expensive, spelling the demise of almost all black-owned, independent filmmaking companies—Oscar Micheaux's was one of the few to survive—so that black performers would subsequently only have the choice of working for whites.

In her survey, which was part of *Close Up*'s special issue on "the Negro and film," Dismond, an African-American reporter for the *Pittsburgh Courier* and the Baltimore *Afro-American* contended that sound pictures were the best yet vehicle for the Negro actor, making possible the display of black musical talent and the distinctive patterns of black voice and speech, showing the "Negro ... at his best."[132] While identifying individual films, Dismond primarily reviewed the film industry, describing prejudicial employment practices, and then suggesting the positive transformations that the new technology of sound might bring. Dismond's optimism in response to King Vidor's planned *Hallelujah* was inseparable from her belief in the efficacy of black filmic representation in both ameliorating the effects of white prejudice and stimulating black "race consciousness and self-respect."[133]

As noted in Part Two, female writers received the coming of film sound with a mixed response, but this view needs to be qualified on racial grounds, for sound may have had a different resonance for black than for white women. In *Their Eyes Were Watching God*, Zora Neale Hurston recalled the powerful rush of speaking, experienced by the inhabitants of Etonville on their porches at sundown, after being "tongueless, earless, eyeless conveniences all day long" in their work.[134] We might speculate on the elation accompanying hearing black voices emanating from the screen, even if the expense of sound technology effectively meant the rapid decline of independent black filmmaking in the United States (while it supported the erratic employment of black choirs for the musical scores of white films), and even as those voices might be ignorantly dismissed by white critics for their colloquialisms and incoherence.

One of the *Close Up* writers critical of the aesthetic possibilities of sound film was Dorothy Richardson, whose review of *Hearts in Dixie*, appearing in the issue of *Close Up* immediately subsequent to Dismond's, offered a negative counterpart to the latter's enthusiasm. Richardson wrote of her initial hope that the freshly audible medium might offer moviegoers a "new Kingdom."[135] Disappointed, the "intermittent dialogue" diminished her pleasure by demanding concentration upon the spoken word, which sapped the faculty of sight; dialogue was far more disruptive than intertitles which, "at the right moment," were "invisible."[136] Where *Hearts in Dixie*'s talk was incomprehensible to Richardson, she applauded its black singing, "rich Negro-laughter," and "Negro dancing," since these inhabited a place outside speech where sound, image, and movement might fuse as one, enhancing the fluency of film viewing rather than fracturing the viewer's focus.[137] Using the image of a growing plant (that figure already familiar from the writings of Dulac, Märten, Field, and Colette), the song of cotton pickers at work "emerged from the screen as naturally as a flower from its stalk," she wrote.[138]

Where Dismond praised the talkies as a new venue for the display of black performers and black life, Richardson concentrated on Dixie's (slim) promise of helping film to retain, if not expand, the kind of spectatorial allure and expressive repertoire it had enjoyed in the silent period. This must have been among the first, if not indeed the first sound film that Richardson was to see, so the question must arise as to how much, or in what ways, black presence in the film invited her dissection of the transforming medium. Rebecca Egger has argued that Richardson's white ears heard black speech at particular analytical cost, propelling her to experience "sound as a technology of miscegenation."[139] Must we infer that, for Richardson, "the Negro" was incompatible with cinema, or that black culture was yet one more of cinema's now many incompatible ingredients, a metonym for the invader sound, and particularly for spoken dialogue?

Richardson indicted talkies through the example of the first all-black cast musical; her complaints about African-American language alongside her praise for black song, dance, and laughter reproduce a classical pattern of racism, in which black talent for musical and physical performance is found "natural" (growing as a flower) while verbal articulation is not. Richardson drew upon this ingrained, stereotyping habit in the new company of a hybridizing art, using it to rank different qualities of sound and movement. In this, her choice of an all-black cast film made her case starker. As with the entire endeavor of this collection, however, we might also recall the historical nature of spectatorship, critical in discussions of the transition to sound. Both Donald Crafton and Alexander Walker have noted the difficulty of imagining or reconstructing audience response to early sound films.[140] Substandard sound screenings were apparently the occasion for laughter, especially in early 1929, in the rush to make films to meet "the unexpectedly strong demand for talkies."[141] Walker describes the British reception of recorded American speech as "acid," while Crafton notes the ideological reasons accompanying preferences for British English, which connoted class and culture.[142] The vernacular dialogue of Hearts in Dixie might well have been received outside the United States as a foreign language, in the way that the London cockney accents of Ken Loach's Riff Raff warranted subtitling in Manhattan. In the light of these possibilities, as well as in the light of Richardson's parsing of sound film in several other essays, and her enormous enthusiasm for music more generally (it is a constant throughout Pilgrimage; she interviewed the composer Antheil), it seems, ultimately, too hasty to dismiss her displeasure at the inadequacy of recorded speech solely on the grounds of racism, even if more work is needed to disentangle the aesthetic and political elements woven together in her discussion.[143]

Dismond had concluded that "the Negro movie actor [was] a means of getting acquainted with Negroes and under proper direction and sympathetic treatment [could] easily become a potent factor in our great struggle for better race relations," but within the African-American press, and elsewhere, there was disagreement as to what "proper direction" and "sympathetic treatment" was, as a comparison of Hazel Washington's and Fay Jackson's reviews of John Stahl's Imitation of Life illustrates.[144] During production, the film had fallen foul of the Production Code Administration

(PCA), since it included a character of black ancestry who might be mistaken for white, Fredi Washington's Peola. As Ruth Vasey's research ascertains, "the PCA was concerned that her light skin indicated a miscegenational relationship among her forebears," miscegenation being proscribed by the Code. (In answer, Universal Studios assured the PCA that this heritage would be explained as impossible through details in the plot, as is indeed the case—Peola's mother describes Peola's father as a light-skinned black man.) The PCA also asserted that such subjects drew fire in Southern states, limiting potential exhibition revenue, although, as it turned out, Imitation of Life had a very successful release overall.[145]

Washington's and Jackson's interest in the film was to reveal other dimensions of this debate. Washington, contributing to Opportunity, the journal of the National Urban League for Social Service Among Negroes, argued that the film's leading black characters were atypical, inconsistent, and untrue. She discerned in the film's treatment of a black woman passing a suggestion that all "Negroes want to be white," which amounted to nothing less than contempt for her race—actual African Americans would never want this.[146] Fay Jackson, writing for the Associated Negro Press, also focused on the film's portrait of the tragic mulatta, but found her to be no literary or dramatic convention. Rather, she was "convincingly TRUE to LIFE," a mirror for the aspirations of twelve million American blacks, her presence on screen a sign that Hollywood's treatment of black themes was improving.[147] In observing that Fredi Washington's performance was "true to her own life" (the actress was a light-skinned black who was taken for white in life) and "more convincing than any mere performer could have voiced," Jackson claimed an intensified reality for the film, for Washington was not acting but being herself.[148] While repeating the tendency of some star discourse to collapse the difference between performer and performance, in this case the conflation served Jackson's opinion that entertainment was not just entertainment when it came to African-American subjects.

Writings by African-American women in "The Critic's Hat" often display a tension between the desire to catalogue the achievement of black performers in the largely white world of cinema on the one hand (Dismond and Jackson), and the consequences of examining the significance of this achievement on the other (Proctor, Hazel Washington, and Goodwin).[149] The first group documents presence; the second finds divergent meaning for that presence. The actress Fredi Washington was representative of general black hope for Jackson; Hazel Washington, writing for Opportunity, was outraged by her role. Writing by white women that dealt with the relationship of women to cinema (such as that discussed earlier from Film Weekly) sometimes manifested similar strains, though arguably less was at stake. British actress Madeleine Carroll, writing in 1931, after the sound revolution, and on the eve of the release of Sarah and Son in Britain (a woman's film directed by Dorothy Arzner), lamented that "talkies [were] almost exclusively a man-made entertainment."[150] In "Making Movies for Women," Beth Brown, a screenwriter at MGM and Paramount, argued that films failed to address women adequately.[151] Writing in 1927, as a woman working in a world dominated by men, she argued that few of these men understood the preferences of the women who comprised "83 per cent" of their audience (preferences for romance, clothes, children, the lives of the rich, "gentle" humor, and "detail, detail, detail").[152] Carroll suggested that filmmakers should concentrate on roles more representative of contemporary women's work. If female performers were freed from the demand that they first appear beautiful, and if more women were involved in film production, representative roles and stories would eventuate. In 1948, Catherine de la Roche also called for film roles that would show women as an "integral part of reality" (an opportunity she felt film noir offered men but denied women) instead of ones that confined them to the business of "personal relationships," making them barely "members of society."[153] She also speculated that the challenge of portraying "modern women" might be met if "women had an equal share" in film production.[154]

Joy Davidman penned the most strident and far-reaching analysis of the poverty of female roles in her 1942 article for the pro-labor New Masses, "Women: Hollywood Version." Female film portrayals were "lagging behind the country" whose "half-unconscious war against the emancipation of women certainly [gave] unintended support to one of the tenets of fascism—the deliberate debasement of womanhood."[155] The answer lay not in hiring more women, however (they were already there, having little effect), nor in stepping up Hays Office efforts. No, the "true corrective" lay in "the education of the American people. When the people at last repudiate completely all expressions of male chauvinism, the movies will hastily follow suit."[156] Muriel Rukeyser's poem "Movie," also published in New Masses, gave a similarly scathing account of American cinema.[157] Using a limited poetic meter, Rukeyser described an artificial femininity—the lifeless female close-up, the hair adorned with a mechanical flower—to characterize the falsity of Hollywood's representation of the Depression. On film, "our country" (the United States) amounted to a conglomeration of stereotypical "Negroes," Western heroes, and ineffectual young lovers.[158] Against this make-believe Rukeyser posited a real America which would rise collectively, ultimately to destroy the lies produced on Hollywood backlots, as well as the sham democratic system that made them; in Rukeyser's poem, the movies' working-class audience recognizes the ideological operations of Hollywood fictions, and will bring about radical change in film production.

In understanding the "detail, detail, detail" so apparently beloved of the female audience, the responses of Harriette Underhill and Colette to the appearance of luxury on screen are instructive.[159] Colette enthusiastically endorsed the excesses of cinema in contrast to an audience's wartime poverty, and applauded the "millionaires who don't look as if they've rented their tuxedos by the week" in DeMille's The Cheat, while Underhill decried the imitation chinchilla rainment and plaster of Paris knickknacks of the on-screen wealthy.[160] Yet, if both writers employed the detail to argue their points, the detail nonetheless presented them with a certain problem. After delighting in the display of "lace, silk, furs" (and, just as importantly, in the restraint of this display), Colette seems to beg the question of the detail's real significance: "Is it only a combination of felicitous effects that brings us to this film and keeps us here? Or is it the more profound and less clear pleasure of seeing the crude "ciné" groping toward perfection...?"[161] Castigating Hollywood for its inability to portray accurately the modes and manners of the rich, and bemoaning the newly wealthy but aesthetically ignorant class that makes pictures (the result of American affluence), Underhill can no longer enjoy films. All she sees in them are errors of taste—the palm beach suit worn on a wintry New York New Year. If Underhill went to the movies to enjoy details, those same details spelled the end of her pleasure.

We can also discern a feminine focus on detail in the appetite for miniaturization of Antonia Dickson's review of the kinetoscope, the earliest critical essay on film included here, written for a popular illustrated monthly. Dickson poses as an eyewitness to the development of "our camera," the new "seeing machine," relishing the illusion of movement itself, its technological underpinnings, and the history of the apparatus, as well as the images and subjects on screen.[162] The languages of infancy and magic inspire her description of film viewing, as well as the lineage she establishes for it, a mixture of archaic knowledge, the sciences of optics and chemistry, and the model-scale toys of "babyland": "Looking into the recesses of this magical casket, bathed in the delicious glow of the incandescent light, the eye takes delighted cognizance of these tiny figures plying the motions of their mimic life with a vim, an ease and celerity which give substance to our fading dreams of elfindom."[163] This individualized show was accompanied, in the kineto-phonograph, by sound on disc, accessible through primitive earphones. Dickson claimed that the union of kinetoscope and phonograph, the goal of each technology's development, was ultimately "so perfect as to obliterate all lines of demarcation," though recent scholarly research suggests she is unlikely to have experienced such synchronic excellence.[164]

Dickson was evaluating cinema before the addition of one of its defining technological features—projection—and its corollary, the mass audience. Nevertheless, her account sets in play the technically oriented teleology that has been the hallmark of many histories of the cinema since. By the end of her essay, the kinetoscope not only exists but has a past and a future, its apogee to be a presentation of grand opera by "artists and musicians long dead."[165] Lucy France Pierce's overview accomplished a similar end thirteen years later by naming, finding ancestry, and sketching the oncoming years for the spectacle now named "the nickelodeon."[166] This renaming is significant, marking a movement in criticism away from a predominant tendency of describing mechanics (pace her account of the truculence of film sound) in favor of one of reviewing the audience and the hall (and the small price paid for admission), as well as the social significance and consequences of the new invention, for, now that "motographs" were "for the most part self-explanatory," making lecturers "superfluous," the question arose as to whether they were replacing the sermon, the newspaper, the saloon, or the schoolroom.[167] Pierce's use of figures—"ten thousand or more" theaters, "more than two hundred thousand people" in New York City—and her depiction of the audience—"the clerk, the mechanic, the student ... the mother with her brood"—were to become standard elements in accounts of the booming urban cinema business, as was the characterization of the nickelodeon as the workingman's academy.[168] But thirteen scant years after Dickson, Pierce made no mention of Edison's role in film's technical development—indeed she claimed French origins for it and noted a multiplicity of subsequent imitations. The article's conclusion, in a shift from patent wars, economics, and machinery to aesthetics, pondered "the curious resemblance to reality" of motographs shot on location, but ultimately preferred theater.[169] Here, in a rhetorical move that was a feature of attempts to discuss the moving picture as art, Pierce classicized her subject, giving it a heritage and a future by comparing the nickelodeon's pantomimic acting style to that of the "world's first plays," and by imagining the likelihood of longer films, more sophisticated shooting locations, and the possibility of literary adaptations.[170]

Another medium was to emerge within the years covered by this volume—television—and in 1938 Marie Seton responded with an early report on developments, one in which she singled out similar traits to those discerned by Dickson for the kinetoscope, but drew different conclusions: miniaturization was distasteful; the essence of the medium lay in the feelings it produced, in the inviting bridge it made between spectator and performer, and not in its technological base; the audience's stance and proximity to the screen were key, not peripheral matters unworthy of comment.[171] The problem was where, and how, to see television (in a department store, at home, in a cinema lobby?), and how to enable makers to manipulate and survive the tension of live broadcasting successfully. It was far too early, argued Seton, to evaluate television shows critically, but, in wondering in conclusion about television's true depths, she alighted on a telling insight, gleaned, paradoxically, from watching the broadcast of a stylized medieval morality play: television, too, had inherently emotional and propagandist properties. It had the power to convince when replicating the real live event, and the civic impact of this might intimidate, or incite, folk to duty.

Where Pierce asked of the new phenomenon, "what is it?" and set out to reply, the writers in the concluding group of Part Four, "The Limits of Criticism," asked of themselves, their craft, and the cinema, "what is the good of it?" They exhibit writerly fatigue with the medium, critical bad faith in the task of reviewing, and an exasperation at the confines of the job. In the words of Winifred Horrabin: "I did not 'assume' the mantle of Film Critic, it was shoved on to me ... all I know is that for the most part my heart is broken and my mind outraged by the stuff I have to go and look at."[172] After Winifred Horrabin asked her Tribune readers in 1941, "What films do YOU like?" she harkened back to her "early so-called Utopian-Socialist days ... [when] 'Comrade' had a real meaning," as did, perhaps, her job of reviewing.[173] Other journalists doubted the effects and value of their work: Elinor Gibbs reported that her views as a critic "often reflect[ed]" her opinion of herself as "a woman of very peculiar habits, or a delayed adolescent, or both."[174] Doubt and self-scrutiny continue in C.A. Lejeune's conversation with herself, during which she admits that, although she likes seeing films, she does not admire them, and in which, in a fit of circularity, she despairs of improving cinema.[175]

Katherine Anne Porter's letter written to the *New Masses* in support of Paul Strand's commissioned documentary on Mexican fishermen (*The Wave*, shot in 1934), indicted journalists for discouraging attendance, and for failing to adjust their criticism according to the particular subject before them. She defended the film's slow-paced, interwoven, and harmonious method of shooting and scoring against those American critics too "speedy" to take in its might. (These critics found the influence of Strand's still photography too strong, and at odds with the film's narrative movement.[176]) Porter had spent much time in Mexico, had met Sergei Eisenstein there while he was shooting *Que Viva Mexico!*, in 1931, and had written "Hacienda" based on this experience.[177] Her metaphor of "old fine Mexican blankets" to praise the woven construction of Strand film's matches Eisenstein's ideal description of film built as a serape.[178]

A final example is Iris Barry's poem "The Challenge," an adept satire of the British film industry.[179] On 8 May 1947, in a climate of severe post-war austerity, and in order to plug the dollar drain from the national economy, the British Labour government had announced a draconian 57 per cent *ad valorem* duty on all films imported from the United States, a measure dealing a dire blow to British film moguls J. Arthur Rank and Alexander Korda, who were each seeking a larger share of the American market at this time. (The tax's imposition alienated their American counterparts, who withdrew American films from the British circuit, effectively restricting British entry into United States territory.) Barry lampooned the seriousness with which the crisis was being discussed, sending up, through exaggeration, the portentous tone of cabinet-level discussions, as well as the idea that the mental health of the British public might be imperiled by withdrawal of American movies. She characterized Rank's and Korda's ambitions as imperialistic anachronisms.

Formally, "The Challenge" is proficient doggerel and Barry, a widely published if "minor" modernist poet, must have relished sharpening her wit in this somewhat debased manner. (We have seen Margaret Anderson engaged in a similar exercise in her mock fan letter to Ibsen.) But "The Challenge" is more than a witty piece of poetic slumming, for, in ridiculing the gravity with which the weak home cinema is being debated and mismanaged—whether as an item of foreign exchange in the Exchequer, or as an unsustainable instrument for morale-boosting in post-war life—Barry seems to imply that this very tone is beneath critical contempt, and that criticism can in fact do nothing against such disproportionate silliness. (If it were not so, one imagines, she would have written a reasoned essay rather than an amusing and "throwaway" piece of verse.)

Assembling "The Critic's Hat" gives an indication of the number of women evaluating films and of the impact of their long careers. A significant proportion of these critics attended to matters that have historically been understood as women's concerns, from the obstetric interests of Parsons and Hopper, to the commentary on fashion and luxury in Colette and Ager, to the analysis of women's film roles in de la Roche, Davidman, Brown, and Deming, to the attention to interior design and detail in Underhill and Brown. While mindful of the multitudinousness of female

Fig. 4.5   Gladys Hall at work, interviewing Peter Lawford in 1950.

opinions on the cinema, it seems worth pondering here whether dubiousness in the critic's role surfaces among women precisely because of their widespread perception of film as bearing crucially on life—because of their lesser inclination to take on film as an autonomous aesthetic system. For the critic does not actually make, but rather responds, albeit sometimes with real urgency. If "one woman goes a long way in any capacity," as Laura Riding put it, and if "activity is the mother of power,"[180] would not a woman rather take off the critic's hat and do something?

Writing on film in the final analysis was a job. Dorothy Richardson titled her regular *Close Up* column "Continuous Performance," meaning the exhibitor's habit of beginning the film again, as soon as it had ended. Moviegoers would sit down at any point during the screening, and leave where they had come in. Elinor Gibbs introduced her article on her job as a critic with a similar sentiment: "This is where I came in."[181] We too can leave where we came in, with Anna Steese Richardson's pointer that reviewing might be a stepping stone to employment in the film business. Writings on this subject are the focus of the next, and concluding, part.

SELECTIONS

Naming the Object

Wonders of the Kinetoscope (1895)
Antonia Dickson

What, broadly stated, without intermediate technicalities, are the nature and functions of [the] kinetoscope and kineto-phonograph? The first is a special application of photography, based upon the appearance of motion, gained by a graded series of images, following each other in rapid succession. Its functions are to give us the representation of life, not as the painting, the photograph or the statue represents it, frozen into a single attitude, but exhibiting all that wealth of movement and expression which makes up the sum of our restless existence. Of this class the kinetograph is the "taking" machine or specially constructed camera, in contradistinction to the kinetoscope or "seeing" machine. The kinetophonograph goes a step further. It is the union of the kinetoscope with the phonograph, the blending of visual impressions with their kindred sounds. The combined effect is life, with all its eloquent and insistent appeals to the senses of man. [...]

The dim suggestions of photography first engage our attention, as furnishing the basis of the kinetoscope. First, we have the exact but reversed image of exterior objects, observed by Porta, the Neapolitan philosopher, and caused by the admission of light through a small circular opening in a shutter, piercing into the recesses of a dark room and projected against a white screen—a veritable picture painted by the golden fingers of the sun.[1] Then the reversal of that image, by means of a convex lens placed in the tiny opening and combined with an ordinary mirror. Next, the innumerable attempts to capture this illusive phantasm [...] relative to the effect produced by light upon certain chemical substances, the selection of chloride of silver as yielding the best results, the application of the discovery in the hands of Fabricius and others [...].[2] Then came the resumption of the old dream by Daguerre and Niépce, the fruitful partnership of the twain, the final capture of the photographic image on a highly polished plate coated with iodized silver, the gradual development or bringing into view of the latent image by exposure to the fumes of vaporized mercury, and the final fixing or definite arrest of the picture by immersing it in a solution of hyposulphite of soda, which, removing the superfluous shadows engendered by the presence of the unaffected salts, left the picture bathed in those delicate gradations of light and shade which had marked the original.[3]

The basis of photography was now firmly established, and the later developments were smoothly progressive. [...]

So far, so good; we have caught the image, vivified its outlines, arrested it permanently and imbued it with the rotundity or angles of life. Still it is insensate and cold, lacking that motion which is the most suggestive feature of existence. The haunt of the enchanter has been laid bare and the imprisoned princesses revealed, but the sleep of enchantment still fetters their limbs, and who shall break the spell?

Curiously enough, the next link in the magic formula was found, not in the laboratories of science, but in the delicious trifles of babyland. Just about this time an ingenious contrivance was launched into the motley kingdom of toys, named the zoetrope, or "wheel of life," consisting of a cylinder, some ten inches wide, open at the top, around the lower and interior rim of which a series of pictures is placed, representing any given phase of animated life.

The cylinder is then rapidly rotated, and the eye of the spectator, being directed to the narrow and vertical slits which are cut in the outer surface, becomes aware of a certain spasmodic movement within. This simulated movement, as the reader probably knows, springs from a substitution of one portion of an attitude for another, so as to produce the effect of continuity upon the retina of the eye [...]. Every movement in life, whether it be a leap in the air, a bow, a courtesy, or a blow, consists of hundreds of intermediate positions, any one of which being omitted causes an awkward hiatus or break in the scale of motion. To this cause the abrupt and automatic movements of the zoetrope are referable. The wood cuts are of the rudest possible type, and taken at such wide intervals of time as to militate against the smooth merging of the one attitude into the other.[4] The idea, however, was powerfully suggestive, and as such commended itself to the attention of many leading photographic experts, who, working upon the plastic surface of the Maddox dry gelatine plate, were enabled to multiply the graded images, and so approximate the desired realism of effect.[5] Gelatine is the most sensitive material in the range of photographic appliances, lending itself when compounded with bromide of silver, with inconceivable swiftness and pliability to the desired results. Dr. Maddox became convinced of the latent possibilities of the compound [...]. After many experiments he succeeded in producing a plate so abnormally sensitive to the action of light as to admit of an impression being taken in a fraction of a second, whereas previously, with Daguerre, Niépce and others, about one minute to twenty seconds per impression was the limit consistent with the attainment of detail—an important stride in the direction of instantaneous photography. Not yet, however, was the goal achieved. Despite the improved facilities the speed was still defective; numbers of intermediate positions were unrecorded, and the gaps

Fig. 4.6   "The Kinetograph—Photographing a 'Serpentine' Dancer,"
from Antonia Dickson, "Wonders of the Kinetoscope."

between the fractions of attitude militated hopelessly against continuity and realism. It was then, in the year of grace 1887, that the exhaustive series of experiments was instituted of which the kinetoscope and kineto-phonograph are the perfected results, the working out of the problem being intrusted to Mr. W.K.L. Dickson, electrical engineer and chief of the electro-mining and photo-kinetographic departments, Edison laboratory, Orange, N.J.[6] The final outcome of these experiments was the adoption of a band of highly sensitive film, especially prepared. An ingenious mechanical device holds the film rigidly in place, while a shutter in the apparatus opens and allows a beam of light to enter. As soon as the shutter closes the film is jerked forward one inch to await the reopening of the shutter, this process being repeated forty-six times a second. [7] It will be seen that two agencies are principally instrumental in securing these swift results, the superior sensitiveness of the film and the smooth and rapid working of the stopping-and-starting device, the source of energy for which is supplied by a high-speed electrical motor.

In this connection it is interesting to note that were these spasmodic motions added up by themselves, exclusive of arrests, on the same principle that a train record is computed, independently of stoppages, the incredible speed of twenty-six miles an hour would be achieved.

The part played by the subjects is more trying and less mechanical. They are exposed either to the untempered glare of the sun, to the blinding effulgence of four parabolic manganese lamps, or to the light of twenty arc lamps, supplied with powerful reflectors, representing a total of fifty thousand candle power. In this searching light they go through their different performances, while our camera is hard at work storing up impressions for future reproduction. The next step after "taking" is to subject the images to the several processes of development, fixing, etc., after which they are connected with the necessary mechanical devices, and placed in a condition to be inspected by the public.

The most familiar adaptation of kinetoscopic methods is embraced in the "nickel and slot," a cabinet containing the electric motor and batteries which energize the mechanism regulating the movements of the film, the latter being in the form of a strip fifty feet long, cemented together at the ends, and making thus an endless band. Each picture when taken is actually only one inch in size, but is several times magnified. It is illuminated by an incandescent lamp whose rays are interrupted forty-six times a second while the pictures shoot past, the latter being only momentarily lighted up just as they reach the centre of the eye. So smooth is the mechanism, however, and so swift is the succession of graded pictures, that the mind or eye is aware of no break any more than would be perceived by the execution of movements in actual life. The effects produced, though more diminutive than when projected on a screen, are essentially realistic. Looking into the recesses of this magical casket, bathed in the delicious glow of the incandescent light, the eye takes delighted cognizance of these tiny figures plying the motions of their mimic life with a vim, an ease and celerity which give substance to our fading dreams of elfindom. Projected sterescopically, the results are finer still; life size is attained, together with a pleasing rotundity lacking in ordinary photographic displays, the general effect being greatly enhanced by a delicate tinting in three colors.[8]

The kinetoscope was complete; the visual impressions were as perfect as the imitative faculties of man could make them; sound alone was conspicuous by its absence, but the means of securing it were not far to seek. A timely accession had meanwhile been made to the ranks of Mr. Edison's scientific progeny—"A young lady," to quote the parent's own words, "who from her birth has spoken all languages, played all instruments and imitated all sounds, cooing with the babies, whistling with the birds, singing with operatic stars and discoursing with the philologists."[9]

This precocious genius was the phonograph, an instrument based upon the acoustic principles of the ear, and giving back with perfect fidelity the vocal footprints impressed upon its wax cylinders. An alliance was set on foot between the animated but soundless image of the kinetoscope and the invisible vocalism of the phonograph, with a view to complementing the deficiencies of each. Apart from the phonograph, the kinetoscope was a mere pantomimic display; divorced from the kinetoscope, the phonograph was a tantalizing suggestion of life, lacking the visible presence of those entities which furnished the sounds. It was as if a mortal should find himself transported to a realm of the Nibelung, balked by the Karnkappe or cap of darkness, which protected the unseen minstrels, and stretching vague hands of entreaty into the eloquent emptiness. It became evident that the means of relieving this painful suggestion of unfed senses lay in promoting a union of the two gifted specialists, Kinetoscope and Phonograph—a union so perfect as to obliterate all lines of demarcation—and to this task the experimental talent of the photographic atelier applied itself. [...] The phonograph is now mechanically and electrically linked with a specially constructed camera in such exact fashion as to admit of the sound record being taken simultaneously with the photographic impressions. Thus, when reproduced, the minutiae of expression or gesture will be found to be harmoniously combined with their appropriate gradations of sound, even to the delicate inflections of the lips in molding speech or song.

The stereoscopic projections are exhibited in an upper story of the main photographic building of the laboratory. The attendant preparations are sufficiently gloomy and mysterious to impress the uninitiate, and to suggest the awe-inspiring adjuncts of a medieval magician. The room is entirely draped with black, for the purpose of preventing any reflection from the circle of light emanating from the screen, and the projector is also concealed behind a curtain of the same ominous hue, a single peephole being left for the lens. A monotonous incantation is sustained, meanwhile, by the invisible electrical motor attached to the projector, and the climax is reached when into your startled scope of vision the figures project themselves, instinct with all the features of life, dancing, singing, gesturing, talking, swinging hammers, or weaving the dangerous intricacies of swordship, with absolute fidelity to life. So complete is the illusion that the mind is totally unprepared for the abrupt vanishing into darkness of these lively phantasmagoria.

The subjects for the kinetograph are taken in the Kinetographic Theatre, which occupies the centre of that cluster of auxiliary buildings which surrounds the laboratory. It is a peculiarly shaped and colored structure, too irregular for architectural classification, covered with paper coated with pitch and studded with numerous tin nails.[10] To the centre a movable roof is attached, which is easily lowered or lifted by a single pair of hands. This adjustable canopy is supplemented by an ingenious mechanical arrangement which admits of the building being swung upon a graphited centre, similar in principle to that of our river swinging bridges, so as to catch the full force of the sun [...]. The interior is as peculiar as the exterior. The lower end of the room is unlit by a single aperture, and is hung with black drapery. Against this sombre background the kinetographic stage is placed in such a position as to meet the fierce light falling down from the movable roof. The effect is marvelous, the figures standing out clear-cut and dazzling against the Stygian gloom of the background. At the other end of the room is a cell, lit by a lurid red window, which lends a Mephistophelian glow to the scene. This compartment is ultilized for the purpose of changing the films from the dark box to the kinetographic camera, and is linked to the rear of the stage by a diminutive railroad.

There is hardly a day affording the necessary solar conditions in which a motley procession may not be seen winding its way toward the Kinetographic Theatre. Boxing cats, performing monkeys, terriers and rats, bucking bronchos, trained bears, form the brute element in this unique company of players [...]. The human subjects are equally diverse. Truculent prize fighters and seductive bacchantes, contortionists and trapezists, jugglers, fencers, swordsmen and artisans are largely represented. Sandow leads the van, a modern Hercules, comely, stately and invincible, the embodiment of our classic ideals.[11] Later he will be seen balancing three-hundred-pound dumbbells as if they were balls of thistle-down on his mighty chest. Buffalo Bill marshals his heterogeneous suite—lustrous-eyed Moors and Arabs, turbaned and bejewelled; dashing Texan cowboys in shadowy sombreros and cavernous boots; sleepy-eyed Celestials and agile Japanese; fierce Cossacks and picturesque Albanians; impassive Indians in pomp of war paint and plumes.[12] These resolve themselves into strange combinations—into the Omaha war dance, the Sioux ghost dance and Indian war council; into wonderful feats of swordsmanship, lassoing and shooting. These scenes, one and all, point decisively to their final development, the kinetographic and kineto-phonographic drama.

Mr. Edison himself has no qualms of uncertainty on this subject. He says: "I believe that in coming years, by my own work and that of Dickson, Muybridge, Marey and others who will doubtless enter the field, grand opera can be given at the Metropolitan Opera House in New York, without any material change from the original and with artists and musicians long dead."[13]

[*Frank Leslie's Popular Monthly* (New York) 39:2, February 1895, pp. 245–51, excerpted.]

The Nickelodeon (1908)
Lucy France Pierce

"What is it?"

"The academy of the workingman, his pulpit, his newspaper, his club."

"Where is it located?"

"On every thoroughfare in every large city."

"Why was it established?

"To afford an inductive method of instructive entertainment for five cents."

"How is it governed and regulated?"

"By me," said the Chief of Police.[1]

"Is the nickelodeon a municipal institution?" finally questioned the investigator, as an officer of the law posted the weekly instruction of the Chief of Police in the entrance.

"It isn't, but it is good enough to be," replied Jane Addams.[2] "It is one of those peculiar mushroom growths in the amusement of a great city that sprang up suddenly, somehow, no one knows why, and it had to grow because the good in it was too big and splendid at rock bottom to allow the little evil to control and destroy it."

A fascinating ribbon of incandescent light wriggles around and around the word "Motion" strung out before the gaudy blue and yellow Moorish entrance, flaming with posters, which leads into the place itself. On the edge of the sidewalk the persuasive notes of the barker rise fitfully above the roar of the elevated trains. His eloquence in many cases stamps him as a person who might have been a United States senator, only he considered the show world less corrupt than politics. One can't miss him. He never permits it. An army of men and women and children, a million strong, march and countermarch past him nightly, past that flaming yellow entrance, as they spring out of the dark to plunge headlong into the dark again. How many thousands know no other light! They pause and look, startled, pleased, drawn by the brilliancy. The eloquence of the barker, the purring of a string band hold them. The conscious thought of relaxation, of recreation, is upon them. The subconscious desire of being a unit in the passing show seizes them. "It is only five cents!" coaxes the barker. "See the moving-picture show, see the wonders of Port Said to-night, and a shrieking comedy from real life, all for five cents. Step in this way and learn to laugh!" And the thousands venture.

Three years ago the nickelodeon was unknown. Cheaply made moving pictures on indifferent topics were utilized to fill up the bills of vaudeville theaters. As the machines became perfected, and every phase of life was drawn upon to enhance the novelty of motography—notice the new word—it was found expedient to create a place devoted solely to the bringing of this practical and inexhaustible form of entertainment to the people.

So vast a field of knowledge, of art, of science, of natural history, of political history, is embraced by motography to-day that it has become a liberal education in itself. In three years' time the nickelodeon has in truth become both a clubhouse and an academy for the workingman. Saloonkeepers have protested excitedly against its permanent establishment as a menace to their trade. The saloon has lost its hypocritical and pious cloak as the workingman's club. The nickelodeon now beckons to the saloon's former patron with arguments too strong to be withstood.

The nickelodeon's grasp on the public, then, is a fact to be reckoned with. It has become a nightly amusement ground of the masses and its influence is widespread and insidious. Ten thousand or more of these little theaters daily open their doors to the working people and the children of the great cities. More than two hundred thousand people find amusement within their doors in New York city every day. More than one hundred thousand pay admission into these theaters daily in Chicago alone.

There is no town of any size in the United States which does not contain at least one nickelodeon. It has become a kind of recreative school for the whole family. On Sunday with its religious subjects it takes the place of the sermon. On week days with its current events of the city, of the world, it takes the place of the newspaper. The clerk, the mechanic, the student, each with his "lady friend," the mother with her brood, young school-children in droves, spend the day and a greater part of the evening loitering in these places. They command a vaster patronage than any school or church. The nickelodeon is more varied than any other type of amusement. It presents its lessons more graphically, more stupendously, reproducing in heroic action life itself without the limitations of art. It is evident that so far-reaching and commanding an institution among the masses may work irreparable evil or boundless good.

Municipal ordinances in New York and Chicago covering the exhibition of what is termed immoral pictures, and a strict police censorship, ever vigilant, are reducing the baneful influences to the minimum.[3] All representation of criminal acts, violent scenes, or questionable social incidents calculated to arouse harmful emotions, is prohibited. Careful inspection is made of every picture which is thrown on the screen. A heavy fine is imposed for every infringement of the law. Its moral tone is thus carefully supervised.

The entertainment is invariably some kind of moving-picture exhibition. Songs and lectures by hired performers sometimes accompany certain series of pictures. Motographs are for the most part self-explanatory, and these interpreters are re-garded as superfluous, and are being done away with, or replaced by phonographic reproduction of the speech of the actors in each moving scene. Decorum in these little theaters is enforced. No persons, not properly attired in conventional business or street dress, are permitted to enter. This rule pertains for the most part to day laborers. Ushers are employed to enforce strict quiet and no smoking.

Few nickelodeons, no matter how gaudy or alluring on the outside, can be described as more than puritanically simple within. They are little more than academic halls, given over to a direct and vital appeal to the eye from the screen alone. Sometimes they are fitted up to look like the interior of a railway car, and the workingman may take a quick, imaginative journey into a strange land.[4] Sometimes it is a submarine boat, and he looks out (through the screen) to behold the giants of the deep hobnobbing with curiously humanlike mermen. And sometimes it is a thick jungle overhung with tangled growths, and by the aid of the phonograph he hears the very scream of almost real monkeys disporting themselves in what looks like a farther glimpse of a tropical wilderness. But usually it is only a plain, neat hall, scrupulously clean, with the usual uniformed group of ushers as in an ordinary theater, and a "ticket-chopper" at the door.

The sentimental side of life is far from being ignored. The *comédie humaine* in all its side-splitting drollery is reproduced from every quarter. It is at this point that art joins hands with science, and the esthetic and human side of life is presented with due regard to the canons of dramatic construction. Motographic comedy is therefore manufactured by a competent stage manager and a group of hired actors. The comedy is always a little incident, or perhaps an episode, devised by an expert, with a certain consideration for artistic development of plot, of natural, amusing climax, of dénouement or retributive justice. It is rehearsed in the open with nature's stage-setting, or with a background deep in a great city's heart with the voices of a great city for orchestral accompaniment. Thrown on the screen, these miniature comedies seem to reproduce life itself with its tender sentiment, its pantomime fun, its buffoonery, its last cry in farce.

The past year has developed a remarkable phase of mechanical amusement, housed in the nickelodeon, which may in time revolutionize the whole amusement world. The action of entire dramas of recogized artistic worth is now being projected to the screen, not in movement alone to satisfy the eye, but with the sound of the voices of living actors speaking the lines. This is accomplished in two ways: first by stationing a group of actual actors behind the screen, and second, by means of the phonograph synchronized with the kinetoscope or projecting machine. In the former case companies of actors are trained to follow the movement of the figures in the motographs, reciting the lines of the action as the play progresses on the screen, but always concealed from sight. In the second place science alone gives the whole show and its cost is then reduced to the minimum. [...]

The nickelodeon is still a novelty to a large portion of the public. Motography itself is still in its infancy. The talking machine is yet to be exactly synchronized with the projecting machine in order to avoid ridiculous lapses between speech and action at the screen. Yet the future is rich with promise. To create complete poise and exact concerted action is the mechanical problem of the hour. Considerable curiosity is being manifested in the possibilities of a device which claims to produce speech at the screen as if emanating from the throats of the figures in the picture. It is operated by electricity on the plan of the telephone. A switchboard erected on the stage behind the screen will receive impressions from a steel ribbon in the projecting cabinet and turn them into sound.

When some such invention has been exactly synchronized with the picture machine, it will materially change the working scheme of the world's theater. The first performance of a new play given in Paris or London will echo around the world in ten thousand simultaneous performances, giving not only the actual movement of the original actors, but the sound of their voices. The modus operandi is simple. Henri [sic] Bernstein will write tragedy for Sarah Bernhardt. The actress will rehearse her company to the point of perfection. A dress rehearsal will be given before the moto-camera and a giant talking machine loaded with blank disks. When the play is over a complete record has been obtained of both speech and action. Then any one may hang up a sheet anywhere, press the button, and the play is re-enacted exactly as the original—and for five cents!

But the dream of the mechanical world does not end there. Inventors behold in the nickelodeon the future forum of the race. With the progress of science it is destined to replace the lecture platform, the pulpit, books and the newspaper. It will become an institution where the people may pause to rest for a few moments, a quiet orderly little hall where silence is wholly enforced and where, on a huge screen, the human activity of the world is being shown almost simultaneously with the action of the event, with the very shouts, the cries, the speeches or what not, all transmitted by telephotography.

To the French nation the world is indebted for the most advanced strides in motography, for France was the pioneer, and all others have been her imitators.

The greatest film-makers in the world are two Parisian brothers whose reels are known and distributed around the globe.[5] The projecting machine has reached some degree of perfection in America. While it is generally known by the generic title of the cinematograph or kinetoscope, there are actually 120 patented machines fundamentally similar in principle, which have been placed upon the market under 120 different names. The result is confusing and misleading to the general public. These 120 patents are moving-picture machines, operated with a crank, an arc light, and a magazine which supports the reel on which the picture film is wound. They are similar in construction and identical in purpose. In the same way five or six variously twisted cognomens have been applied to as many modifications or improvements or inferior imitations (as you will) of the original talking machine known generally as a phonograph.

While it is announced by a famous French firm of moving-picture makers that their output last year reached the seven million dollar mark, it has been roughly estimated that the profits to American manufacturers of films and projecting machines amounted last year to $75,000,000. The middlemen, or rental agents, buy annually from the manufacturer $4,000,000 worth of films, from which they derive a rental from the exhibitor in the nickelodeon of $8,000,000. It requires an army of ninety thousand or more persons to conduct the rental agencies and the theaters proper. It is estimated that four times that number are employed in the manufacturing corps. In the season just past $65,000,000 were spent in paid admissions to the nickelodeon in the United States alone.

Competition has lately become very keen between French and American manufacturers. The American is better able to cope with native demands because he understands the taste of his own countrymen. However, it has been found that while French pictures are often immoral from a social standpoint, American ones have often been found to encourage violent crimes and daring deeds of robbery and brigandage. Such pictures invariably fail to pass the censorship of the police. [...]

Many outdoor productions and spectacles are made, the scenes portrayed being set on a huge outdoor stage, permitting aquatic feats by means of a tank of real water, equestrian feats with mounted riders, circus scenes, wild-west shows and all manner of spectacles impossible on the narrow confines of the stage of a real theater. The pictures when completed have in consequence a curious resemblance to reality, and when thrown on the screen are supposed to be motographs of actual life. Thus it is seen that art is still useful even in this age of growing mechanical amusement, especially since the god of the machine ignores the unities, and fails to regulate dramatic climax to a nicety, and more especially since the law of justice in real life ends the play with its inevitable dénouement of punishment or reward much too deliberately and slowly to suit the expediency of the man who cans the moving drama of life.

"Is this new thing for the theater?" a critical onlooker asked when he observed the process of an entire play being squeezed into a tin and laid on the shelf. "Is it a good thing for the theater?" he continued, thinking no doubt of the pretty inspired art of mere men, against the wonders of the machine. It is new, and yet it is as old as the drama itself. The world's first plays, though acted by living men, were in reality pantomimes. Even in later days when Rome took up the drama, actors depended almost exclusively upon movements of the body rather than facial expression, or tone and inflection of the voice, to convey their meaning. Motography is in fact a modern development in the classic art of pantomime.

[*The World To-day* (Chicago) 15, October 1908, pp. 1052–7, excerpted.]

Television Drama (1938)
Marie Seton

The television receiving set appeared almost furtively in a few large stores and cinema foyers in London about two years ago.[1] Since then it is estimated that some five thousand sets have found their way into private houses situated within the fifty-mile radius of London's highest point, Alexandra Palace, in which the first British television studio is housed.

Unlike the pioneers of the cinema who invested their own money in film production, the British pioneers of television programs are being sponsored by the British Broadcasting Corporation, who, most surprisingly, have made no attempt to graft radio technique onto this new medium.[2] Alexandra Palace is technically independent; the producers are allowed to experiment to their hearts' content. The result is a daily program of two and a half hour transmissions, which consist of outdoor televisings of the Derby, polo and how to plant vegetables, as well as studio productions of cabarets, circus acts, ballet and drama. Most programs also include newsreels and cartoon films, the movement of which I consider too rapid for successful televising.

It is still generally unsatisfactory to see television anywhere but in a private house, for unless the transmission is under the best conditions the present imperfections become so irritatingly obvious that they obscure the possibilities of the medium itself. On account of the nomadic character of shoppers and the excess of light in cinema foyers, almost every public viewing is a strain on the eyes and ears. At Alexandra Palace it is the general opinion that television, at its present stage of development, is intended to be seen at home by a few people who can adjust their chairs to suit their individual vision. This possibility of adjustment is extremely important since the screen is still too small to be comfortably viewed at a greater distance than from 4 to 6 feet. Within this range the essential quality of the medium, that is, its feeling of intimacy and the sense that the thing seen is really happening, is fully impressed upon the spectator. At a greater distance the eye, though it may see the objects on the screen distinctly, receives the impression that these small figures are unpleasantly artificial, like a world of midgets.

It is a waste of time to criticize television as though it were an established form of art or entertainment comparable to the theatre or cinema. Although the experiments in drama alone have been extensive and varied, no definite standards have been established by which to judge even the work of any particular producer.

During the last six months over sixty plays have been transmitted from Alexandra Palace. This does not include revues and cabarets, which are generally popular. A random list of productions suggests the variety of plays and styles: Clemence Dane's *Will Shakespeare*, condensed into the maximum transmitting time for a present program which is an hour and three-quarters; Pirandello's *Henry IV* with Ernest Milton; Eugene O'Neill's *Ah, Wilderness!*, and Elsie T. Schauffler's *Parnell*. Three other successful televisings were a modern-dress version of *Julius Caesar*, an adaptation of Chaucer's *Pardoner's Tale*, produced as a mime with the words spoken by an unseen actor, and Auden and Isherwood's play in verse, *The Ascent of F6*.

Most of the producers working at Alexandra Palace are young. They have come to television from different fields, and independently of radio. For instance, Denis Johnston, who recently joined the studio, has done most of his best work in connection with the Dublin Gate Theatre, while the experimental side of films produced Dallas Bower. Another producer, George More O'Farrell, had had experience in both theatre and film production; and the mime and puppet theatres were the training ground of Stephen Thomas and Jan Bussell. These producers now find themselves faced with certain identical problems no matter how their actual styles of production vary.

Usually four cameras are employed, differently angled. Since the producer must, during a second or two before the public receives the transmitted picture, select the best of two or possibly three of the different camera shots, he must, before rehearsals commence, work out carefully each shot of the four cameras employed and put them on paper.[3] Since the playing area for a scene is often as small as six square feet, and a single movement or gesture outside that range will invalidate the transmission, he must see that every move made by the actor is kept within the prescribed lines during rehearsal. During the actual transmission the producer can communicate from the "bridge" to the cameramen and sound technicians on the studio floor, but not to the actors. He is, therefore, virtually in the position of a conductor who is invisible to the first violinist. For all of these reasons he must be adept in making rapid decisions.

One great limitation imposed not only on every producer at Alexandra Palace, but also on the sole designer, Peter Bax, is the lack of space in the studios. There are only two studios, both 70×30 feet with a height of 25 feet. The maximum number of scenes which can be accommodated in each studio at one time is four, necessitating scenery of the simplest possible design.

With these limitations in mind it is interesting to examine four different types of production illustrated here—a realistic production of Jules Romains' *Dr. Knock*, the stylized mediaeval morality *Everyman*, a ballet which appeared in a cabaret called *Paddle Steamer*, and O'Neill's *The Emperor Jones*, in which camera work and scenery were particularly effective.

The cabaret, *Paddle Steamer*, was made in June 1937. The set, which occupied almost half the studio floor space, shows a stylized pleasure steamer of 1860. It is extremely simply constructed in order that every available foot can be utilized for different turns composed of a singer of sea-chanteys, a patter comedian with properties, as well as a ballet.

For Dr. Knock, produced by Eric Crozier in January 1938, the actors were all drawn from the legitimate theatre and employed a theatre technique more successfully than usual in television. For the fact that he has no audience but still is facing an invisible audience seems to put a great strain upon the stage actor, who is liable to fill the small television screen with too many fleeting movements of face and hands. The result is a blurred impression.

The Emperor Jones is another play in a number of short scenes, but unlike Dr. Knock the impression of space was greatly increased by an ingenious arrangement made by the producer, Dallas Bower. He treated the action as continuous so that after Jones entered the forest he was continually moving. In order to achieve this effect a semicircular set of the forest was constructed around three sides of the studio. Two cameras slowly followed the actor, keeping to a semicircular movement. [...] This method achieved a closely knit performance preventing any break in the mounting emotional intensity. Bower also experimented with trick photography for the appearance of the apparitions, adopting superimposition and other effects used in the cinema, and achieving quite good results.

Everyman, produced on Good Friday by Stephen Thomas, represents yet another type of drama, the masque, in which the speakers are not seen. It is a curious fact that this form, adapted as it is from plays of mediaeval origin, comes nearest to a perfect television performance. The ear can attend to the voice, while the eye concentrating on the independent action on the screen produces a balanced counterpoint. The fact that in Everyman the gestures were stylized and that symbolic masks were used produced a rhythmic impression much more clear and decisive than any so far created by a naturalistic performance. Morality plays such as Everyman and The Pardoner's Tale begin to explore the emotional—and also propagandist—quality inherent in television. They make one wonder if this medium is not the answer to all those theatrical and film theories which have attempted to overcome the barrier between the performer and spectator. Used for an actual event—an air raid, for example—the television camera would become a terrible instrument to convince an audience not only of the reality of something happening elsewhere at the moment they see it, but of such abstractions as "terror", "duty", "good" and "evil".

[Theatre Arts Monthly (New York) 22:12, December 1938, pp. 878–85, excerpted.]

Reviewing

The Cheat (1916)
Colette

In Paris this week, a movie theater has become an art school. A film and two of its principal actors are showing us what surprising innovations, what emotion, what natural and well-designed lighting can add to cinematic fiction. Every evening, writers, painters, composers, and dramatists come and come again to sit, contemplate, and comment, in low voices, like pupils.

To the genius of an Asian actor is added that of a director probably without equal; the heroine of the piece—vital, luminous, intelligent—almost completely escapes any sins of theatrical brusqueness or excess.[1] There is a beautiful luxuriating in lace, silk, furs—not to mention the expanses of skin and the tangle of limbs in the final melee, in which the principals hurl themselves unrestrainedly against each other. We cry "Miracle!"; not only do we have millionaires who don't look as if they've rented their tuxedoes by the week, but we also have characters on screen who are followed by their own shadows, their actual shadows, tragic or grotesque, of which until now the useless multiplicity of arc lamps has robbed us. A monochrome drapery, a sparkling bibelot, are enough to give us the impression of established and solid luxury. In an elegant interior there is no sign (is it possible?) of either a silk-quilted bed in the middle of the room or of a carved sideboard.

Since our French studios don't hesitate to lay on special trains, hire crowds, dam rivers and interrupt railroad service, buy villas and dynamite ships, I wish their magnificence would extend to furniture, women's dresses, men's clothing, to accessories that are stylish, complete, and irreproachable, to everything that the assiduity of the public has given it the right to demand.

Is it only a combination of felicitous effects that brings us to this film and keeps us there? Or is it the more profound and less clear pleasure of seeing the crude "ciné" groping toward perfection, the pleasure of divining what the future of the cinema must be when its makers will want that future, when its music will finally become its inevitable, irresistible collaborator, its interpreter; when the same slow waltz or the same comic-opera overture will no longer accompany, and impartially betray, a tragedy, a love duet, and an attempted murder?

Is wartime not the time, you think, for these frivolities? I disagree. America is building conservatories solely for cinema actors, who will study in them for two years. French commerce, French art, the French economy itself, will have something to worry about and suffer from after the war because of the progress the American cinema is making. Here as elsewhere, a special art of acting, the secret of onscreen walking, onscreen dancing, must inevitably be taught to classes of young actors.

I offer these young actors, as their first model, this Asiatic artist whose powerful immobility is eloquence itself. Let our aspiring ciné-actors hurry to see how, when his face is mute, his hand carries on the flow of his thought. Let them take to heart the menace and disdain in a motion of his eyebrow and how, in the instant when he is wounded, he creates the impression that his life is running out with his blood, without shuddering, without convulsively grimacing, with merely the progressive petrification of his Buddha's mask and the ecstatic darkening of his eyes.

[Originally titled "Cinema," *Excelsior* (Paris), 7 August 1916, p. 2, excerpted. Translated by Sarah W.R. Smith, Collected in *Colette at the Movies: Criticism and Screenplays*, ed. Alain and Odette Virmaux. New York: Frederick Ungar, 1980.]

Matinee (1918)
Jessie Dismorr

The Croisette trembles in the violent matutinal light; shapes quicken and pass;
    the day moves.[1] My nerves spring to the task of quisitiveness.
The secret of my success is a knowledge of the limitedness of time.
Economy is scientific: I understand the best outlay of intention.
Within this crazy shell, an efficient machinery mints satisfactions.
Your pity is a systematic mistake. I may yet grow arrogant on the wastage of
    other lives. The holes of my sack spill treasure.
Who but I should be susceptible to the naked pressure of things?
Between me and apprehension no passions draw their provoking dissimulative
    folds.
I have not clouded heaven with the incense of personal demand.
Myself and the universe are two entities. Those unique terms admit the
    possibility of clean intercourse.
All liaisons smell of an inferior social grade; but alliance can dispense with
    fusion and touch.
I treat with respect the sparkling and gesticulating dust that confronts me: of it
    are compounded fruits and diamonds, superb adolescents, fine manners.

This pigment, disposed by the ultimate vibrations of force, paints the universe in
     a contemporary mode.
I am glad it is up-to-date and ephemeral; that I am to be diverted by a
     succession of fantasies.
The static cannot claim my approval. I live in the act of departure.
     Eternity is for those who can dispose of an amplitude of time.
Pattern is enough. I pray you, do not mention the soul.
Give me detail and the ardent ceremonial of commonplaces that means nothing.
Oh, the ennui of inconceivable space! My travelling spirit will taste too soon of
     emptiness.
I thrill to the microsopic. I plunder the close-packed cells and burrows of life.
The local has always the richness of brocade: it is worth while to explore the
     design.
I spell happiness out of dots and dashes; a ray, a tone, the insignificance of a
     dangling leaf.
Provided it has a factual existence the least atom will suffice my need.
But I cannot stomach shadows. It is certain that the physical round world would
     fit my mouth like a lolly-pop.
You ask: To what end this petty and ephemeral business, this last push of
     human sensation?
Is one then a neophyte in philosophy, demanding reasons and results?
I proclaim life to the end a piece of artistry, essentially idle and exquisite.
The trinkets stored within my coffin shall outlast my dust.

[The Little Review (Chicago) 4:11, March 1918, pp. 31–2.]

Three Russian Movies (1929)
Evelyn Gerstein

Ever since the days of Potemkin, that lyrical and precipitous prelude to revolution,
the Russian films have been more or less vitriolically involved in revolution, to
the bland exclusion of other agents provocateurs in the cinematic dance. There was
Ten Days That Shook the World, Eisenstein's brilliant and crushing panorama of the last
tumultuous days under the provisional government; The End of St. Petersburg, Pudovkin's
more personal recounting of the same cataclysmic happenings; Mother, Pudovkin's
still unpublicized film from Gorki's tale, and others of less violent note.[1]

But the Russian film is now beginning to emerge somewhat from its volcanic
preoccupation with those same ten days and the more literal aspects of revolution.
The mise-en-scène is shifting now, and instead of a St. Petersburg perpetually en route
to becoming Leningrad, and the gargantuan figures of Peter the Great and various
of his lesser kinsmen and their horses shot from every conceivable angle, the motifs

are now the luxuriant wheat fields of the far-lying provinces; the primitive marriage rites of Stravinsky's Les Noces, celebrated cinematically in The Village of Sin; the bare, bleak fastnesses of Mongolia and the temple dances of the Lamas in Storm Over Asia; the French Commune of the brief 1870's in The New Babylon; and the Russian farmers going modern with tractors and such in The General Line—Eisenstein's latest film that will not arrive here until the late fall.

And so while the rest of this animated "movie" world is silhouetting its voice with a theme song, and adulterating its legends to comply with the regimen of artless blue Sundays in the provinces, the Russians have been hard at it evoking folk ballads from all over the steppes and Siberia; ballads with variations, as themes for their questing cameras.[2] Even in the least of their films there is a wildness, a touch of that Rabelaisian ecstasy that only seeps into Hollywood tenth-hand and guaranteed censor pure. The Russian intellectual, after a century of cerebration in Siberia, has gone dynamic, at last, in the kino studios of Moscow.

The Village of Sin, known abroad as The Peasant Women of Riazan, made by one of the first women directors in Russia, Preobrashenskaya, once a disciple of Meyerhold and Tairov, and by turns actress, lecturer, stage manager and director, is one of the first to take to the fields with a camera since Potemkin uncovered the revolution.[3] Although its camera technique belongs to the Eisenstein–Pudovkin school, its motif takes it back to the old pastoral manner of the cruder, more naive Polikushka, Taras Bulba, and Czar Ivan the Terrible.

Eisenstein and Pudovkin are the cinema merchants of war, but Preobrashenskaya has gone back stage in the Ukraine, when the war was on, and only the old men and the young boys were left to reap in the fields with the women. Wheat ripples in the wind, with a swift rhythmic movement; the fields are lush and budding; the reapers stride through the wheat, triumphant and elemental.

War is only something dreamed of. It has no place in this world; in these long sloping fields with the squat, earthy women laying strips of cotton to bleach in the sun or straddling their ancient rafts in the river, to beat their clothes; in the apple orchards where the sun dances impressionist ballets on the grass; with the slim, Russian Ophelia riding to her marriage on a wagon piled high with great, rowdy Katinkas and drunken accordion players and horses wreathed with flowers and ribands.

And then, the village bell tolls. The reapers rush through the shining fields, mere motes of light against the turbulent wheat, figments in a mosaic, insignificant now; no longer gods, but men who go to war. A Russian idyll, like all the other French and German and English idylls, shivered to bits by war.

It is a Russian pastoral into which the figure of Vassilissa enters disconcertingly. Vassilissa, the independent, who refuses to be another of the bartered brides, who takes herself off, in ignominy, with her blacksmith, without benefit of clergy or father's blessing, and rises to heights of feminine dominance in this village of men with the currents of independence the war brings Russian women. Her theme is a triumphant major one, to offset the tragedy of Anna, Ophelia of the steppes. Pudovkin would have carried the tale into the trenches, but Preobrashenskaya is interested only in the women who are left, the blatant seduction of Anna by her father-in-law, lord of his lands and women, and the birth of their child.

It is spring again. The village Katinkas are rowdy and triumphant in the return of the men from the front. Only Anna flees from her husband, hair streaming in the wind, away from the steaming Katinkas, into the river where the girls have thrown their wreaths. Recriminations for the men, but it is Vassilissa, the independent, who sees the future coolly, and takes the child away to the children's home the war has made possible.

Again, in *Storm Over Asia*, it is Pudovkin, that humanist in science in the guise of a film director, who did war with such magnificent fury and agonized lyricism in *The End of St. Petersburg*, who has shifted his camera toward the hills, in this instance of a Mongolia, windblown and strange to the movie screen. And with a fierce and withering clarity, this arch realist has filmed that whole panorama of Mongol types in their febrile struggle to exist.

By a series of swift dissolutions he has his setting: the long barren plains with a solitary round grass hut; the hunter pursuing his fox to the edge of a mound of sand; the chanting, bargaining priest; the bronzed withered old woman, staunch as the tight, windswept trees that cling to the rocks; all that pungent drama of warring races and impact of civilizations and mores. Like *Moana*, *Nanook of the North* and *Chang*, it belongs to the exotic school of ethnography, but it is far more plangent and riddling than any of these. It is all staged and manoeuvred, even to the primitive ritual dances of the Lamas. A swift, picaresque portrait of a hunting people of the hills and the bitter haggle for skins, that ends in a mad symbolical windstorm that sends English generals and soldiers and rocks and sand and rifles and trees all whirling through space to the tune of a Mongol ride to victory.

Pudovkin lacks the stern creative touch of Eisenstein, his ability to think quite abstractly of civilizations and masses. He is more immediate, impetuous and ironical. Eisenstein is the scientist, aloof and unimpassioned. Pudovkin is more personal and flamboyant. Yet there are stretches of dullness in his *Storm Over Asia*, a flagrant literalness that is never in Eisenstein's films. Eisenstein's technique of the mass has dissipated itself in Pudovkin into a mannerism that sometimes degenerates into a formula.

So in turn, this Eisenstein–Pudovkin realism has excited a new school of cinema lefts, with a name, a platform and a policy. Self-styled and labelled the F.E.X.'s, less briefly interpreted as the "school of eccentric cinema," which stems in turn from "the factory of eccentric actors," they are captained and doctrined by Trauberg and Kozintsev, who made *The New Babylon*, and Vertov, whose *Man With the Camera* is still en camera.[4]

The New Babylon, like the *Ballet Mécanique*, *Emak Bakia*, and *The Fall of the House of Usher*, is abstract, but it is an abstract of ideas and associated images, rather than of objects made animate. It is a film that heralds a strange new generation of "movies," in which the accent is on the symbolic and psychological, rather than on the slim, bare facts of a physical shadow reality.

It captures a mood, a galaxy of moods, and the spirit of a people and an age, with a swift and mordant photographic art.

Superficially, it is the Paris of Degas and the impressionists, of ballets and bustles, of cafes and department stores, of the intellectual and the wispy haired slut, of hysterics and debauchery and despair and *élan*. Rows of dancing girls slip in and out of vaporous close-ups; a drunken wag hops madly about on one foot, parasols whirl, and the Germans ride on through the night to Paris. The war is the cello accompaniment in the bass.[5] Here is Paris of the siege and the commune, in a chaotic series of staccato scenes that sear.

One must stand off and let the ballet merge, at a distance, as with the impressionists. For this is imaginative cinema, limning its images subtly and irresistibly, with a continuity that is not that of the drama or narrative, as is Pudovkin's, but of cinema. This is impressionism, the core of the cinema, an impressionism that is choreographic in its feeling for rhythm and the ensemble; a subtler, more fluid symbolism than that of the presiding bronze ghosts of Peter and his descendants. It is really a variation of the stream of consciousness technique, but it is objective, rather than introspective.

The New Babylon marks the entry of a new cinema, that is abstract and satiric, self conscious, selective and cinematic. These young directors have grown sophisticated in the cinema; they have learned from Eisenstein and Pudovkin, but in their whole concept of the "movies" as an art, in the sheer rigor of their photography that has two blacks that have never been achieved before on the screen, they have leaped far ahead. In time, the style may become the *raison d'être*; but all of these Russians, as yet, are too irresistibly grounded in the soil for that.

["Three Russian Movies: Expressionism Gives Way to the Realities,"
Theatre Guild Magazine (New York), October 1929, pp. 14–16.

Metropolis (1927)
Winifred Horrabin

Nobody ever went to see a film hoping as much as I hoped from *Metropolis*. Here, at last, was a treat in store, for not only was the camera work by Freund and Rittau, but Franz [sic] Lang was director, and I have been severely told off lately for not knowing more about these fellows and the work they are doing.[1] Also the story promised much—a drama of exploiters and exploited.... I came away amazed, thrilled, and depressed!

Metropolis must be seen and talked about because it is an amazing piece of work in its appeal to the eye, in its gigantic conception and use of space and light, amazing in the expert and marvellous camera work, and last, but by no means least, amazing in the futility of its story. "The story does not matter," says someone, but I must contradict, in loud and emphatic terms. All that splendid technical work, all that emotion expressed in light and shadow, all those great dominating machines and rushing crowds, are used for one purpose only, to convey to the audience a piece of futility that leaves one's mind slipping its gears!

It is just because the other work is so excellent that one misses so terribly the essential brainwork at the back of the whole thing. The feeling of dismay at the end of the film caused by the poor quality of the film story almost counteracts the emotional value of the camera work. It seems to me stupid to be able to express emotion so well and to use it on a piffling yarn. If this is all that stands between an intelligent public and Hollywood then we are lost indeed; for Hollywood itself never produced anything worse than the end of Metropolis, where capital ("Brain") and Labour ("Hand") shake hands at the door of a cathedral, while the millionaire's son and the "bewtiful" daughter of the people embrace in the background.

It seems incredible that anyone who can use crowds like Lang uses them, can use light and darkness so wonderfully, can realise the strength and cruelty of machinery and the helplessness of man before it, could lend himself and his art for two minutes to the piffle expressed, not only in the captions, but in the whole meaning and drift of the film. The only solution of the mystery must be that Lang, like many another master craftsman, cannot see the wood for the trees. His own work is so superlatively good that he fails to see the badness of the other person's material.

The story is by Thea von Harbou, his wife, and the sooner he is rescued from her the better, if this is the best she can do.[2] Surely Germany, after a war and a revolution, contains some young men and women who understand the gigantic forces that are moving society at the present time, who will write a film story that does not make a futile individual love story the main theme. We need something that has the quality of Toller's Masses and Man, something that has real "roots," and shows us what this film purports to show us, "a vision of the future."[3] Every class conscious worker should try to see Metropolis in spite of what I have said about the story. We know our own story and can read our own lesson into the film. I do not agree with a critic in another Socialist paper who thinks that there is a "message" for the average Daily Mail mis-educated wage-slave in it, unless the message is that it is better to "stay put" than to involve yourself and your family in wasteful revolt.

[Lansbury's Labour Weekly (London), 9 April 1927, p. 4.]

Emasculating Ibsen (1915)
Margaret Anderson

Dear Mr. Ibsen: I hope this letter finds you well as it leeves us the same.[1] The reason why I write you is that I seen your play called Ghosts at the Bijou Movie Theater last night and I thought it was so grand that I had to tell you.[2] I thought it was awful the way poor Mr. Alving is always seeing that hand which was pulling his hair out of the past.[3] And it was awful too the way poor Mr. Alving crawled across the floor on his stomich and pulled the poison offn the icebox before he killed himself. The way his poor, dear mother suffered, that was terrible. She was such a strong, brave woman that I cried for her all the time. And The Rev. Manders he was such a real swell minister that my heart was all torn watching him.[4] It ain't natural for everybody to be so good as ministers because they ain't got so much time and don't read the Bible so often. But he was certainly all there when it came to pureness and kindness. But even if the play was awful it was just grand the lesson that it taught. I sent my friend to see it and he thought it was swell. He said the kissing scenes where the terrible Cap. Alving hugs the different ladies was real stuff and that the lesson against the evils of drink was good for the young. This is what I want to write you about, Mr. Ibsen. We're going to organize a West Side Ibsen Prohibition Club and make you honary president. I wish therefor you will write the club a letter or better if you will write a sequil to the movie play *Ghosts* we will put it on at the club. I know how hard it is to have movie plays accepted because I have done some myself but if you don't write the sequil I will write it and send it to the Mutual people who put the first part on.[5] I am certain they will take it because I will make it just so strong and powerful a sermon against the evils of drink as what you did. With best regards and hopes for your future success, I am your friend,

Mobbie Mag.[6]

P.S. For the reader: The wet nurses who minister to the mob have put our old friend Ibsen into diapers and give him to their patients to play with. The cherubic little fellow is kicking up his dimpled heels and thriving well in all the movie houses.

[Margaret Anderson writing as Mobbie Mag, *The Little Review* (Chicago) 2:5, August 1915, p. 36.]

Personal Eclipses (1930)
Djuna Barnes

The high point of the month, the *Silly Symphonys*, cartoon drawings dealing with Nature and the seasons, bugs, animals, birds & fish.[1] At their best akin to genius, love, sorrow, death, & impinging on that realm in which we are afraid of what we are afraid we are fearing. The fireflies in the symphony *Night* give one that same historic feeling of beauty & murder, lost and gone, that the sight of the Napoleonic bee brings up when it is seen in a tapestry shuddering in the wind of time & tradition.

[From "Playgoer's Almanac," *Theatre Guild Magazine*, September 1930, p. 34, excerpted.]

Fig. 4.7   Djuna Barnes by Berenice Abbott, mid 1920s.

Humoresque (1947)
C.A. Lejeune

In this long rapture of pretence
There is one moment of good sense,
When Crawford (J.), a female souse,
Displays a modicum of *nous*.

On hearing Wagner's *Liebestod*
Performed the way it wasn't wrote,
She proves her musical devotion
By walking straight into the ocean.

[*The Observer*, 6 July 1947, p. 2.[1]]

The Negro Actor and the American Movies (1929)
Geraldyn Dismond

The Negro actor and the part he has played in the development of the American movie is one of the most interesting phases of what is now one of America's greatest industries. Because no true picture of American life can be drawn without the Negro, his advent into the movies was inevitable; but also because of the prejudices which have hampered and retarded him since his coming to America, his debut was delayed. To be perfectly frank, the Negro entered the movies through a back door, labelled "servants' entrance". However, beggars cannot be choosers, and it is to his credit that he accepted the parts assigned to him, made good and opened the door for bigger things.

In order to better appreciate the attitude of the white producer toward Negro talent, we must keep in mind the change in the social status of the group. To put it briefly, at the time of the Civil War, the northern white man considered the Negro a black angel without wings, about whom he must busy himself in spirit and deed.[1] On the other hand, the southern white man detested Negroes in general and liked his particular blacks. After the Negro had been given his freedom, there soon arose the feeling that he was an economic and social menace and we find him depicted everywhere as a rapist. Then the white dilettante, exhausted with trying to find new thrills, stumbled over the Negro and exclaimed, "See what we have overlooked! These beloved vagabonds! Our own Negroes, right here at home!" And voila!—Black became the fad.

These types of thinking have influenced the development of the Negro as part of the moving picture game. Within the remembrance of all of us and still in some pictures and stage productions, we find whites blacked up for indifferent imitations of their dark brothers. But more and more is the practice falling into disrepute.

The old cry that Negroes with ability cannot be found has not held water. In fact, it has been conclusively proven that under the proper director, the Negro turns out some of the best acting on the American screen and stage. A people of many emotions with an inherent sense of humour, and a love for play, they do not find it difficult to express themselves in action, or to bring to that expression the genuineness and enjoyment they feel. Nevertheless, excuse after excuse has been made to keep the Negro off the silver sheet and it was the servants of white stars, who as individuals, first got the breaks.

For example, Oscar Smith, who came to the Paramount Studios nine years ago as the personal servant of Wallace Reid, and at present owns the bootblack stand at the studio, has worked in two hundred pictures and has recently received a contract exclusively for Paramount talking pictures.[2] Stepin Fetchit, who is billed as the star in the William Fox all-talkie Hearts in Dixie was the porter on the Fox lots.[3] Carolynne Snowden, who played opposite Fetchit in In Old Kentucky was also a lady's maid for a prominent star.[4] And so it went. Another point is also true. They worked in the early days in character. By that I mean, often the star's maid went on as her maid, provided she could be made to look homely and black enough. And all Negroes, perhaps with one or two exceptions, were cast as menials and as comedy characters.

As for the exceptions, they were for the most part African chiefs and the members of their tribes. One, however, I do recall from my first experiences with movies. He is Noble Johnson of whom practically nothing is heard now in connection with Negroes.[5] The last time I saw him, he was playing the part of a Mexican bandit, and rumor has it that he owns considerable stock in the company for which he works and is used for all parts calling for a swarthy skin. The other two unusual individuals are Sunshine Sammy and Farina, the juvenile favourites of the Hal Roach—Our Gang Comedies.[6]

Negroes in any great numbers were first used for atmosphere—for mobs, levee and plantation, native African jungle and popular black belt cabaret scenes. Griffith's The Birth of a Nation, which, by the way, employed the old rape idea, and for that reason was so distasteful to Negroes, is an excellent example of the Negro as atmosphere. West of Zanzibar, a popular Lon Chaney film, and the Stanley in Africa pictures used large groups of Negroes for the jungle scenes.

The next move on the part of producers was evident. Isolated Negro characters and Negroes as atmosphere were combined for the Universal feature production, Uncle Tom's Cabin, with James B. Lowe as Uncle Tom.[7] Not all Negro parts, however, even in this picture, were assigned to Negroes. Topsy, Liza, her husband and baby were played by whites, but up to the introduction of the "Talkies", Uncle Tom's Cabin was the outstanding accomplishment of the Negro in the movie world.

It is significant that with the coming of talkies, the first all-Negro feature pictures were attempted by the big companies. White America has always made much of the fact that all Negroes can sing and dance. Moreover, it is supposed to get particular pleasure out of the Negro's dialect, his queer colloquialisms, and his quaint humour. The movie of yesterday, to be sure, let him dance, but his greatest charm was lost by silence. With the talkie, the Negro is at his best. Now he can be heard in song and speech. And no one who has seen the William Fox *Hearts in Dixie*, featuring Stepin Fetchit, Clarence Muse and Eugene Jackson, or Al Christie's *Melancholy Dame*, an Octavus Roy Cohen all-taking comedy with Evelyn Preer, Eddie Thompson and Spencer Williams, will disagree with the fact that the Negro's voice can be a thing of beauty in spite of the mechanics of this new venture in the art of the movies.[8]

Of these two Negro all-talkies which are now playing Broadway, *Hearts in Dixie* is by far the most pretentious. The story as such, is nil. Here indeed, we have the "beloved vagabond". It does embody the idea, however, that some Negroes are not superstitious and are anxious to better themselves, and is a rather entertaining picture of plantation life; but it lacks substance. You were ever conscious of the fact that the producers were not interested in the plot, but rather in the talking and singing sequence. The ensemble singing and the voice of Clarence Muse were decided contributions and well worth the price of admission. *The Melancholy Dame*, a short comedy with little music or dancing, depends principally upon its comic dialogue which is given in the best Octavus Roy Cohen dialect, for its interest. Incidentally, Mr. Cohen, himself, directed the picture.

Of course, it is generally believed that the Metro–Goldwyn–Mayer production, *Hallelujah*, will be the ace of the all-Negro talking pictures. King Vidor is directing. Daniel Haynes, formerly of *Show Boat*, has the principal role and is supported by Nina May McKenney [sic] of the *Blackbirds of 1929*; Victoria Spivey, a "blues" recording artist; Fannie DeKnight, who played in *Lula Belle*; Langdon Grey, a non-professional, and 375 extras.[9] There are forty singing sequences, including folk songs, spirituals, work songs and blues. Eva Jessye, a Negro, who has compiled a book of spirituals and trained the original "Dixie Jubilee Choir", is directing the music.[10] The story, which is devoid of propaganda, is that of a country boy who temporarily succumbs to the wiles of a woman, is beset with tragedy, and ultimately finds peace. It is a known fact that several studios are holding up all-Negro productions until the fate of *Hallelujah* has been pronounced.

In the meantime, *Show Boat*, a talkie using the present American Show Boat Company of both blacks and whites, has been made by Universal and had its première at Miami and Palm Beach, March 17th; Ethel Waters, greatest comedienne of her race, and Mamie Smith, blues singer of note, have been signed up by Warner Brothers for Vitaphone comedies; Sissle and Blake, internationally famous kings of syncopation, have been released by Warner Brothers; Christie Studio is preparing another Negro film; Eric Von Stroheim is working on the Negro sequence of *The Swamp*, and John Ford's *Strong Boy* is using a large number of Negroes.[11]

Three by-products have resulted from this slow recognition of the Negro as movie material—Negro film corporations, Negro and white film corporations, and white corporations, all for the production of Negro pictures. They have the same motives, namely, to present Negro films about and for Negroes, showing them not as fools and servants, but as human beings with the same emotions, desires and weaknesses as other people's; and to share in the profits of this great industry. Of this group, perhaps the three best known companies are The Micheaux Pictures Company of New York City, an all-coloured concern whose latest releases are *The Wages of Sin* and *The Broken Violin*; The Colored Players Film Corporation of Philadelphia, a white concern, which produced three favorites—*A Prince of His People*, *Ten Nights in a Barroom*, starring Charles Gilpin, and *Children of Fate*; and the Liberty Photoplays, Inc., of Boston, a mixed company, no picture of which I have seen.[12] There is a rumor of the formation in New York City of The Tono-Film, an all-Negro corporation, for exclusive Negro talking pictures and that its officers and directors will include Paul Robeson, Noble Sissle, Maceo Pinkard, Earl and Maurice Dancer, J.C. Johnson, F.E. Miller and Will Vodery, all of whom are known in America and abroad.[13] So far, the pictures released by this group have been second rate in subject matter, direction and photography, but they do keep before the public the great possibilities of the Negro in movies.

In conclusion, it must be conceded by the most skeptical that the Negro has at last become an integral part of the Motion Picture Industry. And his benefits will be more than monetary. Because of the Negro movie, many a prejudiced white who would not accept a Negro unless as a servant, will be compelled to admit that at least he can be something else; many an indifferent white will be beguiled into a positive attitude of friendliness; many a Negro will have his race-consciousness and self-respect stimulated. In short, the Negro movie actor is a means of getting acquainted with Negroes and under proper direction and sympathetic treatment can easily become a potent factor in our great struggle for better race relations. And the talkie which is being despised in certain artistic circles is giving him the great opportunity to prove his right to a place on the screen.

[Geraldyn Dismond, "well-known American Negro writer," in *Close Up* (Territet and London) 5:2, August 1929, pp. 90–97.]

Dialogue in Dixie (1929)[1]
Dorothy Richardson

Meekly punctual, clasping our prejudices in what might just possibly prove to be a last embrace, we entered the familiar twilight: the softly-gilded interior twilight, the shared, living quietude, still fresh and morning-new in their strange power. We could not be cheated altogether. We might be about to enter a new kingdom. Curiosity joined battle with fear and was winning when upon the dark screen appeared the silent signal: the oblong of rosy light, net-curtained. In a moment we were holding back our laughter, rueful laughter that told us how much, unawares, we had been hoping. For here was fear to match our own: the steady octopus eye, the absurdly waving tentacles of good salesmanship. The show was condemning itself in advance. We breathed freely, we grew magnanimous. We would make allowances. We were about to see the crude, the newly-born. We grew willing to abandon our demand for the frozen window-sill in favour of a subscription for a comfortable cradle. Ages seemed to have passed since we sat facing that netted oblong, ages since the small curtains has slid apart to the sound of a distressingly animated conversation. We had wandered, moralising; recalled the birth of gramophone and pianola, remember that a medium is a medium, and that just as those are justified who attempt to teach us how to appreciate Music, and the Royal Academy, and Selfridge's so most certainly, how certainly we had not until later any conception, must those be justified who attempt to teach us how to hear Talkies.[2] We remembered also Miss Rebecca West's noble confession of willingness to grow accustomed to listening to speakers all of whom suffer from cleft-palate...

Cleft-palate is a fresher coin of the descriptive currency than the "adenoids" worn almost to transparency by the realists. Nevertheless adenoids, large and powerful, at once mufflers and sounding-boards, were the most immediate obstacle to communication between ourselves and the semi-circle of young persons on the screen, stars, seated ostensibly in council over speech-films. Their respective mouths opened upon their words widely, like those of fish, like those of ventriloquists' dummies, those of people giving lessons in lip-reading. And the normal pace of speech was slowed to match the effort. [...]

The introductory lesson over, the alphabet presumably mastered and our confidence presumably gained by the bevy of bright young people with the manners of those who ruinously gossip to children of a treat in store, we were confronted by a soloist, the simulacrum of a tall sad gentleman who, with voice well-pitched—conquest of medium?—but necessarily (?) slow and laboriously precise in enunciation, and with pauses between each brief phrase after the manner of one dictating to a shorthand-typist, gave us, on behalf of the Negro race, a verbose paraphrase of Shylock's specification of the claims of the Jew to be considered human.[3] He vanished, and here were the cotton-fields: sambos and mammies at work, piccaninnies at play—film, restored to its senses by music. Not, this time, the musical accompaniment possessing, as we have remarked before, the power, be it never so inappropriate provided it is not obtrusively ill-executed, to unify seer and seen and give to what is portrayed both colour and sound—but music utterly lovely, that emerged from the screen as naturally as a flower from its stalk: the voices of the cotton-gatherers in song. Film opera flowed through our imagination. Song, partly no doubt by reason of the difference between spoken word and sustained sound, got through the adenoidal obstruction and, because the sound was distributed rather than localised upon a single form, kept the medium intact. Here was foreshadowed the noble acceptable twin of the silent film.

The singing ceased, giving place to a *dead* silence and the photograph of a cotton-field. The gap, suddenly yawning between ourselves—flung back into such a seat of such a cinema on such a date—and the instantly flattened, colourless moving photograph, featured the subdued hissing of the projector. Apparatus rampant: the theatre, ourselves, the screen, the mechanisms, all fallen apart into competitive singleness. Now for it, we thought. Now for dialogue. Now for careful listening to careful enunciation and indistinctness in hideous partnership. A mighty bass voice leapt from the screen, the mellowest, deepest, tenderest bass in the world, Negro-bass richly booming against adenoidal barrier and reverberating: perfectly unintelligible. A huge cotton-gatherer had made a joke. Four jokes in succession made he, each smothered in sound, each followed by lush chorus of Negro-laughter, film laughter, film-opera again, noble partner of silent film.

And so it was all through: rich Negro-laughter, Negro-dancing, of bodies whose disforming western garb could not conceal the tiger-like flow of muscles. Pure film alternating with the emergence of one after another of the persons of the drama into annihilating speech. Scenes in which only the natural dramatic power of the actors gave meaning to what was said and said, except by a shrill-voiced woman or so and here and there the piercing voice of a child, in a way fatal to any sustained reaction: slow, enunciatory, monstrous. Perhaps only a temporary necessity, as the fixed expressionless eyes of the actors—result of concentration on microphone—may be temporary?

But the hold-up, the funeral march of words, more distracting than the worst achievements of declamatory, fustian drama, was not the most destructive factor. This was supplied by the diminution of the faculty of *seeing*—cinematography is a visual art reaching the mind through the eyes alone—by means of the necessity for concentrating upon hearing the spoken word. Music and song demand only a distributed hearing which works directly as enhancement rather than diminution of the faculty of seeing. But concentrated listening is immediately fatal to cinematography. Imagine, to take the crudest of examples,—the loss of power suffered by representations of passionate volubility—the virago, the girl with a grievance, the puzzled foreigner—if these inimitable floods of verbiage could be heard.... In all its modes, pure-film talk is more moving than heard speech. Concentration upon spoken words reveals more clearly than anything else the hiatus between screen and stage. In becoming suddenly vocal, *locally* vocal amidst a surrounding silence, photograph reveals its photographicality. In demanding for the films the peculiar attention necessary to spoken drama all, cinematographically, is lost; for no gain.

The play featured the pathos and humour of Negro life in the southern States and was, whenever the film had a chance, deeply moving; whenever these people were acting, moving, walking, singing, dancing, living in hope and love and joy and fear. But the certainty of intermittent dialogue ruined the whole. When it was over the brightness of our certainty as to the ultimate fate of the speech-film was the brighter for our sense of having found more in a silent film—seen on the pot-luck system the day before—that happened to be in every way the awful irreducible minimum, than in this ambitious pudding of incompatible ingredients.

The photography was good to excellent. Actors all black and therefore all more than good. A satisfying, sentimental *genre picture*—genuinely sentimental, quite free from sentimentality—might be made of it by cutting out the speeches which served only to blur what was already abundantly clear, and substituting continuous obligato of musical sound.

If the technical difficulties of speech are ultimately overcome, the results, like the results of the addition to silent film of any kind of realistic sound, will always be disastrous. No spoken film will ever be able to hold a candle to silent drama, will ever be so "speaking."

"As we were going to press," the August *Close Up* came in and we read Mr. Herring's notes on *Hearts in Dixie*. Mr. Herring bears a lamp, a torch, electric torch kindly directed backwards, as boldly he advances amongst the shadows of what is yet to be, for the benefit of those who follow *rallentando*. We respect his pronouncements and are filled, therefore, with an unholy joy in believing that for once-in-a-way we may blow a statement of his own down the wind, down a north-easter, *sans façon*. One does not need to temper winds to lambs with all their wool in place. Therefore: As a fair-minded young Englishman Mr. Herring is for giving the Talkies their chance and their due even though his conscience refuses to allow any claim they may make for a place in the same universe as the sound-film proper. He has taken the trouble to consider their possibilities. One of these he finds realised in *Hearts in Dixie* at the moment when the white doctor, having drawn the sheet from the body of the mother who has been treated by a Voodoo woman, and bent for a moment, scrutinising, stands up with his declaration: "All the time," says Mr. Herring, "we see his face. Then his words cut across, 'she's been dead for three days'. Now, in a silent film, the visual thing would have been broken" and he concludes his remarks on the incident by describing it as "the odd spectacle of talkies assisting visual continuity."

We do not deny the possibility here suggested, but if this incident is to stand for realisation then the possibility is not worth pursuing. For though not quite the stentorian announcement of the guest-ushering butler, the doctor's statement inevitably had to be announcement, clear announcement in the first place to us, the audience, and incidentally to the sorrowing relatives to whom, in actuality let us hope, he would have spoken rather differently. The shock got home, not because its vehicle was the spoken word with the tragic picture still there before our eyes, but by virtue of its unexpectedness. It would have lost nothing and, relatively to the method of carefully-featured vocal announcement, have gained much by being put across in sub-title. But since Mr. Herring objects that sub-title would have interfered with visual continuity, we must remind him that the right caption at the right moment is invisible. It flows unnoticed into visual continuity. It is, moreover, audible, more intimately audible than the spoken word. It is the swift voice within the mind. "She's been dead three days" was dramatic, not cinematographic, and the incident would have gained enormously if the white doctor had acted his knowledge of the unknown death, if he had reverently replaced those sheets and shown his inability to help. To be sure we should not have known about the three days. What matter?

["Continuous Performance: Dialogue in Dixie," *Close Up* (Territet and London) 5:3, September 1929, pp. 211–18, excerpted.]

The Star

Is Julian Eltinge, Impersonator of Women, Going to Wed? (1917)
Louella O. Parsons

Julian Eltinge, deft impersonator of feminine charm, has moved his lares and penates to the moving picture studio for keeps, and there he plans to remain.[1] He is not in pictures for the golden shekels pouring into his coffers but because he likes the screen and because he likes to make pictures.

Mr. Eltinge is independently rich and doesn't have to work at anything he doesn't like, and so when he looked me in the eye and said he was in pictures "until death do us part" I believed him.

Out in Hollywood, where a coterie of old friends made pictures during the day and paid social visits in the evening, Julian Eltinge acquired a love of California's sunshine. He liked so much living within a stone's throw of the Tellegens, the Deans and the Elliott Dexters that he decided to build himself a home.[2]

Mme. Farrar Tellegen and Julian Eltinge were childhood friends, and a very delightful grown-up friendship has developed between him and this pictorial prima donna. The stage's most eligible bachelor has charms, brains and a good voice, and is much sought after as a dinner guest. So far he has remained heart whole and fancy free, but he is building a wonderful home in Hollywood, and his parents are remaining behind in New York, all of which leads one to speculate on many things.

*

Will there be a bride to act as hostess in the new Eltinge mansion?

Is Mr. Eltinge planning to steal a march on his friends and take some beautiful lady to the coast on a wedding trip? Or perhaps his dream lady is living in California and he is planning to wed her when he returns to California.

We can only wonder and guess, for Mr. Eltinge is noncommittal and smiles mysteriously when anyone suggests a bride as necessary for the beautiful new home.

Someone asked him one day why he, a man who has so much to offer a woman—wealth, brains, and good looks—has never married. He replied promptly: "Oh, but you see I know what women's clothes cost."

When Mr. Eltinge went West the first time to make his initial appearance in pictures it took him months to get ready. He had a double wardrobe to prepare, and the clothes he took with him for his pseudo lady were no cheap department store bargains.

The clever impersonator is a study of connoisseur in women's wearing apparel. He studies the lady of his creation as carefully as any professional beauty studies her own face and form. For weeks Julian Eltinge visited the most exclusive shops of Fifth avenue to get the sort of frocks and hats he had in mind.

One of the cheerful things about his screen preparation was the hours he spent having these frocks fitted. He thought being a woman had many disadvantages, but standing for hours and being fitted to feminine garb is to his way of thinking the last word in hard work.

❦

But having gowns and other feminine fripperies fitted has its compensation, for it permitted Mr. Eltinge to make his debut in pictures well shod and well groomed. He went to the coast with sixty-four gowns and thirty-two hats, all of them expensive and carefully selected. No actress ever had a better assortment of this woman's weapon than Mr. Eltinge carried with him.

He hasn't begun to wear them all, and it certainly will make some of those little extra girls' hearts beat fast with despair when they think of all of those delectable gowns lying idle. But they will not be idle very long, for Mr. Eltinge hopes to start work very soon, before his frocks have time to go out of style.

His female impersonations are the most unique thing in filmland. There isn't anyone else who has succeeded in bringing to the screen so correct an imitation of a smartly frocked woman, and for that reason Mr. Eltinge has been much in demand by producers. But even so his friends are urging him to make a few pictures without his double character.

He is a good type and could succeed as well, I think, in juvenile leads as in his dual roles. He, like all stars who have made a hit in one particular line, is dying to try his wings and fly in another direction. I could tell when I talked with him the idea of playing a straight part had taken root most strongly, and Julian Eltinge will never be satisfied until he has had a chance to play such a part on the screen.

A lucky man, one might safely say, in summing up all the things Dame Fortune has bestowed upon this actor—good looks, wealth, a mother who studies his every whim, a father who is his constant companion and pal, success, and enough money to carry out his taste in architecture. Everything, one might say, but the chatelaine for his house. Indeed, it looks suspicious, and it would not surprise his host of friends if one day a beautiful lady would sit at the head of that table.

"Only," said one of his friends whimsically, "wouldn't it be the devil's own job to dress in good-looking creations to keep Julian at home. He knows so well what's what in correct gowning."

["Is Julian Eltinge, Impersonator of Women, Going to Wed? New California Home, All Complete Except for a Woman at the Other End of the Table, and Man With 64 Gowns Has a Wise Smile," *Chicago Sunday Herald Features Magazine* 37:32, 16 December 1917, p. 5. Photographs of Julian Eltinge from original article.]

Rudolph Valentino:
The Sheik and *The Son of the Sheik* (1926)
Winifred Horrabin

It seems a curious thing that in the desert, where beards are as plentiful as leaves in Vallombrosa—the desert of the films, that is—no bearded man ever seems to be successful in love. Even an ordinary moustache draws a blank. Only the clean-shaven prosper in the abduction line of business. Perhaps it is that whiskers interfere with romance; and nothing must do that, not even the idiosyncrasies of the local inhabitants.

To those who have read *Arabia Deserta*, and who know therefore that tapeworm, scabies, and ophthalmia are among the minor joys of desert life, the splendiferousness of Rudolph Valentino seems a little exaggerated; but the great British public is not "realist" and has not read Doughty, and to them the desert spells romance with a capital "R."[1]

It is no use being highbrow and sneering at it. Just because of the drabness of the system, just because of the ordinariness of their everyday life, the invincible spirit in the mass of the people craves for something to satisfy its hunger; and so the wide spaces, the moonlit nights, horseriding across glinting sands, for men the all-conquering male seizing in his strong arms the woman he loves, for women the thrill of capture (albeit willing and docile captivity) with a little well designed camouflage to keep up appearances—all are provided by Hollywood's great mass-production machine.

But what a pity that the story of both these films is so similar. A little inventiveness would not have come amiss and the later film would have been better for it.

The photography is good but uninspired—what opportunities are missed in the desert scenes! The acting is efficient. Valentino was deservedly popular as the Young Ladies' Dream of Bliss, and in a world of imperfection perfect riding breeches are something! There is, too, real melancholy in the thought that that sleek brilliantined

Rudolph Valentino

MAY 6, 1895   AUGUST 23, 1926

IN MEMORIAM—By Gladys Hall

Stars shining for their hours—stars we make
    Immortal by our tributary feet—
The teeming skies that never knew a god
    So strangely sweet

As this bright memory that fills our hearts and brims
    Our eyes with tears as bright
As the sharp pain that circled 'round the world
    That death-like night. . . .

Skies filled with stars—one throbbing, empty place
    Gold as the love we bear . . . dark as desire . . .
Shriving from tender mists out of our hearts
    Famine and fire.

Fig. 4.8   Gladys Hall poem and D.G. Shore drawing,
        "Rudolph Valentino: In Memoriam," 1926.

head will no more bow in adoration over the form of his beloved (or beloveds, as the case may be).[2] But Flapperdom can take heart of grace. The Prince of Lovers has a long line of successors.

[Lansbury's Labour Weekly
(London), 16 October 1926, p. 12.]

Mae West Reveals the Foundation of the 1900 Mode (1933)
Cecelia Ager

Out in Hollywood, Mae West smooths her ever-so-gently undulating hips, swells her bosom, and, jiggling easily on one knee, hearkens to the tales of Paris gone Mae West with the quiet equanimity of your true zealot vindicated—a crusader now suddenly become prophet, who can take it.[1] "So Paris is beginning to understand about the freedom of the knees—hmmmm," she murmurs, smiling a little.

"My 'corseted' silhouette—what is it but a return to normal, the ladies' way of saying that the depression is over? Just a tug at the waist-line, and you have it—an optical illusion, really." A little squeeze of the waist, and the passing glance (which Miss West has always accepted as her duty to capture) halts fascinated at the peaks of the curves thereby achieved. There is something about curved lines, Miss West finds, that gets the roving eye. Straight lines, she has noticed, seem to lead it elsewhere. "Indent the waist," she says, "and so accentuate your arcs." Simple, really, and as fundamental as Euclid.

Always, Miss West has believed in fundamentals—honest, straightforward things like Nature. Always, she's appreciated the worth of Nature's beacons. When, as a girl, she used to look upon the Venus de Milo (and she did it often, she says), her whole being fired with the ambition to emulate her celebrated measurements. Even as a little child, she sensed the worth-whileness of a fine figure, a real bosom. "Nightly," she says, "I would spread cocoanut-oil on those areas which I wished to attain prominence." And now look at her. (Everybody does.) Maybe it was the cocoanut-oil, maybe it was plain wish-fulfilment; but, at any rate, Miss West was never one to stop at wishing.

As she herself says: "If they bring corsets back—they'll have to have something to put into them."

It doesn't surprise her that the world is coming around to her way of looking at things; sooner or later, it was sure to happen. "I didn't discover curves, after all," she explains modestly. "I only uncovered them. From the days of Adam and Eve, woman has had breasts and hips. If it weren't intended for her to have them, she never would have been created with them. Why is it you never see men turn around and look at a girl as she passes them on the streets, the way they used to when women were women? Why? Because there's nothing for them to look at any more." Fortunately, this grievous male disinterest may soon be replaced by the lively contemplation Miss West has fought to restore, if, as a result of her persuasive work in *She Done Him Wrong*, it again becomes the fashion for girls to have something to look at.

The Mae West silhouette so unselfishly revealed in *She Done Him Wrong* is not, then, chance—but the ultimate triumph of a lifelong conviction. Miss West's childhood instincts, it turns out, have not betrayed her. Old-fashioned about a great many things, she believes in the Battle of the Sexes—and in being well equipped for the fray.

Foremost of her own weapons is a generous measure of what she delicately characterizes as "that certain element," but, nevertheless, she brings heart to her more scantily endowed sisters. Says she: "That certain element gives a fine foundation to start from, but it must be nurtured. The tiniest bit of it, properly tended and set off, blooms into a passion flower. What can be accomplished by the feminine figure, once it is nipped here and there, but allowed free rein elsewhere, would surprise you."

Her words ringing in your ears, be encouraged then to the best possible enhancement of fore and aft. She suggests corseting, but done only with a clear conception of the results desired, never forgetting that it is just a means to an end. The sole duty of a Mae West corset is the diminishing of the waist-line, thereby accentuating bust and hips, for Miss West admires the figure with hip and bust that measure alike and a waist measure ten inches smaller. (Such, she reminds you, are the Venus de Milo proportions.)

Her *She Done Him Wrong* corset, for instance. Now that was a corset clasped about her waist only after it was found to be all cosy and comfortable above, a short little thing that, no matter what the activities of its wearer, never impeded hip movement, never interfered with easy bending of the knees, never hindered a free swing—and yet withal encouraged an upward curve for the bosom. So convinced is she, in fact, that a corset should place no physical, and consequently mental, constraint upon its wearer that, when her now classic *Diamond Lil* was but the shimmer of an idea teasing her for immortality, she first swayed down to her corsétière (the well-known Madame Binner), had her execute a model to her design, gave it a thorough trial to find out how it would feel—and when she found it utterly cooperative, and not before—she proceeded to write the play.[2] Had that corset come down long over her hips, had it inhibited the characteristic wriggle that is so important a part of Miss West's art—then, she says, might *Diamond Lil* have been lost to American folk-lore.

But Miss West wants it clearly understood that, though that corset reduced the bounds of her waist, there is no artifice elsewhere in the Mae West silhouette. [...]

When she thinks about the now-waning vogue for flat-chested, parallel-thighed girls, she sort of feels the War was to blame. "Starvation, scarcity of food," she says, "women undernourished, and" with an all-inclusive wave of her eloquent hands, "economics." As she sees it, there were all those thin women in France. And fashions originate in Paris. Therefore, the French designers had to create a silhouette to suit the pitiful outlines of their War-lean women. Femininity, alas, languished forgotten.

But now—"No need to diet any more. The depression is over. Let's change the standards of weight compared to height. Let's allow a few pounds' edge, give a girl the assurance, the vitality, the stamina that come from a little judiciously placed heft. A woman should look as well undressed as she does dressed. 'That certain element' is certainly not to be found in skin and bones."

With the return of the corseted silhouette, Miss West half closes her slanting eyes and sees an era of frills and fluffs and feathers. Not, however, as lushly spread as in the Nineties for, she points out, women have entered the business world since then. Obviously, trains, dust ruffles, willow plumes, floor-length skirts would be impractical in an office. Frills and fluffs do change a man's feelings towards a woman, and, during business hours, Miss West believes, his feelings should not be changed.

But frills and fluffs for "social functions" by all means, she says. Excellent psychology. Frills increase a woman's self-confidence, which, by the by, can never be too robust, in Miss West's opinion. They increase too, and this is very important, masculine regard for her.

She remembers when *Diamond Lil* was playing, when *She Done Him Wrong* was being filmed. She says, "When I would swish in, in my devastatingly feminine costumes, and some little girl dressed in a straight little nothing stood by, she'd be knocked down in the rush to serve me. Merely the way the masculine reflexes have been trained since Adam and Eve. And that's the way they should be. Woman simply must be looked up to. Let men see what's coming to them," she adds, "and women will get what's coming to them."

Champion of femininity, befriender of the long-neglected Venus de Milo, philosopher, too, Miss West has found that if you're trig and trim and straight and wiry, you'll travel in a slam-bang sports roadster; but, if you're curved and soft and elegant and grand, you'll ride in a limousine.

[*Vogue* (New York), 1 September 1933, pp. 67, 86, excerpted.]

On Mae West (1934 & 1938)
Colette

1934

[…] I hope that we are not too quick to dismiss the astonishing actress who has only to appear in order to convince us, to gain our vote by means as sure as they are unexpected—I mean Mae West. "And do you know, she's like that in real life!" If that is so, we could rely almost solely on her private life, her authorial independence, her impetuosity—like a wholehearted cavalry charge—even her greediness, to keep her for us just as we see her in *She Done Him Wrong*. However, I'm dubious; in *I'm No Angel* her mastery already seems a bit mechanical.[1] She has not been sufficiently on her guard against the scenario, which lacks bite; the scene with the lions leaves us unmoved. Happily, the beautiful blonde she-devil spirits away all the weaknesses of the film with a sway of her hips, a glance that undermines morals, and a damnable little "hu ... hum" on two notes.

But I feel that she is being pulled in different directions. And moreover—an unforgivable detail, a violation of principle—she is a little thinner.

1938

What's wrong? She's thinner. Nevertheless the film critics, who don't mince their words, reproach her with both the mediocrity of her latest film and her corpulence. One speaks of "fat haunches," another calls her "the adipose beauty," a third makes fun of her age, and the fourth is indignant at her cynicism.

I wanted to see this film, which isn't good, in which Mae West is said to "kill" nobody, though she was so "killing" in *She Done Him Wrong*. But Mae West, ever since *She Done Him Wrong*, has been worth going someplace to see. She alone, out of an enormous and dull catalogue of heroines, does not get married at the end of the film, does not die, does not take the road to exile, does not gaze sadly at her declining youth in a silver-framed mirror in the worst possible taste; and she alone does not experience the bitterness of the abandoned "older woman." She alone has no parents, no children, no husband. This impudent woman is, in her style, as solitary as Chaplin used to be.

Impudence is rare in the cinema. In every country, to ensure its survival it finds itself obliged to borrow the mask of simple grossness and a joviality that dishonors the dialogue. By means of such concessions, it remains an exclusively virile virtue.

If some pretty young American tries to use it for her own ends, the result is desolating. The star has only two ways, both blameworthy, of adopting impudence: to resemble a bad supporting actress in a tragedy, or to have the air of a drunken woman. When we went to see *She Done Him Wrong*, we perceived that Mae West had invented something in the acting art. Since then she has continued, with the nonchalance of a woman of wit and the obstinacy of a trader.

To enlighten my judgement, I would have liked America to send us a great deal of Mae West, since she is the *auteur* and the principal interpreter of her films.[2] It would have interested me to know how, by being insisted upon, the best discoveries spoil, and what is the process that ankyloses and discolors a character so rich, so hardy, so un-American: the woman without scruples, the female rival of the male débauché, the brave enemy of the male, valorous enough to use the same weapons as he.[3] Balzac, who was quick to see things, knew and showed these women warriors. Except for Madame Marneffe, he places them, as is his right and his preference, in the highest ranks of the French peerage.

For Mae West, the age of vice is not 1900 but 1907 or '08: the era of giant hats made popular by Lantelme, the clinging dresses of Margaine-Lacroix, the straight corsets that enclosed the female body from under the arm to the knee—corsets for the sake of which Germaine Gallois stipulated in her contracts that she would not have to sit down on stage. In comparison with such rigors, 1900 was easy, and Mae West's instinct was true when it led her to barricade herself in 1907. Just think of the kind of low drama she acts almost without gestures, except for the local undulations of her backside. Think of the murdered woman, camouflaged by a great head of hair that Mae West combs as she says in her nasal voice to the man calling to her: "Wait a minute, I'm doing something I've never done before." And can you honestly name another artist, male or female, in the cinema whose comic acting equals that of this ample blonde who undulates in little waves, who is ornamented with her real diamonds, whose eye is pale and hard, whose throat swells with the coos of a professional dove?

The only trouble is that since then, due to a major *maladresse*, she is thinner. I am looking at stills of *She Done Him Wrong*. During the short and restrained hand-to-hand struggle between the two women, two breasts, white, powerful, strongly attached to her torso, all but spring nude out of Mae West's bodice. She has the short neck, the round cheek of a young blonde butcher. Her arms are athletic, the cloth of the clinging dress creases, rides up from the well-fleshed thighs onto authentic buttocks.

Through lack of inspiration or good counsel, she has rejected these "advantages" of former days, reducing them all too visibly. In her latest film she is falsely fleshy Her princess-style dresses don't cling to her living flesh but to immobile padding. The short arms have lost their character of compelling force. The essential signification of sensuality and animality abandons the shrunken body, the face barricaded behind makeup and fearing every moment. Thus the dimples in the cheeks, thus the cruel and generous smile she once had, no longer charmingly and infallibly contradict her hard eyes. This implacable gaze, the expression of utter lack of clemency of a Mae West turned to stone—I hardly expected it to remind me, by a resemblance more of inner nature than form, of Castiglione's paralyzed Countess, who, threatened less by mankind than by time, saw her approaching death.

[Originally titled "Les Cinéacteurs" and "Mae West," *La Jumelle Noire* ... *année de critique dramatique*. Paris: J. Ferenczi et fils, 1934–1938. Collected in *Colette at the Movies: Criticism and Screenplays*, ed. Alain and Odette Virmaux, trans. Sarah W.R. Smith (New York: Frederick Ungar, 1980).

Hollywood Gods and Goddesses (1936)
Ruth Suckow

[...] Robert Edmond Jones, I believe, once wrote of the motion picture stars as a new race of gods and goddesses comparable in their symbolic nature and the worship accorded them to the pagan deities of Greece and Rome. The fan magazines frequently, and even matter-of-factly, refer to the feminine stars as "goddesses," while at the same time trying to prove that these shining ones are just like the rest of us.

Just why do the figures of the screen loom so large in our day? A few, a very few, of the great motion picture figures have also been great actors; but it is not through superlative excellence in their profession that they have been raised to mythical heights. It often works the other way. To be an artist is a drawback. It would seem at times that this nation, losing the stern Puritan orthodoxy which it brought with it to the new continent, yet still crude and young in the mass, has turned to the worship of these picture gods, real and yet unreal, common as life and yet larger than life, known in minuter detail than next-door neighbors and yet shiningly remote, because they have come to represent certain national ideals reduced to the lowest common denominator. For that is what the screen does—it reduces while it magnifies, grinds down what it exalts into the typical.

The stories of The Stars, told over and over in those curious Hollywood addenda, the fan magazines, follow the national fairy tale: the overnight rise to fame and material wealth, to social opulence, with Sex and Beauty in headline type, and all turned out in mass quantities with great technical smoothness and ingenuity by machinery. These stories—for the screen dramas and supposedly "real" biographies have been hopelessly mixed—reveal an amazing combination of small-town famil-iarities, front-page magnification, and "glamorous" remoteness. The present status of the motion picture art as an art—at least in Hollywood terms—is reflected in this naïve mixing of the personal with the objective; so that reviews of motion pictures seldom bother with the names of characters of the drama itself, but read something like this, in frank admission of the preponderance of "personality":

> Clark Gable is cast as a director of musical comedies, Joan Crawford again appears as a dancing girl. Clark and Joan don't get along. A young plutocrat, Franchot Tone, falls for Joan and wants to marry her. Joan goes to Franchot's home, where he introduces her to his mother, Mae Robson. And so forth. [...]

It is interesting to try to find the significance of this half-grown and at the same time over-grown mythology in the concrete images of the stars who supply the symbols—the gods and goddesses of the screen.

❧

The early gods of the screen rose out of the good old Westerns, which almost form a mythology in themselves.

Tom Mix was a child's hero—the gaudy circus rider, the fancy cowboy with the wonderful trick horse.[1] The Bill Hart image might be taken to symbolize in some degree a more deeply rooted and less gaudy national ideal: that of the lone cowboy, the modern representation of the hero in the wilderness, personified in legend by Leather Stocking, and in history by Daniel Boone.[2] These are masculine heroes, the sort who figure in books for boys. On the screen, only too characteristically, they are divested of wildness and made fit for family enjoyment. [... Their ...]

follower in the development of motion picture legend is [...] Gary Cooper—no longer a child's idol, but the hero of an adventure-love story with a dude-ranch setting, a sort of modernized and movie-ized version of Leather Stocking who has acquired sex appeal.[3]

There was a juvenile cast even to the greatest romantic heroes of those simpler early days—Wallace Reid, the "clean-cut" type, like a character from a Richard Harding Davis novel, and Douglas Fairbanks, the "athletic" type, sweeping all before him with Teddy Rooseveltian vim and vitality.[4]

But the really great gods of the screen, those who step from airplanes and automobiles into mobs of palpitating women, represent unmistakably some feminine ideal of a perfect lover. [... T]he idea of "the perfect lover" really took on definition with the appearance of Rudolph Valentino as The Sheik.[5]

It was a very ancient ideal which Valentino so completely personified (although he gave it a distinctly contemporary aspect) and one that has proved troublesome to the hard-working males of America from the very start: that of the handsome foreigner, the suave and accomplished Latin lover with a lot of time on his hands, the other man, the eternal gigolo. The appearance of the image was perfectly timed. It came at the very hour when the fevers that followed the World War were hottest, when women were wild to go dancing, and were all scrambling to put on sophistication. The sloe eyes, the smooth approach, the insinuating touch, led them all astray, like the call of the Pied Piper. The funeral of the screen's great lover—for there was never any attempt to separate the screen representation from the individual—has become a hideous classic instance of the orgy of mob adoration.[6] Even now, some years after Valentino's death, it is frequently reported that the middle-aged matrons who were his most hysterical worshipers make pilgrimages to prostrate themselves before his tomb. The morbidity of the Valentino worship belongs almost with the phenomena of sexual insanity. Some of its madness still spills over upon later heroes who most resemble the lost lover.

But in the idolization of the present great god of the screen ordinary American manhood has its innings. The story of the dimming of the Valentino image and the rising of the Gable star is very much on the order of a popular novel of the Graustarkian era in which the plain American six-foot hero wins in the end over the more romantic (but ah, how much less sterling!) foreign prince.[7] There is nothing foreign or morbid about the "appeal" of Clark Gable.[8] It is native American. It goes with popcorn, horseshoe games, and B.V.D.'s.[9] No preliminary publicity campaign was required to put over this hero. The girls themselves picked him out of his obscurity as a minor screen "heavy." Producers, still blinded doubtless by the glory of Valentino, had popularised Gable at first as "a menace"—the term was a hang-over from the overwrought days of the Valentino craze—as a he-man cave-man lover, whose first great popular action on the screen was to give the heroine a sock on the jaw. But the girls were right when they discovered the handsome ice-man, or laundry man, or whatever the role was, and demanded that he be placed among The Stars. [...] For surely that face—ears, eyes, dimples and all—is the face of the good-looking fellow in the next block. It is essentially a small-town face [...]. It bears the unmistakable look of the native good fellow—a Mason, an Elk, who might stand for a popular athletic coach, or be chosen as Scout Master [...]. Although now groomed and made familiar with night clubs, as the movies require, this is the same fellow who used to bring his girl a box of candy every Saturday night. And Clark Gable is almost as popular with masculine as with feminine fans; for in his person, or in his screen image, the ordinary American—whether business man or garage mechanic—long famous as a good husband and a poor lover, and a big child all his days, receives the accolade from the women.

No other American at the moment comes very close to contesting Mr. Gable's supremacy. The appreciation of the elegantly light-footed Fred Astaire is special in comparison. Foreigners are still the chief romantic rivals, though at the moment, the ever-present foreign menace speaks with an Oxford rather than a Latin accent. There is a company of these rivals, who may be said to represent varied aspects of the same general ideal—the ideal of the well-bred English gentleman, whimsical, chivalrous, "spiritual," chock-full of honor, thoughtfully devoted, emotionally restrained: Ronald Colman, with his romantic polish and his little mustache; Leslie Howard, with his attitude of sensitive deference; Herbert Marshall who, with his noble self-effacement, his appealing faint limp, his suffering good-dog eyes, is a hero who has come straight out of a woman's novel.[10] But in none of these figures has this Anglo-Saxon ideal been completely crystallized. It takes the lot of them. [...]

There are some who, although pretty much limited to a single role, have been able to present and stamp with a name a highly typical representation: Harold Lloyd, for example, comic symbol of a well-meaning white-collar boy; or Wallace Beery, who has come to stand for a lovable roughneck with a heart of gold.[11] James Cagney, with his sharply edged characterization of a speedy young twentieth-century tough, is popular not only with the big audiences but is something of an idol to left-wing critics.[12] However, it is a question whether some of these are not praising Mr. Cagney chiefly on the grounds of what they believe to be his intentions, rather than on actual accomplishment. He, like the others, is caught in the mechanics of Hollywood dramatization. In his part of Bottom, in A Midsummer Night's Dream, he certainly did not show himself an actor of any great understanding. W.C. Fields did far better when he stepped over into a "classic" role as Micawber in David Copperfield.[13] The bland clown-face of Fields, which reveals in flashes of ominous irritation the savage mishaps that strew the main-trodden paths of human existence, is that of a genuine artist. [...]

But among all the picture gods, huge as their following is and tempestuous their worship, the image of only one has attained the universality which belongs to genius. The image is that of a tramp—a lost though comic figure wandering through a bewildering world. Too much has been written about Charlie Chaplin for his gift to need description here. It is not inappropriate to note, however, that this pathetic figure does not belong to that movie world in which the slick machine-made heroes, the menaces, the lovers, know all the answers and give them so easily. The little fellow in the battered hat, like Chaplin himself, child of the London slums, is one of the world's dispossessed. He is forever on the outside looking in—that is his place in the great American myth as it flourishes in Hollywood. The happy ending, the kiss in the fade-out, is for the Horatio Alger heroes of the films.[14] The little fellow's fade-out is still that dismal road, with no visible ending, although now his girl takes it with him.

❧

In picture mythology the goddesses have always outnumbered the gods. The very fact that their chances for stardom are greater, however, makes their artistic opportunities less. More even than handsome actors, they are forced into the strict mold of accepted charm. They must all seem worthy to be loved; each be a version of "As You Desire Me." Even the most talented soon loses her appeal as an actress and becomes interesting chiefly for what she reveals and typifies. She appears as the embodiment of some ideal already loosely present in contemporary life and consciousness.

Of the early screen heroines only Mary Pickford has remained in the magnitude of a goddess. Great actresses are remembered as they appeared in great parts: Mrs. Siddons as Lady Macbeth, Sarah Bernhardt as Phaedra, Duse as The Lady from the Sea.[15] But Mary Pickford is simply the representation of "Mary Pickford." The name has the same sort of familiarity as the trade mark upon any famous commercial product. What the name sums up forever is the image of a child-woman with golden curls.

It was fitting that the early days of this new art-industry should have this child-woman as its heroine. It was a pre-war idea which Mary Pickford represented. Present for years in the national consciousness, personified in all the sweetest child heroines from Elsie Dinsmore to Pollyanna, her pretty face gave it concrete finality. This Mary Pickford image was the visible representation of those sunny mottoes and shibboleths, of the posy-framed "Smile, Just Smile" and "Be Glad" which characterized the early fair days of the century. America's Sweetheart was the embodiment of the nation's sexual and spiritual childhood. It has been said truly that a major turning point in national history was reached on the day when Mary Pickford cut her curls.[16]

Miss Pickford at last outgrew the part. The part itself was outgrown. A smaller but also authentic goddess then more briefly ruled the screen. She was Clara Bow, the Brooklyn Bonfire.[17]

The era of which Clara Bow was the popular symbol was known in literature as the era of the Lost Generation. But to motion-picture audiences it went by the name of the Flapper Age, the age of Flaming Youth. In this version its ideas, reduced to the lowest common denominator, became nothing more than Sex Appeal, jauntily abbreviated to S.A.

The central figure of this age had her rivals [...]. But the Clara Bow image was left as its symbol. The image was still that of a child, but of a bad child, not a good child—although of course with the proverbial movie heart of gold. The early innocence was dispelled. The Brooklyn Bonfire appealed to sailors on leave, to boys just out of the army. The child had learned the facts of life. The golden hair had turned to fiery red, the eyes were knowing, the curls were cut and tousled. The childish form had taken on seductive curves. The childish legs were provocatively shapely. (The mental age had not risen in any perceptible degree.) The child had reached the dawn of a precocious adolescence. She was running wild. The high-keyed discussions of Sex in Greenwich Village had come down on the screen to plain It, as defined by the redoubtable Elinor Glyn.[18] There were no refinements upon that raw vitality. It remained for a later era to touch the symbol with the dubious charms of decadence.

All during this brief bright reign another star had been rising. It still shines with an enigmatic luster no one has quite defined. The image of Greta Garbo is the first among the goddesses of the screen with enough subtlety to puzzle anyone; and perhaps to this degree it may be taken to signify the first dawn of a coming age of the picture art-industry.

Perhaps more influence has been exerted by the personality of Greta Garbo herself than by those of earlier stars—in some ways an individuality marked to the degree of bizarre eccentricity. Nevertheless, the picture image is a representative one. Nor is it truly adult. For this goddess' strange charm analyzed proves to be that of adolescence—not the precociously and voluptuously maturing childishness of Clara Bow, but adolescence all the same, strangely childlike, still more strangely mature. The tall figure has an awkwardness sometimes crudely coltish, sometimes divinely odd with its queer off-grace. The long swinging bob of soft light hair, a variation of which is still the favourite coiffure of youth in spite of the hairdressers' efforts to supersede it, is that of a girl just past childhood.

And even about the face—that face so purely marked in its characteristic outlines, with the high cheekbones, the extravagant lashes, the brows curved into a wilful exaggeration of temperamental individuality—there is something immaturely overdone. Immaturity lies in its very enigma. For the peculiar charm and power of this beauty taken as the symbol of "allure" are not those of womanhood but of neurotic adolescence crystallized and held spellbound. This face holds intact the "mysterious" entity of emotional youth, mysterious because not yet yielded. It is a self-centered loveliness. [...]

[T]he screen image and the individual are not really far apart, not even (it seems fair to guess) in the mind of the goddess herself. It has been argued frequently that Greta Garbo is the first great actress of motion pictures. She was dubbed early, with customary grandiloquence, "The Duse of the Screen." But although she has compelling power and intensity, beauty and distinction, it is still, I make bold to state, as a "personality" that Greta Garbo holds her place; and, in a more subtle way than that of the earlier screen goddesses, as a representation and a symbol. The image which she has created out of herself gives a mold to ideal feminine qualities of an era even more than it suggests a unique individual. The way in which girls everywhere have responded to this representation proves the point. The Greta Garbo image has caught their imaginations not so much because it was itself strange and new as because it embodied in thrilling and exquisite form that which they all desired to be.

It was altogether fitting that this more subtle quality of charm should have a foreign flavor; that America's Post-War Sweetheart should bring the conscious "allure" of the Old World. The image came into popularity along with the awareness of "civilized" sophistication which was so much an outgrowth of the mingling of the Old World and the New. It is easy of course to read too much into these symbols; and yet I think the comment holds. Feminine charms were no longer open, but artful—touched with the peculiar glow of decadence in which magic lies. The luminous goddess of this day was no longer a figure of bounding health, but anaemic and almost emaciated, pale, introspective, at once adolescently boyish and ultra-female. America's new sweetheart was distinctly a neurotic girl.

Greta Garbo was the first great popular introvert heroine of a nation of blithe extroverts; and in that shift from earlier and simpler ideals lay the galvanizing shock of change, and perhaps of self-development. This image was the final reduction to the lowest common denominator—glorified of course for screen purposes—of a heroine who had appeared long ago in literature, disturbingly and variously, as the heroine of the Brontë novels, of Russian fiction, of the plays of Ibsen. [...] The It Girl was popularly transformed into the Glamorous One.

Yet it must be repeated that Greta Garbo, although the quality of her acting is indubitably higher, is no more essentially an actress than the goddess who preceded her. An objective artistry is not at the source of her fascination or her power. The truth is that of all the feminine Narcissi who have gazed into the mirror of their own beauty on the silver screen she ranks first. Using the screen as a magic magnifying glass, she like the others, even more than the others, has been acting out her fairy story. For even those famous love scenes with which she won her first popularity had this queer unreality, this lack of human give and take, as if they were being played out alone in a dream. The companion of these scenes is only a shadow prince who never quite comes to life. The drama seems hers alone. She might have created it. [...]

It is this narcissus quality, upon which feminine stardom is still so largely founded, which has kept Miss Garbo from truly earning her title of "The Duse of the Screen." In *Anna Karenina* the dignity of the story gave power to her acting: but it was not the character of Tolstoi's Anna—vital, radiant, unthinking—which she played. She might never have read the book, only the scenario. It was Great Garbo in the situation of the play. [...]

❦

Demi-goddesses have appeared meanwhile during the Garbo reign. They are important enough to offer cause for interesting speculation.

The loveliest is that other foreign beauty, Marlene Dietrich. The German siren is more truly a personification of "feminine allure" than Garbo herself, for there is nothing equivocal about her femininity. The famous trousers set off this voluptuous womanhood comically, like the tights and silk hat worn by the charmer in the music hall. There is no adolescent angularity, but the essence of luxuriant feminine beauty in that delicately rounded figure with the notorious silken legs. The face itself is like either an exaggeration or a more exact rendering of the exotic strangeness of the Garbo face: the cheeks more hollowed, the cheekbones higher, the lips half open, the eyes self-consciously enigmatic, the brows pencilled to a more fantastic sweep. But the mystery of those deep-set eyes and of that husky voice is the age-old mystery of feminine beauty, that and nothing else.

Her image on the screen, no matter what part Miss Dietrich plays, might be called the symbol of a finished ideal of European femininity, ripe, almost overripe in luscious beauty, and heavily charged with disillusionment. In the person of this lovely woman, that ideal, so long a jealously cherished private one, is made visible to outside eyes. It is like drawing back the curtains of the harem. Somewhere behind the masklike smoothness of the face, sculptured yet fascinatingly irregular, there is a frightened and distasteful shrinking, turning slowly to disdain.

But her very excess of femininity has seemed to be Marlene Dietrich's doom as an artist. Obviously too intelligent to be the ridiculous Trilby of her legend, there is, nevertheless, an almost weary passivity about her, a leaning upon authority, an apparent refusal to arouse herself to do her own thinking.[19] The thinking that has been done for her has not overcome that self-placed handicap. Hollywood is prodigally wasteful of talent, but it is doubtful whether it has ever done worse than with the exciting promise and rare beauty of Marlene Dietrich. She was turned into a static image of lorelei charm, frozen in a lovely pose—and to bring the image again to life, there seems to be no proposal except to point again to its over publicized legs, and its—by this time—rubber-stamp "allure."

Joan Crawford is probably the most widely popular of these demi-goddesses. But her own story is more representative than her image on the screen. It is as the heroine of this story, retold in almost every issue of the fan magazines, and not as an actress, not even as a movie star, that Joan Crawford appears as a genuinely significant figure of our times. The story might be called "The Rise of an American Girl." [...] The frank story of a climber, yet it carries an intensity of burning ambition which gives a compelling and moving pathos to a half-shoddy tale.

The same story unrolls, even more clearly, in the pictures in which Miss Crawford appears first as a buxom hoofer with all the obvious charms of burlesque; then as the hungrily ambitious heroine, thin and big-eyed, of the shopgirl's drama; and last as a gorgeously gowned typical star of the screen. The dramas in which she has figured have not been tragic— success stories, rather, although beset with trials. Yet there is a tragic note in the representative history of Joan Crawford as its outline appears through the pictures and beneath the ballyhoo. It is the tragedy of a naïve materialism. A self-made tragedy, it might almost be called. For in the intensity of the effort to Become Someone, to Develop a Personality, the personality itself has become almost wholly externalized. The face has been "groomed" until the earlier interesting and strongly human qualities have been almost entirely ironed out of it; and the image now presented on the screen has become a mask no longer capable of expressing any truly genuine emotion.

Yet the same pathos hovers about this image as about the dramas built round it—and about the movies themselves—that queer pathos of great promise and cheapened accomplishment, the promise nullified by too golden a success. The profile etched for a moment upon the screen gives an effect of nobility, never carried out by the character in the flashy play. A tragic sense of waste is hidden somewhere in the success story.

Katharine Hepburn would undoubtedly be considered by many the strongest contestant for the goddess role, in spite of some spectacular failures. She too has been called "The Duse of the Screen." The Hepburn image, like the Dietrich image, shows a blend of likenesses and contrasts to the Garbo image. Perhaps it is the best American version. But the individuality of the Garbo image has been developed to an exaggerated degree—the face thinned down to genuine oddness, the body to an emaciated angularity. The "personality" is wilfully, even thornily, displayed. It has always seemed to this screen spectator that Katharine Hepburn has missed fire because of a split purpose. It would appear that she is ambitious to stand as a genuine dramatic artist capable of playing varied roles, and that at the same time she must display herself and herself only. As a result, the image which she has given to the screen is provocative, but unsatisfying.

This is offered as guesswork—that in spite of her diffuseness on the one side, the narrowness of her talents on the other, Katharine Hepburn has a capacity for suggesting a representation, slight and brittle, by no means so deeply typical as that summed up in the image of Greta Garbo, or even in the Joan Crawford image, but genuine in its degree—a picture of a debutante, a Junior Leaguer. In her wilfulness, her tomboyishness, her piquant face, her tinny little voice, in her very eccentricities, there might be found a concrete definition of the intense individualism of the spoiled little rich girl of this era. It is a role which Miss Hepburn suggests, but does not play; and in order to play it she would have to deprive herself of that somewhat phony movie "glamour" which, distressingly, she has added even to the roles of Jo March and Alice Adams. Here is another contradiction—versatility where versatility does not exist; a star who has lost, rather than gained, by the lack of that rigid "typing" which most screen actors and actresses rightly dread.

[…] In spite of the greater technical ability of newer actresses, of the influence upon screen acting left by Helen Hayes, and of the influx of opera stars held up as promise, the reigning goddess of the screen, who has stolen up closest to the Garbo throne, represents no great advance in the demands of screen audiences.[20] A backsliding, rather. It is the image of Shirley Temple, curls and grimaces, a summing up of all the ideals of bright, forward, and over-emphasized American childhood.

The screen has no feminine Charlie Chaplin. That old demand of "As You Desire Me" is too strong. The coiffure must still be perfect no matter how hard the winds blow. The clothes must be immaculate even in desert Bar-B.-Q. stands and underworld hide-outs. The fame of Mae West alone is comparable, in a minor way, to that of Chaplin. For Mae West plays a single role, but that role is a conscious representation, not an unconscious typification of an inarticulate ideal. The great exponent of Sex capitalized, she plays not to be loved, not to "keep faith with her fans," but to present the part for all the part is worth. In other words, Mae West is in her degree an artist.

The two consistent artists of the screen, as Hollywood now permits the screen—a slap-stick tramp and a burlesque queen.

❧

How truly are these images, in spite of their worship, the gods of America? How much are they actually and literally "build-ups"? And do they, taken all over the world to represent America and "Americanization" in the deepest sense, represent it at all? [...]

Examine these images, and the bogus element becomes apparent at once. To create them Hollywood has misused rather than used the true power of photography. Look at the faces of the goddesses in the huge close-ups. Artificiality is so much taken for granted that it is almost accepted as a picture convention—the bleached hair, the painted eyebrows, the false eyelashes, the made-to-order mouth, the shining teeth—these are not faces but masks, created to conceal rather than to reveal. [...] To make over the actuality into predetermined types, set to stereotyped and mechanical notions of beauty, is a falsification at the start.

Having examined the images themselves, it is interesting next to try to find the actors and actresses behind the images—the "real" this one and that one.

First of all, let us look into the literature that has been built up round them; those curious contemporary documents, the fan magazines. These are all made to pattern. All are addressed to "the fans" in order to bring them into personal touch with their gods and goddesses. The personal note runs throughout—runs riot. It is in the editorials, intimate and flattering, addressed to "you and you and you," with a chummy air which says, this is *your* magazine, run only for *you*, to bring you news of *your* idols—for we, the writers, and you, the readers, are all common folk together basking in the light of these shining beings. They go into the homes of the deities, leading the readers by the hand, showing them the living rooms, the swimming pools, the playrooms, the kitchens, placing them at the tables (set for guests, menus included), almost in the beds of The Stars.

In all this mass of print, acting itself gets short shrift. The articles are a mixture of highly personal criticism and ballyhoo. The same thing happens over and over again, with nearly all the actors and actresses brought to Hollywood, until it becomes a routine. [...] The glorifying process starts immediately, attempting to lift the actor into mythology through mechanical processes. There were never beings in the world like these; so exciting, so glamorous, so good to the poor, such householders, with such fine cooks, such good dressers on budgets, such parents, such lovers.

But right along with this glorification goes that jeering reduction to the bottom level which runs through American journalism. The fan articles present a curious mixture of adulation and a touchy sense that these deities are no better than the rest of us. The deities are examined first to see if they are "regular"—that is, if they are going to play ball according to Hollywood rules. The first rule is, of course—tell all. You are ours, so open up. A desire to stick to professional instead of personal issues becomes "high-hat," a sign that the actor thinks himself too good to tell. Thus, one magazine spoke of the "vulgar taste" of an actress who refused to "come across" with the intimacies of her marriage. If actors hold out for the conditions under which they can do their best work they are damned with the other bludgeon adjective, "temperamental." [...]

There is little criticism worth the name. This is true not only of the fan magazines. Critics not connected with Hollywood are still too grateful for any favor in the films; either that or they still take the position (fewer of them now) that no good can be expected to come out of Hollywood. In the fan magazines there is such a naïve emphasis upon the personal that acting is called "natural" and "sincere" when it isn't acting at all; when an actor, met face to face, is exactly as he appears upon the screen. When will the producers throw away these siren roles, the complaint runs, and show us the real Marianna, natural, gay, and just a girl at heart?

The blame is by no means entirely on the side of the producers, however. Too many of the actors and actresses themselves very probably come to love the image in the magic looking-glass. Motion pictures constitute the only art in which the players are actually able to see themselves. Nearly everybody prefers a flattering photograph.

Meanwhile, these images which Hollywood has presented have at least the raw value of revealing where the lowest reach of the lowest common denominator seems to lie. That is how they must be read—as a broad typification, half genuine and half imposed, creative only in the tremendous influence which they exert.

With the Hollywood set-up as it is today, we cannot ask for very much else. The stories that Hollywood permits can only scrape the gaudy and tawdry surface of American life and legend. The images of its gods and goddesses are now magnified out of all proportion to their genuine value and significance. So far, American motion pictures, in spite of the skill that goes into their making, form an unconscious social document rather than an art.

[*Harper's Monthly Magazine* (New York) 173, July 1936, pp. 189–200, excerpted.]

Film as the National Barometer

Hollywood: An American State of Mind (1923)
Katharine Fullerton Gerould

It used, as we all know, to be said that Boston was not a place but a state of mind. At the time the epigram was first uttered, it was profoundly true; it is not so true, I fancy, at present. Boston is very much a place; and the minds that kept it in a "state" have perished. But there are cities on our national map that exist for the public rather mentally than physically, which are ideas to us rather than municipalities. Reno, for example, is a symbol; and Butte is a legend. Hollywood, California, you may say, is most often a text. Yet I incline to believe that Hollywood, in the profoundest sense, is a state of mind, as Boston used to be—a very different state of mind, let me hasten to say. I feel sure that when motion-picture stars come on to the eastern studios to produce a film, they bring essential Hollywood with them. [...] But motion-picture stars are few, in comparison with the millions of our population; they do not, in themselves, matter quantitatively any more than Bahaists or Pillars of Flame. Hollywood in itself might be permitted to remain a state of mind, without comment; for it would not necessarily be an American state of mind. But Hollywood is more than itself. As baseball is the national game, so Hollywood is one of the national points of view, and is, therefore, not without interest. [...]

I have never been in Hollywood, and I speak quite without prejudice. The attacks on Hollywood as a sink of iniquity are, I should suppose, as absurd as unfair.[1] I do not even believe that Hollywood, through the medium of the films, is corrupting the American world. Hollywood is an instance, a manifestation of something ubiquitously present in America, not an isolated phenomenon, nor yet a cause. It is not a synonym for the drug habit, or for multiplied divorces, or for mysterious murders, or for drunken orgies. It is, I repeat, a state of mind. Let us get away at once from the conception of it as a hectic town near Los Angeles given over wholly to the production of motion pictures, and consider it as a mental condition, an attitude of some millions of souls. That the motion-picture world offers a good culture for certain germs of which we go spiritually in danger is probably true. Otherwise "Hollywood" would not be the title of this essay. But I wish to make it clear at the beginning that I am not referring to the private lives or the private moralities of motion-picture folk, which, for all I know, are as good as the average. The youth of the country, if it is menaced by Hollywood at all, is menaced less by what it hears of the vices of the film folk than by what it hears of their virtues. The worst phase of the matter is really that the American public should be especially preoccupied with Hollywood at all. That in itself shows that the disease is widespread; that the state of mind is common.

An analysis of this temper which—perhaps rather wickedly—we call "Hollywood" for convenience would be mightily assisted and clarified if I could quote for you, at random, half a dozen paragraphs from almost any of the motion-picture magazines that clutter our news stands. [...] I speak, myself, from a fairly intimate acquaintance with them during the last year. [...] They are perilously easy reading for anyone who likes good films well enough to like to know what is going to be produced and by whom. It is only fair to say that a lot of the criticism of particular films is eminently sane and sound. So are the cooking receipts and the knitting directions in the women's magazines. It is, in both kinds of periodicals, the implied philosophy of life that is appalling—and, I may say, astonishingly similar in the two. [...]

One of the great prices we have paid for being a nation of successful business men is that we have forgotten how to face any facts save financial ones. I am told that the Tired Business Man is a myth; but he has certainly, in all good faith, been made the apology for cheap and easy art. I am inclined to believe that he is real. I am told also that the American woman—having been endowed by her adoring men folk with leisure beyond that of any European woman—is the most cultured in the world. That, I am very disinclined to believe. That she spends more time deliberately looking for culture, I admit. No other country has developed women's clubs and Chautauquas.[2] In no other country do the women habitually attend lectures and "classes" and courses, of a non-academic, but informing nature. But the women of the country at large have made the same mistake which the men have made: they have believed that they could transfer the rules of "efficiency" to the kingdom of the mind, and make up a budget for spirit as they could make it up for food and clothing. [...] Over any mistakes that give us pause we throw the veil of optimism. The fact is that, except in an obvious material sense, we are unwilling to work. The man knows that he must work, in order to make money; the woman knows [...] that she must work in order to keep her household comfortable. Beyond that, neither is willing to toil. They expect knowledge, culture, "standards," to be somehow broadcasted to them while they sit comfortably. The very radio advertisements give us away: the man in the Morris chair, with his feet up, ravished and listening.[3] The fact that the best things cannot be broadcasted is not mentioned in the advertisements. It is not precisely time that we are unwilling to spend; it takes no longer to read an author than to go to a course of lectures upon his work. It is effort that we grudge. We like to have things done for us; and we naively believe [...] that it is possible. [...] Canned food, canned heat, canned music, canned information, canned culture.... [...]

Unfortunately, along with our demand for mental ease, we have developed an inordinate capacity for self-praise. It is the two working together that have produced the state of mind to which I referred earlier. Our vocabulary of eulogy is extraordinary. When we praise, for cause, we know no limit: whether we are praising a statesman, or a motion-picture star. [... I]t is all part of our hectic optimism. We refuse to believe that anything is inaccessible to us; we refuse to believe that there is any intangible good—beauty, or chic, or wisdom—which we cannot acquire by paying a little money for a magic formula.

Why "Hollywood"? Let me quote a few sentences from a recent motion-picture magazine about Charlie Chaplin:

> He has made himself king, and, while to be born a Guelph or a Ghibeline, a Hapsburg or a Hohenzollern might be thrilling or a bore, there can be no doubt as to the romance of making yourself a King! In all history Mr. Chaplin's only rival for that distinction is Napoleon, and Napoleon, after all, died leaving plenty of worlds to conquer. Charles Chaplin has completely conquered his world. He is monarch of all who survey him. There is nothing left for him to vanquish...[...]

"In all history..." Our easy superlatives! This was not an interview, and Mr. Chaplin is not to blame for it. It is only part of our eulogistic habit. The writer probably knew as well as you or I that there are more people in the United States who would not cross the street to see Charlie Chaplin in the flesh than there are people who would. It does not matter: facts do not. Mr. Chaplin, I fancy, comes nearer than most residents of Hollywood to being "universally beloved," but the same kind of praise is meted out to many, many others. No woman since Helen of Troy is so beautiful, no woman since St. Catherine of Siena is so good, as practically all the movie actresses are in the magazines. No marriages are so happy, or so cooed over—until divorce proceedings have been started. Mothers are honored in Hollywood as nowhere else in America; children are nowhere so adored by their parents. The origins of these people are always romantic [...]. They all work hard, and go to bed at nine o'clock, and, when they are at home, live virtuously in Cecil de Mille interiors. [...]

When I said that the youth of the country was more menaced by the accounts of Hollywood's virtues than by any report of its vices, this is what I meant. If Hollywood is the Mecca of thousands of young American men and maidens, it is not because they believe the kind of thing we have been citing, and think that only in Hollywood are so much beauty and virtue met together. It is because they know very well that most of these actors and actresses are very ordinary folk, and that nowhere outside of the motion-picture world does a boy and girl without education, or breeding, or experience of life, or brains, or any of the things that mean toil and trouble, stand such a good chance of getting both cash and adulation over night, as it were. No one, you see, until he or she has been filmed, knows whether or not he or she will film well. There is always a chance. [...] I can think of no other career that comes so near offering the great American desideratum of earning big money without serving a long and arduous apprenticeship. A man does not expect to succeed in the competitive struggles of the business world without giving years of keen thought and service; nor is he always rewarded with wealth at the end. No serious artist in any field expects to master his medium save by unremitting toil; and—genius apart—he knows that the most brilliant promise flickers out unless it is backed up by effort. The real rewards have to be sweated for. But less and less, as a national community, are we willing to sweat for them; and, on the other hand, less and less are we willing to admit to ourselves that all the rewards are not ours. We are materialistic, as everybody says; but we are materialistic after the fashion of children—not so much brutally as foolishly. Our greatest danger lies in believing our own fairy tales, in thinking that Aladdin's lamp exists. We perceive the prestige values without perceiving that no thing can eventually preserve a prestige value if it can be universally possessed with ease—and, I need not say, without perceiving that prestige values themselves are creditable or not creditable ones, according to the intelligence of the community that created them.

It is, I hope, beginning to be clear why I called Hollywood an American state of mind. I read—I cannot, of course, vouch for the truth of it—that a well-known movie star (not yet twenty years old) came recently, for the first time in her life, to New York. Her train slipped into the station, and she alighted. There were no brass bands, no throngs of admiring fans, to greet her; and out of sheer surprise and disappointment—as much surprise, I take it, as disappointment—she wept. The tale is amusing, is even, perhaps, rather engaging; but all the same it is terrifying, if one muses for a little on its implication. A girl of nineteen or so, of whom thousands of the most intelligent American men and women have never even heard, expected to arrive in our greatest city and be greeted as if she were Marshal Foch or the President of the United States—as if, in other words, she had rendered heroic service to mankind, or had been chosen by a great people to control its destinies.[4] Would Mr. Hoover expect to be mobbed on his arrival in the Pennsylvania Station or the Grand Central? Or Paderewski?[5] Or Rudyard Kipling? The story, as we said, may easily not be true; but the motion-picture magazines printed it, not ostensibly as a joke. [...]

I am far from being an enemy to the films or to the film world. I like good films, and have honest belief in the possibilities of the motion picture and honest admiration for the achievements of some of the producers and stars. Nor am I so ignorant of conditions as not to be aware that there is public sanction for these absurdities. Hollywood, I repeat, is a symptom, not a cause; a state of mind, not a geographical entity. [...]. We must cool off; we must readjust ourselves to life; or we are in a state of hysteria. The fact is, I suppose, that a good many of us are in a state of hysteria a large part of the time—but after all, not all of us. I can even understand, intellectually, why Charlie Chaplin or Mary Pickford or Rodolph Valentino [sic] should be mobbed by admirers when it is known that one of them is to appear in person: there is no doubt an element of gratitude for pleasure received, along with the less noble curiosity, in the heart of that crowd. [...]. I, too, am by way of being a Valentino fan, and if I could imagine myself in any of these mobs, I could probably most easily imagine myself in one of which he was the center. Even so—I do not see why Mr. Valentino should have received (as I saw it stated that he did) the freedom of the city of Boston. I do not suppose that Mr. Valentino wanted the freedom of the city of Boston, and I do not doubt it has, in its time, been conferred on individuals less worthy of it, personally, than he, since Boston municipal politics are one of the least creditable features of that beautiful and noble city. But why? On what score? Did they ever give it to Edwin Booth or to Henry Irving?[6] Perhaps they did; I do not know. But I can see that if Mr. Valentino was to have thrust upon him the freedom of one of our most dignified and historic cities, the young lady who did not get even a brass band in the New York station was perhaps, to some extent, justified of her tears. Considering, that is, the unofficial nature of brass bands, and the fact that she is actively in pictures, while Mr. Valentino is not, one might fairly decide that if he was to have all that to-do about him in the Massachusetts State House, she ought in justice to have had two brass bands, and one of them, at least, in costume.

Hollywood, you see, even better than the women's magazines, illustrates our general lack of the sense of proportion, our tendency to distort values. And Hollywood is wherever the young and the ignorant expect to get the triumph without the toil, the reputation without the virtues, the fame without the achievement, the reward without the sacrifice, the knowledge without the study. In the particular sense in which we have used it, Dr. Frank Crane or Mrs. Gene Stratton Porter or any other professional evaders of hard, unpleasant fact represent Hollywood as much as Jackie Coogan.[7] It is not Hollywood, California, that we need to be worried about: it is the Hollywood in the heart of us all. The little high-school girl from mid-Dakota who goes to the Coast in the hope that after a few years she may return, twinkling with jewels, to give her obscure fellow citizens the "once-over," is sister to the woman who believes that if she can find the right complexion clay, she will be an American Venus, to the man who believes that if he will take a correspondence course, he will be truly educated, to all the people who believe that if they buy a certain book, they will develop "personality—charm—power." More and more, you may have noticed, the advertisements insist on the lack of effort demanded of purchasers. We began with labor-saving devices: we have come to labor-eliminating devices. Once, we banted when we were fat; now, "with no hateful walking or rolling or dieting," we grow thin to music, so pleasantly that the whole family insists on joining us. [...]. Fifteen minutes a day of easy application will make you a desirable dinner-guest at any table in the land. You can learn professional dancing in a few lessons by mail. All you need, in fine, is to give up a little of your spare time—those moments when you would not be doing anything, anyhow—to become a Talleyrand, a Madame Récamier, a successful artist, or a captain of industry. [...]

That there is a brave aspect to this optimism of ours is undeniable. In a practical sense, we could not do better, perhaps, than try for all these alleviations of our lot.

[…]. Make-believe often keeps adults happy as well as children. The danger comes when we transfer our make-believe to things of the mind and the spirit. Then abuse of terminology becomes immoral. We are not willing to take the arduous steps necessary to achieving the reality; therefore we do not get it. But, even as we are content with the semblance of effort, so we are content with the semblance of achievement. We do not want the thing itself so much as we want the reputation of having it. The process is relentlessly logical. First, we wanted all the things that had a prestige value; then, knowing that they were hard to come by, we took any short-cut that advertised itself; now, being almost as shrewd as we are sentimental, and realizing uncomfortably that you cannot often get something for nothing, we incline to be satisfied if we can convince some one else that we are what we are not. What the advertisements really promise you is a successful camouflage. And, more and more, we are becoming content with successful camouflage. […]

[*Harper's Magazine* (New York) 146:876, May 1923, pp. 689–96, excerpted.]

Ye Gossips Tayle (1930)
Djuna Barnes

MADAME X—, just back from Hollywood; says contrary to much report, that it is madder than insanity. Eighteen thousand dollar bracelets are tossed about with that simple and Generous gesture with which we folk of MANHATTAN distribute dimes to the poor, if we can't find a nickle.

The Hollywoodite gives the world at large a hint of the magnitude of his income by his choice in architecture. Be you in the "know" you can come within a dollar eighty-nine of an exact estimate. The very rich have marble palaces, like Marion Davies' (no one else has A marble palace like Marion Davies'); next comes the Chinese type, a sprawling affair that takes in many acres; a step lower and there is *ye* Spanish "cottage" with swimming pool and fountain containing enough water to drown Madrid.[1] Getting down to about four thousand cool a week, the grand style disappears. But what the pocket cannot purchase, the wit of man can, and one sees the "Wind blown" home intentional, Chimney awry, gate hanging on one hinge, rafters hither and thither, and doors that can be comfortably entered only on a slant of 85 degrees of Scotch, made more acute by stumbling over a lawn gone "rough" and casual by the nonchalant and partial interment of rocks. Madame X—doth *say* the city looks like a thing *thrown* together to amuse a child given to fits. Shops dealing in orange drinks are built to resemble *oranges*, & the famous Brown DERBY is a brown Derby![2] Everyone is exceeding rich *and* beautiful and sweetly jealous. After three days (unless one meets A producer or two), THE heart sickens for an ugly face. Every postman is an *Adonis*, every waitress a Venus, and appealingly handsome boys, looking for a "break", gaze up at you from the dashboard of *your* car with such eyes as one would leave home for, had one *a* home TO leave!

& then of course, there is the one ENIGMA—who lives like an enigma, in an hotel room—*Greta Garbo*. Everyone wants to know her, and NO one does. Her ambition is the GREAT European stage; perhaps she remembers Sarah Bernhardt.[3] Her castle is already built and stands on a lake in Sweden; her mind is elsewhere. Once she invited someone to dine *chez elle*. He was a young man from whom she buys her tweeds. He hailed a cab. "We walk," she said. They walked, about five miles. Dinner was served, a Swedish dish with sour cream. It was eaten. "Will you have a drink," He would; it was whiskey. Hours later when he came to, he saw Greta sitting apart drinking hers as straight as the CROW flies. He staggered to his feet. She smiled—"You go in a cab now," she said & put him in a cab, and as SHE shut the door on a night now well into the morning she added, "I think I walk now." Yet the boy remembers *that* evening with *love*.

[From "Playgoer's Alamanac," *Theatre Guild Magazine* (New York), September 1930, pp. 34–35, excerpted]

New Secular Forms of Old Religious Ideas (1929)
Rebecca West

One of the most curious experiences which America has to offer the European visitor is the rediscovery in secular forms of ideas which he has always associated with religion. The religious situation will in any case be profoundly puzzling to him. He will find people of the prosperous class who in Europe have most thoroughly abandoned the habits of church going are in America the backbone of the Church. The well-to-do business man of the type that at Gerrard's Cross is the first to give up his morning's worship to a round of golf, that in Berlin or Copenhagen would not even think of himself as making a choice in doing so, that in Catholic countries would look on all that sort of thing as his wife's affair, feels very differently if he lives in the United States, whether he be in New York, or in the Middle West, or in New England, or the South, or in California. The piety of the working-classes is, on the other hand, very regional. In parts, particularly where Methodism rules, forms of religion which originated in Great Britain exercise a domination such as they have not for long exercised over here. I should feel as apprehensive as a turkey at Christmas if I found myself under an obligation to settle down in a small town in New England or in the South or in parts of the Middle West as a declared atheist. Where there are large populations of other than English-speaking races which have kept their identity, they appear to cultivate their religions with as much or more fidelity as if they had stayed at home. One has only to visit the great Greek Church in Buffalo to see that it is a centre of a religious life which could hardly be matched in the Old World for fervour. But a vast population of young Americans who have been born in the great new industrial cities of the United States or have moved there from an actual geographical province or the spiritual province of a non-English-speaking community, and who have not risen high enough to have social ambitions, have virtually no connection with any religious body: which is a condition not at all unlike what obtains in the equivalent class in Europe.

So far the situation is simple enough. It is merely a matter of the contiguity of violently contrasted conditions within the bounds of a single nation. But presently a curious fact impresses itself on the stranger, and that is that American civilisation in its church-going strata, just as much as in its non-church-going strata, is not permeated with Christian symbolism to anything like the same extent as European civilisation. To take the most conspicuous example, the symbol of the cross has nothing like the same power over the popular imagination there as it has here. Some time ago I had occasion to visit the famous cemetery at Woodlawn outside New York, where the price of ground is so high and the standard of mausoleum-building so magnificent, that it costs the rich almost as much to be dead as it did for them to be alive in New York. I was startled to find that, though I walked about among the grounds for about an hour, I came on no tomb that bore a cross or had an image or inscription that made any reference to the Christian religion. The interiors of the mausoleums may have been more Christian but the fact remains that the people belonging to the most church-going class in the country were content to bury their dead in graves that have no relation to the faith in which they had lived, and make no reference to its specific teachings on the subject of immortality, though they have paid them the compliment of listening to them every Sunday. This is an inconsistency I have never seen exhibited in any other country; and I found by visiting cemeteries in other cities that, so far as the graves that have been erected during the lifetime of the new industrial America are concerned, it is a general characteristic of the country.

Another curious example of the difference between the permeation of American and European civilisation by Christian symbolism came under my notice when I was travelling from New York to Albany. I pointed out to my companions, who were an Englishman and an American woman, the advertisements (which since I first went to America have struck me as among the oddest things in the country) of the Three-in-One Oil. The Englishman exclaimed in amazement at this strange reminiscence of the Trinity: the American woman could not see what had attracted our attention. Yet the Englishman was the child of free-thinking parents and had never had any religious instruction save what he had casually acquired through attending prayers at Public School; and the American woman, daughter of a broker and wife of a fashionable doctor, had attended an Episcopal Church on Park Avenue every Sunday since her infancy.[1] This is only one of a hundred examples that I or any intelligent person who has resided for some time in the United States could give you to prove that though a great many Americans are drawn to the practice of religion by personal devoutness or a feeling that it serves the national need for social coherence, and probably human affairs are carried on as much in accordance with Christian precept as they are anywhere, the common mind of the country (at least so far as the white population is concerned) is nothing like so thoroughly saturated with Christian symbolism as the common mind of our continent.

This is apt to make the traveler think that he is going to come in contact with a secular civilisation which will be something quite new to him, which will be quite unlike anything the Old World has to show; and that is where he is certain to find out that he is wrong. For if he examines the common American mind closely enough he will find that though the symbols which are familiar to him in Europe are absent from the New World, the forces which disguise themselves in those symbols are not. Again and again he will be puzzled by beliefs, by custom, by manners, prevalent in the United States, which do not present a straight and simple response to reality. They seem a little fantastic, a little nonsensical. If one questions them, one arouses a certain passion in those who uphold them, which can easily be recognised as the same sort of passion that one may arouse in a devout Christian European if one questions the value of one of his religious symbols. If in the light of this discovery we re-examine the belief or custom or manner that has struck us as not a straight and simple response to reality, we will probably find that it too is a symbol, and probably symbolises in a new secular form exactly the same idea as one of these religious symbols. And it is as likely as not that the idea will prove to be one of those which religion has been accused of inventing and thrusting on the innocent human race.

A conspicuous example of this is the universal American belief which superficially seems at the opposite pole from anything to do with religion, in the extreme brevity of the career of women film stars. Film stars are a constant topic of conversation among the American man and woman in the street. I have hardly ever gone to the hairdresser's without having the attendant female refer to her favourite stars. It would be odd to have lunch with a middle-class American housewife without discussing the movies. They are, since they pass in and out of New York, talked of in New York Society. And always the conversation about them falls into a certain pattern. Their real characteristics, their beauty and their wit, if any, and their sexual lives, and their capacity for acting, if any, are briefly discussed. Then tales are told of their enormous wealth, of their salary, of their augmentation of their savings by investment in real estate, of their jewels, of their colossal homes in Hollywood. Then it is pointed out that their day will soon be over, that the life of a movie actress lasts only a few years, that she is done for after she is in her early twenties, and that her fall into obscurity must be agonisingly full of humiliation. Now, as the most casual student of the films ought to be aware, this last is the sheerest balderdash. To take only ladies who are admittedly near the termination of their career, it is obvious that Miss Lilian [sic] Gish, Miss Mary Pickford, Miss Norma and Miss Constance Talmadge, Miss Gloria Swanson, Miss Mae Murray, Miss Pola Negri, Miss Corinne Griffith, have had careers which are neither brief in relation to the average career in a kindred profession such as stage-playing, nor indeed brief according to any standard.[2] And I have no desire to give away ladies who are still in their heyday, but longstanding visitors to picture palaces must know that should Miss Marion Davies, or Miss Bebe Daniels, or Miss Lya de Putti, or Miss Renée Adorée, elect to appear on the London stage they would not be affected by the L.C.C. regulations regarding the employment of children in theatres.[3] It costs a film corporation far too much to make a star (as those authors know who have been offered fabulous sums to write a scenario that will pull out of failure some actress on whom hundreds and thousands of dollars have been spent in floating) to let her go out again quickly; and the decline of the close-up lets the experienced actress reap the benefit of her years. These facts ought to be at the finger-tips of the American films fans, who many of them keep vast collections of picture-palace programmes and mountainous heaps of film magazines on the subject, yet they can hardly mention a star without sooner or later saying, "Ah, she'll soon be a has-been. Gee, musn't it be tough to be on the crest of the wave, and then have to pack up your traps and go." Though they say this with every appearance of regret, they show signs not of relief but of annoyance if one answers them, "Oh, but you need not be concerned about Miss So-and-So, for she is only twenty-six, and Miss Such-and-Such is still playing that sort of part at thirty-three," and produce facts and figures to prove one's point. One perceived they derive some deep satisfaction from the thought that Miss So-and-So is doomed to early extinction, and one's impression is confirmed by the peculiar tone in which the newspapers announce that some film star (this applies to men as well as women) has lost his or her financial drawing power and is beginning to be a money-loser. I will not say that there is exaltation shown at the expense of the fallen: but the news is given a curious prominence considering its melancholy nature, as if it were the kind of thing people liked to read, and it is told solidly and cheerfully as though part of some wholesome and normal tendency.

Now, when one has heard conversations concerning the short life of film stars in twenty States between the Atlantic and the Pacific seaboards, and has discovered that the contained belief is held with passion and against reason, one begins to perceive that one is in touch with a manifestation of some preferred event in American psychic life. Examination of the subject brings out certain parallels between the attitude of Young America to Hollywood and certain European attitudes towards matters very different from the movies. There is, to begin with, the very obvious parallel between the film fan's hunger for visible tokens of Hollywood—for Miss Dolores del Rio's Spanish shawl, offered as a prize in a journal, for a handbag certified by a department store to be a replica of that Miss Clara Bow always carries, for signed photographs of the stars, for butts of the cigarettes they smoked when making "personal appearances" at the local picture palaces—and the cult of relics in the Roman Catholic churches.[4] I have been into the bed-sitting-room of a film-infatuated shop assistant in Chicago, which with its wall entirely covered with photographs, its vase of flowers set under her favourite one, its burning lamp set in an alcove, its piles of magazines devoted to the system which had excited her piety, might have belonged to some little Catholic girl who had adopted the Little Flower as the object of her devotion; although the lamp was, in fact, a perfume-burner which had been advertised in a screen magazine as part of the arsenal of some peculiarly infallible vamp.[5] The film stars themselves fall into categories which, at any rate if we pass over Christianity and go behind it to older religions, nobody will object to recognise. There is the woman who represents sex with the evil lifted from it by mystically managing to eat her cake and have it too: Mary Pickford, who is the wife of Douglas Fairbanks, the apotheosis of the male on the screen, and yet is completely sexless in quality, clearly plays the part in America's imagination of the virgin wife; or Irene Rich, who has divorced her husband and lives an extremely public life of complete solitude with her two children, and is therefore an image of the Virgin Mother.[6] There is the vamp, the always desired and ill-spoken-of Aphrodite: it is interesting to know that the vamp's press agents find it good policy to circulate stories accusing their clients of bad tempers and inconsiderateness in the studio and vehemence and capriciousness in their homes. The reasonable behaviour of Miss Greta Garbo has, I understand, been a great nuisance from this point of view. There is also the chaste Artemis, Miss Lois Moran or Miss Mary Philbin, whose career would be wrecked by any hint of the indiscretions which are regarded as a public duty on the part of a vamp.[7] Considering the inveterate tendency of film stars to adhere to such easily recognisable types in the mind of the film-loving American public, and considering that that film-loving public is drawn chiefly from the class which has no part in the heritage of either European or pre-Ford American culture, can we doubt that what we are witnessing is a new race starting the business of making a new civilisation at the bottom by making a new mythology? The speculation becomes a certainty if one stays in the country long enough, and meets sufficiently simple people, to hear any of the unwritten legends regarding Hollywood which spread from mouth to mouth across the continent. These are nearly always pure creations of the public mind, and have no relation whatsoever to fact; and they are very often modern versions of the Greek myths, frequently of the kind which are slurred over as much as possible by our teachers. I remember a Spanish archaeologist once telling me of the ecstatic thrill when he went into a cave at the bottom of a cliff and found a primitive painting, many thousand years old, of boys stealing honey from the wild bees from a nest at the top of that cliff: even as they had been doing that afternoon when he made his way down to the cave. I got the same sort of exalted sense of the continuity of human life a year or so ago in Connecticut when an old lady whispered to me as evidence of the depravity of Hollywood, about which good women ought to be prepared to do something, a story alleging that at a beach-party on the Californian coast a certain male film star had performed one of the lesser-known feats of Hercules.

It certainly looks very much as if Hollywood were young America's Olympus, and its stars its gods. Perhaps now that we have recognised the general landscape, we can identify the particular point which puzzles us in the public's desire that the film star shall first be extravagantly pampered, and then destroyed. We are standing in the old sacrificial grove. The civilisation that believes itself headed for life more directly than any other civilisation has ever been, that believes itself held back by no inhibition whatsoever in favour of renunciation and abstinence, nevertheless uses one of its first efforts at creative imagination to make yet another affirmation attributing a mystical value to death and sacrifice. It creates these figures that typify the good things of life, it loads them (at least by imaginative consent) with all the wealth of the world; and then it feels that the best service they can render it is to die. The images of their desire are first dedicated to life and then to death. There could hardly be a more convincing testimony to the reality of the conflict between the will to live and the will to die that rages perpetually in the human mind.

It may be said that the comparison between the imagined destruction of the woman film star with the sacrifice of the deity with which we are familiar in other religions is incomplete to a degree that forbids us to suppose their fundamental identity, because the deity in these Old World instances is usually male. But the sacrificed deity of the Old World is only male because the position of women in the worshippers' minds is so low that it is hard to imagine death as receiving any great satisfaction from a female victim. That point of view would not be anything like so strong in the more feminised civilisation of the United States. Moreover, even there the popular mind would prefer a male victim if it could get it, but the occasions when it can get it are quite rare, since men are not eliminated from the screen on account of age. The only occasions when they can rejoice over the spectacle of a sacrificed male star are if one embroils himself in some moral scandal, for which he can be punished by being barred from the screen—that is, by having his money taken away from him, which is a symbol of his life; or when one dies during his triumph. The wild frenzy of excitement that passes over the country if either of these events takes place is a phenomenon without parallel in any other part of the world. It was interesting, at the time of Charlie Chaplin's divorce, to see the fight that took place between the double value that he has for artistic infantilist America, and America's desire to destroy a famous figure. It was very much a case of an irresistible force meeting an immovable post; and there has ever since been a curious blankness in the film public's attitude towards Mr. Chaplin. When film stars die, the emotions of the public take even more clearly recognisable forms. Two male film stars have died in the very zenith of their glory: Wallace Reid and Rudolph Valentino.[8] Both were decent enough beings, whose lives had been circumscribed by the narrow world of the show business; and that is all one can say. Both died pitiful deaths, Wallace Reid from the effects of taking morphine, a habit into which he had fallen through continual ill-health and overwork, and Rudolph Valentino from a sudden and agonising intestinal disorder, but they were deaths of (so to speak) a thoroughly private and personal kind. In view of these facts, the reaction of the public to their deaths was utterly amazing. From one end of the States to the other the film-loving public flamed up in the deepest emotion. Articles appeared everywhere when Wallace Reid died which would have given any person who read them without knowing who he was the impression that they were the obituaries of some hero who had died while saving his country from great dangers either by land or sea or air and possibly all at once. Girls in beauty parlours talked of "poor Wally" with comfortable tears in their eyes as of gratitude for a benefit received. And that was before film worship had risen to its heights, and it was possible to see the amazing sights that took place when Rudolph Valentino was lying-in-state in New York. For three days and three nights a procession of mourners, most of them men, and those not of an effeminate type, filed in front of the coffin in which there lay the tango-dancer; and their demonstrations of admiration and grief were extravagant.[9] Then, too, one felt the same sort of comfortable feeling about the death, as if it had at any rate not been a wasted sacrifice, as if it had covered everybody with some sort of dignity and a safety. And so, I suppose, it had: the sort of dignity and safety that man has always felt to be conferred on him when a god he has worshipped passes from life into death.

Since we find in this layer of America the idea of the atonement, which is so difficult for a European to conceive as other than specifically religious, translating itself into purely secular terms, it is not surprising that we find many other startling translations of the ideas which are begotten by that idea. We find, for example, some amazing examples of the conversion of that complex of ideas which is known as Puritanism; which springs from a feeling that since a god has sacrificed himself for us we ought to pay him back by sacrificing ourselves to him, through subjection to pain and abstinence from the pleasure that normally might come our way. Mr. G.G. Coulton has written many pages to prove that the common mind is wrong in its conviction that Puritanism is an invention of Protestantism, and that it had been and is manifested just as frequently and unpleasantly in the Roman Catholic Church.[10] But modern conditions in the United States suggest that it can flourish riotously when it is cut off from contact with any religion whatsoever. There is one particular manifestation which I think no European community could beat for fanaticism, which is carried on by people whose minds are blank of all associations with Christianity. That is the movement for promoting and engaging in competitions that involve useless and strenuous trials of strength and endurance. These sprang, I suppose, from the competitions in sheep-shearing and such-like accomplishments that have taken place since time immemorial at village fairs; but they have changed out of all knowledge in the direction of craziness and monstrous misuse of the soul and body.

There are dancing Marathons where wretched creatures totter about without sleep for a week. There are Gabfests where they stand on swelling feet and talk and talk and talk for four days. There are competitions where they cram themselves with food, drinking ninety cups of coffee in a day, eating a hundred slices of pie during a week-end. There are inane contests for championships which make one despair of human nature as one names them. The devoted Christian must, I think, hope that the Divine Powers went to no particular trouble to guarantee the salvation of a species that produces enough competitions to make the flag-pole sitting championship a sporting event. I have heard Europeans sneer at these phenomena as peculiar to the United States, but if one goes and sees for oneself one finds that the extraordinary thing about them is that they reproduce with such perfect exactitude phenomena which are familiar to everybody who knows about Europe of the past or the contemporary East. One has only to look at the competitors to realise that they are not there for the sake of the money prizes, which are usually not very large to begin with according to the scale of American prices and are often cut in half or thirds by a dead-heat. They are there because they find a pride and exhilaration in the torture they are inflicting on their bodies. That is proved by their aspect, and by the fact that many of them go on competing to the last moment, even when they know that because of the rest hours they have taken off they cannot possibly be winners. They are, in fact, the spiritual brothers and sisters of St. Simeon Stylites.[11] There are even those among them who will tell you that they make a practice of going about the country engaging in all these different sorts of competitions; and by the light in their eyes one may see that one is privileged to be present at the birth of a fakir class. Meanwhile the spectators, instead of being disgusted by the sight of human beings wrecking their minds and bodies from sheer folly, are carried off their feet by exultation. They will cheer two crazed creatures staggering to find foothold on a dance-floor among the phantoms of delirium, as if they saw the guarantors of the world's salvation. The people who go in for these competitions, and who witness them, often belong to the urban population which has most completely divorced itself from Christianity. It would probably not occur to most of them to get married in a church, or abstain from getting divorced if they wanted to do so. Yet there they are, as much abandoned to the idea that there is something noble and redeeming in the mortification of the flesh as the most perverse Christian ascetic of the Thebaid.[12]

There are thousands of phenomena like this in the new America which should interest all amateurs of religions. I should imagine that any student of the Gnostic heresies should find a great field of research if he went out to Los Angeles, that great city made up of the retired farmers from the Iowan and Kansan plains, and tried to recognise the specimens he already knows in the innumerable forms of belief (most of them disclaiming all connection with religion and calling themselves New Thought Schools and the like) which there proliferate. It is a historically interesting spectacle; and to find such simplicity developing alongside individuals and societies as sophisticated as any in the Old World affords a dramatic contrast. It has, more-over, a bearing on our own problems. It proves the old-fashioned secularist was grotesquely wrong when he imagined that by shearing the religious institutions of a society he would affect the nature of that society; for here, in a society that should have been the secularists' paradise, the forces he particularly detests have raised their head again, in forms all the stronger because they have not been diverted into the channel of supernatural belief. And it suggests that the interest this generation shows in psychology is not misplaced, since evidently social institutions are only the instruments within the hidden forces of the social mind.

[*The Realist: A Journal of Scientific Humanism* (London) 1:3, June 1929, pp. 25–35.]

Love Through a Film (1946)
Barbara Deming

Hollywood assigns women one perennial role: to get their men. Any other activities they may indulge in are glimpsed out of the corner of the camera's eye. Trivial as these film portraits of modern women are, in isolation, arrayed and observed together they cease to be trivial, shed real light on one aspect of our society.

Those who write of the films refer at regular intervals to the emotional "catharsis" they afford the millions who flock to them. The word is incessantly on the lips of apologists for Hollywood. But neither the apologists, proper, nor the critics, stop to distinguish between this concept as it applies to Hollywood and as it was first applied, by Aristotle, to Greek tragedy. The dramas that Aristotle took as his text afforded release from the emotional drives of that time through a dramatic discipline, in effect educating audiences about these drives by setting them in as deep a perspective as possible.

Hollywood films, with rare exceptions, provide the relief not of discipline but of indulgence, and blind indulgence, for they are so contrived that audiences will not even have to acknowledge to themselves the nature of the drives they are having relieved. (Such comfort is of course easier to sell—and, too, because it opens no eyes it stirs up no trouble.)

Because Hollywood films are so innocuous on the face of them, the deeper story they tell carefully veiled (and it may be veiled even from those who make them), the study of isolated films is unrewarding. But if many films, the good and the bad, are studied together, an underlying pattern begins to clear—exposing the prevailing deep-felt but unanalysed sense of the nature of love in these times.

The first thing one notices about the current movie heroine is her adoption of behaviour once reserved to the villainess: a disdain of coyness in pursuit of the hero, a bold initiative traditionally not hers to take. (The motto reads: boy gets girl.) There was some complaint of the "unorthodox" behaviour of Lauren Bacall toward Humphrey Bogart in To Have and Have Not—walking, bold-faced, into his room in the middle of the night, then refusing to make use of the plane ticket he carefully secures her, bestowing even the first kiss, complete with the suggestion that "It's even better when you help." Her behaviour is not exceptional. In The Lost Weekend, too, it is not the hero who bestows the kisses but the heroine. "Bend down," she says peremptorily, and if he hangs back, draws his face down to hers. It is she who bombards him with notes and with telephone calls—until he cries out, "Stop it. Helen, stop it, stop it!" In Spellbound another heroine walks into a hero's room in the middle of the night: and it is again he who would elude and she who doggedly pursues.

In Pride of the Marines, when letters and telephone calls get her nowhere, the heroine resorts to abducting the hero bodily "home," there, in the face of his desperate "Get me out of here!" to insist that they be married. In Adventure, too, the implication is that the heroine has done the proposing. When Gable remarks of a previous love, "I didn't marry her, did I?" Garson replies, "Maybe she didn't ask it." After their divorce, she is the one to propose re-marriage—this time within our hearing. The heroine of Those Endearing Young Charms also takes things into her own hands: "I'm shameless: I love and want you with me always, even if you don't. I love you, I love you, I love you!" She tells the hero. "You will come back to me (after the war), you'll see," and when he responds, "You made up your mind to spoil my last night, didn't you? You think I love you..." replies, "You've got to." [...]

It is not that the current screen hero is the bashful sort. In the majority of cases he is carefully established as a man of some experience with the ladies, and as of old makes the first advances—to a heroine up to this point inexperienced, even "cold." In *Spellbound* Ingrid Bergman has just been termed cold as a textbook when Gregory Peck arrives, and his persuading her to play hookey from her work gains him the title of "Casanova." Clark Gable in *Adventure* is the sailor with a girl in every port, and teases Greer Garson their first time out for being a "mild tomato." The advertisements of *Those Endearing Young Charms* refer to the hero explicitly as "a young wolf." At the beginning of this film the heroine, who has earned the name Snow White, has to show him the door of her apartment rather rudely. So the pattern goes. The hero is quite capable of making advances. When it comes to suggesting a marriage—then it is that the heroine must take the offensive.

The hero could thus be said to have adopted the behaviour once reserved to the villain—the old-time cad. But he is not the Gay Deceiver. When he walks out on the girl it is with these deep-felt words: "I'd care too much to wish a guy like me off on [a girl I really loved]," "I can't involve you." "I won't be a drag on you." "I'm not what you want; it would be slow murder." "Tell her I left because I'm in love with [her]."

In some of the films the hero offers a very literal reason why he can not "wish himself off on" the heroine. He is an alcoholic (*Lost Weekend*); he is an amnesiac, who fears he is a murderer (*Spellbound*); he has been blinded in the war (*Pride of the Marines*); he is afraid if he marries the heroine he will shatter the "serenity" of her amnesiac state (*Love Letters*). One might say of any one of these films, viewing it singly, that it simply documents a situation not special to our times. Looking at them collectively (and I have not exhausted the examples), the wonder is what makes Hollywood so unfailingly, at the moment, document just those situations in which the hero will feel incapable of marriage. The question is particularly pertinent when the situations are as far-fetched as in *Spellbound* and *Love Letters*. Films which give their heroes no tangible reasons for feeling unable to marry, and yet obey the compulsion to picture them in this state, further mark this image a more than casual one. Why does the reporter in *State Fair* feel he can not marry? Does he believe himself incapable of fidelity? Does he fear he can not offer economic security? We are never enlightened. A film like *Adventure* marks the image with even more finality, a crucial one by the flamboyant manner in which it improvises on the hero's plight, conceiving it not in literal but in highly metaphorical terms, endlessly labouring overtones. Gable's self-explanations are a bit vague too, but here the film-makers intend it. "Are you having a good time?" Garson challenges him. "Rotten! This is no fun! ... Kidding you gets me nothing!" "What do you want?" she probes, "*That's it*," he cries. "What's it?" "Just it!" He doesn't know what he wants, what to want, doesn't dare want anything—for there's nothing on land, he's found, that doesn't "leak itself to death." Like his friend Mudgin, who's seen his soul pop out of his breast like a shiny little seed, a firefly, and drift away, in spite of his efforts to clutch it—he's quite lost. "Both of us," Mudgin raves, "sailing the black ocean without a soul."

The current hero misuses the heroine but it gets him nothing. When he strikes out at her it is from confusion and panic. Garson understands this about Gable. He's like an animal caught in a trap or maze, she explains to Joan Blondell: "You try to help him, he'll turn on you, afraid you'll tear his heart out." (Recall the sequence in *Lost Weekend* where Helen crying out to Don "I want to help you!" goes after the pass-key, and he, though so sick he can hardly stir, drags himself across to the door, to bolt it against her.) The mark of the current hero is this mark of the suffering animal. The new prerequisite for male glamour, one may almost say, is some token of anguish: haunted eyes, slight tremor in the cheek or the hand, sweat on the squinting brow.

And the mark of the heroine is that understanding look, diagnosing his plight, and then chin up, with a battling stance. For she is Ariadne, has the divine itch to lead the poor animal out of the maze. Not an easy labour. [...]. Pretty tough mugs they are, these current heroines, up to tricks and twists of their own. Above all, interminably persistent. Even a little grimly so.

If evidence is needed that this tortuous progress toward a marriage is something other than the traditional love play which makes the final kiss more appetizing, those films may be mentioned in which (even though matters have to be strained to manage the sad effect) the lovers never do attain each other: *Incendiary Blonde, None But the Lonely Heart, Rhapsody in Blue* are a few. And whether the ending given is an unhappy or a happy one, the liveliest sequences in a love film today—those giving rise to the most ambitious cinematic flights—are apt to be the sequences of nightmare separation. There is the dream the heroine suffers in the hotel room in *Shock*, where she hears her husband calling to her from the other side of the door. "Help me! I can't find you!" and struggles to reach the door while it endlessly retreats from her. Or, in *State Fair* where the heroine waits for the hero who does not come and does not come, and all about her workmen dismantle the fair grounds.

This nightmare intensification of the traditional contest between the male who would wander a bit and the female who would have him settle down—this recurrent pattern of a marriage never attained—or attained only, as the heroine of *Love Letters* says, by a "great miracle," shadows forth deep-felt insecurity among us. The values by which men once lived have vanished. The relation of the hero of *Adventure* to the young sailor brought to serve under him is telling. When the boy's grandfather remarks that it will be a good school, Gable counters bitterly: "Yeah, for smart sea-gulls and sharks!" He behaves to the boys as a parent might, obsessed with guilt that he can not offer his son what he should, can not initiate him into an ordered way of life. The boy, appropriately, dies under his care. The end of this film, where Gable breathes life into his own newborn son, is a melodramatic dream-reversal.

The current hero, no longer the man with a Dream, the confident founder of communities, seeks an identity for himself by playing it "tough and lonely." This is how the hero of *Those Endearing Young Charms* describes the pleasures of piloting his plane. Heroes find the nearest thing to a Life far off, above the earth; others sailing his black ocean; others riding his whiskey merry-go-round round and round. The heroine of *Pride of the Marines* accuses the hero: "You want to be lonely"—and is correct. This is the easy way. This is the pattern she must break in upon if she would get her man.

In one entire genre, the Western, she has lost out: the female of the species, in fact, has become virtually extinct. If she does survive, it is not as the girl the hero wins for a wife but only as one on whom he practises a few of his charms, in passing. The Western hero's invariable companion is the comic stooge—who can be counted on not to plague him with the suggestion that he settle down and live anywhere in particular.

The stooge, along with the girls who will setttle for passing flirtations, must be accepted by the heroine in other films than the Westerns. In *To Have and Have Not*, Bacall must give the stooge-friend the right answers to win Bogart. In *None But the Lonely Heart* the introduction of the heroine to the stooge-friend is a solemn moment. She leaves the picture, but the hero says to the stooge. "You'll never leave me, you lopsided old muggins."

The stooge can occasionally be incorporated by the heroine into the family—a sort of mother-in-law figure—but the other women in the hero's life can't quite be reckoned with in this way. These women are very real competition. They and the hero move toward each other not tortuously as hero and heroine do but by a simple affinity: lost soul inclining to lost soul, for a little warmth. And the other woman makes few demands. She's apt like the heroines to take the initiative, but only to state: I'm here if you want me. She will have the hero just as he comes. Even the hardboiled sensation hunters in the thrillers bear little resemblance to the "vamps" of early movies—fatal women who wanted to set their mark on men. They rant of the "Peace" they are looking for. The red-head singer in *State Fair*, who has an affair with the heroine's brother, announces she must be on her way again—she is no would-be wrecker of homes but just a poor lady who "figured she had a right to a little happiness."

The home-wrecker is extinct of course because the hero now lives nowhere in particular. The heroine is the disruptive element—for she would "plant trees in [the hero's] blood" as Gable complains. The other woman is often a warm-hearted type, really more sympathetic than the heroine. She is more relaxed, less grim around the mouth. But the two types blend. There is not the old clear distinction between the type that would be the heroine and the type that would be the "other woman." The heroine isn't invariably the Ariadne, to be distinguished by the set of her chin. Sometimes, like the girl in *None But the Lonely Heart*, she doesn't feel up to it; sometimes, she'd just as soon tag along with the hero wherever he cares to go.

For it's strenuous work, this planting of trees in the blood—hard on the disposition, hard on the whole personality. Gable remarks to a girl who eyes him in *Adventure* that she's a nice red-head but he's looking for a girl with green hair and purple eyes. The image is not far-fetched, for trying to keep hold in her mind's eye of a Vision of a Home and a Life, does incline to put a strain on the face of the heroine, to lend her just a slightly freakish look.

["Love through a film: New attitudes toward men, women, the Other Woman—glimpsed from the corner of the movie camera's eye," *Vogue* (New York), 15 August 1946, pp. 168, 224–27, excerpted.]

The Black Film (1949)[1]
Dilys Powell

It is, I suppose, three or four years since the wave of manliness which now engulfs the cinema began roaring over from America. At the beginning, like landlubbers unused to gale warnings, we did not recognise the signs. In the films of the first 12 months after the war manliness was apt to be confused; sometimes with amnesia, sometimes with what the cultured giants of the screen like to call amour: the new men of the early post-war period demonstrated virility by clipping their sweethearts one over the earhole, or, more simply still, by failing to remember whether or not they had committed a murder.

As time went by, however, amnesia, schizophrenia, and the rest of the psychological decorations were discarded. Forgotten were the arts of love and the casebook; Ovid joined Freud (or possibly Krafft-Ebing) in the dustbin; and the cinema, drumming on its chest, came out with *Brute Force*.[2] Since that day the spread of manliness has been terrific, both on and off the screen; and manliest of all among the spectators have been the intellectuals, who by now can scarcely bear to look at a film unless at least one character in it is beaten to death.

The absence from *Knock On Any Door* of outstanding brutalities may, indeed, prevent the piece from winning the prestige enjoyed by less accomplished work; here we have no more than a scrimmage or two, some violence in the reformatory, a suicide, a murder and a last backward look from the criminal on his way to the electric chair. And here, too, the general manliness of the theme is overlaid by a good deal of democracy and moral sentiment in the handling; if Pretty Boy Romano did in fact murder a policeman, argues his lawyer (excellently played by Humphrey Bogart), that wasn't his fault; it was the fault of society.

❧

One is sometimes tempted to protest that if society is to be held responsible for the goings-on of the gangster, society must be allowed also to take the credit for that section of the public, a minority no doubt, which rejects the life of crime. But let that pass; *Knock On Any Door*, whatever the banality of its message, is an accomplished film; its direction, by Nicholas Ray, has both sensibility and force, the acting of John Derek (as the slum boy), and of a number of secondary players is to be admired, and the detail in many scenes—in, for instance, the judge's chambers at the court-room—is memorable. At the same time the piece is not in the same class with the same director's *They Live By Night*, nor with some of the strictly manly films we have seen lately; to give an example, *The Set-Up*, [...] is much superior in its character-drawing and its social observation.

The truth, I fear, is that the best talent of the American screen is at present going into the cinema of savagery: a fact which has not escaped the critics in France, where the "black" films of Hollywood are greatly admired. In Paris a week ago people were urging one another to visit *Champion*, an American boxing piece admired here too, though overshadowed by *The Set-Up*. Always eager to march with the times, however manly, on my return from holidays I went to see these two stories of the ring. Both imply criticism of a system or of a society; both attack the corruption of the boxing ring, and *The Set-Up* draws a magnificent and horrifying picture of a bloodthirsty audience. I still cannot help thinking that films presenting physical brutality in such intimate detail must tend to debase rather than deter.

❧

It is interesting to compare the savagery of the French cinema with the savagery of the American cinema. While in Paris I saw, among other films, Yves Allegret's extraordinary *Dedée d'Anvers*: a black fog of a film, a dreadful night through which, caught and sharply illuminated now and again in the street-lamps or the lights of the *bordel*, there move the figures of the prostitute and her employer. The piece, which is superbly acted by Simone Signoret as Dedée, Bernard Blier, Dalio and Marcel Pagliero as the man through whom the girl sees the hope of escape, has passages of physical violence: a cold-blooded murder, a fight by the docks which makes the street-brawls of the American cinema look humane. Yet it is not the physical action which one remembers, but the moral violence of the story: the feeling of the savagery of the human spirit. The French film shows us a corruption infinitely older and more experienced than the simple brutality of the gangster; it is the product of a civilisation which knows good and evil, and beside it the violence of the American cinema has a childish and revolting innocence. There is, in some strange way, no sense of guilt in the horrors of the Hollywood screen. [...]

[*The Sunday Times* (London), 24 July 1949, p. 2, excerpted.]

Mr. Deeds and Willie Stark (1950)
Penelope Houston

The films of a nation may not always reflect that nation's mental climate; they do show what its people believe to be the truth about themselves and, most of all, their hopes and their fears. The artist who wishes to light up a corner of the national character must do it in a form that the audience will find acceptable; he must make the same assumptions, although he need not draw the same conclusions from them.

This is especially true of Hollywood in its serious mood. The artist in Hollywood must first satisfy the business man, and the business man has created his power out of a knowledge—soundly based on dollars and cents—of what the public wants, and of how much it is safe to give them. The cinema public will accept big business as a villain but it will not (or is not permitted to) accept Socialism as a solution; it will admit its own tolerance to Negroes, but it will not admit that tolerance could be extended to inter-marriage. Hollywood is often accused of shirking its responsibilities but, especially in recent years, it has made a number of films sociological or political in theme.

This is not a new trend; it was established in the 30's by such films as *Black Legion*, *Fury* and *They Won't Forget*. […]. The social films of the 30's covered a variety of topics—lynching, hysteria, strike problems, slum conditions, miscarriages of justice, gangsterdom—often with more ferocity (due perhaps to more recent memories of the depression and the accession of Roosevelt), than today.[1] In this article, however, an attempt has been made to illustrate points with films fairly fresh in the public mind that have a bearing on the general temper of America today.

Hollywood makes certain basic assumptions in its picture of the national scene. […] They are: power corrupts (*Citizen Kane*, *All the King's Men*); career politicians are very probably dishonest (*Mr. Smith Goes to Washington*); local politics are dominated by crooks (*The Great McGinty*); big business plays at politics for its own dishonest interests (*State of the Union*). In view of these assumptions it is hardly surprising that the fundamental virtue of the good politician, as Hollywood shows him, is always simple honesty; a quality to be found, we are told, not in the big cities, but in the small towns. The ideal American political hero is Longfellow Deeds, overcoming big business by sheer integrity, believing that the will to do good must always conquer.[2]

It is, perhaps, an over simplified view, but it is an understandable one. Hollywood grew to maturity during the twenties when big business was given a free hand during the do-nothing administrations of Harding and Coolidge.[3] Political inertia was at least partly responsible for the crash which destroyed the average American's faith in the virtues of unbridled big business. Roosevelt and Truman embody some of the characteristics of the screen hero; the New Deal was, after all, as much the expression of an ideal as of a policy; hostility to Roosevelt came from just those big financial interests whom Hollywood castigates; support came from those whom Hollywood elevates, the little man who distrusts the cartels and the monopolies of the interests whom (since the slump) he has come to regard as his enemy.[4] To look at America through the eyes of Hollywood is to see a reflection of recent history, and a picture, idealised or realistic, of what the average American wants and fears. In essence, two views of life are reflected: the intellectual and the simple, and although these are very different in origin they are curiously similar in result.

The first is the "unconfused liberalism" (as Thurber expresses it in *The Male Animal*) of the American intellectual.[5] It is an attitude subject to various degrees of confusion and of liberalism. The American intellectual is deeply disturbed by the obvious abuses of American society; he feels for the underdog, he is tolerant, bitter and realistic, but beneath the hard surface he is very probably an idealist. His view of life has reached the screen in a surprising number of films. On the level of pure cynicism, there is the Marx Brothers' *Duck Soup*, the most ruthless exposure of the whole ridiculous political business, and there is Chaplin in his serious mood, notably in *Monsieur Verdoux*, showing the fate of one man who rebels against the murderous pattern of human society in his own private outburst of mass murder. Sturges narrows his cynicism to the American scene; in *The Great McGinty* he tells the story of a man who votes 37 times for a political boss; in Hail the Conquering Hero he shows up the pettiness and dishonesty of small town politics—his simple minded hero is eventually given the office of mayor as a tribute to his honesty, but whether Sturges here bows to the conventional viewpoint, or intends yet another joke at the expense of small town officials, he does not say.[6]

The seaminess of local corruption is revealed in passing in such a film as The Glass Key, a thriller from a Dashiell Hammett novel which gives a ruthless picture of the activities of a political gangster. All the King's Men attempts a detailed study of the effects of large scale corruption. In Robert Rossen's adaptation of Robert Penn Warren's novel, an essentially honest man of high ideals finds that the way to power lies through dishonesty and chicanery, and that these demand their own price. Willie Stark, the gangster governor, becomes an enemy to his people; his only opponents are old, tired politicians who have themselves practised the smaller corruptions. Honesty belongs to another world, but it is implicit in the film that honesty is political virtue.

The reverse side of the same picture is shown in the second point of view, whose greatest exponent is Frank Capra.[7] His films, which stem from the thirties, reflect the fundamental outlook of the "average American". He admires and believes in the little man; he would like to believe that the meek will indeed inherit the earth; in a world dominated by power politics and big business he still finds refuge in idealism. The idealism, however, does not ignore the realities: Capra is always careful to build up a towering structure of dishonesty before he allows his hero to advance against it and knock it down, like the walls of Jericho, with his trumpet call.

The pattern is familiar. We see corruption at work; we see the little man apparently its victim and then, dramatically, we see that if the hero can once reach the ear of the public he will find in them his support. In Mr. Smith Goes to Washington, boy-scout virtues overcome the corrupt senator and the villainous business men. In Mr. Deeds Goes to Town, the hero propounds what seems to be Capra's own solution—a sort of co-operative private enterprise; he is apparently defeated, but once the case comes into the open, the whole of society is on his side. State of the Union (known in Britain as The World and his Wife) had a cutting satirical edge which spared no party; it mentioned actual politicians by name; it created a detailed picture of the methods of political bosses. The hero, a business man built up as a presidential candidate by politicians who want to make use of him, first yields to their promises, believing that if he reaches the White House by dishonest means he can still do good once power is achieved. His realization that the means do not justify the end, his exposure of the interests which have cheated him and the people, is the film's denouement. [...].

Both the points of view briefly described have much common ground. Both accept corruption; the one as a state of affairs from which there is no escape; the other as an enemy which can be destroyed. The opponents of Willie Stark and the opponents of Mr. Deeds belong to the same class; Mr. Deeds' victory is a triumph, Willie Stark's points the way to the still greater dangers of Facism. It is obvious [...] that these films both reflect the American state of mind, and answer a need in the national consciousness: it is important to face the facts, and to be reassured that their implications are less disastrous than they appear. [...].

In its picture of the state of the Union, and of the outside world, Hollywood echoes the thoughts and hopes of its audience. It might seem that in its sociological pictures, notably in the recent Jewish and Negro cycles, the approach was different. These films are propaganda tempered by entertainment; there is no denying the courageous intention and genuine sincerity of their makers. They have shown the tortured violence of the Jew- or Negro-hater (Crossfire, No Way Out); the reactions of a small town to the discovery that their trusted, apparently white doctor had Negro blood (Lost Boundaries); the confused anti-Semitism lurking in the minds of those who pride themselves on tolerance (Gentleman's Agreement). They have brought into the open the ugly conflicts beneath the surface of America, and the fact that the most conservative stronghold in America is prepared to make such films, and to allow them to be shown abroad, is the greatest possible tribute to the strength of a country which has never been ashamed to show its faults.

But these films are made by business men as well as by social reformers; the major concern is to entertain, and for this reason while presenting a problem they must also show its solution. The man half-mad with race hatred is destroyed by society; the small town accepts its Negro doctor, congratulating itself on its charity; in Pinky it is made clear that the place of a trained Negro is with his own people, rather than in the hazards of a mixed community—the final shot of this picture, indeed, was a betrayal of the rest of the film. How much this type of betrayal vitiates the picture's message it is difficult to say, since the effect of the films on American audiences cannot be gauged. Moss Hart (who scripted Gentleman's Agreement) is said to have had an encounter which is at least significant. A minor technician working on the picture told him afterwards that being associated with such a film had made a deep impression on him; when the gratified writer asked for details he said, "I'll be more careful in future; I won't ever ill-treat a Jew in case it turns out that he's really a Christian." [...].

[I]t seems clear that in making sociological pictures Hollywood has the needs of its audience very clearly in mind; just as in a Capra film we are assured that right will triumph, so in a racial discrimination picture we are presented with the facts, and these are then twisted (in varying degrees) to provide a solution for the screen. It is courageous to proclaim that America has its oppressed classes, but it is not essentially controversial: there will always be a happy ending. In the same way, even Willie Stark is not allowed to continue in triumph, his death (however adventitious) gives their chance to those who have learnt their political lesson from his life.

Hollywood, in other words, acts both as the national conscience (Willie Stark) and as the national comforter (Mr. Deeds). To solve the problems of society, at a personal level and on the screen, is to suggest the possibility of a national solution, and so—in accordance with the first rule of showmanship—to send the audience home happy. [...].

[Sight & Sound (London), November 1950, pp. 276–79, 285, excerpted.]

Comments on the Screen (1918)
Janet Flanner

How much most of us owe to the cinema melodrama! What would we know of kidnapping the heroine on a fleet-footed horse, for instance, if it were not for the motion picture "Western?" What would we know of that flip use of two guns at once—the last word in ambidextrous efficiency—if it were not for W.S. Hart, Tom Mix and other kind men who have apparently made it their life work to see that fast riding and hard drinking never die?[1] In our home life we know naught of brigandage, holdups, kidnappings, even of love, and the like. We have been kept completely ignorant of the pleasant use of firearms when shot from both hips, owing, likely, to our parent's timorous dispositions and the fact that our neighbor's houses and yards set close to the right and left of us as we go down the cement walk.

Three meals a day, an honest clerkship and an occasional "see-America-first" trip are about all we know from actual experience. But we have learned enough from the Western cinema to feel that, emotionally, we have lived a rich life indeed.

Most thankful of all are we for the Western cinema bar.

❧

In this day of limited taste, with sarsaparilla and chocolate soda, the extreme outer edges of the government's answer to our thirst, the barroom scene assumes a new responsibility as an entertainer.[2] It has always been a rich field. The chief brigand and his coterie of friends, on whom we Easterners—to a Californian all things are East, even Indiana—have turned rapt eyes at least once a week ever since we were old enough to go to the precinct motion picture house alone, have swaggered up before its wooden counter 100,000 times, surely, and for our entertainment rapped for whisky straight. After drinking down their cold tea they have turned—this they never fail to do—and rested the elbows away from the camera on the bar's edge while they handled the plot. Then they, meaning the hero and his confrere, would stride away from the bar and the hero's mind would be made up. It was always made up when he left the bar with a long, swinging stride.

Of course, if he wabbled [sic] pitifully on leaving the counter, the barroom scene became a little sadder and not so invigorating, for one realised that it indicated the heroine was going to be forced into taking some temperance and reform steps before the end of the sixth reel. The way a hero acted before the bar indicated fairly enough what responsibilities were cut out for him in the play. If he drank recklessly, he was a bad man—see W. S. Hart for details—and would please you for 589 feet with bad-man carryings-on and soothe you for eleven by a change of heart. If he drank, steely-eyed and quiet, he was going to be desperate, maybe, but always just in his shooting. He would look out for the poor and innocent and disdain, even at the last moment, perhaps, actually to kill the villain. The steely-eyed drinker was self-contolled. He took his pleasure sparsely.

The "supers" in a "Western" could drink at the bar any way they pleased, just so they did not thump the wooden counter. They might stick their feet up but thumping was reserved for the leading man.

❧

Cinema bars come in two sorts. There are close-ups and what is called long-shots. The close-ups show the glittering glasses and accompanying bartender's cheery face. The long shots show the backs of the drinkers and produce atmosphere rather than indicate action. They have nothing to do with the plot, but are a customary courtesy.

❧

William Hart, of course, is the hardest drinker on the screen. If the public ever becomes completely in sympathy with the white ribbon movement poor Mr. Hart will have a tight squeeze to earn his living.[3] William Farnum is an occasional taster, but a tendency always to be an older and long-suffering brother, whose younger kin has the privilege of doing all the riotous living, has restricted him in his habits.[4] He appeals to a different class of people in consequence—those who enjoy a steady pillar of virtue, which advances day and night without an interesting falter.

Fairbanks does not drink at bars in the pictures at all any more. He has got to be a healthy ideal of late and has stinted his fullest powers of self-expression. Back in the early days, though, when he did not need to be so cautious, he was known, in a small way, as being quite comic at certain times.

❧

There is nothing in history like the Western cinema dance-hall scenes. How unfortunate history was written before motion pictures were invented. They could have helped color it so. How they could have improved upon every chapter devoted to the growth of all our glorious country between the Pacific and the Mississippi. How they could have livened up some of the duller pages, unillustrated, that we waded through in the sixth grade. The gold rush of '49 has never done so well as it has in the cinemas. Art has improved upon nature. If another gold rush could only be instituted, certainly half the citizens of the country could be relied upon to do the thing up handsomely this time, and get ready for a drive cross the states and a life in the dance halls of the West that would show they had not been asleep at the cinemas or looked upon good advice in vain.

❧

In many ways, the "Western" is a picturization of the country's suppressed desires. It is what the best of America would be if it lived up to its reputation. It is what many of us like to think it is. Being entirely concerned as a rule with the reckless doings of men, it appeals to women and small boys inordinately. It is what a brave life of freedom would be if we only had a good stage manager.

A healthy tradition will go out when the "Western" fails to appeal. A slice of our history out of which we have built a veritable culture will topple at our heels. Surely this will never take place though; at least not so long as the producers keep the tradition going. They have shown us our country as it never was and we can not get along without the vision now.

[*Indianapolis Star* (Indianapolis), 14 July 1918, section 5, pp. 33, 38.]

Imitation Chinchilla (1920)
Harriette Underhill

Imitation chinchilla and a plaster-of-Paris Venus de Milo can effectually spoil any day for us if they are mixed in just the right proportions and administered via the screen.

The first picture we ever saw contained samples of what has since become our *bête noire* and we disliked them on sight. And in the course of three years devoted more or less to sitting through feature pictures we have become so sensitive that, when the heroine is about to be projected into our midst and we read on the screen, "Alice, the spoiled daughter of a millionaire," we involuntarily close our eyes and then open them a little at a time, hoping and praying that Alice will not be clad in a coat with an imitation chinchilla collar. Imitation white fox is also good as a day-spoiler, and a pair of tango slippers worn with a sports suit has been known to send our temperature up three points.

A plaster Venus placed in the center of a library-table has almost the same effect. Three years ago we went into this thing trustingly with all of our ideals intact, but, alas, how soon was our faith blasted! In those early days we felt so keenly on the subject that we went around among our friends bemoaning the fact that bad taste in dress and house-furnishings was rampant in the silent drama. They paid us scant attention!

"How did you like *A House Divided?*" they would ask; and we would murmur, "It was furnished in such atrocious taste!"[1] Or, "Was *The Other Woman* good?" "She must have been," we would answer, "or she would never have dared to wear such dreadful clothes."

Few of our listeners had any sympathy with us. "What do you care what kind of furs she wore if she successfully defended herself against the onslaughts of the villain and married the hero?" was their attitude, and, "Does it matter how the library was furnished when you could never guess until the last reel who shot the millionaire as he sat reading under his night-lamp?" And then one day the editor of this magazine asked: "What do you think the motion-pictures are most in need of?" And without an instant's hesitation we replied:

"A final censor to see that everybody in the east is suitably garbed, and that the interior decorations are not going to offend anyone who knows better." [...][2]

"For, just because a star happens to photograph well and have a trick of pantomime doesn't argue that she knows what to buy and when to wear it; and just because a man can direct a picture and knows all about continuity it doesn't mean that he will know how to collect furniture that will make you think you are really in the library of 'a home on Fifth Avenue.' "

The editor nodded and seemed about to speak, but we gave her no chance.

"That was one nice thing about Madame Petrova's pictures: she used her own sets, and they looked like rooms that people lived in.[3] But you know the words 'Library in the home of Senator Walton' in a scenario are usually the signal for the property man to get out one massive mahogany table with lions carved on the legs, one lamp with a globe made out of irregular pieces of glass like a kaleidoscope, one plaster image of the Venus de Milo, one bronze horse with an Arab on his back carrying a spear rampant, one ormolu clock, one silver vase with natural or paper roses in it, one Chinese-image paper-weight, one ivory paper-knife, one Japanese screen, one bear rug, one tiger rug, one Wilton rug, and one portrait of somebody's ancestor. [...]

"I think it is quite appalling and quite interesting, particularly as I have been told that the poorer people who recently have made a great deal more money than they ever had before, are spending it for interior decorations, and that they have copied as nearly as possible what they see on the screen, both in house-furnishings and in clothes."

"Heaven forbid!" we murmured, "put not your trust in movies." For we couldn't think unmoved of those poor creatures working for a paltry ten or twelve dollars a day and then spending it on Louis chairs and bronze gladiators.

"That is why we insist that they need censors; not for the pictures—they are doing very well—but for the material before it goes into the pictures."

"And how do you account for this indifference on the part of the director?"

"It isn't indifference. He is probably doing his 'darnedest.' It's ignorance, for you know there are a lot of motion-picture directors who can direct but who can not do anything else. Being a motion-picture director is often a matter of environment or accident. In the United States there must be at least a thousand directors, and they can't all be raised in millionaires' homes. Some directors know how to direct a picture, and they also know all about acting, dressing, writing titles, and furnishing homes. But they are the ones who have to be engaged a year ahead if you want them to direct a picture for you, and they command salaries equaled only by the movie stars or the President of these United States."

"But why this melancholy lack?" asked our editor.

"Well, I'll tell you a secret: Many of the motion-picture directors have been something else until quite recently; they have popped in, so to speak, and haven't learned the game thoroughly. [...] There are directors and there are interior decorators, but few directors are also interior decorators.

"The saving grace is that some of the large companies now have art directors, but too often their interiors are 'faultily faultless, icily regular, splendidly null.' One art director, we remember, furnished the heroine's bedroom with a black-velvet bed and nothing else, and in her reception room he stood one chaste marble bench. Such sets never look as though any one used them save to act in. And, really, the easiest way to make a copy of a millionaire's home is to live in one. [...]

❧

"And do you, too, believe that girls who go to the movies (and that means all girls) are influenced in their selection of clothes by what they see on the screen?"

"Do we believe it? We know it. Out best-beloved actress appeared recently on the screen wearing a most striking hat. It was large and white, and had a black buckle on it. We noticed and admired it, and so did others.

"Two days later those hats began to appear everywhere. A walk down Broadway from the Times Building to Herald Square brought to our attention half a dozen copies. Thirty-fourth Street yielded three more, and when we stopped in to have our nails done, Ray, our favorite manicure lady, hurled herself at us with the query: 'Did you see the hat Elsie Ferguson wore at the Rivoli on Sunday?[4] I got one just like it. I drew a picture of it, and my milliner made it, and all the girls in the shop are copying mine.' Now, can you ask if girls who go to the movies are influenced by what they see on the screen?"

The editor nodded, but he didn't seem as much interested as he had been in furniture.

"Do you know," we said confidentially, "that in one of the big pictures which we saw only last week one of the men wore white spats with his evening clothes?"

"No!"

"Yes, and he wasn't ordered off the set nor anything. He stayed and finished dancing with the rest of the guests. And no one seemed to think it was unusual, and perhaps it wasn't, in that gathering, for we spotted two guests with black bow ties and tail-coats, one with chamois gloves heavily stitched in black, and one with what appeared to be a red-bordered handkerchief tucked between his shirt-bosom and his waistcoat.

"We have proof positive that many of those weird things which we see on the screen are directly traceable to the director. [...]

"So, if directors know as little as that about men's clothes, fancy the poor things trying to struggle with the problem of women's clothes! Most of them do not even try; they just trust to luck, and their luck isn't always with them. Statistics show that to the average man white aigrets and a black-velvet gown spell affluence at any time of the day.

"But imitation furs are the worst of all crimes. Women seem to fancy that tabby is going to look exactly like sable on the screen, and that no one is going to recognize that 'Iceland Fox' which curls like an angry rattlesnake when it gets damp.

"Yes, we know furs are expensive things and people who take part in ensemble numbers can't afford them; but let them do without them. Mrs. Vanderbilt's guest might have chosen to call on her wearing no fur at all—rich people do such strange things—but we know, and so does every one else, that she never would call wearing a large white rabbit-skin stole with black tails sewed on it.

"We saw that in a picture not long ago, and we saw the star, who was announced as 'the only daughter of a multi-millionaire,' cross the ocean dressed in gray velvet and wearing an enormous cape of imitation chinchilla, and a large hat of the same fur with velvet streamers hanging almost to the bottom of her gown.

"But of course these are isolated cases (and they should be isolated if there's any danger of contagion). Many of the stars dress exquisitely, and act in perfectly appointed homes which are set up in the studios."

[*The Delineator* (New York) 96, April 1920, p. 27, 107, excerpted.]

The Wanton Playgoer (1931)
Djuna Barnes

The motion picture industry is very anxious that I not tell this. They are trying, and occasionally with success, to rope in the big manufacturers. That is, they say: "For so many thousands, my dear sir, I have a lovely spot in my next film, *The Sands of Desire*—*or what have you*, that could be used to display your product. You are manufacturing a handsome gadget known as the "Day by Night Mattress." Well why should not the heroine, in full view of the audience, do what reclining the story calls for on your Trade-Mark? A close-up will, of course, cost more, but think what it would mean to you. There has never before been a better medium for advertising. Certainly the fee I shall charge will pay half the production costs of the film, but that suits me, and it would bring you bigger and better business, and that suits you." Well, I hope enough of the public will see this and register anger when their favorite moves across the screen, holding on to, trailing about her, leaning against, or just laughing heartily at anything with a trade-mark.

[*Theatre Guild Magazine* (New York), May 1931, pp. 32–33, excerpted.]

La Femme Sihouette: The Bronze Age (1925)[1]
Eulalia Proctor

In the cycle of Vogue, for femininity and feminine devotee, this is the Bronze Age. When Tut's tomb was opened, more than the treasures already described through the Sunday editions were unearthed—jaded Fancy took a new lease on life in a colorful way![2] The Egyptian influence was felt in all circles of style; the smartest set and its sycophants were thrilled infinitely because brown in its varied shades and hues was removed from the ranks of sombre coloring and became a flaunting, exultant thing, which might be honored and admired with obvious respectability remaining intact!

Ere this, Mr. Man had sat up, rubbed his eyes and decided that there was a pre-Volsteadian kick to the presentation of the brown beauty chorus of "Shuffle Along" and similar aggregations.[3] When Milady discovered that friend Man was going back night after night to see and hear "If You've Never Been Vamped by a Brownskin, etc." said Milady being chastely blonde (whether by accident or by design not mentioned in the footnotes) she also sat up—marvelled, trembled and was consumed with jealousy. Rouge and powder, as were, lost their charms, except to conceal the ravages of despairing tears! Milady took to the great outdoors and to the cosmetic expert. New shades of powder and startling effects in rouge are the result! Yet no one dared to intimate it is because Di(a)na of the Brownskin had ascended the throne of Vogue!

The Sheik, (seething from the pen of Mrs. Hull) became the desirable thing in masculinity, particularly if he be the possessor of engagingly dark and sleek hair, insolently glancing dark eyes, was svelte with a tawny glow to his smooth skin![4] Sheba, bronzed and artful, became the popular synonym for all that is attractive and chic in femininity! Harlem and Chicago's South Side became the cynosure and the Mecca of thousands who confess, through action, a desire for a "close-up" of the exponents of the authentic brown on their native heath!

Has Hart, Schaffner & Marks ever produced a living model half so intriguing, (or with the drawing power,) as these scores of suave young negroes, shading from creamy olive to cocoa brown or velvety black as one prefers, who wear immaculately the correct thing, manage to inject just the proper degree of suggestive proposal into the barbaric "perambulating," speak affluently the latest social lingo, and accept with passionate impassivity the offerings of the erstwhile ingenue or her sophisticated sister? Why seek widely advertised Hawaii or Tahiti to "enrich one's experiences?" They offer only a panorama of luxuriant scenery and a sameness of men and women who do dances in native (and censored) fashion. The truly initiated know that there is luxuriant scenery, a variety of men and women, also authentically brown, and native dances, UNCENSORED, to be found at home (Furnishing far more thrills per gallon with less cost per mile!) Then, too, there is an indisputable genuineness about these "made in America" browns that fascinates one. (The exposé of foreigners by the Hearst papers might well be extended to tropical products in bronze.) Frankly, joyously, unmistakably brown, one's assets are increased manifold if one exercises the proper discretion, or lack of it.

Brownskin choruses, wilder wild women, wielders of jazz instruments, all are making "big time." Rumor credited Mr. Ziegfield with preparing to cater to popular taste with a bronze "Follies."[5] Art, drama and literature contribute their portion to this whimsical weaving of laurels! In the wake of an Emperor Jones trails Rosalind and All God's Chilluns with sorry themes, but bronze coloring![6] White Cargo, with a star who does her best to be the brown vampire of the tropics, leaves New York for a run in Chicago where brown vampires long since made their marks: a Viennese artist selects a wee brown maid as a type perfect of beautiful women; Prof. Starr, of the University of Chicago, declares the Liberian maiden the criterion of feminine charm: the Prince of Wales dances with an authentically tinted American made brown in a Parisienne setting and rewards her with a jewelled and monogrammed bauble—and so on, until "Finis" will be scrawled at the bottom of the page.[7]

Some declare that the cycle turns slowly and that a new fad approaches. Reminiscently, Chicago and the hazy, brilliant "Sunset" flash on the screen of memory.

At a nearby table a muchly courted youth blows smoke rings while Milady sends him hastily scribbled telephone numbers by the obliging waiter. He turns his jewelled cigarette holder, musingly, and addressing his remark into the smoky atmosphere yawns—"Before us ... poodle dogs! After us...?" The arched brow and twisted smile remain with me as the rest of the picture fades!

The editor invites introspection as well as prophecy. How has the bronze age affected you? Can you answer the query of the Prince of 35th Street, "After us?" Will it be assimilation of a more intensive nature, or is after us—the deluge?

[*The Messenger* (New York) 7:2, February 1925, p. 93.]

The Color Fad (1929)
Ruby Berkley Goodwin

Every once in a while the whole world adopts a fad. "Day by day in every way," was translated into every language including the Scandinavian. The short dress craze has spread until even in Turkey the women have brazenly pulled the veils from their faces and looked at men without lowering their eyes.[1]

The motor car was a fad at first but now it is a necessity. In fact, the dealers are telling us that every family should have two cars. And so it goes. You never know when a fad is a fad. One fad blows over; almost over night—another becomes a custom.

But this newest fad. Where will it lead to and what will be the consequences of it?

This Color Fad!

Our blue bloods have gone negroid. The smartest thing now is to do a Negro night club or road house.

New York started the fad, probably out of curiosity. Negroes are kings of the art of entertaining and some of the bolder Nordics probably wanted to see what an evening's entertainment would be at a Negro night club. What they saw must have pleased them for they went in ever-increasing numbers to Harlem's clubs until now it is the natural thing to see whites, blacks, varying shades of browns and yellows dancing together and making whoopee.

Even black lovers are considered ultra swank, and so Harlem became the rendezvous for the pedigreed New Yorker who wished to be classed as modern.

But the fad didn't stop there. In Chicago it became the rage and now the Negro night clubs of Los Angeles are filled to overflowing with prominent whites who like dark atmosphere.

A French writer gives us the low-down on the situation in France: "Paris went rather silly over Negro bands when jazz was imported from America some five or six years ago, but Paris has gone absolutely crazy over Negro atmosphere, the smokier the better. At the smartest parties these nights there are always Negro guests invited to be the hit of the evening. Montmartre and Montparnasse are off the night programs of the smartest snobs who would never dream of finishing up their early morning elsewhere than at a Negro cafe and dance hall."[2]

The Negro has invaded Hollywood with his natural charm and his sonorous voice and directors are rejoicing over the invasion! the publicity departments have exhausted their store of adjectives in trying to tell the many wonders the Negro has brought to the screen.

Farina is by far the most popular member of Our Gang.[3] Stepin Fetchit, a dark boy from Dixie is running away with the comic part of the show.[4] Nina Mae McKinney bids fair to rival Clara Bow as a sepia siren.[5] The Metro–Goldwyn–Mayer production Hallelujah will write more history for these people of color.[6]

Phonograph companies vie with each other for Negro singers: radio corporation managers put them on as headliners.

Roland Hayes, internationally famed tenor, shared with Fritz Kreisler, renowned violinist, the distinction of being the only artist to appear three time in Carnegie Hall last season.[7] It is said that no other American born artist has ever held the interest of the music world as he has.

Until the time of his death Bert Williams was king of comedians.[8] Now Al Jolson and the Two Black Crows are cashing in on Negro popularity and are going great guns.[9]

At one time all Negroes were bleaching because it was the smart thing to be high yellow or white, but now![10] Motion picture directors want "pure" Negro types. Society debutantes who were here-to-fore a dainty study in pink and white are now spending days and money to acquire a good healthy tan. That they succeed pretty well is told in a news item. A group of them entered a smart hotel dining room. The management refused them service thinking they were Negroes.

Heretofore black was used for mourning. Now it is used for table cloths, dresses, pillows, rugs, drapes, everything from soup to nuts.

Authors have gone Negro. The year's best seller, Scarlet Sister Mary, is a story of a Negro settlement in Carolina where the people are not immoral but they are unmoral.[11]

In its wake comes Blacker the Berry, Plum Bun, and a flock of others good, bad and indifferent.[12]

On the crest of this wave of color Charles Gilpin, Daniel Haynes and Paul Robeson are starring in Broadway productions and theatregoers are discussing Emperor Jones, Porgy, Earth and the latest sensation, Harlem.[13]

Where will it stop? Or will it stop?

I have never believed that the Negro wanted social equality. Economic and political equality is only right and just. But no matter what color the skin, every nationality feels more at home with its kind be they Jew or Gentile, Scotch or Irish.

The Nordic draws its entertainment from every group. One season they go wild over everything Italian, another season the French have the spotlight, another season everybody is strumming a uke and hula dancing is the vogue.

For years Negroes have fought segregation of public utilities but they have never tried to force themselves upon the social elite of America. It seems that the elite itself has broken down the partition and has shown an over-willingness to mingle with *God's Step-children*.[14]

In Paris some of the Negroes are fighting this. They want to keep their surroundings Negroid.

Our French correspondent, Anita Thompson writes, "For themselves the colored exiles have opened up a sort of community bar and dance hall with a black bruiser at the door to keep smart Paris out."

The social intimacy brings about more serious thoughts. Black lovers might lead to more inter-marriages and inter-marriage brings with it many perplexing and difficult phases.[15] Of course intermixing is as old as the world, hence these different shades from octaroon to jet black. And as I said at first it's a fad now—this color craze.

Or is it a cloud the size of a man's hand that will grow and grow until color equality covers the universe eliminating Nordic superiority and making all me[n] free and equal, endowing them with the same God-given rights of life, liberty and the pursuit of happiness?

[*Flash* (Los Angeles) 2:23, 31 December 1929, p. 11.]

Fredi Washington Strikes a New Note (1934)[1]
Fay M. Jackson

Uncle Tom has dropped his hat; Aunt Jemima has removed her bandana; pickaninnies are wearing shoes and slowly but surely, Hollywood films are growing up.[2]

Witness *Imitations of Life,* [sic] the Universal John M. Stahl production from the book of Fannie Hurst.[3]

But a comparatively short time ago motion pictures seemed to have restricted Negro performers to jungle types. Only the "fat, black and ugly" of the race were able to crash filmdom's gates and become a part of the fabulous payroll associated with production of motion pictures. Directors thought only in terms of plantation themes as a vehicle for featured colored players. Religious fervor was the only emotional expression the Negro seemed to be capable of. Singing and shouting his only mediums.

For great historical roles whose real actors were admittedly Negroes or persons of African descent, motion pictures have persisted in using white performers either under cork or brazenly disregarding historical fact altogether, with no hint as to their true identity.

Fig. 4.9   Photograph of Fay Jackson from mid 1930s.

The most tragic situations, the greatest conflicts, the most dramatic phases of our racial life: those concerning the mulatto, were ignored and overlooked altogether. For what reason, I shall not say. Some think it was because the studios did not wish to admit another type of Negro into its fraternity. Some think it was because this type of Negro is more militant and aggressive. There are numerous conjectures on the subject.

In *Imitations of Life*, Fredi Washington, New York dancer-actress, utters a cry, "I want the same things other people enjoy," that found an echo in the hearts of 12 million smoldering Negroes throughout the United States and probably has been since their so-called emancipation from chattel slavery.[4]

Actress though she be, Fredi Washington expresses the desire for freedom and equal justice in this picture that is more convincing than any mere performer could have voiced. True to her own life, the injustices of color and race prejudices have retarded and prohibited a fuller life and freedom of expression.

You have seen movies showing the persecutions of the Jews; the injustices of imperialistic Russia; the madness of various dictatorships trampling on the rights of human beings. You will feel some of the weight of the bars of race prejudice in this country when you see, probably for the first time, the true symbol of the American Negro struggling against these bars as Fredi Washington portrays the role of "Peola" in *Imitations of Life*.[5]

It may be an accident that Hollywood films are growing up. It may be the demand of the times that social injustices have found a "run" in their scenario departments. Credit Fannie Hurst (or some Negro informant) for conceiving *Imitations of Life*, John Stahl for directing it sympathetically, Fredi Washington, against heavy odds, for presenting the substance of the opus in a manner that is intelligent and convincingly TRUE to LIFE.[6]

["Fredi Washington Strikes a New Note in Hollywood Film: *Imitations*,"
Associated Negro Press (Hollywood), 12 December 1934.]

Imitations: Life, Color and Pancakes (1935)
Hazel Washington

Thank God, Mr. Sterling A. Brown, reviewer and conductor of Chronicle and Comment for *Opportunity*, was not taken in by the motion picture *Imitation of Life*. Neither was I, though I know a full two dozen supposedly intelligent Negroes who are still prattling about the "break" that Hollywood, at last, gave us in this picture.

For me, it was full of subtle irony, partially veiled insult, and a half-hidden, dimly suggested contempt for the whole Negro race. It was all there, behind the scenes if you will, but there for those to see who could see it. When the pancake eater voiced that much repeated expression, "Once a pancake, always a pancake," he did so with a complete deliberation and an unmistakable, emphatic double meaning.[1] My mind went back to the days when grandmother used to tell us stories of life on the plantation. When her master was displeased with something the slaves had or had not done, he would say to them, "You darkies will always be darkies." Now, whether pancakes or darkies, the meaning is the same.

Deliver me from existence, if I am either a Delilah or a Peola. These characters are not only untypical, they are inconsistent and untrue. Where among modern Negro women can you find one who prefers living in a white woman's basement and massaging her mistress' tired feet, (tired either from working or dancing) to making an independent home among her own people, and enjoying the peace and comfort earned by her own ingenuity? Where can you find an intelligent Negro girl, white or black, who would rather work and be white than live in ease and luxury with a loving black mother? If I am not right about this, let us hope that I am.

The scene in which Delilah gave her daughter away when she was "Passing" on the job said this to me: "Negroes want to be white, merely for the sake of being white; they would rather be white and poor than black and rich; they would rather be white and working than black and resting … they would rather be white under any circumstances." I do not believe this, cannot in fact; at least, I am sure it is not typical. I believe that Negroes, who are light enough to pass for white, do so for economic security, the thing which Peola turned away from to be white. Negroes pass in order to obtain the cultural advantages which are denied a black man in these United States of America. If there were no prejudice, no discrimination, why shouldn't one just as soon be black as white?

Now, I don't know why either Mr. Brown or Miss Hurst should have been worried about the shape of Delilah's cap.[2] It was her head that concerned me, and whether clothed in a white chef's cap or a twenty-five dollar marcel, it was decidedly empty.[3]

I suppose the Negro's recognition as, "a definite part of the social pattern of American life," was brought forth in the scene which took place after the party, when Delilah, though not expected to do so, and though clothed in silk and marcel, felt the instinctive urge of the old southern mammy to clean up after the white folks; while poor white black Peola cried her heart out in the basement, because she was denied the privilege of coming upstairs and making her share of the litter that her mother felt duty bound to remove.

I saw neither logical nor an artistic reason why the director took such pains to show us the ladies retreating for the night after that intimate discussion of their daughters' welfare; except to remind us that the Negroes' place in "the social pattern of American life" is downstairs. "The Stairs of Life," I called them. White goes up and black goes down, truly the stairs of life.

The theatre gasped with emotion, though I don't know of what sort, when Peola, under the direction of Hollywood, exclaimed, "Miss Bea, you don't know how it is to look white and be black." How much more dramatic … how much more realistic and true if Fredi Washington had been allowed to say in that cultured and sympathetic voice of hers, "You don't know how it is to feel white and be treated black."[4]

[*Opportunity* (New York) 13:6, June 1935, p. 185.]

Making Movies for Women (1927)
Beth Brown

Entertainment was conceived up in the Garden of Eden. Eve gave the first show the day she slipped into a fig leaf.

Adam, the audience, enjoyed himself so much, that he decided to go into the show business. From then on, shows were made by men for men—the Egyptian festivals, the Greek marathons, the Spanish bull fights, all of them man-made entertainment for men.

And, when a new entertainment developed—the motion picture—it was still man-made entertainment for men. Justly so, because at first, the audiences, in the majority, were men.

Where were the women?

In the kitchen with the dishes, in the parlor with the broom, in the nursery with the children.

Then along came science bringing the electric dishwasher and the vacuum cleaner—and leisure.

And women straightway took their leisure to the movie theatre.

That's how it happened that audiences reversed. Now we find that 83 per cent. of motion picture patrons are women. But they are still being served the man-made entertainment!

I don't argue that men can't make entertainment for women.

Men make fashions for women—and successfully—but they never forget that they're making them for women. Chefs invent pastries, and merchants operate department stores, knowing that their success depends upon their appeal to women.

But, with the motion picture, I've been surprised to notice that the preferences of the 83 per cent. are often overlooked.

Women's main interest lies in clothes, children and romance.

Man's main interest is in achievement, athletics and war. When you feed that a steady diet, you're pleasing 17 per cent. of your audience—what about the 83 per cent. Women prefer stories of young romance and high society, an opportunity to see the homes of the rich, the clothes of the rich, and the manners of the rich. They like photoplays with a pictorial outdoor tone to rest them from their intense indoor existence. [...]

Women notice detail more readily than men, especially details, of costume, homefurnishing, etiquette and love-making. They notice high-heeled slippers of satin on the kitchen slavey, the property man's "dish of dough" that resembles a mess of Portland cement, changes of costume when the story sequence does not permit time for a change, unbecoming hair arrangement of the stars—detail, detail, detail. [...]

If woman's keen eye from the audience can scan the screen so critically, why not have a woman's keen eye at the studio supervise the details that women audiences notice? [...].

When I give a certain twist to a scenario, when I add a seemingly trivial scene to a script, when I cut and re-arrange and re-edit a film, when I prepare a set of titles giving an entirely new slant to a photoplay—man eyes at the studios stare at me with doubt and wonder. Sometimes in the dark of the projection room, a man whisper rises up to question my methods and motives. But staunch defenders—men for whom I have worked—down the whisper with the hoarse retort:

"Remember the 83 per cent.! We're making the movies for the women!"

Then, even though they are man-made movies—they succeed because they are being made—for women!

[Moving Picture World, 26 March 1927, p. 342, excerpted.]

Women: Hollywood Version (1942)
Joy Davidman

In a few ill-chosen words Hollywood not long ago summed up a prevailing attitude toward women. The film was *Tom, Dick, and Harry*; the speaker, Miss Ginger Rogers; the line, approximately:

"It's as natural for a girl to want to make a good marriage as for a man to want to get ahead in business."

The worst offense was that no offense was intended. The picture's producers would have been horrified at an accusation of misogyny; they sincerely believed themselves to be glorifying the American girl, and they did indeed present her as an engaging young lady. *Tom, Dick, and Harry* was an unusually original comedy, with much genuine wit and some genuine tenderness; yet *Tom, Dick, and Harry* accepted as natural and right and healthy the doctrine that the American girl should sell her sex in the most profitable market. Nor does the market end with marriage. Once caught, the husband must be held; and woman's life work, hundreds of films imply, is holding her man with the aid of the beauty parlor and judicious fits of the sulks. The movies dress this doctrine prettily; they adorn it with revealing negligees, demure maidservants, and incredible kitchens that are paradises of labor-saving gadgets. It remains, however, an uncomfortably close relative of the doctrine more succinctly expressed in Germany: *Kinder, Kuche, und Kirche.*[1]

Yet, in the United States, the emancipation of women is part and parcel of the democracy we are fighting for. Increasingly, women succeed along lines once reserved for men; as in the Soviet Union and Britain, women replace men wherever possible in the war effort.[2] Nor are their homes worse run, their children worse cared for. On the contrary; as any psychologist knows, women who have realized their potentialities as creative human beings make better mothers than frustrated women who must take all their ambitions out on their children. Thus the films are lagging behind the country. Their half-unconscious war against the emancipation of women certainly gives unintended support to one of the tenets of fascism—the deliberate debasement of womanhood.

Male chauvinism is a subtler, milder, more easy-going thing than, for instance, race chauvinism. Perhaps for that reason it is singularly persistent. Many a man who judges his own conduct by the most enlightened standards will apply far more primitive ideas to his wife's behavior; many a fighter for freedom has to fight also against the tendency to regard his womenfolk as property. Dominating commercial entertainment as it does, male chauvinism has the power of perpetuating itself. It is able to imply a dozen times a day that the measure of a girl's value to society is her erotic attractiveness. The radio serials and the popular magazines preach something called Love (= sex plus financial dependence) as the only real fruition of a woman's life. And a girl's "personality" itself, according to the films and the ads, is composed of cosmetics, charm, and that Ohrbach dress.[3]

Now and then a movie actually discusses the "woman question," although there is a significant lack of films dealing with the historic fight of women for independence in any spirit but that of mockery. *Tom, Dick, and Harry* was fairly outspoken; it presented this "woman question" in terms of three alternative husbands—a millionaire, a go-getter, and a shiftless screwball. Although the heroine was a working girl, she regarded her work as nothing better than a stop-gap while she prepared for the "real business" of life. At first she chose the millionaire as the man who could most completely relieve her of all responsibility for her own existence; this was offered as the "practical" solution. Eventually, however, she eloped with the screwball, because her physical response when he kissed her was uncontrollable. This was the "romantic" and hence the "correct" solution. For "romance" is an indispensable adjunct of male chauvinism; it is obviously impossible for the films to advocate openly that women marry entirely for cash. The poor men would never stand for it. But *Tom, Dick, and Harry* never made any suggestion that the heroine might have something to offer the world as an individual; she was merely, to put it nakedly, something to be marketed. The salient feature of the film, indeed, was a series of dreams forecasting the girl's probable future with each man. In each case, her life was entirely what the man chose to make it.

☙

A logical development of this thesis is found in the group of films dealing with the misunderstood wife. She is, inevitably, a woman of the idle rich or a prosperous suburbanite; usually with no children, always with no work. She has a genuine grievance, the complete thwarting of all her impulses to be a useful member of society. The wistful reactionaries who exalt the home-keeping woman of more primitive cultures overlook the fact that the home used to be the factory, and the home-keeping woman the most productive worker in existence. She made her bread, she made clothes, she turned out innumerable essential articles; further back she ground the raw grain and carded the raw wool, accomplishing not one but a dozen different productive processes on each article of consumption. The more primitive the culture, the more completely all productive operations were carried on by women, while man went out and shot the raw material with his bow and arrow. Now the work has moved out of the home; but the woman remains. She sits with folded hands, which is good neither for her nor for her family, as anyone can testify who has watched the idle mothers in our parks tormenting their children. And her grievance takes itself out in Mah Jongg, ice-cream sodas, or, in the film, simple dissatisfaction with her husband. He doesn't love her enough, he loves his business more, he actually forgets their wedding anniversary or expects her to be polite to his nasty old boss. Ibsen's Nora, many years ago, simply walked out of her doll's house to get a job. But the films have not caught up to Ibsen yet. Their heroines can think of only one escape—a new man. In *Skylark*, even in the progressive *Male Animal*, in a hundred other movies the heroine tries "romance" briefly, ends by realizing that she loves her husband best, and crawls back chastened among the dolls. Husband, for his part, promises to pet the cute little thing more often. Thus the thesis of these films is teaching woman to "know her place."

When the movies do present a woman with a career, they usually take care to make her suffer for it. Sometimes she has dependents and is consequently "forced to sacrifice herself" by actually doing something useful and interesting with her life. Sometimes an exception is made; she is a member of a "womanly" profession such as acting, singing, nursing, and recently even medicine. Such trades make her glamorous, and, as glamour is the standard by which woman is judged, such trades are excusable. Nevertheless her career always separates her from her man or her child, and after spectacular suffering she comes to realize that she must abandon art for the home. The cardinal point of woman's emancipation—the admission that she can have a successful career and a successful marriage too—is almost never made. *The Men in Her Life* is the latest of this vintage; there have been countless others.

Then sometimes we have such movies as *Woman of the Year*, whose heroine is a pioneer in a profession—journalism—still considered by Hollywood to belong to the male. (The usual girl reporter of the films is only marking time till she can catch an editor.) The cards are therefore stacked against the heroine by making her not a sane journalist but an insane dynamo, and belaboring her with a pathetically frustrated spinster aunt to show the horrors awaiting career women. In defense of this film it has been alleged that the heroine was not meant to retreat into the kitchen, being portrayed as capable of speaking twenty-seven languages simultaneously, but as miserably incapable of making waffles. But this is just as male-chauvinist as the assumption that she belonged in the kitchen in the first place. Career women make very good waffles. So do career men.

To the anti-career list I need only add the endless films caricaturing the schoolteacher—noble but crotchety; caricaturing, as in *Design for Scandal*, the professional woman—thwarted and "unglamorous"; and, above all, caricaturing the unmarried business woman, who appears again and again as that minor comedy character, the office sourpuss. (A mother, presented as such, is on the other hand never-caricatured—she is always all-wise and all-sweet, except when she is a mother-in-law.)

Occasional movies contradicting this tendency should be mentioned: they are such films as *The Silver Cord* and *Craig's Wife*—ancient history now. But these were based on Broadway plays, and their type has almost disappeared in the prevailing conveyor-belt system of film-making. With the decline in film attendance there has come a decline in film quality from the 1935–39 high level. The mass production method throttles the many courageous and original people in Hollywood who might have something valuable to say on this and other subjects. There are, literally, only three plots being used in movies this year.

The Soviet film *Tanya*, whose heroine has career and husband too and makes a rich life for herself with both, is all the refutation necessary to the false husband-or-career alternative. But the deliberate attack on careers for women is only the male chauvinist's second front. It is doubtful whether all the film attacks ever influenced one girl to give up her job. Emotional attitudes, however, are more easily affected by films than are rational decisions; in other words, thousands of adolescent girls have been influenced subtly and perniciously in their expectations of life and their social relations by the antics of their favorite glamour girl. In forcing women into the harem, the important thing is to make the women like it; they must be induced to accept their unhealthy fate as highly moral and emotionally desirable. Consequently we have the whole *Back Street* school of films, glorifying a morbidly passive and self-effacing female type; the great range of movies, superficially quite inoffensive, which never say a word derogatory to women yet present them in a dependent and inferior position as a matter of course; and the still larger group of movies which apparently praise and "glorify" the American girl.

❦

The routine film heroine has no integrity, no sense, no reliability. She is always breaking off her engagement when a more enticing prospect comes along; yielding spinelessly to the blandishment of the brash youth whom she began by resenting; falling among thieves and Nazi spies; dancing helplessly in the background while the villain conks the hero; slapping faces at insults to her imbecile "dignity"; making an idiot of herself at baseball games. But ah, she has beauty! She has SA, she has It, she has Oomph; she has a wonderful apparatus for getting men excited. College students cry for her—according to the studio publicity department. That is all she knows on earth, and all she needs to know.

This phase of the attack on women is not clearly understood even by those who wage it. Producers select film actresses for their physical conformation; decorate them to enhance it; make it the whole point of a film; follow it around with the camera. They publicize a Veronica Lake or a Gene Tierney, whom nobody even pretends to consider actresses. They build movie after movie on the theme that Love is the Ultimate Reward of Life, especially when enhanced by furs and diamonds. In short, they attempt to educate girls for the happy life of the harem. But they do it quite without malice.

There are many reasons for the movie exploitation of sex. The most obvious is, of course, the box office; when you want to please an audience of 60,000,000 or so, it is not easy to find themes which will interest all of them. The most interesting theme of all—the real-life problems of the audience—is taboo in the films except to a group of progressives with the courage and the imagination to tackle such problems. The Frank Capras and the John Fords, the John Howard Lawsons and the Dalton Trumbos, may come to grips with reality.[4] But, to most film-makers, the only subject on which they are sure of interesting a vast audience is sex. It is the one thing that almost everybody has.

More significant than this nakedly financial motive, however, is the plain fact that film-makers write as they think. If they regard woman as a commercial article, that is because pretty girls come to Hollywood from all over the country to trade in their beauty. Beauty is a drug on the market in southern California, with the natural result—the price goes down.

This is still not the whole story, however. After all, film-makers were not born to the celluloid; they have known women in more normal settings, and there are plenty of independent and intelligent women in Hollywood too, to enlighten them. If film society really were a grotesque contrast to the rest of our society, as scandalmongers imply, the harem ideal would not be presented in many movies as a matter of course. But film society is not a contrast; it is an intensification. It concentrates in articulate people most of the prevailing attitudes of our civilization, good and bad. Some of the most devoted and clear-sighted anti-fascists of the country may be found in Hollywood, some of the finest artists, some of the most typical hard-working plain Americans. It is not by accident that southern California has become a Mecca for fighting intellectual anti-fascist refugees from all over Europe. But in Hollywood may also be found some of the most degenerate and parasitic elements of our society—the swamis, the astrologers, the debutantes, the fifth columnists, the reactionaries of every size and shape.[5] Thus, in presenting woman as they do, the films present in intensified form an attitude that exists wherever reaction may be found; an attitude based at least in part on the facts. For there is no denying that thousands of young girls do think of themselves as articles for the marriage market; do track down a husband as the sole end of existence; and do feel cheated when they discover that glamourized Love is not a sufficient full-time occupation. Neither, let it be admitted, is having a baby.

How great a part the movies play in forming girls according to this pattern is not easily measured. Perhaps the greatest single cause of harm is in the compensatory mechanism which women develop, and which the movies encourage, to overcome the unhappiness of their frustration and disappointment—a mechanism which has made the neurotic, attention-getting woman so frighteningly familiar in our society. Taught to value herself only by her reflection in a man's admiring eyes, many a woman spends her whole time in desperate scheming for attention, in frenzied resentment of people or ideas that "come between her and her family"; many a woman clings pathetically to girlishness well into her fifties. These cases are not intrinsically inferior people but poisoned people; the film is not the major source of poison, but an important contributory cause of what amounts to an undermining of the family.

But the whole process of corruption-by-film involves a vicious circle. The movies, out of carelessness or miseducation or corruption, imitate and prettify some of the worst features of daily life; and life promptly imitates the movies. As real life has less money to spend than the movies, however, life imitates without prettifying, and the results of such imitation are hardly satisfactory. Meanwhile young women are miseducated out of respect for themselves as human beings, and—equally deadly—their menfolk are warned not to respect them. A superficial reform of the movie industry is not the corrective. The failure of the Hays Office and the Legion of Decency to achieve anything like intelligent human decency is the failure of the taboo imposed from without.[6] The true corrective is in the education of the American people. When the people at last repudiate completely all expressions of male chauvinism, the movies will hastily follow suit.

[New Masses 44, 14 July 1942, pp. 28–31.]

Women Only (1947)

Cecelia Ager

Women are very much in the minds of movie producers, but especially when producers are planning their pictures. Women key their first decision: Shall we strive for their favor, or do we face the fact that we're going to do without them?

They know full well they're going to do without them any time they go to work on a Western, a kick-'em-in-in-the-groin murder mystery, a Bob Hope—Danny Kaye batch of slapstick, a John Ford chantey of the sea. To boil it down, the matinees will be off for any movie so heartless it fails to stay prostrated before a woman's problems; in other words, for any movie that fails to give the musical score a chance to swell.

So much for the cads among the movie producers who choose to let the women languish at home. They merit none of our compassion; they make their decision with their eyes wide open. However, at this point I'd like to report the case of a certain independent movie producer who tries to straddle the issue.

He happens to be a henpecked fellow in his private life, so the movies he makes always show the man triumphant, picking his way through a clutter of supine female bodies with outstretched arms and submissive eyes. But he also happens to be a knowledgeable little chap who understands why he does what he does. "To stave off my own compulsion," he confesses, "and snatch what women for my audience I can, I make it a practice always to include a singularly articulate character who denounces women unmercifully. Curious, but this always seem to fetch them.

"I stumbled onto it long ago, but I still don't quite understand. Can it be it always works because each woman in the audience knows she's the exception, that the castigation applies to everyone else? Is it because, since every woman is in competition with all other women, it satisfies her sense of feminine justice to hear her ruthless competitors denounced? Or is it because no man has ever said things as bad about women as women say themselves? This I do know: no matter how violent the attack my stock woman-reviling character makes, the women in the audience relish it far more than men. Never do they complain.

"Complain! Shall I tip you off to what they really do? Soon as the picture's over, they telephone their dearest friend, beseech her to go see it quick. Sly minxes, they tell her it's wonderful or unique or stimulating, which of course it is. But the real reason they recommend it is to let their best friend hear from my woman-denouncing character what they themselves secretly think of her."

Let's leave this crafty little producer to his unworthy yet moderately successful devices and return to those who in cold blood set out to please the ladies and let everyone else drop dead.

Well, they all know the rules. They've been scanning each other's box-office grosses for years, figuring out what it is that keeps the girls stomping their feet in zero weather outside Radio City Music Hall, figuring it out the better to make likewise. Thus we have movie cycles. But to the rules. They begin: Garson being ladylike, Dunne being gracious, Colbert being regular, Bergman being natural, Hepburn being steely, Davis being alone.

Now what is there about this Big Six that makes them so irresistible, so dependable, such accomplished unfolders of folding money? The fact that everyone is an expert actress? Helps, but it's not the main thing. That each is a unique personality, herself come rain or come shine? Yes, that contributes, but it's not the nub. Think, girls, think. Excellent, exactly right. Yes, the fact that not one of them is a perfect beauty. Not one of them is capable of launching more than a smattering of small boats. Not one looks like Betty Grable, Lana Turner or even Rita Hayworth. None brings in the boys under her own steam.

No, they are all of them plausible, comprehensible, probable, common—common in the nicest way, of course. Not one of them is more remote from the women in the audience than the woman who lives in the big house on the hill. They make every woman in the theatre feel that with a little fixing up and a little better luck, she could easily change places with them. And since the Big Six usually pulsate through stories that begin with maidenhood and extend until, still unflinching, they're directing the lives of their grandchildren— or start at the end and work back to the beginning—the ladies in the audience can help themselves to any age bracket that fits.

All right. So our producer is able to latch on to Garson, Dunne, Bergman, Colbert, Hepburn, Davis for his movie. Now does he clap his hands and dance up and down? No, now he first begins to worry. For rule two is very subtle. Not only must the story rise and fall with a woman's sacrifice—like the rubber anesthesia bellows in the doctor movies—but she must herself decide to make the sacrifice. The decision must well up from inside her; it cannot be imposed upon her from outside; and still more complicated, nobody but the woman on the screen and the women in the audience can know that she is making the sacrifice. Nobody but the women in the audience may be permitted to see the fox gnawing at her vitals.

It must be arranged for the rest of the actors to go about being big cheery lugs, profiting from her agony, scornful of her patience, misunderstanding her because of her self-imposed reticences no matter how many difficulties they create for others, watching her suffer without seeing, knowing or appreciating that she's doing it, that she chose deliberately to do it and that no power on earth could pry her suffering from her.

The thing is, she's noble. Just like the women in the audience, she's noble, she's long-suffering, nobody appreciates her, nobody understands her. (Often if this isn't quite the case with the women in the audience, when they go home they make it so.)

This is the rapport between star and audience that a sure-fire woman's picture achieves. This is the communication that assures from one choked-back teardrop on the screen a Niagara of them in the audience, a cascade of liquid gold.

The way movie producers calculate it, one chorus of audience nose-blowings is worth a thousand belly laughs. Their heartbreak is what the ladies really enjoy and remember. The happy times they forget even as they're putting on their coats and kicking the bag that held the jelly beans under the seats.

Their heartbreak amidst shining surroundings, of course, with money in the bank, good hairdresser behind the draperies, food on the shelves, neatly pressed clothes in the closets and, no matter how modest the circumstances they're intended to portray, Grand Central Station vistas to the rooms. Rule three says the Big Six must be set in glamour, like cucumbers in aspic.

A few months ago there arrived from England a little bombshell called Brief Encounter, which for one terrorizing moment thought it could upset Hollywood's established, divinely happy and colossal-woman's-picture ways.

Brief Encounter was clearly a woman's picture—it looked at love and a woman's sacrifice from a woman's point of view—yet it had the impudence not to include one single wisp of glamour, not one little little thread. Its protagonists were plain and stayed that way. Their diversions were humdrum: the movies and tea shoppes. The scenes of their rendezvous were available to anybody: railroad stations and public parks. Yet Brief Encounter dared to maintain that this miserable pair were not only capable of romantic love, but were burning up with it as if they were Tristan and Isolde and, even more unsettling, that they were preparing to do the natural thing about it.

You can imagine how quickly Brief Encounter was clapped into the little cinema-art theatres where it could damage only intellectuals, whose box-office potential is of little account anyway, and so leave the good solid woman's audience inviolate, snug and protected in their big gaudy film palaces, safe from foreign heresies.

For it is the conviction of Hollywood movie producers, arrived at from pious study of their box office grosses, that glamour is the opium of the woman's audience. They've got the habit now, they buy the stuff and nobody's going to try to reform them.

[Mademoiselle, April 1947, pp. 234–5, 321–3.]

That "Feminine Angle" (1949)
Catherine de la Roche

Is there anything special to be said about woman and cinema? Usually, to discriminate between men and women in matters which equally concern both is to forget that, as women extend their activities, old distinctions between their interests and men's disappear. And, in essence, there's nothing peculiarly masculine or feminine in cinematography. But movieland, as we know it, is made up of all kinds of elements, real and unreal, and among them we have not one, but many feminine (or is it pseudo-feminine?) angles.

They can be detected, first and foremost, in the calculations of the commerical branch, which plays an initial rôle in determining production policy. […]

[O]n the whole, front-office producers work on hunches, sometimes following trends, sometimes even leading them, but mostly, as we know, aiming to play safe and flooding the market with stereotyped productions, many of which, incidentally, flop as resoundingly as some of the experimental pictures considered so risky. But, if only by sheer weight of numbers, this kind of film cannot have failed to influence picture-goers, so, whatever their reactions, they are the reactions of a public conditioned over a period of years by standardised movies, advertising and journalism. This makes it all the harder to sort things out in the two-way process of supply and demand, to ascertain what the public demand is and, especially, what it might be. The supply, at all events, is largely determined by speculation, and the executives who do the speculating, with very few exceptions, are men.

Aiming at the largest possible audiences, they are, of course, equally interested in both men and women as customers. (Actually, audiences seem to be representative of populations: in Britain, where men are heavily outnumbered by women, 62 per cent of the picture-goers are women; in America, where the figures are almost even, men and women go to the movies in fairly equal numbers.) Nevertheless, backers pay extraordinary attention to this thing called "feminine interest," perhaps even more than to the things that are supposed to attract men, and one of the reasons for this is the widely held belief that it is the citizen's wife who sets the tone for the average film. The point at which their policy gets a thorough airing is when sales pressure is applied to a completed picture, and the trade press starts advising exhibitors of its selling value. The literature provides women with a first-rate opportunity to see themselves as men see them, though, unfortunately, it cannot offer the corresponding advantage to men.

Occasionally a film's appeal for men is made a specific selling point, though showmen are usually reassured that it also has drawing power for women. This applied, for instance, to Naked City, a realistic account of the New York Homicide Bureau at work, and to Body and Soul, an exciting tale about boxing, exposing the evils of the fight racket. From film history one knows that leg shows were evolved with the particular idea of bringing tired business men to the pictures, that horse opera and gunplay are expected to appeal to the boyish elements in men and broad farce to the cap-and-muffler patrons of industrial halls, while feminine glamour of every description should irresistibly attract men of every description. But the points of appeal for men are comparatively rarely singled out. The men who work out film policy know themselves well enough at least to realise that most of their fundamental motives, good and bad, are common to the whole of humanity, and that the few which are peculiar to themselves are usually obvious enough without being stressed. It may occasionally be their policy to appeal to the baser instincts of humanity in general, but they never talk down to themselves as males, never treat themselves as an isolated species. And I have yet to hear of a "sly masculine angle".

"Feminine angles", on the other hand, crop up in startling profusion. Practically every other average movie is supposed to have them. According to trade press reviews the angle was powerful in If Winter Comes, A Woman's Vengeance, The Sign of the

Ram, Homecoming, Nightmare Alley; terrific in Life with Father; good in Bond Street; sly in A Double Life and Calling Paul Temple; obvious in Foxes of Harrow; subtle in My Own True Love; and the occult theme of Night has a Thousand Eyes was considered peculiarly intriguing to women. In a fascinating lecture given a few years ago, W.J. Speakman, an exhibitor, ascribed the success of Now Voyager to the fact that it was psycho-analysis written down for the masses, giving the illusion of high-browism, and classified it as a typical woman's picture. Study advertising and trade press matter, and you will find that sentimentality, lavish and facile effects, the melodramatic, extravagant, naïvely romantic and highly coloured, the flattering, trival and phony—these are the elements in pictures, whatever their overall qualities, that are supposed to draw women. Above all (and not surprisingly, since it's the opinion of men), woman's chief and all-consuming interest is Men. When you find a cliché stubbornly repeated through the decades, make no mistake—it might be a feminine angle: all those remorseful husbands, for instance, trying to atone for having forgotten "what day it is" (wedding anniversary), you see them because once upon a time some business man made the discovery that women long to be appreciated, and his colleagues still think that's one of the most touching ways male appreciation of females can be put over.

That's the standard approach, the routine. Occasionally, however, film business men do manifest their appreciation of women's better qualities, even of their intelligence, by noting the compelling feminine appeal in pictures like Gentleman's Agreement or All My Sons, which were devoted to current social and moral issues. But generally, when it comes to the great serious productions like Oliver Twist or Hamlet, the appeal aimed at is universal and the pictures are recommended without any discriminations for their human interest.

Now, the executives who think up feminine angles are expert and astute. [...]. Undeniably there's a widespread response among women to cheap, sensational or false elements, to the appeal of luxury and the rest. But to know this is to know only a part of feminine nature. Moreover, many of these angles are by no means exclusive to women. I suggest that love of luxury, for instance, and especially sentimentality, are pretty powerful masculine angles. [...]

There is little indication how film production would be affected if women had an equal share in its control. So far, the exceptional few who have become producers have not shown themselves to be of the stuff that pioneers are made of (remember Corridor of Mirrors!)[1] There are hardly any women in the other influential positions, either: they are as exceptional among the directors, though perhaps more promising—I'm thinking in particular of Jill Craigie.[2] Among the writers they are slightly more numerous, though still a small minority, and of these fewer still have any real authority, like the brilliant dramatist and screen-writer Lillian Hellman.[3] Admittedly, a number of pictures have been based on novels written by women—sometimes good, more often second-rate—but the men in charge of production were responsible for their choice and treatment. There are many women, of course, in other departments of film production doing expert but completely subordinate work. What their influence would be if they were given their head is anybody's guess. Not all of it, one imagines, would be to the greater glory of cinema. Especially if one reflects that much of the frivolous fan literature is devised for and flourishes on women readers. Or that some of the most pedantic censoring is attributed to the blue stockings on boards and committees, especially in America, where, I gather, women's organisations play a prominent part in local censorship, exercising an influence which, together with that of the Legion of Decency, sometimes merely encourages those lamentable whitewashing dodges. But it seems beyond question that cinematography can only benefit by giving wider scope to the intelligent and gifted representatives of womankind, especially as it may well be that their lack of pull in the industry is one of the reasons why cinema has given so very few significant portrayals of modern womanhood.

Instead it has developed the phenomenally intricate star system which, though it has undergone many changes in fashion, even in purpose, is of its essence a complex of formulas for producing types. Popular types—and this has meant that, as the film industry expanded, catering for a growing variety of tastes, it concentrated on developing the types that might please everybody—all purpose types, in fact—even more than on increasing their diversity. It was an elaborate process, beginning in the early 1930's, when the Hollywood star system underwent a radical change, and involving colossal expenditure and a lot of hard thinking, with the big chiefs trying to outdo each other in shrewdness and subtlety. The cult of stars as fabulous creatures beyond reach had gone out of fashion, together with the vamps and angelic heroines. Instead of being unattainable, the new stars were supposed to stand closer to the average woman, representing an ideal that she could emulate, and men might admire without being unduly tantalised. Henceforth, the entire system was to depend on the identiy of the stars and the rôles for which they were typed. Publicity saw to it that their private lives were an extension of their film rôles; subjects were chosen and screen-plays written accordingly. To make sure that everybody's likes and dislikes were taken into account, each star was supposed to have it both ways in everything possible (and impossible): she had to cultivate a personality, but seem ordinary; be fashionable, yet exclusive; glamorous, but approachable; intriguing, but understandable; wealthy, but with homely tastes; enviable, but deserving of sympathy; she might even champion some unindentifiable (say philanthropic) cause, yet not be unduly serious. The inevitable result of this studied levelling was that, far from representing the typical features of modern womanhood and portraying average women as diverse individuals, the stars, with some notable exceptions, emerged as synthetic figures possessing less character than real-life women. What's even more serious is that the vehicles chosen for them, whether specially written or adaptations, give a deceptive picture of the part women play in modern society, or ignore it altogether. The effect of the star system on actors isn't quite so bad, in that male characters are at least permitted to have interests, ideals and ambitions outside their private preoccupations. True, the most usual interest is making good, which means making money, but there have also been numerous films of a certain vocational interest, such as the cycle of pictures about doctors, a very good one and still going strong. [...]

Within the star system, [... i]t is impossible to recruit and groom girls with the idea of making them safely non-commital types and yet have brilliant and forceful heroines. So, by way of compensation, pseudo-exciting qualities have been cultivated in the sinful types, and with equal safety, since a story twist invariably provides them with the necessary penalty. "Bad girl makes good box office" is one of the oldest formulae. In consequence, a large proportion of the strongest (and most coveted) rôles are evil characters and, by comparison, heroines are weaker and insipid. Unavoidably this has done much to strengthen the widely spread delusion that it is of the essence of good women to be dull and of bad ones to be thrilling. The latest and, presumably, most subtle bad-girl type (actually a blonde variation of the early vamps, who were mostly dark) is the angelic criminal. She's to be seen in those psycho-analysis thrillers, alluring and gentle, a sweet thing inciting her menfolk to murder or doing the job herself. Lizabeth Scott, Lana Turner and Lauren Bacall are among those who have filled the rôle, and so is Rita Hayworth, turned topaz blonde for the purpose.[4] The British counterpart, I suppose, is the lady spiv, but she's not so angelic. These are the "babies" who are "dynamite".

But what of the élite, the stars who established themselves initially as dynamic artists, defying classification, like Bette Davis, or those who triumphed over the limitations of being typed, like Myrna Loy?[5] What has been their contribution in portraying modern women? Their greatest merit, I think, is that they have preserved and strengthened the integrity of their personalities. Not all the screen-plays in which they appeared have been good, and exceedingly few have touched on the broader issues of the times. Most have been love stories, confining their scope to personal relationships, and the great stars have had almost as little opportunity as the average types to try their strength in characterisations involving serious conflicts and ideas. But they have saved many a trivial story by the compelling reality of their performances and, between the lines, as it were, in an undefinable way, they have often evoked the spirit of the times. To remember Carole Lombard, Greta Garbo, Luise Rainer, Ruth Chatterton, Jean Harlow is to recall personalities somehow belonging to the 1930's, even though, with some exceptions, one has quite forgotten how, if at all, the modern characters they portrayed participated in the social life of the decade.[6] Katharine Hepburn, Bette Davis, Joan Crawford, Claudette Colbert, Irene Dunne, belong to a period spanning the 1930's and 1940's, not because one has understood how the shattering world events of this period affected the modern women they impersonated (though Claudette Colbert and Irene Dunne did give delightful studies of Service-men's wives in war films), but, again, because of something reflected in their personalities.[7] Now and again there have been films giving portrayals of women as active, or at least conscious, members of society, such as Rosalind Russell's in Sister Kenny, Roughly Speaking and The Guilt of Janet Armes, Mary Astor's in A Rich Full Life, Celeste Holm's and Dorothy McGuire's in Gentleman's Agreement or Myrna Loy's and Teresa Wright's in The Best Years of Our Lives, though in the last two pictures the feminine rôles were comparatively passive and subordinate to the men's.[8] But stories of this kind are rare indeed.

Of late they have been comparatively rare in British cinema, too; though during the war our best pictures were inspired by reality and showed women as an integral part of it. New and individual actresses made their mark in British pictures in those years—Celia Johnson, Deborah Kerr, Rosamund John—and since then their numbers have been swelled by fresh recruits.[9] Nowadays our cinema is making better use of available talent, though still, I fear, not enough. Of the few portrayals of contemporary women in recent films, the most noteworthy, I think, were Rosamund John's as a politician in *Fame is the Spur* and Ursula Jeans' as a scheming cadger in *A Woman in the Hall*. But probably the most oustanding recent performances have been in pictures set in the past. In *A Man About the House*, Margaret Johnston gave a splendid study of a domineering Victorian spinster succumbing to the fascination of a younger man.[10] Kay Walsh gave a vivid and highly dramatic performance as Nancy in *Oliver Twist*, and Eileen Herlie revealed herself as a dynamic artist with real temperament in the role of the Queen in *Hamlet*.[11] She is probably the most exciting British discovery of the decade. These and a few other recent portrayals seem to indicate that the vogue for under-acting, at least, is going out.

The rest is speculation, hunches. Will the superb realism of the recent American productions such as *Naked City* or *Boomerang* eventually produce stories that will show with corresponding realism how American women participate in national life, what interests they have besides domestic ones, and will they reveal this, not as deliberate 'women's problems' subjects, but naturally, as an integral part of reality? Will the British cinema recapture the urgent sense of reality it had less than three years ago? Will those ludicrous feminine angles go out of fashion and the star system start encouraging actresses of true individually—the only kind that can achieve universal significance—instead of the all-purpose nonentities? Above all, will screen-plays creating dynamic modern characters be forthcoming? Your guess is as good as mine. So far, at all events, the real story of modern womanhood has not begun to be told. And it cannot be told except as part of the story of modern times.

[*Penguin Film Review* 8 (London), January 1949, pp. 25–34, excerpted.]

Treating Women too Well (1931)
Madeleine Carroll

Have women had a square deal on the screen?

This question is raised in my mind by *Sarah and Son* the remarkable "women's film" [...]

You are doubtless aware that "Sarah and Son" was produced and directed by two talented American women with the great actress, Ruth Chatterton, in the leading role.[1] What you, like myself, may have failed to realise is that, as a feminine enterprise, *Sarah and Son* stands almost alone.

Does it strike other women—as it does strike me rather disturbingly—that there is something wrong in the fact that the talkies are almost exclusively a man-made entertainment? [...].

Do not suppose [...] that I am suggesting the existence of a masculine conspiracy to misrepresent women on the screen. My complaint, if it can be called a complaint, is that the male film producers have treated women too well. Regarding us from the chivalrous standpoint of the opposite sex, they have displayed an unconscious tendency to make light of our faults and idealize our virtues. [...] They have hesitated to tell the plain (and necessarily sometimes unpleasant) truth about us as fellow human beings.

Although it may be very flattering to be treated as a goddess, it is more truly complimentary, and much more satisfying, to be treated as a companion and an equal. [...] I value a man's comradeship more highly than his poems about the beauty of my eyebrows.

My whole criticism of man-produced films is that they have made too much of our eyebrows and too little of our minds and characters. [...]. [O]n the whole the screen inclines to extol woman's physical beauty as her greatest asset at the expense of the intellectual and social qualities which, in real life to-day, she shares with men.

Consider the stuff of which the average screen heroine, as compared with the heroes, is made. She must be attractive at all costs and, in nine cases out of ten, her sex appeal will provide an adequate cover for a multitude of sins. "Be beautiful, sweet maid, and let who will be clever," is her philosophy of life. She may commit bigamy and fraud and even murder. Provided she has nice eyes, all will be forgiven her.

I can recall few screen heroines whose charm did not necessitate good looks. "Lummox" is one of the rare examples—and she was the conception of a woman writer.[2] Yet life is full of "ugly" heroines. Why should we not see occasionally on the screen the feminine counterparts of Disraeli, and other "heroes" whose appeal consists in something more distinctive than *beaux yeux* and a finished drawing-room manner?[3]

Do not think that I dislike beauty or that I associate moral virtue with a distressing physical appearance. My argument is that women on the screen should not be swamped by good looks. I want to see feminine appeal mixed with intellectual charm. I want actresses to be given roles worthy of their mental qualities instead of being wasted in portraying trivial types of womanhood.

Now that women are engaged in practically every form of human activity, I see no reason why they should be depicted on the screen mainly as sweethearts, wives and mothers. Women today are something more important than objects of sex interest. Their achievements in art, business, sport, and even science are as significant as the achievements of men. Why should not women's work figure more prominently in the talkies?

Now and then we do see a film which does pay tribute to other qualities of the modern woman than her physical seductiveness. One such film was Sybil

Thorndike's noble portrait of Nurse Cavell.[4] Every-day life contains numberless other heroines, famous and unknown, whose stories would make inspiring screen entertainment. Whole worlds of interest lie behind the careers of women doctors, women lawyers, women motorists and aviators. Woman's activities in commerce are another enthralling romance which could provide inexhaustible talkie material.

I do not suggest that films should become mere records of material accomplishment with all the emotions cut out. My point is that the emotions of an intelligent woman with a career of her own are more important and more interesting than the sex-life of an empty-headed flapper whose existence (to judge by her screen story) is devoted entirely to "love."

Perhaps I am wrong, but I feel that we should have more "worth-while heroines" if women played a bigger part in the actual production of films. Hitherto, few women have been given an opportunity to show what they can do; but the rare instances of women as directors have been signally encouraging. Many filmgoers will remember the distinctively feminine and unerringly human pictures made by Lois Weber who had a way of introducing all manner of intimate domestic touches that the average male director would never think of.[5] In Dorothy Arzner we have another woman director who proves, in "Sarah and Son," that the creation of talkies is not necessarily an exclusively masculine art.[6]

In London artistic and literary circles I find a growing desire to enter film production among intelligent women of the type from which women dramatists and novelists are drawn. At one of the largest British film studios there is a well-educated girl, the sister of a novelist, who is working as floor secretary without receiving any salary in the hope of qualifying by degrees for direction.

It is true that there are certain technical obstacles in the way of women as directors. Chief among them is the fact that the director's job involves controlling electricians, carpenters, and other male studio workers who might dislike the idea of being 'bossed" by a woman. I feel, however, that sex prejudice would quickly be overcome by a tactful woman as it has been conquered in the many other professions and trades which women have penetrated since pre-war days. Meanwhile, it should be practicable for the woman director to collaborate with a male technical director in control of the staff.

Direction is not the only department in which feminine influence could be brought to bear increasingly upon the screen. I should like to see women writers invited to the studios to collaborate in the production of their own novels, and encouraged to write original stories for the screen. There is a world-shortage of good literary material for the talkies. The present position and future prospects of British films would be greatly strengthened if producers created interest in the possibilities of the screen among professional novelists and playwrights and especially among women writers, such as Ethel Mannin, Mary Borden, F. Tennyson Jesse, and Margaret Kennedy.[7] Seeing that women are by far the greatest "consumers" of films, is it not only logical that they should have a full share in the choice and treatment of the raw material? [...]

[Film Weekly (London), 31 January 1931, p. 9, excerpted.]

Movie (1934)
Muriel Rukeyser

Spotlight her face   her face has no light in it
touch the cheek with light   inform the eyes
press meanings on those lips.
                              See cities from the air,
fix a cloud in the sky, one bird in the bright air,
one perfect mechanical flower in her hair.

Make your young men ride over the mesquite plans   ;
produce our country on film   :   here are the flaming shrubs,
the Negroes put up their hands in Hallelujahs,[1]
the young men balance at the penthouse door.
We focus on the screen   :   look   they tell us
you are a nation of similar whores   remember the Maine[2]
remember you have democracy of champagne —

And slowly the female face kisses the young man,
over his face the twelve-foot female head
the yard-long mouth enlarges and yawns
                              The End
Here is a city   here the village grows
here are the rich men standing rows on rows,
but the crowd seeps behind the cowboy the lover the king,
past the constructed sets America rises
the bevelled classic doorways   the alleys of trees are witness
America rises in a wave a mass
pushing away the rot.

                  The Director cries Cut!
hoarsely CUT   and the people send pistons of force
crashing against the CUT! CUT! of the straw men.

Light is superfluous upon these eyes,
across our minds push new portents of strength
destroying the sets, the flat faces, the mock skies.

[*New Masses*, 11:11, 12 June 1934, p. 28.]

In the Shadow of War

Luxury (1918)
Colette

The manager or the owner of a popular "movie house" in Paris said recently, refusing a very good film:

"That one isn't the sort for my house. There's too much outdoors and nobody in evening clothes."

The story made people laugh and shrug their shoulders. When I was told it, I laughed before thinking. I didn't understand or defend it until later, when I had found in it something other than the expression of an ignorant snobbery and the contempt, still honorable among certain sorts of Parisians, for everything having to do with outdoors or sport.

I was at first tempted to treat my movie-house owner as he seemed to merit. I would have liked to say to him: "Are you the one who educates mass taste by using the cinema? Or are you the one who leads the public toward paperback thrillers in pictures, toward criminals in white ties, and torture chambers made out of painted cardboard? You're the one, aren't you, who demands desperate countesses and bloody marquesses, and high-society adultery in Art Nouveau decors? You're the one … you're the one…" But I didn't say anything at all to him, and it wouldn't take much to make me apologize to this teacher of souls, whose speech is earthy because he can command no better words.

At a time when ramparts of committees, societies, and cinematic leagues are forming to protect a threatened industry, a threatened national art, and are drawing—with what effort—French cinema toward more luminous heights, my manager will bring down on himself curses from the specialists and the technicians. But what is he asking for? People in evening clothes and not so much outdoors. He ought to have added, in his popular language, "Me, I want a thing to be nice-looking, and thy audience likes a little luggsury."

He is not only right in some obscure way, but he has reasons he would be incapable of expressing. He wants luggsury.

And the longer the war lasts, the more we lack sugar and bread and gasoline, the more he will ask, on behalf of his audience in worn-out jackets and spongy, broken-down shoes, for luggsury and still more luggsury. I won't try to explain this need simply by the thirst for superfluity that torments human beings deprived of necessities. The source of it must be found in the progressive impoverishment of the theaters and the music halls. For four years we have lived in an increasing shadow. Artificial light, dimmer every day, no longer inundates the stages or our private homes.[1] By a law of mimicry, bright colors are disappearing from our clothes, in which shades of sand, earth, and troubled water are replacing all the others, and mourning, alas!, we have no lack of, nor of the dark violets and the mauves of half-mourning ... A music hall on the rue Blanche, if it had in its favor only material splendor, would have attracted to its lobby of colors and lights a crowd made anemic by the dark; but the spectacle on stage had no match in the season, or the year. Madame Rasimi can no longer transport from Ba-Ta-Clan to Montrouge and from Montrouge to Grenelle troupes clothed in velvet, glittering with paste jewels; and what is attempted currently in the local café-concerts leaves spectators no illusion about the novelty or the freshness of the refurbished costumes[2]... What is left for the public? Where can it bathe itself in decorative illusion, adventure and romance, high life, society, inexhaustible splendor? At the cinema. Only the cinema spends, wastes, destroys or miraculously builds, mobilizes hordes of extras, rips embroidered cloth, spatters with blood or ink thousand-franc dresses; only there will you see a gentleman in a white tie not giving an instant's thought to his three-hundred-franc evening clothes when he grapples with a bandit—and triumphs, in rags.

So the vote of a public that is worried, tired, badly heated, dimly lighted, suffering in body and tormented in heart, goes first, and logically, and childishly, to the most concrete and tangible luggsury: evening dress and the drawing room, which my movie-house manager was demanding for them. And yet apart from The Cheat and a few others, the finest flower of the cinema is not the high-society dramatic film...

Never mind. In France, should one ever despair? At this awkward moment, we are working again in France at shots taken in the sunlight. I have seen, in one week, films like the Tenth Symphony, overflowing with qualities and defects, with new discoveries and errors, films like L'Ame du Bronze, in which the means of moving the audience operate through their very discretion, and which gained for Henry-Roussell this piquant compliment: "You'll never make this into a propaganda film—it's not boring!" I have seen "documentaries" in which the hatching of an insect, the unfolding of a butterfly outside its chrysalis, set the fairytale quality of stage illusion before our eyes and, thanks to photographic enlargement, open to us the forever-mysterious world where Fabre lived[3] ... Oh, that is the thing itself, luxury, magnificence, fantasy! The feathery and irised material of a butterfly's wing, the palpitations of a minuscule bird, the vibrating bee and its tiny hooked feet, a fly's eye, the flower whose image has been captured on the other side of the world, unknown waters, and also human gestures, human looks brought to us from an unknown world—that is it, that is the thing, inexhaustible luxury! Patience: it will be known at last.

[First published as "Cinema," Excelsior (Paris), 14 May 1918, p. 3.—Collected in Colette at the Movies: Criticism and Screenplays, ed. Alain and Odette Virmaux, trans. Sarah W.R. Smith (New York: Frederick Ungar, 1980).]

A War Film in Berlin (1931)
Dorothy Woodman

Berlin Cinemas   I know no other city in Europe where the cinemas are as much a feature of every main street as they are in London. In Berlin there are comparatively few cinemas, although Germany has contributed so much to the production of films. This is partly the result of the prevailing economic depression. The super cinema like the Regal at Marble Arch, or any of those Astoria "Film Palaces" now springing up in the provinces does not exist. In its place there are Ufa cinemas which are models of good taste, interesting, even thrilling examples of modern lighting and architecture.[1]

I have just visited one such cinema in the northern end of Kurfürstendamm, the "centre animé de la cité," of Berlin. The outer hall is flooded with a straight line light thrown from the walls. Square cubes of light enframe the two girls who sell tickets. There are two severely plain clocks which have bold black lines for the figures on the face. Nothing could be a stranger contrast to the extravagantly—often vulgarly—decorated entrance halls of English super-cinemas. Inside, there is the same striking difference. Beyond the entrance, the cinema resembles a blue and white petunia. There is a bright blue carpet at the base, the walls are painted plain white and blue and an arched line of light is the dividing line between these two colours. The cinema is worked out in the same colour scheme—plain blue walls, and white light radiating from the screen end across the whole ceiling. No other decoration.

Douamont   In such beautiful surroundings the serious realism of the war film "DOUAMONT" became horrible. Douamont, the latest German war film, is a reconstruction of the war round Fort Douamont from February until October, 1916. The screen introduction warns the audience that there will be no comic element introduced. This is interesting. I had always considered that the introduction of comic elements in our war films in England has proved the diversion which has hidden the lessons to be learnt from them.

The film opens with shots of Verdun in February, 1916. In the midst of destruction, people are still carrying on business in the market place. The scene changes to the surrounding country where thousands of German troops are marching to the battlefield. Here they come—the healthy young men who were the counterpart of Germany's youth movement to-day. I was reminded of the crowds of Germans who were sun-bathing at Wann See, just outside Berlin last Sunday. Like the soldiers on march they were singing German folk songs and popular ditties. From time to time there were shots of French supplies which were sent down to the lines.

Finale   Then came the scenes in the trenches and for forty-five minutes the film reproduced the war from the beginning of 1916 to October when the struggle was over. One long series of attacks and counter-attacks. At the end there is a roll call of the Rhineland and Westphalian Regiments which were in the front line. Only three officers and twenty men reply. This scene is followed by gruesome shots which show the fate of some of the men who have been killed. One lies entangled in barbed wire, another is shot to pieces on the field, and so on. These are the realities of war. Here the film ended. Ironically a male-voice choir standing behind the screen ended the performance with one of the most famous German hymns. I recalled the many times I have heard "Abide with me" at the "grand finale" of war films in English cinemas.

Seen in Silence   The reaction of the German audience was interesting. Throughout the performance was no sound of applause and the people sitting round me rarely passed any comment. This attitude of indifference, however, is characteristic of many people in Germany. The pre-war Germans are becoming fatalistic, the post-war generations have already reached a stage of extremism which is as violent as it is disturbing.[2]

It is impossible to sum up the cinema in Germany on the basis of a visit to Berlin and to several provincial cities and towns. But I have the general impression that it has not suffered the American vulgarisation which has spoilt the cinema in England.

[*The New World* (London), 25 September 1931, p. 5.]

War... and the Workers (1932)
Ethel Mannin

Breaking my journey to Palma, in the Balearic Isles—where the pound is worth thirty shillings and you can live for six shillings a day if you don't mind living simply, which, to my mind, is the only decent way of living—I stayed a night in Paris last week and saw a very fine Pabst film, *La Tragédie de la Mine*, which is, I understand, to be shown by the Academy Cinema, London, commencing next Sunday, March 6, under the title, *Kameradschaft*.[1]

The story is based on the terrible Franco-German mine explosion of 1906, in which 1,200 miners lost their lives, and shows a similar fictitious happening in 1919. It is tremendously valuable disarmament propaganda and for the breaking down of national barriers between the workers of different nations. The mine is a frontier mine, and half the cast of the film is German and the other half French. When the disaster occurs the film shows a lorry load of German miners going to the rescue of their French comrades—a spectacle which produced loud applause from the French audience, and wild enthusiasm when the lorry dashes past the frontier regardless of the douane on guard—a subtle way of making the point that in a crisis of the workers the national barriers should not exist, for, as they say in the film, "a miner is a miner," whether he is French, German, British or of any other nation.

A VISION OF THE PAST

The "high spot" of the film is the showing of a German miner going to the rescue of an entombed French miner. Whilst he is groping his way through the débris he has a sudden vision of No-Man's land and the trenches, and French and German soldiers in hand-to-hand fighting surrounded by barbed wire entanglements, shell-holes, and all the horror of warfare. The vision fades... this is 1919; the war is over... and the men who sought to kill each other under the compulsion of political dictatorship a little while ago are now trying to save each other; they are no longer French and Germans who are supposed to hate each other, but workers co-operating for life; they are comrades fighting the common enemy, death — the horrible death to which the capitalist system exposes them, as during the war it exposed them to machine-gun fire....

The film closes showing an iron gate-way, with French officials on one side and Germans on the other.... "It is the law... it is the regulation...." There were cat-calls and hisses from the French audience at these words. For the common people do not want these national barriers any more than they want to kill each other in politician-made wars.

SUBTLE ANTI-WAR PROPAGANDA

The film showed how ridiculous and artificial are these national "hates"—for the workers of the world are, to parody Mr. Kipling, "brothers under the skin." To suggest, as one or two people round me were suggesting, that the showing of the hand-to-hand fighting between French and German soldiers during the war was "unnecessary," is to miss the whole point of the film; nothing could more strikingly demonstrate the stupidity of international hate.

One was reminded of the letters of British soldiers during the war, in which they declared that the Germans were "not at all bad sorts"—a fact to which Douglas Goldring refers in his *Disarmament in War and Peace* pamphlet, a fact which it is as well to remember, for it is as strong a statement of the case for international brotherhood and disarmament as any political consideration. The people don't want war; they never have and never will; why should they? What do they get out of it, when it is they who are called upon to pay the price of it in blood and money?

Fig. 4.10 Photograph of Ethel Mannin in the 1920s by Paul Tanqueray.

This *Tragedy of the Mine* is a great film because it shows the essential brotherhood of man, independent of race and country and national barriers.

EVOLUTION BY REVOLUTION

It is valuable as the subtlest kind of anti-war propaganda, and as a picture of the horrors to which the miner is exposed. There is a remarkable shot of the cage hurtling down at terrific speed, and some terrible shots of the collapse of pit-props following the explosion, and of the trapped men running for their lives before fire and gas and flood—horrors as frightful as those they had to face in the war.

One is reminded of Boden's grim, heart-breaking novel, *Miner*, and Harry Carlisle's *Darkness at Noon*.[2] To see this film after reading those two books is to be filled all over again with that healthy rage which is the life-blood of the Socialist Cause. Rage against the system which requires the workers to face such horrors for less than a living wage, and against the system which requires them to forget the brotherhood of man in politician-made wars. *In peace and war alike the workers are exploited—and will be, so long as the Capitalist system exists.*

The Capitalist system will pass, inevitably, in the course of social evolution—in the meantime the workers suffer, so long as they submit. How many more men must face horrible deaths in mines, how many more wars must make gun-fodder of human life, how much longer must the mass of workers endure "hunger, poverty, dirt," before they rise up to hasten evolution by revolution?

At "the end of everything" on an outlying point of this island, I know nothing of how the international disarmament squabbles are progressing; from the window of the little white-washed room from which I write I look out across the great bay of Palma, utterly beautiful and peaceful ... but in the far distance there are two sinister black monsters ... two British battleships bristling with guns, horrible reminders that disarmament is not yet....[3]

VOLUNTEERING FOR DEATH

And I remember that in far-away Britain thousands of unemployed men are standing listlessly about at street-corners and leaning on the bars of dreary British pubs, wishing to God there was another war because it would at least give them something to do and regular pay for doing it ... If you think that statement is an exaggeration make a little tour of the industrial areas and talk to the men themselves. The people don't want war, but if the peace for which they fought does not grant them the right to live, what is the use of it? *That attitude is a menace of unemployment which is not yet fully recognised.*

I believe that if another war was declared to-morrow thousands of men who hate war and are bitter about the sacrifices demanded of them in the last war would nevertheless enlist at once—out of boredom, out of despair, and because somewhere at the back of their minds something insists that sudden death is preferable to slow starvation of body and spirit. If life is denied them they will volunteer for death.

But what we, who call ourselves revolutionary—as opposed to reformist—Socialists, have to work for is that if there has to be another war it shall be a workers' war—with Capitalism and all it stands for, as the enemy.... Meanwhile, battle-cruisers lie in peaceful foreign harbours ... waiting.

[*The New Leader* (London), 4 March 1932, p. 12.

What Shall You Do in the War? (1933)
Bryher

"To be a Jew is bad, and to be a Communist is worse, but to be a Pacifist is unforgivable."

—Popular German slogan

A year ago this June I returned from Berlin. I came from a city where police cars and machine guns raced about the streets, where groups of brown uniforms waited at each corner. The stations had been crowded: not with people bound for the Baltic with bathing bags, but with families whose bundles, cases or trunks bulged with household possessions. (The fortunate were already going into exile). Everywhere I had heard rumors or had seen weapons. Then I crossed to London and to questions "what is Pabst doing now" or "will there be another film like *Mädchen in Uniform?*"[1] I said "I didn't go to cinemas because I watched the revolution" and they laughed, in England.

But the revolution is a fact now even to people quite uninterested in politics. The *Manchester Guardian* and the *Nation* printed a little of the truth. They have been banned in Germany. Mowrer in *Germany Puts the Clock Back* quoted documents and they tried to turn him out of the country.[2] Actually the real news of the rebellion could not be printed in any newspaper. Tortures are freely employed, both mental and physical. Hundreds have died or been killed, thousands are in prison, and thousands more are in exile.

A great number are Jews. Six hundred thousand, many of them men who were among the finest citizens Germany had, peaceful and hard working, are to be eliminated from the community. In future no Jew is to have the rights of an ordinary citizen.[3] He may be made to fight for Germany but his children are to be denied an education. But besides these Jews and in a way in even worse plight (for they have no other country to which to turn) are the hundreds of liberal minded Protestant Germans who are accused of trying to build up an alliance with France.

"To be a Jew is bad, to be a Communist is worse, but to be a Pacifist is unforgivable." This very popular slogan sums up the revolution. For it is a revolution against the whole conception of peace.

Germany says that she does not want war. This is probably true as far as the statement applies to the present year. She would like first to re-train, re-equip and re-arm the entire folk. But unless her pre-war territory be handed back to her, it is doubtful if she will content herself with any peaceful protest. [...]

For twelve years a liberal and moderate minded section of the German people fought a losing fight. They won popular opinion in England and America over to their side. Treaty revision and the German right to re-arm were discussed in a manner impossible anywhere some years ago.[4] German goods were bought, German films shown and books read, and Germans were welcomed abroad as students and tourists. In exactly three weeks the national socialists smashed what it had taken twelve years of patient and unrewarding work to build.[5] [...]

Books by Heinrich and Thomas Mann, Remarque, Arnold Zweig, Stefan Zweig, Tucholsky, Feuchtwanger, Schnitzler, Glaeser, and many other authors, together with foreign translations have been taken from the libraries and publicly burnt.[6] The writers themselves have been forced into exile and in many cases, their possessions in Germany confiscated.

Heinrich and Thomas Mann both come from a north German non-Jewish family and their work has contributed more than is realised to the overcoming of hostility towards German intellectual life at the end of the war. Heinrich Mann was, we believe, the first German writer to be invited to visit a group of French authors after the Armistice and both his books and those of his brother enjoy an international reputation. [...]

Pabst who did more than any one, to open the cinemas of the world to German films, has been exiled and it is said a price has been put on his head should he approach a German frontier. They will never forgive him the fraternising of French with German workmen in *Kameradschaft*. [7] *All his films have been banned in Germany*. The men who worked with him and under him, have been scattered across Europe. It is said in fact, that barely ten per cent. of the workers in the German studios of last year, are left.

Hundreds of Jewish doctors have been forbidden to practise and have been dismissed from the hospitals. They are unable to obtain work and in several cases known to me personally, they have been left to starve. Einstein and many of their best scientists are in exile. Those who waited too long, or who could not afford a railway ticket, are shot or are in prison.

It is quite possible that a lot of German citizens do not realise what is happening. If a man complains of his treatment or of the new laws, he is beaten to death or sent to a concentration camp. Should he escape across the border, his nearest relative or friend pays the penalty for him. [...]

For the last fifteen years people have used the words peace and war so much that the sound of them means nothing at all. They have read war books, said "how terrible" and gone on to read accounts of life in the south seas or on a farm or stories of a feudal castle, as if all were equally real or perhaps better, unreal. They have signed resolutions and exchanged armistice memories and sighed (if they are old enough) for "the good old days before the war." But very few have ever made a constructive attempt to prevent the months of 1914 from being repeated on a larger and worse scale.

I do not think a pacifism of theories and pamphlets is of any use. The mass of the people desires action. In this respect both fascism and communism alike respond to primitive psychological needs. Ninety per cent. of any nation want deeds and not ideas.

If this point of view is to govern the world, then we can hope only for war, with intervals of peace. But in one of these upheavals (and in spite of speeches how near we are to it at present) the whole of civilisation may disappear. And we shall not return to the Utopia of the machine-less savage, so often evoked by romantic writers, because the native of the Congo say or the south seas is the product of an elaborate scheme of life that has taken generations of peace to evolve. The barbarism to which we should return would be something so cruel and so stark that only the very cunning or the very strong could hope for survival. It would be comparatively easy even to-day, for half Europe to perish from starvation.

It is said that in the Balkan countries not a child is adequately fed, but that every third person is in uniform. They do not organise their food supplies but they find money for their armies. One rash move on the part of desperate young boys, might loose war right across Europe.

I believe peace still to be possible. But on condition only that we fight for it now as hard as we should fight in war.

If we want peace, we must fight for the liberty to think in terms of peace, for all the peoples of Europe. It is useless for us to talk about disarmament when children are being trained in military drill and when every leader of intellectual thought in Germany is exiled or silenced. [...]

If one believes that there is never a justification for war, then it is one's duty to join to a peace organisation and fight for peace, not through the signing of resolutions but through an attempt to help those who are now suffering because they believed in peace. One should try to spread knowledge of other nations among the many English in outlying villages who still believe a foreigner to be not quite as human as themselves. Remember that abstract words about peace mean very little: and that the first impressions that a child receives about another country will be lasting. If you know children find out if their geography lessons are interesting and what they think about other nations.

But it would be advisable to join an organisation and keep in touch with it, not to come with conscientious objections discovered only on the outbreak of war.

On the other hand, those who think that there are times when a resort to arms is justified, should decide what to do if there were war. What training have they? Do they know anything of modern warfare?

Remember that the last war proved to us that we have no right to demand a man who does not believe in war, to be a soldier, for we failed in our war and we have all but failed in our peace. But we have the right to demand that everyone shall choose now, and not when struggle is upon us, whether he or she will fight or not. And if one does not wish to fight, one must think if all is being done now that can make peace possible?

What I write applies to women equally with men. They will be conscripted in the next war: already there is labor conscription for them in Germany and it is said that a similar law would be applied upon the outbreak of hostilities in France.[8]

Let us decide what we will have. If peace, let us fight for it. And fight for it especially with cinema. By refusing to see films that are merely propaganda for any unjust system. Remember that close co-operation with the United States is needed if we are to preserve peace, and that constant sneers at an unfamiliar way of speech or American slang will not help towards mutual understanding. And above all, in the choice of films to see, remember the many directors, actors and film architects, who have been driven out of the German studios and scattered across Europe, because they believed in peace and intellectual liberty.

The future is in our hands for every person influences another. The film societies and small experiments raised the general level of films considerably in five years. It is for you and me to decide whether we will help to raise respect for intellectual liberty in the same way, or whether we all plunge, in every kind and color of uniform, towards a not to be imagined barbarism.

[*Close Up* (London) 10:2, June 1933, pp. 188–92, excerpted.]

On Pickets, *Gone with the Wind*, and "Wolf" (1940)
Lillian Johnson

I crossed a picket line, too!

But I was going to see *Gone with the Wind*, and unlike Mrs. Roosevelt, I wasn't sorry that I had crossed it, although since I am one of the working class, I usually sympathize with the conditions that usually lead people to picket.[1]

But I do feel that there are times when we of the darker race are so sensitive about the prejudices and the insults that we meet so often that we lose sight of our objective and with it our sense of evaluation of wrongs and rights.

It reminds me of a large cat that we used to have. He was so much bigger than any of the other cats in the neighborhood, knew so little about defeat, and was so wrapped up in himself that he used up the larger part of his energy in bristling.

He had practised the art so much that it was super-trigger action with him. If you happen to brush by him unexpectedly, or wake him suddenly from sleep, he came out fighting, every hair on end.

And, of course, in these instances, he didn't know what he was fighting about.

The pickets at the Lincoln Theatre in Washington were a nice looking, intelligent group, until you got to the banners that they were carrying.

Then it was obvious that they either hadn't seen *Gone with the Wind*, or they were attempting to be misleading—both of which is very bad form for those who would persuade others.

It tends to make people feel that they are being taken for a ride—that the would-be swayer of their opinion feels that they are so ignorant that he need not go to the trouble of being clever or subtle, but that he can persuade them by the use of crudely constructed and very evident falsification.

On the other hand, if he shows that he doesn't understand the thing that he is fighting, that gives the impression that perhaps that is the REASON why he is fighting it.

I am as sorry as anyone else that our people are forced to undergo the hardships we do have to undergo because it not only makes it hard for us to get along with other people—but the constant economic pressure makes it hard for us to get along with ourselves.

And no doubt, I know a great deal more about it than many of the pickets who were on the march Saturday in their fur coats and camel hair wraps.

For I came from Georgia, where Sherman and his army cut a swath sixty miles wide from Atlanta to the sea—where he was welcomed by some of my relatives as a saviour, where I was taught from a baby to give him equal honor with Lincoln.[2]

Unlike many of the pickets (who I understand were students), the students in the State where I came from pick cotton and do other types of work all summer to pay their way through school in the fall.

A student in a fur coat in that section is as rare as cold days in August because the students all have a hand in working for their clothes.

I am not attempting to put up a brief for *Gone with the Wind*, any more than I would do for any other picture that has been beautifully done.

I have seen films that I enjoyed as much, some more.

But I do feel that first of all, we should be sure that we don't let a fleeting opportunity, such as "showing" somebody something today, make us do something that will hurt the group for a much longer time.

And then, I believe in being fair.

After all, the picture was a true representation of that period. Its earmarks, its evolution can be seen in the South right now, and, there are no missing links there.

Then, the picture characterized something that has "gone with the wind," even if it would be argued by stretching some points that the writer of the play would like it to return, the picture says in no uncertain terms that those days will never return.[3]

I don't stop to argue here, because I am sure that no one seeing the picture or knowing the conditions would be foolish enough to think that they could.

The film doesn't show the race as we would desire it. If that condition had existed, there would have been no cause for the Civil War.

But on the other hand, it also shows some unhealthy conditions in other races, in other social classes.

Please be fair. Remember that there was once a boy who was told to cry "wolf" in order to get help if wolves came, and the boy cried "wolf," so much for fun that when a real wolf did come, nobody believed his cries, and he was destroyed.

["Light and Shadow: On Pickets, *Gone with the Wind*, and 'Wolf',"
Baltimore *Afro-American*, 9 March 1940, p. 13.]

Gone with the Wind's Place and Prices, and the Public (1940)

Lillian Johnson

Despite the reams and reams which have been written about the film, *Gone with the Wind*, the subject seems to be one of unwaning interest, for in my mail today there came the following letter from Mrs. A.S., of Baltimore:

> I have just learned that the movie, *Gone with the Wind*, is coming to a leading colored theatre in town. From reading the book and from what I have heard of the picture, I have come to the conclusion that no self-respecting member of our race would be seen in a theatre showing this picture.
>
> Certainly, I never expected to see it shown in one of our own theatres. Most of the leading colored newspapers of our own country have taken the position that this is a vicious anti-colored, pro-slavery movie.
>
> It seems to me that this stand on the part of our newspapers is perfectly justified. Therefore, I can see no possible excuse for the action of the Harlem Theatre in bringing this picture into our very midst, and that at prices far above what most of us can pay.[1]
>
> I hope that your paper will lead Baltimore's colored population to take an active stand on this matter. As subscriber to your newspaper, I expect at least this of you.

I am very glad to have this letter, not because the writer condemns *Gone with the Wind*, but because I am sure that only through the alertness and the discriminating forces of the public mind will communities grow into better places in which to live.

But I do not agree with Mrs. A.S. with regard to the film.

An examination of her letter shows, first of all, that she has not seen the film. It is not the best policy to condemn something with which one is not familiar, for it stands to reason that a better job of criticism can be done when one knows all the points which he could criticise.

Now, as to the book. While the theme of the picture has not been changed, it is not nearly as abruptly handled as in the book.

For one thing, most of the racial designations have been removed, and the scene in the book which would be most objectionable to colored audiences—the one in which a colored man attempts to molest Scarlett O'Hara, has been changed.

In the picture it is a white man who is the villain, and it is the former servant from Scarlett's plantation, Big Sam, who comes to her rescue, as he does in the book.

Mrs. A.S. also says that most of the colored newspapers have condemned the movie. This is incorrect. Most of the large newspapers have written reviews praising the picture, a fact that was commented on by *Variety* a few weeks ago.

And certainly, I do not think the Harlem Theatre management should be criticized for bringing the picture to the Baltimore public. This is really a feather in the Harlem's cap, for the best theatres are those who can bring to their patrons the newest and the finest plays and pictures.

Remember that Scarlett's picture won 12 of the 16 major awards recently given by the Motion Picture Academy of Arts and Sciences. So no matter who disagrees, it is 1939's finest film.

The Harlem Theatre is not likely to take sides pro or con in the argument over the picture, for taking sides is not the purpose of good theatre management.

It merely makes it possible for its patrons to make decisions on plays.

The prices are above the Harlem's jurisdiction, too. The picture is being shown at the present time at the same prices everywhere. This is because the film is not being rented to the theatres on the regular price scale, but at a much higher rate.

The picture cost five million dollars and in order to make the production pay, the higher price was necessary. It does seem now that the film will make a tremendous profit.

But then, the men who made it took a gamble on a tremendous amount of money and gambling against such odds is worth high returns.

I was born and reared in Georgia and although I wasn't there at the time that Scarlett was, there are enough earmarks to let me know that the picture is rather authentic.

Of course, there were worse conditions. There were also better conditions. But there is another Georgia play, *Tobacco Road*, in which all of the characters are white, and although these people are worse than the very worst I ever saw, the other race isn't asking that the play be taken off the stage.[2]

Voltaire said once, "I may not agree with what you say, but I will defend to the death your right to say it." This is one of the bases of democracy.[3]

And lest we forget, the theme of the picture is that the old easy living, the slow indolent life of the South has gone with the wind.

It might be worth the price of admission to see what our generation was lucky enough to miss.

["Light and Shadow: *Gone with the Wind*'s Place and Prices, and the Public," Baltimore *Afro-American*, 16 March 1940, p. 13.]

Apollo Comedy Bad for Race (1943)
Fredi Washington

This column has had a great deal to say about the kind of material given colored actors appearing on screen and stage. We have yelled loud and long about the kind of material we want and would like to see done by our actors but after a visit to the Apollo theatre the other day, I was struck with the fact that we, in our indignation, have left our own back yard pretty durn dirty and hopped, skipped and jumped miles away to clean someone else's.[1]

I don't know who is responsible for the material used in the sketches done at the Apollo but I do know it's still the no reading, dumb arguing, razor wielding, name calling, liquor drinking, woman debasing, vulgar, stupid brand of so called comedy which has no place in the new order of the new Negro.

To add to this insulting boredom, it is nothing short of alarming to find an audience made up almost entirely of teen age youngsters and men who should be working or in the army, letting out guffaws of laughter and carrying on an almost constant banter of loud conversation with the performers on the stage.[2] When the orchestra attempts to entertain with a swing tune, these youngsters let out noises which sound inhuman and go through gyrations which make them look moronic.

Witnessing this spectacle it is almost impossible to believe that anyone of these kids have attended school or had any training of any kind. Certainly the life and death struggle which now faces black America, for their rights as citizens, have never entered the minds of this young group.

The combination of offensive sketches on the stage and the rude disgusting behavior of the audience is all a part of the very long rope which we as a minority group have placed around our necks. We, one and all, must face these facts if we are to succeed in our fight to abolish discrimination of our boys in the armed forces, our workers in the factory and all of the other places where it is found in our American set-up. […]

["Headlines, Footlights: Apollo Comedy Bad for Race," *The People's Voice* (New York), 31 July 1943, p. 9, excerpted.]

Tim Moore Replies (1943)
Fredi Washington

This column last week stuck its neck way out on the subject of the kind of material the Apollo theatre uses on its stage and the deportment of its audiences.[1] It tried to show within the confines of limited space, the responsibility placed on the shoulders of Negroes in the theatre, to the progress of all American Negroes, and yes those in foreign lands as well, for after all, we are the yard stick by which freedom and equality will be measured for the oppressed Negroes of British and French rule.

Because of this frank criticism of ourselves, I of necessity stepped on the toes of some individuals. A letter from Tim Moore, comedian, working weekly at the Apollo, has this to say:

"I was indeed surprised when you spoke of razor wielding, woman debasing, etc. That does not happen to be in my repertoire. You also said what we are doing has no place with the New Negro." Mr. Moore continues with a little of my own theatrical background and says: "I have never seen you on the stage but once and that was in *Singing The Blues* and I think they had a little dice shooting and murder. I did not see anything uplifting to the race in the part you played. I also did not see anything uplifting about the part of a colored woman you played in *Imitation of Life*, who was ashamed of her own mother because she was dark." [2]

I should like to point out to Tim that I do not take exception to this criticism of parts I've done in the theatre and on the screen which dates back ten or more years. But I should like to clarify for Tim and all others who are confused on the issue. The fact is that ten years ago, we were a slumbering people standing still with no particular knowledge of the plight of our unfortunate brothers in far off lands or at home for that matter. There was a depression going on and each individual was interested solely in buttering his own bread.

It is hardly necessary to try to point out the terrific world-wide changes which have taken place since that time. Unprecedented attention has been given the Negro since the war began because of the fact that we are theoretically free but actually part slave under a vicious system—a system which allows representatives of our government to stand on the floor of Congress and orate about our lack of responsibility, culture, education, etc., in order to keep us from the polls in the south, to segregate our men and women in the armed forces, to perpetuate the damnable jim-crow laws of the south and which are now invading the north, to keep us in ignorance of the rich history of American Negroes, etc.

These and many more reasons, which certainly we must be acquainted with, are why, what was considered all right in the theatre or on the screen ten years ago, are not all right now. Today we are shedding red blood for democracy which we do not have but for which we are waging a fight on the home front, and culture and education through the medium of every stage, screen and radio is of utmost importance. It is the responsibility of every Negro in the field of amusement to see with clarity his or her relation to this fight. To approach his respective line of endeavor with the thought that I must present something of the rich, Negro culture, something of educational value in all that I do.

This will mean more work. It will mean that Moore for instance will not be able to dig back a few in his book of jokes for material. Instead, it will mean going to the 135th St. library and reading up on some of the magnificent Negro material there—to read the papers more carefully and adapt timely events to his particular style of comedy.[3]

Further, I should like to use the remaining space to assure Tim Moore that all criticism made in this column is made with the thought that all of us in the theatre must do our part toward the realization of our rights as American Citizens in a truly democratic America and not to heckle any one individual.

["Headlines, Footlights: Tim Moore Replies," *The People's Voice* (New York), 7 August 1943, p. 11.]

The Limits of Criticism

The Challenge (1947)
Iris Barry

With our crisis can we cope
If deprived of Mr. Hope?
Is a British working day worth
Nothing without Rita Hayworth?
Clement, Stafford, give the order,
Rally RANKS and SURSUM KORDA!
Prove it in the picture-drome
We can do the job at home,
Prove to all the world we're able
To exist without Miss Grable.[1]

[*The Observer* (London), n.d., cited by C.A. Lejeune
"Can Piccadilly do without Hollywood?" *New York Times*,
24 August 1947, p. 32.]

On *The Wave* (1937)
Katherine Anne Porter

It will be a great pity if people who wish to see a fine picture miss seeing *The Wave* through placing too much confidence in the judgment of certain newspaper reviewers. I spent a beautiful evening at that picture, and I have seen it again, and mean to see it at least once more, for I saw many things at second view I had in my absorption missed at the first. The pictures I have really liked, and I judge them by the vividness of the memory they left, a continuing sense of their qualities, are few: an early comedy of Chaplin's called *Shanghaied*, *Potemkin*, *The Cabinet of Dr. Caligari*, *Chang*, *Man of Aran*, a Zulu picture with Zulu actors speaking their own language, *La Soeur Noire*, a Russian tragi-comedy called *La Frontière* (these last two I saw in Paris, and I fear they may never come here), *Carnival in Flanders*, and *The Wave*. This is a short list, and I know I have missed many fine pictures, but in this company *The Wave* seemed to me as good as the best of them, perhaps the best picture I ever saw. The photography, the actors, the scene, the theme, and the music were all so firmly woven, so harmonious, the effect was as satisfactory as one of those old fine Mexican blankets, a perfect thing of its kind and unassailable on its own grounds.[1]

The light, clean photography, so clear and yet so deep, reminds me of the work of Edward Weston and Tina Modotti, his pupil in Mexico; to my mind it is the very best school, and Strand has added his own gifts to the method.[2] Revueltas has composed his music as Strand composed his scenes; ordinarily the reviewers must be content with less than this.[3] What more did this picture need to draw their praise? They have not always been so hard to please.

Did they not like the acting? How could it have been more suitable for the purposes of this picture? Do you suppose the theme made them vaguely uncomfortable? Maybe these oppressed and struggling Indians were too civilized for them, brought up as they were on gangster films. The political slant? It is a primer, it can hardly be called political at all. It is a story of men asking for bread in exchange for work, then learning slowly that they must not only work for bread, but fight for it. I think I can see why such humane statement of this perpetual worker's predicament might make them uncomfortable. But must they always be comfortable? From the purely visual point of view, could anyone ask anything more beautiful than the scenes of the casting and drawing of the nets, or that hair-raising procession across the water at the end, with the tremendous oar-music? A funeral march for more than just one little defeated man, that music promised a resurrection on earth.

The beauty of the men, the beauty of the woman seated watching the burial of her child, wouldn't you think that should have pleased the reviewers? Or was it the wrong kind of beauty for them?

These are not rhetorical questions. I am asking seriously, not what is wrong with that picture, but what is wrong with most of the reviewers?[4] One of them, after praising everything else, remarked that Americans would be bored with its slow pace. The slow pace, both in action and speech, I believe are right; it is the handsome, deliberate pace of the Indians of the hot countries. If it is too slow for our speedy American reviewer, if he is bored, all the worse for him. If he will consent to slow down a little, he will see more, and better....

[*New Masses*, 18 May 1937, p. 22.]

Me to Myself (1939)
C.A. Lejeune

ME: Do you really like seeing films?

MYSELF: In theory, yes.

ME: Do you generally admire them?

MYSELF: In practice, no.

ME: Why do you like to see them, then?

MYSELF: Like millions of other people, I'm always hoping.

ME: What could be done to improve the standard of pictures?

MYSELF: Give them more human stories about more human people. Use a bit of intelligence and a bit of observation.

ME: Haven't you learnt a great deal from pictures?

MYSELF: Plenty. I've learnt about the milk racket, the truck racket, the taxi-cab racket, the protection racket and the sports racket.... I have mastered the procedure of the courtroom, the campus, the nightclub, the—

ME: Thank you. I take it you have also acquired some knowledge of history?

MYSELF: Certainly. I know how Tyrone Power saw a rainbow in the desert and used it as a blue print for the Suez Canal. I know how Errol Flynn got so mad at the massacre of Chukoti, in India, that he lead the Charge of the Light Brigade in the Crimea. I know how—[1]

MYSELF: Producers have one major obsession.

ME: And what is that?

MYSELF: They think they know what the public wants in pictures.

ME: And don't they?

MYSELF: They haven't the vestige of a notion.

ME: Then why don't you say so?

MYSELF: I will.

ME: When?

MYSELF: Now.

[Theatre Arts Monthly (New York), February 1939, pp. 82–3.]

PART FOUR
Annotations

Wonders of the Kinetoscope

1. Porta (Gianbattista Della Porta) (1535–1615). Italian naturalist who reportedly invented the camera obscura. Some historians suggest Porta probably only improved the device.
2. Fabricius. Either David (1564–1617), German clergyman and astronomer who observed the first known variable star in 1596, or his son Johannes (1587–1615). In 1609, father and son used a modified camera obscura in which light fell upon a piece of paper in order to observe sunspot activity. Johannes is credited with the discovery of sunspots in 1611.
3. Daguerre (Louis Jacques Mandé Daguerre) (1787–1851). French inventor of the diorama (1822). In 1829 he entered into partnership with Joseph-Nicéphore Niépce (1765–1833), a French chemist who had begun photographic experiments in 1814 and had obtained light impressions on bitumen spread on metal plates. In 1837 Daguerre developed the earliest commercial photographic process, daguerreotypy.
4. Woodcuts were used to create the zoetrope's strip of images.
5. Dr Maddox (Richard Leach Maddox) (1816–1902). English chemist who originated the first workable dry-plate photographic process by putting silver-bromide gelatin emulsion on glass plates in 1871. Subsequent improvements on this process, such as the replacement of glass plates by celluloid in 1883, made moving image photography possible.
6. W.K.L. (William Kennedy Laurie) Dickson, the author's brother, was the principal partner in Thomas Edison's iron-ore milling research, and the Edison factory's chief photographer. He worked closely on the development of the kinetograph and the kinetoscope, and received royalties from his contributions to their invention. Some historians claim Dickson was in fact the partner most responsible for their development. He left the Edison laboratory in April 1895.
7. According to recent scholarship, Dickson's figure of forty-six images per second is an exaggeration. In practice, the rate varied and was generally less than forty images, or frames, per second.
8. The stereoscope was a viewing instrument popularized after its exhibition at the Great Exhibition of 1851 in London. Viewers received an illusion of depth when they looked at two still photographs of an object or scene, each taken from a slightly different angle. Dickson suggests that she has seen film images projected to produce this effect, but she is simply referring to film projection itself, since stereoscopic projection of two chains of moving images, though attempted, had been largely unsuccessful. Some early Edison film was hand-tinted using a process similar to that used in coloring stereopticon slides.
9. Edison's scientific progeny included the phonograph (1877), the carbon telephone transmitter (1877–78), and the incandescent lamp (1879).
10. Edison's first purpose-built studio was called "the Black Maria" and took its name from the police patrol wagon it resembled.

11. Sandow (Eugene Sandow) (1867–1925). German-born bodybuilder who featured in a vaude-ville show, "Sandow's Olympia," in 1896, as well as in Edison Kinetoscope films in 1894, and in several other early films.

12. Buffalo Bill (William F. Cody) (1846–1917). American frontiersman, army scout, and show-man. The Buffalo Bill character was the hero of hundreds of dime novels and the central character in Cody's Wild West show, an outdoor exhibition combining Native Americans, buffaloes, and cowboys in a dramatized view of Western life. The Wild West show toured nationally and internationally for thirty years.

13. Muybridge (Eadweard James) (1830–1904). English-born photographer who studied equine locomotion and developed serial photography. In 1879, he synthesized motion by using elongated drawings made from serial photographs, and projecting and turning them on a machine he named the Zoopraxinoscope, producing, in effect, the first animated film.

    Marey (Étienne-Jules) (1830–1904). French physiologist who met Muybridge in 1881, and who also used photography to analyze human and animal locomotion. He pioneered the use of flexible film in moving-image photography.

The Nickelodeon

1. On 4 November 1907, Chicago had passed an ordinance requiring every film shown locally to obtain a film permit. All films were to be first screened at police headquarters, where, under the direction of Major Funkhouser, they were approved or disapproved for exhibition in the city.

2. Jane Addams (1860–1935). American social reformer and settlement house pioneer who co-founded Hull House in Chicago in 1889. For Addams's views on the cinema, see her "The House of Dreams," and her letter to the Laemmle Film Service, both reprinted in this volume.

3. Research so far offers no evidence of clear municipal guidelines regarding immoral films in New York at this time. In New York in 1907, the Children's Aid Society successfully brought suits against several movie exhibitors on the grounds that they showed films unfit for children. One of these films was Lubin's The Unwritten Law (1907), which was banned in many cities. Despite increasing public agitation for some kind of regulation of film exhibition in the period 1907–08, and increased police and private surveillance of the movie business, this did not crystallize into decisive action until 24 December 1908, two months after the publication of Pierce's article, when New York mayor George McClellan revoked the licenses of over five hundred New York movie houses. These events ultimately led to the establishment of the National Board of Censorship by the People's Institute in New York in 1909.

4. Hale's Tours and "Scenes of the World" used a theater made up to look like the interior of a railway carriage. The film was rear-projected onto a screen at the front of the theater, creating the illusion for spectators of being on an observation car. In some theaters, the exhibition was accompanied by the rocking of the carriage and railway sounds.

5. These were not the brothers Lumière, but Pathé Frères, founded by Charles Pathé. The company had opened a New York office in 1904 and in the period 1906–08 was responsible for approximately one-third of the films shown in the United States.

Television Drama

1. The first BBC transmissions took place in November 1936. However, John Logie Baird had first demonstrated his television invention in Selfridge's department store in London in 1925, and Selfridge's had been selling television recordings since 1934.

2. The British Broadcasting Company was set up in 1922 to control radio transmission and receive income from annual radio license fees. In January 1927, the BBC became a public service institution, the British Broadcasting Corporation, and enjoyed both an assured income and a monopoly on the British airwaves.

3. Early television transmission was live and employed multiple cameras simultaneously. The orchestration of images from each camera was handled in the control gallery. This harrying use of multiple, simultaneous cameras and the immediate, sequential arrangement of footage distinguished television from film production.

The Cheat

1. Oriental actor. Sessue Hayakawa (1889–1973), Japanese actor who was to become a popular star of American silent film, best known for his villainous role in Cecil B. DeMille's *The Cheat* (1915).
   The heroine. Actress Fannie Ward.

Matinee

1. The Croisette is the broad elegant promenade bordered by palms and flowers that runs beside the beach at Cannes. At one end of La Croisette is the Palais de Festivals, now site of the Cannes Film Festival. Dismorr may possibly be suggesting this location in her reference to the Croisette.

Three Russian Movies

1. Eisenstein's *Ten Days that Shook the World* (1927) is also known as *October*.
   Vsevolod Pudovkin (1893–1953), Soviet film theorist, writer, actor, and director, whose films include a 1926 film version of Maxim Gorki's novel *Mother* (1919), *The End of St. Petersburg* (1927), and *Storm over Asia* (1928).
2. Artless blue Sundays. From the nineteenth century, and before, Sunday blue laws in many American cities had restricted most forms of entertainment on the Christian Sabbath. The motion picture was no exception, although the popular success of the nickelodeon in the first decade of the twentieth century and the institution of the six-day working week tested the efficacy of these laws.
3. Olga Preobrashenskaya (1881–1971). Russian director, formerly a stage and screen actress. First film directed, *Baryshnya-Krestyanka* (1916). In the 1920s she made films for and about children. In 1927 she directed *The Peasant Women of Riazan* to great acclaim.
   Vsevolod Meyerhold (1874–1940). Leading Russian avant-garde theater director of the twentieth century. He also directed some silent films and founded his own Moscow theater group (1923–1938).
   Alexander Tairov (1885–1950). Russian theater director who co-founded the Moscow Kamerny Theater and advocated theatrical "neo-realism."
4. FEKS or FEX (*Fabrika eksetsentricheskogo aktera*: Factory of the Eccentric Actor), a studio-theater founded by Leonid Zakharovich Trauberg (1902–1990) and Grigori Kozintsev (1905–73) in Leningrad in 1922. Trauberg co-directed, with Kozintsev, *The Overcoat* (1926), *Little Brother* (1927), *The New Babylon* (1929), and the Maxim trilogy, among others. Later, he directed solo and wrote several books on film. Kozinstev also directed solo later in his career.
5. Dmitri Shostakovich composed the score for *The New Babylon*.

Metropolis

1. Günther Rittau (1893–1971). German director and cinematographer who worked with Fritz Lang.
   Karl Freund (1890–1969) Austro-Hungarian cinematographer who is known particularly for his work in the German silent cinema. He later worked in Hollywood, directing *The Mummy* (1932). Freund received the cinematographer credit for *Metropolis* (1926).
2. Thea von Harbou (1888–1954). German scriptwriter whose screenplays include *Dr. Mabuse* (1922), *Niebelungen Saga* (1924), *Metropolis* (1927), *Spione* (1928), and *The Testament of Dr. Mabuse* (1932). When Lang, some of whose films had attracted the ire of the National Socialists and who was of Jewish extraction, emigrated after the National Socialist victory in 1933, von Harbou stayed in Germany and continued working in the film industry.
3. Ernst Toller (1893–1939). German–Jewish dramatist and poet whose 1920 play *Masses and Man* (1920) deals with striking labor.

Emasculating Ibsen

1. Henrik Ibsen (1828–1906). Internationally acclaimed Norwegian dramatist whose works put contemporary social issues on the stage.
2. *Ghosts* (1881), a play by Henrik Ibsen, was filmed in 1915.

3. Mr. Alving. A character in *Ghosts*.
4. Rev. Manders. A character in *Ghosts*.
5. Mutual Film Company. Mutual began as a Chicago-based film exchange. By 1914 it had fifty offices in the United States, Canada, and Europe, handling the films of a number of production companies including Thanhauser, American, Reliance, Majestic, and Keystone, and distributing films by Thomas Ince and D.W. Griffith, among others.
6. "Mobbie Mag" was one of several pseudonyms Margaret Anderson used when writing material for her literary magazine, *Little Review*.

Personal Eclipses

1. The Silly Symphonies were a series of Disney cartoons animated to music. The first in the series was *Skeleton Dance*, made in 1929. *Night*, the ninth in the Silly Symphony series, was released on 28 April 1930. Directed by Walt Disney himself, it is an early black-and-white version of *The Old Mill* (1937).

Humoresque

1. Lejeune reviewed *Humoresque* in *The Observer*, 11 May 1947, p. 2, in the context of discussing a filmed opera, *The Barber of Seville*. Lejeune's text, which contains the germ of her poem, runs as follows:

> Italy, however, isn't the only place where they believe in music. They think it cute in Hollywood, too. In fact, they think it so cute that they end *Humoresque* (Warners), that intense soul-drama of a violinist who rather grumpily puts his art before the love of a female dipsomaniac, with the love-duet from *Tristan* arranged for piano, solo violin and orchestra. The élite of New York take this amazing composition to their hearts, but I was pleasantly surprised to find that it drove Miss Joan Crawford, as the dipsomaniac, straight to suicide. As a result of hearing it over the radio, she mixed her drinks, put on a black sequin gown, and walked straight into the Atlantic. It seemed to me the only sensible thing she or anyone else did in the whole course of the film.

The sound film version of *Humoresque* (1946) (as the earlier 1920 silent version) was based on the title story in a collection of short stories by popular American writer Fannie Hurst, *Humoresque* (1919). Joan Crawford starred.

The Negro Actor and the American Movies

1. The American Civil War lasted from 1861 to 1865.
2. Oscar Smith (1885–1956). Black actor who appeared in such films as Lois Weber's *The Marriage Clause* (1926), *At Yale* (1928), and *Close Harmony* (1929).
Wallace Reid (1891–1923). Silent-era actor, director, and screenwriter who had a small part in D.W. Griffith's *The Birth of a Nation* (1915) and went on to become a star at Paramount before his early death from a drug overdose.
3. Stepin Fetchit (Lincoln Perry) (1902–1985). African-American comic actor, very successful in the 1930s, whose typical roles as the lazy Negro are now considered among the most insulting screen stereotypes of African Americans.
4. Carolynne Snowden. African-American actress who appeared in *In Old Kentucky* (1927) and *The Marriage Clause* (1926) and *The Merry Widow* (1925).
5. Noble Johnson (1881–1978). African-American leading actor and founder of the Lincoln Motion Picture Company in 1916, among the first black-owned film companies.
6. Sunshine Sammy (Ernest "Sunshine Sammy" Morrison) (1912–1989). An original member of the *Our Gang* cast and one of the first African-American actors to sign a long-term Hollywood contract. Also known as Frederick Morrison.
Farina (1920–1980). African-American actor who played "Farina" in the *Our Gang* comedies from 1922 until 1933. Also known as Allen "Farina" Hoskins.
Hal Roach (1892–1992). Oscar-winning American producer, director, and screenwriter, credited with creating the successful *Our Gang* film series of comedy shorts. He also created the Little Rascals, the Charlie Chase comedies, and was responsible for the Laurel and Hardy partnership.

7. James B. Lowe (1879–1963). African-American actor who played Uncle Tom in *Uncle Tom's Cabin* (1927). Lowe got the part after Charles Gilpin resigned over the film's treatment of African Americans.

8. Clarence Muse (1889–1979). African-American character actor, singer, songwriter, and writer and producer of plays whose films include *Hearts in Dixie* (1929), *Cabin in the Cotton* (1932), *Showboat* (1936), and *Tales of Manhattan* (1942). One of the founders of the Lafayette Players of Harlem.

Al Christie (1881–1951). Canadian-born American director and producer of two reel comedies in the 1910s. Christie was the most prolific and best-known producer of silent comedy shorts after Mack Sennett and Hal Roach. Christie, who was white, also directed a number of black-cast comedy films including *Music Hath Charms*, *Lady Fare*, *The Melancholy Dame*, and *Oft in the Silly Night* (all 1929), in addition to white-cast features, the most famous of which was *Charley's Aunt* (1925 and 1930).

Octavus Roy Cohen (1891–1959). Jewish white American writer from Birmingham, Alabama, who was hired by Christie Studios to write scripts for a series of black-cast comedies, among them *Music Hath Charms*, *Lady Fare*, *The Melancholy Dame*, and *Oft in the Silly Night* (all 1929).

Evelyn Preer (1896–1932). African-American actress who starred in Oscar Micheaux's *Within Our Gates* (1920) and *Birthright* (1924), among other films.

Eddie Thompson (1898–1960). African-American actor, married to Evelyn Preer, who appeared in *The Melancholy Dame* (1929) and *Framing the Shrew* (1929).

Spencer Williams (1893–1969). African-American actor, writer, and director who began at the Christie studio in the late 1920s and became best known for playing Andy on the *Amos 'n' Andy* television show from 1951 until 1953.

9. Daniel L. Haynes (1894–1954). African-American actor who played the male lead in *Hallelujah*.

Nina Mae McKinney (1912–1967). African-American actress and dancer who was featured in *Hallelujah* and appeared in *Sanders of the River* (1935), *Dark Waters* (1944), and *Pinky* (1949).

Blackbirds of 1929. African-American touring revue produced by Lew Leslie.

Victoria Spivey (1906–1976). African-American singer and actress who played Missy Rose in *Hallelujah*.

Fannie Belle DeKnight. African-American actress who played Mammy in *Hallelujah*.

10. Eva Jessye. African-American choir director and musician. Her account of working with King Vidor, "The Truth about *Hallelujah*," is printed this volume.

11. Ethel Waters (1896–1977). Legendary African-American singer and actress, best known on film for her roles in *Cabin in the Sky* (1943), *Pinky* (1950), and *The Member of the Wedding* (1952).

Mamie Smith (1883–1946). African-American blues singer who appeared in short films for RCA, including *Jailhouse Blues* (1929).

Sissle and Blake. Noble Sissle (1889–1975): bandleader and songwriter who appeared with his band in black-cast films of the 1930s and 1940s. Eubie Blake (1883–1983): composer, pianist, and bandleader who formed a vaudeville team with Sissle in 1915, also co-writing songs with him.

John Ford's *The Strong Boy* was released in 1929. Eric Von Stroheim's *The Swamp* was never completed.

12. Micheaux Pictures Co., also known as "Micheaux Film Corp." Founded by Oscar Micheaux (1883–1951), this was the most successful black-owned independent film production company of its era, lasting from 1918 until 1928. Micheaux continued to make films until 1948.

Colored Players Film Corp. A white-owned Philadelphia film company founded in 1926 by David Starkman that produced *Scar of Shame* (1929), among other films.

Liberty Photoplays, Boston. Research revealed no reference to this production company, although a Liberty Motion Picture Company and a Liberty Film Manufacturing Company are both indexed by the American Film Institute.

13. Paul Robeson (1898–1976). African-American actor, singer, athlete, and activist who appeared in several Eugene O'Neill plays in the 1920s before appearing in films in the United States and Great Britain, including *Body and Soul* (1925) and *Borderline* (1930). There is no record of the Tono-Film company.

Dialogue in Dixie

1. This essay is a review of one of the first black-cast Hollywood films, *Hearts in Dixie* (1929). At the end of her article, Richardson responds to a commentary on the film by Robert Herring,

in the previous issue of *Close Up*. "Robert Herring Gives Four Points about *Hearts in Dixie*," *Close Up* 5:2 (August 1929), pp. 160–62.

2.   Selfridge's. London department store.

3.   In Shylock's speech, defending the humanity of Jews in William Shakespeare's *The Merchant of Venice* (III:I, ll. 46–66), he asks, for example, "If you prick us, do we not bleed?"

Is Julian Eltinge, Impersonator of Women, Going to Wed?

1.   Julian Eltinge (1882–1941). American film and theater actor who was the most celebrated American female impersonator of his day. Beginning his vaudeville career at the age of ten, playing a young girl, Eltinge portrayed attractive young women with care and sympathy. His crowd-pulling success in musical productions in the first half of the 1910s prompted producer Al Woods to name a theater in Eltinge's honor. Eltinge's film credits include *How Molly Made Good* (1915), *The Countess Charming* (1917), *Over the Rhine* (1918), and *Madame Behave* (1925). Eltinge never married, living with his mother for the last years of his life.

2.   The Tellegens. Lou Tellegen (1881–1934). Dutch-born matinée idol who played opposite Sarah Bernhardt before moving to Hollywood and a successful silent film career in 1914. Film credits include *The Victoria Cross* (1916), *Flame of the Desert* (1919), *The Woman and the Puppet* (1920), *Single Wives* (1924), and others.

   Geraldine Farrar (1882–1967). American opera singer known for her devoted female following, and screen actress who was married to Lou Tellegen. (They subsequently divorced.) Film credits include *Carmen* (1915), *Temptation* (1916), *Joan, the Woman* (1918), *The World and Its Women* (1919, with Lou Tellegen), and others.

   The Deans. Possibly Julia Dean (1878–1952). American screen and stage actress whose film career began in the 1910s and continued until her death. Film credits include *How Molly Made Good* (1915, with Julian Eltinge), *Matrimony* (1916), *Rasputin* (1917), and others.

   The Elliott Dexters. Elliott Dexter (1870–1941). American screen and vaudeville actor married to stage and screen actress Marie Doro (1882–1956) who was one of Adolph Zukor's "Famous Players" and played the title role in *Oliver Twist* (1916). (The Dexters subsequently divorced.) The two appeared together in *The Heart of Nora Flynn* (1916), *Diplomacy* (1916), and *Castles for Two* (1917).

Rudolph Valentino: The Sheik and The Son of the Sheik

1.   *Travels in Arabia Deserta*. Travelogue written by Charles Montagu Doughty (1843–1926), first published in 1888.

2.   Rudolph Valentino (1895–1926), whose first great screen success was in *Four Horsemen of the Apocalypse* (1921), died unexpectedly on 23 August 1926 of a perforated ulcer while in New York for the opening of *The Son of the Sheik*.

Mae West Reveals the Foundation of the 1900 Mode

1.   Mae West (1892–1981). American burlesque star, writer, theatrical producer, and film actress. This article appeared just prior to the American release of *I'm No Angel* in October 1933. In February of that year, West's starring vehicle *She Done Him Wrong* had been released to national controversy and box office success.

2.   Diamond Lil. West's very successful 1928 Broadway show was a nostalgic view of New York's Bowery in the 1890s. It was adapted for screen as *She Done Him Wrong* (1933).

On Mae West

1.   *She Done Him Wrong* was based on *Diamond Lil*, West's successful Broadway show of 1928. When the film was released in the United States in February 1933, it provoked protests by women's groups as well as censorship action in individual American states. Paramount had also been required by the Hays Office to make a last-minute cut to the film. Fearful of further controversy and expensive delays in production, and in spite of the enormous popular appeal and box office success of this film, the studio curtailed West's creative freedom in *I'm No Angel* (1933) and subsequent films. Although West received a screenwriting credit for *I'm No Angel*, Paramount scriptwriter Harlan Thompson was very much involved in its production.

2. West's control over her films declined after *She Done Him Wrong* (1933). Her third Paramount vehicle, *It Ain't No Sin*, was renamed *Belle of the Nineties*, the result of a protracted battle between Paramount and the Hays Office, which tried to force the studio into introducing some "compensating moral value" into the film. During this time, the new Production Code Administration (PCA) had come into operation on 1 July 1934. Studios that failed to comply with the PCA's recommendation were faced with the threat of a $25,000 fine and the denial of the PCA seal of approval, effectively removing any chance of American exhibition. *Belle of the Nineties* was extensively revised at the behest of the Hays Office before its delayed release in September 1934. Paramount, which had just recovered from financial difficulties through a managerial restructuring that had shifted control of the studio away from the West Coast to the more conservative banking-based East, dared not risk the kind of controversy and delays that West's films had caused. In her subsequent vehicles— *Goin' to Town* (1935), *Klondike Annie* (1935), *Go West, Young Man* (1937), and *Every Day's a Holiday* (1938)—the original West character was reworked into something many critics thought to be merely a shadow of its former self.

3. Ankyloses: "stiffens."

Hollywood Gods and Goddesses

1. Tom Mix (1880–1940). American actor who starred in over one hundred low-budget Westerns.

2. William S. Hart (1870–1946). Chiselled-featured American actor and director known for rejecting overly romantic Westerns in favor of an "adult" approach to the genre.
   Leatherstocking, also known as "Hawkeye," and "Natty Bumppo," was an American frontiersman hero who featured in a series of novels by James Fenimore Cooper, published between 1823 and 1841.
   Daniel Boone (1734–1820). American explorer and pioneer.

3. Gary Cooper (1901–1961). Slow-speaking American leading man.

4. Wallace Reid (1890–1923). American leading man of the silent era.
   Douglas Fairbanks (1883–1939). Swashbuckling American star, particularly of the silent period.

5. Valentino appeared in his first "Sheik" role in 1921.

6. Valentino (1895–1926) died unexpectedly of a perforated ulcer while in New York for the opening of *The Son of the Sheik* on 23 August 1926.

7. *Graustark*. Popular novel by George Barr McCutcheon, published in 1901, in which a young, ordinary, democratic American boy wins out over the plots of the decadent, feudal-minded inhabitants of the imaginary European principality of Graustark. McCutcheon's hero marries the princess of the realm and saves the kingdom by reorganizing it along American lines, making it more efficient.

8. Clark Gable (1901–1960). American actor and leading man.

9. BVD's. Brand of American underwear for men.

10. Ronald Colman (1891–1958). Distinguished British romantic actor who worked in Hollywood from 1920. His films include *Beau Geste* (1926), *A Tale of Two Cities* (1935), and *Lost Horizon* (1937).
    Leslie Howard (1893–1943). British actor who also appeared successfully in many American films, including *Gone with the Wind* (1939).
    Herbert Marshall (1890–1966). British actor, often a romantic lead, in Hollywood from the early 1930s. The loss of a leg in World War I did not impair his urbane screen persona.

11. Harold Lloyd (1893–1971). American actor and silent film comedian best remembered for dangling from a clock tower in *Safety Last* (1923), and for *Speedy* (1925).
    Wallace Beery (1885–1949). American character actor who worked in silent and sound film and was long under contract to MGM.

12. James Cagney (1899–1986). American star known for his tough guy roles in the 1930s and 1940s.

13. W.C. Fields (1879–1946). Misanthropic American comedian and writer whose career stretched from vaudeville to the silents and then to sound.

14. Horatio Alger (1832–1899). Popular and prolific American writer of rags-to-riches stories for boys, stories which preached the message of success through virtuous hard work.

15. Mrs. Siddons (Sarah Siddons) (1755–1831). Famed English tragic actress whose portrait was painted by Thomas Gainsborough, and Joshua Reynolds, among others. Her life was dramatized in Josephine Preston Peabody's 1922 play Portrait of Mrs. W.
Sarah Bernhardt (1844–1923). Famous French tragedienne of the stage, known as "the divine Sarah." See interview with her reprinted in this volume.
Duse. Eleanora Duse (1858–1924). Nicknamed "The Duse," Italy's foremost theater actress achieved international fame and was considered a rival to Sarah Bernhardt.
16. Mary Pickford sheared her famous curls in June 1928.
17. Clara Bow (1905–1965). American actress whose films in the 1920s depicted the flapper generation. After appearing in It in 1927, she became known as the "It" girl.
18. Elinor Glyn (1864–1943). English novelist whose daring novel Three Weeks was first filmed in 1914. She coined the word "It" for sex appeal and appeared in the film of that title in 1927.
19. Marlene Dietrich (1901–1992). German actress and singer, in Hollywood from 1930. In Germany she made The Blue Angel (1930) under the direction of Josef Von Sternberg (1894–1969), beginning a productive working partnership. In the Dietrich/Von Sternberg films that followed, Morocco (1930), Dishonoured (1931), Shanghai Express (1932), Blonde Venus (1932), The Scarlet Empress (1934), and The Devil is a Woman (1935), Von Sternberg shaped Dietrich's American image, something Suckow's reference suggests was common knowledge in 1936. George Du Maurier's internationally successful novel Trilby (1894) tells the story of Trilby O'Ferrall, a diva who achieves voice and fame only through the evil machinations of her mesmeric mentor, Svengali.
20. Helen Hayes (1900–1993). Eminent American actress of stage and screen.

Hollywood: An American State of Mind

1. Several scandals in the early 1920s fueled the popular image of Hollywood as a Babylonian city of sin. In September 1920, actress Olive Thomas (Mrs. Jack Pickford) committed suicide. She was subsequently revealed to have been "a dope fiend," with suggestions that husband Jack was similarly afflicted. Actress Virginia Rappe died in September 1921 after attending a wild party hosted by Roscoe "Fatty" Arbuckle, who was charged with her rape and murder. Although Arbuckle was eventually acquitted, his career was ruined. Revelations of drugs and adultery following the unsolved February 1922 murder of Paramount director William Desmond Taylor ended the careers of Mary Miles Minter and Mabel Normand. Later the same year, it was announced that leading man Wallace Reid had been institutionalized for drug addiction. He died in January 1923.
2. Chautauquas. The Chautauqua movement was a broad system of public education seeking to popularize and disseminate culture. It took its name from a program established in 1874 in Lake Chautauqua in New York state. Originally conceived as a training program for Protestant Sunday-school teachers, the movement rapidly expanded to include lectures, discussions, and readings on a wide range of topics for the general population. By 1909, there were 103 local centers nationwide in the United States serving two million course attendees. In addition, summer residential programs were offered and traveling Chautauquas toured the country, giving lectures at meetings where, occasionally, all pretence to intellectual or cultural achievement was abandoned in favor of entertainment.
3. Morris chair. Initially developed by William Morris's Morris, Marshall, Faulkner & Co. in the 1860s, the "Morris Chair" was a sturdy, comfortable, adjustable, capacious armchair, usually made of oak with slatted sides and leather cushioning. Found everywhere in living rooms and dens, it became so popular it was manufactured in the 1890s by virtually every furniture company in the United States, and was still on the lists of over fifty firms as late as 1918.
4. Field-Marshal Ferdinand Foch (1851–1929). French marshal, Supreme Commander of the Allied Armies in France in World War I.
5. Ignace Joan Paderewski (1860–1941). Polish prime minister and classical pianist who was to appear in Moonlight Sonata (1937).
6. Edwin Booth (1833–1893). One of the first American stage actors to be favorably received in Europe, and brother to President Lincoln's assassin, John Wilkes Booth.
Henry Irving (1838–1905). The first English actor to be knighted, Irving dominated the British stage from 1870 until 1900.
7. Dr Frank Crane (1861–1928). American writer and biographer whose works include The Religion

of Tomorrow (1899) and *George Westinghouse* (1925).
Gene (Geneva Grace) Stratton Porter (1863–1924). American photographer, illustrator, and nature writer who specialized in stories for young readers.
Jackie Coogan (1914–84). American child actor of the 1920s whose films include *The Kid* (1920), *Peck's Bad Boy* (1921), *Oliver Twist* (1921), *Trouble* (1922), and *Circus Days* (1923).

Ye Gossips Tayle

1. Marion Davies (1897–1961). American actress in silent and sound films, famous for her long-time affair with press baron William Randolph Hearst, who met her when she was a *Ziegfeld Follies* showgirl. Hearst tried to make her a major star. Davies's "marble palace" is a reference to Hearst's architectural folly, San Simeon.
2. The Brown Derby. A Hollywood eatery, built to look like the headgear of its name.
3. Sarah Bernhardt (1844–1923). Famous French tragedienne of the stage, known as "the divine Sarah." See interview with her reprinted this volume.

New Secular Forms of Old Religious Ideas

1. Public School. English "public" schools are in fact private institutions.
2. Norma Talmadge (1897–1957). American silent film heroine whose films include *Battle Cry of Peace* (1914), *Going Straight* (1915), *Witihin the Law* (1923), and *Camille* (1927).
   Constance Talmadge (1898–1973). American silent film comedian and heroine whose films include *Intolerance* (1916), *The Honeymoon* (1917), *Lessons in Love* (1921), *Her Primitive Lover* (1922), and *The Goldfish* (1924).
   Mae Murray (1883–1965). American leading lady of silent film, formerly a dancer, Murray had become famous for her role in Eric von Stroheim's *The Merry Widow* (1925).
   Pola Negri (1897–1987). Polish-born Appolonia Chalupek took her name from the popular Italian writer Ada Negri and worked in theater and film in Germany before moving to Hollywood where she enjoyed her greatest success in the 1920s. Films include *Madame du Barry/Passion* (1919), *The Flame* (1920), *Forbidden Paradise* (1924), and *Hotel Imperial* (1926).
   Corrine Griffith (1898–1979). American leading lady of the 1920s whose films include *Six Days* (1923), *Lilies of the Field* (1924), *Infatuation* (1925), and *The Garden of Eden* (1928).
3. Marion Davies (1897–1961). American actress in silent and sound films, famous for her long-time affair with press baron William Randolph Hearst, who endeavored to make her a major star.
   Bebe Daniels (1907–71). A child actress, Daniels was an American leading lady of the silent period who played opposite Harold Lloyd and starred in the films of Cecil B. De Mille, becoming a major musical star with the coming of sound. Her films include *Male and Female* (1919), *Why Change Your Wife?* (1920), *Monsieur Beaucaire* (1924), and *42nd Street* (1933). From the mid-1930s she pursued a successful music-hall and radio career in Britain with her husband Ben Lyon, and in the 1950s created the popular radio show *Life with the Lyons*.
   Lya de Putti (1901–32). Hungarian film actress who appeared in German, British and American productions. Her films include *The Phantom* (1925), *Variety* (1925), *The Sorrows of Satan* (1926), *Buck Privates* (1928), and *The Informer* (1929).
   Renée Adorée (1898–1933). French film actress who was formerly a circus horseback raider. In Hollywood from 1920, her career did not survive the transition to sound. Her films include *Monte Cristo* (1922), *Man and Maid* (1925), *The Big Parade* (1925), and *La Bohème* (1926).
4. Dolores del Rio (1905–1983). Mexican leading lady who was a popular Hollywood star in the 1920s and 1930s. Her films include *What Price Glory?* (1927), *The Loves of Carmen* (1927), *Resurrection* (1928), and *Evangeline* (1929).
   Clara Bow (1905–65). American actress whose films in the 1920s depicted the flapper generation. After appearing in *It* in 1927, she became known as the "It" girl.
5. Little Flower. St. Teresa of Lisieux (1873–1897), a Carmelite nun whose posthumous spiritual guide *Histoire d'une âme* (1898) inspired tremendous popular devotion.
6. Irene Rich (1891–1988). American silent screen heroine whose career waned with the arrival of sound. Her films include *Stella Maris* (1918), *Beau Brummell* (1924), *Lady Windermere's Fan* (1925), *So This is Paris* (1926), and *Shanghai Rose* (1921).
7. Lois Moran (1908–90). American-born musical star and actress whose film career began

in France. Her films include *La Galerie des Monstres* (1924), *Feu-Matthaes Pascal* (1925), *Stella Dallas* (1925), *Love Hungry* (1928), and *Men of Her Life* (1931).

Mary Philbin (1902–1993). American leading lady of the silent era whose films include *The Blazing Trail* (1921), *Merry Go Round* (1923), *Phantom of the Opera* (1925), and *The Man Who Laughs* (1928).

8. Wallace Reid (1892–1923), silent-era actor, director, and screen writer, died at the age of thirty on 18 January 1923 as a consequence of drug addiction. Valentino died of a perforated ulcer on 23 August 1926; he was thirty-one.

9. Rudolph Valentino's unexpected death prompted an international outpouring of grief. Fans sent more than 100,000 telegrams, and in New York over 125,000 mourners, described by one contemporary observer as a "frenzied, hysterical mob," lined ten city blocks to pay tribute to the actor. West's observation on the makeup of this crowd is noteworthy because most writers have stressed the predominance of female mourners.

10. G.G. Coulton, *Five Centuries of Religion* (Cambridge: The University Press, 1923).

11. St. Simeon Stylites (c. 390–450). The first of the pillar ascetics, Simeon erected a ten-foot pillar and lived on top of it for twenty-three years, converting the crowds who gathered there and preaching holiness.

12. The Thebaid, Region of Upper Egypt favored by hermits.

The Black Film

1. The French term *film noir* (black film) had been applied to films like *Quai des brumes* (1938) and *Le jour se lève* (1939) by French critics in the late 1930s to describe these films' despairing fatalism. After World War II, British, American and French critics used the term to categorize American urban crime films of the 1940s and later, as in writing by Nino Frank and Jean-Pierre Chartier in 1946, and Raymond Borde and Étienne Chaumeton's 1955 study, *Panorama du film noir américain, 1941–1953* (Paris: Minuit).

2. Krafft-Ebing, R. von (1840–1902). German neuropsychiatrist who was a pioneering student of sexual psychopathology, best known for his groundbreaking study *Psychopathia Sexualis; mit besondere Berücksichtigung der conträren Sexualempfindung* (1886).

Mr. Deeds and Willie Stark

1. President Franklin Delano Roosevelt (1882–1945). American President in office from 1932 until 1945. His administration's social and economic programs, designed to relieve the worst effects of the Great Depression, are known as the New Deal.

2. Longfellow Deeds. A character from Frank Capra's film *Mr. Deeds Goes to Town* (1936), based on the 1935 story by Charence Buddington Kelland.

3. President Warren G. Harding (1865–1923). American president, in office 1921–23.
   President Calvin Coolidge (1872–1933). Thirtieth American president, 1923–29. Republican governor of Massachusetts from 1919 to 1920; vice-president 1921–23; he was appointed president on President Harding's death in 1923, and re-elected in 1924.

4. President Harry S. Truman (1884–1972). In office 1945–52. Truman was president, having succeeded Roosevelt (who died in office), when the Allies defeated Germany and Japan at the end of World War II.

5. James Thurber (1894–1961). American playwright, author, and graphic artist. *The Male Animal* (1940) is one of his plays.

6. Preston Sturges (1898–1959). American director, screenwriter, and playwright. His films as writer/director include *The Great McGinty* (1940), *Christmas in July* (1940), *Sullivan's Travels* (1941), *The Miracle of Morgan's Creek* (1943), and *Hail the Conquering Hero* (1944).

7. Frank Capra (1897–1991). American director, extremely successful from the mid 1930s until the mid 1940s, whose films stress the virtues of the common man. During World War II, he directed the *Why We Fight* documentary series for the Army Signal Corps.

Comments on the Screen

1. William S. Hart (1864–1946). Chiseled-featured American actor and director known for rejecting overly romantic Westerns in favor of an "adult" approach to the genre.
   Tom Mix (1880–1940). Cowboy actor of the silent era and early talkie period.

2. This day of limited taste. During World War I, alcoholic beverage production was restricted in the United States in order to conserve grain. More importantly, in December 1917, both the United States Senate and the House of Representatives approved a resolution to add a constitutional amendment prohibiting the manufacture, sale, or transport of intoxicating liquors. During the next thirteen months, ratification by the legislatures of three-quarters of the American states had been secured, putting the eighteenth amendment, The Volstead Act, into effect and introducing Prohibition. Flanner is writing during the period leading up to the introduction of this amendment.

3. White ribbon movement. The temperance movement.

4. William Farnum (1876–1953). American actor, a leading man of the silent screen who attracted a large salary during his peak period (1917–19).

Imitation Chinchilla

1. *A House Divided.* A reference to the film directed in 1919 by J. Stuart Blackton.

2. In the early 1910s, technical directors or stage managers were responsible for permanent properties and set construction. They were also responsible for ensuring stylistic and historical consistency in the sets. Within a few years, by the mid 1910s, this position was being called the art director by the studios. Research by Anthony Slide has shown that, notwithstanding Underhill's argument that art direction required specifically feminine acumen, there were few, if any, women art directors working in Hollywood up to 1920.

3. Olga Petrova (1886–1977). British-born leading lady who played femmes fatales in silent films, among them *The Tigress* (1914), *The Soul Market* (1916), *The Undying Flame* (1917), and *The Panther Woman* (1918). She formed her own production company.

4. Elsie Ferguson (1883–1961). American leading actress who featured in silent melodramas about the upper classes. Her films include *Song of Songs* (1918), *A Society Exile* (1919), *His House in Order* (1920), *Sacred and Profane Love* (1921).

La Femme Silhouette: The Bronze Age

1. "La Femme Silhouette" was the title of Proctor's occasional column in *The Messenger*. In the column reprinted here, Proctor discusses both theater and film, rarely referring specifically to cinema. However, she describes a cultural climate affecting both stage and screen, and many of the productions she writes about were subsequently filmed.
   "Bronze," like "sepia," is a description of blackness which has faded from use. In the second half of the 1920s African Americans employed it as a form of self-description. Chicago's African-American press used the term "Bronzeville" to identify the city's South Side, a predominantly black neighborhood; and in 1922 Georgia Douglas Johnson published the novel Bronze (1925).

2. Tutankhamen's tomb was discovered by Howard Carter in November 1922.

3. The Volstead Act. The eighteenth amendment to the United States Constitution, prohibiting the manufacture, sale or transport of intoxicating liquors, went into effect in early 1919.

4. *The Sheik* (1919), a novel by Edith Maude Hull, was the basis of the 1921 film of the same name.

5. Florenz Ziegfeld (1867?–1932). American theater manager whose successful revue series, *Ziegfeld Follies*, based on the Parisian *Folies-Bergère*, played almost every year from 1907 until his death.

6. *The Emperor Jones* (1920). Successful play written by Eugene O'Neill, revived three times in the 1920s.
   Rosalind. Play written by J.M. Barrie, first performed in London in October 1912.
   All God's Chillun Got Wings (1924). Controversial play dealing with race, written by Eugene O'Neill, directed by Jamie Light, and starring Paul Robeson.

7. *White Cargo* (1923). Sensationalistic play directed and co-written by Leon Gordon.
   Professor Starr. Frederick Starr, influential American anthropologist who worked in the department of ethnology at the American Museum of Natural History (1889–91), where he was responsible for classifying the department's collection. From 1892 to 1923 he taught at the University of Chicago.
   The Prince of Wales probably first met the African-American dancer and singer Josephine

Baker in 1925 at Le Rat Mort, a nightclub in Pigalle in Paris. Here, after appearing in the sensational review, *La Revue Nègre*, Baker would do a second performance. The Prince of Wales was a regular at Le Rat Mort, where he was known for his drinking and his efforts at drumming.

The Color Fad

1. Under Kemal Atatürk, Turkey became a secular republic in 1923. The sultanate and caliphate were abolished and, among other modernization programs, Turkish women were granted suffrage and were allowed to go unveiled.
2. Goodwin describes a counter-trend to the one commonly noted: by the 1920s, Montmartre and Montparnasse had become destinations for sophisticated American tourists as well as expatriate American writers resident in Paris. Ernest Hemingway noted that, in the 1920s, Montparnasse was full of "lady writers of all sexes."
3. Farina (1920–1980). African-American actor who played "Farina" in the *Our Gang* comedies from 1922 until 1933. Also known as Allen "Farina" Hoskins. The *Our Gang* comedy series was created by white American producer, director, and screenwriter, Hal Roach (1892–1993).
4. Stepin Fetchit (Lincoln Perry) (1902–85). African-American comic actor, very successful in the 1930s, whose typical roles as the lazy Negro are now considered among the most insulting stereotypes of African Americans.
5. Nina Mae McKinney (1913–1967). African-American actress and dancer who featured in *Hallelujah* (1929), and appeared in *Sanders of the River* (1935), *Dark Waters* (1944),and *Pinky* (1949). Clara Bow (1905–1965). American actress whose films in the 1920s depicted the flapper generation. After appearing in *It* in 1927, she became known as the "It" girl.
6. *Hallelujah* (1929). All black-cast sound film directed by King Vidor. For an account of working conditions during the production of the film, see Eva Jessye, "The Truth About *Hallelujah*," reprinted in this volume.
7. Roland Hayes (1887–1977). African-American tenor.
8. Egbert Austin "Bert" Williams (1876–1922). Extremely successful African-American entertainer and songwriter, longtime-featured comedian in the *Ziegfeld Follies* during the 1910s.
9. Two Black Crows. A 1920s radio show starring the comedy duo of George Moran (1882–1949) and Charles Mack (1887–1934). A black-faced white comedy team, Moran and Mack were major vaudeville and review stars from 1927, when they performed their "Two Black Crows" routine on record, although they had been performing together since 1917. They played the *Ziegfeld Follies*. Their first film, *Why Bring That Up* (1929), was written by Octavus Roy Cohen. The duo was apparently popular with both black and white audiences. They also starred in the musical *Anybody's War* (1930), and in *Hypnotized* (1932), the latter a comedy with songs directed by Mack Sennett.
10. African Americans purchased products designed to lighten skin tone and straighten hair throughout the 1920s, as well as earlier and later. Madame C.J. Walker (1867–1919), the African-American beauty products entrepreneur, included hair-straightening products in the Walker system of treatments. Goodwin points to the historical irony of these efforts on the part of African Americans wanting to appear more European, just at the time that Europeans were sporting darker skin tones thanks to the recent fashionability of tanning.
11. *Scarlet Sister Mary* (1928), written by Julia Peterkin (1880–1961).
12. *Blacker the Berry* (1929), written by Wallace Thurman (1902–1934).
    Plum Bun (1928), written by Jessie Redmon Fauset.
13. Charles S. Gilpin (1878–1930). African-American actor who played Brutus Jones in *The Emperor Jones*.
    Daniel L. Haynes (1894–1954). African-American actor who played the male lead in *Hallelujah*.
    Paul Robeson (1898–1976). African-American actor, singer, athlete, and activist who appeared in several Eugene O'Neill plays in the 1920s before appearing in films in the United States and Britain, including *Body and Soul* (1925) and *Borderline* (1930).
    Emperor Jones (1920). Successful play written by Eugene O'Neill, revived three times in the twenties.
    Porgy (1927). Play written by Dorothy and DuBose Heyward (based on their novel), and directed by Rouben Mamoulian.

Earth (1927). Play written by Em Jo Basshe and directed by Russell Wright and Helmsley Winfield.

Harlem (1929). Play written by W.J. Rapp and Wallace Thurman and directed Chester Erskin.

14. *God's Step-children*, Novel by Sarah Gertrude Liebson Millin (1924).
15. Sixteen American states had laws prohibiting intermarriage between blacks and whites (Alabama still did in 1999), and in many other states such marriages were socially, if not legally, unacceptable. These laws were not declared unconstitutional until 1967.

Fredi Washington Strikes a New Note

1. The article reprinted here exists in typescript in the Claude Barnett Papers, Box 298, Folder 15, in the Chicago Historical Society, where it is credited "By Fay M. Jackson for ANP [Associated Negro Press] 12 December 1934." Jackson was a correspondent for the Associated Negro Press and her articles appeared in African-American publications serviced by the ANP. Occasionally her articles appeared without a byline. The article appeared as Fay M. Jackson, "Fredi Washington Strikes New Note in Hollywood Film," *Pittsburgh Courier*, 15 December 1934.
2. Uncle Tom is the title character in Harriet Beecher Stowe's abolitionist novel, *Uncle Tom's Cabin* (1852). Tom is presented as a paragon of pious and long-suffering virtue, a slave who is morally superior to all his masters. Tom refuses to fight against his enslavement and the system that perpetuates it and dies as a result, preferring a spiritual victory in heaven to practical change in the present. Aunt Jemima originated as an advertising trademark for a brand of pancake mix where, depicted as a plump, beaming African-American woman with exaggerated features and a handkerchief knotted on her head, she closely resembled the mammy stereotype. Both the mammy stereotype and Aunt Jemima radiate good-natured smiles, suggesting their willingness to serve. When pancake mix was introduced in the United States in the early 1890s, pre-mixed baking ingredients were a novel idea, and as an advertising gimmick at the 1893 World's Fair the pancake mix company hired an African-American woman named Nancy Green to dress in costume and flip pancakes. Her impact was so great that in 1898 the character was named "Aunt Jemima." The current "Aunt Jemima" logo wears no bandana.
3. *Imitation of Life*, a 1933 novel by the popular American writer Fannie Hurst (1889–1968), was adapted for film in 1934 and directed by John M. Stahl (1886–1950). Her novel was filmed again in 1959.
4. Fredi Washington (1903–1994). African-American actress, dancer, newspaper editor and columnist. Washington's other film appearances include *Emperor Jones* (1933) and *Drums in the Jungle* (1933). For examples of Washington's writings on film while theater editor and columnist for *The People's Voice* (New York) from 1942 to 1947, see her writings included in this volume.
5. In *Imitation of Life* Fredi Washington plays the adult Peola, a light-skinned, black daughter of a darker skinned mother. Peola wants to pass for white.
6. Hurst's "informant" was, in all likelihood, the African-American writer and folklorist Zora Neale Hurston (1891–1960). Hurston was hired in 1925 as Hurst's personal secretary but lacked clerical skills. She stayed on as chauffeur and companion until the end of 1926.

Imitations: Life, Color and Pancakes

1. *Imitation of Life* (1934), directed by John M. Stahl and based on a 1933 novel by popular American writer Fannie Hurst (1889–1968). In this film Delilah is an African-American servant to Miss Bea, a white woman who begins a pancake empire with a recipe for pancake mix that Delilah has given her. In their business negotiations, Delilah shows little interest in the profits that are rightfully hers, undervaluing the worth of her ingenuity and trusting instead in the implicit goodness of her employer. This *naïveté* prompts the remark made by Miss Bea's mordant business advisor, "Once a pancake, always a pancake," with its implication that the "truths" of race will always tell: Delilah is ignorant and gullible because she is black. Peola is Delilah's light-skinned daughter who, trying to pass as white, disdains her heritage and refuses to acknowledge her mother until Delilah is dead.

For passing in the theater, see "The Confessions of an Ex-White Actress," (parts I and II), reprinted in this volume; and for a different view of *Imitation of Life* by another African-

American woman, see Fay M. Jackson, "Fredi Washington Strikes a New Note in Hollywood Film: *Imitations*," reprinted in this volume.

2. Miss Hurst. The popular American writer and novelist Fannie Hurst (1889–1968) whose novel *Imitation of Life* (1933) was adapted for the film.

3. Marcel (wave). A permed bob. In the film, Delilah's distinguishing bandana, a visual reminder of the character's proximity to the "Aunt Jemima" and "mammy" stereotypes, is removed in favor of a European coiffure when she relocates to the city with her now wealthy employer. Despite Delilah's altered appearance, however, she cannot accustom herself to the life of relative ease her new situation has brought. As Washington notes, her faithful subservience wins out against any desire for independence.

4. Fredi Washington (1903–94) plays the part of the adult Peola. For examples of Washington's writings on film while theater editor and columnist for *The People's Voice* (New York) from 1942 to 1947, see her writings included in this volume.

Women: Hollywood Version

1. *Kinder, Küche, und Kirche*: Literally, "children, kitchen, and church"; shorthand for the Nazi ideology of relegating women to the domestic and guardianship spheres.

2. Only the Soviet Union and Great Britain conscripted women to the forces during the Second World War. Germany resorted to female conscription to the forces as a last-ditch effort at the war's end.

3. In the late 1940s and early 1950s, the Ohrbach dress was advertised as an inexpensive make-over outfit with the slogan "Liberal trade-in. Bring in your wife, and for just a few dollars ... we will give you a new woman."

4. Dalton Trumbo (1905–76). American screenwriter who was investigated by the House Committee on Un-American Activities in 1947, cited for contempt for refusing to answer questions about his affiliations with Communist organizations, jailed for ten months and blacklisted.
   John Howard Lawson (1894–1977). American screenwriter who joined the Communist Party in 1934 and was active in the Screen Writers Guild. Investigated by the House Committee on Un-American Activities in 1947. He was cited for contempt and served a one year jail term.

5. Inspired by the isolationism of the America First movement, the Senate Subcommittee on War Propaganda—also known as the Nye–Clark Committee—was established in August 1941 to investigate the charge that the motion picture and radio industries were producing "pro-war" propaganda through their support of the Allied cause in Europe. Although Hollywood's commercial practices (like block-booking) had been subject to prior congressional investigation, and the effects of Hollywood films had been widely (if inconclusively) debated in public, the federal government had never before brought its force to bear on an examination of Hollywood's ideals. (An earlier inquiry, headed by Martin Dies, into movie "subversion" in 1940 was quickly aborted.) Hearings were held in September 1941 and soon revealed the anti-Communist and anti-Semitic basis of the allegations. The bombing of Pearl Harbor a scant three months after the hearings made the Subcommittee redundant, although the anti-Communist and anti-Semitic tenor of its inquiry resurfaced when the Committee founded by Dies, the House Committee on Un-American Activities, pursued investigations of the film industry after the war.

6. The Hays Office. Arm of the Motion Picture Producers and Distributors Association (MPPDA) headed by Will Hays from 1922 to 1945. The Hays Office, which introduced a strengthened Production Code in 1934, was established to forestall federal film censorship, which it did by imposing strict limitations on both the content of pre-production scripts and the finished films themselves.
   Legion of Decency. American Catholic reform movement critical of Hollywood and active in orchestrating public boycotts of supposedly immoral motion pictures. The Legion of Decency hierarchy worked with Will Hays in formulating the Production Code in 1930. This code of practice, which stipulated what could and could not be shown on screen, did not become binding until 1934 when Will Hays established the Production Code Administration to effectively police it. The impetus for Hays at this time was a potential boycott of Hollywood film by several million people that had been orchestrated by women's role in the Legion of Decency. These activities are discussed in Part Three.

That "Feminine Angle"

1. Edana Romney acted in and was the female producer for *Corridor of Mirrors*.
2. Jill Craigie (1914–1999). British journalist, scriptwriter, film producer and director who made *Out of Chaos* (1944) and *The Way We Live* (1947), documentaries for the British company Two Cities Films. With William MacQuitty, she formed her own production company, Outlook, in 1948, and made the feature film *Blue Scar* (1949). Her last film, *To be a Woman* (1951), was a documentary arguing the case for equal pay for women.
3. Lillian Hellman (1905–1984). American playwright who adapted much of her own work for screen in addition to writing other plays. Her autobiographical *Pentimento* (1974) was filmed as *Julia* (1977). Other films based on her work include *The Little Foxes* (1941), *Watch on the Rhine* (1943), *Another Part of the Forest* (1948), and *The Children's Hour* (1962).
4. Lizabeth Scott (1922–). American leading lady of the 1940s with a sultry demeanor. Her films include *The Strange Love of Marta Ivers* (1946), *Dead Reckoning* (1947), *I Walk Alone* (1947), and *Easy Living* (1949).
   Lana Turner (1920–1997). American leading lady of the 1940s whose girl-next-door image became increasingly sophisticated. Films include *Love Finds Andy Hardy* (1939), *Somewhere I'll Find You* (1942), *The Postman Always Rings Twice* (1946), *Peyton Place* (1957), and *Imitation of Life* (1959).
   Lauren Bacall (1924–). American actress with stage experience, who made her screen debut with Humphrey Bogart in *To Have and Have Not* (1944) and went on to play a number of classic film noir roles in the 1940s, continuing to appear on film and stage in the 1990's.
   Rita Hayworth (1918–1987). American leading actress and dancer cast in sultry, tempestuous roles. Her films include *Only Angels Have Wings* (1939), *The Strawberry Blonde* (1941), *Gilda* (1946), and *The Lady From Shanghai* (1948), for which her hair had been bleached.
5. Myrna Loy (1905–1993). American leading actress initially cast in treacherous and mysterious roles, she became famous as William Powell's wife in the witty comedies of the *Thin Man* series (1934–47).
6. Carole Lombard (1908–1942). American leading lady and comedienne of the 1930s whose films include *No Man of Her Own* (1932), *Bolero* (1934), *My Man Godfrey* (1936), and *To Be or Not To Be* (1942).
   Luise Rainer (1910–). Austrian actress with stage experience. In Hollywood from the 1930s, she won Academy Awards for her performances in *The Great Ziegfeld* (1936) and *The Good Earth* (1937).
   Ruth Chatterton (1893–1961). American film actress with stage experience. Popular in the 1920s and 1930s, she was later a successful novelist. Her films include *Madame X* (1929), *Paramount on Parade* (1930), *Sarah and Son* (1930), *Female* (1933), and *Dodsworth* (1936).
   Jean Harlow (1911–37). American actress famous for her platinum blonde hair and wisecracking banter. Her films include *Hell's Angels* (1930), *Public Enemy* (1931), *Dinner at Eight* (1933), and *Bombshell* (1933).
7. Claudette Colbert (1905–96). French-born American leading actress whose career lasted into the 1950s and later. Best remembered for her roles in screwball comedies beginning with Frank Capra's *It Happened One Night* (1934), she also appeared in epics, *Cleopatra* (1934), Westerns, *Drums Along the Mowhawk* (1939), and war dramas, *So Proudly We Hail* (1943). She played a serviceman's wife in *Since You Went Away* (1944).
   Irene Dunne (1898–1990). American actress who starred in screwball comedies, dramas and musicals in the 1930s and 1940s, playing modern women with wit and intelligence. Her films include *Cimarron* (1931), *Back Street* (1932), *Magnificent Obsession* (1935), *Love Affair* (1939), *My Favourite Wife* (1940), and *I Remember Mama* (1948). She played a serviceman's wife in *A Guy Named Joe* (1943).
8. Rosalind Russell (1908–1976). American leading actress of the 1930s and 1940s. Her films include *China Seas* (1935), *The Women* (1939), *His Girl Friday* (1940), *My Sister Eileen* (1942), and *Sister Kenny* (1946).
   Mary Astor (1906–1987). American actress whose career began in the silent era playing opposite John Barrymore. A star from the mid 1920s through the mid 1940s, she later appeared in maternal roles such as those in *Meet Me in St. Louis* (1944) and *Little Women* (1949).
   Celeste Holm (1919–). American stage actress who also worked in films. Her films include *Gentleman's Agreement* (1947), for which she won an Academy Award, *The Snake Pit* (1948), *All About Eve* (1950), and *High Society* (1956).

Dorothy McGuire (1919–2001). American leading lady of the 1940s whose films include *A Tree Grows in Brooklyn* (1944), *The Spiral Staircase* (1945), and *Three Coins in the Fountain* (1954).

Teresa Wright (1918–). American film actress with stage experience, best remembered for her role as Joseph Cotten's niece in Alfred Hitchcock's *Shadow of a Doubt* (1943). Other films include her Academy Award-winning *Mrs. Miniver* (1942), *The Best Years of Our Lives* (1946), and *The Men* (1950).

9. Celia Johnson (1908–1982). Distinguished British actress with stage experience, best known for the three films she made with director David Lean, *In Which We Serve* (1942), *This Happy Breed* (1944), and *Brief Encounter* (1946).

Deborah Kerr (1921–2005). British actress who epitomized the British gentlewoman, Kerr's career was at its height in the mid 1950s. Her films include *Love on the Dole* (1941), *The Life and Death of Colonel Blimp* (1943), *Black Narcissus* (1946), *From Here to Eternity* (1953) and *The King and I* (1956).

Rosamund John (1913–1998). British film actress whose gentle-mannered film performances include *The Gentle Sex* (1943), *Tawny Pippit* (1944), *The Way to the Stars* (1945), *Green for Danger* (1946), and *Fame is the Spur* (1947).

10. Margaret Johnston (1914–2002) Australian-born actress working in British film, particularly during the 1940s. Her films include *The Rake's Progress* (1945), *A Man About the House* (1947), and *The Magic Box* (1951).

11. Kay Walsh (1914–?). British actress who trained in West End revue, and was married to David Lean, whose films include *In Which We Serve* (1942), *This Happy Breed* (1944), *The October Man* (1947), and *Oliver Twist* (1948).

Eileen Herlie (1920–?). Scottish stage actress who made occasional films, among them *Hamlet* (1948), *The Angel with the Trumpet* (1949), and *The Story of Gilbert and Sullivan* (1953).

Treating Women *too* Well

1. *Sarah and Son* (1930) was directed in the United States by Dorothy Arzner for Paramount Famous Players-Lasky. Based on the 1929 novel by Timothy Shea (a pseudonym of Alden Arthur Knipe), the screen adaptation and dialogue were the work of Zoë Akins.

Ruth Chatterton (1893–1961). American film actress with stage experience. Popular in the 1920s and 1930s, and nominated for an Academy Award for Best Actress for her role in *Sarah and Son*, she was later a successful novelist. Her other films include *Madame X* (1929), *Paramount on Parade* (1930), *Female* (1933), and *Dodsworth* (1936).

2. *Lummox* (1923), by the popular American novelist Fannie Hurst, was adapted for film in 1930. Hurst is credited with the film's dialogue.

3. Benjamin Disraeli (1804–1881). British prime minister and novelist who was the subject of a screen biography starring George Arliss in 1921, and again in 1930.

4. In *Dawn* (1929), the distinguished British actress Sybil Thorndike (1882–1976) portrayed Nurse Edith Cavell, a British nurse who aided Allied soldiers in occupied territory in World War I and was executed by the Germans as a spy.

5. Lois Weber (1882–1939). American actress, director, writer and producer who began working in film in 1908. In the 1910s at Universal Studios she was one of the highest-paid directors; and in 1917, formed Lois Weber Productions. Because Weber was keen to use film as a medium of social uplift, her films fared poorly with mid 1920s, jazz-era American audiences. See the writing by Weber and biography of Weber included in this volume.

6. Dorothy Arzner (1900–1979). American editor and director. One of the few American women directors of the classical Hollywood era, Arzner directed seventeen features between 1927 and 1943, among them *Paramount on Parade* (1930), *Working Girls* (1931), *Christopher Strong* (1933), and *Dance Girl, Dance* (1944).

7. Ethel Mannin (1900–1984). Prolific British writer who wrote occasionally about film in the 1930s for the fan magazine *Film Weekly* and, as a member of the Independent Labour Party, for the socialist newspaper, *New Leader*. Her review of G.W. Pabst's *Kameradschaft*, "War... and the Workers," is reprinted in this volume. See the biography of Mannin included this volume.

Mary Borden (1886–1968). American-born English novelist whose 1936 novel *Action for Slander* was adapted for film. Borden later wrote scripts for the BBC's "Saturday Night Theatre."

F. Tennyson Jesse (1889–1959). British journalist and writer whose works include *The Lacquer Lady* (1929), and *A Pin to See the Peepshow* (1934).

Margaret Kennedy (1896–1967). British novelist and playwright whose plays *The Constant Nymph* and *Escape Me Never* were successfully filmed.

Movie

1. In Hallelujahs. A critical reference to the depiction of African-American religion in the 1929 King Vidor film *Hallelujah*.
2. "Remember the Maine!" A war-rallying slogan widely heard during the 1898 Spanish-American War. The US battleship *Maine* was destroyed by a mine in the harbor of Havana, 15 February 1898.

Luxury

1. Colette was writing during World War I, a time of black-outs and brown-outs.
2. Ba-Ta-Clan. The Grand Café Chinois-Théâtre de Ba-Ta-Clan was a Parisian cabaret founded during the Second Empire. In 1910 Madame Rasimi, well-known for her costuming flair, became its manager for the second time.
3. Henri Fabre (1823–1915). French entomologist who wrote the ten volume *Souvenirs Entomologiques* (1879–1907).

A War Film in Berlin

1. Ufa cinemas. The German film production company Universum Film Aktien Gesellschaft (UFA) owned ninety-one theaters throughout Germany in 1925. In Berlin, the nation's moviegoing capital, UFA theaters displayed a variety of architectural styles, from the Romanesque citadel of the Ufa–Palast am Zoo, to the simplified Baroque surfaces of the Gloria–Palast and the streamlined–massive elegance of the Universum am Kurfürstendamm. (This last may be the theater to which Woodman refers.) For a discussion of audiences inside different Berlin movies houses at an earlier point, see Resi Langer, "From Northern Berlin and the Surrounds," and "In the Movie Houses of Western Berlin," both reprinted in this volume.
2. Hitler was to become appointed German chancellor less than eighteen months later, on 30 January 1933.

War... and the Workers

1. G.W. Pabst (1885–1967). Austrian director whose films include *Joyless Street* (1925), *Secrets of a Soul* (1926), *Pandora's Box* (1928), *Diary of a Lost Girl* (1929), *Westfront 1918* (1930), *The Threepenny Opera* (1931), and *Kameradschaft* (1931).
Academy Cinema, London. An early art cinema featuring European films, founded in 1931. For an account of the Academy, see Elizabeth Coxhead, "For a Co-operative Cinema: The Work of the Academy, Oxford Street," reprinted in this volume.
2. Frederick C. Boden, author of *Miner* (1932).
Harry Carlisle, author of *Darkness at Noon* (1931).
3. The League of Nations Conference on the Reduction and Limitation of Arms in Geneva had opened in February in 1932 and was continuing, with diminishing attendance, in the period in which Mannin wrote.

What Shall You Do in the War?

1. G.W. Pabst (1885–1967). Austrian director whose films include *Joyless Street* (1925), *Secrets of a Soul* (1926), *Pandora's Box* (1928), *Diary of a Lost Girl* (1929), *Westfront 1918* (1930), *The Threepenny Opera* (1931), and *Kameradschaft* (1931).
2. *Germany Puts the Clock Back* (1933). Edgar Ansel Mowrer's account of the collapse of German democracy.
3. The first German racial laws were passed in 1933 with the coming to power of the National Socialists.
4. In September 1926, Germany was admitted to the League of Nations and in 1928 signed the Kellogg–Briand Pact, a treaty which promised to outlaw the resort to aggressive war. These efforts to rejoin the world community after the defeat and humiliation of World War I were later repudiated by the Nationalist Socialist government.

5. Hitler had become chancellor of Germany on 30 January 1933. On 27 February of that year, the German Reichstag was set alight, an event understood by many at the time to have been a deliberate act of provocation on the part of the National Socialists. Shortly thereafter, civil liberties were suspended and Communists were arrested. On 7 April, the process of purging the universities and civil service of socialists, democrats and Jews began. (Bryher records the removal of Jews from the medical profession.) On 2 May, trade unions were disbanded.

6. Heinrich Mann (1871–1950). Socially committed German novelist and essayist.
Thomas Mann (1875–1955). German novelist and critic, younger brother of Heinrich.
Erich Maria Remarque (1898–1970). German novelist, known for his realistic fiction and famous for his anti-war novel *All Quiet on the Western Front* (1928).
Arnold Zweig (1887–1968). German novelist, poet, dramatist, and journalist, associated with Zionism and pacifism.
Stefan Zweig (1881–1942). Austrian novelist, dramatist, and essayist.
Kurt Tucholsky (1890–1935). German novelist and socialist journalist.
Leon Feuchtwanger (1884–1958). German poet, novelist, and dramatist.
Arthur Schnitzler (1862–1931). Austrian novelist, dramatist, and essayist.
Ernst Glaeser (1902–1963). German novelist.

7. For a contemporary review of Pabst's *Kameradschaft*, see Ethel Mannin's "War ... and the Workers," reprinted in this volume.

8. Labor conscription for German women. Voluntary labor camps for women were established during the first year of the National Socialist regime. Administered by the Women's Labor Service (*Frauenarbeitsdienst*), these camps were located in both urban and rural settings and operated under the motto: "Be true, Be pure, Be German" (*Sei wahr, Sei klar, Sei deutsch*). The National Labor Service Law, which proclaimed the obligation of both sexes to participate in the National Labor Service, went into effect on 26 June 1935, after Bryher's article was written. The law was not made binding for women until 1939.

On Pickets, Gone with the Wind and "Wolf"

1. Eleanor Roosevelt crossing the picket line. In the June 1941 edition of her regular *Ladies' Home Journal* column, "If You Ask Me," American First Lady Eleanor Roosevelt defended her recent support for a group of women who had struck for better working conditions. Although this post-dates Johnson's essay, Johnson may be referring to this kind of sympathy on the part of Mrs Roosevelt.

2. After setting siege to the city of Atlanta, General William Tecumseh Sherman occupied it on 2 September 1864. From there, as commander of all the Union armies, he conducted his infamous march to the sea, declaring, "I can make Georgia howl." Leading 62,000 men in a broad, ravaging sweep of destruction through the state, he arrived in the city of Savannah at the end of that year.

3. Sidney Howard is credited with writing the script for the film version of Margaret Mitchell's bestselling novel *Gone with the Wind* (1936). The film was released in 1939.

Gone with the Wind's Places and Prices, and the Public

1. The exhibition of *Gone with the Wind* attracted criticism on both sides of the Atlantic for charging inflated ticket prices.

2. The raw, elemental action of Erskine Caldwell's 1932 novel *Tobacco Road* takes place amongst poor white tenant farmers in Georgia. Caldwell's novel was not a best-seller at the time of its publication, but Jack Kirkland's 1933 stage version became a Broadway success.

3. Writing prior to the United States' involvement in World War II, Johnson reiterates the credo that the Allied forces were defending democracy. After America joined the war effort, many more African-American writers treated such appeals to democratic principles critically, noting the incongruity of black Americans being asked to defend a democracy in which they were denied full participation.

Apollo Comedy Bad For Race

1. Apollo Theater. Long a Harlem landmark, the venue opened as Seamon and Hurtig's New Theatre in 1910, featuring films and vaudeville acts, and reopened as the Apollo in 1934.

2. Washington is writing after the United States had declared war on the Axis powers on 11 December 1941.

Tim Moore Replies

1. Washington's previous weekly column is reprinted as "Apollo Comedy Bad For Race" in this volume.
2. Washington had played the part of Peola, a light-skinned black woman who wishes to pass for white, in the 1934 film *Imitation of Life*. For two other views of this film and Washington's role, see Fay M. Jackson, "Fredi Washington Strikes New Note in Hollywood Film *Imitations*," and Hazel Washington, "Imitations: Life, Color and Pancakes," both reprinted in this volume.
3. The 135th Street Library, a branch of the New York Public Library specializing in black history and black materials, is now home to the Schomburg Center for Research in Black Culture.

The Challenge

1. During the 1930s and 1940s, J. Arthur Rank established an empire of film production, exhibition, and distribution, hoping to challenge Hollywood. The second largest film concern in Britain in the late 1940s was Alexander Korda's London Films. Korda, with his two brothers, was known for producing high-production-value imperialist epics. Both operations aspired to fill more British screen time with British-made films and to gain a share of the American market. On 8 May 1947, their efforts were dealt a severe blow when the British government, under the prime ministership of Clement Atlee, announced a massive 75 per cent *ad valorem* duty on all films imported from the United States, an effort to stop the drain of dollars from the country. Atlee favored nationalization of heavy industry and direct government intervention in the economy. In August 1947, in response to a worsening economic situation, a Supplies and Service Act was passed by which the prime minister was authorized to control production of goods and services. Atlee's President of the Board of Trade and Minister of Economic Affairs was Sir Stafford Cripps. The imposition of the 75 per cent film duty alienated Rank and Korda's American counterparts, effectively ending their chances of getting their films into America. After several months of disastrous consequences, Harold Wilson, then President of the Board of Trade, lifted the tax in May 1948.
   Bob Hope (1903–2003). American comedian and actor who was internationally popular during the late 1930s and 1940s in a series of "Road" films with partner Bing Crosby, including *Road to Zanzibar* (1941), and *Road to Morocco* (1942).
   Miss (Betty) Grable (1916–1973). American leading lady at the movies, the most popular pin-up girl of World War II.
   Rita Hayworth (1918–1987). American leading actress and dancer cast in sultry, tempestuous roles. Her films include *Only Angels Have Wings* (1939), *Gilda* (1946), and *The Lady from Shanghai* (1948), for which her hair had been bleached.

On The Wave

1. Porter had visited Mexico on several occasions and her *Outline of Mexican Popular Arts and Crafts* had appeared in 1922 (Los Angeles: Young and McCallister). The motif of the Mexican blanket, or serape, was also used by Soviet director Sergei Eisenstein (1898–1948) to describe the thematic interconnectedness of his uncompleted Mexican film *Que Viva Mexico*. Porter met Eisenstein in Mexico in July 1931 and spent three days observing the film in production. This became the basis of her short story "Hacienda," first published in *Virginia Quarterly Review* in October 1932.
2. Edward Weston (1886–1958). American photographer whose work displays a formal perfection and an enigmatic, subliminal eroticism. In Mexico from 1923 with Tina Modotti, he befriended Diego Rivera and José Clemente Orozco, and in his work developed a new style of candid portraiture and a stark realism.
   Tina Modotti (1896–1942). Italian photographer, active from 1923 to 1932. She met Edward Weston in 1921, who taught her photography in Mexico. In 1927 she joined the Communist Party and began incorporating more overt social content in her work. She was deported from Mexico for political activities in 1929, but returned in 1939.
   Paul Strand (1890–1976). American photographer closely associated with Alfred Stieglitz from

the mid 1910s to the late 1920s and later interested in social issues. From 1933, he devoted all his attention to film. Strand's *The Wave* is a film on the conditions in a Mexican fishing village, made with the assistance of the Mexican government. In 1936 he co-founded a documentary film co-operative, Frontier Films, to produce films on social and political issues.

3. Silvestre Revueltas (1899–1940). Mexican composer and violinist who aligned himself with the Republican cause in Spain in 1937. His mature works acknowledge Mexican folk song and contemporary street music without directly quoting them.

4 In her response to criticism of the pace of *The Wave*, and of the tense relation between its cinematography (which is quite static, drawing on Strand's photographs) and narrative, Porter is probably addressing the reviewers Frank Nugent and Willard Van Dyke.

Me to Myself

1. Tyrone Power (1913–58). American actor who was a popular romantic lead from 1937 onwards.
   Errol Flynn (1909–59). Australian-born Hollywood actor who developed a successful heroic, swashbuckling image during the 1930s and early 1940s.

Cinema as a Job

Fig. 5.1   Women queueing to be extras, 1918.

Introduction

The opening years of cinema saw some of the largest transformations in patterns of women's working lives. If, in the United States, the actual percentage of women working did not alter much between the late nineteenth and early twentieth centuries—poor women, and most women of color continued to work for economic survival, with African-American women twice as likely to be in the labor force as white—what did change was the number of women in the professions, and the number of married and older women working for wages.[1] The numbers in both groups peaked in the 1920s. The proportion of doctorates awarded to women, for example, "after decades of steady gain," and hitting 15 per cent in the early 1920s, slipped down slowly, "plummeting abruptly in the early 1950s to a proportion close to that of 1900 (about 9 per cent)."[2] A decline in the US birth rate, of about one-third for white women between 1891 and 1925, plus longer life expectancy, contributed to the shift of such women into the workforce. Their smaller families, as well as new household technologies and the trend toward manufacturing outside the home, also "helped free daughters to migrate to the city for jobs," or to find higher education.[3] With their entry into the official waged labor force came protective legislation for women, with work periods limited to an hourly maximum, of sometimes ten, sometimes eight hours per day, for example. An inevitable redefinition of leisure accompanied this resegmentation of women's time.[4] And here we come full circle, for, as Kathy Peiss and Elizabeth Ewen have noted, in their breaks from work, girls would go to the movies.[5]

However, the history of change in women's paid work engaged the history of cinema in a more elaborate dance. From an informal, cottage industry before 1910, located primarily in New York, Chicago, Jacksonville (Florida), and a few other spots, cinema rapidly became the fifth largest-grossing business in the United States, with most activity centered in Hollywood. At the beginning of 1913, twenty companies operating thirty-five units were making films in the area, where the previous year there had been only seven.[6] Would this proliferation provide jobs for women as well as entertainment? Would cinema simultaneously repay, in some sense, the massive and still growing investment of its female audiences? Would the ardent appeals to women to attend the movies in order to raise their tone (an appeal that was particularly loud in the 1910s), result in job opportunities? The answer to all these questions was "yes," but other questions must follow.... What kind of work was it? Were women more prominent within certain fields? Where could black women work? When was work available? For how long did opportunities last?

Where Part One suggested the predeliction of female writers for examining women's consumption of film, in the pieces gathered here, taken from business and fan magazines, the film trade press and even an academic journal, women attend to the new employment possibilities, focusing thereby on feminine film production.[7] The essays evidence a wider range of command of language and aim than those found in previous parts of Red Velvet Seat. Writing was not the primary activity of most of these authors, as it was in the case of critics, novelists, and reformers. Even commentary by screenwriters (represented here by Frances Marion, June Mathis and Clara Beranger, among others) betrays a practice and a career that lay elsewhere, based in another medium. Some women write with urgent political purpose (especially Eva Jessye, defending her choir and black extras against Hollywood's discrimination), others to fuel the publicity machine (indirectly in the case of Lois Weber and Anzia Yezierska), and still others through the ironic nuances of fiction (Katherine Mansfield, Resi Langer), or with the leisurely pace of memoir (Lillian Gish).[8] Reflections are brief, or rambling, strategic and forced by circumstance, or rolling with the now painful lilt of the colonial adventure narrative (Osa Johnson's "natives" "grunt," while Frances Flaherty's "half-caste" "savages" lack the "intellectual"). The majority are autobiographical, one of them retaining tantalizing anonymity for dramatic effect: "The Ex-White Actress," writing about her past in 1919, chose an exaggerated melodramatic style to suggest someone near death; her essay is illustrated with an unidentified portrait photograph, as she confesses with the intimacy of the first person to her audience, to the people she calls "my own."[9] And, overall, the writings are of interest as descriptions of female endeavor rather than as pieces of literature.

While hinting at the numbers of women working in film, and the breadth of jobs they held, such a relatively small sampling of essays cannot adequately or accurately illuminate this complex history, or serve directly to convey its scale. For such dimensions future scholars will look to letters, memoirs, business records, and oral histories, as well as published articles, and will cope, as does so much other research on women, with the absence of documents and remembrance. However, we learn here at least that this labor attracted female commentary, and further, of perceptions of the work, in social and cultural terms. At bottom, thirty-one writers confront us with the very existence of this sphere of female activity, much of it long forgotten, and one is left to lament how few of these non-writers published their views.

Feminist research of the 1970s and 1980s argued that women's work in cinema took place "on both sides of the camera."[10] The evidence of the texts in Part Five requires adjustment of this model, in favor of one which allows for the variety of jobs held, which spanned from director, actress, writer, recording musician, conductor, and location assistant, to manager, movie house attendant, and cinema studies scholar. We can better envisage this range as conforming to the figure of an hourglass, with its attendant temporality, the screen hoisted at its waist. In the bell on one side are the jobs done prior to screening, including acting and directing. In the other bell are jobs attendant on the screening and its reception: theater manager, journalist, box office girl, usherette, and academic researcher. The tasks of promotion and distribution funnel the film through the hourglass waist. Perhaps the theater manager and exhibitor inhabit a place at the contours of the waist, depending on the individuality of their programming; if we take our cue from the female theater managers discussed later in this essay, who sought such particular conditions of presentation for their customers, they might even be best placed within the first bell.

To enhance use and comprehension of "Cinema as a Job" in all its incompleteness and idiosyncracy, texts are arranged thematically, following the hourglass template. Starting with screenwriters, actresses, and the topic of breaking into the movies, as well as the female directors' fortunes, we pass to manager and exhibitor before crossing through the screen to the jobs of ticket-taker, critic, and scholar.

The most striking feature of cinema's beginnings may well be the astounding extent and range of female employment it offered, at least in the United States. Half the scenarios written in the silent era were by women, and having a female scenario department head for a "manless Eden" of writers and copiers was common.[11] Anthony Slide claims that more women directors were "at work in the American film industry prior to 1920 than during any period of its history" and that women "virtually controlled" it.[12] As directors and writers, women could earn "handsomely": Henry MacMahon reported in 1920 that *Where Are My Children?*, Weber's controversial film on abortion, was said "to have earned one million dollars. Discount the alleged profit by half, and that famed woman-made story still represents a sum equal to the life-time earnings of the unusually successful man."[13] Weber was also described as "one of the big personalities in the photoplay world," while her renown was held to "open up vistas for other women."[14] Similarly grand statements were made of Frances Marion, who "earned millions in Hollywood entirely by her own efforts.... As a writer, she is unquestioned head of her profession, male and female."[15]

The first major stars were also women, whose immense power enabled them to form (or have formed for them) production companies of their own, even if they were only titular head: by 1921, Mary Pickford, Lois Weber, Corinne Griffith, Mabel Normand, Florence Turner, Nell Shipman, Gene Gauntier, Clara Kimball Young, Anita Stewart, Norma Talmadge, Constance Talmadge, Cleo Madison, Gloria Swanson, Leah Baird, Helen Gardner, Alla Nazimova, and Olga Petrova, among others, had all done so.[16] While all their companies were defunct by 1928, one could still write that "the feminine stars of the screen have exerted a far greater influence upon the movies than their masculine peers."[17] In an era before full rationalization of the industry and its publicity machine, such women were their own auteurs, with the agency to invent; they had, as actresses-cum-directors-cum-producers, a very large hand in shaping their own images.

Scholars have begun to assemble and analyse this legacy of female creativity, but most research remains to be done, particularly beyond the United States.[18] From the filmmaking activity of women in Britain but a few names linger on—Alma Reville, Dinah Shurey, the Countess of Warwick—and there is as yet no adequate or synthetic understanding of their roles.[19] In all likelihood, there was no equivalent scale of female presence within British filmmaking before 1920, at least in part because of British film culture's smaller size, and because the cinema had barely begun to function as an industry there before World War I, and the American competition that followed it struck it a severe blow. (At its lowest point, in November 1923—"Black November"—all studios in Britain were dark). Also, despite women's successful entry into many aspects of theater practice, including writing and staging, in Britain in the last two decades of the nineteenth century, and first decade of this century, Katherine Newey has concluded that "this significant presence was not carried through into the early film industry," except where "negotiated through familial domestic structures," as was the case with Cecil and Mrs Hepworth.[20] The domestic or marital link was certainly important in the United States as well, where Ida May Park co-directed with her husband, Joseph De Grasse for a year at Universal before getting a chance to direct alone in May 1917, and where Elsie Jane Wilson's initial experience was as a stage and screen actress, directed by her husband, Rupert Julian, before she later co-directed with him, and then, in 1917, had opportunities to direct herself at Universal.[21] As Linda Arvidson (as Mrs D.W. Griffith) put it, during the opening years of the century "the general idea of movie directors [was] to use their families in the pictures."[22]

When, and how, did women begin film work? Setting aside, for the moment, their roles as actresses, women were initially most numerous in typically repetitive, meticulous jobs behind the scenes, such as hand-coloring frames, inspecting negatives, assembling prints, and office-keeping.[23] The career of Alice Guy Blaché (who directed actors, and was supervising camerawork as well as staff assistants from 1896) was exceptional.[24] The expansion of female activity into other areas, and particularly into writing titles and scenarios, directing, costuming, and so on, occurred mainly after 1906, as films themselves became longer, and more complex, and as they demanded more elaborate staffing as well as devices such as the continuity script for keeping control during longer shooting schedules. At that time, a combination of factors "temporarily lowered barriers for entry in the field of motion picture production"[25] so that *Views and Films Index* could comment in 1908 that "women's chances of making a living have been increased by the rise of the cinematograph machines."[26]

Filmmaking developed after 1906 into a business that was, for the short term, relatively open, unprofessionalized, and unstructured. This was especially so after 1912, when the Motion Picture Patents Company (MPPC) lost a decisive court case, diminishing its power and giving more room to the so-called "Independents," companies where women had greater access to job range.[27] Job positions were not clearly defined, so that many women (as well as men) worked in several capacities, moving between them: Gauntier was a writer, director, and actress; Weber was written up as "author–actor–director"; actress Lillian Gish once directed, in 1919; writer Rinehart described shooting her own films; and the long list of stars noted above worked as producers.[28] "Near-director" was Henry MacMahon's term for the successful female scenario writer.[29] As Charles Musser has put it, "hyphenates (whether producer–director or writer–star) were as important—and more common—in the American film industry of 1913 as they are today."[30] Another form of multitasking, the doubling up of roles ("doubling in brass") was common, and also had its roots in stock company practice, being the method by which the poor theater troop had habitually economized on bodies.

Besides giving opportunity to women in general, film attracted political groups, including labor unions, suffragists, socialists, reformers, and some ethnic minority groups, many of whom had female membership.[31] Among the fascinating list of titles produced by such groups and linked to women were Birth Control, scripted by Margaret Sanger in 1917, showing her work, her clinic, and her arrest;[32] Your Girl and Mine, a suffrage melodrama released in 1914 through a contract with World Film Corporation by the National American Woman Suffrage Association;[33] The Dangerous Age (Das gefährliche Alter) (1910/11), a scandalous personal book on menopause by Karin Michaëlis made into a film in 1927 starring Asta Nielsen; Maisie's Marriage (1923), largely authored by Marie Stopes, and at least implicitly about the links between marital happiness and birth control; and Motherhood: Life's Greatest Miracle (1925), an hour-long film written and produced, and possibly also directed, by Lita Lawrence, which contrasted how two women from different social classes coped with unplanned pregnancies.[34] To this idiosyncratic list we can add poet Ella Wheeler Wilcox's "Humanology Films," made by the "Humanology Company" in 1915;[35] the autobiographical Deliverance, supervised by Helen Keller and made by the Helen Keller Film Corporation in 1919;[36] and a 1916 clay animation of, among other subjects, "two scrub-women arguing" by New York sculptress Helene Smith Dayton.[37]

In this expansion, apart from acting, one strand of female film employment flourished above all others—that of writer. Wendy Holliday has pointed out that so many women found employment as writers in early Hollywood because they had been hired into positions likely to produce this effect; they worked in the steno pool, as secretaries, and in reading departments, to assess unsolicited manuscripts, prepare synopses and reports. Also, before the establishment of scenario departments in the early 1910s, last-minute scenarios were often needed, and actresses were as likely to supply them as anyone. Even beyond that date, "the sheer number of actresses who wrote the occasional screenplay is staggering," comments Holliday.[38] A further reason for this high number of women writers lay in the enormous pressure for new stories suddenly needed to fill production demand, especially after the 1911 litigation against the Kalem Company over copyright infringement of Ben-Hur (adapted by Gene Gauntier). The suit made companies more wary of "borrowing" from previously published material.

Floods of submissions from amateur writers poured in, in response to company advertisements in fan and trade magazines,[39] and typewriters in Hollywood were, according to Anne Walker, "as scarce and as hard to rent as houses in other towns."[40] Margaret Anderson, writing as fan Mobbie Mag, commiserated in her mock fan letter to playwright Ibsen in 1915 that "I know how hard it is to have movie plays accepted because I have done some myself."[41] The craze of writing may have swept up as many as one in three citizens at its peak,[42] and every now and again "The young lady from Oshkosh or Hartford who had mailed in several clever scripts was sent for and installed as scenario writer."[43] As Holliday explains, "Amateur scenario writing, with its lack of requirements and structure, was work that did not discriminate against women." Women "latched onto the accessibility of the free-lance world and turned it to their own use ... [it was] a good place from which to launch a profession." Most of the contests run in magazines were won by women, their primary readership, women who might well have drafted stories at the kitchen table.[44] Mary Roberts Rinehart and the sixteen-year-old Anita Loos had such a beginning. (Writing might then lead to other opportunities, as it did for Ida May Park when she took on directing, or for Lois Weber, who, in 1915, lay her own success as a director at the door of her writing.[45]) This freelance market had shrivelled by the early 1920s since by then most studios had strongly established scenario departments as well as authors under contract, although these included women.[46]

Many of the contemporary commentators struck by the "vast army" of women writers in Hollywood focus on a "natural" explanation for the phenomenon: the majority of filmgoers are female, and female writers are better able to meet their wishes in a screenplay. This opinion suggests that female experience is shared, and the women writer can and will tap common emotional experience, using her capacity to analyse familial dynamics and convey their centrality to human life through stories.[47] Frances Marion, many years on, put forth, if more soberly, an equivalent logic for the significant presence of women writers:

> A very large proportion of the motion picture audiences is composed of women, and the studios therefore are compelled to produce pictures which satisfy them. A woman scenario writer would seem to have an advantage in that she more easily can determine and understand women's likes and dislikes, and thus be able to give them the kind of pictures they enjoy. If she can do this, she will reap a correspondingly great reward.[48]

Clara Beranger gave this logic of inter-female empathy a more cutting turn. She recounted in an interview that,

> It is an old truism that love to a woman is her story ... [whereas to] man it is a mere incident in his life. This is one of the reasons why a woman writing drama for the screen gives to her story the sincerity that no man can lend. With this sincerity the audience gets plausibility and probability. Men writers in developing their story have to create artificial emotions which they delude themselves into believing is inspiration.[49]

Marion Fairfax similarly argued that "countless ages" as a "trained observer" of men (on which skill women have long depended for their "safety and comfort") have made women highly appropriate and talented as writers.[50] "Development of Photodramatic Writing," an article by Jeanie Macpherson—Cecil B. DeMille's long-time chief scenarist—illustrates the way certain attributes of femininity explained the craft of story-telling. She gave the following advice to writers: "If the writer will take a single theme, then work up the detail, decorate it with embroidery and lace, every little bit different from the last, but have each bit of trimming pertain directly to the main theme he will have a much better story."[51]

Yet another strand of argumentation tapped heterosexual congress as a metaphor: from the complementarity of the sexes working together—female as writer, male as director—the complete "psychology of the story" would issue forth on the screen.[52] Interested in spiritualism, June Mathis held seances with Alla Nazimova and Rudolph Valentino and believed that "a woman's spiritual qualitites must be fully incorporated into human affairs for the world ever to achieve peace and harmony." On account of all this feminine advantage, gained through years and generations of psycho-social training, Beranger predicted that "women are going to come into the writing end of the picture industry in greater numbers than ever before."[53]

Against these discussions which specifically separated writing and directing skills according to gender, we should also remember Jane Murfin's contrary view, for whom the androgynous mind (that with a "mixture of the qualities" of both sexes) is the ideal one for picture-making, be it in writing or directing.[54] Or Mathis's opinion that screenwriting is at its best when the feminine qualities of the writer come to the fore, but that such qualities are also to be found in men.[55]

As already indicated in the General Introduction, these new opportunities for work for women, and the ways in which they came about, must be understood within a wider economical and historical context, as indeed they were by women themselves. Exercise and bodily strength in women became a sign of their moder-nity. As one female reporter wrote of this woman in 1910, "she has grasped at the splendid possibility of physical perfection, which implies a resulting mental strength heretofore classed as masculine.... The day of the interesting feminine invalid is gone."[56] World War I, with its recruitment of men and patriotic appeal to women to take up new activities was a period marked by fluid gender boundaries, with expectations of transformation in women's roles, partly because jobs vacated by men became accessible to women.[57] During the same years the passing of divorce laws and the campaign for women's suffrage (won in California in 1911, in the federal United States in 1920, and in Britain in stages from February 1918) led conserva-tives to fear emasculation via the "so-called equality of the sexes, ... a monstrous inversion, robbing woman of her essential flower and charm."[58] While most women in early Hollywood might not explicitly have named themselves feminist, as young women, almost all in their early twenties, they expected generational change, and took on the spirit of modern womanhood in its dynamism, physical challenge, and search for career. As Gladys Hall unexpectedly put it, "One of the first principles of modernism is that women should be economically independent."[59]

Jeanie Macpherson and Frances Marion had flying licenses.[60] Long before them, in 1898, Gertrude Bacon, daughter of balloonist John Bacon, had collaborated with him in aerial filming.[61] The theme of daring, associated with aviation and other novel activities for women, was present both in films of the day, especially in serial queen exploits—Gauntier wrote and starred in one of the earliest ones, The Girl Spy series, in 1909—and in women's descriptions of their emergent careers—in Gish's ice-cake float, or Gauntier's "plunge" into motion pictures, both borne by New England rivers.[62] Evelyn Preer related she was "nearly drowned" filming Birthright in 1922, and "still [had] a scar on [her] ankle which linger[ed] from the many bruises" she received rolling down a hill. She continues: "I am not complaining about it, because Mr Oscar Micheaux, the director, wanted to use a dummy for the scene, but I said 'No.' You see I must have my thrills. Then, too, the dummy couldn't have gotten up at the bottom of the hill, and waded through the pond of water" (in which she was shortly further imperiled).[63] In press coverage, "pluck" was the preferred adjective for actress and director Margery Wilson,[64] and producer and screenwriter Mrs Sidney Drew.[65] The headlines "A Nervy Movie Lady," and "I Went Among Savages for 'Movies,'" convey the same spirit in actresses Kathlyn Williams (of The Adventures of Kathlyn) and Meg Gehrts ("the first white woman to penetrate into the hinterland of Togo" to make "African dramas"), as does the discouraging application form confronting the aspiring actress Miss Moss, in Katherine Mansfield's "The Pictures": "Can you aviate—high-dive—drive a car—buck-jump—shoot?"[66] Harriet Quimby, queen of pluck, was a movie actress-flyer-cum-journalist; the first American woman to hold a pilot's license, and the first woman to fly a monoplane across the English Channel, she wrote for Sunset: the Pacific Monthly before moving to New York where she became drama critic and feature writer for Leslie's Weekly (which had, as Frank Leslie's Popular Monthly, published Antonia Dickson's report on the kinetoscope), heightening through her articles her fame as an aviatrix. In 1909, she played the village fishermaiden in D.W. Griffith's film Lines of White on a Sullen Sea, but was to crash to her death while attempting to fly over Boston harbor in 1912.[67]

A related suite of literature recorded the extreme conditions of filmmaking in the field, where Osa Johnson, Frances Flaherty, Jessica Borthwick, and Nell Shipman directed footage, set up outdoor projection screens and faced everything from photographing prison executions and improvising darkrooms (if as a kitchen variant) to rescuing their spouses from poisoning, frostbite delirium, and animal attacks.[68] Nell Shipman published a three-part gruelling essay on the toil of shooting in a North Idaho winter with a menagerie of over a hundred animals.[69] Twenty-two-year-old Borthwick, traveling alone in the footsteps of her father in the war-torn Balkans of 1913–14, lost many exposed reels to inquisitive officials who unraveled them, ruining them. These women's modernity also expressed itself in the roles they sought, and in their recorded opinions of their work; in her memoir of her Middle Eastern tour, Gene Gauntier recorded researching the segregation of women in "oriental customs," as well as the lowly feminine status of Mary Magdalen, in order to develop the script of Kalem's film From the Manger to the Cross, for which she took the role of the Virgin Mary.[70]

Occasionally this backdrop of emancipation evidences itself in more obviously feminist terms—as separatism. In 1913 a "movement among the women engaged in the producing end of the industry to form an organization of their own" was reported, although apparently nothing came of it; the plan in 1916 to form a feminist film company named The American Woman Film Company, financed entirely by women, and led by the writer May Whitney Emerson, also left no evidence of having released any productions.[71] More possible, particularly as described in Cari Beauchamp's account of the lives of Frances Marion and her female co-workers, was the era's networking among professional women, enhanced through their substantial numbers in the 1910s and early 1920s.[72]

Fan and trade magazines found women's presence as film workers well worth a story, and their accounts give some indication of women's actual activities, as well as of how these publications made sense of them. Edna Ferber, for example, a highly successful novelist and screenwriter, penned one of umpteen articles describing the hard hours of toil entailed in the star's life.[73] Myrtle Gebhardt's 1923 "Business Women in Film Studios" was practically oriented and feminist in tone: it ended with a clarion call to sisters and sisterhood.[74] She started with the familiar reminder that "catering to women as the pictures do, it is only natural that a very vital part in their production depends on woman." She then discussed twenty-nine jobs open to women besides acting, including that of fan-mail reader, musician (for setting "actors' histrionic moods"), "doctor" (for smoothing continuity), plasterer, and director. She concluded that "the usual route to almost any studio-job for women is through the stenographic ranks.... Stenographers become script-holders and cutters, secretaries to the executives and stars, readers and—some of them—scenario-writers.... A sort of sublimated stenographer is the 'script-girl,' sometimes called 'the continuity-girl-on-the-set.'" (She warned, however, that this was the "one job in the studio that I would not take for love nor riches," for its low pay, pressure, and endless hours.)[75] The large number of work advice columns found in magazines and "How To" manuals written by women also treated jobs squarely as labor.[76] By contrast, fairy-tale chronicles detailed the rise from humbleness of Henrietta Cohn, Dorothy Arzner, and Grace Haskins, chronicles which feminized the Horatio Alger myth, a founding image of American capitalism. Company business manager at Paramount, Cohn had started there as a stenographer in 1914, and had worked her way up, via the Independents, in four years; Arzner had started as a stenographer at the Lasky studio, graduating to script girl, cutter, scenario writer, and then director; producer, writer, and director Grace Haskins had formerly been a telephone operator and stenographer, and then fan mail reader, cutter, and continuity girl.[77] These career patterns appear yet more remarkable when we remember that the stenographer was essentially the copier (duplicating scripts for a cast, for example) in the days before roneostat and xerox brought her obsolescence. Other articles, many written by women, discussed women's work as wardrobe mistress,[78] costume designer,[79] librarian,[80] film exchange manager,[81] cashier,[82] usherette,[83] producer,[84] concert mistress,[85] song writer,[86] caption and continuity writer,[87] scenario reader,[88] Floor Secretary (Continuity Girl),[89] cinematographer,[90] talent scout,[91] editor,[92] censor,[93] diction coach,[94] and "movie teacher" for stars' children.[95] One observer noted that, after stenographer and file-keeper, manicurist and hair-dresser were the most numerous jobs for women.[96]

Jobs were not as accessible to black women, and the work of black women was rarely covered in the white press. One exception was that of "Hattie the Hairdresser," whose making of coiffures for Paramount actresses Agnes Ayres (in *The Sheik*), Gloria Swanson (in *The Great Moment*), and Lois Wilson (in *Miss Lulu Bett*) was "set down" in black-inflected speech—"Hattie's own trenchant style"—in *Filmplay* magazine. In a typical, prejudicial obliteration of her person, the article began: "Whence Hattie came, and what her real name is, nobody knows," although Hattie somehow managed to insert a candid description of her status vis à vis her white clients: "I feel like one of them movie-subtitles that says, 'I am enslaved to a pretty woman.'"[97]

The black press paid more attention to such labor. In "They Made Good in the Movie Capital," *Opportunity* described the success of Mrs Hazel Washington, a glovemaker and artist in leatherwork, who supplied props and also sold to stars, and milliner Miss Mildred Blount, who made hats for *Gone with the Wind*, among other titles, and whose byword was "accept no limitations because of color."[98] Bernice L'Tanya, a Hollywood couturier who had studied in Paris, and whose gowns were donned by Ida Lupino in *Love of Innocence*, as well as by Lena Horne, Rochelle Hudson, and "other movieville starlets," was reported to be the first black woman to receive a fashion screen credit.[99] The success in scenario writing of Birdie Gilmore and Mrs M. Webb was also noted in the black press.[100] As might be expected, the career for black women most frequently reported in the black press was that of actress, although these columns most typically detailed the failure of their careers, as in Avenelle Harris's autobiographical report.[101] Musical director Eva Jessye wrote in a letter to Etta Moten (singer, broadcaster, actress, and wife of Associated Negro Press director Claude A. Barnett) of the following extreme obstacle:

> I'm told that *Lost in the Stars* is being made into a movie soon ... shot in South Africa ... AND ... listen to this! ... the Negro actors must be registered as bonded servants of Alex Korda, the Director in order to be permitted to live in South Africa ... if true, and I'm sure my source of information is reliable,... it is abominable ... and one can see why such a ruling was made ... to keep the native from seeing what freedom is ... and in what dastardly slavery they are being held. It should be investigated and exposed if true.[102]

Directorships for black women were the scarcest of all jobs within the industry; black women who directed during cinema's first half-century (including Zora Neale Hurston, Laura Bowman, Katherine Dunham, and Madame Eloyce Gist) did so at most at the periphery of Hollywood, and they have sadly left no published writings of their view of filmmaking or cinema from the period.[103]

Another type of article, paralleling those combing the innards of the business, was the cautionary tale, warning of star-struck daughters going "movie mad" in the "pathetic breadline of waiting actresses anxious for 'extra' work," or of negotiating the complex pressures of the casting couch.[104] As Dorothy Gish regretted, despite her own success: "I could not let a daughter or niece or any other child close to me go on the stage or in the pictures"[105] A particularly chilling account—"Don't Go to Hollywood"—explained how, having failed in the search, "many a disillusioned girl reache[d] home by acting as chaperon to a corpse. The dead are not supposed to travel alone. So when a body must be shipped out from Hollywood, the railroad lets the Chamber of Commerce know, and some girl gets a free ticket for performing this gruesome job."[106] Miriam Leuck gave a similarly grim description when considering "Motion Pictures" in her 1926 survey of fields of work for women: "Every civic agency of Hollywood is worked overtime caring for the hundreds of girls who come here without any reason to believe they will succeed beyond their own good opinion of themselves and the advice of judicious friends."[107] She warned of the "hundreds of fakirs [who] have found a gold mine in establishing ostensible moving picture companies, taking 'tests' (for a fee) and offering to teach the applicant and to get an engagement for another large fee."[108] Adela Rogers St. Johns titled her series of articles on this theme "The Port of Missing Girls."[109] Journalists collectively assembled the miserable picture of a city awash with floundering young women of dashed hopes, an urban problem of epidemic proportions, and a sufficiently large public relations challenge to inspire the intervention of Will Hays, who funded a new building to house extras who had insisted on coming to Hollywood nevertheless, among other clean-up measures.[110] These very women, however, also constituted the flow of unskilled labor, and audience cinema needed: "Because of the millions of movie-struck girls in America, the moving-picture theaters flourish," the Universal Company's general manager had commented in 1918.[111] His studio had also learned to fear them after the radical group International Workers of the World (IWW) had begun organizing film workers, Maude Thompson leading protests against low wages and poor conditions at the Edison Company in 1913. The following year this union had organized movie extras at Universal for higher daily pay, leading them out on strike when Universal refused. The IWW supported striking extras again in 1916.[112]

The "victims" lured to Hollywood were "not all screen-struck girls by any means," but actors of both sexes and their mothers, dubbed by one critic the "mother-moth."[113] An essay of 1928, "Do Women Rule the Movies?" first noted the absence of any promoting fathers among would-be stars, and then devoted several paragraphs to the energy and ambition of aspirants' mothers (focusing on those of the Gishes, Jeanie Macpherson, Mary Pickford, and the Talmadges) who sustained the "reign of petticoat politics" through matriarchal effort.[114] A later essay defined them: "the movie mama has a thick hide like an aligator's, the sharp eye of a condor, and is a mammal.... It is believed to have originated in Southern California, where a prehistoric specimen was recovered in the La Brea Pits, well-preserved, holding a scrapbook of clippings in its mandibles."[115] When jobs were in the offing, "Herds of movie mamas gather[ed] at the salt licks in Culver City or Fox Hills."[116] (Occasionally movie mamas made it onto screen, where, as poet Nancy Nadin put it, "their hair is always white, and generally they've erring sons who open safes at night."[117])

Critic Resi Langer's 1919 journalistic foray into acting—whether in fact or in fiction is not clear—and the two short stories by Zelda Fitzgerald (1925) and Katherine Mansfield (1918) stand squarely in this sourcebook for the chorus of voices warning away wishful extras, as well as those interested in examining their psychology. Mansfield's "The Pictures," written and set during World War I, presents an unsuccessful wannabe actress whose inability to secure employment leads her to possible prostitution, while Fitzgerald's story is a stirring fantasy of female power where a woman's vengeance, enacted through her alteration of a film, brings her marriage, happiness, and respect. Fitzgerald's twenty-year old Gracie Axelrod entertains visions of stardom after winning a popularity contest in the store where she works. The contest is rigged, and Gracie, unbeknownst to her, must play second fiddle to the store owner's daughter in a film lauding the merits of their hometown. On realizing her pathetic rank in the film while attending its première, Gracie vows retaliation and effectively remakes the film. In her version, she takes the starring role and puts her rival in her place. Unlike Mansfield's Ada, Gracie's fantasy of stardom to some extent comes true. She is the small-town girl from the wrong side of the tracks who makes good, not by bowing to social convention but by subverting it, in this case through cinema. Gracie may not be bright, but at the end of Fitzgerald's tale she is still buying movie magazines and watching with ironic interest for new opportunity contests.

Fitzgerald explores the American dream of becoming "somebody" through mimimum effort, a dream that Hollywood was particularly suited to realize with the luck-borne fame that it conferred, as Gerould had ruefully noted.[118] Regionalism fuels her tale's satirical edge: Gracie's achievement of success is through her own vengeful engagement with the cinematic apparatus in Minnesota, far from Hollywood, rather than through the random anonymity of the studio star system. By literally taking apart and remaking a film in which she played a minor role, Gracie has re-created herself. "Our Own Movie Queen" suggests perhaps that only provincial cinema with its local audience could be the agent of such transformation, where today public-access television or perhaps the Internet would do the job.

Katherine Mansfield models another kind of aspirant. Ada Moss is a plump, college-educated, ageing singer anxious for film work because her singing career has evaporated. Rejected by closed teashops as well as the "Backwash Film Co." and "The Bitter Orange Company," Ada lacks the pluck and shape needed for film (although she has pluck of another sort in sailing off with a pick-up from the Café de Madrid to pay the rent). Ada's vaguely cultured aspirations come to nought in an anonymous London of bedsits and cheap tearooms, and she is further marginalized by a cinema Mansfield shows to be interested only in the young and lithe. Indeed, cinema is less the writer's concern than Ada herself—the cinema is simply another of Ada's oppressors. In this regard, Mansfield's short story accords the cinema less importance than Fitzgerald's does.

Novelist Anzia Yezierska also needed to pay the rent, and did so, eventually, by selling her writing.[119] Both Mansfield's tale and Yezierska's autobiographical column, describing her voyage from impoverished immigrant novelist to Hollywood scenarist, include the figure of the beautiful stenographer hoping for a break into film writing. With her "youthful grace and up-to-dateness," Yezierska's Hollywood steno "can't get along on [her] wages." "But a lot they care," she responds resignedly. "It's take it or leave it with them. A dozen girls are ready to step into my job." The ravishing woman who *did* make it against the odds was a feature of Yezierska's fiction, and a stand-in for Yezierska herself.

Equally to be pondered, alongside the staggering facts of women's occasional vigorous earning presence in this phase of cinema, are their sudden appearances and disappearances from film work, most particularly from the role of director.[120] Anne Walker wrote in 1921 that, "just as girls are making places for themselves in other lines of industry, so they are finding profitable employment in the manufacture of motion pictures, which now ranks fifth among the industries of this country," but a director was not among the many women she interviewed, who ranged from a continuity girl, "technical dresser," researcher and librarian, to a fan-mail sorter and hairdresser.[121] Recent research suggests that there were extremely few female directors working anywhere in the world before 1907, and none in the United States.[122] In the chaos of the nickelodeon boom, which peaked in 1908 and which brought with it the need for more, longer, and cleaner movies, opportunities came; generally speaking, women began to direct films at the moment at which features (be they three-reelers or longer) and serials (a sort of compromise between the short film and the feature) began to be made. As early as 1923, however, the number of female directors had dimished almost to nil, and Dorothy Arzner was the only prominent American woman making a successful transition to sound cinema, directing in Hollywood into the 1940s. In 1934 she could be referred to as "the only woman director in the world worth mentioning" (a characterization which overlooks Leni Riefenstahl and Esther Schub, but few others).[123] How do we make sense of this see-sawing of the female director's fortunes?

Several explanations have been offered. One came from Gene Gauntier, who described the last months of 1912 as "the end of an epoch in picture-making. The old order of things passed ... the trust had been beaten in the higher courts and Independents had sprung up all over the land.... Multiple reels were becoming numerous and 'feature pictures' were in demand."[124] Gauntier herself was to set up as an Independent, as the Gene Gauntier Feature Players, in December 1912.[125] The demand for more films to slake the thirst of burgeoning audiences, in combination with the breaking of the Trust's motion picture monopoly (after patent wars, chiefly fought between the Edison and Biograph companies), fostered a climate supportive of many independent, small companies, making room for women. (The Trust was fairly resistant to making films of feature length, leaving the field open for Independents.) However, the imbalance between supply and demand, which had created an explosive, unplanned, uncontrolled state of creativity, eventually settled down as the Big Five motion picture studios began to consolidate after 1920 (Famous-Players, later Paramount; Fox; Loew's; Warner Bros.; and RKO) and were firmly in place by 1929 as sound arrived and as filmmaking became a fully stream-lined business.[126] Under this newly rationalized climate, doors to women closed.

In sum, the growing professionalism of the new industry, including unionization, and the establishment of the Academy of Motion Picture Arts and Sciences in 1927, was to disempower women. Karen Mahar details most convincingly the typical exclusion of women from clubs and unions associated with the business, starting with the all-male Screen Club founded in New York in 1912, and Marsha McCreadie makes the general point that the slowly ebbing female population diminished the potentially positive consequences of female networking.[127] By 1936, Julie Lang Hunt could report that there were "eight studio trades open to women" besides that of actress: seamstress, decorator, designer, secretary, singer, writer, hairdresser, and, yes, waitress.[128]

Another type of explanation speculated on the egalitarianism of the newest industry on the block, one growing up alongside the struggle for universal suffrage. Clara Beranger saw the work in this light, remarking in 1920 (the year that votes for women were federally approved) that the film industry was giving women more opportunities than any other.[129] Reporter Frances Denton, visiting the Universal lot in 1918, observed while watching directors Ida May Park and Elsie Jane Wilson that there will soon "be no question as to whether some particular work belongs more to a man than to a woman, but each will do whatever he or she can do the best."[130] Ida May Park herself concurred, arguing that both men and women could direct films, even if women's superior emotional and imaginative capacity gave them an advantage.[131] However, she erroneously suggested that women wait before entering the field since the climate would certainly become still more advantageous to them.[132] Such commentators understood the film business, in its youthful modernity, to reflect the aspirations of suffrage, and as somehow escaping, or refashioning, typical sex-role stratification.

Anthony Slide has put forth an alternative emphasis, proposing that Carl Laemmle's Universal Studio, which employed more women directors than any other studio in the 1910s, and which at one time "had nine women directors at work on its lot," had committed itself in the late 1910s to a heavy shooting and release schedule, and had found itself with an insufficient number of directors.[133] According to Slide, instead of hiring new directors, which would have been expensive, Universal drew on personnel already under contract such as editors, writers, and actors, all of which were areas dominated by women.

The commercial pragmatism of Slide's solution is found again in the far more elaborate and, to date, most thorough analysis, put forward by Mahar.[134] She argues that the film industry, "like other 'new' industries, was gendered from the beginning" as a masculine place of work, which only permitted female contributions where and when economic and cultural pressures demanded it.[135] According to Mahar, the abundance of women working as film inspectors, cutters, and hand tinters (in other words in repetitive jobs associated with the traditionally feminine traits of neatness and tidiness) merely continued a trend established in the photographic trade.[136] Explaining the "late" arrival of women to other aspects of filmmaking including directing, Mahar argues that they entered "only after 1906, when competition over patents and cameras gave way to competition based on dramatic quality."[137] As the cinema "battled censorship and sought a middle-class audience, the woman filmmaker gained additional status as a symbol of propriety and uplift," so that "by 1910, women were solidly placed in all facets of the industry."[138] Mahar emphasizes that the centrality of the camera to filmmaking (the camera both shot and projected film, and was heavy and unwieldy), discouraged full feminine participation.[139]

Accounting for the subsequent disappearance of women, particularly from the role of director, Mahar, like other scholars, has asserted that female employees suffered as the Big Five "majors" took hold, since these vertically integrated companies squeezed out competition from the Independents, making them too unprofitable. Mahar develops this point by reminding us that, following a brief but severe recession in 1921, and in order to keep up with the escalating prices of film production, the film industry was to reorganize itself in the early 1920s, and, among other things, woo Wall Street banking for support. Women filmmakers were incompatible with this newly emerging image of an efficient, big-business Hollywood, particularly in the eyes of New York capital; Wall Streeters would trust their dollars only to other men.[140]

The arrival of sound also seems to have contributed to the statistic of female decline. Vyvyan Donner's career as an "independent producer came to an end in 1928 with the advent of sound pictures. The cost of talkies was prohibitive," and she joined Fox Movietone News.[141] Clara Beranger complained of the fragmentation of writing conditions in Hollywood after the coming of sound when multiple writers were assigned to one project, authorial control was diluted, and enthusiasm waned.[142] There was a further thinning of jobs for women in the 1930s, even though some new opportunities returned, briefly, with the Second World War, as they had with the First.

The decline of female workers in the film business, particularly from the high-profile roles of director and producer, can also be understood as linked to a postwar anti-feminist climate that re-emphasized sexual difference and separate spheres for men and women, and eroded many of the gains women had made in previous years.[143] After the First World War, many women, particularly volunteer women, had left activities that had in any case only been temporarily open to them.[144] In addition, there was disillusionment with the outcomes of feminist campaigning, for, by the mid 1920s, it was evident that being able to vote, in itself, had not and would not change women's lives; the content of votes, their implementation, and cultural and political attitudes towards relations between the sexes in general mattered just as much. Fannie Hurst was not alone in her open indignation at some women's irresponsibility, post-suffrage:

> No thinking woman can look at the picture of women since they got the vote with-out a sinking heart. Too many women's organizations still seem a kind of superficial bridge-playing. Some women join them to do constructive social work, but to other women they afford a valid reason for absence from home, or for getting one's name

into favored columns of the newspaper, or for satisfying the human longing for praise and achievement.[145]

Just a year earlier, in 1934, Beryl de Querton, a voice-over artist for newsreel commentaries, wrote that she had won her "first chance as a commentator by saying 'I can do this job as well as any man,'" adding "and even in 1934 that is not a statement to get away with easily," her phrase indicating again the slowness, or reversal, of progress for women, also in non-directing fields.[146]

Already during the First World War we can detect negative reactions to women whose success extended beyond acting: a *Photoplay* editorial of 1916 forgave Mary Pickford and Clara Kimball Young for forming their own companies, since "such is their movie greatness that each is inherently an organization in herself." But the same writer added that "at present, four more producing companies headed by women are actually grinding out plays.... In six months there will be an avalanche of these demi-star manufactories choking up the exhibitor's every avenue.... The motion picture star-system now imminent is as preposterous, anarchistic and insidious an evil as has ever been introduced into dramatic art in America."[147] As Mahar suggests, such commentary evidences an early industry push against the autonomy of actresses.[148] Regularizing, seven-year contracts were one of many measures soon to be taken to tame stars generally, and by the mid 1920s such female directing power, feared as well as observed, was evaporating into thin air.

The research and explanations presented here shape a picture of precipitous fluctuation in female film activity, particularly in directing, that most sensitive indictator of job range. Broadly speaking, women started directing in 1908, experienced an increase in opportunity in around 1912, a peak in the years 1918–23, and a dramatic decline thereafter. Indeed, women have at no time since regained numerical prominence in the role of director. This periodization helps us interpret the "woman director" debate that took place in the 1920s (to recur during feminism's second wave in the 1970s), documents from which are reprinted here.[149] It helps us see, for example, that when Lillian Gish in 1925, or, better yet, Nerina Shute in 1929 proposed that directing was not a woman's job, they were writing after the horse had bolted—the female director was no more.[150]

The mid 1920s appear as pivotal years in the fortunes of the woman director. Up to this time, her work was widely described as if it were a threatening "invasion,"[151] while by the 1930s we find a powerful case of forgetting, forgetting that so many women had even held the posts of director and producer. By 1933 Adela Rogers St. Johns could call Dorothy Arzner "a pioneer, because as a woman she broke down an age-old tradition against women" directing, and erroneously claim, in an instance of this amnesia, that only three women had ever directed pictures in motion picture history: Weber, Marion, and Arzner.[152] We have moved from a world in which directing and producing were imaginable (if feared) as the province of women, to the opposite condition.

In 1920 *Kinematograph Weekly* remarked that "Woman is challenging the supremacy of man in every branch of the kinema Industry, and she is getting away with it too. We have had feminine film-joiners, film-printers, operators, Press agents, and scenario writers; and now the male producer is to be pulled from his pedestal."[153] In Carolyn Lowrey's *The First 100 Noted Men and Women of the Screen*, also of 1920, thirty-six of the one hundred selected were women, among them several writers, directors, and editors, as well as actresses.[154] In 1923, E. Leslie Gilliams, in an essay hoping female presence would bring reform more ably than the Hays Office, speculated about the female "invasion" and its potential for moral improvement and concluded that women's "extraordinary success seems to indicate that they have come in to stay, and that the movies must be counted as the field which they have made their own."[155] But in 1925 Florence M. Osborne, writing as "The Editor" of *Motion Picture Magazine*, asked "Why Are There No Women Directors?", pondering that "There have been a few ... [but] for some reason or other they do not seem to be doing it now."[156] "The invasion of motion pictures by women" had led to domination in the scenario field, but had fallen short of the role of director.[157] From 1925 onwards, the more typical comment was to note the absence of the female director, and offer explanation. This is Mary Field in 1931: "At present the woman directors can be counted almost on the fingers of one hand, but there seems to be no reason why many more women should not take up film directing as a career."[158] In 1934 Reina Wiles Dunn also evaluated women working in film and remarked, when discussing the make-up department, that "women appear to have been unable to break into the ranks of the make-up directors to any extent, though there is one woman picture-director and one co-director, Wanda Tuchock, as well as several who have directed children's pictures."[159]

Much writing suggests the strain of incompatibility between the work of directing and womanhood itself, through the coining of terms such as "directress" or "mistress director," in the argument that "woman cannot construct," in the characterization of events as an "invasion," or a form of imposture analagous to cross-dressing, or in the finding of female direction such a revolutionary prospect as to invite comparison with ancient Babylonian matriarchies and the first stirrings of the new millennium.[160] In Leontine Sagan's words, in 1931, "the world looks wonderingly at a woman who directs a film."[161] We can better understand these conflicted perceptions by remembering and analysing how and where women and the apparatus, particularly the camera, have historically coexisted.

Images of Victorian women operating magic lanterns at home, projecting scenes from slides by way of entertaining or educating children, were not uncommon.[162] Women are also to be found entwined with, or alongside, equipment in promotional images, as a way of expressing, allegorically, the wonder of the machines, as well as their attraction as spectacles in themselves (like the women) irrespective of the film content they projected.[163] Sometimes the contraption was completely abandoned so the projected image could simply spring magically from the woman's body, from under her cloak.[164] (See Fig. 3) But we should distinguish between associations of women with the apparatus in the capacity of projectionist, teacher, or manager—reproducing images already dormant on slide or film—and those scarce associations which broach her agency in taking and making the initial picture, perhaps by cranking the camera, or in some other way directing its formation. An example of the former is misogynist mock report and cartoon of the fictional opening of a "School for Lady Operators." This made sure "the ladies ma[d]e exhibitions of themselves" by describing and illustrating them as failing to absorb lecture material, being scared of mice in the training room, accidentally setting film on fire, rejecting fondling by male instructors, and being frightened of switches.[165] (Fig. 5.2) Among the putative students learning the ways of the camera-projector Bioscope was a suffragist, "Isa...b...a P...nk...rst" (on a soapbox in the top right-hand corner of the cartoon, sporting a hat labeled "Votes for Women"), who, according to this fiction, first campaigned for the "right to operate at once," shaking a banner in the movement's colors, but then abruptly dropped her cause. All in all, the conjunction of woman and camera is presented as unthinkable and chaotic, so much so that a strident feminist will learn by experience to abandon a claim to this right.

As with the amateur still camera, the amateur film market often used images of women running camera-projectors to advertise the latter's operational facility.[166] But woman and camera barely appeared together in the professional filmmaking set, except in the context of domestic partnership, as in the examples of Osa and Martin Johnson, and Frances and Robert Flaherty, distaff accounts of which partnerships are reprinted in this collection.[167] As these examples suggest, as well as those of Jessica Borthwick and Mrs Ditmars, this "woman director" is most commonly found in accounts of adventure filmmaking in the field, a circumstance whose difficult and unpredictable conditions increased the chance of contact between the woman and the apparatus, and through which several women came close to the role of film director. In a 1919 article on "educational films" Mrs Raymond L. Ditmars was illustrated standing behind a light stand in the laboratory, on the far side of the camera from her husband. We read that their "intricate camera ... may be thrown into various ratios of gear in order to photograph and portray types of motion that are too quick for the eye to follow," and then Mr Ditmars describes "our method" of filming. Through her position alongside both him and the camera, we might surmise Mrs Ditmar's assistant director role in shooting wildlife films for "The Living Book of Nature" series he mentions.[168] Ethnologist M.W. Hilton-Simpson wrote of his wife's contribution in "persuad[ing] the natives to submit to the camera" in Algeria when filming the segregated Berber tribes. In the course of six visits to the region she had made "Shawiya women friends," whose cooperation only she could assure.[169] Filming in another Islamic context—outside a mosque in Constantinople—Mr H.M. Lomas reported that "the presence of a lady with him ... was a decided assistance," again apparently for her mediating role between the camera and the subject before it.[170] Lomas spoke in terms of exercising tact, as if local perceptions of the apparatus were modified through the female figure standing by it—as if it became less threatening and more acceptable through her presence.

A fascinating detail of this history lies in the fate of a photographic portrait of the petite Osa Johnson. This shows her standing by her camera, an African male interpreter standing alongside her holding the tripod leg, with the subject matter (a

Fig. 5.2 "Grand Opening of the School for Lady Operators," cartoon by A. Glossop, *The Bioscope*, 24 June 1909, p. 7.

group of tribesmen with spears) gathered beyond.[171] This configuration was altered for the cover of *Camera Trails in Africa*, the book of their travels authored for posterity by her husband Martin. On the book's cover, Osa becomes Martin's assistant, in that her husband's silhouette, with its signature, brimmed bush hat and commanding, open stride, substitutes for the figure of the black man—the hierarchy of gender now overrules that of race.

When we turn to female direction in Hollywood, we find more extreme clashes in stereotypes of masculinity and femininity, where the relation to race consisted in total segregation; no black man or black woman directed within Hollywood during these years. In the search for language and metaphors for discussing the female director, one phrase was the "dynamo with dimples" syndrome,[172] inspired by, as Anne Wagner puts it, bald displays of a "female person who is the equivalent of the male."[173] One of the first questions to arise was, "Does film directing 'make a woman unfeminine'?"[174] Carrying a megaphone and wearing puttees seemed to answer in the affirmative. The very need to ask the question stemmed from the general crisis in concepts of femininity arising from changes wrought through industrialization, immigration, and the more specific pressures of wartime life, all of which challenged habitual gender distinctions. During the First World War most American women were not entitled to vote, and yet were asked to do war work. Not only were women officially asked not to act like women, they were also not

Fig. 5.3   Osa Johnson filming in Africa, an illustration
from *Camera Trails in Africa* (1924)

looking like women. Women of pluck manned planes; post-war flappers bound
their breasts and cut their hair, donned male clothing, and generally dressed in
designs that de-emphasized femininity. The female director enjoined this fashion
trend, inviting reporters to study her attire.

By 1920 certain conventions of (male) directorial working gear had been
established; in 1920 Rinehart referred to "the breeches and puttees the directors
wear" in terms of cliché.[175] Analysis of the female director's femininity typically
focused on the masculinization of her clothing, so that we learn that on Jeanie
Macpherson "you can almost see the directorial lace boots"[176] just out of picture,
and that puttees are Elsie Jane Wilson's "working togs."[177] Fan magazine writer
Frances Denton's article actually offered two divergent wardrobes for Wilson: one
illustrated in the two photographs of her at work, legs astride, feet in lace-up boots
and puttees; the other provided by Denton's prose, which evokes Wilson directing
pictures from the height of fragile femininity, a woman "all in white, except for
her dainty black French-heeled shoes. Also, she wore a broad-brimmed hat and
white silk gloves." Denton concludes by urging that female film directors (including
Lois Weber, "Mother" Lule Warrenton, Ruth Stonehouse, and "Peggy" Baldwin, as
well as Park and Wilson) are anything but unfeminine.[178]

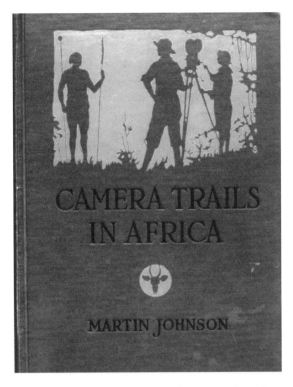

Fig. 5.4 The cover of *Camera Trails in Africa*.

Decor also provided clues to answering the question. Remont found Weber's studio to be more a home than a manufactory of mass-produced dreams, a point she supports through Weber's voice—"'I made up my mind that when I had my own studio everything about it would be harmonious and beautiful, and free from that business air which pervades studios generally'"—and by describing the "books, pictures and flowers [that] brightened every corner. On the desk lay the cutest bouquet of straw flowers in pale pink, blue, yellow and white, with a big paper-lace collar and streamer of pastel-colored ribbons—they looked as if they had just been plucked and brought in fresh from the garden."[179] Aline Carter, reviewing Weber's career in 1921, was relieved "that she [had] retained all her womanly charms," listing dahlias, pillows, flames in the fireplace—"the definite touch of a woman's hands"—as signs of femininity's survival.[180] Despite her huge range of responsibilities (mayor, director, writer, author, editor), we learn at the end of Bertha Smith's article that Weber also "directs her household," cooking and hosting, and caring for a menagerie including everything from a pet butterfly and fox, to an English husband.[181]

That there was some kind of fundamental contradiction between directing and womanhood constituted Ida May Park's reason for turning down the first company she was offered to direct.[182] Beranger found women lacked "physical endurance," and the "generalship ... more natural to a man than to a woman" needed for directing (although Murfin regarded these obstacles more as patriarchal values than actual biological limitations).[183] What were the implications of this new role? Would it turn men into slaves, or women into partners?[184] Would a balance between men and women be found in their taking up like activities, or would the upheavals of suffrage catapult women into the role of master and oppressor? These were worries surrounding suffrage in general, now focused and flourishing in the debate over the female director. Her wearing of puttees suggested her energy, and spirit of adventure; it was a garb redolent of boundary-breaking and colonization. Worn by women, these clothes expressed her command of the West, that geographical and cultural frontier of filmmaking which surprisingly, and for a short while, was hers to explore.

Several women writers give reasons why women *should* direct, some of which have already arisen in the earlier discussion of female screenwriters: to meet the needs of the largely female audience; "to take the raw edges off men's work"; and because there were particular experiences that made women's interpretations different to those of men.[185] Rogers St. Johns held that "there should be women motion picture directors [because] ... [t]hey have certain qualities which might have a great meaning in the interpretation of life—the presentation of women and their problems—which no man can have."[186] Similarly, Weber should direct because she could bring her "infinite knowledge of girls and girlhood" to the screen.[187] Leontine Sagan argued that film, "as an artistic medium" (which was how she saw its mission, rather than in commercial terms), could "express better than any other the love and strife and sorrow of humanity," and, further, that there were particular subjects for which a female director was far more suitable, such as the story of "a girl who conceives an illegitimate child," even though, as she subsequently acknowledged, "no big company would dare to employ a director, particularly a woman director" who subscribed to these priorities.[188]

The female aptitude for detail (a leitmotiv of this book) also lent itself to directing, in the opinion of Park as well as Mary Field, who singled out "a quick grasp of detail, and [being able to] see in a flash if things are right or wrong" as the first qualifications that women possessed for becoming directors; Kathlyn Williams felt that "women can direct just as well as men, and in the manner of much of the planning they often have a keener artistic sense and more of an eye for detail" which can save spoiling a picture.[189] Just as often, however, the gift for detail was felt to suit women to other filmmaking tasks: to writing, technical direction and set dressing, and studio supervision, in the views of Osborne, Beth Brown, and June Mathis.[190] Indeed, following the inferior status which attention to detail generally has, many found this trait to equip women precisely for lowlier roles than that of director: it was the job of *secretary* to "stand at the director's elbow, indoors or out, and catch mistakes, small details that might escape his eye"; she must "remember details, for mistakes in details spell waste in production ... [for] you and every other film fan would notice the mistake."[191] Anne Walker devoted one of her articles on women in the film business to the "infinite care" that went into making a film, contributed by women who were secretaries, technical dressers, librarians, mail sorters, and other "'average' girls doing 'average' but interesting things.'"[192] The message was clear: having a command of detail would not meet the greater challenges of directing. Where Beth Brown might emphasize women's unique worth on set for paying attention to design items, Clara Beranger could carve away that significance: "the successful motion picture is dependent on numerous mechanical devices; it requires accurate knowledge of period furniture and interior decoration. But these come under the category of crafts rather than of art, and as such are not included in this discussion [of] ... motion pictures as a fine art."[193] The double bind for women emerged thus: they might get into directing through their feminine talent of noticing detail, but this would be devalued as a minor gift, appropriate for clearing up after, and around, a male director.[194] Mastery of detail became feminized as fastidiousness, pernicketiness, being unable to see the grand design in a process of gendered trivialization that Dorothy Richardson succinctly summarized: women are those who "see without looking," while men are those who "look without seeing."[195]

One contribution to the debate over the woman director, Osborne's editorial "Why Are There No Women Directors?", invites comparision with Linda Nochlin's later influential essay, "Why Have There Been No Great Women Artists?" (if only at the level of its title's reference to women's absence).[196] Nochlin examined the ideological curdling arising from the term "woman painter," a term that mixed nature with culture, biological reproduction with artistic production. She noted the logistical barriers to women who could not work in a mixed-sex studio to paint the nude (the *sine qua non* of an eighteenth- or nineteenth-century training in art) and concluded that education, class, and institutions were of more significance than genius in determining who, and what, became great.[197] Further, "while art-making has traditionally demanded the learning of specific techniques and skills—in a certain sequence, in an institutional setting outside the home, as well as familiarity with a specific iconography and motifs—the same is by no means true for the poet or novelist." This gave a clue, according to Nochlin, "as to the possibility of the existence of an Emily Dickinson or a Virginia Woolf, and their lack of counterparts (at least until quite recently) in the visual arts."[198]

Becoming a film director in the period between 1906 and the early 1920s did not require a prior institutional training, nor the acquisition of a formalized sequence of skills. The position and its attributes were sketchily defined, and still evolving. A firming up of the terms and conditions for taking up the role (equivalent to that which Nochlin described for the visual artist and involving the exclusion of women from unions and clubs, as they had earlier been excluded from painting studios and exhibitions) emerged by the mid 1920s, consolidating just at the point at which the female director more or less vanished.[199] Where Nochlin described the socio-cultural affront performed by the woman who painted—who, in so doing, demonstrated no disjunction between biological and cultural creation—the woman who made films challenged not only this but also another facet of understandings of femininity, for she paired biological with mechanical reproduction. The conjunction of woman with the apparatus—not a pairing at issue in Nochlin's discussion—was uncomfortable enough, as discussion has already made evident, to severely limit the overall number of female directors there could be, for even at their peak there were still very few.[200]

Just at the moment at which women were experiencing failure in becoming directors, in the mid 1920s, Dorothy Richardson was to write her suite of three highly articulate *Vanity Fair* essays on the woman question, essays so suggestive of reasons for female decline from professional positions (as in the demise of the female Hollywood career) that one of them is reprinted here, even though it does not directly discuss film.[201] In 1925 Richardson raised the question later treated by Nochlin, what to make of "the absence of first-class feminine art,"[202] a topic that Rebecca West was also shortly to take up.[203] The aspirations of suffrage, combined with women's newly acquired opportunities for public life, stimulated such female intellectuals to reflect on conditions, and to ask if anything indeed was changing. Like Nochlin, both West and Richardson aimed to explain the almost total absence of famous creative women. The two earlier writers are interested in causes lying nearer biology, and in the home, as well as in general economic structures and working trends. West first establishes that there is nothing in the female constitution (she mentions brain cortices) preventing women "equal[ing] the performance of man as thinker and artist," but that "there are factors in her environment which choke back whatever potentialities she may have," factors such as segregation from opportunity, or the demand to overbreed, or refrain from breeding, depending on the era.[204] Sexism itself was a huge deterrent: "it is obviously extremely difficult to work when one is constantly being bitten by mosquitoes in the form of criticisms of the female sex in general," so that to survive and succeed "women must learn to go on their way without caring overmuch for the judgements passed on their work by men."[205] However, in conclusion, West urges that there is a rare, feminine type of art, realized by Jane Austen, Colette, Willa Cather, and Virginia Woolf among others, "who have not adopted masculine values as the basis for their work" so that their "art is different in essence from man's."[206] This difference lay in men being "on the side of death, women on the side of life"; where men cut through life with a knife, women carried a box "in which to shut up things and preserve them."[207] These tendencies were equivalently matched, yet sufficiently pronounced to make sure all civilizations ended in ruins, and to explain "why the work of woman since it springs from the will to live, is fundamentally repugnant to [man]."[208]

Richardson would have straightforwardly disagreed with Nochlin and West when addressing the question of means: "Always women have had access to the pen, the chisel and the instrument of music." For greatness in artistic achievement one needed, rather, "quiet, and solitude in the sense of freedom from preoccupations" (an echo of Virginia Woolf's recipe in *A Room of One's Own*). The first problem for the woman artist, according to Richardson, "and particularly the woman painter, going into the world of art," was that one was "immediately surrounded by masculine traditions. Traditions based on assumptions that are largely unconscious and whose power of suggestion is unlimited."[209] But this obstacle was as nothing compared to the ones that lay at home; there this artist was "left in an environment such as has surrounded no male artist since the world began."[210] That is, she had no "devoted wife or mistress, or neglectful char ... someone who will either reverently or contemptuously let [her] be." Somehow, through such ministering, a man "will be tended and will live serenely innocent of the swarming detail that is the basis of daily life."[211] Help and service occurring between women—given from one to another—also provided no antidote, Richardson asserted, concluding that "Art demands what, to women, currently civilization won't give.... Neither motherhood nor the more continuously exacting and indefinitively expansive responsibilities of even the simplest housekeeping can so effectively hamper her as the human demand, besieging her where ever she is, for an inclusive awareness, from which men, for good or ill, are exempt."[212] What Richardson terms "inclusive awareness" is tantamount to the female aptitude for detail, that immersive training she might turn to good at the movies, on either side of the screen. It is that capacity to sense, grade, and respond to multiple, simultaneous, disparate events and ingredients, and that attention to other people's needs and wants, qualities developed under women's historical roles as mothers and care-givers.

By way of concluding, let us try to pass through the waist of the hourglass into the auditorium, by taking up an issue already amply explored within studies of cinema: the prospect of women as objects to view. But the transition from invisibility (behind the camera) to visibility (in front of it) itself demands a story. A further dimension of the woman director debate lay in the perception that something was amiss when a woman opted against "sensitizing the camera" with her own body, and stood instead outside its viewing range.[213] As John Berger and others have cogently argued, there seems, in industrial culture, always a tendency for the woman to become the image, even when she is trying to make it.[214] When interviewed in 1914, Alice Guy Blaché described the nuisance of this inversion, an especial liability when on location:

> while enthusiastic about her own sex in this sort of vocation, [Madame] dwelt upon the fact that at present a woman director or photographer being unusual would attract much attention and curiosity.... "It is necessary," she said "that work be carried on with a[s] little interruption or notice as possible, and I fear the sight of a woman turning the crank of the camera or directing in the city streets would cause the attraction of a great crowd of sight seers and draw from the value of the picture."[215]

In describing Hollywood cinema, Laura Mulvey has observed that often the spectacle of the female star interrupts the film story's flow, threatening to undo the fiction's illusions.[216] Here Guy Blaché is describing the way in which the tendency for the woman to become a spectacle threatens to undo the production; in becoming the image, she is stopped from creating it. Mulvey posited her insight as a textual operation realized in reception; for Blaché the interruption shaped material production.

From discourse of the time we learn that women's choices to remain off-camera were in constant need of explanation.[217] Apparently, one "old-time picture man" was delighted when he recognized in an isolated close-up of held water tumblers "Lois' hands!" in a film Weber was directing but not appearing in.[218] It is hard to imagine similar satisfaction being reported in sighting manual traces of the male director of this era (although later it was apparently well known within the industry that Preston Sturges used his own hands when a close-up of hands was required). There was no such pressure to locate him as an image, to pin down a body part for him; it is as if this hand, reaching through the hourglass's waist into the auditorium to appear on the screen reassured by finally having the woman show up at the more appropriate site. With its links to the feminine profession of fortune-telling and notions of feminine touch, the female hand has long been something to be read, but, enlarged on screen, as Louella Parsons noted when assessing Theda Bara's "slender, sinuous, and alluring" hand (one "dual in its tendencies"), female hands amassed additional power as "the means of describing graphic emotional scenes in the language of silent pictures."[219]

When Nerina Shute suggested women could not direct films because they did not combine brawn, artistic power, and business brain, her newspaper was sued for libel by Dinah Shurey—the female director damned—and lost.[220] Dismissing overall arguments of inferior physical strength, or lack of sufficient aggression, Jane Loring, in 1935, preferred instead that the reason women had not "equalled the achievements of men in the field of film production" lay in the amount of scrutiny they suffered. Her vocabulary is above all visual:

> she has had to fight against unfair handicaps arising from her sex. From the moment that women began to direct films, they were under critical contemplation, not merely as film directors, but as *women*. They had to face a new and peculiar standard of judgement. Because they were women they were watched especially.... The woman film director hasn't got to be *as good* as the men. She has to be better.[221]

June Mathis used similar visual patterns of speech: "When a woman takes the megaphone in her hand, the eyes of the entire industry are focused upon her."[222] And when we pursue this theme across the racial divide into "Sepia Hollywood," the discussion of invisibility and appearance takes yet another turn.[223]

Scarce though African-American published views on filmmaking are from the silent period, those we have regularly refer to the question of visibility in two respects: representativeness (that every crowd should have black faces since they do in reality), and skin tone's relation to professional opportunity (as in the ex-white actress's discussion of passing, or darkness being a white fashion item in Proctor and Goodwin).[224] The Hollywood star needed to glow, to radiate light, qualities amplified by white skin, porcelain make-up, fair hair, film stock calibrated for light skin, and strategic lighting.[225] With the coming of sound, women such as Avenelle Harris and Theresa Harris, among others, continued to describe white Hollywood's barriers to screen-acting, but another dicussion began, over the reception of visualized black sound.[226] Dorothy Richardson dissected (and rejected) most of its consequences in *Hearts of Dixie*, as discussed in Part Four, despite the contrasting optimistic welcome by some writers of black performers singing and acting on screen. It seems that, as opposed to experiencing cultural pressure to stand before the camera (rather than of remaining out of sight behind it), as in the discussion of the white female director, African Americans, including black women, were preferred heard rather than seen. On the image track, prejudical attitudes kept black women, as well as black men, out of sight, or forced them to pass as white. Black choirs were invisible, as well as cheaper, and often better than their white counterparts, and would not necessarily betray their racial identity.[227] Black women were rarely to attain the position of director—theirs was the invisibility of lack of recognition, rather than the invisible omnipotence of the director. But because racial divisions were and are based principally on visible difference, a segregated industry could more easily tolerate the invisible, audible presence of African Americans than either their silent on-screen image, or the utterly disembodied off-screen power of the directorial role.[228] The singing voice was still of the body, corporeal, if not visible.

Verna Arvey, in her regular column "Worth While Music in the Film," wrote of the significant presence of black musicians in Hollywood, usually uncredited, unacknowledged, and unseen.[229] She described racially determined hiring stratifications in which white choirs were on studio contract, while black choirs were rented on a per-film basis. She also wrote on the black voice passing as white, dubbed onto soundtracks, a theme Julie Dash was later to examine in her film *Illusions* (1982), and of "shadow Hollywood"'s opportunities for black women in choir mastery and musical directorship. The career of singing or music teacher was a possible trade for black women, an extension of the religious music traditions of black worship. Eva Jessye itemized the behind-the-scenes racist practices of Hollywood in the making of *Hallelujah*, for which she was musical director, particularly the camouflaging of black musical work as white, or the leaving of it as uncredited. The film, MGM's first all-black talkie, while garnering high praise in the white press, had brought a mixed response in the black; like *Imitation of Life* and *Hearts of Dixie*, it was a film about which racial questions, especially those of truthfulness of representation, raged.[230]

The requirement for visibility among white women brought with it a discourse on youth and ageing still heard in the film industry. The cautionary tale against stardom warned that women of a surfeit of years or pounds would fail; there was no equivalent rhetoric for male prospects.[231] Already by 1917, actress Cora Drew was complaining (with the support of many letters from readers) of imbalances in the casting of the sexes:

> Men can be and are cast for leading men and lovers and the public is treated to the same old story of "May and December." ... Are women given opportunities to play important parts that suit their age? Rarely. Stories written for such capable women are not purchased—the producers seem to believe that the public cares only for youth represented by *woman!*... When a producer does give an opportunity to a woman of years he usually makes her a "Vampire."[232]

The enduring youthfulness of Mary Pickford prompted endless discussion: such professional actresses learned expertise in the expression of emotions and took "heed not to let ugly lines mar the harmony" of their play of features, wrote one magazine writer.[233] As mentioned in Part Four, Lejeune's short essay on Pickford (written after the "crisis" provoked when Mary cut her curls in Jone 1928 for her first talkie, Coquette, an event widely covered in fan magazines and the press) understood her career to map the span of the public's entire history of reception, since film began; Pickford was ageing with the cinema's audience. For D.W. Griffth in 1921, the young industry possessed (and required) the qualities of the young American maiden, while by the 1940s there was a thoroughgoing popular understanding of Hollywood's make-over procedures.[234] In the earlier discussions, make-up was explicitly denied as a means to continued youth; the camera was said to be pitiless, rendering a star old at twenty-five years. Youth had to be genuine.

Rebecca West intervened dramatically in this discussion in 1929. She was searching for the reason for America's paradoxical investment "in the extreme brevity in the career of women film stars," which she took as her primary example in her comparative analysis of "New Secular Forms of Old Religious Ideas," the title of an article which identified manifestations of European rituals across the Atlantic. After pointing to the impressively lengthy careers of Pickford, Gish, and others, who, in 1929, had been film actresses for twenty years, West concluded that this belief, "held with passion and against reason," was "a manifestation of some preferred event in American private life," effectively a brand of relic cult, "a new mythology."[235] The ubiquitous "imagined destruction of the woman star" that West encountered at the hairdresser's as at dinner was a female sacrifice suited to the "more feminized civilization of the United States" where men were "not eliminated from the screen on account of age."[236] West helps us understand that women were to stay but not change on the screen. Ageing put them in tension with the medium's power to preserve looks against the ravages of time; the professed desire that West observed, of disposing of the female star while she was still in use revealed the gendered base for the urge to cling to the screen as youthful balm.

A further aspect of being seen, or not (a pairing also at work in the writings gathered in Part One), arose in the writing profession, that area of filmmaking which women had inhabited with most success and promise. Sonya Levien specifically recommended this career, because "an age limit" did not come into consideration, since the writer was not to be displayed.[237] But a further level of invisibility was in play, since, in writing, the act of creation went on largely invisibly, in the mind, with small, consequent motions of fingers and hand, on a typewriter, or with pen; the means were minimal, almost illusory, and the activity disproportionately internal, when compared with acting or directing. Communicating the practice of writing is always challenging to the reporter, but we can detect a particular awkwardness in efforts to signify women's acts of film writing, given the cultural desire to make her an object of visual study. A pair of fan magazine photographs of Jeanie Macpherson were captioned, "The powder puff is only a bluff, as the scenarios are written with the pencil."[238] In the first image Macpherson holds a compact and puff, in the second a pad and pencil; the first pair covers for the second, helping to make feminine sense of them. The point is that writing is invisible as a process, but that feminine accoutrements can frame and designate this disconcertingly cerebral trade, especially when the writer has also appeared on the screen, as in Macpherson's case.[239]

Another option was to photograph or draw the author at her typewriter.[240] The typewriter, now a dinosaur of scriptural production, was, in the opening years of film, a veritable weapon of dynamic femininity.[241] Clerical work prior to the 1880s had been a male occupation, but starting in the late nineteenth century a rapid feminization of this world had taken place until, by 1920, 90 per cent of all typing and stenographic work in the United States was accomplished by women.[242] This machine, wrote Anne Morgan in 1927, had proved "skillful enough to prove woman's open sesame. Its keys gave her the chance she longed for to come out into the world."[243] Morgan credited the typewriter's inventors with transforming women's options, and bringing them opportunities which threatened the status quo. (Others recorded the erotic opportunity the typewriter wrought.)[244] Michael Monahan held an extremely bleak view of all this. For him, the plight of the United States in 1914 was a consequence of women's entry into journalism, to which the typewriter was handmaiden. He lamented that women read women's writings eagerly; that department stores followed with advertising; that in a short time the male view, and male literary polish, would be rubbed out; and that men would become fit "only to escort women to poll or public office."[245] While male antagonism towards literary women was long known—Nathaniel Hawthorne had groaned to his publisher in 1855 that "America is now wholly given over to a d———d mob of scribbling women," adding "and I should have no chance of success while the public taste is occupied with their trash"—the conjunction of the typewriter and suffrage intensified this discontentment.

The many publicity shots of film women writing, with and without their typewriter—in log cabins (Jeanie Macpherson), living rooms (Fredi Washington), tree desks (Frances Marion), by swings (Sarah Y. Mason), with cats (Colette), on office (Pickford) or breakfast table chairs (Loos), or in the garden (Weber, Mason, Marion)—give a sense of the fascination generated by the woman writer and how she worked, and make in some way concrete and material, even domestic and pastoral, the elusiveness of her acts (while they also explore and expand on the captivating figure of the female stenographer).[246] But how are we to understand the unholy constellation of Mildred Harris, sixteen-year-old actress for Lois Weber, "trying to clean … the camera with the stenographer's typewriter brush," sending into orbit in one gesture female director, starlet, typist, and camera?[247]

The theme of visibility and invisibility continues to affect discussion of those jobs that usher the film through the hourglass's waist into the auditorium, jobs such as those of manager, cashier, ticket-taker, and piano player. The picture palace typically provided a glass box on the street in front of the theater for its cashier, whose exhibition was redolent of promised offerings within. In Ina Rae Hark's

Fig. 5.5   Lois Weber at her garden typewriter in 1918.

Fig. 5.6   Frances Marion at her tree desk in 1917.

Fig. 5.7 Sarah Y. Mason typing by her children's swing in about 1926.

Fig. 5.8 Caricature of Anita Loos typing, by Ralph Barton, 1927.

5.9   Mary Pickford seated at the typewriter in 1922.

Fig. 5.10   Mildred Harris dusting Lois Weber's
camera in 1918.

Aesteticism
and Dimes

A BOSTON SOCIETY WOMAN
HAS MADE A SUCCESS
OF A PLAYHOUSE JUST
TO PROVE THAT RE-
FINEMENT PAYS IN
DOLLARS AND CENTS

ENTRANCE
OF LADIES.
ROOM OF THE
BIJOU
DREAM; AND
MRS.
JOSEPHINE
CLEMENT,
THE
THEATER'S
MANAGER

BOSTON has a picture playhouse with a temperament, where the announced "Refinement" in the box-office really means all that the dictionary says it is to mean, where flourish cut flowers and marble statuary and velours, and where for ten cents one buys a real æsthetic tidbit.

More than two years ago, Josephine Clement, society matron of Brookline, and wife of Edward H. Clement, for years editor of the Boston *Transcript*, announced that she had decided to assume the management of a combination motion-picture and vaudeville playhouse, and prove that refinement would pay.

1030

Fig. 5.11   Entrance to the Ladies' Room of the Bijou Dream, in Boston, in 1914, a Motion-Picture and Vaudeville Playhouse run by Mrs Clement (in foreground).

words, "The girl in the box office was to use her appearance and demeanor to sell tickets in the same way the gaudy, incandescent marquee or titillating poster might."[248] Richly described in Resi Langer's essays on filmgoing in Berlin, she was as sex-typed female as the projectionist, enclosed in an opaque box, was male.[249] This archetypical female employee absorbed some of the housewifely aspects of theater management, including "expertise in 'feminine' concerns like housekeeping, interior decoration, and gracious social interaction," deflecting them away from the managerial persona.[250] The usherette, who sometimes wore trousers in the 1920s' movie palaces, and who took over from male ushers during both world wars, also served to shelter the male manager from too strong an association with domesticity in his job.[251] Female ushers were introduced into movie theaters as a refining element as early as 1910; in 1931, one described her working equipment as a "torch in hand" and a "smile unshackled."[252] The usherette was strikingly visible to film critic Winifred Horrabin, who promoted her as a courageous figure of morale-boosting, national fortitude when evaluating her in her appreciative blitzkrieg report.[253]

Robert Siodmak, in his memorial scene to the silent cinema auditorium (from his 1946 film Spiral Staircase), remembered the live pianist as a woman; her accompaniment wafts up through the floorboards of a hotel room where a young woman is being murdered in the opening moments of the film. The female accompanist was a familiar feature of the silent era, for, as with the usherette and female manager, her presence brought salubriousness.[254] Further, piano-playing and musical proficiency were areas in which women (including black women) were trained as part of social finishing, or by way of participating in religious life, and they were talents adaptable to the exhibition business for pay.[255] Actress Margery Wilson's first job, at age fourteen, was "playing the piano in a cheap little picture house"; a character for a short story published in 1913 was a "girl ... chewing gum" who "came along and struck up the piano" in the orchestra pit of a Maine cinema; and Marian Bowlan pictures a "girl at the piano" in her stage monologue about filmgoing.[256] By the 1920s movie theaters were annually hiring "nearly 20,000 musicians—a third of the nation's musical workforce," some of whom were women.[257] (In her survey of women's film options in 1923, Gebhart claimed that every studio director employed an orchestra or "at least a piano-player and violinist, one of whom is a girl" to set the mood.)[258] In 1915 Kinematograph Weekly celebrated the female pianist in its first Kinema Ballad, "Types of Pianists,"[259] while many more recently collected oral histories of the movies recall the pianist as female, just as Siodmak had.[260]

As with the female pianists, ushers, and ticket-takers, female management brought respectability to the movies, and indeed some women entered the profession after having served on censor boards or in other film-reforming activities (as mentioned in Part Three); the moral tone set by Boston society woman Mrs Clement, who programmed classical music to accompany her shows, and who decked her interiors with "cut flowers and marble statuary and velours," was certainly in tune with that of reformers.[261] One manageress described the financial rewards of politeness: "I always greet people as they enter the theater and at the close of every performance, I invite every patron, man, woman, or child to come again."[262] Another recorded that "the development of moving pictures has opened a field to women managers" because "picture theaters have become more or less family affairs. Of course, families attend theaters run by men, but the woman manager can infuse the atmosphere of home and refinement into the place."[263] She can do this not only through her manners and the films she selects, but also through her musical taste: "Even where women managers are not musical performers, they frequently have sufficient artistic ability to see that pictures are put on with appropriate music, though not necessarily elaborate."[264] A third female manager advised that "men follow women's notion of entertainment" so that managers should pick films for exhibition accordingly.[265] Another article, of 1930, described an old-fashioned cinema manager in the Old Kent Road (London), who knew her audience by name, and babysat Mrs Green's two sons for her until nine o'clock; here the female manager doubles the nanny function of the film itself.[266]

Management had been a well-established female role in the fairground and traveling lantern trades, one that re-emerged with the cinema.[267] Mary Ellen Hitchcock, American author and explorer, traveled in 1898 to Dawson City, Alaska from San Francisco with her long-term companion Edith van Buren and their two Great Danes, Ivan and Queen, to set up an "animatoscope" show for prospectors.[268] Mrs S.C. Sloan, who ran The Searchlight Theater in Tacoma, Washington, in 1900–02 was among the few women operating a storefront picture show in the pre-nickelodeon era.[269] However, several nickelodeon owners were female, and later black women theater managers were not that unusual, another indirect result of discrimination: as the New York Dramatic Mirror reported in 1912, "Resenting the treatment accorded them at some of the moving picture houses, the colored people have opened one of their own, operated by Mrs Laura Hill, a social leader among the negroes of Denver, Colo."[270] In 1917, Alta Davis, who ran the Empire Theater in Los Angeles, could still find the field sufficiently "unexplored by my own sex" to invite entrepreneurs.[271]

A number of individual women developed distinctive entertainment programs and sometimes significantly influenced trends of film exhibition. Mrs A.C.M. Sturgis, manager of the Lafayette Theater in Washington D.C., aimed to "increase the attendance of women and the young folks" by using "big exhaust fans," "hourly spraying with a perfumed deodorizer," and by screening the National American Woman Suffrage Association's brand-new 1914 film Your Girl and Mine, whose political content she hoped would particularly draw women.[272] Mrs Clement offered a "lounging room for women, with a maid in attendance," while the overall ambience made her Bijou "a women's theater throughout."[273] All attendants were women, "gowned in uniform gray nun's veiling, with white trimmings. Suffusing the auditorium at all times during the performance [was] a delicate violet light."[274] Interviewed in 1910, Clement favored "scenic, industrial, and scientific kind[s] of picture."[275] Her varied programming, including one-act plays intermixed with lantern slide lectures (called "camera talks" or "camera chats") and "suitable" musical accompaniment, were to "aestheticalize" the house, making up for shortcomings in "technical and artistic excellence," and helping to cope with constraints in exhibition generated by the Trust's closed market which limited Mrs Clement to their pictures only.[276] In another report, two years later, Mrs Clement was offering a chorus "of thirty voices for Sunday night programmes," seeking films of "illustrated songs" to no avail, and finding her "audience at the Bijou listening with unmistakable enjoyment to the music of Florina, to solos from La Bohème, Tosca, Madame Butterfly and many other operas."[277]

By interleaving slides, variety acts, and playlets among films (and perhaps even re-editing short films) into a unique program shaped for particular audiences, Mrs Clement was exercising a relatively high degree of editorial control over what the public saw and heard, and how they did so.[278] Such editorial power waned after cinema's first fifteen years, as the vertically integrated industry emerged, and as the individual film became an unvarying, canned, circulated commodity. The exhibitor's influence survived to some extent, however, in the specialist cinemas that cropped up in Europe and the United States from the 1920s onwards.

While film critic for the *Spectator*, Iris Barry co-founded the London Film Society in 1925, together with Ivor Montagu and others. The Society's high annual membership fees excluded working-class patrons, and because it was organized as a club, it could conduct separate licensing negotiations with the British Board of Film Censors, which enabled it to show rare and sometimes banned films in Sunday screenings.[279] Its highly varied programs (scientific films alongside newsreels, art films, and travelogues, for example) nourished London's film culture until the Second World War, although Barry had, in the meantime, left for the United States, where she was to co-found the New York Film Society in 1930.[280] Germaine Dulac was secretary-general and co-founder of the Club français du cinéma (CFC) in 1922, later co-founding the Ciné-Clubs de France in 1924. Her organization assisted in bringing non-commercial and foreign films (from the Soviet Union, Germany, and Sweden, for example) to French audiences, but also in arranging debates, discussions, and lecture series in coordination with screenings.[281] Margaret Larkin, secretary to the Film *Forum*, reported on the founding and goals of this venture in 1933, explaining its niche between commercial movie houses and "the 'arty' standard of the Little Theater," as well as its alliance with workers newsreel groups and its intent of showing "pictures of keen social and cinegraphic importance" at a New York venue, also on Sundays.[282] Lastly, Irene Nicholson co-organized the Forum Cinema in Villiers Street in the mid 1930s, a venue once described as London's "Advance-Guard Cinema."

The Little Film Theater movement (named after the Little Theater movement for stage) was mooted as an idea in the United States in 1922, although the first houses were only programmed in 1926. These theaters again were to offer venues to avant-garde and European art cinema. Marguerite Tazelaar reported on the history of these developments (describing links to the London Film Society and the French ciné-club movement), while women such as Mrs Regge Doran of the Filmarte cinema in Hollywood were founders of such theaters.[283] Another group of women, including Mrs Henry Griffin, Miss Anne Morgan, Miss Elizabeth Perkins, and Miss Sophie Smith, directed the Little Picture House, which planned to offer a morning program of educational talks and films intended for school children and for "women who go to lectures, who go on shopping expeditions, and many who go nowhere and are bored."[284]

Elizabeth Coxhead described the pioneering work of film manager Elsie Cohen as one of forging "new relations between exhibitor and audience."[285] Cohen, after a full career as a film journalist, distributor, publicist, and producer, founded the Academy Cinema, Oxford Street, in 1931, which specialized in screening the latest German and Soviet pictures as well as silent classics. (Winifred Holtby recorded watching Carl Dreyer's *The Passion of Joan of Arc* there in the cinema's opening season and later named Cohen's "enterprising and perspicacious" entry "into the world of cinema management ... one of the joys of London."[286]) Eschewing the industry practice of the double feature bill, she teamed features with documentaries and shorts and contributed substantially to London's lively film culture until the Second World War when the cinema was bombed.[287]

All these women, from those who developed sophisticated film programs for urban centers to those manageresses and usherettes who recorded being on personal terms with their patrons shaped the culture of the auditorium, that sector of cinema most thoroughly inhabited by women, and the place, or at least the perspective, from which most of the women in this collection wrote. We have now stepped fully out of the hourglass's waist and into the bell of film's reception, where some women were watching professionally: the journalist, the reformer, the budding film scholar, and the educator planning her classes. Critic Elinor Gibbs surveyed the peculiar extremes of her work, from assessing films too early in the day, practically alone, to evaluating them in the steamy crush of a premier.[288] Frances Taylor Patterson took over Victor Freeburg's courses at Columbia University when he was called up during World War I, and taught screenwriting and film appreciation there. Alice Guy Blaché lectured at this venue in 1917, and Iris Barry was also later to teach there (in 1937–38).[289] Clara Beranger had become a lecturer in screenwriting at the University of Southern California by the 1940s, writing in 1947 that "The cinema is now figuratively and literally ready for college," advocating courses in "the theory and practice of the art of picture-making."[290] Iris Barry wrote in an academic quarterly, The College Art Journal, in 1945, of the newly possible job of "research worker in film."[291] Her tools were finally available: films could be rented, circulated to schools, reseen in collections; one no longer needed to rely on memory or on "dead scrabbling through the inept film criticism of yesteryear."[292] Barry had laid much of the groundwork for this herself. Through her work as a journalist in Britain in the 1920s, writing for both the highbrow Spectator and the lower-middle class Daily Mail (the highest circulating newspaper in Britain), she had reached the widest possible audience with her opinions on film.[293] She had brought both an intellectual and a populist passion to her task, putting the desires of women filmgoers squarely on the map while also sketching the contours of the characteristics of different national cinemas. By looking to other cinemas, to documentaries, and by calling for change in types of plot, she had hoped women might expand their experience of art and the world, and develop critical faculties to demand better film. Through her film society work, but more particularly in becoming museum librarian at the Museum of Modern Art in 1932, then the first film curator of its Film Library in 1935 (and later its director), she had created non-commercial institutions for cinema, and was a founding member of the film archive movement. She had made possible a whole range of educational programs and alternative exhibition settings. As Mary Lea Bandy reminds us, in 1936–37 "the Film Library was in correspondence with 1,520 universities, colleges, preparatory schools, museums, film societies, high schools, hospitals, the Works Progress Administration projects, Jewish centers, drama groups, and prisons, of which more than one hundred organizations rented film series."[294] In her essay, "Motion Pictures as a Field of Research," as in her career, Barry ultimately asserted that film was worthy of a kind of intellectual work upon it, an effort and sentiment therefore of direct ancestory to *Red Velvet Seat*. Indeed, *The Film Index*, published in 1941, which Barry supervised from the Museum of Modern Art, was a starting point for researching this book. If it was to be in the roles of censor, writer, ticket-taker, usherette, and cinema-goer that women would survive the mid 1920s crunch, the coming of sound, and even, to differing extents, the 1950s, the seeds of women's fascination with the professional study of cinema, fully realized only from the 1970s, were nevertheless planted in cinema's first half-century, as the writings here attest.

A Job for Whom?

The Confessions of an Ex-White Actress (1919)[1]
Anonymous

Are you one of the many who believe that the life of an actress is one of ease and pleasure? Do you think that the Colored actress receives a big, fat salary for bowing and smiling at you over the footlights each night, and that her extensive wardrobe is donated to her by the management? Are you one of those who believe that "actin' beats scrubbin'" and you get more for it? If you have ever given the young Colored women on the American stage any consideration whatever, just read what this actress has to say about it.

Pasadena, Cal., May 20, 1919

The Half-century Magazine,
  5202 Wabash Avenue,
    Chicago, Illinois.

Gentlemen:—It is with reluctance that I comply with your request of recent date regarding my stage life. A feeling of despair grips me when I review my career, when I sit here in my luxury and span the meadows of time. My life has been blotted with a great sin. With the exception of a few intimate friends and relatives my racial identity has been a closed book to my race. My nerves are shattered and as the finger of death points at me and beckons me Home, my innerself says "give a message," if such it may be called, "to my own."

The story runs thus: My love for art was innate. In fact, for three generations my ancestors on my paternal side, which was white, were actors and actresses of rare deportment. When my mother, a Colored lady from Mississippi, with great ambition for her child, confided to me that she was going to renounce me when I became six years of age, I accepted it as my share and went to live at a boarding school. To make a long story concise, I finally reached the stage. It was the desire that I become an actress; that is why my mother turned me over to white people to become a part of them before I became too attached to Colored people. I grew up, then, and gave the best years of my life to white ideals.

My mother, who is with me now, saw the weaknesses, pitfalls and small future for a Colored girl in high-class drama. I formed the acquaintance of some of the Colored actresses throughout the country at the beginning of my career twenty years ago and to this day these acquaintances occupy a warm place in my heart. They always confided in me, for they knew that I could not afford to talk. I succeeded and made money, they succeeded in a limited way only, and have hardly made a living. I could and did "pass" for white and today my mother and I are on "easy street." My friends could not "pass" and today are fighting to keep up their front.

What I have to say below was written with reluctance because of the black cloud it throws about the stage which my Colored friend actresses have attempted to purify and elevate. It is not written out of bitterness or disrespect. You asked me to write candidly what were my views concerning the stage to which my fellow Colored actresses are bound.

My observations will be briefly made and I trust they may be a lighthouse steering your thoughts and endeavors to great power; to the end which your magazine has dedicated itself as the apostle of clear and wholesome stage life.

I find fault with the unlicensed boldness with which the Colored actress is approached both by Colored and white men. It wounds me deeply as I turn over in my mind the many cases which have been brought to my attention over a stretch of a score of years from Colored girls. The young and undeveloped actresses, with their futures far distant, seem to be the ones who have these snares laid for them most often. If they resent them they are branded as lacking in tact, as being out of harmony with the spirit of the stage. How often they have told me in tears about the traps set to dash their careers to pieces.

The Colored actress in stock and vaudeville is also under a great handicap because of the requirement that she furnish her own costumes for the stage. Of course, clothes for the street must be bought. My mind teems with the cases which my friends have brought me regarding their salaries being cut into so heavily by this requirement. Oftentime it exceeds 75 per cent of their weekly earnings. In those companies which put on a new show each week the costumes must be changed weekly and three cases out of four the actress must buy the costume, hat, dress and shoes. When an actress in a stock show does not have a part to play in a particular engagement, she receives only half pay. This half-pay custom happens about twice a month for the average actress who attempts to play in stock.

Another burden upon an actress' shoulders is the wrong impression the public has about Colored actresses. It imagines that the Colored actress' purse has no bottom, that a ham sandwich, when eaten by an actress, is worth twice as much to her as it is to the ordinary civilian. The hotelkeepers and private homes in which the actresses stay contract the "get-rich-quick" fever as soon as a Colored actress seeks accommodations.

The actresses have struggled for a generation to remove the uncertainty in their working conditions. Only the brightest stars receive contracts. The mediocre actress merely works from day to day and a trip which has begun in New York City and bound for the Pacific Coast may terminate for her in a train-shed in Black Hills, South Dakota, or on the deserts of Utah. How an actress could put her best efforts into her work I could never see with such shadows forever hanging over her head. The actresses deserve unbounded praise for the success they have attained with only this as part of their theatrical intimidation.

My amazement mounts when I consider the lack of Colored dramatists. This reveals the barren spot in my own stage life where I was under the thumb of white ideals. One function of the white stage is to paint the ideals, passions and love of the white race. I did my best to drink in white ideals. To a certain extent I succeeded; to a larger extent I failed. I paced up and down in my room many an hour in great anxiety when the struggle was on within me—a Colored woman vs. white ideals. But to whom could I confide the inner struggle? I had friends among the dramatists. It was no use to lay bare my mind to them. Granted that they could sympathize with me, they could do me no good. They could not write a great play about Colored people if they tried ever so hard. White people are ignorant about the life of Colored people, even though they try to flatter themselves that they know more about us than we do about ourselves. I do hope the day will soon arrive when a Colored dramatist will present himself who can portray the sweet love and holy ambitions of the Colored people. He can pave the way for great art among our people, who, without doubt, are the most aesthetic people in America. I know: I have been on both sides of the fence.

Another great drawback to the Colored actress is one which our own race could partly control. It is the conduct of our own theatrical promoters. Colored promoters have been a dismal failure. One would think that their intimate knowledge of our own and a desire to excel in a field in which Colored men have fallen down would drive them on to greater endeavors. It is quite to the contrary. Those whom I have known were only carbuncles so far as qualifications of a director of a theatrical venture is concerned. Most of them would lay aside almost any business engagement if a good time were in sight. Many a mother, who had ambitions for her daughter in the theatrical world, has withdrawn her when she was made familiar with the struggle a noble-minded woman has on the stage. Do not consider what I say as too harsh. It is not. Were I to tell you some of the hair-raising truths about the shabby way Colored men have treated their own, you would wish you were not of our stock. Low wages, irregular wages, insults, and ungentlemanly conduct are a few of the mild accusations against them.

I trust this inexhaustive article will be of interest to you and your readers. I am having a few memories compiled for the use of Colored stage-lovers. It will be released shortly and will be placed at your disposal if you so desire.
With wishes for success, I am
   Yours very truly,
      (She asked us not to use her name, as yet.)

[*The Half-century Magazine* (Chicago), July 1919, p. 16.]

The Confessions of an Ex-White Actress—concluded (1919)
Anonymous

In the July issue of the Half-century the actress told us why she spent the greater portion of her life as white rather than with the people of her own race. She told of the hardships and disappointments that are the lot of Colored actresses and their sufferings even at the hands of their own people. So interested were most of our readers in her story that she has agreed to a little more about herself.

Pasadena, California,
July 10th, 1919

The Half-century Magazine,
    5202 Wabash Avenue,
        Chicago, Ill.

Dear Editor: I feel much elated that you and your readers enjoyed the manuscript I submitted to you for the July issue of the magazine. My mother was overjoyed at the appreciation and response my few remarks evoked. A pang darts through my heart as I attempt to dig up a chapter in my past life and as I rehearse it, the wail of the poet tingles in my ears:

"O, Death in Life, the days that are no more."

Oh, if I could recall the days which have gone by and live the life the way I feel now that it should be lived! In a measure fickleness has been too much of a part of me, for had womanhood sat more seriously on my brow, say fifteen years ago, today I would not be playing hide-and-go-seek with heaven in order that I might put a few impressions on paper. Anyone can dream of what ought to have been done but if I am successful in cheating the Grim Reaper I will attempt to get down among my own, cast my lot with the coming people of the stage and the world and do my bit in elevating the Colored stage.

It was pointed out in the previous article that pitfalls of a deep order are abroad for the Colored actress: this time I will mention an incident drawn at random from many similar ones in my life.

I was sitting on the veranda of my Newport home about ten years ago in deep conversation with a playwright who had just returned from northern Mexico where he had spent eighteen months studying the life of the Peon Indians in particular and witnessing excavations which were being made in Chihuahua to reveal the early civilization of those people. Why, the man's soul burned with enthusiasm as he waded into every angle of their life, like a child into a creek, with unbounded joy, his face lit up with a sweetness magnificent in its charm. He carried me up and down the valleys and mountains with a sweep of description worthy of a poet. When he arrived at the Rio Grande he lost his fervor. I asked him why he did not stop in the south to study the Negro at first hand.

"Oh, it's a waste of time," he said with a tinge of impatience in his voice.

"I would imagine that their life is studded with as much interest as the Mexican Peons."

"Not for a minute," he said, shaking his head in deep earnestness.

"You mean to say that ten million people possess no virtues worthy to be studied at first hand?"

"Exactly so, when the Negro is to be studied."

"But you spent more than a year and a half studying the life of less than a million semi-civilized Indian Peons?"

"Yes, but the white people know that they are a people who can never cut much of a figure in the affairs of the world."

"You mean the white people never give much attention to races who are likely to challenge the supremacy of the white race?" I interrupted.

"You know," he continued, "when too much interest is directed towards a race or races which thrive rather than deteriorate when in contact with our race, they begin to feel themselves and of course that makes our race apprehensive."

"Is this only a whim of the dramatists?" I asked.

"It is ground in us, haven't you ever had it brought to your attention?" he asked with surprise.

"Not in so many words," I maneuvered.

"There is no angle of professional or business life in which this is not a common understanding. The Negroes had more favorable attention paid to them in Uncle Tom's Cabin days than they ever will have again.[1] They were chattels in those days and of course demanded the sympathy of mankind but now they have their freedom and must work out their own destiny. To be candid, it's queer about those people, they are only fifty years out of bondage and on my word, they are thriving in their contact with the white race. As a matter of history their population has trebled since Civil War days; their wealth increased a hundred fold and their illiteracy has decreased a thousand per cent."

"What do you think of their possibilities in the theatrical world?" I interrupted.

"Not much. You see it's like this. The writer must ante-date the actor. They have no dramatic writers, not even mediocre ones."

"Are you certain about that?"

"My fellow writers had a warm argument recently about this matter. And one writer who was raised in the heart of the South admitted it was queer that those who have attempted to write, "write like icebergs" even though they possess the imaginations of so many DeQuincys."[2]

"Have you spent any time in the South and seen the Colored people at the end of a hard day's labor?" I interrupted again.

"No, I haven't," he said.

"Of all the sweet music which comes welling straight from the heart, I never heard the like before in my life. I remember distinctly the evening that we spent not long ago at the foot of Lookout Mountain when the sun was about to drop over the western horizon. A lanky fellow in his twenties, lay with his feet stuck up the trunk of a tree playing a banjo which poured out his soul. If ever in my life I felt as if I was living in an earthly paradise, it was those few minutes that

that man made his banjo talk with tunes sweet enough for Elysium." I hesitated and the dramatist picked up the thread of conversation.

"I'll admit there is something in the Negro nature which bears the stamp of the real stuff, but it cannot be developed," said my company.

We ended our conversation when he was summoned to his cottage where some magazine owners had gathered to make him offers for his impressions in Mexico.

I mentioned the above incident at length because it was the best expression of white people's view of Colored people that it has ever been my good fortune to hear. He was fair and spoke candidly what he really believed.

I said above if I am the winner in my struggle with death, I would strive to do some worthy service. In the first place I would secure several competent teachers in every angle of theatrical life,—dancing, music, writing, management, etc., and solicit students who would be willing to give two years of concentrated and diligent study to theatricals. At the end of that time I am certain I would have around me a set of actors and actresses that would be a credit to any race.

Furthermore, I would start a big advertising campaign with the object in view of hounding the cheap, coarse, wild music that is being fed to the race, out of existence. Why the white people associate such music with the islanders of the South Pacific. And the dancing, it is reproachful! Those break-down, inconsistent distortions of the body are the most shocking things I have witnessed. Whoever possesses the creative genius in this line must have taken lessons from monkeys.

I would also attempt to organize race opinion against this "monkey shine" business which so many Colored shows produce.

I must close for this time but as announced in the previous issue, I am writing some memoirs for my race and when completed, will place a part of them, at least, at your disposal.

Dear reader, do not misconstrue my cutting remarks for I feel that my days are too few to arouse any one's anger against me. I am merely giving my impressions in order that the bright spots of my race's theatrical life may be made brighter and more light shed on the obstructions which are keeping us from bequeathing to the world's history, Colored theatrical artists of whom any one would be proud.

Hoping I am still in the good graces of all, and with best wishes for your success, I am

Sincerely yours,

The Ex-White Actress.

[The Half-century Magazine (Chicago), August 1919, pp.16, 19.]

The Truth about *Hallelujah* (1930)[1]

Eva Jessye

The players in *Hallelujah* worked under many disadvantages on the Metro lot. In the first place, it was a long time before we received dressing rooms, and the stars never received the consideration that they deserved.

Many days we were called out to work and had no place to go to await the call. All projection rooms and sets were filled, and we stood around for hours like lost sheep.

The Dixie Jubilee Singers were required to sing the opening chorus for the big special, *The Hollywood Revue*, working all night and doing a mighty fine job of the singing.[2] Promised pay for it by the casting office and later refused by the executives. This had no connection with our *Hallelujah* contract—just another advantage taken. They are not given credit on the screen for this contribution, it being attributed to "The Hollywood Ensemble."

Eddie Connors was called upon to do a bit in a short, received no pay for it. One of the singers was called out to the lot one day to play the piano so Nina Mae might rehearse.[3] Now they had been paying outside piano players to rehearse the leading lady, and paying them well. But the idea struck them that money could be saved by demanding this extra service within the group. The boy refused to do it without pay, and was promptly fired by "Red" Golden, assistant director. I put the matter before Mr. Vidor and he, seeing the importance of every voice, reinstated him.[4]

When I approached Golden about the matter, he refused to consider further, raging in altogether more fury than the episode called for and finally blurted out, "Well, you know what that guy had the impertinence to say? He said he wouldn't do it, and no WHITE man will talk to ME that way." Of course he wanted to add, "Much less a 'nigger'," and his expression did say it.

Well, Golden hailed from Georgia and all through his connection with the group demonstrated an utter lack of respect for Negroes, a coarseness and familiarity that were disgusting in the extreme.

It was heartrending to see the leading characters, after a gruelling day's work, having to pull up on the bus and street car, no conveyances for them, and the studio lot full of cars. There were days when Haynes and Nina were ready to collapse, yet had to get home the best way they could or spend the money for a taxi out of their meager salary.[5] It was a shame.

Of course, we ordinary singers and assistants did no exhausting work and no such heavy demands were made on our nerve supply, but we resented such neglect of the others. Had they been receiving salaries that permitted such an expenditure, nothing would have been thought of it: but when [you?—illeg.] remember that directors are given expenses for bringing out a production [within?—illeg.] the allowance, it makes your blood boil with indignation.

Once there was a tacit understanding between Vidor and cast that there was to be whole-hearted co-operation in the making of *Hallelujah*, a co-operation far beyond

Fig. 5.12 Eva Jessye (second from left) with members of her choir in 1929.

that called for from any other cast in any other production, we expected response from him in the same measure that we gave our sincere co-operation.

There was no kindly word or card of greeting to the cast at Christmas time. There was no final statement of appreciation when the cast was discharged. They were dropped like one drops a sponge after squeezing it dry. The cast was sent home on tourist tickets and with the minimum allowance for meals. I think one or two of the stars refused to accept the tourist fare and thus secured first class accommodations.

Although in all publicity the matter of singing in the picture was stressed, and although it played an outstanding part in the picture, the singers were not mentioned in the cast when it was run off at the Metro projection room. Therefore I was receiving no credit whatever for my part in composing much of the music, arranging the spirituals, as director of the now famous Dixie Jubilee Singers, or my service in directing all synchronised singing, timing and vocal sequences, etc., for which ability I had been engaged by contract.

King Vidor evaded the issue, and Wanda Tuchok informed me that since [it was?—illeg.] not stated in the contract that credit was to be given for the music, I could not hope to successfully demand recognition. But I knew that the principle of Metro–Goldwyn–Mayer is to do the fair thing if it be presented and I carried the matter to Mr. Cohen, one of the executives. Recognition was given the Dixie Jubilee Singers on the screen immediately.

Also, I might add that Metro–Goldwyn was square enough, upon my solicitation, to grant the singers a raise in salary early after their arrival on the lot. This deviation from their contracts was made in appreciation of their unstinted service and co-operative spirit, also in the realization that the salaries they were receiving were inadequate for their upkeep.

In the first matter there was no other course for the company to take in the recognition of our services, so perhaps it should not be mentioned as generosity, but in the latter case it was a marked departure from an iron-clad rule, and the singers deeply appreciated the consideration.

I wish to state that no hurt is intended to any individual by this article. It is sincerely hoped that it will do some good to all concerned, and serve as a warning to all Negroes who have the opportunity to go into moving pictures. There is one thing that I wish to stress, something that the *Hallelujah* cast will readily understand.

Always, fellow actor, keep your dignity in your dealings with your white associates or superiors. Don't get familiar. The old saying that "familiarity breeds contempt" was never more true. He will laugh and joke with you until you are off your guard. [When?—*illeg.*] he gets a change of heart and doesn't feel inclined to play, what are you going to do? A straw shows which way the wind blows and a chance word or phrase should put you on the alert.

Be sure of your knowledge and [ability?—*illeg.*] and give them just valuation. Take nothing for granted. Whatever you should have, see that it is put on paper. Give nothing away. If you are hired to sing, sing and don't be dancing around to entertain the crowd. First thing you know they will demand you to dance also and you won't want to do it unless you are paid. They will resent the inconsistency and you will hit the walk.

That is what happened to our bass singer. He had been playing the piano every day on the set, entertaining. But when they had use for his ability and called on him he balked. Of course he was right, in a way, but he HAD been playing for nothing, so they couldn't see the sudden importance. And they were right, too.

If things go wrong, or you think they are wrong, don't stand around complaining and gumming the works. Go to the proper parties and state your grievance, which is a man's way of doing things. Whatever the troubles or indignities heaped upon you, there is never any excuse or justification for a poor performance. Remember that.

The biggest thing in the world is your work. It is bigger than your feelings, the director, and the whole shootin' match. Be patient with the director's moods. The birth of an idea is sometimes exceedingly painful and there's no telling when he is trying to figure something out.

You will find it hard to refrain from giving suggestions when they are not asked for. Find out what type of man he is before offering any idea you may have. If he is vain, superficial, newly-arrived, or a trifle unsteady on his directorial feet, he will resent it. Or if he does accept it, will do so surreptitiously as if too stubborn or ashamed to acknowledge your contribution. You will be surprised at finding such littleness among men who should be above any kind of fear or jealousy, but when you should be surprised is when you discover a big man among them.

I have heard it said by experienced executives and officials that directors are as a rule a painful lot—know too much to be told anything about anything under the sun. In the director ranks broad men are rare as in other professions. What they should remember is, that only the short man fears to bend over, and pretends to be taller than he is. The man who towers above the common herd stoops with a smile of assurance, for he knows that the world is aware that he has but to lift his head to gaze down upon the pigmies about his feet.

We both suffered and profited in the making of *Hallelujah*. There was not much hallelujah in it for the cast, but they learned a great deal they could have learned no other way. It is to be hoped that motion picture companies will consider carefully the man who is appointed to direct a Negro aggregation—by all means he should be fair, human, and have respect for the sensitive race with which he has to deal.

[Baltimore *Afro-American*, 2 August 1930, p. 8.]

I Tried to Crash the Movies (1946)
Avenelle Harris

I suppose everybody in America, especially girls, dreams about the movies and Hollywood.

And the way the stars get discovered, it just sends shivers into a girl—Lana Turner was sipping a malted on a high stool.[1] Yes, it might even happen to you—except if you're colored!

Sure, there's Lena Horne—but only one Lena Horne.[2] Go through the names of all the directors, writers, blacksmiths, painters, carpenters, actors—the 28,000 people in the movie industry. You know how many Negroes you'll find? About 400! As far as they are concerned at the present moment, they work in the studios as maids, porters, butlers, cleanup men or play the same roles on the screen.

I know. I've been around Hollywood 20 of my 25 years and been in 18 movies—but it's always a dancer, extra, chorus girl. I've learned that as far as Negroes and star roles are concerned, it can't happen here.

I came to Hollywood when I was 5. The studios were still making silent pix, *Our Gang* stuff.[3]

I'm still not sure how it happened—one day I was a kid in St. Paul giving my mother a kick with keeping rhythm to a piano—then we decided I was going to be a movie star! We came to Hollywood and quick as a bunny I got wiggled into a Mack Sennett comedy as a little vamp.[4] Bless me! I played that part (the hardest acting I have ever done) for two years and made $125 a week.

You know the pressure they manufacture here. Hundreds of movie magazines. Glamour! Super-colossal! Everybody had a chance! A nobody today! Tomorrow your profile is caught by somebody as you walk the street! And sister, you're in.... That's the air I breathed as I grew up here.

I took all of the acting classes in public school, the glee club work, but I liked dancing best. Laurette Butler chuckled me under her wing, started to teach me really how to dance. The excitement grew and grew. I was going to be a movie gal, a movie queen!

At last I was old enough to "be seen" and did a week's work at the Paramount Theatre in the girlie line behind the Mills Brothers.[5] Then I got a singing job in the little White Horse Tavern, working 'till close to midnight all the time.

People encouraged me and I worked carefully, doing gymnastics to keep a good figure, stretching myself to meet the chorus girl's average height, brushing my hair a hundred strokes a night. Yeah, I followed all the tricks.... It meant more now because my mother had been a seamstress ever since we came to Los Angeles, in order that I could make the movies.

I moved into the Cotton Club chorus line, with a bit of singing in a few spots and then hit my first musical show, Sepia Bells of 1938, which went on tour to Mexico.[6]

Finally it came, it came! My first grown-up movie call, The Singing Kid, starring Al Jolson. About twenty of us gals were called for the Save Them Sinners number, if you remember. We were way in the background, but we were there!

The same studio gave us another call for a chorus line in New Faces of 1938. Once again we were background decoration. Then I got two breaks with Ronald Colman.[7] I was an Algerian slave dancer in Kismet and I graced a pillar in The Light That Failed.

It was a funny thing, my young eyes were growing accustomed to the fact that there was a steady group of gals the studios called whenever they wanted colored extras, chorus cuties, or dancers. But some of us, because our skin was too black or even brown, were called very rarely. And others got the same treatment because they were too light-skinned! When these gals did go before the camera they were ordered to 'color down' one or two whole tones!

Take Alice Keyes who is one of the most beautiful and personable colored gals in the entertainment business. She's got great talent. But Alice has red hair and light features... she's just out, that's all, hasn't a chance.

Then too, many times the studios took jobs that were rightly ours and gave them to white girls. Katherine Dunham, you know the dancer?—was hired by Universal Studios to teach white chorines how to be South Sea Island babes![8] So Dunham spent two months working, even though her group of colored dancers knew the authentic routines and were the exact color wanted. No—the studio put wigs and body leg makeup on the white girls simply because they didn't want to use Negroes....

A major studio dickered for the screen rights to The Street, the fine story of Harlem by Ann Petry.[9] But here was the condition—that the Negroes all be changed to Spaniards, Swedish, or Italian people! And that's not a joke, son!

In the main, because we had only been doing maid and porter and chorus work before the war, we were hardest hit by Hollywood going war-conscious. The studios cut budgets, (out go the chorines), concentrated on war ideas that automatically excluded butlers and porters. I guess it would be too ridiculous even for the movies, to have a butler follow his employer through the war.

I didn't stay ignorant of the reasons. Did you know that 30 per cent of the movie houses are in the South?[10] Well, that's all brother. [...].

When Lena Horne got picked up singing at the Little Trocadero out here and inked a contract at MGM, I shouted for joy.

Old Charley Butler who handles all Negro movie calls for Central Casting picked up the rumor that Metro was going to ink about ten of us to studio deals to back Lena's singing. You see, every major studio has some white cuties on contract. So... we were excited, on edge. Sure enough, we got called for Lena's first, Cabin In The Sky, but although Arthur Freed, Lena's producer, was more than cooperative, there was only talk, talk, talk, and there are still no Negroes on contract as extras.

But we came back for all of Lena's work. I was her stand-in for awhile, so was Juliette Ball, so was Artie Young, another one of the "hounds" that kept up the fight. We danced or looked nice or did both in Stormy Weather, but it became bitterly clear that all Lena was ever going to do was sing, do spot numbers. And pretty soon they just used classy drapes as background, and that, girls, was the end of that dream!

The system is just changing but do you see how vicious and unfair it is? The studios only want us to play Negroes with a capital N but we could play any number of roles depending on how we photograph, light, dark, or whatnot. The camera doesn't have a white man's eye! Why with a little makeup I could do a French barmaid or an Italian street girl or even a Southern belle![...]

The NAACP, and some of the Negro press, are trying to force the studios to give us colored a better break. Not especially we who work, but in the writing, the characters we portray. It isn't important that I do more work standing in front of a pillar but it is important that there are parts written about Negro pilots, engineers, or just plain ordinary people! Our life is as rich, our problems as important, and our music and comedy as good, if not in many instances, a lot better than the trash they put before a camera many times!

Oh-yes... some people, colored, are starting all-Negro films. But I think this is just as bad as all-white films.... This country is a mixture, isn't it?

The movies are a big business. They're very sensitive to the B.O. (that's box office). If people could be organized to protest to the movie house managers, to write to the studios protesting or demanding certain changes, if they'd boycott certain films to show their displeasure—ah, then there'd be some changes made, yes sirree!

Before the war there were about 300 of us paying dues regularly to the Screen Actors or Screen Extras Guild. Now—there are less than half that number left. The simple fact is there hasn't been one call from a studio for any Negro dancers or singers in over two years! How can you keep trying in a dead silence? [...]

[Ebony (Chicago) 1, August 1946, pp. 5–10, excerpted.]

The Actress and Adventuress

"Sarah" Talks to Us About the Cinema (1914)
Interview with Sarah Bernhardt

It was one of the last evenings, after a matinée in which the great tragedienne had played *La dame aux camélias* to perfection yet again. We talked about Antoine's resignation and the candidates to replace him as director of the Odéon.[1] Madame Sarah Bernhardt indignantly condemned the indifference of the public, who had for seven years come to see the efforts of the founder of the Théâtre Libre without ever assisting him, and who were now letting him leave the stage where he had produced such beautiful plays without offering him the least help.

Someone says, smiling, "A movie producer is offering his services to direct the Odéon."

Mrs. Bernhardt smiles too, and then adds in a more serious tone, "France is losing its taste for the theater! But I am not one of those for whom the progress of cinema is a cause for this turn. The theater and the cinema offer such different kinds of entertainment that it's impossible that the popularity of one impedes the development or success of the other. The two can very easily live side by side, and here's the proof: I remember that, in a recent tour I made in America with *La dame aux camélias*, our troupe was followed by a cinema company.[2] Everywhere I stopped, and frequently in a theater right next door to where I was playing, the movie version of *La dame aux camélias* was also showing. It so happened that the posters for the two events were sometimes put up right next to each other. However, every night both theaters were full—but in the one you paid only fifteen or twenty sous while in the other it cost fifteen or twenty francs.

"Furthermore, isn't it natural that the cinema appeals to the public? It offers, for a modest price, pictures that are often very beautiful. It demands no intellectual effort of its spectator. It seduces him with strange or picturesque images. It entertains. It instructs. Thanks to the cinema, we're now acquainted with landscapes we never could have seen otherwise. It shows the natural behavior of wild animals. It makes it possible for us to witness scenes of life of the most exotic and extraordinary kinds. And lastly, it can record historical events—kings' processions, battle preparations. It provides a varied documentation, always precise, accurate and infinitely repeatable.

"Now you see that I'm not an enemy of the cinema and that I even give it more credit than it perhaps deserves. I'm less enthusiastic about cinema that tries to imitate the theater and reproduce famous plays. For this sort of thing, I find cinema frankly inferior.

"Have you noticed how it works? The décor never gets bigger along with the actor. At first, actors appear in proportion with the frame that surrounds them; then, as the action proceeds, they find themselves propelled into the foreground. They become enormous, while the objects around them keep their original dimensions. The actor soon dominates the décor, he reaches the borders of the screen, he outgrows them. You only see him. Theatrical verisimilitude is lost.

"The same goes for the art of the actor. Stage acting comprises numerous elements: pronunciation, intonation, voice, gestures, movements. The cinema uses only gestures. How could it ever give a really complete and artistic impression? It's already quite difficult to act and to bring out all that is in a text using all of the elements of dramatic art. But to reduce them to one is to condemn oneself to a mediocre result.

"As for me, I've played in a number of films, among them *La dame aux camélias*, an act of *Hamlet*, *Adrienne Lecouvreur*.[3]

"I thought that they would offer me the filming of other plays that belong to my repertoire, like *L'Aiglon*, *La Samaritaine* and *La princesse lointaine*.[4] I was surprised to learn that they had already given up the rights, and that *L'Aiglon* will appear very soon.[5]

"How do I act in films? It's simple. I act exactly as I do on the stage. I say the text of the play without leaving out a single word. I don't exaggerate the gestures. I merely do what I usually do. It would be impossible to act otherwise, since, for me, there's only one way to make a character come alive.

"I shot the act of Hamlet's death in 1900, during the Universal Exposition. So it was at the very beginnings of cinema. It has advanced much since then. Nevertheless, it seems to me, from a theatrical point of view, that it remains a far cry from dramatic beauty and grandeur.

"I don't doubt, however, that certain pantomimes, with uncomplicated action, as well as certain sketches, can provide comic or tragic spectacles capable of arousing emotions. I understand that certain playwrights now work for the cinema. But they have to push themselves in a totally different direction than that of the theater. Cinematic pantomime has its laws. I believe that artists can derive interesting effects from it.

"The same goes for actors. But it's a very delicate question. I'd say, though, that it would seem damaging to me for a good actor to take screen roles too often. I'll speak first of all as a theatrical director. Do you know what time one shoots? Film directors summon their subjects at six in the morning. They make them work hard and long hours. That's how the morning goes. And then the actor, hardly having had the time to eat lunch, runs off to his theater for rehearsal. He arrives feverish, tired. When he's played the night before and gone to bed late—which is often the case—he's falling over with fatigue. He rehearses badly, and everyone suffers from it: the actor, the director, and the other actors.

"But that's a rather personal point of view. More generally, I believe that a talented artist wastes his gifts in the cinema. I'm saying this, I'm only thinking of real, professional artists, for whom the theater represents an ideal and who are devoted to their art like priests to their god. For the others, who aren't of the faith, the dangers are less.

"I think that the division from the serious artists of the theater will soon occur naturally: between those possessed by the demon of the boards, and those, also very respected, who work as readily in theater or cinema. There are already actors who specialize in film, and they're sure to grow in numbers. They'll push this specialized craft to the point of perfection that only the celebrated few reach now. And everything will work out for the better, for both the stage and the screen.

"Besides, I'm wrong to malign the cinema. Isn't it thanks to the cinema that so many artists can live almost grandly? The theater pays little. The cinema pays nice wages. To forget its generosity would be ingratitude."

Madame Sarah Berhardt has talked to us about the cinema with her burning passion, with that vibrant eloquence that she brings to the art that she has made famous. Her fair and profound criticisms clarify certain points that need to be further studied in this new art form. Her predictions open up a wide field.

[Jean Levèque, "En Ecoutant 'Sarah' Parler du Cinéma," Le Journal (Paris), 17 April 1914, p. 7, translated by Andrew Broan.]

My Film Debut (1919)
Resi Langer

"Hopping from branch to branch, the squirrel searches laboriously for his meal." I had to take these words to heart in relation to my own life when I found myself standing among the props and dazzling light of a film studio.

Oh, how many "hopes" had passed over me, like doves of happiness bearing their green olive branches. The "world-renowned boards"[1] had been a bundle of firewood to me—the "boards" had bounced too wickedly for my rubbery frame. But now the screen winked promisingly at me: here is fame!

And I was once again ready to believe.

My voice, which was supposedly too small for the stage, would here be entirely eliminated—it would be no barrier to success. And singing, which isn't my forte either, also wasn't required. Here everything was to be done plastically—mimicry, gestures, poses. That's got to be easy, I reassured myself. That's silent, fine work! Sure—my foot!

During the first rehearsal, I already noticed that it's not as easy as it seems at night on the silver screen. And I had to agree with the director when he said that I didn't walk like a human being, but rather hopped like a sparrow. I would have to think about it, and "walk flatly," if I didn't want to resemble a seismographic line, because the lens would render only eighteen of my movements a second. I was prepared to accept that, and paid attention from then on to the "flatness" of my steps; but then my arms, which I moved too rashly, emerged as a new stumbling block to my budding career. Oh, God! So I moved my arm in a "dignified" manner, nearly "pastoral," full of form, and forgot in the process that I also had a face that had to match the legs and arms! It was really hard!

Here I saw for the first time how little actual gesture is required of stage actors and how much more is required of film actors. It takes an immense amount of expressive ability to arrange the face in telling lines, and to work with it so that it looks like a "physical study" and not a "silly grimace" on screen. Regretfully, during my many visits to the movies I have noticed that the audience has broken out in gales of laughter at the most serious moments. Most of the time this response was in fact caused by the actor's unusual, humorous facial expression, whose intended seriousness appeared on screen like a deliberately bad joke. Anyway, because fame beckoned from the screen, I did my best. Still, the director was not completely satisfied. I managed to console myself with the expectation that my success would come with practice; one needs as much practice in film as on the stage.

Extremely tired and rather depressed, I made my way out of the studio on the afternoon of this eventful day and down onto the street. The good advice of the director stayed with me, and I feverishly internalized it as I incessantly thought about "walking flatly." I didn't notice anyone turning around to look at me, and attributed it already perhaps to imminent fame. Crossing the road, I wanted to flag the approaching chauffeur with my prettiest "film arm movements," so as to indicate which side of the street I was headed for, when I got a powerful blast from a cyclist coming up behind, which forced me quickly onto the sidewalk. Both their curses followed me, but they faded from my ears, like noise behind a window pane.

Finally, I reached our regular café where my friends and acquaintances were already expectantly awaiting me, wanting to hear news of my experiences as a film diva. I saw them whispering, and sink back astonished as I approached, slowly and "flatly." When I didn't speak, but only nodded my head and offered them my hand with an "aristocratic" gesture, some made wide eyes, others laughed. Softly, from the far end of the table, the comment "She's cracked!" reached my ear. I finally came to my senses and recovered my voice. "No, you, you don't see that this is part of my new profession: 'walking flatly,' 'noble poses,' and 'remaining silent,' you stupid cattle!!'" Putting up with my well-meaning epithet, they swarmed about me like hornets, grilling me about film. I recovered my bourgeois equilibrium eating *Wiener Schnitzel*, and now look confidently into the future. The silver screen, whether lying in the closet, or acting as a projection surface, is absolutely the pride and joy of the German woman.

["Mein Filmdebut," *Kinotypen vor und hinter den Filmkulissen (Zwölf Kapitel aus der Kinderstube des Films)* (Hanover: Der Zweemann Verlag, 1919), pp. 56–60; translated by Patti Duquette, with the assistance of Christine Haas and Sarah Hall.]

The Pictures (1918)
Katherine Mansfield

Eight o'clock in the morning. Miss Ada Moss lay in a black iron bedstead, staring up at the ceiling. Her room, a Bloomsbury top-floor back, smelled of soot and face powder and the paper of fried potatoes she brought in for supper the night before.

"Oh, dear," thought Miss Moss, "I am cold. I wonder why it is that I always wake up so cold in the mornings now. My knees and feet and my back—especially my back; it's like a sheet of ice. And I always was such a one for being warm in the old days. It's not as if I was skinny—I'm just the same full figure that I used to be. No, it's because I don't have a good hot dinner in the evenings."

A pageant of Good Hot Dinners passed across the ceiling, each of them accompanied by a bottle of Nourishing Stout ...

"Even if I were to get up now," she thought, "and have a sensible substantial breakfast ... " A pageant of Sensible Substantial Breakfasts followed the dinners across the ceiling, shepherded by an enormous, white, uncut ham. Miss Moss shuddered and disappeared under the bedclothes. Suddenly, in bounced the landlady.

"There's a letter for you, Miss Moss."

"Oh," said Miss Moss, far too friendly, "thank you very much, Mrs. Pine. Its very good of you, I'm sure, to take the trouble."

"No trouble at all," said the landlady. "I thought perhaps it was the letter you'd been expecting."

"Why," said Miss Moss, brightly, "yes, perhaps it is." She put her head on one side and smiled vaguely at the letter. "I shouldn't be surprised."

The landlady's eyes popped. "Well, I should, Miss Moss," said she, "and that's how it is. And I'll trouble you to open it, if you please. Many is the lady in my place as would have done it for you and have been within her rights. For things can't go on like this, Miss Moss, no indeed they can't. What with week in week out and first you've got it and then you haven't, and then it's another letter lost in the post or another manager down at Brighton but will be back on Tuesday for certain—I'm fair sick and tired and I won't stand it no more. Why should I, Miss Moss, I ask you, at a time like this, with prices flying up in the air and my poor dear lad in France?

"My sister Eliza was only saying to me yesterday—Minnie, she says, you're too soft-hearted. You could have let that room time and time again, says she, and if people won't look after themselves in times like these, nobody else will, she says. She may have had a College eddication and sung in West End concerts, says she, but if your Lizzie says what's true, she says, and she's washing her own wovens and drying them on the towel rail, it's easy to see where the finger's pointing. And its high time you had done with it, says she." Miss Moss gave no sign of having heard this. She sat up in bed, tore open her letter and read:

Dear Madam,

Yours to hand. Am not producing at present, but have filed photo for future ref.
Yours truly,

BACKWASH FILM CO.

This letter seemed to afford her peculiar satisfaction; she read it through twice before replying to the landlady.

"Well, Mrs. Pine, I think you'll be sorry for what you said. This is from a manager, asking me to be there with evening dress at ten o'clock next Saturday morning."

But the landlady was too quick for her. She pounced, secured the letter.

"Oh, is it! Is it indeed!" she cried.

"Give me back that letter. Give it back to me at once, you bad, wicked woman," cried Miss Moss, who could not get out of bed because her nightdress was slit down the back. "Give me back my private letter." The landlady began slowly backing out of the room, holding the letter to her buttoned bodice.

"So it's come to this, has it?" said she. "Well, Miss Moss, if I don't get my rent at eight o'clock to-night, we'll see who's a bad wicked woman—that's all." Here she nodded mysteriously. "And I'll keep this letter." Here her voice rose. "It will be a pretty little bit of evidence!" And here it fell, sepulchral, "My lady."

The door banged and Miss Moss was alone. She flung off the bedclothes, and sitting by the side of the bed, furious and shivering, she stared at her fat white legs with their great knots of greeny-blue veins.

"Cockroach! That's what she is. She's a cockroach!" said Miss Moss. "I could have her up for snatching my letter—I'm sure I could." Still keeping on her nightdress she began to drag on her clothes.

"Oh, if I could only pay that woman, I'd give her a piece of my mind that she wouldn't forget. I'd tell her off proper." She went over to the chest of drawers for a safety-pin, and seeing herself in the glass she gave a vague smile and shook her head. "Well, old girl," she murmured, "you're up against it this time, and no mistake." But the person in the glass made an ugly face at her.

"You silly thing," scolded Miss Moss. "Now what's the good of crying: you'll only make your nose red. No, you get dressed and go out and try your luck—that's what you've got to do."

She unhooked her vanity bag from the bed post, rooted in it, shook it, turned it inside out.

"I'll have a nice cup of tea at an ABC to settle me before I go anywhere," she decided. "I've got one and thrippence—yes, just one and three."

Ten minutes later, a stout lady in blue serge, with a bunch of artificial "parmas" at her bosom, a black hat covered with purple pansies, white gloves, boots with white uppers, and a vanity bag containing one and three, sang in a low contralto voice:

Sweet-heart, remember when days are forlorn
It al-ways is dar-kest before the dawn.

But the person in the glass made a face at her, and Miss Moss went out. There were grey crabs all the way down the street slopping water over grey stone steps. With his strange, hawking cry and the jangle of the cans the milk boy went his rounds. Outside Brittweiler's Swiss House he made a splash, and an old brown cat without a tail appeared from nowhere, and began greedily and silently drinking up the spill. It gave Miss Moss a queer feeling to watch—a sinking, as you might say.

But when she came to the ABC she found the door propped open; a man went in and out carrying trays of rolls, and there was nobody inside except a waitress doing her hair and the cashier unlocking the cash-boxes. She stood in the middle of the floor but neither of them saw her.

"My boy came home last night," sang the waitress.

"Oh, I say—how topping for you!" gurgled the cashier.

"Yes, wasn't it," sang the waitress. "He bought me a sweet little brooch. Look, it's got 'Dieppe' written on it."

The cashier ran across to look and put her arm round the waitress' neck.

"Oh, I say—how topping for you."

"Yes, isn't it," said the waitress. "O-oh, he is brahn. 'Hullo,' I said, 'hullo, old mahogany'."

"Oh, I say," gurgled the cashier, running back into her cage and nearly bumping into Miss Moss on the way. "You are a treat!"

Then the man with the rolls came in again, swerving past her.

"Can I have a cup of tea, Miss?" she asked.

But the waitress went on doing her hair. "Oh," she sang, "we're not open yet." She turned round and waved her comb at the cashier.

"Are we dear?"

"Oh, no," said the cashier. Miss Moss went out.

"I'll go to Charing Cross. Yes, that's what I'll do," she decided. "But I won't have a cup of tea. No, I'll have a coffee. There's more of a tonic in coffee ... Cheeky, those girls are! Her boy came home last night; he brought her a brooch with 'Dieppe' written on it." She began to cross the road ...

"Look out, Fattie; don't go to sleep!" yelled a taxi driver. She pretended not to hear.

"No, I won't go to Charing Cross," she decided. "I'll go straight to Kig and Kadgit. They're open at nine. If I get there early Mr. Kadgit may have something by the morning's post ... I'm very glad you turned up so early, Miss Moss. I've just heard from a manager who wants a lady to play ... I think you'll just suit him. I'll give you a card to go and see him. It's three pounds a week and all found. If I were you I'd hop round as fast as I could. Lucky you turned up so early..."

But there was nobody at Kig and Kadgit's except the charwoman wiping over the "lino" in the passage.

"Nobody here yet, Miss," said the char.

"Oh, isn't Mr. Kadgit here?" said Miss Moss, trying to dodge the pail and brush. "Well, I'll just wait a moment, if I may."

"You can't wait in the waiting room, Miss. I 'aven't done it yet. Mr. Kadgit's never 'ere before 'leven-thirty Saturdays. Sometimes 'e don't come at all." And the char began crawling towards her.

"Dear me—how silly of me." said Miss Moss. "I forgot it was Saturday."

"Mind your feet, *please*, Miss," said the char. And Miss Moss was outside again.

That was one thing about Beit and Bithems; it was lively. You walked into the waiting-room, into a great buzz of conversation, and there was everybody; you knew almost everybody. The early ones sat on chairs and later ones sat on the early ones' laps, while the gentlemen leaned negligently against the walls or preened themselves in front of the admiring ladies.

"Hello," said Miss Moss, very gay. "Here we are again!"

And young Mr. Clayton, playing the banjo on his walking-stick, sang: "Waiting for the Robert E. Lee."

"Mr. Bithem here yet?" asked Miss Moss, taking out an old dead powder puff and powdering her nose mauve.

"Oh, yes, dear," cried the chorus. "He's been here for ages. We've all been waiting here for more than an hour."

"Dear me!" said Miss Moss. "Anything doing, do you think?"

"Oh, a few jobs going for South Africa," said young Mr. Clayton.

"Hundred and fifty a week for two years, you know."

"Oh!" cried the chorus. You *are* weird, Mr. Clayton. Isn't he a cure? Isn't he a *scream*, dear? Oh, Mr. Clayton, you do make me laugh. Isn't he a *comic*?"

A dark, mournful girl touched Miss Moss on the arm.

"I just missed a lovely job yesterday," she said. "Six weeks in the provinces and then the West End. The Manager said I would have got it for certain if only I'd been robust enough. He said if my figure had been fuller, the part was made for me." She stared at Miss Moss, and the dirty dark red rose under the brim of her hat looked, somehow, as through it shared the blow with her, and was crushed, too.

"Oh dear, that was hard lines," said Miss Moss trying to appear indifferent. "What was it—if I may ask?"

But the dark mournful girl saw through her and a gleam of spite came into her heavy eyes.

"Oh, no good to you, my dear," said she. "He wanted someone young, you know—a dark Spanish type—my style, but more figure, that was all."

The inner door opened and Mr. Bithem appeared in his shirt sleeves. He kept one hand on the door ready to whisk back again, and held up the other.

"Look here, ladies—" and then he paused, grinned his famous grin before he said—"*and bhoys*." The waiting room laughed so loudly at this that he had to hold both hands up. "It's no good waiting this morning. Come back Monday; I'm expecting several calls on Monday."

Miss Moss made a desperate rush forward. "Mr. Bithem, I wonder if you've heard from ... ."

"Now let me see," said Mr. Bithem slowly, staring; he had only seen Miss Moss four times a week for the past—how many weeks?

"Now, who are you?"

"Miss Ada Moss."

"Oh, yes, yes; of course, my dear. Not yet, my dear. Now I had a call for twenty-eight ladies to-day, but they had to be young and able to hop it a bit—see? And I had another call for sixteen—but they had to know something about sand-dancing. Look here, my dear, I'm up to the eyebrows this morning. Come back on Monday week; it's no good coming before that." He gave here a whole grin to herself and patted her fat back. "Hearts of oak, dear lady," said Mr.Bithem, "hearts of oak!"

At the North-East Film Company the crowd was all the way up the stairs. Miss Moss found herself next to a fair little baby thing about thirty in a white lace hat with cherries round it.

"What a crowd!" said she. "Anything special on?"

"Didn't you know, dear?" said the baby, opening her immense pale eyes. "There was a call at nine-thirty for *attractive* girls. We've all been waiting for *hours*. Have you played for this company before?" Miss Moss put her head on one side. "No, I don't think I have."

"They're a lovely company to play for," said the baby. "A friend of mine has a friend who gets thirty pounds a day .... Have you *arcted* much for the fil-lums?"

"Well, I'm not an actress by profession," confessed Miss Moss. "I'm a contralto singer. But things have been so bad lately that I've been doing a little."

"It's like that, isn't it, dear," said the baby.

"I had a splendid education at the College of Music," said Miss Moss, "and I got my silver medal for singing. I've often sung at West End concerts. But I thought, for a change, I'd try my luck..."

"Yes, it's like that, isn't it, dear?" said the baby.

At that moment a beautiful typist appeared at the top of the stairs.

"Are you all waiting for the North-East call?"

"Yes!" cried the chorus.

"Well, it's off. I've just had a phone through."

"But look here! What about our expenses?" shouted a voice.

The typist looked down at them, and she couldn't help laughing.

"Oh, you weren't to have been *paid*. The North-East never *pay* their crowds."

There was only a little round window at the Bitter Orange Company. No waiting room—nobody at all except a girl, who came to the window when Miss Moss knocked, and said: "Well?"

"Can I see the producer, please," said Miss Moss, pleasantly. The girl leaned on the window-bar, half shut her eyes and seemed to go to sleep for a moment. Miss Moss smiled at her. The girl not only frowned; she seemed to smell something vaguely unpleasant; she sniffed. Suddenly she moved away, came back with a paper and thrust it at Miss Moss.

"Fill up the form!" said she. And banged the window down.

"Can you aviate—high-dive—drive a car—buck-jump—shoot?" read Miss Moss. She walked along the street asking herself those questions. There was a high, cold wind blowing; it tugged at her, slapped her face, jeered; it knew she could not answer them. In the Square Gardens she found a little wire basket to drop the form into. And then she sat down on one of the benches to powder her nose. But the person in the pocket mirror made a hideous face at her, and that was too much for Miss Moss; she had a good cry. It cheered her wonderfully.

"Well, that's over," she sighed. "It's one comfort to be off my feet. And my nose will soon get cool in the air ... It's very nice in here. Look at the sparrows. Cheep. Cheep. How close they come. I expect somebody feeds them. No, I've nothing for you, you cheeky little things..." She looked away from them. What was the big building opposite—the Café de Madrid. My goodness, what a smack that little child came down! Poor little mite. Never mind—up again... By eight o'clock to-night... Café de Madrid. "I could just go in and sit there and have a coffee, that's all," thought Miss Moss. "It's such a place for artists too. I might just have a stroke of luck... A dark handsome gentleman in a fur coat comes in with a friend, and sits at my table, perhaps. 'No, old chap, I've searched London for a contralto and I can't find a soul. You see, the music is difficult; have a look at it.'" And Miss Moss heard herself saying: "Excuse me, I happen to be a contralto, and I have sung that part many times... Extraordinary! 'Come back to my studio and I'll try your voice now.'... Ten pounds a week... Why should I feel nervous? It's not nervousness. Why shouldn't I go to the Café de Madrid? I'm a respectable woman—I'm a contralto singer. And I'm only trembling because I've had nothing to eat to-day....'A nice little piece of evidence, my lady'... Very well, Mrs. Pine. Café de Madrid. They have concerts there in the evenings... 'Why don't they begin?' The contralto has not arrived... Excuse me, I happen to be a contralto; I have sung that music many times."

It was almost dark in the café. Men, palms, red plush seats, white marble tables, waiters in aprons, Miss Moss walked through them all. Hardly had she sat down when a very stout gentleman wearing a very small hat that floated on the top of his head like a little yacht flopped into the chair opposite hers.

"Good evening!" said he.

Miss Moss said, in her cheerful way: "Good evening!"

"Fine evening," said the stout gentleman.

"Yes, very fine. Quite a treat, isn't it?" said she.

He crooked a sausage finger at the waiter—"Bring me a large whiskey"—and turned to Miss Moss. "What's yours?"

"Well, I think I'll take a brandy if it's all the same."

Five minutes later the stout gentleman leaned across the table and blew a puff of cigar smoke full in her face.

"That's a tempting bit o' ribbon!" said he.

Miss Moss blushed until a pulse at the top of her head that she never had felt before pounded away.

"I always was one for pink," said she.

The stout gentleman considered her, drumming with his fingers on the table.

"I like 'em firm and well covered," said he.

Miss Moss, to her surprise, gave a loud snigger.

Five minutes later the stout gentleman heaved himself up. "Well, am I goin' your way, or are you comin' mine?" he asked.

"I'll come with you, if it's all the same," said Miss Moss. And she sailed after the little yacht out of the café.

[*Art and Letters* (London), 2:1 (New Series), Winter 1918–19, pp. 153–62.]

Our Own Movie Queen (1925)[1]
Zelda Fitzgerald

The Mississippi River came carelessly down through the pine forests and phlegmatic villages of Minnesota to the city of New Heidelberg, for the express purpose of dividing the ladies and gentlemen of the town from their laundresses and their butchers and their charioteers of the ash can—who dwelt in sodden bad taste upon thither bank. On the high and fashionable side an avenue lined with well bred trees pushed itself out to where the river, by a series of dexterous swoops, brought the city to a tidy end.

On the low side there were huge chalk cliffs where the people grew mushrooms and made incompetent whisky, and there were cobblestone streets where casual water lay incessantly in dull little pools. Here, too, was the morgue, with its pale barred windows, and here were rows of sinister, dull red houses that no one was ever seen entering or leaving. Back further from the water were railroad yards and stockyards and the spot (mark it now with an X) where Gracie Axelrod lived—Gracie who backed into local publicity a short year since as "our movie queen." This is the story of her screen career, and of a picture the memory of which still causes bursts of crazy laughter, but which, alas, will never be shown again in this world.

Gracie's neighbors were fat Italians and cheerless Poles and Swedes who conducted themselves as though they were conversant with the Nordic theory.[2] Her father may or may not have been a Swede. He did not speak the language certainly, and his deplorable personal appearance cannot with justice be ascribed to any nationality. He was the sole owner of a tumbledown shanty where fried chicken of dubious antecedents might be washed down by cold beer, any time between ten o'clock at night and eight o'clock in the morning. Gracie fried the chicken with such brown art that complaints were unknown.

For seven months a year New Heidelberg was covered with sooty snow, and mere zero weather was considered a relief from the true cold: citizens were glad to get home at night and there was little inducement to linger late around the streets. But dances were given in the best hotel and even Gracie had heard tales about the gaiety of the dwellers on the upper river bank. She had seen them, too, arrive in closed automobiles and come shouting into the shanty at small hours, behaving as if it were a daring thing to do.

❧

Gracie was pretty, but too full blown for a girl of twenty. Her flaxen hair was a glorious smooth color, and would have been beautiful if she had not snarled it and brushed it out over her ears until the shape of her head was entirely distorted. Her skin was radiantly pale, her large blue eyes were faintly inclined to bulge. Her teeth were small and very white. There was a warm moist look about her, as if she had materialized out of hot milk vapor—and perhaps she had, for no one had ever seen or heard of her mother. Her whole appearance was as voluptuous as that of a burlesque show prima donna—that was the way Gracie felt about it anyhow, and if Mr. Ziegfeld (of whom she had never heard) had wired her to join his show, she would have been only faintly surprised.[3] She quietly expected great things to happen to her, and no doubt that's one of the reasons why they did.

Now on Gracie's side of the river Christmas eve was celebrated with no more display than the Dante centennial. But on the high bank where the snow lay along the fashionable avenue as if it had just been unwound from a monster bolt of cotton batting, every model home set out a tree adorned with electric bulbs. It was a gorgeous sight, and Gracie and her father always came every year and walked a few blocks in the icy cold. They compared each tree to the last one, and were scornful and superior toward the trees that had no stars on top.

Tonight was the fifth time that Gracie could remember having taken this walk, and as she bustled about after the excursion and filled the shack with greasy, pleasant smelling smoke, she discussed it thoroughly with her vague parent.

"Honest," she complained, "if people ain't going to have better trees than them, I don't see why they want to get you out on a cold night like this for. There was only one place that didn't look like somebody was dead in it."

The place to which she referred was a great white house adorned with stone animal heads and Greek friezes which tonight had had suspended proudly from its arched porte-cochere, a huge electric sign which wished the passers-by a Merry Christmas.

"Who lives there, daddy?" she asked abruptly.

"B'longs to the feller that owns the Blue Ribbon," elucidated Mr. Axelrod. "I guess he must be worth a good lot of money."

"Who says so?" demanded Gracie.

"O, some people told me," her father answered vaguely. He was propped up back of the stove, his hat shading his eyes as he read the evening pink sheet. Just at the moment the paper was open over his knees at a full page advertisement: the Blue Ribbon Department store wished every one a happy New Year, and hoped they would attend the sale of white goods immediately after the holidays.

Mr. Axelrod read the composition to his daughter. He always read her everything in the big type. They liked to hear each other's voices, and as Gracie was too busy with the chicken and her father with the reading to pay much attention to the content, it was a successful arrangement. To Mr. Axelrod reading in itself was enough and he would have enjoyed a Chinese newspaper just as much had the hieroglyphics aroused as familiar and soothing a sensation.

"He's a swell looking fella, too," Gracie remarked after a moment. "Every time I go in there I see him walking up and down the store. B'lieve me, I'd just as soon marry a man like that. Then you could just walk in the store and say gimme this or gimme that and you wouldn't have to pay nothing for 'em."

This was worth thinking about apparently, for Mr. Axelrod discontinued his reading, and looked Gracie over appraisingly.

In the long interval between the completion of the evening's preparation and the appearance of the first customer they speculated upon the advantages of being married to a man who owned a store like the Blue Ribbon. No wonder Gracie was as surprised and as disconcerted as if she had been caught breaking his huge plate glass window when Mr. Blue Ribbon himself walked into the shack, demanding, in a loud and supercilious voice, chicken that was all white meat.

❧

I say that this respectable gentleman walked in, but perhaps this is an understatement, for what he literally did was to reel in. And Gracie recognized the man she had seen walking up and down the Blue Ribbon's gorgeous aisles.

He was an officious little man, fat in spots and not unlike one of those bottom-heavy dolls which refuse to lie down. Tonight the illusion was increased, for he swayed faintly with no partiality as to direction, as though if some one removed the weights from his great round abdomen he would keel permanently over and never again stand on his own initiative. There was a small cranium, a large jaw, and two superhuman ears—a comic valentine of a man with a pig's head. But he was affable, and tonight he was obsessed with the idea of himself, not as a comic valentine, but as a person of importance.

He announced that he was celebrating, and asked at large if it were possible that Gracie and her father did not know him.

"I should say," answered Gracie reassuringly, "why, you own the Blue Ribbon. I always notice you around every time I go in there."

If Gracie had made this speech in full possession of the facts in the case, it would have indicated an extraordinary subtlety and tact. For Mr. Albert Pomeroy did not own the city's biggest and best department store. But from eight in the morning until six at night he owned the departments of which he was in charge—notions, perfumes, hosiery, gloves, umbrellas, dress goods, and men's wear. Gracie has flattered not only him but his position in life. He beamed. For a moment he stopped bobbing around and focused unblinking eyes on Gracie.

"Not exactly," he managed, resuming his teetering. "I don't exactly own it. I run it. Blue Ribbon's got the money and I got the brains." Mr. Pomeroy's voice rose to a sort of confidential shout and Gracie was impressed in spite of her disappointment.

"You any relation to him?" she asked curiously.

"Not exactly relation," explained Mr. Pomeroy, "but close—very, very close." He implied that they were in all but complete physical juxtaposition.

"Can you just go and say, 'This looks pretty good to me. I guess I'll take it,' and walk right out of the store with anything you want?"

She was now engrossed by the man himself. Her father was also listening intently.

"Not exactly," admitted Mr. Pomeroy. "I can't exactly take things, but I can get 'em for about twenty or twenty-five dollars less than the people who don't have the influence and don't work there."

"O, I see." Gracie enthusiastically handed a platter of chicken to her important customer. "I suppose that's why them girls work in there. I'd like to try it for awhile myself. I'd get what I wanted cheap and then quit."

Mr. Pomeroy's head waggled and his cheeks blew out, and he busied himself with his food.

"O, no, you wouldn't," he managed to say. "You wouldn't quit. You just say you'd quit." He waved a greasy drumstick in Gracie's face.

"How do you know I wouldn't quit, I'd like to know?" cried Gracie indignantly. "If I say I'm gonna quit, I'm gonna quit. I guess I can quit if I want to quit."

She became animated by the thought of quitting. She wanted passionately to quit, and doubtless would have done so immediately had there been anything to quit. Mr. Pomeroy, on his part, was incredulous toward the idea. It was inconceivable and beyond all reason to him that Gracie should quit.

"You just come down and see," he insisted. "Come down tomorrow and I'll give you a job. Just between you and me—our candidate's gonna win the Grand Popularity contest. Mr. Blue Ribbon says to me, 'Albert, old man, you pick out the girl and I'll make her the Grand Popularity queen.'"

❧

Now one of the news items which Gracie's father had habitually read aloud of late bore always the headline, "Our City's Queen." The reading matter which followed explained how the Blue Ribbon, our largest department store, together with the *New Heidelberg Tribune*, our city's foremost newspaper, and the Tick-tock Jewelry emporium, and a dozen other business establishments were going to give some lucky young woman the opportunity for which every girl has always longed. She would be selected from the whole city of New Heidelberg, would "lead" all the affairs which centered around the winter carnival and, last and best of all, would win a chance to distinguish herself in the movies.

"Who's your girl and how do you know she's gonna win?" Gracie demanded.

"Well, the folks from all the stores that's in on the thing each choose their own girl. Mr. Blue Ribbon, he says to me, 'Albert, the jane that represents this store wins the whole contest.' Everybody can't win, can they?"

Mr. Pomeroy was growing eloquent. He would probably have talked about himself through the waning night, but Gracie's interest was aroused in another direction.

"Aw, can it!" she interrupted. "I bet I'd quit anyhow, whether you or Mr. Blue Ribbon wanted me to or not. I'd just quit and show you I'd quit."

Mr. Pomeroy had finished his chicken, and an automobile horn was blowing furiously outside the shanty demanding Gracie's attention, so he spoke one parting line.

"You come in tomorrow and see, Miss—Miss Quit," he remarked oracularly, and reeled out into the cold just as he had reeled in—with all the motion above the knees.

And that was how it happened that on Christmas night Gracie retired early and left Mr. Axelrod to shift for himself. She slept as determinedly as she usually fried chicken, and for about the same length of time. She was drinking coffee when she heard the first trolley pass a block below her house and, putting on a coat of some indeterminate fur that in damp weather smelled like a live animal, she minced over the ice and crusted snow to the trolley stop. The street she came along was steeply down hill, and if she had been an exuberant person she might have taken a little skip and slid all the way. But she didn't—she walked sideways to keep from falling.

The car was filled with steamy heat and melted snow, and workingmen puffing their ways to far parts of the city. Gracie reached the Blue Ribbon at the opening hour, and after some wandering among aisles and elevators located Mr. Albert Pomeroy.

He was more pompous and less verbose than when she had seen him before—but he remembered her perfectly and for the best part of an hour he initiated her, with severe finger shakings, into the art of being a saleslady.

Before Gracie had time to consider the question of quitting, a momentous occasion arose that drove the thought out of her head. She had been a participant in the activities of the store for less than a week when a general massmeeting of all the employés was held in the restroom after hours. Mr Pomeroy standing on a bench, acted as general chairman.

"We are gathered here," he announced from his rostrum, "for the purpose of discussing the subject of selecting the Blue Ribbon's representative in the popularity contest now being held under the auspices of Mr. Blue Ribbon, one of the town's leading business men, and several other of the town's leading business men." He paused here and took a long breath as one slightly dizzy.

"We must choose our queen—with honesty," he went on, and then added surprisingly, "which is always the best policy. Everybody knows that we have here in this store the most beautiful ladies that can be found in this town, and we must choose the best one among them all to represent us. You have until this time tomorrow to decide who you will vote for. I want to thank you on behalf of myself and Mr. Blue Ribbon for your attention and—" he had prepared a strong finish for his speech, but it was considerably marred by the fact that just at this moment a stray thought of the haberdashery department flashed into his mind.

"In clothing, I wish to say—" He paused. "In clothing, I wish—" Then he gave up and ended somewhat tamely with, "And that's the way it is."

As Gracie went out through the employés' entrance behind the tittering file of females she saw Mr. Pomeroy on the corner under the white arc light. She walked quickly over and spoke to him.

"Honest," she said, "that was a great speech you made. I don't see how some people can all of a sudden just make up a speech."

She smiled and disappeared into the winter lights and the furry crowds and hurried toward her street car. Unwittingly, she had made up a good speech herself. Mr. Pomeroy, though impervious both to ridicule and insult, was a sensitive man to compliments.

❦

The next afternoon in the Blue Ribbon restroom, Gracie was somehow being heralded as a leading candidate for the honor of representing the store. She was surprised—and in the same breath she was not surprised. She never doubted that she would win, although she was a newcomer and there were five girls competing against her. Two of the five were prettier than Gracie and the other three were not pretty at all. But the ballot found a spirit of irritable perversity in possession. The pretty women were jealous of each other and voted for the ugly ones. The ugly ones were jealous of the pretty ones and voted for the newcomer, Gracie—and ugly ones were in the majority. No one was envious of Gracie, for no one knew her. And no one believed she could possibly win the contest—but she did.

And Mr. Blue Ribbon was as good as Mr. Pomeroy's indiscreet and intoxicated word. He "fixed it," and at the end of a month came the day of the coronation. It was to proceed up the main business street and then along the fashionable avenue to the river. In effect Queen Gracie Axelrod, in her royal coach, was to be borne through shouting mobs of faithful citizenry.

On a cold noon the cohorts gathered in front of the New Heidelberg hotel, where there was much scraping of fenders and blowing of horns. Gracie sat in her car beside Mr. Pomeroy, whose title was "Blue Ribbon Courtier Dedicated to the Queen of Popularity." Behind Gracie a blue pole arose, balancing over her head a bright, insecure star. She carried a sceptre and wore a crown made by the local costumer, but due to the cold air the crown had undergone a peculiar chemical change and faded to an inconspicuous roan. Of this Gracie was unaware.

From time to time she glanced tenderly at Mr. Pomeroy, and it occurred to her how nice it would be if his gloved hand should hold hers under the heavy robe. The thought was delicious, and she reached out experimentally until her finger barely touched his, just faintly suggesting an amour of digits to take place later in the ride.

The less important cars—loaded with representatives of fraternal orders and assistant queens from other stores—had begun to move slowly off, following the brass band, and now the chauffeurs of the principal floats were coaxing roars of white steam from their engines. The mayor's car set up a cloud of noise and vapor.

"What's the matter?" demanded Mr. Pomeroy anxiously of Gracie's chauffeur. "We don't want to be left behind."

"I'm afraid it's a little bit froze up." The chauffeur was unscrewing the radiator cap. "I guess I'd better get some hot water from the hotel."

"Well, hurry up, then," complained Gracie. The car ahead of them was pulling out. "Let's start anyhow," she went on excitedly. "You can fix it when we get back."

"Start!" exclaimed the chauffeur indignantly. "Start! How can I start when it's froze up?"

The tail of the procession was a hundred yards up the street, and several automobiles that had no connection with the celebration had turned in and followed behind it.

Another car, containing a stout young man in the back seat, drove up alongside Gracie.

"Are you stuck?" asked the young man politely.

"Of course we are, you crazy fool!" shouted Gracie, whereupon the crowd laughed.

"You better get in this here car," suggested the young man, unabashed.

"Maybe we better jump in," said Mr. Pomeroy uncertainly. "When these things freeze up—"

"But how about all them decorations?" interrupted Gracie.

*

Willing onlookers began to tug at the ornamental star with the idea of transferring it to the other automobile, whereupon the support creaked, groaned, and collapsed neatly into four pieces.

The tail of the parade had by this time rounded a bend and was passing out of sight far up the street; the music of the band was already faint and faraway.

"Here!" commanded Mr. Pomeroy, breathing hard, "get in!"

Gracie got in, and someone threw the star in after her for good luck. The young man drew the robe over them and they set off at full speed—but in less than a block the long-delayed cross traffic brought them to another halt. When they overcame this obstacle a quarter of a mile of tight-packed cars still interposed between Gracie and the procession ahead.

"Tell your chauffeur to honk!" said Gracie indignantly to the fat young man.

"He isn't mine. They gave me this car. I just got into town, you see. I'm Joe Murphy, the assistant director."

"We got to get up to our place, ain't we?" shouted the queen. "What do you suppose everybody's going to say when they don't see me?"

The chauffeur obediently honked, but as everybody else was honking, too, it produced little effect. The other cars, having attained a place in line, were not disposed to relinquish it to an undecorated machine containing an obviously intoxicated young woman who kept threatening them with a long blue stick.

When the procession turned into the fashionable avenue Gracie began to bow right and left to crowds that should have lined the way. She bowed to groups or individuals impartially, to babies, to responsive dogs, and even to several of the more pretentious houses, which answered her with cold plate glass stares. Here and there some one nodded back at her politely, and one group gave her a short cheer—but they obviously failed to connect her with the colorful display ahead.

Gracie bowed for over a mile. Then two young men on a corner yelled something that was perfectly audible to her. They yelled it over and over again, and several small boys on the sidewalk took up the cry:

"Where'd you get the gin, sister? Where'd you get the gin?"[4]

Then Gracie gave up and burst into tears and told Mr. Murphy to take her home.

The movie, New Heidelberg, the Flowery City of the Middle West, was being filmed in the outskirts of the city. On a morning of February thaw. Gracie stepped gingerly from the street car at the end of the line and, with the other city queens, navigated the melted snow and mud puddles that almost obliterated the ground. The lot was already crowded and Gracie, as leading lady, tried to locate those in charge. Someone pointed out a platform in the center, and told her that the active little man who was pacing nervously back and forth upon it was the director, Mr. Decourcey O'Ney. Gracie elbowed her way in that direction.

Mr. Decourcey O'Ney had come early into the pictures and back in 1916 had been known as a "big" director. Then, due to one of those spasms of hysteria which periodically seize upon the industry, he had found himself suddenly out of work. His acquisition by the "Our Own Movie" committee was especially played up by the New Heidelberg Tribune.

He was commenting to his assistant director on the undeniably swampy condition of the ground when a plump young lady with a big suit box under her arm appeared beside him on the platform.

"What can I do for you?" he asked absently.

"I'm the movie queen," announced Gracie.

Mr. Joe Murphy, "assistant director" and man of all work, confirmed this fact.

"Why, sure," he said warmly, "this girl was elected the most popular girl in the city. Don't you remember me, Miss Axelrod?"

"Yeah," said Gracie grudgingly. She had no wish to be reminded of the late fiasco.

"Have you any experience in pictures?" inquired Mr. O'Ney.

"O, I seen a lot of 'em and I know just about how the leading lady ought to act."

"Well," murmured Mr. O'Ney, alarmingly, "I think I'll have you gilded to start with."

"Mr. O'Ney means that he'll show you how to do," said Joe Murphy, hastily.

"By the bye," said Mr. O'Ney politely. "Can you scream?"

"What?"

"Have you ever done any screaming?" And then he added in explanatory fashion, "The only reason I ask you is because I want to know."

"Why—sure," answered Gracie hesitantly, "I guess I can scream good enough, if you want somebody to scream."

"All right." Mr. O'Ney seemed greatly pleased. "Then scream!"

Before Gracie could believe her ears, much less open her mouth, Joe Murphy again interjected: "Mr. O'Ney means later. You go over to that house and put on your costume."

Somewhat bewildered, Gracie set out for the ladies' dressing rooms, and Joe Murphy looked after her admiringly. He liked blondes as full blown as himself—and especially those who seemed to have materialized out of the vapor from warm milk.

The picture, written by a local poetess, commemorated the settling of New Heidelberg by the brave pioneers. Three days were spent in the rehearsal of the mob scenes. Gracie, relieved from work at the store, came every morning and sat shivering in the back of a prairie schooner. It was all very confusing, and she had little idea of what her part was to be. When the day came for the actual shooting she acted as she had never acted before. Entering the covered wagon, she violently elevated her eyebrows and crooked her little fingers into grotesque hooks. During the Indian attack she rushed about in the center of a blank cartridge bedlam, waving her arms and pointing here and there at the circling redskins as if to indicate startling tactical dispositions. At the end of the second day Mr. O'Ney announced that the shooting was done. He thanked them all for their willingness, and told them their services were no longer required. Not once during the whole course of the picture had Gracie been required to scream.

❧

Since Gracie had been "working days," Mr. Axelrod's business had fallen off. He went to bed at midnight just when he should have been most alert. It was lonely when Gracie wasn't there to fill the shack with warm chicken smoke, and he had no one to read the newspaper at. But he was vaguely proud of his daughter, and his drowsy mind grasped the fact that something apart from him was going on in her life.

He was flattered when Gracie asked him to accompany her one Thursday night to the private showing of the picture. Only the people closely concerned were to be there. The real showing would take place in grand style at the city auditorium.

The preliminary showing was at the Bijou, and when the small, select audience was seated and the red velvet curtains parted to show the screen, Gracie and her father became rigid with excitement. The first title flashed suddenly on.

NEW HEIDELBERG

THE FLOWERY CITY OF THE MIDDLE WEST
AN EPIC OF PAST AND PRESENT
GROWTH AND PROSPERITY
BY
HARRIET DINWIDDIE HILLS CRAIG
DIRECTED BY
DECOURCEY O'NEY

There followed a cast of characters. Gracie thrilled when she found her name:

MISS GRACE AXELROD
WINNER OF THE POPULARITY CONTEST

And, after a line of dots:

AS AN EARLY QUEEN OF NEW HEIDELBERG

The word "Prologue" danced before her eyes, and Gracie felt in her stomach the sinking sensation that preceded dental work. She looked steadfastly at the clumsy covered wagons creeping across the plain and she gasped as there was a sudden close-up of herself, acting, in the canvas oval at a wagon's back.

LET US NEVER FORGET THE NOBLE MEN AND
WOMEN WHOSE SUPREME SACRIFICE MADE
POSSIBLE OUR GLORIOUS CITY

There were the Indians in the distance now—it was much more exciting than it had been on the suburban lot. The battle, looking desperately real, was in full swing. She sought herself anxiously amid the heat of conflict, but she might have been any one of a score of girls who it seemed had been acting just as violently as herself.

And here was the climax already. A savage rode up threateningly. Bang! And Gracie, or some one who looked like Gracie, sank wounded to the ground.

"See that? See that?" she whispered excitedly to her father. "That was hard to do let me tell you!"

Some one said "Sh!" and Gracie's eyes again sought the screen. The Indians were driven off, a hearty prayer was said by all, and the fields were expeditiously plowed for corn. Then, to Gracie's astonishment, the whole scene began to change. The surburban plain disappeared, and one of the covered wagons faded before her eyes into a handsome limousine. From the limousine stepped out a modern young girl in a fur coat with hat to match. It was none other than Miss Virginia Blue Ribbon, the pretty daughter of the owner of the Blue Ribbon store.

Gracie stared. Was the pioneer part over, she wondered—in less than fifteen minutes? And what did this limousine have to do with the picture?

"They must of left out some," she whispered to her father. "I guess they'll have me doing some more in a minute. But they shouldn't have showed so soon how I got wounded."

Even now she did not realize the truth—that she was in the prologue and the prologue was over. She saw Miss Blue Ribbon standing in front of her father's store and then she saw her shopping in the Blue Ribbon aisles. Now she was in a limousine again bound for the fashionable avenue, and later in a beautiful evening dress she was dancing with many young men in the ballroom of the big hotel.

In the dim light Gracie looked at her program. "Miss Virginia Blue Ribbon," it stated, "representing the Queen of Today."

"They must be saving some of that western stuff for the end," Gracie said in an uncertain voice.

Two reels flickered by. Miss Blue Ribbon manifested an unnatural interest in factories, jewelry stores, and even statistics. Gracie's bewilderment was fading now and a heavy, burning lump had arisen in her throat. When the parade itself was thrown on the screen she watched through a blurry glaze that had gathered over her eyes. There went the automobiles through the cheering crowds—the minor queens, the mayor, Mr. Blue Ribbon, and his daughter in their limousine—then the scene ended—and she thought of her car, lost somewhere back two miles in the crowd.

Gracie wanted to leave, but she still felt that all the audience were watching her. She waited, stunned and unseeing, until in a few minutes more the screen flashed white and the movie was over.

Then she slipped into the aisle and ran quickly toward the exit, trying to bury her head in her coat collar. She had hoped to evade the crowd, but the closed door detained her and she came out into the lobby simultaneously with a score of people.

"Let me by," she said gruffly to a portly person who had wedged her against a brass rail. The portly person turned, and she recognized Mr. Blue Ribbon himself.

"Isn't this the carnival queen?" he asked jovially.

Gracie straightened up and seemed to draw the half ejected tears back into her eyes. She saw Mr. Pomeroy just behind his employer, and she realized that the floorwalker's leer was but a copy, on a small scale, of Mr. Blue Ribbon's business grin.

Then rage gave her dignity, gave her abandon, and Mr. Blue Ribbon and his employé started back as they saw the expression that transformed her face.

"Say!" she cried, incredulously, "just let me tell you one thing right to your face. I think the picture was rotten and I wouldn't pay a cent to see anything so rotten as that."

A lobby full of people were listening now; even the fountain in the center seemed puffing with excitement. Mr. Pomeroy made a move forward as if he would have seized her, but Gracie raised her hand threateningly.

"Don't you touch me!" she shouted. "I told you if I didn't like your old store I'd quit, and now I quit! When they go out and elect somebody queen they ought to make her queen of something except an old broken-down wagon." Her voice was soaring now to the highest pitch it had ever reached.

"I resign from the moving pictures!" she cried passionately, and with the gesture of one tearing up a million dollar contract, she pulled a program ferociously from her pocket, tore it once, twice—and hurled the white segments into Mr. Blue Ribbon's astonished face.

❧

Two o'clock that night. There were no customers in the chicken shanty and Mr. Axelrod, worn out with the excitement of the evening, was long gone to bed when the door opened suddenly and a stout young man with a baby's face stepped inside. It was Joe Murphy.

"Get out of here!" cried Gracie quickly. "You go on out of this chicken joint!"

"I want to speak to you about the movie."

"I wouldn't be in another movie if you gave me a million dollars! I hate movies, see? I wouldn't dirty my hands being in one. And, besides, you get out!"

She looked wildly about her, and as Joe Murphy saw her eyes fall on a dish of sizzling chicken gravy he took an instinctive step toward the door.

"I didn't have nothing to do with it. They fixed up the whole thing. Say, I wouldn't keep you out of a picture," and then he blurted out suddenly, "Why—why, I'm in love with you."

Gracie's plate rattled to the floor, where it vibrated for a moment like a top.

"Well," she snapped, "this is a fine time of night to come telling me about it!"

But she indicated that he should come in.

"Look here, Gracie," he began, "that was a dirty trick they did you and I was wondering wouldn't you like a chance to get back at 'em?"

"I'd like to smash 'em in the face."

"That's the way Decourcey O'Ney feels about it," confided Joe. "He ain't a good business man, you see, and they beat him out of some of the cash they said they'd pay him."

"Why didn't he let me be the leading lady when I should of been?" demanded Gracie.

"He says they told him not to," said Joe eagerly. "They said you was just an accident and wasn't important at all and not to waste any footage on you."

"O, they did, did they?" cried Gracie, red with rage. "Wait till the people who elected me queen see what they done to that picture!"

"That's what I think," agreed Joe, "and my idea is that we ought to fix that picture up. Because, like you say, I been thinking how sore those people are going to be."

"Gosh, they're going to be sore," said Gracie, drawing a pleasant warmth from the idea. "I bet they'll get after old Blue Ribbon. They'll all get together and never buy nothing more in his store," she added, hopefully.

"That's right," agreed Joe with tact, "and that's why I think the thing for us to do is to try and fix that picture up. Mr. O'Ney, he's so mad he don't care what happens. He says for me to go ahead and do anything I want to. He don't care."

Gracie hesitated.

"I'd rather have it so nobody would ever go to the Blue Ribbon no more."

She visualized Mr. Pomeroy, out of a job, bobbing into the shack after a scrap of charity chicken. But Joe shook his head.

"I got a better scheme," he insisted. "I'll come around tomorrow morning at nine o'clock. Have your costume in a box—the one you wore in the movie."

When he went out, she stood in the doorway and followed his retreating figure with her eyes. The roofs were dripping, and the stars were out, and there was a soft, moist breeze. An earlier remark he had made was reverberating persistently in her head.

"Say," Gracie called after him, "what did you mean when you said all that stuff about being in love with me?"

Joe stopped and turned.

"Me? Why—I just meant it, that's all!"

"That's funny," and then she added, "Say, come back here a minute, will you—Joe?"

Joe came back.

❦

As the public performance drew near, the pavements grew sloppier and the snow in the gutters melted into dirty sherbet. On the great Saturday night the auditorium was jammed to capacity. There was a big orchestra this time, which played a stupendous overture, after which Mr. Blue Ribbon himself appeared on the lighted stage and advanced to the footlights.

"Fellow New Heidelbergians!" he began in an inspiring voice, "to make a long story as short as possible, this movie is a real—a real epoch in the life of our city. It shows first in a great sweeping epic a picture of what I may call an epic of our pioneer days when our grandfathers and grandmothers yoked up their oxen and came over here from—from Europe—looking for gold!"

He seemed to realize that there was some slight inaccuracy in his last observation, but as there was a burst of applause from a line of old, deaf, white-haired people in the middle of the house, he let it pass, and now turned to those without whose efforts this picture could never have been made. He wanted to thank first of all the splendid spirit of everyone who participated. This spirit had convinced Mr. Blue Ribbon that New Heidelberg could act as a unit. Next he turned to that distinguished director, Mr. Decourcey O'Ney. After constant triumphs in Hollywood Mr. O'Ney had come here because he had heard of the splendid spirit of the inhabitants.

Applause! Everyone turned to look at Mr. O'Ney. Mr. O'Ney on being located stood up and bowed. It was afterwards remarked by those nearest him that he glanced somewhat nervously around and that his eyes fell with most approval upon the red exit lamps over the doors.

"Then," continued Mr. Blue Ribbon, and this was true magnanimity, "let us not forget the young lady who was chosen by public acclaim as the fairest in our city and who adorns this work of art with her graces—Miss Grace Axelrod—Our Own Movie Queen!"

Fig. 5.13   Line drawing by Raymond Sisley, "'I resign from the moving pictures,' she cried passionately." Original illustration to "Our Own Movie Queen."

There was a storm of applause. Gracie stood up, bowed, and then sat down quickly, uttering a subdued ironic sound.

Mr. Blue Ribbon rambled on for some moments. Finally he ceased with a benign smile and, bobbing off the stage, took his seat down in front. The house grew dark, the orchestra struck up the national anthem, and the silver rectangle appeared upon the blue screen:

NEW HEIDELBERG, THE FLOWERY CITY
OF THE MIDDLE WEST

The preliminary titles were all as before. The wagons set off on the journey to outbursts of applause as the passengers were recognized by proud relatives and friends.

Then, to the surprise of those who had witnessed the private showing, a brand-new title flashed on:

MISS GRACE AXELROD

CHOSEN BY EVERYBODY IN THE CITY

TO BE QUEEN AND STAR OF THE PICTURE.

A PIONEER GIRL ... MISS AXELROD

Mr. Blue Ribbon gasped faintly. The audience, unconscious of a change, applauded.

Here were the Indians now, shading their eyes with their hands and beginning their immemorial tactics of riding around their prey in concentric circles. The battle began, the wagon train was brought to a stop, the bedlam of blank cartridges was so real as to be almost audible. Clapping broke out. A title:

WHEN THE WHITE PEOPLE WERE GETTING
BEATEN, MISS GRACE AXELROD, THE CITY'S
QUEEN, SHOOTS THE INDIAN CHIEF WITH A
GUN SHE GOT.

The applause which greeted this was punctuated with an occasional gasp and somebody snickered. But the action which followed was even more curious. It showed Miss Axelrod snatching a rifle from some one who leapt quickly out of the picture, but who gave the undeniable impression of having been a young man in a derby hat. Miss Axelrod knelt and fired the gun in the direction of a telegraph pole, which had sprung up suddenly on the prairie. There followed a scene, so short as to be scarcely distinguishable, of a man falling down. This was obviously the Indian chief shot by Miss Axelrod, but again the realists in the audience perceived that the aborigine, though he wore feathers in his hair, was dressed in modern trousers rolled up above modern garters.

This time a long restrained titter broke out, but the audience were still far from the suspicion that this was not the film as originally planned.

AS THE INDIANS WERE NOT YET BEATEN OFF
BY MISS GRACE AXELROD'S ATTACK, SHE
SHOOTS THE SECOND IN COMMAND AND THUS
COMPLETES THEIR DISMAY.

The shooting of the second in command was remarkably like the shooting of the chief. There was the lean telegraph pole in the distance, and there was the be-gartered Sioux who in the next flash fell to the ground. The resemblance indicated that the second in command might be the chief's twin brother.

The whispering had now thickened to a buzz, and a suspicion was abroad that somewhere, somehow, something had gone awry.

On the screen, however, the action had returned to normality. The Indians, dismayed by the fall of the second in command— apparently he was the real power behind the throne—began to retreat in earnest, and the settlers, after embracing each other with shouts of joy, sang a hymn of thanksgiving and went about building New Heidelberg.

Mr. Blue Ribbon had for some time been stirring wildly in his seat, casting distraught glances rearward and then glaring back at the screen with unbelieving eyes. The prologue was over, and Miss Virginia Blue Ribbon's triumphant progress among the marts and emporiums should now have been recorded.

MISS GRACE AXELROD, WINNER OF THE CITY'S POPULARITY'S CONTEST,
GOES ON A TOUR TO THE CITY'S BIG STORES.

And as the flickering letters flashed out, Mr. Blue Ribbon found himself gazing on an episode that was so cut as to expose only a back view of his daughter. She entered the shops as before, she fingered materials, she admired jewelry—but whenever she seemed about to turn to her face to the audience the scene ended.

Then the astounding information blazed across the silver sheet that:

> MISS GRACE AXELROD LOOKS THINNER HERE
> BECAUSE SHE'S GOT ON A BETTER CORSET
> THAN YOU COULD EVER BUY
> AT THE BLUE RIBBON STORE.

For a moment there was no sound except a long sigh from Miss Virginia Blue Ribbon as she fainted away. Then with a low flabbergasted roar that increased to a din, pandemonium burst forth in the auditorium. Mr. Blue Ribbon rose choking from his seat and dashed for the back of the house, leaving a little path of awe that marked his passage through.

To the rest of the audience, history was being made before their eyes. A full close-up of Miss Blue Ribbon appeared, following the comment:

> ONE WHO STUCK HER NOSE IN

After that the picture went on, but no one cared. It was a crazed howl from the gallery for "More Gracie!" which really terminated the entertainment. No one saw the end of the picture, in which the schoolchildren's black and white handkerchiefs spelled out the name of the city. The crowd was on its feet looking up at the balcony, where Mr. Blue Ribbon and other inarticulate, half-crazy citizens were trying to climb over the operator's back and stop the projector. A mob had gathered around Mr. Decourcey O'Ney, who stood calmly trembling. The only remark he was heard to make was that it would have been a bigger picture if he could have had everyone gilded.

Joe Murphy turned and whispered to Gracie,

"We better beat it before they turn up the lights."

"Do you think it went off good?" she asked anxiously, as they came out by a side exit into the almost warm night. "I thought it was a swell picture, and I guess anybody would of but a lot of soreheads."

"Poor O'Ney," said Joe thoughtfully as they walked toward the streetcar.

"Do you suppose them people will put Mr. O'Ney in prison?"

"Well, not in prison." He pronounced the last word so that Gracie demanded: "Where will they put him?"

Joe took Gracie's hand and squeezed it comfortably.

"They'll put him in a nice, quiet asylum," he said. "He's a good director, you know, when he's right. The only trouble with him is that he's raving crazy."

❧

Gracie Axelrod and Joe Murphy were married late in March, and all the department stores, except the Blue Ribbon, sent her elaborate wedding presents. For their honeymoon they went to Sioux City, where every night they went to the picture show. Since they've been back in New Heidelberg and started the restaurant, which has made them rather more than prosperous, Gracie has become the neighborhood authority on the subject of pictures. She buys all the movie magazines, *Screen Sobs*, *Photo Passion*, and *Motion Picture Scandal*, and she winks a cynical eye when a new opportunity contest is announced in Wichita, Kansas.

Mr. Decourcey O'Ney has been released from the asylum and engaged by "Films Par Excellence," at two thousand a week. His first picture is to be called *Hearts A-Craze*. Gracie can hardly wait to see it.

[*Chicago Sunday Tribune* (Chicago), 7 June 1925, Magazine Section, pp. 1–4.]

Beginning Young (1925)
Lillian Gish

[...] When anyone asks me to pick out from the many I have been in, the picture I like best, I answer without hesitation and without much thought, *Broken Blossoms*. I say this not because the picture was an artistic picture, which it was. I say this not because it was a compelling or tragic story with no clearing away, no laying of tracks, no getting ready for the tragedy—it was exactly all this; but because the picture was quickly and smoothly accomplished. It took only eighteen days to film. As I was just recovering from the influenza, I was not asked to rehearse. The scenes in which I could sit down were taken first, and the worries of production and detail were kept from me.

My idea of a really uncomfortable picture was *Way Down East*, one of the most successful of all moving pictures. This was rehearsed eight weeks before a foot of it was recorded by the camera. From the minute I read the play I knew that the picture was going to be an endurance test, and I went into training for it. During that winter there was very little snow, and as we had had only eight or ten days on which we could take snow pictures, a permanent call had gone up in the studio that if there were to be a blizzard, night or day, all the actors in the snow scenes were to report to the studio. The memorable day of March sixth arrived and with it a snowstorm and a ninety-mile-an-hour gale. As I was living at Mamaroneck, near the studio, I quickly reported and was made up as Anna Moore, ready, but not eager for the work to be done.[1] The scene to be taken was the one just after the irate Squire Bartlett turned Anna out of the house into the storm. Dazed and all but frozen, she wanders about through the snow and finally to the river.

The Griffith studio is on a point, or arm, which runs well out into Long Island Sound. The wind simply swept across this narrow neck of land with fury. I had to face it, but the cameras had their backs to the gale. I had only been out a short time before my face became caked with snow. Around the eyes this would melt and my eyelashes became small icicles. They wanted this, and they would bring the cameras up close and photograph my face. My eyes were so heavy I could scarcely keep them open. When I could stand no more and was half unconscious, they would pull me into the studio on a little sled and give me some hot tea. After a short rest I went back again to the gale. It was not safe to count upon another blizzard that season.

But this pleasant day was as nothing compared with the taking of the ice scenes. The whole company journeyed to White River Junction, Vermont, where the Connecticut River and the White River flow side by side. If all the thrills experienced by all the people all around the world when they have seen the ice scenes of *Way Down East* on the screen could be condensed or compressed into one great thrill, I doubt whether it would equal my thrill that day when I floated on a cake of ice down the waterfall, only to be rescued just in time by David Bartlett, the character played by Richard Barthelmess.[2]

We could not wait for the ice to go out of the river, so with a big ice saw the cake upon which I was to float was cut and then holes were drilled in a section of the river and the ice was dynamited. We did this day after day. In a moment of enthusiasm, which I had cause to regret later, I suggested that I thought it would be effective if one hand were trailing in the water. This turned out to be very painful and the sensation was, of course, just like putting the hand in fire.

Finally, the big day arrived, and with it some work that it was not necessary to repeat. A camera stand, swung as a bridge, was built over the waterfall, and upon this eleven cameras were placed and trained on the river. The cake of ice upon which I was to float toward the falls was selected. I got into position on my strange craft under the bridge and was turned adrift in the rapids. Richard Berthelmess was in waiting at the side as I floated toward the rapids. Upon a given signal from Mr. Griffith he was, by successive jumps, to reach the cake of ice nearest me and grab me off my ice cake just as it went over the falls. The roar of the water and the confusion were so great that Richard did not hear the signal and he waited too long. Then in somewhat of a panic, for fear that he would not have time to get me before I went over the falls, he fell and was only just in time to save me. A second later the rescue would have been impossible.

No part that I have ever played on the screen has been liked, I suppose, by so many people as that of Anna Moore in *Way Down East*. Here was a story that might be said to be typically American and one that would find neither sympathy nor understanding abroad, and yet everywhere the record is one of great success. [...]

["Beginning Young: The Story of Lillian Gish," *Ladies' Home Journal* (Philadelphia) 42, September 1925, pp. 19, 117–120, excerpted.]

Blazing the Trail (1928)
Gene Gauntier

It was in June, 1906, that I literally jumped into the moving pictures. And from that day to this I have been connected with them as an actress, scenario writer, producer and critic. In these different capacities I have watched the very birth-pangs

Fig. 5.14   Gene Gauntier as "The Girl Spy" in 1909.

of the industry. I helped to develop and guide it, I cried and laughed over it, and was part of it as it was part of me.

In these reminiscences I make no attempt to write a history of moving pictures. I merely set forth what I recall of those early days in the few companies with which I was associated.

The impulse which led me to fling myself into a Connecticut river from which I issued forth leading lady of a small picture company destined to become a power in the industry was characteristic of the hour.

On the stage melodrama was in its heyday, and from the ranks of melodramatic actors were drawn the players for the first pictures. *Why Girls Leave Home: or A Danger Signal on the Path of Folly* gave us Lois Weber, Phillips Smalley, Anne Schaeffer and me.[1] *The Worst Woman in London* was the play that graduated James Kirkwood.[2] *Billy the Kid*, starring the boy Joseph Santley, produced three men who eventually became great directors, Sidney Olcott, Robert Vignola and George Melford; also Marion Leonard, the original "Biograph Girl," and Fred Santley who afterward starred in the Bertie series for Kalem.[3] Mary Pickford had already appeared in *The Fatal Wedding* and Laurette Taylor had been leading woman for young Santley in *The Boy of the Streets*, written by her husband, Charles Taylor.[4] Plays like *Bertha the Sewing-machine Girl*,

Across the Pacific, and *Nellie the Beautiful Cloak Model* were coming fortunes for Al Woods, Sullivan and Harris, the Mittenthal Brothers, and the Blaneys.[5] The public's appetite for thrillers seemed insatiable.

Like all players of the day, I came to New York each year at the close of the road season in search of an engagement for the next season. In 1906 I arrived with sufficient money to take a delightful little apartment on 101st Street near Central Park West for which I paid thirty-two dollars a month.

About June first I realized that my funds were running low and in a vague way I thought of the new opening for actors, moving pictures. But like the rest of the legitimate profession I looked on them with contempt and felt sure that my prestige would be lowered if I worked in them. I knew only one person who did work in them regularly, Sidney Olcott, whom I had met at the home of Mrs. Santley, mother of Tommie, Fred and Joe, and my own "New York mother." He was then with the Biograph Company. Today he is one of our outstanding directors.

One noon Sid came from Forty-second Street to 101st Street by surface car, as this was before the day of subways and we had no telephone.

"How would you like to come on a picture tomorrow with Biograph?" I stalled for I did not want to go. He went on to explain:

"It's a water picture. If you can swim—"

"But I can't," I cried, relieved.

"That's all right. You'll only have to get your feet wet. We are going up to Sound Beach, Connecticut, and it will give you a long day in the country. I know you'll enjoy it and it'll put three berries in your pocket. Probably will mean more work too. Now, Dot, I think you are foolish not to seize such an opportunity. It's all going out and nothing coming in with you, and that is no right way for anyone to live—just to lie around waiting for something to turn up."

Good old Sid, how many times has he guided not only me but all of his confrères along the road of his wisdom!

*

So the next morning at eight-five I met the company at the Grand Central Station and we took a train for Sound Beach. Mr. Harrington was the director but the life of the party was a good-looking, enthusiastic man of vivid personality who seemed to take matters into his own hands. He was Frank J. Marion, sales manager for the Mutoscope, a subsidiary of the Biograph.[6]

Arrangements had been made for our reception at a farmhouse smothered in roses and lilacs and set down in a field of daisies. Beyond the winding dirt road flowed a river some fifty feet wide which, a few hundred yards below, had been dammed to give power to a woolen mill, dilapidated and abandoned. Here on one side of the dam was a great pool thirty feet deep and on the other a sheer drop of thirty or forty feet.

"A wonderful place for the plunge," announced Marion and turning to me he added, "You swim of course!"

"Never was in water in my life except a bathtub," I said cheerfully.

"I told you we must have someone who could swim," railed Marion at Olcott.

"You didn't say 'swim,'" said Sid; "you said someone to go in the water."

"That's a fine way to get out of it. The next time you do as I say. All right, folks, take off your make-up and we'll go home and come back again tomorrow."

This would never do. Mentally I made a calculation—ten people at three dollars a day, railroad fares and so forth. I spoke up:

"What do you want me to do?"

"The girl must be thrown into the mill dam."

"All right, I'll do it if you make sure someone will save me."

"It's impossible. The water is thirty feet deep. I won't risk it."

"Well, I will. Just have rescuers near and I'll take the chance."

It took some persuading, Sid adding his voice to mine, and in the end Marion agreed.

The picture, The Paymaster, proceeded on its criminal way until noon and I quickly caught on to the knack of facing the camera. But in the back of my mind lurked the fear of the big scene. For I was afraid—horribly so. But I was going through with it if it killed me. We had a rehearsal, all except the plunge. I came running across the stone dam until I reached the center when Jim Slevin, the villain who was pursuing, caught me. There was a fierce struggle and he lifted me bodily, whispering: "Hold your breath. Now—one—two—three—!" and hurled me head downward into the water. Just outside the camera lines, in boats, waited the other members of the cast, tense and ready to plunge in should it be necessary. Slevin, frightened at what he had done, stared with mouth open and arms hanging.

"Get out, you fool," roared Marion, holding back Gordon Burbe, the hero, who strained to run into the scene and make the rescue. It was too good! Marion gripped him until my body rose and disappeared again. In the meantime I felt as if I were plumbing the bottom of the river. Ten feet down I went, with the strength of Slevin's arm. I thought I would never stop going and start up again. My lungs were bursting. It seemed impossible to hold my breath another second. I felt the air on my face and wondered why I wasn't rescued; then down I went again. I was panic-stricken. Something had gone wrong. I was going to drown! Just then I felt firm arms under me and remembered not to struggle. A few strong strokes and I was laid on the damhead while the camera ground out the last few feet.

It was quite a triumph. Marion seized my hands and all but kissed me. Sid laughed and cried in his excitement and the cast gathered around showering me with congratulations. As for me, I have never before nor since been so exhilarated and self-satisfied. The plunge was my open sesame to the film world, for Mr. Marion was so grateful that for several years he would not even consider another leading woman. Moreover I was presented with five dollars for my day's work instead of the customary three.

[Woman's Home Companion (Springfield, Ohio) 55, October 1928
(first installment of six), pp. 7–8, 181–84, 186, excerpted.]

A Girl Cinematographer at the Balkan War (1914)[1]
Interview with Jessica Borthwick

Miss Jessica Borthwick, the English girl of twenty-two who returned in January last from the Balkans, where she had spent the whole of the previous year studying the war and taking cinematograph pictures thereof, is a very remarkable personality. Youthful in appearance and of rather slender build, she nevertheless gives one an immediate impression of great strength, both physical and mental—an impression which is confirmed when one listens to the story of her adventures—whilst her voice, beautiful, deep and like a resonant organ note, is vibrant with the enthusiasm and determination of one whose indomitable spirit will endure every rebuff and hardship in the achievement of a worthy end. Idealist, thinker, and practical woman of action, Miss Borthwick has a unique individuality, and the history of her life, short as it has been to the present, is already a record such as few men of any age could match.

"I had two objects in going to the war," Miss Borthwick told us during the exceedingly interesting interview she was kind enough to give us last week in her South Kensington studio, which she had fitted up with projector and screen as a temporary picture theatre. "Firstly, curiosity pure and simple, and secondly the great interest the Balkans have for me through my father's (the late General Borthwick) connection therewith. In the eighties my father was employed by Bulgaria to reorganise and command the army in Eastern Rumelia, and all the country I went over last year he had been over before.[2] His name, I found, was known everywhere, and the fact that I was 'General Borthwick's daughter' helped me many times to overcome what might otherwise have proved insurmountable difficulties. Among the other spots holding memories of my father which I visited was the place where a famous brigand, Spanos, dwelt, living by loot and by taking people for ransom. (His practice was to send little bits of them to their relatives until such time as the latter forwarded a sufficient sum to justify his releasing them.) Spanos was a cripple, and one day my father, while he was searching for this notorious rascal, came upon the pony which the brigand used to ride upon, together with the ram which he employed as a decoy in stealing herds from the villagers. Confiscating both animals, my father shortly afterwards received a letter from Spanos, stating that he had watched him for years, and describing in detail different occasions on which he could have shot him. 'You have taken my food and my legs,' he concluded. 'If you give them back you may go free, otherwise I will surely kill you.' My father replied that he would return neither, and that, on the other hand, he wanted Spanos's head. And a little later he captured the brigand and brought him to justice.

"I took out with me to the Balkans one small plate camera and one cinematograph camera, which was made for me by Mr. Arthur Newman, who taught me in three days how to use it. This cinematograph camera of Mr. Newman's lasted me the whole twelve months, in spite of the fact that it underwent terribly hard usage and received no repairs whatever except for my amateurish effort to mend it with bits of wire. I was occasionally able to supplement my photographic outfit with cameras taken from the dead bodies of officers on the battlefield, but most of these I lost again. Rather a curious incident happened, by the way, in connection with the little plate camera I took out with me. Shortly after I arrived it was either mislaid or stolen, together with 200 plates. Four months later, while sitting in bivouac with some soldiers in quite another part of the country, I found it in the possession of a private, who stated that he had picked it up, and was keeping it in the hope of being able to sell it to a war correspondent. Needless to say, I promptly reclaimed it.

"The difficulties of taking cinematograph pictures on the battlefield, especially when quite alone and unaided by any assistant, are, as you can imagine, tremendous. The use of a tripod is a particular embarrassment. Things happen so quickly in time of war that, unless one can be ready with one's camera at a few seconds' notice, the episodes one wishes to record will probably be over. During the Servian war in Macedonia my tripod was smashed by a shell, and although the camera was intact, the film which I was taking at the time got hopelessly jumbled up, and had to be cut away from the mechanism with which it had become entwined.[3]

"Another great difficulty was the want of a dark room. One day, while taking films in the Rhodope Mountains, I came to a strange village of wooden huts inhabited by a nomadic race called Vlaques. Something went wrong with my camera and I tried to make the people understand that I wanted some place which would serve as a dark room. It was impossible to get them to grasp what I meant, however, until eventually I found a man making rugs out of sheep's wool. After much persuasion, I induced him to cover me up with his rugs, and in this unusual and very stuffy 'dark room' I managed to open my camera in safety. Having no film box with me at the moment, I wrapped the negative up in pieces of paper and stowed it away in my pocket, carrying it thus for fifteen days until I returned to Sofia. Occupied with other matters, I forgot the film, and handed my coat to a servant who, being of an inquisitive nature, unwrapped the negative, and finding it uninteresting, put it back in the pocket without the paper, afterwards hanging up the coat to air in the sun. Subsequently I developed the film—and found it one of the best I had!

"The want of a technical dictionary, combined with the natives' ignorance of photography, brought about several rather amusing situations. On one occasion, in Adrianople, I lost a screw from my tripod. There were shops of most other kinds, but no ironmonger's, and at last, in despair, I tried to explain to an officer what I wanted in dumb show, not knowing the word for 'screw.' Having followed my actions for some moments with apparent intelligence, he suddenly hailed a cab and bundled me hastily in. We drove and drove right across the city, until eventually we entered some massive gates and drew up—inside the prison! However, I turned the misconception to advantage by securing some excellent snapshots and having some very interesting talks with the prisoners. One convict—a German of considerable education—invited me to go and see him hanged the next morning, and gave me a souvenir. I saw two executions in that prison.

"During the cholera rage in Adrianople everything connected with that terrible disease was painted black. The carts in which the dead bodies were carried away were black, for example, as were the coffins in which cholera victims were buried. While the scourge was at its height I went down into the gipsy quarter to take a small film. The people in this part of the city had never seen a camera before, and when they saw me pointing my little black box at various objects they thought that I was operating some wonderful new instrument for combating the disease which was destroying them. Quickly surrounding me, they came and knelt upon the ground, kissing my feet and clothing, and begging with dreadful pathos that I should cure them. It was a task as sad as it was difficult to explain that their hopes were mistaken, and that I was impotent to help them.

"I brought back with me about 2,500 ft. of film and a large number of photographs. I should have had a great deal more had the Customs authorities not been so suspicious of me when I left the country. They refused to believe that nothing was visible on the undeveloped negatives I carried in my film boxes, and insisted on opening many of the latter, with the result, of course, that the pictures were ruined. In this way I lost many hundreds of feet of film and more than 250 plates. It was particularly annoying, in that I had sacrificed innumerable comforts and even necessities throughout the whole of the war in order that I might always have my cameras with me.

"What are my present and future plans? Well, in a few days time I hope to start a month's engagement at the Polytechnic to lecture twice daily on the war.[4] My lecture will be illustrated by my films and by lantern slides from my plates. I am also writing two books on the Balkan War.[5]

"With regard to the future, I shall leave England in June next for the Arctic regions, where I want to start a colony for the cure of consumption and other diseases. This is the great dream of my life. The great open spaces of the North are God's sanatorium, and I believe that, when once their possibilities are known, their value will be recognised. I have been in the Arctic regions before. Yes, I shall take two or three cameras with me, including Mr. Newman's wonderful new hand cinematograph camera. When shall I return? That I cannot say. Perhaps at the end of a year—perhaps never."

["A Girl Cinematographer at the Balkan War: Interview with Miss Jessica Borthwick," The Bioscope (London), 7 May 1914, pp. 625, 627, 629.]

Filming Moana of the South (1925)[1]
Frances Hubbard Flaherty

SETTING UP HOUSE AND SHOP IN SAMOA: THE STRUGGLE TO FIND SCREEN MATERIAL IN THE LYRIC BEAUTY OF POLYNESIAN LIFE

[...] Of course the cave had been the chief object of interest, far more important than the house. Almost as soon as we set foot on Savai'i, we went off to inspect it. What if the cold water should prove a myth after all?[2] In many of the Samoan villages there is nothing but rain-water, which the people collect in big galvanized iron tanks, for drinking and cooking. The trader Bauer, our temporary host, undertook to banish all our forebodings. "Cold? Ho! you vait und try your thermometer. I tell you it's der coldest water in der South Seas!"

Five minutes' walk inland, past the scattered *fales* of the village folk, through groves of mangoes and coconuts and oranges, brought us not to one but to two caves, facing each other across a space of twenty yards. The larger cave had little air of mystery. A gradual descent from the outside brought us to the brink of a subterranean stream. The water was clear, yes and cool—heaven be praised! Little fishes, very much like tiny trout, swam about in it. Here, it seems, the Samoans were in the habit of bathing and washing their *lavalavas*. But the mouth of the second cavern, much smaller than the entrance of the first, was nothing but a gaping black hole in black lava. Into this hole disappeared the broad back of the German trader. We followed, one by one, and by the faint beams of his flash-light slowly and cautiously picked our way downward. Within a few yards of the entrance it was pitch-dark. The ceiling was low, the descent sharp, the footing uncertain. Little birds that made a noisy, clicking sound with their wings flew past us toward the cave door, alarmed by this rare invasion of their retreat.

"Ho!" announced the trader. "Here is der water you are looking for. Come, feel it, put your thermometer in. Cold water like dot you don't find anywhere else in Samoa."

I felt the water—it was cold! Bob thrust in the thermometer and by the light of the torch we all read it.[3] Seventy-two degrees! The cavern resounded with a shout of joy. He drank some and pronounced it sweet. As far as we could see in the dim light, that heaven-sent, mysterious pool reached back into the dark interior. Where we stood, at the brink of the water, it must have been fully five feet deep. The underground tunnel was spacious, too. Its solid lava ceiling cleared our heads by several feet, and from wall to wall it measured nearly fifteen feet—ample space for a workroom.

Within a month the half-caste carpenters had finished their work. The mouth of the cave, carefully boarded up, was provided with a door. To make doubly sure of absolute darkness, a second bulwark with a door was built a few yards inside the cave. A long stairway led from the entrance to the water's edge, where now stood a substantial platform. At the edge of this the large wooden developing-tanks were set so that the cold, clear water of the cave formed a jacket around them. The boxes for the development of still films, the safe-light and the timing-clock rested on a long table. Electric lights, the first on Savai'i, the current carried a hundred fifty yards from our generator, hung from a roughly constructed ceiling. And the dark room was complete.

Our occupation of the cave put to flight the little birds, and their alarmed exodus filled the simple natives with wonder; for, as the trader explained: "Those little birds are the spirits of the dead." Just above this cave was the old graveyard of the village.

Outside, on the eminence between the two caves, rose the newly built laboratory, a commodious shed of imported Oregon pine and New Zealand kauri, with a peaked roof of corrugated iron. The branches of one huge breadfruit-tree almost overspread it. Here we kept the big drying-drums and stored our film and chemicals. In one corner we partitioned off a little room for the printing-machine.

In surroundings idealized by Melville, Stevenson, O'Brien and others, before the wondering eyes of these gentle Samoans, the papalangi—the white men from heaven—prepared to perform miracles.

We breathed a sigh of relief when the machinery of our living and our work was all in order. It had meant long, wearisome and expensive labor. There are fine woods in Samoa but no saws; every plank for our building had come two thousand miles from New Zealand.

But now we looked upon our work and found it adequate. The house was not beautiful. But just to live in the open all day and sleep in the open all night, with nothing to hem us in but invisible screens, was comfort and romance, too. The big porch contained two heavily laden shelves of a not ignoble library of Polynesiana, the Encyclopaedia Britannica and several books on photography. Part of the shelf-room was given over to our victrola records, and the victrola stood on the table just below, easily accessible. There was a center-table for magazines and smoking accessories, with plenty of comfortable chairs. At one end of the porch was a long deal work-table; at the other, our dining-table. Here, on this porch, was the center of our little universe. Here, day by day, unfolded the drama of our existence.

We looked down from our porch through gray coconut stems beyond the big, high fale tele, the village guest-house, to the beach and far out to the white line of the reef. Before the guest-house ran the pathway where all Safune walked by and all the malagas, the visiting-parties that came to the village—a continuous panorama of figures silhouetted against the glittering sea. At the side we looked upon what was by day only a close-cropped sward but by night, alive and illuminated, the arena of our trials and our triumphs. For here at one end of the field stood our projector-house and projector and at the other end, facing it, the all-revealing screen. [...]

From the time we first set foot on Savai'i, our one desire, of course, was to find the chief character for the new film. Which was the face that was going to be the face for the screen? Nanook was not handsome, but he had strength and kindliness. His character shone out of his face. Our idea was to find a man like Nanook, whose character would shine out of his face in the same way. We looked and we looked and we looked. From this point of view, the faces were very, very discouraging—very, very disappointing. They were all, as Bob said, "soft," even those of the old men. They were gentle, but they were gentle without strength. All the chiefs looked as if they had done nothing but sit and make sennit—the braided rope of coconut-fiber used in the building of Samoan houses—all their lives. As time went on, dejection settled down upon us. I remember one particularly black day when Bob and I were sitting on the sand by the lagoon, talking it all over. But we had talked it over a hundred times before. We knew that our white compatriots could not see any film material in these people and their simple lives. The Samoans were neither interesting nor attractive to them. What did we think we could find in them? And, God help us, through the blackest months that ever darkened our lives, we tortured ourselves with the same question.

Unfortunately we had come to Samoa with preconceived notions about the necessary element of struggle for a film. We did not have any scenario, but we had the idea that we were going to make just such another film as *Nanook*, with the drama of struggle to be found in the element of the sea.[4] And for the "animal sequences" we expected to use octopuses, sharks, turtles and robber-crabs—those big land crabs that climb the coconut trees and clip off the nuts.

Here was the hitch, however. In the North the whole of life is a very grim affair, an endless struggle for existence. Not only that, but the drama is one of action that we understand because it comes close to our own lives and the eternal competition for daily bread. In the South there is no struggle for existence. The mere getting of food is as incidental as a game. The environment is perfect as it is. It has never demanded of the people the development of any intellectual life, any ingenuity, any adaptation to change. Drama exists, but it is a very subtle thing, quite apart from anything that we understand. It is to be found in nothing more nor less than *fa'a-Samoa*. Therein the people build their whole lives. If you break *fa'a-Samoa*, you break their lives to pieces and they die.

As we realized the problem we were facing, black despair settled over every one of us. We could not make a picture, à la *Nanook*, out of the heroic things the people did not really do. As for *fa'a-Samoa*, that was something psychological. It expressed itself in mass ceremonies, in set forms and endless dances, most particularly simply in talking. How in heaven's name are you going to get a picture out of that? How are you going to photograph talk? The only thing we could do, as we saw it, was just to make the best of a very bad business and get home as soon as possible.

That we did, in the end, get something else came about simply through bungling and accident and a happy technical discovery. When we projected our first experiments on the screen, the people came out black like negroes, and there was nothing pleasant about them at all. The orthochromatic film we were using did not give the proper color-value to their beautiful light brown skin. An orthochromatic film takes red as black, and wherever red enters into a color, it is seriously distorted. We had brought with us a color-camera, however, with the idea of making some experiments in motion-picture color-work.[5] In color-photography panchromatic film is used—a color-corrected film, sensitive to red. It was an experimental use of this film with our ordinary camera that threw the first gleam of light on our difficulty. We found that the panchromatic film, used in direct sunlight, gave an extraordinary, stereoscopic effect. The figures jumped right out of the screen. They had roundness and modeling and looked alive and, because of the color correction, retained their full beauty of texture. The setting immediately acquired a new significance. There are a hundred different tones of green in a tropical island—the dark, shiny green of the breadfruit, the sage-green of the taro, the clear, brilliant green of the coconuts. With the orthochromatic film, green, like red, is always dark. Our new process gave the proper color-value of each leaf. We could make even a fish look interesting because it was as beautiful in the photograph as it was in reality.

In the past photographers have made use of panchromatic film for outdoor shots, particularly for cloud effects, but sparingly. It requires an entirely different technique in the laboratory. In an ordinary laboratory a red light is considered safe, because the orthochromatic film is not sensitive to red. Panchromatic film has to be developed in absolute darkness. The obvious difficulty of handling it in the laboratory is one reason why it has been so little used up to the present time. Within the next five years it is likely to come into general use in motion-picture work.

We first made our discovery about the middle of November, six months after our arrival in Safune. Under the date of November 19, I have this record in my diary, "Something grows a little every day. Got a new basis for working in full sunlight." The next day I note: "Bob radiant, trying out panchromatic exposures."

At last we had the solution of our problem. The drama of our picture should lie in its sheer beauty, the beauty of fa'a-Samoa, rendered by panchromatic film. And the characters should be no other than our friends in Safune and the neighboring villages. [...]

FA'A SAMOA: THE OLD, PRIMITIVE POLYNESIAN LIFE—A FLEETING[6] GHOST—CAUGHT FOR THE AMERICAN SCREEN

In many ways the Samoans are curiously like us. Physically, I have no sense of difference, color notwithstanding. I want to hug Pe'a like my own, rock him in my arms—only, boylike, he would squirm; I know that. Sometimes when we have been in a strange village, the chiefs squatting about us, naked to the loins, I have noted that there was not a facial type among them that I could not recognize as familiar to Wall Street or Broadway—but for the expression of the eyes. There was the difference, the gulf, the chasm. These people have no thought-life, no intellect. They are back in the days before the Fall; they have not tasted of the Tree of Knowledge. By that deep chasm are we—all of us whites—separated from them. To put it figuratively, for us are the rough, rugged heights, the struggle, the slipping, the falling, the heartache, the pain, the vision, the hope, the faith, the despair; for them, a beautiful plain, sun-blessed, fertile, flower-spread, balm-kissed, a plain where life runs in and out and in and out like an unending repetition of a song. Why, their singing is the very epitome of their life—never a solo, ever in chorus, instinct with harmony and a rhythm as absolute as nature herself and as unemotional.

They mate as the birds mate, for the purpose and period of reproduction. Under their social system, in which every child is a welcome pair of hands for planting taro, for spearing fish, for weaving mats, there is no denial of motherhood; the love and bearing of children is whole-souled and free. The first cry of a new-born child is heralded by a shout that echoes through the whole village. The families meet for mutual congratulation with an exchange of mats and presents. The man, following his instincts, later on may take another wife; the woman, following hers, will bring back to her father's house the crown of motherhood and in peace and dignity unhampered and the fulness of her strength rear her young. Nature, satisfied, takes no toll in "problems."

We were making a film of this wonderful life so different from our own. We had tried to mold it into a dramatic form, a form of struggle and danger, into which it fitted not at all. Our spirits were worn out with the struggle we had made; and they were bowing down and worshipping and weeping with the beauty of these people and our love for them. We were in despair. Could any of this that we saw, could any of this that we felt, be translated into terms of motion for the screen? That thing typical of their lives in which there was the most expression through action was the *siva*, the dance. We had tried to film the dance before. We had tried with orthochromatic film, and our disgust with the results had put the siva as a screen possibility far from our minds. But now, with panchromatic film to work with, we had a whole new palette for our brush. We wrote out a siva sequence. We had come to know the siva as the people themselves felt about it, and it was this, and not merely its outward form, that we wanted to portray.

Our sequence called for a house as setting. "Any old house" would not do. We wanted one that was typically *fa'a-Samoa*, according to Samoan style, that is, with rounded beams and fine proportions and real rhythmic beauty. We wanted to see those bodies in the siva framed as we had seen the sitting figures of the chiefs, so beautifully set in the spacing of posts and roof as to be like a piece of music. At the same time, we must have a house that we could adapt to the practical requirements of our photography. We should have to remove a portion of the roof to let in the light.

[...] As it happened, [...] there was a house in Safune that seemed exactly suited to our needs. It was a good house, but old, abandoned, its roof already full of holes. As luck would have it, it belonged to Taulelea, Pe'a's father and our good friend. We offered him the usual rental for a house, two pounds a month, with additional compensation for any damage we might do to it. Taulelea immediately started taking off the thatch for us. We felt elated. Soon we should be at work on our siva picture, entering upon our adventure in the dramatization of beauty and charm as against danger and struggle. [...]

[W]e filmed the little sequence—all in the hottest heat of the hot season, perspiration pouring off us in bucketfuls, the rubber gaskets melting out of the cameras.

And what was the result? It was *good*, beyond all expectation good. Never had a Ta'avale danced like that before, and, blessed be panchromatic film and sunlight, he and Fa'angase stood out from the screen bodily. They were living and beautiful and dramatic. We looked at one another, hardly believing. [...]

We gloated over our siva negative. It had a beautiful photographic quality. The photographer loves his negative. He has seen a vision of something beautiful and exciting and interesting. He has caught it. He has watched his vision coming out in the developer—there it is, as beautiful! It is magic! He has watched it fixed. It is a permanent record now for other people to see. It is no longer ephemeral. It is a fact, a new contribution to the sum of human knowledge and feeling ....

We ran the negative through our hands. Clark, our laboratory assistant, held it up to the light. He kept unrolling it, holding it up to the light and unrolling it. "Look here!" said he, suddenly. Faint but unmistakable, at regular intervals, were dark flashes on the film. Here we were, after a year's work in Samoa, face to face with the most cruel thing that could possibly have happened to us—a flaw in our negative. After a whole year of searching and experimenting and at last finding, we were at the beginning again.

The cave, our dark room, with the beautiful clear, cold water that had first brought us to Safune, now became our research laboratory. Above it still lay the graves of past generations; in and out of it still clicked the little birds that the villagers thought were the spirits of the dead. Entering through the door of the bulkhead that boarded its mouth, down a winding flight of stairs through another doorway, you groped your way to a subterranean chamber. Here, by a dim red light, you became aware of the shapes of table, bench, winding-frames, racks, great bottles and, at the ghostly edge of the platform, of gleaming black water and the tops of wooden tanks poking up from it. Echoing from the blackness beyond came a steady drip, drip. Somewhere here lurked the ghost that was spoiling our film.

We made experiments innumerable. Nothing we could think of was too far-fetched or too obvious, too simple or too complicated, to try and try again. Night after night I sat up alone until cockcrow, my lamp the single spot of light in the village of dark fales and darker bush, waiting for Bob to bring the final test from the laboratory. At last footsteps sounded on the laboratory path. Stillness again. A momentary gleam of the projector, a flickering on the screen under the coco-palms, and it was all over—another test had run. June, July, week after week, day and night and night and day, we worked, and always the result was the same—always the test showed the same baffling waver.

And now the season came when go westward we must to the other side of Savai'i to catch the big seas of the trades for our reef sequence. An Australian engineer, a recruit to our forces, from Apia, was to build a new developing device in our absence. Three weeks later we returned to Safune with thousands of feet of film. We found that Hall, the Australian, had been ill and almost died and that the new device was a failure. The film taken on the malanga would not keep—exposed film deteriorates very rapidly, particularly in a climate like that of Samoa. There was but one thing left to do. Clark packed up the film and with it shipped off to Hollywood. [...]

Was it the cave that was responsible for the flashing of the film? We thought that perhaps its walls of solid rock were not light-tight. Stay in there a little while, and you could see your hand before your face—not always, but sometimes—just a faint, ghostly luminosity. The walls were lava, porous, full of worms most likely, a sort of sieve. Bob called in our developing corps, Sam and Imo. They squatted gravely on the floor of the veranda. Earnestly we questioned them. Light in the cave—had they ever seen it? Yes. We looked at one another. When? After rain.

Again I sat waiting, alone. Twelve ... one ... two o'clock. What a long time they were gone! It was uncannily still. I jumped at the sound of a voice almost under my feet. "Ti moni, ti moni, ti moni"—"Good morning, good morning, good morning" ... it was only Tilesa, the village madwoman, who had stolen in under the porch and fallen asleep. At last they were coming. Bob marched up on to the veranda and spun a tin cover on the table. In it was a little pile of crumbly black dirt ... the ghost ... phosphorus!

Who would have dreamed of such a thing? Every day we had sat and dabbled our feet in the water of our romantic cave and loved it. Now I watched the bulkheads being torn away, the big tanks coming out on the shoulders of the men. What a job it all was! And how could we ever develop in the hot laboratory above ground, with solutions at 89 degrees? I need not have worried. A week later the big tanks were trundling back again. The phosphorus ghost was laid. It was not, after all, the real ghost.

Besides our cave was another one, bigger and more open. This cave was usually filled with chattering and splashing women and children and the sound of the slapping clothes. Suddenly it was deserted, and a sign was posted, forbidding its use. As an experiment, we washed a test in this second cave, and the strip of negative showed no queer streaks or waver. We washed another test and another ... all were good. Was there, then, something the matter with the clean, clear, perfect water of our cave? We remembered that at low tide it often had a peculiar smell. Rotten timber, Bob had said—just the same smell as in a mine.

It was not long before the laboratory table displayed a row of test-bottles. They were filled with cave water—some of it blackening to a purplish color in the sun, some of it throwing down a white flaky precipitate, some of it murky with a fine black powder suspended in it. We tore up the platform that had been put down in the cave. Bob pointed to a white deposit on the rocks at the bottom of the pool. The water evidently had not flushed out, as we had supposed, with the regular rising and falling of the tides, which somehow caused the fresh water in the cave to rise and fall likewise. From the washing of the negative after developing, a deposit of silver nitrate had formed in the pool. Our fresh negative, washed in water chemically tainted with nitrate, had been regularly retoned with disastrous results.

This was not all. The Encyclopaedia gave the symptoms of nitrate poisoning. They were exactly the symptoms of Bob's strange illness while we were on our malanga in search of animal and sea sequences and the strange attack that had almost killed Hall. Both men had been drinking the cave water. Moreover the fumes of nitrous gases produce bleeding of the lungs. Imo, our laboratory boy, had been afflicted with this trouble. We had sent him to Apia to be examined there but the doctor had reported that he showed no signs of tuberculosis in a laboratory test. Much was now clear to us besides the fearful difficulty with the film.

As we walked up to the laboratory after our inspection of the cave, my eyes fell on the forbidding sign posted near the second cavern. The village well is connected with the caves. Of late the well-water had been tasting. Too much soap, the chiefs said. I stared at the sign, I stared at Bob, I stared at the test-tubes on the table. The village well! Good God ... I shut my eyes ... the people at the well, filing by, filing by ... their pails, their pails ... oh, merciful heavens!

As a matter of fact, the village did not die, and fortunately for us we continued to enjoy the liberty of Sava'i'. But I think that Bob had a very close shave and Mr. Hall a closer.

["Filming *Moana of the South*: Setting Up House and Shop in Samoa" *Asia* (New York) 25, August 1925, pp. 640–41, 644, 710–11, excerpted; and "Fa'a-Samoa," *Asia*, December 1925, pp. 1085–1090, 1096.]

I Married Adventure (1940)
Osa Johnson

[...] Early the next morning a score of natives appeared on the beach yelling and waving their arms.[1] Paul and Martin went ashore. When they returned to the ship they said my presence was required. Nagapate had sent yams, coconuts and wild fruit—not to Martin or the men—but to me. It was unbelievable. Here, as is the case with nearly all primitive people, a woman does not count in the scheme of things except as a slave, to do the work of the village and bear the children, and this with kicks and abuse for reward.

Paul was plainly confounded by the whole thing and I was doubtful until Nagapate's men laid the offerings of their chief at my feet.

"I suppose he figured it out," Paul said, "that because we all treat you with respect that that's how it is with white people—that our women hold some sort of position black people don't know about."

Martin laughed: "No, it's simpler than that. The old boy can see that Osa's the boss of the expedition, and this is his way of opening diplomatic relations."

Paul, Perrole and Stephens agreed with Martin and me that the sooner we could show Nagapate and his people the motion pictures we had taken of them on our first trip, the quicker we would have them awed into an acquiescent mood that would permit us to move on up into the village and really settle down to the purpose of our expedition. To attract as many of them to the beach as possible we spread out our trade stuff. Martin set up his cameras, and we began to take pictures. By dusk it seemed to me we must have had the larger part of the male population on the beach. Nagapate himself didn't come until almost last. Apparently, after that slip in which he yielded to the temptation to sing with me, he had felt the need of retrieving his dignity.

Rapidly, now, Martin worked to set up the screen and projection machine. Nagapate and his men seemed to think that with night coming on they might as well get back to their village. To hold them became a problem. I played the ukulele, distributed more trade stuff, jabbered to Nagapate in my poor *bêche-de-mer*.

"For goodness' sake, Martin," I cried out finally. "It's dark enough, isn't it? Why don't you start the picture?"

"Because I can't!" he shouted back. "The damned generator won't work!"

He was sick with disappointment and so was I. The generator of necessity was run by man-power; two boys on each side turning the handles. For what seemed hours Martin drove them frantically in relays without the faintest glow from the lights.

The natives showed not the slightest curiosity about the machinery or the screen. Nagapate grew suspicious of my obvious efforts at detaining him on the beach. The boys continued to grind the generator. It was no use. Martin wiped his forehead, shook his head and signalled them to stop turning. Misunderstanding the gesture, the boys doubled their efforts, the generator spun, and the miracle happened! The lights flashed on!

The bright beam of light shot through the darkness with such suddenness and sharpness that the natives grunted and drew back.

With no means of knowing how the savages would react when the pictures appeared, Paul had placed armed guards around the projector, and because of this it now became a problem to get the natives to face the screen. Plainly they didn't want the guards and the machine that shot light at their backs.

There seemed only one thing to do. I took Nagapate by the arm and, with as imperious a manner as I could summon, sat on the ground facing the screen and indicated that I expected him to do likewise. Clearly he didn't like being pushed around by a woman, but he sat down beside me, apparently to think it over. The rest of the savages, trained to do whatever their chief did, followed suit. At last we were ready for the show to begin.

Through the titles the natives divided their attention between the screen and the shafts of light over their heads. They looked from one to the other, chattering like mad, until my picture faded in on the screen. Their chatter stopped short. They were literally struck dumb. Here I was on the beach sitting beside Nagapate—and there I was on the screen as big as a giant. Then the picture of me winked at them. This threw them into a furore. They shrieked with laughter. They howled and screamed.

They were silent again as they saw Martin and me leaving the Waldorf-Astoria, and the silence deepened when they saw the mad throngs of New York on Armistice Day; glimpses of the great metropolitan centers of the world; flashes of steamers, racing automobiles and airplanes. Where we expected excitement, there was an uncomprehending silence.

Only once did Nagapate stir, and that was during the pictures of Armistice Day. This troubled him, and he said afterwards he didn't know there were so many white people in the world. He added that we must live on a pretty large island.

Martin wanted to get a picture of the savages as they saw themselves on screen. So he showed Paul how to crank the projector and gave Perrole and Stephens the flares. Then he focused his camera on our strange audience.

After a hundred feet of titles Nagapate's face loomed before the natives. Again a great roar went up. Over and over they yelled: "Nagapate—Nagapate—Nagapate." Martin gave the signal for the radium flares. They went off—a bomb of light, and I caught a glimpse of Martin's elated grin as he cranked the camera and recorded the mingled fear and amazement on the faces of the blacks.

Some two-thirds of the natives, terrified by the flares, scrambled for the bush. I touched Nagapate's arm and gave him my most reassuring and nonchalant smile. This sort of business, I indicated, was an every day occurrence in the lives of white people. Nagapate wavered for an instant then sat back on his haunches again, setting the example for his people.

The flares lasted only about two minutes and, after we had gradually coaxed the runaways back to their places, we started the reel all over again.

Practically every savage shown in the picture was in the audience. As each man appeared on the screen the audience shrieked his name and roared with laughter. They had not changed a bit except perhaps to add another layer of dirt. Suddenly the roar became a hushed murmur as the figure of a man who had been dead for a year was shown. The natives were awe-struck. Martin's "magic" had brought a dead man from his grave.

After this we felt a definite change in the attitude of the Big Numbers people towards us. No longer was there a feeling of treachery or defiance. Instead they gathered around quietly and respectfully. It was apparent, however, that they were waiting for something else to happen. Inquiry revealed they wanted tobacco as pay for looking at the pictures. As I handed out the sticks each one grunted the same phrase. I tried to learn what it was, but I never did.

At last everything was packed. We were ready to return to the schooner and about to leave when a savage came running down the beach waving his arms and yelling at us. He had come back with a message which said: "Nagapate, he big fellow master belong Big Numbers. He, he wantem you, you two fellow, you lookem picannimy belong him, you lookem Mary belong him. He makem big fellow sing—sing. More good you, you two fellow come. He no makem bad, he makem good altogether."

All of which was meant as an invitation from Nagapate to visit his village and the assurance that we would not be used as the main dish of a savage feast.

Martin hid his elation and said, "We'd love to come."

[Excerpt from I Married Adventure: The Lives and Adventures of Martin and Osa Johnson (New York: J.B. Lippincott, 1940), pp.134–37.]

The Hats in My Life (1940s)
Hedda Hopper

Only once in my life did I really take a hat seriously. That was my first "bought" one, when I was just fourteen. Up to this point my hat-life had been quiet and home-made, but, after months of saving pennies and nickels, I walked to church on Easter Sunday with my head covered by the most elegant hat in the world.

It was green straw and its huge red velvet geraniums, with life-like green leaves, highlight my most vivid and awesome millinery memory. On that triumphal march, I looked neither to the left nor the right, nor deigned to speak to any of the boys in the neighborhood. Wasn't I wearing the most beautiful hat in the parish? Wasn't I superior to the whole world?

I was!

That's when I decided to make a career of hats. I was very shy, very unsure of myself. We were quite poor, and even at fourteen I knew I would have to sing for my supper. Well, if a hat could give me that much confidence, then I'd hitch my wagon to a smart chapeau.

So I learned early what every smart woman knows. A becoming hat is a worthwhile investment—not a screwy hat, or a nondescript piece of felt clapped on to keep off the beat of the rain or the heat of the sun, but an eye-filling hat, a hat whose personality is a deft foil for the wearer's own. In woman's parlance, a hat that "does" something for her.

A hat like that will bring fabulous dividends per dollar. It will help a gal reach her goal, whether it's a husband, a job, a raise or the envy of her female contemporaries.

Always when I was depressed, when I couldn't get a job or when I had just lost one, I would buy myself a new hat. I'm the kind of woman who will walk four blocks to save a 50-cent parking fee, then go around the corner and pay $50 for a new hat.

That hat, however, may net returns of $5,000 or $50,000.

By the same reasoning, a bad hat... a hat cursed with mediocrity... a stupid dullard of a hat... can scare away that potential husband, job or raise.

I believe that now, and I believed it the day I tiptoed in to try out for my first fling at fame and fortune in the theater. Inspired by the ravishing spectacle of Ethel Barrymore in *Captain Jinks of the Horse Marines*, I had run away from home to seek a career behind the footlights. [1] When I reached Broadway, the only opportunity that beckoned was a call for chorus girls. But if it had been a command performance at Buckingham Palace, the thrill couldn't have been greater.

My best dress, pressed within an inch of its already advanced life, wasn't too discouraging. But my one and only hat!

I dusted it, and shook it, twisted it, patted it. It was hopeless. If my experience was one strike against me, that hat would provide the other two, to put me out of the ballgame.

No hat at all would be better than that one, I told myself in the mirror. So I braided my hair in a coronet, dropped that awful millinery monstrosity in the ash can on my way out and got my first job-bare-headed.

I had some stiff competition that day. More than a hundred girls showed up, in their best bibs and tuckers *and* their flashiest noggin pieces. The only thing that made me stand out was my bare head. The director told me so later.

Selecting the girls who were to stay, he designated lucky me with a bellowing, "And you, Kid—you with the hair!"

That was my kindergarten course in hat psychology. From then on, through chorus jobs to bit parts, to leading-lady roles, I kept my mind and the public eye on my head. I bought my bonnets with the same studied eye-to-business of a sculptor selecting a block of perfect marble.

I like to remember a particularly lush winter long ago when I was reaching on tiptoe for my first real chance at a leading role on the stage. The French Room buyer at Saks–Fifth Avenue asked whether I would wear his salon's hats exclusively, and free of charge! *Would* I? Would a budding young pianist appear with the Philadelphia Symphony? Would a Hollywood extra share top billing with Charles Boyer?[2]

That season was one long dream of the most beautiful hats in the world. I would call the salon and report my color scheme for the day — for luncheon, tea, dinner. A hat for each costume would arrive practically with my morning milk and newspaper. This daily shuttle service between me and Saks–Fifth Avenue kept me in dazzling millinery for the whole season. I never wore the same hat twice — to the bewilderment and annoyance of my contemporaries.

I never divulged my guilty secret.

One hat I owned turned out to be a band-box Frankenstein. It was a black Persian lamb dunce cap two and a half feet high. As I walked down Fifth Avenue, a growing crowd followed me, and when small boys took up the cry of "Where did you get that hat?" dancing and jeering in my wake, I took refuge is a passing taxi and fled home.

In the old days, when the first movies were made in New York, I snared a role in Louis B. Mayer's debut production, *Virtuous Wives*, in gray chiffon, climaxed with a gray hat, plumed and bejeweled.[3]

"Perfect for the part," Director George L. Tucker enthused when I swept into his office, fairly dripping gray ostrich feathers.[4]

"But," he squelched, "I'm sure you won't get it."

Then he explained that Anita Stewart, star of the picture, had the final say-so as to cast, and that I "looked too well" for her approval.[5]

Needless, to say, when I called on Miss Stewart I didn't wear the gray chiffon, but the sorriest outfit and the dowdiest hat I could find. She said she thought I'd "do."

At the time, I used to get all my hats at Mercedes on 40th Street in New York, and she would always save her choicest millinery tidbits for me. One day she emerged from her workroom with a tricky little thing she'd rigged up for $150.

"You just *must* have this one," she announced.

My alter ego—the one that vetoes the 50-cent parking splurge—tried to demur. But the hat was too beautiful. I couldn't resist buying it. I wore it to the Ritz that day for tea, and met a producer who gave me a role in a picture that brought me $20,000.

Extravagant? Not when your hat pays off like that.

Literally and truly, just as surely as my new John Frederics is a foot high, my hat is my fortune. Maybe it would give me a more righteous feeling to attribute any success I may have earned to my face or my talents or my weakness for hard work. But it's time I took off my bonnet and confessed...

IT'S ALL DONE WITH THE HATS!

[*The Woman Magazine*, c. 1940s. Held as an undated typescript, marked *The Woman Magazine*, "Autobiographical File," Hedda Hopper Collection, Margaret Herrick Library, Academy of Motion Picture Arts and Sciences.]

The Screenwriter

This is What $10,000 Did to Me (1925)
Anzia Yezierska

I was very poor. And when I was poor, I hated the rich. Now that I too have some means, I no longer hate them. I have found that the rich are as human as any of us.

When I lived in Hester Street, I could feel life only through the hurts and privations of Hester Street. Why were we cramped into the crowded darkness of dingy tenements? Because the heartless rich had such sunny palaces on Fifth Avenue. Why were we starving and wasting with want? Because the rich gorged themselves with the fat of the land.

And then it happened. I who thought myself doomed to Hester Street had the chance to move myself up to Fifth Avenue. And now where are the horns and hoofs that I always seemed to see at sight of the well-fed, the well-dressed? Where's the righteous indignation that flared up in my breast when I saw people ride around in limousines? Where's the hot sureness with which I condemned as criminals those who dared to have the things we longed to have but never could hope of having—furs and jewels and houses?

It began five years ago, just a few days before Christmas. Shivering with cold, I walked up and down the shopping district of Fifth Avenue. I caught a glimpse of myself in the mirror of a passing shop window. What a pinched, starved thing! Worried, haunted eyes under a crumpled hat. Faded, ragged old coat. Overpatched shoes, pulling apart at the patches.

All about me fine ladies, sleek and warm in fur coats, stepping in and out of their cars. All about me shop windows glittering with ball gowns and gorgeous wraps. Riches and luxury everywhere, and I so crazed with want!

In one window a dazzling Christmas tree blinded me with rage. Why should there be Christmas in the world? Why this holiday spirit on Fifth Avenue when there's no holiday for Hester Street? Why these expectant, smiling faces of the shoppers buying useless presents for each other, when we didn't know from where would come our next meal?

I had been writing and starving for years. My stories, which appeared in the magazines from time to time, had been gathered together and published in a book called Hungry Hearts.[1] Although reviewers praised it, my royalties were so small that it brought me little money and almost no recognition. People who read a book little know what small reward there is for the writer while he is still unknown—of his often solitary, starved existence. A book read in one evening may have taken the author years and years of the most agonizing toil to create.

On and on I walked through the gay street, shoved and elbowed by the hurrying crowd. Wild thoughts raced in the corner of my brain. If I could only throw a bomb right there in the middle of Fifth Avenue and shatter into a thousand bits all this heartlessness of buying and buying! The slush of the sidewalk creeping into the cracks of my shoes made me feel so wretchedly uncomfortable. Exhausted with the bitterness and hatred of my thoughts, my futile rebellion gradually settled into a dull melancholy. If I could only kill myself as a protest against the wrongs and injustices I had suffered! I did not really want to die. But I did so much want to shock the world out of its indifference.

Almost a sense of exaltation stole over me as I went on imagining the details of my death. I could see the beautiful limousine wrenched to a sudden stop. The pale chauffeur lifting my crushed, bleeding body in his arms. The whole world crowding around me, dumb, horrified. Then a voice breaking the hush of the crowd.

"This was the author of Hungry Hearts, and we left her to languish and die in want!"

Already I saw the throngs mobbing the bookstores for my book. My last letter and my picture in the front page of every newspaper in the country. Everywhere people reading and talking "Hungry Hearts." The whole world shaken with guilty sorrow for my tragic death—but too late!

Yes, on that dark day there seemed no way to take revenge for the cruel neglect of a heartless world but to blow out my brains or plunge under the wheels of the crowded traffic. My last letter was already shaping itself in my head as I hastened back to my room to write it.

How I dreaded to meet the landlady on the stairs! I could not bear to hear her nagging for the rent in my last tragic hour. Trembling with fear, I sneaked into my room.

There on the table lay a little yellow telegram!

I stared at it. Who in the world would send me a telegram?

I tore it open and read uncomprehendingly. It was from a well-known moving picture agent, saying that he could get for the film rights of my book the unheard-of sum of ten thousand dollars.

In a flash the whole world changed! And I was changed. It changed still more when, after negotiations for the book had been made, they offered to send me to California to collaborate on the screen version of Hungry Hearts.[2]

There followed a wonderful trip across the continent, in a private compartment. I had to pinch myself to make sure that I was not dreaming when I entered the diner and ordered roast duck, asparagus, endive salad and strawberries with cream. I could treat myself with a full hand because a millionaire corporation was paying the bills.

"And this is no accident of good fortune, no matter of luck," I kept telling myself. "*Hungry Hearts* has earned it for me."

Arrived in Los Angeles, I was greeted with overwhelming friendliness by a representative of the company. In a gorgeous limousine, one of those limousines that I always condemned as a criminal luxury of the hated rich—in one of these limousines I was driven to a hotel.

Flowers filled my room. Flowers for me! I looked around, dazzled out of my senses. Luxurious comfort beyond dream all about me. I felt dizzy drunk with this sudden plunge into the world of wealth.

For the first day I stayed in my room struggling to pull together my bewildered wits. I wanted to let go and be happy. But I could not let go, nor be happy. All my Hester Street past rose up in arms against me. "Betrayer! Deserter!" my soul that once was cried accusingly.

The following morning a limousine called to take me to the studio in Culver City.[3] A private office and a secretary were assigned to me. And that secretary! I wondered, would I have to get myself new clothes to match up to her style?

I suddenly became aware of my frumpy, old-fashioned dress against her youthful grace and up-to-dateness. I had heard of newly rich people who were always scared that their servants would look down on them out of the corners of their eyes. And I wondered, would I let myself get shamed out of being what I am by the proud condescension of my grand secretary? Before I could finish my thought, Julian Josephson, that great scenario man, came in.[4] One look of his eyes, the smile on his face, and I felt at home, among my own. Then other members of the scenario department joined us to discuss the plot for *Hungry Hearts*.

The minute we got busy, I was myself again. Happy for the first time since my good luck. *Ach*, what a heart-filling thing is work! In poverty or wealth, work has been to me the one escape from the storms of soul within or the struggles with the world without.

At luncheon time I met the "eminent authors" that were working about the lot—Rupert Hughes, Gertrude Atherton, Leroy Scott, Alice Duer Miller, Gouverneur Morris and many others.[5] What a thrilling experience it was to see them for the first time face to face, to talk to them as they were eating luncheon, just as if they were plain human beings!

One of the "eminent authors" invited me to dinner at his house that evening. Such things as dinner clothes or evening clothes never came into my mind. It seemed to me even if I had such fancy things I'd never know how to wear them. I stayed around the lot that afternoon, visiting the different sets. Before I knew it, it was time to go.

Again the company's limousine drove me to the place. A grave, dignified butler opened the door for me. Through the hall beyond I saw ladies almost half naked, in what seemed to me dressy, gay-colored night-gowns, and all the men in wedding suits.

"So these are evening clothes!" I pondered.

I wanted to rush back to my hotel, but my host saw me as he passed the hall and hastened over to welcome me.

"I might as well stay and see how 'eminent authors' dine," I thought. "How do they behave themselves at a party, these shining lights of the world?"

Up-stairs, a fancy maid in a black uniform helped me take off my things. She gave me one look that said as plain as words, "From where do you come? You here—among 'eminent authors'?"

But the "eminent authors" themselves were such lively, plain people. They greeted me with such natural friendliness that I almost forgot I was different.

Cocktails were served. And then we seated ourselves about the table. Such a millionaire wedding feast! And that's what "eminent authors" called just dinner.

Four butlers were busy waiting on a dozen guests. Champagne—it would be impossible to count the bottles. As one rich dish after another was served, I thought of the people in Hester Street, starving, thrown in the street for unpaid rent. The cost of the champagne for that one dinner would be enough to feed a whole tenement house full of people... I remembered the picture of Nero fiddling before the fall of Rome. I had touched the two extremes of life—Hester Street—Hollywood.

At first there was a lot of educated talk about literature, art, Freud and other high things over my head. Then, warmed by the champagne, they began to talk about other authors. I felt happy just as if I were among my own people in Hester Street. Of course they didn't yell and holler or get excited like the people in Hester Street. They sat quite still in their chairs—ladies and gentlemen. But by the tones in their voices, the looks in their eyes, I saw again the tenants sitting on the stoop, tearing their neighbors to pieces behind their backs. These two "eminent" evening gowns were like those two girls with uncombed hair and flashing eyes fighting over some man. And that grand author lady, so proud of her best-selling books, made me think of that frowzy herring woman with a shawl over her head, nodding and talking behind her hand what was cooking in the neighbors' pots.

In the morning, still elated with the gay party of the night before, I awoke to the delicious feel of my soft, smooth bed. Such fresh, clean-smelling sheets! Warm wool blankets finer than silk. Fresh air and sunshine flooded my room.

How far away was that dark hole in the tenements whence I came—six lodgers on one hard mattress on the floor, and the landlady with all her children in that narrow bed!

At the push of a button, a Japanese maid brought me my breakfast on a silver tray. Hot-house grapes—great purple ones, big as plums they looked to me. And the smell of that coffee in that silver pitcher and the fresh, buttered toast!

I laughed aloud at myself—crazy from Hester Street! You playing lady? You breakfasting in bed? You served on a silver tray? … Well, I'm only finding out how it feels. I'm only doing it for experience.

The limousine called to take me to my office. I felt so fine, so in love with the whole world as I relaxed against the cushions of the car. How much more comfortable than the crowded trolley! Would I ever be able to stand the elevated or subway after this?

My secretary was waiting for me as usual. I greeted her gaily.

"Don't you love it out here?" I laughed.

"Love it! When they don't pay me enough to live?" Then she poured out to me her bitter story. "In my home town in Iowa I got thirty-five a week. But I was crazy to work with the movies. I left a good job to come here. And all they pay is twenty-five dollars a week. I asked for a raise of five dollars. They refused it. It's impossible to get along on my wages. But a lot they care. It's take it or leave it with them. A dozen girls are ready to step into my job."

At every word my spirits sank. The joy over my good luck was over. In the next few days I met other stenographers, clerks, readers, stage hands. So many were horribly underpaid. The "eminent authors," the screen stars, the directors got fortunes for their work; the others drudged from morning till night for less than their bread.

Like a ghost at a feast, my secretary, and behind her a whole army of under-dogs at the studio, rose up before me every time I stepped into the limousine. There was no peace for me at my hotel.

I could stand it no longer. At the end of the week I went to the president of the company. "I'm so miserable in this grand hotel," I said.

"What? Aren't you comfortable?"

"I'm too comfortable—so comfortable it makes me nervous. I've got to live plain like I'm used to. How much does it cost the company to keep me here?"

"About two hundred a week."

"Good heavens!" I cried. "Seven families with a dozen children each could live on that sum. Give me that money. I can live like a queen on fifty a week."

I left Hollywood a few months later; a tortured soul with a bank account. I had the money now to live securely for a few years. Security buys peace of mind to develop a soul. And here I was losing the very soul that my security was giving me. For now I was a capitalist—one of the class that I hated.

The moving picture company saw in my sudden fortune a good human interest story for the papers, to advertise *Hungry Hearts* throughout the country without cost. And I, new to the game of publicity, gave out one interview after another. And every interview was twisted and distorted. Soon the ten thousand dollars for the picture rights of *Hungry Hearts* grew to twenty-five thousand. The two hundred a week I was paid while assisting on the scenario became two thousand. And then from lips to lips it leaped to ten thousand a week. Such were some of the headlines in the ghetto papers—"From Want to Wealth—From Hester Street to Hollywood."

People who have been always comfortable can't know what it means to come into sudden wealth. My mail was full of begging letters. Poor relatives besieged me for money. And my conscience told me that if I were true to my soul I'd give all. I had hated the rich because they kept their wealth and refused to share it with the rest of the world. But how was I to begin to share?

[*Hearst's International–Cosmopolitan* (New York), October 1925, pp. 40–41, 154.]

Why Do They Change the Stories on the Screen? (1926)
Frances Marion

[...] I have translated several hundred books and plays to the screen.[1] Authors have fainted when they have seen their "brain-children" in fantastic new garb, authors have threatened, and authors have written appreciative letters, many endorsing and applauding the free translation of their books.

The latter authors are in closer touch with the making of pictures, and they have begun to understand why these revisions are necessary.

For an example, let me explain why I changed The Dark Angel. It was a very successful play, a very successful picture; yet the plots of the play and picture are divorced.[2]

A play reaches several thousand, a picture is shown to millions. So it is that a successful picture must appeal to every type of mind, and to every age.

In The Dark Angel, a difficult problem lay before us. The play of The Dark Angel told the story of an English girl who was so infatuated with an officer that she gave herself to him on the eve of his departure for Flanders. He was reported killed.

Five years passed. She loved another. It was no infatuation, but a deep-rooted and tender love. To her the past stood between them. Her secret was locked in her heart: she wanted to marry the man she loved, but she had given herself to another.

Then she found that the officer wasn't killed, but blinded and that he had hidden himself away from the world under an assumed name.

She went to him. He successfully pretended that he could see because he feared she would, out of pity, sacrifice her life to him. She told him that she loved another, that she would be happy with the man of her choice if he would release her from the bond of their old promise.

He feigned indifference to her and wished her good fortune. When she did discover that he was blind, she told him she would give up her life and remain with him, to watch over him and comfort him as long as he lived.

He protested gloriously against this.

He convinced her that he no longer cared, and sent her away with the man that she loved, while he faced a life of loneliness and unfathomable longing.

Now, for the reason of the changes: In the first place we must convince our audiences how much a girl really loves a man in order to push aside the barriers of conventional marriage. It takes at least two reels to run through these scenes.

And, as "All the world loves a lover," we do not slight their romance. We see them together, in springtime happiness.

Then war-clouds gather. Follows their long emotional parting. Few have not sent forth men they loved on dangerous missions. It is no hurried gesture, this tearing of hearts, this slow agonized release from arms of love.

Now that we have revealed this great emotion between two people, we cannot shock our audiences by saying in a cold title, "Five years later," and introduce another man with whom our heroine is in love.

Especially not with such a hero as Ronald Colman playing the role of the officer![3] We are much more interested in following him—through battle; we see him wounded, we see his heart-struggle not to return to the girl he loves and be a burden to her. Truly a great and worthy love.

The other man comes into her life. He is kind, he loves her. He pleads with her not to deny herself a woman's birthright: a husband to protect her, children to fill her empty life with work and happiness.

She cannot live forever with the ghost of a remote sorrow. Reluctantly she consents to marry him. But all the time Fate is weaving the threads of the lovers into one pattern. They find each other again; she is sent to him by the man who would make her his wife.

As it was in the play, he hides his blindness. It is a poignant, dramatic scene where he sends her away, then releases himself to his grief. She returns, guided instinctively back to him, because love is the vital force of life and it cannot be denied.

When we leave them in each other's arms we feel that the veil of his sorrow is lifted and that through her he will see with his blind eyes all the divine beauties of life.

This ending permits us to carry away a remembrance of his happiness, and so we no longer pity but rejoice with him.

Of course there is a percentage who would have preferred the unhappy ending of the play. But most of us know sorrow, and disillusion, and weariness from work. Our daily life is sometimes inexorable. The screen beckons us and offers us amusement and forgetfulness. To weep a little is pleasant relaxation, but few of us like to carry away the burdens of a heavy heart.

Stella Dallas, which I also wrote for the screen, has what is technically called an "unhappy ending."[4] It is the story of a gross, common mother who gives up her sensitive flower-like child (born of an aristocratic father) that she may blossom in a better environment than the mother can ever provide.

Upon close analysis it isn't an unhappy ending. There is glory and touching beauty in self-sacrifice. A mother, though we may feel sorry for her, knows divine joy if she can serve the child of her heart.

The screen story of Stella Dallas is basically like the book. It is a great story of mother-love. The scenes as they unfold upon the screen are different from the actual narrative in the book, but the feeling is exactly the same.

It was necessary to invent picturable situations which would express the types, their relations to each other, and the motives for their acting as the author saw them. These changes extend through the first half of the picture. In the latter half of the picture the author had written scenes which with slight changes could be brought to the screen.

The effect of the whole gives the impression of a careful translation of the book into screen language. Students of screen technique might be interested in comparing them.

If we successfully interpret books or plays, the public seems scarcely aware of the minor changes.

There were many who saw *Pollyanna, Rebecca of Sunnybrook Farm, Stella Maris, The Poor Little Rich Girl* (which were among the twelve scenarios I wrote for Mary Pickford) who think they remember having read in the books many of the scenes they saw on the screen, which in fact were never in the books at all.[5] I never contradict them. It is a compliment to our work; we know then that we have interpreted well the author's idea.

Fanny [sic] Hurst pays a great tribute to the scenario-writers.[6] She admits that she has seen several pictures which photographed the narrative of the books she had enjoyed and that she was frankly bored to death with them. She wanted the skeleton of those stories in new garb especially designed for the screen. This is because she has of late carefully studied moving pictures.

It has been several years since we did *Humoresque*.[7] I remember how disappointed I was when she reviewed the film. She was indignant. She wanted her name taken off the screen and mine left on. It was in such small measure her short story as she had written it. She couldn't understand why that little girl had been added, why we went further and brought the soldier back to his sorrowing mother. She had sent him away never to return.

Now Miss Hurst knows why we make these changes; because of that vast audience of ours, an American audience whose inspiration is founded on the optimism of hope. Isn't it interesting to note that all the PHOTOPLAY Gold Medal pictures have happy endings? All save *Abraham Lincoln*, though who can deny that Abraham Lincoln's martyrdom does not hold forth an eternal and all-inspiring hope?

❧

Now hearken to the scenario-writer's complaint! The star system has forced us to make changes in stories we do not always agree with. But often we are under contract and the voice of our protest is a wee one.

A producer buys a story because it is a "big seller." Sometimes it is a splendid story for a man. The woman plays an important role in it, but a passive role.

He hands it over to us poor picked-on scribes and says: "Make this into a great vehicle for Norma Talmadge, or Gloria Swanson, or Mae Murray!"[8] When the smelling-salts revive us we go to work.

What happens to the author's story? !!!!****!!!—We tear it down, we reconstruct it, we make the woman dominate, and the male character as passive as every woman would like to have her own husband. We end up with a splendid vehicle for a woman star—and the cyclone-wrecked story.

Take *Graustark!*[9] Many have criticized the changes. Perhaps it would have been a better picture if we had followed the book, but not a better picture for Norma. It was a man's story. The American dominated every scene.

Norma is a positive character; we go to the theater to see her magnificent interpretation of human emotions. She is a great actress, so we want to see her *act*; not be a passive figure.

The director, the producing-organization, and the scenarist were not considering *Graustark* as a book, but were concentrating on Norma Talmadge. Those who read the book were disappointed to see a free translation of the story upon the screen, but those who had not read the story were delighted with Norma's fine treatment of the character of the Princess who dominated every scene and every situation.

The proof we have of this is the theaters; for records of attendance have been smashed wherever this picture has been shown.

As I am writing this, the small boy who lives across the street is standing on the curb and crying out, when he is safely alone, "Come on out everybody, I can lick you! I could lick the world if I wanted to!"

He is whistling in the dark to keep up his courage. I am afraid the scenario-writers are, too! We would like to please everybody, authors, stars, public, but we just can't lick everybody, except when we are alone! So come on, now, with your bouquets and brickbats!

[*Photoplay* (Chicago), March 1926, pp. 38–39, 144–5, excerpted.]

An Author is the Person Who Wrote the Story (1929)
Fannie Hurst

By no stretch of the imagination can I conceive of myself as ever writing, or desiring to write, directly for the motion-picture screen.

I am first and last, by preference, and I hope by equipment, a writer of narrative fiction. By that very token, however, the screen encroaches to no small extent upon my literary destiny.

It is apparent to me, from the authentic reason that my work is constantly being sought by motion-picture producers, that my work has "screen possibilities." These possibilities, in the past, when translated to the screen, have caused me no little mental anguish. Perhaps only an author can fully understand the kind of torture that assails the creator of a character or a situation when he sees the one or the two of them distorted by the feeble or wilful imagination of another.

Surely it is not egregious ego for an author to feel that his interpretations of his own characters are superior to the hired interpretations of just anybody.

There came a time, however, after years of walking out on one after another of nauseating distortions of my stories, when I realized that I was doing a great deal of bellowing without trying to acquaint myself with actual conditions. The mere idea of a motion-picture studio where these outrages upon my work were perpetrated was noxious. But either, I now concluded, it was up to me to refuse to sell another one of my novels, stories or plays to the movies, or take the time to pause in my own work long enough to study and at least partially understand this important by-product of fiction.

I have just returned from a two-months sojourn in Hollywood.

I am wiser. No sadder. I have come away, convinced of one outstanding fact. The intelligent, first-rate directors who are making today's first-rate pictures are those who tamper least with the original idea of the author; a discovery which relieves me, and many of my colleagues who think as I do, of the onus of the undue ego.

Men like Brabin, Lubitsch, William de Mille, Robert Milton, Lester Lonergan, George Fitzmaurice, Frank Borzage, Herbet Brenon have veered sharply away from what they consider the old-fashioned legend that it improves a story to jerk it as far as possible from the author's original idea.[1]

There is, of course, no evading the fact that there are certain translations from the narrative to the cinema word that are impossible without change and sometimes radical change. But in the main, allowing for these divergencies in the technique of the two mediums, it is the men who believe in adherence to the author's fundamental idea who have risen to the first-rank in their profession.

No one but an artist could have faced and surmounted the difficulties and yet retained the subtle flavor of The Bridge of San Luis Rey.[2] The changes and concessions to screen made by Mr. Brabin were the inevitable ones that will always exist while the narrative word is what it is and the screen is what it is. One feels that whatever the shortcomings of this picture, they were due to the inevitable difficulties of transcription of this particular material from stage to screen. Mr. Brabin did not fail.

This recent visit of mine to Hollywood, for no other purpose than to watch from the side-lines the picturization of my novel, Lummox, turned out to be an experience well worth the time gratuitously expended.[3]

At last it has been my good fortune to see both a scenarist and a director bring to a work of mine fidelity, understanding and intelligence.

Mr. Herbert Brenon, already noted and notable as a director who has achieved splendid pictures, in spite of adhering to the text of his stories (Peter Pan, Sorrel and Son, etc.) to the extent of journeying overseas for the purpose of conferring with his authors, actually holds a volume of Lummox in his hand while directing.

From a certain angle, a man like Brenon is not only a king-pin director, but an excellent business man as well. He purchased a product from an author and he intends to get his money's worth. In his careful study of Lummox he has lost no opportunity to squeeze the book dry of its essence, and not content with that, he storms the portals of the author's brain for more information. His intellectual curiosity about an author's meaning is without limit; his respect for the author's ideas as wide as his intelligence. It was likely due to his desire to carry fidelity of interpretation to its limit that I journeyed to Hollywood, although previous to that Mr. Brenon and Miss. Meehan, his scenarist, had spent months in New York conferring with me.[4] Not content with even the finished scenario in hand, Mr. Brenon wanted the author as near to the sound stage as possible.

Should Lummox, for one reason or another, fall short of expectations, it will not be because the director failed to exert every one of his talents in an effort to faithfully interpret the author, so few and far between are the points upon which our judgements diverged.

It has been the sort of experience that pours balm on old wounds and makes one feel sanguine for the dawn of the author's new era in the motion-picture world.

As men like the afore-mentioned continue to buy Peter Pans, Bridges of San Luis Rey, Doctor's Dilemmas and translate them faithfully and without hokus pokus to the screen, it seems fair to assume that the smaller-fry directors may take a leaf from the books of these wiser men of Hollywood and cease trying to protect their feeble creative talent. [5]

Even assuming that they have bought and paid for a feeble product—and legion they are—the chances are that even then they are better than the snide concoctions of the literary Toms, Dicks and Harrys around the "lots."

As an author who has, time and time again, lifted voice against the machine-stitched, third-rate hokum that has been dished out in her name and of which she protests and protests she was innocent, Herbert Brenon, to whom an author is the person who wrote the story, seems too good to be true.

["An Author is the Person Who Wrote the Story: Assuming Which, a Few Intelligent Picture Directors Have the Gumption to Seek His Cooperation," Theatre Magazine (New York) 50, August 1929, pp. 14, 66.]

Women Scenario Writers (1918)
Interview with Clara Beranger

Clara S. Beranger, scenario and continuity writer, who has just completed the continuity for Heart of Gold, says that women are going to come into the writing end of the picture industry in greater numbers than ever before. "The motion picture as an entertainment," declares Miss Beranger, "appeals more to women than to men. This fact is bound to be admitted if the exhibitors' statistics are credited as they deserve. To appeal to the female patrons the photoplay must display the feminine point of view and no one is better able to project this angle than women writers.

"It needs no cursory glance at the current releases and those of even six months ago to prove that there are more writers among the feminine sex than the male persuasion.

"The heart throb, the human interest note, child life, domestic scenes and even the eternal triangle is more ably handled by women than men because of the thorough understanding our sex has of these matters. It is an old truism that love to a woman is her story the sincerity that no man it is a mere incident in his life [sic]. This is one of the reasons why a woman writing drama for the screen gives to her story the sincerity that no man can lend. With this sincerity the audience gets plausibility and probability. Men writers in developing their story have to create artificial emotions which they delude themselves into believing is inspiration."

[*The Indianapolis Star* (Indianapolis), 1 September 1918, Section Five, p. 1.]

Feminine Sphere in the Field of Movies is Large Indeed (1919)
Interview with Clara Beranger

"Of all the different industries that have offered opportunities to women, none have given them the chance that motion pictures have," says Clara S. Beranger, scenario and continuity writer.

"In every department of the industry women have shown an aptitude that has earned for them the appreciation of their superiors in the form of substantial salaries.

"If women had shown that their sphere was limited in pictures then the number employed outside of purely clerical positions would have been no greater than what holds in other commercial lines. But women have scored as directors. They have shown a marked value in the creation of scenic ideas and artistic stage settings. It is also true that women who have invaded the hitherto sacred precincts given over to men of handling exchanges, have more than succeeded.

"In passing judgement on the value of pictures for foreign markets, women are now being employed and so down the list. But in one particular branch women are more than holding their own and in many instances proving that the female angle is worth serious consideration and that is in the contriving of situations in building up a continuity. It is also true that women are the equal of men in writing original stories just as it is true that women today in the field of fiction are holding the reins. No man among the current successful authors has a larger following than Mary Roberts Rinehart or Gertrude Atherton.[1]

"In the writing of picture stories women seem to have the call and just why this should be is easily understood. The largest proportion of motion picture 'fans' are women. Women writers know better what pleases their sisters than men for has it not been true since time immemorial that men never understood women but the baby girl just beginning to toddle knows men?"

[*The Moving Picture World* (New York), 2 August 1919, p. 662.]

Fig. 5.15 Photograph of Jeanie Macpherson in her mud and log scriptorium on the Paramount lot. "Even the desk is a huge log," explains the accompanying article.

The Feminine Mind in Picture Making (1925)
Marion Fairfax[1]

[…] Personally, I think that writing is one game in which being a woman is far from being a handicap and as pictures are the universal language of mankind today, and over half of mankind is "womankind." I think woman's point of view is not only valuable in pictures, but necessary.

It will probably be admitted that women know more about women than do men, and our pictures are largely about woman—her home, her struggles, her love as sweetheart, wife or mother. And our audiences are about 75 per cent. women.

As for woman's insight into a man's problems, the struggle of the hero toward success in the field of business, love, adventure or ambition, she may not understand the strictly masculine phases of life of a man—but she very often understands the man. For generations she has helped develop and train the minds of men, as well as taken care of their bodies. Moreover, men habitually confide in women when in need either of encouragement or comfort. Women see men at their most emotional, most self-revealing moments.

For countless ages woman's very existence—certainly her safety and comfort—hinged upon her ability to please or influence men. Naturally, she has almost unconsciously made an intensive study of them. Therefore, if she is a writer at all, she should not only be able to write with insight and sympathetic understanding about women, but at least the authority of a "trained observer" about men.

These appear to me to be fairly good reasons for using whatever we can find of feminine insight and understanding in creating or editing our pictures.

[The Film Daily (New York), 7 June 1925, p. 9, excerpted]

The Director

Alice Blaché, a Dominant Figure in Pictures (1912)
Interview with Alice Blaché

[…] "Perhaps I should not have been able to accomplish so much in any other country, particularly in France. […]

"I am a woman. Do you understand? […]

"Here, in a general way, the fight and victory is to the strong, irrespective of sex. It is not so where I came from. In France we are women, just women, to be treated with all due deference by the men of breeding and to be pampered and showered with affection.[1] Women are commonly in a state of dependence, and are not likely to exercise their reason with freedom. Art in some forms is practically the only field open to them. There are exceptions, of course, but they are rare.

"It is so different here and never for once have I been sorry that my husband brought me with him—to live, to associate and to grow among such nice cosmopolitan people.[2] They talk of French chivalry. Yes, it does exist, but mostly it is superficial. So long as a woman remains in what they term, her place, she suffers little vexation. Yet let her assume the prerogatives usually accorded to her brothers and she is immediately frowned upon. The attitude towards women in America is vastly different.

"During my first experience with a film stock company in this country, I did not fully realize this and I put into practise wrong tactics. I ruled with an iron hand. I soon learned my mistake, and ever since then I have progressed more rapidly. An American gentleman, on joining my company, presumes that I know what I am doing and that I have a right to be where I am. It is a constant conflict when a woman in a French studio attempts to handle and superintend men in their work. They don't like it, and they are not averse to showing their feelings." […]

[Harvey H. Gates, "Alice Blaché, a Dominant Figure in Pictures: How a French Woman Came to this Country and Built up a Big Business," *The New York Dramatic Mirror* (New York), 6 November 1912, p. 28, excerpted.]

Woman's Place in Photoplay Production (1914)
Alice Blaché

It has long been a source of wonder to me that many women have not seized upon the wonderful opportunities offered to them by the motion-picture art to make their way to fame and fortune as producers of photodramas. Of all the arts there is probably none in which they can make such splendid use of talents so much more natural to a woman than to a man and so necessary to its perfection.

There is no doubt in my mind that a woman's success in many lines of endeavour is still made very difficult by a strong prejudice against one of her sex doing work that has been done only by men for hundreds of years. Of course this prejudice is fast disappearing, and there are many vocations in which it has not been present for a long time. In the arts of acting, music, painting, and literature, woman has long held her place among the most successful workers, and when it is considered how vitally all of these arts enter into the production of motion pictures, one wonders why the names of scores of women are not found among the successful creators of photodrama offerings.

Not only is a woman as well fitted to stage a photodrama as a man, but in many ways she has a distinct advantage over him because of her very nature and because much of the knowledge called for in the telling of the story and the creation of the stage setting is absolutely within her province as a member of the gentler sex. She is an authority on the emotions. For centuries she has given them full play while man has carefully trained himself to control them. She has developed her finer feelings for generations, while being protected from the world by her male companions, and she is naturally religious. In matters of the heart her superiority is acknowledged, and her deep insight and sensitiveness in the affairs of cupid give her a wonderful advantage in developing the thread of love that plays such an all-important part in almost every story that is prepared for the screen. All of the distinctive qualities which she possesses come into direct play during the guiding of the actors in making their character drawings and interpreting the different emotions called for by the story. For to think and to feel the situation demanded by the play is the secret of successful acting, and sensitiveness to those thoughts and feelings is absolutely essential to the success of a stage director.

The qualities of patience and gentleness possessed to such a high degree by womankind are also of inestimable value in the staging of a photodrama. Artistic temperament is a thing to be reckoned with while directing an actor, in spite of the treatment of the subject in the comic papers, and a gentle, soft-voiced director is much more conducive to good work on the part of the performer than the overstern, noisy tyrant of the studio.

Not a small part of the motion-picture director's work, in addition to the preparation of the story for picture-telling and the casting and directing of the actors, is the choice of suitable locations for the staging of the exterior scenes and the supervising of the studio settings, props, costumes, etc. In these matters it seems to me that a woman is especially well qualified to obtain the very best results, for she is dealing with subjects that are almost a second nature to her. She takes the measure of every person, every costume, every house, and every piece of furniture that her eye comes into contact with, and the beauty of a stretch of landscape or a single flower impresses her immediately. All of these things are of the greatest value to the creator of a photodrama, and the knowledge of them must be extensive and exact. A woman's magic touch is immediately recognized in a real home. Is it not just as recognizable in the home of the characters of a photoplay?

That women make the theatre possible from the box-office standpoint is an acknowledged fact. Theatre managers know that their appeal must be to the woman if they would succeed, and all of their efforts are naturally in that direction. This being the case, what a rare opportunity is offered to women to use that inborn knowledge of just what does appeal to them to produce photodramas that will contain that inexplicable something which is necessary to the success of every stage or screen production.

There is nothing connected with the staging of a motion picture that a woman cannot do as easily as a man, and there is no reason why she cannot completely master every technicality of the art. The technique of the drama has been mastered by so many women that it is considered as much her field as a man's and its adaptation to picture work in no way removes it from her sphere. The technique of motion-picture photography, like the technique of the drama, is fitted to a woman's activities.

It is hard for me to imagine how I could have obtained my knowledge of photography, for instance, without the months of study spent in the laboratory of the Gaumont Company in Paris at a time when motion picture photography was in the experimental stage, and carefully continued since [in] my own laboratory in the Solax Studios in this country. It is also necessary to study stage direction by actual participation in the work, in addition to burning the midnight oil in your library, but both are as suitable, as fascinating, and as remunerative to a woman as to a man.

[Madame Alice Blaché, "Woman's Place in Photoplay Production," *Moving Picture World* (New York), 11 July 1914, p. 195.]

How I Became a Motion Picture Director (1915)
Lois Weber

The opportunity to enter the director's field came through my ability to write photoplays. I had abandoned the legitimate stage for the shadowy drama, and was appearing in leading parts on the Gaumont films. Mr. Smalley played opposite to me, and Mr. Herbert Blaché was the director.[1] This was six years ago, and I was dissatisfied with the quality of many of the scenarios submitted. They lacked the force—the "punch," as the expression goes—and were sadly deficient in technique and construction. The general idea seemed to consider a jumble of melodrama and stage tricks, hastily thrown together, quite adequate to meet the demands of the public. Little thought was accorded to the boundless art essential to a real photodrama. The writers were satisfied to keep the characters moving through a thin plot, insipid in conception, and pathetic in sentiment. It occurred to me that the public would welcome something better. The many undeserved criticisms of the work of screen folks were an indication of this desire; for no amount of clever acting can redeem a character poorly drawn, or a play that is hopelessly deficient in plot and execution. So I began to write scenarios around the personalities of Mr. Smalley and myself.

It was not such a difficult matter for one with my experience in legitimate and motion picture drama to improve on the scenarios of that period. I submitted my efforts to Mr. Smalley and Mr. Blaché, who gave me every encouragement.

When they came up for production I learned a lot of things. No one knows more about a scenario worthy of the name than the originator of it; and yet, few scenario writers have the faculty to visualize a scene with every detail polished to a sparkling brilliancy. Many vague ideas away back in the mind struggle for expression, but can not work into the concrete mental picture. So they are sketched in roughly, and may suggest nothing at all in the way of elaboration to the director, who has little time to puzzle over a writer's unrecorded conceptions. Therefore, as we came to each scene, and the mental pictures were acted out by real characters, I discovered little defects here and there; a chance to improve the action occasionally; a new line to etch in that strengthened a character, and a hundred and one other things that enlarged the scene and gave it a finish.

I was fortunate in being associated with broad-minded men. Both Mr. Smalley and Mr. Blaché listened to my suggestions. They approved or disapproved as the suggestions were good or bad, and I did the same with the ones they offered. The work became a real pleasure when we brought our individual talents into an effective combination, and we were enabled to turn out many original and successful photoplays.

That is the way I acquired my first experience in arranging the drama for the screen. Our combination worked in perfect harmony, and would have continued to the present day but for the natural growth of the organization. I know that each of us shared the same regret when the change was made, even though it gave us separate directorships in the larger company.

Since then I have been associated in a business way with Mr. Edwin Porter, of the old Rex Company; Mr. Carl Laemmle, of the big Universal concern; with Mr. Frank A. Garbutt and Mr. Hobart Bosworth, of Bosworth, Inc., and now I have again joined the big Universal organization with Mr. Smalley. In all my dealings with these men the quality of my work alone has counted.

There may be some truth in the opinion that a good director, like other artists, is born and not made. The position seems to require certain talents that it is impossible to acquire. There is that infinite capacity for detail; an apparent sixth sense that intuitively recoils from the inartistic, and the faculty to visualize, from the artificial workings of the studio, how a play will appear on the screen. But given all the natural talent in the world, one must develop it by persistent study, or complete failure will result. The illusions that are possible of creation with the camera must be learned; the little tricks of light and shadows; the limitations of photography; and then the assistance that may be rendered by skilful mechanical devices which enlarge the scope of the pictures. One may possess natural good taste in harmonious effects, and may be able to produce them without much effort in the studio; but the matter of how to convey them to the screen is a matter of deep study.

A director cannot afford to slight a detail of the groupings, the acting, the lighting—anything; for upon the details depend the atmosphere so necessary to bring an audience en rapport with the play on the screen. The "feel" that they are in the plot, and undergoing the emotional suspense of the characters as the story develops, does not lie entirely in the skill of the scenario writer. The director must act as the medium between his work and the audience, to transmit the subtle influence from the studio to the screen. There is no royal road to this knowledge. It is acquired only by a diligent study of the many intricate details of cause and effect that makes the conscientious director an artist to the finger tips.

It then becomes a labor of love; and the spur to greater effort is the promise that the future motion picture will develop into a source of universal knowledge and influence. The discovery of new marvels that come within the scope of reproduction endows the film with endless possibilities for doing good; and to know that one is benefiting others is the supreme pleasure of work.

The feature films alone have added to the amusement and education of millions of people. The range of literature and drama had its limitations until the motion picture came along; but now the boundary lines of ignorance and poverty are taken down, and the intellectual reservations of centuries are thrown open to millions of new settlers.

It is good to be a director.

[Mrs Phillips Smalley, How I Became a Motion Picture Director," *Static Flashes* (Los Angeles) 1:14, 24 April 1915, p. 8.]

Motion-Picture Work: The Motion-Picture Director (1920)
Ida May Park

Description of occupation and qualifications necessary

The vocation of the motion-picture director is one that commands so comprehensive a knowledge of the arts and sciences, economics and human nature, that it is particularly difficult to describe. To the almost unlimited mental demands on the director is added the necessity of an invulnerable physique. Perhaps that is why the number of consistently successful directors, both male and female, is relatively so small. But having these things there is no one, man or woman, who might not take up the profession with a certain degree of confidence in his or her ultimate success.

Because it is so obvious, I have not mentioned the necessity for a well-developed dramatic instinct. Perhaps more than anything else that instinct is the deciding factor of the success or the failure of the motion-picture director. Like acting, this ability to direct is an inborn talent, but it can be cultivated to a certain degree through the mediums of training, proper reading, and environment. But again, as it is with acting, the cultivated art can never equal the natural; it will always lack the fire of genius. From the beginning of the production, when the story is being moulded to scenario requirements, the director is the supervisor, the dominant note of the production, and (I am now writing to women alone) it is her sense of dramatic value that imparts to, or withholds from, the picture that indefinable something which can raise it to the ultimate peak of picture perfection or relegate it to the vast scrapheap of "rubber-stamp" productions.

Second to this in importance is the artistic eye, for at all times the picture must be perfect in its angles, composition, and grouping. Our chief aim is to please, first and foremost, through the vision.

Preparation necessary

Preparation, since the demands on knowledge of all kinds is boundless, must necessarily be very general. A college education is a great help if it has not been concentrated on any particular subject to the detriment of others. The whole motion-picture industry is so young and the recognition of the value of good direction so recent that, so far as I know, there is yet no school established which teaches the strictly technical side. Knowledge of camera operation, of lightning effects, and of all the hundred and one less important mechanical details must be gained through work in the studio itself. The difficulty of obtaining a position as apprentice or assistant is unfortunately very great.

Opportunity for advancement

Once in the game the aspirant to a directorship will find the opportunities limitless. Such a statement is not half so extreme as it sounds. The perfect picture is still a thing of dreams. An industry can develop only as the intelligence which directs it develops. The interest of big minds is a thing that until recently has been glaringly absent from the motion picture. But now converts, intelligent converts, are flocking to the banner and results are bound to come in the form of better pictures.

Financial returns

The financial return is likewise unlimited. A thousand dollars a week is a small income for a successful director. It might well be called a minimum. There is no maximum.

Advantages and disadvantages

While production is on there is no rest. No eight-hour day is known to the director. Often work extends far into the night, many times through it, and the next day brings no respite. Given a certain number of weeks, a certain number of dollars, and a troupe of actors, you are under a terrific nervous and physical strain that does not let up until you have completed the work. The obstacles which arise are frequently enough to try the greatest patience. The director must never lose her poise, must never betray the slightest annoyance unless she wishes to jeopardize the success of her picture. In all the world there is no more difficult lot of people to handle than a company of actors. When vacation finally does come, it is never more than two or three days. For the first time in six years I am taking a ten-day vacation, and even now the tentacles of the great cinema octopus reach out at intervals and threaten to drag me back, my vacation half over, into the maelstrom of the studio.

As for the natural equipment of women for the rôle of director, the superiority of their emotional and imaginative faculties gives them a great advantage. Then, too, the fact that there are only two women directors of note in the field to-day leaves an absolutely open field.[1] But unless you are hardy and determined, the director's rôle is not for you. Wait until the profession has emerged from its embryonic state and a system has been evolved by which the terrific weight of responsibility can be lifted from one pair of shoulders. When that time comes I believe that women will find no finer calling.

[From *Careers for Women*, ed. Catherine Filene (Boston: Houghton Mifflin, 1920), pp. 335–7.]

Harmony in Picture-Making (1923)
June Mathis

Successful motion pictures are made in an atmosphere of harmony.

Great stories shape themselves like beautiful, perfect crystals—in a mind or medium undisturbed by jars, free from the shocks of jealousies and intrigues.

In the studio, there must be harmony between the writer and the director, or, according to my observation, something goes wrong with the picture.

There is, to me, a very striking analogy between creation in the biological sense and the creation of a work of art such as we try to, and sometimes do, achieve on the screen. Biological creation takes two elements: male and female. It is a significant fact that most of the best-known and most successful scenario writers are women. The greatest directors are men, and the harmonious endeavors of a man and a woman have resulted in the best pictures.

Parenthetically, this is said in no disparagement of masculine scenario writers. The great artists, surgeons, authors and musicians have the feminine quality in their nature, and the successful scenarist also has this enviable quality, or reflects it from a home in which the feminine influence is strongly felt in the person of wife or mother.

Two people working together is usually a better arrangement than one working alone. Even the work of the great author must pass through the hands of an
editor.

To continue our figure of speech, let us say that the woman writer takes the
fundamental theme of a great story or play, and by her art translates it into the
pictorial medium. What she hands the director is only a bundle of typed scenes—but
it contains the sleeping soul of drama.

The director interprets, renders the idea, the theme, into form for the celluloid.
His masculine touch activates the written words, and they grow from latency into
life on the screen. So it was in the beginning, is now, and ever shall be.

The proof that harmony must enter into creation is shown by the wonderful
improvement in the effect of a picture when shown with music. Perfect construction
and synchronization only come with the thought of harmony.

There is also a more practical side to this question of the feminine influence in
picture-making. The great majority of picture-goers are women, and the picture
director, to be successful, must reflect their viewpoint. The best way for him to
do this is by having a feminine collaborator.

[Film Daily (New York) 24:36, 6 May 1923, p. 5.]

The Feminine Mind in Picture Making (1925)
June Mathis[1]

My first introduction to this phrase in connection with the motion picture industry
was just prior to taking up the writing of motion pictures seriously—and that was
really the reason I was admitted into the ranks of the industry. A certain director
felt he needed just that one thing to help him in his work.[2] In his argument with
the general manager when he explained why he wanted a special writer (and that
writer a woman) added to his personal staff, the general manager's reply was to
the effect: "What good can a woman possibly be—but if you want her, Okay;
she'll soon prove a nuisance, and you'll [let] her go." A year later I became the
same general manager's assistant, helping him in all his productions and the head
of the scenario staff. This was because he, too, felt through the experience of a
year the value of a woman's viewpoint. There were only a few women at that time
who were working in the industry—I mean, working side by side, or rather as
silent aides to the directors and production heads. Somehow, these men prospered
and succeeded in quite a remarkable way, outstripping most of the others: and it
was half-heartedly acknowledged throughout the industry that a woman could do
something to aid in the great development of the motion picture business. And
why? The question has often been asked.

First, because in the scenario field, where stories are formed, and the chrysalis
[sic] of an idea becomes a great motion picture that is expected to appeal to millions

of people throughout the country; and of those millions the hand that rocks the cradle is the ruling spirit. Women must be pleased, and a woman understands the inner workings of a woman's brain better than any man. Men may think they do, but many men have met their Waterloo in thinking they know women better than women know themselves.

And so women seem to succeed in the careful, fine detail work of scenario writing.

Added to the scenario writer in the studio is the woman technical or art director and set dresser. Again the reason: They understand the decoration of the home, the setting of tables, the arrangement of flowers. Late years I have heard many big directors say they would not attempt to "shoot" a set until a woman had looked it over and lent her final touch to it, just to establish the "home" quality.

After some little time there appeared the woman script clerk, for just the same reason; because women watch the smaller details better than men. Again I am quoting some eminent directors. Late years a few women film cutters have appeared, and some excellent title writers have also come into the industry; but as yet I have to find a woman turning a camera crank. For some reason or other they have balked at this. Perhaps for the reason that we have never had very many world famous women painters.

And last of all, I have to mention the directorial field for women. So many women have attempted this and have given it up. I won't say, have failed—because where is there a man who has directed his first picture entirely alone, without a great deal of experienced technical assistance, and made a knock-out of that same first picture?

When a woman takes the megaphone in her hand, the eyes of the entire industry are focused upon her. She makes her first picture, and people say, "Well, it wasn't so much." and so the woman sits down and allows some man to take the megaphone away from her.

But this we all know: Women in general are playing an important part in the American production of films, and America is first in the world's market, and picture-making is the fourth industry in the United States.

While in Europe recently my official position was the subject of much curiosity on the part of foreign film men. They could not quite grasp just what part a woman could play, from the standpoint of an executive. And I was surprised to learn that women play little or no part in foreign production. And after thinking over the matter, reasoning out the few foreign motion pictures that have come to us, I have come to the conclusion that perhaps this may be the "nigger in the woodpile." The great cry of the American producers in their complaint against foreign motion pictures has been "Wonderful spectacles! Settings remarkable! Scenery beautiful!"—but they lack the human quality that makes a motion picture commercial. Hence, from out of Europe there comes to us a wonderful man-made motion picture spectacle or drama, produced with great finesse—but lacking in human quality. And perhaps that same human quality lurks behind the woman's view point. Women in Europe are more or less kept in the background; the man is the mouth-piece of the family; at home and abroad. While here, a woman pokes her nose into nearly everything, and makes herself heard. So even when the man who does not, or will not acknowledge that there is such a thing as a woman's viewpoint that is possibly commercial, it's bound to creep in, anyway, through the voice of the home; and perhaps it is this same thing—this same magic something—that has made American films supreme in the world's market.

[Film Daily (New York), 7 June 1925, p. 115.]

Why Are There No Women Directors? (1925)
Florence M. Osborne

The invasion of motion pictures by women has been complete except for one last remaining citadel. There are no women directors who are helping to make motion picture history. In every other department, they have been pre-eminently successful. Women writers may almost be said to dominate the scenario field. There is a deep scientific reason for this. Some years ago a series of psychological experiments were made in a German university town—long before motion pictures were heard of. School children of both sexes were required to write fiction stories. One fact was established as a result of the experiment: the girl children were not so logical in their plots: they didn't bother so much how they "got there": but they showed a superior sense of picturization to the boy children. Also their stories had more interesting detail and more sentiment and more emotion.

So it would seem that women were naturally fitted for the work of writing for the screen. Experience of motion picture companies has shown that the combination of a woman, with her quick, alert sense of invention and her ability to "see in pictures," and a director with a logical sense of construction, is the ideal working team for movies.

Among the greatest "cutters" and film editors are women. They are quick and resourceful. They are also ingenious in their work and usually have a strong sense of what the public wants to see. They can sit in a stuffy cutting-room and see themselves looking at the picture before an audience.

They have been successful as producers: some of the best film "salesmen" are women: they have, in rare cases, been conspicuously successful as studio executives.

But they do not seem to have "left their nick" on the industry as directors. There have been a few like Ida May Park, Mary Jane Wilson, and Lois Weber who were good directors—more than ordinarily good directors.[1] For some reason or other, they do not seem to be doing it now.

A good director has to be a singularly versatile individual. He has to have the physical endurance of a bull buffalo; the patience of a saint. He has to be at once a good executive and a good diplomat. A company of temperamental actors can't be handled like a company of Prussian dragoons. He has to be an artist with a comprehensive knowledge of color and composition; an actor of enough technical knowledge to show actors the fine points of their art; and most of all a good showman who knows instinctively what audiences like and want.

Where is it along this line that women fail to qualify? Probably it is in the matter of physical strength. The strain of picture production usually wears out the strongest man in a few years. The casualties even among men of the most robust physique and nerve force is appalling. It is a devastating pace. It would have to be a superwoman to stand up under the strain.

[*Motion Picture Magazine* (Jamaica, NY) 30:4, November 1925, p. 5. The article is signed "The Editor."]

Sex and the Screen (1924)
Jane Murfin

The above title may sound alluring but it is like many of those grafted upon our picture productions—its object is to arrest attention while I tell you about something you wouldn't otherwise be interested in.

I have observed that Jill must know her business, not only as well, but just a little better than Jack, if she is going to "get by" at all. The more jobs she has filled, the more she knows of the business as a whole, the better chance she has of making a real place for herself. Her sex is her chief handicap, not as a playwright nor as a continuity writer—for it is the general belief that both of these need the feminine slant—but as a producer or director of pictures.

A producer is necessarily involved in endless business details. Now, men don't really like to do business with women. In the first place, they don't trust them. Perhaps as husbands they have so often had their pockets picked while taking the morning shower that they have ceased to expect a woman to play the game, man to man. And even if the men have confidence in a woman's financial integrity, they are never quite sure she won't take advantage of their masculine gallantry and get something she isn't entitled to just because she is a woman. After all, it is a bit precarious to do business with someone you suspect will fall back on her sex and get all the sympathy of the onlookers if you ever have to fight her. And what business man in the world doesn't look forward to an occasional good row, given an even break! Then, men don't expect women to understand the intricacies of business, the cost of production and distribution, the percentage of overhead, locked up capital and liquid assets, and especially the complications of banking transactions. I admit I've sometimes wondered just how clearly the men themselves understood them, and one or two unwisely frank gentlemen have even admitted that they were congenitally hazy about "earned and unearned profits" and the "circuit velocity of money," doubtless due to the parental influence of their mothers.

As a director, too, Jill's sex is a handicap. There is a general impression that her physical strength is not sufficient to meet the demands of such work. The answer to this is—it depends entirely upon the individual. I know several women who can out-work most men. To be sure there are some types of pictures I would not advise a woman to direct. The great out-of-doors productions with thousands of extras or animals seem to belong more naturally to men.

There is always the question as to whether or not an actress responds to a woman director as readily and with as good results as to a man director. That, too, depends upon the individuals. Some women respond emotionally to the opposite sex more easily than to their own. These women need a man to direct them. Other women are stimulated through the mind and the imagination and can create their own emotions regardless of the director, and so respond as quickly to one sex as the other.

I have found that the first impulse of an actor is to mentally question the ability of a director—does he know his business—and until the actor is fairly certain the director does know, nothing much happens in the way of a response of any kind. I think a woman is faced by a bigger question mark in the minds of actors than a man, which brings me back to my original statement—Jill has to know her business quite as well and perhaps a little better than Jack to "get by."

[From *The Truth About Movies by the Stars*, ed. Laurence A. Hughes (Hollywood: Hollywood Publishers, 1924), pp. 459–61.]

Beginning Young (1925)
Lillian Gish

[...] While the successful appeal of moving pictures is to women and girls, I want to say emphatically from my own experience that there is one part of the business of the making of pictures which I do not believe a woman can do. I do not believe that women can direct pictures. I say this in spite of the excellent work done by Lois Weber, who was assisted by her husband in the making of some very successful releases.[1] Directorship requires a combination of qualities that women do not possess. I would not have believed this until I tried. While Mr. Griffith was waiting for his Mamaroneck studio to be completed he took two films in Florida. I was not in either of these, and Dorothy was a picture behind on her schedule. I suggested to Mr. Griffith that we get a story and that while he was in Florida I would direct Dorothy in a picture. "What do you want to do," Mr. Griffith asked me—"disrupt your whole family?"

"I think I can do it. I want to try."

"You better not. You two girls and your mother have been the best of companions through the years you have worked on the stage and in the films. Why do you want to spoil it all now?"

But I persisted and went to work on a story called *Remodeling Her Husband*.[2]

In spite of Mr. Griffith's prediction the family circle was not disrupted. On the contrary it was added to, for shortly after *Remodeling Her Husband*, my sister became Mrs. Rennie.

When released, the picture did quite well and caused the price of Dorothy's pictures to be doubled thereafter. As a director, however, I was and am through.

[*Ladies' Home Journal* (Philadelphia) 42, September 1925, p. 120, excerpted.]

Can Women Direct Films? (1929)
Nerina Shute[1]

It is pathetically obvious that women can't produce films. In England only one lady has had the temerity to try. Dina Shurey (who will go to heaven by reason of her great courage) has created several appalling pictures. Critics have bowed with sad courtesy to the gentle creator of such films as *The Last Post*. They can't fail to admire her good intentions, and yet...

In America, the situation is very nearly as distressing. There are, perhaps, three women directors in existence, but no one of them has made an outstanding picture.

What, then, is the answer?

Down at the Archibald Nettlefold studios I put this question to Mrs. Walter Forde, wife of the actor–director, and a lady whose guidance is sought constantly by her brilliant husband.[2]

"I've been in the picture business for years," she told me. "I started before the war at the very bottom of the ladder. And I think I know pretty thoroughly the technicalities that make a good director.

"Nevertheless I wouldn't take on the post. A woman isn't fitted for direction. As you know, I am Walter's assistant, and he comes to me after every scene and asks my advice.

"A woman of ideas can be invaluable to a director, lending all sorts of feminine subtleties to his work, but *she cannot do the work herself*. You see, a really fine director is a mixture of artist and business magnate. He must have a commercial brain, and he must be able to handle men. Physically, he must endure all kinds of hardships, and mentally he must be a creative genius.

"If a woman is fitted artistically for the post, she has never the temperament to endure 15-hour days of hard mental and physical exertion.

"Although some women are strong enough to swim the Channel, and others sufficiently artistic to paint famous pictures or write famous books, they can't hope to combine the two qualities. They can't possibly comply with the demands made on an average director." [...]

[*Film Weekly* (London), 10 June 1929, p. 12. excerpted.]

Women in the Arts: Some Notes on the Eternally Conflicting Demands of Humanity and Art (1925)

Dorothy Richardson

It is only lately that the failure of women in the fine arts has achieved pre-eminence in the *cause célèbre*, Man versus Woman, as a witness for the prosecution. In the old days, not only was art not demanded of women, but the smallest sign of genuine ability in a female would put a man in the state of mind of the lady who said when she saw the giraffe: "I don't believe it."

Thus Albrecht Dürer, travelling through the Netherlands in 1521 and happening upon the paintings of Susanne Horehout, makes appreciative notes in his diary, but is constrained to add: "Amazing that a she-creature should accomplish so much." And some three hundred years later, Gustave Flaubert, standing at the easel of Madame Commanville, smiles indulgently and murmurs: "Yes, she has talent: it is *odd*."

✿

But today, under pressure of the idea that women in asserting equality, have also asserted identity with men, the demand for art as a supporting credential has become the parrot-cry of the masculinists of both sexes. A cry that grows both strident and hoarse. For this pre-eminent witness for the prosecution is, poor fellow, shockingly over-worked. And not only over-worked but also a little uneasy. Feeling no doubt, since most of his fellows have been hustled away in disgrace and those that remain are apt to wilt in the hands of defending counsel, that his own turn may be at hand.

But though towering a little insecurely still he towers, at once the last refuge of all who are frightened by anything that disturbs their vision of man as the dominant sex, and the despair of those feminists who believe fine art to be the highest human achievement.

There are of course many, an increasing band, who flatly deny that art is the highest human achievement and place ahead of it all that is called science, which they are inclined to regard as the work of humanity's post-adolescence. But it is a curious and notable fact, a fact quite as curious and notable as the absence of first-class feminine art, that all these people, whenever they want to enlighten the layman on the subject of the scientific imagination, are at pains to explain that the scientific imagination, at its best, is the imagination of the artist. It is not less odd that the man of science if he is masculinist, will, when hard-pressed, seize, to belabour his opponent, not the test-tube, but the mahlstick. (It is of course to be remembered that while the mahlstick is solid and persists unchanging, the test-tube is hollow and its contents variable.) And the rush for the mahlstick goes on in spite of the fact that the witness for science does not, on the whole, have a bad time. He has perhaps lost a little of his complacency. But he can still, when counsel for the defense reminds the jury how recently women have had access to scientific material and education, point to the meagre, uninstructed beginnings of some of the world's foremost men of science.

Side by side with the devotees of science we find those who count religion the highest human achievement. They are a house divided. In so far as they set in the van the mystic—the religious genius who uses not marble or pigment or the written word, but his own life as the medium of his art—they supply a witness for the defense who points to Catherine and Teresa walking abreast with Francis and Boehme.[1] But their witness is always asked what he makes of the fact that Jesus, Mahomed, and Buddha are all of the sex male. His prompt answer: that he looks not backward but ahead, leaves things, even after he has pointed to Mrs. Eddy and Mrs. Besant, a little in the air.[2] For Catholic feminists there is, always the Mother of God. But they are rare, and as it were under an editorial ban. Privately they must draw much comfort from the fact that the Church which, since the days of its formal organization has excluded woman from its ultimate sanctities, is yet constrained to set her above it, crowned Queen of Heaven.

Last, but from the feminist point of view by no means least of those who challenge the security of the one solidly remaining hope of the prosecution, are the many who believe, some of them having arrived at feminism via their belief, that the finest flowers of the human spirit are the social arts including the art of dress. In vain is their witness reminded of the man modiste, the pub and the club. He slays opposition with lyrics, with idylls of the Primitive Mother forming, with her children, society, while father slew beasts and ate and slept. And side by side with the pull at its best he places the salon at its best, and over against Watt and his dreamy contemplation of the way the light steam plays with the heavy lid of the kettle—a phenomenon, thunders the prosecution, that for centuries countless women have witnessed daily in animal stupidity—he sets Watt's mother, seeing the lifting lid as tea for several weary ones.[3]

❧

But in all this there is no comfort for the large company of feminists who sincerely see the fine arts as humanity's most godlike achievement. For them the case, though still it winds its interminable way, is settled. There is no escape from the verdict of woman's essential inferiority. The arraignment is the more flawless because just here, in the field of art, there has been from time immemorial, a fair field and no favour. Always women have had access to the pen, the chisel and the instrument of music. Yet not only have they produced no Shakespeare, no Michelangelo and no Beethoven, but in the civilization of today, where women artists abound, there is still scarcely any distinctive feminine art. The art of women is still on the whole either mediocre or derivative.

There is, of course, at the moment, Käthe Kollwitz, Mother and Hausfrau to begin with, and, in the estimation of many worthy critics, not only the first painter in Europe today but a feminine painter—one that is to say whose work could not have been produced by a man.[4] She it may be is the Answer to Everything. For though it is true that one swallow does not make a summer, the production by the female sex of even one supreme painter brings the whole fine arts argument to the ground and we must henceforth seek the cause of woman's general lack of achievement in art elsewhere than in the idea that first-class artistic expression is incarnate in man alone.

Let us, however suppose that there is no Käthe Kollwitz, assume art to be the highest human achievement, accept the great arraignment and in the interest of the many who are driven to cynicism by the apparent impossibility of roping women into the scheme of salvation, set up the problem in its simplest terms. Cancel out all the variable factors; the pull of the home on the daughter, celibacy, the economic factor and the factor of motherhood, each of which taken alone may be said by weighting the balance to settle the matter out of court and taken all together make us rub our eyes at the achievements of women to date—cancel out all these and imagine for a moment a man and a woman artist side by side with equal chances and account if we can for the man's overwhelming superiority.

◆

There is before we can examine our case one more factor to rule out—isolated here because it grows, in the light of modern psychological investigation, increasingly difficult to state, and also because as a rule it is either omitted from the balance, or set down as a good mark to the credit of one party. This elusive and enormously potent factor is called ambition. And its definition, like most others, can never be more or less than a statement of the definer's philosophy of life. But it may at least be agreed that ambition is rich or poor. Childishly self-ended or selflessly mature. And a personal ambition is perhaps not ill-defined as the subtlest form of despair—though a man may pass in a lifetime from the desire for personal excellence, the longing to be sure that either now or in the future he shall be recognized as excellent, to the reckless love of excellence for its own sake, leaving the credit to the devil—and so on to becoming, as it were behind his own back, one with his desire. And though the ambition of the artist need not of necessity be personal, he is peculiarly apt to suffer in the absence of recognition—and here at once we fall upon the strongest argument against fine art as the highest human achievement. These are altitudes. But we are discussing high matters. And though the quality of a man's ambition takes naught from the intrinsic value of his work, an ambition to the extent that it remains a thirst to be recognized as personally great, is a form of despair. And it is a form of despair to which men are notoriously more liable than are women. A fact that ceases to surprise when one reflects that, short of sainthood, a man must do rather than be, that he is potent not so much in person as in relation to the things he makes.

And so with ambition ruled out and our case thus brought down to the bare bones of undebatable actuality, back to our artists of whom immediately we must enquire what it is that they most urgently need for the development of their talents, the channels through which their special genius is to operate. The question has been answered by genius—on its bad days and always to the same effect. Da Vinci, called simultaneously by almost everything that can attract the mind of man, has answered it. Goethe, the court official, answered it. And by way of casting a broad net we will quote here the testimonies of an eleventh century Chinese painter and a modern writer, a South African.

"Unless I dwell in a quiet house, seat myself in a retired room with the window open, the table dusted, incense burning and the thousand trivial thoughts crushed out and sunk, I cannot have good feeling for painting or beautiful taste, and cannot create the you" (the mysterious and wonderful—Fennelosa's translation) Kakki.

"It's a very wise curious instinct that makes all people who have imaginative work (whether it's scientific or philosophic thinking, or poetry, or story-making, of course it doesn't matter so it's original work, and has to be spun out of the texture of the mind itself) try to creep away into some sort of solitude."... "It's worry, tension, painful emotion, anxiety that kills imagination out as surely as a bird is killed by a gun." Olive Schreiner.[5]

Quiet, and solitude in the sense of freedom from preoccupations, are the absolute conditions of artistic achievement. Exactly, it may be answered, and your male artist will pay for these things any price that may be asked. Will pay health, respectability, honour, family claims and what not. And keep fine. And there are in the world of art women who make the same payments and yet do not achieve supremacy and, indefinably, do not remain fine. What is the difference? Where is it that the woman breaks down? She should with a fair field and her fascinating burdensome gift of sight, her gift for expansive vicarious living, be at least his equal. She should. But there are, when we come down to the terms of daily experience, just two things that queer the pitch. One abroad and one at home. For the woman, and particularly the woman painter, going into the world of art is immediately surrounded by masculine traditions. Traditions based on assumptions that are largely unconscious and whose power of suggestion is unlimited. Imagine the case reversed. Imagine the traditions that held during a great period of Egyptian art, when women painters were the rule—the nude male serving as model, as the "artist's model" that in our own day is the synonym for nude femininity.

But even the lifting away from our present gropings after civility in the world at large of the diminishing shadow of that which, for want of a more elegant term, is being called men-state mentality, would do nothing towards the removal of the obstruction in the path of the woman artist at home. She would still be left in an environment such as has surrounded no male artist since the world began. For the male artist, though with bad luck he may be tormented by his womankind, or burdened by wife and family, with good luck may be cherished by a devoted wife or mistress, or neglectful char, by someone, that is to say, who will either reverently or contemptuously let him be. And with the worst of luck, living in the midst of debt and worry and pressure, still somehow he will be tended and will live serenely, innocent of the swarming detail that is the basis of daily life.

It is not only that there exists for the woman no equivalent for the devoted wife or mistress. There is also no equivalent for the most neglectful char known to man. For the service given by women to women is as different from that given by women to men as is chalk from cheese. If hostile, it will specialize in manufacturing difficulties. If friendly, it will demand unfaltering response. For it knows that living sympathy is there. And in either case service is given on the assumption that the woman at work is in the plot for providing life's daily necessities. And even vicarious expansion towards a multitude of details, though it may bring wisdom, is fatal to sustained creative effort.

Art demands what, to women, current civilizations won't give. There is for a Dostoyevsky writing against time on the corner of a crowded kitchen table a greater possibility of detachment than for a woman artist no matter how placed. Neither motherhood nor the more continuously exacting and indefinitely expansive responsibilities of even the simplest housekeeping can so effectively hamper her as the human demand, besieging her wherever she is, for an inclusive awareness, from which men, for good or ill, are exempt.

[*Vanity Fair* (New York), May 1925, pp. 47, 100.]

Working in the Auditorium

Great Field for Women (1917)

Alta M. Davis

In a letter to the Balboa Company, Miss Alta M. Davis,
manager of the Empire Theater at Los Angeles, Cal., says in part:[1]

"It seems to me that there is a great field in the movie business, as yet practically unexplored by my own sex, for women of the progressive type who are not satisfied to let the masculine element of every community dominate, plan, manage, and originate everything—and, of course, reap all the benefits that naturally accrue to those who have initiative, a quality possessed by women as well as men.

"It is a known fact that women and children form the greater part of every moving picture audience, and it is but natural that a woman manager should be better qualified than a man to judge the kind of pictures the majority of her patrons like, when most of them are of her own sex.

"After all, the meat in the cocoanut of successful management, so to speak, is in obtaining the right kind of pictures—pictures that appeal to the greatest number."

["Great Field for Women: Lady Manager of Theater Writes to Balboa Company," *New York Dramatic Mirror* (New York), 10 February 1917, p. 24.]

Towards a Co-operative Cinema:
The Work of the Academy, Oxford Street (1933)
Elizabeth Coxhead

Everyone knows the Academy Cinema.[1] When we say Academy, it is as often as not, (and how shocked our grandfathers would be to hear it) that one we mean. It is more than a cinema; it is a policy, a promise, a guarantee. Something one has in common with other people, a topic of conversation, a means of making friends.

To understand the Academy and its aims, one has to go back more than three years, back, in fact to 1916, when Elsie Cohen, a young woman fresh from college, and rather interested in films, found Wardour Street open to women, as so many fields were then which now are not.[2] She walked into a post on the *Kinematograph Weekly*, and began, from the excellent vantage-point of a technical paper, her apprenticeship to the oddest trade in the world.

She soon observed that there were a good many interesting film happenings in other countries besides America. There was Germany, for instance, and there was also Holland, where a small company was making films specifically for the English market. The difficulty of getting information about them suggested to her that the company needed a good publicity manager. She wrote offering her services, and by return—those were the happy, haphazard days—was invited.

Her work for this company included, in the end, everything except actual direction. She managed the studio, sold films, travelled everywhere, even getting to the States and selling the first European film. When the company was dissolved, she already knew her way about the film world; she went to Berlin, coming in at the end of the great silent period. She stood over *Vaudeville* and *Manon*, and had her fingers in many interesting pies. So far, just the chequered career anyone might have in the Trade.

But already she saw in it more than a trade. She grew yearly more convinced that the most important film work was scarcely heard of in England, let alone seen; but that there were people at home who would be interested, people who never went to films at all, but would be won over by the new kind of film, which struggled for a footing against the old. The audiences of Germany and France appreciated and understood; and so would the right audience in England.

She came home, and found films in a state of apathy. For a time she worked as floor-manager in English studios, but the lack of organisation made a too painful contrast with those of Germany. Everyone, she said, spent their time hanging around waiting.

The idea of catering for an intelligent film public was growing in her mind. People seemed interested. She was constantly asked about her experiences in Germany, about the new films from Russia, about the chances of getting old films revived. Only the Trade was not interested at all. She could find no one to finance her.

For years she waited, being discouraged and laughed at with a dreary persistence. It was not till 1929 that she had any kind of opportunity; the little Windmill Theatre fell vacant for six months, and she was allowed to try out a highbrow season which was a success. But then the theatre was taken for other purposes, and her pilgrimage in the Trade wilderness began again. Finally she secured the support of Eric Hakim; in 1931 the Academy opened with *Earth*. Everyone gave the scheme a six weeks' run. But it seems likely that of all London's film policies, it will have the longest life.

The policy of the Academy, like all living ideas, has developed since its birth, and one change is notable. At first it was definitely a repertory cinema, and showed interesting pictures without regard to their age or the number of times they had been seen before. The audience clamoured for revivals, and the difficulty of seeing again in an ordinary cinema a picture one has once liked was, and for that matter still is, acute. The Academy worked off a good many of the great silent pictures during 1931, and then the audience began to show an interest in new work and to ask for it. This accorded with Miss Cohen's own desire to encourage fresh ideas, and the Academy changed over to a policy of premieres and longer runs. The new sound films *Westfront 1918*, *Kameradshaft*, *The Blue Express* were shown, and their immense success established the cinema as important. Even the Trade noticed it, and was uneasily stirred.

From the beginning, Miss Cohen realised that the ordinary clamorous methods of film publicity were useless; the public she worked for had long been deafened by them; it had to be approached quietly, rationally, told the really important thing about each new picture, the director, the technical staff, the country and place of origin, the artistic aim. Only circularising could convey all this information. She started a mailing list, quite a small one. The names on it now run into thousands and a good many of them are people who live far away, but like to know what is going on and come up to London specially for a particular film. Ten of the Academy circulars are posted each week to China. The recipients intend to come up too, in time.

So the co-operative spirit of the Academy began. The audience began to write in its turn, asking for this and that, criticising and suggesting. Gradually the Academy became a nucleus of intelligent film thought, a meeting-ground and a clearing house for ideas. All the interest which had been floating in the air for a year and more before it opened, it gathered, and in some sense interpreted by its programmes. It was a very great service to the cinema. Small groups and film societies, valuable though they are, cannot by their very nature do such a work; because their members constitute, finally, a clique, and a clique, do what it may, is always in the end driven into an attitude of intellectual conceit; and also because they are so often dominated by one strong personality. The Academy has been broad enough to escape intellectual snobbery, and Miss Cohen sufficiently wise, experienced and wholehearted to efface herself and see her audience as a whole. Her years on the Continent and up and down Wardour Street did that for her; they fitted her to guide, and to guide impersonally, what is fast becoming a national movement.

The Academy films have included three Pabsts, five Clairs, the Dutch Pièrement, the Swedish En Natt, the American Quick Millions, the Russian Blue Express and Road to Life, the German Hauptmann von Köpenick, Mädchen in Uniform, Barberina, Emil and the Detectives; that gives some idea of the breadth of choice. Not all these films have pleased everyone; they have not all pleased Miss Cohen equally; but that is the point. Each one had some new and particular merit, and for that it was shown, regardless of the prejudices of any particular section of the audience. Only by encouraging a wide appreciation can such work as the Academy keep its educative value.

On the other hand, its relations with the amateur film societies all over the country have been more than friendly; in many cases it has kept them alive. Miss Cohen is at present acting as a quite unpaid agent and source of supply to these rather bewildered amateurs; she passes on to them her films, supplies them with endless information and advice regarding the securing of films, and listens with amazing patience to all their long and often unreasonable demands. As she is very well aware, the new intelligence and understanding of cinema which they represent is tremendously valuable to her. It is preparing the ground for a chain of Academies in every big town, and this, of course, is her ideal. Not until her work is national can it really be said to have succeeded. When she can again find the capital and the encouragement, this chain will be established, for her plans have a way of working themselves out. The further plan of a film club and social centre at the Academy itself is at present held up for lack of space; but the need for it is great, and Miss Cohen is undoubtedly the person to carry it through.

Of course there has been criticism of her programmes; but apart from her deliberate policy of broad-mindedness, the extreme difficulty she finds in getting the right films at the right time must be taken into account. Her market is the whole world, and this gives plenty of room for the rapaciousness and obstinacy which seem everywhere to characterise the renter of films. Over and over again she is held up in the most urgent negotiations, because huge sums are demanded for first British rights of films which would have no appeal in the ordinary commercial market. A chain of cinemas would, of course, help matters here.

In my opinion, the greatest work of the Academy is the establishment of quite new relations between exhibitor and audience. As its ideas spread, the theatre itself will become less important; it will end as just one of a wide circle of theatres working on the same plan. But the spirit of co-operation which it has fostered will increase; the ideal of a thinking audience, as opposed to an audience which is spared all thought by the exhibitor's own policy, may finally become the most powerful factor in the Trade. And it will be high time. Not until that happens can we expect a consistently high standard of film production. For we know well enough that in the last instance it is the audience, not the artist, that makes the film; the artist can only supply a demand which is already there. The film is our responsibility, and the co-operative film theatre our best way of creating a film that is worth while.

[Close Up (London) 10:2, June 1933, pp. 133–37.]

Salute to the Usherettes (1940)
Winifred Horrabin

I have now been in about ten cinemas when the banshees have wailed their weary warnings. And I would like to add my little chirp of praise to the chorus of admiration going up for all workers in London—and the provinces—who carry on.

Cinema usherettes have much to put up with, not the least being the silly costumes they have to wear. But I shall never see one of those extravagantly cocked hats, or a pair of those baggy breeches covering a jaunty behind, and want to giggle again. I shall remember the time when, as synthetic drama unfolded inside the cinema, suddenly real drama came in through the window and there was no ducking for cover, no trembling of those attractive knees, just an added reassuring swagger down the center aisle, an encouraging normality about the flick of a torch, even a friendly, if tremulous, whisper of "You are safer in here."

I give Priestley cinema attendants to add to his list of those little women who will ultimately help to defeat the Nazis.[1]

[*The Tribune* (London), 11 October 1940, p. 14.]

This Is Where I Came In... (1946)
Elinor Gibbs

The metropolitan cinema critic, a label that fits me as loosely as a shroud, leads an absurd and rather demoralizing life, especially when female. For some reason, she is usually summoned to look at pictures in the morning, either at a trade showing in a projection room or else in a regular theatre on Broadway. This unnatural entertainment at an hour when her friends are either still in bed or else decently employed in their offices inevitably gives her a sense of mingled depravity and foolishness.

A girl peering at a succession of animated photographs at ten o'clock in the morning may be able to persuade herself that she is working, though it is necessarily a humourless fantasy, but she is not likely to convince anybody else. When she comes blinking out into the unspeakable brightness of Times Square at noon, with her hair ruffled and her complexion damp with concentration, she is automatically classified by the civilized passer-by as either a woman of very peculiar habits or a delayed adolescent or both, and since she is very apt to share this opinion herself, it is often reflected in her work.

In addition to this moral uneasiness, there is also a certain amount of physical stress. A projection room, while infinitely preferable to a theatre crowded with the unemployable and mad, is nevertheless an unlikely place to dream of art. It is generally small, airless, and inaccessible, altogether dismaying to the claustrophobe.

The reviewer usually sits in it with only three or four others of her kind and this makes it almost unthinkable for her to leave before the picture is over, no matter how shattering to her nervous system it may be. According to my male colleagues, who seem to know a lot about the facts of life, it costs only ten or twelve dollars to run off a film; just the same, the inevitable impression is that you are a guest at an exclusive and extremely expensive dinner and that it would be inexcusable to leave before the dessert, obliging your host to eat it by himself.

An opening at a big Broadway house, especially when it is accompanied by the appearance of some popular idol in the flesh, is an imp's-eye view of hell. On one occasion, in the legitimate theatre, I sat beside Mr. Frank Sinatra and he seemed a meagre, amiable young man, obviously in mortal terror because at the moment I happened to have a very bad cold in my head. There can be no question, however, that his effect on moving picture audiences is real and cataclysmic, and the same thing to a lesser extent applies to various others. Too many clichés have been written about the symptoms produced in my sex by Mr. Sinatra and similar demon lovers, and I won't add mine. It is enough to say that a conviction that your neighbours are all crazy hardly leads to level, orderly thought.

Even without the stimulus of a living celebrity, these première audiences are of an eccentric turn of mind, sometimes laughing maniacally at nothing in particular, sometimes relapsing into a profound and melancholy stupor though all hell may be breaking loose on the screen, always breathing alarmingly in the sacred presence of Love. They are not helpful to a reviewer anxious to observe the effect of an entertainment on the public for which it was theoretically designed. According to the late Edmund Pearson, Miss Mary Pickford, in her acting days, was wont to refer uneasily to her admirers as "Lizzies": I can only say that, taken on top of an only partially digested breakfast, the audience sometimes makes me feel very queer indeed. [...]

["This Is Where I Came In......: Notes on the Movies, 'an innocent medium'—and the Critic's demoralizing Life," *Vogue* (New York), 15 March 1946, p. 157, excerpted.]

Motion Pictures as a Field of Research (1945)
Iris Barry

It was the president of a large eastern college who, in a moment of discouragement, said not long ago that his new crop of students appeared to be genuinely interested in little but swing music and the movies. He very much welcomed the idea, therefore, of providing them with material for a considered study of motion picture aesthetics and history since, as he put it somewhat wryly, by inducing them first to cerebrate about films he might afterwards more readily induce them to use their native intelligence about other subjects.

This is a rather desperate attitude for an educator, yet it indicates that the idea of motion pictures as a new field for research, for scholarship and scholarly publication, is not a wholly unknown one. Once upon a time, of course, study of popular novels, or lithographs, or the early history of printing must have seemed equally novel and extra-academic, and there is no longer much opposition to the choice of any particular subject for study merely because it happens to interest the student.

The motion picture, a comparatively new form of communication, is now fifty years old. As an innovation a great many claims were made for it, and many have been made since. At the turn of the century, sober persons were contending that films would revolutionize education, prove to be the obedient handmaid of science, and mitigate if not entirely dispel international misunderstandings and antagonisms. These dreams seem rather pathetic now, except for the fact that they are still being dreamed and might, conceivably, even come true in some part. They are like the dreams of those who believe that the use of gunpowder and explosives might well be employed exclusively for the purpose of blasting and of firework celebrations: only it is simply not sufficient merely to dream of these things.

When we turn instead to see what in fact motion pictures have accomplished during the past half-century, their achievements turn out to be along very different lines. The spontaneous growth of this almost unimaginably popular form of entertainment has been nourished by an odd combination of genuine creative impulse, of marked technical progress, and of bald commercial expansion and exploitation. The true financial history of American motion pictures, or of French or German, alone would offer to a research student as fascinating a job as has ever been done on the Borgias: and the basic material lies almost untouched. We are all accustomed to hear that films like *The Birth of a Nation* or *The Great Train Robbery* constituted big steps forward in the expressiveness and complexity of the new medium: but we have yet to be told clearly of what this advance really consisted, whether it was accidental or conscious, and what was actually achieved by attempting to relate action or communicate ideas by joining together now one, now another series of images to be projected upon a screen. Is it great editing that makes great films and if so what is great editing? Are there few styles or many? What counter-philosophies led to the abandonment of the methods introduced in the U.S.S.R. by men like Vertov and Pudovkin and Eisenstein after their examination of the work of earlier American directors like Griffith and Ince, in favour of the very different style of films like *Chapayev*? Why has one production company alone in this country, rather than all companies, shown an interest in making films with a socially-conscious or political theme? Is it the function of the motion picture to re-narrate fiction, as in *Gone with the Wind*, and if so can we measure the merit of the picture by its fidelity to the original? Or, as seems most likely, is the motion picture not as different from fiction as is a symphony, in which case the merit of films possibly lies not in their fidelity to a plot derived from a totally different medium, such as fiction or the drama, but on their originality and power as motion pictures? Has fiction itself changed under the influence of the movies and if so how? By what means is the impact upon the senses provided by *The Fighting Lady* made different from that of *Thirty Seconds Over Tokio?*

The realm of enquiry is endless. Until recently, it would have been difficult to undertake it, since the motion pictures to be examined would have been inaccessible: films were produced, ran though the cinemas of the world, and then vanished. Today this is no longer true, since the Film Library of the Museum of Modern Art has already collected many hundreds of films of all types and periods and from many countries, and these are available for study.[1] More than that, they *are being studied* though, as yet, insufficiently. Colleges and museums throughout the country make use of them and, if they are sometimes seen rather as "old films" with a quaint period flavor, they are increasingly seen by a whole new generation of serious film-students who, however, often lack any particular encouragement or guidance from their local teachers. Even now, from Pacific islands, naval bases and Europe's battlefields a steady trickle of letters comes in to the Museum today from men in uniform who were formerly and hope again to be numbered among such students. Educators will have to reckon with this new appetite for learning in a new field.

If I have mentioned the aesthetic element in motion pictures earlier, as a particularly enticing avenue for exploration, it is because during the last ten years—since the founding of the Museum's Film Library opened up any such possibilities—a much keener interest in the sociological implications of the motion picture has been elicited than in its aesthetic content, and it would be unfortunate if this unbalance were to persist. However this sociological eye to films, too, continues to present infinite possibilities. That they do have an immense influence on public thinking and public feeling is by now commonly agreed and it would seem well, therefore, to discover and measure what this influence is. For the psychologist as well as the sociologist there is a storehouse of material here. Nor is the interest necessarily confined to the fictional film alone, or to the behaviour patterns which gangster films and Superman serials have stamped upon the youthful psyche. We know that the Nazi party was conscious of what it was doing when it harnessed the motion picture to its propaganda service. I suspect that the English official film-makers were much less conscious of the effect *Desert Victory* would have abroad; yet a careful and scientific study instituted by the U.S. Army itself conclusively proved that this one film did much to make the American fighting man respectfully conscious of Britain's contribution to the united war effort. Practical results, as well as the honors and pleasures of scholarship, attend the future research worker in film.

For fear I am suggesting that nothing in serious research has yet been attempted, rather than suggesting how much could be done, I should instance here Barbara Deming's illuminating analysis of the content of last year's Hollywood films, "Exposition of a Method" in *The Library of Congress Quarterly Journal*, v.2, no.1 (1944).[2] And, as a stimulating example of pioneer work in analysis in another field, there is also Siegfried Kracauer's valuable pamphlet "Propaganda and the Nazi War Film" lithoprinted by the Museum of Modern Art a couple of years ago. In a quite different realm, a great art historian threw brilliant light on the iconography of early motion pictures when Erwin Panofsky published (under the title "Style and Medium in the Moving Picture," *Transition*, No. 26, 1937) the text of a lecture he had addressed to a possibly startled audience at the Metropolitan Museum of Art. It is not that these excellent jobs were done that is surprising, but that many more excursions into a field so fertile and so illimitable have not as yet been undertaken. For it is no longer a question of feeble conjecture, hearsay and memory, of dead scrabbling through the inept film criticism of yesteryear: the authentic raw material for research awaits the new expert's eye.

[*College Art Journal* (New York) 4:4, May 1945, pp. 206–9.]

PART FIVE

Annotations

The Confessions of an Ex-White Actress

1. Although the writer speaks mainly about theatrical conditions, her "Confessions" are relevant to African-American actresses working in film as well. Despite research, and the presence of a photograph accompanying this article, the author so far remains unidentified.

The Confessions of an Ex-White Actress (concluded)

1. *Uncle Tom's Cabin*. Best-selling abolitionist novel by Harriet Beecher Stowe, first published in 1852.
2. The English writer Thomas De Quincey (1785–1859) recalled the experiences of opium-induced reveries in *Confessions of an English Opium Eater*, first published in 1821.

The Truth About *Hallelujah*

1. This is the fifth of a five-part series of articles published in the *Baltimore Afro-American* written by black performers involved in the production of *Hallelujah*.
2. Dixie Jubilee Singers. An African-American choral group of between sixteen and twenty members founded by Eva Jessye in the mid 1920s. The Singers' repertoire included spirituals, work songs, mountain ballads, ragtime, jazz, and opera. Later known as the Eva Jessye Choir.
3. Nina Mae McKinney (1909–1967). African-American actress, dancer, and singer who featured in *Hallelujah*. She joined the chorus line of Lew Leslie's *Blackbirds of 1928* and toured France and London with a production of the *Congo Raid* featuring Paul Robeson. Later appeared in *Sanders of the River* (1935), *Dark Waters* (1944), and *Pinky* (1949).
4. King Vidor (1894–1982). Famous American director whose career began in the silent period. Films included *The Big Parade* (1925), *The Crowd* (1928), *Billy the Kid* (1930), *Stella Dallas* (1937), *The Fountainhead* (1949), and *War and Peace* (1956), as well as *Hallelujah* (1929).
5. Daniel L. Haynes (1894–1954). African-American actor who played the male lead in *Hallelujah*.

I Tried to Crash the Movies

1. Lana Turner (1920–97). American leading lady of the 1940s whose original girl-next-door image became increasingly sophisticated as her career progressed. Films include *Love Finds Andy Hardy* (1939), *Somewhere I'll Find You* (1942), *The Postman Always Rings Twice* (1946), *Peyton Place* (1957), and *Imitation of Life* (1959).
2. Lena Horne (1917–). African-American singer and actress who appeared in a number of Hollywood musicals in the 1940s.

3. The first *Our Gang* films, short slapstick comedies featuring child performers, were created and directed by Hal Roach in the mid 1920s. Although the cast changed over time, the films remained in production and popular through the 1930s and 1940s.
4. Mack Sennett (1880–1960). American producer responsible for hundreds of slapstick shorts in the 1910s and 1920s, including those featuring the Keystone Cops.
5. Mills Brothers. An African-American singing group who appeared in films, including the black-cast *Ebony Parade* (1947).
6. The Cotton Club. A popular Harlem nightclub located at 142nd Street and Lennox Avenue, in operation from 1923 to 1936. It was advertized as a "window on the jungle ... a cabin in the cotton," with a lineup of "tall, tan and terrific" African-American chorus girls.
7. Ronald Colman (1891–1958). Distinguished British romantic actor who worked in Hollywood from 1920. His films include *Beau Geste* (1926), *A Tale of Two Cities* (1935), and *Lost Horizon* (1937), as well as *Kismet* (1944) and *The Light that Failed* (1939).
8. Katherine Dunham (1909–2006). Popular and acclaimed African-American dancer, dance scholar and choreographer who, with her troupe the Katherine Dunham Dancers, performed internationally in the 1940s and 1950s, choreographing Caribbean, African, and African-American movement for a variety of audiences.
9. Ann Petry's *The Street* was published in 1946 (Boston: Houghton Mifflin).
10. Shots of black actors were regularly cut from prints of mixed-cast films in distribution in the American South into the 1950s. Producers worked around this fact by limiting African-American screen presence to musical interludes which could be cut with no loss to a film's narrative structure.

"Sarah" Talks to Us about the Cinema

1. The director André Antoine had managed the Odeon since 1906.
2. Bernhardt had been appearing in the title role in *La dame aux camélias* (Alexandre Dumas fils, 1852) since her first American tour, which lasted from October 1880 to May 1882.
3. According to Sabine Lenk, Bernhardt's filmography comprises: *Hamlet* (1900), a recording (with sound) of her performance in the title role during the Paris World Fair; *Tosca* (1908, Film d'Art); *La dame aux camélias* (1911, Films d'Art); *Adrienne Lecouvrer* (1912, Urban Trading Co.); *Les amours de la reine elizabeth* (1912, Urban Trading Co.); *Jeanne Doré* (1916, Eclipse); and *Mères françaises* (1917, Eclipse).
4. Bernhardt first performed the role of Mélissinde in *La princésse lontaine*, written by Edmond Rostand in 1895, in that year. Two years later, in 1897, Rostand wrote *La Samaritaine* expressly for her and she performed it immediately. As Herzog, in Rostand's *L'Aiglon* of 1900, Bernhardt achieved one of her greatest successes.
5. *L'Aiglon* was filmed in 1914.

My Film Debut

1. The phrase *weltbedeutenden Bretter* alludes to the theater from the expression *die Bretter, die die Welt bedeuten* (the boards that mean the world) (Trans.).

Our Own Movie Queen

1. This was first published in the *Chicago Sunday Tribune*, 7 June 1925, Magazine Section, pp. 1–4, under the authorship of F. Scott Fitzgerald but, according to Matthew J. Bruccoli, the editor of Zelda Fitzgerald's collected writings, F. Scott's "Ledger" notes: "Two thirds by Zelda. Only my climax and revision." Matthew J. Bruccoli, *Zelda Fitzgerald: The Collected Writings* (New York: Charles Scribner's Sons/Macmillan, 1991), p. 273 n. 1. The story was part of the "Blue Ribbon Fiction" series published by the *Chicago Sunday Tribune*.
2. The Nordic Theory. In *The Races of Europe* (New York: D. Appleton, 1899), William Z. Ripley offered a theory of European racial development. According to Ripley, the European "races" were divided into three, descending groups: the Teutonic (at the apex of development), the Alpine, and the Mediterranean (at the bottom). Ripley's theory gained currency as American society debated the consequences of a liberalized immigration policy in the 1900s and 1910s. Following Ripley's eugenic views, Madison Grant's *The Passing of the Great Race* (New York: C. Scribner, 1916) argued that the superiority of old-stock Americans, which Grant described as

"Nordic," was in danger of "racial extinction" by the immigration of millions of southern and eastern Europeans, and Jews. These arguments continued into the 1920s, with the publication of Carl Brigham's *A Study of American Intelligence* (Princeton: Princeton University Press, 1923), which purported to prove the eugenicist theory through the use of intelligence tests. (Fitzgerald clearly uses the term ironically here.)

3. Florenz Ziegfeld (1867?–1932). American theater manager who perfected the American revue form in his *Ziegfeld Follies* from 1907 on. Modeled on the Parisian Folies-Bergère, the *Ziegfeld Follies* combined scenic grandeur, comedy, vaudeville, and beautiful show girls, some of whom, such as Marion Davies, went on to Hollywood careers.

4. Fitzgerald was writing during Prohibition.

Beginning Young

1. D.W. Griffith bought his studio at Mamaroneck, on Long Island, in 1919 and sold it in 1925. Griffith shot his first film there—*Way Down East*—in 1920. The first film shot there was Lillian Gish's *Remodelling Her Husband* (1919).

2. Richard Barthelmess (1895–1963). American film actor who first appeared in Herbert Brenon's *War Brides* (1916) and was known for his outstanding performance in *Broken Blossoms* (1919), in which Gish played the female lead.

Blazing the Trail

1. Fred Summerfield's *Why Girls Leave Home: or A Danger Signal on the Path of Folly* (1904) was later made into a film by William Nigh in 1921. Lois Weber appeared in Summerfield's play before beginning her film career. Weber (1881–1939), an American writer, director and producer, was extremely successful in the silent period. She began directing in the early 1910s and although she originally shared the directing credit with her husband Phillips Smalley (1865–1939), whom she married in 1905, Weber became increasingly recognized for her own merit. Her films often focused on social issues. See also her writing reprinted in this volume.
    Anne Schaeffer (1870–1957). Actress who joined Vitagraph from the stage in the early 1910s and often appeared in features as a supporting character in a variety of roles. Her first film was the Western *Angels of the Desert* (1913), opposite George Stanley.

2. James Kirkwood (1875–1965). Actor and director who began his career as D.W. Griffith's leading man in 1909 and rose to the status of matinée idol.

3. Billy the Kid. The 1910 film of the life of American gunslinger William Bonney (c. 1860–1881) was possibly based on Patrick F. Garrett's 1882 account of Bonney's capture and subsequent death.
    Joseph Santley (1889–1971). American director, vaudevillian, and child actor. Billed as "America's greatest boy actor" on stage, Santley continued his career in film and became a film and television producer. His biggest role was in *Billy the Kid*.
    Sidney Olcott (1872–1949). Irish-Canadian director who pioneered location shooting. Working for Kalem, he co-directed the original one-reel *Ben-Hur* (1907) and filmed in Florida, Ireland, and the Middle East.
    Robert Vignola (1882–1953). A friend of Sidney Olcott's, Vignola was an actor and director who produced the Frances Marion-authored film *The World and His Wife* (1920).
    George Melford (1877–1961). American actor and director who began as a leading man for Kalem in 1911. At Famous-Players Lasky in the twenties he became one of the most successful directors with *The Sheik* (1921).
    Marion Leonard (1881–1956). American screen actress for the Biograph company, who was active from 1908 to 1915. Her films include *The Lonely Villa* (1909) and *Pippa Passes* (1909).
    Fred Santley (1888–1953). Brother of director and actor Joseph, Fred Santley acted on stage, screen and in vaudeville. He made his first film appearance for Kalem in 1911.

4. The Fatal Wedding. A 1914 film based on Theodore Kremer's 1901 play *The Fatal Wedding, or, The Little Mother: A Comedy Drama in a Prologue and Three Acts*.
    Laurette Taylor (1884–1946). American stage actress who appeared in a few films. Married to playwright Charles Taylor (1864–1942) who wrote *Rags to Riches* for her.

5. Bertha the Sewing Machine Girl. A 1927 film based on Theodore Kremer's undated play of the same title. In 1906, Mrs. Helen Burell D'Apery, writing as "Olive Harper," adapted the play for

fiction, writing *Bertha, the Sewing Machine Girl, a Romantic Story Based upon Theodore Kremer's Great Play of the Same Title.*
Across the Pacific. Melodrama by Charles E. Blaney (1904), adapted for film in 1924.
Nellie the Beautiful Cloak Model. Play by Grace Miller White (c. 1906), adapted for film in 1924.
Al Woods (1870–1951). Broadway producer of *Hokey Hits and Flops"*

6. Frank J. Marion. Co-founder, with George Kleine and Samuel M. Long, of American film production company Kalem, in 1907. The company took its name from the initials of the three principals.

A Girl Cinematographer at the Balkan War

1. Balkan War (1912–1913). The first Balkan war began on 8 October 1912 between the Balkan League (Bulgaria, Serbia, Greece, Montenegro) and Turkey. It ended with the recognition of Albanian independence in 1913. The second Balkan war lasted from 29 June until 30 July 1913, when Greece, Serbia, Montenegro, Romania and Turkey fought Bulgaria. A treaty was reached in Bucharest on 10 August 1913.
2. Eastern Rumelia. Part of the former Ottoman Empire, Eastern Rumelia was recognized as an autonomous province in 1878 and annexed by Bulgaria in 1885.
3. Servian War. Fighting Turkey and then Bulgaria in the two wars known as the Balkan Wars of 1912 and 1913, Servia acquired much of Macedonia as a consequence. During World War I, Servia's name was changed to Serbia and in 1918 it became known as Yugoslavia.
4. Polytechnic. This was probably the Regent Street Polytechnic, founded in 1838, known expecially for spectacular illustrated lantern lectures, and the first location at which films were publicly screened in the United Kingdon, in 1896. The Polytechnic was rebuilt in 1910–12, and began a focus on education rather than exhibition, conferring degrees through the University of London.
5. We have found no evidence that these books were published.

Filming *Moana of the South*

1. These excerpts are taken from a series of five articles about filming *Moana of the South*, published in *Asia* in 1925.
2. Cold water was necessary for the processing of motion-picture film.
3. Bob. Robert J. Flaherty (1884–1951). American documentary pioneer who was originally an explorer. Husband to Frances. His films include *Nanook of the North* (1922), *Moana* (1926) and *Tabu* (1931) (co-directed with F.W. Murnau), *Man of Aran* (1934), *The Land* (1942), and *Louisiana Story* (1948).
4. Nanook's famous struggle with the seal in Flaherty's *Nanook of the North* (1922) was staged for the camera.
5. Flaherty's use of panchromatic stock in *Moana* was quite revolutionary. Panchromatic stock was a black and white stock which was sensitive to all the colors of the spectrum, unlike the more widely used orthochromatic stock, which was not sensitive to reds, and particularly sensitive to blues and greens. Flaherty's use of it in Samoa, where it registered the texture of vegetation and the muscular activity of his subjects, prompted the subsequent general adoption of panchromatic stock worldwide after 1926.
6. This third and final excerpt is taken from the concluding installment to Frances H. Flaherty's series on filming *Moana*, "Filming *Moana of the South*: Fa'a-Samoa," *Asia* (December 1925), pp. 1085–1090, 1096.

I Married Adventure

1. In 1917, Osa and Martin Johnson traveled to the island of Malekula in the New Hebrides. Here they met Nagapate, the hereditary chief of a tribe reputed to be cannibals. While on Malekula, Martin Johnson shot *Cannibals of the South Seas*. According to Osa, this film did include footage showing the remains of a feast involving human flesh. Several years later, the couple returned and screened their film to Nagapate and his group. (It is this event that Osa is recounting). In 1918, Martin Johnson produced a film based on the couple's visits to the region, *Among the Cannibal Isles of the South Pacific*, and, in 1922, *Head Hunters of the South Seas*.

The Hats in My Life

1. Ethel Barrymore (1879–1959). American actress on stage from 1894 to 1940 and member of an American acting dynasty. She scored her first Broadway success in Clyde Fitch's *Captain Jinks of the Horse Marines* in 1901.
2. Charles Boyer (1899–1978). French romantic actor who went to Hollywood in 1929. Boyer was known as the screen's "great lover." His films included *Red-headed Woman* (1932), *Caravan* (1934), and *All This and Heaven Too* (1940).
3. Louis B. Mayer (1885–1957). American film executive who formed Metro–Goldwyn–Mayer with Sam Goldwyn in 1924. In 1917 he began production of *Virtuous Wives* for Metro, Marcus Loew's film production company based in New York; however, legal problems arising from the fact that the film's leading lady, Anita Stewart, was still under contract to Vitagraph, delayed completion of the film until 1918.
4. George Loane Tucker (1872–1921). American actor, director, and producer of the silent period. He directed *Traffic in Souls* (1913), and *The Prisoner of Zenda* (1915), among others, the latter being one of many films he directed in Britain.
5. Anita Stewart (1895–1961). American stage and screen actress who also produced films. Her films include *The Web* (1913), *Diana's Dress Reform* (1914), *The Goddess* (1915), and *Whispering Wives* (1926), as well as *Virtuous Wives* (1918).

This is What $10,000 Did to Me

1. *Hungry Hearts* was published in 1920 by Houghton Mifflin, Boston.
2. The Goldwyn film version of *Hungry Hearts* premiered in 1922.
3. Studio in Culver City. The Goldwyn Studio, later MGM, and now the Sony Pictures Studio.
4. Julian Josephson. A screenwriter who headed the scenario department at Thomas H. Ince's studio in the late 1910s and who presumably held a similar position with Goldwyn. Josephson worked with Yezierska on the script for *Hungry Hearts* and received a credit as the film's scenario writer. Montague Glass is credited with the film's titles.
5. Eminent Authors. A group of well-known writers brought together by Samuel Goldwyn for the purposes of producing material suitable for film and elevating the image of the studio's films. Authors were awarded a three-year contract at $15,000 per year. In addition to the authors listed by Yezierska, the group included Mary Roberts Rinehart and Rex Beach. See Rinehart's account of cinemagoing in Vienna, "My Experience in the Movies," reprinted in this volume.

Why Do They Change the Stories on the Screen?

1. Marion is credited with writing about 200 scripts.
2. The 1925 film *The Dark Angel* was based on the 1924 play *The Dark Angel; a play of yesterday and today* by Guy Bolton, writing as "H.B. Trevelyan."
3. Ronald Colman (1891–1958). Distinguished romantic British actor who worked in Hollywood from 1920. His films include *Beau Geste* (1926), *A Tale of Two Cities* (1935), and *Lost Horizon* (1937).
4. *Stella Dallas*, by Mrs. Olive Higgins Prouty, was published in 1923. A film version was made in 1925, as well as in 1937 (starring Barbara Stanwyck) and 1990 (starring Bette Midler).
5. *Pollyanna*, Eleanor H. Porter (1913); *Rebecca of Sunnybrook Farm*, Kate Douglas Smith Wiggin (1903); *Stella Maris*, William John Locke (1912); *The Poor Little Rich Girl*, a play by Eleanor Gates (c. 1916).
6. Fannie Hurst (1889–1968). Popular American novelist whose romantic works, often with a tragic ending, have often been adapted for film. See her contribution to this volume.
7. Hurst's collection of short stories titled *Humoresque* was published in 1919, and the title story adapted for film by Marion the following year.
8. Norma Talmadge (1893/7–1957). American silent film heroine whose films include *Battle Cry of Peace* (1914), *Within the Law* (1923), and *Camille* (1927).
   Gloria Swanson (1897–1983). American silent film star who began as a Mack Sennett bathing beauty, worked with Cecil B. DeMille, and made a number of successful comebacks in the course of her career.

Mae Murray (1883–1965). American silent screen star, formerly a dancer, who became famous for her role in Eric von Stroheim's film The Merry Widow (1925).

9. The 1901 novel Graustark; a Story of a Love behind a Throne by George Barr McCutcheon was adapted for film in 1925. Norma Talmadge played the princess in the film.

An Author is the Person Who Wrote the Story

1. Charles Brabin (1883–1957). British-born film director and screen writer who worked in Hollywood. He directed La Belle Russe (1919), While New York Sleeps (1920), So Big (1924), and The Bridge of San Luis Rey (1929), among other films.

    Ernst Lubitsch (1892–1947). German director, renowned for his distinctive approach to sophisticated sex comedies, who moved to Hollywood in 1922. His films include Madame Du Barry (1919), The Marriage Circle (1924), The Love Parade (1929), To Be or Not to Be (1944), and many more.

    William de Mille (1878–1955). American director, producer, playwright, and screenwriter, brother to Cecil B. His directorial credits include Miss Lulu Bett (1921), What Every Woman Knows (1921), and Nice People (1922).

    Robert Milton (1886–1956). American director whose films include The Dummy (1929), Outward Bound (1930), Devotion (1930), and Westward Passage (1932).

    Lester Lonergan (1869–1931). Irish-born screen and stage actor who also produced for the stage and directed films. He began his film career with Thanhauser Company.

    George Fitzmaurice (1885–1940). French-born actor, director, and screenwriter. His directorial credits include Son of the Sheik (1926), Mata Hari (1931), and As You Desire Me (1932).

    Frank Borzage (1883–1962). American director of gently sentimental romantic dramas. His films include Humoresque (1920), Seventh Heaven (1927), A Farewell to Arms (1932), Desire (1936), and many others.

    Herbert Brenon (1880–1958). Irish-born director who worked in Hollywood, and later in England. His films include Ivanhoe (1913), War Brides (1916), Peter Pan (1924), A Kiss For Cinderella (1924),and Beau Geste (1926).

2. The Bridge of San Luis Rey. Novel by Thornton Wilder published in 1927. Charles Brabin directed the 1929 film version.

3. Fannie Hurst's Lummox (1923) was adapted for film in 1930. Hurst is credited with the film's dialogue.

4. Elizabeth Meehan (1905–1967). Screenwriter who often worked with Herbert Brenon. Her film credits include Lummox (1930), Transgression (1931), Oliver Twist (1933), and Harmony Lane (1935).

5. J.M. Barrie's Peter Pan (1905) was filmed in 1924 by Herbert Brenon. The Doctor's Dilemma (1909), by George Bernard Shaw, was filmed in 1958 by Anthony Asquith, but there seems to be no evidence of a film adaptation from 1929, the year in which Hurst is writing.

Feminine Sphere in the Field of Movies is Large Indeed

1. Mary Roberts Rinehart (1876–1958). Successful American novelist, short-story writer, and journalist whose fiction was adapted for film. A member of Samuel Goldwyn's "Eminent Authors" group. See her writing included in this volume.

    Gertrude Atherton (1857–1948). Popular American novelist who was noted for her fictional biographies and historical writing. A member of Samuel Goldwyn's "Eminent Authors" group.

The Feminine Mind in Picture Making

1. Fairfax was one of nine women working in the film industry responding to Film Daily's survey of female effort in filmmaking. The other eight were: Mary Pickford, Anita Loos, Jane Murfin, Clara Beranger, Josephine Lovett Robertson, Eve Unsell, Leah Baird, and June Mathis. Mathis's response is also reprinted in this volume.

Alice Blaché, a Dominant Figure in Pictures

1. Unlike in the United States, Germany, or Great Britain, where women were granted suffrage after World War I, French women had to wait until October 1945 to vote.

2. After working for Léon Gaumont for twelve years, during which time she rose from secretary

to writer and director, Alice Guy married cameraman Herbert Blaché in 1907. The couple emigrated to the United States, where Herbert worked for Gaumont. After a two-year hiatus, Guy returned to work in film, establishing the Solax film company in 1910. See the biography of Guy Blaché included in this volume.

How I Became a Motion Picture Director

1. Mr. (Phillips) Smalley. Born in 1865, the British Smalley was a protégé of English stage actor Sir Henry Irving. In 1904, Smalley met Weber while she was performing in the musical play *Why Girls Leave Home*, which he was stage-managing. They married early in 1905 and worked together for several years in stock theater before Weber directed, wrote, and acted in a film for the Gaumont Chronophone Company (c. 1908). The two joined the Reliance Motion Picture Company in 1910, moving to Rex in 1912. Smalley is credited with directing forty-one films on his own for the New York-based Crystal Company between 1912 and 1913. While he worked closely with his wife at Rex, his real contribution to her directorial work remains unclear. The Smalley/Weber credits vary during the 1910s, although by 1917 Weber generally took sole credit, a practice that continued into the 1920s.
Herbert Blaché (1882–1953). English cinematographer and director who married Alice Guy in 1907. The couple then emigrated to the United States where he worked for the Gaumont Chronophone Company. It was there that Weber got her first chance to write, direct, and perform on film, working there for about eighteen months. There is no record of a meeting between Alice Guy Blaché and Lois Weber during this time.

Motion Picture Work: The Motion Picture Director

1. Only two women directors of note. It is not clear to whom Park refers—perhaps Elsie Jane Wilson and Lois Weber.

The Feminine Mind in Picture Making

1. Mathis was one of nine women working in the film industry responding to *Film Daily*'s survey of female effort in filmmaking. The other eight were: Mary Pickford, Anita Loos, Jane Murfin, Clara Beranger, Josephine Lovett Robertson, Eve Unsell, Leah Baird, and Marion Fairfax. Fairfax's response is also excerpted and reprinted in this volume.
2. A certain director. In 1916 Mathis worked for Edwin Carewe at B.A. Rolfe Company. Carewe is presumably the director she refers to here.

Why Are There No Women Directors?

1. Ida May Park (1879-1954). American director of silent film. One of a number of women directors to work at Universal in the late 1910s, she began by teaming up with her husband actor Joseph de Grasse and eventually directed some of the biggest stars at the studio, including Lon Chaney. Her films include *Bondage* (1917), *Bread* (1918), *Broadway Love* (1918) and *The Butterfly Man* (1920).
Mary Jane Wilson. Park is probably referring here to Elsie Jane Wilson (1890–1965), a New Zealand-born actress and director who worked in the United States from 1913. At Universal she appeared in several films directed by her husband, Rupert Julian, whom she began to assist in a directorial capacity. In 1917 she directed four films for Universal starring the child actress Zoe Rae, and in 1918 she directed *The City of Tears*, *The Dream Lady*, and *The Lure of Luxury*. Wilson's last film was *The Game's Up* (1919), six years before Osborne's editorial. The confusion over her name might indicate how much she had been forgotten.
Lois Weber (1881–1939). American screenwriter, actress, and director whose evangelism in early life prompted her successful move to theater. At Gaumont Chronophone Company, she directed her first film in 1908. By 1916, she was the top-salaried director at Universal. Her films often addressed controversial issues, such as religious hypocrisy, in *Hypocrites* (1914); abortion, in *Where Are My Children?* (1916); and capital punishment, in *The People vs John Doe* (1916). In 1920 Weber moved to Paramount and a $50,000-per-picture contract, but her interest in using film as a platform for social and moral reform did not sit well with the 1920s audience. See her writing included in this volume.

Beginning Young

1. By 1925 Lois Weber had divorced her husband, director Phillips Smalley, and after directing *A Chapter in Her Life* for Universal, a remake of her 1915 film *Jewel*, underwent a period of relative inactivity and some personal difficulty before returning to the studio in the 1930s.
2. This 1919 film is now lost. See also Lillian Gish, "Lillian Gish… Director," interview with Anthony Slide, *Silent Picture* 6 (Spring 1970), pp. 12–13, for further discussion by Gish on her experience directing.

Can Women Direct Films?

1. This article prompted a libel suie against English Newspapers Ltd., the publishers of *Film Weekly*, brought by the British film producer and director Dinah Shurey in early February 1930. Shurey, who had worked in the British film industry for over a decade and who had produced *Every Mother's Son*, *Second to None*, *Carry On*, *The Last Post* and *Red Sea to Blue Nile*, claimed damages for libel and demanded an apology from the magazine. After hearing argument from Norman Birkett, K.C. and Sir Patrick Hastings, K.C., a jury awarded Shurey £500 damages.
2. Walter Forde (1897–1984). English music-hall pianist and comedian, on stage from 1918, and later film director. His films include the "Walter" series of two-reelers from 1922 to 1926, *Wait and See* (1928), *You'd Be Surprised* (1930), and *Jack's the Boy* (1932).
   Mrs Walter Forde. Adeline Culley, who edited some of Walter Forde's films in the 1920s, and then became his script girl. He credited her with much of his success.

Women in the Arts: Some Notes on the Eternally Conflicting Demands of Humanity and Art

1. Catherine. The Italian St. Catherine of Siena (1347–1380), patroness of the city of Rome who, as ambassadress of Florence, persuaded Pope Gregory XI to abandon Avignon for Rome.
   Teresa. The Spanish St. Teresa (1515–1622), only woman to whom the title Doctor of the Church is popularly, though not officially, given. A great mystical writer who founded a convent.
   Francis. The Italian St. Francis of Assisi (1181–1226) who founded the Friars Minor in 1209 and who, in 1224, received the stigmata of the Passion on his body, the first recorded example of this phenomenon.
   Boehme. Jacob Boehme (1575–1624). German mystical writer and shoemaker whose more than thirty books describe his revelations on the "divine order of nature." Among the persecutions he suffered for his beliefs were five years of silence.
2. Mrs. Eddy (Mary Baker Eddy) (1821–1910). American founder of the Church of Christ, Scientist and author of its textbook, *Science and Health with Key to the Scriptures* (1875). In 1908 she established the international newspaper *Christian Science Monitor*.
   Mrs. Besant (Annie Besant) (1847–1933). English social reformer, Theosophist and Indian independence leader who for more than sixty years was at the forefront of liberal movements on behalf of intellectual freedom, social justice, and women's rights.
3. In 1765 Scottish engineer James Watt (1736–1819) invented a separate condensing vessel for the steam engine, a device that greatly improved it.
4. Käthe Kollwitz (1867–1945). German artist who worked in lithography, woodcuts, etching and sculpture. The first woman member of the Prussian Academy of Fine Arts, from which she resigned as head of its graphic section in 1933, her work dealt with social oppression, death, and war, and often represented women and children.
5. Olive Schreiner (1855–1920). South African writer, pacifist, socialist, and feminist whose works include *The Story of an African Farm* (1883), *Dream Life and Real Life* (1893), *Woman and Labour* (1911), and the posthumous *From Man to Man, or, Perhaps only…* (1926).

Great Field for Women

1. Balboa Company. The Balboa Amusement Producing Co., Long Beach CA, a very successful movie studio, 1913–1918, which closed its doors in 1923. In its heyday it had distribution agreements with Pathé and fox, among others, through which Alta Davis would have been supplied.

Towards a Co-Operative Cinema: The Work of the Academy, Oxford Street

1. Academy Cinema, Oxford Street, London. An early art cinema, founded in 1931 by Elsie Cohen.
2. Elsie Cohen (Mrs. Elsie Kellner). British film writer, promoter, producer, and pioneer of art cinema exhibition. In 1915 Cohen became junior sub-editor of *The Kinematograph Weekly*, rising to associate editor in 1917. She was also editor for *Pictures and Picturegoer*, and film correspondent for *National News*. During this time she was known to the trade as "Kinet." In 1919 she was publicity manager for the Anglo-Hollandier Company, an Anglo-Dutch production company based in Haarlem, Holland. In this capacity she traveled to New York, securing a distribution contract for Hollandia films in 1922. During her year in America she also negotiated the sale of the British film *Bulldog Drummond*. Returning to Europe, she was briefly head of the Hollandier Company, then worked for the British firm Ideal Film Company, doing publicity and production. In 1927 she was general manager, Wien House Film Studio in Teddington, and responsible for *His House in Order*, a film starring Tallulah Bankhead. In 1928 she organized a season of European films at the Palais de Luxe in London, and in 1931 established the Academy Cinema in Oxford Street, beginning with an international program of silent films. Cohen gave weekly press shows, had an international mailing list, eschewed the industry practice of showing two features by running a feature and a shorter, often documentary, film, and developed a new audience for European cinema. In the 1930s, she briefly managed the Cambridge Theatre at Cambridge Circus and, from 1934 to 1937, Cinema House in London. Cohen planned a further eight Academys across England when the Second World War intervened. During the war she worked for the Overseas Recorded Broadcasting Service. (Some of this information comes from two interviews Cohen gave to Anthony Slide in *Silent Picture* 10 and 11 when she was in her seventies; it differs, at some points, from Coxhead's more contemporaneous account of her career.)

Salute to the Usherettes

1. John Boynton Priestley (1894–1984). English novelist, playwright, and critic who commented on radio and in essays on the role of British women during World War II. His *British Women Go to War* was published in 1944.

Motion Pictures as a Field of Research

1. The Museum of Modern Art Film Library was founded in 1935 with Barry as its first curator.
2. Barry's activities at the Museum of Modern Art Film Library facilitated the work of other scholars. The eminent art historian Erwin Panofsky was a member of the Museum of Modern Art's Film Library Advisory Committee. He was also a guest lecturer in the course on motion pictures that Barry delivered at the invitation of Columbia University 1937–38. From 1942 to 1945, the Film Library worked with the Library of Congress on the Motion Picture Project, a study funded by the Rockefeller Foundation, whose goal was the establishment of a national film collection. To that end, Barry, and other experts, developed a set of criteria for film selection, and acquired and stored copies of the chosen titles. Among those working with Barry were Barbara Deming (who was part of the Library of Congress team and subsequently published a lengthy analysis of the selection criteria), and, in an informal capacity, the German film scholar Siegfried Kracauer. The Film Library's holdings of German documentaries and propaganda, all of which were made available to various Allied intelligence agencies during the war, facilitated Kracauer's study *Propaganda and the Nazi War Film* (1942). Kracauer acknowledged his debt to Barry and the Film Library in the conception and realization of his *From Caligari to Hitler: A Psychological History of the German Film* (1947). Barbara Deming, "Love Through A Film," reprinted in this volume, an example of popular film criticism, bears the mark of the style of analysis of the Library of Congress team.

Biographies

The information for these biographies has been culled mainly from standard sources. The lives of many if not most of these women would reward original research, by which errors of fact no doubt would be revealed. The scope of this book did not allow for this additional work.

Minnie Adams (no dates found). African-American reporter for *Chicago Defender*, who is also recorded in that paper to have written *The Retribution* (c. 1911–14), a play for a Chicago church dramatic group.

Jane Addams (1860–1935). In 1889 founded, with Ellen Starr, Hull House settlement in Chicago's 19th Immigrant Ward; helped to found American Civil Liberties Union (1920). Author of several books, including *Democracy and Social Ethics* (1902) and *Peace and Bread in Time of War* (1922). Vice-President of National American Women Suffrage Alliance (1911–14). President of Women's Peace Party in the United States (1915), and then co-founded Women's International League for Peace and Freedom (1919). President of Women's International Peace Congress at The Hague (1915), in Zurich (1919), and attended the Congress in Vienna (1921). Shared Nobel Peace Prize in 1931 with Nicholas Murray Butler (an educator). In 1910 became first woman to receive an honorary degree from Yale, while in 1920s called "the most dangerous woman in America today" by Daughters of the American Revolution. Appeared in the National American Woman Suffrage Association film melodrama *Votes for Women* in 1912.

Cecelia Ager (1902–81). American film critic, best known as a commentator on the foibles and personalities of the entertainment world. Early writings in *Variety* concentrated on fashions in film. Her pithy style also appeared in *PM*, *Harper's Bazaar*, *Vogue*, and the *New York Times*.

Emilie Altenloh (1888–1985). Pioneering German film scholar, trained in political economy and law, whose Heidelberg doctorate on the sociology of cinema, covering taste, class, and gendered consumption, *Zur Sociologie des Kino*, was completed under the national economist and cultural sociologist Alfred Weber in 1913. Published in 1914, this was the first film book in German by a woman, and the first sociology dissertation on film there. In 1919 became director of a welfare agency in Schleswig–Holstein. She also founded a welfare school for women. A parliamentarian in the German Reichstag for the Deutsche Demokratische Partei (1930–33). In 1934 she began studies in Natural Science, and from 1940 assumed leadership of the Department of Environmental Studies at the University of Hamburg. In 1945 she co-founded the FDP (Freie Demokratische Partei/Liberal Democratic Party); thereafter a senator for many years. In 1963 honored with the Medal of the Freedom of the City of Hamburg.

Margaret Anderson (1886–1973). American writer, magazine founder, and editor. Ardent feminist. Book reviewer, *Chicago Evening Post* (1906); later joined *Dial* magazine. Literary editor, *Continent* (1913). Founded *Little review* (1914) in Chicago for "the best conversation the world has to offer," unprecedented magazine of avant-garde literature and arts. She initially published Emma Goldman, Vachel Lindsay, H.D., Sherwood Anderson, Ben Hecht; the magazine moved to Greenwich Village, New York (1917); Ezra Pound, foreign editor (1917–19); published T.S. Eliot, Wyndham Lewis, W.B. Yeats, Hart Crane, Ford Madox Ford, and Pound. Serialized Joyce's *Ulysses* (1918). Prosecuted for obscenity; four issues featuring Joyce's text burnt by US Post Office. Also published Djuna Barnes, Gertrude Stein, Hemingway, Cocteau, Louis Aragon, Breton, Francis Picabia. Moving the magazineto Paris (1922), Anderson's companion, Jane Heap, assumed primary editorship (1924–27). *Little review* ceased publication in 1926, with single issue in 1929. Close friend of Chicagoan Janet Flanner. In later life, Gurdjieff disciple.

Lou Andreas-Salomé (1861–1937). Russian/German novelist, literary critic, and psychoanalyst. Lover of Rainer Maria Rilke (on whom she wrote a study in 1928), and Friedrich Nietzsche (whose proposal she declined). Her *Im Kampf um Gott* (1884) recounts her experience with Nietzsche, and her *Friedrich Nietzsche in seinen Werken* (1894) is an evaluation of his thought. After attending a conference on psychoanalysis in 1910, she met Sigmund Freud, and in 1913 began taking patients. These experiences produced two memoirs: *Mein Dank an Freud* (1931), and *Lebensrückblick: Grundriss einiger Lebenserinnerungen* (1933). Her autobiography was posthumously published in 1951.

Betty Balfour (1903–1979). Popular British comedienne of silent films and theater, later in character parts. West End début in 1914 at the age of eleven. Film début in George Pearson's *Nothing Else Matters* (1920), in whose films she primarily acted until 1927. Dubbed "Britain's Queen of Happiness," a British Mary Pickford. Her 1921 title role of Squibs enjoyed great success and launched a series of films based on this character, a Piccadilly flower girl. First talking film, *The Brat* (1930). Directed by Marcel l'Herbier in *Le diable au coeur* (1927), and Alfred Hitchcock in *Champagne* (1928). Her career suffered as a consequence of the transition to sound, which seemed to challenge her youthful type. Her papers are held at the British Film Institute.

Djuna Barnes (1892–1982). American poet, journalist, playwright, novelist, illustrator, theatrical columnist, short-story writer. First poems, *Harper's Weekly* (1911). Studied Pratt Institute; Art Students League, New York (1915–16). Began writing journalism, *Brooklyn Daily Eagle* (1913), and others. Lived Greenwich Village; first volume poetry, *The Book of Repulsive Women* (1915). Contributor to avant-garde journals, *Little review*, *transition*, *Dial*, and fashionable magazines, *Smart Set*, *Charm* (late 1910s). Three one-act plays staged, Provincetown Playhouse (1919, 1920). Traveled to Paris (1920), interviewed Joyce for *Vanity Fair* (1922). First novel, *Ryder* (1928). *Ladies Almanack* (1928), self-illustrated, satirical portrait of Natalie Barney's Parisian lesbian circle. During 1930s moved between Paris and London. *Nightwood* (1936) established her place in modernist canon, with its discontinuous temporalities and multiple stylistic references. Returned to New York (1940). Little published during next forty years except *The Antiphon* (1958), a verse play, later translated and produced in Swedish with Dag Hammarskjöld's assistance.

Iris Barry (1895–1969). British-born film historian, curator, feminist, poet, and writer, living in the United States (1932–50/51). Co-founder of London Film Society (1925) and New York Film Society (1930). Film critic for *The Spectator* (1924–29), and for *Daily Mail* (1925–30. Member of Wyndham Lewis's and Ezra Pound's circles. Joined the Museum of Modern Art in 1932 as museum librarian, becoming first curator of the brand new Film Library in 1935, where she directed the first successful effort anywhere in the world to preserve films. Taught course at Columbia University in 1937–38, "The History, Aesthetic, and Technique of the Motion Picture." Founding member of International Federation of Film Archives (FIAF) in 1938. Lectured and taught on cinema, wrote program notes and the pioneering *D.W. Griffith: American Film Master* (1940). During Second World War assisted fleeing European political refugees including Siegfried Kracauer, whose *From Caligari to Hitler* was written in the MoMA Film Library. Henri Langlois consulted her in founding the Cinémathèque Française. Moved from the US to France in 1950/51. Received Chevalier of French Légion d'Honneur, and reputedly saw more than fifteen thousand films. Her papers are held at the Museum of Modern Art.

Clara Beranger (1886–1956). Author of over sixty scripts, her movie career spanned over thirty years, primarily with Paramount and MGM. Writing first for magazines and newspapers, she then embarked, in the 1910s, on freelance screenwriting for Edison, Vitagraph, Famous Players, Kalem, Pathé Frères, and Fox, where she worked as staff writer, and adapted *Anna Karenina* (1915). Her *His Chinese Wife*, written with Forrest Halsey, was a hit in 1919–20 on Broadway. In the early 1920s went to Hollywood, hired by William de Mille for Paramount—a very successful writer–director professional association resulted, as did a Hollywood scandal when both left marriages for the other. She had written for de Mille for seven years before their wedding in 1928, and continued for several years thereafter. Lectured on screenwriting at the University of Southern California after retiring. Authored the classic *Writing for the Screen* (1950).

Sarah Bernhardt (1844–1923). Internationally acclaimed French actress, renowned for her voice, beauty, and grace of movement. Debuted Comédie française (1862). Equally at home in classical and modern repertoire, achieved popular and critical success in *Adrienne Lecouvreur, Phèdre, Hernani*, and *Ruy Blas*. Sensational success in American début, *La dame aux camélias* (1880). Toured Russia, United States, Australia, and England. Established Théâtre Sarah-Bernhardt (1899), opening with her performance as Hamlet. Played several male roles, including Napoleon's son, *L'Aiglon* (1900). Many roles written especially for her. Appeared in seven films: *Hamlet* (1900); *Tosca* (1908); *La dame aux camélias* (1911); *Adrienne Lecouvreur* (1912); *Les amours de la reine Elizabeth* (1912); *Jeanne Doré* (1916); *Mères françaises* (1917). Amputation of leg (1914) did not restrict performing life. Bernhardt also sculpted and wrote.

Marguerite Bertsch (1889–1967). Head of Vitagraph's scenario division for many years, where she scripted *The Wreck* (1913), *Captain Alvarez* (1914), *A Million Bid* (1914), and *My Official Wife* (1916). She co-directed *The Law Decides* (1916). Her first solo directorial job was *The Devil's Prize* (1916). She wrote the guide *How to Write for Moving Pictures* (1917).

Alice Guy Blaché (1873/5–1968). Alice Guy, French-born film director and producer, was effectively the first woman director. Began as secretary to Léon Gaumont (1895), but soon found the opportunity to make *The Fairy of the Cabbages* (*La fée aux choux*) (1896) in his garden. Subsequently chief producer, supervising all Gaumont films to 1905, and directing many of them. Hired director Ferdinand Zecca, head writer and later artistic director Louis Feuillade, and assistant Victorin Jasset (1905). Made scores of musical sound films from 1902, using the Gaumont Chronophone process, making her the first director to produce a significant body of work using a sound technology. Married former Gaumont cameraman Herbert Blaché (1907), leaving with him for Cleveland in the States in 1907. Founded independent company Solax in New York (1910), supervising production of its 300-plus films before it closed (1914), having relocated to New Jersey. Herbert founded Blaché Features (1913)—Alice directed half its productions. For Popular Plays and Players, she directed Olga Petrova's films including the first two: *The Tigress* (1914) and *The Heart of a Painted Woman* (1915). Lectured on film at Columbia University (1917). In 1917 left independent production to direct for Pathé Exchange and Metro.

After her 1922 divorce she returned to France but found no further film work. Received French Légion d'Honneur (1953).

Lillie Devereux Blake (1833–1913). American novelist, lecturer, and suffragist. Wrote novels, novellas, hundreds of short stories, and essays on women's rights. War correspondent during Civil War. Wrote for *The Galaxy* (thereafter *Atlantic Monthly*) as "Tiger Lily." Began her lifelong crusade for women's rights in 1869. President, New York State Woman Suffrage Association (1879–90). President, New York City, Woman Suffrage League (1886–1900). Founded and led the National Legislative League (1900–05). Chair, Committee on Legislative Advice, National American Woman Suffrage Association (NAWSA), in which capacity she won women the right to be school trustees, police station matrons, census takers, and physicians in insane asylums. Through her influence, war nurses received pensions. *Woman's Place To-Day* (1883), four collected lectures calling for women's right to study at Columbia University responding to a misogynist Columbia trustee and theologian. Contributed to Elizabeth Cady Stanton's controversial *Woman's Bible* (1895). *Fettered for Life* (1874), novel of wife abuse, unjust marriage laws, and job discrimination, features a heroic reporter, later revealed to be female, who rescues female characters.

Louise de Koven Bowen (1859–1953). American social worker and writer. Author of *Safe Guards for City Youth at Work and at Play* (1914) and *Growing Up with a City* (1926). Founded Juvenile Protective Association of Chicago (1907), of which she was President for thirty-five years. Trustee and Treasurer of Hull House (see Jane Addams) for forty years, succeeding Addams as President. Very close friend of Addams, who dedicated *The Spirit of Youth and the City Streets* (1909) to her. President and co-founder, the Woman's City Club (Chicago) for ten years. A US delegate to the Pan-American Conference (1922). President, Board of Directors, Woman's World Fair (1925). Chairman, Woman's Committee, Council of National Defense, during World War I.

Elizabeth Bowen O.B.E. (1899–1973). Successful and critically acclaimed Anglo-Irish author whose writings, often on the moral dilemmas posed by contemporary society, have been adapted for radio and television. Worked in a shell-shock hospital near Dublin during World War I, and for Ministry of Information in London during World War II, during which time she was also an Air Raid Precautions warden. Wrote radio scripts for BBC. Wrote essays and reviews for *Tatler*, *New Statesman and Nation*, *New Republic*, *New York Times*, *Harpers*, among others. Honorary member of American Academy of Arts and Letters, and awarded honorary degrees from Trinity College, Dublin, and Oxford University. In 1923 married Alan Cameron, first chairman of British Film Institute. Her circle included Rose Macaulay and, later, Virginia Woolf. Among her best-known novels are *The Death of the Heart* (1938), *The Heat of the Day* (1949), *The Little Girls* (1964), and *Eva Trout* (1968). She also completed a literary study, *Anthony Trollope: A New Judgement* (1946).

Marian Bowlan (no dates found). Chicago-based American woman playright. Author of the following monologues: *Teena Stars on Tag Day* (1911); *Elevating the Drama*, *Up in the Air*, and *Why Shoe Clerks Go Insane* (1912); *In the Life Class*, *Minnie at the Movies*, and *Popular Music Hath Charms* (1913). These were collected in *City Types*, a 1916 book of monologues sketching the city woman. Contributed to the Chicago *Journal*, and sent a series of written sketches from the Ford Peace Ship during World War I.

Jessica Borthwick. No information found.

Beth Brown (no dates found). Manhattan-based American writer and newspaperwoman, who also wrote songs, animal stories, and a radio show—*Hotel for Pets*. May have worked with D.W. Griffith. Hired by Cecil B. DeMille in 1928 as a "gagman," in Hollywood she also wrote scenarios for Metro–Goldwyn–Mayer and Paramount Pictures, including science fiction. Gathered material for specific books by working as: nursemaid in an orphanage (for *Little Girl Blue*, 1926, written under the pseudonym Beth A. Retner); and stripper with a burlesque troop (for *Applause*, 1928, the basis of Mamoulian's 1929 film).

Bryher (1894–1983). British writer, critic, and poet, born Annie Winifred Ellerman, who lived mostly outside Britain. Wrote twenty-five books. Took her name from her favorite island of the Scillies, off Cornwall, a childhood haunt. In 1918 began her lifelong friendship and companionship with the poet H.D., whose daughter Perdita she adopted. Author of two film books, *Film Problems of Soviet Russia* (1929), and *Cinema Survey* (1937, co-author). Aided Jewish and other refugees in the 1930s. With her first husband, Robert McAlmon (whom she divorced in 1927), she moved in the Parisian literary and artistic circle of the early 1920s that included Gertrude Stein, James Joyce, and Picasso. With her second husband, Kenneth McPherson (whom she married in 1927 and divorced in 1947), she co-founded and co-edited the film journal *Close Up* (1927–33), H.D. being the third editor. Author of several well-received historical novels, and of poetry, articles, and reviews for numerous periodicals including *Transition*, *Little review*, and *Life and Letters Today*. Spent the last years of her life living somewhat hermitically in Territet, Switzerland.

Mary Ellen Bute (1909–1983). Award-winning American abstract filmmaker. Studied painting at Pennsylvannia Academy in early 1920s. Yale School of Drama graduate (1925). Interested in absolute film, which synthesized sound and image in a non-representational fusion through new technologies. Influenced by association with Thomas Wilfred (developer of color organ instrument), Russian physicist Leon Theremin (Theremin inventor), and composer Joseph Schillinger (analyst of music's relation to mathematics). Began filming with documentarian Lewis Jacobs. First films, *Synchrony No. 2* (1935) and *Rhythm in Light* (1936). Founded and headed company, Expanding Cinema in mid 1930s. Worked with future husband Ted Nemeth and Norman McLaren. Helped pioneer the oscilloscope in early 1950s. Completed two live-action narrative films, *The Boy Who Saw Through* (1958) and *Passages from Finnegans Wake* (1967), in addition to fifteen absolute films, produced singly and collaboratively. Musical sources for her films included Wagner, Milhaud, Bach, Liszt, Copland, Rimsky-Korsakov, Shostakovich, and Saint-Saëns.

Madeleine Carroll (1906–87). British-American actress, imported to Hollywood for John Ford's *The World Moves On* (1934). Earned B.A. Hons., French from University of Birmingham, England, and then taught French. After a theatrical beginning, she had entered British film scene in 1928 for *The Guns of Loos*. Returned to England for Hitchcock's *The 39 Steps* (1935) and *The Secret Agent* (1936). From 1941 until war's end she was engaged exclusively in war activities: helped refugee orphans in the United States; was entertainment director for merchant seamen in New York; worked for the Red Cross in France and Italy (1943–45); and subsequently worked with UNESCO, making documentary films for the United Nations, including *Children's Republic* and *The Eternal Fight*. After the war, and until the early 1950s, re-established a successful film and stage career. Recipient of the French Légion d'Honneur and the United States Medal of Freedom.

J. Cogdell (1900–?). According to the African-American journal *The Messenger* (April 1923), Ms J. Cogdell was a student, magazine writer, and art critic. In its March 1923 issue the journal states that she writes from the Pacific Coast and is twenty-three years of age.

Colette (1873–1954). Successful French novelist, editor, columnist, musical hall performer (briefly), and critic, born Sidonie Gabrielle Colette. Her first books, the Claudine novels, published under her husband's name, Willy. Ffirst woman in the Académie Goncourts (1945). First woman to attain Grand Officier of French Légion d'Honneur (1953). Wrote scenarios, dialogue, adaptations, and film criticism (in two principal bouts, 1914–19, 1931–35). Wrote for *Le Matin*, *Le Film*, *Excelsior*, *Vogue*, and *Le Figaro*. Adapted her own story for *La Vagabonde* (1917), starring Musidora. Other novels were adapted to the stage and screen later in life (*Gigi*, translated into English by Anita Loos, in 1951, and directed for the screen by Minnelli, in 1958; and *Chéri*, translated by Loos for Broadway in 1959). On account of her bisexuality and multiple marriages, she had a reputation for sensuality and exoticism, if not questionable morality.

(Eileen) Elizabeth Coxhead (1909–79). Journalist, critic, novelist, and broadcaster. First-class honors degree in French from Somerville College, Oxford. Novels include *A Wind in the West* (1949), *One Green Bottle* (1951), *The Midlanders* (1953), *The Figure in the Midst* (1955). Other works include a 1961 pamphlet, *Women in the Professions*, and *Daughters of Erin* (1965), an account of the women of the Irish Literary Revival. In 1962, edited *Selected Plays* of Lady Augusta Gregory, one of the co-founders of the Abbey Theatre in Dublin, and, in 1966, wrote *Lady Gregory*, a biographical study. Was film critic for the *Liverpool Daily Post*, 1949–50. A keen mountaineer, she spent time regularly in France.

Joy Davidman (1915–60). American poet and poetry editor, critic, and novelist. Attended Columbia University Graduate School. First volume of poetry, *Letter to a Comrade* (1938), won Yale Series of Younger Poets Award. A Communist in her early years, she wrote criticism for *New Masses* (1941–43), and edited an anthology of anti-fascist poetry. Later turned to Christianity, and began correspondence with Oxford theologian C.S. Lewis, whom she married shortly after her cancer diagnosis. (Their relationship was the subject of the film, *Shadowlands*.) Works include *Anya* (1940), *Weeping Bay* (1950), and *Smoke on the Mountain: An Interpretation of the Ten Commandments* (1954).

Alta M. Davis. No information found.

Barbara Deming (1917–84). American writer, pacificist, feminist, and lesbian activist. Co-director of Bennington Stock Theater (1938–39). Teaching Fellow, Bennington School of the Arts (1940–41). Film analyst for the Library of Congress Film Project (1942–44), developed with advice from Siegfried Kracauer and Iris Barry. Associate editor of *Liberation* magazine (1962–69). She also contributed poems, stories, and essays on politics, film, and theater, to *The New Yorker*, *Partisan Review*, *Paris Review*, *Nation*, *Vogue*, and *Hudson Review*. Commited to nonviolent pacifist activism after reading Gandhi's writings. Between 1959 and 1960, joined the Committee for Non-violent Action. Her participation in many peace and civil rights actions resulted in jail, in 1963, 1964, and 1967. Visited Cuba in 1960 and spoke with Fidel Castro. Traveled to North and South Vietnam during the Vietnam War. Author of *Running Away from Myself: A Dream Portrait of America Drawn from the Films of the Forties* (1969).

Maya Deren (1917–1961). Russian-American avant-garde filmmaker and theorist. Interested in socialism in the 1930s. Fascination with dance (becoming Katherine Dunham's secretary in 1941) led to studies in Haitian culture—travelled to Haiti (four trips between 1947 and 1955), filming Voudoun ceremonies. Wrote *Divine Horsemen: The Living Gods of Haiti* (1953). With Alexander Hammid (whom she married, 1942) made *Meshes of the Afternoon* (1943). Deren features in *Meshes*, her *At Land* (1944), and *Ritual in Transfigured Time* (1946), films which, with *A Study in Choreography for Camera* (1945), *Meditation on Violence* (1948) and *The Very Eye of Night* (1952/59), extended her interest in the human body in motion. Received the first Guggenheim award for film (1946). First woman and first American to receive Cannes Grand Prix Internationale for Avant-Garde Film (16 mm) (1947). A tireless advocate for film as art, founded Creative Film Foundation, to assist independent filmmakers (1954).

Antonia Dickson (1856–1903). Probably French-born, musician, poet, and writer, oldest of three children, the elder sister of only brother William Kennedy Laurie Dickson, Edison's chief assistant in the laboratory at Menlo Park, New Jersey. Younger sister, Eva. Child musical prodigy and performer, received conservatoire education in Leipzig, Germany, accompanied by William. In 1879, received associate diploma from College of Organists, now the Royal College of Organists, and later became a Fellow of the Royal Organ Society, London. Poems published in *Living Age*, *Current Literature*, and *Eclectic Magazine*. Spoke German, French (probably), and English. In Orange (now West Orange), New Jersey, in the 1890s she gave performances and yearly lectures on musical history. With William, wrote a hagiographical account of Edison's life, *The Life and Inventions of Thomas Alva Edison* (1894), and *History of the Kinetograph, Kinetoscope and Kinetophonograph* (1895). Died in London.

Frances White Diehl (Mrs Ambrose N.) (1888–?). American leader of women's organizations. Executive at Elizabeth Arden. National Field Commander of the Red Cross Motor Corps, World War I, France. In Pittsburgh, after 1921 marriage to President of Carnegie Steel, Ambrose N. Diehl organized numerous civic activities. Helped found Pittsburgh Opera. *Men of Steel* (1926) based on her script. Chairman, Motion Pictures, General Federation of Women's Clubs. *Ladies' Home Journal* motion picture reviewer (1932). Advocated economic pressure against poor films, rather than censorship, to raise standards. During World War II active in Red Cross (San Francisco), served on National Advisory Board of Women's Section, United States Army Public Relations, and coordinated war activities of National Council of Women. Elected president of National Council of Women (1946). Attended first post-war executive council meeting of International Council of Women, Brussels; as a member, she deplored paucity of women in the United Nations. International Relations Chairman, General Federation of Women's Clubs (1947).

Geraldyn Dismond (Gerri Major) (1894–?). African-American journalist, educator, nurse, and columnist. Teacher (1915–17). Red Cross nurse (1917–23). From 1925, contributor to *Pittsburgh Courier* with columns "New York Social News" and "Through the Lorgnette." Columnist for *Chicago Bee* (1926–27) with "In New York Town." From 1927 managing editor for *Inter-State Tattler*, publication covering black social life in small and large cities. Here she chronicled nightly excitement of Harlem Salon, "Dart Towers" of A'Lelia Walker, daughter of cosmetics millionaire, Madame C. Walker. Organizer of Geraldyn Dismond Bureau of Specialized Publicity. From 1928 writing for *The Baltimore Afro-American*. In later life edited social pages of *Jet* magazine. Editor, *The Negro Actor*, publication of the Negro Actors League. Published *Gerri Major's Black Society* (1977).

Jessie Dismorr (Jessica) (1885–1939). British poet and artist. Studied at Slade School of Art, London. Part of British Fauve circle, then the Vorticists. An associate and possible mistress of Wyndham Lewis, she was one of two women to sign the Vorticist manifesto (1914). Contributed poems and drawings to *Tyro*, *Rhythm*, *Blast*, *Little review*. Exhibited abstract works with the Seven and Five Society in London in the 1920s. A posthumous retrospective of her paintings and drawings was held at Mercury Gallery, London, 1974. Appears in William Roberts's well-known painting *The Vorticists at the Restaurant de la Tour Eiffel: Spring 1915* (1962).

Germaine Dulac (1882–1942). French writer, film director, journalist, and film theorist. After writing for French feminist journal *La Française*, as drama critic and interviewer (1906–13), she formed her own production company, D.E.L.I.A. Film, among other names, with her companion and future screenwriter Irène Hillel-Erlanger in 1916. First film, *Les soeurs ennemies* (1917). Best-known film, *The Smiling Madame Beudet* (1923). Meets Louis Delluc in 1917, and, with him, in association with other Impressionists (a group of filmmakers including Abel Gance, Marcel l'Herbier, and Marie and Jean Epstein), formed the first French film avant-garde, devoted to promoting the seventh art by establishing ciné-club circuits using a screening plus lecture and discussion format. Founded her own, short-lived journal *Schémas* (1927). Her *The Seashell* and the *Clergyman* (1928) (screenplay by Antonin Artaud) particularly evidences her interest in surrealism. Some later films such as *Disque 957* and *Etude cinématograph sur une Arabèsque*, both made in 1929, are "musical accompaniments" to pieces by Chopin and Debussy, though intended to be projected without music. From 1930, made newsreels for Gaumont–Franco-Films—Aubert (GFFA), launching the newsreel *France-Actualités-Gaumont* in 1932. Made her last film as individual director, *Le Cinéma au service de l'histoire* in 1935. Artistic and technical consultant for *France-Actualités* until 1939. Participated in the founding and administration of the Cinemathèque Française. Her papers are held in the Bibliothèque du film, Paris.

Olivia Howard Dunbar (1873–1953). American journalist, biographer, and short-story writer. Writer for the New York *World* c. 1894–1902. Wrote for *Harper's Weekly*. Wrote "That Neglected Age," on periods in child development, for *The Dial*, June 1920.

Mabel Dwight (1875/6–1955). American printmaker of popular works of social observation, sharpest in 1930s. Attentive to particularity of urban life, and quality of human contact. First exhibition 1897. Moved to New York (1903). Prints regularly included in Whitney Studio Club (from 1918); in Society of Independent Artists Exhibition (1921); at National Academy of Design (1922, 1925); in First Biennial, Whitney Museum of American Art (1933–34); in "Against War and Fascism," American Artists' Congress (1936); in "Prints for the People," Federal Art Project (1937); in XXII Biennial International, Venice (1940). Traveled and worked in Paris (1926–27). First one-person exhibition (1928). Late 1920s published in *Vanity Fair*, *Theatre Guild Magazine*, *The New Freeman*, *Fortune*. Affiliated with John Reed Club (1933). Works for Public Works of Art Project (1934), WPA Federal Art Project (1939). One-person lithograph exhibition (1938). Eleven images, Federal Writers' Project, *WPA Guide to New York City* (1939).

Eva Elie (no dates found). Probably Swiss. In 1932 Elie was appointed chief sub-editor of *L'Effort cinégraphique suisse*, official organ of the Association Cinématographique Suisse Romande.

Marion Fairfax (1879–70). Successful American playwright, of *The Builders* (1907), her first work; *The Chaperon* (1908), which had a run on Broadway and at The Strand, London; *The Talker* (1912); and *A Modern Girl* (1914). Appeared on stage, and played in summerstock with her husband, actor Tully Marshall. Entered film industry around 1915 as screenwriter for Lasky, at the suggestion of William de Mille, head of the scenario department there. Wrote *The Immigrant* (Chaplin, 1917). Director of Marion Fairfax Productions. In 1920 signed with Marshall Neilan to write and edit his productions. During the 1920s, she wrote, supervised, and edited more than thirty features, and directed *The Lying Truth* (1922), which treated drug addiction. In 1930 she wrote a column, "Marionettes," for the Los Angeles-based weekly *Rob Wagner's Script*.

Mary Field (1896–1968). Award-winning British nature filmmaker, writer, lecturer, and expert on films and television for children. M.A. in Imperial History, Bedford College, University of London. After school teaching, worked checking facts on commonwealth films at university, beginning association with British Instructional (1926), where she was variously responsible for scenario, production, and direction in *The Secrets of Nature* (1922–33) films with Percy F. Smith. Pioneered children's matinée movement. Directed *The King's English* (1932), and one dramatic film, *Strictly Business* (1932). Pioneered use of moving diagrams in educational film. At Gaumont British Instructional from 1934, contributed to making *The Secrets of Life* nature film series (1933–44). Reputation as Britain's most distinguished, if singular, female director. Established Children's Film Department of J. Arthur Rank (1944), producing hundreds of films until 1950. Member, British Board of Film Censors (1950–51). Executive officer, Children's Film Foundation (1951–58). In 1950s, traveled internationally as an advocate for children's film. Consultant to UNESCO on children's films. O.B.E. (1951). Supervisor of children's programs for ABC Television and Associated Television, Britain (1959).

Zelda Fitzgerald (1900–1948). American writer. With F. Scott Fitzgerald, her husband, was part of American expatriate group in Europe, which included Ernest Hemingway. From 1928 to 1930, tried to develop her talent in dancing, writing, and painting. This contributed to her first breakdown in 1930. The remainder of her life is checkered with periods of insanity. In 1920s and early 1930s, wrote several articles and short stories, some of which were revised by, or written with, her husband. Some appear with a joint byline. Others were printed under his name alone, but his private ledger records Zelda's authorship, as in the case of "Our Own Movie Queen." Her only published novel is *Save Me the Waltz* (1932), written while a patient in a psychiatric clinic.

Frances Hubbard Flaherty (1886–1972). American filmmaker, photographer, lecturer, writer. Married Robert J. Flaherty (1914), collaborating with him on many films, and documenting their production in still photographs and essays. Co-edited their film *Moana of the South* (1926), assistant scenarist and photographer for *Man of Aran* (1934), and co-wrote *Louisiana Story* (1948). With Ursula Leacock, wrote children's novel *Sabu, the Elephant Boy* (1938), subsequently filmed. After Flaherty's death (1951), lectured on his work at universities and film clubs, and co-founded the Robert J. Flaherty Foundation (later International Film Seminars). In 1960 wrote an account of Flaherty's work, *The Odyssey of a Filmmaker: Robert Flaherty's Story*.

Janet Flanner (1892–1978). American writer, translator, and correspondent, best known for her columns for *The New Yorker*, "Letter from Paris" (1925–39) and "Paris Journal" (1944–78), written under *nom de plume* "Genet" (given her by *New Yorker* editor Harold Ross). Her Paris report spanned more than fifty years. Film critic for *Indianapolis Star* (1917–18). Co-founder, with Ruth Hale, of Lucy Stone League, organization advocating women's rights to use their maiden names on passports (1921). In Paris from 1922, part of Left Bank artistic and literary scene (which included Margaret Anderson, Gertrude Stein, Djuna Barnes, Ernest Hemingway). Translated two of Colette's novels. French Légion d'Honneur (1947). Her letters to long-term companion Natalia Danesi Murray were posthumously published as *Darlinghissima: Letters to a Friend* (1985).

E. Margery Fox (no dates found). British (probably), educator with an interest in the moral and social aspects of the cinema. Headmistress of County School for Girls, Gravesend, near London, c. 1916. Expert witness for the Cinema Commission of Inquiry, National Council of Public Morals, 1917, representing the Headmistresses' Association. Member, Commission on Educational and Cultural Films (1930–1932/3). Vice-Chairman of the Cinema Sectional Committee of the National Council of Women (1932). Headmistress, County School for Girls, Beckenham, c. 1932.

Gene Gauntier (1885–1966). American actress, screenwriter, director, film producer. Acted briefly in Lois Weber's theater company, in *Why Girls Leave Home*. Wrote over five hundred scenarios, starring in many, going on location and undercover for research. Began film career with Kalem Company (founded 1907), forming long creative partnership with head Sidney Olcott. Did her own stunt work. Write possibly first film adaptation of *Ben-Hur* (1907), which, after a law suit, established American film copyright procedures. Moved to Biograph as scenario writer/editor (1908); purportedly responsible for D.W. Griffith's first directing opportunity. Returned to Kalem (1908), and began writing and performing for the serial *The Adventures of a Girl Spy* (1909). Toured Ireland, Germany (1909), Egypt and Holy Land (1911), the latter trip resulting in Kalem's *From the Manger to the Cross* (1912). Gauntier and Olcott broke with Kalem to form short-lived Gene Gauntier Film Players; joined Bison (1915). War correspondent.

Katharine Fullerton Gerould (1879–1944). American short-story writer, essayist, and novelist. A.B. and A.M., Radcliffe College. Won *Century Magazine* prize, best short story by college graduate (1900). Taught English composition, Bryn Mawr, inaugurating narrative writing course (1901–10). Wrote for Century, Atlantic Monthly, Harper's, Scribner's. Scorned many twentieth-century modernist writers, vigorously defended "the life of the mind and the spirit" against twentieth-century materialism, defended older Eastern universities against state universities of the West. Argued for philosophy and art against science, and against leveling effects of massive immigration and widespread acceptance of "the democractic fallacy." Eschewed literary circles. Novels include Lost Valley (1922), The Light that Never Was (1931). Her "Conquistador" adapted by Fox as the film Romance of the Rio Grande. Published two collections of travel sketches, and two collections of critical essays, Modes and Morals (1920) and Ringside Seats (1937), featuring her once-famous coverage of the Tunney–Dempsey fight as Greek tragedy.

Evelyn Gerstein (no dates found). American (?) journalist and critic. Film and theater critic for The Boston Herald; New York film correspondent for the Boston Evening Transcript; film editor, Theatre Guild Magazine (New York) in the late 1920s and 1930s. Published reviews in Nation and New Republic. Traveled to Soviet Union in 1935.

Elinor Gibbs (born Elinor Mead Sherwin) (no dates found). American? Attended Wellesley College for one year. Acted briefly in silent films in California. Returning to the East Coast, worked as a fashion model in Depression New York, paid by getting to keep the clothes she modeled. Became third wife of Wolcott Gibbs, drama critic for The New Yorker, 14 October 1933, regularly accompanying him to opening nights. Began movie reviewing during the Second World War, and, after the war, wrote some of the "Briefly Noted" reviews (mostly about mysteries) in The New Yorker. Also after the war, she wrote for Vogue, and for Harper's Junior Bazaar. Committed member of Democratic Party, and cat lover.

Catheryne Cooke Gilman (1880–1954). American social worker, pacifist, feminist. Wrote over two hundred pamphlets and articles. Began as teacher. Studied at University of Chicago, where she learned of Hull House. Took up residence at East Side House Settlement, New York (1913). Moved to Northeast Neighborhood House settlement, Minneapolis (1914), lived there over thirty years. Civic work for babies, mothers, in child welfare, and juvenile delinquency. Appointed to Minnesota Child Welfare Commission (1916). Worked, Minneapolis' Women's Co-operative Committee (renamed Alliance), writing sex education program seeking to prevent juvenile deliquency and protect morals of children and young women. Group worked with immigrants and African Americans, publishing in several languages. Supported Prohibition. Alliance efforts led to establishment of Women's Bureau, Minneapolis Police Department. Monitored movie regulation from 1915. Chairman, Motion Picture Committee, National Council of Women (1927). President, Federal Motion Picture Council (1928). Chairman, Motion Picture Committee, the National Congress of Parents and Teachers (1932).

Charlotte Perkins Gilman (1860–1935). American feminist, economist, author, lecturer. Trained at Rhode Island School of Design. Worked as teacher, greeting card designer. Married, 1884. Suffered depression after birth of daughter (1885), and sought medical treatment. The experience formed the basis of The Yellow Wallpaper (1892). Separated from husband, moved to California (1888). Wrote and lectured widely on women, labor, social reform. Publications include In This Our World (1893, verse); Concerning Children (1900); The Home (1903); Human Work (1904); Man-Made World (1911); His Religion and Hers (1923); acclaimed Women and Economics (1898), attacking women's financial dependency, translated into seven languages. Met Jane Addams, 1895. Attended International Social and Labour Congress, London, 1896. Argued women's nature was peaceful and cooperative. From 1909 to 1916 published The Forerunner, most of which she wrote, two hundred short stories, and three utopian novels, one, Herland (1915), describing all-female society with collective childrearing and parthenogenetic reproduction. Diagnosed with breast cancer in 1932; took chloroform, 1935.

Lillian Gish (1893–1993). Renowned American stage and screen actress, directed once. Performed with mother and sister (Dorothy) on stage from early age. Introduced to D.W. Griffith at Biograph while visiting fellow child actress, Mary Pickford (1912). Entire family given parts by Griffith. Appeared in twenty Griffith shorts (1912–14), developing into expressive, utterly compelling actress. Left Biograph with Griffith (1914). Persona as frail, innocent, but determined heroine, evident in *Broken Blossoms* (1919) and *Way Down East* (1920). Directed sister in *Remodeling Her Husband* (1919). Broke with Griffith over salary, made films in Europe, joined MGM (1925). Insisted on right to vet scripts and directors. Acted under King Vidor, Victor Sjöstrom, Fred Niblo. Refused to adapt to 1920s flapper mood. From 1930s until 1970s, appeared successfully, if intermittently, on Broadway. Made occasional films into her nineties. Undertook lecture tours of Europe and United States, 1969–70. In later life she actively supported film preservation and respect for silent cinema.

Ruby Berkley Goodwin (1903–61). African-American writer, publicist, actress. Daughter of coal miner, married and had five children, took B.A. in 1949 from San Diego State College. Maintained a dual career as syndicated columnist on black Hollywood, "Hollywood in Bronze" (1936–52); and publicist and secretary to actress Hattie McDaniel (1936–52). Contributed "Stories of Negro Life" to *Twelve Negro Spirituals* (1937), and contributed writings to *Negro Voices* (1938) and *Ebony Rhythm* (1938). Two collections of poems, *From My Kitchen Window* (1942) and *A Gold Star Mother Speaks* (1944). Award-winning autobiography, *It's Good to Be Black* (1953). Appeared in films *The View from Pompey's Head* (1955), *Strange Intruder* (1956), *The Alligator People* (1959), and *Wild in the Country* (1961). In 1940 secretary of Federated Council of Church Women. Known as an authority on interrracial matters, and much in demand as a lecturer.

Gladys Hall (1892–1977). Hollywood fan magazine interviewer and writer. Began professional career (1912) writing poems and fan magazine articles, also publishing novelettes and short stories. Syndicated newspaper column, "The Diary of a Professional Movie Fan," began 1922. Moved to Los Angeles (1927). Wrote for *Photoplay, Modern Screen, Screenland, Motion Picture Classic* and others. Helped found Hollywood Women's Press Club (1928). Interviewed most of the major movie stars from the 1920s through the 1950s; was dubbed "undisputed queen of the cosy confession" and "one of the principal architects of the wondrous Hollywood myth." Returned to New York (1943), continuing to write for fan magazines. Papers deposited at Academy of Motion Picture Arts and Sciences.

Avenelle Harris (1881–1966). African-American actress, singer, and dancer who appeared infrequently in Hollywood films from the early sound era to the immediate post-war period, after which her name disappears from view. Occasionally credited as "Avarel Harris" in cast lists.

H.D. (Hilda Doolittle) (1886–1961). American-born writer, poet, playright, novelist, translator, editor, actress. Attended Bryn Mawr, wooed by Ezra Pound. Traveled Europe (1911), met D.H. Lawrence, W.B. Yeats, Richard Aldington (married 1913). Early poems inspired Pound's term "Imagism." First poems published, began translating Greek poetry (1913). Editor, *The Egoist* (London, 1916). Met Bryher (1918), beginning lifelong liaison. Bryher, with husband Kenneth MacPherson, founded *Close Up* film journal (1927–33), for which H.D. was contributing editor. The three, as Pool Films, produced *Foothills* (1927), *Wingbeat* (1927), and *Borderline* (1930), the latter featuring Paul (in his first screen role) and Eslanda Robeson. Never wrote directly about film again after 1929. Analysis with Freud (Vienna, 1933 and 1934), resulted in memoir, *Tribute to Freud* (1956). Interest in classical myth and history. Wrote *Trilogy* (three-part verse work, 1944–46), affirming life's resurrection from wartime London, and long poem, *Helen in Egypt* (1961). Award of Merit Medal for Poetry from American Academy of Arts and Letters (1960).

Winifred Holtby (1898–1935). English feminist, pacifist, novelist, journalist, and lecturer. Member of the Women's Auxiliary Corps in World War I, a service interrupting her history degree at Somerville College, Oxford (1917–21), where she met Vera Brittain. Moved to London, setting up house with Brittain (1922). Lectures for the Six Point Group, a women's rights organization, and the League of Nations Union. A prolific journalist, wrote for the *Manchester Guardian*, *News Chronicle*, and *Time and Tide*, of which she became a director in 1926. Was involved in a variety of feminist and pacifist activities including the unionization of black workers in South Africa, which she visited in 1926, the year before writing "Missionary Film." Fiction includes *Anderby Wold* (1923), *The Land of Green Ginger* (1927), *Poor Caroline* (1931), *Mandoa Mandoa!* (1933), and *South Riding* (1936), which was filmed in 1938. Non-fiction work includes *Virginia Woolf* (1932) and *Women in a Changing Civilization* (1934).

Hedda Hopper (1885–1966). American actress, radio, and newspaper columnist renowned for cattiness, reactionary politics, and headgear. Born Elda Furry, inspired to act on seeing Ethel Barrymore. Worked summer stock; Broadway début 1909; married actor DeWolf Hopper 1913; screen début *The Battle of Hearts* (1916). Moved to Hollywood (1923), film work spotty, worked in real estate, cosmetics, radio. Hollywood gossip column (1937) soon picked up by *Los Angeles Times* and others. Touted rivalry with fellow columnist Louella Parsons boosted her notoriety; column syndicated worldwide. *Los Angeles Times* "Woman of the Year" (1955). Books, *From Under My Hat* (1952) and *The Whole Truth and Nothing But* (1963). Papers depisited at Academy of Motion Picture Arts and Sciences.

Winifred Horrabin (1887–1970). English writer, socialist feminist, and journalist. Film reviewer *Lansbury's Labour Weekly* (1925–27), *Tribune* (1940–45), and *Manchester Evening News* (1944–48), writing there under the name "Freda Wynne." In late 1920s had a woman's page in the Independent Labour Party newspaper, *The New Leader*. Known to Ethel Mannin and Minnie Pallister. After World War I, active in Workers' Education, as well as in theater and art. With husband Frank Horrabin (Independent Labour MP, 1929–33) wrote a primer, *Working Class Education* (1924), and, as sole author, a pamphlet, *Is Woman's Place in the Home?* (1935). Unpublished reminiscences, "The Summer of a Dormouse."

Penelope Houston (1927–). English film critic whose long career has been a significant influence on British film culture. B.A. Oxford. Associate Editor of publications for British Film Insititute (1950–56), thereafter General Editor. Editor, *Sight and Sound*, from 1956. Film critic for the *Observer*, *Manchester Guardian*, *Spectator*, *International Film Annual*, *Sequence*, and others. Author of three books, *The Contemporary Cinema* (1963), *Went the Day Well?* (1992), and *Keepers of the Frame: The Film Archive* (1994).

Fannie Hurst (1889–1968). Highly successful American writer of popular fiction. Graduated from Washington University (1909), moved to New York to establish writing career (1910). In 1925–26, employed Zora Neale Hurston as her secretary. Works include the bestselling *Backstreet* (1931), *Apassionata* (1926), *Five and Ten* (1929), *We are Ten* (1937), *Anywoman* (1950), and the autobiographical *Anatomy of Me* (1958). Her stories *Humoresque*, *Back Street*, and *Lummox* were successfully adapted for the screen. One of her best-known books, *Imitation of Life* (1933), which was filmed in 1934 and 1959, was a study in racial identity, and showed professional success to be unfulfilling to women without male companionship; her novels frequently suggest women are conditioned to be emotionally dependent on men. Unlike many of the characters in her books, however, Hurst combined a successful career with marriage, maintaining a separate residence, and rendezvousing with her husband three nights a week, according to reports.

Fay M. Jackson (no dates found—still alive in 1957). African-American journalist, syndicated through Associated Negro Press (ANP), for which she was Pacific Coast correspondent from about 1934. Editor and publisher, *California News* (Los Angeles) from late 1935 to 1937. Column,

"Hollywood Stardust" for the Baltimore Afro-American (1935). Traveled to London for ANP to cover coronation of George VI (1936), only African-American woman to sit in Westminster Abbey. Spent six months in Europe in spring 1937, aided by Nancy Cunard (Paris ANP correspondent)—though the two did not meet—writing on Robeson, Europe, Haile Selassie, and color bar in England. IN 1937, she declared to her ANP boss "I am rabid on the question of women's rights." Of coronation she wrote, "Africa was there, but not the Africans, Indians were there, but not India..." (Africa was represented by the white masters of various African colonies and but "two reactionary black chieftains"; India, although represented by Indian royal families and thousands of Indian troops, was not present as a political entity, still being a British colony. (Mahatma Gandhi and others were agitating for this to end, arguing that "India" could comprise a single nation-state—this was not the case with Africa.) See Box 288, Folder 1, Chaude A. Barnett Collection, Chicago Historical Society.) Left ANP in late 1937 to write for California Eagle, successor to California News. In 1950s worked as realtor in Los Angeles.

Milena Jesenská (1890–1944). Czech journalist, humanist. Moved to Vienna upon marriage, correspondent for Czech papers. Interested in Kafka's works, she wrote to him seeking translation permission (1920). Correspondence and relationship developed; Jesenská generally accepted as Frieda's model in Kafka's The Castle. Kafka's letters to her published posthumously as Briefe an Milena (1952). Returning to Prague, edited Narodny Listy women's page, worked as translator, wrote children's books, and associated with Devetsil circle. Edited compilation of reader's recipes (1925), and collection of own articles (1926). Later wrote for a provincial daily and an illustrated arts magazine. Briefly a member of the Communist Party, writing for leftist journals (1935). Traveled and reported on the Sudetenland (1938). Defiant against Nazism, she assisted refugees and wrote for the underground press. Deported to Ravensbruck, where she died. An ardent Czech nationalist, Jesenská's name was expunged from public record during the Communist takeover of Czechoslovakia (1948).

Eva Alberta Jessye (1895–1992). African-American composer, musical editor and arranger, choir director, conductor, teacher, columnist, and poet. Musical director of Hallelujah (1929), one of the first Hollywood all-black-cast sound films. Studied choral music and music theory, Western University, Kansas, graduating 1914. M.A. degree, with medals in poetry, oratory, and music. Director, Music Department, Morgan College (Baltimore), and, in 1922, staff writer, the Baltimore Afro-American. Moved to New York (1926). Formed Original Dixie Jubilee Singers (later called Eva Jessye Choir), with between sixteen and twenty singers, singing spirituals, work songs, mountain ballads, ragtime jazz, and light opera. Choir sang for Vidor's Hallelujah, performed on Broadway, and did World War II benefits, for which it received government citations. Sang Porgy and Bess (George Gershwin) and Four Saints in Three Acts (Virgil Thomson). Official choir, 1963 "March on Washington" Freedom March led by Martin Luther King, and toured United States and Europe. Official choral group to sing at Martin Luther King's funeral. Jessye's folk oratorio Paradise Lost and Regained (1931) sets Milton's poem to black spirituals. Her primary work, My Spirituals (1927), was a combination book and musical score. Artist-in-Residence, Pittsburgh State University (1979–80). Awarded several honorary degrees, including a doctorate. Throughout her career as a film and stage musical director, Jessye managed a training school for performers in New York. Papers at the University of Michigan, Ann Arbor.

Lillian Johnson (no dates found). African-American journalist. Reported on film for the Baltimore Afro-American in the early 1940s. Also had a column, "A Woman Talks," in the same newspaper.

Osa Johnson (1894–1953). American writer–adventurer. In 1912, with husband Martin, began a series of explorations which resulted in many feature-length documentaries such as

Headhunters of the South Seas (1922), *Simba, the King of Beasts* (1928), *Congorilla* (1932), and *Across the World with Mr and Mrs Johnson* (1930). In their first trip they traveled to the New Hebrides seeking cannibals. Returning to the US, they toured their footage on the Keith–Albee vaudeville circuit where Osa danced "Hawaiian" numbers while Martin lectured. Subsequent trips made to the South Pacific, Africa (where they lived for several years), and Borneo. A crack shot, Osa was Martin's camera assistant, and established and ran base camp. Badly injured in the plane crash that killed Martin, Osa assisted on *Stanley and Livingstone* (1939). Produced a 1940 film from her biography I Married Adventure and *African Paradise* (1942). Wrote *Bride in the Solomons* (1944) and many animal stories. Papers at Martin and Osa Johnson Safari Museum, Chanute, Kansas, and at teh Leonard H. Axe Library, Pittsburg, Kansas.

Resi Langer (1890–?). German writer, actress, and lecturer. Born in Breslau. Published *Kinotypen: Vor und hinter den Filmkulissen. Zwölf Kapitel aus der Kinderstube des Films* (1919). Evening lectures and performances written and compiled by Langer, on contemporary verse, lyric poetry of the German rococo, farce, and grotesques (1912–13, but possibly at other times), to positive critical response.

C.A. Lejeune (1897–1973). Prolific, respected, and influential British film critic—sometimes credited as first female film critic in Britain. First class honours degree in English, Manchester University (1921). Began reviewing opera for the *Manchester Guardian*, and started writing on film *c*. 1921. Regular film column, *Manchester Guardian*, 1922–28, after she had moved to London, where she also studied for a PhD. Film critic, *Sunday Observer* (1928–60). Honorary doctorate of literature (1961). Also wrote for *Picturegoer, New York Times Magazine, The Sketch, Good Housekeeping, Theatre Arts Monthly, Penguin Film Review*, and *Sight and Sound*, being a member of its first editorial board in 1932. Published a survey of film, *Cinema* (1931), and a collection of her criticism, *Chestnuts in Her Lap* (1947). With her son, Anthony Lejeune, wrote television play, *Vicky's First Ball*. Her lively and witty reviewing style rejected both jargon and high-falutin language.

Hattie M. Loble. No information found.

Anita Loos (1893–1981). American satirist, screenwriter, film producer, diminutive beauty. Briefly child actress. First scenario, *The New York Hat*, submitted by post to D.W. Griffith (1912). Subsequently wrote over one hundred scenarios for Biograph Company. Credited with writing comic subtitles for *Intolerance* (1916). Wrote for Keystone Cops. With Douglas Fairbanks and husband, John Emerson, worked as unit in Griffith's company from 1915. Emerson and Loos wrote for various studios, and Loos scripted several scenarios for the Talmadges. Her *Gentlemen Prefer Blondes* (1925) published to great success, and adapted for screen (1928 and 1953). Screenwriter, MGM, from 1931; first MGM screenplay *Red-Headed Woman* (1932), which she had taken over from F. Scott Fitzgerald, provoked protests from women's clubs and Church groups. Other MGM screenplays included *San Francisco* (1936) and, with Jane Murfin, *The Women* (1939), an adaptation of Clare Booth Luce's successful play. Later translated Colette's *Gigi* (1951) and *Chéri* (1959) for Broadway.

Barbara Low (1877–1955). British feminist, pedagogue, Fabian, and psychoanalyst. Correspondent for the suffragist journal *The New Freewoman* (1913). Worked for the Labour Party in the 1910s. Abandoned a teaching career to study psychoanalysis. Freud credited her for originating the "Nirvana Principle." Was a founding member of the London Association of Psycho-Analysis (*c*. 1920), and published in the *International Journal of Psycho-Analysis*, and in *National Health*. Wrote one of the first accounts of psychoanalysis for the general public, *Psycho-Analysis: A Brief Account of the Freudian Theory* (1920). Reported on the 1925 International Psycho-Analytic Congress. Translated Anna Freud's *Psycho-Analysis for Teachers and Parents* (1931). Her circle included H.D., George Bernard Shaw, H.G. Wells, Rebecca West, and Dorothy

Richardson. Maintained a strong interest in education, being active in the Institute for the Study and Treatment of Delinquency until her death.

Rose Macaulay, DBE (1881–1958). Prize-winning English Catholic satirical novelist, biographer, and essayist. Read history at Somerville College, Oxford. Moved to London, 1916. Early novels explore the war's consequences, as in *Non-Combatants and Others* (1916) and *Told by an Idiot* (1923). In the 1920s published essays in *The Daily Mail, Evening Standard,* and an Anglican High Church weekly known as *Guardian.* A member of various literary coteries in London from the 1910s through the 1930s, her circle included Virginia Woolf, Rupert Brooke, Edith Sitwell, Storm Jameson, Arnold Bennett, and Aldous Huxley. During World War II voluntary part-time ambulance driver. After World War II wrote a number of travel books.

Ethel Mannin (1900–1984). Working-class English leftist, writer of novels, short stories, children's fiction, travelogues, and nonfiction works. Began work at age fifteen as a stenographer. Then wrote pulp novelettes, edited *The Pelican,* and wrote articles for women's pages. She penned almost a hundred books and travelled widely. Her novels were socially and politically engaged works, sensitive to women's plight. Among her publications, *Red Rose* (1941), based on Emma Goldman's life; *Women and the Revolution* (1938), a long, nonfiction polemic against capitalism; and several volumes on child-rearing, including *Common Sense and the Child: A Plea for Freedom* (1931). Active for Republican forces during Spanish Civil War. An atheist and member of the Independent Labour Party in the 1930s, during which time she wrote for *The New Leader,* she was later attracted to anarchism and pacifism. She wrote seven volumes of autobiography.

Mrs Henry Mansergh (also wrote as Mrs de Horne Vaizey) (1857–1917). British romantic and historical novelist and short-story writer. Published in *English Illustrated Magazine, Living Age, Blackwoods, Cornhill Magazine, Windsor Magazine.* Many of her novels published by the Religious Tract Society (London) or the romance specialists, Mills & Boon. Works addressed to women and often feature active heroines although she disapproved of female suffrage. Some stories first serialized in *Girl's Own Paper. Pixie O'Shaughnessey* (1903), and *About Peggy Saville* (1900) initiated popular series of novels. Works include *A Girl in Spring-Time* (1897), *A Rose-Coloured Thread* (1898), *Tom and Some Other Girls: A Public School Story* (1901), *A Houseful of Girls* (1902), *Flaming June* (1908), *The Conquest of Chrystabel* (1909), *A Honeymoon in Hiding* (1911), and *An Unknown Lover* (1913).

Katherine Mansfield (1888–1923). New Zealand-born short-story writer and novelist. Student in London (1903–06). Settled in London (1908), feeling limited by the provincial, colonial climate of home. First published in *New Age* (1910). First volume of stories, *In a German Pension* (1911), most openly feminist work. Other works include *Prelude* (1918) and *The Garden Party* (1922). Suffered from tuberculosis, which eventually killed her; from 1918 onwards wintered in Southern France. Posthumous publications: *The Doves' Nest* (1923); *Bliss* (1923); *Something Childish* (1924); *Poems* (1924); extracts from her journals (1927); selected letters (1928); *Collected Stories* (1945). Assisted in translating Gorky's *Reminiscences of Leonid Andreyev* (1922) and *Reminiscences of Tolstoy, Chekov, and Andreyev* (1934). Virginia Woolf confessed that Mansfield's work was the only writing that made her jealous.

Frances Marion (1887–1973). Extremely successful American screenwriter, as well as journalist, director, and commercial artist. Wrote over 70 westerns; completed over 130 produced screenplays. First woman to win Academy Award for screenplay writing (1930`); first woman to win Academy Award for original story (1932). Began as cub reporter for *San Francisco Reporter* (c. 1906). Commissioned by General Pershing to cover World War I. Arrived Hollywood (1913). Worked for Lois Weber. Stunt woman, extra, script reader, and editor for Bosworth Studios. First scenario *The Foundling* (1916) was first of many for Mary Pickford. Directed and wrote *The Love Light* (1921) starring Pickford, and *Just Around the Corner* (1921). Formed Frances

Marion Pictures (1925), writing *Love* (1927) starring Garbo. Wrote *The Son of the Sheik* (1926) adapting Edith Hull's sequel to her popular novel *The Sheik*; adapted *Stella Dallas* for screen (1925). Contract writer, MGM, 1930s. Wrote several novels, an autobiography, and guide, *How to Write and Sell Film Stories* (1937). Accomplished sculptor.

Lu (Luise) Märten (1879–1970). German dramatist, poet, essayist, reporter, and film critic. Interested in workers' movement and women's rights from 1900, when she began to write and live as a free socialist in Berlin, member of SPD (Sozialdemokratische Partei Deutschlands) from 1903. First collection of verse, *Meine Liedsprachen* (1906). Also wrote children's stories, and essays on women artists Käthe Kollwitz and Ricarda Huch. Her one-act play, *Bergarbeiter (Miners)*, a portrayal of miner and strike leader Jakob Burger, achieved international fame (1909). *Torso: das Buch eines Kindes* (1904) is an account of her childhood. Thereafter dedicated herself to writing on socialist and feminist issues. Works include *Die Künstlerin (The Woman Artist)* (1914), *Die wirtschaftliche Lage der Künstler (The Economic Position of the Artist)* (1914), a historical-materialist analysis of artistic form (1924), and a catalogue of writings on the history and theory of socialism. Joined the Communist Party (1920). After 1924, lectured publicly and gave readings. Wrote and presented radio talks. Her writings on film appeared in *Die neue Bücherschau* (1928). In the 1930s wrote film scripts, though none realized. After the Second World War lived in East Berlin and worked for Verlag Volk und Wissen.

June Mathis (1887–1927). Prolific American screenwriter, producer, actress, casting director, and editor. Child actress. Published magazine stories from 1913, entered scenario competition—Hollywood offers followed. Credited with 113 films over her eleven-year career. Worked for Metro from c. 1919, writing original stories and adaptations, becoming head of scenario department. Wrote roles for Ethel Barrymore and Nazimova. Adapted *The Four Horsemen of the Apocalypse* (1921) for screen, insisting on Valentino's starring role, his first break; also wrote *Blood and Sand* (1922) for him, a film which catapulted editor (later director) Dorothy Arzner to fame. As production executive moved to Famous Players (1921), and then to Goldwyn (1922), easing the merger of Metro–Goldwyn–Mayer, setting studio policy, running the story division and developing continuity in production as we know it today. Approved the script of Von Stroheim's *Greed* (1923), and made editorial decisions re-editing it. Scriptwriter and producer for *Ben-Hur* (1922). Production executive at First National (1924–26).

Mrs Charles E. Merriam (Elizabeth Hilda née Doyle) (no dates found). Married professor and political scientist Charles E. Merriam (1874–1953) in 1901. Chairman, Better Films Committee of the National Congress of Parents and Teachers (1924).

Maboth Moseley (1906–?) Journalist and author. Editor for various industrial trade publications, including *Instrument Practice* and *Automation and Automatic Equipment News*. Wrote for *The Daily Mail*, *The Daily Express*, *Sunday Dispatch*, *Sunday Graphic*, *Punch*, *Queen*, *Lady*, *West African Review*, *Notes Africaines*, and others. Books include *War Upon Women* (1934), a science fiction novel, and a biography of computer pioneer Babbage, *Irascible Genius: The Life of Charles Babbage, Inventor* (1964).

Jane Murfin (1893–1955). American writer. Started playwrighting 1908, often co-writing with Jane Cowl, who also acted in these works. First play, *The Right to Lie* (1908), subsequently filmed (1919); *Daybreak* (1918), filmed that year; *Smilin' Through*, filmed at least three times. Began writing scripts for Famous Players Lasky in New York, completing sixty odd, directing or producing some, before moving to Hollywood (late 1910s). Between 1921 and 1924 wrote and co-produced five films for First National (including extremely popular pictures for "Strongheart," a German Shepherd dog who had served in an Army Red Cross Unit, predecessor to Rin-Tin-Tin). Co-directed *Flapper Wives* (1924) there, credited as "her own production," thereafter writing and adapting mostly romantic comedies and dramas, for RKO and MGM, including *Little Women* (RKO, George Cukor, 1933). Appointed first female production supervisor at RKO in 1934. In 1935 joined MGM, co-adapting *The Women* with Anita Loos, and *Pride and Prejudice* with Aldous Huxley. Wrote *Andy Hardy's Private Secretary* (1940).

Ada Negri (1870–1945). Italian popular poet, short-story writer, and novelist. Her working-class background and poverty-stricken childhood informed many of her works. Trained as a teacher, first poems published 1892–95, both with humanitarian themes. A collection of rapturous poetry *Maternità* (1904), inspired by her daughter's birth, as well as the tragic *Dal profondo* (1910) and *Esilio* (1914). Volume of patriotic prose (1918). Attracted a substantial critical following, and earned a number of literary prizes. Translated *Manon Lescaut* (1931). Received Mussolini Prize (1931). First woman admitted to the Academia d'Italia (1940). Wrote an autobiographical novel, *Stella mattutina* (1921). Writings translated into fourteen languages, including Romanian, Catalan, and Serbo-Croat. Her critical reputation is clouded as a consequence of her friendship with Mussolini.

Irene Nicholson (no dates found). British film critic, magazine editor, and avant-garde filmmaker who wrote on Mexico and Mexican film in later life, from the 1950s. With B. Vivian Braun made the silent film *Beyond This Open Road* (1934). She also made the silent seven-minute film poem *Ephemeral* (c. 1934). Visited Trinidad with Brian Montagu to make a film (unfinished) for the *Trinidad Guardian* (1937). Co-editor of the magazine *Film Art* for issues 6 through 10 (1935–37). With B. Vivian Braun and M. Hatzfeld organized the Forum Cinema in Villiers Street, described as "London's Advance-Guard Cinema" (mid 1930s). In 1967 her *Mexican and Central American Mythology* was published, followed by her edited compilation, *The Conquest of Mexico: A Collection of Contemporary Material* (1968).

Mary Ellis Opdycke (Mrs John DeWitt Peltz) (1896–1981). Writer and poet, published in *Harper's Monthly Magazine, Poetry*, and *New Republic* (1924–29).

Florence M. Osborne (no dates found). Editor of *Motion Picture Magazine* in 1925.

Minnie Pallister (no dates found). British socialist writer and critic associated with the Independent Labour Party, active in 1920s and 1930s. Author of "Socialism for Women" in *Independent Labour Party Study Courses no. 8* (1923?); *The Orange Box: Thoughts of a Socialist Propagandist* (1924); "Socialism, Equality, and Happiness" in *Independent Labour Party Guild of Youth and Young Labour Library no. 2* (1925); *Mrs Smith of Wigan* (1926); and *A Cabbage for a Year* (1934).

Ida May Park (1879–1954). American director of silent films in the 1910s. Began as a theater actress at age fifteen, then wrote and directed with husband, actor Joseph De Grasse. Couple worked on features at Universal Studios. Solo direction, *Fires of Rebellion* (1917) and *The Grand Passion* (1918). Park's directorial credits disappear after 1921. She is credited with writing *The Hidden Way* (1926), directed by De Grasse.

Louella O. Parsons (1884–1972). American scenario-writer and movie critic who perfected the gossip column format and became a household name. Did local journalism while teenager; sold *Chains* script to Essanay (1912); hired as story editor; wrote *How to Write for the Movies* (1915). Movie columns, *Chicago Record Herald* and *Tribune* (c. 1915–17); *New York Morning Telegraph* (c. 1918). Praise of Marion Davies (1922) attracted W.R. Hearst's attention; began column in Hollywood at his suggestion (1926); national, then international, syndication followed. Radio programs (1928–38) with domestic audience of twenty million; columns printed in 372 papers internationally (early 1930s). Played herself, *Hollywood Hotel* (1938). Books, *The Gay Illiterate* (1944) and *Tell it to Louella* (1962). Scrapbooks at Academy of Motion Picture Arts and Sciences.

Lucy France Pierce (1877–?). Wrote on theater as journalist and reviewer for *The World To-day* (1905–11). Also published in *Review of Reviews* (1917).

Katherine Anne Porter (1890–1980). American short-story writer and novelist. Left first husband to pursue movie actress career in Chicago (1914); performed briefly, Lyceum circuit (1915). Newspaper work, *Rocky Mountain News*, and others. Moved to Greenwich Village (1919), worked in film publicity, ghostwriting. Traveled to Mexico (1919–20, 1922). Short story "The Martyr," based on Diego Rivera, published *Century* (1923). Visited Boston to protest Sacco and Vanzetti execution (1927). Traveled to Mexico (1929–31), met Eisenstein filming *Que Viva Mexico!*, the subject of Porter's 1932 short story *Hacienda*. Awarded Guggenheim Fellowship (1931), traveled in Europe, met Goering. Lived in Paris until 1936, which sparked memories of Texas youth, later fictionalized. Returned to United States (1936), briefly Hollywood scriptwriter (mid 1940s). Taught at American universities. Works include *Flowering Judas* (1930), *Pale Horse, Pale Rider* (1936), *The Leaning Tower* (1944), *A Defense of Circe* (1955), and bestselling *Ship of Fools* (1956), adapted for film.

Emily Post (1873–1960). American novelist, short-story writer, broadcaster, and etiquette expert. Began as society journalist. Her *Etiquette: The Blue Book of Social Usage* (1922), a guide to manners ranging from the use of cutlery to the address of royalty, was an instant hit, revised ten times in her lifetime, and is to this day revised and reissued. The Emily Post Radio Program began in 1929; the Emily Post Institute for the Study of Gracious Living was founded in 1946. She had a syndicated newspaper column (1932–60). Wrote a cookbook, a book on home decoration, a guide to weddings, and contributed to numerous publications. Posthumous autobiography, *Truly Emily Post* (1961).

Dilys Powell (1901/2–1995). Influential English film critic. Read Modern Languages at Oxford. Began as a book reviewer for the *Sunday Times* in 1926, starting film reviewing there in 1936. Between 1926 and 1936 divided her time between Oxford and Athens. Was *Sunday Times* chief film critic between 1939 and 1976, continuing to write her regular 1,200-word column throughout these thirty-seven years. After 1976 was film critic for *Punch*. Regular broadcaster on cinema for the BBC Third Programme and, later, Radio Three. Wrote for *Sight and Sound* among other publications. Was on Board of Governors of the British Film Institute and the Cinematograph Film Council. Championed Penguin's publication of *Lady Chatterley's Lover* in 1960. Longtime admirer of westerns, disliked post-war cinema's increasing violence. Wrote *Descent from Parnassus* (1934), a study of D.H. Lawrence, Edith Sitwell, T.S. Eliot, and Siegfried Sassoon; *Films Since 1939* (1946); and several books on Greece.

Eulalia Proctor (no dates found). African-American writer, editor, activist, and newspaper representative. At some point before March 1925, city editor, *The Freeman*, an African-American weekly published in Indianapolis. From late 1910s, active in the mobilization of African-American women voters against the Ku Klux Klan in Indiana. In Chicago, worked as a school teacher, and for the Red Cross (c. 1918–24). Chairman of the Committee on Public Opinion of the Interracial Committee of Indianapolis, and representative of *The Messenger* there (c. 1925). Occasional column in *The Messenger* titled "La Femme Silhouette" in mid 1920s. In Indianapolis in 1925 ran a public stenographic and notary public office.

Lotte Reiniger (1899–1981). German pioneer of film animation with strong interest in music. Briefly studied with Max Reinhardt. Made hand-cut silhouette titles for Paul Wegener's film *The Pied Piper of Hamelin* (1916). Using cardboard, tin, and paper, made her first silhouette film, *The Ornament of a Loving Heart* (1919). Circle included Walter Ruttmann, Hans Richter, and Carl Koch, whom she married. Created animated sequence for Lang's *Die Niebelungen* (1923), and shadowplay interlude for Renoir's *La Marseillaise* (1937). Made first full-length animated feature ever (for which she developed the multi-plane camera), *The Adventures of Prince Achmed* (1926), ten years before Disney's *Snow White* (1937), often wrongly credited as the first. In mid 1930s left Germany for Britain, working for the Crown and GPO Film Units. After the war, made many short films for children's television. Her last film produced in 1980, concluding six-decade career. Her other films include *Carmen* (1933), and *Papageno* (1935).

Malwine Rennert (1856–?). Well-known German writer and film critic from the period before the First World War, writing for *Bild und Film*, 1912–1915. From her articles it appears she was particularly partial to the new Italian feature cinema, undersigning many of her reviews as if she were writing from Rome, and writing an important appraisal of the Italian film *Padre* which she compared to the work of D.W. Griffith. She appealed for good entertainment cinema, always reflecting on the needs and conditions of audiences, believing cinema to be the art of the masses. Developed theories of silent acting, of film physiognomy, and of the unique montage potential of the film medium through her columns. Nothing more is known of Rennert's life and career.

Agnes Repplier (1855–1950). Eminent American essayist, satirist, literary critic, biographer, observer of American social life. Career spanned six decades. Wrote as teenager for Philadelphia newspapers to support family. Published in *Catholic World* (1881), *Atlantic Monthly* (1886). First of many collected essays, *Books and Men* (1888). Lectured across America (1890–1920). "The Eternal Feminine" in *Varia* (1897) dissected foibles of contemporary feminism. Skeptical of sentimentalism, suspicious of philantropists' motives, she disliked Jane Addams. With J.W. White, *Germany and Democracy* (1914), strongly anti-German tract. Vocally interventionist before American involvement in World War I, she then preached isolationism. *Counter-Currents* (1916) collects war-inspired essays. Anti-Puritan, opposed Prohibition. Works include poetry, a sketch of Philadelphia, memoirs of convent life, a history of humor, and study of tea. Committee, Ibero-American Exposition (1929). Honorary degrees: University Pennsylvania (1902), Notre Dame (1910), Yale (1925), Columbia (1927), Princeton (1935). Member, National Institute of Arts and Letters (1926).

Dorothy Miller Richardson (1873–1957). English novelist, feminist, translator, short-story writer, poet, columnist. Taught in Germany, then moved to London (1896), frequented various intellectual and bohemian circles. Met H.G. Wells (1896), with whom she had a lifelong, if complex, friendship. Worked in dentist's practice (1896–1908), thereafter precarious living as freelancer. First piece of journalism published in 1902. Published in *The Dental Record*, *Saturday Review*, *Adelphi*, *Life and Letters*, *London Magazine*, *Crank*, *Vanity Fair*, and others. Contributor, the suffragist *The Freewoman* and *The Egoist*. In 1917 married Alan Odle. Met Bryher in 1923, and supported by her. Film column, "Continuous Performance," ran in *Close Up* 1927–33. Her massive semi-autobiographical novel *Pilgrimage* published in thirteen volumes (1915–67), begun in 1912. Reviews of early volumes linked Richardson's technique to stream-of-consciousness styles of Joyce and Proust. Virginia Woolf, however, described her style as the creation of a specifically feminine sentence. An early observer of the cultural constraints limiting women's artistic achievement, her 1925 essay, "Women and the Arts" (reprinted in this volume) stands comparison with Woolf's better-known argument about the same in *A Room of One's Own* (1929). Wrote two books on the Quakers.

Mary Roberts Rinehart (1876–1958). American novelist, short-story writer, and journalist. Trained as nurse. Began writing to fight debt. First mystery novel, *The Circular Staircase* (1908), initiated her line of independent, adventurous female protagonists, and her career as leading US popular writer. Many works serialized; over twenty filmed. Also wrote popular romances, plays, and articles on travel, war, and women's roles. Reported from front line in France and Belgium for *Saturday Evening Post* (1915). First reporter to interview Queen Mary, although copy censored in Britain (1915). Championed rights of Blackfeet Indians. In 1919 started three-year writing contract with Goldwyn. Averaged one book per year for over forty years. Her published account of breast cancer (1947) broke silence on the subject. In 1910 created intrepid problem-solving spinster "Tish," whose adventures *The Saturday Evening Post* carried for nearly thirty years. Had sold over ten million books by her death.

Alice Rix (no dates found). San Francisco society woman who wrote for *San Francisco Examiner's* colorful Sunday supplement (Hearst's flagship newspaper) around the turn of the century, publishing sensational stories. "Alice Rix at the Veriscope" is one of these. Went to Honolulu to cover annexation of Hawaii in 1899. Wrote for *Sunset* magazine in 1918. The Rix family had moved from New Hampshire to the Bay Area after the 1849 Gold Rush and were prominent in San Francisco life. An Alice Rix had four daughters between 1855 and 1863, the last of whom was Harriet Hale Rix, a socialist suffragist and teacher. Author Alice Rix was in all likelihood Harriet's sister however, which would make her about forty years old at the time of writing her Veriscope article in 1897.

E. Arnot Robertson (Eileen Arbuthnot Turner) (1903–61). British novelist, broadcaster, and film critic. First novel, *Cullum* (1928); *Four Frightened People* (1931) filmed by Cecil B. DeMille (1934); *Ordinary Families* (1933). Worked as an adviser on films during World War II. Became a BBC radio film critic. Her unfavorable 1946 radio review of MGM's *The Green Years* led to a battle with MGM in which the House of Lords reversed her libel-suit victory. Public sympathy supported her heavy legal costs. She continued to be a popular broadcaster until her suicide. Later novels unfold in exotic locations: *Devices and Desires* (1954); *Justice of the Heart* (1959); *Strangers on My Roof* (1964); and *Spanish Town Papers* (1959).

Catherine de la Roche (no dates found). Russian-born British film critic, broadcaster, and writer, authority on Soviet cinema. Active in Russian-speaking amateur dramatic society (1929–39). Scenario writer, researcher at Korda's London Film Productions. Contributor to *Penguin Film Review*, *Soviet Cinema*, *The Leader*, *Good Housekeeping*, and others. Film critic, *British Ally*, the only British newspaper published in the Soviet Union; a fluent Russian speaker, she often visited the Soviet Union. During World War II, Films Officer to Soviet Relations Division of the Ministry of Information. Broadcaster, "Women's Hour" and "The Critic's Programme" for BBC. Books include *René Clair* (1953); a survey of stars, *Made in Sweden* (1953); *British Cinema: A Survey of 1957*; and *Vincente Minelli* (1966). From late 1950s she worked in New Zealand. Also wrote about cats, and wrote against cruelty to animals.

Muriel Rukeyser (1913–80). American poet, feminist, teacher, biographer, screenwriter, translator (Swedish, German, Spanish, Italian, French), dramatist, author of children's books, and political activist. First poems *Theory of Flight* (1935). In 1930s protested in Alabama on behalf of black defendants in Scottsboro trials; briefly jailed. Documented mine workers' conditions in West Virginia (1936). Poems in *U.S.* (1938) based on these experiences. Assistant editor, *Decision* (1941). Guggenheim Fellowship (1943). Published in *New Masses*, *Nation*, *New Republic*, *Poetry*, and *Saturday Review*. Vice-president, House of Photography, New York (1946–60). Taught Sarah Lawrence College (1946, 1956–57). In 1960s translated poems of Octavio Paz and Gunnar Ekeloef. Documentary film scripts include *A Place to Live* (1941). Biographies, *Willard Gibbs* (1942); *The Traces of Thomas Hariot* (1971); and a study of Wendell Wilkie, *One Life* (1957). Jailed for anti-Vietnam War protests. Visited Hanoi and South Korea. President of PEN (1975–76). *Collected Poems* (1979).

Leontine Sagan (Leontine Schlesinger) (1899–1974). Austrian film director and theater actress; spent childhood in South Africa. Trained with Max Reinhardt, worked successfully on stage in Austria and Germany. First film, *Mädchen in Uniform* (1931) co-operatively produced, giving shares, not salaries, to crew and all-female cast. The film was banned by Goebbels as "unhealthy" because of its frank depiction of repressed homosexuality and anti-authoritarian values at an all-girls boarding school. Sagan moved to England and directed *Men of Tomorrow* (1932) with Zoltan Korda. A plan to work for David O. Selznick in the United States failed.

Active in South African theater during World War II, she co-founded the National Theatre, Johannesburg.

Matilde Serao (1856–1927). Neapolitan newspaper woman, novelist, and writer of popular fiction. Several of her novels were adapted for film. Trained as a teacher and worked in telegraph office, experiences fictionalized in *Telegrafi dello Stato* (1885) and *Scuola Normale Feminile* (1885). Wrote for newspapers, *Giornale di Napoli* (1876), *Il Piccolo*, and *Cronaca Bizantina*. With husband Edoardo Scarfoglio ran *Corriere di Roma*, *Il Mattino*, and *Corriere di Napoli*. Founded *La Settimana* and *Il Giorno*, writing under the name Gibus, about film among other subjects. An opponent of female suffrage, Serao's journalism has been called reactionary. Her fiction combined elements of sentimental, melodramatic, and gothic genres although it is her realist work, associated with *verismo*, that is most critically acclaimed. Writings include *Fantasia* (1883), *La conquista di Roma* (1885), *Il paese di cuccagna* (1891), *La mano tagliata* (1921), and *Mors tua* (1926), as well as *Il ventre di Napoli* (1884) and *Sterminator Vesevo* (1906).

Marie Seton (c. 1892/1910–85). British journalist, biographer, film producer, and film critic. Met Eisenstein in the Soviet Union in late 1920s. Possibly spent time in India. Wrote for *Sight and Sound*, *Soviet Studies*, *Painter and Sculptor*, *World Film News*, *Prompt Box*, and others. Authored *Sergei M. Eisenstein, a Biography* (1952); *Paul Robeson* (1958); *Film as an Art and Film Appreciation* (1964); *Paditji: a Portrait of Jawaharlal Nehru* (1967); and *Portrait of a Director: Satyajit Ray* (1971).

Nerina Shute (1908–?). English journalist, novelist, publicity agent. With her mother, the adolescent Shute moved to Los Angeles in 1920. Befriended by distant relative, Elinor Glyn. First short story published in *McClure's* at age sixteen. Returning to England at age nineteen, worked as typist, *The Times Book Club*, then studio correspondent, *Film Weekly*. First novel, *Another Man's Poison*. Wrote for *The Sunday Graphic*, *Daily Express*, *Sunday Dispatch*. Film critic for three years, *Sunday Referee*, fired for negative review of film produced by paper's parent company. Visited Soviet Union twice in 1930s. Publicity manager, Max Factor, late 1930s. Red Cross Nurse during World War II. Samaritan work, mid 1960s, handling suicide calls, and helping unwed mothers. Memoirs, *We Mixed Our Drinks* (1945), *Come into the Sunlight* (1957); novels, *Georgian Lady* (on Fanny Burney), *Poet Pursued* (on Shelley), *Victorian Love Story* (on D.G. Rossetti); also books on London's villages.

Jane Elliot Snow (1837–1922). American poet, teacher, writer, lecturer. Lectured frequently on women's rights and other subjects. Published a family history, and *Bits of Verse* (1916).

Marie Stopes (1880–1958). British paleobotanist, coal expert, poet, playwright, birth-control pioneer. At University College London, simultaneous degrees in geology, geography, and botany. First woman, Manchester University science faculty, Ph.D. (1904); youngest British woman D.Sc. (1907). Research, Japan (1907–08). Fellow, University College London (1910). Published *Ancient Plants* (1910), *Cretaceous Flora* (1913–15), *The Constitution of Coal* (1918). Member, National Council of Public Morals, Cinema Commission, representing Society of Authors (1917). Books on contraception and sexual fulfilment, *Married Love* (1918), *Wise Parenthood* (1918), widely translated and controversial. Began birth-control clinic (1921); vilified by a public-health official, undertook ultimately unsuccessful libel suit. Developed cervical cap, called "pro-race cap." Member of Eugenics Society. *Maisie's Marriage* (1923), film version of *Married Love*. Plays, *Don't Tell Timothy* (pseudonymously written, 1925) and *Vectia* (banned, 1926). After World War II, campaigned for birth control in Asia. Edited volume of letters by women seeking birth-control advice, *Mother England* (1929). Wrote several volumes of poetry and novels. Corresponded with H.G. Wwlls, G.B. Shaw, Walter de la Mare, E.M. Forster, Margaret Sanger. Her papers are held at the British Museum.

Ruth Suckow (1892–1962). American short-story writer, poet, novelist, and essayist known for her regionalist fiction. First poems published 1918, studied and practiced beekeeping (1918–26). Short story "Uprooted" published *The Midland* (1921), thereafter she served as its assistant editor. Wrote for Mencken's *The Smart Set* (1921–23), and *The Century* (1924). First volume of short stories, *Iowa Interiors* (1926), praised for its unsentimental view of rural life. Moved to New York (1926–29), wrote novels *The Bonney Family* (1928), *Cora* (1929), *The Kramer Girls* (1930). Long novel, *The Folks* (1934). A friend of Norwegian novelist Sigrid Undset, Suckow's work appeared in translation throughout Scandinavia. *New Hope*, her most lyrical vision of rural community (1942). A pacifist during World War II, supported conscientious objectors. After war, joined Society of Friends. Last novel, *The John Wood Case* (1959).

Harriette Underhill (no dates found). Pioneer woman sports writer, who began covering horseracing for the *New York Tribune* in 1908, reporting also on dog shows. Appeared on the stage, touring the United States and Mexico with a Shakespearean company. In 1910s began theater and film criticism for the *Tribune*. In 1919 was seriously crippled by a car accident. Continued her Broadway coverage undaunted, with an interlude in Hollywood, which she hated. Wrote for film magazines and wrote a number of scenarios. Producers considered her an authority and frequently consulted her on technical matters.

Mary Heaton Vorse (1874–1966). American labor journalist, foreign correspondent, union activist, popular writer, feminist, peace activist, and egalitarian socialist. Published eighteen books, hundreds of short stories, and newspaper reports. Founded experimental housing co-operative in Greenwich Village, and Montessori school in Provincetown, where she later helped establish Provincetown Players. Took part in Lawrence textile strike (1912). A founding editor of *Masses*. Charter member, Liberal Club. Reported from pre-World War I Europe. Covered International Congress of Women (Amsterdam, 1915) and International Woman Suffrage Convention (Budapest, 1915). Toured Soviet famine (1921). Novels, *Passaic* (1926) and *Strike!* (1930), based on actual strikes, stressing working-class women's strength. Nonfiction, *Men and Steel* (1921), *Labor's New Millions* (1938). Labor activism continued into old age. At age seventy, official war correspondent (1944). Post-war, served with UN, Italy. Published exposé of crime in waterfront unions, a source for the film *On the Waterfront* (1954).

Lillian D. Wald (1867–1940). American public health nurse, social reformer, and pioneer of the Settlement House Movement. Studied at New York Hospital training school for nurses (1889–90) and Women's Medical College, New York (1891). Organized home nursing classes for immigrant families on New York's Lower East Side (1893). Established Nurses' Settlement at 265 Henry Street (1895). By 1913, the ninety-two nurses of the Henry Street Visiting Nurses Service were making over 200,000 visits annually. Services included civic, philanthropic, and educational activities which integrated health care with neighborhood life and made Henry Street Settlement a force for community improvement. Pioneered organization of nursing work in schools. With Florence Kelly, founded National Child Labor Committee (1904); worked for legislation outlawing child labor, and led campaign for a governmental Children's Bureau, which was created in 1908. Autobiography, *The House on Henry Street* (1915).

Fredi (Frederika) Washington (1903–94). Savannah-born African-American actress, singer, casting consultant, executive secretary, journalist. Chorus dancer, including in *Shuffle Along* (1922–26). Played female lead opposite Paul Robeson in *Black Boy* (1926). Formed ballroom dance team "Moiret and Fredi" and toured Europe (1927–28). Film appearances included Cab Calloway musical short (1933); *Emperor Jones* (1933); *Drums in the Jungle* (1935); *Imitation of Life* (1934). Co-founded Negro Actors Guild and served as first executive secretary (1937). Played opposite Ethel Waters in *Mamba's Daughters* (1939–41). Theater editor and columnist, *The People's Voice* (1942–47); without byline, wrote "Odds and Ends" column. In Women's Voluntary

Service during World War II. Between 1942 and 1947 appeared in all-black *Lysistrata*. Worked with Actor's Equity on hotel accommodation for black performers (1948–51). Inducted into Black Filmmaker's Hall of Fame (1975).

Hazel Washington (no dates found). African-American writer. According to *Opportunity* magazine, Washington was a college student in 1935.

Lois Weber (1881–1939). American screenwriter, actress, and prolific filmmaker with forty or so features and many short subjects to her credit, most of which she wrote. One of the most famous American filmmakers of the 1910s. Attracted to the motion picture's missionary potential. A trained pianist at age sixteen, toured as prodigy. Later, street-corner hymn singer in Pittsburgh, evangelism prompting her move to theater (c. 1904). Married Phillips Smalley (1905), with whom she often co-directed until 1917. Recalled 1908 as year of entry into films: writing, directing, and acting in a film for Gaumont Chronophone in New York City. Worked for Reliance with Smalley (1910), then briefly for Edwin S. Porter at Rex (c. 1911–12), where she made *Suspense* (1913). Made only dramatic film to star Pavlova, *The Dumb Girl of Portici* (1916). Top-salaried director, Universal (1915–17), then formed Lois Weber Productions (1917). Her films maintained a staunch Christian Science faith while addressing controversial issues—anti-Semitism, in *The Jew's Christmas* (1913); religious hypocrisy, in *Hypocrites* (1915), which displayed female nudity; birth control and abortion, in *Where Are My Children?* (1916); capital punishment, in *The People vs John Doe* (1916)—and were themselves controversial. Moved to Paramount for $50,000-per-picture contract (1920), where her interest in moral reform meshed badly with relaxed 1920s mores. Other films include *The Hand that Rocks the Cradle* (1917), *The Doctor and the Woman* (1918), *Forbidden* (1920), *The Blot, Too Wise Wives, What do Men Want?* (all 1921), and, her last film, *White Heat* (1934). Suffered both a personal and a professional collapse in mid 1920s; resumed work as script consultant for Universal in 1930s.

Rebecca West D.B.E. (1892–1983). British novelist, biographer, journalist, critic. Born Cicely Fairfield, took pseudonym from Ibsen's *Rosmerholm*. Early journalism for suffragist *The Freewoman* (1911) and socialist *Clarion*, (1912), earned respect of G.B. Shaw, who acknowledged her superiority, and H.G. Wells, her lover of ten years. Reviewer, *New Yorker, New York Herald-Tribune, Time and Tide, New Republic*, and others. Published critical accounts of Henry James, D.H. Lawrence, and Arnold Bennett; biography of St. Augustine, and two-volume study of Yugoslavia, *Black Lamb and Grey Falcon* (1942). This last led to her superintending BBC broadcasts to Yugoslavia during World War II. Her reports of the Nuremberg and other trials published as *The Meaning of Treason* (1947) and *A Train of Powder* (1955). Chevalier of the Legion of Honour (1957), Companion of Literature (1968), Honorary Member of American Academy of Arts and Letters (1972).

Mrs J.E. Whitby (no dates found). Published in *Cassell's Magazine of Art* (London) at around the turn of the century, and may have traveled to Belgium with her husband at this time.

Alice Ames Winter (1865–1944). American woman's club leader, author. Studied Pennsylvania Academy Fine Arts and Wellesley College (M.A. in Greek and Political Science, 1889). Teacher (1890–1892). President, Minneapolis Kindergarten Association (1890s). Romantic novels, *The Prize to the Hardy* (1905) and *Jewel Weed* (1906). First president, Woman's Club Minneapolis (1907–15). Director, Minneapolis chapter, American Red Cross, World War I. Active, General Federation of Women's Clubs (1914), elected president (1920–24). During presidency promoted federal reforms supporting women and children. Helped establish Women's Joint Congressional Committee (1920), Indian Welfare Committee (1921), International Relations Committee (1922). Appointed by President Harding to advisory committee, Washington Conference on naval disarmament (1921–22). Contributing editor, *Ladies' Home Journal* (1924–28). Published *The Business of Being a Club Woman* (1925), *The Heritage of Women* (1927). Appointed liaison between women and film industry by Motion Picture Producers and Distributors of America (1929–42). Honorary D.Litt., University Southern California, 1938.

Dorothy Woodman (1902–1970). British socialist, labor writer, and organizer. Studied Sanskrit and the organ, attending Exeter University. Worked for Women's International League; Union of Democratic Control. Co-worker and companion of *New Statesman* editor Kingsley Martin. Fought against fascism and imperialism in 1930s; attended and reported on meeting of Union of British Fascists at Olympia; organized China Campaign Committee; worked with Krishna Menon and the India League; with Jomo Kenyatta; and for Spanish Republicans. During World War II assisted refugees and reported on resistance movements for *New Statesman*. Organized support for Tito in Yugoslavia. Involved in independence struggles in India, Burma, Indonesia, and Vietnam. Close to Nehru, she and Martin were the only unofficial British guests at Rangoon ceremony hoisting new Burmese flag (1948). An authority and author on the Far East. At Indira Gandhi's invitation, traveled to India to present Martin's Indian library to Nehru University (1969).

Virginia Woolf (1882–1941). British novelist, biographer, short-story writer, and literary critic. Taught briefly at Morley College, South London. A central figure of the Bloomsbury Group and one of the most important writers of the twentieth century. With husband Leonard Woolf, founded the Hogarth Press (1917) and was instrumental in the careers of T.S. Eliot, E.M. Forster, Sigmund Freud, Katherine Mansfield, Maxim Gorky, Christopher Isherwood, and others. Formally innovative, the fictional techniques of *Mrs Dalloway* (1925), *The Waves* (1931), *Jacob's Room* (1922), *The Years* (1937), and *To the Lighthouse* (1927) have often been described in cinematic terms. *Orlando* (1928), a fantasy based on lover Vita Sackville-West that crosses genders and centuries, was filmed by Sally Potter (1992). The feminist inquiry of *A Room of One's Own* (1929) and *Three Guineas* (1938) has inspired a generation of women scholars and writers. Struggling with mental illness since her teens, Woolf committed suicide during the Battle of Britain.

Anzia Yezierska (1885?-1970). Polish-born Jewish American writer who chronicled tenement life and immigrant aspirations. Emigrated America (1901). Worked days in sweatshops while studying English at night. Scholarship, Columbia University. Taught domestic science (c. 1908–10). Through John Dewey, her mentor and possible lover at Columbia, worked as translator for university project, Philadelphia (1917–1918). First publication in *Forum* (1915). Her short story *The Fat of the Land* awarded prize for best of the year, 1919. Relocated briefly to Hollywood to work on 1922 adaptation of *Hungry Hearts*, a collection of short stories published 1920. Disliking Hollywood milieu, declined a $10,000 Hollywood writing contract to return to New York. First novel, *Salome of the Tenements* (1923, filmed in 1925); others include *Bread Givers* (1925), an indictment of life with her Talmudic scholar father; *All I Could Never Be* (1932), a disguised version of her romance with Dewey; and the autobiographical *Red Ribbon on a White Horse* (1950).

Notes

Introduction

1. Dorothy Richardson, "Continuous Performance VI: The Increasing Congregation," *Close Up* 1:6 (1927): 64.
2. C.A. Lejeune, "The Week on the Screen: *The Women*," *Manchester Guardian*, 16 January 1926, p. 9, reprinted in this volume. As Iris Barry opined in 1926, in *Let's Go to the Pictures* [American title: *Let's Go to the Movies*] (London: Chatto & Windus, 1926), p. 6, "pictures are made to please women." This theme is developed in Part One. Shelley Stamp discusses the complexities of the recruitment of women to the movies in the 1910s in *Movie-Struck Girls: Women and Motion Picture Culture after the Nickelodeon* (Princeton: Princeton University Press, 2000).
3. See, for example, *Eve's Film Review*, a Pathé Cinemagazine produced for female viewers from 1921 to 1933, covering fashion, stage, sport, home and boudoir. See Jenny Hammerton, *For Ladies Only? Eve's Film Review: Pathé Cinemagazine, 1921–1933*. Hastings: The Projection Box, 2001. *News Pictorial No. 19*, a Hearst–Selig newsreel showing fashiion pictures prepared by Lady Duff-Gordon is cited in "Lures Feminine Patronage with 'Pictorial Fashions,'" *Motion Picture News*, 27 March 1915: 50; see also L.C., interview with Abby Meehan, "Fashiions on the Film," *The Picturegoer*, 22 November 1913, pp. 211–13.

   For collections of essays by women see, for example, C.A. Lejeune, *Cinema* (London: Alexander Maclehose, 1931), and *Chestnuts in Her Lap* (London: Phoenix House, 1947); and Barry, *Let's Go to the Pictures*. Female-authored film textbooks, and "how to" books, on screenwriting in particular, were slightly more numerous, although these are also almost all out of print. See, for example, Louella O. Parsons, *How to Write for the 'Movies'* [1915] rev. ed. (Chicago: A.C. McClurg, 1917); Marguerite Bertsch, *How to Write for Moving Pictures: A Manual of Instruction and Information* (New York: George H. Doran, 1917); and Frances Taylor Patterson, *Cinema Craftsmanship: A Book for Photoplaywrights* (New York: Harcourt, Brace, 1921), and *Scenario and Screen* (New York: Harcourt, Brace, 1928), as well as others noted in Part Five.

   This absence of collections has not been true for women's male contemporaries, whose reflections, often initially written in article form, soon began to be anthologized, or synthesized, sometimes quite rapidly. Sergei Eisenstein, Siegfried Kracauer, Rudolph Arnheim, Hugo Münsterberg, Terry Ramsaye, and Béla Balázs all wrote short pieces on cinema during this period, with published collections or books following by the mid 1940s. See Sergei Eisenstein, *The Film Sense*, trans. Jay Leyda (Harcourt, Brace, Jovanovich: New York, 1942); Siegfried Kracauer, *From Caligari to Hitler: A Psychological History of the German Film* (Princeton: Princeton University Press, 1947); Rudolph Arnheim, *Film as Art* [1932] (a translation and adaption of *Film als Kunst* [Berlin: Ernst Rowohlt Verlag 1932]) (Berkeley: University of California Press, 1957); Hugo Münsterberg, *The Photoplay: A Psychological Study* [1916] (New York: Dover, 1970); Terry Ramsaye, *A Million and One Nights* (New York: Simon & Schuster, 1926); and Béla Balázs, *Theory of the Film: Character and Growth of a New Art* [1945], trans. Edith Bone (London: Dobson,

1952). As Peter De Cherney has pointed out in discussion, Vachel Lindsay is the exception to this rule. Before publishing *The Art of the Moving Picture* [1915] (New York: Dover, 1970), Lindsay had only written poetry about the cinema, not criticism.

4. In England, the popular newspaper the *Daily Mail* was founded in 1896, and the first tabloid, the *Daily Mirror*, in 1903. The first tabloid in the United States is usually regarded to be William Randolph Hearst's *San Francisco Examiner*, founded in 1895.

5. Lindsay, *The Art of the Moving Picture*, pp. 22 and 211. Rebecca West, visiting the United States in 1929, found American hoardings "among the oddest things in the country." See Rebecca West, "New Secular Forms of Old Religious Ideas," *Realist* 1:3 (June 1929), p. 26, reprinted in this volume.

6. For remarks on posters and lobbies see, for example, Resi Langer, "From Northern Berlin and the Surrounds," translation of "Aus dem Berliner Norden und da Herum," in *Kinotypen: Vor und Hinter den Filmkulissen (Zwölf Kapitel aus der Kinderstube des Films)* (Hannover: Der Zweemann Verlag, 1919), p. 21, reprinted in this volume; Lucy France Pierce, "The Nickelodeon," in *The World To-day*, 15 (October 1908), p. 1052, reprinted in this volume; Louise de Koven Bowen, "Theatres," in *Five and Ten Cent Theatres: Two Investigations* (Juvenile Protective Association of Chicago, 1909 and 1911), p. 1, reprinted in this volume; Jane Addams, *The Spirit of Youth and the City Streets* (New York: Macmillan, 1909), p. 91, reprinted in this volume; and "The Moving Picture Show: What It Ought to Mean in Your Town, and What It Really Does Mean," *Woman's Home Companion* 38 (October 1911), p. 22. E. Margery Fox presenting evidence in *The Cinema: Its Present Position and Future Possibilities*, Report and chief evidence of the Cinema Commission of Enquiry to the National Council of Public Morals (London: Williams & Norgate, 1917), p. 135. By "the real thing," Fox refers to the film advertised by the poster. According to David Nasaw's research, discrepancy of the kind observed by Fox was a common advertising strategy of the nickelodeon period. (See David Nasaw, *Going Out: The Rise and Fall of Public Amusements* (New York: HarperCollins, 1993), p. 155.) See also Dorothy Richardson, who wrote of finding herself in one of those cinemas "whose plaster frontages and garish placards broke a row of shops in a strident, north London street," in "Continuous Performance," *Close Up* 1:1 (July 1927), p. 35, reprinted in this volume.

7. Suffrage was won: in the United States, in stages, from 1869 to 1918; in the United Kingdom from 1918 to 1928; in Italy and France in 1945; and in Germany in 1918.

8. For further discussion of work and leisure, see Kathy Peiss, *Cheap Amusements: Working Women and Leisure in Turn-of-the Century New York* (Philadelphia: Temple University Press, 1986); Elizabeth Ewen, *Immigrant Women in the Land of Dollars: Life and Culture on the Lower East Side, 1890–1925* (New York: Monthly Review Press, 1985); Roy Rosenzweig, *Eight Hours for What We Will: Workers and Leisure in an Industrial City, 1870–1920* (Cambridge and New York: Cambridge University Press, 1983); and Lizabeth Cohen, *Making a New Deal: Industrial Workers in Chicago, 1919–1939* (New York: Cambridge University Press, 1990).

9. Will Durant, "The Modern Woman," *Century Magazine*, February 1927, p. 418.

10. For a history of these trends, see Robert Sklar, *Movie-Made America: A Cultural History of American Movies Revised and Updated* (New York: Vintage Books, 1994). James C. Robertson has estimated that "sound entrenched the importance of the cinema in Britain" so that by September 1939, approximately half of the adult population were attending the cinema at least once a week. See James C. Robertson, *The British Board of Film censors: Film Censorship in Britain, 1896–1950* (Beckenham: Croom Helm, 1985), p. 45.

11. Julie Burchill, *Girls on Film* (Pantheon Books: New York, 1986), who writes on p. 4, "perhaps the women's films were people's films after all."

12. See Tino Balio, *Grand Design: Hollywood as a Modern Business Enterprise, 1930–1939* (Berkeley: University of California Press, 1993), pp. 1–12, 235–55, on the central significance of appealing to female viewers in the 1930s; Thomas Doherty, *Teenagers and Teenpics: The Juvenilization of American Movies in the 1950s* (Boston: Unwin Hyman, 1988).

13. "Women and the Box Office," *Good Housekeeping* 130 (May 1950), p. 254.

14. Peter Krämer, citing *Variety*, 3 June 1996, p. 70, in "A Powerful Cinema-Going Force?" in *Identifying Hollywood's Audiences: Cultural Identity and the Movies*, ed. Melvyn Stokes and Richard Maltby (London: British Film Institute, 1999), p. 103.

15. The black press flourished in the period between the Civil War and the civil rights movement; that is, its decline coincided with the end point of this collection. Ironically, the latter movement weakened the black press both because the best black writers started to be

hired by white papers to cover events (mainstream white papers could pay more, had more prestige, and reached more readers), and because the white press could no longer ignore black activity—previously, white papers had acted as if black life did not exist.

16. Addams, *The Spirit of Youth and the City Streets*, p. 5.
17. Hugo Münsterberg, *American Traits* [1901] (Port Washington, NY: Kennikat Press, 1971), pp. 129–30. It seems that Münsterberg had Gertrude Stein, then a student at Harvard, particularly in mind here.
18. Ibid., p. 164.
19. Ibid., p. 157. Here Münsterberg is discussing stage plays. Münsterberg, who published *The Photoplay: A Psychological Study* in 1916, had perhaps not been to the cinema by the time he completed *American Traits*.
20. Münsterberg, *American Traits*, p. 164. This female spectator of Münsterberg's points forward to one described by Dorothy Richardson in "Continuous Performance VIII," *Close Up* 2:3 (March 1928), p. 52; and another described by Marian Bowlan, in *Minnie at the Movies: A Monologue* (Chicago: T.S. Denison, 1913), pp. 3–8, both reprinted in this volume.
21. Münsterberg, *American Traits*, pp. 138, 139, 160.
22. In her tour of Victorian culture, Ann Douglas has written a history of this phenomenon, revealing feminization to have seeped not only through writing, education, and entertainment, but also along the interstices of religious and emotional culture, as American society turned to feast on affect. In establishing this feminization to be part of a "process of sentimentalization," involving the forces of anti-intellectualism, commercialism, and the "exaltation of the average," Douglas builds the broadest possible setting for Münsterberg's remarks, so wide is the parcel of life she finds to be under the female sign. See Ann Douglas, *The Feminization of American Culture* [1977] (New York: Noonday Press, 1998), pp. 7, 398, 2.
23. See Andreas Huyssen, "Mass Culture as Woman: Modernism's Other," in Tania Modelski, ed., *Studies in Entertainment: Critical Approaches to Mass Culture* (Bloomington: University of Indiana Press, 1986), pp. 192, 193.
24. See especially Walter Benjamin, "The Work of Art in the Age of Mechanical Reproduction" [1935–36], in *Illuminations*, ed. Hannah Arendt, trans. Harry Zohn (New York: Schocken Books, 1969), pp. 217–51; and Siegfried Kracauer, *The Mass Ornament: Weimar Essays*, trans. and ed. Thomas Y. Levin (Cambridge: Harvard University Press, 1995). These essays were written from 1921 into the early 1930s, and edited by Kracauer himself in 1963. "This our period," wrote Gertrude Stein, "was undoubtedly the period of the cinema and series production." Gertrude Stein, "Portraits and Repetition," in *Lectures in America* (New York: Random House, 1935), p. 177, quoted in Miriam Bratu Hansen, "The Mass Production of the Senses: Classical Cinema as Vernacular Modernism," *Modernism/ Modernity* 6:2 (1999), p. 65.
25. Antonia Dickson and W.K.L. Dickson, *The Life and Inventions of Thomas Alva Edison* (London: Chatto & Windus, 1894), pp. 361–2, although their account of these transformations is still based in "the junction of woman's perceptive wisdom with the rational wisdom of man."
26. Lejeune, "The Week on the Screen: *The Women*," p. 9. Clare Booth Luce's play *The Women* dates from 1936, George Cukor's film following in 1939.
27. Patrice Petro discusses the way Siegfried Kracauer was necessarily confronted and distracted by modern womanhood when visiting the cinema to write his columns. See Patrice Petro, *Joyless Streets: Women and Melodramatic Representation in Weimar Germany* (Princeton: Princeton University Press, 1989), pp. 26, 67. Heide Schlüpmann has argued, in the context of Wilheminian cinema, that "Cinema exposed the rights of a female audience" who "became the impetus for the narration of stories in the cinema and for the introduction of stars, above all actresses." See Heide Schlüpmann, "Cinema as Anti-Theater: Actresses and Female Audiences in Wilhelminian Germany," in Richard Abel, ed., *Silent Cinema* (New Brunswick, NJ: Rutgers University Press, 1996), pp. 133, 135.
28. Violet M. Taylor, "Women and Films," *Film Weekly*, 3 January 1931, p. 9. The reasons for this impact lay, for Taylor, in the representation of famous women and attractive men on the screen, but also in the more intangible effects of "developing woman's mind, broadening her outlook, and ... assist[ing] in eliminating to an appreciable extent the 'inferiority complex.'"
29. Alma Taylor, "How Films Have Changed Women," *Film Weekly*, 21 March 1931, p. 9.
30. Ibid., p. 9. Taylor continues:

For a few pence women were able to taste the unaccompanied pleasures of theater-going while their menfolk were still at work. The picture palaces were cheap and convenient. If you went during the afternoon, they gave you a cup of tea. And the films appealed strongly to women. In this manner the great new force of the screen became imbued immediately with feminine influence. Because women were the keenest patrons of the early movies—and have remained so ever since—it was natural that film producers should pay special attention to feminine tastes. Women, who are much less conservative than men, demanded novelty. The film-makers accordingly combed the world for the latest fashions—not only in dress but also in manners and ideas. Thus it happened that the screen became a mirror of all that was newest in life—with women always in the forefront of the picture.

31. Cinema set designer Paul Iribe found his own metier to be an important channel for bringing the feminine (if European) realm into the nation's focus:

All the great periods of decorative art came into being to harmonize with women's dress. But America has no distinctive homes up to the present day, because it is essentially a country of masculine interests in which the emphasis has been laid upon machinery, sky-scrapers, business offices, efficiency. Now, thanks to the pictures, the attention of the country is being turned toward the feminine interests, romance, light, color, beauty of living—harmonious homes and gracious hospitality.

See Paul Iribe in Dorothy Donnell, "Movie Modes and Manners," *Motion Picture Classic* 21 (March 1925), p. 79.

32. Catherine de la Roche, "That 'Feminine Angle,'" *Penguin Film Review* 8 (January 1949), p. 29; Cecelia Ager, "Women Only," *Mademoiselle*, April 1947, pp. 234–5, 321–3; E. Arnot Robertson, "Women and the Film," *Penguin Film Review* 3 (August 1947), pp. 31–5; and Joy Davidman, "Women: Hollywood Version," *New Masses* 44 (14 July 1942), pp. 28–31, all reprinted in this volume.

33. Catherine de la Roche, "The Mask of Realism," *Penguin Film Review* 7 (September 1948), p. 37.

34. For drudgery, see Minnie Pallister, "Sunday Cinemas," *New Leader*, 19 December 1930, p. 5; for relief from motherhood, see Leonora Eyles, "The Woman's Part: V. Amusements," *Lansbury's Labour Weekly*, 28 March 1925, p. 14. See also Lejeune, "The Week on the Screen: *The Women*," p. 9, reprinted in this volume.

35. Barbara Low, "Mind-Growth or Mind-Mechanization? The Cinema in Education," *Close Up* 1:3 (September 1927), p. 46, reprinted in this volume.

36. June Head, *Star Gazing* (London: Peter Davis, 1931), p. 147. Further research is needed to establish whether this is the same June Head who worked as Rebecca West's secretary.

37. Barry, *Let's Go to the Pictures*, pp. 31, 33. Barry also describes the cinema as "a drug," on pp. 53 and 54.

38. Dorothy Richardson, "Continuous Performance X: The Cinema in the Slums," *Close Up* 2:5 (May 1928), pp. 61–2, among other examples in Richardson's writing; Maboth Moseley, "Films Have Taught Us What Life Means," *Film Weekly*, 25 July 1931, p. 9, reprinted in this volume.

39. Dorothy Richardson, "Continuous Performance: This Spoon-Fed Generation?" *Close Up* 8:4 (December 1931), p. 306.

40. Miriam Hansen, *Babel and Babylon: Spectatorship in American Silent Film* (Cambridge MA: Harvard University Press, 1991), p. 40. See also Petro, *Joyless Streets*, p. 19, who discusses cinema as an aspect of popular culture that "served a crucial function in mediating women's experiences of modernity," and a similar point made by Hansen, *Babel and Babylon*, p. 118, concerning female working-class and immigrant audiences going to the cinema.

41. *New York Sun*, 28 May 1891, pp. 1–2, cited in Charles Musser, *Edison Motion Pictures, 1890–1900: An Annotated Filmography* (Washington, DC: Smithsonian Institute Press, 1997), pp. 75–8. The motion picture loop the clubwomen saw displayed W.K.L. Dickson, Antonia Dickson's brother.

42. Maxim Gorky, "A Review of the Lumière Program at the Nizhni-Novogorod Fair [The All Russian Fair of Industry and Art], as printed in the *Nizhegorodski Listok* newspaper (4 July 1896)," trans. Leda Swan, in Jay Leyda, *Kino: A History of the Russian and Soviet Film* (New York: Collier Books, 1960), p. 408.

43. *Who's Who of Victorian Cinema: A Worldwide Survey*, ed. Stephen Herbert and Luke McKernan (British Film Institute: London, 1996), p. 89.

44. These images may have exaggerated female presence to engender salubriousness, but they also built the expectation that women would and should go. Such female viewers are illustrated in David Robinson, *From Peep Show to Palace: The Birth of American Film* (New York: Columbia University Press, 1996), pp. 45 and 49. See also the poster for "The Vitascope," 23 April 1896, and for the "Cinématograph Lumière," 1896, illustrated as Robinson's color plates 6 and 7.

45. For examples of such juxtapositions of the female body and film equipment, see *Cinéma: Premières Affiches (1895–1914)*, coordinator Elizabeth Chopin (Chaumont: Bibliothèque Municipale de Chaumont, 1991).

46. See for an example of a very early female film subject the illustration of "The Serpentine Dance" in Antonia Dickson's "Wonders of the Kinetoscope," *Frank Leslie's Popular Monthly* 39:2 (February 1895), pp. 245–51, reprinted in this volume. (The factory workers appearing in the Lumière's film, *Workers Leaving the Factory* (1895) were also mostly women.) Female stars outnumbered male ones at least until the early 1930s. See, for example, Bosley Crowther, "Male Movie Stars Outshine the Female," *New York Times*, 16 February 1941, pp. 10–11, 17. Crowther writes, on p. 10: "In every year since 1934 (excepting 1938, when the score was tied) [polls have] clearly disclosed a predominance of masculine stars among the box office toppers."

47. Dorothy Calhoun, "Do Women Rule the Movies?" *Motion Picture Classic* 27 (August 1928), p. 88; for Mae West's power, see Marybeth Hamilton, *When I'm Bad I'm Better: Mae West, Sex, and American Entertainment* (New York: HarperCollins, 1995), p. 195, although Hamilton notes the hyperbolic nature of this claim on the part of West's fans.

48. "If the Strike Fever Hits the Movies," cartoon illustration by Ethel Plummer, *Shadowland*, December 1919, pp. 56–7, reproduced in this volume.

49. This centered at one point on actress Fredi Washington's performance as a mulatta in John Stahl's 1934 film about passing, *Imitation of Life*. See discussion of this film in Hazel Washington, "Imitations: Life, Color, and Pancakes," *Opportunity* 13:6 (June 1935), p. 185; and see also The Ex-White Actress, "The Confessions of an Ex-White Actress," *Half-century Magazine*, July 1919, p. 16, and August 1919, p. 16, 19, both reprinted in this volume.

50. The films referred to in the article (Editor [Marcus Garvey], "White Movies not Shown in Africa. African Natives as Film Stars," *Black Man* 1:10 (October 1935), (London: Universal Negro Improvement Association), p. 19) were part of the Bantu Kinematograph Experiment, which was the first example of complete film production—including processing and editing—in Africa. The Vugiri studio was based in an old sanitorium left behind by the Germans. The missionaries, Major L.A. Notcutt and G.C. Latham, wrote up their experiment in *The African and the Cinema: An Account of the Bantu Educational Cinema Experiment during the Period March 1935 to May 1937* (London: Edinburgh House Press, 1937).

51. Editor [Garvey], "White Movies Not Shown in Africa. African Natives as Film Stars," p. 19.

52. The work of an actress was almost inevitably associated with diminished reputation for the African women the filmmakers were trying to recruit. This might well have discouraged their participation. While we might also consider the role played by the Islamic context in the eventual absence of women before the camera, Vugiri was an inland hill station and therefore unlikely to be a Muslim area, since these were located more on the coast in Tanganyika. Thanks to Brian Larkin for his help in interpreting this article.

53. Donnell, "Movie Modes and Manners," p. 16. Alma Taylor's view was similar: "the example of film has taught women to give more intelligent attention to the details of their appearance." Taylor, "How Films Have Changed Women," p. 9.

54. A topic discussed further in Parts Four and Five, particularly in the context of Katherine Mansfield's short story "The Pictures," *Art and Letters* 2:1 (New Series) (Winter 1918–19), pp. 153–62; and Zelda Fitzgerald's "Our Own Movie Queen," *Chicago Sunday Tribune*, 7 June 1925, pp. 1–4, both reprinted in this volume.

55. Margaret Turnbull, *The Close-Up* (New York: Harper & Brothers, 1918). Margaret Turnbull wrote the story for the film *My Cousin* (1918) specifically for Enrico Caruso.

56. Ibid., p. 98.

57. Ibid., pp. 72–3.

58. Fitzgerald, "Our Own Movie Queen," p. 3; Richardson, "Continuous Performance VIII," p. 53.

59. For celebrations of the close-up among cinema's first avant-garde see, for example, Dziga Vertov, *Kino-Eye: The Writings of Dziga Vertov*, trans. Kevin O'Brien, ed. Annette Michelson (Berkeley: University of California Press, 1984), p. 17, and elsewhere; Balázs, "The Face of Man" [first published largely in 1924], in *Theory of the Film*, pp. 60–88; and Jean Epstein, "Magnification" [1921], in *French Film Theory and Criticism 1907–1939: A History/Anthology*, Vol. 1, 1907–1929, ed. Richard Abel (Princeton: Princeton University Press, 1988), pp. 235–41.

60. Fox, in *The Cinema: Its Present Position and Future Possibilities*, p. 136. Nielsen's and Balfour's views of the close-up are discussed in Part Two.

61. See Antonia Lant, "Haptical Cinema," *October* 74 (Fall 1995), pp. 59–63, for more on this point.

62. Thank to Annette Michelson for this well-known reference to Jean Cocteau. On femininity and death, see Katherine Stern, "What is Femme? The Phenomenology of the Powder Room," *Women: A Cultural Review* 8:2 (1997), pp. 183–96. thanks to Mary Hamer for this reference.

63. Lejeune, "Mary Pickford," in *Cinema*, pp. 56–62.

64. West, "New Secular Forms of Old Religious Ideas," p. 28, reprinted in this volume.

65. Durant, "The Modern Girl," p. 425.

66. The work of Elaine Showalter, Sandra M. Gilbert and Susan Gubar, and Hélène Cixous suggests different ways of approaching the question of a distinctly feminine literary practice. Showalter's "gynocriticism" seeks to study women writers in the context of female tradition rather than in relation to the male canon. Gilbert and Gubar have elaborated modes of this tradition, suggesting patterns of affiliation whereby women writers consciously select female antecedents or literary "foremothers." Cixous's work on "l'écriture féminine" explores sexual difference within language and textuality itself. See Elaine Showalter, *A Literature of Their Own* (Princeton: Princeton University Press, 1977); Sandra M. Gilbert and Susan Gubar, *No Man's Land: The Place of the Woman Writer in the Twentieth Century*, Vol. 1, *The War of the Words* (New Haven: Yale University Press, 1988); Hélène Cixous, "Castration or Decapitation?" trans Annette Kuhn, *Signs* 7:1 (Fall 1981), pp. 41–55; and "The Laugh of the Medusa," *Signs* 4:1 (Summer 1976), trans. Keith Cohen and Paula Cohen, pp. 875–93.

67. This investigation might also shed further light on the old question of whether there is a feminine art practice, or mode of reception. The method used in *Red Velvet Seat* was advocated by Sylvia Bovenschen when asking the question, "Is There a Feminine Aesthetic?"

> There is no proof of a different (female) relationship to detail and generality, to motionlessness and movement, to rhythm and demeanor. At present, this is all still conjecture. I find the only sensible approach to be the search for evidence within individual, concrete texts (pictures, films, etc.), as Virginia Woolf once attempted with Dorothy Richardson's writing.

See Silvia Bovenschen, "Is There a Feminine Aesthetic?" trans. Beth Weckmueller, *New German Critique* 10 (Winter 1977), p. 135.

68. Pallister, "Sunday Cinemas," p. 5; Marie Stopes, "The Unsuspected Future of the Cinema," *New East* 3:1 (July 1918), p. 26, both reprinted in this volume.

69. Matilde Serao, "A Spectatrix is Speaking to You," translation of "Parla una Spettatrice," *L'Arte Muta* 1:1 (15 June 1916), pp. 31–2, reprinted in this volume.

70. This was ironic in Hurst's case, since she was such a popular writer. Many of her stories, including *Humoresque* and *Imitation of Life*, were adapted for the screen. See Fannie Hurst, "New Films for Old," *Theatre Guild Magazine*, January 1929, pp. 11–13; and Harriette Underhill, "Imitation Chinchilla," *Delineator* 96 (April 1920), pp. 27, 107, both reprinted in this volume. Writings by Mary Heaton Vorse and Olivia Howard Dunbar exhibit this interest in the observation of class. See Mary Heaton Vorse, "Some Picture Show Audiences," *Outlook* 98 (24 June 1911), pp. 441–7, and Olivia Howard Dunbar, "The Lure of the Films," *Harper's Weekly* 57 (18 January 1913), pp. 20, 22, both reprinted in this volume. African Americans were seldom let in to nickel theaters, whose humble dimensions had no galleries or balconies for segregation, as would later be the case. As David Nasaw puts it, in *Going Out*, p. 172, "mixing blacks and whites in the cramped, darkened storefronts was beyond the bounds of possibility." This absence of black Americans from film audiences until the 1910s freed the screen for particularly virulent racial representations.

71. Barry, *Let's Go to the Pictures*, p. 68.

72. Dorothy Sayers, interview with R.B. Marriott, "Dorothy Sayers Joins the Fray," *Film Weekly*, 14

May 1938, p. 9. In this interview Sayers is reported as saying "authors must take a determined stand and absolutely refuse to give in to producers. It is the only way." Sayers was, most famously, author of the Lord Peter Wimsey detective stories.

73. Richardson, "Continuous Performance," *Close Up* 1:1 (July 1927), p. 37, reprinted in this volume. Richardson also discussed the possible threats of cinema to literature in "Continuous Performance: Almost Persuaded," *Close Up* 4:6 (June 1929), pp. 31–7.

74. In Leslie Kathleen Hankins' words, "cinema served as intellectual common ground for theorizing about aesthetics in general." See Leslie Kathleen Hankins, "'Across the Screen of My Brain': Virginia Woolf's 'The Cinema' and Film Forums of the Twenties," in Diane F. Gillespie, ed., *The Multiple Muses of Virginia Woolf* (Columbia MO: University of Missouri Press, 1993), p. 148.

75. Rebecca West, *Black Lamb and Grey Falcon: The Record of a Journey through Yugoslavia in 1937* (London: Macmillan, 1942; reprinted Harmondsworth: Penguin, 1982).

76. West, *Black Lamb and Grey Falcon*, p. 15. Early editions of West's book included a photograph of the dying Alexander opposite West's description of the same, as if to illustrate her problem, the resistance of the image.

77. Ibid., p. 17.

78. Margaret Anderson (writing as "Mobbie Mag"), "Emasculating Ibsen," *Little Review* 2:5 (August 1915), p. 36; Djuna Barnes, "Playgoer's Almanac," *Theatre Guild Magazine* (September 1930), pp. 34–5, among other examples. Both are reprinted in this volume.

79. Earl J. Morris quoting Jesse A. Graves, "Says Negro Should Be in All Pictures," *Pittsburgh Courier*, 15 April 1939, p. 20, cited in Alfred Singer Buchanan, *A Study of the Attitudes of the Writers of the Negro Press Towards the Depiction of the Negro in Plays and Film, 1930–1965*, dissertation (Ann Arbor: University of Michigan, 1968), p. 74.

80. Fredi Washington, "Fredi Says…" *People's Voice* (9 August 1947), p. 22. In the same year another journalist, also writing for a publication with a black audience, commented similarly: "We do notice that Hollywood has taken a nebulous sort of cognizance of the Negro as part of the American scene in filming crowd sequences. This is done in the Academy Award winner, *The Best Years of Our Lives* where Negro servicemen are shown along with others. It seems so natural however, that it goes unnoticed by the audience; and that is as it should be. While this is not much by way of the employment and treatment of Negroes on the screen, it is a step forward from the day when usually the only time Negroes were pictured as part of groups was in jail sequences." See "The Screen," *Opportunity*, July 1947, p. 174. The recurring argument was that films could and should be made "realistic" by including blacks, even if only in their crowd scenes.

We should note the striking difference between this and Rose Macaulay's view, a white woman, who, writing in the mid 1930s, argued against a realist vocation for cinema, on the grounds that there was enough real in the world. She found cinema "ludicrous," but valued it for this quality, especially now that it talked "like women preaching or dogs walking on their hind legs." For Macaulay, cinema was not, and should not be, a mirror of life. Rose Macaulay, "Cinema," in *Personal Pleasures* (London: Macmillan, 1936), p. 136.

81. Minnie Adams, "In Union is Strength," *Chicago Defender*, 24 February 1912, p. 6; The Observer, "Here and There," *Half-century Magazine* 17:3 (November–December 1924), p. 6. For "sepia Hollywood" see Joan Jackson, "Role of Queenie in film Showboat Dangling," *Baltimore Afro-American* (28 December 1935), p. 8; for "sepia Cinderella" see Fay Jackson, "Hollywood Stardust," *Baltimore Afro-American*, 19 January 1935, p. 8.

82. Marian Spitzer, "The Modern Magic Carpet," *Saturday Evening Post* 197 (28 March 1925), p. 60. For more on women's tastes in the eyes of Hollywood during these years, see Janine Basinger, *A Woman's View: How Hollywood Spoke to Women, 1930–1960* (New York: Knopf, 1993).

83. See Janet Flanner, "Comments on the Screen," *Indianapolis Star*, 14 July 1918, pp. 33, 38; the typist in Ada Negri's short story "The Movies" [1928] enjoys going to Westerns. See Ada Negri, "The Movies," *Corriere della Sera* 27 November 1928, p. 3, reprinted in *Unspeakable Women: Selected Short Stories by Italian Women during Fascism*, trans., with an Introduction and Afterword by Robin Pickering-Iazzi (New York: Feminist Press of the City University of New York, 1993), p. 60, reprinted in this volume. Frances Marion wrote over seventy Westerns. Anita Loos enjoyed writing Westerns (see, for example, Loos's script for *Wild and Woolly* (1917), starring Douglas Fairbanks), as did Adela Rogers St. Johns, who wrote early Westerns for Tom Mix. On the early popularity of Westerns, including Queen Victoria's love of Buffalo Bill's Wild

West Show, see Ian Christie, *The Last Machine: Early Cinema and the Birth of the Modern World* (London: British Film Institute, 1994), pp. 138–41. Emilie Altenloh records women only moderately liking Westerns in Emilie Altenloh, *Zur Soziologie des Kino: Die Kino-Unternehmung und die sozialen Schichten ihrer Besucher* (Jena: Eugen Diedrichs, 1914), p. 89, excerpts reprinted in this volume.

84. Barry claimed that "the majority of films of sentiment are false and correspond to nothing in the actual erotic experience of anyone"; Barry, *Let's Go to the Pictures*, p. 68. See Cecelia Ager, "Mae West Reveals the Foundation of the 1900 Mode," *Vogue*, 1 September 1933, pp. 67, 86; Underhill, "Imitation Chinchilla," pp. 27, 107; Colette, on luxury, "Cinema," *Excelsior* (Paris), 14 May 1918, p. 3, in *Colette at the Movies: Criticism and Screenplays*, trans. Sarah W.R. Smith, ed. Alain and Odette Virmaux (New York: Frederick Ungar, 1980), pp. 43–6; Colette, two writings on Mae West, from 1934 and 1938, from *Colette at the Movies*, pp. 62–4, all reprinted in this volume. E. Arnot Robertson, "Woman and the Film," *Penguin Film Review* 3 (August 1947), pp. 31–5; Madeleine Carroll, "Treating Women too Well," *Film Weekly*, 31 January 1931, p. 9; de la Roche, "That 'Feminine Angle,'" pp. 25–34; Ager, "Women Only", pp. 234–35, 321–23; Davidman, "Women: Hollywood Version," pp. 28–31; Barbara Deming, "Love Through a Film," *Vogue*, 15 August 1946, pp. 168, 224–7, all reprinted in this volume.

85. Allene Talmey, "Gloria Swanson ... Mirror of the Movies," *Vogue*, 15 August 1941, p. 104.

86. For prohibition, see Flanner, "Comments on the Screen," 14 July 1918, pp. 33, 38; and Anderson (writing as Mobbie Mag), "Emasculating Ibsen," p. 36. See Marie Stopes's line, written in 1918: "He who held the Cinema shows in his power could at will create a revolution," in "The Unsuspected Future of the Cinema," p. 26, reprinted in this volume; Margherita G. Sarfatti, "The Revolutionary Fifth Estate," *International Review of Educational Cinematography* 5:1 (January 1933), p. 6. Sarfatti, who was Mussolini's paramour and cultural editor of *Il Popolo*, writes:

> The cinema's influence is enormous. Perhaps it is only the Russians who have understood its social power. It used to be said in the last century that the press was the fourth estate. We may certainly say of the cinema with even more truth that it is the revolutionary 'fifth estate.' It comes after the press and has the same relation to it as the 'fourth' estate, the proletariat, the people has to the third estate, the *bourgeoisie* of the eighteenth century. In fact, the revolution effected by the cinema is much more widespread and vaster, and reaches deeper levels among the people and may be likened to the Russian Bolshevist revolution as compared with the bourgeois revolution of 1789

87. In "The Art of Cineplastics," Elie Faure illustrated the particular primitivism of the cinema by comparing the apparent crudity of an African-American jazz band to the complexity of a symphony conducted and written by Beethoven. See Elie Faure, "De la Cinéplastique" [1922], translated as "The Art of Cineplastics" and reprinted in Abel, ed., *French Film Theory and Criticism*, Vol. I, p. 261. On these themes in the fine arts, which have themselves been heavily debated, see Elazar Barkan and Ronald Bush, eds, *Prehistories of the Future: The Primitivist Project and the Culture of Modernism* (Stanford: Standford University Press, 1995); "Primitivism" in Twentieth Century Art: Affinity of the Tribal and the Modern, ed. William Rubin (New York: Museum of Modern Art, 1984); and, for a critique, Hal Foster, "The 'Primitive' Consciousness of Modern Art," *October* 34 (Fall 1985), pp. 45–70.

88. H.D., "The Cinema and the Classics I: Beauty," *Close Up* 1:1 (July 1927), pp. 22–33; H.D., "The Cinema and the Classics II: Restraint," *Close Up* 1:2 (August 1927), pp. 30–39; and H.D., "The Cinema and the Classics III: The Mask and the Movietone," *Close Up* 1:5 (November 1927), pp. 18–31. For the attic temple and the star idol, see H.D., "The Cinema and the Classics III: The Mask and the Movietone," pp. 22–3. Betty Bergson Spiro Miller's novel, *The Mere Living* (New York: Frederick A. Stokes, 1933), p. 81.

89. Lillian Gish, "A Universal Language," *The Theatre and Motion Pictures: A Selection of Articles from the New 14th Edition of the Encyclopaedia Britannica* (New York and London: Encyclopaedia Britannica, c. 1933), p. 33.

90. Barbara Low wrote of the "enormous hold the 'Pictures' exert upon the minds and interest of the adult population—whether white, black, or of any intervening shade." See Low, "Mind-Growth or Mind-Mechanization?" p. 45, reprinted in this volume.

91. Writing about the overwhelming reception that she had received when traveling, Mary Pickford described those "foreign peoples [who] have a warm spot in their hearts for our

pictures ... such incongrous peoples as the stevedores of Alexandria, the students of Luxor, the tourists at the Parthenon, the great grinning mobs of Tokio and Kyoto, the calm, scholarly Chinese...", in Mary Pickford, "Ambassadors," *Saturday Evening Post* 203 (23 August 1930), p. 7.

92. See Antonia Lant, "The Curse of the Pharaoh, or How the Cinema Contracted Egyptomania," *October* 59 (Winter 1992), pp. 86–112, for further discussion of this point.

93. Barry, *Lets Go to the Pictures*, p. 27.

94. West, "New Secular Forms of Old Religious Ideas," pp. 25–35; Deming, "Love Through a Film," p. 168; Ruth Suckow, "Hollywood Gods and Goddesses," *Harper's Monthly Magazine* 173 (July 1936), pp. 189–200, all reprinted in this volume.

95. Barry, *Let's Go to the Pictures*, p. 33; Charlotte Perkins Gilman, "Mind-Stretching," *Century Magazine* 3 (December 1925), pp. 218, 222–23.

96. Münsterberg, *American Traits*, p. 164.

97. Elizabeth Bowen, "Why I Go to the Cinema," Charles Davy, ed., *Footnotes to the Film* (London: Dickson, 1937), p. 219, reprinted in this volume.

98. "The End of the Line," *Etude* 52, 1934, p. 450.

99. Virginia Woolf, "The Movies and Reality," *New Republic*, 4 August 1926, p. 308, reprinted in this volume.

100. Ibid. Note also Irene Nicholson's "degenerate audiences" in Irene Nicholson, "Film—Its Basic Structure," *Film Art* 2 (Autumn 1935), p. 56.

101. Dorothy Richardson, "Continuous Performance: Dialogue in Dixie" (a review of *Hearts in Dixie*), *Close Up* 5:3 (September 1929), pp. 211–18, which has been criticized by Rebecca Egger in "Deaf Ears and Dark Continents: Dorothy Richardson's Cinematic Epistemology," *Camera Obscura* 30 (May 1992), pp. 5–33.

102. Adams, "In Union is Strength," p. 6. This colonial legacy is also amply evident in Bowlan's slighting references to Arabs, and Vorse's to Italian Americans, to name but two further instances.

103. For examples of recent treatments of this topic, see Daniel Bernardi, ed., *The Birth of Whiteness: Race and the Emergence of U.S. Cinema* (New Brunswick, NJ: Rutgers University Press, 1996).

104. Recent historical work has done much to illuminate the relationship of war to the early cinema. See, for example, the discussion of the significance of the Spanish–American War of 1898 for film history, in Charles Musser, *The Emergence of Cinema: The American Screen to 1907* (New York: Charles Scribner's Sons, 1990), pp. 225–62.

105. Rachael Low, *The History of the British Film*, Vol. 3 [1948] (1914–1918) (London: British Film Institute, 1973), p. 24. Edgar Middleton, in an article arguing that women should be film censors, reminded his readers of the "two million surplus women" in Britain whose tastes films should accommodate. See Edgar Middleton, "Should Women Be Film Censors?" *Film Weekly*, 10 February 1933, p. 7. Rising rates of employment, triggered by war, both in the United States and Great Britain, helped swell cinema audiences.

106. Rebecca West was actually to apply this distinction to a topology of creativity in general—aligning men with death, and women with life and preservation—to the extent that men's and women's art-making, she argued, evolved along two, parallel tracks, destined never to converge, as if it were made by separate species awkwardly inhabiting the same planet. See Rebecca West, "Woman as Artist and Thinker," in *Woman's Coming of Age: A Symposium*, ed. Samuel Schmalhausen and V.F. Calverton (Horace Liveright: New York, 1931), pp. 379, 381.

107. Mary Losey mentions her forthcoming study, "Films for the Community at War," in "Making Films Work," *National Board of Review Magazine*, November 1942, p. 17, although research has been unable to locate this publication. Stopes, "The Unsuspected Future of the Cinema," p. 27, reprinted in this volume.

108. This theme is discussed in Part Three.

109. Lillie Devereux Blake, "Brutality in Prize Fight Pictures," *New York Journal*, 21 November 1899, p. 7, reprinted in this volume.

110. Colette, on luxury, "Cinema," in *Colette at the Movies*, pp. 43–6; Mansfield, "The Pictures," pp. 153–62, both reprinted in this volume.

111. Malwine Rennert, "The Onlookers of Life at the Cinema," translation of "Die Zaungäste des Lebens im Kino," *Bild und Film* 4:2 (1914/15), pp. 217–18, reprinted in this volume.

112. Florence Kiper Frank, "War Impressions: The Moving Picture Show" *Little Review* 2:5 (August 1915), p. 11.

113. Lu Märten, "Kunst und Proletariat," *Die Aktion* 15 (1925), pp. 667–8, translated and quoted in Sabine Hake, *The Cinema's Third Machine: Writing on Film in Germany, 1907–1933* (Lincoln: University of Nebraska Press, 1993), p. 203.

114. Lu Märten's "Workers and Film" [1928], translation of "Arbeiter und Film," in Lu Märten, *Formen für den Alltag: Schriften, Aufsätze, Vorträge*, with selection, commentary, bibliography, and afterword by Rainard May (Dresden: Verlag der Kunst, 1982), p. 120, reprinted in this volume.

115. Märten, "Workers and Film," translation of "Arbeiter und Film," p. 121, reprinted in this volume.

116. Woolf, "The Movies and Reality," p. 308, reprinted in this volume. When Woolf writes of the cinema, at times she evokes an elegiac wonder related to that expressed by André Bazin and Roland Barthes in their discussions of the nature of photography. See André Bazin, "The Ontology of the Photographic Image" [1945], in *What is Cinema?* 1, trans. Hugh Gray (Berkeley: University of California Press, 1967), pp. 9–16; and Roland Barthes, *Camera Lucida*, trans. Richard Howard, (New York: Hill & Wang, 1981). Both Bazin and Barthes likened the photographic image, in slightly different ways, to death and preservation.

117. Woolf, "The Movies and Reality," p. 308, reprinted in this volume. As Samuel Hynes describes it, a "sense of radical discontinuity of present from past" was part of the imaginative construction of the war written largely after the event, a construction he calls the Myth of the War. However, Hynes writes further that, "Even more than the still photographs, though, it was the motion picture that made the war imaginable for the people at home." See Samuel Hynes, *A War Imagined: The First World War and English Culture* (New York: Atheneum, 1991), pp. xi, 121. It is instructive to compare and contrast this with Resi Langer's 1919 foreword to her essays on pre-war cinema, *Kinotypen*, which cautions on their näive exuberance: "These sketches were made about two years before the start of the war, when film and cinema were still almost cosy, leisurely, Biedermeier-ish, and not, unfortunately, as today, almost exclusively the stomping ground of racketeers and the demimonde. These are, therefore, fond memories of a better time" (trans. Antonia Lant).

118. Woolf, "The Movies and Reality," p. 308, reprinted in this volume.

119. Quoted in Ian Christie, "Has the Cinema a Career?" *Times Literary Supplement*, 17 November 1995, pp. 22–3. Christie is quoting from John Carey, *The Intellectuals and the Masses: Pride and Prejudice among the Literary Intelligensia, 1880–1939* (London: Faber & Faber, 1992), p. 8; Carey is quoting from D.L. LeMahieu, *A Culture for Democracy: Mass Communication and the Cultivated Mind in Britain Between the Wars* (Oxford: Clarendon Press, 1988), p. 265.

120. Dickson and Dickson, *The Life and Inventions of Thomas Alva Edison*, p. 361. Only W.K.L. Dickson worked at Edison's laboratory.

121. June Mathis, "Harmony in Picture-Making," *Film Daily* 24:36 (6 May 1923), p. 5; Florence M. Osborne, The Editor, "Why Are There No Women Directors?" *Motion Picture Magazine* 30:4 (November 1925), p. 5; Barry, *Let's Go to the Pictures*, p. 176; Alice Guy Blaché, "Woman's Place in Photoplay Production," *Moving Picture World*, 11 July 1914, p. 195, all reprinted in this volume. Blaché writes of woman: "she takes the measure of every person, every costume, every house and every piece of furniture that her eye comes into contact with." See also Henry MacMahon, "Women Directors of Plays and Pictures," *Ladies' Home Journal*, 20 December 1920, p. 140, who comments that, "to a very large extent in motion-pictures to-day the art vision is the woman's, the executive force and direction the man's."

122. In offering a model of how the mind worked, Gilman and Low referred to "the subconscious," as well as to the way in which our thoughts stem from the past, a habit cinema could help us break by "Mind-Stretching" (Gilman), or pushing us into thinking forwards. Anzia Yezierska, in 1925, recalled the "eminent authors" at Goldwyn (established novelists recruited by Goldwyn to elevate screenplay writing) discussing Freud alongside art and literature. See Gilman, "Mind-Stretching," pp. 218, 221; Low, "Mind-Growth or Mind-Mechanization?" p. 46; Anzia Yezierska, "This is What $10,000 Did to Me," *Hearst's International–Cosmopolitan*, October 1925, p. 154, all reprinted in this volume.

123. See Dr. M.D. Eder and Dr. J. Rickman in "Report of the British Psychoanalytic Society, Fourth Quarter, 1924," *International Journal of Psychoanalysis* 6 (1925), p. 238. Dr. Rickman reports on case where "the processes of taking a photograph were substitutes for the sexual act." Dr. Eder discusses the still "camera as a phallic symbol" in dream analysis, but adds that it is "also a bisexual symbol, like the eye." Dr. Eder was Barbara Low's brother-in-law.

For more on the importance of psychoanalysis for the journal *Close Up*, see Laura Marcus, "Cinema and Psychoanalysis," in James Donald, Anne Friedberg, and Laura Marcus, eds., *Close Up, 1927–1933: Cinema and Modernism* (London: Cassell, 1998), pp. 240–46.

124. West, "New Secular Forms of Old Religious Ideas," reprinted in this volume; Helene Deutsch, *The Psychology of Women: A Psychoanalytic Interpretation*, Vol. I [1944] (New York: Grune & Shatton, 1979), p. 222.

125. Dilys Powell, "The Black Film," *Sunday Times*, 24 July 1949, p. 2. Many more recent feminist scholars have drawn on psychoanalytic theory to develop their arguments as to cinema's meaning in terms of gender. See, for example, Laura Mulvey, *Visual and Other Pleasures* (Bloomington: Indiana University Press, 1989); Mary Ann Doane, *The Desire to Desire: The Woman's Film of the 1940s* (Bloomington: Indiana University Press, 1987); Hansen, *Babel and Babylon*; Linda Williams, *Hard Core: Power, Pleasure and the "Frenzy of the Visible"* (Berkeley: University of California Press, 1989).

126. For "feminine slant," see Jane Murfin, "Sex and the Screen," in Laurence A. Hughes, ed., *The Truth About Movies by the Stars* (Hollywood: Hollywood Publishers, 1924), p. 459; for "feminine angle" see de la Roche, "That 'Feminine Angle,'" p. 25, and elsewhere. See also Eve Unsell's remark that, "In spite of the fact that woman's curves, rather than her angles, are believed to be of more general interest to the motion picture public, it is also a fact that she may have an angle or so, especially as regards picture-making, that can be deemed worthy of serious consideration." See Eve Unsell on "The Feminine Mind in Picture Making," *Film Daily*, 7 June 1925, p. 113.

127. Ager, "Mae West Reveals the Foundation of the 1900 Mode," p. 67, reprinted in this volume. We might remember also Richardson decrying those male, "straight-line thinkers" who had brought synchronized sound to the movies. Dorothy Richardson, "Continuous Performance: The Film Gone Male," *Close Up* 9:1 (March 1932), p. 36, reprinted in this volume.

128. Colette, two writings on Mae West, from 1934 and 1938, in *Colette at the Movies*, pp. 62–4; Lotte Reiniger, "Film as Ballet," *Life and Letters Today* 14:3 (1936) p. 161, both reprinted in this volume.

129. Bowen, "Why I Go to the Cinema," p. 212; Fitzgerald, "Our Own Movie Queen," p. 3; Lejeune, "The Week on the Screen: *The Women*," p. 9, all reprinted in this volume.

130. Lejeune, "The Week on the Screen: *The Women*," p. 9, reprinted in this volume.

131. Pierce, "The Nickelodeon," p. 4; Woolf, "The Movies and Reality," p. 309. For Woolf this quivering form "seemed to be fear itself," and not a description of fear. Jessie Dismorr, "Matinee," *Little Review* 4:11 (March 1918), p. 31, although Dismorr may not be describing the cinema *per se*, as discussed in Part Four. All reprinted in this volume.

132. We might compare the picture of the auditorium being built up here with that developed later by film theorist Jean-Louis Baudry, who, in 1975, described the cinema as a feminine space, but one pertaining less to sex than to the breast or womb—the cinema offered a return to a site of maternal repose and plenitude. For Taylor, Bowen, Lejeune, Fitzgerald, and others, the cinema was for the Modern Girl's good time, where she might finally find a space of her own, one promising sensuality, and alive with feminine intensity and desire. For Baudry, all watchers had the chance of experiencing again, in seeing the screen, a false recompletion of themselves, by regressing to the pre-Oedipal phase, to not perceiving their separateness from the mother. See Jean-Louis Baudry, "The Apparatus: Metapsychological Approaches to the Impression of Reality in Cinema," *Communications* 1975, reprinted in *Narrative, Apparatus, Ideology: A Film Theory Reader*, ed. Philip Rosen (New York: Columbia University Press, 1986), pp. 313, 308.

Baudry's account also invites comparison with Woolf and Bowen for its primitivist overtones. As discussed earlier, the prior developmental stage aroused in spectators by cinema was analysed by Woolf and Bowen in terms of racial primitivism. Baudry also found his spectators regressing, but, using the framework of psychoanalysis, this was to a prior psychosexual developmental stage.

133. Kay Sloan discusses films treating birth control made in 1916 and 1917 in her chapter "Sexual Politics," in *The Loud Silents: Origins of the Social Problem Film* (Urbana: University of Illinois, 1988), pp. 86–94.

134. Stopes, letter protesting the screening of Lois Weber's film *Where Are My Children?*, drafted in July 1917, reprinted in this volume. This manuscript is marked "re: *Where Are My Children?*",

and is held in the British Library, Department of Manuscripts, as item number Add. MS 58545, ff.56–56v.

135. Winifred Ray, "Kultur-Film," *New Masses* 5:4 (September 1929), p. 14; Bryher, *Film Problems of Soviet Russia* (Territet, Switzerland: Pool, 1929), p. 124; "Norma Mahl" [Robert Herring], "Second-rate Sex, September 1929," *Close Up* 5:6 (December 1929), pp. 471–9. (Laura Marcus has sleuthed that "Norma Mahl" was a pseudonym for Robert Herring, a *Close Up* regular.)

  Abortion, directed by G. Lemberg and N. Baklin, is praised in two contemporary sources reprinted in *The Film Factory: Russian and Soviet Cinema in Documents, 1896–1939*, ed. Ian Christie and Richard Taylor (Cambridge MA: Harvard University Press, 1988), pp. 124, 150. The film showed the newly liberalized Soviet law on abortion in operation, through a combination of documentary and fiction. It featured the chief commissioner for health, Semaschko, in the role of medical prosecutor. Dziga Vertov refers to "our first scientific picture, *Abortion*," in two essays, of 1925 and 1926 (see *The Film Factory*, p. 130, and *Kino-Eye: The Writings of Dziga Vertov*, ed. Annette Michelson (Berkeley: University of California Press, 1984), p. 78), a "Cine-Pravda" film for which his group, the Cine-Eyes (kinoks) shot the factual footage, which was then linked, to his dismay, to "a bad romantic drama of a low order." (See *Kino-Eye*, p. 78). Vertov mentions that I. Belyakov played a significant part in shooting the film. It seems likely that all the above references are to one and the same film.

  "Mahl"'s long and critical review of a specific, unlicensed screening of the film as part of the Third Sexual Reform Congress in London in September 1929 pokes fun, in poetic form, via the adoption of a metered female voice, at lesbians, birth control advocate Marie Stopes, German film censorship, members of the Men's Dress Reform Society, and the World League for Sexual Reform. Outlining the location, mechanics, and the audience's falsely libertarian rhetoric, "Norma Mahl" finds this one, particular instance of viewing to be an index of a prurient, life-denying and, finally, pathological advanced film culture.

136. Dr. Marthe Ruben Wolff, "Introduction to the Russian Film About Abortion," in *Sexual Reform Congress, London 8–14 September 1929: World League for Sexual Reform, Third Congress Proceedings*, ed. Norman Haire (London: Kegan Paul, Trench, Trubner, 1930), p. 238. The film had attracted eager audiences, one of which Wolff recalled witnessing in Rostow on the Don in 1927, after some 150 screenings in that town: "It was shown to us in a club which belonged to a trade union of domestic servants, waiters, etc. They were all earnest and full of attention. They were all ripe to see it, and to learn from it..." Wolff, "Introduction to the Russian Film About Abortion," p. 239, emphasis in original.

  At around the same time that the Sexual Reform Congress conference was being held in London, Sergei Eisenstein was, in fact, participating in making a film on abortion in Switzerland, where he was attending the International Independent Filmmakers Conference. The film, *Frauennot–Frauenglück*, is normally credited to Eduard Tissé, Eisenstein's cinematographer, with Eisenstein receiving credit as advisor. (Thank you to Ian Christie for advice on this point.)

137. Joyce Milton discusses this practice in the context of Joan Barry's paternity suit against Charles Chaplin, citing the investigative journalism of Florabel Muir, Hollywood columnist for the *New York Daily News*. See Joyce Milton, *Tramp: The Life of Charlie Chaplin* (New York: HarperCollins, 1996), pp. 419–20. Gloria Swanson describes the pressure under which she had an abortion while at Paramount Studios in 1925, rather than break her contract. See Gloria Swanson, *Swanson on Swanson* (New York: Random House, 1980), ch. 1. Anthony Slide's research suggests that trade papers frequently referred to star abortions as appendectomies, the organ sometimes being removed from an individual star more than once.

138. "Bed and Sofa," *Close Up* 1:6 (December 1927), p. 72 (the editorial triumvirate at *Close Up* were H.D., Bryher, and Kenneth McPherson). Bryher, *Film Problems of Soviet Russia*, pp. 27, 74, 75.

139. Agnes Smedley, "The Cultural Film in Germany," *Modern Review* (Calcutta) (July 1926), pp. 61–6.

140. Ibid., p. 65.

141. E.H.M. [possibly Edith How Martyn], "Europe and Birth Control" (letter), *The Birth Control Review*, May 1927, p. 155.

142. Winifred Holtby, "Reforms and Films," *The Schoolmistress*, 16 February 1933: 537.

143. Bryher, "A Private Showing of *Cosmos*," *Close Up* 4:5 (May 1929), p. 44. The original German title of *Cosmos* was *Natur und Liebe*. See also Trude Weiss, "Film Review," *Close Up* 9:3 (September

1932), pp. 207–8, a review of *Das keimende Leben*, a documentary film on human prenatal development.

144. Field's film was *Life of a Plant* (1926), of which she made another version in 1932. Smedley, "The Cultural Film in Germany," p. 63.

145. Mary Field, interview with Lawrence Murray, "The Movies Come to the Schoolroom: An Interview with Mary Field of *Secrets of Nature* Fame," *Film Weekly*, 6 April 1934, p. 12.

146. Colette, "Cinéma," from *Aventures Quotidiennes* (Paris: Flammarion, 1920), in *Colette at the Movies*, p. 61.

147. Bonnie R. Ginger, "The Prodigal Nephew's Aunt," *Delineator*, September 1913, p. 7.

148. Märten, "Workers and Film," translation of "Arbeiter und Film," p. 119, reprinted in this volume.

149. Balázs, *Theory of the Film*, p. 55, and elsewhere; Benjamin, "The Work of Art in the Age of Mechanical Reproduction," pp. 236–7. See also Marcus, "Cinema and Psychoanalysis," in Donald et al., eds, *Cinema and Modernism*, on this theme. Germaine Dulac, in "The Music of Silence," translation of "La Musique du Silence," *Cinégraphie* 5 (15 January 1928), p. 77, writes that cinema makes visible "the invisible, the materially existent that lies beyond our visual perception."

150. Germaine Dulac, "From Sentiment to Line," translation of "Du Sentiment à la Ligne," *Schémas* 1 (February 1927), p. 28.

151. Dulac, "The Music of Silence," p. 77. Le Corbusier, "The Spirit of Truth [Esprit de Verité]" [1933], in Richard Abel, ed., *French Film Theory and Criticism: A History/Anthology* Vol. II, 1929–39 (Princeton: Princeton University Press, 1988), pp. 112–13.

152. Mary Field, "Can the Film Educate?" in *For Filmgoers Only*, ed. R.S. Lambert (London: Faber & Faber, with the British Institute of Adult Education, 1934), pp. 59–60.

153. After publishing *On the Origin of Species by Means of Natural Selection* (London: John Murray, 1859), Charles Darwin wrote, as his next book, a massive treatise titled *The Various Contrivances by Which British and Foreign Orchids are Fertilized by Insects* (London: John Murray, 1862).

154. Isabel Bolton, *Do I Wake Or Sleep* (New York: Charles Scribner's Sons, 1946), p. 58. Isabel Bolton was the pseudonym of Mary Britton Miller.

155. Bolton, *Do I Wake Or Sleep*, pp. 58, 59–60.

156. Colette, "Luxury," in *Colette at the Movies*, pp. 45, 46, reprinted in this volume. It is also more than likely that Colette had read something of Maurice Maeterlinck's discussion of animal life and life forces, which popularized Fabre's work, such as *Das Leben der Bienen* [*The Life of Bees*] (Jena: E. Diederichs, 1905), or *The Double Garden* (New York: Dodd, Mead, 1911). Maeterlinck's wife was Georgette Leblanc, who wrote on cinema (see, for example, "Propos sur le Cinéma," *Mercure de France*, 16 November 1919, p. 275–90) and who was to be the star of Marcel l'Herbier's *L'Inhumaine* (1923), L'Herbier being one of the most prominent members of the French Impressionist circle of filmmakers, and a person well-known to Germaine Dulac. See Stuart Liebman, "French Film Theory, 1910–1920," *Quarterly Review of Film Studies* (Winter 1983) p. 9.

157. For an overview of natural history films, with mention of the popularity of Maeterlinck's essays "The Life of the Bee" (1901) and "The Intelligence of Flowers" (1907), see also Christie, *The Last Machine*, p. 100.

158. Albert Renger-Patzsch began publishing his plant photographs in 1923, while his *Die Welt ist Schön*, a collection of one hundred of his photographs, including many examples of plants, was published in Munich in 1928. Karl Blossfeldt, *Urformen der Kunst/Art Forms in Nature* (Berlin: Wasmuth, 1928; London: Zwemmer, 1929).

159. Field, "The Movies Come to the Schoolroom," p. 12.

160. Among the letterheads checked, in the hope of finding leads to writings by women, were those of "Cinema 16," where Mary Losey and Helen van Dongen, among other women, are listed, and that of "Frontier Films," whose advisory board in 1939 were "vitally interested in dramatizing the vast cultural contributions of the Negro people to American life," and whose participants included Dorothy Parker, Lillian Hellman, Muriel Rukeyser, and Catherine Bauer, among other women. (Quotation taken from Arnold Perl, in a letter to Walter White, 24 April 1939. Manuscript Division, Library of Congress, NAACP papers, Part 1, Container C299, File "Films and Plays—General," January–June 1939).

While the history of women's contribution to the first fifty years of cinema is still largely unknown, Anthony Slide's pioneering scholarship on female biography and material culture in the silent cinema era (conducted outside the academy) has provided a wealth of guidance. See especially his many edited collections of republished materials, including: *The Picture on a Dancing Screen: Poetry of the Cinema* (Vestal, NY: Vestal Press, 1988); *They Also Wrote for the Fan Magazines: Film Articles by Literary Giants from e.e. cummings to Eleanor Roosevelt, 1920–1939* (Jefferson, NC: McFarland, 1992); and his *Selected Film Criticism*, 7 vols (Metuchen, NJ: Scarecrow Press, 1982–1985). Also important have been Anthony Slide, *The Idols of Silence* (South Brunswick and New York: A.S. Barnes/London: Thomas Yoseloff, 1976); *Early Women Directors* [1977] (New York: Da Capo Press, 1984); *The Memoirs of Alice Guy Blaché*, ed. Anthony Slide (Metuchen, NJ: Scarecrow Press, 1986); Anthony Slide, *Lois Weber: The Director Who Lost Her Way in History* (Westport, CT: Greenwood Press, 1986); *International Film, Radio, and Television Journals*, Anthony Slide, ed. (Westport, CT: Greenwood Press, 1985); and *100 Rare Books from the Margaret Herrick Library of the Academy Foundation: An Annotated Bibliography*, annotator Anthony Slide (Beverly Hills: Academy of Motion Picture Arts and Sciences, 1987).

Myron O. Loundsbury, *The Origins of American Film Criticism, 1909–1939* (New York: Arno Press, 1973), was valuable in suggesting sources, as were several collections of writings on cinema: George C. Pratt, ed., *Spellbound in Darkness: A History of the Silent Film* (Greenwich, CT: New York Graphic Society, 1973); Richard Koszarski, *Hollywood Directors, 1914–1940* (New York: Oxford University Press, 1976); *American Film Criticism: From the Beginnings to Citizen Kane*, ed. Stanley Kauffmann, with Bruce Henstell (New York: Liveright, 1972); *The Movies in Our Midst: Documents in the Cultural History of Film in America*, ed. Gerald Mast (Chicago: University of Chicago Press, 1982); and *Voices of Film Experience: 1894 to the Present*, ed. Jay Leyda (research by Doug Tomlinson and John Hagan) (New York: Macmillan, 1977).

Marsha McCreadie's *Women on Film: The Critical Eye* (New York: Praeger, 1983) discusses several of the writers collected in *The Red Velvet Seat* including C.A. Lejeune, Bryher, Maya Deren, and Hortense Powdermaker, but it does not reprint any of their writings, and most of its emphasis lies outside the period up to 1950. Also very helpful have been *The Women's Companion to International Film*, ed. Annette Kuhn and Susannah Radstone (London: Virago, 1990); Ally Acker, *Reel Women: Pioneers of the Cinema, 1896 to the Present* (New York: Continuum, 1991); *Sexual Stratagems: The World of Women in Film*, ed. Patricia Erens (New York: Horizon Press, 1979); and Gwendolyn Audrey Foster, *Women Film Directors: An International Bio-Critical Dictionary* (Westport, CT: Greenwood Press, 1995). Similarly valued was the guidance of *The Gender of Modernism: A Critical Anthology*, ed. Bonnie Kime Scott (Bloomington: Indiana University Press, 1990); Susan J. Leonardi, *Dangerous by Degrees: Women at Oxford and the Somerville College Novelists* (New Brunswick, NJ: Rutgers University Press, 1989); and Gillian Hanscombe and Virginia L. Smyers, *Writing for Their Lives: The Modernist Women, 1910–1940* (London: Women's Press, 1987). Particularly helpful indexes were, of course, *The Reader's Guide to Periodical Literature*, the WPA Writer's Project *The Film Index: A Bibliography Vol. I: The Film as Art* (New York: Museum of Modern Art and H.W. Wilson, 1941), and *The New Film Index: A Bibliography of Magazine Articles in English, 1930–1970*, ed. Richard Dyer MacCann and Edward S. Perry (New York: E.P. Dutton, 1975), as well as *A Guide to Negro Periodical Literature, 1941–46*, compiled by A.P. Marshall (Winston-Salem NC, 1946), typescript held at the Schomburg Library, New York Public Library. Other relevant bibliographies included: Frances Christeson, *A Guide to the Literature of the Motion Picture* (Los Angeles: University of Southern California Press, 1938); John C. and Lana Gerlach, *The Critical Index: A Bibliography of Articles on Film in English, 1946–1973, Arranged By Names and Topics* (New York: Teachers' College Press, 1974); and Rosemary Ribich Kowalski, *Women and Film: A Bibliography* (Metuchen, NJ: Scarecrow Press, 1976). Lastly, *Who's Who of Victorian Cinema*, ed. Luke McKernan and Stephen Herbert (London, British Film Institute, 1996), was a stimulating source.

161. The following film periodicals were carefully examined: *Close Up, Penguin Film Review, The Cinegoer, Cinema Quarterly, Film Art, Film Weekly, Experimental Cinema, International Review of Educational Cinematography and Intercine*. Other film magazines and film trade papers, such as *Moving Picture World, New York Dramatic Mirror, Picturegoer, Sight and Sound, Show World* (up to 1908), *Filmplay, Motion Picture Director, Shadowland, Motion Picture Magazine, Photoplay, National Board of Review Magazine*, and *Screen Pictorial* were sampled. The following women's magazines were thoroughly examined: *Delineator* (1920–37), *Vogue* (New York, up to 1950), *Vogue* (London, up to 1930), *Vanity Fair* (up to 1950), *Woman's Journal*, and *Englishwoman* (volumes 5–17). Among African-American publications the following were researched: *Half-century Magazine, Brown American, Negro World, Race Relations, Crisis, Color Line, Harlem Quarterly, Fire!, New Challenge, Race, Negro Quarterly, Black Man, Negro Liberator, Negro Story, Ebony* (up to 1950), *Messenger, Flash*, and *Phylon*. The following Little Magazines were fully

studied: *Accent* (up to 1950), *transition, Little Review, Dial, Contact, Broom, Hound and Horn, Egoist, Life and Letters Today*, and *Arts and Letters*, as were the suffrage journals *Freewoman* and *New Freewoman*. The *Southwest Review* (1915–35), *Lansbury's Labour Weekly, New East, New Leader*, and *New World* were also researched, as were *Masses, New Masses, Theatre Guild Magazine*, and *Rob Wagner's Script*.

162. Chief among these collections were those of Marie Stopes (at the British Library), Muriel Box and Elsie Cohen (at the British Film Institute Library), Gladys Hall, Louella Parsons, and Hedda Hopper (all at the Library of the Academy of Motion Picture Arts and Sciences), and the W.I.F.E. (Women's Independent Film Exchange) collection of Cecile Starr, held at Bobst Library, New York University. Michael Balcon's papers at the British Film Institute Library held correspondence with E. Arnot Robertson. The Claude A. Barnett collection at the Chicago Historical Society, and the NAACP Collection at the Library of Congress, not women's collections, were also consulted.

163. "Why I go to the Cinema" was missing from Elizabeth Bowen's bibliography; "The Unsuspected Future of the Movies" was missing from Marie Stopes's; and "New Secular Forms of Old Religious Ideas" was missing from Rebecca West's. See J'nan M. Sellery and William O. Harris, *Elizabeth Bowen: A Bibliography* (Austin: Humanities Research Center, University of Texas, 1981); Peter Eaton and Marilyn Warnick, *Marie Stopes: A Checklist of Her Writings* (London: Croom Helm, c. 1977); and Joan Garrett Packer, *Rebecca West: An Annotated Bibliography* (New York: Garland Publishing, 1991). Among the most obscure items was Laura Riding's *Literal Solutions: Len Lye and the Problem of Popular Films* (London: Seizin Press, 1993), which, while included in the Laura Riding bibliography, is not to be found in the British Library, nor in Cornell University's Laura Riding Collection. Once this work had finally been located (at the University of Minnesota Library, Minneapolis), Riding's estate denied permission to reprint it.

164. On the subject of research on black women writers, it might be noted that only three issues of the Los Angeles journal *Flash*, and one (January 1923) of the Philadelphia-based monthly *Woman's Voice* ("By woman—of woman—for woman") could be consulted. Many other texts remained materially impossible to retrieve; a few words from Eva Jessye's essay remain illegible despite repeated inquiries to likely depositories for paper originals over inferior, blotchy microfilm copies of the Baltimore *Afro-American*.

165. For the "Fifth Estate" see: Hampton Del Ruth, "Developing the 'Fifth Estate,'" *New York Dramatic Mirror*, 10 February 1917, p. 28; Elizabeth Richey Dessez, "The Fifth Estate," *American Hebrew*, 16 March 1928), pp. 656, 670–71; and Sarfatti, "The Revolutionary Fifth Estate," pp. 5–7. Lillian D. Wald, "A Grave Injustice to Colored People," in *Fighting a Vicious Film: Protest Against "The Birth of a Nation"* (Boston: NAACP, Boston Branch, 1915), p. 18, reprinted in this volume; Janet Flanner, "Comments on the Screen," *Indianapolis Star*, 21 July 1918, p. 33, reprinted in this volume; Dickson, "Wonders of the Kinetoscope," p. 249, reprinted in this volume; Blake, "Brutality in Prize Fight Pictures" p. 7, reprinted in this volume; Addams, *The Spirit of Youth and the City Streets*, pp. 86, 89, 93, reprinted in this volume; Pierce, "The Nickelodeon," p. 4, reprinted in this volume. "Motography" was also the name of an early trade periodical for the film industry.

166. This editorial structure also engenders a more coherent and feasible project. Indian women writing in the English-language Anglo-Indian press have not been included due to limited resources.

167. Altenloh, *On the Sociology of Cinema* [*Zur Soziologie des Kino*], cited in, for example Miriam Hansen, "Early Cinema: Whose Public Sphere?" in *Early Cinema: Space/Frame/Narrative*, ed. Thomas Elsaesser, with Adam Barker (London: British Film Institute, 1990), pp. 228–46; and Petro, *Joyless Streets*, p. 3 and elsewhere. Altenloh's reputation had been significant among writers on film much earlier. Rudolf Harms describes *Zur Soziologie des Kino* as "ein kluges Buch" in his own *Philosophie des Films* (Leipzig: Felix Meiner, 1926), p. 3. Altenloh is also mentioned or discussed at several other points (see pp. 12, 57, 62, 167).

168. As a child Pola Negri was "passionately fond of the writings of Ada Negri, the late Victorian poetess, and adopted her name for professional use as a tribute for veneration, and because of its euphonious sound," according to *The Blue Book of the Screen*, ed. Ruth Wing (Hollywood: The Blue Book of the Screen, 1923), p. 195.

169. Six exceptions should be mentioned: Jessie Dismorr's poem "Matinee" is possibly about theater, if not life itself; Marie Seton's contribution is about television; Minnie Adams's "In Unity is Strength" considers theater as much as film; Eulalia Proctor treats theater more

than film; "Confessions of an Ex-white Actress" is above all about the stage, but describes problems also paramount for film actresses; and Dorothy Richardson's "Women in the Arts" does not treat film, but profoundly illuminates women's engagement with film through its arguments.

170. For an example of this, see Laura Lee Hope (the pseudonym of Edward Stratemeyer and Stratemeyer Syndicate Writers), who wrote a series of girls' adventure stories about the movies, including *The Moving Picture Girls at Oak Farm* (New York: Grosset & Dunlap, 1914). Thanks to David Francis for pointing out these books. Robert Herring took the pseudonym "Norma Mahl" to write on the reception of a film about abortion, a topic further discussed above. See Mahl, "Second-rate Sex," pp. 471–9.

171. According to Anthony Slide, Herb Sterne ghostwrote Lillian Gish's article "Screen" for *Rob Wagner's Script* 32:738 (14 September 1946), pp. 10–11; indeed, Sterne chaimed that all pieces published under her name were ghosted. In a parallel instance, publicists (usually male) at the studios would generally write Hedda Hopper's Sunday column (which usually featured a specific film or star) for her. To have excluded pseudonymic writings actually by men from this collection would also have meant reaching several research impasses, since it is often impossible to trace authorship among such materials.

172. See annotation 1 to Fitzgerald, "Our Own Movie Queen," reprinted in this volume, giving details of the authorship of this short story.

173. Winifred Holtby, "Missionary Film" [1927], in *Truth is Not Sober* (London: William Collins, 1934; Freeport, NY: Books for Libraries Press, 1970, reprint), pp. 108–13, reprinted in this volume. See, for example, Bowen, "Why I Go to the Cinema"; Janet Flanner, "The Movies, Montmartre and Main Street," *Filmplay*, May 1922, pp. 10–11, 51; and Richardson, "Continuous Performance VIII," pp. 51–5. The Bowen and Richardson essays are reprinted in this volume.

174. Margaret Sanger and Marie Stopes wrote scenarios as well, of course, as did many important Hollywood-based women. Nettie Palmer, "Readers and Writers," *Argus* (Melbourne), 3 February 1917, p. 4. Winifred Holtby's 1932 critical study *Virgina Woolf* employed the metaphor of the cinema to describe the imagistic quality of Woolf's prose. Winifred Holtby, *Virginia Woolf* [1932] (Folcroft, PA: Folcroft Press, 1969).

175. L.L. and L.R. (Len Lye and Laura Riding), "Film-Making: Movement as Language," *Epilogue; a Critical Summary* 1 (Autumn 1935) (Deya, Majorca: Seizin Press; and London: Constable, 1935), pp. 231–35. See Martha Wolfenstein and Nathan Leites, "An Analysis of Themes and Plots," *Annals of the American Academy of Political and Social Science*, Philadelphia, November 1947; and Martha Wolfenstein and Nathan Leites, *Movies: A Psychological Study* (New York: Free Press, 1950).

176. Two other criteria required winnowing out writings whose interest would not sustain "a three-page undergraduate essay," or whose meanings would have required too much "reading against the grain" to have become intriguing.

177. Zora Neale Hurston used film in her anthropological study of black communities in Florida in 1928–29, and again in South Carolina in 1940, and was employed as a story consultant by Paramount Pictures from October 1941 to January 1942, but research has so far been unable to find any published material by Hurston about these experiences, or about the cinema generally.

178. But see the three, somewhat arbitrary, exceptions: Marie Stopes's letter destined for *The Times*; Lou Andreas-Salomé's diary entry "Movies" [1913], in *The Freud Journal of Lou Andreas-Salomé*, trans. Stanley A. Leavy (New York: Basic Books, 1964; London: Quartet Books, 1987), pp. 100–101; and Maerten's "Workers and Film," translation of "Arbeiter und Film," pp. 116–22, which, while unpublished, was probably delivered as a radio broadcast in Berlin in 1928. Stopes's letter may have been published, but research was unable to establish this. See annotation to the letter, as published here, for further discussion.

Also not included are women's views solicited as written questionnaires or collected orally and subsequently published in sociological studies; also not included are diary entries later published in studies such as those of Mass-Observation in England. Such material is to be found in the Payne Fund study of Herbert Blumer, *Movies and Conduct* (New York: Macmillan, 1933). Blumer is known to have altered identifying autobiographical data, even switching the sex of subjects. See Garth S. Jowett, Ian C. Jarvie, and Kathryn H. Fuller, *Children and the Movies: Media Influence and the Payne Fund Study Controversy* (New York: Cambridge University Press, 1966), p. 238. Mass-Observation, founded in 1937 by Tom Harrison, Humphrey Jennings, and Charles Madge, was an enterprise that facilitated, collected, and ensured the survival of a great deal of women's record-taking, on cinema and other topics. Several collections of these diary reports were published at the time, and others have been published subsequently, most notably for this project, *Mass-Observation at the Movies*, ed. Jeffrey Richards and Dorothy Sheridan (New York: Routledge & Kegan Paul, 1987).

The criterion of only including previously published work places the bar quite high. Different, hierarchichally ordered regimes of power surround the publication of a book, as opposed to that of a fan magazine article, or indeed a private handwritten jotting in a diary, or a casual conversation in a movie theater. Most female response to the movies probably took the latter two forms, so that only assembling previously published writing *a priori* disqualifies the bulk of expressed female opinion. This criticism can be answered as follows: a significant amount of women's opinions on film *was* published, and we have lost awareness even of this; once republished, these writings will insist on being compared to published writing by men (the majority of that which we know of cinema from cinema's first fifty years), writings with which these women's texts once rubbed shoulders. (One is comparing like with like, as opposed to comparing private with published writing.) One consequence of this choice is to heighten the interest of making other kinds of collection, which might include film scenarios, diaries, memories, and letters, as well as writings in other languages.

179. This criterion of only reprinting previously published work stems also from the need to manage the task of research. Diary entries, while occasionally revelatory, are also time-consuming to find—in the five published volumes of Virginia Woolf's diary, covering a period of twenty-six years, cinema attendance is mentioned only twelve times, and film titles specified on only two occasions.

To suggest the personal and professional associations among the women collected here, in support of the proposition that there was discussion among them about cinema, and that they were aware of each other's opinions, here is a lengthy, if inadequate footnote. (It would take another book to make this point properly...)

A number of the women republished here were linked through their work on "little magazines" on both sides of the Atlantic: Rebecca West, Dorothy Richardson, H.D., and Barbara Low all contributed to the suffrage journal *The Freewoman*, or its later incarnation, *The New Freewoman*. Richardson, H.D., and Low subsequently wrote for *Close Up*, as did H.D.'s partner Bryher, who was, with H.D., one of its editors. Through the *Egoist* circles, and particularly through Ezra Pound, Iris Barry met H.D. in the 1910s. Margaret Anderson's *Little Review* published H.D. and Djuna Barnes.

Psychoanalysis was another connecting thread. H.D. was introduced to Sigmund Freud's work by Havelock Ellis, and was analysed by Freud in 1933 and 1934. (Lou Andreas-Salomé had studied with Freud in the 1910s, and Bryher attended a number of European psychoanalytic conferences.) Freud knew of the work of Barbara Low and Marie Stopes.

Literary friendships, inside and outside Bloomsbury, brought together other women. Dorothy Richardson's work was known to Virginia Woolf, who reviewed it at several points. Woolf knew Elizabeth Bowen and Rose Macaulay as well as their writing, and she met Winifred Holtby at least once; the latter wrote a critical study of Woolf's work. Woolf also knew Rebecca West's writing, and they corresponded and on occasion met. Katherine Mansfield knew Woolf and the latter admired the former's literary talent. Through D.H. Lawrence, Katherine Mansfield and H.D. were linked: Mansfield's correspondence illustrates her friendship with the Lawrence's, while H.D. fictionalized her experience of Lawrence in *Bid Me to Live* (New York: Grove Press, 1960). T.S. Eliot was known to many of this group of writers, and was instrumental in getting Barnes's *Nightwood* published. Leonard and Virginia Woolf's Hogarth Press published a book on Lotte Reiniger (Eric Walter White, *Walking Shadows: An Essay on Lotte Reiniger's Silhouetter Fillms*. London: L. and Virginia Woolf at the Hogarth Press, 1931). Lotte Reiniger, at one period of her life, was friendly with H.D. and Dorothy Richardson; from 1928 to 1932, when Bryher was regularly visiting Berlin, Reiniger and Bryher went to the cinema together. In Paris, Barnes was also friendly with Robert McAlmon, Bryher's first husband. In her Greenwich Village days, Barnes had performed at the Provincetown Playhouse, when it was a pier building owned by Mary Heaton Vorse. She also quoted Vorse in the mid 1910s in one of her early pieces of journalism. Barnes's and Flanner's mutual friend Nancy Cunard assisted Fay Jackson on the latter's trip to Europe in 1937. (Cunard also contributed a single essay to *Close Up*.) The group of left-wing British women knew of each other's writing, especially since Holtby, Winifred Horrabin, and Ethel Mannin all contributed to *The Tribune*; Horrabin certainly knew Mannin and Minnie Pallister.

Rebecca West and Dorothy Richardson had affairs with H.G. Wells within the period of a decade or so. Similarly, Iris Barry and Jessie Dismorr shared the affections of Wyndham Lewis in the 1910s. Iris Barry knew C.A. Lejeune's work—their early careers as film critics in England were parallel—and the latter included one of Barry's poems in one of her articles. Catherine de la Roche was familiar with both these women's work, and vice versa, and they probably met. Similar links existed between Dilys Powell and Penelope Houston. Iris Barry had a friendship with Elizabeth Bowen before moving permanently to the United States in 1932, where, through her work as a film curator, she got to know Lillian Gish. Gish, Frances Marion, Fannie Hurst, Mary Roberts Rinehart, Jane Murfin, and Anita Loos were among the powerful women connected with early Hollywood, and acquainted with one another, if not firmer friends; Rinehart helped Marion find work as a war reporter in Europe during the First World War, while Lois Weber gave her her start in the film industry (and Marion is credited with paying for Weber's funeral, though there is no proof of this). And Gish, Marion, Mary Roberts Rinehart, Jane Murfin, and Anita Loos all came to know Louella Parsons and Hedda Hopper.

Many of the women on occasion worked together: Iris Barry with Barbara Deming; Jessie Dismorr with Margaret Anderson; E. Margery Fox with Marie Stopes; Fannie Hurst with Frances Marion; Frances Marion with Lillian Gish (on *The Scarlet Letter*); Anita Loos with Jane Murfin (on *The Women*); Anita Loos wrote for Lillian Gish; Lillian Wald, with Jane Addams; and Jane Addams with Louise De Koven Bowen. Fredi Washington wrote for *The Negro Actor*, for which Geraldine Dismond was editor. Marie Stopes, Ethel Manin, and Barbara Low made presentations at the Third Sexual Reform Congress in London in September 1929. Both Germaine Dulac and Frances White Diehl gave papers at the meeting of the International Council of the Women's Commission of the Cinema in Rome in October 1931. Pacifism linked Charlotte Perkins Gilman, Jane Addams, and Lillian Wald who were all members of the Women's International League for Peace and Freedom; Addams certainly met both C. P. Gilman and C. C. Gilman. Marie Seton wrote her biography of Eisenstein at the home of Elsie Cohen in Rottingdean. Janet Flanner translated two of Colette's novels, perhaps meeting her at Natalie Barney's salon, where she socialized with Margaret Anderson and Djuna Barnes as part of the Left Bank circle of Paris. Germaine Dulac, working as a journalist in the 1910s inParis, wouold, in all likelihood, have been aware of the coverage of the paris film scene in the writing of Colette and Flanner at the time, while, in the later 1930s it is probable that she interacted with Iris Barry in the establishment of the Cinémathèque Française. (The Fitzgeralds belonged to another expatriate American community in Paris after World War I.)

180. Such links between one section and another include the "Don't Go to Hollywood" maxim of Part Three resurfacing in Part Five; women's written reception of sound persisting from Part One until Part Four; and women's reception of prize fight films cropping up in both Parts One and Three.

181. "How the Cinema Could Help with Lessons," by a Governess, *The Cinegoer*, 11 March 1916, p. 2.

182. The latter point is particularly evident in the group of writings gathered under the subheadings "Why We Go to the Movies" and "The Spectatrix."

183. For the "gent" and "the salesman," see Langer, "In the Movie Houses of Western Berlin," translation of "In den Lichtspielhäusern des Berliner Westens," pp. 27 and 30, reprinted in this volume; for front row boys, see Dorothy Richardson, "Continuous Performance VII: The Front Rows," *Close Up* 2:1 (January 1928), p. 59; and Barry, *Let's Go to the Pictures*, p. 3; and Bowlan, *Minnie at the Movies*, p. 3. (But see also the "ragged news boys" and "chattering group of girls, evidently clerks in some big department store" in Robert G. Bachman, "The Popularity of Film Grows," *Show World*, 13 July 1907, p. 10.)

184. For Gracie Fields country, see Bowen, "Why I Go to the Cinema," p. 209, reprinted in this volume; for the Tuscan hill town cinema, see Vorse, "Some Picture Show Audiences," p. 441, reprinted in this volume; the particular song is from Dorothy Woodman, "A War Film in Berlin," *The New World*, September 1931, p. 5, reprinted in this volume.

185. This is a gendered observation tied to other, somewhat more familiar, insights into cinema's modernity: the movies as a site of distraction; as an opportunity for the assembly of the crowd. See Siegfried Kracauer, "The Cult of Distraction: On Berlin's Picture Palaces," in *The*

Mass Ornament: Weimar Essays, trans. and ed. Thomas Y. Levin (Cambridge: Harvard University Press, 1995), pp. 323–8, among other relevant writings.

186. See Mary Ann Doane, "Film and the Masquerade: Theorizing the Female Spectator," *Screen* 23:3–4 (1982), pp. 74–88, for a discussion of distance and the female viewer.

187. Vorse, "Some Picture Show Audiences," p. 441, reprinted in this volume.

188. Bazin, *What is Cinema?* vols I and II.

189. Marie Seton, "Television Drama," *Theater Arts Monthly* 22:12 (December 1938), p. 885, reprinted in this volume.

190. Texts especially relevant here include Epstein, "Approaches to Truth" [1928], "Art of Incidence" [1927], "For a New Avant-Garde" [1925], "Magnification" [1921], "On Certain Characteristics of 'Photogenie'" [1924], and "The Senses I (b)" [1921], all translated and reprinted in *French Film Theory and Criticism*, Vol. I, pp. 422–5, 412–14, 349–53, 235–41, 314–18, and 241–6, respectively. Arnheim, *Film as Art*.

191. Rebecca West, "Preface," in Bernard Caston and G. Gordon Young, *Keeping it Dark, or the Censor's Handbook* (London: Mandrake Press, c. 1929), pp. 7–13; Anita Loos, contribution to "In Defense of Hollywood: Prominent Figures in the Film World Rise to Refute the Exaggerated Reports of Motion Picture Morals," *Filmplay* 1:2 (May 1922), p. 21, both reprinted in this volume.

192. "The End of the Line," *Etude* 52 (August 1934), p. 450.

193. Among particular uses of cinema, see Mrs J. E. Whitby, "The Future of the Cinematograph," *Chambers's Journal*, 1 June 1900, pp. 391–2, who promoted making scientific films; and Mary Field, "Can the Film Educate?" p. 57, both reprinted in this volume.

     For education from the most mundane films see, for example, Field, "Can the Film Educate?" p. 61, where she records a nine-year-old boy having learned "the Art of Making Love" from the screen; and Moseley, "Films Have Taught Us What Life Means," p. 9, both reprinted in this volume. Mary Field also writes, in "Can the Film Educate?" p. 49, that films give "a sense of experience."

194. See, for example, C.A. Lejeune, "'Eyes and No Eyes': What to Look for in Films," in *For Filmgoers Only*, ed. R.S. Lambert (Faber & Faber, with the British Institute of Adult Education: London, 1934), pp. 80–95; and Alice Ames Winter, "And So to Hollywood," *Woman's Journal* 15:3 (March 1930), pp. 7–9, 45–6, reprinted in this volume.

195. Dorothy Arzner, unpublished, typed lecture notes titled "Starlight," held in the Arts–Special Collections, Dorothy Arzner Papers, University of California, Los Angeles. The lecture is typed on Department of Theater Arts letterhead, and was delivered in the late 1950s, or possibly in the 1960s.

196. See de la Roche, "That 'Feminine Angle'"; Ager, "Women Only"; Davidman, "Women: Hollywood Version"; Deming, "Love Through a Film," reprinted in this volume. De la Roche speculated that this state of affairs had developed in part through the lack of women working in production, so that the literature of advertising, for example, "provides women with a first-rate opportunity to see themselves as men see them," but not vice versa. See de la Roche, "That 'Feminine Angle'," p. 26, reprinted in this volume.

197. André Bazin, *Orson Welles: A Critical View* [1950], trans. Jonathan Rosenbaum, (New York: Harper & Row, 1978), p. 94.

198. Among second women's movement books on film the reference here is especially to Majorie Rosen, *Popcorn Venus: Women, Movies, and the American Dream* (New York: Coward, McCann & Geoghegan, 1973), and Molly Haskell, *From Reverence to Rape: The Treatment of Women in the Movies* (Baltimore: Penguin Books, 1974).

199. Lotte Eisner reflected on methods of writing film history in article form, starting in the early 1930s in Germany, and then in exile in France after 1933, before eventually penning her better known books on Expressionist cinema and individual directors in the 1960s. See Lotte H. Eisner, "Film History: Like That of Other Arts, It Requires Integrity," *Films in Review* 2:10 (December 1951), pp. 18–21. As mentioned in note 3, early film histories were usually developed from journal columns.

200. See Joan Scott, "Women's History," in Peter Burke, ed. *New Perspectives on Historical Writing* (University Park, PA: Pennsylvannia State University Press, 1992), p. 49.

201. George Eells, *Hedda and Louella: A Dual Biography of Hedda Hopper and Louella Parsons* (New York: G.P. Putnam's Sons, 1972), p. 12, although Eells adds that this figure was probably an exaggeration. Jules Dassin remembered Hedda Hopper and Louella Parsons as ball-busters, as recounted by Eells, *Hedda and Louella*, p. 16.

202. As Ruth Vasey puts it, "pressures arising from sections of the audience, both national and international, were incorporated into Hollywood's mode of representation." See Ruth Vasey, *The World According to Hollywood, 1918–1939* (Madison: University of Wisconsin Press, 1997), p. 7.

203. This increase was to signal the improved morals of the industry, argued Leah Baird, in "The Feminine Mind in Picture Making," *Film Daily* (7 June 1925), p. 115.

204. Mathis on "The Feminine Mind in Picture Making," p. 115, reprinted in this volume.

Part One

1. See Richard Koszarski, *An Evening's Entertainment: The Age of the Silent Feature Picture, 1915–1928* (Berkeley: University of California Press, 1990), p. 30, who writes "there are few reliable statistics on the proportion of women in silent film audiences." For additional discussion of women's presence in film audiences, see Eileen Bowser, *The Transformation of Cinema, 1907–1915* (Berkeley: University of California Press, 1990), pp. 2–3. It is usually argued (see Nasaw, *Going Out*, p. 233) that women were not in the majority in film audiences until the 1920s, though this too may be a result of the sources used to gain an impression of who was in the audience. Leo Handel, *Hollywood Looks at Its Audience* (Urbana: University of Illinois, 1950), p. 90, suggests that Hollywood often operated "under the impression" that women were a majority of the American film audience, noting that "it is even possible, though not probable, that this proportion (of 65%-70% women) held true at some time in the past." Cited in Gaylyn Studlar, "The Perils of Pleasure? Fan Magazine Discourse as Women's Commodified Culture in the 1920s," *Wide Angle* 13:1 (1991), reprinted in *Silent Film*, Ed. Abel, p. 293 n1.

2. Throughout the silent era, on account of the absence of synchronized sound, it was relatively easy for exhibitors to cut and re-edit prints. To this day, intermissions are frequently added, by exhibitors by simply turning off the projector.

3. For more on this history, see the three aforementioned studies by Musser, Bower, and Koszarski in the Charles Scribner's Sons series of volumes, *History of the American Cinema*, as well as Douglas Gomery, *Shared Pleasures: A History of Movie Presentation in the United States* (Madison: University of Wisconsin Press, 1992); Bowen, "Why I Go to the Cinema," p. 212, reprinted this volume Bowen's is a longer version of her essay published in *Screen Pictorial* (Winter Annual 1937?), pp. 12, 52.

    For most people in the United States, their first contact with air-conditioning was probably in a movie theater, where refrigerated air-conditioning took off from 1917 onwards, and was widespread by the 1920s. (See Gail Cooper, *Air-Conditioning America: Engineers and the Controlled Environment, 1900–1960* (Baltimore: Johns Hopkins University Press, 1998), especially pp. 80–109.)

4. Dunbar, "The Lure of the Films," p. 20; Bowlan, *Minnie at the Movies*, pp. 5–6.

5. Shelley Stamp, in *Movie-Struck Girls*, p. 7, discusses historical documentation that indicates that in downtown areas, men preferred afternoon screenings, concluding with the general comment that men and women engaged in different patterns of cinema attendance.

    There is much recent research into the historical make-up of audiences, in terms of location, class, nationality, ethnic identity, race, and gender. See, for example, Gregory Waller, *Main Street Amusements: Movies and Commercial Entertainment in a Southern City, 1896–1930* (Washington, DC: Smithsonian Institution Press, 1995); Mary Carbine, "'The Finest Outside the Loop': Motion Picture Exhibition in Chicago's Black Metropolis," in *Silent Film*, ed. Abel, pp. 234–62; Ben Singer, "Manhattan Nickelodeons: New Data on Audiences and Exhibitors," *Cinema Journal* 34:3 (Spring 1995), pp. 5–35; Sumiko Higashi, Robert Allen, and Ben Singer, "Dialog: Manhattan Nickelodeons," *Cinema Journal* 35:3 (Spring 1996), pp. 72–128; William Uricchio, Roberta Pearson, Judith Thissen, and Ben Singer, "Dialog: Manhattan Nickelodeons," *Cinema Journal* 36:4 (Summer 1997), pp. 98–112. See also Vorse, "Some Picture Show Audiences," and Dunbar, "The Lure of the Films," on the micro-geography of New York, reprinted in this volume. Nasaw, *Going Out*, p. 164, describes "nooning" as "an exhilarating—and slightly scandalous—break from routine" for women. Koszarski writes of "an increasing feminization of film audiences beginning in the high school years," *An Evening's Entertainment*, p. 30.

6. Beth Brown, "Making Movies for Women," *Moving Picture World*, 26 March 1927, p. 342.

7. Elizabeth Symes, "A Woman's View of British Films and Players," *Film Weekly*, 5 April 1935, p. 50. Other estimates include: 65 per cent, in Spitzer, "The Modern Magic Carpet," p. 60; "almost 80 per cent," in Auriol Lee, "Women Are Needed in British Films," *Film Weekly*, 5 August 1932, p. 7; "the majority of film goers," in Laura Whetter, "Give Us Back Our Lost Gods," *Film Weekly*, 3 May 1930, p. 6; "three out of every four" filmgoers, in Barry, *Let's Go t' the Pictures*, p. 59; "more than seventy-five per cent of audiences," in Myrtle Gebhart, "Business Women in Film Studios," *Business Woman*, December 1923, p. 27; and "a very large part, perhaps a majority, of picture audiences," Alice Ames Winter, letter to Williams Hays, 21 September 1934, Hays papers, Indianapolis Public Library, Indiana. Thanks to Lea Jacobs for her reference to this correspondence.

Among male writers who shared this impression, see L'Estrange Fawcett, *Writing for the Films* (London: Pitman, 1932), p. 43, who thought women were "the bulk of audiences," and D.W. Griffith, who wrote that "nearer two-thirds of all movie audiences" were female. See D.W. Griffith, "Youth, the Spirit of the Movies," *The Illustrated World* 36 (October 1921), p. 195.
8. Lillie Messinger, "New Stars are My Job," *Film Weekly*, 5 April 1935, p. 24. See also L'Estrange Fawcett, who summarized the situation, in c.1927, as follows: "Women in the cinema must bear the responsibility to a large extent for the fare, good and bad, provided. It is for them that the films are generally created, for they form the backbone of the audiences." L'Estrange Fawcett, *Films: Facts and Forecasts* (London: G. Bles, 1927), p. 238.
9. Miles Mander, "The Feminine Touch," *Film Weekly*, 4 May 1934, p. 29. For a discussion of the opposite situation, apparently pertaining in the early 1910s by which exhibitors appealed to men to bring women to the movies, see Stamp, *Movie-Struck Girls*, p. 12.
10. Susan Ohmer, *Measuring Desire: Gallup and the Origins of Market Research in Hollywood* (dissertation, New York University, 1997), pp. 6–7. Thanks to Robert Sklar and Susan Ohmer for discussions and advice on the question of the scale of the female film audience.
11. See Dan Streible, "Female Spectators and the Corbett-Fitzsimmons Fight Film," in Aaron Baker and Todd Boyd, eds., *Out of Bounds: Sports, Media, and the Politics of Identity* (Bloomington: Indiana University Press, 1997), p. 29, and elsewhere, for a discussion of this rhetoric of summoning up female viewers for this boxing film in 1897; Anna Steese Richardson, "Who Gets Your Dime?" *McClure's Magazine* 46 (November 1915), p. 21. Richardson is quoting Jim Stone, manager of The Colonial Photo-Playhouse in "a prosperous town in northern New England," who is complaining that he cannot fully take women's taste into account in his programming because he is hamstrung by agreements with exchanges and distributors, who predetermine the films he should screen. Richard Abel stresses the significance of the actual female audience for exhibitors in the first decade of this century in *The Red Rooster Scare: Making Cinema American, 1900–1910* (Berkeley: University of California Press, 1999), pp. 66–7. This topic also centrally concerns Stamp's *Movie-Struck Girls*.
12. For "the preview huntress" see Cecilia Ager, "Native Customs of Hollywood," *Vogue*, 1 July 1934, p. 60; for "the shop girl," see Langer, "In the Movie Houses of Western Berlin," translation of "In den Lichtspielhäusern des Berliner Westens," *Kinotypen*, p. 30, reprinted in this volume; for Mrs Fitton's hat, see Holtby, "Missionary Film," p. 109, reprinted in this volume; for the typist "in search of a thrill," see Barry, *Let's Go To the Pictures*, p. 8; for another typist, see Negri, "The Movies," reprinted in this volume; for the Austrian woman, see Vorse, "Some Picture Show Audiences," p. 443, reprinted in this volume.
13. Dorothy Richardson, "Continuous Performance VI: The Increasing Congregation," *Close Up* 1:6 (December 1927), p. 64.
14. Winifred Holtby, "The Street Cinema," from "My Weekly Journal 9: Rain Over Brittany," *Schoolmistress* 50:2592 (13 August 1931), p. 533, reprinted in this volume. According to Gregg Bachman's research, open-air silent cinema venues were not uncommon. See Gregg Bachman, "Still in the Dark—Silent Film Audiences," *Film History* 9:1 (1997), pp. 40–43.
15. Langer, "In the Movie Houses of Western Berlin," p. 31; Serao, "A Spectatrix is Speaking to You," p. 32, both reprinted in this volume.
16. Vorse, "Some Picture Show Audiences," p. 445.
17. Winifred Horrabin, "What Films Do YOU Like?" *Tribune*, 24 January 1941, p. 11.
18. Dunbar, "The Lure of the Films," pp. 20, 22. She found this crowd neither bored nor enthralled. Barry, *Let's Go to the Pictures*, p. 30.
19. For "incidental interests," see Dorothy Richardson, "Continuous Performance VII: The Front Rows," *Close Up* 2:1 (January 1928), p. 63; for "goats" and "seat phones," see Cecilie Leslie,

"Sedate Edinburgh and Superior Manchester," Film Weekly, 20 June 1931, p. 17; for "lead helmets," see Flanner, "The Movies, Montmartre and Main Street," p. 11; for "warm humanity," see Holtby, "Missionary Film," p. 109, reprinted in this volume.

According to Koszarski, An Evening's Entertainment, p. 9, in a certain sense this was the case for most moviegoers; in the period up to the arrival of sound, and arguably up to 1950, patrons went for the entire event, rather than for a particular film.

20. "Adolescence of an oyster," in Flanner, "The Movies, Montmartre and Main Street," p. 51; "The Drama of the Dessert [sic]," in Bowlan, Minnie at the Movies, p. 4, reprinted in this volume.

21. The atmosphere of many of these women's writings belongs with Roland Barthes' "Leaving the Movie Theater," an essay unusual for a male writer in its graphic embedding of the author within the physics of the crowd. See Roland Barthes, "Leaving the Movie Theater" [1975], The Rustle of Language, trans. Richard Howard (New York: Hill & Wang, 1986), pp. 345–49. Also relevant here is Hanns Zischler, Kafka geht ins Kino (Hamburg: Rowohlt Verhag, 1996).

22. Sally Benson, "The Screen in Review: Criticism of the Important Film Productions of the Month," Picture-Play Magazine 22:5 (July 1925), p. 53. She is describing a screening of The Fool, dir. Harry Millarde.

23. Langer, "From Northern Berlin and the Surrounds," translation of "Aus dem Berliner Norden und da Herum," and "In the Movie Houses of Western Berlin," translation of "In den Lichtspielhäusern des Berliner Westens," both from Kinotypen and reprinted in this volume. Western Berlin was an area of new suburbs, the subject of a film shot on location there in 1913 (Das Recht auf dasein), as well as of Langer's pen. Cecilie Leslie, "A Thousand Miles of Filmgoing," Film Weekly, 13 June 1931, p. 9. Later in the article, she notes that, "At the 6:30 performance … there is music—a panatrope accompaniment by Mrs. Sowerby," the manager's wife, and that this cinema was owned by an Oxford undergraduate who aimed to cultivate an audience for quality silent films at the Black Cat. (Panatrope was a trade name of Brunswick and refers to a 1925/26 phonograph model with amplifier—and sometimes radio receiver—that was used in concert halls and cinemas to supply recorded music and sound effects.)

24. Cecilie Leslie, "The Best and Worst of British Cinemas," Film Weekly, 11 July 1931, p. 9. The other two articles in her survey are "Making a Cinema Pay," Film Weekly, 27 June 1931, p. 22; and "Sedate Edinburgh and Superior Manchester," p. 17.

25. Flanner, "The Movies, Montmartre and Main Street," p. 11; Janet Flanner, "The Turkish Fez and the Films," Filmplay 1:10 (April 1922), pp. 10–11, 54, reprinted in They Also Wrote for the Fan Magazines: Film Articles by Literary Giants from e.e. cummings to Eleanor Roosevelt, 1920–1939, ed. Anthony Slide (London: McFarland, 1992), pp. 59–63; Vorse, "Some Moving Picture Audiences." Lower East Side spectators also feature in the writing of Dunbar, who mentions "youthful East Side" boys seeking to view a prize-fight film, while Yezierska starts her review of her film career with her origins on Hester Street in the Lower East Side, New York. See Dunbar, "The Lure of the Films," p. 22; Yezierska, "This is What $10,000 Did to Me," p. 40, both reprinted this volume.

26. The Matinee Girl, "The Matinee Girl," New York Dramatic Mirror, 12 June 1897, p. 14; Alice Rix, "Alice Rix at the Veriscope," San Francisco Examiner, 18 July 1897, p. 22. The first boxing films were shot in May 1891 at Thomas Edison's New Jersey Laboratory, but were not commercially exploited. See Charles Musser, Edison Motion Pictures, 1890–1900: An Annotated Filmography (Washington, DC: Smithsonian Institution Press, 1997), p. 75.

27. Rix's would have been received as a sensational story, one only deliverable by a female reporter, whose very presence could have become the center of an exposé. See Streible, "Female Spectators and the Corbett–Fitzsimmons Fight Film," p. 36. As Streible suggests, "The Matinee Girl's insider knowledge, of who Jim's manager was, for example, also suggests that her account was 'driven more by publicity than reportage.'" A press package had been circulated beforehand stressing feminine appetite for the event. It turned out that the film's promoters had hyped the numbers of women attending, to give prizefighting a more refined stamp, to suggest its broad new audience, and to answer protestors, among whose loudest voices were other women, from the Women's Christian Temperance Union, and the Federation of Women's Clubs, among other groups. See Streible, "Female Spectators and the Corbett–Fitzsimmons Fight Film," pp. 26, 34; and Dan Streible, "A History of the Boxing Film, 1894–1915: Social Control and Social Reform in the Progressive Era," Film History 3 (1989), p. 241. Lawmakers were also working to censor both the sport, and films of fights—prizefights

were illegal in most states in the USA by 1896, and legalized in New York State only in 1896. See also Streible, "Female Spectators and the Corbett–Fitzsimmons Fight Film," p. 23. See the commentary on Blake's "Brutality in Prize Fight Pictures," p. 7, discussed in Part Three. Prizefight pictures were one of the first readily identifiable film genres (along with films of passion plays). This discussion of prizefight films is deeply indebted to Streible's research, which is collected in Dan Streible, *Fight Pictures: A History of Prizefighting and Early Cinema* (forthcoming).

28. On the film stock, see Luke McKernan, "Sport and the Silent Screen," *Griffithiana* 64 (October 1998), p. 93.

29. Streible, "Female Spectators and the Corbett–Fitzsimmons Fight Film," p. 18.

30. Streible recounts how female viewing of live fights was "represented as an act of transgression" in journalism and cartoons of the late nineteenth century. See Streible, "Female Spectators and the Corbett–Fitzsimmons Fight Film," p. 31.

31. Musser, *The Emergence of Cinema*, p. 200; Streible, "Female Spectators and the Corbett–Fitzsimmons Fight Film," p. 33. See also Miriam Hansen, "Individual Response," *The Spectatrix*, special issue of *Camera Obscura* 20/21 (May–September 1989), p. 171; and Hansen, *Babel and Babylon*, p. 10.

32. Dan Streible has pointed out the exclusion of black fighters from the first fight films, noting how the "all-white cast of boxers on-screen reference the legendary black fighters who were being banned," particularly by Corbett, "an active race baiter." See Dan Streible, "A Return to the 'Primitive': One Hundred Years of Cinema … and Boxing," *Arachne* 2:2 (1995), p. 316.

33. Corbett was not unique among screen men in sporting such scanty costume—strongman Eugene Sandow had also performed practically naked before Edison's Kinetoscope camera, in 1894. In a related set of discussions, Tom Waugh has examined the appeal of this imagery to gay male viewers, in *Hard to Imagine: Gay Male Eroticism in Photography from their Beginnings to Stonewall* (New York: Columbia University Press, 1996).

34. See, for example, Kathleen Box and Louis Moss, *The Cinema Audience*, Wartime Social Survey, June–July 1943, conducted for the Ministry of Information, Great Britain (New Series No. 37b). Fifty-three out of the fifty-four investigators for this report were women. Between 1933 and 1935, the (American) Payne Fund Studies published twelve volumes of audience analysis, with a particular emphasis on the effects of filmgoing on children. Gender and age differences were used to differentiate sections of the audience. See, for example, Blumer, *Movies and Conduct*. *Ladies' Home Journal* conducted surveys in which "a cross-section of the opinions of America's thirty-seven million female citizens is given every month." In one, "What do the Women of America Think About Entertainment?" women were evenly divided as to whether they objected or not to movie scenes showing women drinking, while only 36 per cent objected to scenes of them smoking. Mary Cookman, "What do the Women of America Think About Entertainment?" *Ladies' Home Journal* 56 (February 1939), pp. 20, 63–4. Some surveys developed elaborate mathematical equations to obtain answers. Mary Ellen Abbott, in "Motion Picture Preferences of Adults and Children," *School Review* 41 (April 1933), p. 278, explained her rating system, in which boys and girls were assessed separately:

> M represents the films liked the most and D the films liked the least. M was given a weight of 3; neutral (a film seen but not marked either M or D), 2; and D, 1. T represents the number of persons who saw the films. The formula is as follows:

$$\frac{(3 \times M) + 2[T-(M+D)]+(1 \times D)}{T}$$

> For example, *All Quiet on the Western Front* was seen by 21 men, was liked by 10, and was not liked by 4.

$$\frac{(3 \times 10) + 2[21-(10+4)] + (1 \times 4)}{21} = 2.28$$

35. Mary Field, "Unfinished Project," *Sight & Sound* 18:69 (Spring 1949), pp. 8–11.

36. See for example, Jacqueline Bobo, *Black Women as Cultural Readers* (New York: Columbia University Press, 1995); and Taylor, *Scarlett's Women*. Both these authors interview filmgoers, almost all women, about their film preferences, focusing on one or two titles in particular. See also Jackie Stacey, *Star Gazing: Hollywood Cinema and Female Spectatorship* (New York: Routledge, 1994), who used letters, over three hundred questionnaires (advertised in *Women's Realm* and *Women's*

Weekly), and other ethnographic material, to seek to understand what stars of the 1940s and 1950s had meant to women in Britain.

37. Altenloh, *Zur Soziologie des Kino* (*On the Sociology of Cinema*), parts of which have been translated and reprinted in this volume. In her article "Cinematographic Enlightenment versus 'The Public Sphere': A Year in Wilheminian Cinema," *Griffithiana* (May 1994), p. 78, Heide Schlüpmann stresses the significance of the year 1913, for this was when film criticism fully emerged in Germany.

38. See Robert Michael Brain, "The Ontology of the Survey: Max Weber on Measurement and Mass Investigation," *Studies in the History and Philosophy of Science* 32:4, December 2001: 676–77.

39. See Helmut H. Diederichs, "Emilie Altenloh—Filmwissenschaftlerin," in *Cinegraph: Lexikon zum deutschsprachigen Film* (Hamburg: Edition Text und Kritik, 1984), pp. D1–2. Thank you to Roland Cosandey for this reference. For the success of French cinema internationally in this period, see Abel, *The Red Rooster Scare*.

40. Hansen, "Early Cinema: Whose Public Sphere?" p. 239. For further discussion of Altenloh, see Heide Schlüpmann, "Kinosucht," *Frauen und Film* 33 (October 1982), pp. 45–52; Petro, *Joyless Streets*, pp. 18–20; Hake, *The Cinema's Third Machine*, pp. 45–8.

41. See Anthony Kaes, "Literary Intellectuals and the Cinema: Charting a Controversy, 1909–1929," *New German Critique* 40 (Winter 1987), pp. 7–34.

42. Altenloh argued that Nielsen films (mostly romances and social dramas), and indeed all cinema, took women out of their everyday lives. Heide Schlüpmann has suggested that they might equally have appealed for a contrary reason, in that they "afforded female spectators a kind of mirror in which they could see their imprisonment" within a patriarchal world. See Heide Schlüpmann, "Cinema as Anti-Theater," in Abel, ed., *Silent Cinema*, p. 138. Nielsen, one of the most renowned actresses of the silent era, had a career which began in 1910 in Danish cinema and flourished during the following decade in Germany. See annotation 3 of Altenloh, *On the Sociology of Cinema*, for more on Nielsen.

43. And of those six, all but that by Barnes are by British writers (Holtby, Bowen, Macaulay, and E. Arnot Robertson). Perhaps the significance of movie congregations remained potent in Britain longer.... this disproportation had significance for Dorothy Richardson, as discussed below, and for Miriam Hansen, whose research argues for the greater instability and contestation of reception in the silent era, due in part to the persistence of older forms of exhibition practice alongside film (including vaudeville elements), which "lent the show the aura of a live performance ... preserving a link between the isolated viewing subject and the audience as a collective term," as well as inhibiting the segregated conditions necessary for classical spectatorship. See Hansen, "Individual Response," p. 171.

44. It has become a cliché to note that the silent cinema was never silent. Among other sounds, there were the various sound systems of the first decade of the twentieth century, the singing accompaniment for the illustrated song-slide (a type of sound which died out during the same decade), and live musical performance, frequently by female pianists. On sound in the silent cinema, see Rick Altman, *Silent Film Sound* (New York: Columbia University Press, 2005).

45. H.D., "Conrad Veidt: The Student of Prague," *Close Up* 1:3 (September 1927), p. 44.

46. Bowlan, *Minnie at the Movies* [1913], later collected in *City Types: A Book of Monologues Sketching the City Woman* (Chicago, S.T. Denison, 1916), a publication which also included "Why Shoe Clerks Go Insane" [1912], "In the Life Class" [1913], and "Popular Music Hath Charms [1913]."

47. "Flickers," *The Picturegoer*, May 1921, p. 8.

48. Richardson, "Continuous Performance VIII," p. 52, reprinted in this volume. Rebecca Egger gives a different account of Richardson's female spectator in Egger, "Deaf Ears and Dark Continents," pp. 4–33. The female chatterer remained a cliché of filmgoing. See, for one example, Kay Riley, "—And So I'm Movie-Mad!" *Good Housekeeping* 108 (April 1939), p. 13. Riley's cartoon is accompanied by the caption, which seems to be being spoken by a male cinemagoer: "I enjoy the talkies/ When I can hear them;/ But there's another kind,/ And I sit near them." See also the deriding of the female viewer in one of the series called "Cinema Pests." The text runs: "She didn't seem to be a pest,/ But then I couldn't know/ She'd used my hat as her footrest/ Throughout the whole darned show." "Cinema Pests: No. 2," *Film Weekly*, 19 December 1931, p. 19.

See Stamp's discussion of the denigrated female natterer in *Movie-Struck Girls*, pp. 26–27, a figure whom Stamp understands as a symptom of the difficulty of integrating women into motion picture culture.

49. Richardson, "Continuous Performance VIII," p. 51, reprinted in this volume. Laura Marcus, drawing on *Windows on Modernism: Selected Letters of Dorothy Richardson*, ed. Gloria Fromm (Athens, GA: University of Georgia Press, 1995), p. 141, has noted that Richardson's Latin epigraph, "*animal impudens*," which might be translated as "shameless creature," recalls, mockingly, Juvenal's satire on women, and that Richardson here writes a satire on satires of women. See *Close Up, 1927–1933: Cinema and Modernism*, ed. Donald et al., p. 157.

50. See, for example, Lejeune, "The Week on the Screen: *The Women*," p. 9; and C.A. Lejeune, "Humoresque," *Observer*, 6 July 1947, p. 2. Altenloh, "Girl's Taste," translation of "Geschmack der Mädchen," in *Zur Soziologie des Kino*, p. 62, reprinted in this volume. Altenloh notes that this may be because opera was closer to these audiences' tastes than plays were. Richard Koszarski's research has uncovered two surveys done in the United States in the 1920s which reveal that patrons favored music as the most important feature of an evening out (over the picture, and the lighting, which also come near the top, with seating comfort also ranking high). The subjects of one of the surveys were 58 per cent male. See Koszarski, *An Evening's Entertainment*, pp. 30–31. Vachel Lindsay remarked in 1915 that continuous music in the cinema encouraged a sense of emotional community, while its absence invited intellectual response and critical exchange, observations which may also illuminate women's attractions to film music as an aid to relaxation. See Lindsay, *The Art of the Moving Picture*, pp. 224–5, cited in Altman, "The Silence of the Silents," pp. 687–8.

51. Flanner, "Comments on the Screen," *Indianapolis Star*, 21 July 1918, pp. 33, 38. In Martin Marks, "The First American Film Scores," *Harvard Library Bulletin* 2:4 (Winter 1991), pp. 78–100, Marks discusses scores from 1912. His research confirms Flanner's account in that "scores follow the story closely from beginning to end" (p. 85) and that usually "all of the film's changes of title and shot [are matched] with changes in the music." Marks also notes that "lyrics associated with … tunes [recommended on the cue sheet] help the audience to interpret the settings and actions of the story" (p. 87).

52. Mary Lea Bandy, "Nothing Sacred: 'Jock Whitney Snares Antiques for Museum': The Founding of the Museum of Modern Art Film Library," *Studies in Modern Art* (New York: Museum of Modern Art, December 1995), p. 13, quoting Iris Barry, "The Film Library and How it Grew," typescript, n.d., p. 1, the Museum of Modern Art, Film Study Center, Iris Barry Collection.

53. See the discussion of this theme in Part Four, and particularly concerning Richardson's "Continuous Performance: Dialogie in Dixie," pp. 211–18.

54. Grace Kingsley, "Little Journeys Around the Studios," *Motion Picture Director* 2:11 (August 1926), p. 38. By 1930, Ursula Bloom could remark that, "today it is seldom that I see [a picture] that I really enjoy. To my mind the talkie has taken the thrill out of it." She is not explicit about how this has happened, but sorrows for the diminishment of romance in pictures, and the new emphasis on chorus lines and "more spectacular endeavors," and is nostalgic about the way in which she used to wipe "sentimental tears" from her eyes and say, as "the End" flashed on the screen, "Well, wasn't that just too lovely." See Ursula Bloom, "The Films that Women Want," *Film Weekly*, 31 May 1930, p. 7.

55. Whetter, "Give Us Back Our Lost Gods," p. 6. She continues: "We are sick of the ninnies, the nitwits, the nincompoops." See Richardson, "Continuous Performance: Dialogue in Dixie," pp. 214, 216, reprinted this volume, and the further discussion of this text in Part Four.

56. Dorothy Richardson, "Continuous Performance: A Tear for Lycidas," *Close Up* 7:3 (September 1930), p. 200, reprinted this volume,.

57. Richardson, "Continuous Performance: A Tear for Lycidas," p. 200.

58. Djuna Barnes, "Playgoers Almanac," *Theatre Guild Magazine*, January 1931, p. 35.

59. There is relatively little record of the extent of food sales accompanying the silent cinema, but Greg Bachman's research suggests quite widespread vending of popcorn, and other snacks and drinks. See Bachman, "Still in the Dark," pp. 39–40. Andrew F. Smith, in *Popped Culture: The Social History of Popcorn in America* (Columbia: University of South Carolina Press, 1999), discusses the growth of popcorn selling in movie theaters, which he describes as beginning in the early 1930s (see pp. 100–103).

60. For "gum" see Dunbar, "The Lure of the Films," p. 22, reprinted this volume; "Comment and Review," *Close Up* 1:2 (August 1927), pp. 63, 64, for "peeling" and "sucking" and "frenzy." This article in *Close Up*, while it pays significant attention to feminine presence in the cinema, has no byline, and so may not be by H.D., nor Bryher, but rather perhaps by the third editor, Kenneth McPherson.

61. Winifred Horrabin, "*Lady Hamilton* and *Target for Tonight*," *Tribune* (London), 29 August 1941, p. 8.
62. Miller, *The Mere Living*, pp. 266–7. Thank you to Katie Trumpener for this reference.
63. E. Margery Fox, "Children and Picture Palaces," *Parents' Review* 27:9 (September 1916), p. 703, reprinted in this volume.
64. Lady Correspondent of the *Boston Journal*, "Picture Shows Popular in the 'Hub,'" *Moving Picture World* (16 May 1908), p. 433, reprinted in this volume; Flanner, "The Movies, Montmartre and Main Street," p. 11.
65. Bowen, "Why I Go to the Cinema," reprinted in this volume.
66. Fannie Hurst, "Bitter-Sweet," in her short-story collection *Gaslight Sonatas* (New York: Harper & Bros., 1918), p. 5; Ginger, "The Prodigal Nephew's Aunt," p. 7.
67. Dorothy Richardson, "Continuous Performance VI: The Increasing Congregation," *Close Up* 1:6 (1927), p. 62. Here Richardson is comparing film to theater.
68. Lejeune, "The Week on the Screen: *The Women*," p. 9.
69. Spitzer, "The Modern Magic Carpet," p. 47; Miller, *The Mere Living*, p. 266; Langer, "In the Movie Houses of Western Berlin," p. 26, reprinted in this volume; Hurst, "New Films for Old," p. 11; Macaulay, "Cinema," p. 135, both reprinted in this volume. Jackie Stacey has collected many further recollections of plush seating from female British filmgoers of the 1940s and 1950s, which she explains in terms of the cinema being a site of comparative luxury for most of the audience. See, for example, Stacey, *Star Gazing*, pp. 96, 99. The importance of "deep red seats" still thrives in cinema memory. The manager of the recently renovated Cinerama Theater in Seattle, a project funded by Microsoft billionaire Paul Allen, disclosed to a reporter his sad, ultimate fear that soon, inevitably, "buttered popcorn or soda" would make their way into the velvety pile. See Mark Matassa, "A Billionaire's Great Save: Cinerama," *Boston Globe*, 19 April 1999, p. A3. Thank you to Steffen Pierce for this cutting.
70. Winifred Holtby, "My Weekly Journal 21—Trader Horn's Africa," *Schoolmistress*, 5 November 1931, p. 153.
71. Celia Harris, "The Movies and the Elizabethan Theater," *Outlook* 130 (4 January 1922), p. 29.
72. Woodman, "A War Film in Berlin," p. 5, reprinted in this volume; Hurst, "New Films for Old," p. 11, reprinted in this volume. H.A. Potamkin was also intrigued to describe the modern, chandelierless Berlin cinemas, with their "dimmed wall, or alcove lighting," some cinemas being "lighted through squares cut into the ceiling—a severe, appropriate pattern of squares." See H.A. Potamkin, "The Movie Palace," *Billboard*, 24 December 1927, p. 51, reprinted in *The Compound Cinema: The Film Writings of Harry Alan Potamkin*, ed. Lewis Jacobs (New York: Teachers College Press, 1977), p. 549.
73. For the fly see Richardson, "Continuous Performance VII: The Front Rows," p. 60; Dorothy Richardson, "A Note on Household Economy," *Close Up* 2:2 (February 1928), pp. 61, 62. Richardson continues by lamenting (p. 62) that, in the average movie theater, "The greater part of that hindmost region of barriers, curtains, draughts, arrivals and departures, that should be the ultimate, undisturbed wall-backed paradise of the film-lover, is sheer wasteland."
74. Nell Shipman, *Abandoned Trails* (New York: Dial Press, 1932), p. 116. Thank you to Kay Armatage for pointing out Shipman's novelized autobiography.
75. Ibid., p. 116.
76. Flanner, "The Movies, Montmartre and Main Street," p. 11; Winifred Holtby, "My Weekly Journal 4—An Indian Week," *Schoolmistress*, 9 July 1931, p. 417.
77. Langer, "From Northern Berlin and the Surrounds," p. 23, reprinted in this volume; Mary Roberts Rinehart, "My Experience in the Movies," *The American Magazine*, October 1920, p. 76, reprinted in this volume.
78. Jean Rhys, *Voyage in the Dark* [1934] (New York: Norton, 1982), p. 107. Rhys is describing a visit to a silent cinema, to see a serial, "Three-Fingered Kate." Dunbar, "The Lure of the Films," p. 20.
79. Langer, "In the Movie Houses of Western Berlin," p. 28; Langer also writes of "tasteful lamps" that "stream brightness over excited faces" at the close of a show, in Langer, "In the Movie Houses of Western Berlin," p. 31, reprinted in this volume.
80. Holtby, "Missionary Film," p. 110.
81. Miller, *The Mere Living*, pp. 81–2.
82. Langer, "From Northern Berlin and the Surrounds," pp. 21–2, reprinted in this volume. With modern air conditioning, this literal thickness, which hit you as you pulled back the curtain

to enter the cinema, and which built up in women's writings, was now gone—pointing to yet another reason why women might have had less to say about the cinema after 1930. Dunbar, "The Lure of the Films," p. 20, comments on the cinema's "air" too, but differently, referring to the cinema's perpetually "stagnant and misleading air of a holiday."

83. Dickson and Dickson, *The Life and Inventions of Thomas Alva Edison*, p. 362.

84. Adams, "In Union is Strength," p. 6. But compare this to Lillian Johnson's somewhat contrary view, expressed twenty-eight years later, on the question of whether black audiences should refrain from seeing *Gone with the Wind*, discussed in Part Four. See Lillian Johnson, "Light and Shadow: On Pickets, *Gone with the Wind*, and 'Wolf,'" Baltimore *Afro-American*, 9 March 1940, p. 13, reprinted in this volume.

85. Henry T. Sampson, *Blacks in Black and White: A Sourcebook on Black Films* (Metuchen, NJ: Scarecrow Press, 2nd edn 1997), p. 7, referring to the numbers of films released. Rose Atwood, "Rose Atwood in the *Pittsburgh Courier*, 'Noted Writer Tells of Amazing Growth of Movie Industry,'" *Western Dispatch*, 1 December 1921, p. 6, held in George P. Johnson Collection, Special Collections, University of California at Los Angeles, Box 50. Other black writers called for audiences to refrain from assembling in movie houses to protest the cinema's abundant racist stereotypes: "It is, therefore, up to the colored people to set the manager right by making an insistent demand for up-to-date Negro pictures and making known in no uncertain terms that razor- crap shooting, watermelon 'comedy' is no longer desired." Editorial in an article about Dr. W.S. Smith titled "The Difficulties of a Pioneer Film Company," *New York Age*, 8 August 1917, p. 6, quoted in Sampson, *Blacks in Black and White*, 2nd edn, p. 7.

86. This segregation was challenged however. For an example of one effort to secure non-discriminatory seating, see "Motion Picture Men are Given Another Lesson: Another Colored Woman Wins Her Suit Against a Federal Street Place: White Lawyer Flunked," *Philadelphia Tribune*, 2 June 1915, p. 1. Nasaw, in *Going Out*, p. 240, concludes that segregation enabled the democratic mingling of some audiences in the cinema.

87. Mrs Charles E. Merriam, "Solving the Motion Picture Problem," *Journal of the National Education Association* 13:5 (May 1924), p. 167. These arguments are discussed further in Part Three.

88. Bryher, "What Shall You Do in the War?" *Close Up* 10:2 (June 1933), p. 191, reprinted in this volume; Lejeune, "'Eyes and No Eyes,'" p. 95; Barry, *Let's Go to the Pictures*, p. ix.

89. Harris, "The Movies and Elizabethan Theater," p. 29. Harris did not make this comparison with theater to bring prestige and status to the cinema, or to secure its validity, but rather to claim that the public's intense enthusiasm for the movies was part of a longer history.

90. Addams, *The Spirit of Youth and the City Streets*," p. 76. Altenloh, in "The Cinema Theater [Die Kinematographentheater]," *Zur Soziologie Des Kino* [*On the Sociology of Cinema*], writes: "Both the cinema and its audience are typical products of our time, which is characterized by constant activities and nervous agitation. Locked into their jobs during the daytime, people cannot even shake off this haste when they want to relax. Passing by a movie theater, they enter it to seek diversion and distraction for a short time, already worried about how to fill the next hours." This translation is taken from Hake, *The Cinema's Third Machine*, p. 46.

91. E. Arnot Robertson, "They Call It 'Box Office,'" *Vogue*, 15 October 1949, p. 134. In late-1946, Robertson's own position as a radio film critic for the BBC had been in jeopardy after the radio network received a letter of complaint from MGM about her reviewing of their films. Robertson successfully sued MGM for libel, although the House of Lords later reversed her victory. The case was closely watched as an indicator of the latitude film critics had to speak their minds. See Ernest Betts, *Inside Pictures: With Some Reflections from the Outside* (London: Cressel Press, 1960), pp. 78–9, and "'Privilege' Defence in Critic's Suit," *Today's Cinema* 69:5519 (16 July 1947), pp. 3, 46.

92. The manichean perfection of cinema's types and their fates offered temporary relief, in the view of Milena Jesenská, in "Cinema," translation of "Kino," *Tribuna*, 15 January 1920, reprinted in Milena Jesenská, *Alles ist Leben* (Hamburg: Verlag Neue Kritik, 1984), pp. 16–19, reprinted in this volume. (For further information on Jesenská's writings, see Jana Cerná, *Kafka's Milena*, trans. A.G. Brain, with an introduction and translation of Milena Jesenská's work by George Gibian (Evanston: Northeastern University Press, 1993.) Rennert, "The Onlookers of Life at the Cinema," translation of "Die Zaungäste des Lebens im Kino," pp. 217–18, reprinted in this volume. According to Dunbar, in "The Lure of the Films," p. 22, reprinted in this volume, cinema made of its audience "no demand whatsoever." For Helen Brown Norden costume pictures—the "masquerade boom"—were a key instance of this

escapism: "movies quite naturally never had the social or the mental stamina to portray the actual problems which existed." The only way out, then, was the historical epic. See Helen Brown Norden, "Passion for the Past," *Vogue*, 1 March 1947, p. 124.

93. Miller, *The Mere Living*, pp. 267–8.

94. Hattie M. Loble, "A Western Woman's Opinion of Pictures," *Moving Picture World* 12:9 (1 June 1912), p. 820, selected poem reprinted in this volume.

95. In his book on the industrialization of light in the nineteenth century, Wolfgang Schivelbusch remarks that "light-based media" (from the diorama to the cinemascope screen) invite a contemplation like that of the candle flame. "In this respect," he comments, "the film is closer to the fire than to the theater." See Wolfgang Schivelbusch, *Disenchanted Night: The Industrialization of Night in the Nineteenth Century*, trans. Angela Davis (Berkeley: University of California Press, 1988), pp. 220, 221. Perhaps the tone of Loble's text smacks of its trade press venue, for she concludes that the cinema's reverie is superior because images of the screen are renewed every day, while embers of the fire "fade and die away."

96. Dunbar, in "The Lure of the Films," p. 22, if less gracefully, also concluded that people visited this cheap "lounging place" for "social contact." As mentioned in Part Three, Margaret Mead found cinema to be marked by a collective dream, so she went for "indications of the way our national daydreams are developing and changing." See Margaret Mead, Cecile Starr, and Others, "What I Look for in a Film," *Films in Review* 1:3 (April 1950), p. 12.

97. Bowlan refers to the thicket of baby carriages parked in front of the nickelodeon in *Minnie at the Movies*, p. 5. Vorse describes the armloads of babies and children being brought to the cinema, "Some Picture Show Audiences," pp. 445–6. The following vignette, as recounted by a box office cashier of a super cinema in London, is not unusual:

> You would be amazed to see some of the stalwart infants in arms of Forest Hill, who, after shouting and climbing off the trams and buses outside the door, miraculously become delicate, soulful-eyed babes in their mothers' arms as soon as they are under our canopy. But, bless them, we don't begrudge these hard-working housewives their little subterfuge to get Sidney, aged seven, in on the nod.

See Irene Wright, "Life Looks Funny Through a Grille," *Film Weekly* (4 July 1931), p. 19.

98. See Eyles, "The Woman's Part," p. 14, on the use of the cinema for coping with domestic demands:

> Some of them [women] go to the movies. But I know from my own experience that when I took my three youngsters to the cinema, I was asleep within ten minutes, simply because the seat was comfortable and the music soothing, and—blessed relief!—no little voices to keep saying "Mum!" because the kiddies were being entertained by the screen while I slept. Later, when I was a programme girl at a cinema, I saw row after row of sleepy women at the afternoon performances, and knew that this was pretty general. Most mothers, if they have enough energy to dress themselves and the kiddies and go to the pictures, are too tired to take any interest in them. They come back home with their minds just as unfed as they were when they set out.

99. See Stamp, *Movie-Struck Girls*, p. 17. Stamp also discusses the significance of baby contests, and the projecting of photographs of competing babies on screen, in this regard (p. 22).

100. See Peiss, *Cheap Amusements*, p. 152. This was particularly the case for the first two decades of the twentieth century. Many other scholars have researched the significance of filmgoing for women in this era. See especially Ewen, *Immigrant Women in the Land of Dollars*; Hansen, *Babel and Babylon*; Lauren Rabinovitz, *For the Love of Pleasure: Women, Movies, and Culture in Turn-of-the-Century Chicago* (New Brunswick, NJ: Rutgers University Press, 1998); Janet Staiger, *Bad Women: Regulating Sexuality in Early American Cinema* (Minneapolis: Minnesota University Press, 1995); and Stamp Lindsey, "Is Any Girl Safe? Female Spectators at the White Slave Films," *Screen* 37:1 (Spring 1996), pp. 1–15, reprinted in a revised version in Stamp, *Movie-Struck Girls*.

101. "The Lonely Girl," *Photoplay* 16:3 (August 1919), p. 27, reproduced this volume.

102. See Lois Banner, *American Beauty* (New York: Alfred Knopf, 1983), pp. 187–90, cited in Stamp, *Movie-Struck Girls*, p. 15.

103. See, for example, Colette, "Cinema," *Excelsior* (14 May 1918), p. 3, translated in *Colette at the Movies*, pp. 43–6, reprinted in this volume. Jackie Stacey's research documents the extreme importance of cinema as a form of escape from the Second World War in Britain for women. See Stacey, *Star Gazing*, ch. 4.

104. Antonia Lant, *Blackout: Reinventing Women for Wartime British Cinema* (Princeton: Princeton University Press, 1991), pp. 22–4.

105. E. Vaughan Smith, "Munition Workers and the Cinema," *The Cinegoer*, 15 April 1916, p. 16.

106. See "Navy Week Films," *The Times*, 26 July 1917, p. 3; "Captured Austrian Films," *The Times*, 6 July 1917, p. 9.

107. Bloom, "The Films That Women Want," p. 7. Leonora Eyles describes the same privation for working-class women, regarding the Sunday paper, in "The Woman's Part," p. 14.

108. See Richardson, "Continuous Performance VI: The Increasing Congregation," p. 64. Dunbar is unusual among women writers in attributing "little or no emotional outlet" to the cinema, although this may be a consequence of the relatively early date of Dunbar's article (1913 was the first year in which longer, more involving narrative films began to dominate). Dunbar, "The Lure of the Films," p. 22, reprinted in this volume. She is comparing cinema with live melodrama here, and explains of cinema that "the interest that it excites, when it excites any, is shallow, fleeting, two-dimensional, like the pictures themselves," and that the "self-protective surface of apparent torpor" that spectators acquire before the screen results from this thinness and dissatisfaction. See *The Year 1913*, Special Issue, *Griffithiana* 50 (May 1994). One oral history study of the silent era records that, "In our theater it was nothing for the women to sob right out loud." See Bachman, "Still in the Dark," quoting Harry Fischer, recorded 13 February 1993, p. 27.

109. Sue Harper and Vincent Porter, in "Moved to Tears: Weeping in the Cinema in Postwar Britain," *Screen* 37:2 (Summer 1996), have summarized and analysed a Mass-Observation survey of British audience responses to film, conducted in August 1950. The results indicate that women have tended to be more affected by the emotions of others in the movie theater, while "men who found themselves on the verge of tears reported their sense of isolation from others in the audience." (p. 157) In general, men cried less, or chose a definition of crying which did not include their own particular form of emotional response. The Second World War "made both men and women more liable to weep in the cinema. But the impact on the traditionally reticent males was more noticeable than that on women, who in any case tended to be far less reserved." (p. 171) Fir "separate cinemas," see A Woman Reader, "Keep Men Out of Cinemas," *Film Weekly*, 30 September 1932, p. 18. One reason she gives is that men "cannot lose themselves in a film" and so embark on other, distracting activities: coughing, grunting, dropping cigarette ash on one's clothes, and inflicting their lovemaking. She concludes, "If men had cinemas to themselves they probably would not go, which only shows how much they care about films." From "Just A Man," see the opposite argument: "Women Cannot Appreciate Films," *Film Weekly*, 28 July 1933, p. 26. There is one report of a cinema segregated by sex, run by an English "bioscope attaché," employed by "the Sultan," to show "the women of the harem … motion pictures of various parts of the world." See Dwight Elmendorf, "Novel and Useful Applications of Motion Photographs," *Views and Films Index* 1:21 (15 September 1906), p. 4. Langer writes of women's "bitter contempt" for those who laugh during "sentimental moments," in "In the Movie Houses of Western Berlin" p. 30, reprinted in this volume.

110. Gabriel Costa, "The Jew on the Screen: What the Ghetto Likes," *Kinematograph and Lantern Weekly*, 14 January 1915, p. 75.

111. Djuna Barnes, "The Wanton Playgoer," *Theatre Guild Magazine*, September 1931, p. 21; Langer, "In the Movie Houses of Western Berlin," p. 31; both reprinted in this volume.

112. Barry, *Let's Go to the Pictures*, pp. viii, ix.

113. Taylor, "How Films have Changed Women," p. 9.; Riding, *Literal Solutions*, p. 30.

114. Barry, *Let's Go to the Pictures*, p. 68; Maya Deren, "Magic is New," *Mademoiselle*, January 1946, pp. 260, 263, both reprinted in this volume.

115. Riding, *Literal Solutions*, p. 26; Woolf, "The Movies and Reality," p. 309, reprinted in this volume.

116. Langer, "In the Movie Houses of Western Berlin," p. 31; Altenloh, *Zur Soziologie des Kino* [On the Sociology of the Cinema], p. 94, both reprinted in this volume. In Altenloh's text, the sight of women was attractive to men.

117. For "pallid ovals" and "the half light," see Vorse, "Some Picture Show Audiences," p. 443, reprinted in this volume; for "self-protective surface" see Dunbar, "The Lure of the Films," p. 22, reprinted in this volume. Here Dunbar is contrasting the attitude of a filmgoer to that of

someone before a live melodrama; this protection had been developed before the film screen. For "sheened" and lifting "a foolish gaze," see Richardson, "The Front Rows," p. 59.

118. "Pallor" in Holtby, "Missionary Film," p. 109; Macaulay, "Cinema," p. 138; Dunbar, "The Lure of the Films," p. 20.

119. This theme is developed in Parts Two and Three. For an example of appeal to the eye over the intellect, see Low, "Mind-Growth or Mind-Mechanization?" p. 47; "the moving-picture eye" is from Edward Lyttleton, "Note on the Educational Influence of the Cinematograph," *Hibbert Journal*, July 1913, p. 855; "the movin' pitcher squint" is from Bowlan, *Minnie at the Movies*, p. 4; the "permanently injur[ed]" eye is from Addams, *The Spirit of Youth and the City Streets*, p. 93.

120. "The too synthetic eye," which cannot see the very small, or things happening very slowly or very fast (things revealed in the processes of magnification, and slow- and fast-motion) is found in Germaine Dulac, "The Meaning of Cinema," *International Review of Educational Cinema* 3 (December 1931), p. 1093; the "English unaesthetic eye" is in Woolf, "The Movies and Reality," p. 308; the practical, injury-avoiding eye is in Barry, *Let's Go to the Pictures*, p. 37, reprinted in this volume.

121. Stamp, *Movie-Struck Girls*, p.20.

122. Streible, "Female Spectators and the Corbett–Fitzsimmons Fight Film," p. 39.

123. Ibid., p. 35. Musser argues that women's attendance at boxing pictures waned, partly as nickelodeons became more carefully managed and watched, but also no doubt because in general the pleasures of viewing remained limited and circumscribed, making the Corbett–Fitzsimmons Veriscope event isolated and unique. See Musser, *The Emergence of Cinema*," p. 208; and Streible, "Female Spectators and the Corbett–Fitzsimmons Fight Film," p. 41. See also Dunbar's discussion of the attraction of fight films for boys, in "The Lure of the Films," p. 22.

124. See Doane, *The Desire to Desire*; and Anne Friedberg, *Window Shopping: Cinema and the Postmodern* (Berkeley: California University Press, 1993) for further discussion of these themes.

125. Virginia, "The Diary of a Daughter of Eve," *Black and White*, 4 April 1896, p. 442, reprinted in this volume. The cinematograph she wanted would have been capable of both projecting and shooting films. Readers are reminded in an editorial footnote that patterns for the lavishly illustrated costumes in the article can be purchased by mail. (Nothing about the cinema is illustrated.) The Matinee Girl, "The Matinee Girl," p. 14, reprinted in this volume.

126. Lady Correspondent of the *Boston Journal*, "Picture Shows Popular in the 'Hub,'" p. 433, reprinted in this volume.

127. Rix, "Alice Rix at the Veriscope," p. 22.

128. See, for example, Addams, *The Spirit of Youth and the City Streets*, p. 8.

129. Margaret Deland, "The Change in the Feminine Ideal," *Atlantic Monthly* 105 (March 1910), p. 290.

130. Rinehart, "My Experience in the Movies," p. 76. The hat-and-ladder glass slide is illustrated in Robinson, *From Peepshow to Palace: The Birth of American Film*, p. 52. Also relevant here is the Biograph short film directed by D.W. Griffith, *Those Awful Hats* (1909), in which women are asked to remove their hats.

131. Mr F.H. Richardson, "Those Hats," *Moving Picture World* 6 (9 April 1910), p. 549. Richardson is disparaging about the lack of refinement of "ladies" insensitive enough to wear large hats, and adds that he "cannot possibly agree with the Atlanta managers in their unique position. He [Richardson] holds that both men and women should be obliged to remove their hats or else leave the theater. When a manager sells me a ticket, it is supposedly a guarantee that I will see a show, not someone's hat.... In Atlanta the women might, got a time, cease to attend the theater as often as they did before (that is to say, some of them might), but it won't last very long, believe me, especially if convenient mirrors be installed." Earlier "High Hat" bills, passed in the 1890s in New York and Chicago had prohibited such apparel. See Ann Douglas, *Terrible Honesty: Mongrel Manhattan in the 1920s* (New York: Farrar, Straus, & Giroux, 1995), p. 380.

132. "How to Buy a Hat," *Vogue*, 15 January 1941, p. 43. This article does not discuss the cinema.

133. Recalling the era of the mid 1910s, when she was a schoolgirl, C.A. Lejeune wrote: "When I first went to the pictures, I remember how my friends and I used to hide behind the billboards outside the theatre, in case one of our relations came by and discovered us in the

queue, or some other girl from school told tales about the way we spent our evenings." See Lejeune, "'Eyes and No Eyes,'" pp. 82–3.

134. See Anke Gleber, "Women on the Screens and Streets of Modernity: In Search of the Female Flâneur," *The Art of Taking a Walk: Flanerie, Literature, and Film in Weimar Culture* (Princeton: Princeton University Press, 1999), pp. 171–89.

135. Mabel Dwight, "Mott Street Movies," pencil and black crayon drawing from 1929, reproduced in *Theatre Guild Magazine* 7 (October 1929), p. 26 and captioned "In the motion pictures theatres of Mott Street in New York, Hollywood films alternate with Chinese reels. Miss Dwight has sketched one of the latter, called *The Spiders*, an oriental thriller about a secret order of criminals." Reproduced in this volume.

136. Mabel Dwight, "The Clinch," (1928), lithograph on stone, published in "Scenes from the Cinema—by Mabel Dwight," *Vanity Fair* 32 (March 1929), p. 54, among other sites. Reproduced in this volume. Another one of Dwight's lithographs of film audiences was of a masked bandit looming out of the screen, over the heads of audiences, called "Stick 'em Up," or "'Stick 'em Up,' Cinema," or "A 'Western.'" This was published in *The Philadelphia Record*, 20 January 1929, as "Scenes from the Cinema," p. 29, as well as in *New Masses* 11:13 (26 June 1934), p. 23.

137. Mabel Dwight printed two states of this work, as far as is known, although only the second state was published. In the first state the couple embrace to the right instead of the left, and the clock on the wall reads 12:15 instead of 9:55. Dwight conveyed even in her use of the medium the contingencies of each screening—was this a matinée, or an evening event?

138. For "celluloid twilight," see Bolton, *Do I Wake or Sleep*, p. 57. See especially the essays in this section by Loble, Negri, Holtby, Langer, and Bowlan, for this trait, as well as Flanner, "The Movies, Montmartre and Main Street," pp. 10–11, 51.

139. Macaulay, "Cinema," p. 135.

140. Flanner, "The Movies, Montmartre and Main Street," p. 11.

141. Richardson, "Continuous Performance VI: The Increasing Congregation," p. 64; Barry, *Let's Go to the Pictures*, p. viii.

142. Negri, "The Movies," p. 59, reprinted in this volume. Emily Post, *Etiquette: in Society, in Business, in Politics, and at Home.* (New York: Funk & Wagnalls, 1923), pp. 40–1, reprinted in this volume.

143. Ibid.

144. This may be usefully compared with descriptions of flânerie penned by Georg Simmel and Walter Benjamin, among others. See, for example, Georg Simmel, "The Metropolis and Mental Life," in *The Sociology of Georg Simmel*, ed. Kurt H. Wolff (New York: Free Press, 1950); and Walter Benjamin, "The Flâneur," in *Charles Baudelaire: A Lyric Poet in the Era of High Capitalism* (London: Verso, 1983), pp. 35–66.

145. Gertrude Koch, "Why Women Go to the Movies," trans. Marc Silberman, *Jump Cut* 27 (July 1982), pp. 51–3. First published as "Warum Frauen ins Männerkino gehen," in *Frauen in der Kunst*, vol. 1, ed. Gislind Nabakowski et al. (Frankfurt am Main: Suhrkamp, 1980), 15–29.

146. Lejeune, "The Week on the Screen: The Women," p. 9. Dorothy Richardson, "Talkies, Plays, and Books: Thoughts on the Approaching Battle Between the Spoken Pictures, Literature and the Stage," *Vanity Fair*, August 1929, p. 56, an article comparing film with stage and opera, Richardson writes that the significance of "fair face, exquisite toilet, shimmering jewels," staples of a theater or opera outing, are transformed, even threatened with cancellation in cinema conditions, for there "all these are invisible in darkness" (p. 56). In the same article, Richardson describes the "atmosphere" of the cinema as "not social," unlike that of the theater or opera, for its interval is not for "paying calls" and "'seeing the house.'" On the contrary, "there is no occupation for the opera-glass, the inseparable companion of the real stage addict."

147. Post, *Etiquette*, p. 293, reprinted in this volume; Taylor, "How Films have Changed Women," p. 9.

148. *The Spectatrix*, special issue of *Camera Obscura* 20/21 (May–September 1989), p. 17, and elsewhere.

149. See Hansen, *Babel and Babylon*; Doane, *The Desire to Desire*; and Helen Taylor, *Scarlett's Women: Gone with the Wind and Its Female Fans* (New Brunswick, NJ: Rutgers University Press, 1989).

150. Laura Mulvey, "Visual Pleasure and Narrative Cinema," *Screen* 16:3 (Autumn 1975), pp. 6–18. According to the theory, this state of affairs pertained in the "classical Hollywood film," the dominant filmmaking style characterizing mainstream cinema from about 1917 onwards.

151. Christian Metz and Jean-Louis Baudry are among the most important of writers who have described identification in the cinema in these terms. See Christian Metz, *The Imaginary Signifier: Psychoanalysis and the Cinema*, trans. Celia Britton et al. (Bloomington: Indiana University Press, 1982); Jean-Louis Baudry, "Ideological Effects of the Basic Cinematographic Apparatus" [1970], in Philip Rosen, ed., *Narrative, Apparatus, Ideology: A Film Theory Reader* (New York: Columbia University Press, 1986), pp. 286–98, and Jean-Louis Baudry, "The Apparatus: Metapsychological Approaches to the Impression of Reality in Cinema" [1975], also in Rosen, ed., *Narrative, Apparatus, Ideology*, pp. 299–318.

152. See, for example, E. Ann Kaplan, "Is the Gaze Male?" in *Women and Film: Both Sides of the Camera* (New York: Methuen, 1983), pp. 23–35.

153. Gaylyn Studlar, *In the Realm of Pleasure: Von Sternberg, Dietrich, and the Masochistic Aesthetic* (Urbana: University of Illinois Press, 1988).

154. Laura Mulvey, "Afterthoughts on 'Visual Pleasure and Narrative Cinema' inspired by *Duel in the Sun*," *Framework* 6 (Summer 1981), p. 15.

155. Doane, "Film and the Masquerade: Theorizing the Female Spectator," p. 78. See also Mary Ann Doane," Masquerade Reconsidered: Further Thoughts on the Female Spectator," *Discourse* 11:1 (Fall–Winter 1988–89): 42–54. Joan Rivière, "Womanliness as a Masquerade" [1929], reprinted in *The Inner World and Joan Rivière: Collected Papers, 1920–1958* (London: Karnac Books, 1991), pp. 90–101.

156. See Linda Williams, "Introduction," in Linda Williams, ed., *Viewing Positions: Ways of Seeing Film* (New Brunswick, NJ: Rutgers University Press, 1995), pp. 1–20, for a clear survey of these developments; see also Stacey, *Stargazing*, ch. 2, "From the Male Gaze to the Female Spectator."

157. Annette Kuhn, "Women's Genres: Melodrama, Soap Opera and Theory" [1984], in Christine Gledhill, ed., *Home is Where the Heart Is: Studies in Melodrama and the Woman's Film* (London: British Film Institute, 1987), pp. 339–49.

158. See, for example, Lorraine Gamman and Margaret Marshment, eds., *The Female Gaze: Women as Viewers of Popular Culture* (Seattle: Real Comet Press, 1989); E. Deidre Pribram, ed., *Female Spectators: Looking at Film and Television* (London and New York: Verso, 1988); bell hooks, "The Oppositional Gaze: Black Female Spectators," in *Black Looks: Race and Representation* (Boston: South End Press, 1992); Mulvey, *Visual and Other Pleasures*; Doane, *The Desire to Desire*; Taylor, *Scarlett's Women*; Hansen, *Babel and Babylon*; Stacey, *Star Gazing*; Bobo, *Black Women as Cultural Readers*.

159. *Red Velvet Seat* has been shaped by research into women's history generated in other fields, such as via the collection of oral records, and in reader-response criticism, both of which aim to secure access to specific historical moments of consumption, often those of understudied consumers. See *Enter the Dream House: Memories of Cinemas in South London from the Twenties to the Sixties*, ed. Margaret O'Brien and Allen Ayles (London: Museum of the Moving Image, 1993); Ian Breakwell and Paul Hammond, *Seeing in the Dark: A Compendium of Cinema-Going* (London: Serpent's Tail, 1990); and Bachman, "Still in the Dark," pp. 23–48, for examples of collecting oral history and testimonies of memory for knowledge of the cinema. This method, a hallmark of cultural studies, had among its forerunners the Mass-Observer diarists operating in Britain from 1937 onwards. For reader-response criticism, see Janice Radway, who, for her study *Reading the Romance*, made an "ethnographic examination of an actual community of romance readers," submitting a "lengthy questionnaire" to forty-two women in 1980–81, and interviewing sixteen others. Through this procedure she intended to countermand a theoretical position which, as she put it, "reifies human activity, ignores the complexities of sign production and semiosis, and transforms interactive social process into a confrontation between discrete objects." Through this method, the divergence between women's interpretations of romance novels and those of cultural critics would finally be noticed, and the former would necessarily challenge the idea that all possible meanings reside within a text, independently of the person reading. See Janice Radway, *Reading the Romance: Women, Patriarchy, and Popular Literature* (Chapel Hill: University of North Carolina Press, 1984), p. 8.

160. Dunbar, "The Lure of the Films," p. 20; Lejeune, "The Week on the Screen: *The Women*," p. 9; Serao, "A Spectatrix is Speaking to You," pp. 31–2; Bowen, "Why I Go to the Cinema," pp. 208, 210; all reprinted in this volume.

161. For "pulse," see Hermine Rich Isaacs, "Whistling in the Dark: Every Soldier a Movie Critic," *Theatre Arts* 27 (December 1943), p. 730; for "casual glance," see Richardson, "Continuous Performance VIII," p. 54, reprinted in this volume.

162. Ager, "Women Only," p. 321, reprinted in this volume.

163. For her writing Negri drew on her origins in Lodi's working class of the north, and indeed, she has been described as the first Italian writer from that class. See Bruce Merry, "Ada Negri," in Rinaldina Russell, ed., *Italian Women Writers: a Bio-bibliographical Sourcebook* (Westport, CT: Greenwood Press, 1994), p. 295. Negri, "The Movies," p. 62, reprinted in this volume. Anzia Yezierska contemplates a similar fate to Negri's fictional Bigia, that of throwing herself under a limousine, when pondering the lack of recognition she suffers in New York. See Yezierska, "This is What $10,000 Did to Me," p. 41, reprinted in this volume.

164. Woolf, "The Movies and Reality," p. 308, reprinted in this volume. Mary Ann Doane writes of the record of a skeptical female spectator, remembered by early British filmmaker William Friese-Greene, who "poked her fingers at the image on the screen of a girl's face, convinced that the whole thing was an impossible illusion, and that there were holes in the screen for the eyes of a real girl standing behind it." Mary Ann Doane, "Technology's Body: Cinematic Vision in Modernity," *differences* 5:2 (Summer 1993), p. 1, quoting Michael Chanan, *The Dream That Kicks: The Prehistory and Early Years of Cinema in Britain* (London: Routledge, 1980), p. 15.

165. *Views and Film Index* 3:49 (19 December 1908), p. 5; "Filmaniac?" *Views and Film Index* 2:32 (22 August 1908), p. 8.

166. For "poor moth," see Richardson, "Continuous Performance VII: The Front Rows," p. 61, where the moth is a young boy; and Anne Walker, "Movie Moths," *Woman's Home Companion* 47 (December 1920), p. 14, in which there are "movie moths" of both sexes and "every age and station in life"; for "Photobia," see Elizabeth Lonergan, "Danger! Go Slow!," *Picturegoer*, April 1921, p. 21. "Photobia" was "a new disease ... afflicting the male population of the United States," who were "staring too intently at dazzling objects ... Such as Blondes!" For "cinemania," see Madame Sylviac, "Cinemania—the Dire Disease: A Few Reflections on the Silver Screen," *Vogue*, 15 August 1927, p. 64. ("Cinemania" can affect the whole family, including fathers and sons, although daughters seem most at risk.) For "filmitis," see A.S. Richardson, "'Filmitis,' the Modern Malady—Its Symptoms and Its Cure," *McClure's Magazine*, January 1916, pp. 12–14, 70. ("Filmitis," a disease of wanting to be in pictures, affects both men and women, "David" and "Betty," according to Richardson.) See also Epes W. Sargent, "Flimflamming the Film Fans," *Woman's Home Companion* 51 (November 1924), pp. 26, 94, on the latter topic, with reference to both sexes.

167. Fannie Hurst described this ritual in "Nothing Ever Happens" [1937]. There, Mrs Nevada, with an "air of complete relaxation ... day after day ... settled herself beside her child's perambulator, mulled or dozed over her multi-colored motion picture magazines, changed her baby or crooned to it, and then just sat with her long, narrow feet in their high heels stretched out before her, her blanched-looking, uncommunicative face recalling newspaper pictures of the past." See Fannie Hurst, "Nothing Ever Happens," *We Are Ten* (New York: Harper & Bros, 1937), p. 357. Hurst's short stories contain several other filmgoers, among them a delinquent shopgirl, Miss Ruby, who "comes into the store at nine o'clock 'cause she runs to the picture show all night." See Hurst, "Other People's Shoes," *Just Around the Corner: Romance en Casserole* (New York: Harper & Bros., 1914), p. 34. Goldie Flint writes white slave dramas that promise "the free advertising of censorship," and is, perhaps working for the screen as well as the stage, in Hurst, "The Other Cheek," *Just Around the Corner*, p. 73. In "Nightshade," Hanna Burkhardt rejects John's proposal that they go to a moving picture with the remark: "That's a fine enjoyment to try to foist off on a woman to make up for eight years of being so fed up on stillness that she's half-batty!" See Hurst, "Nightshade," *Gaslight Sonatas*, p. 192. Lastly, there is Charley, Lilly's husband, who earns a measly living playing "pianer" to silent films and vaudeville acts at the Gem, Third Avenue, New York, in Fannie Hurst, "The Squall" in *Just Around the Corner*, p. 338.

168. "These Fans Are Dangerous," *Screen Pictorial*, September 1939, p. 9. This article describes the "fan hysteria" that attends any public appearance of a film star. See also Helen Beal, "Confessions of a Photoplay Fan," *Photoplay* 50:1 (July 1936), pp. 32–3, 100, 102, in which the fan is imagined as female. Elinor Gibbs, in "This is Where I Came In...", *Vogue*, 15 March 1946, p. 157, feminizes all Mary Pickford's "admirers as 'Lizzies.'"

169. Holtby herself was a radical campaigner, and active against apartheid in South Africa, often writing and lecturing on racial questions. (See, for example, her essay on Paul Robeson, "Does Colour Really Matter," *The New World*, July 1930, p. 7.) She makes reference to the cinema in another of her fictional writings, which takes an African setting, *Mandoa, Mandoa!*

A Comedy of Irrelevance (London: Collins, 1933), a satire on colonialism in which an indigenous African population (located in the Sudan region) captures films from a travelling American film crew (which is making the sound picture "Siren of the Swamps"), and, endlessly rescreening the booty, develops a film culture of its own at its "Hollywood Hall," while learning American slang from the talkies. The topic of the encounter of Africa with cinema is also discussed in the General Introduction, in relation to film coverage in The Black Man, edited by Marcus Garvey.

170. The theme of the intrusion of the strange and foreign into the everyday, a description applicable to the effects of cinema itself, links Holtby's stories together in the "Exotic" section. In one, a training camp for African soldiers, and their graveyard, with its Chinese ornamentation, is located in Southern France ("Dragons at Fréjus" [1928]); in another, Mr Matsyama petitions for Japanese earthquake relief to bureaucrats in Geneva, overwhelmed by loneliness amongst all the foreigners of the League of Nations ("Earthquake at Geneva" [1923]); and in "Missionary Film" a movie brings South Africa into the English village of Market Brindle, with life-changing consequences.

171. Dunbar, "The Lure of the Films," pp. 20, 22.

172. Richardson, "Continuous Performance VIII," p. 52, reprinted in this volume.

173. Richardson, "The Front Rows," p. 63; Dorothy Richardson, "Continuous Performance: Narcissus," Close Up 8:3 (September 1931), p. 185, reprinted in this volume.

174. Richardson, "Talkies, Plays, and Books," p. 56.

175. In "Continuous Performance VIII," p. 54, Richardson writes that film offers "the possibility of escape via incidentals into the world of meditation or of thought." On contemplation as a form of viewing, see Richardson, "Continuous Performance: Narcissus," p. 185; and Dorothy Richardson, "Continuous Performance X: The Cinema in the Slums," Close Up 2:5 (May 1928), p. 61. In the former article Richardson writes: "In this single, simple factor rests the whole power of the film: the reduction, or elevation of the observer to the condition that is essential to perfect contemplation." For "the imagination of the onlooker," see Dorothy Richardson, "Continuous Performance: Pictures and Films," Close Up 4:1 (January 1929), p. 56.

176. Richardson, "Continuous Performance X: The Cinema in the Slums," p. 61.

177. In "Continuous Performance: The Film Gone Male," p. 37, Richardson writes of women sensing cinema as "the changeless being at the heart of all becoming." See also Patrice Petro writing on contemplation as a feminine mode of consuming Weimar films in Joyless Streets, pp. 69 n. 54, 186, and elsewhere.

178. In her essay, "Continuous Performance: Almost Persuaded," p. 36, Richardson fears that the "onlooker [will be] too overwhelmingly conducted" before the sound film, worrying of the sound film experience, "Is it that the interference between seer and seen is to be too complete? The expressionism, the information, the informatory hint altogether too much of it?"

179. Richardson, "Continuous Performance VI: The Increasing Congregation," p. 64.

180. Ibid., p. 63.

181. Stacey, in Star Gazing, has noted a similar richness of detail in memory in women's recollections of moviegoing of the 1940s and 1950s.

182. Naomi Schor, Reading in Detail: Aesthetics and the Feminine (New York: Methuen, 1987), p. 4, 6.

183. Ibid., p. 16.

184. Dorothy Richardson, "Women in the Arts: Some Notes on the Eternally Conflicting Demands of Humanity and Art," Vanity Fair 24 (May 1925), p. 100. Richardson describes the social and historical effort of women to keep men "innocent of the swarming detail that is the basis of daily life."

185. Schor writes of "the alleged femininity of the detail" (in Reading in Detail, p. 5) but writes to insist on the detail as an item of "aesthetic dignity and epistemological prestige" (p. 7).

186. Mary Ann Doane, "Screening Time," in Jeffrey Masten, Peter Stallybrass, and Nancy Vickers, eds., Language Machines: Technologies of Literary and Cultural Production (New York: Routledge, 1997), p. 151.

187. For "the gardener," see Woolf, "The Movies and Reality," p. 309, reprinted in this volume. Doane discusses cinema as "a technology which appears to be capable of representing the contingent, of providing the ephemeral with a durable record," in "Screen Time," p. 155. Underhill, "Imitation Chinchilla," pp. 27, 107, reprinted in this volume. For "aesthetic sensations," see Altenloh, "Female Shop Assistants," in Zur Soziologie Des Kino [On the Sociology of the Cinema], p. 89, reprinted in this volume.

Part Two

1. See Ann Friedberg's impressive study of the work of Dorothy Richardson, Bryher, and H.D. (among others) for *Close Up* in *Writing About Cinema: "Close Up," 1927–1933* (Ph.D. dissertation, New York University, 1983). See also Donald et al., *Close Up, 1927–1933*.
2. Deren's writings have been published as *The Legend of Maya Deren: A Documentary Biography and Collected Works, Volume I*, ed. VéVé A. Clark, Millicent Hodson, and Catrina Neiman (New York: Anthology Film Archives/Film Culture, 1988). Volume II is expected to be published in 2003, and the third, and final, volume is still in preparation. *The Legend of Maya Deren* includes juvenilia, fiction, correspondence, excerpts from grant applications, production ledgers, and photos, a collection of memorial letters, essays and interviews, and a bibliography of Deren studies, in addition to film scripts and articles Deren wrote on filmmaking. Dulac's collected writings are published in French in *Germaine Dulac: Écrits sur le Cinéma (1919–1937)*, ed. Propser Hillairet (Paris: Éditions Paris Expérimental, 1994).
3. Arnheim, *Film as Art*; Münsterberg, *The Photoplay: A Psychological Study*.
4. While Irene Nicholson, in "Film—Its Basic Structure," attempted to set out a taxonomy of the arts in order to adumbrate film's formal potential, her essay is anomalous. There are two other exceptions reprinted here—essays by filmmakers Maya Deren and Lotte Reiniger, in which they both expound on their working methods and aesthetic principles—but even these display a disinclination toward the abstracted elaboration of general schemas. The two women use a chatty format in which there is a pronounced sense of the filmmaker's personal presence: Deren begins her essay with a conversation structured as a series of questions addressed to herself, and Reiniger outlines her filmmaking practice through a dialogue format with a "familiar." See articles by Nicholson, Deven, and Reininger reprinted in this volume.
5. J. Cogdell, "Truth in Art in America," *The Messenger*, March 1923, pp. 634–6.
6. Ibid., pp. 636, 635.
7. Ibid., p. 635.
8. Ibid., p. 636.
9. Ibid., p. 635.
10. Betty Balfour, "The Art of Cinema," *English Review* 37 (September 1923), pp. 388–91; Leontine Sagan, "Courage in Production," *Cinema Quarterly* 1 (Spring 1933), pp. 140–43; both excerpted and reprinted in this volume. Asta Nielsen, *The Silent Muse* [1946], trans. Elsa Gren Wright, ts, Museum of Modern Art, Film Study Center, Asta Nielsen files, pp. 124–7.
11. Balfour, "The Art of Cinema," p. 389, reprinted in this volume.
12. In "The Work of Art in the Age of Mechanical Reproduction [1935–36]," Walter Benjamin also writes that, thanks to editing, and the camera, "the performance of the actor is subjected to a series of optical tests." Benjamin suggests that the movie audience also tests the performer, because it takes the same position as the camera. Walter Benjamin, in *Illuminations*, trans. Harry Zohn (London: Jonathan Cape, 1970/Fontana, 1973), pp. 230–31.
13. Balázs, "The Face of Man," in *Theory of the Film*, pp. 60–88; Dziga Vertov, "The Birth of Kino-Eye" [1924], in *Kino-Eye*, pp. 40–42; Jean Epstein, "On Certain Characteristics of 'Photogénie'" [1924], in Abel, *French Film Theory and Film Criticism*, pp. 314–18.
14. Balfour, "The Art of Cinema," pp. 388, 389, reprinted in this volume.
15. Nielsen, *The Silent Muse*, p. 127, translation modified.
16. Langer, "Mein Film Debut/My Film Debut," in *Kinotypen*, pp. 56–60, reprinted in this volume.
17. Nielsen, *The Silent Muse*, p. 125, emphasis in original.
18. Balfour, "The Art of Cinema," pp. 389–90, reprinted in this volume.
19. Sagan, "Courage in Production," pp. 142–3, reprinted in this volume.
20. Or, as Iris Barry wrote, presaging Bazin's proposal that realism is created through artifice: "is it not a curious thing that realism is often achieved by cunning...?" Barry, "Art?", in *Let's Go to the Pictures*, p. 42, reprinted in this volume.
21. See Frances Hubbard Flaherty's account of finding suitable "types" in Samoa while working with her husband, Robert, on *Moana of the South* (1926). Flaherty, "Filming *Moana of the South*: Setting Up House and Shop in Samoa," *Asia Magazine* 25 (September 1925), pp. 710–11, reprinted in this volume. Sagan cites Robert Flaherty's films as good examples of the use of untrained performers. See Sagan, "Courage in Production," p. 142, reprinted in this volume.

22. Ibid., p. 142.

23. Ibid.

24. Ibid., p. 143.

25. Beatrice Corrigan, "Harlequin in America," *Canadian Forum* 14 (March 1933), pp. 62–5; Harris, "The Movies and Elizabethan Theater," pp. 29–31.

26. Janet Flanner, "Comments on the Screen," *Indianapolis Star*, 7 July 1918, Section Six, p. 1, excerpted and reprinted in this volume.

27. Ibid., p. 1.

28. Virgina Woolf, "The 'Movie' Novel," originally published in *Times Literary Supplement*, 29 August 1918, reprinted in *The Essays of Virginia Woolf, Volume II (1912–1918)*, ed. Andrew McNellie (New York: Harcourt Brace Jovanovich, 1987), pp. 290–91. Iris Barry quotes a similar story-line to Woolf's description of a hectic Sylvia Scarlett chase involving cars, chickens, and women ("The 'Movie' Novel," p. 290), this time in a film:

    A woman is riding in a limousine that is racing with a roadster. As the race leads over uneven ground, the woman is tossed gracelessly about in the tonneau of the big car and her antics as she tries vainly to maintain a dignified position on the rear seat, and remonstrates with the reckless driving of her speed-mad chauffeur, are very funny. A white chicken tossed from the wheel of the roadster into the big car adds to the woman's confusion, and the delight of any spectator.

    Barry writes that while this is "really dreadful stuff," it is saved by the acrobatic skill of the performers. Barry, *Let's Go to the Pictures*, p. 11.

29. See Barry, "Art?"; Mary Ellen Bute, "Light*Form*Movement*Sound," *Design* 42:8 (April 1941), p. 25; Deren, "Magic is New," pp. 180–81, 260–65; Dulac, "From Sentiment to Line," p. 28, all reprinted in this volume. Dance has continued as an aesthetic concern for female filmmakers, many of whom, like Deren, had been trained as dancers. Doris Chase, a pioneering American videomaker, has combined dance and sculpture in her videos. Shirley Clarke, a founding figure in the American independent film and video movement, trained as a dancer. Sally Potter has worked as a dancer and choreographer, in addition to making films. Wendy Toye appeared in ballet films while a teenager, founded her own ballet company, and was one of the few women in Britain to work as a film producer in the 1950s and 1960s. Yvonne Rainer trained with Merce Cunningham before co-founding the Judson Dance Workshop. Her influence on modern dance continued through the 1970s, when, in 1975, she devoted herself to filmmaking.

30. Altenloh, *On the Sociology of Cinema*, excerpted and reprinted this volume.

31. Lotte Reiniger, "Moving Silhouettes," *Film Art* 3:8 (1936), p. 15.

32. Ibid., p. 15.

33. Reiniger, "Film as Ballet," p. 161, reprinted this volume. Reiniger writes that the cinema employs a unique "space–time diagonal" (ibid.), echoing Eisenstein's conceptions of filmic spatio-temporality. (It is arguable that it is in his explanation of the use of music in film that Eisenstein most directly addresses filmic temporality. See "Form and Content: Practice," in Eisenstein, *The Film Sense*, pp. 157–216.) Eisenstein's ruminations on the diagonal, and on Baroque aesthetics more widely can be found in Sergei Eisenstein, *Non-Indifferent Nature: Film and the Structure of Things*, trans. Herbert Marshall (New York: Cambridge University Press, 1987). See particularly his discussions of Piranesi and El Greco.

34. Janet Flanner, "Comments on the Screen," *Indianapolis Star*, 21 July 1918, Section Five, pp. 33, 38, reprinted in this volume.

35. Ibid., p. 33.

36. Mary Ellis Opdycke, "What the Movies have Done to Music: A New View of the Relationship Between Music and the Screen," *Filmplay*, July 1922, pp. 16–17, reprinted in this volume.

37. Ibid., p. 16.

38. Ibid.

39. Ibid.

40. Iris Barry, "Dolls and Dreams," pp. 21–33, and "Art?", pp. 37–49, in *Let's Go to the Pictures*; Nicholson, "Film—Its Basic Structure," pp. 54–6, Bute, "Light*Form*Movement*Sound," p. 25, all reprinted in this volume.

41. Barry, *Let's Go to the Pictures*, p. ix.

42. Ibid., p. 26.

43. Ibid.
44. Ibid, p. 27.
45. Ibid., p. 32.
46. Barry, Let's Go to the Pictures, p. 38, reprinted in this volume.
47. Ibid., pp. 43, 39.
48. Ibid., pp. 42, 25, 41.
49. Ibid., p. 31.
50. Nicholson, "Film—Its Basic Structure," p. 54, reprinted this volume.
51. Ibid., p. 55.
52. Ibid., p. 56.
53. Bute, "Light*Form*Movement*Sound," p. 25, reprinted in this volume. Arguments in favor of purifying the cinema were made by many filmmakers and theoreticians in the French Impressionist film movement of the 1920s, including Jean Epstein, Germaine Dulac, and Marcel l'Herbier. See, for example, Jean Epstein, "The Senses I(b)" [1921], pp. 9–16; "On Certain Characteristics of 'Photogenie'" [1924], pp. 20–23, Afterimage 10 (Autumn 1981), trans. Tom Milne, reprinted Abel, French Film Theory and Criticism, vol I, 1907–1929, pp. 241–46, and pp. 314–18, respectively; and, in the same volume, Germaine Dulac, "Aesthetics, Obstacles, Integral 'Cinégraphie'" [1926], pp. 389–97.
54. Ibid., p. 25.
55. Mary Ellen Bute, "Abstronics," Films in Review, June–July 1954, p. 263.
56. Barry, Let's Go to the Pictires, p. 43, reprinted this volume.
57. Ibid., p. 43.
58. Dulac, "From Sentiment to Line," p. 27, reprinted this volume.
59. Ibid., pp. 29, 30.
60. Balfour, "The Art of the Cinema," p. 388, reprinted in this volume.
61. Gish, "A Universal Language," pp. 33–4. Clayton Hamilton, "Esperanto of the Eye," New York Evening Post, 11 August 1923, pp. 889–90. Hamilton is reviewing the optimistic claims advanced on behalf of the silent film in Edward S. Van Zile's That Marvel the Movie (New York: G.P. Putnam's Sons, 1923). See also Stuart Liebman's discussion of "Film as Visual Esperanto" in "French Film Theory, 1910–1921," Quarterly Review of Film Studies (Winter 1983), pp. 1–23.
62. Umberto Eco, The Search for the Perfect Language, trans. James Fentress (Oxford and Cambridge, MA: Blackwell, 1995), p. 325.
63. "Motion Picture as Peacemaker," Literary Digest, 3 March 1917, p. 556; John Freuler in World Court, February 1917, cited in "Motion Picture as Peacemaker," p. 556. See also "The Motion Picture is Esperanto," Motion Picture News, 14 February 1914, p. 23.
64. "The League of Sunshine," Photoplay 16:2 (July 1919), p. 27.
65. Ibid.
66. "The League of Sunshine," Photoplay 16:2 (July 1919), pp. 52–3.
67. Proponents argued that the simple act of showing diverse races and nationalities promoted mutual understanding through a recognition of commonality, while the rapid transmission of matters of record through newsreels increased general levels of public awareness. See for instance Bernard Edelhertz, "Cinema: the Universal Eye," American Hebrew, 15 March 1929, pp. 647, 679; and Harry M. Warner, "The New Ambassadors of Good-Will," American Hebrew, 15 March 1929, p. 666.
68. Lillian Gish, with Ann Pinchot, The Movies, Mr. Griffith, and Me (Englewood Cliffs, NJ: Prentice-Hall, 1969), p. 358.
69. Pickford, "Ambassadors," p. 117.
70. Ibid. Here Pickford noted the "hopeful outlook of the average American story" (p. 7) as further reason for the worldwide popularity of American films.
71. Laura Dreyfus-Barney, "The Cinema and Peace," International Review of Educational Cinematography 6:4 (April 1934), p. 252. Dreyfus-Barney perhaps alludes to multi-language versions, or to renewed interest in artificial languages such as Esperanto, a constructed language whose goal was international intelligibility. E. Sylvia Pankhurst's account of the development of such a language, Delphos: The Future of International Language (London: Kegan Paul, Trench, Trubner, 1927) lists the telegraph, telephone, and television as means of communication but does not mention cinema.
72. The convention was held in Oxford. Henrietta Grayne, "Reversing Babel," Film Weekly, 19 July

1930, p. 8. See also Mary Bray, "Interlingua: Can the Movies Use an Artificial Language?" *Films in Review* 3:8 (October 1952), pp. 380–81, for a later revival of this idea.

73. G. Moulan, "The Cinema and International Amity," *International Review of Educational Cinematography* 4 (December 1932), pp. 907, 911. In 1931, actress Norma Talmadge clung to these ideas, despite the silent era's extinction, heralding the motion picture as the most important agent of a new "Dawn of Understanding":

> When nations comprehend the motives back of [i.e. behind] another nation's proce-dure, they cease to be intolerant. For centuries the printed word has been the only universal method of explaining the beliefs, habits and customs of one race or nation to another. All too frequently words breed misunderstanding.... But motion pictures are a medium of expression universally understandable. And, aside from their entertainment value, there is the far more important angle of authentic information regarding the customs of alien races which the motion picture carries to the far corners of the earth.

Norma Talmadge, "The Mission of Motion Pictures," in *Who's Who in Filmland*, 3rd edn, ed. Langford Reed and Hetty Spiers (London: Chapman & Hall, 1931), p. xxiv.

74. H.D., "Projector," *Close Up* 1:1 (July 1927), pp. 46–51, reprinted in this volume. See also H.D., "Projector II (Chang)," *Close Up* 1:4 (October 1927), pp. 35–44.

75. "The Cinema and the Classics III: The Mask and the Movietone," *Close Up* 1:5 (November 1927), p. 23, reprinted in this volume.

76. H.D., "Projector," p. 51.

77. According to Gillian Hanscombe and Virginia L. Smyers, in 1912, H.D.'s former fiancé Ezra Pound had written "H.D. Imagiste" at the bottom of a group of poems she had written. Three of these poems were subsequently published in Harriet Monroe's *Poetry* magazine, but only one with "Imagiste" appended to H.D.'s initials. Two anthologies of poems, one edited by Pound (*Des Imagistes*) and one by Amy Lowell (*Some Imagist Poets*), helped to popularize the word. Poets associated with Imagism included H.D., Pound, Lowell, May Sinclair, Richard Aldington, T.E. Hume, D.H. Lawrence, F.S. Flint, and John Gould Fletcher. See Hanscombe and Smyers, *Writing for their Lives: The Modernist Women, 1910–1940* (London: Women's Press, 1987), pp. 23–4, 199, 202.

78. See "The New Laocoon: Artistic Composites and the Talking Film," in Arnheim, *Film as Art*, pp. 164–89.

79. H.D., "The Cinema and the Classics III," pp. 20, 21.

80. Ibid., p. 22.

81. Ibid., p. 23.

82. H.D., "The Cinema and the Classics III," reprinted this volume. Barry also makes use of the language of religion. In an effort to describe both the particular investment of the viewer and the singularly affective power of the cinematic image, she writes that film creates a world where the audience is transported to "a region that other ages found to lie somewhere about an altar." (Barry, "Dolls and Dreams," p. 33, reprinted in this volume. Sound may indeed have made the stars less divine, "democratised" them, as Alexander Walker suggests. He cites the upsurge in fan mail to stars of the new talkies in 1929–30 as evidence of the way recorded dialogue made performers less elements of a dream and more like "identifiable parts of the audience's consciousness." Alexander Walker, *The Shattered Silence: How the Talkies Came to Stay* (London: Elm Books/Hamish Hamilton, 1978), pp. 99, 204.

83. H.D., "The Cinema and the Classics," p. 26. H.D.'s suggestion runs counter to the argument made on behalf of silent cinema's universality which privileged vision, because it privileges sound as the locus of ecumenical potential. Mussolini speechifying was the subject of an early Movietone short.

84. Dorothy Richardson, "Foreword" to *Pilgrimage* (London: Dent, 1967), pp. 9–12, reprinted in *The Gender of Modernism: A Critical Anthology*, ed. Bonnie Kime Scott (Bloomington: Indiana University Press, 1990), p. 430.

85. Virginia Woolf, "Romance and the Heart" (19 May 1923), cited by Dianne Gillespie in "Dorothy Richardson," in Kime Scott, *The Gender of Modernism*, p. 396. In 1939, at the beginning of World War II, Richardson returned to her interest in voice and talking: "A Talk About Talking," *Life and Letters Today* 23 (Winter 1939), pp. 286–8.

86. Richardson, "The Film Gone Male," p. 38, reprinted this volume.

87. Ibid., p. 38.

88. Ibid., p. 36.
89. Ibid., p. 37.
90. Ibid., p. 38.
91. Ibid., p. 37.
92. Julia Kristeva, "Women's Time" [1981], trans. Alice Jardine and Harry Blake, in *Feminisms: An Anthology of Literary Theory and Criticism*, ed. Robyn R. Warhol and Diane Price Herndl (New Brunswick, NJ: Rutgers University Press, 1991), pp. 443–59.
93. Ibid., p. 446. Kristeva links this rejection of linear time to the profound distrust of politics and the refusal of the idea of a historical project on the part of the post-1968, psychoanalytically informed generation of European feminists. Richardson's own skepticism of the sound film's promise of a vast "council chamber" of humanity might be viewed in a related, if generationally different, light. Richardson, "The Film Gone Male," p. 38.
94. Richardson, "The Film Gone Male," p. 36, reprinted in this volume.
95. Ibid., p. 37.
96. Ibid., p. 38.
97. Opdycke, "What the Movies Have Done to Music," p. 16, reprinted this volume.
98. Ibid., p. 16.
99. Ibid., p. 16. This painted and peroxided virgin also recalls the Movietone doll in H.D.'s essay, "The Cinema and the Classics III," pp. 18–31.
100. For an interesting discussion of Lord Leighton's painterly depiction of music as feminine (or castrated), see Richard Leppert, *The Sight of Sound: Music, Representation, and the History of the Body* (Berkeley: University of California Press, 1993), pp. 217–27.
101. Hurst, "New Films for Old," pp. 11–13, reprinted in this volume.
102. Ibid., p. 11.
103. Ibid., p. 12.
104. Ibid., p. 11.
105. Ibid.
106. Dulac, "The Music of Silence," pp. 77–8, reprinted in this volume.
107. Dulac, "Fron Sentiment to Line," p. 30, reprinted this volume.
108. Dulac, "The Music of Silence," p. 78, reprinted in this volume. The use of music as a model for film form is based, in part, on the formal similarities of the two media. Opdycke notes that while film and music both have continuous motion, they "flow" in different ways. She writes that music's principles are repetition, development, and contrast, and that film has limited means of deploying the first two of these. For an account of the use of music as an analogy to film, see David Bordwell, "The Musical Analogy," *Yale French Studies* 60 (1980), pp. 141–56.
109. Dulac, "The Music of Silence," p. 77, reprinted in this volume. Laura Riding, "Sound Accompaniments," *Literal Solutions*, pp. 25–34. Her booklet is ostensibly dedicated to the work of New Zealand-born animator Len Lye.

    Riding, sometimes known as Riding Jackson (1901–1992), was an American-born poet, critic and writer, who, with Robert Graves, produced *A Survey of Modernist Poetry* in 1926, and founded the Seizin Press (1926–1939). From 1929 to 1936 Riding and Graves lived in Majorca, and, during this period, initiated *Epilogue*, a literary journal. Riding's publication on Lye was the first in a projected series of booklets called *Literal Solutions*, intended to deal with a variety of practical subjects, including furniture-making, novel-writing, and education. It is an extremely rare text. Given its intrinsic interest, plus the scant awareness of Riding's film-writing generally, and her somewhat contentious status in literary modernism, it was disappointing to be denied permission to reprint the excerpt, "Sound Accompaniments." During her lifetime, Riding did not allow her work to be included in gender-based anthologies, and her Board of Literary Management continues to respect these wishes after her death. (Correspondence from Elizabeth Friedmann, for the Laura (Riding) Jackson Board of Literary Management, 24 July 1998). Riding herself produced a study of woman, published posthumously as *The Word Woman and Other Related Writings* (New York: Persea Books, 1993).
110. Riding, *Literal Solutions*, p. 26.
111. Ibid., p. 32.
112. Ibid., p. 31.
113. Ibid., p. 31.
114. Ibid., p. 25.

115. Ibid., p. 26.
116. Ibid., pp. 27, 25.
117. Ibid., p. 27.
118. It is arguable that Riding fails to understand jazz's musical complexity and that she effectively primitivizes it here, though she accords it a positive value over contemporary, non-jazz music for film purposes.. She writes:

> Jazz, even because of its unaffected emotional crudeness, is more adaptable to film use, capable of more subtle integration with a film, than formal music.... Jazz song ... can be peculiarly apt for conveying a stress of nostalgia or abandon at moments of complex significance in a film plot, where people need a simple reminder to guide their feelings among the implications crowding them at that point. Honest jazz music can assist in the simplification of the feelings aroused by a film, by its power to cut away superfluous or dishonest emotional reactions.

Riding, *Literal Solutions*, p. 27.
119. Ibid., p. 29.
120. Ibid. These remarks raise questions about the way the introduction of sound changed the perception of film's diegesis. For a historical account of the way musical accompaniment and sound effects contributed to a sense of immediacy and audience participation in several "silent" films by Abel Gance, see Norman King, "The Sound of Silents," in Abel, ed., *Silent Film*, pp. 31–44.
121. Riding, *Literal Solutions*, p. 33.
122. Ibid., p. 33.
123. Colette, "Black and White" [1935], reprinted in *Colette at the Movies*, p. 66.
124. Riding, *Literal Solutions*, p. 30.
125. Richardson, "Continuous Performance: A Tear for Lycidas," p. 198; Clara Beranger, "Motion Pictures as a Fine Art," *Theatre Magazine* 29 (May 1919), p. 304.
126. Woolf, "The Movies and Reality," p. 308, reprinted this volume; Barry, *Let's Go to the Pictures*, p. 37.
127. Bute, "Light*Form*Movement*Sound," p. 25; Barrry, "Dolls and Dreams," p. 25; Woolf, "The Movies and Reality," p. 309; Deren "Magic is New," p. 263, all reprinted this volume.
128. In his discussion of what he calls the psychology and the aesthetics of the photoplay in *The Film: a Psychological Study*, Hugo Münsterberg tries to establish the interrelationship of film form and human intellection. Eisenstein, in "Word and Image," describes the work of art as "the process of arranging images in the feelings and mind of the spectator." Reprinted in Eisenstein, *The Film Sense*, p. 17.
129. Lou Andreas-Salomé, "Movies" [1913], *The Freud Journal of Lou Andreas-Salomé*, trans. Stanley A. Leavy (London: Quartet Books, 1987), p. 101, reprinted in this volume.
130. Richardson, "Continuous Performance: Narcissus," p. 184, reprinted in this volume.
131. Ibid., p. 185.
132. Woolf, "The Movies and Reality," p. 309; Hurst, "New Films for Old," pp. 11–12.
133. Deren. "Magic is New," p. 264, reprinted in this volume.
134. For an account of the many activities undertaken by Deren in order to create a context in which her own films could be made, exhibited, and understood, see "Maya Deren and an American Avant-garde Cinema," in Lauren Rabinovitz, *Points of Resistance: Women, Power and Politics in the New York Avant-garde Cinema, 1943–71* (Urbana: University of Illinois Press, 1991), pp. 49–91. See Reiniger, "Film as Ballet," p. 162, reprinted this volume.
135. Maya Deren, *An Anagram of Ideas on Art, Form and Film* (Yonkers, NY: The Alicat Book Shop Press, 1946), reprinted in *Film Culture* 39 (Winter 1965), and in *The Legend of Maya Deren*.
136. In her preface to the booklet, Deren writes: "Each element of an anagram is so related to the whole that no one of them may be changed without effecting its series and so effecting [sic] the whole." Deren, *An Anagram of Ideas on Art, Form and Film*, p. 5.
137. Deren, "Magic is New," p. 262, reprinted in this volume.
138. Ibid., pp. 262–3.
139. Ibid., p. 263.
140. Ibid., p. 264.
141. Woolf, "The Movies and Reality," p. 309.
142. Ibid.

143. Eisenstein's project of a film version of *Capital* would be the most ambitious instance of this legacy. These questions are at the root of Eisenstein's enquiries into modes of sensuous understanding and play no small part in the more recent interest of cinema studies in cognitive psychology. See Annette Michelson, "Reading Eisenstein Reading *Capitalm*" *October* 2 (Summer 1976): 27–38.

144. Woolf, "The Movies and Reality," p. 309, reprinted in this volume. Siegfried Kracauer, *Theory of Film: The Redemption of Physical Reality*, (London: Oxford University Press, 1960) p. 60.

145. Woolf, "The Movies and Reality," p. 309.

146. Ibid., p. 309.

147. Ibid.

148. Ibid., p. 308.

149. Ibid.

150. It has not been possible to identify this film, and indeed it may be that Woolf is speaking hypothetically, and that this is a fictional account of film viewing.

151. Woolf, "The Movies and Reality," p. 309.

152. Ibid., p. 309.

153. If Woolf's phrase suggests a particular style of film practice, it would be the art cinema, as characterized by David Bordwell in "The Art Cinema as a Mode of Film Practice," *Film Criticism* 4:1 (Fall 1979), pp. 56–64.

154. Roger Cardinal, "Pausing over Peripheral Detail," *Framework* 30/31 (1986), p. 113, 118, 128.

155. Ibid., pp. 124, 129.

156. Richardson, "Continuous Performance: Narcissus," p 185, reprinted this volume.

157. Ibid.

158. Some of the relevant texts here include Baudry, "Ideological Effects of the Basic Cinematographic Apparatus," pp. 299–318; and Jean-Louis Commoli, "Technique and Ideology: Camera, Perspective, Depth-of-Field," *Film Reader* 2 (1977), pp. 128–40.

159. Richardson, "Continuous Performance: Narcissus," p 183, reprinted this volume.

160. Richardson, "Continuous Performance: A Tear for Lycidas," p 198, reprinted this volume.

161. Ibid., p. 200.

162. Ibid.

Part Three

1. Part Three borrows its title from the original title of Marie Stopes's essay "The Unsuspected Future of the Cinema," reprinted in this volume, which is held as a manuscript titled "Cinema as a Power" in the British Library, Department of Manuscripts, Stopes Papers, Add. 58545.

2. Stopes, "The Unsuspected Future of the Cinema," p. 26, reprinted in this volume. This essay appeared in a Japanese translation in the same issue of *The New East*.

3. Edison's idea appears in a facsimile reproduction of a handwritten statement by the inventor which introduces Antonia and W.K.L. Dickson's account, "Edison's Invention of the Kineto-Phonograph," *Century Magazine* 48:2 (June 1894), p. 206. Edison's comment is repeated in Dickson, "Wonders of the Kinetoscope," p. 251, reprinted in this volume. The Dicksons also suggested that the development of the kinematograph was part of the general trajectory of scientific progress that would result, in the twentieth century, in a new relationship between the sexes. See "L'Envoi," the short, final chapter of their hagiographical study of Edison, *The Life and Inventions of Thomas Alva Edison*.

4. The National Council of Public Morals Cinema Commission of Inquiry reported average weekly attendance in the United Kingdom in 1917 at over 20 million. Tom Gunning has reassessed the response of the audience in the Salon Indien of the Grand Café, Paris, and he argues that it ran not from fear of the image but from astonishment at the fact that still images had started to move. See his "An Aesthetic of Astonishment: Early Film and the (In)Credulous Spectator," *Art & Text* 34 (Spring 1989), pp. 31–45. See also Stephen Bottomore, "The Panicking Audience? Early Cinema and the 'Train Effect,'" *Historical Journal of Film, Radio, and Television* 19:2 (1999), pp. 177–216.

5. See, for example, Mrs William Dick Sporborg, "A Clubwoman Chats on Films for the Family," *Motion Picture and the Family* (15 November 1936), pp. 4, 6; Mary Roberts Rinehart, "Your Child and the Movies," *Ladies' Home Journal* 48 (April 1931), pp. 8–9, 96, 99; Laura Dreyfus-Barney, "What Woman Can Offer the Cinema," *International Review of Educational Cinematography* 4 (June 1932), pp. 471–2; Mrs Ambrose A. (Frances White) Diehl, "The Moral Effect of the Cinema on Individuals," *International Review of Educational Cinematography* 3:12 (December 1931), pp. 1123–37; Florence Jacobs, "Tremendous Influence of Films on Family Life of Today," *International Review of Educational Cinematography* 2:10 (October 1932), pp. 1189–90. Young female adolescents were interviewed in contemporary studies of film's effects conducted by the Payne Fund. The Payne Fund Studies produced eleven volumes of results between 1933 and 1935. These included Blumer, *Movies and Conduct*, which incorporated such interview material, although biographical data was often altered; Ruth Peterson and L. I. Thurstone, *Motion Pictures and the Social Attitudes of Children* (New York: Macmillan, 1933); and Samuel Renshaw, Vernon L. Miller, and Dorothy F. Marquis, *Children's Sleep* (New York: Macmillan, 1933). J.P. Mayer, *Sociology of Film: Studies and Documents* (London: Faber & Faber, 1946), includes extensive responses to questionnaires by female adolescents and young women. Debate about the effect of moving images upon audiences has in no way abated. New technologies, New Right conservatism, and the feminist inquiry into pornography have all extended its long shelf life. Belief in the special fitness of women to involve themselves in a non-professional and voluntary capacity in matters concerning children and youth has also continued to the present, given prominence in the examples provided by America's First Ladies (and aspirants to that position): Nancy Reagan's contribution to the "Just Say No" anti-drug program; Barbara Bush's literacy work; Hillary Rodham Clinton's primer on community responsibility in child-rearing; and Tipper Gore's spearheading of the attack on obscene rock lyrics. See Hillary Rodham Clinton, *It Takes a Village, and Other Lessons Children Teach Us* (New York: Simon & Schuster, 1996).

For these women, Eleanor Roosevelt was an important precursor. A First Lady with strong interests in social reform, race relations, and education, she also wrote occasionally on the cinema, as in "Why We Roosevelts Are Movie Fans," *Photoplay*, July 1938, 16–17, 84–5, in which the First Lady wrote approvingly of the newsreel's educational value, as well as of the virtue of film as general entertainment. See Giuliana Muscio, *Hollywood's New Deal* (Philadelphia: Temple University Press, 1996), p. 37, and, for further discussion on Roosevelt's writing on the cinema, see Slide, ed., *They Also Wrote for the Fan Magazines*, pp. 129–36.

6. Whether as the child's teacher at school—as members of a profession in which their numbers were dramatically increasing—or as the child's first teacher at home, women were expected to express their concerns regarding cinema, and especially enter debates on education and censorship.

7. Agnes Repplier, "The Unconscious Humor of the Movies," *Atlantic Monthly* 136 (November 1925), p. 604, reprinted in this volume.

8. The following studies on the role of the church in American film censorship address women's activities to various degrees: Gregory D. Black, *Hollywood Censored: Morality Codes, Catholics, and the Movies* (Cambridge: Cambridge University Press, 1994); Gregory D. Black, *The Catholic Crusade Against the Movies, 1940–1975* (Cambridge: Cambridge University Press, 1998); Francis G. Couvares, "Hollywood, Mainstreet, and the Church: Trying to Censor Movies Before the Production Code," in Francis G. Couvares, ed., *Movie Censorship and American Culture* (Washington, DC: Smithsonian Institution Press, 1996), pp. 129–58; Lea Jacobs, *The Wages of Sin: Censorship and the Fallen Woman Film, 1928–1942* (Madison: University of Wisconsin Press, 1991); James M. Skinner, *The Cross and the Cinema: The Legion of Decency and the National Catholic Office for Motion Pictures, 1933–1970* (Westport: Praeger, 1993); Frank Walsh, *Sin and Censorship: The Catholic Church and the Motion Picture Industry* (New Haven: Yale University Press, 1996); and Mary L. McLaughlin, *A Study of the National Catholic Office for Motion Pictures*, dissertation, University of Wisconsin–Madison, 1974. For an account of the Women's Christian Temperance Union's activities in film reform, see Alison M. Parker, "Mothering the Movies: Women Reformers and Popular Culture," in Couvares, ed., *Movie Censorship and American Culture*, pp. 73–96, and Alison Parker, *Purifying America: Women, Cultural Reform, and Pro-Censorship Activism, 1873–1933* (Urbana: University of Illinois Press, 1997).

Lea Jacobs speculates on the proto-feminist orientation of the Film Reform Movement of the 1930s (a movement concerned with demanding cleaner and better pictures) in "Reformers and Spectators: The Film Education Movement in the Thirties," *Camera Obscura* 22

(January 1990), pp. 29–49. For writing on the child audience as a special audience category requiring extra safeguarding, see also Richard de Cordova, "Ethnography and Exhibition: The Child Audience, The Hays Office, and Saturday Matinees," *Camera Obscura* 22 (January 1990), pp. 29–50.

9. Jacobs, in "Reformers and Spectators," p. 45, lists the following women's groups to whom the MPPDA made viewing facilities available: International Federation of Catholic Alumnae; the American Association of University Women; the Daughters of the American Revolution; and the National Council of Jewish Women.

10. Marina Warner, *Monuments and Maidens: The Allegory of the Female Form* (London: Weidenfeld & Nicolson, 1985; Vintage, 1996), p. 52.

11. Rebecca West, "These American Women," *Harper's Monthly Magazine* (1925), 728, quoted in Sophonisba P. Breckenridge, *Women in the Twentieth Century: A Study of Their Political, Social, and Economic Activities* (New York: McGraw-Hill, 1933, reprinted New York: Arno, 1972), p. 94.

12. Deland, "The Change in the Feminine Ideal," p. 291.

13. Karen J. Blair, *The Clubwoman as Feminist: True Womanhood Redefined, 1868–1914* (New York: Holmes & Meier, 1980), p. 74. Two other recent studies of feminism and the political efficacy of American club women are: Margit Misangyi Watts, *High Tea at Halekulani: Feminist Theory and American Club Women* (Brooklyn: Carlson, 1993); Darlene Rebecca Roth, *Matronage: Patterns in Women's Organizations, Atlanta, Georgia, 1890–1940* (Brooklyn: Carlson, 1994).

14. See, for example, "California Women Discuss Pictures," *Motion Picture Director* 2:5 (December 1925), p. 64; Anna Steese Richardson, "Better Films a Community Asset," *Woman's Home Companion*, January 1923, pp. 17, 82; Catheryne Cooke Gilman, "Better Movies—But How?" *The Woman's Journal*, February 1930, pp. 10–12, 34–5. In 1929, theater critic Creighton Peet wrote that although women's "committees [had] no legal right to cut a film, ... their suggestions [were] almost invariably followed to the letter by the producers. The fact is that our women's clubs, by mere suggestion, probably achieve more changes in the films which you and I see in our theatres than all the state boards together." See Creighton Peet, "Our Lady Censors," *Outlook and Independent*, 25 December 1929, p. 645.

15. Mrs Winter was a former president of the General Federation of Women's Clubs. According to correspondence in the Hays papers held in the Indianapolis Public Library, Indiana, Mrs Winter tendered her resignation at least once during her tenure on this committee, which began in 1929 (see also note 152). Many thanks to Lea Jacobs for this reference. For more on the Studio Relations Committee, see Jacobs, *The Wages of Sin*, pp. 27–51.

16. See Anne Meis Knupfer, *Toward a Tenderer Humanity and a Nobler Womanhood: African American Women's Clubs in Turn-of-the-Century Chicago* (New York: New York University Press, 1997). Knupfer lists over two hundred African-American women's clubs operating in Chicago from 1890 to 1930 (Appendix I, pp. 139–43). African Americans were concerned about the influence of movies on youth as well as on audiences generally. See, for example, the editorial, "The Theatres and Our Problems," *Negro American* (San Antonio, Texas) 6:8 (December 1928), pp. 3, 11; and Rayford W. Logan, "Negro Youth and the Influence of the Press, Radio, and Cinema," *Journal of Negro Education* 9:3 (July 1940), pp. 425–34.

17. Mrs William A. Corbin, "Urges Women to Attend Third International Convention," *Negro World*, 15 July 1922, p. 8.

18. Glenda Elizabeth Gilmore, *Gender and Jim Crow: Women and the Politics of White Supremacy in North Carolina, 1896–1920* (Chapel Hill: University of North Carolina Press, 1997). See also Stephanie J. Shaw, *What a Woman Ought To Be and To Do: Black Professional Women Workers During the Jim Crow Era* (Chicago: University of Chicago Press, 1996). Only further research into the scattered archival holdings of African-American response to cinema will produce an adequate answer to this matter.

19. The color bar to keep black women's clubs out of the General Federation of Women's Clubs, applied in 1900, dissolved over the issue of suffrage in about 1912. To date, the most clearly documented response by black club women to cinema is their protesting of D.W. Griffith's *The Birth of a Nation*, an effort in which black and white women's voices joined together. See, for example "Women of Race Fighting Against Birth of a Nation," *Chicago Defender*, 26 June 1915, p. 3; "Birth of a Nation Barred by Mayor in Cedar Rapids," *Chicago Defender*, 3 June 1915, p. 1, recounting the efforts of Mrs Fred H. Gresham, president of the Women's Club of Cedar Rapids, to ban *The Birth of a Nation*, *The Clansman*, and *The Nigger* from that city; "Police Beat and Arrest Boston Women Protesting Against Birth of a Nation," *Chicago Defender*, 19 June 1915, p. 1,

describing the arrest of men and women of "the Race" for protesting the film; and, for a related protest, "Rev. Thomas Dixon Jr., Will Appear in his Anti-Negro Play, *The Sins of the Father*, Sunday, March 26," *Broad Ax* (Chicago), 25 March 1911, p. 1, noting the failure of Ida B. Wells-Barnett (Ida B. Wells) and others to prevent Dixon from performing in his play at the Princess Theater, Chicago.

Knupfer cites an example of the cooperation between black and white women in the effort to curtail the impact of *The Birth of a Nation*: Celia Parker Wooley, a white Unitarian minister and clubwoman, and president of the Frederick Douglas Settlement Center in Chicago (a settlement co-founded in 1906 with Ida B. Wells) conducted strenuous lobbying to receive assurance from Chicago's mayor that the film would be withdrawn from Chicago (a promise not kept). See Knupfer, *Toward a Tenderer Humanity*, p. 60. Further research on the reception of and organized protest against *The Birth of a Nation* on the part of black women is needed.

According to Henry Sampson, in 1924 Miss Sadie Dorsey was the first African-American appointed to the Maryland Board of Film Censors, where her responsibilities were limited to the inspection of theaters catering to blacks. However, Dorsey's work suggests prior activity and agitation on the part of black women over film. See Sampson, *Blacks in Black and White*, p. 16. Knupfer cites evidence of several club women recorded as protesting against segregation of theaters and demanding immediate action, as reported in *Broad Ax*, 19 August and 4 November 1911, and 22, 25 May 1915. See Knupfer, *Toward a Tenderer Humanity*, p. 60.

20. Whitby, "The Future of the Cinematograph," reprinted in this volume; also reprinted in Colin Harding and Simon Popple, *In the Kingdom of Shadows: A Companion to Early Cinema* (Madison, NJ: Farleigh Dickinson University Press, 1996), pp. 21–2.
21. Mrs Henry Mansergh, "An Idyll of the Cinematographe," *Windsor Magazine* 7 (February 1898), pp. 363–8, reprinted in this volume.
22. Miss May, the female protagonist, remarks on Mr John Webb's second drink "in the last half hour" while watching the surreptitiously made film of her fiancé. While the 1897 Veriscope film of the *Corbett–Fitzsimmons Fight* was feature-length, (and one film that quite a number of women had seen, according to the historical record, as discussed in Part One), and while some passion play films were also about twenty minutes long (and about two hours long in a mixed slide and film program), they were the result of joining several sequences together. In Mansergh's story, a continuous film of thirty minutes' length is described; this was not yet a part of cinema culture. See Musser, *The Emergence of Cinema*, p. 218. During the early years of cinema, lantern slides were often part of the same program as a film projection, magic lanternists often entered the film business, and trade papers of the magic lantern profession evolved to cover matters of the cinema. In all these ways, Mansergh's fusion of the cinematograph with the magic lantern might be explained, but the machine she describes is certainly the motion picture camera rather than a still slide projector. The tsar and tsarina visited Paris on 5–9 October 1896, and the Lumière brothers made several films of their activities during their stay.
23. For discussions of the detective genre in early film and in literature from the time, see Stephen Bottomore, "Le thème du témoignage dans le cinéma primitif," in *Les Premiers Ans du Cinéma Français* (Perpignan: Institut Jean Vigo, 1985), pp. 155–9; and Tom Gunning, "Tracing the Individual Body: Photography, Detectives, and Early Cinema," in Leo Charney and Vanessa R. Schwartz, eds., *Cinema and the Invention of Modern Life* (Berkeley: University of California Press, 1995), pp. 15–45.
24. Gunning, "Tracing the Individual Body," p. 36, makes a similar observation.
25. Gilman, "Mind-Stretching," pp. 217–24, reprinted in this volume.
26. Ibid., p. 217, 218, 219.
27. Charlotte Perkins Gilman, "Public Library Motion Pictures," *Annals of the American Academy of Political and Social Science*, November 1926, p. 144.
28. Woolf's phrase (in Woolf, "The Movies and Reality," p. 309, reprinted in this volume) is "it was thus." Gilman, "Public Library Motion Pictures," p. 144.
29. Ibid.
30. Gilman's domestic metaphors are carefully considered; elsewhere in this essay she writes critically of the "kitchen-minded mother." (See Gilman, "Mind-Stretching," p. 217.) As a proponent of feminist apartment hotels and kitchenless suburban homes, she was keen to get women out of the kitchen, mentally and physically. See Dolores Hayden, "Domestic Evolution or Domestic Revolution," *The Grand Domestic Revolution: A History of American Feminist Designs*

for *American Homes, Neighborhoods, and Cities* (Cambridge, MA: MIT Press, 1981), particularly pp. 186–97.

31. Bertsch, *How to Write for Moving Pictures*, whose concluding chapter, "Motion Pictures: The Greatest Educational Force of All Times," pp. 272–5, is reprinted in this volume.

32. Ibid., p. 274.

33. Gilman suggests, in her example of a film showing the folly of women's fashion history, that the cinema can also provide a retrospective vision that will influence the future. Dress reform was a frequent topic of feminist endeavor, and might be compared with Fannie Hurst's contemporary argument in "Let's Not Wear Them!" *New Republic*, 30 October 1929, pp. 293–4.

34. This emphasis on the uniquely cinematic aspects of the motion picture's power, its capacity to suggest motion, was also to be found in the writings of Jean Epstein (among others) in France in the 1920s, as noted in Part Two. See also Münsterberg, *The Film: A Psychological Study*, for another, contemporary, analysis of cinema as following the contours of the human mind.

35. Stopes, "The Unsuspected Future of the Cinema," p. 28, reprinted in this volume. In contrast to Gilman, who saw the subject matter of formal education, particularly history, as contributing little to the future life and imaginative capacity of children—indeed, she claimed most of this knowledge was ultimately relegated to the "basement" of the mind or otherwise forgotten—Stopes found the study of history and literature valuable precisely because it facilitated the development of imagination.

36. Stopes, "The Unsuspected Future of the Cinema," p. 26, reprinted in this volume. Stopes had addressed the instructional value of film in a slightly earlier article, "A Real Use for the Cinema," *Bioscope*, 2 September 1915, pp. 1028–9. In 1915, the Cinema Sub-Committee of the Authors' Society, of which Stopes was a "distinguished member," polled a group of British professors and educational authorities, asking them about their current or anticipated use of the cinema in the classroom and lecture hall. Stopes reported on the results in her article. The raw data are held among her papers at the British Museum.

37. This observation is made by other writers discussed here. See, for example, Richardson, "Continuous Performance X: The Cinema in the Slums," pp. 58–62; and Moseley, "Films Have Taught Us What Life Means," p. 9, both reprinted in this volume.

38. Diehl, "The Moral Effect of the Cinema on Individuals," pp. 1125–6.

39. Talmadge referred to the "cheap thriller of a few years ago [which] gave false impressions of the lives and customs of other peoples." Talmadge, "The Mission of Motion Pictures," p. xxiv.

40. A fuller account of the activities of Hull House can be found in *Eighty Years at Hull House*, ed. Allen F. Davis and Mary Lynn McCree Bryan (Chicago: Quadrangle Books, 1969); Addams's own history can be found in her *Twenty Years at Hull House, with Autobiographical Notes* (New York: Macmillan, 1910). Chicago was the first city in the United States to institute a juvenile court, in 1899. The Chicago Women's City Club was very active in this development.

41. Addams, *The Spirit of Youth and the City Streets*, p. 45. Among adolescents' plights, Addams listed their exploitation as cheap labor, and their attraction to petty criminal activities. Although Addams had published much of the material previously in periodicals, she presented it in book form, "in the hope that it may prove of value to those groups of people who in many cities are making a gallant effort to minimize the dangers which surround young people and to provide them with opportunities for recreation." Addams, in her Foreword, *The Spirit of Youth and the City Streets*.

42. Ibid., p. 77.

43. Ibid., p. 78.

44. Ibid., p. 103, reprinted in this volume. In addition, wrote Addams, films made a conscious appeal to emotions whose force young audiences were ill-equipped to manage. In fact, thrills such as love, revenge, and jealousy weakened their already underdeveloped judgement; the call to a primitive code of morality did not foster the sense of participatory brotherhood that baseball, for instance, did.

45. Ibid., pp. 79–80.

46. Jane Addams, *A New Conscience and An Ancient Evil* (New York: Macmillan, 1912), p. 118.

47. For further discussion, including discussion of the unenforceability of this ordinance, see Rabinovitz, *For the Love of Pleasure*, pp. 122–36. Women were to continue to shape Chicago film

culture, buoyed by the momentum of the suffrage movement. While Louella Parsons was launching her career and making her name there in the 1910s, other women's groups fought for cinema reform. A report on cinemas by the Chicago Political Equity League was reviewed as follows: "One very tangible effect of the women's influence, backed by their voting power, in Chicago politics, is visible in the clean up campaign under way in moving picture houses." See "Chicago Women Voters Clean Up Film Plays," *Woman's Journal*, 1 April 1916, p. 106.

48. This point has been recognized in much recent scholarship. See Lindsay, "Is Any Girl Safe? Female Spectators at the White Slave Films"; Hansen, "Early Audiences: Myths and Models," *Babel and Babylon*, pp. 60–89; and Lauren Rabinovitz, "Temptations of Pleasure: Nickelodeons, Amusement Parks, and the Sights of Female Sexuality," *Camera Obscura* 23 (May 1990), pp. 71–89, now part of her *For the Love of Pleasure*.

49. Bowen, *Five and Ten Cent Theaters*, reprinted in this volume. See, for another example of such monitoring, Edward H. Chandler, "How Much Children Attend the Theatre, the Quality of the Entertainment That They Choose and Its Effect upon Them," *Proceedings of the Children's Conference for Research and Welfare* 1 (New York: G.E. Stechert, 1909), pp. 55–9; and George Esdras Bevans, *How Workingmen Spend Their Spare Time*, Ph.D. thesis, Columbia University, New York, 1913. In 1911, de Koven Bowen authored a study, "Our Most Popular Recreation Controlled by the Liquor Interest," also for the Juvenile Protective Association of Chicago, a forerunner of the Juvenile Protection Agency.

50. Addams's dedication read: "To my dear Friend Louise de Koven Bowen— with sincere admiration for her understanding of the needs of city children and with warm appreciation of her service as president of the Juvenile Protection Agency of Chicago."

51. Bowen, *Five and Ten Cent Theatres*, pp. 2, 9, reprinted in this volume.

52. Ibid., p. 10. Measures such as raising lighting levels during screenings, the use of deodorizing sprays, better ventilation, the addition of restrooms, and refreshments stands, and the toning down of posters all contributed to elevating the nickelodeon's reputation, changes recorded across the country at this time, as well as in Chicago. See Bowser, *The Transformation of Cinema*, p. 39. Lucy France Pierce notes some of these recent improvements in her "The Nickelodeon in *The World To-Day*," *Film Index* 3:41 (24 October 1908), pp. 4, 6, reprinted in this volume.

53. Fox, "Children and Picture Palaces," p. 706, reprinted in this volume.

54. Addams did not directly address the issue of the cinema's inducement to passivity, although her own pedagogical enterprises, described in *Twenty Years at Hull House*, clearly favored activity on the part of the child.

55. Addams also notes the overstimulation provided by the cinema and she discusses it, in the larger context of *The Spirit of Youth and the City Streets*, as but one facet of urban life's general bombardment of the senses.

56. E. Margery Fox's evidence, in *The Cinema, Its Present Position and Future Possibilities*, p. 132.

57. Ibid., pp. 132–33.

58. Fox, "Children and Picture Palaces," p. 703.

59. Louis Dop, "The Role and The Purpose of the International Educational Cinematographic Institute," *International Review of Educational Cinematography* 1:1 (July 1929), p. 19. The IIEC conceived its mission grandly:

> By the cinema language frontiers and even the limits of civilizations are overcome. The customs, the manner of living, the fashions, the ideas with which the public conceives social or private relations, all in fact, is material for the cinema that penetrates through various peoples, and if the films produced and presented to the public have for their object the elevation of the intellectual and moral level of the individual, it follows that the film exerts in this way its educational mission and contributes largely to create a solidarity of sentiment amongst the different peoples.

See Dop, "The Role and Purpose," p. 21. Although under the authority of the League of Nations, the Institute was juridically distinct from it as it had been created by a member state (Italy) rather than the League itself. The Institute's predecessor was L'Unione Cinematografica Educativa (LUCE), founded in Rome in September 1924, the first educational cinematographic organization under direct control of the state. Mussolini took an active interest in the affairs of LUCE and the subsequent Institute. Italy withdrew from the League of Nations in 1937.

Many references to the Institute give its title as the International Institute of Educational Cinematography. This appears to be the practice for articles written originally in English.

Articles originally written in French or Italian generally refer to the Institute as Dop does and use the acronym IECI. Here the practice of the English articles which use IIEC is followed.

60. The *Review* was published by the League of Nations Secretariat from July 1929 to December 1934. In January 1935, the journal was renamed *Intercine* and published under this title until December 1935. The August–September 1935 issue signaled a change in policy, being published in two and not five language editions: Italian, and "international" (English, French, German and Spanish combined). This policy continued until the final issue, in which it was announced that the IIEC was suspending publication of the international edition, "En raison de la situation internationale, et surtout à cause des difficultés résultant des restrictions apporteés, dans la plupart des pays, à l'exportation des divises." See *Intercine* 12 (December 1935), p. 1.

61. Previous meetings of the Commission, had been held in London in 1929, and Vienna in 1930. The Rome meeting was reported in *The International Women's News*, December 1931, p. 22, as "International Council of Women: Conference on Cinematography and Broadcasting."

62. "Director's Note," *International Review of Educational Cinematography* 3:12 (December 1931), p. 1067.

63. Ibid., p. 1069.

64. Harriet Hyman Alonso, *The Women's Peace Union and the Outlawry of War, 1921–1942* (Knoxville: University of Tennessee Press, 1989), p. 133.

65. Women's activism in such areas had grown out of the suffrage campaign. The Women's Peace Party (soon renamed the Women's International League for Peace and Freedom) had been founded in January 1915, with Jane Addams as its first head. Charlotte Perkins Gilman, Mary Heaton Vorse, and Lillian Wald were also members. Pacifism had divided the British suffrage movement during World War I, but afterwards many were to work for peace. Susan Kingsley Kent suggests that the experience of the First World War further divided the profile of British post-war feminism, splitting it between the "old" feminists (i.e. those with war experience of nursing or ambulance driving) and the "new" (those who remained at home). See "The Vote: Sex and Suffrage in Britain, 1916–1918," in Kent, *Making Peace: The Reconstruction of Gender in Interwar Britain* (Princeton: Princeton University Press, 1993), pp. 74–96. Historian Hyman Alonso has suggested that, in America, "a significant part of the larger peace movement of the interwar era was the women's peace movement," and that peace activism channeled much of the female energy that had, in the 1910s, been directed at suffrage. See Hyman Alonso, *The Women's Peace Union*, p. xvi.

66. Mme. La Contesse Apponyi, "The Cinema, Instrument of General Culture and Human Solidarity," paper for the Cinema Commission of the International Council of Women, *International Review of Educational Cinematography* 3:12 (December 1931), pp. 1138, 1139. La Contesse, President of the National Council of Hungarian Women, was married to Count Albert Apponyi, Hungarian chief delegate to the League of Nations, disarmament champion, pacifist, Hungarian Member of Parliament, and cabinet minister.

67. Ibid., p. 1138.

68. Note appended to ibid., p. 1139.

69. Ibid. This resolution was again made the following year by the Cinema and Broadcasting Commission of the International Women's Council at its October 1932 meeting in Rome. See Dreyfus-Barney, "The Cinema and Peace," p. 256. The 1931 meeting had been presided over by Dreyfus-Barney.

70. A similar inquiry was conducted by *La Revue du cinéma* (Paris) in 1931; also note the investigation of the Special Cinema Inquiry Committee of Birmingham, in England, and that of Sir James Marchant, also in England.

71. Eva Elie, "Should War Films Be Seen By Children?" *International Review of Educational Cinematography* 2:10 (October 1930), p. 1177, reprinted in this volume.

72. Eva Elie, "Open Letter to the Director of the IIEC," *International Review of Educational Cinematography*, 4 (August 1932), p. 604. See also her "Casus belli," *International Review of Educational Cinematography* 3:6 (June 1931), pp. 556–7.

73. Elie, in what appears to be a complete *volte-face* from her 1930 position, now wrote that while no child would desire war after having seen its horrors on-screen, "if the film exalt[ed] on the other hand the sense of heroism in defence against an aggressor, why not rejoice in such a proof of vitality." Elie, "Open Letter to the Director of the IIEC," p. 606.

74. Maria Martinez Sierra, "Internationalism and the Film," *International Review of Educational Cinematography* 5 (March 1933), pp. 175–6. Sierra was also a member of the International Committee for

the Protection of Infancy, another of the League of Nations' Committees, as well as a member of the Council of the IIEC. César Santelli noted a similar absence of pity in young children watching the film *Verdun, visions d'histoire*. His report of a Belgian inquiry into the impression of war films on children and adolescents was originally published in the *Mercure de France* and translated as "Children and War Films," *Living Age*, 1 August 1930, pp. 664–70.

75. Sierra, "Internationalism and the Film," p. 176. Here Sierra sees these weaknesses as also shared by "ignorant masses of peasants," "the masses" themselves, and women, who after all "copy the fashions which actresses launch in films."

76. Ibid.

77. Blake, "Brutality in Prize Fight Pictures," p. 7; Wald, "Grave Injustice to Colored People," p. 18; Marie Stopes, manuscript draft of a letter marked "re: Where Are My Children?", intended for publication in *The Times* (London), 1917, possibly published; and Fredi Washington, "Headlines, Footlights: Uncle Tom's Cabin," *People's Voice*, 5 February 1944, p. 22, all reprinted in this volume. (*Imitation of Life* (1934), discussed in Part Four, was such a film.)

78. In her memoir of campaigning against *The Birth of a Nation* in Chicago, Ida B. Wells lamented the paucity of protesters who had actually seen the film, for the recounting of second-hand reports had weakened the NAACP's case. Ida B. Wells, *The Crusade for Justice* (Chicago: Chicago University Press, 1970), pp. 342–3. See also Lillian Johnson's related comments on *Gone with the Wind*, discussed in Part Four.

79. On the reception of *The Birth of a Nation*, see Thomas Cripps, "The Reaction of the Negro to the Motion Picture Birth of a Nation," in Fred Silva, ed., *Focus on Birth of a Nation* (Englewood Cliffs, NJ: Prentice-Hall Inc., 1971), pp. 111–24; and Janet Staiger, "The Birth of a Nation: Reconsidering its Reception," in *Interpreting Films: Studies in the Historical Reception of American Cinema* (Princeton: Princeton University Press, 1992), pp. 139–53. Ida B. Wells described the successful rescinding of the film's permit in Philadelphia, in *Crusade for Justice*, p. 344.

80. See Streible, "A History of the Boxing Film, 1894–1915," pp. 235–57, for a discussion of legislation against boxing and boxing films. The Women's Christian Temperance Union, among other groups, pushed for a bill to stop fight films in 1897. Streible writes that "the most often heard voices of opposition came from women's groups" (see p. 241).

81. Wald's protest was based on first-hand experience of the consequences of racism for African Americans. Her account of her work, *The House on Henry Street* (New York: Henry Holt, 1915) is illustrated with a photograph of a playground of predominantly black children staffed by black nurses. On the neighboring pages Wald discusses "the difficulty of proper placement in industry experienced by the ordinary boy and girl [being] intensified in the case of colored juveniles" (p. 162). (African-American Florence Jacobs Edmonds worked at the Settlement as a visiting nurse in the late 1910s. See Shaw, *What a Woman Ought to Be and To Do*, p. 226.) NAACP correspondence mentioning Jane Addams's viewing of *The Birth of a Nation* in New York, as well as her negative views of the film, is held in the Julius Rosenwald Collection, University of Chicago.

82. Reconstruction (1865–77) was the political process by which Southern States were restored to normal relations in the Union after the American Civil War.

83. Washington, "Headlines, Footlights: Uncle Tom's Cabin," p. 22, reprinted in this volume. *Uncle Tom's Cabin* had been filmed many times by the time of Washington's response: Lubin Film Manufacturing Company, USA, 1903, one reel; Thanhouser, USA, 1910, 1,000 feet; Vitagraph, USA, 3 reels, 1910; Imp, USA 1913, 3 reels, directed by Otis Turner; Kalem, USA, 1913, 2 reels, directed by Sidney Olcott; World Producing Company, USA, 1914, 5 reels, directed by William Robert Daly; Famous Players Lasky, USA, 1918, 5 reels, directed by J. Searle Dawley; Universal Pictures, USA, 1927, 13,000 feet, directed by Harry Pollard, later revived with sound effects. Edwin S. Porter made a one-reel version in 1903 in the USA titled *Uncle Tom's Cabin; or, Slavery Days*. Geza von Radvanyi directed a wide-screen European version in 1965. Most of this information is taken from Lea Jacobs and Ben Brewster, *Theater to Cinema: Stage Pictorialism and the Early Feature Film* (Oxford: Oxford University Press, 1997), p. 232.

84. In *The Souls of Black Folk* (Chicago: A.C. McClurg, 1903), W.E.B. DuBois had described the non-acceptance of black emancipation.

85. The National Council of Public Morals (NCPM) had set up an inquiry into the declining British birth rate in 1913. The findings of this inquiry, the Report of the National Birth-Rate Commission, were published in June 1916. According to Annette Kuhn, the NCPM was interested in Weber's film firstly because it supported the findings of their inquiry, namely

that fertility decreased according to increase of income (suggesting that birth control was indeed practiced by the middle and upper classes), and secondly because it was indicative of the cinema's potential for socially useful purposes. In Great Britain, thanks to the patronage of the NCPM, the film was shown non-commercially. When a certificate for theatrical exhibition was applied for, it seems from all the evidence that it was denied by the British Board of Film Censors and the Home Office. A consequence of the NCPM's involvement with the Weber film was the NCPM's establishment of a Cinema Commission of Inquiry in late 1916. (Weber's film premièred in England on 8 November 1916.) See Annette Kuhn, *Cinema, Censorship and Sexuality 1909–1925* (London: Routledge, 1988), pp. 38–45. Stopes represented the Society of Authors, Playwrights and Composers on this Commission, and, in 1919, in recognition of the success of her book, *Married Love*, she was appointed to the National Birth-Rate Commission. The consequences of the connections between Stopes's antagonism towards Weber's film in 1917, her friendship with the widowed Bishop of Birmingham, president of the Cinema Commission of the NCPM, whom she had first met on this Commission, and her own role in the Cinema Commission remain unclear.

Anthony Slide reports that the Birth Control League in the United States objected to Weber's film on the same grounds that Marie Stopes had. See Slide, *Lois Weber*, p. 82.

86. This raises the very difficult question of how film can show something that did not or does not happen, a question that had been critical in discussions of the use of film to promote peace. In her chapter "War Films," published in 1931, C.A. Lejeune explained the issue this way:

> The time for films of war, even films to convince the public of the horrors of war, is definitely past. If the cinema is to serve its age, it must move with the age, and we are living in a world to-day that has got to build towards peace ... that has got to tackle the job of living without arms rather than recall the horrors of dying under arms....
> It may sound a little crazy to say that peace is good film stuff. We doubt it because we have inherited from our arts and histories a false idea of peace; as just not fighting; as a pause between action; as something ... a little bit dull. But the real peace is a fact of terrific energy.... It is our job ... to make peace as thrilling and urgent on the screen as war has been made by our predecessors. We have got to supply a positive to the negative of the war film....

Lejeune, *Cinema*, pp. 222, 223, 224. French Prime Minister and Minister for War during World War I, Georges Clemenceau had set the agenda here, on 11 November 1918, when he announced, "We have won the war ... now we must win the peace, and that will be perhaps more difficult."

87. *Married Love: A New Contribution to the Solution of Sex Difficulties*, first appeared on 26 March 1918, published by A.C. Fifield, London. It subsequently sold over a million copies and was translated into thirteen languages. June Rose, in *Marie Stopes and the Sexual Revolution* (London: Faber & Faber, 1992) p. 115, quotes from a letter written to Stopes shortly after the publication of *Married Love* :

> As a 30-years married and, I hope, broadminded woman, mother of six children, I read your *Married Love* and was disgusted with the filth.... You take upon yourself to teach us what surely nature herself does is [sic] an insult to all decent people and I fail to see the use at all except to excite people and cause a great deal of immorality.

Stopes's book formed the basis of a film, initially titled *Married Love*, retitled *Maisie's Marriage*, for which Stopes had written the script with Walter Summers, a prominent director of British films of the 1920s. The story advocated birth control within marriage. The film had a rocky ride past the British Board of Film Censors, incurring cuts of all references to birth control, a new title, and removal of Stopes's name from the credits.

88. In America, during the period 1933–34, approximately 89 per cent of teachers in public kindergartens and elementary schools were women, according to Mary L. Ely and Eve Chappell, *Women in Two Worlds* (New York: American Association for Adult Education, 1938), p. 48.

89. Richardson, "Continuous Performance: This Spoon-Fed Generation?" p. 306.

90. Loble, "A Western Woman's Opinion of Pictures," p. 820.

91. A Governess, letter, "How the Cinema could Help with Lessons," *Cinegoer*, 11 March 1916, p. 2.

92. Ibid., p. 2.
93. Colette, "Cinéma," from *Aventures Quotidiennes*, reprinted in *Colette at the Movies*, p. 61.
94. Mary Field. Interview with Lawrence Murray, "The Movies Come to the Schoolroom: An Interview with Mary Field of *Secrets of Nature* Fame," *Film Weekly*, 6 April 1934, p. 12.
95. Winifred Aydelotte, "The Little Red School House becomes a Theatre," *Motion Picture Magazine* 47 (March 1934), p. 34, and Weber, quoted in ibid., p. 85. According to Anthony Slide's study of Lois Weber, there is no evidence of these educational films having been made. See Slide, *Lois Weber*, p. 146.

The emphasis placed on the role of experience in the educational process, the value attached to the vividness of that experience, and the importance of the child's imagination and creative power are hallmarks of the Progressive tenor of American educational reform.
96. Jane Elliott Snow, "The Workingman's College," *Moving Picture World* 7:9 (27 August 1910), p. 458, reprinted in this volume. The trade press (where Jane Elliott Snow was published), keen to legitimate a medium that was still disparaged, eagerly embraced the argument for education (as had Laemmle, in his use of Addams's imprimatur). Late in 1911, *Moving Picture World* announced that, after a year of reporting items on cinema and education, it was establishing a special department to foster the spread of "the educational movement." See "The Moving Picture Educator," *Moving Picture World* (16 December 1911), p. 822. Specific articles relating to film and education were previously published in the "Education and Science" page, or in the section titled "In The Educational Field." Education and cinema had been treated by the publication since at least 1908, in "Moving Pictures as an Educator," *Moving Picture World* 3:21 (21 November 1908), p. 397, for example.
97. Snow, "The Workingman's College," p. 458, reprinted this volume.
98. Ibid.
99. In a slightly earlier article Snow made this connection between instruction and amusement explicit. She wrote of the cinema: "let us hope ... that it will eventually have a place in our schools, and in all our penal, reformatory, and philanthropic institutions, where both amusement and instruction are so much needed." See Jane Elliott Snow, "The Workingman's Theater," *Moving Picture World* 6:14 (9 April 1910), p. 547. See also Joseph Medill Patterson, "The Nickelodeons, the Poor Man's Elementary Course in the Drama," *Saturday Evening Post*, 23 November 1907, p. 10, reprinted in *Spellbound in Darkness: A History of the Silent Film*, ed. George C. Pratt (Greenwich, CT: New York Graphic Society, 1973), p. 46.

Constance Leupp, reporting in 1910 on a co-production of the Edison Company and the New York Milk Committee on a film designed to teach the virtues of clean milk, also noted this twofold nature of filmic education. She wrote: "The greatest difficulty in the use of the picture pantomime as an instrument of propaganda will be that of making the scenario serve the double duty of holding interest and giving instruction within the scope of its limited mechanism." Constance D. Leupp, "The Motion Picture As a Social Worker," *Survey* (27 August 1910), p. 740.
100. Field, "Can the Film Educate?", pp. 49–50.
101. Richardson, "Continuous Performance X: The Cinema in the Slums," pp. 58–62, reprinted in this volume.
102. Ibid., p. 61.
103. Barbara Low, "The Cinema in Education: Some Psychological Considerations," *Contemporary Review* (London) 128 (November 1925), p. 630; Richardson, "Continuous Performance: This Spoon-Fed Generation?" p. 307.
104. Richardson, "Continuous Performance: This Spoon-Fed Generation?" p. 307.
105. Ibid., p. 308.
106. Repplier, "The Unconscious Humor of the Movies," pp. 601, 605.
107. Ibid., p. 603.
108. Ibid., p. 607.
109. As Patrick A. Henry reported, "Her readiness to discuss the benefits of the moving picture industry has astounded many, who expected she would not dare advocate this particular form of amusement after it had been attacked by the press." See Patrick A. Henry, "Motion Views Win Jane Addams," *Show World* 1:2 (6 July 1907), p. 1.
110. Addams, *A New Conscience and an Ancient Evil*, p. 111. She countenanced screenings on topics such as tuberculosis and infant care when opening the Chicago Child Welfare Exhibit in 1911.

See "Child Welfare Exhibit in Chicago," *Moving Picture World*, 27 May 1911, p. 1185. (Thanks to Stephen Bottomore for this reference.)

111. See "Social Workers Censor Shows," *Chicago Tribune*, 3 May 1907, p. 3, cited in Rabinovitz, *For the Love of Pleasure*, p. 131; Addams, *Twenty Years at Hull House*, p. 386. For the opening of the Hull House nickelodeon, see *The Chicago Tribune*, 16 June 1907, p. 3. For a brief, three-month period, from 16 June 1907, Mrs Gertrude Britton ran a nickelodeon at Hull House, Jane Addams's response to the reforming debates of that year. Lee Grieveson points out that Addams conceived of the theater "mainly as a means of educating young boys, in line with the Boys Club at Hull House, which aimed to shape the 'moral codes' of boys in line with those of the 'more fortunate boys' who read the 'chivalric tales of Homer and Stevenson.'" Lee Grieveson, personal communication, quoting Addams, *Twenty Years at Hull House*, p. 172. Grieveson also points out that Mrs Gertrude Britton was quoted by the *Moving Picture World* as noting that "Funny pictures of the kind desired by the Hull House theater were difficult to find. Those of the 'slap-stick' and vulgar variety were numerous but not wanted"; she goes on to quote a young boy disaffected with the show. See *Moving Picture World*, 29 June 1907, p. 262. Addams's Hull House "theatorium of the higher class" is also reported in the Chicago trade paper *Show World* 1:2 (6 July 1907), p. 12, in which Addams's taste in film is taken to be indicative of a general upgrading of standards in cinema, and in which *Cinderella*, *Alladin* [sic] *and His Wonderful Lamp*, *Little Statue Seller*, and *Travels in Japan* are listed among the titles screened. This matter is expanded in Henry, "Motion Views Win Jane Addams," p. 1.

112. Jane Addams, letter printed in *Show World*, 3 August 1907, p. 32, reprinted in this volume. The advertisement also appeared in *Views and Films Index*, 10 August 1907, p. 10. See Rabinovitz on the advantages of Addams' name to Laemmle in *For the Love of Pleasure*, pp. 170–77. Laemmle had opened his first nickelodeon in February 1906 in Chicago, building up his film exchange thereafter. (See Musser, *The Emergence of Cinema*, p. 422). Addams was also named by H. H. Buchwalter as endorsing motion pictures. See *Views and Films Index* 2:52 (11 January 1908), p. 3.

113. Elie had (initially) suggested a similar spectatorial response to war films, where the viewer, recoiling in horror, would become convinced of war's folly. Both Field's and Elie's spectators identify with the victims of catastrophe—"this could be me"—the film potentially enhancing a moral edification, a recognition of self in the other, and, thence, the essential connectedness of mankind.

114. Germaine Dulac, "The Educational and Social Value of the News-reel," *International Review of Educational Cinematography* 6 (August 1934), p. 546, reprinted in this volume.

115. Ibid. Dulac calls such films the "mirror of any country." According to Richard Abel, these newsreel theaters began in 1931 with the five "Cinéac–Le Journal" theaters. By 1934 there were nearly twenty theaters devoted to newsreels throughout Paris. Richard Abel, *French Film Theory and Film Criticism: A History/Anthology, 1929–1939*, Volume II, (Princeton: Princeton University Press, 1988), p. 86 n8.

116. Ibid., p. 548.

117. Dulac, "The Meaning of Cinema," p. 1091.

118. The original form of Field's essay was presented as part of a series of public lectures organized by the British YWCA on the topic, "Are Films Worthwhile?" lectures subsequently published in a volume intended for the wider audience of "intelligent filmgoer[s]." See R. S. Lambert, "Introduction," in *For Filmgoers Only*, pp. 9, 10, a volume published in conjunction with the British Institute of Adult Education. Dulac delivered "The Meaning of the Cinema" at the 1931 Rome Conference, that women's forum formed for developing an international audience with a keen interest in the social and educational potential of cinema, while her news-reel essay was, in all likelihood, the paper she delivered as representative of France–Actualités–Gaumont at the April 1934 Teaching and Educational Conference sponsored by the IIEC in Rome, an international forum (with seven hundred delegates representing forty-five nations) also promoting the educational use of cinema, one opened by Mussolini. For a brief discussion of Dulac's role in French film culture of the 1920s and 1930s, see Sandy Flitterman-Lewis, *To Desire Differently: Feminism and the French Cinema* (Chicago: University of Illinois Press, 1990), pp. 86–9.

119. For Field, interview with Murray, "The Movies Come to the Schoolroom," p. 12. Dulac had also worked in the French commercial cinema for the Société des Cinéromans at different

points during the 1920s. Late in the 1920s she worked for Pathé Journal, and, in 1931, she became editor-in-charge of a new news-reel, France–Actualités–Gaumont.

120. In 1935 Dulac completed her montage of documentary scenes from the period 1905–35, *Le Cinéma au Service de l'Histoire*, a synthetic work developed from her experience in both actualities and the avant-garde, an amalgamation also to be detected in her "The Meaning of Cinema" speech.

121. See Field, "Can the Film Educate?" pp. 48–4, reprinted in this volume. Germaine Dulac made a similar plea in her "The Meaning of Cinema," p. 1089, and elsewhere. Field subsequently used infra-red photography to document the reaction of children in the cinema. See her "Unfinished Project," *Sight & Sound* 18:69 (Spring 1949), pp. 8–11. The filming of nature so that it can be made visible is also hard work, as Field explains in "Making Nature Films," *Sight & Sound*, Autumn 1932, pp. 70–71. For another instance of musical instruction via the camera, see Louise Kimball Baker, "Music Teachers and Movie Cameras," *Etude* 58 (March 1940), p. 166.

122. Dulac, "The Meaning of Cinema," pp. 1091, 1092. She writes that through film, "a plant is no longer simply a vegetable that charms ... but a sensitive organism ... whose reflexes we know."

123. Ibid., p. 1094.

124. Ibid.

125. For a discussion that links educational reform, the development of British cinema, and an intellectual cinematography, see Bryher, "Danger in the Cinema," *Close Up* 7:5 (November 1930), pp. 299–304. Bryher, who wrote one of the earliest books on Soviet cinema, was interested in Soviet film precisely because it understood its mission as an educational one. See also Bryher, "Children and the Cinema," *Outlook* (London), 21 August 1926, pp. 173–4.

126. Low, "Mind-Growth or Mind-Mechanization?" pp. 44–51. In an earlier article discussing two British reports on cinema's role in education, Low had already distinguished between these two aspects of cinema's potential educational force (its factual content, and its spectatorial affect), which together constituted "a method by which the human mind can be affected and directed," and had agreed with the reports' reservations about the passivity that the cinema may induce in children. Citing conclusions drawn from an experiment at Birmingham, she added: "The Cinema may even be fostering a quick and careless way of looking at things, develop[ing] the habit of the unseeing eye which never gets beyond the obvious." See Low, "The Cinema in Education," pp. 628–9, 630. The two reports were the Report of the Committee on the Use of the Cinematograph in Education (1924, Imperial Education Conference), and a "Report of the psychological investigation conducted by special sub-committees appointed by the Cinema Commission of Inquiry established by the National Council of Public Morals (NCPM)," *The Cinema in Education*, James Marchant (1925), secretary to the NCPM. Marie Stopes had earlier served as representative of the Society of Authors for the Cinema Commission of Inquiry, in 1917, as mentioned above.

127. Low, "Mind-Growth or Mind-Mechanization?" p. 51.

128. Ibid.. This occurred "both in the production and the spectator."

129. For a discussion of the figure–ground relationship in terms of spectatorial response, see Cardinal, "Pausing over Peripheral Detail," pp. 112–30. Gloria Waldron Grover's "Documentary Values in Fiction Films," *Films in Review* (May–June 1950), pp. 7–8, 47, tests the figure–ground relationship in fiction films.

130. In a 1934 pamphlet for high school students, Sarah MacLean Mullen gives the aims of photoplay appreciation. She writes:

> the motion picture habits of young Americans could be greatly improved in the English class; ... desirable attitudes could be developed through photoplay discussions; ... in a word, the cinema could give boys and girls worthwhile literary experiences and lead them to a fine selection of books.... The photoplay appreciation movements combines well with two new educational trends—the teaching of the proper use of leisure time and the new emphasis on social attitudes in the teaching of literature. If our millions of school students learn good standards for judging the photoplays they will inevitably see, there is likely to be at least a slight advance along the entire front of human thought.

Sarah MacLean Mullen, *How to Judge Motion Pictures and How to Organise a Photoplay Club* (New York:

Scholastic: The National High School Weekly, 1934), pp. 5–6. Mullen was the Head of the English Department at Abraham Lincoln High School, Los Angeles. The Film Education Movement in general saw watching films as an extremely active exercise, and in high schools in the 1930s film appreciation classes were widespread. Besides Mullen's, textbooks of instruction included Edgar Dale, *How to Appreciate Motion Pictures* [1933] (New York: Arno Press, 1970), and William Lewin, *Photoplay Appreciation in American High Schools. A Publication of the National Council of Teachers of English* (New York: D. Appleton Century, c 1934).

131. See, for example, British writer C.A. Lejeune advising: "Remember that the box-office controls the studio all the time and you—not the critics—not the exhibitors, but *you*—control the box-office" (emphasis in original). Lejeune, "'Eyes and no Eyes,'" p. 95. Field also expresses this view in "Can the Film Educate?"

132. *Extension Magazine* 29 (November 1934), p. 27, cited in Black, *Hollywood Censored*, p. 167.

133. See "Film Censorship in Italy," *International Review of Educational Cinematography* 2:4 (April 1930), pp. 500–505; "Film Censorship in Australia," *International Review of Educational Cinematography* 2:1 (January 1930), pp. 89–92. For the British case, see James C. Robertson, *The British Board of Film Censors: Film Censorship in Britain, 1896–1950* (Beckenham: Croom Helm, 1985), p. 5. The BBFC was in operation from 1913.

Elizabeth J. Clapp defines and discusses maternalism as follows:

> The kind of gender consciousness that prompted women to become involved in social welfare reform during the Progressive Era has recently been named 'maternalism' by a number of historians of women. Maternalism accepted, even idealized, women's traditional role as wife and mother but at the same time insisted that women had a duty to extend their female skills and concerns beyond their own houses. The discourse of maternalism insisted on women's role as universal mothers, making it the duty of all mothers to look after children.

See Elizabeth J. Clapp, *Mothers of All Children: Women Reformers and the Rise of Juvenile Courts in Progressive Era America* (University Park, Pennsylvannia: The Pennsylvannia University Press, 1998), pp. 3–4. As an ideology, maternalism was not dependent on the fact of biological maternity. As Clapp notes (p. 4), a number of women active in child welfare reform were not mothers.

134. "'Redfords of the Screen: Censors of Living Pictures,' the Work of the New York Board of Censors at the People's Institute," *Illustrated London News*, 22 April 1911, p. 585. Drawn by Jay Hambidge. This drawing is also illustrated in Harding and Popple, *In the Kingdom of Shadows*, p. 65, although the editors incorrectly suggest that it is an image of British censors at work. "Redfords" refers to Mr. G.A. Redford, who was to become director of the British Board of Film Censors on its establishment in late 1912, and who was to be assisted by a team of four examiners.

135. "Motion Picture Patents Company," *Moving Picture World* 4:12 (20 March 1909), p. 335, cited in Bowser, *The Transformation of Cinema*, p. 49.

136. Middleton, "Should Women Be Film Censors?" p. 7. Women's work in screenwriting is amplified in Part Five.

137. Like the American film industry, the British one was largely self-policing, through the work of the BBFC, although ties to Government were always closer than in the American case. The Cinematograph Act of 1909 had been the first piece of British legislation designed to regulate film exhibition. Ostensibly a safety measure (which required the licensing of theaters showing flammable films), it was soon being used by local authorities to restrict exhibition of films considered undesirable. By 1912, local government hold over film content was so strong as to invite centralized censorship. Trying to forestall this situation, the film industry approached Parliament and the BBFC was set up, an agency without legal status but with strong liaisons to Government. It classified, cut, or rejected films, while local authorities retained statutory power to reverse these rulings. (In the mid 1920s the Home Office intervened to establish uniformity regarding censorship, among the BBFC and local authorities, and this seems to have been successful until the early 1930s, when a number of authorities refused or cut films passed by the Board.) The habit of the BBFC meeting individual producers and distributors in advance, to anticipate the censorable consequences of projected films, began in around 1919.

There were four British censors for most of the period covered by this book, but, despite the 1912 recommendation mentioned above, the "first lady censor" of the BBFC, Mrs Redford, wasn't officially appointed until 1922. Later Mrs Crouzet would serve, as well as Madge Kitchener and Mary Field (1950–51). There was a suggestion in 1917 that the four-person team should expand, to four male censors and two female ones, with the assumption that each film would be viewed by at least two male censors and one female. See Robertson, *The British Board of Film Censors*, p. 30, and elsewhere.

The National Council of Public Morals' inquiry into the cinema, running for six months in 1917, supported by Government and done in cooperation with the BBFC, called on female opinion, including that of Stopes and Fox. Pressure groups on the BBFC included the right wing British Women's Patriotic League, and The National Association of Head Teachers, an organization with strong female representation. Robertson, *The British Board of Film Censors*, p. 38, and elsewhere. The British Women's Patriotic League protested directly to Prime Minister Stanley Baldwin for the suppression of *The Unknown Soldier* (1926), an American film which had, in their view, wrongly presented the "unknown soldier" as American and not British.

Among other women who might be mentioned as intervening in assessing or protesting cinema's power in Britain during this period are the National Council of Women in Birmingham; the National Union of Women Teachers of Bristol; Dr. Edith Summerskill, parliamentary secretary to the Ministry of Food; Labour MP Ellen Wilkinson, secretary to the Parliamentary Films Committee, which challenged the restrictiveness of BBFC rulings in 1930; and a British official wartime social survey conducted in 1943, 53 out of whose 54 investigators were women. See Kathleen Box and Louis Moss, *The Cinema Audience* (Wartime Social Survey, June–July, 1943, conducted for the Ministry of Information, Great Britain (New Series, No. 37b). (The National Council of Women in Birmingham had protested the exhibition of Weber's *Where Are My Children* in 1916, and, according to Robertson's research (see Robertson, *The British Board of Film Censors*, p. 152), also protested the certification of films by the BBFC in 1930.) Charles W. Key, in "Children and the Films," *Lansbury's Labour Weekly*, 9 January 1926, p. 14, refers to the "Conference of the National Union of Women Teachers of Bristol, where a resolution was passed calling attention to 'the evil effects on growing children of attendance at picture-houses, where undesirable films are exhibited.'" For Summerskill, who spearheaded public protest of *No Orchids for Mrs Blandish* in 1948, see Robertson, *The British Board of Film Censors*, p. 174; for Wilkinson, see Robertson, *The British Board of Film Censors*, p. 152.

For women in England writing against censorship and in favor of a liberalization of laws governing film exhibition, see also Dorothy M. Richardson, "The Censorship Petition," *Close Up* 6:1 (January 1930), pp. 7–11, an account of the Petition for the Revision of Film Censorship that the film magazine inaugurated in 1928. Richardson was actively involved in the work associated with the petition. She also wrote against censorship in "A Note on Household Economy," p. 58. Winifred Holtby protested the censoring of Eisenstein's *Battleship Potemkin* by the reactionary conservative Sir William Joynson-Hicks (popularly known as "Jix") of the Home Office, as did many other public figures, including Ivor Montagu. See Winifred Holtby, "JIX: His Refusal of a Private Showing of *Potemkin*," *New Leader*, 12 April 1929, p. 5; and the letters, including one by Ivor Montagu, collected under "Is 'Jix' Bluffing?", *New Leader*, 29 March 1929, p. 6. The possibility of involvement in film by the Co-operative Women's Guild, the largest women's organization in the Labour Party, would be a subject for further investigation.

138. Winifred Holtby, "Author's Note," *Poor Caroline* [1931] (New York: Penguin, 1986), p. vii.
139. Kuhn, *Cinema, Censorship and Sexuality*, p. 14.
140. In September 1923, Hays visited Liberal MP T.P. Connor (conceptual head of the BBFC) in Britain as well as British film producers; in 1937 there were discussions of installing a permanent representative of Hays's Production Code Administration in Britain. See Anthony Slide, *Banned in the USA: British Films in the United States and Their Censorship* (New York: I B. Tauris, 1998), p. 10.
141. Though further research may turn up more writings, there is no reference to the cinema in the collection of West's early journalism edited by Jane Marcus, *The Young Rebecca: Writings of Rebecca West 1911–1917* (New York: Viking Press in association with Virago, 1982), and a complete search of two of the journals for whom West wrote, *The Freewoman* and its subsequent reincarnation *The New Freewoman*, also reveals nothing by West on cinema. West's other non-fiction essay on film is "New Secular Forms of Old Religious Ideas," reprinted in this volume. Later, West returned to the question of censorship in her essay "Censorship," in *Censorship: For and Against*, ed. Harold Hart (New York: Hart Publishing, 1971), pp. 124–40, finding censorship

necessary in cases of literature or other media containing sadistic pornography involving children.

Although West's brief reference to cinema appears something of an afterthought in the *Keeping it Dark* essay, the overall structure of her text indicates that she believed that debates over film censorship belonged within other, larger discussions. Indeed, with both Radclyffe Hall's lesbian novel *The Well of Loneliness* and Eisenstein's *Potemkin*, these years must count as among the most contentious for British censorship, no doubt boosting sales of Holtby's *Poor Caroline* (set in London in the latter 1920s), as well as precipitating the founding of several new film societies (for both middle- and working-class patrons) to get around BBFC rulings, and liberal rallies for film, such as the one backed by Lady Cynthia Mosley in 1930. (For Mosley, see Robertson, *The British Board of Film Censors*, p. 51.)

Dorothy Knowles wrote her book on the political nature of censorship, *The Censor, the Drama, and the Film, 1900–1934* (London: Allen & Unwin, 1934), at this time.

(*Battleship Potemkin* was banned by the BBFC on 30 September 1926, following the nine-day General Strike in Britain of 1926, a decision only reversed at the BBFC in 1954. A second cycle of banning of showings at film societies took place in 1929, to which Dorothy Richardson and Winifred Holtby, among others, responded.)

142. West, "Preface," in Causton and Young, *Keeping it Dark*, p. 13, reprinted in this volume.
143. Williams, *Hard Core*, pp. 51–2.
144. West, "Preface," p. 8.
145. Rebecca West, "Concerning the Censorship," in *Ending in Earnest: A Literary Log* [1931] (Freeport, NY: Books for Libraries Press, 1967), p. 6.
146. West's essay would reward a much closer reading than can be given it here, particularly in light of its general pathologizing of homosexuality, apparently mapped onto a distaste for the corporeal in cinematic sound. Perhaps West did not care for the cinema, but this would not necessarily explain the revulsion evidenced in her essay. Some biographical dimension may be in play here. In later life, West wrote: "If I were young again, I would deliberately (and against my nature) choose to be a lesbian" (quoted in Victoria Glendinning, *Rebecca West: A Life* (New York: Alfred A. Knopf, 1987), p. 132). In another essay she described "the homosexual woman" as "neurotic." (See Rebecca West, "Woman as Artist and Thinker," in *Woman's Coming of Age: A Symposium*, ed. Samuel Schmalhausen and V. F. Calverton (New York: Horace Liveright, 1931), p. 371.) Regarding the *Well of Loneliness* obscenity trial, Arnold Bennett, E.M. Forster, and Leonard and Virginia Woolf rallied support for Radclyffe Hall's novel by organizing a petition protesting the work's suppression by the Home Office. The signatories included George Bernard Shaw, Lytton Strachey, T.S. Eliot, Storm Jameson, Rose Macaulay, Vera Brittain, Victor Gollancz, Julian Huxley, Sheila Kaye-Smith, John Middleton Murray, and Hugh Walpole. In addition, many writers agreed to testify in court including Vera Brittain, E.M. Forster, Sheila Kaye-Smith, Winifred Holtby, Rose Macaulay, Storm Jameson, Naomi Mitchison, John Middleton Murray, Leonard and Virginia Woolf, and Desmond MacCarthy. Rebecca West's name did not appear on either list. According to a recent biography of Radclyffe Hall, West was "appalled at the Home Office action but did not feel this was a good case on which to fight censorship." (Sally Cline, *Radclyffe Hall: A Woman Called John* (Woodstock, NY: Overlook Press, 1998), pp. 256.) West did, however write a response against the censor ("Jix") in *Time and Tide* during the trial's proceedings: "A Jixless Errand," *Time and Tide*, 15 March 1929, pp. 282–6. She also indirectly defended the absence of her name among those protesting the censorship of the book in "Concerning the Censorship," where she proposed that *The Well of Loneliness* was of insufficient literary quality to support such a fight. See West, "Concerning the Censorship," pp. 6–12.
147. Loos, contribution to "In Defense of Hollywood," p. 21; Katharine Fullerton Gerould, "Hollywood: An American State of Mind," *Harper's Magazine* 146:876 (May 1923), pp. 690, 694, both reprinted this volume.
148. "Deluded Women," *Christian Century*, 6 December 1933, pp. 1527–29; "Revamping the Vampires," *Nation* 113: 2927 (10 August 1921), p. 140; Otis Ferguson, "Weep No More, My Ladies," *New Republic* 102:23 (3 June 1940), pp. 760–61. Gerould found these women smug, dogmatic, and needing to be "psychoanalysed" (Katharine Fullerton Gerould, "The Nemesis of the Screen," *Saturday Evening Post*, 8 April 1922, p. 12); Cogdell labelled them weak and "neurotic" (Cogdell, "Truth in Art in America," p. 634, reprinted this volume); Loos dubbed them "citizens of saintly" towns (Loos, contribution to "In Defense of Hollywood," p. 21, reprinted in

this volume); and Ethel Mannin, writing in London, on "Films Which Cheapen Love," hoped she didn't sound like "a member of a Middle West purity league" (Ethel Mannin, "Films Which Cheapen Love," Film Weekly, 24 May 1930, p. 7). The reputation of such women was well known to Catherine de la Roche who, writing in England, in 1949, commented: "Some of the most pedantic censoring is attributed to the bluestockings on boards and committees, especially in America, where, I gather, women's organizations play a prominent part in local censorship, exercising an influence which, together with the Legion of Decency, sometimes merely encourages those lamentable white-washing dodges." (See de la Roche, "That 'Feminine Angle,'" p. 29, reprinted in this volume.) With the intertitle "the church board investigates," Loos had already, in her first screenplay, The New York Hat, filmed by D.W. Griffith in 1912, disparaged elderly female reformers who snoop on an apparently unseemly liaison. (Elderly female reformers also play a crucial part in the modern story of D.W. Griffith's film Intolerance (1916).) "Women Fail to Halt Sunday Shows," Motion Picture News, 6 June 1917, p. 31; Merriam, "Solving the Motion Picture Problem," pp. 167–8, reprinted in this volume; A. S. Richardson, "Better Films a Community Asset," Woman's Home Companion, January 1923, p. 17.

149. "The Kinetograph," New York Sun, 28 May 1891, p. 1, quoted in Musser, Edison Motion Pictures, p. 76.

150. "A Tribute to Moving Picture Shows," Moving Picture World 3 (7 March 1908), p. 181, cited in Black, Hollywood Censored, p. 13.

151. "Motion Picture Patents Company," p. 335, cited in Bowser, The Transformation of Cinema, p. 49. The New York Board of Censorship was renamed the National Board of Review in 1915, although its goal of national scope was not realized. Chicago regularly refused films carrying the Board's seal of approval, and a number of regions established their own censorship bodies with power to override the New York-based Board. Mutoscopes, kinetoscopes, and illustrated lectures using motion pictures had been subject to occasional, local censorship in the United States right from the beginning, in 1896. For more on the New York Board of Censorship and the National Board of Review, see Robert Fisher, "Film Censorship and Progressive Reform: The National Board of Censorship of Motion Pictures, 1909–1922," Journal of Popular Film and Television 4:2 (1975), pp. 143–56; Charles Matthew Feldman, "The National Board of Censorship (Review) of Motion Pictures, 1909–1922 (New York: Arno Press, 1977), pp. 20–87; and Shelley Stamp, "Moral Coercion, or the Board of Censorship Ponders the Vice Question," in Matthew Bernstein, ed., Regulating Hollywood: Censorship and Control in the Studio Era (New Brunswick, NJ: Rutgers University Press, 1999), pp. 41–58.

152. A 1920 study commissioned by the General Federation of Women's Clubs had found that 80 per cent of all motion pictures examined were either "bad" or "not worth while." Ruth Inglis, Freedom of the Movies: A Report on Self-Regulation from the Commission on Freedom of the Press (Chicago: University of Chicago Press, 1947), p. 63.

153. Vasey, The World According to Hollywood, p. 28.

154. Cooperation with women's groups was not always successful. In 1926, the General Federation of Women's Club's was to resign from Hays's Public Relations Committee. The National Congress of Parents and Teachers also resigned from the Committee in 1926. See Walsh, Sin and Censorship, p. 30. Two competing histories of Hollywood's relations with women's groups are provided in Gilman, "Better Movies—But How?", and Winter, "And So to Hollywood," both reprinted in this volume.

155. See Jacobs, The Wages of Sin, pp. 106–31.

156. See Richard Maltby, "The Genesis of the Production Code," Quarterly Review of Film and Video 15:4 (1995), pp. 5–32. Producers were now required to submit film scripts or plans to the PCA before beginning production, and any films screened without the PCA seal of approval risked a $25,000 penalty. The system worked as a public relations activity, and as a method of self-censorship, for about twenty years, petering out from 1952 onwards with the challenge of Otto Preminger's The Moon is Blue. The PCA finally closed its doors in 1968.

157. Motion Picture Producers of America, The "Open Door," (New York: Motion Picture Producers of America, 1924), cited in Vasey, The World According to Hollywood, p. 37.

158. Maltby, "The Genesis of the Production Code," p. 5.

159. Winter had already had some years of experience with Will Hays, having been appointed to the MPPDA's Committee on Public Relations in 1922. Josephine Littlejohn, "What Ten Million Women Want," Motion Picture 40 (December 1930), pp. 66, 100, 112. Hays himself was known as "the Czar of the Movies." Hays's wooing of women continued throughout the early 1930s.

See Florence Fisher Parry, "The Friendly Movies," *Delineator*, April 1933, p. 34, for an appeal to the readers of this woman's magazine to become "participants" rather than critics in efforts to improve the industry.

160. Mrs. Ambrose A. Diehl, "Women and the Cinema," *International Review of Educational Cinematography* 6 (1934), pp. 400–405, reprinted in this volume; the earlier speech was published as Mrs Ambrose A. Diehl, "The Moral Effect of the Cinema on Individuals," *International Review of Educational Cinematography* 3 (1931), pp. 1123–37. Diehl was also chairman of the Motion Picture Department of the League of American Pen Women, and, in 1932, wrote a regular column titled "Recommended Motion Pictures" for *Ladies' Home Journal*.

161. Diehl, "The Moral Effect of the Cinema on Individuals," p. 1123. Here Diehl also writes that women's common maternal role makes them guardian of the "atmosphere of the family," that "Unit of Civilization."

162. Diehl, quoted in "Women Present Plea for Film Progress to League Institute," *Motion Picture Herald*, 17 October 1931, p. 20, cited in Richard Maltby, "The Cinema and the League of Nations," in Andrew Higson and Richard Maltby, eds., *"Film Europe" and "Film America": Cinema, Commerce, and Cultural Exchange, 1920–1939* (Exeter: University of Exeter Press, 1999), p. 103.

163. Diehl, "The Moral Effect of the Cinema on Individuals," p. 1125. To this end she endorsed the homeopathic theory of war films (shortly to be abandoned by Elie), citing several studies on the effects of motion picture viewing on children.

164. Diehl, "The Moral Effect of the Cinema on Individuals," p. 1127.

165. Diehl listed some of the programs of public education organized by the General Federation of Women's Clubs: advance previews of new releases; the development of family and children's screening programs; protest against or support for selected films; and the development of a motion picture study program covering the "history, business, art, personalities and moral standards" of foreign and domestic film. See Diehl, "The Moral Effect of the Cinema on Individuals," pp. 1129 and 1132.

166. Diehl, "The Moral Effect of the Cinema on Individuals," p. 1132; Diehl, "Women and the Cinema," p. 400.

167. Headlines are cited in *Daily Report*, K.L. Russell to Will Hays, 19 October 1931, Hays Papers, quoted in Maltby, "The Cinema and the League of Nations."

168. Maltby, "The Cinema and the League of Nations," pp. 102–3, citing a memo from Frederick Herron to Will Hays, 10 October 1931, Will H. Hays Papers, Department of Special Collections, Indiana State Library, Indianapolis..

169. Diehl, "The Moral Effect of the Cinema on Individuals," p. 1135.

170. The Better Films Movement was an offspring of the National Committee for Better Films, formed in 1914, itself a child of the National Board of Review.

171. Anon, "Louise Connolly" [obituary], *National Board of Review Magazine* 2:8 (August 1927), pp. 3, 9.

172. Koszarski, *An Evening's Entertainment*, pp. 208, 209.

173. Pare Lorentz and Morris Ernst, *Censored: The Private Life of the Movie* (New York: Cape & Smith, 1930), p. 110, quoted in Koszarski, *An Evening's Entertainment*, p. 208.

174. Richardson, "Better Films a Community Asset," p. 17. The service started at least as early as 1922. For two very different examples of Richardson's writing on the motion picture, from the time before her work with the Good Citizenship Bureau, see her "Who Gets Your Dime?", *McClure's Magazine* 46 (November 1915), pp. 21–22; and "'Filmitis,'" pp. 12–14, 70.

175. Richardson, "Better Films a Community Asset," p. 17.

176. Cited in Larry May, *Screening Out the Past: The Birth of Mass Culture and the Motion Picture Industry* (Oxford: Oxford University Press, 1980), p. 53.

177. Janet Priest, "Films—And Your City's Welfare," *Photoplay* 16:3 (August 1919), p. 53. According to an editorial article in *Photoplay* 14:4 (September 1918), pp. 75, 117, titled "The Photoplay League of America,""The Photoplay League of America" was established by 1918, with Myra Kingman Miller, president of the National Federation of College Women and "one of the foremost feminists and public workers in the United States," as its secretary. The same article also announces that *Photoplay* was the League's official journal, and that it had, at last, become a national organization.

178. Published as Scott F. Fitzgerald, "Our Own Movie Queen," *Chicago Sunday Tribune*, 7 June 1925, pp. 1–4 (Magazine Section), reprinted in this volume.

179. Baird, "The Feminine Mind in Picture Making," *Film Daily*, 7 June 1925, p. 115.

180. According to Ellen Anderson, *Guide to Women's Organizations: A Handbook About National and International Groups* (Washington, DC: Public Affairs Press, 1949–50), pp. 52–3, as of 1949–50 IFCA had approximately 500,000 members. IFCA published the *Quarterly Bulletin of the International Federation of Catholic Alumnae.*

181. Inglis, *Freedom of the Movies*, pp. 100–103. See also Mary Harden Looram, "National Recognition for our Motion Picture Bureau," *Quarterly Bulletin of the International Federation of Catholic Alumnae* 5 (March 1936), pp. 15, 22.

182. Walsh, *Sin and Censorship*, p. 33.

183. A.S. Richardson, "Talking Pictures and Community Taste," *Woman's Home Companion* 57 (January 1930), p. 32. For a discussion of IFCA activities and the training of its reviewing staff, see Skinner, *The Cross and the Cinema*, pp. 40–50. IFCA was generally cooperative with the Hays Office, in part because it worked on the principle of educated consumption (rather than trying to affect film production per se), and the precept "praise the best and ignore the rest" (an approach encouraged by the industry). By contrast, the male-dominated Legion of Decency, founded in 1934 on a policy of blacklisting objectionable films, and a huge force behind the establishment of the PCA, was highly critical of Hays. The Legion was also, if more quietly, critical of the reviewing efforts of its Catholic sisters, who, in 1936, were recognized by the Catholic Church as the Legion's official reviewing group. (The Legion of Decency worked at a pastoral level through a pledge system in which the Catholic faithful were exhorted to boycott films the Legion deemed immoral. In addition to these efforts to direct film consumption, the Legion became an active force in shaping film production through its historical ties to the Production Code Administration (PCA). The Production Code of 1930 had been the work of an influential Catholic layman, the film trade publisher Martin Quigley, and a Jesuit priest, Daniel A. Lord. When the PCA was founded, in 1934, Catholic bishops associated with the Legion supported the appointment of Joseph I. Breen as the PCA's head. For the negative views expressed by bishops associated with the Legion of Decency, and directed towards IFCA's film reviewing, see Walsh, *Sin and Censorship*, pp. 118, 119). While the two Catholic organizations ran parallel to one another for a time, it was the Legion, intent on modifying scripts, cutting, and the like, that was to became more intimately integrated into Hays Office practices in the long run.

184. *Endorsed Films* is discussed by Richard de Cordova in "The National Congress of Parents and Teachers, the Cinema, and the Agenda of Reform, 1920–1940," paper delivered 2 March 1995, Society for Cinema Studies Annual Conference, New York City.

185. Merriam, "Solving the Motion Picture Problem," pp. 167–68, reprinted in this volume.

186. Anon, "The End of the Line," p. 450.

187. De Cordova, "The National Congress of Parents and Teachers."

188. "Deluded Women," pp. 1527–9.

189. Gilman, "Better Movies—But How?", pp. 10–12, 34–5.

190. Ibid., p. 12.

191. Block-booking and blind-bidding did not finally end until 1948, when the US federal government divested film companies of their vertically integrated monopolies, in what was known as the Paramount Decree.

192. Memo, Herron to Hays, 10 October 1931, Hays Archive, quoted in Maltby, "Cinema and the League of Nations."

193. Elizabeth Gilman, "Catheryne Cooke Gilman, Social Worker," *Women of Minnesota: Selected Biographical Essays*, ed. Barbara Stuhler and Gretchen Kreuter (St. Paul: Minnesota Historical Society Press, 1977), pp. 190–207.

194. Catheryne Cooke Gilman, "Government Regulations for the Movies," *Christian Century* 48 (26 August 1931), pp. 1066–8.

195. Catheryne Cooke Gilman, "The Movie Problem: The Program of the National Congress of Parents and Teachers," *Ladies' Home Journal*, July 1934, p. 104.

196. Winter, "And So to Hollywood," pp. 7–9, 45–6, reprinted in this volume.

197. Ibid., p. 46.

198. Ibid.

199. Rinehart, "How About the Movies," pp. 21, 77–80. Roberts Rinehart held a three-year screenwriting contract with Samuel Goldwyn from 1919 onward, during which time she co-wrote one feature that was produced. Over twenty of her novels and short stories were adapted for the screen.

200. Ibid., p. 79.
201. Ibid., p. 80.
202. Ibid.
203. Gerould, "The Nemesis of the Screen," pp. 12, 157, reprinted in this volume.
204. Gerould wrote as a parent, rather than as a mother. The question of a parent's control over children's viewing was also an aspect of the debate over the effect of war films. Eva Elie wrote:

> And let us in this matter hear no more of parental rights as opposed to those of the State. How about 'the rights of the child,' which Victor Hugo called 'even more sacred than the paternal right and identical with the rights of the State'? For the State has the right of every community to protect itself against any influences that aim at its destruction.

Elie, "Casus Belli," p. 557.
205. For a slightly different argument about the Hollywood-ization of America, see Gerould, "Hollywood: An American State of Mind," pp. 689–96, reprinted in this volume.
206. Loos, contribution, "In Defense of Hollywood," p. 21, reprinted in this volume.
207. A.S. Richardson, "It's Up to the Box Office," Woman's Home Companion, November 1931, p. 54.
208. Ibid. She added, "so long as less discriminating theater-goers dominate the box office ... the stupid and salacious picture of crime and sex, sex and crime, will continue to besmirch the silver screen."
209. Laura Whetter, "The Triumph of Screen Virtue," Film Weekly, 22 March 1930, p. 6.
210. Film censor Helen Tinguely, a member of the Maryland State Board of Motion Picture Censors, described this process. She doubted that film viewing had any real effect on children, and argued that censors could not make movies "fit" for children; labeling films "Adults Only" increased children's desire to see them and encouraged them to "read all sorts of suggestive meanings into innocent lines and situations." When censorship justified itself by arguing the need to protect children, it created a false alarm. See Helen Tinguely, quoted in Stanley Frank, "Headaches of a Movie Censor," Saturday Evening Post 220 (27 September 1947), p. 72.
     Mary Field wrote of the capacity of children to make informed, independent judgements about motion pictures, while Lady Allen of Hurtwood, in reviewing children's Saturday cinema clubs in post-World War II Britain, argued that children could easily accommodate themselves to the conventions of genre films "far removed from their everyday life" while being "intensely critical" of films "dealing with people or situations familiar to them." See Mary Field, "The Child-Mind and the Screen," radio broadcast for "Britanskyi Soyusnik," a Soviet Radio program, transcript, British Film Institute, n.d. (c. 1944–45); Lady Allen of Hurtwood, "Children and the Cinema," Fortnightly, July 1946, p. 5; "Report of the International Cinematographic Institute," School and Society 34:864 (18 July 1931), p. 84; as well as Mary Field, "The Audience," in Good Company: The Story of the Children's Entertainment Film Movement in Great Britain, 1934–50 (London: Longmans, Green, 1952), pp. 58–77.
211. Breckenridge, Women in the Twentieth Century, p. 92.
212. Adela Rogers St. Johns, The Honeycomb (Garden City, NY: Doubleday, 1969), pp. 17–26. According to St. Johns's recollection, this debate would have taken place shortly after women won the vote, between 1920 and 1924, years in which Mrs Winter was president of the GFWC.
213. Barbara Low, "The Cinema in Education," p. 630.
214. Agnes Repplier, "The Repeal of Reticence," Atlantic Monthly 113 (March 1914), pp. 297–304.
215. William Leach, True Love and Perfect Union: The Feminist Reform of Sex and Society (New York: Basic Books, 1980).
216. Douglas, The Feminization of American Culture.
217. Rabinovitz, For the Love of Pleasure, p. 122.
218. Blair, The Clubwoman as Feminist, pp. 102–5. Giuliana Muscio suggests that the Paramount decree, which finally stopped block booking and the related practice of blind bidding in 1948, was one of the legacies of Franklin Delano Roosevelt's New Deal. See Muscio, Hollywood's New Deal, p. 195. Her study does not cover women's earlier efforts to secure this legislation.
219. See Nancy K. Bristow, Making Men Moral: Social Engineering During the Great War (New York: New York University Press, 1996). Bristow argues that the Progressively informed CTCA, a federal agency created shortly after the United States joined the war, worked against ethnic and

working-class leisure habits in favor of more homogenous "American" types of recreational and social practice.

220. Marie Stopes, *Ancient Plants* (London: Blackie, 1910); Marie Stopes, co-authored with Professor J. Sakurai, *Plays of Old Japan, the No* (London: Heinemann, 1913); *The Sportophyte* lasted from 1910 to 1913.

221. Andreas Huyssen has assessed this history, "noting the persistent gendering as feminine of that which is devalued," and the repeated habit of naming mass culture "feminine" and thereby inferior, from the late nineteenth century onwards, and indeed up to the decline of modernism in the 1950s and 1960s. Andreas Huyssen, *After the Great Divide: Modernism, Mass Culture, Postmodernism* (Bloomington: Indiana University Press, 1986), p. 53.

Part Four

1. Addams, *The Spirit of Youth and the City Streets*, p. 8.

2. Underhill, "Imitation Chinchilla," p. 107, reprinted in this volume. See Charles Eckert, "The Carol Lombard in Macy's Window," *Quarterly Review of Film Studies* (Winter 1978): 1–21, for a study of the phenomena of tie-ins and fashion sales.

3. Pauline Kael, *The Citizen Kane Book* (Boston: Little, Brown, 1971), pp. 40, 58. Kael argues that female reporters in newspaper films were all based on Rogers St. Johns, Hearst's star woman reporter, a regular columnist for *Photoplay*, and an influential writer on the film industry, who famously observed that Hollywood celebrity was like "living in a goldfish bowl." Adela Rogers St. Johns's striped suits were cut, in the 1910s at least, by Eddie Schmidt, a man's tailor. The wearing of hats by critics continues: *Los Angeles Times* columnist Pat Morrison wears a trademark hat, and when she is attacked, she is often compared to Hedda Hopper.

4. Hedda Hopper, *From Under My Hat* (Garden City, NY: Doubleday, 1952). Hedda Hopper also wrote "The Hats in My Life," (undated, c. 1940s), a four-page typescript (marked *The Woman Magazine*) held in the "Autobiographical File," Hedda Hopper Collection, Margaret Herrick Library, Academy of Motion Picture Arts and Sciences Library, Los Angeles (reprinted in this volume), and wrote a weekly column on fashion for the *Washington Herald* in 1935.

5. In "Fan Discourse in the Heartland: Gertrude Price and the *Des Moines News*, 1912–14," a paper given at the conference *Women and the Silent Screen*, November 2001. Richard Abel proposes that Gertrude Price was the earliest syndicated writr on the movies.

6. "Vultures of Hollywood," *American Mercury*, March 1943, p. 345. *Variety* constitutes a notable exception to this trend. While Cecilia Ager wrote for *Variety*, and while it supported the notion of feminine authorship with the column byline "The Skirt," relatively few of its writers have been women.

7. "Irene Thirer, 59, Movie Reviewer" [obituary], *New York Times*, 20 February 1964, p. 29.

8. Flanner wrote for the *Indianapolis Star* from 1917 to mid 1918. Her film column, "Comments on the Screen," ran in the *Indianapolis Star* for the last two months of this period. (She later became Paris correspondent for the *New Yorker*, and, writing under the pseudonym "Genêt," covered that city for almost fifty years.) George Eells quotes Louella Parsons's report of Flanner's seven-week trip to the West "exploit[ing] the advantages of *The Heart of Humanity*," in around 1918. Eells, *Hedda and Louella*, pp. 49–50. For more examples of Flanner's film writing see Slide, *They Also Wrote for the Fan Magazines*, as well as examples reprinted in this volume. Mollie Panter-Downes wrote occasional articles for *Film Weekly* during the 1930s and then became the London correspondent for the *New Yorker* for several decades. Two collections of her popular wartime reporting for this magazine were published as *Letter From England* (Boston: Little, Brown, 1940) and *London War Notes* (London: Longman: 1972). For an early example of Porter's writing about film, see "The Week at the Theaters," *Critic* (and) *Camp Bowie Texahoma Bugler* [Fort Worth, Texas] 3:5 (12 January 1917), p. 3. Katharine Anne Porter worked in film publicity (as had Flanner) to supplement her income from fiction, joining the Arthur S. Kane Pictures Corporation in 1920 to help with promotion. (See Slide, *They Also Wrote for the Fan Magazines*, p. 115.) Sally Benson, whom Louella Parsons befriended while in New York in the late 1910s, turned to novels and screenplays after writing film criticism for *Picture-Play Magazine* and elsewhere. She was the original author of the work that was adapted for the screen as

Meet Me in St. Louis (1944), and co-wrote *Shadow of a Doubt* (1943), *Anna and the King of Siam* (1946), *The Farmer Takes a Wife* (1953), and *The Flying Nun* (1966), among others.

9. For "spectatorium," see Patterson, "The Nickelodeons, the Poor Man's Elementary Course in the Drama," p. 10, reprinted in Pratt, *Spellbound in Darkness*, p. 46; "Gladys Glycerine, Theater Owner, Banker, Cry Real Tears Together," *Business Week*, 10 August 1932, p. 14; "Films of the Soil," in Lejeune, *Cinema*, pp. 232–39.

10. Evelyn Gerstein, "Three Russian Movies: Expression Gives Way to the Realities," *Theatre Guild Magazine*, October 1929, pp. 14–15; Madeleine Carroll, "Treating Women too Well," *Film Weekly* (31 January 1913), both reprinted this volume. Winifred Holtby, "Children in the Spotlight," *The Schoolmistress*, 19 January 1933, pp. 425, 447; Winifred Holtby, "Reforms and Films," *The Schoolmistress*, 16 February 1933, p. 538.

11. Elsie Cohen. Interview with Anthony Slide. "Elsie Cohen, in an Interview with Anthony Slide," *Silent Picture* 10 (Spring 1971), not paginated.

12. Eells, *Hedda and Louella*, p. 50.

13. See Kauffmann, *American Film Criticism*, pp. 5–6. See also Loundsbury, *The Origins of American Film Criticism, 1909–1939*. It is generally agreed that, in the United States, Frank Woods, writing for the *New York Dramatic Mirror* from 1908 onwards as "The Spectator," was the first film critic to build a personal identity through his columns, in this case through championing D.W. Griffith's films.

14. According to Anthony Slide, Henry Hart assumed female names as pseudonyms for his film reviews published in *Films in Review*, names taken from headstones in a Brooklyn cemetery. From speaking with Adela Rogers St. Johns, and others, Slide also concludes that "Cal York" was a pseudonym, since the column was a collection of paragraphs by various authors (conversation with Slide, 24 June 1994). See also Mae Tinee, *Life Stories of the Movie Stars* (Hamilton, OH: Presto Publishing, 1916); "The Letters of Morphia Money," *Film Weekly*, 4 January 1930, p. 20; and "Norma Mahl" [Robert Herring], "Second-Rate Sex, September 1929," pp. 471–9.

15. "Filmore's Inside Film Talk," *Moving Picture News*, 2 September 1911, p. 17. Thanks to Iris Cahn for this reference.

16. Fay M. Jackson's "Pay of 'Green Pastures' Cast Irks Hollywood," *Baltimore Afro-American*, 25 January 1936, p. 11, is collected as a typescript, with Jackson's name on it, titled "Fear *Green Pastures* New Yorkers May Spoil Hollywood: Claim Connolly Scrimps on Salaries," Associated Negro Press, *California News* 1935/36, Claude A. Barnett Papers, Box 287, Folder 20, and microfilm reel 01071, Chicago Historical Society, while it appears without a byline in the *Baltimore Afro-American*. According to Heywood Hale Broun, his mother, Ruth Hale, began her career as a professional journalist at eighteen, in 1904. She wrote uncredited film reviews beginning some time after 1910 for the Philadelphia *Public Ledger*, before moving to New York where she worked for *Vogue* and the *New York Times* (and gained renown as the co-founder and president of the Lucy Stone League in 1921, an organization of women dedicated to retaining their "maiden" names after marriage). See Heywood Hale Broun, *Whose Little Boy Are You? A Memoir of the Broun Family* (New York: St. Martin's/Marek, 1983). According to Ishbel Ross, Hale successfully fought her battle with the US State Department on the passport issue, becoming "the first woman to go abroad under her maiden name." Ishbel Ross, *Ladies of the Press: The Story of Women in Journalism by an Insider* (New York: Harper & Bros., 1936), p. 259.

17. On Nellie Bly, born Elizabeth Jane ("Pink") Cochran, see Brooke Kroeger, *Nellie Bly: Daredevil, Reporter, Feminist* (New York: Times Books, 1994). Bly got her first newspaper job on the *Pittsburgh Despatch* in 1885, after writing an angry letter protesting the newspaper's stand against women's suffrage. Djuna Barnes, "How It Feels To Be Forcibly Fed," *New York World Magazine*, 6 September 1914, reprinted in Djuna Barnes, *New York*, ed. with a commentary by Alyce Barry (Los Angeles: Sun & Moon Press, 1989), pp. 174–9. This collection also includes a reprint of Barnes's account of women attending prize fights, "My Sisters and I at a New York Prizefight," originally published in *New York World Magazine*, 23 August 1914. See Barnes, *New York*, pp. 168–73. Jeanie Macpherson, chief scenario writer for Cecil B. DeMille, was arrested, convicted, and went to jail for three days to prepare herself for scripting the film *Manslaughter*. See Jeanie Macpherson, "'I Have Been in Hell'—Or in Search of Prison Knowledge," *Movie Weekly*, 19 August 1922, pp. 10, 27, 29.

18. Dorothy Dix and Annie Laurie were leading representatives here. See Barbara Bedford, *Brilliant Bylines: A Biographical Anthology of Notable Newspaper Women in America* (New York: Columbia University Press, 1986), p. 3.

19. Mabel Condon covered mainly West coast filmmaking, while Alison Smith covered mainly the East coast. For Mabel Condon see, among others: "Keystone: The Home of Mack Sennett and the Film Comedy," *New York Dramatic Mirror*, 9 September 1916, pp. 32, 36; "The Lasky Studio," *New York Dramatic Mirror*, 28 October 1916, pp. 34–6, 38, 42–3; "Yorke-Metro Studios—Hollywood's Home of Artistic Picture Production," *New York Dramatic Mirror*, 2 December 1916, pp. 34, 40. For Alison Smith, see "Little Journeys to Eastern Studios I—Astra," *New York Dramatic Mirror*, 14 July 1917, p. 10; "Little Journeys to Eastern Studios II—Metro," *New York Dramatic Mirror*, 21 July 1917, p. 10; "Little Journeys to Eastern Studios III—Biograph," *New York Dramatic Mirror*, 28 July 1917, p. 11; "Little Journeys to Eastern Studios IV—Goldwyn," *New York Dramatic Mirror*, 4 August 1917, p. 11; "Little Journeys to Eastern Studios V—Vitagraph," *New York Dramatic Mirror*, 8 August 1917, p. 11; "Little Journeys to Eastern Studios VI—Paramount," *New York Dramatic Mirror*, 18 August 1917, p. 10; and "Little Journeys to Eastern Studios VII—World Film," *New York Dramatic Mirror*, 1 September 1917, p. 13. In 1917, Louella Parsons was sent by the Chicago *Record-Herald* to report on studios in New York, and across the Hudson, in New Jersey.
20. Richard Abel, *French Cinema: The First Wave, 1915–1929* (Princeton: Princeton University Press, 1984), p. 242.
21. Agnes Smedley, "The Cultural Film in Germany," *Modern Review* (Calcutta), July 1926, pp. 61–6. Smedley lived with Communist-led Chinese troops from 1939 to 1940—the Chinese Revolution lasted from 1926 to 1949. See Jan and Steve MacKinnon, "Introduction" in Agnes Smedley, *Portraits of Chinese Women in Revolution* (Old Westbury, NY: The Feminist Press, 1976), pp. ix–xxxv. For examples of Dunnigan's writing, see Alice A. Dunnigan, "D.C. Downtown Movie Theaters End Ban on Negroes," Associated Negro Press, 17 January 1953 and Alice A. Dunnigan, "Approximately 400 Attend Premiere of *Prejudice* in Washington," Associated Negro Press, 1 February 1950, both held in the Claude A. Barnett Papers, Box 298, Folder 1, Chicago Historical Society. See Roger Streitmatter, *Raising Her Voice: African-American Women Journalists Who Changed History* (Lexington: University of Kentucky Press, 1994), pp. 107–17.
22. Dilys Powell, "Introduction," in Helen Fletcher, *Bluestocking* (London: Pandora Press, 1986), p. v. Thanks to Anthony Slide for information on Edith Nepean, Adele Whitely Fletcher, Radie Harris, and Ruth Waterbury. Radie Harris, *Radie's World* (New York: G.P. Putnam's Sons, 1975).
23. Anna Steese Richardson's speech quoted in Mary Kelly, "Women Journalists Attend Selznick Luncheon to Anna Steese Richardson," *Moving Picture World* 53:8 (24 December 1921), p. 930, cited by Wendy Holliday, "Hollywood's Modern Women: Screenwriting, Work Culture, and Feminism, 1910–1940" (Dissertation, New York University, 1995), p. 126.
24. Stanley Kauffmann lists three male critics who crossed over to work in the film industry: Epes Winthrop Sargent, a scenario writer who wrote articles about film and scenario writing; Robert E. Sherwood, a dramatist and scenario writer, who was the film critic for the pre-Henry Luce *Life*, from 1920 to 1928; and Frank S. Nugent, film critic of the *New York Times* from 1936 to 1940, who became a screenwriter. Kauffmann, *American Film Criticism*, p. 52 for Sargent, p. 337 for Nugent, p. 112 for Sherwood. Julian Johnson, former editor of *Photoplay*, later wrote titles for many important silent films and, in 1932, became a story editor at Fox. See "Preface," by Anthony Slide, ed., *Selected Film Criticism Vol. II, 1912–1920* (Metuchen, NJ: Scarecrow, 1982), p. xii.
25. Vicki Baum, *Falling Star*, trans. Ida Zeitlin (Garden City, NY: Doubleday, 1934).
26. Winifred Horrabin, "Rudolph Valentino: The Sheik and The Son of the Sheik," *Lansbury's Labour Weekly*, 16 October 1926, p. 12; and "Metropolis," *Lansbury's Labour Weekly*, 9 April 1927, p. 4, both reprinted in this volume.
27. Colette, "Luxury," *Filma*, 15–30 August 1918, first published as "Cinema" in *Excelsior*, 14 May 1918, p. 3, reprinted as "The French Cinema in 1918" in *Colette at the Movies*, pp. 42–6, reprinted in this volume.
28. Djuna Barnes, "The Wanton Playgoer," *Theatre Guild Magazine*, May 1931, p. 32; and Muriel Rukeyser, "Movie," *New Masses*, 12 June 1934, p. 28, both reprinted in this volume.
29. Eells, *Hedda and Louella*, p. 187. Eells is citing a critical essay on Parsons by Richard Watts in the *New York Herald Tribune*, 16 April 1939, a response to her article of 7 April 1939. As Neal Gabler notes in his study of Walter Winchell, a Broadway gossip columnist employed by the Hearst press and occasional rival to Louella Parsons and Hedda Hopper, Hearst directed his gossip columnists to avoid issues he deemed controversial. Gabler reports that when Winchell used

his column to denounce foreign dictators shortly after Hitler had annexed Austria, Hearst gave all his editors *carte blanche* to cut Winchell's columns. Neal Gabler, *Walter Winchell: Gossip, Power and the Culture of Celebrity* (New York: Alfred A. Knopf, 1994), pp. 272–3.

30. Graves, quoted in Morris, "Says Negro Should Be in All Pictures," p. 19; cited in Buchanan, *A Study of the Attitudes of the Writers of the Negro Press*, p. 74.

31. See Washington, "Imitations: Life, Color, and Pancakes," p. 185; and Fay Jackson, "Fredi Washington Strikes New Note in Hollywood Film: *Imitations*," Associated Negro Press, 12 December 1934, Typescript, Claude A. Barnett Papers, Box 298, Folder 15, Chicago Historical Society, both reprinted in this volume.

32. Ross, *Ladies of the Press*, pp. 409–10.

33. According to Ross, Irving Cobb is credited with inventing the phrase "sob sister," which "in time [became] the hallmark of the girl reporter." Ross, *Ladies of the Press*, p. 65. "Flicker" is the term the film journalist-cum-detective Asphodel Smythe uses for herself in Anthony Asquith's 1928 film about film, *Shooting Stars*; for "vulture," see "Vultures of Hollywood," pp. 345–50. Another term was "hack," as in Carl F. Cotter, "The Forty Hacks of the Fan Magazines," *Coast*, February 1939, pp. 18–21. These opprobrious terms were not always restricted to women.

34. Cotter, "The Forty Hacks," p. 21.

35. Eells, *Hedda and Louella*, p. 12, although Eells adds that they probably exaggerated the figures.

36. See, for example, *American Film Criticism*, which includes fifty-six male authors, six female authors, six anonymous ones, and three with initials only, and Slide's multi-volume series, *Selected Film Criticism*, which runs up to 1960, and which includes one hundred men, nineteen women, thirty anonymous items, and eight with initials only. Of course, many factors shape selection in such collections—copyright status, quality, informative value, previous republication use—and these have a large impact on sex ratio, the balance of which may not have been under consideration by the editors. (Thanks to Talitha Espiritu for tallying these figures). Cecelia Ager is the only woman included in Alistair Cooke's 1937 collection of film criticism, *Garbo and the Night Watchmen*. In his preface to the 1971 edition, Cooke writes of his regret in omitting the work of *Observer* critic C.A. Lejeune. *Garbo and the Night Watchmen* ed. Alistair Cooke (New York: McGraw-Hill, 1971), p. 8. On the question of anonymity, see *American Film Criticism*, pp. 13, 19.

37. See Washington, "Imitations: Life, Color, and Pancakes," for the latter.

38. Deming was working with a group of scholars responsible for recommending films for preservation by the Library of Congress, Siegfried Kracauer being consulted on the project, as mentioned above. The group's headquarters was the Museum of Modern Art, where Iris Barry, curator of the Museum's Film Library, had established a set of selection criteria. See Barbara Deming, "The Library of Congress Film Project: Exposition of a Method," *Library of Congress Quarterly Journal of Current Acquisitions* 2:1 (November 1944) pp. 3–36.

39. Powell's cultivation of her critical persona included a measure of self-deprecation. In an April 1959 column devoted to the art of criticism, titled "Criticism is not an Exact Science," she recalled receiving her first fan letter, in April 1944:

> I opened the letter with girlish optimism. "Your 'criticism,'" it began, "strikes me as being rather cheap and crude. I realise, of course, that being a 'critic' and a woman, it is your natural desire to appear to your readers as 'intellectual' a type as possible, and to show yourself as *thoroughly appreciative* of all foreign films, particularly those having the ever-fashionable theme of a good, interested, as-twisted-as-possible sex complex as a basis, so dear to the hearts of the majority of women. Your judgement bears as much crude resemblance to a really fair, decent, and constructive criticism as a lump of butter to a howitzer. Please," the writer thoughtfully concluded, "do not bother to reply."

Powell adds, "For sentimental reasons I have treasured the letter." See *The Dilys Powell Film Reader*, ed. Christopher Cook (Oxford: Oxford University Press, 1992), p. 417. Powell began reviewing films for the *Sunday Times* in 1939. In his Preface to a collection of Powell's writings, Christopher Cook cites Powell's recollections of a film-viewing rate of nine films per week for a decade in 1949, at a reviewing length of 1,200 words per column. *The Dilys Powell Film Reader*, p. xi.

40. Meaghan Morris, "Indigestion: A Rhetoric of Reviewing," *The Pirate's Fiancée: Feminism, Reading, Postmodernism* (London: Verso, 1988), pp. 117, 118.

41. Dismorr, "Matinee," pp. 31–2, reprinted in this volume. Thanks to Tom Gunning for discussion about this poem.

42. At one end of La Croisette is the Palais de Festivals, site now of the Cannes Film Festival. Sophie Croisette was also a famous young French actress of this time.

43. Richardson, "Continuous Performance: Dialogue in Dixie," pp. 211–18, reprinted in this volume.

44. Djuna Barnes, "Playgoer's Almanac," *Theatre Guild Magazine* (September 1930), p. 34.

45. Djuna Barnes, *Ladies Almanack* (Paris, 1928) (New York: Harper & Row, 1972).

46. Iris Barry, [poem] "The Challenge," included in C.A. Lejeune, "Can Piccadilly Do Without Hollywood?" *New York Times*, 24 August 1947, p. 32 (original source *London Observer*, n.d.), reprinted in this volume.

47. Lejeune, "At the Films," p. 2; Lejeune, "Humoresque," p. 2.

48. Anthony Slide has collected over one hundred examples in his *The Picture Dancing On the Screen*. See also *The Faber Book of Movie Verse*, ed. Philip French and Ken Wlaschin (London: Faber & Faber, 1993). Two important American poets who wrote extensively on the cinema were Vachel Lindsay, author of one of the earliest studies of film aesthetics (*The Art of the Moving Picture*), and Carl Sandburg, who reviewed films for the Chicago *Daily News* from 1920 to 1927. A selection of Sandburg's criticism can be found in *Carl Sandburg at the Movies: A Poet in the Silent Era, 1920–1927*, ed. Dale and Doug Fetherling (Metuchen, NJ: Scarecrow Press, 1985).

49. Anderson, "Emasculating Ibsen," p. 36, reprinted in this volume. (Jane Heap, co-editor of the *Little Review*, was later a member of the Board of Directors of Associated Film Audiences (AFA), a pro-labor group promoting the production of progressive films. AFA published *Film Survey*.)

50. Evelyn Gerstein, "What I Saw in the Film Studio," *Moscow News*, 10 October 1935, pp. 3, 9 (Thanks to Peter Decherney for this reference). Many women mentioned in this collection were particularly attracted to writing about Soviet film, to wit Bryher, Catherine de la Roche, Marie Seton, June Head, Nerina Shute, and C.A. Lejeune. Thyra J. Edwards discussed the Russian experience of African-American performer Wayland Rudd, one of a group of twenty-two African Americans who had sailed to the Soviet Union in 1932 to make a film about "Negro life" for the Mezhrapbom Studios, in "American Negros in Soviet Plays and Films," *Negro Liberator*, 22 December 1934, p. 2. Writers Langston Hughes and Dorothy West were also among the group, although the film, *Black and White*, was never made. A fuller account of this venture is to be found in Marjorie Smith, *From Broadway to Moscow* (New York: Macaulay, 1934).

51. *The Cheat* was widely praised for its stylistic invention on its release, particularly its experimental lighting and color tinting. However, the film had a controversial reception in Great Britain, where it was banned because the villain's identity was Japanese and Japan was fighting on the Allied side during the First World War. The villain's ethnic identity was altered in the 1918/19 reissue of the film, so that the actor Sessue Hayakawa was now "a Burmese ivory king" rather than a Japanese one. It is this latter version that is now in circulation. See also the brief discussion of *Potemkin*'s fate in Britain, noted in Part Three.

52. Louella O. Parsons, *Tell it to Louella* (New York: G.B. Putnam's Sons, 1962), p. 7.

53. Louella O. Parsons, *How to Write for the "Movies"* (Chicago: A.C. McClurg, 1915, rev. edn, 1917). Parsons's book was serialized after it was initially sold to the publisher.

54. Fetherling and Fetherling, *Carl Sandburg at the Movies*, pp. 5–6.

55. Eells, *Hedda and Louella*, p. 45.

56. Ibid., p. 50.

57. Ibid., p. 92, and elsewhere.

58. Cari Beauchamp, *Without Lying Down: Frances Marion and the Powerful Women of Early Hollywood* (New York: Lisa Drew/Scribner's, 1997), p. 333.

59. Gladys Hall, "The Lady Who Knows It All: Hollywood Can't Keep Any Secrets From Hedda Hopper," *Motion Picture Magazine*, June 1931, pp. 47, 93, 113.

60. Eells, *Hedda and Louella*, p. 21.

61. In Billy Wilder's *Sunset Boulevard* (1950), an allegory of Hollywood, Hedda Hopper appeared as herself.

62. Eells, *Hedda and Louella*, pp. 122, 130, 210, 246.

63. Beauchamp, *Without Lying Down*, p. 337.

64. Parsons was reported to have been privy to a Hearst cover-up of events surrounding the death

of the director Thomas Ince, shortly after he had attended a sailing party on Hearst's yacht in 1924. Eells refutes this suggestion. See Eells, *Hedda and Louella*, pp. 84–8.

65. Jules Dassin, quoted in Eells, *Hedda and Louella*, p. 16.

66. Eells, *Hedda and Louella*, p. 199. See also, however, Anthony Slide, "Hedda Hopper's Hollywood," *Los Angeles Reader*, Section 1, 4 April 1986, pp. 1, 8–9, 12, for a discussion of the contents of the Hedda Hopper holdings at the Academy of Motion Picture Arts and Sciences Library. As Slide concludes, "Those files prove that Hopper, unlike her rival Louella Parsons, was a major political figure in Hollywood. Louella's only interest was in a scoop; Hedda's was in protecting her country against communism" (p. 12).

67. For Janet Flanner's report on the international media frenzy that surrounded the subsequent birth of Bergman's child, Renato Roberto Giusto Giuseppe Rossellini, see her "Movie Scandal," originally published in the *New Yorker* (April 1950), and reprinted in *Janet Flanner's World: Uncollected Writings 1932–1975*, ed. Irving Drutman (New York: Harcourt Brace Jovanovich, 1979), pp. 276–86. For a discussion of forced abortions, see Milton, *Tramp*, pp. 419–20.

68. Olwen Hufton, *The Prospect Before Her: A History of Women in Western Europe*, Vol. 1, 1500–1800 (New York: Alfred A. Knopf, 1996), pp. 56, 192.

69. Parsons, *Tell It To Louella*, p. 316.

70. Gerould, "The Nemesis of the Screen," p. 157, reprinted in this volume.

71. Eells, *Hedda and Louella*, p. 12. Unfortunately, Eells does not specify when this was. Grover Jones gives the figure of 306 accredited reporters in Hollywood in 1938. See Grover Jones, "Knights of the Keyhole," *Collier's*, 16 April 1938, p. 25. "100,000 words a day," according to Daniel J. Boorstin, *The Image: A Guide to Pseudo-Events in America* (New York, Atheneum, 1961; 25th Anniversary Edition, 1987), p. 154. Boorstin claims a figure of 300 reporters for Hollywood in its heyday of newsworthiness.

72. Slide, "Preface," *Selected Film Criticism: 1912–1920*, p. xii. See Richard de Cordova, *Picture Personalities: The Emergence of the Star System in America* (Urbana: Illinois University Press, 1990), who argues that the American film star system emerged from 1909 onwards.

73. Gaylyn Studlar, "The Perils of Pleasure? Fan Magazine Discourse as Women's Commodified Culture in the 1920s," *Wide Angle* 13.1 (1991) Reprinted in *Silent Film*, ed. Richard Abel (New Brunswick, NJ: Rutgers University Press, 1996), p. 264. Studlar later notes that "a more realistic circulation figure is probably 500,000," p. 293 n. 4. She also argues in this article that scandal was the province of the daily press rather than the fan magazine, which often worked to contain or diffuse potentially harmful information about the star by concentrating on aspects of domestic and romantic life.

74. For "mash note," see Fredda Dudley, "Usually They Want Something," *Ladies' Home Journal*, January 1941, p. 79, which refers to many more male fan writers than female; for "hypnotized," see Ernest A. Dench, "Strange Effects of Photoplays on Spectators," *Illustrated World* 27 (July 1917), p. 788. This article gives a ribald account of the misfortunes of filmgoers, including the example of a woman who, while watching Svengali in *Trilby*, went into a trance.

75. As an example of the kind of reader response fostered by the fan magazine, see Helen Beal's prize-winning essay, "Confessions of a Photoplay Fan," *Photoplay* 50:1 (July 1936), pp. 32–3, 100, 102. For another example of the invitation for reader participation see the advertisement in *Hearst's International-Cosmopolitan*, July 1925, p. 169, asking girls to write in with a photograph, saying why they're suited to a part in a Pathé serial film. Joan Crawford's article, "The Job of Keeping at the Top," *Saturday Evening Post* 205 (17 June 1933), p. 75, illustrates for readers their supposed impact on the screen by recounting how she, Crawford, after receiving umpteen letters from fans urging her to use less lipstick, had complied.

76. *Girls' Cinema* was a British fan magazine, one twinned with *Boys' Cinema* (1919–40). According to Ross Ballaster, Margaret Beetham, Elizabeth Frazer, and Sandra Hebron, *Women's Worlds: Ideology, Femininity, and the Woman's Magazine* (London: Macmillan Education, 1991), p. 119, *Women's Filmfare* began publication in London in 1935.

77. Ivy Crane Wilson was Hollywood correspondent for *Star* (London) and published her album in London from the 1940s to the 1960s. (Thanks to Anthony Slide for this information.)

78. *Film Weekly*'s discourse on femininity and the cinema included a debate on women's directorial capabilities (discussed in Part Five), as well as one on the more familiar topics of beauty and personal charm—Marthe Troly-Curtin, "Beauty is an Art—and a Science," *Film Weekly*, 6 May 1929, p. 17, is one of the many articles on feminine appearance. Others were flip in tone, such as that by actress Anne Grey anticipating "badder—and better—vamps" on screen

(Anne Grey, "Badder—and Better—Vamps," *Film Weekly*, 25 March 1932, pp. 7, 26), and that by Nerina Shute explaining the specialized vocabulary of current Hollywood speech. (Nerina Shute, "A Vulgar Film Dictionary," *Film Weekly* (26 July 1930), p. 19.)

79. Moseley, "Films Have Taught Us What Life Means," p. 9; Taylor, "How Films Have Changed Women," p. 9; Violet M. Taylor, "Women and Films," p. 9. For a critical view, see Mannin, "Films Which Cheapen Love," p. 7, and her solution, in "Screen Love As I Would Treat It," *Film Weekly*, 28 September 1931, pp. 8–9.

80. Bloom, "The Films that Women Want," p. 7; Anony"Do Films Libel Women?: Famous Writers Reply to Madeleine Carroll," *Film Weekly*, 7 February 1931, p. 6; Carroll, "Treating Women too Well," p. 9, reprinted in this volume. For examples beyond *Film Weekly*, see Brown, "Making Movies for Women," p. 342, reprinted in this volume; de la Roche, "That 'Feminine Angle,'" pp. 25–34, reprinted in this volume; Davidman, "Women: Hollywood Version," pp. 28–31, reprinted in this volume.

81. May Edginton, "The IT-Less British Girl," *Film Weekly* (17 December 1928), p. 9.

82. See Anthony Slide, *The Encyclopedia of Vaudeville* (Westport, CT: Greenwood Press, 1994), p. 160. For more on Julian Eltinge, see Laurence Senelick, "Lady and the Tramp: Drag Differentials in the Progressive Era," in *Gender in Performance: The Presentation of Difference in the Performing Arts*, ed. Laurence Senelick (Hannover and London: University Press of New England, 1992), pp. 26–45 (Thanks to Anna McCarthy for this reference). Gladys Hall, starting out on her career as an interviewer of stars, was also intrigued by the Eltinge phenomenon, as she discusses in *Motion Picture Classic*, March 1918, pp. 21–3, 79–80. Gladys Hall Collection, Margaret Harrick Library, Academt of Motion Picture Arts and Sciences.

83. Hopper, "The Hats in My Life," reprinted in this volume.

84. Richard Dyer introduces this notion in *Heavenly Bodies: Film Stars and Society* (New York: St. Martin's Press, 1986), p. 13: "Stars not only bespeak our society's investment in the private as the real, but also often tell us how the private is understood to be the recovery of the natural 'given' of human life, our bodies." See Colette, "Mae West," in *Colette at the Movies*, pp. 62–3; Ager, "Mae West Reveals the Foundation of the 1900 Mode," pp. 67, 86, both reprinted in this volume.

85. Freda Bruce Lockhart, "This Was Jean Harlow," *Film Weekly*, 28 August 1937, p. 27.

86. See Joan Crawford explaining the hard work of stardom to a general audience during the Depression in Crawford, "The Job of Keeping at the Top," pp. 14–15, 75. De la Roche, "That 'Feminine Angle,'" reprinted in this volume.

87. Simone de Beauvoir, *Brigitte Bardot and the Lolita Syndrome*, trans. Bernard Fretchman (New York: Reynal, 1960); first published in *Esquire*, August 1959.

88. Ibid., pp. 16–32.

89. Suckow, "Hollywood Gods and Goddesses," pp. 192, 193, reprinted in this volume; Lejeune, "Mary Pickford" in *Cinema*, pp. 56–62. Lejeune's text oddly occludes Pickford's notoriously swift divorce and remarriage to Douglas Fairbanks.

90. Allene Talmey, "Gloria Swanson ... Mirror of the Movies," *Vogue*, 15 August 1941, pp. 79, 104, 111.

91. Suckow, "Hollywood Gods and Goddesses," p. 189.

92. Ibid., pp. 199, 200.

93. Ibid.

94. Gerould, "Hollywood: An American State of Mind," p. 693, reprinted in this volume.

95. Ibid., p. 694. Compare Gerould's comments with those of Pauline Kael in "Zeitgeist and Poltergeist: Or, Are Movies Going to Pieces? Reflections from the Side of the Pool at the Beverly Hills Hotel" [1964], reprinted in Kael, *I Lost It at the Movies* (New York: Little, Brown, 1965; Bantam edition 1966), pp. 3–5. Kael writes: "What 'sensible' people have always regarded as the most preposterous, unreal and fantastic side of life in California—the sun palace of Los Angeles and its movie-centered culture—is becoming embarrassingly, "fantastically" actual, not just here but almost anywhere. It embodies the most common, the most widespread dream...."

96. Djuna Barnes, "Ye Gossips Tayle" in "Playgoers Alamanac," *Theatre Guild Magazine*, September 1930, p. 35, reprinted in this volume.

97. Janet Flanner, "Comments on the Screen," *Indianapolis Star*, 14 July 1918, Section 5, p. 38, reprinted in this volume.

98. One might make comparisions here, in terms of method, to Robert Warshow's "The Gangster

as Tragic Hero," *Partisan Review* 15:2 (February 1948), reprinted in Robert Warshow, *The Immediate Experience* (Garden City, NY: Doubleday, 1962), pp. 127–33, and to Kracauer's *From Caligari to Hitler*.

99. Penelope Houston, "Mr Deeds and Willie Stark," *Sight and Sound*, November 1950, pp. 276–9, 285, reprinted in this volume.

100. Ibid., p. 277.

101. Ibid., p. 276.

102. West, "New Secular Forms of Old Religious Ideas," reprinted in this volume.

103. Gladys Hall poem, "Rudolph Valentino: In Memoriam," 1926, Rudolph Valentino Files, Motion Picture Department, George Eastman House, Rochester, reproduced in this volume.

104. Deming, "Love through a Film," p. 168, 225, reprinted this volume. Powell, "The Black Film," p. 2, reprinted this volume. In a review of Walt Disney's *The Three Caballeros* (1945), Deming similarly found that the film invited the scrutiny of the "psychoanalyst, or the social analyst—the inquirer into the mythos, the ethos of the times." Disney revealed, in his artlessness, the predominant wartime mood and opinion that the world was falling apart. See Barbara Deming, "The Artlessness of Walt Disney," *Partisan Review* 12:2 (Spring 1945), p. 226.

105. Powell, "The Black Film," p. 2, reprinted in this volume. It is possible that in this title, Powell (or the London *Sunday Times* editorial office) is translating the French term "film noir," given her knowledge and affiliation with French publication on film. She had published in the wartime, London-based, Free French publication *La France Libre*, in 1945, for example (Dilys Powell, "Le cinéma anglais en temps de guerre," *La France Libre* 9:53 (15 March 1945), pp. 349–52), and had a lifelong interest in French cinema, holding French film criticism to have the highest standard. See section titled "The French," for a grouping of Powell's writing on French cinema, in *The Dilys Powell Film Reader*, pp. 159–82. It is also possible that this title, "The Black Film," refers to the race of Willard Motley, the author of the novel *Knock on Any Door* (and co-author of the screenplay), a connection which would contribute an interesting detail to critical work currently underway investigating the presence of questions of race in *films noir* of the 1940s and 1950s. For an example of this work, see Eric Lott, "The Whiteness of Film Noir," in Mike Hill, ed., *Whiteness: A Critical Reader* (New York: New York University Press, 1997), pp. 81–101.

106. Deming, "Love through a Film," pp. 225, 226, reprinted in this volume. Deming's writings are collected as *Running Away From Myself: A Dream Portrait of America Drawn from the Films of the Forties* (New York: Grossman, 1969). Two other important works in this regard are Parker Tyler, *The Hollywood Hallucination* [1944] (New York: Simon & Schuster, 1970), and Parker Tyler, *Magic and Myth of the Movies* [1947] (New York: Simon & Schuster, 1970). The later study approaches myth as an imaginative process rooted in human desire. Tyler calls his method "psychoanalytic-mythological," aiming to show "the frequently unconscious magic employed by Hollywood—a magic of dream creation that far transcends its literal messages." Tyler, "Preface," *Magic and Myth of the Movies*, pp. xx, xxviii, xxix. Martha Wolfenstein and Nathan Leites also use the dream analogy, arguably de-Freudianizing it by calling it the "day-dream." They analyse contemporary American films in order to determine "what are the recurrent day-dreams which enter into the consciousness of millions of moviegoers." See their *Movies: A Psychological Study* (New York: The Free Press, 1950; reprinted 1971), p. 14.

107. Deming, "Love through a Film," p. 168, reprinted in this volume.

108. Siegfried Kracauer's contribution to Deming's "The Library of Congress Film Project" is acknowledged in her footnotes. See Deming, "The Library of Congress Film Project," p. 3.

109. Margaret Mead, in Margaret Mead, Cecile Starr, et al., "What I Look for in a Film," *Films in Review* 1:3 (April 1950), p. 12.

110. Hortense Powdermaker, *Hollywood, the Dream Factory: An Anthropologist Looks at the Movie-Makers* (Boston: Little, Brown, 1950; reprinted Arno Press, 1979). Because Powdermaker's 300-plus page volume does not permit any satisfactory excerpting, it is not represented in this anthology. Readers seeking a distilled truncation of her argument might refer to Hortense Powdermaker, "Celluloid Civilization," *Saturday Review of Literature*, 14 October 1950, pp. 9–10, 43–5.

111. Powdermaker, *Hollywood, the Dream Factory*, p. 307.

112. Ibid., p. 332. For a contemporary report on Hollywood society which hints at the clique-ridden and prestige-conscious fears outlined by Powdermaker, see Cecelia Ager, "The New

Hollywood," *Flair* 1:2 (March 1950), pp. 21–2, 119, the second in that magazine's series of "social studies of our times." While Powdermaker later expressed some dissatisfaction with her working method, she did not retract her conclusions. On this dissatisfaction, which she described as an unrecognized envy that clouded her professional anthropologist's objectivity and made her attitude towards her object of study "holier-than-thou," see her autobiography, *Stranger and Friend: The Way of An Anthropologist* (London: Secker & Warburg, 1962), pp. 225–9. Powdermaker hated the year she spent in Hollywood. (Thanks to Robert Sklar for his help in this area.)

113. Bryher, "What Shall You Do in the War?" p. 192, reprinted in this volume.
114. Ibid., pp. 188, 189.
115. Bryher, "Berlin April 1931," *Close Up* 8:2 (June 1931), p. 126.
116. She wrote: "In time of danger the 'We Want War' crowd psychology may destroy a nation. We want a race that understands what acceptance of warfare means. By all means let us have war films. Only let us have war straight and as it is; mainly disease and discomfort, almost always destructive." Bryher, "The War From More Angles," *Close Up* 1:4 (October 1927), p. 45.
117. Bryher, "What Shall You Do in the War?" p. 191.
118. Woodman, "A War Film in Berlin," p. 5. *The New World* was the official organ of the War Resister's League.
119. Ethel Mannin, "War ... and the Workers," *New Leader* (London), 4 March 1932, p. 12, reprinted in this volume. The League of Nations Conference on the Reduction and Limitation of Arms in Geneva had opened in February 1932 and was continuing, with diminishing attendance, in the period in which Mannin wrote.
120. Ibid., p. 12.
121. Johnson, "Light and Shadow: On Pickets, *Gone with the Wind*, and 'Wolf'," p. 13; Lillian Johnson, "Light and Shadow: *Gone with the Wind*'s Place and Prices, and the Public," Baltimore *Afro-American*, 16 March 1940, p. 13; Fredi Washington, "Headlines, Footlights: Apollo Comedy Bad for Race," *People's Voice*, 31 July 1943, p. 9; Fredi Washington, "Headlines, Footlights: Tim Moore Replies," *People's Voice*, 7 August 1943, p. 11, all reprinted in this volume. Johnson's column in the Baltimore *Afro-American* was titled "Light and Shadow."
122. Balio, *Grand Design*, p. 1.
123. Washington, "Headlines, Footlights: Tim Moore Replies," p. 11, reprinted in this volume.
124. For two examples in this collection, see Cogdell, "Truth in Art in America," and Adams, "In Union is Strength."
125. Loren Miller, "The Screen: No 'Escape' for Negro Artists," *New Masses*, 16 July 1935, p. 29. Miller is reviewing *Sanders of the River*, challenging Paul Robeson to return home from England, since the problems facing "the Negro people in [America] cannot be solved by the flight of talented artists."
126. Washington, "Headlines, Footlights: Tim Moore replies," p. 11, reprinted in this volume.
127. Eulalia Proctor, "La Femme Silhouette: The Bronze Age," *Messenger* 7:2 (February 1925), p. 93; Ruby Berkley Goodwin, "The Color Fad," *Flash* 2:23 (31 December 1929), p. 11, both reprinted in this volume. *Flash* (A Weekly Newsmagazine) was published in Los Angeles, Fay Jackson Robinson being one of its editors. For an example of white, high fashion discourse on tanning and the questionable appeal of darker skin, see the editorial, "The Sun and Our Daughters," which asks, "Does the Shadowed Livery of the Burnished Orb Become Young Females as the Preserved Niceties of the Rose-Leaf Complexion Did Their Forebears?" *Vogue* 60 (New York), 1 June 1923, p. 55.
128. Many other writers have speculated on the reasons for, and significance of, this fashion for blackness. Michael Rogin, in *Blackface, White Noise: Jewish Immigrants in the Hollywood Melting Pot*, Berkeley: University of California Press, 1998, argues that such Jazz Age admiration, by whites for blacks, was part of an effort to construct a myth of American origins.
129. Geraldyn Dismond, "The Negro Actor and the American Movies," *Close Up* 5 (July–December, 1929), pp. 90–97, reprinted in this volume.
130. Robert Benchley, "*Hearts in Dixie*: The First Real Talking Picture," *Opportunity* 7:4 (April 1929), p. 122, quoted in John Kisch and Edward Mapp, *A Separate Cinema: Fifty Years of Black-Cast Posters* (New York: Farrar, Straus & Giroux, 1992), pp. xix-xx.
131. Kisch and Mapp, *A Separate Cinema*, pp. xviii-xx, has further discussion of this material.
132. Dismond, "The Negro Actor and the American Movies," p. 94, reprinted this volume. A

useful comparison might be made with Harry Alan Potamkin, "The Aframerican Cinema," *Close Up* 5:2 (July–December 1929), pp. 107–17. Potamkin downplays the possibilities afforded African-American performers by the sound film, favoring instead cinema "at the source of its content" (p. 109). This "source" sounds surprisingly like Hollywood's "pure Negro types" referred to by Goodwin. Potamkin writes:

> I want cinema and I want cinema at its source. To be at its source, cinema must get at the source of its content. The Negro is plastically interesting when he is most negroid. In the films he will be plastically interesting only when the makers of the films know thoroughly the treatment of the Negro structure in the African plastic, when they know of the treatment of his movements in the ritual dances, like the dance of the circumcision, the Ganza. (p. 109)

133. Dismond, "The Negro Actor and the American Movies," p. 97, reprinted in this volume. For an account of the working conditions of the African-American singers during the production of this film, see Eva Jessye, "The Truth about *Hallelujah*," Baltimore *Afro-American*, 2 August 1930, p. 8, reprinted in this volume.
134. See Claudia Roth Pierpont, "A Society of One: Zora Neale Hurston, American Contrarian," *New Yorker*, 17 February 1997, p. 91.
135. Richardson, "Continuous Performance: Dialogue in Dixie," p. 211, reprinted in this volume.
136. Ibid., pp. 215, 217.
137. Ibid., p. 214.
138. Ibid., p. 213.
139. Egger, "Deaf Ears and Dark Continents," p. 17. On page 15, Egger finds Richardson guilty of "glorifying in the failure of the Black actors."
140. Donald Crafton, *The Talkies: American Cinema's Transition to Sound, 1926–1931* (Berkeley: University of California Press, 1999), p. 536; Alexander Walker, *The Shattered Silents: How the Talkies Came to Stay* (London: Harrap, 1978; 1986), p. viii.
141. Crafton, *The Talkies*, p. 14.
142. Walker, *The Shattered Silents*, pp. 48, 98, 88; Crafton, *The Talkies*, p. 451.
143. See Richardson's "Continuous Performance: The Film Gone Male," reprinted in this volume, as well as Dorothy Richardson, "Antheil of New Jersey," *Vanity Fair* 25 (November 1925), pp. 136, 138. Egger's "Deaf Ears and Dark Continents" gives only brief attention to the historical facets of spectatorship.
144. Dismond, "The Negro Actor and the American Movies," p. 97, reprinted in this volume.
145. Vasey, *The World According to Hollywood*, p. 139.
146. Jackson, "Fredi Washington Strikes New Note in Hollywood Film: Imitations," reprinted this volume.
147. Ibid. In a survey of black roles in film, Paul Robeson concurred that *Imitation of Life* was one of the few films "which had a strong Negro interest handled in a worthwhile manner." See Paul Robeson, "New Hope for the Negro Hero," *Film Weekly*, 23 May 1936, p. 9.
148. Jackson, "Fredi ... Imitations."
149. Buchanan, *A Study of the Attitudes of the Writers of the Negro Press*, p. 1, articulates this distinction.
150. Carroll, "Treating Women Too Well," reprinted in this volume.
151. Brown, "Making Movies For Women," p. 342, reprinted in this volume.
152. Ibid.
153. De la Roche, "That 'Feminine Angle,'" pp. 34, 33, 32, reprinted in this volume.
154. Ibid., pp. 32, 28.
155. Davidman, "Women: Hollywood Version," p. 28.
156. Ibid., p. 31.
157. Rukeyser, "Movie," p. 28, reprinted in this volume.
158. Ibid.
159. Colette, "The Chea," (originally published as "Cinema," *Excelsior*, 7 August 1916, p. 2), reprinted in *Colette at the Movies*, pp. 19–20, and reprinted in this volume. See also Colette, "Luxury," reprinted in this volume. Underhill, "Imitation Chinchilla," pp. 27, 107. Underhill also criticized misleading details in Ernst Lubitsch's *Passion*, in "*Passion at the Rivoli Shows Life of DuBarry*," *New York Tribune*, 13 December 1920, p. 8. In this case, the extinguishing of each flame of a three-candle candalabrum (in which each flame had stood in for one of DuBarry's

lovers) misrepresented a far greater scale of promiscuity in DuBarry's life. (Cited in David B. Pratt, "'O, Lubitsch, Where Wert Thou?' Passion, the German Invasion and the Emergence of the Name 'Lubitsch,'" Wide Angle 13:1 (January 1991), p. 53.)

160. Colette, "The Cheatt [Cinema]," p. 2, and reprinted in this volume. Underhill was writing in 1920, just as wardrobe and art departments were in the process of becoming standard components of the Hollywood mode of production. See David Bordwell, Janet Staiger, and Kristin Thompson, The Classical Hollywood Cinema: Film Style and Mode of Production to 1960 (New York: Columbia University Press, 1985) pp. 147–9. Underhill's attentiveness to decor suggests the influence of Elsie de Wolfe's The House in Good Taste (New York: Century, 1915), a popular guide to interior decoration that was reprinted several times in the five years following its publication. De Wolfe defined taste largely in terms of authenticity; she abhorred the sham, which would presage Underhill's fixation on the imitation.

161. Colette, "The Cheat [Cinema]," p. 2, reprinted in this volume. Colette discussed cinematic luxury further in "Luxury in the Movies," Part IV of "A Short Manual for the Aspiring Scenario Writer" [1918], reprinted in Colette at the Movies, pp. 54–56.

162. Dickson, "Wonders of the Kinetoscope," pp. 248, 245, reprinted in this volume.

163. Ibid., pp. 247, 248. Dickson's brother, W.K.L. Dickson, was Edison's chief assistant in the development of the kinetoscope and kineto-phonograph and had, with Antonia, written a study of Edison, The Life and Inventions of Thomas Alva Edison.

164. Dickson, "Wonders of the Kinetoscope," p. 250, reprinted in this volume. See Musser, Edison Motion Pictures, pp. 177–8.

165. Dickson, "Wonders of the Kinetoscope," p. 251, reprinted in this volume.

166. Pierce, "The Nickelodeon, in 'The World To-day,'" pp. 4, 6. This was published in a slightly different version as "The Nickelodeon," World To-day (Chicago) 15 (October 1908), pp. 1052–7, reprinted in this volume.

167. Ibid. p. 1053.

168. Ibid., pp. 1052, 1053. See Snow, "The Workingman's College," p. 458, reprinted in this volume. Several articles in Part One, among them those by Vorse and Dunbar, evoke the crowd in terms used by Pierce.

169. Ibid., p. 1057.

170. Ibid., p. 1057. See also Corrigan, "Harlequin in America," pp. 62–5, and Harris, "The Movies and the Elizabethan Theater," pp. 29–31, for later comparisons of film with pre-modern forms of expression.

171. Seton, "Television Drama," pp. 878–85, reprinted in this volume.

172. Winifred Horrabin, "Highbrow to the Rescue," Lansbury's Labour Weekly, 5 March 1927, p. 5. Winifred Horrabin's work came to our attention through the scholarship of Ian Taylor, whose article "The Film Reviews of Winifred Horrabin, 1927–1945," Screen 33:2 (Summer 1992), pp. 174–83 has guided the research and selection of Horrabin's work for this volume.

173. Horrabin, "What Films do YOU Like?", p. 11. As already mentioned, Horrabin sometimes disowned her job. See Horrabin, "Highbrow to the Rescue," p. 5.

174. Gibbs, "This is Where I Came In…," p. 157, reprinted in this volume.

175. C.A. Lejeune, "Me to Myself," Theatre Arts Monthly, February 1939, pp. 82–83, reprinted in this volume. Lejeune began film reviewing at the Manchester Guardian in 1922 and was arguably the first established female film critic in England.

176. Katherine Anne Porter, "On The Wave," New Masses, 18 May 1937, p. 22, reprinted in this volume. Following on from William Alexander's research, it seems that Porter is taking aim particularly at Frank Nugent, who had reviewed the film in his column "The Screen," New York Times, 21 April 1937, p. 18, and Mark Van Doran, who had included it in "Films: on Horror's Head," Nation, 8 May 1937, p. 545. See William Alexander, Film on the Left: American Documentary Film from 1931 to 1942 (Princeton: Princeton University Press, 1981), pp. 78–79.

177. Katherine Anne Porter, "Hacienda," Virginia Quarterly Review 8:4 (October 1932), pp. 556–69.

178. In the outline for his uncompleted Mexican film project, Que Viva Mexico!, Eisenstein used the serape as a motif to explain the principles of the film's construction. See Sergei Eisenstein, "First Outline of Que Viva Mexico!," Film Sense, p. 251.

179. Barry, "The Challenge," p. 32, reprinted in this volume.

180. Laura Riding, "Answers to an Enquiry," New Verse 11, October 1934, p. 5, cited in Deborah Baker, In Extremis: A Life of Laura Riding (New York: Grove Press, 1993), p. 349.1934; Charlotte Wilbour, 1869, addressing the Members of Sorosis, the New York women's club devoted to

the study of culture, quoted in *New York World*, 23 March 1869, cited in Blair, *The Clubwoman as Feminist*, pp. 37–38..

181. Gibbs, "This is Where I Came In...," p. 157, reprinted this volume.

Part Five

1. Nancy Cott, *The Grounding of Modern Feminism* (New Haven: Yale University Press, 1987), p. 132, and p. 217 onwards; Alice Kessler-Harris, *Out to Work: A History of Wage-Earning Women in the United States* (New York: Oxford University Press, 1982), p. 109.
2. Cott, *The Grounding of Modern Feminism*, p. 218.
3. Kessler-Harris, *Out to Work*, pp. 111, 113.
4. Ibid., pp. 188–9, and elsewhere. Kessler-Harris discusses the mixed blessings of this legislation, which, while protecting women, also sometimes resulted in lower wages, and was construed in terms of women's weakness as compared with men. See also Rosenzweig, *Eight Hours for What We Will*.
5. Peiss, *Cheap Amusements*; Ewen, *Immigrant Women in the Land of Dollars*.
6. Charles Musser, "On 'Extras,' Mary Pickford, and the Red Light Film: Filmmaking in the United States, 1913," *Griffithiana* 50 (May 1994), p. 149.
7. However, as Part One has shown, female filmgoing, and writing about it, were themselves kinds of production—of cinema culture.
8. Note that many women who worked during the period of this collection—1895–1950—only published their memoirs after 1950, thereby escaping the discourse of the period (Frances Marion, Anita Loos, and Louise Brooks are examples).
9. Research has not been able to locate the memoir "The Ex-White Actress" promises she will write in her "Confessions." As mentioned in the General Introduction, this actress reflects on a stage rather than a screen career.
10. See, for example, Kaplan, *Women and Film*.
11. Lizzie Francke, *Script Girls: Women Screenwriters in Hollywood* (London: British Film Institute Publishing, 1994), p. 6. See also Ann Martin and Virginia Clark, *What Women Wrote: Scenarios 1912–1929* (University Publications of America, Cinema History Microfilm Series, 1987), p. v; Holliday, "Hollywood's Modern Women"; and Marsha McCreadie, *The Women Who Write the Movies: From Frances Marion to Nora Ephron* (New York: Birch Lane Press, 1994). All researchers come to more or less this conclusion about the proportion of women writers in the silent era. For "manless Eden," see MacMahon, "Women Directors," p. 140. The career of June Mathis represents the significant power of the female Hollywood writer, in that she was not only head of the scenario department at Metro by 1918, at age twenty-seven, but then became a production executive, being in sole charge of production at Goldwyn in 1923. (See McCreadie, *The Women Who Write the Movies*, pp. 9–11). She is singled out for her success across these two areas of filmmaking in Wing, ed., *The Blue Book of the Screen*, p. 329, at which time she was adapting Ben-Hur.
12. Slide, *Early Women Directors*, p. 9.
13. MacMahon, "Women Directors," p. 13. Gebhart, in "Business Women in Film Studios," p. 68, wrote that it was as writers "that woman reaps the greatest financial harvest." This article is cited in Slide, *Early Women Directors*, p. 13.
14. Ernestine Black, "Lois Weber Smalley," *Overland Monthly* 68:3 (September 1916), p. 198.
15. Adela Rogers St. Johns, "The One Genius in Pictures: Frances Marion, She is One of Hollywood's Six Greatest Women," *Silver Screen*, January 1934, p. 22. St. Johns admitted her bias in reporting, since Marion was one of her dearest friends. But equivalent statements of her earning power are found throughout coverage of her career; in 1934 Miles Mander suggested that, in the field of writing, she was "the most successful woman in Hollywood." See Mander, "The Feminine Touch," p. 29.
16. See Slide, *Early Women Directors*, p. 9. See also Karen Ward Mahar, "Women, Filmmaking, and the Gendering of the American Film Industry, 1896–1928" (Ph.D. dissertation, University of Southern California, 1995), pp. 307–08, for further names and discussion. Ivy Close, an actress for the Hepworth Film Co. in England in the 1910s formed Ivy Close Films. (Thanks to Anthony Slide for this information.) Elinor Glyn, author, formed Elinor Glyn Productions

Ltd. in England in 1929, and directed two features: *Knowing Men* (1930) and *The Price of Things* (1930).

17. Calhoun, "Do Women Rule the Movies?", p. 88. Mahar discusses the numerical dominance of female stars in "Women, Filmmaking," p. 109 and elsewhere.

18. See Mahar, "Women, Filmmaking"; Ally Acker, *Reel Women: Pioneers of the Cinema, 1896 to the Present* (New York: Continuum, 1991); Beauchamp, *Without Lying Down*; as well as Francke, *Script Girls*, Holliday, "Hollywood's Modern Women,", Slide, *Early Women Directors*, and McCreadie, *The Women Who Write the Movies*, noted above.

19. This footnote suggests some of this activity of women in Britain, although the sources pose the usual problem of the factual unreliability of some film journalism. Future scholars will obviously need to make substantial further researches to bring the commentaries cited in this footnote into sharper historical perspective.

Female aristocrats were attracted to the field in Britain (as was the aristocracy in general)—see several accounts of such interest in Herbert and McKernan, eds, *Who's Who of Victorian Cinema*. The Marchioness Townshend wrote cinematograph plays for the Clarendon Film Company (of Croydon, Surrey) including *The Convent Gate* (1913), *The Love of An Actress* (1914), and *House of Mystery* (1913), all starring Dorothy Bellew, and Baroness Blanc performed voice accompaniments to pictures from behind the screen (see "Interview with the Marchioness Townshend," *The Bioscope*, 30 July 1914, p. 429; "A Chat with Baroness Blanc," *Moving Picture News*, 3 September 1910, pp. 5–6). The Countess of Warwick wrote scenarios, beginning with *The Eleventh Commandment* in 1913; one, *The Great Pearl Affair*, was reported as in "a highly sensational vein." See *The Bioscope*, 18 September 1913, p. 891. On a visit to New York she discussed motion pictures and their educational promise with Thomas Edison (see Frances, Countess of Warwick, *Afterthoughts* (London: Cassell and Company, Ltd, 1931), pp. 116–18). From the context, it seems that this meeting took place some time before 1917. Later, her daughter Mercy married the producer Basil Dean, and Lady Warwick often made Warwick Castle available for location shooting. See Frances, Countess of Warwick, *Life's Ebb and Flow* (New York: William Morrow, 1929), p. 192. (Thanks to Stephen Bottomore for the aforementioned references.)

Actress, writer, and director Ethyle Batley made over eighty silent dramas and comedies in the four years between 1912 and 1916, some alone, with her own production company, and some together with her husband, Ernest G. Batley. (See Caroline Merz, "The Tension of Genre: Wendy Toye and Muriel Box," *Film Criticism* 16:1–2 (Fall–Winter 1991–92), p. 85. Merz also mentions Jill Craigie and Kay Mander as British women directors of the 1940s.) Alma Reville, later Mrs Alfred Hitchcock, had already had long experience as an editor, producer, and assistant director when she accompanied Hitchcock to Munich in 1925 to make *The Pleasure Garden* as his chief assistant director. See "Alma In Wonderland," *Picturegoer*, December 1925, p. 48. (Thanks to Anthony Slide for drawing our attention to this reference.) Director and producer Dinah Shurey worked for a small company, Britannia Films Ltd., which she managed and organized, after being assistant director of the Master Film Co., Twickenham. By 1930 she had produced four films (*Every Mother's Son, Second to None, Carry On*, and *The Last Post* (1929)) and had organized the production of Mrs Rosita Forbes's film of Abyssinian life, *Red Sea to Blue Nile*. In the *London Film Society Program Notes*, 1930, p. 150 (held in the Iris Barry Collection, Museum of Modern Art), written for the Society's screening of her film *The Last Post*, Shurey's *Carry On* was described as having wide circulation, and she was characterized as a specialist in patriotic melodrama. Shurey was the subject of Nerina Shute's attack in June 1929, "Can Women Direct Films? A Decided Negative." In the interim the latter had been sued by Shurey and lost. See Nerina Shute, "Can Women Direct Films? A Decided Negative from a Woman Who Knows," *Film Weekly*, 10 June 1929, p. 12, reprinted in this volume; N.S. "Can Women Direct Films? Elinor Glyn's Emphatic 'Yes'" *Film Weekly*, 7 October 1929, p. 1; for information on the law suit see "*Film Weekly* Sued for Libel," *Film Weekly*, 8 February 1930, p. 25.) Elinor Glyn, author of *It*, among other novels adapted for the screen, directed her own *Knowing Men*, with Shute's confident endorsement in October 1929.

This outline of a British history of female film directing suggests a context for Auriol Lee's reactions to visiting England to direct films with British International Pictures in 1932. Although she was "not a raging feminist," she found it a "great surprise" that so few women were working in the British industry, as compared with in the United States. She could name only two other female directors at work beside herself—Mary Field and Leontine

Sagan, who had recently come from Germany after completing *Mädchen in Uniform* there in 1931—and one assistant director, Marjory Gaffney. See Lee, "Women Are Needed in British Films". L'Estrange Fawcett gives a different view: "Americans are always surprised to find how few women write in our studios where, strangely enough, they have penetrated more frequently as assistant directors." See Fawcett, *Writing for the Films*, p. 43. He continues: "There is one notable exception here. Alfred Hitchcock's wife has written most of his scripts and it is worth noting that he occupies one of the premier positions among English directors." The juxtaposition of such views points out the need for further research.

Gaffney is also discussed in Mander, "The Feminine Touch." Mary Field herself wrote that women should have more influence on filmmaking, in "Why Women Should Make Films," *Film Weekly*, 10 October 1931, p. 8.

20. Katherine Newey, "Women, Theater, and Film: Finding a Screen of her Own," Linda Fitzsimmons and Sarah Street, eds, *Moving Performance: British Stage and Screen, 1890s–1920s*, (Trowbridge: Flick Books, 2000), pp. 151–65. One might also note the "familial structure" of early film production more generally, where the two Gish sisters, Lillian and Dorothy, and their mother, were taken in by the patriarch D.W. Griffith, or the three generations of de Milles, the two sons of Beatrice, William and Cecil, and Agnes, daughter of William, who first acted in William's first film as director, *The Ragamuffin* (1916), at age ten. Cecil's daughter Cecilia appeared as a baby in his film *The Virginian*. Clara Beranger had written scenarios for William for seven years, when, in 1927, she became his second wife, after his divorce from Anna de Mille, mother of Agnes and Margaret de Mille. Lastly, one could add the three McDonagh sisters in Australia: Isobel (1899–1982), Phyllis (1900–1978), and Paulette (1901–1978). Based in Sydney, the three women produced four features between 1926 and 1933: *Those Who Love* (1926), *The Far Paradise* (1928), *The Cheaters* (1930), and *Two Minutes' Silence* (1933). Paulette wrote and directed, Isobel starred, appearing under her stage name "Marie Lorraine," and Phyllis served as business manager, art director, and publicist.

21. See Slide, *Early Women Directors*, pp. 57, 60–61. Screenwriter Sarah Y. Mason was married to director-screenwriter Victor Heerman, and they often worked together in the 1930s. The theme of women's contributions in marital and family collaboration in filmmaking is also covered in: Paul Thompson, "They're Married *and* Work Together," *Motion Picture* 36 (October 1928), pp. 47, 106; Faith Service, "The Tortures of Cutting," *Motion Picture Classic* 28:10 (November 1924), pp. 20, 86–7; and Beatrice de Mille, "The De Mille Family in Motion Pictures," *New York Dramatic Mirror*, 4 August 1917, p. 4.

22. Mrs D.W. Griffith (Linda Arvidson), *When the Movies Were Young* (New York: E.P. Dutton, 1925); reprinted with a new introduction by Edward Wagenknecht (New York: Dover, 1969), p. 37.

23. See illustration of women assembling prints at the Biograph laboratory in Hoboken, New Jersey, in Bowser, *The Transformation of Cinema*, p. 32.

24. Herbert and McKernan, eds, *Who's Who of Victorian Cinema*, pp. 80–81, also lists Elizabeth Alice F. Le Blond as one of the first women filmmakers, who shot alpine subjects in early 1900, making her the world's first mountain filmmaker. Stephen Bottomore's research has turned up records of an even earlier woman in the movies, Madame Labarthe (veuve), née Cusac, who applied for two French patents for film devices in February 1896, nos 254071 and 254298.

25. Musser, "On 'Extras,' Mary Pickford," p. 159.

26. *Views and Films Index* 3:38 (3 October 1908), p. 9, cited in Slide, *Early Women Directors*, p. 14. This article refers primarily to acting however, and the desire for dynamic actresses who can accomplish physical feats: "'The woman with a beautiful face gets no more than the plainer women. Action, not looks, is what recommends a woman for employment with us,' says a manager."

27. Musser, "On 'Extras,' Mary Pickford," p. 159. See also n124.

28. For Weber, see Bertha H. Smith, "A Perpetual Leading Lady," *Sunset: the Pacific Monthly* 32:3 (March 1914), p. 634. See Rinehart, "My Experience in the Movies," pp. 19, 76, 78, 80, excerpted in this volume. Jeanie Macpherson started on the stage, singing musical comedy in Chicago and New York, acted for D.W. Griffith at the Biograph Company, and then went West for Universal, where she began writing, including scenarios for herself, one of which was *The Tarantula*, which she also directed after the first negative, directed by Edwin August, was accidentally destroyed. (She returned, once, to acting, fighting in a bit part in the cigarette factory in Cecil B. De Mille's *Carmen*, starring Geraldine Farrar.) See Slide, *Early Women Directors*,

p. 60; Alice Martin, "From 'Wop' Parts to Bossing the Job," *Photoplay*, October 1916, pp. 95–7. "Wop" parts are emotional roles in front of the camera.

29. MacMahon, "Women Directors," p. 140.

30. Musser, "On 'Extras,' Mary Pickford," p. 167.

31. See Steven J. Ross, *Working-Class Hollywood: Politics, Class, and the Rise of the Movies* (Princeton, NJ: Princeton University Press, 1998) and Steven J. Ross, "The Unknown Hollywood," *History Today* 40 (April 1990), pp. 40–46; Sloan, *The Loud Silents*; and Sampson, *Blacks in Black and White*. For a discussion of the ethnicity of employees, see Musser, "On 'Extras,' Mary Pickford," pp. 163–4. The first black-owned film production company is usually considered to be that of William Foster, called the Foster Photoplay Company, founded in Chicago in 1913.

32. "An Honest Birth Control Film at Last," *The Birth Control Review* 1 (April–May, 1917), p. 11. See also "Exploiting Falsehood and Boycotting Truth," *The Birth Control Review* 1 (April–May, 1917), p. 10; the advertisement for "Birth Control," (through B.S. Moss Company) in the same issue; and Margaret Sanger, "Superwoman—an Idea of a Movie" (1914–15), a manuscript sketch, Margaret Sanger and the Movies, Reel 76, New York University Margaret Sanger Papers Microfilm Project.

33. "Bring Out Picture Play," *The Woman's Journal*, 10 October 1914, p. 276. For more on the commercial fate of this film, see Sloan, *The Loud Silents*, pp. 120–21, Stamp, *Movie-Struck Girls*, pp. 175–7.

34. Thank you to Marguerite Engberg for reference to Karin Michaëlis. Information on *Motherhood* comes from Rick Worland's notes for "Treasures from the G. William Jones Film-Video Collection," Society for Cinema Studies Conference Special Event Screenings, Southern Methodist University, Dallas TX, 1995).

35. "Ella Wheeler Wilcox's Humanology Films," *The Kinematograph and Lantern Weekly*, 7 January 1915, p. 69. Poems by Ella Wheeler Wilcox were published in 1919 as *Cinema Poems and Others* (London: Gay & Hancock, 1919). However, the six "Cinema Poems" were poems she had written earlier, which had subsequently formed the bases of films, or, as the foreword notes, are poems "now being shown on the films" (titled "A Married Coquette," "Lais When Young," "Divorced," "Angel or Demon," "Meg's Curse," and "Lord, Speak Again") rather than poems about the cinema.

36. "Miss Keller's Own Work," *New York Times*, 24 August 1919, p. 4, cited in Mahar, "Women, Filmmaking," p. 301.

37. "Motion Picture Comedies in Clay," *Scientific American* 115 (16 December 1916), p. 553.

38. Holliday, "Hollywood's Modern Women," p. 130.

39. Louella Parsons' experience as Scenario Editor, Essanay Film Company, was typical. She writes: "The Essanay Film Company receives approximately six hundred scenarios a week, most of which are absolutely worthless. However, in the hope of discovering an occasional good story, editors carefully wade through this mass of manuscripts.... With the increased demand for three and four reel subjects, scenario writing appears to be evolving into more of an art." See Louella Parsons, "A Message to Scenario Writers" in Catherine Carr, *The Art of Photoplay Writing* (New York: Hannis Jordan, 1914), pp. 116, 119.

40. Walker, "Movie Moths," p. 14.

41. Anderson,, "Emasculating Ibsen," p. 36, reprinted in this volume.

42. Holliday, "Hollywood's Modern Women," pp. 86–89.

43. MacMahon, "Woman Directors," p. 140.

44. Holliday, "Hollywood's Modern Women," pp. 104, 106, 123.

45. Lois Weber, "How I Became a Motion Picture Director," *Static Flashes*, 24 April 1915, p. 8., reprinted this volume.

46. In 1923 Gebhart wrote "women scenarists are increasing in number" (Gebhart, "Business Women in Film Studios," pp. 67–8), while 1924, in "Flimflamming the Film Fans," pp. 26, 94, Sargent writes of the hundreds of disappointed men and women traveling to Hollywood in the hope of breaking into the careers of writing and acting. Further research will reveal more precise datings and reasons for these fluctuations.

47. See, for example, Mathis, "Harmony in Picture-Making," p. 5, reprinted in this volume; Mathis "The Feminine Mind in Picture Making," p. 115, reprinted in this volume; and Jane Murfin's comment that the "feminine slant" is an advantage in screenwriting in "Sex and the Screen," p. 459, reprinted in this volume. For "vast army" see Movie Margerie, "The

Feminine Touch on the Film, which is—Wanted," *Pictures and Picturegoer*, 2–9 November 1918, p. 449.

48. Frances Marion, "Scenario Writing," in Stephen Watts, ed., *Behind the Screen: How Films Are Made* (London: Arthur Barker, 1938), p. 39. Producer B.P. Schulberg seconded this view, in that he "prefer[ed] that a woman write the script, for women understand character delineation and the innuendos of human relationships far better than do men." (See B.P. Schulberg, quoted in Gebhart, "Business Women in Film Studios," p. 27). In 1933, noting recent successes and past trends, Herbert Harris also commented that women "seem far better than men for writing screen stories. Perhaps it is that there is more emotion, analysis, and understanding in their situations and characters." (See Herbert Harris, "Women as Screen Authors: Do They Write the Best Screen Stories?" *Film Weekly*, 15 September 1933, p. 34). Screenwriter and journalist L'Estrange Fawcett commented in his 1932 writing guide that "In America practically all the work of Treatment, Script, and Dialogue is done by women.... The studios employ mainly women for the work because the bulk of audiences is women and their point of view is vitally important." See Fawcett, *Writing for the Films*, p. 43. Mary Pickford, for whom Marion had written many successful screen parts (as well as ghost-written articles), noted that "all of [her] outstanding pictures [had] been written by women" because they were less egotistical than a man, who would always "write himself" into his stories. See Mary Pickford on "The Feminine Mind in Picture Making," *Film Daily* (7 June 1925), p. 9.

49. Clara Beranger, interview, "Women Scenario Writers," *Indianapolis Star*, 1 September 1918, sect. 5, p. 1, reprinted in this volume. (The original contains syntactical errors.)

50. Marion Fairfax on "The Feminine Mind in Picture Making," *Film Daily*, 7 June 1925, p. 9, reprinted in this volume.

51. Jeanie McPherson, "Development of Photodramatic Writing," *Moving Picture World* 33 (21 july 1917), p. 393.

52. Clara Beranger on "The Feminine Mind in Picture Making," *Film Daily* (7 June 1925), p. 9. See also, in the same article, Eve Unsell on "teamwork," also in "The Feminine Mind in Picture Making," p. 115, as well as related comments by Leah Baird on p. 116.

53. Thomas J. Slater, "June Mathis: A Woman Who Spoke Through Silents," *Griffithiana* 53 (May 1995), p. 141. Beranger, "Women Scenario Writers," p. 1, reprinted in this volume.

54. Jane Murfin on "The Feminine Mind in Picture Making," *Film Daily*, 7 June 1925, p. 9.

55. Mathis, "Harmony in Picture-Making," p. 5, reprinted in this volume.

56. Deland, "The Change in the Feminine Ideal," p. 293.

57. Ella Fabrique, manager of a Detroit photoplay theater, got her job because of the scarcity of men, according to an article on her career, "We Have with Us Today," *Moving Picture World* (17 April 1920, p. 395). In his discussion of women directors of plays and pictures, MacMahon also mentions this factor, particularly strong in France: "the war profoundly affected society by temporarily withdrawing manpower and permitting women to tackle the jobs." (See MacMahon, "Women Directors," p. 144.) See also David Williams, "Ladies of the Lamp," *Film History* 9:1 (1997), pp. 116–27 on women working as projectionists during the First World War in Britain. By contrast, in X, "The 'All-British' Firm," *Pictures and Picturegoer*, 26 October–2 November 1918, p. 422, Mrs Smalley, a film distributor, insists that she is not "working for the duration," but will continue after the war.

Winifred Holtby describes modern life as "more hurried, complex, rich and bewildering. All barriers are more fluid—morals, classes, economic groups, even time and space. We are eliminating distance. We are packing more into time." (Winifred Holtby, "My Weekly Journal 25: Through Fifty Years," *The Schoolmistress*, 24 December 1931, p. 382.)

58. A.S.B. (the initials of Alice Stone Blackwell), "The American Peril," *The Woman's Journal*, 4 July 1914, p. 210. Michael Monahan, speaking of America, is being quoted.

59. Gladys Hall, "Rot," *Metropolitan Magazine*, n.d., p. 11, Folder 536, Gladys Hall Collection, Margaret Herrick Library, Academy of Motion Picture Arts and Sciences, Los Angeles. Gladys Hall did a series of four articles for *Filmplay* in 1922 on the theme of "film feminists," interviewing Madge Kennedy, Olga Petrova, Elsie Ferguson, and Lillian Gish. In the fourth and final article of the series, "The Serious Side of the Women on the Screen: Lillian Gish," Hall and Gish (then aged 29) discuss the word "feminism," and decide it doesn't exist since it isn't in the dictionary. The text runs as follows:

> "I came to talk with you about feminism," I reminded her. "I am not supposed to know anything about such matters," said Miss Gish, with severe amusement. "I am a

juvenile!" "There are juveniles and juveniles..." "I am not even sure," pursued Miss Gish, thoughtfully, "that 'feminism' is not a coined word." She procured the ponderous family dictionary and looked it up. It was not there. It was then decided between us that feminism is a coined word.

(Gish went on to say that women "*have always ruled the world.*") (See *Filmplay* 2:1 (July 1922), pp. 20–21.)

Other examples of film women's feminism include Anita Loos's authorship of *A Cure For Suffragettes* (1913), and perhaps Dorothy Gish's starring role in *The Suffragette Minstrels* (1913). Writer Sonya Levien was a suffrage campaigner and managing editor of *The Woman's Journal* from 6 July 1912 to 28 September 1912. (See Larry Ceplair, *A Great Lady: A Life of the Screenwriter Sonya Levien* (Metuchen, NJ: Scarecrow, 1996.) Adela Rogers St. Johns and Mary Roberts Rinehart participated in suffrage marches. Olga Petrova was an active campaigner for birth control and legal abortion, declaring "I am a feminist" in a *Photoplay* interview. (See Randolph Bartlett, "Petrova—Prophetess," *Photoplay*, December 1917, p. 27.) Florence Lawrence marched in a suffrage parade in the early part of 1913 in Washington DC (See *Motion Picture World*, 5 April 1913, p. 689, cited in Musser, "On 'Extras, Mary Pickford," p. 165.) Nell Shipman described becoming interested in "'Feminism,' 'Socialism,' and other 'Isms'" in the 1910s. (See Nell Shipman, "Me," *Photoplay* 15:3 (February 1919), p. 48.) In contrast, Aline Carter assured readers in 1921 that Lois Weber, regarding "the feminist movement ... has never marched in a parade, carried a banner nor made speeches in its support," although she had been politically active: in 1913 she had been elected mayor of Universal City. (See Aline Carter, "The Muse of the Reel," *Motion Picture* 21:2 (March 1921), p. 62.)

One dynamic female activity rarely recorded on film, in either fictional or documentary form, was the thousands-strong suffrage march. Louella Parsons reviewed such a film, *The Fight*, which she described as showing "a woman's struggle for political supremacy in a country where women have the right to hold office," a right not yet realised across the United States. See Margaret Herrick Library, Academy for Motion Picture Arts and Sciences, Los Angeles, Louella Parsons Scrapbooks, 1915–1917, "Seen on the Screen: *The Fight*," *Chicago Herald*, n.d.. See also Sloan, *The Loud Silents*, and Stamp, *Movie-Struck Girls*, on suffrage films.

60. Jeanie Macpherson was the only woman to pilot Lt. Ormer Locklear, a wing walker and stunt pilot who pioneered mid-flight airplane to airplane transfers in November 1918. Locklear was killed during the filming of an air stunt for *The Skywayman*, on 2 August 1920, at DeMille Field (named after Cecil B. DeMille, an avid flyer who had established the airfield in 1919).

61. See Gertrude Bacon, *The Record of an Aeronaut: Being the Life of John M. Bacon* (London: John Long, 1907), cited in Herbert and McKernans, eds, *Who's Who of Victorian Cinema*, pp. 19–20.

62. On *The Girl Spy* series, see *Motion Picture World*, 22 May 1909, p. 672, as well as Gene Gauntier, "Blazing the Trail," *Woman's Home Companion* 55 (November 1928), p. 170. For Gauntier's "plunge," see Gene Gauntier, "Blazing the Trail," *Woman's Home Companion* (October 1928), p. 8, reprinted in this volume; for Gish's ice-cake float, see Lillian Gish, "Beginning Young," *Ladies' Home Journal* 42 (September 1925), pp. 118, 120, reprinted in this volume. Such brisk baptisms are still relevant: an article on young Iranian director Samira Makhmalbaf's second film, *Blackboards* (Joan Dupont, "A Woman Pushes the Broders of Iranian Film," *International Herald Tribune*, 13–14 May 2000, p. 22) reports that "during filming, she took a plunge into a cold river as an example to the old men she was directing. 'It's hard for men to be directed by a woman and I couldn't ask them if I wasn't willing to take the dive myself—they were very old men, and the water was icy.'"

See Ben Singer, "Female Power in the Serial-Queen Melodrama: The Etiology of an Anomaly," *Camera Obscura* 22 (January 1990), pp. 91–129; and Nan Enstad, "Dressed for Adventure: Working Women and Silent Movie Serials in the 1910s," *Feminist Studies* 21:1 (Spring 1995), pp. 67–90, for further discussion of serial queen films. As Mahar has suggested, in "Women, Filmmaking," Ch. 5, it seems possible that with further research we might find a correlation between the demise of the dynamic serial queen heroine and commedienne, and the decline of the female director.

63. Evelyn Preer, "Evelyn Preer Nearly Drowns in Realistic Movie Scene—Screen Star, writing 'Thrills' for Courier, Had to Hold Out Meat for Bloodhounds To Chase—Pond of Water She Thought Only Waist Deep Came Up To Neck and Nearly Drowned Her," *Pittsburgh Courier*, 11

June 1927, Second Section, p. 2. See Pearl White, *Just Me* (New York: George H. Doran, 1919) for similar examples. In her fictionalized autobiography, *Abandoned Trails*, Nell Shipman, as Joyce Jevons, also a veteran of river dramas, indignantly insists, "I've never been doubled," when viewers, watching her pull "some crazy stunt, ... say: 'She didn't *really* do that! It's a trick! They do it with the camera!'" (p. 53). Elsewhere, she reports on thrilling a Woman's Club with her feats, an audience who "admired the slapdash of her sudden exit," for "it seemed to glimpse, for them, another, more magic world—far from dishpans and baby diapers" (p. 100). The thrill aspect of filmmaking for the film actress seems generally to have tapered off by the late 1910s; Cleo Madison expressed the opinion in 1916, for example, when she was directing her own films for Universal, that "the days of 'stunt photography' are just about over and ... stories of modern life are the popular thing." (See William M. Henry, "Cleo, the Craftswoman," *Photoplay*, January 1916, p. 111.)

64. Helen Norton, "Brains, Brown Eyes, and Buttons," *Motion Picture Magazine* 17:2 (March 1919), p. 30.

65. MacMahon, "Women Directors," p. 140.

66. Miss Meg Gehrts, "I Went Among Savages for 'Movies'," *Pearson's Weekly*, 1 August 1914, p. 154 (Thank you to Stephen Bottomore for this reference). See also Meg Gehrts, *A Camera Actress in the Wilds of Togoland* (London: Seeley Service, 1915). Bertha H. Smith, "A Nervy Movie Lady," *Sunset: the Pacific Monthly* 32 (June 1914), pp. 1323–5. "Kathlyn Williams, the Jungle Actress," *Picture-Play Weekly* 1:2 (17 April 1915), pp. 1–4, recounts, partly in the first person, her experiences with "untamed beasts" for the screen. In describing the "bunk" surrounding the creation of the star in 1918, a process of "manufacturing stars at low wages," William A. Page considered an act of pluck (in this case the rescue of the leading man from accidental drowning during filming) a mandatory element. See Page, "The Movie-Struck Girl," *Woman's Home Companion* 45 (June 1918) p. 18. Anne Walker also referred to this standard element of star-construction when describing a conversation between a director and the young actress who had come into his office to offer him an idea for a screenplay: "What's the matter? Not getting enough work? Or did someone drop you in the tank?" Later Walker proposed that the "unusual, thrilling thing" that was obligatory for a star was being replaced by more absorbing stories that provided for more than "mere effects." See Walker, "Movie Moths," pp. 14 and 130. Mansfield, "The Pictures," p. 161, reprinted this volume.

67. For more on Quimby and other aviatrixes, see: Robert Wohl, *A Passion for Wings: Aviation and the Western Imagination, 1908–1918* (New Haven: Yale University Press, 1994), pp. 279–82; Valerie Modman, *Women Aloft* (Alexandria, VA: Time:Life, 1981), pp. 7–29.

68. See the essays by Jessica Borthwick, Osa Johnson and Frances Hubbard Flaherty included in this volume. See Natalie Barkas, *Thirty-Thousand Miles for the Films* (London and Glasgow: Blackie and Son, 1937) for another example. Mrs Barkas travels to India and Africa with her husband, director Geoffrey Barkas, "once more to help to make a film in a far country" (p. 1). For a description of one of Osa Johnson's acts of marksmanship to protect her husband, see Martin Johnson, *Camera Trails in Africa* (New York: Grosset & Dunlap, 1924), p. 330. Osa Johnson published an additional discussion of difficulties of filming in the field in Osa Johnson, "Africans Rebel at Playing Slaves," *New York Times*, 17 October 1937, p. 29. Nell Shipman describes rescuing her partner from the snow in *The Silent Screen and My Talking Heart* (Boise ID: Boise State University Press, 1987).

69. Nell Shipman, "The Movie that Couldn't Be Screened," *Atlantic Monthly* 135 (March 1925), pp. 326–32; 135 (April 1925), pp. 477–82; 135 (May 1925), pp. 645–51. This was precisely the kind of directorial task, "great out-of-doors productions with thousands of extras or animals," which Murfin advised women to avoid. See Murfin, "Sex and the Screen," p. 461, reprinted in this volume.

70. Gene Gauntier, "Blazing the Trail," *Woman's Home Companion* 56 (February 1929), p. 98.

71. "Doings in Los Angeles," *Moving Picture World*, 11 January 1913, p. 142, cited in Mahar, "Women, Filmmaking," p. 400; Slide, *Early Women Directors*, p. 13, and Sloan, *The Loud Silents*, p. 78, who both cite G. P. von Harleman and Clarke Irvine, "Women Start Something," *Moving Picture World*, 27 May 1916, p. 1515. In 1923 Gebhardt reported another "first all-woman motion picture company," organized by Mrs Lule Warrenton, which had produced one film. (Gebhardt, "Business Women in Film Studios," p. 68.) *Story World* also ran the story: "The special significance of this move may be interpreted in a number of ways. It is certainly a triumph for women in general." ("An All-Woman Film Company," *Story World* 5:1 (July 1923), p. 79,

cited by Holliday, "Hollywood's Modern Women," p. 277.) More research is needed to clarify the implications of these reports.

72. Lois Weber had herself given Marion a helping hand. See Fritzi Remont, "The Lady Behind the Lens," *Motion Picture Magazine* 15:4 (May 1918), p. 60. McCreadie discusses this aspect of feminine film culture in *The Women Who Write the Movies*, p. 6, and elsewhere. It is also a prominent theme in Beauchamp, *Without Lying Down*. This climate of cooperation among women was not experienced by Ida Lupino. Her negative view of women, as gossips, is hinted at in Ida Lupino, "Who Says Men Are People?" *Silver Screen* 18:8 (June 1948), p. 23, while Annette Kuhn refers to Lupino's experience that "other women could not be counted on as allies," in *Queen of the B's: Ida Lupino Behind the Camera*, ed. Annette Kuhn (Westport CT: Greenwood Press, 1995), p. 8. Than k you to Richard Kozsarski for discussions about Ida Lupino's career.

73. Edna Ferber, "They Earn Their Million," *Collier's*, 4 December 1920, pp. 7–8, 24, 26, 28. See also Crawford, "The Job of Keeping at the Top," pp. 14–15, 75.

74. She concludes her detailed essay with: "We are here, sisters, and we're so stubborn that we're going to make our mark—indeed, many of our sisterhood are already making it, and indelibly, too." See Gebhart, "Business Women in Film Studios," p. 68.

75. Ibid., pp. 28, 66, 67. William Page discussed appealing to gullible stenographers far from Hollywood with "acting through the mail" courses. See Page, "The Movie-Struck Girl," p. 18. Reina Wiles Dunn, in "Off-stage Heroines of the Movies," *Independent Woman* 13:7 (July 1934), p. 202, described a similar journey from stenographer to script-girl. Julie Lang Hunt described Virginia van Upp's route through stenography to writing in "They Aren't All Actresses in Hollywood: Eight Little Girls Went to Hollywood. Before You Follow Them, Read What Happened...", *Photoplay*, September 1936, p. 93.

76. Anita Loos and John Emerson ran an advice column on screenwriting in *Photoplay*, titled "Photoplay Writing," running from February to July 1918. Jeanie Macpherson ran a column titled "Hints to Scenario Writers" for *Movie Weekly* in Fall 1921. (See bibliography for complete references to these columns.) Early manuals by women included Parsons, *How to Write for the "Movies"*; Carr, *The Art of Photoplay Writing*; Bertsch, *How to Write for Moving Pictures*; Patterson, *Cinema Craftsmanship*; Inez Klump and Helen Klump, *Screen Acting: Its Requirements and Rewards* (New York: Falk, 1922); Mae Marsh, *Screen Acting* (New York: Frederick A. Stokes, 1921); Agnes Platt, *Practical Hints on Acting for the Cinema* (New York: E.P. Dutton, 1923); and Frances Agnew, *Motion Picture Acting* (New York: Reliance Newspaper Syndicate, 1913).

77. Carolyn Rosenberg, "Only Woman to Manage Film Company," *American Hebrew*, 16 March 1928, p. 663; Adela Rogers St. Johns, "'Get Me Dorothy Arzner!'", *Silver Screen* 4:2 (December 1933), p. 24. On Haskins, see Janet Reid, "From Telephone Operator to Motion Picture Producer: With Apologies to Horatio Alger," *Motion Picture Magazine*, May 1923, pp. 66, 100; and Sydney Valentine, "The Girl Producer," *Photoplay*, July 1923, pp. 55, 110, cited in Mahar, "Women, Filmmaking," p. 399. See Mahar's discussion of Haskins, pointing out that she was one of the last female directors to work in Hollywood for the next forty years. Mahar, "Women, Filmmaking," pp. 349–50.

78. The sumptuous wares of Jane Lewis, Vitagraph's wardrobe mistress, were reported to protect the studio from the accusation that it gathered workers "from a class of women who are using the picture business as either a cloak or a pastime" (in other words from women who, for whatever reason, could afford such clothes), and not from the typical extra girl who "can't dress in sables and velvets on the money she makes." See Nance Monde, "A Fitting Finish, Or a Day with the Wardrobe Mistress," *Motion Picture Magazine* 15 (August 1918), pp. 58–9. Joyce Auberon, Dress Controller at Elstree discussed her job in "Dressing a New Film is No Joke," *Film Weekly*, 26 September 1931, p. 8.

79. The work of Claire West, designer for Cecil B. DeMille's productions, and Sophie Wachner, chief of the costuming department at Goldwyn in Culver City is covered in Anne Walker, "Dressing the Movies," *Woman's Home Companion*, May 1921, p. 24. See also Edith Head, "A Costume Problem: From Shop to Stage to Screen," *Hollywood Quarterly* 2:1 (October 1946), pp. 44 ff. (remaining four pages not numbered).

80. Dunn, "Off-stage Heroines of the Movies," p. 203. Dunn wrote that women were in almost exclusive charge of reference departments in Hollywood.

81. See, for example, the announcement of Miss M.E.M. Gibsone joining the Mabel Condon Exchange, in "Mabel Condon Exchange Grows," *Motography*, 24 March 1917, p. 651. For an

earlier record of a female film exchange manager, see mention of Miss E.M. Murphy, who successfully ran the Troy, New York, office of the United Film Company in 1911, in Anon, "A Woman Exchange Manager," *Moving Picture World*, 19 August 1911, p. 460. The job of exchange manager arose in the nickelodeon period once film reels were no longer bought but rented by exhibitors.

82. Wright, "Life Looks Funny Through a Grille," p. 19
83. David J. Murphy, "People of the Pictures: No. 1—The Usherette," *Screen Pictorial*, November 1938, p. 29.
84. See Murfin, "Sex and the Screen," p. 459, reprinted in this volume. Female producers headed two short-lived companies catering to Asian Americans: Mrs E.L. Greer headed the Fujiyama Feature Film Company, which was formed in 1916 to make films in Japan for US release, and Marion E. Wong headed the Mandarin Film Company, set up in Oakland in 1917. See Mahar, "Women, Filmmaking," p. 299. Mahar is citing sources given in *The American Film Institute Catalog of Motion Pictures Produced in the United States, Feature Films, 1911–1920*, ed. Patricia King Hansen (Berkeley: University of California Press, 1988), pp. 140, 204. See also "Edith Ellis Discusses the Pictures," *New York Dramatic Mirror* (26 May 1917), p. 23, for another example of a woman (playwright and producer, chief of Goldwyn literary staff) writing about her production work in the business.
85. Eudice Shapiro's work as concert mistress at RKO is discussed in Hildegard Level, "Women Behind the Screen," *Independent Woman* 27 (June 1948), p. 172.
86. W. John Elton, "A Miss Who Writes 'Hits,'" *Film Weekly*, 12 April 1935, p. 10.
87. See Jeanie Macpherson, "Functions of the Continuity Writer," *Opportunities in the Motion Picture Industry*, Vol. 2 (Los Angeles: Photoplay Research Society, 1922), pp. 25–35, and Laura Kent Mason, "Capturing the Caption," *Motion Picture Magazine* 24 (January 1923), pp. 39–40, 90. Mason discusses Anita Loos and Jeanie Macpherson in particular. Speaking as a continuity writer about her work, Eve Unsell, of the Lasky staff in London, gave a talk to the Cinema Composers' Club, on 24 January 1919, titled "The 'Routine' of Film Adaptation," published in Patterson, *Cinema Craftsmanship*, pp. 86–95. See also Thompson, "They're Married and Work Together," pp. 47, 106, about Harry H. Caldwell and Katherine Hilliker.
88. Kate Corbaley, "Duties and Qualifications of the Scenario Reader," *Oportunities in the Motion Picture Industry*, vol. 2 (Los Angeles: Photoplay Research Society, 1922), pp. 61–3.
89. See Billie Bender, "The Director's Right Hand," *Screen Pictorial*, September 1937, pp. 44–5.
90. Nancy Naumberg, cinematographer since 1934, edited a collection of essays on film jobs, *We Make the Movies* (New York: Norton, 1937).
91. Marion Robertson, "I am a Talent Scout," *National Board of Review Magazine* 13 (December 1938), pp. 4–7; Messinger, "New Stars are My Job," p. 24.
92. See "She Cuts the Kisses," *American Magazine* 147 (January 1949), p. 99, about Barbara McClean, editor for Twentieth-Century Fox; and Margaret Booth, who wrote that she "penetrated into film-making on a side which is generally regarded as exclusively masculine," in Margaret Booth, "The Cutter," *Behind the Screen: How Films Are Made*, ed. Stephen Watts, (London: Arthur Baker, 1938), pp. 149–50. In another article, an interview, Booth could recollect only four female cutters in Hollywood; she said she aspired to become a director, and could recall only one other of these (presumably Dorothy Arzner). She never succeeded. See Freda Bruce Lockhart, "Lady with Scissors," *Film Weekly*, 9 October 1937, p. 14; see also the oral history with Margaret Booth held at the Academy of Motion Picture Arts and Sciences. The work of Hattie Gray Baker, film editor, was discussed in Ruth-Dorothy Block, "A Movie Stepmother: Hattie Gray Baker, Film Editor, Brings the Author's Brainchild to Its Full Development," *Filmplay* 1:11 (May 1922), pp. 18–19. She put forward the interesting thesis that film was a child that grew up, in the course of editing, awith the diurector or writer (it is not clear which) being its mother, and the editor its stepmother. Baker, as the film's final editor, prepared it for the censor. See also Anne Bauchens, "Cutting the Film," Naumberg, ed., *We Make the Movies*, pp. 199–215. Bauchens was, at the time, cutter for Cecil B. DeMille at Paramount. Service, "The Tortures of Cutting," pp. 20, 86–7, discussed the film-editing career of Josephine Lovett (Mrs John Robertson).
93. Margaret Ann Young, director of the title registration bureau of the Motion Picture Association of America in 1948, is described in "Lady of Many Titles," *American Magazine*, 1 April 1948, p. 119.
94. Diction coaches and voice trainers converted "shadows into sounds" in the words of Clara

Novello Davies, matinée star Ivor Novello's mother. See Clara Novello Davies, "Making Screen Voices," Film Weekly, 27 May 1929, p. 13.

95. See E. Leslie Gilliams, "Will Woman Leadership Change the Movies?" Illustrated World 38 (February 1923), p. 861. Gilliams lists many other kinds of jobs women held.

96. Dunn, "Off-stage Heroines of the Movies," p. 203. The results of Anthony Slide's research into the Metro payroll records of the early 1920s paint a slightly different picture of employment patterns: more male stenographers are listed than female ones, and there are more women working in other areas of the studio than as stenographers.

97. A Representative, "Hattie the Hairdresser Speaks," Filmplay, April 1922, p. 24.

98. William Smallwood, "They Made Good in the Movie Capital," Opportunity 19 (March 1941), p. 77. Blount's was a principle also held by Opportunity.

99. "L'Tanya. First Negro Woman to Receive Fashion Screen Credit," 31 August 1949, typescript, Claude A. Barnett Papers, Box 298, Folder 1, Chicago Historical Society. L'Tanya was awarded a Rosenwald scholarship and studied at L'Ecole de Chambre-Coutier in Paris.

100. "Our Growing Importance in the Amusement World" by J.A. Jackson in The Competitor 3:4 (June 1921), p. 38, notes: "Birdie Gilmore, author of the Jungle God, now being produced by the Delsarte Film Co. She has also had a story accepted by the Metro Company." According to Sampson, Blacks in Black and White, p. 183, in 1916 the Unique Film Company (an African-American film production company) was organized in Chicago. Its first and only production was Shadowed by the Devil, based on an original story by Mrs M. Webb, wife of the company's director, Miles M. Webb.

101. Avenelle Harris, "I Tried to Crash the Movies," Ebony 1 (August 1946), pp. 5–10, reprinted in this volume.

102. Eva Jessye, letter of 20 August 1950 to Etta Moten, Claude A. Barnett Papers, Box 297, Folder 3, Chicago Historical Society. (Moten played the black wife in the "My Forgotten Man" finale of The Golddiggers of 1933 (1933).

103. Perhaps future research will turn up such writings... See John Thompson, "Laura Bowman, Noted Actress, Revives Haitian Folklore and Puts it on Screen and Stage," Chicago Defender, 15 July 1939, p. 17. This article described Laura Bowman's role in the history and realization of the Warner Bros. film Voodoo Fires. Zora Neale Hurston worked as Fannie Hurst's personal assistant from 1925 until the end of 1926, and worked as a staff writer at Paramount Studios in 1941. See Zora Neale Hurston, "Fannie Hurst, by her ex-amanuensis," Saturday Review of Literature 16:15–16 (9 October 1937), pp. 15–16. Hurston shot films in Florida in 1928–29, and in South Carolina in 1940 as part of her anthropological and folkloric research.

104. Page writes, "Stardom is merely a rainbow-like illusion which fascinates and attracts, only to bring, in the long run, unhappiness, disappointment and failure to many thousands of girls every year." Page, "The Movie-Struck Girl," p. 18. For the couch, and the view that "the films breed more immorality than the stage ever did," see Irene Wallace, "The Woman on the Screen," The Green Book Magazine (December 1914), 983. (Thank you to Stephen Bottomore for this reference.)

105. Dorothy Gish, "And So I am a Comedienne," Ladies' Home Journal 42 (July 1925), p. 7.

106. Ruth Waterbury, "Don't Go to Hollywood," Photoplay, March 1927, p. 50. A decade later Clara Beranger gave the same advice in "Let Hollywood Discover You," Delineator 128 (April 1936), pp. 4, 14–15.

107. Miriam S. Leuck, "Motion Pictures," Fields of Work for Women (New York: Appleton, 1926), pp. 132–3.

108. Ibid., p. 133.

109. Ruth Biery referenced St. Johns's title in her "Haven in the Port of Missing Girls," Photoplay, February 1928, p. 39, 102, an article on the Los Angeles judge Georgia Bullock, apparently the only female judge in Los Angeles, who sent seventy-five "movie mad girls" home from Hollywood in 1927.

110. Ruth A. Inglis reports that the Hays Office cooperated in financing a new building, named the Studio Club, "a dormitory for young women connected with the industry in minor capacities" attached to the Young Women's Christian Association. (See Inglis, Freedom of the Movies, p. 98.) The Hollywood Studio Club had been founded in 1916 by the YWCA to provide low-cost housing for young women trying to enter the film industry, and the new building, added in 1926, erected with funds raised by Mrs. Cecil B. DeMille, and others, was sponsored by the Motion Picture Producer's Association, and run by the YWCA as a kind of sorority. (See

Anthony Slide, *New Historical Dictionary of the American Film Industry* (Lanham, MD, and London: Scarecrow Press, 1998), p. 95.) Hays also oversaw the establishment of the Central Casting Corporation in late 1925, which was to "replace the many private movie employment agencies which charged fees." (Inglis, *Freedom of the Movies*, p. 98.) See Heidi Kenaga, "Making the 'Studio Girl': The Hollywood Studio Club and Industry Regulation of Female Labor," paper delivered at the conference Women and the Silent Screen, November 2001, University of California at Santa Cruz, for further discussion of these themes. Kenaga points out that Hays' benevolence also drew a veil across the fact of the extras' activities as industrial labor.

111. Joseph Brandt, general manager of the Universal Film Company, quoted in Page, "The Movie-Struck Girl," p. 18.

112. This discussion of the IWW is taken from Ross, *Working-Class Hollywood*, pp. 61–2. The cartoon by Plummer, called "If the Strike Fever Hits the Movies," illustrated this volume, published at the end of the year of "red summer," also suggests the vital role female minions could and did play (as consumers and extras) in the functioning of Hollywood's business.

113. Walker, "Movie Moths," p. 14. Mary Roberts Rinehart also wrote about the "exploiting" movie mother in "How About the Movies," *Ladies' Home Journal* 38 (June 1921), p. 21.

114. Calhoun, "Do Women Rule the Movies?" p. 31. In Calhoun's view, movie mothers had "the real power."

115. Gordon Kahn, "Mother and Brat," *Atlantic Monthly* 174:4 (October 1944), p. 110.

116. Kahn, "Mother and Brat," p. 110.

117. Nancy Nadin, "The Movie Ma," *Picturegoer*, April 1921, p. 46. Another couplet of Nadin's poem runs: "(A Movie Papa is a thing I've never seen, so far,/ You never see a real white-haired, pathetic Movie Pa)".

118. See Gerould, "Hollywood: An American State of Mind," reprinted in this volume. Fitzgerald may also be responding to the operations of the Better Films Movement, discussed in Part Three, whereby local groups tried to affect what got made and screened. She may additionally have been referring to film companies that made a living shooting local movies using local talent, also a feature of the film landscape of the 1920s. Thanks to Richard Rogers for discussion of the latter type of local filmmaking.

119. Yezierska, "This is What $10,000 Did to Me," pp. 40–41, 154, reprinted in this volume.

120. On the history of the woman director, see Louise Heck-Rabi, *Women Filmmakers: A Critical Reception* (Metuchen, NJ: Scarecrow Press, 1984); Richard Henshaw, "Women Directors: 150 Filmographies," *Film Comment* 8:4 (December 1972), pp. 33–45; Slide, *Early Women Directors*; Barbara Koenig Quart, *Women Directors: The Emergence of a New Cinema* (New York: Praeger, 1988); Gwendolyn Foster, *Women Film Directors: An International Bio-Critical Dictionary* (Westport, CT: Greenwood Press, 1995); Acker, *Reel Women*; Sharon Smith, *Women Who Make Movies* (New York: Hopkinson & Blake, 1975); Sharon Smith, "Women Who Make Movies," *Women and Film* 1:3–4 (1973), pp. 77–90; Gerald Peary, "Sanka, Pink Ladies, and Virginia Slims," *Women and Film* 1:5–6 (1974), pp. 82–4; Martin F. Norden, "Women in the Early Film Industry," *Wide Angle* 6:3 (1984), pp. 58–67; Gretchen Bataille, "Preliminary Investigations: Early Suffrage Films," *Women and Film* 1:3–4 (1973), pp. 42–4. For more on individual women filmmakers one can also consult Geoffrey Donaldson, "Caroline van Dommelen," *Silent Picture* 15 (Summer 1972), pp. 33–4; Joseph and Harry Feldman, "Women Directors Seem to Go More Often Than They Come," *Films In Review* 8 (November 1950), pp. 9–12; Judith Mayne, *Directed by Dorothy Arzner* (Bloomington: Indiana University Press, 1994); and contributions to Patricia Erens, ed., *Sexual Stratagems: The World of Women in Film* (New York: Horizon Press, 1979).

121. Anne Walker, "The Girls Behind the Screen," *Woman's Home Companion* 48 (January 1921), p. 14.

122. Lois Weber joined the Gaumont Talking Pictures Company in about 1907, where she acted, wrote, and directed. See Remont, "The Lady Behind the Lens," p. 126; see also Slide, *Lois Weber*.

123. Mander, "The Feminine Touch," p. 29. By comparison, Mary Field, who began filmmaking in the silent era, was the only woman directing feature films in England in 1939.

124. Gene Gauntier, "Blazing the Trail: Conclusion," *Woman's Home Companion* 56 (March 1929), p. 146. Gene Gauntier's unpublished memoir, "Blazing the Trail," is held in the Film Study Center at the Museum of Modern Art, New York. Several sections of this were published in 1928–29 in *Woman's Home Companion*. Gauntier also sent "letters" on her filmmaking adventures with the Kalem Company and Gauntier Players to the *Moving Picture World*. See, for example,

Gene Gauntier, "A Voice from the Desert," *Moving Picture World*, 2 March 1912, p. 771; "Picture Players at a Turkish Wedding," *Moving Picture World*, 20 July 1912, p. 253; and "Gauntier Players in Ireland," *Moving Picture World*, 4 October 1913, p. 39. The so-called "Trust," formed in December 1908 included members of the Motion Picture Patents Company (MPPC)—Biograph, Edison, Essanay, Kalem, Lubin, Méliès, Pathé, Selig, and Vitagraph were the most important of these, Biograph being the last to join. These had all been established producers in the United States market since at least 1907. The "Independents" were more recently formed companies. For more information on this history, see Bowser, *The Transformation of Cinema*, pp. 21–36.

125. In January 1915 Mabel Condon reported visiting Gauntier and discussing her work at the Gauntier Feature Players Studio. See Mabel Condon, "Hot Chocolate and Reminiscences at Nine in the Morning," *Photoplay*, January 1915, p. 69. Gauntier also opened the Gene Gauntier Theater in Kansas City, her hometown.

126. Close on the heels of the Big Five were the Little Three (Universal, Columbia, and United Artists) who had production and distribution units but not exhibition circuits. Already in 1920, Anne Walker could suggest this professionalization as it affected writers. She wrote: "time was that, knowing a star, a director, even a photographer, you could sell a crude idea, crudely written, provided it had action and spirit. But to-day, experience as a writer is almost necessary to secure a hearing"—she listed Edna Ferber, Mary Roberts Rinehart, Gertrude Atherton, Jeanie Macpherson, and Fannie Hurst among those who had survived the competition. Walker, "Movie Moths," p. 130.

127. Mahar, "Women, Filmmaking," p. 353; McCreadie, *The Women Who Write the Movies*, p. 6, although McCreadie emphasizes a decline among screenwriters occuring in the mid 1940s. See also Beauchamp, *Without Lying Down*, p. 12, and the contrasting comments on Ida Lupino's experience of Hollywood noted above.

128. Hunt, "They Aren't All Actresses in Hollywood," p. 50.

129. "Feminine Sphere in the Field of Movies is Large Indeed, says Clara S. Beranger," *Moving Picture World*, 2 August 1919, p. 662, reprinted in this volume and quoted in Mahar, "Women, Filmmaking," p. 2. In 1919 Beranger was embarking upon her Hollywood career, and starting to write scripts for William de Mille. She had already had considerable success in New York writing for film and theater.

130. Frances Denton, "Lights! Camera! Quiet! Ready! Shoot!" *Photoplay*, February 1918, p. 48.

131. Ida May Park, "Motion-Picture Work: The Motion Picture Director," in *Careers for Women*, ed. Catherine Filene (Boston: Houghton Mifflin, 1920), pp. 335–37.

132. As Richard Koszarski has pointed out, by the time Filene's compendium on careers for women was reissued in an expanded and updated version in 1934, motion picture directing had been cut out. See Richard Koszarski, *Hollywood Directors, 1914–1940* (New York: Oxford University Press, 1976), p. 71.

133. Slide, *Early Women Directors*, p. 52.

134. Mahar, "Women, Filmmaking."

135. Ibid., abstract, p. viii; see also p. 6.

136. Ibid., p. 35.

137. Ibid., abstract, p. viii.

138. Ibid., abstract, p. viii and p. 55. This moral climate contributed to making Lois Weber the most successful of all women directors of the silent period, even while many of her films aroused controversy, as discussed in Part Three.

139. Ibid., pp. 25–30. Overall, Mahar has provided the most thorough explanation of women's changing roles in the early film industry, even if her explanation of the arrival of women through the association of cinema with the stage remains insufficiently supported. This would require further research and justification, especially given the evidence that a reviewer in 1918 could make precisely the opposite claim: "Following stage traditions, moving-picture directing was considered a work exclusively the property of men." Denton, "Lights! Camera!" p. 48. In reviewing women directors on stage and in the movies, MacMahon makes a related statement: "The professional stage director of the feminine sex is something new in Stage Land." See MacMahon, "Women Directors," p. 143.

140. Mahar, "Women, Filmmaking," p. 3 and elsewhere. In 1923 Grace Haskins apparently took the credit "G.S. Haskins presents" because "she didn't want anyone to know, at first, that the "G." stood for Grace instead of George. It's a fact, she says, that people are less likely to put confidence in a Grace than a George." See Valentine, "The Girl Producer," p. 110.

141. Jean Sarthe, "She Makes Movies," *Independent Woman* 13:10 (October 1934), p. 315.

142. Clara Beranger, "The Unused Asset," *Rob Wagner's Script*, 27 June 1931, p. 20.

143. For such an argument, based on the case of the United Kingdom, see Kent, *Making Peace*. See also Maureen Honey, *Breaking the Ties That Bind: Popular Stories of the New Woman, 1915–1930* (Norman, OK: Oklahoma University Press, 1992). In 1931, Winifred Holtby referred to the fierce "but hidden campaign against women's equality being fought." (See Holtby, "My Weekly Journal 26: Through Fifty Years," p. 382.

144. Writing in 1927, Anne Morgan claimed that 90 per cent of the volunteer women "did go back [home], and many of the 90 per cent are discontented today." See Anne Morgan, as told to Mary Margaret McBride, "Sidelights on the Woman Question," *Saturday Evening Post*, 26 March 1927, p. 189. See also n57.

145. Fannie Hurst, "Fannie Hurst Advises a Plan," *Christian Science Monitor*, Magazine Section, 7 August 1935, p. 13. During World War II, Hurst wrote again of her disappointment in the historical lack of "woman-push," and urged women to contemplate what they wanted for their futures, whether to "step aside," as after the last war, or push for something better after the current one. See Fannie Hurst, "A Crisis in the History of Women," *Vital Speeches of the Day* 9:15 (1 June 1943), pp. 479–80.

146. Beryl de Querton, "My Voice Makes News," *Film Weekly*, 8 June 1934, p. 13. In newsreels, female voice-overs were typically reserved for topics specifically geared towards women (e.g. fashion), while male voice-overs accompanied all other kinds of news items.

147. "Close-Ups: Editorial Expression and Timely Comment," *Photoplay*, December 1916, pp. 63, 64. This editorial fears that through this trend filmmaking will be dragged "back to its days of solitary, suspicious, feudal inefficiency." Quoted in Mahar, "Women, Filmmaking," p. 307.

148. Ibid., pp. 306–07 and 128–9.

149. A central document here is *Film Daily*'s survey in which nine women (Eve Unsell, Mary Pickford, Clara Beranger, June Mathis, Marion Fairfax, Leah Baird, Jane Murfin, Anita Loos, Josephine Lovett Robertson) respond to the issue of "The Feminine Mind in Picture Making," in *Film Daily*, 7 June 1925, pp. 9, 113, 115–16. Three of the nine responses are reprinted here.

150. Miles Mander took up the question in 1934, asking "Why should not women direct films, which are mainly a women's entertainment?" He implied that there was a feminine "point of view," which had a "seventy-five per cent value in picture making," since that was the proportion of the cinema audience "representative of the selective decision of the female mind." (As mentioned in Part One, 10 per cent of this 75 per cent were men influenced by women to attend shows.) Also dismissing notions of women's physical limitations, he begins modestly by writing: "I will not attempt to answer the question because I cannot. I wish only to examine it. Why are there not more women directors?" He scans European countries as well as the United States, commenting on the prominence of female writers but finding (almost) no directors. As so many others, he then argued that a female mind was more able to handle "romance and sentiment" on the screen, but that these were tendencies frightening to British men—"the Englishman is so notoriously afraid of showing that he, too, has feelings." (See Mander, "The Feminine Touch," p. 29.) In 1932, Harry Alan Potamkin had pondered the scarcity of female directors, finding the only point of optimism in Soviet Russia, where "we may expect to see many more women directors [because] ... There is a State School of Cinema which accepts women in its courses." His article concentrates on Germaine Dulac. He also mentions by name the following women directors: Lois Weber, Olga Tschehowa, Jacqueline Logan, Dorothy Arzner, Esther Schub, Olga Preobrashenskaya, Lucie Derain, Mme J. Bruno-Ruby, and the daughter of Eugene Chen. See Harry Alan Potamkin, "The Woman as Film-Director," *American Cinematographer* 12:9 (January 1932), p. 10.

151. For "invasion," see Gilliams, "Will Woman Leadership Change the Movies?" p. 859; "The New Woman Director," *Motion Picture Director* (October 1926), p. 70; and Osborne, "Why Are There No Women Directors?" p. 5, reprinted in this volume. Mahar cites a headline stating "A Woman Invades The American Moving Picture Industry," printed in 1909, although, according to the article, this woman was foreign, an invader in a second sense. See Mahar, "Women, Filmmaking," p. 54. The *Motion Picture Director* article continues: "Just now there is imminent danger of a 'mistress director' as well as a 'master director.' Danger? Well, perhaps that's not the proper word to use. Yet it is looming danger for the mere male megaphoner."

152. St. Johns, "'Get Me Dorothy Arzner!'", p. 22. Similarly, in 1923, Sydney Valentine wrote that

there were only two "women producers in motion pictures," Grace Haskins and Lois Weber. For the work of Dorothy Davenport Reid as a director in 1933–34 see Valentine, "The Girl Producer," p. 55. See Slide, *Early Women Directors*, pp. 79–82.

153. This challenging female "producer" was Frances Grant, who, from the context of the rest of the article, would be better described as a director. The article erroneously claims she is the "first British woman producer." See "The New Woman Discovered," *Kinematograph Weekly*, 11 November 1920, p. 83. Another example of the use of the word "producer" for the role of director, as we would now understand it, comes from 1918, in an article on Lois Weber, who is described as "the biggest woman producer in the Motion Picture field." See Remont, "The Lady Behind the Lens," p. 59.

154. Carolyn Lowrey, *The First 100 Noted Men and Women of the Screen* (New York: Moffat, Yard, 1920).

155. Gilliams, "Will Woman Leadership Change the Movies?" p. 860. Gilliams's essay is full of factual errors, but is of historical interest nevertheless. In the same year, Jessie Lasky recorded that "the ambition evinced by the girl and women workers is really astounding, and there is much work here that only women can do." Lasky quoted in Gebhart, "Business Women in Film Studios," p. 27.

156. Osborne, "Why Are There No Women Directors?" p. 5, reprinted this volume.

157. Ibid.

158. Mary Field, "Why Women Should Make Films," p. 8.

159. Dunn, "Off-stage Heroines of the Movies," p. 203.

160. "Directress" is used to describe Jeanie Macpherson in Martin, "From 'Wop' Parts," p. 97; "mistress director" and the reference to cross-dressing are in "The New Woman Director," p. 70; "Woman cannot construct" is from MacMahon, "Women Directors," p. 12; Babylonian and millenial references are in Denton, "Lights! Camera!" p. 48.

161. Leontine Sagan, "Why I Defy the Film Conventions," *Film Weekly*, 12 March 1932, p. 7.

162. See one illustrated example in *The Magic Lantern Society Newsletter* 43 (November 1995), p. 7; see also David Robinson, compiler, *Lantern Images: Iconography of the Magic Lantern, 1420–1880* (Nutley, East Sussex: Magic Lantern Society, 1993).

163. Tom Gunning discusses the attraction of the apparatus as spectacle in "The Cinema of Attractions: Early Film, Its Spectator, and the Avant-Garde," in Thomas Elsaesser, ed., *Early Film: Space, Frame, Narrative* (British Film Institute Publishing: London, 1990), p. 58.

164. See, for example, the advertisement for "The Royal Biograph," where a woman naked from the waist up seems to crank a film of the military; or "Projections animées," in which a woman cranks a projected beam out of the projector. These are illustrated in *Affiches Françaises du Cinéma Muet: Une Exposition du Service des Archives du Film* (Lyon: Institut Lumière, 1987), p. 52, cat. no. 122, and p. 48, cat. 87 respectively. Such impressions precede the cinema, and were used in promoting magic lanterns.

165. "Grand Opening of the School for Lady Operators (WE DON'T THINK)," *The Bioscope*, 24 June 1909, p. 7, article illustrated by Glossop. "P...nk...rst" in the accompanying text is a reference to the suffrage activism of the Pankhurst women, Emmeline (mother), Christobel and Sylvia (daughters). Thank you to Stephen Bottomore for this reference.

166. See J.K. Cramer-Roberts, "Our Inventions Corner: The First Description of the 'Biokam,'" *The Golden Penny*, 3 June 1899, p. 476, in which the Biokam is accompanied by such an example. Thank you to Stephen Bottomore for this reference. For still cameras see, for example, the Kodak Brownie of 1900.

167. We should not forget, however, the early and widespread interest of royalty and aristocracy in motion pictures, by which several women came to participate in filmmaking and viewing. See, for example, Elmendorf's mention "that the queen mother of the reigning King of Italy owns a Bioscope," in his "Novel and Useful Applications of Motion Photographs," p. 4.

168. Henry MacMahon, "Educational Films," *Photoplay* 15:2 (January 1919), p. 40. Thank you to Stephen Bottomore for this reference.

169. M.W. Hilton-Simpson and J.A. Haeseler, "Cinema and Ethnology," *Discovery* 6 (London) September 1925, p. 325. Haeseler operated the camera. Thank you to Stephen Bottomore for this reference.

170. "The Cinematograph on Tour—Filming East and West," *The Amateur Photographer and Photographic News*, 9 December 1912, p. 574. Thanks to Stephen Bottomore for this reference.

171. Photograph opposite p. 160 in Johnson, *Camera Trails in Africa*, titled "Reinforcement of porters, raw savages from the hills." From Martin's discussion on p. 170 it seems that the Africans

on either side of Osa might be Zabenelli (on her left), and an Askari interpreter behind her, also to her left.

172. This phrase crops up in discussing Jeanie Macpherson's work as a director. Martin, "From 'Wop' Parts," p. 95.

173. Anne Wagner, *Three Artists (Three Women)* (Berkeley: University of California Press, 1996), p. 8.

174. Denton, "Lights! Camera!," p. 48.

175. Rinehart, "My Experience in the Movies," p. 78. By 1932, Rinehart observes that this attire is only a memory, and has been replaced with "anything from soiled flannels to a neat business suit." (See Mary Roberts Rinehart, "Sounds in Silence," *Ladies' Home Journal* 49 (July 1932), p. 10.) In 1922, the "Mae Murray Fashion Page," *Filmplay* 1:2 (May 1922), p. 41, examined the wearing of jodhpurs. Holliday discusses writers' working clothes, including puttees, in "Hollywood's Modern Women," p. 309, and elsewhere.

176. Martin, "From 'Wop' Parts," p. 96.

177. See Denton, "Lights! Camera!," p. 48

178. Ibid., p. 50.

179. Remont, "The Lady Behind the Lens," pp. 59–60. In fairness to Remont, she describes Weber in very varied terms, as aspiring to Utopia, and as a worker as well. MacMahon also discusses the "homey appearance" of Weber's studio, and her custom of treating "her coworkers as a family." (See MacMahon, "Women Directors," pp. 12, 13.) Jean Sarthe brings together a similar combination when describing the work of Vyvyan Donner, animator and newsreel director:

> Her only ambition is to be a better moving picture director. To look at her against the vivid red and blue background of her charming apartment with its masses of flowers, one would hardly dream of the experiences and ambitions inside the dark bobbed head and behind the glowing dark eyes. Serene, soft-spoken, yet feminine— yet she does a man's job and does it well.

(See Sarthe, "She Makes Movies," p. 331.)

180. Carter, "The Muse of the Reel," p. 62.

181. Smith, "A Perpetual Leading Lady," p. 636.

182. Park remarked that "directing seemed so utterly unsuited to a woman." See Denton, "Lights! Camera!" p. 49.

183. Beranger on "The Feminine Mind in Picture Making," p. 9; Murfin, "Sex and the Screen," pp. 459–60.

184. Denton, "Lights! Camera!" p. 50.

185. Lee, "Women are Needed in British Films," p. 7.

186. St. Johns, "'Get Me Dorothy Arzner!'", p. 73.

187. Josephine MacDowell, "Lois Weber Understands Girls," *Cinema Art* 5:18 (January 1927), p. 18. (The late 1920s were a low point in Weber's career.) In the context of discussing plans for Weber to direct a film of *Uncle Tom's Cabin*, MacDowell makes this her case for Weber's particular talent as a director.

188. Sagan, "Why I Defy the Film Conventions," p. 7.

189. Park in Denton, "Lights! Camera!" p. 49; Field, "Why Women Should Make Films," p. 8; Kathlyn Williams, interview for *Feature Movie Magazine* (April 15, 1915), cited in Slide, *Early Women Directors*, p. 102. Williams continues: "and often it is just one tiny thing, five feet of film maybe, that quite spoils a picture, for it is always the little things that go wrong that one remembers." Williams directed only one film, *The Last Dance* (1912). She also starred in, and wrote it. MacMahon noted that Mrs Sidney Drew "mastered every detail of the studio" when she and her husband transferred their talents from stage to screen. (See MacMahon, "Women Directors," p. 13.) This theme was reiterated by producer B.P. Schulberg, who insisted: "I am absolutely sold on the idea of women workers in many departments of studio activity, inasmuch as they possess a greater gift for detail and application than men," while the reporter interviewing him here, Myrtle Gebhart, stressed that "the inattentive girl" would receive scant encouragement. (Schulberg quoted in Gebhart, "Business Women in Film Studios," p. 27; and Gebhart, "Business Women in Film Studios," p. 66.)

190. See Osborne, "Why Are There No Women Directors?" p. 5; Brown, "Making Movies for Women," p. 342; and Mathis, "Harmony in Picture-Making," p. 5, and "The Feminine Mind in Picture Making," p. 115, all reprinted in this volume.

191. Walker, "The Girls Behind the Scenes," p. 14. Rose Kurland, in her autobiographical summary "The Script Girl," *How Talkies Are Made*, ed. Joe Bonica (Hollywood: Joe Bonica, 1930), no folio, starts out with the sentence: "Any girl who has a natural aptitude for details and can list them accurately, will make a script girl." Mathis also notes that feminine attentiveness to detail lends success to the "script clerk." See Mathis, on "The Feminine Mind in Picture Making," p. 115, reprinted this volume.

192. Walker, "The Girls Behind the Scenes," p. 14.

193. Brown, "Making Movies for Women," p. 342, reprinted this volume. Clara Beranger, "Motion Pictures as a Fine Art," *Theatre Magazine* 29 (May 1919), p. 300. It is precisely this knowledge that Mary Roberts Rinehart also noted as being located largely in women; she described one woman visitor she received who saw "so many things that need[ed] correcting [on the screen]. And I know something about decorating. Everybody likes my house." Such a woman knows "form," claims Rinehart, and is needed on the film set—"an intelligent, observant woman would be a highly useful addition" to the film board. (See Rinehart, "My Experience in the Movies," pp. 76, 78.)

194. The job of the secretary to the director is to "catch mistakes, small details that might escape his eye.... He sees a picture, grouping, dramatic action, effects. She sees a tear in the lace of the star's dress, a picture or rug which has slipped out of place, an American magazine in an English setting.... Mistakes in details spell waste in production." The technical dresser "must have artistic taste, feeling for the drama, as expressed even in a sofa cushion or bit of Chinese embroidery." Walker, "The Girls Behind the Screen," p. 14.

195. Dorothy Richardson, "Talent and Genius: Is not Genius Actually Far More Common than Talent," *Vanity Fair*, October 1923, p. 120. (This article was published in an incomplete form as Dorothy Richardson, "Talent and Genius: A Discussion of Whether Genius is not Actually Far More Common than Talent," *Vanity Fair*, May 1923, p. 65.)

196. Linda Nochlin, "Why Have There Been No Great Women Artists?", *Art and Sexual Politics: Why Have There Been No Great Women Artists?*, ed. Thomas B. Hess and Elizabeth C. Baker (New York: Collier, 1973; originally published by Newsweek, 1971), pp. 1–43. On this debate, see also Potamkin, "The Woman as Film-Director," pp. 10, 45; Jane Loring, in an interview with W.H. Mooring, "Women as Directors," *Film Weekly*, 1 November 1935, p. 7; and Mander, "That Feminine Touch," p. 29.

197. On the question of women's access to the culture of art-making, and its consequences, see also Bovenschen, "Is there a Feminine Aesthetic?" pp. 111–37.

198. Nochlin, "Why Have There Been No Great Women Artists?" p. 27. Nochlin continues by saying that to run an atelier (à la Rubens) required "an enormous amount of self-confidence and worldly knowledge, as well as a natural sense of dominance and power," unfeminine traits in their focus on excelling in one thing, as opposed to the ladylike elegance of having competence in all, but an overall lack of committment. To have a full career the woman artist must have "total inner confidence, that absolute certitude and self-determination" (p. 36), and must "adopt, however covertly, the 'masculine' attributes of single-mindedness, concentration, tenaciousness" (p. 31).

199. Kay Armatage treats these issues in "Nell Shipman: A Case of Heroic Femininity," in Laura Pietropaolo and Ada Testaferri, eds., *Feminisms in the Cinema* (Bloomington: Indiana University Press, 1995), p. 127.

200. And at least one commentator, June Mathis, remarked that there might be parallel causes for the absences of female cinematographers and great women painters. See Mathis on "The Feminine Mind in Picture Making," p. 115, reprinted in this volume.

201. Richardson, "Talent and Genius" pp. 118, 120; Dorothy Richardson, "Women and the Future," *Vanity Fair* (April 1924) p. 39; and Richardson, "Women in the Arts," pp. 47, 100. In "Women and the Future" Richardson dissected the idea that there was a "new species of woman," comparing it to other female types, such as "the womanly woman," the "'intelligent' woman," and "the daughters of the horse-leech."

202. Richardson, "Women in the Arts," p. 47.

203. West, "Woman as Thinker and Artist," pp. 369–82.

204. Ibid., p. 371.

205. Ibid., pp. 374, 382.

206. Ibid., p. 381.

207. Ibid., pp. 378, 381.

208. Ibid., p. 380.
209. Richardson, "Women in the Arts," p. 100.
210. Ibid., p. 100.
211. Ibid.
212. Ibid. Morgan, in "Sidelights on the Woman Question," approached the same question, and called on "what must so far be called a man's mind," that is, a habit of thinking logically, and "thinking through and acting accordingly." She suggested by the words "so far" that a feminine or masculine mind was created through accumulated experience, over generations. With new changes in women's lives, their minds too will change, over time: "Most women skip nimbly from one idea or task to another without finishing anything. Again we can blame evolution. Women have not yet the race experience that makes for consecutive purpose and accomplishment. Experience of the world outside her home will accumulate from generation to generation." (See Morgan, "Sidelights on the Woman Question," p. 7.)
213. MacMahon, "Women Directors," p. 140, in a discussion of Lillian Gish.
214. John Berger, *Ways of Seeing* (London: British Broadcasting Corporation and Penguin, 1972), especially ch. 3, and p. 47.
215. Alice Guy Blaché, interview, "The First Motion Picture and Its Producer, Madame Blaché" (8 August 1914), clipping file, Billy Rose Collection, New York Public Library. Research suggests that this article is not from the *New Jersey Star*, as is usually cited. The site of publication remains unclear.
216. Mulvey, "Visual Pleasure and Narrative Cinema," pp. 6–18.
217. Here are some examples of writings that oppose appearing on the screen to other film work women were performing: "Girls are learning that if they do not photograph well, they can find something else to do on the motion picture lot, something that keeps them near the film world they love," wrote Walker in "The Girls Behind the Scenes," p. 14; Gebhart began her essay on women in the film business by reminding her readers that women "are not all imbued with a desire to see their faces pictured on the screen," in Gebhart, "Business Women in Film Studios," p. 26. Beryl de Querton, newsreel commentator wrote: "To the filmgoer I am just a voice. I am the first woman newsreel commentator. I got the job by gate-crashing a studio and asking bluntly to be taken on as a commentator. They were so surprised to find a woman who did not want her picture on the screen that they gave me some fashion commentaries to speak" (de Querton, "My Voice Makes News," p. 13). Gilliams's treatment of the career of Blanche Sewell, film editor, is similar: "She is very pretty and charming and when one day, five years ago, at a Hollywood studio, she went into the employment office, everybody remarked 'another would-be-star.' When she approached the employment manager and told him that she wanted a job in the 'works' he was nearly bowled over with astonishment." Gilliams, "Will Woman Leadership Change the Movies?" p. 956. Florence L. Strauss recommended the career of Scenario Editor to women because it had "no hampering time limits, because, while the screen demands youth and beauty in women, editorial work has the advantage of requiring brains and personality and these qualities usually increase with the years." See Florence L. Strauss, "The Scenario Editor," in *Careers for Women*, ed. Catherine Filene (Boston, MA: Houghton Mifflin, 1934), p. 440. Of Frances Marion, Adela Rogers St. Johns wrote: "They pay her at the rate of five thousand a week … ; yet she has never appeared on the screen," in St. Johns, "The One Genius in Pictures," p. 22. (Marion *did* appear on film. She started in Hollywood by being tested as an actress and being given a new name, and classified as a "refined type," even though she was insisting on her preference for writing. See Beauchamp, *Without Lying Down*, p. 37.
218. MacDowell, "Lois Weber Understands Girls," p. 19. Remont, in "The Lady Behind the Lens," captions a photograph of Weber's isolated hand with "a close-up of her artistic hand" (p. 60).
219. See Louella Parsons, "Miss Theda Bara's Expressive Hand," *Chicago Tribune*, 9 October 1915, and Louella Parsons, "Seen on the Screen," *Chicago Tribune*, both held in Louella Parsons Scrapbooks, Scrapbook no. 1, Special Collections, Margaret Herrick Library, Academy of Motion Picture Arts and Sciences, Los Angeles.
220. Shute, "Can Women Direct Films?" p. 12, reprinted in this volume. (For an account of the case, in which Dinah Shurey was awarded £500 damages from *Film Weekly*'s parent company, English Newspapers, see "'Film Weekly' Sued for Libel," p. 25.) Shute later changed her tune in optimistically assessing Elinor Glyn's forthcoming first effort at directing: "If *Knowing Men*

should prove, as I imagine, a spectacular British success, Elinor Glyn will not only have aided the British Film Industry, she will have done something else of almost equal importance. She will have destroyed the notion that women cannot direct films." See Shute, "Can Women Direct Films?", p. 1, reprinted in this volume.

221. Loring, "Women as Directors," p. 7. Loring discusses Dorothy Arzner in this interview. According to Richard Koszarski, Loring worked as a film editor at Paramount in the late 1920s. (See Koszarski, *An Evening's Entertainment*, p. 136.) Jane Murfin echoed Loring's point in writing, "Jill must know her business, not only as well, but just a little better than Jack, if she is going to 'get by' at all." See Murfin, "Sex and the Screen," p. 459, reprinted in this volume.

222. Mathis, on "The Feminine Mind in Picture Making," p. 115, reprinted in this volume.

223. Jackson, "Role of Queenie in Film 'Showboat' Dangling," p. 8.

224. For the crowd, see Morris, "Says Negro Should Be in All Pictures," p. 20; The Ex-White Actress, "The Confessions of an Ex-White Actress," pp. 16, 16, 19, reprinted in this volume; Goodwin, "The Color Fad," p. 11, reprinted in this volume; Proctor, "La Femme Silhouette: The Bronze Age," p. 93, reprinted in this volume.

225. See Richard Dyer, "The Colour of Virtue: Lillian Gish, Whiteness, and Femininity," in *Women and Film: A Sight and Sound Reader*, ed. Pam Cook and Philip Dodd (London: British Film Institute, 1993), pp. 1–9.

226. Harris, "I Tried to Crash the Movies," pp. 5–10, reprinted in this volume; Theresa Harris interviewed in the *Pittsburgh Courier*, 27 August 1937, cited in Sampson, *Blacks in Black and White*, pp. 490–91. See also Lena Horne, "My Life Story," *Negro Digest* 7:9 (July 1949), pp. 3–13; and the counterpoint piece, "She Passed for Negro ... in the Movies," by Jeanne Crain, *Negro Digest* 8 (March 1950), pp. 26–7, in which the white Crain discusses acting the part of a black woman who passes for white.

227. Rogin, in *Blackface, White Noise*, writes of the ethnic and racial significance of film's transition to sound.

228. See Kaja Silverman, *The Acoustic Mirror: The Female Voice in Psychoanalysis and Feminism* (Bloomington: Indiana University Press, 1988), for more on the theme of the power of the disembodied voice, which in cinema has nearly always been male.

229. See, for example, Verna Arvey, "Worth While Music in the Film," *The Etude* 57 (March 1939), pp. 152, 205. We might note also that some black opera singers, male and female, were beginning to develop professional careers that crossed racial barriers at this time. See John Dizikes, *Opera in America: A Cultural History* (New Haven: Yale University Press, 1993), p. 493 and elsewhere.

230. See Claude A. Barnett Papers, Chicago Historical Society, Box 298, Folder 1, for articles on *Hallelujah*: Thomas Walker Wallace, "Here and There"; The Editor, "Adding to the Mirth of a Nation"; and "*Hallelujah!*—A Disgrace to the Race," *Chicago Whip*. No further references are attached to these clippings.

231. Walker, "Movie Moths," p. 14. Katherine Mansfield's Ada Moss, from "The Pictures," failed to make the grade as a film actress on these grounds.

232. Cora Drew, "Again—the Question of 'Types' on the Screen," *New York Dramatic Mirror*, 5 May 1917, p. 26. On the theme of older women in film see also Karen M. Stoddard, *Saints and Shrews: Women and Aging in Popular American Film* (Westport, CT: Greenwood Press, 1983); and Lucy Fischer, *Cinematernity: Film, Motherhood, Genre* (Princeton, NJ: Princeton University Press, 1996). And see Mrs W.B. Meloney, "A Mother of the Movies," *Delineator* 87 (August 1915), p. 9, which described Mary Maurice as "The Oldest Motion Picture Actress," who, at age seventy (her movie career had begun when she was sixty-five, preceded by an early career on the stage), played "old mother" roles for Vitagraph.

233. Troly-Curtin, "Beauty is an Art—and a Science," p. 17.

234. Griffith, "Youth, the Spirit of the Movies," p. 195; see, for example ,Howard Whitman, "What Hollywood Doesn't Know about Women," *Collier's* (March 1949), pp. 18–19, 46, illustrated with a cartoon of a "Swedish film star" having a "new face and form" superimposed upon her by her studio.

235. West, "New Secular Forms of Old Religions Ideas," pp. 29, 30, reprinted in this volume.

236. Ibid., p. 31.

237. Sonya Levien, "The Screen Writer," Catherine Filene, ed., *Careers for Women* (Boston : Houghton Mifflin, 1934), p. 437.

238. Martin, "From 'Wop' Parts," p. 95. For another example of this process of making the work

of writing visible, see Fannie Hurst, "The Author and His Home Environment: Where and How I Write my Two-Thousand Dollar Short Stories," *Arts and Decoration* 19:9 (June 1923), pp. 9, 55, 62. In this article Hurst does not discuss writing for the movies in particular, but describes the setting she requires for hatching her stories, contained within her gothic house on Central Park West:

> My writing-desk and paraphenalia are unpicturesque. No colored quills. No rosemary for remembrance. No socratic bust to help me muse. Familiar objects, yes. The warmth of dear, shabby old books on their accustomed shelves. Objects that are loved chiefly because they are mine own, and have gathered here, there and everywhere. Wood-carvings, old wall fabrics, a couple of good cryptics. Chairs that I have searched for and found in queer places—just the worn, mellow things that make a room a place in which to dream and relax. I think I work most comfortably in such surroundings, but a hotel room and a bit of ugly wall paper for outlook will suffice at a pinch. (p. 9)

239. In her fictionalized autobiography, *Abandoned Trails*, Nell Shipman (taking the name Joyce Jevons) opposes the *typewriter* to the make-up box, as female symbols of writing and acting in film: "she cheerfully pitched her typewriter overboard and bought a make-up box," when getting her break as a leading lady (p. 13).

240. See Jill Krementz, *The Writer's Desk* (New York: Random House, 1996), for more on the image of the writer writing.

241. See J.M. Barrie, "The Twelve-Pound Look," for a short story on the liberatory potential of the typewriter for women, in which a woman escapes a stiffling bourgeois marriage once she has proved to herself her capacity to earn £12 typing, with which she buys her rented machine. Barrie's work became particularly famous as a one-act play starring Ethel Barrymore, in which she toured in vaudeville. Thanks to Annette Michelson for this reference. J.M. Barrie, "The Twelve-Pound Look," first performed in London in 1910, published in J. M. Barrie, *Half Hours* (New York: Charles Scribners' Sons, 1914), pp. 43–85. In Dorothy West's "The Typewriter" (*Opportunity*, July 1926, pp. 220–22, 233–34), the rented typewriter not only releases the young African-American Millie from home into a job as a stenographer but also feeds the fantasy life of her janitor father, who imagines himself to be various grand businessmen as he dictates fictional letters to help her practise.

Friedrich Kittler sees a link between film, the phonograph, and the typewriter, the "three storage media" which "can neither amplify nor transmit." He continues, "the historical synchronicity of cinema, phonography, and typewriter separated the data flows of optics, acoustics, and writing and rendered them autonomous," whereas recent technologies brought them "back together" to "combine them." See Friedrich Kittler, "Gramaphone, Film, Typewriter," *October* 41 (Summer 1987), pp. 103, 114.

242. Breckenridge, *Women in the Twentieth Century*, p. 177; Ellen Lupton, *Mechanical Brides: Women and Machines from Home to Office* (New York: Princeton Architectural Press, 1993), p. 43.

243. Anne Morgan took the occasion of the opening of the headquarters in New York of the America Women's Association (of which Mary Pickford was a member) to address irritations and opportunitites in "the achievements of today's woman." See Morgan, "Sidelights on the Woman Question," p. 7. Morgan proposed that new members being put up for election should have "ambition, pluck, and energy" (p. 190).

244. For the typewriter and erotic opportunity, see Rabinovitz, *For the Love of Pleasure*, p. 16, where she invokes George Ade's 1903 story, "The Stenographic Proposal." See also Christopher Keep, "The Cultural Work of the Typewriter Girl," *Victorial Studies* (Spring 1997), p. 416.

245. Michael Monahan quoted in A.S.B., "The American Peril," p. 210.

246. The photograph of Sarah Y. Mason is illustrated in Holliday, "Hollywood's Modern Women," p. 332. Anita Loos later claimed that Barton's caricature was a "figment of the artist's imagination" since, as she put it, "I never learned to type, having always found it more cosy to loll on a chaise longue and write on a clipboard." Anita Loos, *Cast of Thousands* (New York: Grosset & Dunlap, 1977), p. 73.

247. Remont, "The Lady Behind the Lens," p. 61.

248. Ina Rae Hark, "The 'Theater Man' and 'The Girl in the Box Office': Gender in the Discourse of Motion Picture Theater Management," *Film History* 6 (1994), p. 180.

249. Langer, "In the Movie Houses of Western Berlin," pp. 26–7, reprinted in this volume. See

also Wright, "Life Looks Funny Through a Grille," p. 19, for journalism on the cashier's role, a study of a cashier at the Capitol Super Cinema, Forest Hill, London, in 1931. Women had the opportunity to work as projectionists chiefly during the male labor shortages of the First and Second World Wars; during the latter they were referred to as "projectionettes." See Williams, "Ladies of the Lamp," and letter to the Editor, 18 November 1997.

250. Hark, "The 'Theater Man' and 'The Girl in the Box Office,'" p. 180.

251. For more on ushers and usherettes, see Ben M. Hall, The Best Remaining Seats: The Golden Age of the Movie Palace (New York: C.N. Potter [1961], 1975, reprinted 1987). Female ushers are discussed in Bowser, The Transformation of Cinema, pp. 45, 123, 127–8, 135.

252. "In the Dark, by a West End Cinema Attendant," Film Weekly, 7 February 1931, p. 14.

253. Winifred Horrabin, "Salute to the Usherettes," The Tribune, 11 October 1940, p. 14, reprinted in this volume.

254. One trade writer recommended that the ticket-taker be "ladylike" and that the "piano player and vocalist preferably [be] a young lady." See F.G. Aiken, in "The Business of Exhibiting," Views and Films Index 3:22 (13 June 1908), p. 6. See also Mahar, "Women, Filmmaking," p. 64. A photograph of "The Star" nickelodeon in Bradford, Pennsylvannia shows the employees standing in front of the theater. The pianist and two ticket-takers are women. See Views and Films Index 3:19 (23 May 1908), p. 8. Altman's research has also turned up female pianists. See Altman, "The Silence of the Silents," pp. 680, 682. Remember also the female cellist-cum-organist appearing in the tea rooms and then movie theater in David Lean's Brief Encounter (1945).

255. A perusal of advertisements in the Chicago Defender of the 1920s reveals several women's names accompanying films being shown to black audiences. Frances Marion and Lois Weber were both accomplished pianists.

256. Norton, "Brains, Brown Eyes and Buttons," p. 30; Ginger, "The Prodigal Nephew's Aunt," p. 7; Bowlan, Minnie at the Movies, p. 6, reprinted in this volume.

257. Statistic taken from James P. Kraft, "Stage to Studio: American Musicians and Sound Technology," Dissertation, University of Southern California, 1990, pp 39–40, 60, and cited in Ross, Working-Class Hollywood, p. 190.

258. Gebhart, "Business Women in Film Studios," p. 68.

259. Momus, "Kinema Ballads. No. 1—Types of Pianists," Kinematograph and Lantern Weekly, 18 February 1915, p. 2. The poem discusses three types of pianist, in three verses. The female pianist is described in the central verse, sandwiched by two men, a verse which runs as follows:

> Then the lady rather haughty, with a touch extremely forte,
>   Who admits her age is nearly thirty-two,
> Is devotionally sturdy in her love for Grieg and Verdi
>   Irrespective of the incidents on view.
> She is pretty ma non troppo, guaranteed to never stop oh!
>   Of melody perpetual the queen;
> And she's elegantly booted, if her music is unsuited
>   To the action of the drama on the screen.

260. See, for example, Bachmann, "Still in the Dark," pp. 35, 36, 37, 38 39.

261. See, for example, "Woman Educator on Moving Pictures," Moving Picture World, 19 August 1911, p. 452, which reports on Mrs R.G. Dolese, former member of the Board of Censors, who had given "a moving picture entertainment for a ladies' club" in a hotel and who had found that many there knew practically nothing about pictures, and had never seen one. For a related development in film distribution, see: Katherine F. Carter, formerly head of the General Film Company's educational division, who founded the Katherine F. Carter Educational and Motion Picture Service Bureau in New York, in mid 1914 (cited in Norden, "Women in the Early Film Industry," p. 61); and Elizabeth Richey Dessez, Director of the Educational Department, Pathé Exchange in 1928. (In Anthony Slide, Before Video: A History of Non-Theatrical Film (Westport, CT: Greenwood Press, 1992), p. 11, we read that a Mrs Catherine Carter contributed to the founding of the Educational Films Corporation in New York in May 1915.) In Josephine Clement, Interview, "Mrs Clement and Her Work," Moving Picture World, 15 October 1910, p. 859, we read that "the influence of good women in the moving picture field is of incalculable advantage and value in hastening the date when the picture will come into its right and full inheritance of being the principal means of entertaining and amusing

the Plain People." See also Bowser, *The Transformation of Cinema*, pp. 45–6. For "cut flowers," see Josephine Clement, Interview, "Aestheticism and Dimes: A Boston Society Woman has made a Success of a Playhouse just to Prove that Refinement Pays in Dollars and Cents," *The Green Book Magazine*, December 1914, p. 1030. Thank you to Stephen Bottomore for this reference.

262. Mrs T.H. Swenson, Grand Theater, Hastings, Minnesota, "The Value of Courtesy," *New York Dramatic Mirror*, 16 June 1917, p. 24. For another female exhibitor, see "Woman Exhibitor Welcomes Ass'n," *New York Dramatic Mirror*, 15 September 1917, p. 22, an item on the establishment of the American Exhibitor's Association. In this, Dolly Spurr, president and general manager of the Mutual Theater Company, Marion, Indiana, is described as "one of the foremost women exhibitors of the industry."

263. Bessie F. Baker, manager, Northport Theater, Northport, Long Island, "The Woman Manager in the Small Community," *New York Dramatic Mirror*, 28 April 1917, p. 24.

264. Baker, "The Woman Manager in the Small Community," p. 24.

265. "We Have with Us Today" (about Ella Fabrique, Detroit manager of a photoplay house), p. 395.

266. Leslie Wood, "Where the Clock has Stopped," *Film Weekly*, 5 July 1930, p. 19. Murphy, "People of the Pictures," p. 29, recounts an usherette, Mary, saying "I have been at the same cinema for some years now, and I know the regular clients and they know me."

267. See Vanessa Toulmin, "Women Bioscope Proprietors: Before the First World War," *Celebrating 1895: The Centenary of Cinema*, ed. John Fullerton (London: John Libbey, 1999), pp. 55–65. This trend is also discussed in Mahar, "Women, Filmmaking," pp. 65–70.

268. Herbert and McKernan, eds, *Who's Who in Victorian Cinema*, p. 66. Their operation lasted one short season. See also pp. 62–3 for discussion of three other female film exhibitors of c. 1898: Sophie Hancock, Elizabeth Crecraft, and Annie Holland, and p. 103 for traveling showwoman Madame Olinka, presenting films in Germany, Holland, and Poland.

269. See Musser, *The Emergence of Cinema*, pp. 299–301. Mrs Sloan's theater ran for eighteen months from November 1900.

270. For Mrs Laura Hill, see "Motion Picture Notes," *New York Dramatic Mirror*, 24 January 1912, p. 40, cited in Bowser, *The Transformation of Cinema*, p. 124. Sampson, *Blacks in Black and White*, lists several black female managers in his Appendix C, Table 4, "Theaters Owned and Operated by Blacks, 1910–1930," pp. 644–9. Bowser, *The Transformation of Cinema*, pp. 47, 124, lists several female managers working in 1912 and 1913. Mahar, "Women, Filmmaking," p. 66, cites several female nickelodeon owners and managers from the period 1907 to 1910, published on the pages of *Moving Picture World*. *Views and Films Index* 3:19 (23 May 1908), p. 8, reports two women managing the Olympic Theater in Topeka, Kansas.

271. Alta M. Davis, "Great Field for Women: Lady Manager of Theater Writes to Balboa Company," *New York Dramatic Mirror*, 10 February 1917, p. 24, reprinted in this volume.

272. *Motion Picture News*, 19 December 1914, p. 37, cited in Bowser, *The Transformation of Cinema*, p. 124.

273. Clement, Interview, "Aestheticism and Dimes," p. 1030. For "the busy man," she offered a smoking room, with magazines, writing materials, and a stenographer.

274. Ibid.

275. Clement, Interview, "Mrs Clement and Her Work," p. 859. This article is discussed in Bowser, *The Transformation of Cinema*, pp. 45–7.

276. Interview with Josephine Clement, "Mrs Clement and Her Work," p. 859. "Aestheticalize" is not Mrs Clement's word, but that of the *World* reporter.

277. Josephine Clement, interviewed by "The Film Man," "Comment and Suggestion," *New York Dramatic Mirror*, 13 November 1912, pp. 25–6, cited in Bowser, *The Transformation of Cinema*, pp. 123–4.

278. See Musser, *The Emergence of Cinema*, pp. 193–293.

279. In all likelihood, Virginia Woolf saw *The Cabinet of Dr. Caligari* (which she analyses so provocatively in her essay on the cinema "The Movies and Reality," reprinted in this volume) in a revival screening at the London Film Society.

280. See Bandy, "Nothing Sacred," p. 10. Barry settled in the United States in 1932.

281. See Flitterman-Lewis, *To Desire Differently*, pp. 86–8.

282. "The Film Forum," *New Masses* 8:7 (February 1933), p. 29. The venue was the New School for Social Research, New York.

283. Marguerite Tazelaar, "The Story of the First Little Film Theater," *Amateur Movie Makers* 3:7 (July

1928), pp. 441–2; see also Jan-Christopher Horak, "The First American Film Avant-Garde, 1914–1945" in *Lovers of Cinema: The First American Film Avant-Garde, 1914–1945*, ed. Jan-Christopher Horak (Madison: University of Wisconsin, 1995), pp. 20–29.

284. Elizabeth Perkins, "The Civic Cinema: A Unique Movie Move Planned for Manhattan," *Amateur Movie Makers* 3:4 (April 1928), p. 254.

285. Elizabeth Coxhead, "Towards a Co-operative Cinema,' *Close Up* 10:2 (June 1933), p. 137.

286. Winifred Holtby, "My Weekly Journal: Life and Art," *Schoolmistress* (16 July 1931), p. 441. Holtby also notes that *Turksib* and *The Marriage of Figaro* are playing; Holtby, "Children in the Spotlight," p. 425.

287. See Coxhead, "Towards a Co-operative Cinema," reprinted in this volume, as well as "Elsie Cohen in an interview with Anthony Slide," not paginated.

288. Gibbs, "This is Where I Came In...", p. 157.

289. Notes for Iris Barry's course held at Columbia, titled "The History, Aesthetic, and Technique of the Motion Picture," are housed at the Museum of Modern Art, Film Study Center, Iris Barry Collection. See Frances Taylor Patterson, "A New Art in an Old University," *Photoplay*, January 1920, pp. 65, 124, and Patterson, *Cinema Craftsmanship* (one of her course text books), for information on her teaching and intentions at Columbia University. For Alice Guy Blaché, whose lecture notes do not survive, see Blaché, *The Memoirs of Alice Guy Blaché*, pp. 68–69.

290. Clara Beranger, "The Cinema is Ready for College," *Theatre Arts* 31 (January 1947), p. 62.

291. Iris Barry, "Motion Pictures as a Field of Research," *College Art Journal* 4:4 (May 1945), pp. 206–9.

292. Ibid., p. 9.

293. Many of the opinions expressed in this journalism are to be re-found in Barry's *Let's Go to the Pictures*, some chapters of which are reprinted in this volume.

294. Bandy, "Nothing Sacred," p. 18.

Primary Bibliography

NOTE: This bibliography includes writings by women on cinema published up to 1950, and a few unpublished items, or items published after 1950, where the inclusion seems helpful, as in the case of volumes which reprint earlier writings by women, and autobiographies by women writers on cinema. Certain genres and formats, such as the fan magazine, the trade press, the weekly critical review, and the gossip column, are poorly represented, so that a number of women who wrote voluminously on cinema (such as Edith Gwynne, a gossip columnist for *Hollywood Reporter* in the 1930s, or prolific fan magazine writer Jane Ardmore) receive no entry. For other women, such Olga Petrova, Dora Albert, and Adele Whitley Fletcher, a single entry might stand in for their extensive contributions.

Abbott, Mary Allen. "Children's Responses to the Motion Picture *The Thief of Bagdad*." *International Review of Educational Cinematography* 3 (1931): 65–80, 157–64, 241–6, 469–82.

——. "Motion Picture Classics." *English Journal* [Chicago] 21 (1932): 624–8.

——. "Motion Picture Preferences of Adults and Children." *School Review* 41 (1933): 278–83.

Adams, Mildred. "Talkies in the Making." *Woman's Journal* June 1930: 16–17+.

Adams, Minnie. "In Union is Strength." *Chicago Defender* 24 February 1912: 6.

Addams, Jane. "Jane Addams Condemns Race Prejudice Film." *New York Evening Post* 13 March 1915: 4.

——. Letter included in an advertisement for the Laemmle Film Service. *Show World* 3 August 1907: 32. It also appeared in *Views and Films Index* 10 August 1907: 10.

——. *The Spirit of Youth and the City Streets*. New York: Macmillan, 1909.

Ager, Cecelia. "Cecelia Ager" [a collection of her essays]. *Garbo and the Night Watchmen*. Ed. Alistair Cooke. 1937. London: Secker & Warburg, 1971. 227–52.

——. "Mae West Reveals the Foundation of the 1900 Mode." *Vogue* [New York] 1 September 1933: 67, 86.

——. "Native Customs of Hollywood." *Vogue* [New York] 1 July 1934: 23, 60, 76.

——. "The New Hollywood." *Flair* March 1950: 21–22, 119.

——. "Women Only." *Mademoiselle* April 1947: 234–35, 321–23.

Agnew, Frances. *Motion Picture Acting*. New York: Reliance Newspaper Syndicate, 1913.

Albert, Dora. [A prolific writer for fan magazines.] "Child's Year in Hollywood." *American* July 1945: 122–23.

Alden, Mary. "The Woman Making Up for the Screen." *Opportunities in the Motion Picture Industry*. Vol. 3. Los Angeles: Photoplay Research Society, 1922: 13–17.

Aldrich, Maude M. "The Motion Picture Problem." *Union Signal* 25 January 1930: 12–13.

Alexander, Norah. "Frustrated, Lonely and Peculiar." *Diversion: Twenty-Two Authors on the Lively Arts*. Ed. John Sutro. London: Max Parish, 1950. 70–77.

Lady Allen of Hurtwood. "Children and the Cinema." *Fortnightly* [London] July 1946: 1–6.

Allen, Gertrude M. "The Hidden People." *Film Weekly* 15 February 1930: 6.

——. "Painting the Stars With Moonshine." *Film Weekly* 8 March 1930: 6.

Alsberg, Grete. "Films and Biology." *Life & Letters Today* 15 (1936): 170.

Altenloh, Emilie. Zur *Soziologie des Kino: Die Kino-Unternehmeung und die sozialen Schichten ihrer Besucher* [On the Sociology of the Cinema: Film Entertainment and the Social Classes of its Patrons]. Jena: Eugen Diederichs, 1914.

——. "Theater und Kino." *Bild und Film* 11–12 (1912–13): 264–6.

Anderson, Margaret (writing as "Mobbie Mag"). "Emasculating Ibsen." *Little Review* 2.5 (1915): 36.

Andreas-Salomé, Lou. "Movies" [1913]. *The Freud Journal of Lou Andreas-Salomé*. Trans. Stanley A. Leavy. New York: Basic Books, 1964. London: Quartet, 1987. 100–101.

Andrus, Edythe F. "Ladies, Please Remove Your Hats." *Christian Science Monitor Magazine* 31 December 1949: 15.

Appleton, Dorothy. "Speed the March of Improvement." *Moving Picture World* 9 April 1910: 547.

Apponyi, Mme la Contesse. "The Cinema, Instrument of General Culture and Human Solidarity." *International Review of Educational Cinematography* 3 (1931): 1138–39.

Arledge, Sara Kathlyn. "The Experimental Film: A New Art in Transition." *Arizona Quarterly* Summer 1947: 101–12.

Arthur, Charlotte. "In the Old Days." *Close Up* 6.4 (1930): 297–303; 6.5 (1930): 369–77.

Arvey, Verna. Regular columns titled "Music of Worth to the Movies." "Worth While Music in the Film." *Etude* 1932–1942.

——. "Hall Johnson and His Choir." *Opportunity* 19 (1941): 151, 158–9.

——. "Present-Day Musical Films and How They Are Made Possible." *Etude* 49 (1931): 16–17.

Arzner, Dorothy. "Starlight." [c. Late 1950s–1960s], unpublished lecture notes, UCLA Arts——Special Collections, Dorothy Arzner Papers.

Attasheva, Pera. "The Michurinsky Nursery Garden." *Close Up* 7.1 (1930): 65–70.

——. "News of Soviet Cinema." *Close Up* 5.4 (1929): 309–18; 7.3 (1930): 177–83.

——. "A Soviet Film Star: Martha Lapkina." *Close Up* 4.2 (1929): 48–52.

——. "The Stump of an Empire." *Close Up* 5.5 (1929): 372–5.

Atwood, Rose. "Rose Atwood in the *Pittsburgh Courier*: 'Noted Writer Tells of Amazing Growth of Movie Industry'." *Western Dispatch* 1 December 1921: 6. George P. Johnson Collection, Special Collections, UCLA, Box 50.

Auberon, Joyce. "Dressing a New Film is No Joke." *Film Weekly* 26 September 1931: 8.

Aydelotte, Winifred. Interviewing Lois Weber. "Little Red School House Becomes a Theater." *Motion Picture magazine* March 1934: 34–5, 85, 88.

Ayres, Agnes. "Advice." *The Truth About the Movies by the Stars*. Ed. Laurence A. Hughes. Hollywood: Hollywood Publishers, 1924. 137.

Bacon, Gertrude. *The Record of an Aeronaut: Being the Life of John M. Bacon*. London: John Long, 1907.

Baird, Leah. "The Feminine Mind in Picture Making." *Film Daily* 7 June 1925: 115–16.

Baker, Besse F. "The Woman Manager in the Small Community." *New York Dramatic Mirror* 28 April 1917: 24.

Baker, Louise Kimball. "Music Teachers and Movie Cameras." *Etude* 58 (1940): 166.

——. "Music Teachers, etc." *Careers for Women*. Ed. Catherine Filene. Boston: Houghton Mifflin, 1934. 166.

Balaban, Carrie. *Continuous Performance: The Story of A.J. Balaban as Told to his Wife, Carrie Balaban*. New York: G.P. Putnam's Sons, 1942.

Balfour, Betty. "The Art of the Cinema." *English Review* [London] 37 (1923): 388–91.

——. "I'm Telling You." *Picturegoer* July 1928: 20–21.

Bankhead, Tallulah. "Not Three-D, But No-T." *New York Times Magazine* 31 January 1954: 14+.

Bannister, Edith. "Britain on the Screen" *Special Libraries* 35 (1944): 452–4.

Bara, Theda. "How I Became a Vampire." *Forum* June–July 1919: 715–27.

——. "The Curse on the Moving-Picture Actress." *Forum* 62 (1919): 83–93.

Barkas, Natalie. *Thirty-Thousand Miles for the Films*. London and Glasgow: Blackie & Son, 1937.

Barnes, Djuna. "Playgoer's Almanac." *Theatre Guild Magazine* July 1930: 26–7, September 1930: 34–5, October 1930: 34–5, November 1930: 34–5, January 1931: 34–5.

——. "The Stage Sets the Style." *Theatre Guild Magazine* October 1930: 38–9.

——. "The Wanton Playgoer." *Theatre Guild Magazine* April 1931: 30–31; May 1931: 32–3; June 1931: 36–7; July 1931: 18–19; August 1931: 24–25; September 1931: 20–21.

Barry, Iris. 'The Lure of the Films." *Daily Mail* 9 October 1925: 8.

——. "Cowboy Films for 'High brows'." *Daily Mail*, 10 August 1927: 8

——. "The Prince of Hollywood." *Daily Mail* 23 March 1927: 10.

——. "America's Giant Cinema." *Daily Mail* 21 November 1927: 10.

——. "Hollywood's English Colony." *Daily Mail* 18 November 1927: 10.

——. "Pity the Extras of Hollywood." *Daily Mail* I November 1927: 10.

——. "Actors Who Dream of Films." *Daily Mail* 24 November 1927: 10.

——. "The New Art." *Daily Mail* 15 April 1926: 8.

——. "New Blood for British Films." *Daily Mail* 17 December 1925: 7.

——. "Films Made on a Girder." *Daily Mail* 23 April 1928: 2 1.

——. "Films the Public Want." *Daily Mail* 21 November 1925: 8.

——. "Films We Do Not Want." *Daily Mail* 21 september 1926: 8.

——. "Nelson and Three Bad Men." *Daily Mail* 4 October 1926: 8.

——. "Do-Everything Filmmakers." *Daily Mail* 22 february 1927: 17.

——. "Music-Making Films: Will They Displace Orchestras?" *Daily Mail*, 17 May 1927: 17.

——. "This Week's Films: Miss Beatrice Lillie on the Screen." *Daily Mail*, 6 June 1927: 17.

——. "Season of Poor Films." *Daily Mail*, 20 June 1927L 17.

——. "Fraining for Film Work." *Daily Mail*, 21 June 1927: 17.

——. "Why they Go to 'The Pictures.' *Daily Mail*, 10 April 1928: 17.

——. "The Cinema: American Prestige and British Films." *Spectator* 11 July 1925: 51–2.

——. "The Cinema: Back to Simplicity." *Spectator* 17 July 1926: 88.

——. "*The Beggar's Opera.*" *National Board of Review Magazine* June 1931: 11–13.

——. "Ben-Hur at the Tivoli." *Spectator* 20 November 1926: 898.

——. "Ben-Hur at the Tivoli. *Mademoiselle from Armetières* at the Marble Arch Pavilion." *Spectator* 13 November 1926: 43–4.

——. "Jean Benoit-Levy: A Film Historian." *Documentary News Letter* [London] 4 (1946): 11–13.

——. "*The Big Parade.*" *Spectator* 5 June 1926: 946–4.

——. "A Brief History of the American Film, 1895–1938." *Trois siècles d'art aux États-Unis*. Paris: Éditions des Musées Nationaux, 1938. 97–101.

——. "The British Film Situation I: Decline and Fall." *Spectator* 9 January 1926: 43.

——. "The British Film Situation II: The Plight and the Remedy." *Spectator* 23 January 1926: 123–4.

——. "The British Film Weeks." *Spectator* 2 February 1924: 171.

——. "The Cinema: Of British Films." *Spectator* 14 November 1925: 870–71.

——. "British Films, The Quota and Reciprocity." *Spectator* 24 April 1926: 755–6.

——. "The Challenge" [poem]. Included in C.A. Lejeune, "Can Piccadilly do Without Hollywood?" *New York Times* 24 August 1947: 32. (Original source London *Observer*, n.d.)

——. "Challenge of the Documentary Film." *New York Times Magazine* 6 January 1946: 16–17, 46.

——. "A Change for the Better." *Spectator* 2 January 1926: 10.

——. "Christmas Films." *Spectator* 19 December 1925: 1137–38.

——. "The Cinema." *Vogue* [London] early February 1926: 53.

——. "The Cinema." *Spectator* 18 June 1927: 1062–63.

——. "The Cinema: Hope Fulfilled." *Spectator* 19 May 1924: 788.

——. "The Cinema: *Greed*—A Film of Realism." *Spectator* 14 March 1925: 402.

——. "Cinema Notes." *Spectator* 2 August 1924: 158; 18 April 1925: 629.

——. "Common Sense About Movies." *Journal of Adult Education* 12 (April 1940): 191–2.

——. "The Cinema: A Comparison of Arts." *Spectator* 3 May 1924: 707.

——. "*Dante's Inferno.*" *Spectator* 31 January 1925: 152.

——. "*A Diary for Timothy.*" *Film News* [New York] November 1945: 20.

——. "The Documentary Film in War Time." Unpublished ts., n.d., Museum of Modern Art, Film Study Center, Iris Barry Collection.

——. "Documentary Film: Prospect and Retrospect." *Bulletin of the Museum of Modern Art* 13 (1945): 2–5.

——. "Editorial Postscript (1935–1938) [as editor and translator]." *The History of the Motion Pictures*. By Maurice Bardeche and Robert Brasilliach. New York: W.W. Norton and the Museum of Modern Art, 1938.

——. "The Cinema: *The Epic of Everest* at the Scala." *Spectator* 20 December 1924: 982.

——. "Fairbanks Triumphant." *Spectator* 20 March 1926: 525.

——. "Farewell to Griffith." *Spectator* 11 April 1925: 590.

——. "*Faust.*" *Spectator* 8 January 1927: 39.

——. "The Film: A Review of Film History in a Cycle of Seventy Films" *Art in Our Time*. Exhibition catalog. New York: Museum of Modern Art, 1939: 335–48.

——. "A Film of the American War of Independence." *Spectator* 13 September 1924: 354.

——. "The Film of Fact." *Town & Country* September 1946: 142, 253–4, 256.

——. "Film Library, 1935–1941." *Bulletin of the Museum of Modern Art* 8.5 (1941): 3–13.

——. "The Film Library and How it Grew." *Film Quarterly* 22.4 (1969): 12–27.

——. "The Film Library and How it Grew." ts. nd. Museum of Modern Art, Film Study Center, Iris Barry Collection.

——. "Film Notes—Part 1: The Silent Film." *Bulletin of the Museum of Modern Art* 16.2/3 (1949): 1–68.

——. "The Film and Reality." *Home and Food* Museum of Modern Art, Film Study Center, Iris Barry Collection. n.d.

——. "Film as Recording Machine." *Saturday Review* 12 August 1939: 12.

——. "Films for the Empire." *Spectator* 30 October 1926: 736–7.

——. "Films for History." *Special Libraries* 30 (1939): 258–60.

——. "Foreign Coast." *New Yorker* 16 September 1933: 46–8.

——. Foreword. *The Film Index: A Bibliography*, Vol. 1, *The Film as Art*. For the WPA Writer's Project. New York: Museum of Modern Art and H.W. Wilson, 1941.

——. "From Caligari to Hitler." Review of *From Caligari to Hitler*, by Siegfried Kracauer. *New Republic* 19 May 1947: 28–9.

——. "The German Film." *New Republic* 19 May 1947.

——. "The Gold Rush." *Calendar* 2.8 (1925): 129–31.

——. *D.W. Griffith: American Film Master*. New York: Museum of Modern Art, 1939. Rpt. New York: Museum of Modern Art, 1965, with an annotated list of films by Eileen Bowser.

——. "A Guide to New Films." *Spectator* 16 May 1925: 804–5.

——. "History in the Movies." *National Board of Review Magazine* April 1941: 4–7.

——. "Hollywood is Not America." *Sunday Review* 11 March 1934: 8–9.

——. "Hotel Imperial." *Spectator* 29 January 1927: 147–8.

——. "Hunting the Film in Germany." *American-German Review* June 1937: 40–43.

——. "The Last Laugh." *Spectator* 28 March 1925: 497.

——. "The Cinema: Laughter-Makers." *Spectator* 19 September 1925: 444–5.

——. "Lecture Notes [1937–1938]." For "The History, Aesthetic and Technique of the Motion Picture" course taught by Iris Barry at Columbia University, ms. Museum of Modern Art, Film Study Center, Iris Barry Collection.

——. "The Cinema: Lesser Glories." *Spectator* 6 March 1926: 415.

——. *Let's Go to the Pictures*. London: Chatto & Windus, 1926. American title *Let's Go to the Movies*. New York: Payson & Clarke, 1926. New York: Arno Press and New York Times, 1972.

——. "Looking Backward Through Films." *Tricolor* 3 (1944): 115–24.

——. "Manon Lescaut at the New Gallery." *Spectator* 11 September 1926: 376.

——. "Les Miserables." *Spectator* 18 September 1926: 413.

——. "Metropolis." *Spectator* 26 March 1927: 540.

——. "Michael Strogoff." *Spectator* 5 February 1927: 184–85.

——. "Mons." *Spectator* 25 September 1926: 471.

——. "The Motion Picture." *Art in America in Modern Times*. Ed. Holger Cahill and Alfred H. Barr. New York: Reynal & Hitchcock, 1934. 91–3.

——. "Motion Pictures in Adult Education." Review. *Journal of Adult Education* 7 (1940): 191–93.

——. *The Motion Picture 1914–1934*. Wadsworth Atheneum, Hartford, CT. 1934. Program notes for the ten-part screening program, "The Motion Picture 1914–34." 28 October–30 December 1934. Wadsworth Atheneum, Hartford, CT.

——. "Motion Pictures as a Field of Research." *College Art Journal* 4.4 (1945): 206–9.

——. "Museum Festival of Documentaries." *Film News* November 1945: 10–.

——. "The Museum of Modern Art Film Library: Last Year & This." *Magazine of Art* 30 (1937): 41.

——. "A National or International Cinema?" *Bioscope* 28 January 1924: 29.

——. "The Necessity for Good Films." *Spectator* 24 October 1925: 692.

——. "Neglected Master." *Saturday Review* 30 May 1953.

——. "New Projects of the Cinema." *Spectator* 5 September 1925: 362.

——. "The Niebelungs." *Spectator* 14 June 1924: 955.

——. "No More Classics." *Spectator* 6 February 1926: 214.

——. "Of British Films." *Spectator* 14 November 1925: 870–71.

——. "The Peter Pan Film." *Spectator* 24 January 1925: 115.

——. Preface. *The Rise of the American Film: A Critical History*. By Lewis Jacobs. New York: Harcourt, Brace, 1939.

——. "Progress is Being Made." *Spectator* 11 February 1925: 235–6.

——. "Retrospect with Lament & Motto." *Saturday Review* 6 August 1949: 138–41.

——. "The Right British Films." *Spectator* 14 May 1927: 843–4.

——. "Russia's Master Film Maker: Sergei Eisenstein Expounds His Cinema Technique." Rev. of *The Film Sense*, by Sergei Eisenstein. Possibly published *New York Herald Tribune*. Museum of Modern Art, Films Study Center, Iris Barry Collection.

——. "Satire and History." *Spectator* 21 February 1925: 281.

——. "The Screen Talks." *Spectator* 27 April 1929: 645–46.

——. "In Search of Films." *Sight and Sound* 16 (Summer 1947): 65–7.

——. "Siegfried." *Spectator*, 14 June 1924: 955.

——. "Sublimity versus Vulgarity." *Spectator* 11 October 1924: 501–2.

——. "Symposium: Do Films Have a Pedagogical Mission for the Masses?" *Decision* [New York] 1.3 (1941): 65–6.

——. "It Talks and It Moves." *Spectator* 7 June 1924: 915–16.

——. "Thunder Over Mexico." *Bulletin of the Museum of Modern Art* 2:2 (October 1933); 4.

——. "Warning Shadows." *Spectator* 15 November 1924: 734–5.

——. "We Enjoyed the War." *Scribner's Magazine* November 1934: 279–83.

——. "What Price Glory?" *Spectator* 19 March 1927: 480.

——. "Work and Progress." *Museum of Modern Art Film Library Bulletin* January 1937: 1. Museum of Modern Art, Film Study Center, Iris Barry Collection.

——. "Why Wait for Posterity?" *Hollywood Quarterly* 1.2 (1946): 131–37.

——. "On Writing for Films." *Spectator* 7 August 1926: 208.

Barry, Iris, with John Abbott. "An Outline of a Project for Funding the Film Library of the Museum of Modern Art" [17 April 1935]. Rpt. *Film History* 7 (1995): 325–5.

Barry, Iris, with Helen F. Conover and Helen Fitz-Richard. *The Motion Picture: A Selected Booklist*. Chicago: American Library Association and Warner Bros. 1946.

Barry, Iris, with Richard Griffith. "The Film Library and the Film of Fact." *Museum of Modern Art Film Library Bulletin* 1942: 1–5.

Bauer, Leda V. "Movie Critics." *American Mercury* January 1929: 71–4.

Bauchens, Anne. "Cutting the Film." *We Make the Movies*. Ed. Nancy Naumberg. New York: Norton, 1937. 199–215.

Beal, Helen. "Confessions of a Photoplay Fan." *Photoplay* July 1936: 32–3, 100, 102.

Bearden, Bessye. "Miss McKinney Bids Farewell Fond America." *Chicago Defender* 13 December 1930: 7.

de Beauvoir, Simone. *Brigitte Bardot and the Lolita Syndrome*. New York: Reynal, 1960. First published in *Esquire* August 1959. Trans. Bernard Fretchman.

Bellamy, Madge. "Art v/s Gold." Letter. *New York Times* 22 March 1931. Rpt. *A Darling of the Twenties: Madge Bellamy*. Madge Bellamy. Introduction by Kevin Brownlow. Vestal, NY: Vestal Press, 1989. 184.

Bender, Billie. "The Director's Right Hand." *Screen Pictorial* September 1937: 44–5.

Bennett, Isadora. "The Stage Door Canteen." *Pulse* June 1946: 6–7.

Benson, Sally. "The Screen in Review: Criticism of the Important Film Productions of the Month" *Picture-Play Magazine* July 1925: 52–5, 111.

Beranger, Clara. "The Cinema is Ready for College." *Theatre Arts* January 1947: 61–3.

——. "The Feminine Mind in Picture Making." *Film Daily* 7 June 1925: 9.

——. "Feminine Sphere in the Field of Movies is Large Indeed, Says Clara S. Beranger." *Moving Picture World* 2 August 1919: 662.

——. "Let Hollywood Discover You." *Delineator* April 1936: 4, 14–15.

——. "The Secret of Good Pictures." *The Truth About the Movies by the Stars*. Ed. Laurence H. Hughes. Hollywood: Hollywood Publishers, 1924. 392.

——. "Motion Pictures as a Fine Art." *Theatre Magazine* May 1919: 300, 304.

——. "The Unused Asset." *Rob Wagner's Script* [Los Angeles] 27 June 1931: 20.

——. Interview. "Women Scenario Writers." *Indianapolis Star* 1 September 1918, sec. 5: 1.

——. *Writing for the Screen*. Dubuque, IA: William C. Brown, 1950.

Berg, Clara de Lissa. "The Title Editor." *Careers for Women*. Ed. Catherine Filene. Boston: Houghton Mifflin, 1920. 337–9.

Bergman, Ingrid. "Films as Ambassadors." *Scholastic* 14 April 1947: 36.

Bernhardt, Sarah. Interview. "'Sarah' Talks to Us About the Cinema." Translation of Jean Levèque, "En écoutant 'Sarah' parler du cinéma." *Le Journal* 17 April 1914: 7.

Bertsch, Marguerite. *How to Write for Moving Pictures: A Manual of Instruction and Information*. New York: George H. Doran, 1917.

Besant, Annie. "Theosophy and Dramatic Art." *Show World* 5 October 1907: 1.

Best, Camilla. "Teaching Americanism Through the Use of the Film Strip." *Education* 61 (1941): 333–6.

Biery, Ruth. "Haven in the Port of Missing Girls." *Photoplay* February 1928: 39, 102.

——."It's the Easiest Job in the Movies." *Photoplay* December 1927: 42, 94, 138–39.

Biery, Ruth, and Eleanor Packer. "England Challenges Hollywood." *Saturday Evening Post* 29 June 1933: 12–13+.

Binger-Cantor, Mme. "Cinema and Taxation." *International Review of Educational Cinematography* 3 (1931): 1110–12.

Blaché, Alice Guy. "An Interesting Statement by Madame Alice Blaché of the Solax Company." *Motion Picture News* 28 December 1912: 17.

——. *The Memoirs of Alice Guy Blaché*. Ed. Anthony Slide. Trans. Roberta Blaché and Simone Blaché. Metuchen, NJ: Scarecrow Press. Rev. edn. 1986.

——. "Woman's Place in Photoplay Production." *Moving Picture World* 11 July 1914: 195.

——. Interview. "Alice Blaché, a Dominant Figure in Pictures: How a French Woman Came to this Country and Built up a Big Business." By Harvey Gates. *New York Dramatic Mirror* 6 November 1912: 28.

——. Interview. "The First Motion Picture and its Producer, Madame Blaché." Incorrectly marked as *New Jersey Star* 8 August 1914. New York Public Library. Billy Rose Collection.

Black, Ernestine. "Lois Weber Smalley." *Overland Monthly* September 1916: 198–200.

Blair, Patricia. "Ideas on Film." *Saturday Review* 11 June 1949: 34–6.

——. "Treatment, Storage and Handling of Motion Picture Film." *Library Journal* 71 (1946): 333–6.

Blake, Frances. "Something New in the Motion Picture Theatre." *Close Up* 10.2 (1933): 154–7.

Blake, Lillie Devereux. "Brutality in Prize Fight Pictures." *New York Journal* 21 November 1899: 7.

Blanc, Baroness. Interview. "A Chat with Baroness Blanc." *Moving Picture News* 3 September 1910: 5–6.

Blanchard, Phyllis. "The Motion Picture as an Educational Asset." *Pedagogical Seminary* September 1919: 284–7.

Block, Maxine. "Films Adapted From Published Works." *Wilson Library Bulletin* 10 (1936): 394–5.

Block, Ruth-Dorothy. "A Movie Stepmother: Hattie Gray Baker, Film Editor, Brings the Author's Brain Child to its Full Development." *Filmplay* 1:11 (May 1922): 18–19.

Bloom, Ursula. "The Films That Women Want." *Film Weekly* 31 May 1930: 7.

Bogan, Louise. "True to the Medium." *New Republic* 26 October 1927: 263–4.

Bolton, Isabel [Mary Britton Miller]. "At a Newsreel Theatre." *Films in Review* June–July 1951: 15–17, an excerpt from *Do I Wake or Sleep*. New York: Charles Scribner's Sons, 1946.

Booth, Margaret. "The Cutter." *Behind the Screen: How Films Are Made*. Ed. Stephen Watts. London: Arthur Baker, 1938. 147–53.

Borthwick, Jessica. Interview. "A Girl Cinematographer at the Balkan War: An Interview with Miss Jessica Borthwick." *Bioscope* [London] 7 May 1914: 625, 627, 629.

Bow, Clara. "Evoking Emotions is No Child's Play." *Theatre Magazine* November 1927: 42.

Bowen, Elizabeth. "Why I Go to the Cinema." *Screen Pictorial* [London], Winter Annual, 1937(?): 12, 52. A longer version of this article is printed in *Footnotes to the Film*. Ed. Charles Davy. London: Lovat Dickson, 1937. 205–20.

Bowen, Louise de Koven. *Five and Ten Cent Theatres: Two Investigations*. Chicago: Juvenile Protective Association of Chicago, 1909 and 1911.

Bower, Mrs. Robert. *Children in the Cinema: A Summary of the Main Aspect of the Report on Children and the Cinema and Comments on Points of Importance to Parents*. Newport, Mon.: R. H. Johns, nd. Noted in the British Film Institute Library catalog, listed as "missing."

Bowlan, Marian. *Minnie at the Movies: A Monologue*. Chicago: T.S. Denison, 1913.

——. *City Types: A Book of Monologues Sketching the City Woman*. Chicago: T.S. Denison, 1916.

Box, Muriel. *Odd Woman Out: An Autobiography*. London: Leslie Frewin, 1974.

Brady, Alice. "Movies and Mummers." *Drama* November 1923: 46–7.

——. "Myself and the Shadow." *Picturegoer* January 1921: 55, 60.

Brande, Dorothea. "A Letter on the Movies." *American Review* May 1934:. 148–60.

Bray, Mary. "Interlingua: Can the Movies Use an Artificial Language?" *Films in Review* October 1952: 380–81.

Brazier, Marion Howard. *Stage and Screen*. Norwood, MA: The Plimpton Press, 1920.

Brenon, Aileen St. John. "Three Thousand Puppets in Motion Pictures." *Design* May 1936: 22–3.
Brooks, Louise. "Charlie Chaplin Remembered." *Film Culture* Spring 1966: 5–6.
——. "Gish and Garbo: The Executive War on Stars." *Sight and Sound* Winter 1958–59: 13+.
——. *Lulu in Hollywood.* New York: Alfred Knopf, 1983.
——. "Why I Will Never Write My Memoirs." *Film Culture* 67–68–69 (1979): 216–220.
Brown, Beth. "Making Movies for Women." *Moving Picture World* 26 March 1927: 342.
Browne, Alice B. "How Our Town Got Better Movies." *Parents Magazine* January 1932: 28+.
Bruce, Margaret B. "Librarians à la Hollywood." *Wilson Library Bulletin* 22 (1948): 692–3.
Brush, Katherine. "It's Not My Hollywood." *Good Housekeeping* November 1941: 43+.
Bryher. "The American Season 1934–1935." *Intercine* 7.8/9 (1935): 23–7.
——. "Berlin April 1931." *Close Up* 8.2 (1931): 126–33.
——. "A Certificate of Approval." *Close Up* 5.6 (1929): 483–7.
——. "Children and the Cinema." *Outlook* [London] 21 August 1926: 173–4.
——. "Criticism from Within." *Close Up* 1.4 (1927): 48–56.
——. "Danger in the Cinema." *Close Up* 7.5 (1930): 299–304.
——. "Defence of Hollywood." *Close Up* 2.2 (1928): 44–51.
——. "Dope or Stimulus." *Close Up* 3.3 (1928): 59–61.
——. "East and West of the Atlantic." *Close Up* 9.2 (1932): 131–3.
——. Note on "The Educational Influence of the Cinema." In "Comment and Review" section, *Close Up* 6.5 (1930):429–31."
——. "Film in Education." *Cinema Survey.* In Bryher, Robert Herring, and Dallas Bower. London: Blue Moon Press, 1937: 11–16.
——. *Film Problems of Soviet Russia.* Riant Chateau, Territet: Pool, 1929.
——. "Films for Children." *Close Up* 3.2 (1928): 16–20.
——. "Films in Education: The Complex of the Machine." *Close Up* 1.2 (1927): 49–54.
——. "A German School Film." *Close Up* 6.2 (1930): 128–33.
——. "G.W. Pabst: A Survey." *Close Up* 1.6 (1927): 56–61.
——. "The Hollywood Code." *Close Up* 8.3 (1931): 234–8.
——. "The Hollywood Code II." *Close Up* 8.4 (1931): 280–82.
——. "How to Rent a Film." *Close Up* 3.6 (1928): 45–51.
——. "How I Would Start a Film Club." *Close Up* 2.6 (1928): 30–36.
——. "An Interview: Anita Loos." *Close Up* 2.4 (1928): 12–15.
——. "*Mechanics of the Brain.*" Review in "Six Russian Films" (continued). *Close Up* 3.4 (1928): 27–31.
——. "A New Commission." *Close Up* 6.3 (1930): 223–4.
——. "Notes on Some Films." *Close Up* 9.3 (1932): 196–9.
——. "Pre-view of *The General Line.*" *Close Up* 6.1 (1930): 34–9.
——. "A Private Showing of Cosmos." *Close Up* 4.5 (1929): 42–5.
——. "The War From More Angles." *Close Up* 1.4 (1927): 44–8.
——. "The War From Three Angles." *Close Up* 1.1 (1927): 16–22.
——. "*Westfront 1918.*" *Close Up* 7.2 (1930): 102–11.
——. "What Can I Do." *Close Up* 2.3 (1928): 21–5.
——. "What Can I Do!" *Close Up* 2.5 (1928): 32–37.
——. "What Shall You Do in the War?" *Close Up* 10.2 (1933): 188–92.
Bryher, Robert Herring and Dallas Bower. *Cinema Survey.* London: Blue Moon Press, 1937.
Buck, Pearl, et al. "What I Look For in a Film." *Films in Review* March 1950: 1–2.
Burgess, Marjorie A. Lovell. *A Popular Account of the Amateur Ciné Movement in Great Britain.* London: Simpson, Low, Marston, 1932.
Bute, Mary Ellen. "Abstronics," *Films in Review* June–July 1954: 263–6.
——. Interview with Gretchen Weinberg. "An Interview with Mary Ellen Bute on the Filming of *Finnegans Wake.*" *Film Culture* Winter 1964: 25–8.
——. "Light * Form * Movement * Sound." *Design* April 1941: 25.
Byrd, Pauline Flora. Letter. "*Imitation of Life.*" *Crisis* March 1935: 91–2.
Calhoun, Dorothy. "Do Women Rule the Movies?" *Motion Picture Classic* August 1928: 30–31, 88.
Callimachi, Princess Anne-Marie, et al. "What I Look for in a Film." *Films in Review* April 1950: 13.
Cameron, Kate. "The Movie Critic." *Careers for Women.* Ed. Catherine Filene. Boston: Houghton Mifflin, 1934. 422–6.
Candler, Martha. "The Rutherford Experiment in Motion Pictures as a Community Service." *American City* 23 (1927): 457–8.

Canfield, Mary Cass. "Letter to Garbo." *Theatre Arts* 21 (1937): 951–60.

Carr, Catherine. *The Art of Photoplay Writing.* New York: Hannis Jordan, 1914.

Carroll, Madeleine. "Treating Women too Well." *Film Weekly* 31 January 1931: 9.

Carter, Aline. "The Muse of the Reel." *Motion Picture* March 1921: 62–3, 105.

Cenkalski, Christina, and Eugene Cenkalski. "Polish Film Builds for the Future." *Hollywood Quarterly* 2.3 (1947): 294–6.

Cerminara, Gina. "Little Black Angels. *Crisis* 57 (1950): 221–5, 266–8.

Chadwick, Mary. "Commission on Educational and Cultural Films." *Close Up* 8.1 (1931): 55–60.

Chauvel, Elsa. *My Life with Charles Chauvel.* Sydney: Shakespeare Head Press, 1973.

"Chicago Teacher in Movies." *Chicago Defender* 5 August 1939, weekend edn.: 22.

Christeson, Frances. *A Guide to the Literature of the Motion Picture.* Los Angeles: University of Southern California Press, June 1938. Cinematography Series No. 1.

Chute, Margaret. "Hollywood's Girl Photographer." *Modern Woman* [London] 4 August 1928: 804–7.

Clarke, Edith. "Designing Clothes for the Movie Folk." *Opportunities in the Motion Picture Industry.* Vol. 3. Los Angeles: Photoplay Research Society, 1922: 79–82.

Clark, Jacqueline. "Report From the Argentine." *Films in Review* March 1950: 16+.

Clement, Mrs. Interview. "Comment and Suggestion." *New York Dramatic Mirror* 13 November 1912: 25–26.

——. Interview. "Aestheticism and Dimes: A Boston Society Woman Has Made a Success at a Playhouse Just to Prove that Refinement Pays in Dollars and Cents." *Green Book Magazine* December 1914: 1030–31.

——. Interview. "Mrs. Clement and Her Work." *Moving Picture World* 15 October 1910: 859–60.

Cochran, Mary Luc. "Movies and Young Criminals." *National Education Association Journal* 21 (1932): 169.

Codd, Elsie. "Modes & Movies." *Picturegoer* June 1921: 8–9.

Cogdell, J. "Truth in Art in America." *Messenger* 5 (March 1923): 634–36.

Cohen, Elsie. Interview with Anthony Slide. "Elsie Cohen in an Interview with Anthony Slide." *Silent Picture* 10 (Spring 1971) N. pag.

——. Interview with Anthony Slide. "Elsie Cohen Talks to Anthony Slide About the Academy Cinema, Political Censorship and the British Scene in the Thirties." *Silent Picture* 11 (Summer 1971): 9–13.

——. "Seeking Expression in the Films." *Studio* [London] May 1939: 196–201.

Colette. *Colette at the Movies: Criticism and Screenplays.* Edited and with an introduction by Alain Virmaux and Odette Virmaux. Trans. Sarah W. Smith. New York: Frederick Ungar, 1980.

Compson, Betty. "Acting in Talking Pictures." *How Talkies Are Made.* Ed. Joe Bonica. Hollywood: Joe Bonica, 1930: n.p. (article on what would be page 9)

Conde, Carmen. "The Children's Cinema." *International Review of Educational Cinematography* 5 (1933): 331–2.

——.——. "The Educational Cinema and the Spanish Pedagogic Mission." *International Review of Educational Cinematography* 5 (1933): 476–9.

Condon, Mabel. "Hot Chocolate and Reminiscences at Nine in the Morning." *Photoplay* January 1915: 69.

——. "Keystone: The Home of Mack Sennett and the Film Comedy." *New York Dramatic Mirror* 9 September 1916: 32, 36.

——. "The Lasky Studio." *New York Dramatic Mirror* 28 October 1916: 34–6, 38, 42–3.

——. "The Primitive in Pictures." *New York Dramatic Mirror* 9 September 1916: 40.

——. "The Real Perils of Pauline." *Photoplay* October 1914: 59–64.

——. "Yorke-Metro Studios: Hollywood's Home of Artistic Picture Production." *New York Dramatic Mirror* 2 December 1916: 34, 40.

——. "Mabel Condon Exchange Grows." *Motography* 24 March 1917: 651.

Connolly, Louise. "The Library and the Motion Pictures." *National Board of Review Magazine* March–April 1926: 4–6, 8.

Connolly, Vera C. "Backstage in the Talkies." *Delineator* March 1930: 14+.

Coogan, Mrs. John. "The Child's Opportunity in the Movies." *Opportunities in the Motion Picture Industry.* Vol. 2. Los Angeles: Photoplay Research Society, 1922: 79–83.

Cookman, Mary. "What do the Women of America Think About Entertainment?" *Ladies' Home Journal* February 1939: 20, 63–64.

Cooper, Gladys. *Gladys Cooper.* London: Hutchinson, 1931.

Corbaley, Kate. "Duties and Qualifications of the Scenario Reader." *Opportunities in the Motion Picture Industry.* Vol. 2. Los Angeles: Photoplay Research Society, 1922. 61–63.

——. *Selling Manuscripts in the Photoplay Market.* Los Angeles: Palmer Photoplay Corporation, 1920.

Coromilas, Mrs. G. "Cinema Theatres." *International Review of Educational Cinematography* 3 (1931): 1074–9.

Corrigan, Beatrice. "Harlequin in America." *Canadian Forum* March 1933: 62–5.

Costa, Gabriel. "The Jew on Screen: What the Ghetto Likes." *Kinematograph and Lantern Weekly* [London] 14 January 1915: 75.

Coxhead, Elizabeth. "A Film Actor." *Close Up* 10.1 (1933): 47–9.

——. "Towards a Co-operative Cinema." *Close Up* 10.2 (1933): 133–7.

Craig, Anne Throop. "Community Pageantry in the Films." *National Board of Review Magazine* August 1928 3–9.

Crain, Jeanne. "She Passed For Negro… in the Movies." *Negro Digest* March 1950: 26–27.

Crawford, Joan. "The Job of Keeping at the Top." *Saturday Evening Post* 17 June 1933: 14–15, 75.

Crocker, Phyllis. "The Continuity Girl." *Working for the Films.* Ed. Oswell Blakeston. London: Focal Press, 1947: 143–51.

Crone, Berta. "Occupations, Today and Tomorrow." *New Outlook* June 1933: 2+.

Cross, Elizabeth. "Film Commentary." *Sight and Sound* May 1944: 7–8.

——. "It Won't Last Forever." *Sight and Sound* Summer 1943: 22–2.

——. "Large as Life—Twice as Natural." *Sight and Sound* January 1944: 97–8.

——. "A Little More Nonsense!" *Sight and Sound* Autumn 1940: 45.

——. "More Carping." *Sight and Sound* October 1944: 70–71.

——. "The Pace that Kills." *Sight and Sound* Autumn 1942: 36–7.

.——. "Plain Words to the Exhibitor." *Sight and Sound* Autumn 1941: 44–5.

——. "Rural Plea." *Sight and Sound* Winter 1940–41: 65.

Croughton, Amy. "Scanning the Screen." *Library Journal* 71 (1946): 908.

Cullman, Marguerite W. "Double Feature—Movies and Moonlight." *New York Times Magazine* 1 October 1950: 22.

Cunard, Nancy. "*The New Gulliver.*" *Film Art* (Autumn 1935): 78.

——. "Nancy Cunard discusses *Un Monde qui se Meurt.*" *Film Art* (Second Quarter 1936): 32.

——. "Nancy Cunard discusses *Tarass Boulba.*" *Film Art* (Second Quarter 1936): 32

——. "Scottsboro." *Close Up* 10:3 (September 1933): 274–8.

Cussler, Margaret. *Not By a Long Shot: Adventures of a Documentary Film Producer.* New York: Exposition, 1952.

D.L.H. "An Outburst on an Old Subject." *Close Up* 6.2 (1930): 150–52.

——. "Films in the Provinces." *Close Up* 4.6 (1929): 52–7.

——. "Finds." *Close Up* 5.5 (1929): 415–17.

Daly, Rosemary. "Films for Fledglings." *Saturday Review of Literature* 19 November 1949: 58.

Dane, Clarence. "What is Love? Is it What We See in the Movies?" *Forum and Century* 94 (1935): 335–8.

Danilova, Alexandra. "Classical Ballet and the Cinema." *Sight and Sound* 4.15 (1935).

Danischewsky, Monja, ed. *Michael Balcon's 25 Years in Films.* London: World Film Publications, 1947.

Davidman, Joy. "Before the Talkies." *New Masses* 5 May 1942: 28.

——. "Cameras as Weapons." *New Masses* 8 December 1942: 28–9.

——. "*Citizen Kane.*" *New Masses* 13 May 1941. Rpt. *American Film Criticism: From the Beginnings to Citizen Kane.* Ed. Stanley Kauffmann, with Bruce Henstell. New York: Liveright, 1972. 411–13.

——. Reply to letter from Lester Cole. "Miss Davidman replies." *New Masses* 20 April 1943: 29–30.

——. "Deaths and a Warning." *New Masses* 18 May 1943: 30–31.

——. "Masquerade." *New Masses* 25 May 1943: 29–31.

——. "Mission of Sabotage." *New Masses* 1 June 1943: 29.

——. "Monopoly Takes a Screen Test." *New Masses* 24 June 1941: 28–30.

——. "The War Film: An Examination." *New Masses* 24 November 1942: 29–30.

——. "The Will and the Way." *New Masses* 27 October 1942: 28–31.

——. "Women: Hollywood Version." *New Masses* 14 July 1942: 28–31.

Davies, Mary Carolyn. "At the Movies in New York." *Chicago Ssunday Herald* 10 February 1918, section 5:6.

——. "My Favorite Screen Hero." *Motion Picture Classic* October 1918: 75.

Davis, Alta M. "Great Field for Women: Lady Manager of Theater Writes to Balboa Company." *New*

York Dramatic Mirror 10 February 1917: 24.

Davis, Bessie. "The Comparative Value of Fixed and Motion Pictures." International Review of Educational Cinematography 5 (1933): 811–13.

Davis, Bette. "Hollywood Canteen." Collier's 2 January 1943: 10–11.

Davis, Bette, and David Chandler. "On Acting in Films." Theatre Arts 25 (1941): 632–9.

Defries, Amelia. "Criticism from Within." Close Up 1.4 (1927): 48–56.

Deming, Barbara. "The Artlessness of Walt Disney." Partisan Review 12 (1945): 226–31.

——. "The Library of Congress Film Project: Exposition of a Method." Library of Congress Quarterly Journal of Current Acquisitions 2 (1944): 3–36.

——. "Love Through a Film." Vogue [New York] 15 August 1946: 168, 224–7.

——. "Non-Heroic Heroes: II." Films in Review April 1951: 32–8.

——. Running Away from Myself: A Dream Portrait of America Drawn from the Films of the Forties. New York: Grossman, 1969.

——. "The Villain-Hero: I." Films in Review March 1951: 32–6.

Denton, Frances. "Lights! Camera! Quiet! Ready! Shoot!" Photoplay February 1918: 48–50.

——. "Real Folks from the Scenario of the Original Story by Kate Corbaley." Photoplay April 1918: 83–86.

De Putti, Lya. "Bad Girls in Pictures." Breaking Into the Movies. Ed. Charles Reed Jones. New York: The Unicorn Press, 1927. 68–75.

Deren, Maya. The Legend of Maya Deren: A Documentary Biography and Collected Works. 3 vols. Eds. VéVé A. Clark, Millicent Hodson, and Catrina Neiman. New York: Anthology Film Archives/Film Culture. Vol. 1. 1988. Vol. 2. 2003. Vol. 3.

——. "Magic is New." Mademoiselle January 1946: 180–81, 260–65.

Dessez, Elizabeth Richey. "Educational Films, The United States." The Theatre and Motion Pictures: A Selection of Articles from the New 14th Edition of the Encyclopaedia Britannica. New York and London: Encyclopaedia Britannica, 1929–33. 34.

——.——. "The Fifth Estate." American Hebrew 16 March 1928: 656, 670–71.

Dickson, Antonia. "Wonders of the Kinetoscope." Frank Leslie's Popular Monthly 39.2 (1895): 245–51.

Dickson, Antonia, and W.K.L. Dickson. "Edison's Invention of the Kineto-Phonograph." Century Magazine [New York] 48 (1894): 206–14.

——. History of the Kinetograph, Kinetoscope and Kinetophonograph. New York: Albert Bunn, 1895. Rpt. Salem, NH: Ayer Company Publishers, 1984. Rpt. New York: Museum of Modern Art, 2000.

——. The Life and Inventions of Thomas Alva Edison. London: Chatto & Windus, 1894.

Diehl, Mrs. Ambrose A. [Frances White]. "The Moral Effect of the Cinema on Individuals." International Review of Educational Cinematography 3 (1931): 1123–37.

——. Regular column titled "Recommended Motion Pictures." Ladies' Home Journal (1932).

——. "Women and the Cinema." International Review of Educational Cinematography 6 (1934): 400–404.

Dietrich, Marlene. "La Belle Dame Sans Merci." Saturday Review [London] 15 August 1931: 209–10.

——. Marlene Dietrich's ABC. Garden City, NY: Doubleday, 1962.

Dismond, Geraldyn. "The Negro Actor and the American Movies." Close Up 5.2 (1929): 90–97.

Dismorr, Jessie. "Matinee." Little Review 4.11 (1918): 31–2.

Dix, Beulah Marie. "An Essential of Writing." The Truth About the Movies by the Stars. Ed. Laurence H. Hughes. Hollywood: Hollywood Publishers, 1924. 397.

van Dongen, Helen. "How I Edited Robert Flaherty's Louisiana Story." Screen Director October 1949: 8–11.

——. "Joris Ivens in America." Film Art Autumn 1936: 15–16.

van Dongen Ivens, Helen. "Plan for the Dutch Indies." Film News October 1945: 24.

——. "Robert J. Flaherty 1884–1951." Film Quarterly 18.4 (1965): 2–14.

——. "Three Hundred and Fifty Cans of Film." The Cinema 1951. Eds Roger Manvell and R. K. Neilson Baxter. Harmondsworth: Penguin Books, 1951. 57–78.

Donnell, Dorothy. "Movie Modes and Manners." Motion Picture Classic March 1925: 16–18, 79–80.

Doolittle, Hilda. See H.D.

Dove, Billie. "Physical Culture and Poise." Breaking Into the Movies. Ed. Charles Reed Jones. New York: Unicorn Press, 1927. 83–9.

Drew, Cora. "Again—the Question of 'Types' on the Screen." New York Dramatic Mirror 5 May 1917: 26.

Dreyfus-Barney, Laura. "The Cinema in Education." International Review of Educational Cinematography 6 (1934): 184–8.

———. "The Cinema and Peace." *International Review of Educational Cinematography* 6 (1934): 252–6.

———. "Cinema and the Protection of Infancy: Summary Report of the Cinema and Broadcasting Commission of the International Women's Council." *International Review of Educational Cinematography* 6 (1934): 280–84.

———. "Cinéma d'occident et peuples d'orient." *Intercine* 7.10 (1935): 55–6.

———. "Cinema, Technical Training and Women's Work." *International Review of Educational Cinematography* 6 (1934): 104–6.

———. "Considerations on 'The International Conference of Cinema and Broadcasting' held by the International Council of Women." *International Review of Educational Cinematography* 3 (1931): 1071–3.

———. "Public Hygiene and the Cinema. "*International Review of Educational Cinematography* 6 (1934): 161–3.

———. "What Woman Can Offer the Cinema. "*International Review of Educational Cinematography* 4 (1932): 471–2.

Dudley, Fredda. "Usually They Want Something." *Ladies' Home Journal* January 1941: 79.

Dulac, Germaine. "Aesthetics, Obstacles, Integral Cinegraphie [1926]." Trans. Stuart Liebman. *French Film Theory and Criticism: A History/Anthology 1907–1939*. Vol 1. Ed. Richard Abel. Princeton: Princeton University Press, 1988. 389–97.

———. "The Avant-Garde Cinema [1932]." Trans. Robert Lamberton. *The Avant-Garde Film: A Reader of Theory and Criticism*. Ed. P. Adams Sitney. New York: Anthology Film Archives, 1987. 43–8.

———. "The Educational and Social Value of the News-Reel." *International Review of Educational Cinematography* 6 (1934): 545–50.

———. "The Essence of the Cinema: The Visual Idea [1925]." Trans. Robert Lamberton. *The Avant-Garde Film: A Reader of Theory and Criticism*. Ed. P. Adams Sitney. New York: Anthology Film Archives, 1987. 36–42.

———. "The Expressive Techniques of the Cinema [1924]." Trans. Stuart Liebman. *French Film Theory and Criticism: A History/Anthology 1907–1939*. Vol 1. Ed. Richard Abel. Princeton: Princeton University Press, 1988. 305–14.

———. *Germaine Dulac: Écrits sur le Cinéma (1919–1937)*. Ed. Prosper Hillairet. Paris: Éditions Paris Experimental, 1994

———. "The Meaning of Cinema." *International Review of Educational Cinematography* 3 (1931): 1089–1108.

———. "The Music of Silence." A translation of "La Musique du Silence." *Cinégraphie* 15 January 1928: 77. Rpt. *Germaine Dulac: Écrits sur le Cinéma (1919–1937)*. Ed. Prosper Hillairet. Paris: ´Éditions Paris Experimental, 1994. 106–8.

———. "From Sentiment to Line." A translation of "Du Sentiment à la Ligne." *Schémas* 1 (February 1927): 26–31. Rpt. *Germaine Dulac: Écrits sur le Cinéma (1919–1937)*. Ed. Prosper Hillairet. Paris: Éditions Paris Experimental, 1994. 87–9.

———. "From 'Visual and Anti-Visual Films' [1928]." Trans. Robert Lamberton. *The Avant-Garde Film: A Reader of Theory and Criticism*. Ed. P. Adams Sitney. New York: Anthology Film Archives, 1987. 31–5.

Dunbar, Olivia Howard. "Blockade." *Theatre Arts Magazine* 7 (1923): 127–42.

———. "The Lure of the Films." *Harper's Weekly* 18 January 1913: 20, 22.

Duncan, Catherine. "As Others See Us." *Sight and Sound* Spring 1948: 12–14.

———. "The First Years." *Sight and Sound* March 1950: 37–9.

Dunn, Reina Wiles. "Off-stage Heroines of the Movies." *Independent Woman* 13 (1934): 202.

Dunnigan, Alice A. "Approximately 400 Attend Premiere of *Prejudice* in Washington." Associated Negro Press, 1 February 1950, ts. Box 298, File 1, Claude A. Barnett Papers, Chicago Historical Society.

———. "D.C. Downtown Movie Houses End Ban on Negroes." Associated Negro Press, 17 January 1953, ts. Box 298, File 1 Claude A. Barnett Papers, Chicago Historical Society.

Dwight, Mabel. "The Clinch" [1928] (lithograph on stone), reproduced in "Scenes from the Cinema—by Mabel Dwight," *Vanity Fair* March 1929: 54.

———. "Mott Street Movies" (pencil and black crayon drawing, 1929), reproduced *Theatre Guild Magazine* October 1929: 26.

———. "Stick 'm Up" or "Stick 'em Up, Cinema," or "A Western," (lithograph on stone, 1928), reproduced *New Masses* 26 June 1934: 23, and *Philadelphia Record* 20 January 1929.

Eads, Laura Kreiger. "Talking Pictures in Primary Education." *International Review of Educational Cinematography* 6 (1934): 18–19.

Eames, Marian. "Gray Thoughts on *Red Shoes*." *Films in Review* October 1950: 20–24.

Eastman, Elaine Goodale. "Handmaidens of Hollywood?" *Christian Century* (48) 1931: 268–70.

Edginton, May. "The IT-Less British Girl." *Film Weekly* 17 December 1928: 9.

Edwards, Catherine C. "Family Films Are Box Office." *Parents' Magazine* May 1949: 34–5.

Edwards, Thyra J. "American Negroes in Soviet Plays and Films." *Negro Liberator* 22 December 1934: 2.

Eisner, Lotte. "Ach, the Kammerspiel." Trans. David A. Mage. *Films in Review* May 1952: 229–32.

——. "Film History: Like That of Other Arts, It Requires Integrity." *Films in Review* December 1951: 18–21.

——. "The German Cinema Loses its Way." *Film* 12 (1957): 9–12.

——. "The German Films of Fritz Lang." *Penguin Film Review* 6 (1948): 53–61.

——. "Homage to an Artist." *Film Culture* 4.18 (1958): 7–8.

——. *The Haunted Screen: Expressionism in the German Cinema and the Influence of Max Reinhardt.* [1952]. Trans. Roger Greaves. London: Thames & Hudson, 1969.

——. *Fritz Lang.* Trans. Gertrud Mander. Ed. David Robinson. London: Secker & Warburg, 1976.

——. "Meeting with Pabst." *Sight and Sound* Autumn 1967: 209.

——. *Murnau.* [1964]. London: Secker & Warburg, 1973.

——. "Notes on Some Recent Italian Films." *Sequence* 8 (1949): 52–8.

——."Notes on the Style of Stroheim." *Film Culture* 4.18 (1958): 13–19.

——. "The Passing of the First Film Star." *Film* 11 (1957): 4.

——. "Some Notes on Lost German Films." *Silent Picture* 8 (1970): 20–21.

——. "Style of René Clément." *Film Culture* 3. 12 (1957): 21; 3. 13 (1957): 11.

——. "A Witness Speaks." Afterword. *Lulu in Hollywood.* By Louise Brooks. New York: Alfred A. Knopf, 1983. 107–9.

Elie, Eva. "A quasi-fairy-tale." *International Review of Educational Cinematography* 3 (1931): 29–31.

——. "Alleluia!" *International Review of Educational Cinematography* 3 (1931): 237–9.

——. "Casus belli." *International Review of Educational Cinematography* 3 (1931): 556–7.

——. "Dubbing." *International Review of Educational Cinematography* 4 (1932): 764–6.

——. "Non Olet." *International Review of Educational Cinematography* 2 (1930): 267–8.

——. "Open Letter to the Director of the I.I.E.C." *International Review of Educational Cinematography* 4 (1932): 604–6.

——. "Should War Films Be Seen By Children?" *International Review of Educational Cinematography* 2 (1930): 1177–8.

——. "The Reign of the Documentary." *International Review of Educational Cinematography* 4 (1932): 348–50.

Ellis, Edith. "Edith Ellis Discusses the Pictures." *New York Dramatic Mirror* 26 May 1917: 23.

Elston, Laura. "What and Why of Movie Censorship." *Canadian Magazine* 79.5 (1933): 6+.

Enters, Angna. "A Mime and the Movies." *California Arts and Architecture* 58.10 (1941): 18+.

Evans, Ernestine. "Films Tell Your Story Better." *Independent Woman* 27 (1948): 350–52+.

——. "Much Could Be Done." *Virginia Quarterly Review* 14 (1938): 491–501.

——. "New Jobs in New Films." *Independent Woman* 28 (1949): 6–8+.

——. "Potemkin." *Nation* 15 September 1926. Rpt. *American Film Criticism: From the Beginnings to Citizen Kane.* Ed. Stanley Kauffmann, with Bruce Henstell. New York: Liveright, 1972. 181–3.

——. "The Soviet Idea in the Kino." *Asia* 26 (1926): 698+.

Ex-White Actress, The. "The Confessions of an Ex-White Actress." *Half Century Magazine* July 1919: 16; August 1919: 16, 19.

Eyles, Leonora. "The Woman's Part: V. Amusements." *Lansbury's Labour Weekly* [London] 28 March 1925: 14.

Fairfax, Marion. "Marionettes." Regular column. *Rob Wagner's Script* [Los Angeles] early 1930s.

——. "The Feminine Mind in Picture Making." *Film Daily* 7 June 1925: 9.

——. "Our Industry." *The Truth About the Movies by the Stars.* Ed. Laurence H. Hughes. Hollywood: Hollywood Publishers, 1924. 35.

Fazenda, Louise. "The Comedienne." *Breaking Into the Movies.* Ed. Charles Reed Jones. New York: Unicorn Press, 1927. 95–100.

Ferber, Edna. "I Usually Walk Out on Them." "Good Bad Pictures and Those Just Bad." By Ferber and Anita Loos. *Theatre Magazine* (New York) July 1927: 41.

——. "They Earn Their Million. " *Collier's* 4 December 1920: 7–8, 24, 26, 28.

Field, Mary. "Can the Film Educate?" *For Filmgoers Only.* Ed. R.S. Lambert. London: Faber & Faber with the British Institute of Adult Education, 1934. 48–61.

——. "The Child-Mind and the Screen." 1–4 [c. 1944/1945]. ts. with the notation, "sent to the U.S.S.R. for Britanskyi Soyuznik." British Film Institute Library.

——. "Children in Cinema," Films and Filming 4.7 (1958): 9–10.

——. "Children and the Entertainment Film." Sight and Sound Summer 1946: 46–47.

——. Children and Films: A Study of Boys and Girls in the Cinema: A Report to the Carnegie United Kingdom Trustees on an Enquiry into Children's Response to Films. Dunfermline, Fife: Carnegie United Kingdom Trust, 1954.

——. "The Children's Film Foundation." Financial Times 23 September 1957: 5.

——. "Children's Films: A New International Approach and Some Suggestions." Times Educational Supplement 20 October 1950: 804; 27 October 1950: 820.

——. "Children's Taste in Films." Quarterly of Film, Radio, and Television 11 (1956): 14–23.

——. "Cinemas for Children." Film News October 1945: 21.

——. "The Film in the Museum." Museums Journal 33 (1934): 348–50.

——. "The Film in the Teaching of Biology." The Road to Maturity. Ed. Edward Griffith. 1947. 128–33.

——. Good Company: The Story of the Children's Entertainment Film Movement in Great Britain, 1934–1950. London: Longmans, Green, 1952.

——. "Instructional Film." Photography Journal [London] April 1935: 204–7.

——. "Making Nature Films." Sight and Sound Autumn 1932: 70–71.

——. "Making the Past Live." Sight and Sound Autumn 1935: 132–4.

——. Interview. "The Movies Come to the Schoolroom: An Interview with Mary Field of Secrets of Nature Fame." Interview with Lawrence Murray. Film Weekly 6 April 1934: 12.

——. "Moving Pictures and How They Move." Junior. London: Children's Digest Publications, 1945. 70–78.

——. "Unfinished Project." Sight and Sound Spring 1949: 8–11.

——. "Why Women Should Make Films." Film Weekly 10 October 1931: 8.

Field, Mary, and J.V. Durden, and F. Percy Smith. See How They Grow: Botany Through the Cinema. Harmondsworth: Penguin, 1952.

Field, Mary, and J. Valentine Durden, and F. Percy Smith. Cine-Biology. London: Pelican, 1941.

Field, Mary, and Maud M. Miller. The Boys' and Girls' Book of Films and Television London: Burke, 1961.

Field, Mary, and Maud M. Miller. The Boys' and Girls' Film Book. London: Burke, 1947. Rev. ed. 1948.

Field, Mary, and F. Percy Smith. Secrets of Nature. London: Faber & Faber, 1934. Rev. ed. The Scientific Book Club, 1939.

Fitzgerald, Zelda. "Our Own Movie Queen" (fiction). Chicago Sunday Tribune 7 June 1925, magazine sec.: 1–4. Originally published with the byline of F. Scott Fitzgerald.

——. Zelda Fitzgerald: The Collected Writings. Ed. Matthew J. Bruccoli. New York: Charles Scribner's Sons/Macmillan, 1991.

Flaherty, Mrs. Robert J. [Frances Hubbard]. "The Camera's Eye." National Board of Review Magazine April 1927: 4–5.

——. "Explorations." Film: Book 1, The Audience and the Filmmaker. Ed. Robert Hughes. New York: Grove Press in cooperation with the American Federation of Film Societies, 1959.

——. "Filming Moana of the South." Asia (1925). "Setting Up House and Shop in Samoa." August 1925: 638–51, 709–11; "Behind the Scenes With Our Samoan Stars." September 1925: 746–53, 795–6; "Serpents in Eden." October 1925: 858–69, 895–8 (this installment written by David Flaherty, with photographs by Frances); "A Search for Animal and Sea Sequences." November 1925: 954–62, 1000–1004; "Fa'a-Samoa." December 1925: 1085–90, 1096.

——. The Odyssey of A Film-Maker Dummerston, VT: Threshold Books with the Dummerston Historical Society, 1960.

Flaherty, Miriam R. "Sentimentality and the Screen." Commonweal 5 October 1934: 522–523.

Flanner, Janet. A regular columnist for the New Yorker for fifty years, where, under the name 'Genêt' she wrote her "Letter from Paris", and other cities. Flanner occasionally discussed film. Several collections of her columns have been published.

——. An American in Paris. New York: Simon & Schuster, 1940.

——. "Bette Davis." New Yorker 20 February 1943: 19–29.

——. "Comments on the Screen." Indianapolis Star 7 July 1918, sec. 6: 1.

——. "Comments on the Screen." Indianapolis Star 14 July 1918, sec. 5: 33, 38.

——. "Comments on the Screen." Indianapolis Star 21 July 1918, sec. 5: 33, 38.

——. Janet Flanner's World: Uncollected Writings, 1932–1975. Ed. Irving Drutman. New York: Harcourt Brace Jovanovich, 1979.

——. "The Movies, Montmartre, and Main Street." *Filmplay* May 1922: 10–11, 51.

——. *Paris Journal: 1944–1965.* Ed. William Shawn. New York: Atheneum, 1965.

——. *Paris Journal: 1965–1971.* Ed. William Shawn. New York: Harcourt Brace Jovanovich, 1971.

——. *Paris Was Yesterday: 1925–1939.* Ed. Irving Drutman. New York: Viking, 1972.

——. "Thumbs Down on the Roman Movies." *Filmplay* July 1922: 12–13, 56. Rpt. *They Also Wrote for the Fan Magazines: Film Articles by Literary Giants from e.e. cummings to Eleanor Roosevelt, 1920–1939.* Ed. Anthony Slide. London: McFarland, 1992. 64–9.

——. "The Turkish Fez and the Films." *Filmplay* April 1922: 10–11, 54. Rpt. *They Also Wrote for the Fan Magazines: Film Articles by Literary Giants from e.e. cummings to Eleanor Roosevelt, 1920–1939.* Ed. Anthony Slide. London: McFarland, 1992. 59–63.

Fletcher, Adele Whitely. Prolific fan-magazine writer whose work appeared in *Motion Picture Magazine, Movie Weekly, Photoplay* and others over a fifty-year period.

——. with Gladys Hall. "We Interview" series. *Motion Picture Magazine* 1920's.

——. "Adele Whitely Fletcher." Interview with Anthony Slide. *Film Fan Monthly* February 1974. Rpt. *The Idols of Silence.* Ed. Anthony Slide. South Brunswick, NJ: A.S. Barnes, 1976. 111–14.

Formiggini-Santamaria, Emilia. "The Educational Function of the Cinema." *International Review of Educational Cinematography* 4 (1932): 923–5.

Foster, Inez Whitely. "Partners and Pioneers." *Christian Science Monitor Magazine* 15 January 1949: 5.

Fox, E. Margery. "Children and Picture Palaces." *Parents' Review* [London] 27.9 (September 1916): 700–706.

——. "Minutes of Evidence." Given to the National Council of Public Morals Cinema Commission of Inquiry (19 February 1917). *The Cinema: Its Present Position and Future Possibilities.* (Report and chief evidence, National Council of Public Morals Cinema Commission of Inquiry) London: William & Norgate, 1917. 132–38.

Frakes, Margaret. "Drinking in the Movies" *Christian Century* 60 (1943): 325–7.

——. "Time Marches Back: Propaganda for Defense" *Christian Century* 57 (1940): 1277–8.

——. "Why the Movie Investigation?" *Christian Century* 58 (1941): 1172–4.

Francis, Kay. "Don't Try Your Luck Out Here!" *Pictorial Review* January 1933: 16–17+.

Frank, Florence Kiper. "The Movies." (poem) *The Faber Book of Movie Verse.* Eds. Philip French and Ken Wlaschin. London: Faber & Faber, 1993. No original source listed.

——. "War Impressions: The Moving Picture Show." *Little Review* 2.5 (1915): 11.

Fuller, Loïe. *Fifteen Years of a Dancer's Life.* London: Herbert Jenkins, 1913.

Garbo, Greta. "What the Public Wants." *Saturday Review* [London] 13 June 1931: 39–46.

Garden, Mary. "Music Comes to Hollywood. " *Cinema Arts* 1 (1937): 19.

Garrett, Lula Jones. "Nothing 'Delilah-Like' in Real Louise Beavers." *Baltimore Afro-American* 18 May 1935: 9.

Garrison, Gretchen. "Forgetting a Thousand Cares; Library-Film Cooperation." *Library Journal* 64 (1939): 87–90.

——. "The Library and the Films." *National Board of Review Magazine* October 1937: 3–5.

Gauntier, Gene. "A Voice from the Desert." *Moving Picture World* 2 March 1912: 771.

——. "Blazing the Trail." *Woman's Home Companion* October 1928: 7–8, 181–84, 186; November 1928: 25–6, 166, 168–70; December 1928: 15–16, 132, 134; January 1929: 13–14, 94; February 1929: 20–21, 92, 94, 97–8; March 1929: 18–19, 142, 146.

——. "Gauntier Players in Ireland." *Moving Picture World* 14 October 1913: 39.

——. "Picture Players at a Turkish Wedding." *Moving Picture World* 20 July 1912: 253.

Gebhart, Myrtle. "Business Women in Film Studios." *Business Woman* December 1923: 26–28, 66–8.

——. "The Chocolate Comedy." *Extension Magazine* November 1929: 17–18, 42, 44.

Gehrts, Meg. *A Camera Actress in the Wilds of Togoland.* London: Seeley Service, 1915.

——. "I Went Among Savages for 'Movies.'" *Pearson's Weekly* 1 August 1914: 154.

Genauer, Emily, and Dorothy Thompson. "Art of Fantasia." *Art Digest* 15 (1940): 10–11.

Gerould, Katharine Fullerton. "Hollywood: An American State of Mind. " *Harper's Magazine* 146 (May 1923): 689–96.

——. "The Lost Art of Motion Pictures." *Century Magazine* 118 (1929): 496–506.

——. "Movies." *Atlantic Monthly* April 1921: 22–30.

——. "The Nemesis of the Screen." *Saturday Evening Post* 8 April 1922: 12, 157.

Gerstein, Evelyn. "English Documentary Films." *New Theatre Magazine* [New York] January 1936: 7, 38.

——. "Four Films of New Types." *Theatre Arts Monthly* April 1927: 295–98.

——. "Metropolis." *Nation* 23 March 1927: 323–24. Rpt. *American Film Criticism: From the Beginnings to Citizen Kane*. Ed. Stanley Kauffmann, with Bruce Henstell. New York: Liveright, 1972. 186–7.

——. "Musical Talkies." *Nation* 14 October 1931: 407–8.

——. "The Passion of Joan of Arc." *New Republic* 10 April 1929. Rpt. *American Film Criticism: From the Beginnings to Citizen Kane*. Ed. Stanley Kauffmann, with Bruce Henstell. New York: Liveright, 1972. 214–16.

——. "Potemkin." *New Republic* 20 October 1926: 243–4.

——. "Russia's Film Wizard: A Study of the Career and Achievements of Eisenstein." *Theatre Guild Magazine* February 1930: 44–7.

——. "Three Russian Movies: Expressionism Gives Way to the Realities." *Theatre Guild Magazine* October 1929: 14–16.

——. "Variety." *New Republic* 28 July 1926: 280–81. Rpt. *American Film Criticism: From the Beginnings to Citizen Kane*. Ed. Stanley Kauffmann, with Bruce Henstell. New York: Liveright, 1972. 175–7.

——. "What I Saw in the Film Studio." *Moscow News* [New York] 10 October 1935: 3, 9.

Gibbs, Elinor. "This is Where I Came In…" *Vogue* [New York] 15 March 1946: 157, 189–90, 192.

Gilman, Catheryne Cooke. "Better Movies—But How?" *Woman's Journal* February 1930: 10–12, 34–5.

——. "Government Regulations for the Movies. " *Christian Century* 48 (1931): 1066–68.

——. "The Movie Problem: The Program of the National Congress of Parents and Teachers." *Ladies' Home Journal* July 1934: 104–5.

——. *Responsibility for Better Motion Pictures*. Minneapolis: Women's Cooperative Alliance, May 1929.

Gilman, Charlotte Perkins. "Mind-Stretching." *Century Magazine* 3 (December 1925): 217–24.

——. "Public Library Motion Pictures." *Annals of the American Academy of Political and Social Science*. Philadelphia, November 1926. 143–45.

Ginger, Bonnie R. "The Prodigal Nephew's Aunt." (fiction) *Delineator* September 1913: 7–8.

Gish, Dorothy. "And So I Am a Comedienne." *Ladies' Home Journal* July 1925: 7, 57–8.

——. "Largely a Matter of Love." *Photoplay* March 1922: 37–8, 99.

——. "Lillian Gish, the Most Thoughtful Girl I Know." *Filmplay* April 1922: 6, 55.

Gish, Lillian. "Are We Creating Art?" *National Board of Review Magazine* July 1928: 8–9.

——. "Beginning Young." *Ladies' Home Journal* September 1925: 19, 117–18, 120.

——. "On Behalf of the Silent Film." *Revolt in the Arts*. By Oliver M. Sayler. New York: Brentano, 1930. 225–30.

——. "Dorothy Gish, the Frankest Girl I Know." *Filmplay* April 1922: 7, 56.

——. Foreword. *Sounds for Silents*. By Charles Hoffmann. New York: DBS Publications/Drama Book Specialists, 1970.

——. "Lillian Gish… Director." Interview with Anthony Slide. *Silent Picture* 6 (Spring 1970): 12–13.

——. "I Made War Propaganda." *Scribner's Commentator* November 1941: 7–11.

——. "Screen." *Rob Wagner's Script* [Los Angeles] 14 September 1946: 10–11.

——. "Silence Was Our Virtue." *Films and Filming* December 1957: 9.

——. "My Sister and I." *Theatre Magazine* November 1927: 14–15.

——. "A Universal Language." *The Theatre and Motion Pictures: A Selection of Articles from the New 14th Edition of the Encyclopaedia Britannica*. New York and London: Encyclopaedia Britannica, 1929–33. 33–4.

Gish, Lillian, with Josie P. Lederer. "Lillian Gish Says that Talkies are Imitations." *Film Weekly* 9 August 1930: 9.

Gish, Lillian, with Ann Pinchot. *The Movies, Mr. Griffith and Me*. Englewood Cliffs, NJ: Prentice-Hall, 1969.

Glencross, Barbara. "The Film and Native Cultures." *East and West Review* [London] 14 (1948): 125–7.

Glick, Annette. "The Habit of Criticizing Motion Pictures." *Educational Screen* January 1934: 10–12.

Glyn, Elinor. *The Elinor Glyn System of Writing*. 4 vols. Albany: Author's Press, 1922.

——. "In Filmdom's Boudoir." *Photoplay* March 1921: 28–30. Rpt. *They Also Wrote for the Fan Magazines: Film Articles by Literary Giants from e.e. cummings to Eleanor Roosevelt, 1920–1939*. Ed. Anthony Slide. London: McFarland, 1992. 76–9.

——. "Gloria Swanson as a Mother." *Pictures and Picturegoer* 13 August 1932: 12.

——. "Rudolph Valentino as I Knew Him." *Modern Screen* May 1931: 26–29.

——. "Sex and the Photoplay." *Motion Picture Magazine* June 1921: 21. Rpt. *They Also Wrote for the Fan Magazines: Film Articles by Literary Giants from e.e. cummings to Eleanor Roosevelt, 1920–1939*. Ed. Anthony Slide. London: McFarland, 1992. 80–81.

Goodwin, Ruby Berkley. "The Color Fad." *Flash* 2.23 (31 December 1929): 11.

——. "Negro Pioneers in the Field of Sound Movies." *Pittsburgh Courier* 4 May 1929, sec. 2: 1, 7.

——. "When Stepin' Fetchit Stepped into Fame." *Pittsburgh Courier* 6 July 1929: 7, 11.

Gorney, Sondra. "On Children's Cinema: America and Britain." *Hollywood Quarterly* 3.1 (1947): 56–62.

——. "The Poppet and the Muppet." *Hollywood Quarterly* 1.4 (1946): 371–5.

Governess, a. Letter. "How the Cinema Could Help With Lessons." *Cinegoer* [London] 11 March 1916: 2.

Grant, Elspeth. "From Pearl White to Pearl Harbour." *Sight and Sound* Winter 1942–43: 61–2.

——. "Those Critics!" *Sight and Sound* May 1944: 12–13.

Graves, Janet. "Hollywood Trademarks." *Cinema Arts* 1.3 (1937): 39.

Gray, Barbara. "Social Effects of the Film." *Sociological Review* [London] 42 (1950): 135–44.

Grayne, Henrietta. "Reversing Babel." *Film Weekly* 19 July 1930: 8.

Green, Alice. "Discovering the Middle Class." *Film Weekly* 7 June 1935: 30.

——. "Picture-House Beethoven—And then the Gramophone." *Gramophone* 6 (1928): 101–102.

Gregory, Yvonne. "They Laughed at Hattie." *Baltimore Afro-American* 17 January 1942: 15.

Grey, Anne. "Badder—and Better Vamps." *Film Weekly* 25 March 1932: 7, 26.

Griffith, Mrs. D.W. [Linda Arvidson]. *When the Movies Were Young*. New York: E.P. Dutton, 1925. Rpt. with a new introduction by Edward Wagenknecht. New York: Dover, 1969.

Grover, Gloria Waldron. "Documentary Values in Fiction Films." *Films in Review* May–June 1950: 7–8, 47.

Guy, Alice. See Alice Guy Blaché.

H.D. "An Appreciation." *Close Up* 4.3 (1929): 56–68.

——. "Boo." *Close Up* 2.1 (1928): 38–50.

——. *Borderline: A Pool Film with Paul Robeson* London: Pool, 1930.

——. "The Cinema and the Classics I: Beauty." *Close Up* 1.1 (1927): 22–33.

——. "The Cinema and the Classics II: Restraint." *Close Up* 1.2 (1927): 30–39.

——. "The Cinema and the Classics III: The Mask and the Movietone." *Close Up* 1.5 (1927): 18–31.

——. "Conrad Veidt: *The Student of Prague*." *Close Up* 1.3 (1927): 34–44.

——. "Expiation." [By the Law.] *Close Up* 2.5 (1928): 38–49.

——. "Joan of Arc." *Close Up* 3.1 (1928): 15–23.

——. "The King of Kings Again." *Close Up* 2.2 (1928): 21–32.

——. "Projector." (poem) *Close Up* 1.1 (1927): 46–51.

——. "Projector II (Chang)." (poem) *Close Up* 1.4 (1927): 35–44.

——. "Reply to questionnaire." *Little Review* 12.2 (1929): 22.

——. "Russian Films." *Close Up* 3.3 (1928): 18–29.

——. "Turksib." *Close Up* 5.6 (1929), pp. 488–92.

Hackett, Hazel. "The French Cinema During the Occupation." *Sight and Sound* Spring 1946: 1–3; Summer 1946: 48–52.

——. "Jean Grémillon," *Sight and Sound* Summer 1947: 60–62.

Hale, Louise Closser. "The New Stage Fright: Talking Pictures." *Harper's Monthly Magazine* September 1930: 417–24.

——. "Tragedy and Comedy in the Talkies." *Woman's Journal* October 1930: 18–19+.

Hall, Gladys. [Prolific film critic. A sampling of her film writing includes:]

——. "Does Hollywood Believe in the Hereafter?" 9 January 1941, ts. Gladys Hall Collection, Margaret Herrick Library, Academy of Motion Picture Arts and Sciences.

——. "Elsie Ferguson—A Film Feminist," *Filmplay* April 1922: 22–3.

——. "Haunted by the Camera." 28 February 1931, ts. Gladys Hall Collection, Margaret Herrick Library, Academy of Motion Picture Arts and Sciences.

——. "How Sex Appeal is Manufactured in Hollywood." 27 May 1932, ts. Gladys Hall Collection, Margaret Herrick Library, Academy of Motion Picture Arts and Sciences.

——. "I Am a Star." *Motion Picture Classic* November 1918: 6.

——. "If the Worst That Can Be Has Been Done?" n.d., ts. Gladys Hall Collection, Margaret Herrick Library, Academy of Motion Picture Arts and Sciences.

——. "The Lady Who Knows it All: Hollywood Can't Keep Any Secrets from Hedda Hopper." *Motion Picture Magazine* June 1931: 47, 93, 113.

——. "Olga Petrova—A Film Feminist." *Filmplay* May 1922: 34–5.

——. "Recurrent Dreams." 31 May 1934, ts. Gladys Hall Collection, Margaret Herrick Library, Academy of Motion Picture Arts and Sciences.

——. "Rot." *Metropolitan Magazine* nd.: 11. Gladys Hall Collection. Margaret Herrick Library, Academy of Motion Picture Arts and Sciences, Folder 536.

——. "Rudolph Valentino in Memoriam." (poem) 1926. Rudolph Valentino Files, Motion Picture Department, George Eastman House, Rochester.

——. "The Serious Side of the Woman on the Screen: Madge Kennedy." *Filmplay* July 1922: 20–21.

——. "The Serious Side of the Woman on the Screen: Lillian Gish." *Filmplay* July 1922: 20–21.

——. "The Star Diggers—Sam Goldwyn Chooses Women Trained to Please Men." *Motion Picture Magazine* October 1928: 50–51, 106–7.

——. "The Widow's Might," *Motion Picture Classic* March 1918: 21–23, 79–80.

Hall, Gladys, with Adele Whitely Fletcher. "We Interview" series. *Motion Picture Magazine* 1920's.

Hammon, Mary. "Adventures of a Baby Star." *Good Housekeeping* November 1939: 42–3+.

Harper, Patricia. "Your Minimum Basic Flat Deal." *Screen Writer* 1 (1946): 19–25.

Harriman, Margaret Case. "Gloria Swanson." *New Yorker* 18 January 1930: 24–27.

——. "Mary Pickford." *New Yorker* 7 April 1934: 29–33.

Harris, Avenelle. "I Tried to Crash the Movies." *Ebony* August 1946: 5–10.

Harris, Elizabeth M. "The Functions of the Specialized Cinema." *Penguin Film Review* 6 (1948): 80–86.

Harris, Celia. "The Movies and the Elizabethan Theater." *Outlook* 4 January 1922: 29–31.

Harrison, Stella. "Letter from London." *Canadian Forum* April 1948: 6–7.

Hawkes, Jacquetta. "The Beginning of History: A Film." *Antiquity* 20.78 (1946): 78–82.

——. "Space, Time, and the Possible." *Sight and Sound* April 1950: 67, 73.

Head, Edith. "A Costume Problem: From Shop to Stage to Screen." *Hollywood Quarterly* 2.1 (1946): 44ff.

Head, June. *Stargazing*. London: Peter Davies, 1931.

Hilliker, Katharine. "Writing the Titles." *Opportunities in the Motion Picture Industry*. Vol. 2. Los Angeles: Photoplay Research Society, 1922: 49–53.

Hoffmann, Marianna. "Children and the Cinema." *International Review of Educational Cinematography* 2 (1930): 1071–5.

Holmes, Winifred. "Bill Smith and Mrs. Brown Like the Latest Documentaries." *Sight and Sound* Spring 1940: 10–11.

——. "British Films and the Empire." *Sight and Sound* Autumn 1936: 72–74.

——. "China and the Cinema." *Life & Letters Today* 16.7 (1937): 121–24.

——. "Evil Eye in Belgium." *Sight and Sound* Autumn 1938: 113–11.

——. "Forty Years." *Sight and Sound* Summer 1938: 57–59.

——. "Hamburg Cinema." *Sight and Sound* Spring 1939: 18–20.

——. "Kalpana." *Sight and Sound* Spring 1949: 47–49.

——. "Postscript to India." *Sight and Sound* Summer 1946: 43–45.

——. "The New Renaissance." *Sight and Sound* Summer 1936: 79.

——. "Two Films from the U.S.S.R." *Life & Letters Today* 21.21 (1939): 124–25.

——. "What's Wrong with Documentary?" *Sight and Sound* Spring 1948: 44–5.

——. "Your Freedom is at Stake!" *Sight and Sound* Winter 1946–47: 117–20.

Holtby, Winifred. *Mandoa, Mandoa! A Comedy of Irrelevance*. London: Collins, 1933.

——. "Does Colour Really Matter?" *New World* [London] July 1930: 7.

——. "JIX: His Refusal of a Private Showing of *Potemkin*." *New Leader* [London] 12 April 1929: 5.

——. "Children in the Spotlight." *Schoolmistress* [London] 19 January 1933: 425, 447.

——. "Missionary Film [1927]." (fiction) *Truth is Not Sober*. London: William Collins, 1934. Rpt. Freeport, NY: Books for Libraries Press, 1970. 108–13.

——. "My Weekly Journal": regular column for *Schoolmistress*, including:

——. "My Weekly Journal 4. An Indian Week." *Schoolmistress* [London] 9 July 1931: 417.

——. "My Weekly Journal 5: Life and Art." *Schoolmistress* [London] 16 July 1931: 441, 458.

——. "My Weekly Journal 7: A Russian Week." *Schoolmistress* [London] 30 July 1931: 493.

——. "My Weekly Journal 8: The Emerald Coast." *Schoolmistress* 6 Augst 1931: 513, 528.

——. "My Weekly Journal 9: Rain Over Brittany." *Schoolmistress* 13 August 1931: 533, 539. (Contains "The Street Cinema.")

——. "My Weekly Journal 13 : England Again." *Schoolmistress* [London] 10 September 1931: 633.

——. "My Weekly Journal 21: Trader Horn's Africa." *Schoolmistress* [London] 5 November 1931: 153.

——. "My Weekly Journal 25: Through Fifty Years." *Schoolmistress* 24 December 1931: 369, 382.

——. *Poor Caroline*. (fiction) New York: Robert M. McBridge, 1931. Rpt. London: Virago Press, 1985.

——. "Reforms and Films." *Schoolmistress* [London] 16 February 1933: 537, 562.

——. "So This is Hollywood!" *Schoolmistress* [London] 13 April 1933: 29.

Hopper, Hedda. "The Hats in My Life." ts., n.d. (c. 1940s), marked *The Woman Magazine*. "Autobiographical File." Hedda Hopper Collection, Margaret Herrick Library, Academy of Motion Picture Arts and Sciences.

——. Scrapbooks of columns syndicated through the *Chicago Tribune—New York Daily News* Syndicate. Hedda Hopper Collection, Margaret Herrick Library, Academy of Motion Picture Arts and Sciences.

——. *From Under My Hat*. Garden City, NY: Doubleday, 1952.

Hopper, Hedda, and James Bough. *The Whole Truth and Nothing But*. Garden City, NY: Doubleday, 1963.

Horn, Florence. "Formidavel, Fabulosissimo." *Harper's Magazine* December 1941: 59–64.

Horne, Lena. "My Life Story." *Negro Digest* July 1949: 3–13.

Horrabin, Winifred. "Filming the Golden Eagle." *Lansbury's Labour Weekly* [London] 18 June 1927, p. 2.

——. "From Old Baghdad to New Russia." *Tribune* [London] 1 August 1941: 6–7.

——. "Go West, Young Mormon." *Tribune* [London] 7 February 1941: 7.

——. "Good Men v. Bad Men." *Tribune* [London] 24 October 1941: 16.

——. "Good, So-So and Fine." *Tribune* [London] 7 November 1941: 18–19.

——. "Highbrow to the Rescue." *Lansbury's Labour Weekly* [London] 5 March 1927: 5.

——. "Lady Hamilton and Target for Tonight." *Tribune* [London] 29 August 1941: 8–9.

——. "Major Barbara." *Tribune* [London] 4 July 1941: 10–11.

——. "Metropolis." *Lansbury's Labour Weekly* [London] 9 April 1927: 4.

——. "Rudolph Valentino: The Sheik and The Son of the Sheik." *Lansbury's Labour Weekly* [London] 16 October 1926: 12.

——. "Salute to the Usherettes." *Tribune* [London] 11 October 1940: 14.

——. "Shows." *Tribune* [London] 25 August 1944. [This was a regular column.]

——. "So this is Paris." *Lansbury's Labour Weekly* [London] 13 November 1926, p. 2.

——. "What Films do YOU Like?" *Tribune* [London] 24 January 1941: 11.

——. "The Worker's Film Association." *Tribune* [London] January 1943: 11.

Houston, Penelope. *The Contemporary Cinema*. Baltimore: Penguin Books, 1963.

——. "Mr. Deeds and Willie Stark." *Sight and Sound* November 1950: 276–9, 285.

——. "Hollywood Warning." *Sequence* 2 (1947): 15–17.

——. "Interview with Flaherty." *Sight and Sound* December 1949: 16–18.

——. *Keepers of the Frame: The Film Archive*. London: British Film Institute, 1994.

——. "Leading the Blind." *Sight and Sound* 18: 69 (1950): 42–3.

——. "Scripting." *Sight and Sound* January 1951: 376; March 1951: 442.

——. *Went the Day Well?* London: British Film Institute, 1992.

Huettig, Mae D. *Economic Control of the Motion Picture Industry*. Philadelphia: University of Pennsylvania Press, 1944. Pages 34–39, "The Battle for Theaters." Rpt. in *The First Tycoons*. Ed. Richard Dyer MacCann. Metuchen, NJ: Scarecrow Press in association with Image and Idea, Iowa City, 1987. 168–73.

Hunt, Julie Lang. "They Aren't All Actresses in Hollywood: Eight Little Girls Went to Hollywood. Before You Follow Them, Read What Happened..." *Photoplay* September 1936: 50–51, 92–4.

Hunt, Marsha. "A Hollywood Actress Looks at the Negro." *Negro Digest* September 1947: 14–17.

——. *The Way We Wore: Styles of the 1930s and 1940s and Our World Since Then, Shown and Recalled by Marsha Hunt*. Falbrook, CA: Fallbrook Publishing, 1993.

Hurst, Fannie. "New Films for Old." *Theatre Guild Magazine* January 1929: 11–13.

——. "The Author is the Person Who Wrote the Story." *Theatre Magazine* 50 (1929): 14, 66.

Hussey, Nancy. "Talkies Set Them Talking." *Sight and Sound* October 1943: 61–63.

Hutchins, Patricia. "The Mountains and the Swan." *Sight and Sound* Autumn 1939: 107–108.

——. "News from Ireland." *Sight and Sound* Winter 1947–1948: 159–60.

——. "Puppets on Parade." *Sight and Sound* Autumn 1936: 69–71.

Hyer, Martha. "What it Takes To Be a Starlet." *American* February 1948: 136–40.

Inglis, Ruth. *Freedom of the Movies: A Report on Self-Regulation from the Commission on Freedom of the Press*. Chicago: University of Chicago Press, 1947.

——. "Freedom to See and Hear." *Survey* 35 (1946): 477–81+.

——. "Need for Voluntary Self-Regulations." *Annals of the American Academy of Political and Social Science*. Philadelphia, November 1947. 153–9.

Irvin, Katherine. "Here and There." *Half-Century Magazine* November–December 1924: 6.

Isaacs, Edith [J.R.], ed. "Artists of the Movies." *Theatre Arts* 23 (1939): 424–8.

——. "Let's Go to the Movies." *Theatre Arts* 19 (1935): 399–410.

Isaacs, Hermine Rich. "Beauty and the Beast of Berlin." *Theatre Arts* 27 (1943): 283–90.

——. "Citizen Kane." *Theatre Arts* 25 (1941): 427–34.

——. "Escape to Films." *Theatre Arts* 28 (1944): 25–8.

——. "Face the Music." *Theatre Arts* 28 (1944): 718–27.

——. "Film in the Court." *Theatre Arts* 22 (1938): 907–9.

——. "The Film Critic's Quest." *Films in Review* 1.3 (1950): 19–20.

——. "Fine Spirits: Eric Johnston and the Hays Office." *Theatre Arts* 29 (1945): 637.

——. "Laugh, and You Laugh Alone." *Arts* 29 (1945): 226.

——. "The Movies Murder Illusion." *Sight and Sound* Spring 1947: 27–9.

——. "New Horizons; *Fantasia* and Fantasound." *Theatre Arts* 25 (1941): 55–60.

——. "Presenting the Warner Brothers." *Theatre Arts* 28 (1944): 99–101+.

——. "Profits and Prestige." *Theatre Arts* 25 (1941): 666–72.

——. "Shadows of War." *Theatre Arts* 26 (1942): 689–96.

——. "Two Way Traffic." *Theatre Arts* 29 (1945): 32–3.

——. "War Fronts and Film Fronts." *Theatre Arts* 28 (1944): 343–8.

——. "War and Love." *Theatre Arts* 29 (1945): 273–80

——. "When is a Fiction a Fact?" *Theatre Arts* 31 (1947): 51–4,

——. "Whistling in the Dark: Every Soldier a Movie Critic." *Theatre Arts* 27 (1943): 727–33.

——. "William Wyler, Director with a Passion and a Craft." *Theatre Arts* 31 (1947): 20–24.

Jackson, Fay. "Edna Harris Chosen as Joe Louis' Leading Lady." *Pittsburgh Courier*, 6 November 1937: 21.

——. "Fear *Green Pastures* New Yorkers May Spoil Hollywood: claim Connolly Scrimps on Salaaries." Associated Negro Press, *California News* 1935/1936, ts. Claude A. Barnett Papers, Chicago Historical Society, Microform Reel #01071, and Box 287, Folder 20.

——. "Fredi Washington Strikes New Note in Hollywood Film: *Imitations*." Associated Negro Press, 12 December 1934, ts. Claude A. Barnett Papers, Chicago Historical Society, Box 298, Folder 15. Published as "Fredi Washington Strikes New Note in Hollywood Film," *Pittsburgh Courier* 15 December 1934: 8.

——. "Hollywood Lowdown." Unidentified clipping, marked 1934. Claude A. Barnett Papers, Box 228, Folder 1, Chicago Historical Society.

——. "Hollywood Stardust." Baltimore *Afro-American* 19 January 1935: 8.

——. "'Imitation' Nearest to Authentic Negro." Associated Negro Press, 22 May 1935, ts. Claude A. Barnett Papers, Box 298, Folder 15, Chicago Historical Society. This ts does not carry Fay M. Jackson's name, but its style and content indicate her authorship.

——. "Pay of *Green Pastures* Cast Irks Hollywood." Baltimore *Afro-American* 25 January 1936: 11. Published article appears without by-line but the same article exists as a typescript by Jackson in the Claude A. Barnett Papers, Chicago Historical Society, under the title listed above.

——. "People Talked About." *California News* c.1935/1936. ts. Claude A. Barnett Papers, Chicago Historical Society.

——. "Topical Types in Filmland." Associated Negro Press, 12 December 1934, ts. Claude A. Barnett Papers, Box 298, Folder 15, Chicago Historical Society.

Jackson, Joan. "Role of Queenie in Film *Showboat* Dangling." Baltimore *Afro-American* 28 December 1935: 8.

Jacobs, Florence. "The Motion Picture Will Preserve Historical Events for Future Generations." *International Review of Educational Cinematography* 5 (1933): 734–44.

——. "Tremendous Influence of Films on Family Life of Today." *International Review of Educational Cinematography* 2 (1930): 1189–90.

——. "Wholesome Pictures for Children a Great and Growing Need." *International Review of Educational Cinematography* 4 (1932): 767–8.

Jennings, Amy S. "An Extra in Hollywood." *Atlantic Monthly* May 1927: 634–41.

Jesenska, Milena. "Cinema." A translation of "Kino." *Tribuna* [Prague] 15 January 1920. Rpt. *Alles ist Leben*. Frankfurt: Verlag Neue Kritik, 1984: 16–19.

Jessye, Eva. "The Truth about *Hallelujah*." Baltimore *Afro-American* 2 August 1930: 8.
——. Letter to Etta Moten, 20 August 1950. Claude A Barnett Papers, Box 297, Folder 3, Chicago Historical Society.
Johnson, Lillian. "Light and Shadow: *Gone with the Wind*'s Place and Prices, and the Public." Baltimore *Afro-American* 16 March 1940: 13.
——. "Light and Shadow: On Pickets, *Gone with the Wind*, and 'Wolf'." Baltimore *Afro-American* 9 March 1940: 13
Johnson, Osa. "Africans Rebel at Playing Slaves." *New York Times* 17 October 1937: 29.
——. *Bride in the Solomons*. Boston: Houghton Mifflin, 1944.
——. *I Married Adventure: The Lives and Adventures of Martin and Osa Johnson*. New York: J.B. Lippincott, 1940.
Johnston, Winifred. *Memo on the Movies: War Propaganda, 1914–1939*. Norman, OK: Cooperative Books, 1939.
Jones, Dorothy B. "Is Hollywood Growing Up?" *Nation* 3 February 1945: 123–25.
——. "The Hollywood War Film: 1942–1944." *Hollywood Quarterly* 1.1 (1945): 1–19.
——. "Quantitative Analysis of Motion Picture Content." *Public Opinion Quarterly* 6 (1942): 411–28.
Jones, Isabel Morse. "Photographed Music." *Harlequinade: A Miscellany of Notes on the Visual Arts, Life, and Letters* Ed. Maude Home. 1 (1931). Los Angeles: M. Hume, 1931. n.p.
Jüer-Marbach, Franziska. "The Comparative and Complementary Value of Fixed and Animated Projections." *International Review of Educational Cinematography* 5 (1933): 807–10.
——. "Difficulties Experienced in Understanding Films." *International Review of Educational Cinematography* 4 (1932): 692–8.
——. "Grammar." *International Review of Educational Cinematography* 3 (1931): 432–9.
——. "Language Teaching and the Talking Film." An I.I.E.C. Inquiry. *International Review of Educational Cinematography* 4 (1932): 779–89, 857–66, 927–33; 5 (1933): 113–17, 191–6, 339–46, 487–95, 547–53.
——. "Language and the Talking Film." *International Review of Educational Cinematography* 5 (1933): 27–32.
Justice, Maibelle Heikes. "A Garden of Allah Impression." *New York Dramatic Mirror* 4 August 1917: 8.
Kalmus, Natalie M. "Color Consciousness." *Journal of the Society of Motion Picture Engineers* August 1935: 139–47.
Katz, Nancy, and Robert Katz. "Documentary in Transition: Part I—The United States." *Hollywood Quarterly* 3.4 (1949): 425–33.
Katz, Nancy, and Robert Katz. "Documentary in Transition: Part II—The International Scene." *Hollywood Quarterly* 4.1 (1949): 51–64.
Kay, Charlotte. "Tooting Lena's Horn." *Negro Digest* September 1945: 25–9.
Keir, Gertrude. "Children and the Cinema." *British Journal of Delinquency* 1 (1951): 225–9.
——. "Psychology and the Film." *Penguin Film Review* 9 (1949): 67–72.
Keliher, Alice V. "Children and Movies: A Critical Summary of the Scientific Literature." *Films* [New York] 1.4 (1940): 40–48.
——. "Literature of the Film: Children and Movies." *Films* [New York] 1.4 (1940): 40–48.
Kelly, Mary. "Do Dramas Cater Exclusively to Women? Roy L. Manker Sees Possible Danger." *Moving Picture World* 11 February 1922: 615.
——. "Women Journalists Attend Selznick Luncheon to Anna Steese Richardson." *Moving Picture World* 53.8 (25 December 1921): 930.
Kennedy, Margaret. *The Mechanized Muse*. London: George Allen & Unwin and P.E.N., 1942. Rpt. *Film: An Anthology*. Ed. Daniel Talbot. Berkeley: University of California Press, 1959. 80–109.
Kennedy, Minnie E. *The Home and Moving Pictures* New York and Cincinnati: Abingdon, 1921.
Kerr, Sophie. "Censorship a Step Backward." *National Board of Review Magazine* February 1929: 5–6.
Kingsley, Grace. "Little Journeys Around the Studios." *Motion Picture Director* August 1926: 38.
Kinross, Martha. "The Screen, From This Side" *Fortnightly Review* 136 (1931), pp. 499–512.
Klump, Inez and Helen Klump. *Screen Acting: Its Requirements and Rewards*. New York: Falk, 1922.
Knowles, Dorothy. *The Censor, the Drama, and the Film, 1900–1934*. London: Allen & Unwin, 1934.
Krasne, Belle. "Sound Tracks to Art Appreciation." *Independent Woman* 27 (1948): 176–8.
Kuhn, Irene. "Rainbow 'round the Screen." *Cinema Arts* 1 (1937): 28–32.
Kurland, Rose. "The Script Girl." *How Talkies Are Made*. Ed. Joe Bonica. Hollywood: Joe Bonica, 1930, n.p.
Kutner, Nanette. "Box-Office Babies" *Collier's* 25 March 1939: 74–7.

Lachmund, Marjorie Glevre. "Irony of Fate." *Picture-Play Weekly* [London] March 1916: 119.

Lady Correspondent of the *Boston Journal*. "Picture Shows Popular in the 'Hub.'" *Moving Picture World* 16 May 1908: 433.

Laine, Juliette. "Operetta and the Sound Film: Interview with Jeanette MacDonald." *Étude* 56 (1938): 359–60.

Laing, Nora. "*Cavalcade* at Hollywood: The Casting of the Film." *Review of Reviews* [London] 10 December 1932: 53–7.

Langer, Resi. *Kinotypen: Vor und hinter den Filmkulissen (Zwölf Kapitel aus der Kinderstube des Films)*. Hannover: Der Zweemann Verlag, 1919.

La Plante, Laura. "Breaking In as an Extra." *Breaking Into the Movies*. Ed. Charles Reed Jones. New York: Unicorn Press, 1927. 13–20.

Lawrence, Florence. "Growing Up with the Movies." *Photoplay* November 1914: 28–41; December 1914: 91–100; January 1915: 95–107; February 1915: 142–46.

Leblanc, Georgette. "Propos sur le Cinéma." *Mercure de France* 16 November 1919: 275–90.

Lee, Auriol. "Women are Needed in British Films." *Film Weekly* 5 August 1932: 7.

Lejeune, C.A. [A prolific writer who was the London *Observer*'s film critic for over thirty years, and wrote for numerous other publications. A selection of her writing includes:]

——. "Qualities of the Good Lay Critic." *Guardian* 4 February 1922: 7

——. "The Test of Truth." *Guardian* 25 February 1922: 9.

——. "What the Public Wants." *Guardian* 18 March 1922: 7.

——. "Film We Could Do Without." *Guardian* 27 May 1922: 7.

——. "On Mixing the Arts." *Guardian* 8 July 1922: 9.

——. "On Footage." *Guardian* 15 July 1922: 7.

——. "On Naturalism." *Guardian* 30 September 1922: 7.

——. "Arthur Joins the Film Wagon!" *Screen Pictorial* April 1939: 14–15, 36.

——. "At the Films." *Observer* 11 May 1947: 2.

——. "The Best is Good Enough Says Sam Eckman Jr." *Picturegoer* 26 January 1935: 12–13.

——. "The British Film and Others." *Fortnightly Review* May 1935: 285–94.

——. *The C.A. Lejeune Reader*. Ed Anthony Lejeune. London: Carcanet, 1991.

——. "Can Piccadilly do without Hollywood?" *New York Times Magazine* 24 August 1947: 16–17, 32.

——. *Chestnuts in Her Lap*. London: Phoenix House, 1947.

——. *Cinema*. London: Alexander Maclehose, 1931.

——. "The Days of the West are Back!" *Screen Pictorial* August 1939: 20–21, 37.

——. "'Eyes and No Eyes': What to Look for in Films." *For Filmgoers Only*. Ed. R.S. Lambert. London: Faber & Faber, with the British Institute of Adult Education, 1934. 80–95.

——. "Film Report from London." *Theatre Arts* 30 (May 1946): 663–6.

——. "The Film as an Art Form." *Fortnightly Review* January 1943: 43–9; February 1943: 127–33; March 1943: 194–9.

——. "The Film: International Medium." *Theater Arts* 3.1 (1942): 336–43.

——. "Films You Ought to See." *Sight and Sound* Spring 1932: 25.

——. "Humoresque." *Observer* 6 July 1947: 2.

——. "Korda's Three." *Screen Pictorial* March 1939: 20–21, 38.

——. "Laughton." *Screen Pictorial* September 1938: 20–21, 61.

——. "Making Movies Amid the Blitz." *New York Times Magazine* 11 May 1941: 15, 24.

——. "Me to Myself." *Theatre Arts Monthly* February 1939: 82–3.

——. "Stick to Your Hobbies: A Message to All Boys and Girls." *Teachers World & School Mistress* [London] 11 March 1936: 1051.

——. "Muni—A Fugitive From Life." *Picturegoer* 21 April 1934: 10–11.

——. "The Private Lives of London Films." *Nash's Pall Mall Magazine* [London] December 1936: 108–17; January 1937: 96–104; February 1937: 98–104.

——. "Stroheim the Craftsman." *Hollywood Scapegoat: The Biography of Erich von Stroheim*. Ed. Peter Noble. [1950]. Rpt. New York: Arno, 1972: 187–90.

——. "Two English Films" *Theatre Arts Anthology*. Eds. Rosamund Gilder, et al. New York: Theatre Arts Bookshop, 1950: 564–69.

——. *Thank You for Having Me*. London: Hutchinson, 1964.

——. "The Week on the Screen: *The Women*." *Manchester Guardian* 16 January 1926: 9.

Leslie, Cecilie. "The Best and Worst of British Cinemas." *Film Weekly* 11 July 1931: 9.

——. "A Home of British Films." *Film Weekly* 4 July 1931: 22.

——. "Making a Cinema Pay." *Film Weekly* 27 June 1931: 22.

——. "Sedate Edinburgh and Superior Manchester." *Film Weekly* 20 June 1931: 17.

——. "A Thousand Miles of Filmgoing." *Film Weekly* 13 June 1931: 9.

——. "Where the Clock has Stopped." *Film Weekly* 5 July 1930: 19.

Leuck, Miriam S. "Motion Pictures." *Fields of Work for Women*. New York: Appleton, 1926. 132–34.

Leupp, Constance D. "The Motion Picture as a Social Worker." *Survey* 27 August 1910: 739–41.

Level, Hildegard. "Women Behind the Screen." *Independent Woman* 27 (1948): 170–72, 188–89.

Levien, Sonya. "New York's Motion Picture Law." *American City* 9 (1913): 319–21.

——. "The Screen Writer." *Careers for Women*. Ed. Catherine Filene. Boston: Houghton Mifflin, 1934. 433–7.

Levèque, Jean. See Sarah Bernhardt.

Littlejohn, Josephine. "What Ten Million Women Want." *Motion Picture* December 1930: 66, 100, 112.

Livingstone, Beulah. *Remember Valentino: Reminiscences of the World's Greatest Lover*. New York: Strand Press, 1938.

Loble, Hattie M. "A Western Woman's Opinion of Pictures." *Moving Picture World* 1 June 1912: 820.

Locher, Harriet Hawley. "Making the Neighborhood Motion Picture Theater a Community Institution." *Educational Screen* April 1926: 203–205; May 1926: 264–66; June 1926: 331–34; July 1926: 397–401, 409; August 1926: 457–60.

Locket, Margery. "Educational Films, Great Britain." *The Theatre and Motion Pictures: A Selection of Articles from the New 14th Edition of the Encyclopaedia Britannica*. New York and London: Encyclopaedia Britannica, 1929–33. 34–35.

Lockhart, Freda Bruce. "Catholics and the Cinema: A Conference of the Catholic Film Society." *Tablet* 28 August 1948: 136–37.

——. "Costume Sets a New Language Problem." *Film Weekly* 23 November 1934: 10.

——. "Lady with Scissors." *Film Weekly* 9 October 1937: 14.

——. "This was Jean Harlow." *Film Weekly* 28 August 1937: 27.

Lonergan, Elizabeth. "Danger! Go Slow!" *Picturegoer* April 1921: 21.

Looram, Mary Harden. "National Recognition for Our Motion Picture Bureau." *Quarterly Bulletin of the International Federation of Catholic Alumnae* March 1936: 15, 22.

Loos, Anita. "This Brunette Prefers Work." *Woman's Home Companion* March 1956: 4, 6

——. *Cast of Thousands*. New York: Grosset & Dunlap, 1977.

——. Contribution to "In Defense of Hollywood: Prominent Figures in the Film World Rise to Refute the Exaggerated Reports of Motion Picture Morals." *Filmplay* May 1922: 21.

——. *Fate Keeps on Happening: Adventures of Lorelei Lee and Other Writings*. London: Harrap, 1984.

——. "The Feminine Mind in Picture Making" *Film Daily* 7 June 1925: 9.

——. *A Girl Like I*. New York: Viking, 1966.

——. *Kiss Hollywood Good-By*. New York: Viking, 1974.

——. "I Like 'em When They're Bad." "Good Bad Pictures and Those Just Bad." By Loos and Edna Ferber. *Theatre Magazine* July 1927: 41.

——. *The Talmadge Girls: A Memoir* New York: Viking, 1978.

——. "Women Do a Lot for the Screen, Anita Loos Says, Besides Act on It." *New York Herald Tribune* 16 September 1940. Clipping, Anita Loos folder, Billy Rose Theater Collection, Lincoln Center Library, New York.

Loos, Anita, and John Emerson. "How to Write Movies." *Photoplay* February 1920.

——. "Photoplay Writing," *Photoplay* February 1918: 51–52; March 1918: 53–54; April 1918: 81–82; May 1918: 81–82; June 1918: 78–79; July 1918: 88–89, 121.

——. *Breaking into the Movies*. New York: James A. McCann, 1921.

——. *How to Write Photoplays*. New York: James A. McCann, 1921.

——, with Lillian Montanye. "The Play's the Thing ('But Collaboration Between Author and Director is Just the Thing,' Say Anita Loos and John Emerson)." *Motion Picture* April 1918: 67–8, 123.

Loring, Jane. Interview with W.H. Mooring. "Women as Directors." *Film Weekly* 1 November 1935: 7.

Losey, Mary. "Filming Great Britain in War." *Travel* December 1942: 17–19.

——. "Films for the Community at War," a forthcoming study mentioned in "Making Films Work." *National Board of Review Magazine* November 1942: 17. Unlocated.

——. "Joris Ivens's *Power and the Land*." *Direction* [New York] November 1940.

——. "Making Films Work." *National Board of Review Magazine* November 1942: 17–18.

——. "More Seeing, Less Selling." *Saturday Review* 9 October 1948: 61–66.

Loverman, Amy. "Knowledge and the Image." *Saturday Review of Literature* 8 February 1941: 8.

Lovett, Josephine. Interview with Faith Service. "The Tortures of Cutting." *Motion Picture Classic* November 1924: 20, 86–7.

Low, Barbara. "The Cinema in Education: Some Psychological Considerations." *Contemporary Review* [London] 128 (1925): 628–35.

——. "Mind-Growth or Mind-Mechanization? The Cinema in Education." *Close Up* 1.3 (1927): 44–52.

Low, Rachael. "Audience Research." *Sight and Sound* Winter 1946–47: 150–51.

——. *The History of the British Film, Vol.* 2 (1906–1914). London: George Allen & Unwin, 1948. Rpt. British Film Institute, 1973.

——. *The History of the British Film, Vol.* 3 (1914–1918). London: George Allen & Unwin, 1948. Rpt. British Film Institute, 1973.

——. "The Implications Behind the Social Survey." *Penguin Film Review* 7 (1948): 107–12.

Low, Rachael, with Roger Manvell. *The History of the British Film* (1896–1906). London: George Allen & Unwin, 1948. Rpt. British Film Institute, 1973.

Lowrey, Carolyn. *The First 100 Noted Men and Women of the Screen.* New York: Moffat, Yard, 1920.

Loy, Mina. "Film-Face" (poem). n.d. *The Lost Lunar Baedeker: Poems of Mina Loy.* Comp. and ed. Roger Conover. New York: Farrar Straus Giroux, 1996. 125.

Luce, Candida. "Incoherence in Italian Films." *Films in Review* October 1950: 15–18.

Lucht, Mrs. William A. "Time for a Movies Movement?" *Rotarian* March 1949: 3.

Lupino, Ida. "I Cannot Be Good." *Silver Screen* June 1949: 42.

——. "Me, Mother Directress." *Action* 2:3 (1967): 14–15.

——. "My Fight For Life." *Photoplay* February 1946: 58.

——. "My Secret Dream." *Photoplay* October 1943: 54.

——. "New Faces in New Places: They Are Needed Behind the Camera, Too." *Films in Review* September 1950: 17–19.

——. "The Trouble With Men is Women." *Silver Screen* April 1947: 36.

——. "Who Says Men Are People?" *Silver Screen* June 1948: 23.

Mabie, Janet. "Pictorial Journalism." *Christian Science Monitor Magazine* 30 October 1935: 35.

Macaulay, Rose. "Cinema." *Personal Pleasures.* London: Macmillan, 1936. 135–8.

——. "Films and Instincts." *Weekend Review* [London] 3 May 1930: 256–7.

——. "Marginal Comments." *Spectator* 25 January 1935: 117; 29 May 1935: 976.

MacDowell, Josephine. "Lois Weber Understands Girls." *Cinema Art* January 1927: 18, 38.

Mack, Grace. "You at Center Stage." *Ladies' Home Journal* December 1933: 23+.

Mackenzie, Catherine. "Movies and Superman." *New York Times Magazine* 12 October 1941: 22.

MacLean, Helen. "Movies, the Radio and the Library." *Library Journal* 63 (1938): 550–55.

Macpherson, Jeanie. "Building the Dramatic Scenario." *The Truth About the Movies by the Stars.* Ed. Laurence A. Hughes. Hollywood: Hollywood Publishers, 1924: 382–84.

——. "Development of Photodramatic Writing." *Moving Picture World* 21 July 1917: 393.

——. "Functions of the Continuity Writer." *Opportunities in the Motion Picture Industry.* Vol. 2. Los Angeles: Photoplay Research Society, 1922. 25–35.

——. "'I Have Been in Hell'—Or in Search of Prison Knowledge." *Movie Weekly* 19 August 1922: 10, 27, 29.

——. "Hints to Scenario Writers." Column. *Movie Weekly* 15 October 1921: 23; 22 October 1921: 25; 29 October 1921: 14; 5 November 1921: 26; 12 November 1921: 28; 26 November: 29; 3 December 1921: 27; 17 December 1921: 31; 24 December 1921: 31; 31 December 1921: 31.

——. *The Necessity and Value of Theme in the Photoplay.* Los Angeles: Palmer Photoplay Corporation, 1920.

——. "The Subtitle—Friend and Foe." *Motion Picture Director* December 1926: 32, 74.

Macpherson, Jeanie, with Edward Weitzel. "Jeanie Macpherson in Film Limits and the Joys of Unbounded Space." *Moving Picture World* 17 January 1920: 401.

Märten, Lu. "Von Charlie Chaplin" *Ebenda* 4 (1928): 201–2.

——. "Filmkategorisches." *Ebenda* 5 (1928): 231–5.

——. "Kunst und Proletariat," *Die Aktion* 15 (1925): 667–8.

——. "Die Rolle des Films im Theater," *Die Neue Bücherschau* 1 (1928): 3–5.

——. "Rundfunk und Film." *Deutsche Welle* [Berlin] 2: 36–7.

——. "Workers and Film." [1928] A translation of "Arbeiter und Film." *Formen für den Alltag: Schriften, Aufsätze, Vorträge.* Selection, commentary, bibliography, and afterword by Rainard May. Dresden: Verlag der Kunst, 1982. 116–22.

Magny, Claude-Edmonde. "The American Novel and the Movies." *The Age of the American Novel: The Film Aesthetic of Fiction Between the Two Wars*. Trans. Eleanor Hochman. New York: Frederick Ungar Publishing Co., 1972. 1–101. Trans. of *L'Age du romain américain*. Paris: Éditions du Seuil, 1948.

"Norma Mahl" [Robert Herring]. "Second-Rate Sex, September 1929." *Close Up* 5.6 (1929): 471–79.

Manners, Dorothy. "Do You Talk Hollywood?" *Motion Picture Magazine* November 1933: 54–5, 98.

——. "Enter the Dixies." *Motion Picture Classic* February 1929: 63, 88.

Mannes, Marya. "Bad Men: Six-year-old's Reaction to Italian Mob Portrayal." *New Yorker* 25 November 1944: 75–7.

——. "Vogue's Spot-Light." *Vogue* [New York] 15 November 1935: 57, 98.

Mannin, Ethel. "Films Which Cheapen Love." *Film Weekly* 24 May 1930: 7.

——. "*I Was a Spy*: Is it an Anti-War Film?" *New Leader* [London] 22 September 1933: 3.

——. "Screen Love as I Would Treat It." *Film Weekly* 28 September 1931: 8–9.

——. "War ... and the Workers." *New Leader* [London] 4 March 1932: 12.

——. "Wasting the Screen's Best Brains." *Film Weekly* 30 December 1929: 7.

Mansergh, Mrs. Henry. "An Idyll of the Cinematographe." *Windsor Magazine* [London] February 1898: 363–8.

Mansfield, Katherine. "The Pictures." *Art and Letters* [London] ns 2:1 (Winter 1918–1919): 153–62.

Margerie, Movie. "The Feminine Touch on the Film, Which is—Wanted." *Pictures and Picturegoer*. 2–9 November 1918: 449.

Marion, Frances. "The Cinema in Art and Education." *International Review of Educational Cinematography* 6 (1934): 535–8.

——. *How to Write and Sell Film Stories*. New York: Covici, Friede, 1937.

——. "Scenario Writing." *Behind the Screen: How Films Are Made*. Ed. Stephen Watts. London: Arthur Barker, 1938. 27–39.

——. "Why Do They Change the Stories on the Screen?" *Photoplay* March 1926: 38–39, 144–45.

Marion, Frances, with Mary B. Mullet. "Frances Marion: A Girl Who Has Won Fame and Fortune Writing Scenarios." *American Magazine* May 1924: 18–19, 126–7, 134–6.

Marion, Frances, with Leslie Wood. "Writing 400 Films." *Film Weekly* 11 October 1935: 7.

Marsh, Mae. *Screen Acting* New York: Frederick A. Stokes, 1921.

Marshall, Margaret. "*A Nous la Liberté*." *Nation* 8 June 1932: 659–60. Rpt. *American Film Criticism: From the Beginnings to Citizen Kane*. Ed. Stanley Kauffmann, with Bruce Henstell. New York: Liveright, 1972. 265–6.

Martin, Alice. "From 'Wop' Parts to Bossing the Job." *Photoplay* October 1916: 95–7.

Martin, Olga. *Hollywood's Movie Commandments: A Handbook for Motion Picture Writers and Reviewers*. New York: Wilson, 1937. Rpt. New York: Arno Press, 1970.

Mason, Laura Kent. "Capturing the Caption." *Motion Picture Magazine* January 1923: 39–40, 90.

Mathis, June. "Elements of a Screen Story." *The Truth About the Movies by the Stars*. Ed. Laurence H. Hughes. Hollywood: Hollywood Publishers, 1924. 378–79.

——. "European-Made American Pictures." *Motion-Picture Director* February 1925: 7, 30–31.

——. "The Feminine Mind in Picture Making." *Film Daily* 7 June 1925: 115.

——. "Harmony in Picture-Making." *Film Daily* 6 May 1923: 5.

——. "June Mathis Confers with Ibanez on *Four Horsemen of the Apocalypse*." *Moving Picture World* 17 January 1920: 431.

——. "Scenario Writers Must Find Theme." *New York Times* 15 April 1923, sec. 7: 3.

——. "Symbolism in the Silent Drama." *Motion Picture Director* December 1925: 31–32.

——. "Tapping the Thought Wireless." *Moving Picture World* 21 July 1917: 409.

——. "The Wavelength of Success." *Motion Picture Director* February 1927: 22.

The Matinee Girl, "The Matinee Girl." *New York Dramatic Mirror* 12 June 1897: 14.

Matz, Elsa. "Film Censorship." *International Review of Educational Cinematography* 3 (1931): 1113–22.

McCall, Mary. "A Brief History of the Guild." *Screen Writer* 3 (1948): 25–31.

——. "Hollywood Close-Up." *Review of Reviews* May 1937: 44.

——. "Facts, Figures on Your Percentage Deal." *Screen Writer* 1 (1945): 32–5.

——. "The Unlick'd Bear Whelp." *Screen Writer* 2 (1946): 27–33.

McCormick, Mrs. Medill. "Your Girl and Mine." *Woman's Journal* 7 November 1914.

McGoldrick, Rita. "School and Screen: Cry of the World." *Motion Picture Herald* 14 May 1932: 38–9.

Mead, Margaret, Cecile Starr, and Others. "What I Look for in a Film." *Films in Review* April 1950: 12–13.

Meloney, Mrs. W.B. "A Mother of the Movies." *Delineator* August 1915: 9.

Merriam, Mrs. Charles E. "Solving the Moving Picture Problem." *Journal of the National Education Association* 13 (1924): 167–8.

Messinger, Lillie. "New Stars are My Job." *Film Weekly* 5 April 1935: 24.

de Mille, Agnes. *Dance to the Piper*. Boston: Little, Brown, in association with the Atlantic Monthly Press, 1952.

de Mille, Beatrice. "The De Mille Family in Motion Pictures." *New York Dramatic Mirror* 4 August 1917: 4.

Miller, Betty Bergson Spiro. (fiction) *The Mere Living*. New York: Frederick A. Stokes, 1933: 80–82, 265–68.

Mistral, Gabriela. "The Poet's Attitude Toward the Movies." *The Movies on Trial*. Ed. William J. Perlman. New York: Macmillan, 1936. 141–52.

Mitchell, Alice Miller. *Children and Movies*. Chicago: University of Chicago Press, 1929.

——. "Movies Children Like." *Survey* 15 November 1929: 213–15.

Modern, Klara. "Young Workers Film Their Own Life." *Close Up* 9.1 (1932): 53–4.

Monde, Nance. "A Fitting Finish, Or, A Day with the Wardrobe Mistress." *Motion Picture Magazine* (August 1918): 58–9.

Moore, Beatrix. "Censor the Censor!" *Sight and Sound* Winter 1938–39: 149.

Moore, Colleen. *Silent Star*. Garden City, NY: Doubleday, 1968.

——. "Up From the Extra Ranks." *Breaking Into the Movies*. Ed. Charles Reed Jones. New York: Unicorn Press, 1927. 21–7.

——. "Flappers and the Movies." *The Truth About the Movies by the Stars*. Ed. Laurence H. Hughes. Hollywood: Hollywood Publishers, 1924. 145.

Moore, Marian. "Fiction or Nature?" *Close Up* 10.3 (1933): 260–65.

——. "Lot in Sodom." *Close Up* 10.4 (1933): 318–19.

Morris, Virginia. "Women in Publicity." *Breaking Into the Movies*. Ed. Charles Reed Jones. New York: The Unicorn Press, 1927. 202–8.

Moseley, Lillian. "Secrets of a Movie Maid." *Ebony* November 1949: 52–6.

Moseley, Maboth. "Films Have Taught Us What Life Means." *Film Weekly* 25 July 1931: 9.

Moten, Etta. "Negro Actors Put on the Spot." *New Vistas* March 1946: 61–4.

Moulan, G. "The Cinema and International Amity." *International Review of Educational Cinematography* 4 (1932): 907–14.

Mount, Laura. "Designs on Hollywood." *Collier's* 4 April 1931: 21.

Muir, Florabel. "They Risk Their Necks for You." *Saturday Evening Post* 15 September 1945: 26–7+.

Muir, Jean. "How to Become a Star." *American* May 1935: 63, 102, 104.

Mullen, S[arah]. M[cLean]. "All that Flickers is not News." *Scholastic* 23 May 1936: 11ff.

——. "Following the Films: All Motion Pictures Have a Basic Theme." *Scholastic* 23 March 1935: 28.

——. *How to Judge Motion Pictures and How to Organize a Photoplay Club. A Pamphlet for High School Students with a foreword to Teachers by William L. Lewin*. New York: Scholastic, The National High School Weekly, 1934.

——. "Motion Pictures, A Twentieth Century Art." *Scholastic* 18 April 1936: 7–8+.

——. "From Paper to Celluloid." *Scholastic* 17 October 1936: 17–18.

Murfin, Jane. "The Feminine Mind in Picture Making." *Film Daily* 7 June 1925: 9.

——. "Sex and the Screen." *The Truth About Movies by the Stars*. Ed. Laurence A Hughes. Hollywood: Hollywood Publishers, 1924. 459–61.

Musidora. "Ce que je suis devenue." *Pour Vous* 8 June 1938: 38.

——. "La vie d'une vamp." *Ciné-mondial* 12 June 1942: 6–7; 19 June 1942: 6–7; 26 June 1942: 12; 3 July 1942: 12; 10 July 1942: 13; 17 July 1942: 10; 24 July 1942: 13.

——. "Dialogues de jadis." *Cahiers du Cinéma* November 1964.

Nadin, Nancy. "If Life Resembled the Movies." *Picturegoer* May 1921: 46.

——. "The Movie Ma." (poem) *Picturegoer* April 1921: 46.

Naumberg, Nancy. Ed. *We Make the Movies*. New York: Norton, 1937.

Negri, Ada. "The Movies." *Corriere della Sera* 27 November 1928: 3. Rpt. *Unspeakable Women: Selcted Short Stories by Italian Women During Fascism*. Translated and with an introduction and afterword by Robin Pickering-Iazzi. New York: The Feminist Press of the City University of New York, 1993. 58–62.

Negri, Pola. "I Become Converted to the Happy Ending." *Motion Picture Director* March 1926. 35–6, 80.

——. *Memoirs of a Star*. Garden City, NY: Doubleday, 1970.

——. "The Autobiography of Pola Negri." A series. *Photoplay* January 1924: 32, February 1924: 50–53,

106, March 1924: 56–57, 86, 118–20; April 1024: 38–39, 114.
——. "What is Love?" *Photoplay* November 1924: 30.
Nicholson, Irene. [editor of and regular contributer to *Film Art*] "Film Art Activities in Trinidad." *Film Art* Autumn 1936: 23.
——. "Film—Its Basic Structure." *Film Art* 2 (1935): 54–6.
——. "Memoirs of a Mexican—An Historic Film." *Sight and Sound* July-September 1953: 13–15.
——. "Mexican Films—Their Past and Their Future." *Quarterly of Film, Radio and Television* 10 (1956): 248–52.
——. "Negro and Film, a reply from Irene Nicholson." *Film Art* Winter 1934: 24.
Nielsen, Asta. *Den tiende Muse*. Kobenhavn: 1946. German trans. *Die schweigende Muse*. Berlin: Henschverlag, 1977. English trans. *The Silent Muse*. Elsa Gren Wright. ts. Museum of Modern Art, Film Study Center, Asta Nielsen files.
Norden, Helen Brown. "Passion for the Past." *Vogue* [New York] 1 March 1937: 84, 124.
Normand, Mabel. "Myself—by the Seaside." *Pictures and the Picturegoer* 8 August 1914: 547–8.
Norton, Helen. "Brains, Brown Eyes, and Buttons." *Motion Picture Magazine* March 1919: 30.
Nott, Mabel. "Ubiquitous Eve: Her Place in the Kinema Sun." *Picturegoer* January 1921: 12–13, 56.
Novello Davies, Clara. "Ivor Novello by His Mother." *Film Weekly* 20 June 1931: 9.
——. "Making Screen Voices." *Film Weekly* 27 May 1929: 13.
Oglesby, Catherine. "The Movie Problem." *Ladies' Home Journal* May 1934: 142.
——. "Toward Federal Censorship of Movies?" Letter. *Theatre Arts* April 1934: 314.
Oliver, Maria Rose. "Cantinflas." *Hollywood Quarterly* 2.3 (1947): 253–6.
——. "The Native Film of Mexico." *Penguin Film Review* 6 (1948): 73–9.
Opdycke, Mary Ellis. "What the Movies have Done to Music: A New View of the Relationship between Music and the Screen." *Filmplay* July 1922: 16–17.
Orczy, Baroness [Mrs Montagu Barstow], with J. Danvers Williams. "The 'Pimpernel' Lives Again." *Film Weekly* 12 October 1934: 7–8.
Ormsbee, Helen. "No Tear Drops for Her." *Negro Digest* November 1943: 49–50.
Osborne, Florence M., signed as The Editor. "Why Are There No Women Directors?" *Motion Picture Magazine* November 1925: 5.
Pallister, Minnie. "Sunday Cinemas." *New Leader* [London] 19 December 1930: 5.
Palmer, Greta. "Screen Appeal: Our Highest Priced Commodity." *Reader's Digest* October 1945: 93–5.
Palmer, Nettie. "Readers and Writers." *Argus* [Melbourne] 3 February 1917: 4.
Panter-Downes, Mollie. "Commit Murder First!" *Film Weekly* 16 February 1929: 9.
Park, Ida May. "Motion-Picture Work: The Motion-Picture Director." *Careers for Women*. Ed. Catherine Filene. Boston: Houghton Mifflin, 1920. 335–7.
Parker, Claire, and A. Alexeieff, "New Abstract Process." *Cinema Quarterly* 3 (1935): 34.
Parker, Gudrun. "A Comment on Canadian Films." *Canadian Art* Autumn 1950: 24–8.
de Parks, Mercedes Gallagher. "The Cinema Censorship in Peru." *International Review of Educational Cinematography* 4 (1932): 631–5.
Parry, Florence Fisher. "The Friendly Movies." *Delineator* April 1933: 34, 68+.
——. "Mary and the Movies." *Delineator* May 1933: 12+.
——. "Are Movie Stars Actors?" *Delineator* September 1933: 4+.
Parsons, Harriet. "What Producers Do." *Films in Review* 5 (1954): 404–8.
Parsons, Louella O. [Prolific writer about film and syndicated columnist. Her many scrapbooks of cuttings are held in Special Collections, Margaret Herrick Library, Academy of Motion Picture Arts and Sciences, Los Angeles. A selection of her work includes:]
——."Briny Record Set by Sylvia Bremer, Who May Be Called on to Weep a Full Pound of Salt." *Chicago Herald* 6 January 1918. Louella Parsons Scrapbooks, Special Collections, Academy of Motion Picture Arts and Sciences, Los Angeles.
——. "Essanay Days." *Theatre Arts* July 1951: 33.
——. "Fate of Birth of a Nation Will Be Decided Today." *Chicago Herald* (ca. 1915). Louella Parsons Scrapbooks, Special Collections, Academy of Motion Picture Arts and Sciences, Los Angeles.
——. *The Gay Illiterate*. Garden City, NY: Doubleday, Doran, 1944.
——. "Girl Who Made Fairbanks Famous." *New York Herald* (?) 24 March 1918. Louella Parsons Scrapbooks, Special Collections, Academy of Motion Picture Arts and Sciences, Los Angeles.
——. "D.W. Griffith in Plea for His Greatest Film." *Chicago Herald* (ca. 1915). Louella Parsons Scrapbooks, Special Collections, Academy of Motion Picture Arts and Sciences, Los Angeles.

——. "Hollywood and Censorship." *Cosmopolitan* April 1954: 8.

——. *How to Write for the 'Movies'.* Chicago: A.C. McClurg, 1915. Rev. ed. 1917.

——. "A Message to Scenario Writers." *The Art of Photoplay Writing.* Ed. Catherine Carr. New York: Hannis Jordan, 1914. 116–19.

——. "Miss Theda Bara's Expressive Hand." *Chicago Tribune* 9 October 1915. Louella Parsons Scrapbook no. 1, Special Collections, Academy of Motion Picture Arts and Sciences, Los Angeles.

——. "Movies Solve Puzzle That Vexed 'Kittens.'" *Chicago Tribune* n.d. Louella Parsons Scrapbooks, Special Collections, Academy of Motion Picture Arts and Sciences, Los Angeles.

——. "Is Julian Eltinge, Impersonator of Women, Going to Wed? New California Home All Complete Except for a Woman at the Other End of the Table, and Man with 64 Gowns has a Wise Smile." *Chicago Sunday Herald eatures Magazine* 37.32 (16 December 1917): 5.

——. "Propaganda: An Earnest Consideration on the Inestimable Part Being Played by the Motion Picture in the Great War." *Photoplay* September 1914: 43–5, 110.

——. "Seen on the Screen." Regular columns. *Chicago Herald* and *Chicago Tribune* 1915–1918. Louella Parsons Scrapbooks, Special Collections, Margaret Herrick Library, Academy of Motion Picture Arts and Sciences, Los Angeles.

——. "Society Girl Quits Gay Season to Seek Fame and Fortune Before Motion Picture Cameras." *Chicago Tribune* 18 November 1915. Louella Parsons Scrapbooks, Special Collections, Academy of Motion Picture Arts and Sciences, Los Angeles.

——. "Seen on the Screen: *The Fight.*" *Chicago Herald* n.d. Louella Parsons Scrapbooks 1915–1917, Special Collections, Margaret Herrick Library, Academy of Motion Picture Arts and Sciences, Los Angeles.

——. *Tell it to Louella.* New York: G.B. Putnam's Sons, 1962.

——. "Wilbur is Tied Up to His Leading Lady." *Chicago Herald* 15 October 1915/16/17 (?). Louella Parsons Scrapbooks, Special Collections, Academy of Motion Picture Arts and Sciences, Los Angeles.

Parsons, Louella O., with Monte M. Katterjohn. "Thumbnail Biographies." *Photoplay* September 1914: 166.

Patterson, Ada. "Blacktown Measures Upward Career By Landings." *New York Dramatic Mirror* 17 November 1917: 10–11.

Patterson, Frances Taylor. "The Author and Hollywood." *North American Review* September 1937: 77–89.

——. "Bread and Circuses." *North American Review* December 1938: 259–66.

——. *Cinema Craftsmanship: A Book for Photoplaywrights.* New York: Harcourt, Brace, 1921.

——. "Descent into Hollywood." *New Republic* 14 January 1931: 239–40.

——. *Motion Picture Continuities: A Kiss for Cinderella, The Scarlet Letter, The Last Command.* New York: Columbia University Press, 1929.

——. "Nanook of the North." *New Republic* 9 August 1922: 306–307. Rpt. *American Film Criticism: From the Beginnings to Citizen Kane.* Ed. Stanley Kauffmann, with Bruce Henstell. New York: Liveright, 1972. 133–36.

——. "A New Art in an Old University." *Photoplay* January 1920: 65, 124.

——. *Scenario and Screen.* New York: Harcourt and Brace, 1928.

——. "The Sedulous Ape." *New Republic* 1 July 1927: 177–9.

——. "Signs and Portents." *Exceptional Photoplays* April 1923: 4.

——. "Swedish Photoplays." *Exceptional Photoplays* December 1922: 3–4.

——. "Teleview." *Exceptional Photoplays* January 1923: 2–3.

——. "Will Hollywood Move to Broadway?" *New Republic* 5 February 1930: 297–9.

——. "Writing and the Motion Picture." *National Board of Review Magazine* November 1938.

Pelswick, Rose. "*Craig's Wife.*" *New York Evening Journal* 2 October 1936: 24.

——. "Dancing Daughters Outranks Flaming Youth Films." *New York Evening Journal,* 2 October 1928. Clipping, Billy Rose Collection, New York Public Library, Scrapbook 1548.

——. "On the Lot with Lois Weber." *Photoplay* October 1917: 89–91.

Peltret, Elizabeth. "My Experience in the Academy of Motion Picture Art." *Photoplay* February 1919: 57–8.

Perkins, Elizabeth. "The Civic Cinema: A Unique Movie Move Planned for Manhattan." *Amateur Movie Makers* 3 (1928): 254.

Peterson, Ruth Camilla, and Louis Leon Thurstone. *Motion Pictures and the Social Attitudes of Children.* New York: Macmillan, 1933.

Petrova, Olga. *Butter With My Bread*. Indianapolis and New York: Bobbs-Merrill, 1942.
——. "Mme. Petrova Interviews Theda Bara." *Shadowland* March–April 1920: 43–44, 74.
——. "Thus Speaks Woman." (poem) [c. 1919] *Silent Picture* 18 (1973): 4.
Pickford, Mary. "Ambassadors." *Saturday Evening Post* 23 August 1930: 6–7, 117.
——. "The Feminine Mind in Picture Making." *Film Daily* 7 June 1925: 9.
——. "Greatest Business in the World." *Collier's* 10 June 1922: 7–8, 22–3.
——. "Mary is Looking for Pictures." *Photoplay* June 1925: 39, 109.
——. "Mary Pickford Awards." *Photoplay* October 1925: 45, 109.
——. "My Own Story." *Ladies' Home Journal* September 1923: 9.
——. "Pickfordisms for Success." *Opportunities in the Motion Picture Industry*. Vol. 1. Los Angeles: Photoplay Research Society, 1922. 93–8.
——. "Stay Away from Hollywood." *Good Housekeeping* October 1930: 36–7+
——. *Sunshine and Shadow*. Foreword by Cecil B. DeMille. Garden City, NY: Doubleday, 1955.
——. "The Best-Known Girl in America: Mary Pickford Tells What it Means to Be a 'Movie' Actress." *Ladies' Home Journal* January 1915: 9.
Pierce, Lucy France. "The Nickelodeon." *World To-day* 15 (October 1908): 1052–7.
——. "The Nickelodeon in *The World To-day*." *Film Index*, 24 October 1908: 4, 6.
Platt, Agnes. *Practical Hints on Acting for the Cinema*. New York: E.P. Dutton, 1923.
Ploeger, Eva, "The Motion Picture and the Adolescent Girl." Paper written for E.W. Burgess's course, "Social Pathology" (270), Fall Quarter, 1928, 13 pp. ts. University of Chicago, Joseph Regenstein Library, Ernest Burgess Collection.
Plummer, Ethel. "If the Strike Fever Hits the Movies." (illustration) *Shadowland* December 1919: 56–7.
Podselver, Judith. "Motion Pictures in Central Europe." *Screen Writer* 2 (1947): 30–34.
Pollano, Etta. "The Importance of Being Angry." *Sight & Sound* Autumn 1939: 112–13.
Pollard, Elizabeth Watson. *Motion Picture Study Groups: A Handbook for the Discussion Leader*. Columbus, OH: Bureau of Educational Research, Ohio State University, 1934.
——. *Teaching Motion Picture Appreciation: A Manual for Teachers of High-School Classes*. Columbus, OH: Bureau of Educational Research, Ohio State University in co-operation with the Payne Fund, 1935.
Pool, Rosey E. "The Negro Actor in Europe." *Phylon* Fall 1953: 258–67.
Popkin, Zelda F. "Camera Explorers of the New Russia." *Travel* December 1931: 37–40+.
——. "Russia Goes to the Movies." *Outlook* 28 May 1930: 129–31+.
Porter, Katherine Anne. "On Communism in Hollywood" [Westwood, Los Angeles] *Daily* 1947. Rpt. *The Collected Essays and Occasional Writings of Katherine Anne Porter*. New York: A Seymour Lawrence Book, Delacorte Press, 1970. 205–8.
——. "Hacienda" *Virginia Quarterly Review* 8 (1932): 556–69. Rpt. *Flowering Judas and Other Stories* New York: Harcourt Brace, 1935: 223–85.
——. "On *The Wave*." *New Masses* 18 May 1937: 22.
——. "The Real Ray." *Motion Picture Magazine* October 1920: 36–7, 102. Rpt. *They Also Wrote for the Fan Magazines: Film Articles by Literary Giants from e.e. cummings to Eleanor Roosevelt, 1920–1939*. Ed. Anthony Slide. London: McFarland, 1992. 117–20.
——. "The Week at the Theaters." *Critic* (and) *Camp Bowie Texahoma Bugler* [Fort Worth, TX] 12 January 1917: 3.
Post, Emily. *Etiquette, in Society, in Business, in Politics and at Home*. New York: Funk & Wagnalls, 1923.
Powdermaker, Hortense. "An Anthropologist Looks at the Movies." *Annals of the American Academy of Political and Social Science*. Philadelphia: November 1947. 80–87.
——. "Celluloid Civilization." *Saturday Review of Literature* 14 October 1950: 9–10, 43–5.
——. *Hollywood, the Dream Factory; An Anthropologist Looks at the Movie-Makers*. Boston: Little, Brown, 1950.
Powell, Dilys. [Prolific film critic who wrote for the London *Sunday Times* for over thirty years. A sample of her writing for this, and other publications, includes:]
——. "The Black Film." *Sunday Times* [London] 24 July 1949. 2.
——. "La cinéma anglais en temps de guerre." *La France Libre* [London] 15 March 1945: 349–52.
——. "Colour and the Film." *Sight and Sound* Autumn 1942: 36–7.
——. "Credo of a Critic." *Sight and Sound* Summer 1941: 26–7.
——. "The Development of the Film in Educational and Social Life." [Peter La Neve Foster Lecture.] *Journal of the Royal Society of Arts* 14 January 1949: 120–29.
——. *The Dilys Powell Film Reader*. Ed. Christopher Cook. Oxford: Oxford University Press, 1992.

——. *Films Since 1939*. London and New York: Published for the British Council by Longmans, Green, 1947.

——. *The Golden Screen: Fifty Years of Film*. Ed. George Perry. London: Pavilion Books, 1989.

——. "H for Horriplant." *Diversion: Twenty-Two Authors on the Lively Arts*. Ed. John Sutro. London: Max Parrish, 1950. 128–33.

——. "The Importance of International Film Festivals." *Penguin Film Review* 3 (1947): 59–61.

——. "Introduction" in Helen Fletcher, *Bluestocking*. London: Pandora, 1986.

——. "Variable Stars." *Sight and Sound* Winter 1940–1941: 66–7.

Preer, Evelyn. "Evelyn Preer Nearly Drowns in Realistic Movie Scene:." *Pittsburgh Courier* 11 June 1927, sec. 2: 2.

——. "My Thrills in the Movies." *Pittsburgh Courier* 18 June 1927, sec 2: 2; 25 June 1927, sec. 2: 2.

Price, Miriam Sutro. "More on Motion Pictures." *Woman's Journal* May 1930: 48–9.

Price, Mona. "Aesthetic of the Film." *Dublin Magazine* April 1928: 48–52.

Priest, Janet. "Films—and Your City's Welfare." *Photoplay* August 1919: 53–4, 120.

Pring, Beryl. "Shakespeare and Russian Films." *Adelphi* April 1932: 469–73.

Prinzlau, Olga. "Virtue vs. Vice." *Motion Picture Director* May 1925: 15.

Proctor, Eulalia. "La Femme Silhouette: The Bronze Age." *Messenger* 7.2 (February 1925): 93.

Prolo, Maria Adriana. "Naissance d'un Musee [Birth of a Museum: Turin's Museum of Cinema]." *Cahiers du Cinéma* March 1954. Rpt. *Le Dragon et l'Alouette*. Ed. S. Toffetti. Turin: Museo Nazionale del Cinema di Torino, 1992. 212–14.

de Querton, Beryl. "My Voice Makes News." *Film Weekly* 8 June 1934: 13.

Radinoff, Florence. *The Photoplaywright's Handy Text Book*. New York: Manhattan Motion Picture Institute, 1913.

Radnor, Leona. *The Photoplay Writer*. New York" L. Radnor, 1913.

Rall, Pearl. "Women's Clubs and the Movies." *Motion Picture Director* September-October 1926: 35, 80.

Rambova, Natacha. *Rudy: an Intimate Portrait of Rudolph Valentino*. London: Hutchinson, 1926.

Ray, Winifred. "The Japanese Cinema." *Close Up* 6.2 (1930): 92–8.

——. "Kultur Film." *Close Up* 5.1 (1929): 51–6. Rpt. as "Kultur-Film." *New Masses* September 1929: 14.

Read, Jan. "Box Office or Bust." *Penguin Film Review* January 1948: 64–72.

Reef, Betty. "Avant-Garde Artists Make a Surrealist-Abstract Movie." *Vogue* [New York] 15 April 1946: 156–7, 174, 176, 178, 180.

Reid, Janet. "From Telephone Operator to Motion Picture Producer: With Apologies to Horatio Alger." *Motion Picture Magazine* May 1923: 66, 100.

Reiniger, Lotte. "The Adventures of Prince Achmed." *Silent Picture* 8 (1970): 2–4.

——. "Film as Ballet." *Life and Letters Today* 14.3 (1936): 157–63.

——. "Film Magic in Scissors." *Film Weekly* 5 April 1930: 7.

——. "Moving Silhouettes." *Film Art* 3.8 (1936): 14–18.

——. "Scissors Make Films," *Sight and Sound* 5.17 (1936): 13–15.

Remont, Fritzi. "The Lady Behind the Lens." *Motion Picture Magazine* May 1918: 59–61, 126.

Rennert, Malwine. "Ein Abgrund, der nicht zu überbrücken ist." *Bild und Film* 1 (1912/1913): 18–19.

——. "Gabriele d'Annunzio als Filmdichter." *Bild und Film* 9/10 (1913/14): 210–13.

——. "Ein Besuch im Kino." *Bild und Film* 1 (1912): 2–3.

——. "Maria Carmi." *Bild und Film* 12 (1914/15): 241–5.

——. "Der Film Julius Cäsar. Die ewige Wiederkehr aller Geschehnisse." *Bild und Film* 4/5 (1914/15): 84–7.

——. "Film und Schauspielkunst." *Bild und Film* 8 (1912/1913): 179–81.

——. "Heureka." *Bild und Film* 5 (1912/13): 112–14.

——. "Victor Hugo und das Kino. Französische und deutsche Filmkunst." *Bild und Film* 6 (1912/13): 129–31.

——. Rev. of *Kino und Bühne*, book by Willy Rath. *Bild und Film* 2 (1913/14): 46–7.

——. "Zur Kinofrage." *Kölnische Volkszeitung* 6 October 1912, sec. 3: 1–2.

——. "Kleopatra, die Herrin des Nils. Die letzten Tage von Byzanz." *Bild und Film* 3/4 (1913/14): 65–8.

——. "Kriegslichtspiele." *Bild und Film* 4 (1914/15): 217.

——. "Die Kunst des Lichtspieltheaters." *Bild und Film* 6 (1913/14): 128–30.

——. "Asta Nielsen im Kinodrama *Die Suffragetten.*" Bild und Film 6 (1913/14): 137.
——. "The Onlookers of Life at the Cinema." A translation of "Die Zaungäste des Lebens im Kino."
   Bild und Film 4 (1914/15): 217–18.
——. "*Quo vadis?*" Bild und Film 10 (1912/13): 227–30.
——. "Der Todestritt." Bild und Film 4 (1912/13): 98–9.
——. "*Die Tote.*" Bild und Film 8 (1913/14): 203–4.
——. "Der Totentanz." Bild und Film 1 (1912/1913): 26–7.
Repplier, Agnes. "The Unconscious Humor of the Movies." *Atlantic Monthly* November 1925:
   601–7.
A Representative. "Hattie the Hairdresser Speaks." *Filmplay* April 1922: 24.
Rhys, Jean. *Voyage in the Dark* [1934] (fiction) New York: Norton, 1982: 107–09.
Richardson, A[nna]. S[teese]. "Better Films, Better Children." *Woman's Home Companion* September
   1926: 4, 84.
——. "Better Films A Community Asset." *Woman's Home Companion* January 1923: 17, 82.
——. "'Filmitis,' the Modern Malady—Its Symptoms and Its Cure." *McClure's Magazine* January 1916:
   12–14, 70.
——. "The Good Citizenship Bureau: Prize Winning Letters on How We Get Better Films in Our
   Town." *Woman's Home Companion* January 1927: 28, 92.
——. "It's Up to the Box Office." *Woman's Home Companion* November 1931: 54.
——. "Pleasure, Publicity and Profits." *Woman's Home Companion* February 1926: 32.
——. "Talking Pictures and Community Taste." *Woman's Home Companion* January 1930:. 32.
——. "Who Gets Your Dime?" *McClure's Magazine* November 1915: 21–2.
See also interview with Mary Kelly, under Mary Kelly.
Richardson, Dorothy. "Antheil of New Jersey." *Vanity Fair* November 1925: 136, 138.
——. "The Censorship Petition." *Close Up* 6.1 (1930): 7–11.
——. "Continuous Performance." *Close Up* 1.1 (1927): 34–7; 10.2 (1933): 130–32.
——. "Continuous Performance II: Musical Accompaniment." *Close Up* 1.2 (1927): 58–62.
——. "Continuous Performance III: Captions." *Close Up* 1.3 (1927): 52–7.
——. "Continuous Performance IV: A Thousand Pities." *Close Up* 1.4 (1927): 60–64.
——. "Continuous Performance V: There's No Place Like Home." *Close Up* 1.5 (1927): 44–7.
——. "Continuous Performance VI: The Increasing Congregation." *Close Up* 1.6 (1927): 61–5.
——. "Continuous Performance VII: The Front Rows." *Close Up* 2.1 (1928): 59–64.
——. "Continuous Performance VIII." *Close Up* 2.3 (1928): 51–5.
——. "Continuous Performance IX: The Thoroughly Popular Film." *Close Up* 2.4 (1928): 44–50.
——. "Continuous Performance X: The Cinema in the Slums." *Close Up* 2.5 (1928): 58–62.
——. "Continuous Performance XI: Slow Motion." *Close Up* 2.6 (1928): 54–8.
——. "Continuous Performance XII: The Cinema in Arcady." *Close Up* 3.1 (1928): 52–7.
——. "Continuous Performance: Almost Persuaded." *Close Up* 4.6 (1929): 31–7.
——. "Continuous Performance: Dialogue in Dixie." *Close Up* 5.3 (1929): 211–18.
——. "Continuous Performance: The Film Gone Male." *Close Up* 9.1 (1932): 36–38.
——. "Continuous Performance: Narcissus." *Close Up* 8.3 (1931): 182–5.
——. "Continuous Performance: Pictures and Films." *Close Up* 4.1 (1929): 51–7.
——. "Continuous Performance: This Spoon-Fed Generation?" *Close Up* 8.4 (1931): 304–8.
——. "Continuous Performance: A Tear for Lycidas." *Close Up* 7.3 (1930): 196–202.
——. "Films for Children." *Close Up* 3.2 (1928): 21–7.
——. "A Note on Household Economy." *Close Up* 2.2 (1928): 58–62.
——. "Talent and Genius: Is Not Genius Actually Far More Common than Talent?" *Vanity Fair*
   October 1923: 118, 120. This article appears under the title, "Talent and Genius: A Discussion of
   Whether Genius is not Actually Far More Common than Talent," in *Vanity Fair* May 1923: 65, but
   is incomplete.
——. "A Talk about Talking." *Life & Letters Today* 23 (1939): 286–8.
——. "Talkies, Plays and Books: Thoughts on the Approaching Battle Between the Spoken Pictures,
   Literature and the Stage." *Vanity Fair* August 1929: 56.
——. "Women in the Arts: Some Notes on the Eternally Conflicting Demands of Humanity and Art."
   Vanity Fair May 1925: 47, 100.
——. "Women and the Future." *Vanity Fair* April 1924: 39, 40.
Riding, Laura. "A Film Scenario." *Epilogue: A Critical Summary* 2. Deya, Majorca: The Seizin Press; London:
   Constable, 1936. 162–90.

——. *Literal Solutions: Len Lye and the Problem of Popular Films*. London: The Seizin Press, 1938.
Riding, Laura, and Len Lye. "Film-Making: Movement as Language." *Epilogue: A Critical Summary* 1 (Autumn 1935). Deya, Majorca: The Seizin Press; London: Constable, 1935. 231–5.
Riefenstahl, Leni. *Hinter den Kulissen des Reichsparteitagfilms*. Munich: Zentralverlag der NSDAP, 1935.
——. *Kampf in Schnee*. Leipzig: Hesse & Becker, 1935.
——. "Meine Arbeit am Triumph des Willens." *Interciné* 7 (1935): 189–91.
——. "'This Picture is Entirely Ours': The Sound-and-Picture Outline for Leni Riefenstahl's *Triumph of the Will*." *Film Comment* 3 (1965): 16–22.
——. *Schönheit im Olympischen Kampf*. Berlin: Deutsch, 1937.
——. *The Sieve of Time: The Memoirs of Leni Riefenstahl*. New York: St Martin's Press, 1993.
——. "Why I am Filming *Penthesilea* [1939]." *Film Culture* 56 (1973): 192–215.
Riefenstahl, Leni, with Kevin Brownlow. "Leni Riefenstahl." *Film* Winter 1966: 14–19.
Riefenstahl, Leni. Interview with Michel Delahaye. "Leni and the Wolf: Interview with Leni Riefenstahl." *Cahiers du Cinéma in English* 5 (1966): 48–55.
Riley, Kay. "—And So I'm Movie-Mad!" *Good Housekeeping* April 1939: 13.
Riley, Rosa. "Louise Beavers: Graciously Plain, Interested in Juvenile Problems." *Los Angeles Sentinel* 31 January 1946: 17.
Rinehart, Mary Roberts. "Faces and Brains." *Photoplay* February 1922: 47–48, 107. Rpt. *They Also Wrote for the Fan Magazines: Film Articles by Literary Giants from e.e. cummings to Eleanor Roosevelt, 1920–1939*. Ed. Anthony Slide. London: McFarland, 1992. 121–8.
——. "My Experience in the Movies." *American Magazine* October 1920: 18–20, 76, 78.
——. "How About the Movies." *Ladies' Home Journal* June 1921: 21, 77, 79–80.
——. "Sounds in Silence." *Ladies' Home Journal* July 1932: 10.
——. "Your Child and the Movies." *Ladies' Home Journal* April 1931: 8–9, 96, 99.
Ring, Frances Kroll. "The Case of the Cream Puffs." *Hollywood Quarterly* 2.1 (1946): 30–34.
del Rio, Dolores. "Achieving Stardom." *Breaking Into the Movies*. Ed. Charles Reed Jones. New York: The Unicorn Press, 1927. 28–35.
Rix, Alice. "Alice Rix at the Veriscope." *San Francisco Examiner* 18 July 1897: 22.
Robbins, Michela. "Films for the Church." *Hollywood Quarterly* 3.2 (1947–1948): 178–84.
Roberts, Katharine. "Acting in a Business Way." *Collier's* 16 March 1935: 14+.
Robertson, E. Arnot. "£1,500 Damages For Critic in Film Suit." *To-day's Cinema* 18 July 1947: p. 18.
——. "The Cinema." *Cultural Forces in British Life Today: Addresses to the 20th Annual Conference*. London: British Institute of Adult Education, 1946. 36–42.
——. "Intruders in the Film World." *Fortnightly* [London] February 1936: 194–8.
——. "'Privilege' Defence in Critic's Suit." *To-Day's Cinema* 16 July 1947: 3, 46.
——. "They Call it 'Box Office.'" *Vogue* [New York] 15 October 1949: 89, 134.
——. "Woman and the Film." *Penguin Film Review* 3 (1947): 31–35.
Robertson, Josephine Lovett. "The Feminine Mind in Picture Making." *Film Daily* 7 June 1925: 113.
Robertson, Marion. "I am a Talent Scout." *National Board of Review Magazine* December 1938: 4–7.
Robinson, Corienne. "At the Regal." *Chicago Defender* 18 January 1930: 8.
Robson, Flora. "Why Not Film the Heroines of History." *Film Weekly* 30 November 1935: 10.
de la Roche, Catherine. "Actors of the Soviet Cinema." *Penguin Film Review* 6 (1948): 104–10.
——. "Animals and the Cinema." *Sight and Sound* Summer 1955: 44–7.
——. "British Cinema, 1950." FIPRESCI Lecture at 1951 Cannes Film Festival, ts. British Film Institute Library.
——. "British Film Comedy." *Central Office of Information* 1957, ts. British Film Institute Library.
——. "British Mystery Films." *British Ally* August 1946, ts. British Film Institute Library.
——. "Charles Dickens Films." *British Ally* June 1946, ts. British Film Institute Library.
——. "The Cinema in the U.S.S.R." *BBC Third Programme* [London] 10 June 1947: 1–9, ts. BBC Archives, London.
——. "The Cinema—Mirror of our Times?" *Film* 11 January-February 1957.
——. "The Cinematograph Films Act." BBC 1947. BBC Archives, London.
——. "Design in the Soviet Cinema." *Penguin Film Review* 3 (1947): 76–80.
——. "The Development of Soviet Cinema." *Sight and Sound* Winter 1945–1946: 111–13.
——. "The Director's Approach to Filmmaking: John and Roy Boulting." BBC 1947. ts. BBC Archives, London.
——. "The Director's Approach to Filmmaking: David Lean." BBC 1947. ts. BBC Archives, London.

——. "The Director's Approach to Filmmaking: Carol Reed." BBC 1948. ts. BBC Archives, London.

——. "Don't Shoot the Censor!" *Films and Filming* April 1955: 12.

——. "Escapism in Soviet Cinema." *Sight and Sound* Winter 1946–47: 141–2.

——. "That 'Feminine' Angle." *Penguin Film Review* 8 (1949): 25–34.

——. "First Royal Command Performance." *British Ally* November 1946, ts. British Film Institute Library.

——. "Front Line Cameraman." *British Ally* January 1944, ts. British Film Institute Library.

——. "H. G. Wells and the Cinema." *Central Office of Information* 1949, ts. British Film Institute Library.

——. "Hue and Cry." *Central Office of Information* November 1947, ts. British Film Institute Library.

——. "Launder and Gilliat." *British Ally* June 1946, ts. British Film Institute Library.

——. "Launder and Gilliat." *Sight and Sound* Autumn 1946: 94–5.

——. "Mark Donskoi." *Sequence* 5 (1948): 20–27.

——. "The Mask of Realism." *Penguin Film Review* 7 (1948): 35–43.

——. "Men of Two Worlds." *British Ally* August 1946, ts. British Film Institute Library.

——. "The Moscow Script Studio and Soviet Screenwriting." *Penguin Film Review* 2 (1947): 64–9.

——. "New Documentaries." *British Ally* August 1946, ts. British Film Institute Library.

——. "No Demand for Criticism?" *Penguin Film Review* 9 (1949): 88–94.

——. "Odd Man Out." *British Ally* November 1947, ts. British Film Institute Library.

——. *Performance*. Palmerston North, NZ: Dunmore Press, 1988.

——. "Personal Opinion: *Les Parents Terribles*." *The Cinema* 1951. Eds. Roger Manvell and R.K. Neilson Baxter. Harmondsworth: Penguin Books, 1951: 86–90.

——. "Recent Developments in Soviet Russia." *Penguin Film Review* 1 (1946): 84–9.

——. *René Clair: An Index*. London: British Film Institute, 1958.

——. "School for Secrets." *British Ally* November 1946, ts. British Film Institute Library.

——. "Soviet Cinema." *Spectator* 6 July 1945: 7.

——. "The Soviet Cinema." *Film News* November 1945: 22, 25.

——. "Soviet Cinema in London." *British Ally* August 1946, ts. British Film Institute Library.

——. "The Soviet Cinema and Science." *Penguin Film Review* 5 (1948): 77–81.

——. "The Soviet Cinema and Youth." *Penguin Film Review* 4 (1947): 109–13.

——. "The Soviet Sound Film." *Soviet Cinema*. By de La Roche and Thorold Dickinson. London: Falcon Press, 1948: 39–78.

——. "Stars." *Sight and Sound* April-June 1953: 172–4.

——. "The State Institute of Cinema and the Film Actors' Theatre in Moscow." *Sight and Sound* Summer 1948: 101–2.

——. "That 'Feminine Angle'." *Penguin Film Review* 8 (January 1949): 25–34.

——. "Swedish Films." *Films in Review* 4 (1953): 461–4.

——. "Truth and Propaganda in the Cinema." *Film* 12 (March–April 1957): 25–29.

——. *Vincente Minnelli*. Ed. L P. Lee. Wellington: New Zealand Film Institute, 1959.

——. *Vincente Minnelli*. Lyon: SERDOC, 1966; Paris: Premier Plan No. 40, 1966.

de la Roche, Catherine, and Thorold Dickinson. *Soviet Cinema*. London: Falcon Press, 1948.

Roosevelt, Eleanor. "Film Folk I Have Known." *Photoplay* January 1939: 10–11, 83. Rpt. *They Also Wrote for the Fan Magazines: Film Articles by Literary Giants from e.e. cummings to Eleanor Roosevelt, 1920–1939*. Ed. Anthony Slide. London: McFarland, 1992. 131–5.

——. "Why We Roosevelts Are Movie Fans." *Photoplay* July 1938: 16–17, 84–85.

Rosenberg, Carolyn. "Only Woman to Manage Film Company." *American Hebrew* 16 March 1928: 663.

Ross, Betty. "Mexico's Chaplin." *Sight and Sound* Summer 1948: 87–9.

Ross, Lillian. "Onward and Upward with the Arts: Come in, Lassie!" *New Yorker* 21 February 1948: 32–5, 38, 40, 42, 44, 46, 48.

——. *Picture*. New York: Rinehart, 1952. Serialized in five parts, "Onward and Upward with the Arts." *New Yorker* 24 May 1952: 32–87; 31 May 1952: 29–71; 7 June 1952: 32–79; 14 June 1952: 39–65; 21 June 1952: 31–81.

Ross, Nellie Tayloe. "Public Service on Motion Pictures." *National Board of Review Magazine* February 1930: 5–7.

Rukeyser, Muriel. "Gauley Bridge: Four Episodes from a Scenario." *Films* [New York] 1 (1940): 51–64.

——. "Movie." (poem) *New Masses* 12 June 1934: 28. Rpt. *Theory of Flight* New Haven: Yale University Press, 1935: 87.

——. "*The River Damned.*" *World Film News* [London] July 1938: 121.

Rumbold, Charlotte. "Against *The Birth of a Nation.*" Letter. *New Republic* 5 June 1915: 125.

Russell, Evelyn. "Films of 1941." *Sight and Sound* Spring 1942: 70–72.

——. "Films of 1942." *Sight and Sound* Spring 1943: 99–101.

Russell, Rozalind. "They Still Lie About Hollywood." *Look* 3 July 1951: 36–43.

Sabine, Lillian. "That Elusive Something." *Independent Woman* 13 (1934): 70–71, 95.

Sagan, Leontine. "Courage in Production." *Cinema Quarterly* 1 (Spring 1933): 140–43.

——. "The Miscellany." *Cinema Quarterly* 1 (1933): 229–30.

——. "Why I Defy the Film Conventions." *Film Weekly* 12 March 1932: 7.

Sand, Sevigné. "The Female Epicurus." *Motion Picture Director* September 1924: 24–25.

Sanger, Margaret. "Superwoman—an Idea of a Movie" (1914–15), a manuscript sketch, Margaret Sanger and the Movies, Reel 76, Nwe York University Margaret Sanger Papers Microfilm Project.

Sarfatti, Margherita G. "The Cult of 'Stars.'" *International Review of Educational Cinematography* 5 (1933): 703–5.

——. "The Revolutionary Fifth Estate." *International Review of Educational Cinematography* 5 (January 1933): 5–7.

Sarthe, Jean. "She Makes Movies." *Independent Woman* 13 (1934): 315, 330–31.

Sayers, Dorothy L. "Detective Stories for the Screen." *Sight and Sound* Summer 1938: 49–50.

Sayers, Dorothy L., interview with R. B. Marriott. "Dorothy Sayers Joins the Fray." *Film Weekly* 14 May 1938: 9.

Sayre, Gertrude, and Joel Sayre. "What We Liked About Hollywood" *Scribner's* March 1938: 24–5.

Schemke, Irmgard. "Documentary To-Day." *Sequence* 3 (1948): 12–14.

Schoeni, Helen. "Production Methods in Soviet Cinema." *Cinema Quarterly* 2 (1934), pp. 210–14.

Schooling, Patricia. "Children's Entertainment Films." *Sight and Sound* Winter 1947–48: 172–75.

Schuler, Marjorie. "The Bard of Hollywood." *Christian Science Monitor Magazine* 20 October 1935: 5.

See, Hilda. "Actors Steal 'Imitation.'" *Chicago Defender* 12 January 1935: 9.

——. "Hattie McDaniel Weds." *Chicago Defender* 29 March 1941: 12.

——. "'Imitation.'" *Chicago Defender* 16 February 1935: 6.

——. "Louise Beavers." *Chicago Defender* 23 November 1935: 12.

——. "Oscar Polk Brings Movies to the Stage and Scores." *Chicago Defender* 31 October 1931: 7.

——. "You Can Thank Georgia for Fredi Washington." *Chicago Defender* 23 February 1935: 6.

Serao, Matilde. "Duse in the Movies." *Literary Digest* 54 (1917): 1702–703.

——. "A Spectatrix is Speaking to You." Translation of "Parla una Spettatrice." *L'Arte Muta* [Naples] 15 June 1916: 31–2.

Service, Faith. See Lovett, Josephine.

Seton, Marie. [regular contributor to Film Art] "Ancient Rome in Gangster Town." *Sight and Sound* June 1950: 176–7.

——. "Basil Wright's *Song of Ceylon.*" *Film Art* Autumn 1935: 76–7.

——. "British and Canadian Films in America's Middle West." *Sight and Sound* October 1945: 94–5.

——. "The British Cinema." *Sight and Sound* Spring 1937: 5–8.

——. "The British Cinema 1907–1914." *Sight and Sound* Summer 1937: 64–7.

——. "The British Cinema 1914." *Sight and Sound* Autumn 1937: 126–8.

——. "Contemporary Problems of Soviet Cinema." *Film Art* Spring 1934: 15.

——. "A Conversation with V. I. Pudovkin." *Sight and Sound* Spring 1933: 13–14.

——. "Drawings that Walk and Talk." *Listener* [London] 18 August 1938: 344–5.

——. *Sergei M. Eisenstein.* London: The Bodley Head, 1952.

——. "Eisenstein Aims at Simplicity." *Film Art* Summer 1933: 27–8.

——. "Eisenstein's Images and Mexican Art." *Sight and Sound* July–September 1953: 8–13.

——. "The Indian Film." *Film* 4 (1955): 22–6.

——. "Jottings for *Que Viva Mexico.*" *Film Art* Spring 1934: 79–80.

——. "Lovers on the World's Screens." *Screen Pictorial* October 1937.

——. "The Making of a Russian 'Star.'" *Close Up* 10.2 (1933): 163–6.

——. "Memorial to Méliès." *Life and Letters Today* Spring 1938: 4–5.

——. "New Trends in Soviet Cinema." *Cinema Quarterly* 3 (1935): 149–52; 210–14.

——. "George Pal." *Sight and Sound* Summer 1936: 13.

——. "Prague: The Window Between East and West." *Theatre Arts* November 1947: 60–65.

——. *Paul Robeson.* London: Dennis Dobson, 1958.

——. "Silent Shadows." *Sight and Sound* Spring 1938: 31–3.

——. "Teaching Film in Russia." *Film Art* Winter 1934: 24–26.

——. "Television Drama." *Theater Arts Monthly* 22.12 (1938): 878–85.

——. "Three Songs of Lenin." *Film Art* Winter 1934: 41.

——. "Treasure Trove." *Sight and Sound* Autumn 1939: 89–92.

——. "Turkish Prelude." *Close Up* 10.4 (1933): 309–15.

——. "Vignettes of Eisenstein." *Films in Review* April 1952: 29–31.

——. "War." *Sight and Sound* Winter 1937–38: 182–5.

——. "Yugoslav Films: The First Two Years." *Sight and Sound* Summer 1947: 47–9.

Seton, Marie, with Karel Reisz and Lewis McLeod. "Editing Unfair to Eisenstein." *Sight and Sound* June 1951: 54–5+

Seyler, Athene. *The Craft of Comedy.* London: Muller, 1943.

Shaver, Anna Louise. "New Art and the Old Artisans." *Catholic World* 154 (1941): 306–10.

Shearer, Norma. "The Leading Woman." *Breaking Into the Movies.* New York: Unicorn Press, 1927. Ed. Charles Reed Jones. 42–51.

Shipman, Nell. *Abandoned Trails.* New York: Dial Press, 1932.

——. "This Little Bear Went Hollywood." *Good Housekeeping* January 1931: 30–31+.

——. "Me." *Photoplay* February 1919: 47–48.

——. "The Movie That Couldn't Be Screened." *Atlantic Monthly* March 1925: 326–32; April 1925: 477–82; May 1925: 645–51.

——. *The Silent Screen and My Talking Heart.* Boise, IH: Boise State University Press, 1987.

Shub, Esther. "Esther Shub [1959]." *Dziga Vertov by His Contemporaries.* Moscow, 1976. Rpt. *Dziga Vertov Revisited.* Program notes. New York: Collective for Living Cinema, April-May 1984. 14.

——. "Road from the Past." *Isskustvo Kino* 11–12 (1934).

N.[erina] S.[hute]. "Can Women Direct Films? A Decided Negative From a Woman Who Knows." *Film Weekly* 10 June 1929: 12.

——. "Can Women Direct Films? Elinor Glyn's Emphatic 'Yes.'" *Film Weekly* 7 October 1929: 1.

——. "Films Have Changed the Art of Making Love." *Film Weekly* 7 March 1931: 8.

——. "Ivor Novello's Mother." *Film Weekly* 1 March 1930: 20.

——. "My Personal Experiences at Shepherd's Bush as 'One of the Crowd.'" *Film Weekly* 3 June 1929: 9, 11.

——. "Race for the First British Talkie." *Film Weekly* 20 May 1929: 13.

——. "A Vulgar Film Dictionary." *Film Weekly* 26 July 1930: 19.

Sierra, Maria Martinez. "Internationalism and the Film." *International Review of Educational Cinematography* 5 (1933): 175–6.

Simonson, Lucy Clarke. "Cinematograph and the Neglected Child." *International Review of Educational Cinematography* 6 (1934): 181–3.

Sitwell, Edith. "Film People I Would Like to Massacre." *Film Weekly* 29 April 1929: 9.

Smedley, Agnes. "Cinéma aus Schanghai." *Frankfurter Zeitung* 15 June 1930: 1–2.

——. "The Cultural Film in Germany." *Modern Review* [Calcutta] July 1926: 61–6.

Smith, Alison. "From Monastery to Picture Studio." *New York Dramatic Mirror* 21 July 1917: 13.

——. "Little Journeys to Eastern Studios I—Astra." *New York Dramatic Mirror* 14 July 1917: 10.

——. "Little Journeys to Eastern Studios II—Metro." *New York Dramatic Mirror* 21 July 1917: 10.

——. "Little Journeys to Eastern Studios III—Biograph." *New York Dramatic Mirror* 28 July 1917: 11.

——. "Little Journeys to Eastern Studios IV—Goldwyn." *New York Dramatic Mirror* 4 August 1917: 11.

——. "Little Journeys to Eastern Studios V—Vitagraph." *New York Dramatic Mirror* 11 August 1917: 11.

——. "Little Journeys to Eastern Studios VI—Paramount." *New York Dramatic Mirror* 18 August 1917: 10.

——. "Little Journeys to Eastern Studios VII—World Film." *New York Dramatic Mirror* 1 September 1917: 13.

Smith, Bertha H. "A Nervy Movie Lady." *Sunset: The Pacific Monthly* [San Francisco] 32 (1914): 1323–5.

——. "A Perpetual Leading Lady." *Sunset: The Pacific Monthly* [San Francisco] 32 (1914): 634–46

Snow, Jane Elliott. "The Elusive Quality." *Moving Picture World* 15 October 1910: 860.

——. "The Workingman's College." *Moving Picture World* 27 August 1910: 458.

——. "The Workingman's Theater." *Moving Picture World* 9 April 1910: 547.

Speare, Dorothy. "Hollywood Madness." *Saturday Evening Post* 7 October 1933: 26–7+.

Spiess, January "Life Can Be Terrific!" *Vogue* [New York] 11 November 1941: 118–20.

Spinola, Helen. "That Terrible Talkie Test." *Delineator* May 1931: 17+.

Spitzer, Marian. "The Modern Magic Carpet." *Saturday Evening Post* 28 March 1925: 47, 60, 62.

Sporborg, Mrs. William Dick. "A Clubwoman Chats on Films for the Family." *Motion Picture and the Family* 15 November 1936: 4, 6.

St. Johns, Adela Rogers. [Prolific writer about film who regularly contributed to *Photoplay*, and other publications. A sampling of her film writing includes:]

——. "'Get Me Dorothy Arzner!'" *Silver Screen* December 1933: 22–4, 73.

——. *The Honeycomb*. Garden City, NY: Doubleday, 1969.

——. "Matrimony and Meringues." *Photoplay* July 1919: 80–82.

——. "The One Genius in Pictures: Frances Marion, She is One of Hollywood's Six Greatest Women." *Silver Screen* January 1934: 22–3, 53–4.

——. "Why do Great Lovers Fail as Husbands?" *Photoplay* July 1927: 28–30, 116–17.

——. *How to Write a Story and Sell It*. Garden City, NY: Doubleday, 1956.

——. *Some Are Born Great*. Garden City, NY: Doubleday, 1974.

Starr, Helen. "Putting it Together." *Photoplay* July 1918: 52–5.

Starr, Cecile. "Animation: Abstract & Concrete." *Saturday Review* December 1952: 46–8.

——. "Film as Education." *Films in Review* May–June 1950: 1–2+.

——. "Films with a Purpose." *Saturday Review* 8 April 1950: 34.

——, ed. *Ideas on Film*. New York: Funk and Wagnalls, 1951.

——. "Ideas on Film." *Saturday Review of Literature* 15 October 1949: 31.

——. "Ideas on Film: Kid's Stuff." *Saturday Review of Literature* 18 November 1950: 44–5.

——. "Looking Forward." *Saturday Review of Literature* 14 January 1950: 37.

——. "Through the Psychiatric Looking Glass." *Saturday Review of Literature* 12 May 1951: 38, 40.

Stecker, Dora. "More on Motion Pictures." *Woman's Journal* May 1930: 48.

——. *Some Desirable Goals for Motion Pictures*. Chicago: University of Chicago Press, 1927.

Sternberger, Estelle M. "What Should an Anti-War Film Contain?" *Film Survey* September 1937: 1

Sterner, Alice P., and P. Bowden. *A Course in Motion-Picture Appreciation*. Newark, NJ: Educational and Recreational Guides, Incorporated, produced with the cooperation of the Finer Films Federation of New Jersey, 1936.

Stevens, Jeanne. "Mediocre Pictures—The Remedy." *Photodramatist* September 1922: 8.

Stopes, Dr. Marie C. "Cinema as a Power." ms version of Stopes's "The Unsuspected Future of the Cinema." British Library, Department of Manuscripts, Stopes Papers, Add. 58545.

——. "A Real Use for the Cinema." *Bioscope* [London] 2 September 1915: 1028–9.

——. "The Unsuspected Future of the Cinema." *New East* [Tokyo] July 1918: 26–8.

——. draft of letter protesting the screening of Lois Weber's film *Where Are My Children?* intended for publication in *Times* [London] July 1917. British Library, Department of Manuscripts, Stopes Papers, Add. MS 58545, ff. 56–6v.

Storm, Leslie. "Tragedies of Youth." *Film Weekly* 25 November 1932: 13.

Strand, Edith. "You Ought to Be in Pictures." *American* June 1936: 24–5+.

Strauss, Florence L. "The Scenario Editor." *Careers for Women*. Ed. Catherine Filene. Boston: Houghton Mifflin, 1934. 437–41.

Strick, Anne. "Peck on Prejudice." *Negro Digest* July 1948: 17–20.

Stuart, Betty Thornley. "Movie Set-Up." *Collier's* 30 September 1933: 20+.

Stuart, Isobel. "Shooting Pains." *Collier's* 1 January 1938: 19–20+.

Suckow, Ruth. "Hollywood Gods and Goddesses." *Harper's Monthly Magazine* 173 (July 1936): 189–200.

Svilova, Elizaveta. "Elizoveta Svilova." *Dziga Vertov by His Contemporaries*. Moscow, 1976. Rpt. *Dziga Vertov Revisited*. Program notes. New York: Collective for Living Cinema, April–May 1984. 15.

Swanson, Gloria. *Swanson on Swanson*. New York: Random House, 1980.

——. "There is No Formula for Success." *Photoplay* April 1926: 32–3, 117–19.

——. "A Week with the Star: Wednesday." *Photoplay* November 1921: 48–9.

——. "What is Love?" *Photoplay* November 1924: 28–30, 123.

Sweet, Blanche. "Keep Your Public Guessing." *Motion Picture Director* August 1926: 21–3.

Swenson, Mrs. T.H. "The Value of Courtesy." *New York Dramatic Mirror* 16 June 1917: 24.

Sylviac, Madame. "Cinemania—The Dire Disease: A Few Reflections on the Silver Screen." *Vogue* [New York] 15 August 1927: 64–5, 106.

Symes, Elizabeth. "A Woman's View of British Films and Players." *Film Weekly* 5 April 1935: 50.

Talmadge, Constance. "What Am I?" *Motion Picture Magazine* August 1918: 47.

Talmadge, Margaret L. *The Talmadge Sisters: An Intimate Story of the World's Most Famous Screen Family*. Philadelphia: Lippincott, 1924.

Talmadge, Norma. "Close Ups: An Autobiography." *Saturday Evening Post* 12 March 1927: 6–7; 26 March 1927: 26–7; 9 April 1927: 30–33; 7 May 1927: 34–5; 21 May 1927: 41–3; 25 June 1927: 43–6.

——. "How Men Strike Me." *Photo-Play Journal* March 1919: 9.

——. "The Mission of Motion Pictures." *Who's Who in Filmland*. Ed. Langford Reed and Hetty Spiers. 3rd ed. London: Chapman & Hall, 1931. xxiv.

——. "My Lucky Break." *Picturegoer* July 1928: 69.

——. "What 'Fashion' Really Means." *Photoplay* June 1920: 64–5, 112.

Talmey, Allene. *Doug and Mary and Others*. New York: Macy-Masius, 1927.

——. "Gloria Swanson … Mirror of the Movies." *Vogue* [New York] 15 August 1941: 79, 104, 111.

Taylor, Alma. "How Films Have Changed Women." *Film Weekly* 21 March 1931: 9.

Taylor, Violet M. "Women and Films." *Film Weekly* 3 January 1931: 9.

Tazelaar, Marguerite. "Amateurs Point the Way." *Amateur Movie Makers* 6 (1929): 599–600.

——. "On the Screen: *The Wave*—Filmarte." *New York Herald Tribune* 21 April 1937: 18.

——. "The Story of the First Little Film Theatre." *Amateur Movie Makers* 3 (1928): 441–42.

Temple, Gertrude. "Bringing up Shirley." *American* February 1935: 26–27+.

Terlin, Rose. *You and I and the Movies*. New York: Woman's Press, 1936.

Thomas, Yvonne. "The Foreign Films Return." *Sight and Sound* Spring 1939: 28–9.

Thornborough, Laura, and D.C. Ellis. *Motion Pictures and Education*. New York: Crowell, 1923.

Thornton, Clare. "The Art of Conversation." *Picture Theatre Magazine* 1 (1914): 395–7.

Thorp, Margaret Farrand. *America at the Movies*. New Haven: Yale University Press, 1939.

——. "The Motion Picture and the Novel." *American Quarterly* 3 (1951): 195–203.

——. "The Vampire Art." *Saturday Review* 21 October 1939: 13–14, 16.

Tildesley, Alice. "The Road to Fame." *Motion Picture Magazine* April 1926: 43, 94–5.

Tildesley, Beatrice. "The Cinema in Australia." *International Review of Educational Cinematography* 3 (1931): 683–7.

Tildesley, Ruth M. "Directing Directors." *Hollywood Life* August 1926: 58, 93.

——. "Filming Children for Children." *National Board of Review Magazine* December 1929: 5–7.

Tinee, Mae (Frances Smith). *Life Stories of the Movie Stars*. Hamilton, OH: Presto Publishing, 1916.

Tommasi, Miss A. "Projectors, Films and Film Libraries." *International Review of Educational Cinematography* 3 (1931): 1081–8.

de la Torre, Matilde. "The Cinematographic Education of the Rural Masses." *International Review of Educational Cinematography* 5 (1933): 321–3.

Townshend, Marchioness. "A Coroneted Filmer: A Marchioness Picture-Playwright." *Sketch* 10 September 1913: 291.

——. "Interview with the Marchioness Townshend." *Bioscope* [London] 30 July 1914: 429, 431.

Treat, Ida. "China Makes Its Own Movies." *Travel* June 1936: 32–5.

Troly-Curtin, Marthe. "Beauty is an Art—and a Science." *Film Weekly* 6 May 1929: 17.

——. "Woman to Woman." *Film Weekly* 22 October 1928: 9.

——. "Screen Sirens—and the Talkies." *Film Weekly* 3 June 1929.

Turnbull, Margaret. *The Close-Up*. (fiction) New York: Harper & Brothers, 1918.

Underhill, Harriette. "Imitation Chinchilla." *Delineator* April 1920: 27, 107.

——. "*Passion* at the Rivoli shows life of Du Barry." *New York Tribune* 13 December 1920: 8

——. Appreciation by Walter Conley. "Harriette Underhill." *Silent Picture* 13 (1972): 24–30.

Unsell, Eve. "The Feminine Mind in Picture Making." *Film Daily* 7 June 1925: 113, 115.

——. "The 'Routine' of Film Adaptation." *Cinema Craftsmanship: A Book for Photoplaywrights*. Frances Taylor Patterson. New York: Harcourt Brace, 1921. 86–95.

Védrès, Nicole. "Criticism and French Cinema." *Penguin Film Review* 4 (1947): 105–108.

——. "French Cinema." *Penguin Film Review* 2 (1947): 70–73.

——. "The French Cinema Since 1944." *Penguin Film Review* 1 (1946): 74–9.

——. "French Cinema Takes Stock." *Penguin Film Review* 3 (1947): 81–3.

——. "It's Typically French." *Penguin Film Review* 5 (1948): 73–6.

——. "Risques et Chances du Cinéma Français." *La France Libre* [London] 15 December 1945: 157–63.

Virginia. "The Diary of a Daughter of Eve." *Black and White* [London] 4 April 1896: 440, 442.

Vorse, Mary Heaton. "Some Picture Show Audiences." *Outlook* 24 June 1911: 441–47.

Wald, Lillian D. "A Grave Injustice to Colored People." *Fighting a Vicious Film: Protest Against "The Birth of a Nation"*. Boston: N.A.A.C.P., Boston Branch, 1915. 18.

Walker, Anne. "Dressing the Movies." *Woman's Home Companion* May 1921: 24.

——. "The Girls Behind the Screen." *Woman's Home Companion* January 1921: 14.

——. "Movie Moths." *Woman's Home Companion* December 1920: 14, 130–31.

Walker, Hannah Reid. "How We Got Better Movies in Glen Ellen." *Rotarian* November 1948: 14–16.

Wallace, Irene. "The Woman on the Screen." *Green Book Magazine* December 1914: 981–6.

Walsh, Ann. "Music in the Film: Its Possibilities and Uses." *British Journal of Photography.* 18 February 1949: 73–4; 11 March 1949: 110–11.

Ward, Luci, and Jack Natteford. "Economics of the Horse Opera." *Screen Writer* 3 (1948): 21–4.

——. "Problems of the Outdoor Action Writer." *Screen Writer* 2 (1946): 15–19.

Warner, Virginia. "The Negro Soldier: A Challenge to Hollywood." *People's World* [San Francisco] 8 April 1944: 5.

Warwick, Countess of. Interview. *Bioscope* [London] 18 September 1913: 891, 893.

"Lady Warwick as Author of Film-Plays." *Sketch* [London] 24 September 1913: 359.

Washington, Fredi. "Fredi says…" *People's Voice* [New York] 9 August 1947: 22.

——. "Headlines, Footlights: Apollo Comedy Bad for Race." *People's Voice* [New York] 31 July 1943: 9.

——. "Headlines, Footlights: Letter from a White Soldier." *People's Voice* [New York] 29 April 1944: 22.

——. "Headlines, Footlights: *Uncle Tom's Cabin*." *People's Voice* [New York] 5 February 1944: 22.

——. "Headlines, Footlights: Tim Moore Replies." *People's Voice* [New York] 7 August 1943: 11.

Washington, Hazel. "Imitations: Life, Color, and Pancakes." *Opportunity* 13.6 (June 1935): 185.

Waterbury, Ruth. [Prolific writer on film whose work for *Photoplay* spanned fifty years. A selection of her writings includes:]

——. "Don't Go to Hollywood." *Photoplay* March 1927: 50–51, 125–8.

——. "The Final Fade-Out." *Photoplay* March 1926: 34–5, 121–2.

——. "Gloria, Connie and the Marquis." *Photoplay* August 1930: 32–3, 118–19.

——. "Wedded and Parted." *Photoplay* December 1922: 58–9, 117–20.

——. "Ruth Waterbury." Interview with Anthony Slide. *Film Fan Monthly* March 1973. Rpt. *Idols of Silence*. Ed. Anthony Slide. South Brunswick, NJ: A.S. Barnes, 1976. 115–18.

Weber, Lois. Interview with Arthur Denison. "A Dream in Realization." *Moving Picture World* 21 July 1917: 417–18. Rpt. *Hollywood Directors 1914–1940*. Richard Koszarski. Oxford: Oxford University Press, 1976.

——. "How I Became a Motion Picture Director." *Static Flashes* 24 April 1915: 8.

Epes Winthrop Sargeant, interview, "Lois Weber on Scripts." In Epes Winthrop Sargeant, "The Photo Playwright." *Moving Picture World* 19 October 1912: 241.

See also Winifred Aydelotte.

Wehberg, Hilla. *Films of Everyday Life*. New York: Production Committee, Metropolitan Motion Picture Council, 1938.

——. *Pan-American Films* New York: Metropolitan Motion Picture Council, 1939.

——. "Some Recent Developments in the Educational Film Field." *Journal of Educational Sociology* November 1938: 163.

Weil, Peggy. "Race Tolerance Newest Box Office Hit." *Negro Digest* August 1948: 46–9.

Weiss, Trude. "Film Review." *Close Up* 9.3 (1932): 207–8.

——. "The First Opera-Film." *Close Up* 9.4 (1932): 242–5.

——. "Kurble." *Close Up* 4.5 (1929): 78–80.

——. "Motion Pictures in the Class Room." *Close Up* 7.4 (1930): 260–63.

——. "*Mutter Krausens Fahrt ins Glück*." *Close Up* 6.4 (1930): 318–21.

——. "The Primeval Age of Cinema." *Close Up* 10.4 (1933): 326–8.

——. "A Starring Vehicle." *Close Up* 7.5 (November 1930): 333–5.

Wellesby, Norah. "Temple Rocking in the Movies." *North American Review* August 1931: 166–72.

Wells, Ida B. *Crusade for Justice*. Chicago: University of Chicago Press, 1970. [Chapter 38 is on Birth of a Nation.]

West, Rebecca. "New Secular Forms of Old Religious Ideas." *Realist* [London] June 1929: 25–35.

——. Preface. *Keeping it Dark, or The Censor's Handbook*. Bernard Caston and G. Gordon Young. London: Mandrake Press, c. 1929. 7–13.

——. "Woman as Artist and Thinker." *Woman's Coming of Age: A Symposium*. Ed. Samuel Schmalhausen and V.F. Calverton. New York: Horace Liveright, 1931. 369–82.

Whetter, Laura. "Give Us Back Our Lost Gods." *Film Weekly* 3 May 1930: 6.

——. "Peril, Perfidy—and Papers!" *Film Weekly* 8 March 1930: 21.

——. "The Triumph of Screen Virtue." *Film Weekly* 22 March 1930: 6.

Whitby, Mrs. J.E. "The Future of the Cinematograph." *Chambers's Journal* 1 June 1900: 391–2.

White, Lilliam McKim. "Better Week-End Movies." *Parents Magazine* March 1933: 28.

White, Pearl. "Always Just Escaping Death." *Picturegoer* 27 July 1918: 111.

——. *Just Me*. New York: George H. Doran, 1919.

——. "Pearl White." *Picturegoer* 9 October 1920: 412. 421.

——. "Putting It Over." *Motion Picture Magazine* February 1917: 61–2.

——. "Why I Like to Work for Uncle Sam." *Pictures and Picturegoer* 5 October 1918: 343.

Wilcox, Ella Wheeler. *Cinema Poems and Others*. London: Gay and Hancock, 1919.

Williamson, Alice M. *Alice in Movieland*. New York: D. Appleton, 1928.

Wilson, C. M. "Children and War Films: An Enquiry." *Educational Survey* (Geneva) January 1929: 12–57.

Wilson, Lois. "Good Girls in Pictures." *Breaking Into the Movies*. Ed. Charles Reed Jones. New York: The Unicorn Press, 1927. 59–67.

Wilson, Margery. *I Found My Way* Philadelphia: J.P. Lippincott, 1956.

Wing, Ruth, ed. *The Blue Book of the Screen*. Hollywood: The Blue Book of the Screen, 1923.

Winship, Mary. "When Valentino Taught Me to Dance," *Photoplay* May 1922: 45, 118.

Winslow, Thyra Samter. "Color Takes the Stage." *Negro Digest* May 1946: 43–45.

Winter, Alice Ames. [Mrs. Thomas G.] "And So to Hollywood." *Woman's Journal* March 1930: 7–9, 45–6.

——. "Cinematography as an Agency for World Unity." *Proceedings of the Institute of World Affairs* [Los Angeles] 11 (1934): 245–7.

——. "Motion Picture's Self-Correction." *Woman's Journal* June 1930: 49+.

——. "Taking the Movies into the Community." *Ladies' Home Journal* February 1927: 31, 186, 188.

——. "The Thrill of the Movies," *Motion Picture* December 1930: 4, 8, 12.

——. Letter to William Hays, 21 September 1934, Hays Papers, Indianapolis Public Library, Indiana.

Winter, Alice Ames, with Alice Evans Field. *A Motion Picture Study Program*. Hollywood: Association of Motion Picture Producers, 1931.

Winter, Marian Hannah. "The Function of Music in Sound Film." *Musical Quarterly* [New York] April 1941.

Withers, Googie. "Acting for Stage and Screen." *Penguin Film Review* 4 (1947): 36–40.

Wolf, Julia. "The Continental Film in Britain." *Penguin Film Review* 4 (1947): 89–94.

Wolfenstein, Martha, and Nathan Leites. "An Analysis of Themes and Plots." *Annals of the American Academy of Political and Social Science*. Philadelphia: November 1947. 41–48.

——. *Movies: A Psychological Study*. New York: The Free Press, 1950.

——. "Trends in French Films." *Journal of Social Issues* 11.2 (1955): 42–51.

——. "The Unconscious Versus the 'Message' in an Anti-Bias Film—Two Social Scientists View *No Way Out*." *Commentary* 10 (1950): 388–91

Wolff, Marthe Ruben, Dr. "Introduction to the Russian Film About Abortion." *Sexual Reform Congress, London 8–14* (September 1929): *World League for Sexual Reform, 3rd Congress Proceedings*. Ed. Norman Haire. London: Kegan Paul, Trench, Trubner, 1930. 238–9.

Woman Reader. "Keep Men Out of Cinemas." *Film Weekly* 30 September 1932: 18–19.

Woodman, Dorothy. "Do War Films Make Pacifists?" *New World* [London] March 1931: 8.

——. "War—as Seen on the Screen." *New World* [London] January 1931: 7.

——. "A War Film in Berlin." *New World* [London] September 1931: 5.

Woolf, Virginia. "Cinema." *Arts* [New York] 9 (1926): 314–16.

——. "The Cinema." *Nation and Athenaeum* [London] 3 July 1926: 381–3.

——. "The Movies and Reality." *New Republic* 4 August 1926: 308–10.

——. "The Movie Novel [1918]." *The Essays of Virginia Woolf, Volume II* (1912–18). Ed. Andrew McNellie (New York: Harcourt Brace Jovanovich, 1987. 290–91).

Wright, Irene. "Life Looks Funny Through a Grille." *Film Weekly* 4 July 1931: 19.

Yezierska, Anzia. "A Hungry Heart and—$10,000." *Literary Digest* 24 October 1925: 44, 46, 48.

——. "This is What $10,000 Did to Me." *Hearst's International—Cosmopolitan* October 1925: 40–41, 154.

Young, Clara Schermerhorn. "Movie Mother." *Delineator* February 1934: 4+.

Zeitlin, Ida. "'Great Women of Motion Pictures'—Natalie Kalmus, the Technicolor Girl." *Screenland* February 1939: 64–5, 74.

Zetterling, Mai. "Some Notes on Acting." *Sight and Sound* October–December 1951: 83, 96.

Other Works Cited

A.S.B. [Alice Stone Blackwell]. "The American Peril." *Woman's Journal* 4 July 1914: 210.

Abel, Richard. *French Cinema: The First Wave, 1915–1929.* Princeton: Princeton University Press, 1984.

——, ed. *French Film Theory and Criticism, 1907–1939: A History/Anthology.* 2 vols. Princeton: Princeton University Press, 1988.

——. *The Red Rooster Scare: Making Cinema American, 1900–1910.* Berkeley: University of California Press, 1999.

——, ed. *Silent Film.* New Brunswick, NJ: Rutgers University Press, 1996.

Acker, Ally. *Reel Women: Pioneers of the Cinema, 1896 to the Present.* New York: Continuum, 1991.

Addams, Jane. *A New Conscience and An Ancient Evil.* New York: Macmillan, 1912.

——. *Twenty Years at Hull House, with Autobiographical Notes.* New York: Macmillan, 1910.

Affiches Françaises du Cinéma Muet: Une Exposition du Service des Archives du Film. Lyon: Institut Lumière, 1987.

Aiken, F.G. "The Business of Exhibiting." *Views and Films Index* 13 June 1908: 6.

Alexander, William. *Film on the Left: American Documentary Film from 1931 to 1942.* Princeton: Princeton University Press, 1981.

"Alma in Wonderland." *Picturegoer* [London] December 1925: 48.

"An All-Woman Film Company." *Story World* July 1923: 79.

Alonso, Harriet Hyman. *The Women's Peace Union and the Outlawry of War, 1921–1942.* Knoxville: University of Tennessee Press, 1989.

Altman, Rick. "The Silence of the Silents." *Musical Quarterly* 80.4 (Winter 1996): 648–718.

Anderson, Ellen. *Guide to Women's Organizations: A Handbook About National and International Groups.* Washington, DC: Public Affairs Press, 1949–50.

Armatage, Kay. "Nell Shipman: A Case of Heroic Femininity." *Feminisms in the Cinema.* Eds. Laura Pietropaolo and Ada Testaferri. Bloomington: Indiana University Press, 1995. 125–145.

Arnheim, Rudolf. *Film as Art.* Berkeley: University of California Press, 1957. A translation and adaption of *Film als Kunst.* Berlin: Ernst Rowohlt Verlag, 1932.

Bachman, Gregg. "Still in the Dark—Silent Film Audiences," *Film History* 9 (1997): 23–48.

Bachman, Robert G. "The Popularity of Film Grows." *Show World* 13 July 1907: 10.

Balázs, Béla. *Theory of the Film: Character and Growth of a New Art.* [1945] Trans. Edith Bone. London: Dobson, 1952.

Balio, Tino. *Grand Design: Hollywood as a Modern Business Enterprise, 1930–1939.* Berkeley: University of California Press, 1993.

Ballaster, Ross, Margaret Beetham, Elizabeth Frazer, and Sandra Hebron. *Women's Worlds: Ideology, Femininity, and the Woman's Magazine.* London: Macmillan Education, 1991.

Bandy, Mary Lea. "Nothing Sacred: 'Jock Whitney Snares Antiques for Museum': The Founding of the Museum of Modern Art Film Library." *Studies in Modern Art* (New York: Museum of Modern Art, December 1995). 2–32.

Banner, Lois. *American Beauty.* New York: Alfred Knopf, 1983.

Barkan, Elazar and Ronald Bush, eds. *Prehistories of the Future: The Primitivist Project and the Culture of Modernism.* Stanford: Stanford University Press, 1995.

Barnes, Djuna. *Ladies Almanack.* Paris: 1928. New York: Harper & Row, 1972.

——. *New York.* Edited and with a commentary by Alyce Barry. Los Angeles: Sun & Moon Press, 1989.

——. *Nightwood.* London: Faber & Faber, 1936.

Barrie, J.M. "The Twelve-Pound Look." *Half Hours.* New York: Charles Scribner's Sons, 1914. 43–85.

Barthes, Roland. *Camera Lucida.* Trans. Richard Howard. New York: Hill & Wang, 1981.

——. "Leaving the Movie Theater [1975]." *The Rustle of Language.* Trans. Richard Howard. New York: Hill & Wang, 1986. 345–9.

Bartlett, Randolph. "Petrova—Prophetess." *Photoplay* December 1917: 26–7, 112.

Basinger, Janine. *A Woman's View: How Hollywood Spoke to Women, 1930–1960.* New York: Knopf, 1993.

Bataille, Gretchen. "Preliminary Investigations: Early Suffrage Films." *Women and Film* 1. 3–4 (1973): 42–4.

Baudry, Jean-Louis. "The Apparatus: Metapsychological Approaches to the Impression of Reality in Cinema." *Communications* (1975). Rpt. *Narrative, Apparatus, Ideology: A Film Theory Reader.* Ed. Philip Rosen. New York: Columbia University Press, 1986. 299–318.

——. "Ideological Effects of the Basic Cinematographic Apparatus" [1970]. *Narrative, Apparatus, Ideology: A Film Theory Reader.* Ed. Philip Rosen. New York: Columbia University Press, 1986. 286–98.

Baum, Vicky. *Falling Star.* Trans. Ida Zeitlin. Garden City, NY: Doubleday, 1934.

Bazin, André. "The Ontology of the Photographic Image [1945]." *What Is Cinema?* Vol. 1. Trans. Hugh Gray. Berkeley: University of California Press, 1967. 9–16.

——. *Orson Welles: A Critical View* [1950]. Trans. Jonathan Rosenbaum. New York: Harper & Row, 1978.

Beauchamp, Cari. *Without Lying Down: Frances Marion and the Powerful Women of Early Hollywood.* New York: Lisa Drew/Scribner's, 1997.

"Bed and Sofa." *Close Up* 1.6 (1927): 69–74.

Bedford, Barbara. *Brilliant Bylines: A Biographical Anthology of Notable Newspaper Women in America.* New York: Columbia University Press, 1986.

Benchley, Robert. "Hearts in Dixie: The First Real Talking Picture." *Opportunity* 7.4 (1929): 122.

Benjamin, Walter. *Charles Baudelaire: A Lyric Poet in the Era of High Capitalism.* London: Verso, 1983.

——. "The Work of Art in the Age of Mechanical Reproduction" [1935–36]. *Illuminations.* Ed. Hannah Arendt. Trans. Harry Zohn. New York: Schocken Books, 1969. 217–51.

Berger, John. *Ways of Seeing.* London: British Broadcasting Corporation and Penguin, 1972.

Bernardi, Daniel, ed. *The Birth of Whiteness: Race and the Emergence of U.S. Cinema.* New Brunswick, NJ: Rutgers University Press, 1996.

Bernstein, Matthew, ed. *Regulating Hollywood: Censorship and Control in the Studio Era.* New Brunswick, NJ: Rutgers University Press, 1999.

Bertetto, Paolo and Gianni Rondolino, eds. *Cabiria e il suo Tempo.* Milan: Museo Nazionale del Cinema/ Editrice il Castoro, 1998.

Betts, Ernest. *Inside Pictures: With Some Reflections from the Outside.* London: Cressel Press, 1960.

Bevans, George Esdras. *How Workingmen Spend Their Spare Time.* New York: Ph.D. Thesis, Columbia University, 1913.

"Birth of a Nation Barred by Mayor in Cedar Rapids." *Chicago Defender* 3 June 1915: 1.

Black, Gregory D. *The Catholic Crusade Against the Movies, 1940–1975.* Cambridge: Cambridge University Press, 1998.

——. *Hollywood Censored: Morality Codes, Catholics, and the Movies.* Cambridge: Cambridge University Press, 1994.

Blair, Karen J., *The Clubwoman as Feminist: True Womanhood Redefined, 1868–1914.* New York: Holmes & Meier, 1980.

Blossfeldt, Karl. *Urformen der Kunst.* Berlin: Wasmuth, 1928; *Art Forms in Nature.* London: Zwemmer, 1929.

Blumer, Herbert. *Movies and Conduct.* New York: Macmillan, 1933.

Bobo, Jacqueline. *Black Women as Cultural Readers.* New York: Columbia University Press, 1995.

Bonica, Joe, ed. *How Talkies Are Made.* Hollywood: Joe Bonica, 1930.

Boorstin, Daniel J. *The Image: A Guide to Pseudo-Events in America.* New York, Atheneum, 1961. 25th Anniversary Edition, 1987.

Bordwell, David. "The Art Cinema as a Mode of Film Practice." *Film Criticism* 4.1 (1979): 56–64.

———. "The Musical Analogy." *Yale French Studies* 60 (1980): 141–56.

———. *Narration in the Fiction Film.* Madison: University of Wisconsin Press, 1985.

Bordwell, David, Janet Staiger, and Kristin Thompson. *The Classical Hollywood Cinema: Film Style and Mode of Production to 1960.* New York: Columbia University Press, 1985.

Bottomore, Stephen. "The Panicking Audience? Early Cinema and the 'Train Effect.'" *Historical Journal of Film, Radio, and Television* 19.2 (1999): 177–216.

———. "Le thème du témoignage dans le cinéma primitif." *Les Premiers Ans du Cinéma Français* (Perpignan: Institut Jean Vigo, 1985).155–9.

Bovenschen, Silvia. "Is There a Feminine Aesthetic?" Trans. Beth Weckmueller, *New German Critique* 10 (1977): 111–37.

Bowen, Louise de Koven. "Our Most Popular Recreation Controlled by the Liquor Interest." Chicago: Juvenile Protective Association of Chicago, 1911.

Bowser, Eileen. *The Transformation of Cinema, 1907–1915.* Berkeley: University of California Press, 1990.

Box, Kathleen and Louis Moss. *The Cinema Audience.* Wartime Social Survey, June–July 1943, conducted for the Ministry of Information, Great Britain. New Series No. 37b.

Brain, Robert Michael. "The Ontology of the Questionnaire: Max Weber on Measurement and Mass Investigation," *Studies in the History and Philosophy of Science* 32.4 (December 2001): 647–84.

Breakwell, Ian, and Paul Hammond. *Seeing in the Dark: A Compendium of Cinema-Going.* London: Serpent's Tail, 1990.

Breckenridge, Sophonisba P. *Women in the Twentieth Century: A Study of Their Political, Social, and Economic Activities.* 1933. New York: Arno, 1972.

"Bring Out Picture Play." *Woman's Journal* 10 October 1914: 276.

Bristow, Nancy K. *Making Men Moral: Social Engineering During the Great War.* New York: New York University Press, 1996.

Broun, Heywood Hale. *Whose Little Boy Are You? A Memoir of the Broun Family.* New York: St. Martin's Press/Marek, 1983.

Buchanan, Alfred Singer. *A Study of the Attitudes of the Writers of the Negro Press Towards the Depiction of the Negro in Plays and Film, 1930–1965.* Dissertation, University of Michigan. Ann Arbor: UMI, 1968.

Burchill, Julie. *Girls on Film.* New York: Pantheon, 1986.

"California Women Discuss Pictures." *Motion Picture Director* December 1925: 64.

"Captured Austrian Films." *Times* 6 July 1917: 9.

Carbine, Mary. "'The Finest Outside the Loop': Motion Picture Exhibition in Chicago's Black Metropolis." *Silent Film.* Ed. Richard Abel. New Brunswick, NJ: Rutgers University Press, 1996. 234–62.

Cardinal, Roger. "Pausing over Peripheral Detail." *Framework* 30/31 (1986): 112–30.

Carey, John. *The Intellectuals and the Masses: Pride and Prejudice among the Literary Intelligentsia, 1880–1939.* London: Faber & Faber, 1992.

Ceplair, Larry. *A Great Lady: A Life of the Screenwriter Sonya Levien.* Metuchen, NJ: Scarecrow, 1996.

Cerná, Jana. *Kafka's Milena.* Trans. A.G. Brain. With an introduction and translation of Milena Jesenska's work by George Gibian. Evanston, IL: Northeastern University Press, 1993.

Chanan, Michael. *The Dream That Kicks: The Prehistory and Early Years of Cinema in Britain.* London: Routledge, 1980.

Chandler, Edward H. "How Much Children Attend the Theatre, the Quality of the Entertainment That They Choose and Its Effect upon Them." *Proceedings of the Children's Conference for Research and Welfare* 1. New York: G.E. Stechert, 1909: 55–9.

Charney, Leo and Vanessa R. Schwartz, eds. *Cinema and the Invention of Modern Life.* Berkeley: University of California Press, 1995.

"Chicago Women Voters Clean Up Film Plays" *Woman's Journal* 1 April 1916: 106.

"Child Welfare Exhibit in Chicago." *Moving Picture World* 27 May 1911: 1185.

Chopin, Elizabeth, Coordinator. *Cinéma: Premières Affiches (1895–1914).* Chaumont: Bibliothèque Municipale de Chaumont, 1991.

Christie, Ian. "Has the Cinema a Career?" *Times Literary Supplement* 17 November 1995: 22–3.

———. *The Last Machine: Early Cinema and the Birth of the Modern World.* London: British Film Institute, 1994.

Christie, Ian and Richard Taylor, eds. *The Film Factory: Russian and Soviet Cinema in Documents, 1896–1939.* Cambridge: Harvard University Press, 1988.

The Cinema: Its Present Position and Future Possibilities. Report, National Council of Public Morals Cinema Commission of Inquiry. London: William & Norgate, 1917.

"Cinema Pests: No. 2." *Film Weekly* 19 December 1931: 19.

"The Cinematograph on Tour—Filming East and West." *Amateur Photographer and Photographic News* 9 December 1912: 574.

Cixous, Hélène. "Castration or Decapitation?" Trans. Annette Kuhn. *Signs* 7.1 (1981): 41–55.

Cixous, Hélène, "The Laugh of the Medusa." Trans. Keith Cohen and Paula Cohen. *Signs* 4.1 (1976): 875–93.

Clapp, Elizabeth J. *Mothers of All Children: Women Reformers and the Rise of Juvenile Courts in Progressive Era America.* University Park, PA: Pennsylvannia University Press, 1998.

Claude A. Barnett Collection, Chicago Historical Society, Box 298, Folder 1, for articles on *Hallelujah*: Thomas Walker Wallace, "Here and There"; The Editor, "Adding to the Mirth of a Nation"; and "*Hallelujah!*—A Disgrace to the Race," *Chicago Whip*.

Cline, Sally. *Radclyffe Hall: A Woman Called John.* Woodstock, NY: Overlook Press, 1998.

Clinton, Hillary Rodham. *It Takes a Village, and Other Lessons Children Teach Us.* New York: Simon & Schuster, 1996.

"Close-Ups: Editorial Expression and Timely Comment." *Photoplay* December 1916: 63, 64.

Cohen, Lizabeth. *Making a New Deal: Industrial Workers in Chicago, 1919–1939.* New York: Cambridge University Press, 1990.

"Comment and Review," *Close Up* 1.2 (1927): 63–4.

Commolli, Jean-Louis. "Technique and Ideology: Camera, Perspective, Depth-of-Field." *Film Reader* 2 (1977): 128–40.

Cook, Christopher, see Dilys Powell.

Cook, Pam, and Philip Dodd, eds. *Women and Film: A Sight and Sound Reader.* London: British Film Institute, 1993.

Cooke, Alistair, ed. *Garbo and the Night Watchmen.* New York: McGraw-Hill, 1971.

Cooper, Gail. *Air-Conditioning America: Engineers and the Controlled Environment, 1900–1960.* Baltimore: Johns Hopkins University Press, 1998.

Corbin, Mrs. William A. "Urges Women to Attend Third International Convention." *Negro World* 15 July 1922: 8.

Le Corbusier. "The Spirit of Truth" [Esprit de Verité] [1933]. *French Film Theory and Criticism, 1907–1939: A History / Anthology.* Vol. II, 1929–39. Ed. Richard Abel. Princeton: Princeton University Press, 1988. 112–13.

de Cordova, Richard. "Ethnography and Exhibition: The Child Audience, The Hays Office, and Saturday Matinees." *Camera Obscura* 22 (1990): 29–50.

——. "The National Congress of Parents and Teachers, the Cinema, and the Agenda of Reform, 1920–1940." Unpublished paper delivered at Society for Cinema Studies Annual Conference. Hilton Hotel, New York City. 2 March 1995.

——. *Picture Personalities: the Emergence of the Star System in America.* Urbana: Illinois University Press, 1990.

Cott, Nancy. *The Grounding of Modern Feminism.* New Haven: Yale University Press, 1987.

Cotter, Carl F. "The Forty Hacks of the Fan Magazines," *Coast* February 1939: 18–21.

Couvares, Francis G., ed. *Movie Censorship and American Culture.* Washington, D.C.: Smithsonian Institution Press, 1996.

Crafton, Donald. *The Talkies: American Cinema's Transition to Sound, 1926–1931.* Berkeley: University of California Press, 1999.

Cramer-Roberts, J.K. "Our Inventions Corner: the First Description of the 'Biokam.' *Golden Penny* 3 June 1899: 476.

Cripps, Thomas. "The Reaction of the Negro to the Motion Picture Birth of a Nation." *Focus on Birth of a Nation.* Ed. Fred Silva. Englewood Cliffs, NJ: Prentice-Hall, 1971. 111–24.

Crowther, Bosley. "Male Movie Stars Outshine the Female." *New York Times* 16 February 1941: 10–11, 17.

Dale, Edgar. *How to Appreciate Motion Pictures.* 1933. New York: Arno Press, 1970.

Darwin, Charles *On the Origin of Species by Means of Natural Selection.* London: John Murray, 1859.

——. *The Various Contrivances by Which British and Foreign Orchids are Fertilized by Insects.* London: John Murray, 1862.

Davis, Allen F. and Mary Lynn McCree Bryan, eds. *Eighty Years at Hull House.* Chicago: Quadrangle Books, 1969.

Del Ruth, Hampton. "Developing the 'Fifth Estate'." *New York Dramatic Mirror* 10 February 1917: 28.

Deland, Margaret. "The Change in the Feminine Ideal." *Atlantic Monthly* March 1910: 289–302.

"Deluded Women." *Christian Century* 6 December 1933: 1527–29.

Dench, Ernest A. "Strange Effects of Photoplays on Spectators." *Illustrated World* July 1917: 788.

Destrée, Jules. "Une illusion pacifiste." *Le Soir* [Brussels] 16 April 1932.
Deutsch, Helene. *The Psychology of Women: A Psychoanalytic Interpretation*. Vol. I. 1944. New York: Grune & Shatton, 1979.
De Wolfe, Elsie. *The House in Good Taste*. New York: Century, 1915.
Diederichs, Helmut H. "Emilie Altenloh—Filmwissenschaftlerin." *Cinegraph: Lexikon zum deutschsprachigen Film*. Hamburg: Edition Text und Kritik, 1984: D1–2.
"The Difficulties of a Pioneer Film Company." *New York Age* 9 August 1917: 6.
"Director's Note." *International Review of Educational Cinematography* 3 (1931): 1067–70.
Dizikes, John. *Opera in America: A Cultural History*. New Haven: Yale University Press, 1993.
Doane, Mary Ann. *The Desire to Desire: The Women's Film in the 1940s*. Bloomington: Indiana University Press, 1987.
———. "Film and the Masquerade: Theorizing the Female Spectator." *Screen* 23.3–4 (1982): 74–88.
———. "Masquerade Reconsidered: Further Thoughts on the Female Spectator," *Discourse* 11:1 (Fall–Winter 1988–89): 42–54.
———. "Screening Time." *Language Machines: Technologies of Literary and Cultural Production*. Eds. Jeffrey Masten, Peter Stallybrass, and Nancy Vickers. New York: Routledge, 1997: 137–59.
———. "Technology's Body: Cinematic Vision in Modernity." *differences* 5.2 (1993): 1–23.
"Do Films Libel Women?: Famous Writers Reply to Madeleine Carroll." *Film Weekly* 7 February 1931: 6.
Doherty, Thomas. *Teenagers and Teenpics: The Juvenilization of American Movies in the 1950s*. Boston: Unwin Hyman, 1988.
"Doings in Los Angeles." *Moving Picture World* 11 January 1913: 142.
Donald, James, Anne Friedberg, and Laura Marcus, eds. *Close Up, 1927–1933: Cinema and Modernism*. London: Cassell, 1998.
Donaldson, Geoffrey. "Caroline van Dommelen." *Silent Picture* 15 (1972): 33–34.
Dop, Louis. "The Role and The Purpose of the International Educational Cinematographic Institute." *International Review of Educational Cinematography* 1 (1929): 12–25.
Douglas, Ann. *The Feminization of American Culture*. 1977. New York: Noonday Press, 1998.
———. *Terrible Honesty: Mongrel Manhattan in the 1920s*. New York: Farrar, Straus, and Giroux, 1995.
DuBois, W.E.B. *The Souls of Black Folk*. Chicago: A. C. McClurg, 1903.
Dupont, Joan. "A Woman Pushes the Borders of Iranian Film." *International Herald Tribune* 13–14 May 2000: 22.
Durant, Will. "The Modern Woman." *Century Magazine* February 1927: 418–29.
Dyer, Richard. "The Colour of Virtue: Lillian Gish, Whiteness, and Femininity." *Women and Film: A Sight and Sound Reader*. Eds. Pam Cook and Philip Dodd. London: British Film Institute, 1993. 1–9.
———. *Heavenly Bodies: Film Stars and Society*. New York: St. Martin's Press, 1986.
E.H.M. [possibly Edith How Martyn]. "Europe and Birth Control." Letter. *Birth Control Review* May 1927:155.
Eaton, Peter and Marilyn Warnick. *Marie Stopes: A Checklist of Her Writings*. London: Croon Helm, c. 1977.
Eckert, Charles. "The Carol Lombard in Macy's Window." *Quarterly Review of Film Studies* (Winter 1978): 1–21.
Eco, Umberto. *The Search for the Perfect Language*. Trans. James Fentress. Oxford and Cambridge, MA: Blackwell Publishers, 1995.
Edelhertz, Bernard. "Cinema: the Universal Eye." *American Hebrew* 15 March 1929: 647, 679.
Eder, M.D. see "Report of the British Psychoanalytic Society, Fourth Quarter, 1924."
Eells, George. *Hedda and Louella: A Dual Biography of Hedda Hopper and Louella Parsons*. New York: G.P. Putnam's Sons, 1972.
Egger, Rebecca. "Deaf Ears and Dark Continents: Dorothy Richardson's Cinematic Epistemology." *Camera Obscura* 30 (1992): 5–33.
Eisenstein, Sergei. *The Film Sense*. Trans. Jay Leyda. 1942. New York: Harcourt Brace Jovanovich, 1970.
———. *Non-Indifferent Nature: Film and the Structure of Things*. Trans. Herbert Marshall. New York: Cambridge University Press, 1987.
"Ella Fabrique," *Moving Picture World* 17 April 1920: 395.
"Ella Wheeler Wilcox's Humanology Films," *Kinematograph and Lantern Weekly* 7 January 1915: 69.
Elmendorf, Dwight. "Novel and Useful Applications of Motion Photographs." *Views and Films Index* 15 September 1906: 4.

Elsaesser, Thomas, ed., with Adam Barker. *Early Cinema: Space, Frame, Narrative.* London: British Film Institute, 1990.

Elton, W. John. "A Miss Who Writes 'Hits'." *Film Weekly* 12 April 1935: 10.

Ely, Mary L. and Eve Chappell. *Women in Two Worlds.* New York: American Association for Adult Education, 1938.

"The End of the Line." *Etude* 52 (1934): 450.

Enstad, Nan. "Dressed for Adventure: Working Women and Silent Movie Serials in the 1910s." *Feminist Studies* 21.1 (1995): 67–90.

Epstein, Jean. "Approaches to Truth [1928]." Rpt. *French Film Theory and Criticism, 1907–1939, A History/Anthology.* Vol. 1, 1907–1929. Ed. Richard Abel. Princeton: Princeton University Press, 1988: 422–25.

——. "For a New Avant–Garde [1925]." Rpt. *French Film Theory and Criticism, 1907–1939, A History/Anthology.* Vol. 1, 1907–1929. Ed. Richard Abel. Princeton: Princeton University Press, 1988: 349–53.

——. "Art of Incidence [1927]" Rpt. *French Film Theory and Criticism, 1907–1939, A History/Anthology.* Vol. 1, 1907–1929. Ed. Richard Abel. Princeton: Princeton University Press, 1988: 412–14.

——. "On Certain Characteristics of 'Photogenie'" [1924]. *Afterimage* 10 (1981): 20–23. Trans. Tom Milne. Rpt. *French Film Theory and Criticism 1907–1939, A History/Anthology.* Vol. I, 1907–29. Ed. Richard Abel. Princeton: Princeton University Press, 1988. 314–18.

——. "Magnification [1921]." *October* 3 (1977): 9–15. Trans. Stuart Liebman. Rpt. *French Film Theory and Criticism, 1907–1939: A History/Anthology.* Vol. I, 1907–29. Ed. Richard Abel. Princeton: Princeton University Press, 1988. 235–41.

——. "The Senses I (b) [1921]." *Afterimage* 10 (1981): 9–16. Trans. Tom Milne. Rpt. *French Film Theory and Criticism 1907–1939, A History/Anthology.* Vol. I, 1907–29. Ed. Richard Abel. Princeton: Princeton University Press, 1988. 241–6.

Erens, Patricia, ed. *Sexual Stratagems: The World of Women in Film.* New York: Horizon Press, 1979.

Ewen, Elizabeth. *Immigrant Women in the Land of Dollars: Life and Culture on the Lower East Side, 1890–1925.* New York: Monthly Review Press, 1985.

"Exploiting Falsehood and Boycotting Truth." *Birth Control Review* April–May 1917: 10.

"These Fans Are Dangerous." Editorial. *Screen Pictorial* September 1939: 9.

Faure, Elie. "De la cinéplastique" [1922]. *The Art of Cineplastics.* Trans. Walter Pach. Boston: Four Seas, 1923. Rpt. *French Film Theory and Criticism 1907–1939, A History/Anthology.* Vol I, 1907–29. Ed. Richard Abel. Princeton: Princeton University Press, 1988. 258–67.

Fawcett, L'Estrange. *Films: Facts and Forecasts.* London: G. Bles, 1927.

——. *Writing for the Films.* London: Pitman, 1932.

Feldman, Charles Matthew. *The National Board of Censorship (Review) of Motion Pictures, 1909–1922.* New York: Arno Press, 1977.

Feldman, Joseph and Harry Feldman. "Women Directors Seem to Go More Often Than They Come." *Films In Review* November 1950: 9–12.

Ferguson, Otis. "Weep No More, My Ladies." *New Republic* 3 June 1940: 760–61.

Fetherling, Dale and Doug Fetherling, eds. *Carl Sandburg at the Movies: A Poet in the Silent Era, 1920–1927.* Metuchen, NJ: Scarecrow Press, 1985.

Filene, Catherine, ed. *Careers for Women.* Boston: Houghton Mifflin, 1920. 2nd ed. Boston: Houghton Mifflin, 1934.

"Film Censorship in Australia." *International Review of Educational Cinematography* 2 (1930): 89–92.

"Film Censorship in Italy." *International Review of Educational Cinematography* 2 (1930): 500–05.

"The Film Forum." *New Masses* February 1933: 29.

"Film Weekly Sued for Libel." *Film Weekly* 8 February 1930: 25.

"Filmaniac?" *Views and Film Index* 22 August 1908: 8.

"Filmore's Inside Film Talk." *Moving Picture News* 2 September 1911: 17.

Fischer, Lucy. *Cinematernity: Film, Motherhood, Genre.* Princeton: Princeton University Press, 1996.

Fisher, Robert. "Film Censorship and Progressive Reform: The National Board of Censorship of Motion Pictures, 1909–1922." *Journal of Popular Film and Television* 4 (1975): 143–56.

Fletcher, Helen. *Bluestocking.* London: Pandora Press, 1986.

"Flickers." *The Picturegoer* May 1921: 8.

Flitterman-Lewis, Sandy. *To Desire Differently: Feminism and the French Cinema.* 1990. Expanded ed. New York: Columbia University Press, 1996.

Foster, Gwendolyn Audrey. *Women Film Directors: An International Bio-Critical Dictionary.* Westport, CT: Greenwood Press, 1995.

Foster, Hal. "The 'Primitive' Consciousness of Modern Art." *October* 34 (1985): 45–70.

Francke, Lizzie. *Script Girls: Women Screenwriters in Hollywood.* London: British Film Institute, 1994.

Frank, Stanley. "Headaches of a Movie Censor." *Saturday Evening Post* 27 September 1947: 20–21, 70–72.

French, Philip and Ken Wlaschin, eds. *The Faber Book of Movie Verse.* London: Faber & Faber, 1993.

Friedberg, Anne. *Window Shopping: Cinema and the Postmodern.* Berkeley: California University Press, 1993.

——. " Writing About Cinema: *Close Up, 1927–1933*." Dissertation, New York University, 1983.

Fromm, Gloria, ed. *Windows on Modernism: Selected Letters of Dorothy Richardson.* Athens, GA: University of Georgia Press, 1995.

Fullerton, John, ed. *Celebrating 1895: The Centenary of Cinema.* London: John Libbey, 1999.

Gabler, Neal. *Walter Winchell: Gossip, Power and the Culture of Celebrity.* New York: Alfred A. Knopf, 1994.

Gamman, Lorraine and Margaret Marshment, eds. *The Female Gaze: Women as Viewers of Popular Culture.* Seattle: Real Comet Press, 1989.

Garrett Packer, Joan. *Rebecca West: An Annotated Bibliography.* New York: Garland Publishing, 1991.

Garvey, Marcus, Ed. "White Movies Not Shown in Africa. African Natives as Film Stars." *Black Man* (London: Universal Negro Improvement Association/Blackman) October 1935: 19.

Gerlach, John C. and Lana Gerlach. *The Critical Index: A Bibliography of Articles on Film in English, 1946–1973, Arranged By Names and Topics.* New York: Teachers College Press, 1974.

Gilbert, Sandra M. and Susan Gubar. *The War of the Words.* Vol. 1 of *No Man's Land: The Place of the Woman Writer in the Twentieth Century.* New Haven: Yale University Press, 1988.

Gilliams, E. Leslie. "Will Woman Leadership Change the Movies?" *Illustrated World* February 1923: 859–61, 956–7.

Gilman, Elizabeth. "Catheryne Cooke Gilman, Social Worker." *Women of Minnesota: Selected Biographical Essays.* Eds. Barbara Stuhler and Gretchen Kreuter. St. Paul: Minnesota Historical Society Press, 1977. 190–207.

Gilmore, Glenda Elizabeth. *Gender and Jim Crow: Women and the Politics of White Supremacy in North Carolina, 1896–1920.* Chapel Hill: University of North Carolina Press, 1997.

"The Girl Spy." *Motion Picture World* 22 May 1909: 672.

"Gladys Glycerine, Theater Owner, Banker, Cry Real Tears Together." *Business Week* 10 August 1932: 14, 15.

Gleber, Anke. *The Art of Taking a Walk: Flanerie, Literature, and Film in Weimar Culture.* Princeton: Princeton University Press, 1999.

Gledhill, Christine, ed. *Stardom: Industry of Desire.* New York: Routledge, 1991.

Glendinning, Victoria. *Rebecca West: A Life.* New York: Alfred A. Knopf, 1987.

Gomery, Douglas. *Shared Pleasures: A History of Movie Presentation in the United States.* Madison: University of Wisconsin Press, 1992.

Gorky, Maxim. "A Review of the Lumière Program at the Nizhni-Novogorod Fair [The All Russian Fair of Industry and Art], as printed in the *Nizhegorodski Listok* newspaper (4 July 1896)." Trans. Leda Swan in Jay Leyda, *Kino: A History of the Russian and Soviet Film.* New York: Collier Books, 1960. 408.

"Grand Opening of the School for Lady Operators (WE DON'T THINK)." *Bioscope* 24 June 1909: 7.

Graves, Jesse A. "Says Negro Should Be in All Pictures." *Pittsburgh Courier* 15 April 1939: 20.

Griffith, D.W. "Youth, the Spirit of the Movies" *Illustrated World* October 1921: 194–6.

Gunning, Tom. "An Aesthetic of Astonishment: Early Film and the (In)credulous Spectator." *Art & Text* 34 (1989): 31–45.

——. "The Cinema of Attractions: Early Film, Its Spectator, and the Avant-Garde." *Early Film: Space, Frame, Narrative.* Ed Thomas Elsaesser. London: British Film Institute, 1990: 56–62.

——. "Tracing the Individual Body: Photography, Detectives, and Early Cinema." *Cinema and the Invention of Modern Life.* Eds. Leo Charney and Vanessa R. Schwartz. Berkeley: University of California Press, 1995. 15–45.

H.D. *Bid Me to Live.* New York: Grove Press, 1960.

Haire, Norman, ed., *Sexual Reform Congress, London 8–14 September 1929: World League for Sexual Reform, Proceedings of the Third Congress.* London: Kegan Paul, Trench, Trubner, 1930.

Hake, Sabine. *The Cinema's Third Machine: Writing on Film in Germany, 1907–1933.* Lincoln: University of Nebraska Press, 1993.

Hall, Ben M. *The Best Remaining Seats: The Golden Age of the Movie Palace.* New York: C.N. Potter [1961], 1975. Rpt. 1987.

Hall, Gladys. "Rot," *Metropolitan Magazine*, nd., p.11. In Folder 536, Gladys Hall Collection, Margaret Herrick Library, Academy of Motion Picture Arts and Sciences, Los Angeles.

Hamilton, Clayton. "Esperanto of the Eye." *New York Evening Post* 11 August 1923: 889–90.

Hamilton, Marybeth. *When I'm Bad I'm Better: Mae West, Sex, and American Entertainment*. New York: Harper-Collins, 1995.

Hammerton, Jenny. *For Ladies Only? Eve's Film Review: Pathé Cinemagazine, 1921–1933*. Hastings: The Projection Box, 2001.

Handel, Leo. *Hollywood Looks at Its Audience*. Urbana: University of Illinois Press, 1950.

Hankins, Leslie Kathleen. "'Across the Screen of My Brain': Virginia Woolf's 'The Cinema' and Film Forums of the Twenties." *The Multiple Muses of Virginia Woolf*. Ed. Diane F. Gillespie. Columbia, MO: University of Missouri Press, 1993. 148–79.

Hanscombe, Gillian and Virginia L. Smyers. *Writing for Their Lives: The Modernist Women, 1910–1940*. London: Women's Press, 1987.

Hansen, Miriam. "Early Cinema Audiences: Myths and Models," in *Babel and Babylon: Spectatorship in American Silent Film*. Cambridge, MA: Harvard University Press, 1991. 60–89.

——. "Early Cinema: Whose Public Sphere?" *Early Cinema: Space/Frame/Narrative*. Ed. Thomas Elsaesser, with Adam Barker. London: British Film Institute, 1990. 228–46.

——. "Individual Response," *The Spectatrix*. Special issue of *Camera Obscura* 20/21 (1989): 169–74.

Hansen, Miriam Bratu. "The Mass Production of the Senses: Classical Cinema as Vernacular Modernism." *Modernism/Modernity* 6.2 (1999): 59–77.

Hansen, Patricia King, ed. *The American Film Institute Catalog of Motion Pictures Produced in the United States, Feature Films, 1911–1920*. Berkeley: University of California Press, 1988.

Harding, Colin and Simon Popple. *In the Kingdom of Shadows: A Companion to Early Cinema*. Madison, NJ: Farleigh Dickinson University Press, 1996.

Hark, Ina Rae. "The 'Theater Man' and 'The Girl in the Box Office': Gender in the Discourse of Motion Picture Theater Management." *Film History* 6 (1994): 178–87.

von Harleman, G.P. and Clarke Irvine. "Women Start Something." *Moving Picture World* 27 May 1916: 1515.

Harms, Rudolf. *Philosophie des Films*. Leipzig: Felix Meiner, 1926.

Harper, Sue and Vincent Porter. "Moved to Tears: Weeping in the Cinema in Postwar Britain." *Screen* 37.2 (1996): 152–73.

Harris, Herbert. "Women as Screen Authors: Do They Write the Best Screen Stories?" *Film Weekly* 15 September 1933: 34.

Harris, Radie. *Radie's World*. New York: G.P. Putnam's Sons, 1975.

Hart, Harold, ed. *Censorship: For and Against*. New York: Hart Publishing Company, 1971.

Haskell, Molly. *From Reverence to Rape: The Treatment of Women in the Movies*. Baltimore: Penguin, 1974.

Hayden, Dolores. "Domestic Evolution or Domestic Revolution?" *The Grand Domestic Revolution: A History of American Feminist Designs for American Homes, Neighborhoods, and Cities*. Cambridge, MA: MIT Press, 1981. 183–205.

Heck-Rabi, Louise. *Women Filmmakers: A Critical Reception*. Metuchen, NJ: Scarecrow Press, 1984.

Henry, Patrick A.. "Motion Views Win Jane Addams." *Show World* 6 July 1907: 1.

Henry, William M. "Cleo, the Craftswoman." *Photoplay* January 1916: 111.

Henshaw, Richard. "Women Directors: 150 Filmographies." *Film Comment* 8.4 (1972): 33–45.

Herbert, Stephen, and Luke McKernan, eds. *Who's Who of Victorian Cinema: A Worldwide Survey*. London: British Film Institute, 1996.

Hess, Thomas B. and Elizabeth C. Baker, eds. *Art and Sexual Politics: Why Have There Been No Great Women Artists?* New York: Collier, 1973.

Higashi, Sumiko, Robert Allen, Ben Singer. "Dialog: Manhattan Nickelodeons." *Cinema Journal* 35.3 (1996): 72–128.

Hill, Mike, ed. *Whiteness: A Critical Reader*. New York: New York University Press, 1997.

Hilton-Simpson, M.W., and J.A. Haeseler. "Cinema and Ethnology." *Discovery* [London] 6 (1925): 325.

Holliday, Wendy. "Hollywood's Modern Women: Screenwriting, Work Culture, and Feminism, 1910–1940." Dissertation, New York University, 1995.

Holtby, Winifred. *Virginia Woolf*. 1932. Folcroft, PA: Folcroft Press, 1969.

"An Honest Birth Control Film at Last." *Birth Control Review* 1 (April–May 1917): 11.

Honey, Maureen. *Breaking the Ties That Bind: Popular Stories of the New Woman, 1915–1930*. Norman: Oklahoma University Press, 1992.

hooks, bell. "The Oppositional Gaze: Black Female Spectators." *Black Looks: Race and Representation*. Boston: South End Press, 1992. 115–31.

Hope, Laura Lee [Edward Stratemeyer, and others]. *The Moving Picture Girls at Oak Farm*. New York: Grosset and Dunlap, 1914.

Horak, Jan-Christopher. "The First American Film Avant-Garde, 1914–1945." *Lovers of Cinema: The First American Film Avant-Garde, 1914–1945*. Ed. Jan-Christopher Horak. Madison: University of Wisconsin, 1995. 20–29.

"How to Buy a Hat," *Vogue* 15 January 1941: 43.

Hufton, Olwen. *The Prospect Before Her: A History of Women in Western Europe*. Vol. 1, 1500–1800. New York: Alfred A. Knopf, 1996.

Hughes, Laurence A., ed. *The Truth About Movies by the Stars*. Hollywood: Hollywood Publishers, 1924.

Hurst, Fannie. "The Author and His Home Environment: Where and How I Write my Two-Thousand Dollar Short Stories." *Arts and Decoration* June 1923: 9, 55, 62.

——. "Bitter-Sweet." *Gaslight Sonatas*. New York: Harper, 1918. 1–39.

——. "A Crisis in the History of Women." *Vital Speeches of the Day* 9 (June 1, 1943): 479–80.

——. "Fannie Hurst Advises a Plan." *Christian Science Monitor* (Magazine Section) 7 August 1935: 10, 13.

——. "Nightshade." *Gaslight Sonatas*. New York: Harper & Bros., 1918.

——. "Let's Not Wear Them!" *New Republic* 30 October 1929: 293–4.

——. "Nothing Ever Happens." *We Are Ten*. New York: Harper & Bros., 1937: 351–400.

——. "The Other Cheek." *Just Around the Corner: Romance en Casserole*. New York: Harper, 1914. 72–109.

——. "Other People's Shoes." *Just Around the Corner: Romance en Casserole*. New York: Harper, 1914. 31–71.

——. "The Squall." *Just Around the Corner: Romance en Casserole*. New York: Harper, 1914. 329–361.

Hurston, Zora Neale. "Fannie Hurst, by her Ex-amanuensis." *Saturday Review of Literature* 9 October 1937: 15–16.

Huyssen, Andreas. "Mass Culture as Woman: Modernism's Other." *Studies in Entertainment: Critical Approaches to Mass Culture*. Ed. Tania Modelski. Bloomington: University of Indiana Press, 1986: 188–207. Rpt. *After the Great Divide: Modernism, Mass Culture, Postmodernism*. By Andreas Huyssen. Bloomington: Indiana University Press, 1986. 44–62.

Hynes, Samuel, *A War Imagined: The First World War and English Culture*. New York: Atheneum, 1991.

"In the Dark, by a West End Cinema Attendant." *Film Weekly* 7 February 1931: 14.

"Irene Thirer, 59, Movie Reviewer" [obituary]. *New York Times* 20 February 1964: 29.

"Is 'Jix' Bluffing?" Letters. *New Leader* 29 March 1929: 6.

Jackson, J.A., "Our Growing Importance in the Amusement World," *Competitor* 3:4 (June 1921): 36–9.

Jacobs, Lea. "Reformers and Spectators: The Film Education Movement in the Thirties." *Camera Obscura* 22 (1990): 29–49.

——. *The Wages of Sin: Censorship and the Fallen Woman Film, 1928–1942*. Madison: University of Wisconsin Press, 1991.

Jacobs, Lea, and Ben Brewster. *Theater to Cinema: Stage Pictorialism and the Early Feature Film*. Oxford: Oxford University Press, 1997.

Johnson, Martin. *Camera Trails in Africa*. New York: Grosset & Dunlap, 1924.

Jones, Grover. "Knights of the Keyhole." *Collier's* 16 April 1938: 25–6, 28.

Jowett, Garth S., Ian C. Jarvie, and Kathryn H. Fuller. *Children and the Movies: Media Influence and the Payne Fund Study Controversy*. New York: Cambridge University Press, 1996.

Jura, Jean-Jacques and Rodney Norman Bardin II. *Balboa Films: A History and Filmography of the Silent Film Studio*. Jefferson, NC: McFarland, 1999.

Kael, Pauline. *The Citizen Kane Book*. Boston: Little, Brown, 1971.

——. "Zeitgeist and Poltergeist: Or, Are Movies Going to Pieces? Reflections from the Side of the Pool at the Beverly Hills Hotel" [1964]. *I Lost It At The Movies*. New York: Little, Brown, 1965. Bantam, 1966. 3–5.

Kaes, Anthony. "Literary Intellectuals and the Cinema: Charting a Controversy, 1909–29." *New German Critique* 40 (1987): 7–34.

Kahn, Gordon. "Mother and Brat." *Atlantic Monthly* October 1944: 110, 113, 115.

Kandinsky, Wassily. *Concerning the Spiritual in Art* [1912]. New York: Dover, 1977.

Kaplan, E. Ann, "Is the Gaze Male?" *Women and Film: Both Sides of the Camera*. New York: Methuen, 1983. 23–35.

"Kathlyn Williams, the Jungle Actress." *Picture-Play Weekly* 1.2 (17 April 1915): 1–4.

Kauffmann, Stanley, ed., with Bruce Henstell. *American Film Criticism: From the Beginnings to Citizen Kane.* 1972. New York: Liveright, 1972.

Keep, Christopher. "The Cultural World of the Type-writer Girl," *Victorial Studies* (Spring 1997): 401–26.

Kent, Susan Kingsley. *Making Peace: The Reconstruction of Gender in Interwar Britain.* Princeton: Princeton University Press, 1993.

Kessler-Harris, Alice. *Out to Work: A History of Wage-Earning Women in the United States.* New York: Oxford University Press, 1982.

Key, Charles W. "Children and the Films." *Lansbury's Labour Weekly* 9 January 1926: 14.

"The Kinetograph." *New York Sun* 28 May 1891: 1.

King, Norman. "The Sound of Silents." *Silent Film.* Ed. Richard Abel. New Brunswick: Rutgers University Press, 1996. 31–44.

Kisch, John and Edward Mapp. *A Separate Cinema: Fifty Years of Black-Cast Posters.* New York: Farrar, Straus & Giroux, 1992.

Kittler, Friedrich. "Gramaphone, Film, Typewriter." *October* 41 (1987): 101–18.

Knupfer, Anne Meis. *Toward a Tenderer Humanity and a Nobler Womanhood: African American Women's Clubs in Turn-of-the-Century Chicago.* New York: New York University Press, 1997.

Koch, Gertrude. "Why Women Go to the Movies." Trans. Marc Silberman. *Jump Cut* 27 (1982): 51–53. "Warum Frauen ins Männerkino gehen." *Frauen in der Kunst.* Vol 1. Ed. Gislind Nabakowski et al. Frankfurt am Main: Suhrkamp, 1980: 15–29.

Koszarski, Richard. *An Evening's Entertainment: The Age of the Silent Feature Picture, 1915–1928.* Berkeley: University of California Press, 1990.

———. *Hollywood Directors, 1914–1940.* New York: Oxford University Press, 1976.

Kowalski, Rosemary Ribich. *Women and Film: A Bibliography.* Metuchen, NJ: Scarecrow Press, 1976.

Kracauer, Siegfried. *From Caligari to Hitler: A Psychological History of the German Film.* Princeton: Princeton University Press, 1947.

———. *The Mass Ornament: Weimar Essays.* Trans. and ed. Thomas Y. Levin. Cambridge, MA: Harvard University Press, 1995.

———. *Theory of Film: The Redemption of Physical Reality.* Oxford: Oxford University Press, 1960.

Kraft, James P. "Stage to Studio: American Musicians and Sound Technology." Dissertation, University of Southern California, 1990.

Krämer, Peter. "A Powerful Cinema-Going Force? Hollywood and Female Audiences Since the 1960s." *Identifying Hollywood's Audiences: Cultural Identity and the Movies.* Ed. Melvyn Stokes and Richard Maltby. London: British Film Institute, 1999. 98–112.

Krementz, Jill. *The Writer's Desk.* New York: Random House, 1996.

Kristeva, Julia. *Revolution in Poetic Language.* New York: Columbia University Press, 1984.

———. "Women's Time" [1981]. Trans. Alice Jardine and Harry Blake. *Feminisms: An Antholgy of Literary Theory and Criticism.* Eds. Robyn R. Warhol and Diane Price Herndl. New Brunswick: Rutgers University Press, 1991. 443–59.

Kroeger, Brooke. *Nellie Bly: Daredevil, Reporter, Feminist.* New York: Times Books, 1994.

Kuhn, Annette. *Cinema, Censorship and Sexuality 1909–1925.* London: Routledge, 1988.

———. "Women's Genres: Melodrama, Soap Opera and Theory" [1984]. *Home is Where the Heart Is: Studies in Melodrama and the Woman's Film.* Ed. Christine Gledhill. London: British Film Institute Publishing, 1987. 339–49.

———, ed. *Queen of the B's: Ida Lupino Behind the Camera.* Westport, CT: Greenwood Press, 1995.

———, and Susannah Radstone, eds. *The Women's Companion to International Film.* London: Virago, 1990.

L.C. Interview with Abby Meehan "Fashions on the Film." *Picturegoer* 22 November 1913: 211–13.

"Lady of Many Titles." *American Magazine* 1 April 1948: 119.

Lambert, R.S., ed. *For Filmgoers Only.* London: Faber & Faber, with the British Institute of Adult Education, 1934.

Lane, Ann J. *To Herland and Beyond: The Life and Works of Charlotte Perkins Gilman.* New York: Pantheon Books, 1990.

Lant, Antonia. *Blackout: Reinventing Women for Wartime British Cinema.* Princeton: Princeton University Press, 1991.

———. "The Curse of the Pharaoh, or How the Cinema Contracted Egyptomania." *October* 59 (Winter 1992): 86–112.

———. "Haptical Cinema." *October* 74 (Fall 1995): 59–63.

——. "Spazio per la Razza in *Cabiria*" ["Space for the Race in *Cabiria*"]. *Cabiria e il suo Tempo*. Eds. Paolo Bertetto and Gianni Rondolino. Milan: Museo Nazionale del Cinema/Editrice il Castoro, 1998. 212–22.

Leach, William. *True Love and Perfect Union: The Feminist Reform of Sex and Society*. 1980. Middletown, CT: Wesleyan University Press, 1989.

"The League of Sunshine." *Photoplay* July 1919: 27.

LeMahieu, D.L. *A Culture for Democracy: Mass Communication and the Cultivated Mind in Britain Between the Wars*. Oxford: Clarendon Press, 1988.

Leonardi, Susan J. *Dangerous by Degrees: Women at Oxford and the Somerville College Novelists*. New Brunswick, NJ: Rutgers University Press, 1989.

Leppert, Richard. *The Sight of Sound: Music, Representation, and the History of the Body*. Berkeley: University of California Press, 1993.

"The Letters of Morphia Money," *Film Weekly* 4 January 1930: 20.

Lewin, William. *Photoplay Appreciation in American High Schools. A Publication of the National Council of Teachers of English*. New York: D. Appleton Century, c. 1934.

Leyda, Jay. *Kino: A History of the Russian and Soviet Film*. New York: Collier Books, 1960.

——, ed. with research by Doug Tomlinson and John Hagan. *Voices of Film Experience: 1894 to the Present*. New York: Macmillan, 1977.

Liebman, Stuart. "French Film Theory, 1910–1921." *Quarterly Review of Film Studies* 7.3 (1983): 1–23.

Lindsay, Vachel. *The Art of the Moving Picture*. 1915. New York: Dover, 1970.

Lindsey, Shelley Stamp. "Is Any Girl Safe? Female Spectators at the White Slave Films." *Screen* 37.1 (1996): 1–15. Rpt. in a revised version in Shelley Stamp. *Movie-Struck Girls: Women and Motion Picture Culture after the Nickelodeon*. Princeton: Princeton University Press, 2000.

Logan, Rayford W. "Negro Youth and the Influence of the Press, Radio, and Cinema." *Journal of Negro Education* 9 (1940): 425–34.

"The Lonely Girl." *Photoplay* August 1919: 27.

Lorentz, Pare and Morris Ernst. *Censored: The Private Life of the Movie*. New York: Cape & Smith, 1930.

Lott, Eric. "The Whiteness of Film Noir." *Whiteness: A Critical Reader*. Ed. Mike Hill. New York: New York University Press, 1997. 81–101.

"Louise Connolly" [obituary]. *National Board of Review Magazine* August 1927: 3,9.

Loundsbury, Myron O. *The Origins of American Film Criticism, 1909–1939*. New York: Arno Press, 1973.

Lupton, Ellen. *Mechanical Brides: Women and Machines from Home to Office*. New York: Princeton Architectural Press, 1993.

"Lures Feminine Patronage with 'Pictorial' Fashions," *Motion Picture News* 27 March 1915: 50.

Lyttleton, Edward. "Note on the Educational Influence of the Cinematograph." *Hibbert Journal* July 1913: 851–5.

MacCann, Richard Dyer and Edward S. Perry, eds. *The New Film Index: A Bibliography of Magazine Articles in English, 1930–1970*. New York: E.P. Dutton, 1975.

MacKinnon, Jan, and Steve MacKinnon. "Introduction." *Portraits of Chinese Women in Revolution*. By Agnes Smedley. Old Westbury, NY: The Feminist Press, 1976. ix–xxxv.

MacMahon, Henry. "Educational Films." *Photoplay* January 1919: 40–42.

——. "Women Directors of Plays and Pictures." *Ladies' Home Journal* 20 December 1920: 12–13, 140, 143–144.

"Mae Murray Fashion Page." *Filmplay* May 1922: 41.

Maeterlinck, Maurice. *Das Leben der Bienen* [The Life of Bees]. Jena, Germany: E. Diederichs, 1905.

——. *L'Intelligence des Fleurs*. Paris: Fasquelle, 1928.

——. *The Double Garden*. New York: Dodd, Mead, 1911.

Mahar, Karen Ward. "Women, Filmmaking, and the Gendering of the American Film Industry, 1896–1928." Dissertation, University of Southern California, 1995.

Maltby, Richard. "The Cinema and the League of Nations." *"Film Europe" and "Film America": Cinema, Commerce, and Cultural Exchange, 1920–1939*. Eds. Andrew Higson and Richard Maltby. Exeter: University of Exeter Press, 1999. 82–116.

——. "The Genesis of the Production Code." *Quarterly Review of Film and Video* 15.4 (1995): 5–32.

Mander, Miles. "The Feminine Touch." *Film Weekly* 4 May 1934: 29.

Marchant, Sir James, *The Cinema in Education*. National Council of Public Morals, Cinema Commission of Inquiry, London: Allen & Unwin, 1925.

Marcus, Jane, ed. *The Young Rebecca: Writings of Rebecca West 1911–1917*. New York: Viking Press/Virago, 1982.

Marks, Martin. "The First American Film Scores." *Harvard Library Bulletin* 2.4 (1991): 78–100.

Marshall, A.P., compiler. *A Guide to Negro Periodical Literature, 1941–46*. Winston-Salem, NC: 1946, Typescript, Schomburg Library, New York Public Library.

Martin, Ann and Virginia Clark. *What Women Wrote: Scenarios 1912–1929*. Frederick, MD: University Publications of America, Cinema History Microfilm Series, 1987.

Mast, Gerald, ed. *The Movies in Our Midst: Documents in the Cultural History of Film in America*. Chicago: The University of Chicago Press, 1982.

Masten, Jeffrey, Peter Stallybrass, and Nancy Vickers, eds. *Language Machines: Technologies of Literary and Cultural Production*. New York: Routledge, 1997.

Matassa, Mark. "A Billionaire's Great Save: Cinerama." *Boston Globe* 19 April 1999: A3.

May, Larry. *Screening Out the Past: The Birth of Mass Culture and the Motion Picture Industry*. Oxford: Oxford University Press, 1980.

May, Rainard. See Lu Märten in Primary Bibliography.

Mayer, J.P. *Sociology of Film: Studies and Documents*. London: Faber & Faber, 1946.

Mayne, Judith. *Directed by Dorothy Arzner*. Bloomington: Indiana University Press, 1994.

McCreadie, Marsha. *Women on Film: The Critical Eye*. New York: Praeger, 1983.

——. *The Women Who Write the Movies: From Frances Marion to Nora Ephron*. New York: Birch Lane Press, 1994.

McDonald, James, Anne Friedberg, and Laura Marcus, eds. *Close Up, 1927–1933: Cinema and Modernism*. London: Cassell, 1998.

McKernan, Luke. "Sport and the Silent Screen." *Griffithiana* 64 (1998): 80–141.

McLaughlin, Mary L. *A Study of the National Catholic Office for Motion Pictures*. Diss. University of Wisconsin-Madison, 1974. Ann Arbor: UMI, 1974.

Merry, Bruce. "Ada Negri." *Italian Women Writers: a Bio-bibliographical Sourcebook*. Ed. Rinaldina Russell. Westport, CT: Greenwood Press, 1994. 295–301.

Merz, Caroline. "The Tension of Genre: Wendy Toye and Muriel Box." *Film Criticism* 16.1–2 (1991–92): 84–94.

Metz, Christian. *The Imaginary Signifier: Psychoanalysis and the Cinema*. Trans. Celia Britton et al. Bloomington: Indiana University Press, 1982.

Middleton, Edgar. "Should Women Be Film Censors?" *Film Weekly* 10 February 1933: 7.

Miller, Loren. "The Screen: No 'Escape' for Negro Artists." *New Masses* 16 July 1935: 29.

Milton, Joyce. *Tramp: The Life of Charlie Chaplin*. New York: HarperCollins, 1996.

"Miss Keller's Own Work." *New York Times* 24 August 1919: 4.

Modman, Valerie. *Women Aloft*. Alexandria, VA: Time:Life, 1981.

Momus. "Kinema Ballads. No. 1—Types of Pianists." *Kinematograph and Lantern Weekly* 18 February 1915: 2.

Morgan, Anne, as told to Mary Margaret McBride. "Sidelights on the Woman Question." *Saturday Evening Post* 26 March 1927: 6–7, 186, 189–90.

Morris, Earl J. "Says Negro Should Be in All Pictures." *Pittsburgh Courier* 15 April 1939: 19.

Morris, Meaghan. "Indigestion: A Rhetoric of Reviewing." *The Pirate's Fiancée: Feminism, Reading, Postmodernism*. London: Verso, 1988. 105–21.

"Motion Picture Comedies in Clay." *Scientific American* 16 December 1916: 553.

"The Motion Picture is Esperanto." *Motion Picture News* 14 February 1914: 23.

"Motion Picture Men are Given Another Lesson: Another Colored Woman Wins Her Suit Against a Federal Street Place: White Lawyer Flunked." *Philadelphia Tribune* 2 June 1915: 1.

"Motion Picture Notes." *New York Dramatic Mirror*. 24 january 1912: 40.

"Motion Picture Patents Company." *Moving Picture World* 20 March 1909: 335.

"Motion Picture as Peacemaker." *Literary Digest* 3 March 1917: 556.

"Motion Picture Producers of America. The Open Door*. New York: Motion Picture Producers of America, 1924.

"The Moving Picture Educator." *Moving Picture World* 16 December 1911: 822.

"The Moving Pictures as an Educator." *Moving Picture World* 21 November 1908: 397.

"The Moving Picture Show: What It Ought to Mean in Your Town, and What It Really Does Mean." *Woman's Home Companion* October 1911: 21–2.

Mulvey, Laura. "Afterthoughts on 'Visual Pleasure and Narrative Cinema' inspired by *Duel in the Sun*." *Framework* 6 (1981): 12–15.

——. *Visual and Other Pleasures*. Bloomington: Indiana University Press, 1989.

——. "Visual Pleasure and Narrative Cinema." *Screen* Autumn 1975: 6–18.

Münsterberg, Hugo. *American Traits*. 1901. Port Washington, NY: Kennikat Press, 1971.

———. *The Photoplay: A Psychological Study*. 1916. New York: Dover, 1970.

Murphy, David J. "People of the Pictures: No. 1—The Usherette." *Screen Pictorial* November 1938: 29.

Muscio, Guiliana. *Hollywood's New Deal*. Philadelphia: Temple University Press, 1996.

Musser, Charles. *Edison Motion Pictures, 1890–1900: An Annotated Filmography*. Washington DC: Smithsonian Institution Press, 1997.

———. *The Emergence of Cinema: The American Screen to 1907*. New York: Charles Scribner's Sons, 1990.

———. "On 'Extras,' Mary Pickford, and the Red Light Film: Filmmaking in the United States, 1913." *Griffithiana* 50 (1994): 149–75.

Nasaw, David. *Going Out: The Rise and Fall of Public Amusements*. New York: HarperCollins, 1993.

"Navy Week Films." *Times* 26 July 1917: 3.

"The New Woman Discovered." *Kinematograph Weekly* 11 November 1920: 83.

"The New Woman Director," *Motion Picture Director* October 1926: 70.

Newey, Katherine. "Women and Early British Film: Finding a Screen of Her Own." *Moving Performance: British Stage and Screen, 1890s–1920s*. Eds. Linda Fitzsimmons and Sarah Street. Trowbridge: Flick Books, 2000. 151–165.

Nochlin, Linda. "Why Have There Been No Great Women Artists?" *Art and Sexual Politics: Why Have There Been No Great Women Artists?* Eds. Thomas B. Hess and Elizabeth C. Baker. New York: Collier, 1973. 1–43.

Norden, Martin F. "Women in the Early Film Industry" *Wide Angle* 6.3 (1984): 58–67.

Notcutt, Major L.A. and G.C. Latham. *The African and the Cinema: An Account of the Bantu Educational Cinema Experiment during the Period March 1935 to May 1937*. London: Edinburgh House Press, 1937.

Nugent, Frank. "The Screen." *New York Times* 21 April 1937: 18.

O'Brien, Margaret and Allen Ayles, eds. *Enter the Dream House: Memories of Cinemas in South London from the Twenties to the Sixties*. London: Museum of the Moving Image, 1993.

Observer, The. "Here and There." *Half-century Magazine* November–December 1924: 6.

Ohmer, Susan. "Measuring Desire: Gallup and the Origins of Market Research in Hollywood." Dissertation, New York University, 1997.

Packer, Joan Garrett. *Rebecca West: An Annotated Bibliography*. New York: Garland Publishing, 1991.

Page, William A. "The Movie-Struck Girl," *Woman's Home Companion* 45 (June 1918) 18, 75.

Panter-Downes, Mollie "Letter from London." *New Yorker* 10 December 1949: 126–8.

Pankhurst, Sylvia. *Delphos: The Future of International Language*. London: Kegan Paul, Trench, Trubner, 1927.

Panter-Downes, Mollie. *Letter from England*. Boston: Little, Brown, 1940.

———. *London War Notes*. London: Longman, 1972.

Parker, Alison M. "Mothering the Movies: Women Reformers and Popular Culture." *Movie Censorship and American Culture*. Ed. Francis G. Couvares. Washington, D.C.: Smithsonian Institution Press, 1996. 73–96.

———. *Purifying America: Women, Cultural Reform, and Pro-Censorship Activism, 1873–1933*. Urbana: University of Illinois Press, 1997.

Patterson, Joseph Medill. "The Nickelodeons, the Poor Man's Elementary Course in the Drama." *Saturday Evening Post* 23 November 1907: 10. Rpt. *Spellbound in Darkness: A History of the Silent Film*. Ed. George C. Pratt. Greenwich, CT: New York Graphic Society, 1973. 46.

Peary, Gerald. "Sanka, Pink Ladies, and Virginia Slims." *Women and Film* 1.5–6 (1974): 82–4.

Peet, Creighton. "Our Lady Censors." *Outlook and Independent* 25 December 1929: 645–7, 678–9.

Peiss, Kathy. *Cheap Amusements: Working Women and Leisure in Turn-of-the Century New York*. Philadelphia: Temple University Press, 1986.

Perl, Arnold, letter to Walter White, 24 April 1939. Manuscript Division, Library of Congress, NAACP papers, Part 1, Container C299, File "Films and Plays—General," January–June, 1939.

Petro, Patrice. *Joyless Streets: Women and Melodramatic Representation in Weimar Germany*. Princeton: Princeton University Press, 1989.

"The Photoplay League of America," *Photoplay* September 1918: 75, 117.

Pierpont, Claudia Roth. "A Society of One: Zora Neale Hurston, American Contrarian." *New Yorker* 17 February 1997: 80–91.

Pietropaolo, Laura and Ada Testaferri, eds. *Feminisms in the Cinema*. Bloomington: Indiana University Press, 1995.

"Police Beat and Arrest Boston Women Protesting Against *Birth of a Nation*." *Chicago Defender* 19 June 1915: 1.

Potamkin, Harry Alan. "The Movie Palace," *Billboard*, 24 December 1927: 51. Rpt in *The Compound Cinema: The Film Writings of Harry Alan Potamkin*. Ed. Lewis Jacobs. New York: Teachers College Press, 1977.

——. "The Aframerican Cinema." *Close Up* 5.2 (July–December 1929): 107–17.

——. "The Woman as Film-Director." *American Cinematographer* January 1932: 10, 45.

Powdermaker, Hortense. *Stranger and Friend: The Way of An Anthropologist*. London: Secker & Warburg, 1962.

Powell, Dilys "Introduction." *Bluestocking*. By Helen Fletcher. London: Pandora Press, 1986. v–xii.

Pratt, David B. "'O, Lubitsch, Where Wert Thou?' *Passion*, the German Invasion and the Emergence of the Name 'Lubitsch.'" *Wide Angle* 13.1 (1991): 34–70.

Pratt, George, C., ed., *Spellbound in Darkness: A History of the Silent Film*. Greenwich, CT: New York Graphic Society, 1973.

Pribram, E. Deidre. *Female Spectators: Looking at Film and Television*. New York: Verso, 1988.

"'Privilege' Defence in Critic's Suit." *Today's Cinema* 16 July 1947: 3, 46.

Quart, Barbara Koenig. *Women Directors: The Emergence of a New Cinema*. New York: Praeger, 1988.

Rabinovitz, Lauren. "Maya Deren and an American Avant-garde Cinema." *Points of Resistance: Women, Power and Politics in the New York Avant-garde Cinema, 1943–71*. Urbana: University of Illinois Press, 1991. 49–91.

——. "Mary Ellen Bute," in Jan Christopher Horak, ed. *Lovers of Cinema: The First Americ an Avant-Garde*. Madison, WI: University of Wisconsin Press, 1995, 315–34.

——. "Temptations of Pleasure: Nickelodeons, Amusement Parks, and the Sights of Female Sexuality." *Camera Obscura* 23 (1990): 71–89; now part of her *For the Love of Pleasure: Women, Movies, and Culture in Turn-of-the-Century Chicago*. New Brunswick, NJ: Rutgers University Press, 1998.

Radway, Janice. *Reading the Romance: Women, Patriarchy, and Popular Literature*. Chapel Hill: University of North Carolina Press, 1984.

Ramsaye, Terry. *A Million and One Nights*. New York: Simon & Schuster, 1926.

"'Redfords of the Screen: Censors of Living Pictures,' the Work of the New York Board of Censors at the People's Institute." *Illustrated London News* 22 April 1911: 585.

Renger-Patzsch, Albert. *Die Welt ist schön*. Munich: K. Wolff, 1928.

Renshaw, Samuel, Vernon L. Miller, and Dorothy F. Marquis. *Children's Sleep*. New York: Macmillan, 1933.

"Report of the British Psychoanalytic Society, Fourth Quarter, 1924." *International Journal of Psychoanalysis* 6 (1925): 236–39.

Report of the Committee on the Use of the Cinematograph in Education. London: Imperial Education Conference, 1924.

"Report of the International Cinematographic Institute." *School and Society* 18 July 1931: 84.

Repplier, Agnes. "The Repeal of Reticence." *Atlantic Monthly* March 1914: 297–304.

"Rev. Thomas Dixon Jr., Will Appear in his Anti-Negro Play, *The Sins of the Father*, Sunday, March 26." *Broad Ax* [Chicago] 25 March 1911: 1.

"Revamping the Vampires." *Nation* 10 August 1921: 140.

"'Richard Dehan': The Woman Who Wrote the Dop Doctor." *Cinegoer* [London] 25 March 1916: 7.

Richards, Jeffrey and Dorothy Sheridan, eds. *Mass-Observation at the Movies*. New York: Routledge & Kegan Paul, 1987.

Richardson, Dorothy. Foreword. *Pilgrimage*. London: Dent, 1967. 9–12. Rpt. *The Gender of Modernism: A Critical Anthology*. Ed. Bonnie Kime Scott. Bloomington: Indiana University Press, 1990. 429–32.

Richardson, F.H. "Those Hats." *Moving Picture World* 9 April 1910: 549.

Rickman, J. See "Report of the British Psychoanalytic Society, Fourth Quarter, 1924."

Riding, Laura. *The Word Woman and Other Related Writings*. New York: Persea Books, 1993.

"Robert Herring Gives Four Points about *Hearts in Dixie*." *Close Up* 5.2 (August 1929): 160–62.

Rivière, Joan. "Womanliness as a Masquerade" [1929]. Rpt. *The Inner World and Joan Rivière: Collected Papers, 1920–1958*. London: Karnac Books, 1991. 90–101.

Robertson, James C. *The British Board of Film Censors: Film Censorship in Britain, 1896–1950*. Beckenham: Croom Helm, 1985.

Robeson, Paul. "New Hope for the Negro Hero." *Film Weekly*, 23 May 1936: 9.

Robinson, David. *From Peepshow to Palace: The Birth of American Film*. New York: Columbia University Press, 1996.

———, compiler. *Lantern Images: Iconography of the Magic Lantern, 1420–1880.* Nutley, East Sussex: Magic Lantern Society, 1993.

Robinson, Susan Barnes. *Mabel Dwight: A Catalogue Raisonné of the Lithographs.* Washington; Smithsonian Institution Press, 1997.

Rogin, Michael. *Blackface, White Noise: Jewish Immigrants in the Hollywood Melting Pot.* Berkeley: University of California Press, 1998.

Rose, June. *Marie Stopes and the Sexual Revolution.* London: Faber & Faber, 1992.

Rosen, Majorie. *Popcorn Venus: Women, Movies, and the American Dream.* New York: Coward, McCann & Geoghegan, 1973.

Rosenzweig, Roy. *Eight Hours for What We Will: Workers and Leisure in an Industrial City, 1870–1920.* Cambridge and New York: Cambridge University Press, 1983.

Ross, Ishbel. *Ladies of the Press: The Story of Women in Journalism By an Insider.* New York: Harper & Bros., 1936.

Ross, Steven J. "The Unknown Hollywood." *History Today* 40 (1990): 40–46.

———. *Working-Class Hollywood: Politics, Class, and the Rise of the Movies.* Princeton: Princeton University Press, 1998.

Roth, Darlene Rebecca. *Matronage: Patterns in Women's Organizations, Atlanta, Georgia, 1890–1940.* Brooklyn: Carlson Publishing, 1994.

Rubin, William, ed. *"Primitivism" in Twentieth Century Art: Affinity of the Tribal and the Modern.* New York: Museum of Modern Art, 1984.

Sampson, Henry T. *Blacks in Black and White: A Sourcebook on Black Films.* Metuchen, NJ: Scarecrow Press, 2nd ed. 1997.

Santelli, César. "Children and War Films." *Living Age* 1 August 1930: 664–70.

Sargent, Epes W. "Flimflamming the Film Fans." *Woman's Home Companion* November 1924: 26, 94.

Schivelbusch, Wolfgang. *Disenchanted Night: The Industrialization of Light in the Nineteenth Century.* Trans. Angela Davis. Berkeley: University of California Press, 1988.

Schlüpmann, Heidi. "Cinema as Anti-Theater: Actresses and Female Audiences in Wilhelminian Germany." *Silent Cinema.* Ed. Richard Abel. New Brunswick, NJ: Rutgers University Press, 1996. 125–41.

———. "Cinematographic Enlightenment versus 'The Public Sphere': A Year in Wilheminian Cinema." *Griffithiana* 50 May 1994: 75–85.

———. "Kinosucht." *Frauen und Film* October 1982: 45–52.

Schmalhausen, Samuel and V.F. Calverton, eds. *Woman's Coming of Age: A Symposium.* Horace Liveright: New York, 1931.

Schor, Naomi. *Reading in Detail: Aesthetics and the Feminine.* New York: Methuen, 1987.

Scott, Bonnie Kime, ed. *The Gender of Modernism: A Critical Anthology.* Bloomington: Indiana University Press, 1990.

Scott, Joan. "Women's History." *New Perspectives on Historical Writing.* Ed. Peter Burke. University Park, PA: Pennsylvannia State University Press, 1992. 42–66.

"The Screen." *Opportunity* July 1947: 167, 174–75.

Sellery, J'nan M. and William O. Harris. *Elizabeth Bowen: A Bibliography.* Austin: Humanities Research Center, University of Texas, 1981.

Senelick, Laurence. "Lady and the Tramp: Drag Differentials in the Progressive Era." *Gender in Performance: The Presentation of Difference in the Performing Arts.* Ed. Laurence Senelick. Hannover and London: University Press of New England, 1992. 26–45.

Shaw, Stephanie J. *What a Woman Ought To Be and To Do: Black Professional Women Workers During the Jim Crow Era.* Chicago: University of Chicago Press, 1996.

"She Cuts the Kisses." *American Magazine* January 1949: 99.

Showalter, Elaine. *A Literature of Their Own.* Princeton: Princeton University Press, 1977.

Silva, Fred, ed. *Focus on Birth of a Nation.* Englewood Cliffs, NJ: Prentice-Hall, 1971.

Silverman, Kaja. *The Acoustic Mirror: The Female Voice in Psychoanalysis and Feminism.* Bloomington: Indiana University Press, 1988.

Simmel, Georg. "The Metropolis and Mental Life." *The Sociology of Georg Simmel.* Ed. Kurt H. Wolff. New York: Free Press, 1950. 409–24.

Singer, Ben. "Female Power in the Serial-Queen Melodrama: The Etiology of an Anomaly." *Camera Obscura* 22 (1990): 91–129.

———. "Manhattan Nickelodeons: New Data on Audiences and Exhibitors." *Cinema Journal* 34.3 (1995): 5–35.

Skinner, James M. *The Cross and the Cinema: The Legion of Decency and the National Catholic Office for Motion Pictures, 1933–1970.* Westport, CT: Praeger, 1993.

Sklar, Robert. *Movie-Made America: A Cultural History of American Movies.* Rev. and Updated. New York: Vintage Books, 1994.

Slater, Thomas J. "June Mathis: A Woman Who Spoke Through Silents. *Griffithiana* 53 (1995): 133–57.

Slide, Anthony, annotator. *100 Rare Books from the Margaret Herrick Library of the Academy Foundation: An Annotated Bibliography.* Beverly Hills: Academy of Motion Pictures Arts and Sciences, 1987.

——. *Banned in the USA: British Films in the United States and Their Censorship.* New York: I.B. Tauris, 1998.

——. *Before Video: A History of Non-Theatrical Film.* Westport, CT: Greenwood Press, 1992.

——. *Early Women Directors.* 1977. Metuchen, NJ: Scarecrow Press, 1986.

——. *The Encyclopedia of Vaudeville.* Westport, CT: Greenwood Press, 1994.

——. "Hedda Hopper's Hollywood." *Los Angeles Reader* 4 April 1986, sec. 1: 1, 8–9, 12.

——. *The Idols of Silence.* South Brunswick and New York: A.S. Barnes/London: Thomas Yoseloff, 1976.

——, ed. *International Film, Radio, and Television Journals.* Westport, CT: Greenwood Press, 1985.

——. *Lois Weber: The Director Who Lost Her Way in History.* Westport, CT: Greenwood Press, 1996.

——, ed. *The Memoirs of Alice Guy Blaché.* Metuchen, NJ: Scarecrow Press, 1984.

——. *New Historical Dictionary of the American Film Industry.* Lanham, MD, and London: Scarecrow, 1998.

——. *The Picture on a Dancing Screen: Poetry of the Cinema.* Vestal, NY: The Vestal Press, 1988.

——, ed. *Selected Film Criticism.* 7 vols. Metuchen, NJ: Scarecrow, 1982–1985.

——, ed. *They Also Wrote for the Fan Magazines: Film Articles by Literary Giants from e.e. cummings to Eleanor Roosevelt, 1920–1939.* London: McFarland, 1992.

Sloan, Kay. *The Loud Silents: Origins of the Social Problem Film.* Urbana: University of Illinois, 1988.

Smallwood, William. "They Made Good in the Movie Capital." *Opportunity* March 1941: 76–7.

Smith, Andrew F. *Popped Culture: The Social History of Popcorn in America.* Columbia: University of South Carolina Press, 1999.

Smith, E. Vaughan. "Munition Workers and the Cinema." *Cinegoer* 15 April 1916: 16.

Smith, Marjorie. *From Broadway to Moscow.* New York: Macaulay, 1934.

Smith, Sharon. "Women Who Make Movies." *Women and Film* 1. 3–4 (1973): 77–90.

——. *Women Who Make Movies.* New York: Hopkinson & Blake, 1975.

"Social Workers Censor Shows," *Chicago Tribune* 3 May 1907: 3.

Stacey, Jackie. *Star Gazing: Hollywood Cinema and Female Spectatorship.* New York: Routledge, 1994.

Staiger, Janet. *Bad Women: Regulating Sexuality in Early American Cinema.* Minneapolis: Minnesota University Press, 1995.

——. "*The Birth of a Nation:* Reconsidering its Reception." *Interpreting Films: Studies in the Historical Reception of American Cinema.* Princeton: Princeton University Press, 1992. 139–53.

Stamp, Shelley. "Moral Coercion, or the Board of Censorship Ponders the Vice Question." *Regulating Hollywood: Censorship and Control in the Studio Era.* Ed. Matthew Bernstein. New Brunswick, NJ: Rutgers University Press, 1999. 41–58.

——. *Movie-Struck Girls: Women and Motion Picture Culture after the Nickelodeon.* Princeton: Princeton University Press, 2000.

Stein, Gertrude. "Portraits and Repetition." *Lectures in America.* New York: Random House, 1935. 165–206.

Stern, Katherine. "What is Femme? The Phenomenology of the Powder Room." *Women: A Cultural Review* 8.2 (1997): 183–96.

Stoddard, Karen M. *Saints and Shrews: Women and Aging in Popular American Film.* Westport, CT: Greenwood Press, 1983.

Stopes, Marie. *Ancient Plants.* London: Blackie, 1910.

——. *Married Love: A New Contribution to the Solution of Sex Difficulties.* London: A.C. Fifield, 1918.

Stopes, Marie, and Professor J. Sakurai. *Plays of Old Japan, the No.* London: Heinemann, 1913.

Streible, Dan, "Female Spectators and the Corbett-Fitzsimmons Fight Film." *Out of Bounds: Sports, Media, and the Politics of Identity.* Eds. Aaron Baker and Todd Boyd. Bloomington: Indiana University Press, 1997. 16–47.

——. *Fight Pictures: A History of Prizefighting and Early Cinema.* Washington, D.C.: Smithsonian Institution Press, 2002.

——. "A History of the Boxing Film, 1894–1915: Social Control and Social Reform in the Progressive Era." *Film History* 3 (1989): 235–57.

——. "A Return to the 'Primitive': One Hundred Years of Cinema ... and Boxing." *Arachne* 2.2 (1995): 297–323.

Streitmatter, Roger. *Raising Her Voice: African-American Women Journalists Who Changed History*. Lexington: University of Kentucky Press, 1994.

Studlar, Gaylyn. *In the Realm of Pleasure: Von Sternberg, Dietrich, and the Masochistic Aesthetic*. Urbana: University of Illinois Press, 1988.

——. "The Perils of Pleasure? Fan Magazine Discourse as Women's Commodified Culture in the 1920s." *Wide Angle* 13.1 (1991). Rpt. *Silent Film*. Ed. Richard Abel. New Brunswick: Rutgers University Press, 1996. 263–97.

"The Sun and Our Daughters." *Vogue* [New York] 1 June 1923: 55.

"L'Tanya First Negro Woman to Receive Fashion Screen Credit." 31 August 1949. ts Claude A Barnett Papers, Box 298, Folder 1, Chicago Historical Society.

Taylor, Helen. *Scarlett's Women: Gone with the Wind and Its Female Fans*. New Brunswick, NJ: Rutgers University Press, 1989.

Taylor, Ian. "The Film Reviews of Winifred Horrabin, 1927–1945." *Screen* 33.2 (1992): 174–83.

"A Theatre Built for Mothers." (illustration) *Photoplay* November 1919: 50.

"The Theatres and Our Problems." *Negro American* 6.8 [San Antonio, Texas] December 1928, 3, 11.

"These Fans Are Dangerous." *Screen Pictorial*. September 1939: 9.

Thompson, John. "Laura Bowman, Noted Actress, Revives Haitian Folklore and Puts it on Screen and Stage." *Chicago Defender* 15 July 1939: 17.

Thompson, Paul. "They're Married and Work Together." *Motion Picture* October 1928: 47, 106.

Toulmin, Vanessa. "Women Bioscope Proprietors: Before the First World War." *Celebrating 1895: The Centenary of Cinema*. Ed. John Fullerton. London: John Libbey, 1998. 55–65.

"A Tribute to Moving Picture Shows." *Moving Picture World* 7 March 1908: 181.

Tyler, Parker. *The Hollywood Hallucination*. 1944. New York: Simon & Schuster, 1970.

——. *Magic and Myth of the Movies*. 1947. New York: Simon & Schuster, 1970.

Uricchio, William, Roberta Pearson, Judith Thissen, Ben Singer, "Dialog: Manhattan Nickelodeons." *Cinema Journal* 36.4 (1997): 98–112.

Valentine, Sydney. "The Girl Producer." *Photoplay* July 1923: 55, 110.

Van Doran, Mark. "Films: on Horror's Head." *Nation* 8 May 1937: 545.

Van Zile, Edward S. *That Marvel the Movie*. New York: G.P. Putnam's Sons, 1923.

Vasey, Ruth. *The World According to Hollywood, 1918–1939*. Madison: University of Wisconsin Press, 1997.

Vertov, Dziga. *Kino-Eye: The Writings of Dziga Vertov*. Trans. Kevin O'Brien. Ed. Annette Michelson. Berkeley: University of California Press, 1984.

Views and Film Index 19 December 1908: 5.

Virmaux, Alain and Odette Virmaux, eds. *Colette at the Movies: Criticism and Screenplays*. Trans. Sarah. W.R. Smith. New York: Frederick Ungar, 1980.

"Vultures of Hollywood." *American Mercury* March 1943: 345–50.

Wagner, Anne. *Three Artists (Three Women)*. Berkeley: University of California Press, 1996.

Wald, Lillian. *The House on Henry Street*. New York: Henry Holt, 1915.

Walker, Alexander. *The Shattered Silents: How the Talkies Came to Stay*. 1978. London: Harrap, 1986.

Waller, Gregory. *Main Street Amusements: Movies and Commercial Entertainment in a Southern City, 1896–1930*. Washington, DC: Smithsonian Institution Press, 1995.

Walsh, Frank. *Sin and Censorship: The Catholic Church and the Motion Picture Industry*. New Haven: Yale University Press, 1996.

Warner, Harry, M. "The New Ambassadors of Good-Will." *American Hebrew* 15 March 1929: 666.

Warner, Marina. *Monuments and Maidens: The Allegory of the Female Form*. 1985. London: Vintage, 1996.

Warshow, Robert, "The Gangster as Tragic Hero." *Partisan Review* 15.2 (1948). Rpt. *The Immediate Experience*. Garden City: Doubleday, 1962. 127–133.

Warwick, Frances, Countess of. *Afterthoughts*. London: Cassell, 1931.

——. *Life's Ebb and Flow*. New York: William Morrow, 1929.

Wasson, Haidee. *Modern Ideas/Old Films: The Museum of Modern Art's Film Library and Film Culture, 1935–39*. Berkeley: University of California Press, 2005.

Watts, Margit Misangyi. *High Tea at Halekulani: Feminist Theory and American Club Women*. Brooklyn: Carlson Publishing, 1993.

Watts, Stephen, ed. *Behind the Screen: How Films Are Made*. London: Arthur Barker, 1938.

Waugh, Tom. *Hard to Imagine: Gay Male Eroticism in Photography from their Beginnings to Stonewall*. New York: Columbia University Press, 1996.

"We Have with Us Today" (about Ella Fabrique).. *Moving Picture World* 17 April 1920: 395.

West, Dorothy. "The Typewriter." *Opportunity* July 1926: 220–22, 233–4.

West, Rebecca. *Black Lamb and Grey Falcon: The Record of a Journey through Yugoslavia in 1937*. London: Macmillan, 1942. New York: 1982.

——. "Censorship." *Censorship: For and Against*. Ed. Harold Hart. New York: Hart Publishing, 1971. 124–40.

——. "Concerning the Censorship." *Ending in Earnest: A Literary Log*. 1931. Freeport, NY: Books for Libraries Press, 1967. 6–12.

——. "A Jixless Errand." *Time and Tide* 15 March 1929: 282–6.

——. "These American Women." *Harper's Monthly Magazine* (1925): 722–30.

White, Eric Walter. *Walking Shadows: An Essay on Lotte Reiniger's Silhouette Films*. London: Leonard and Virginia Woolf at the Hogarth Press, 1931.

Whitman, Howard. "What Hollywood Doesn't Know about Women." *Collier's* March 1949: 18–19, 46.

Wilcox, Ella Wheeler. *Cinema Poems and Others*. London: Gray & Hancock, 1919.

Williams, David. "Ladies of the Lamp." *Film History* 9.1 (1997): 116–27.

Williams, Linda. *Hard Core: Power, Pleasure and the "Frenzy of the Visible"*. Berkeley: University of California Press, 1989.

——, ed. *Viewing Positions: Ways of Seeing Film*. New Brunswick, NJ: Rutgers University Press, 1995.

Wohl, Robert. *A Passion for Wings: Aviation and the Western Imagination, 1908–1918*. New Haven: Yale University Press, 1994.

"Woman Educator on Moving Pictures." *Moving Picture World* 19 August 1911: 452.

"A Woman Exchange Manager." *Moving Picture World* 19 August 1911: 460.

"Woman Exhibitor Welcomes Ass'n." *New York Dramatic Mirror* 15 September 1917: 22.

"Women and the Box Office." *Good Housekeeping* May 1950: 254–6.

"Women Cannot Appreciate Films." *Film Weekly* 28 July 1933: 26.

"Women Fail to Halt Sunday Shows." *Motion Picture News* 6 June 1917: 31.

"Women Present Plea for Film Progress to League Institute." *Motion Picture Herald* 17 October 1931: 20.

"Women of Race Fighting Against Birth of a Nation." *Chicago Defender* 26 June 1915: 3.

Wood, Leslie. "Where the Clock has Stopped." *Film Weekly* 5 July 1930: 19.

Worland, Rick, Notes for "Treasures from the G. William Jones Film-Video Collection" Southern Methodist University, Dallas TX, Society for Cinema Studies Conference Special Events Screenings, 1995.

X, "The 'All-British' Firm," *Pictures and Picturegoer* 26 October–2 November 1918: 422.

The Year 1913. Special issue of *Griffithiana* 50 (1994).

Zischler, Hanns. *Kafka geht ins Kino*. Hamburg: Rowohlt Verlag, 1996.

Index

Film Titles